J. W. M

12 Stoneleigh Park Road
Ewell, Epsom, Surrey KT19 0QT
England

Tel: 0011 44 208 393 7700   Fax: 0011 44 208 393 1694
email: jwmck@netcomuk.co.uk
website: www.mckenzie-cricket.co.uk

*Specialists in Antiquarian,
Secondhand Cricket Books
Wisdens, and Memorabilia*

Catalogues Issued

*We are always pleased to hear of Books and
Collections for Sale*

4TH EDITION

WISDEN

CRICKETERS' ALMANACK

AUSTRALIA

2001-02

HARDIE GRANT BOOKS

Published in 2001 by
Hardie Grant Books
12 Claremont Street, South Yarra, Victoria 3141, Australia
www.hardiegrant.com.au

Cased edition ISBN 1 876719 85 0
Leather bound edition ISBN 1 876719 86 9
(Limited edition of 100)
ISSN 1441-1725

Typeset by Melbourne Media Services
Printed in Australia by McPherson's Printing Group

PREFACE

In last year's Preface Gideon Haigh referred to the contemporary obsession with quantification and the inescapable part that *Wisden* plays in this process. Of course our readers want to know the statistical dimensions of the game contained in scorecards, records and figures which are an integral part of our publication. By themselves, though, they are just inert marks on a page, and it is a necessary part of our job to provide a context which will give life and meaning to the raw figures.

It has become fashionable to talk of the way in which we live in an "information-rich" society, but this alleged bounty can quickly become the tawdry dross of the 30-second sound grab, the instantly formed opinion of a child prodigy on the workings of the stock market, the endless chatter of talk-back radio and the sleazy deception of so-called reality television. In contrast, it is our task to take the longer, more thoughtful, perspective on the happenings of cricket, to be serious without being pompous, to be informative without being pedantic and to be entertaining without being frivolous. In our pages, readers have the opportunity to savour and relish the players, matches and moments of the past year which will become part of the fabric of cricket. So, in the frosty reaches of a winter's night, we can rekindle the surgical precision of a Glenn McGrath hat-trick, the ripe abundance of the batting of Jamie Cox, the elegant heroism of V. V. S. Laxman and Rahul Dravid, whose deeds made the film *Moulin Rouge* look like a tamely conventional documentary.

The most significant cricket event of the year was one which was also of national significance: the death of a man who played his last Test match over half a century ago. That man was Sir Donald Bradman, whose absolute dominance with the bat was complemented by his crucial role in shaping modern Australian cricket as an administrator, and whose long life saw him come to be regarded as a national treasure. The farewell to him in Adelaide's St Peter's Cathedral was an occasion where the personal and the public were blended with moving effect, and Richie Benaud has kindly permitted us to reprint his moving and poignant eulogy in which restrained understatement became an instrument of enormous power. Philip Derriman's obituary is a cogent account by a thoughtful analyst of the Australian sporting scene which records and analyses the many facets of Bradman's life and achievements. Brett Hutchins has drawn on the research which he has undertaken for a doctoral dissertation at the University of Queensland to explore some of the factors which went into the making of the Bradman legend. Through meditating on Bradman as an Australian hero, we have the opportunity to understand more about what it means to be Australian.

Charles Davis has taken his training in statistics and applied it to cricket. No scientist is interested in statistics for their own sake but, rather, for what they reveal and what they mean, and Davis explores and interprets the statistics of Bradman's batting in a fascinating and original way.

In the next Ashes series after Bradman retired, David Frith saw his first Test match. That small boy who saw the Sydney Test against the redoubtable Freddie Brown's team has become one of the most substantial and discerning of contemporary cricket writers, and one whose organisational energy saw him become the founding editor of *Wisden Cricket Monthly*. He is uniquely positioned to celebrate his golden jubilee of Test match watching by, as ever, understanding the present through the light offered by cricket's past.

Sir Donald Bradman remained a potent presence in Australian cricket because he was vitally concerned with the present and the future of the game. One of the most imposing features of contemporary Australian cricket has been the run of successes by the Queensland team. Gone are the days when the northern state was synonymous with struggle, uneven playing standards, and the corrosive disappointment of failure to win the Sheffield Shield. Instead, Queensland now stands for professionalism, depth of talent, and success, and local journalist Martin Rogers charts the reasons for this dramatic change.

The Australian tour to India provided pulsating and memorable Test cricket of the highest order. In passing, I might note that free-to-air television viewers were denied any coverage of this momentous series, continuing the well-established tradition of contempt which commercial television has for the game and its followers outside of the Australian summer. Tony Wilson reminds us that while cricket has its mountain peaks of Test cricket, it is dependent on its grass or asphalt roots in parks and streets around the world. Wilson moves outside the air-conditioned and homogenised world of the international hotel into the frenetic streets of Kolkata. His observations are as sharp as his wit is illuminating; administrators and players could well ponder that it is on the enthusiasm, support and money of the people that Wilson met that they depend for their existence.

The same observation could be made after reading Jim Young's delightful recent book *Any Old Eleven* with its evocative account of the trials and tribulations of playing park cricket in Melbourne. It also leads me to point to the sheer diversity of the cricket recorded in these pages. While it is right and proper to highlight the achievements of the national side, we are also reminded of the pleasures of watching old and new faces in the Pura Cup, the substantial and exciting achievements of women's cricket and the infinite variety of games contained under the bland heading of Minor Cricket. John Polack discusses the importance of minor competitions, such as the ACB Cup, in nurturing the talents of young cricketers for the step up to state, and even national, level. Of such is Australian cricket made, and sufficient, I hope, to satisfy the figure-conscious and nourish the memory.

My pleasure in being given the honour of becoming the Executive Editor of *Wisden Australia* is balanced by my regret that the inaugural editor, Gideon Haigh, resigned in order to pursue his many writing projects. Gideon's compendious knowledge of the really important things both inside and outside cricket, his effortless artistry as a writer, and his meticulous attention to detail, set a standard to which I can only aspire. As evidence of the large task which he had shouldered, I now share Gideon's duties with copy editor George Thomas, whose critical sense and ability to create readable and interesting English are evidence of the learning and skill which he wears so deftly. The production of this volume was also dealt a blow by the departure of Amanda Finnis of Hardie Grant Books. Her enthusiastic energy and indefatigable competence were a huge loss and it was fortunate that I had the experience and calm wisdom of John Ross as her replacement. I also thank Graeme Wright, Christine Forrest and Christopher Lane, our colleagues at John Wisden & Co Ltd, statistician Ross Dundas, whose ability to work at speed without ever sacrificing accuracy puts him in the Dennis Lillee class, proof-reader and fact-checker Nabila Ahmed, style and typesetting wizards Neil Conning and David Spratt.

WARWICK FRANKS
Executive Editor

CONTRIBUTORS

Nabila Ahmed is a trainee journalist with the *Age*, Melbourne.

Richie Benaud was Australian Test captain (1958-1964) and is now a journalist and the doyen of TV commentators.

Simon Briggs is a cricket writer for the *Daily Telegraph*, London.

Alex Buzo is an author, humourist and cricket lover, and captain of The Metros in Sydney.

Ken Casellas was chief cricket writer for the *West Australian* for 27 years. He covered three Ashes series in England and World Cup tournaments, and has been on two tours of South Africa.

Colin Chung is a cricket writer for Hobart's *Mercury* newspaper.

Lawrie Colliver, a former grade cricketer for Tea Tree Gully, South Australia, is a broadcaster for 5AA.

Mike Coward is a cricket commentator for the *Australian* and is a broadcaster for both radio and television.

Michael Crutcher is an AAP sports writer, based in Brisbane.

Charles Davis is a sports historian with a special interest in statistics. His recent book *The Best of the Best* is a unique comparison of sporting abilities.

Philip Derriman writes on cricket for the *Sydney Morning Herald* and is the author of a number of cricket books and the compiler of two anthologies. He edited the *Australian Cricket Almanac* from 1990 to 1996.

Ross Dundas is Australia's only full-time cricket statistician.

Ric Finlay is a cricket statistician and historian, and a senior secondary college mathematics teacher.

Warwick Franks teaches English and Sports History at Charles Sturt University, Bathurst, NSW, and is co-editor of the *Oxford Companion to Australian Cricket*.

David Frith is a former editor of *The Cricketer* and *Wisden Cricket Monthly* and has written or edited more than 20 books on cricket.

Stephen Gibbs is a cricket bibliophile, and co-editor of *Early Cricket in Sydney*.

Jamie Grant is a poet, reviewer and editor of *The Longest Game*.

Stephen Gray is media manager for Queensland Cricket.

Gideon Haigh is a Melbourne journalist.

Peter Hanlon is a cricket writer for the *Age*, Melbourne.

Brett Hutchins has just completed his doctorate in sociology at the University of Queensland, with the thesis 'Bradman: representation, meaning and Australian culture'.

Ian Jessup is a sports writer for AAP.

Greg McKie is a secondary school teacher, VCA delegate and the Australian Cricket Board's statistician for under-age cricket.

Valkerie Mangnall is a journalist with AAP, based in Adelaide.

Adam Morehouse is the statistician for the ACT Cricket Association and the author of *From Country to Comets*.

Ken Piesse is a journalist and author, and former editor of *Cricketer* and *Australian Cricket*.

John Polack is Australian editor of CricInfo.

Martin Rogers is a former Fleet Street journalist who has covered Queensland and Australian Cricket for the *Gold Coast Bulletin* since 1989. He has written or edited 16 books on a variety of sports.

Erica Sainsbury is the statistician for Women's Cricket Australia and scorer for the Commonwealth Bank Southern Stars.

David Stockdale is a senior sports journalist with the Hobart *Mercury*.

Warwick Torrens is a statistician and author of a history of the National Country Cricket Championships.

Adrian Warren is a Sydney-based freelance sports writer, who has written about cricket for AAP since 1987.

Phil Wilkins has been chief cricket writer for the *Sydney Morning Herald* and the *Sun-Herald* and the *Australian* and now writes on cricket and rugby for the John Fairfax Group of papers.

Ken Williams assists the Victorian Cricket Association with club and first-class records and is one of the principals of the First Class Cricketers Project, which aims to produce a biographical register of all Australian first-class players.

Tony Wilson is a freelance writer and documentary maker and wrote features on the 2001 Australian tour of India for the Melbourne *Age*.

CONTENTS

Part One: Comment

Part Two: The Players

Part Three: Records

Part Four: Australian Cricket in 2000-01

Part Five: Australians Overseas in 2000-01

Part Six: Administration and Laws

Part Seven: Miscellaneous

Index of Fillers and Inserts

ACKNOWLEDGEMENTS

Black and white photographs
ALLSPORT, pp 89, 91, 92, 94, 95, 402, 438 © Tony Lewis, p 310 © Tony McDonough, p 322, 405, 644, 670 © Hamish Blair, p 113 © Darren England; Cricket New South Wales, pp 70, 72, 73, 379, 381; Prahran CC/David Dukes 108; Queensland Cricket pp 80, 82, 83, 85, 86 , 390, 393; Rick Smith pp 96, 98, 100, 101, 102, 414, 417, 832, 835, 838, 440; St George CC/John Jobson 76; Victorian Cricket Association p 105; Western Australian Cricket Association, pp 115, 118, 119; Women's Cricket Australia p 706

Colour photographs are credited in the colour section.

The publisher acknowledges the work done over many years by the Association of Cricket Statisticians and Historians and offers thanks for the assistance of members in compiling information for *Wisden Australia*.

PART ONE: COMMENT

NOTES BY THE EDITOR

Cricket after Condon

It is a truism in politics that a government never establishes a Royal Commission or calls for an expert report unless it is confident that it already knows what the recommendations will be. When, in June 2000, the International Cricket Council appointed Sir Paul Condon, former commissioner of London's Metropolitan Police, to direct its Anti-Corruption Unit, with a brief to examine and report on the issue of corruption in cricket by April 30, 2001, expectations were not high. Because of its own previous reluctance to move on the issue, the ICC itself had produced a mixture of pessimism and cynicism among cricket followers. After all, there were the names that had come to dominate cricket news such as Salim Malik, Mohammad Azharuddin, M. K. Gupta, Jagmohan Dalmiya, Justice Qayyum, the Indian Central Bureau of Investigation, Hansie Cronje, and the King Commission. On the Australian scene, there had been the sobering revelation that, back in 1994, Shane Warne and Mark Waugh had been fined for their dealings with a book-maker, but that both the Australian Cricket Board and the ICC had chosen to keep the matter secret until 1998. Yet, it was against this background that, last year, one of the panjandrums of the ICC in-sisted to a television interviewer that corruption was not a major issue in world cricket. Thus, there was ample justification for feeling that we would get an anodyne document with enough platitudes to satisfy the pious but little else.

Instead, the Condon Report, having described the role and work of the Anti-Corruption Unit, goes on to give a lucid analysis of the origins, development and nature of corruption in international cricket and culminates in a series of clear and challenging recom-mendations. Central to them is Condon's unequivocal challenge to the ICC to transform itself from "a loose and fragile alliance" into an "open, transparent and accountable ... modern regulatory body with the power to lead and direct international cricket". Of course, this transformation cannot occur without the backing of the con-stituent members of the ICC, and the commitment that they bring to this task will be a clear indication of their sincerity and their seriousness about cleaning up cricket.

Condon gives a clear diagnosis of a controlling body which has lacked both the ability and the willingness to exercise its responsibilities to the game, but his ultimate indictment is the way in which the issue of corruption became enmeshed in "a climate of silence, apathy, ignorance and fear". The issue grew and festered because of a view, genuinely held by the many and cynically exploited by the few, that the ethos of cricket made corrupt practices unthinkable. The ICC, by the very commissioning of this report, has taken a first crucial step towards replacing ignorance with knowledge, but this knowledge must be based on clear understanding and must lead to considered action. Such a process will destroy the apathy that breeds the silence in which fear can flourish.

The initial reaction gives cause for some optimism. The ICC's Code of Conduct Commission, whose five-member panel includes former Australian captain Richie Benaud, met immediately and endorsed all of Condon's recommendations. In June, the Executive Board of the ICC met and fully endorsed the findings and recommendations. Malcolm Gray, recently elected president of the ICC, has shown a willingness to be refreshingly candid, with such comments as: "The ICC and all the national boards … were slow to react. They didn't act strongly enough or robustly enough or quickly enough." He is being joined by the new Chief Executive Officer of the ICC, Malcolm Speed, who will bring to the position a record of purpose and action at the ACB. One of Speed's initial tasks is the development of a process to put these recommendations into action. The Condon Report warns that corrupt malpractice in cricket is a continuing problem for which the Anti-Corruption Unit has a brief to sustain its investigations until the World Cup in South Africa in 2003. The rest is up to the constituent members of the ICC, bearing in mind that, as ever, actions will speak louder than words. If sluggish inaction and narrow self-interest prevail, Australians have the stark precedent of the sport of sculling to ponder. In the 1890s it was a major spectator sport, but after disclosures of rigged races and the presence of shady bookmakers, the public turned its back on the sport totally and permanently.

An episode from the apparently remote history of Australian cricket provides a useful perspective on the issue. In December 1875 at the Melbourne Cricket Ground, Victoria had made 136, to which New South Wales had replied with 171. A prominent figure sent several messages to the New South Wales captain, asking him to ease the pressure on the Victorians because, it was later revealed, he had wagered against New South Wales winning by an innings. The Victorians were dismissed for 34 and the punter is alleged to have said to James Coates, the victorious captain, "You might have obliged an old friend, as I would have done the same for you." The New South Wales Cricket Association Committee investigated the incident, but took no action. This inaction was severely criticised by the press, and after a public outcry, the Committee was stung into action and revealed the culprit's name as Alfred Leath Park, treasurer of the Association until 12 months before the incident. His identity was written into the minutes and his immediate resignation as Trustee of the Domain Ground was sought and gained.

The Park episode has all the familiar ingredients: avarice, improper attempts to influence the outcome of a game of cricket, official inaction, public demands for action, and the departure of a once-respected figure from the cricket scene. One response to the Condon Report might be a collective and weary sigh and a reflection that it was ever thus, and that the issue is just too difficult to rectify. Or, the game's administrators – and players – can read and digest its contents, and then act with vigour and purpose on its recommendations.

The M word

One of Condon's early recommendations is that the ICC should follow a number of American sports by producing a video as a part of training programme for young professional cricketers aimed at deterring corruption. While it is tempting to reflect on a society in which we have to explain to our youth that it is wrong to be on the take, it does raise the issue of what we expect from our cricketers.

The reality of contemporary cricket is that it is packaged and promoted as a commercial and increasingly global commodity. It has also become so profitable that as a result of a new financial deal struck between the ACB and the Australian Cricketers' Association in May 2001, an Australian cricketer will be paid $1 million within the next two years. But sport cannot be divorced from its social and political context, and for the past decade and a half, Australia, like many western countries, has lived through the mania for deregulation and so-called flexibility. It has been stressed that the user pays, the only important bottom line is the financial one, and that cricket has to be part of this ethic or it will die. Accompanying this process has been the increasing pressure on standards of public behaviour and the sense that propriety is infinitely adjustable.

Yet, an important component of cricket is a sense of morality, unfashionable though the word is in these post-modern times. Part of this component is a specific sense of a code of behaviour which is separate from what is legally enforceable – for example, the fact that a bowler will generally not Mankad a batsman without first warning him. Its other part is a general approach which is reflected in the expression of something being "not cricket", a notion that there is an agreed ethical standard which imbues the game itself and is at the heart of what makes it worthwhile and satisfying as a sport.

Condon issues a clear warning to administrators about the unrestrained pursuit of money, which has seen the mushrooming of meaningless cricket, particularly the limited-overs form. The dreary routine of yet another fancifully named competition on which nothing hangs, except money, provides almost laboratory conditions for the growth of apathy and the compromising of morality. And who knows, in our world morality might even be a great marketing concept.

Australia: triumphant or triumphalist?

In the Second Test against West Indies at Perth, Australia set a new record of 12 successive Test victories, a number which was eventually extended to 16, before India's V. V. S. Laxman defied credulity and brought the run to an unforgettable end in the Second Test at Kolkata. These successes generated plenty of discussion as to whether this was the best-ever Australian team, discussion which, like a fire in a hollow log, often generated more heat than light. There is much entertainment, and even some instruction, to be had from such discussions, as long as we remember the capacity of statistics to mislead, and treat the issue as essentially a question of philosophical speculation.

There is no doubt as to the extent and the conclusiveness of this string of victories. Its most crucial element was that it was a team achievement; there were no dominating individuals but, rather, a team with the capacity to produce a wide variety of individual performances in the service of a collective effort, combined with total self-belief. Thus, at some stage, each team member made crucial contributions to victory, contributions which underlined the team's enormous self-belief. So, for example, against West Indies in Brisbane, when there was a minor stutter in the Australian innings, Brett Lee revealed himself as a batsman who could make runs with skilful bravado. Similarly, Colin Miller, who is very much the capable journeyman cricketer, was always likely to weigh in with crucial wickets.

Yet, behind the admiration for successful and tough cricket, there has been a sense of unease at some of the more unpleasant player behaviour and actions. The often-boorish words of the sledge have sometimes been transformed into actions such as the bullet-like return of the ball past the batsman's nose to remind him of Australian displeasure at his presence or as a comment on an umpiring decision. This aspect of the game was encapsulated in Michael Slater's performance during the First Test against India at Mumbai, when he dressed down Rahul Dravid for not automatically leaving the crease after the third umpire disallowed a catch that Slater claimed to have taken. Umpire Srinivas Venkataraghavan also came in for some Slater criticism that was not only free but gratuitous. Many observers found it pungently ironic that this sense of moral outrage came from one who had chosen not to head for the pavilion after a palpable nick to the keeper when he had been batting. The episode brought into focus a feeling that, while Australian cricket followers respected the skill and success of the team, there was not a great deal of affectionate warmth in their response, a feeling which was evident in the muted reaction to the end of the winning sequence at Kolkata.

Interestingly, at the beginning of the Ashes tour, Steve Waugh signalled a desire to rectify this situation, citing adverse response from the public over such incidents as one of the reasons for wanting his team to be seen as less abrasive, particularly with umpires. While Waugh is the epitome of cricketing toughness, he is also steeped in a wider knowledge of both cricket's history and its place in the Australian scheme of things. His comments followed his team's visit to Gallipoli on its way to England, a visit which initially produced in observers the queasy sensation of its being a piece of gormless image construction of the team as the lineal descendants of the Anzacs. Thankfully, it seems to have made a profound impact on the players, and there was much talk among them of its significance for the cricket that was to come. If that significance produces an Australian team which is successful, respected and warmly regarded, Australian cricket will be the better for it.

Generational change in the Australian team ...

With the majority of the Ashes touring team having passed the age of 30, it is on the verge of a period of generational change. Professionalism, of course, means that Australian cricketers can now extend their time in the game compared to the players of preceding times but, even so, the need to deal with changes in personnel cannot be far off. The perils of not addressing the issue, or mismanaging it, are starkly evident in the calamities which have befallen the West Indian game.

Australian cricket faces different challenges. Its organisation is thorough and complete but a consequence has been that it has produced a lock-step structure that means many players are serving an apprenticeship until they are in their mid-twenties. A decade of success at the national level has made the selectors properly chary of changing a winning combination, so opportunities for new players have been limited. For example, the next to last specialist batsman to be selected for the Test team was Darren Lehmann back in March 1998, while Simon Katich, who was chosen for his first Test in England, is already 26. Greg Chappell has argued that the supreme virtue of the best young cricketers is that they exude an air of invincibility that springs from the fearlessness of youth. By contrast, he asserts that older new players are already aware of the possibility of failure and have in them the canker of self-doubt.

This is not an argument for a revolving-door policy of selection; but the national selectors are faced with the problem that the most obvious contenders for the Test side are themselves players of substantial maturity. Despite the proven ability of the present system to produce a range of substantial players, there needs to be a willingness to think outside the circle and to consider backing hunches about young players of real promise such as Shane Watson or Cameron White.

... and at the ACB

Malcolm Speed's replacement as Chief Executive Officer of the ACB is James Sutherland, a 35-year-old chartered accountant who played four matches for Victoria in the early 1990s as a fast-medium bowler and had an extensive and successful career as a district player. His combination of youth, professional qualifications and experience should be a positive addition to Australian administration. Writing in last year's edition on the board's abandonment of the Sheffield Shield, I drew the distinction between the need for administrators to be businesslike and the dangers of treating the game as just a business. Administering cricket is not the same as running a fast-food franchise or a chicken-processing factory. It requires an understanding of the history, culture and contemporary condition of Australian cricket, so that the creative meshing of the past and present will offer successful ways into the future.

Sutherland's appointment is part of a generational change which is under way in Australian administration. In earlier times, our administrators tended to be men who had given decades of honorary service to the game, but the very length of this service made them convinced that they were the sole guardians of the spirit of cricket, a guardianship which they often exercised in an autocratic and insensitive manner. One consequence of this belief was the development of a gulf between administrators and players, the latter often being seen as chattels whose main functions were to play well and do as they were told. The Condon Report regards this gulf as still a feature of the contemporary game and recommends its speedy bridging as a crucial way of driving forward the best interests of the game. The report urges, in particular, the more direct incorporation of players into administration. The challenge facing the ACB is to manage its own generational change and thus be able to provide creative leadership in a world of flux.

Men in white coats

The pressure to turn the umpire into a clothes horse mounts steadily. It comes in a kind of pincer movement, which starts with a number of allegedly or demonstrably poor decisions, as was the case in the Sri Lanka–England series of February and March 2001. Authorities are then bombarded with the "use it if you've got it" argument on technology, and so the quest to introduce yet another electronic intervention into the game gets another boost. So we have the gee-whizzery of such developments as snickometers and leg-before-wicket detectors, which offer the illusion of certainty and are part of the entertainment package of cricket.

Cricket, though, is a human game, and extending the intervention of technology will compromise its flesh-and-blood dimension. The search for total accuracy could be fruitless and self-defeating as the replay screen becomes the focus of attention, and the game becomes a kind of replica of itself. The inevitable consequence of this process is the further slowing of the game in order to allow time for electronic adjudication. American football offers a view down the road which cricket might travel towards technological domination.

There are also the umpires themselves. Standards of umpiring will not rise if we undertake a process of what amounts to de-skilling. Rather than opting out by giving umpires less to do, a more positive move is to continue trying to enhance standards, so that we see a game where competent adjudication is the norm, but in a human context.

Indigenous cricket

Despite the tragic peaks of men such as Jack Marsh and Eddie Gilbert, cricket has not generally proved congenial to Aboriginal Australians. Historians such as Colin Tatz and Bernard Whimpress have traced the complex of reasons for this, but the ACB has made a fresh start in trying to address the issue. After a skilful game between the ATSIC Chairman's XI and the Prime Minister's XI at Manuka Oval, Canberra in April 2001, an Aboriginal Cricket Working Party was formed. Set up under the aegis of the ACB's Game Development Program, its largely indigenous members are settling on a small number of cricket projects to be developed in indigenous communities. After 12 months, the forum will consider the projects and assess their significance. A related but separate development is a three-week tour of England in August 2001 of an Aboriginal youth cricket team, coached by former Australian off-spinner Ashley Mallett.

Given the deeds of groups such as the 1868 Aboriginal team to England, and individuals such as Sam Anderson, whose batting skill dominated cricket on the far-north coast of New South Wales for decades in the first half of the 20th century, this is an appropriate practical start to establishing a significant cricket presence among indigenous Australians. Wider than that, however, it has an important moral dimension to it, as cricket has the opportunity to be a force for inclusiveness in Australian society.

Brightly fades the Don

Sir Donald Bradman had achieved immortality before his death on 25 February, 2001. As a batsman, he set standards of achievement and dominance by which all others will be measured, and after he retired from the field he gave a significant portion of his life to the administration of the game. His long life ensured that these qualities would make him a venerable and venerated elder figure both in the world of cricket and in Australian society. In May 2001, John Carroll, in one of the Alfred Deakin Lectures devoted to exploring what is distinctive in the Australian people, argued that Bradman has been our one national hero. This heroic status changed him from the boy from Bowral into a figure through whom we could explore what it means to be Australian, crystallised in the fact that the post office box number of the national broadcaster is Bradman's Test batting average. We stand in his debt for the richness of his talents, his tough-minded modesty and the breadth of his influence on Australian life.

CRICKET'S SUPERMAN

By CHARLES DAVIS

The commonly held view in cricket – that statistics can never give us a complete picture of a player – contains more than a grain of truth, and has remained relevant well into this computer age. But there are occasions where statistics, properly handled, can reveal more about the great players than is normally recognised. Anyone wishing to argue for the fundamental importance of statistics in cricket need go no further than the unique career of Donald George Bradman. Bradman was a man of many admirable qualities, but it is his achievements as a batsman which truly set him apart: to define his uniqueness, we must turn to the stats.

Statisticians have devoted enormous energy into analysing Bradman's career, none more so than B. J. Wakley, whose *Bradman the Great* examined, over 300 pages, every first-class innings of the Don. The challenge for modern statisticians is to tease out an instructive story from this mass of detail. What new can be said about the career of Don Bradman?

In an ever-expanding world of first-class and Test cricket, Bradman's most extreme one-off records have been whittled away. (There are still a few major records where his name tops the list, such as his Test series record of 974 runs in 1930.) But when it comes to measuring batting prowess through averages, the Don remains peerless. His Test average of 99.94, and the huge gap between this and any other player's, must be known to every true-blue Australian cricket fan. His average in other first-class matches, at 93.6, is lower, and this is a little surprising, given that Australian first-class bowling was not especially strong in this period. Wakley comments that in lesser matches Bradman frequently threw his wicket away (or tried to) after reaching high scores. In one sense Bradman's abilities sometimes made him too big for his sport, in that his huge scores often generated far more runs than were needed. In such a high-scoring era, there were exceptions, such as the match where he scored 349 runs (124 and 225) only to finish on the losing side, but in general a big century from Bradman put paid to the opposition.

Bradman's double-centuries in Tests and non-Tests follow different patterns. In lesser matches, the pattern is often of remorseless acceleration, with runs after 200 coming more than 50 per cent faster than his first 50. This is accompanied by an increasing number of chances dropped and catches taken. By contrast, in Tests Bradman usually remained much more circumspect when in the batting stratosphere, with far less acceleration when well set. Bradman sixes were rarities – in Tests he hit just six, or about 0.5 per cent of his runs – but his ability to hit fours, 40 per cent of his runs, was superior to his contemporaries. The modern standards are more like 4 to 5 per cent from sixes and 45 to 50 per cent from fours.

Double-centuries in abundance were the hallmark of Bradman's career. His total of 12 Test double-centuries is one of his most formidable records. Even in an age where Tests are two or three times more frequent than they once were, no modern player has scored even half as many. If we ignore smaller unbeaten innings, Bradman reached 200 in 17 per cent of his Test innings, and 100 in 38 per cent. Only a dozen other batsmen in history have ever hit centuries as often as Bradman reached 200.

It is surprising to find that in spite of his reputation and steely determination never to loft the ball, Bradman fell to catches more often than most of his contemporaries. In Tests 56 per cent of his dismissals were catches: the standard in those days was 45 to 50 per cent. (In fact, an outstanding technique provides better protection against being bowled than being caught.) Bradman made minimal demands on Lady Luck. According to Wakley, only six of his 29 Test centuries included missed chances in the first 100 runs. Even if all the chances Bradman offered had been taken, his average would still have been 78. About 80 per cent of Bradman's centuries were chanceless in the first 100; compare this to the modern pattern of about 60 to 65 per cent.

The profusion of Bradman double-centuries has led, understandably, to the idea that he had a special ability to carry on to huge scores. In one sense this is true, but it is really just an inevitable outcome of his extraordinary ability. Bradman's "century average" in Tests, that is the number of runs he was likely to add after reaching 100, was 108.4 (Table 1). This is the highest on record, of course, but Bradman's lead in this department is much less than might be expected.

Table 1: Highest Test Century Averages

	100s	100 Avge
D. G. Bradman (Australia)	29	108.4
F. M. M. Worrell (West Indies)	9	105.0
W. R. Hammond (England)	22	99.0
D. L. Amiss (England)	11	97.4
Zaheer Abbas (Pakistan)	12	95.8
A. Flower (Zimbabwe)	*9*	*86.3*
D. M. Jones (Australia)	11	82.7
V. T. Trumper (Australia)	8	77.8
G. S. Sobers (West Indies)	26	77.5
B. C. Lara (West Indies)	*15*	*75.1*
E. R. Dexter (England)	9	73.7
S. R. Waugh (Australia)	*25*	*71.7*
Javed Miandad (Pakistan)	23	71.3
L. Hutton (England)	19	71.1
Hanif Mohammad (Pakistan)	12	69.4

100 Avge = number of runs beyond 100 divided by number of dismissals.
Minimum 8 Test centuries. Current careers in italics.

We can see, from the fact that his century average is only slightly higher than his overall average, that Bradman's superior ability to concentrate was something he applied from early in his innings, not just after reaching 100. If we look at this aspect more closely, it can reveal a little more about Bradman the player; it suggests that psychological dominance was a critical part of Bradman's achievements. Bradman's likelihood of getting out changed in an unusual way as his innings progressed, quite different than for any other batsman.

For scores below about 15, his chance of dismissal was still within the range of other great batsmen. Jack Hobbs, for example, was more reliable at reaching double figures. Once set, however, Bradman's chance of dismissal plummeted, and above a score of 50 he is way ahead of anyone else in Test history. Specifically, Bradman's chance of dismissal before his next run stayed constant at about 0.5 per cent, whether his score was 50, 100 or 150. No other batsman in history has approached this, and for the typical top Test batsman the rate is closer to 1.5 per cent. It is only at scores above 150 that Bradman's dismissal rate begins to rise and return to the mortal realm, unlike most other top batsmen who enjoy reduced dismissal chances above 150. The fact that Bradman's chance of dismissal is so low, and constant, specifically between 50 and 150, suggests a psychological factor. This is supported by some statements from opposing captains (such as George Grant and "Gubby" Allen) to the effect that they expected the "customary" century from Bradman, and once he looked like getting one they preferred to focus on the other batsmen while he went about it.

Further evidence comes from the only two series where Bradman did not enjoy psychological dominance: 1928-29 (before he established his reputation) and 1932-33 (Bodyline). Bradman exceeded a score of 40 in these two series just as often as he did in all his other Tests, but he did not reach 150 once. In short, his scoring looks much like that of a typical superior batsman. His psychological dominance over bowlers in other series appears to have applied only to good batting conditions, and may also explain his almost complete failure to score well on poor pitches. Pick out the six worst pitches he had to bat on, pitches which are rare to non-existent today, and Bradman's total is just 27 runs. Without these innings, his average would have been 109!

Bradman could not have exploited his dominance over opposing bowlers if he did not possess great reserves of mental strength. This strength is manifested in aspects of his personality which have been often remarked on: his self-reliance, his semi-reclusive nature, and the social distance he maintained from colleagues. It was also shown in his return to Tests after World War II. By convincingly outscoring, in spite of his advancing years and health problems, a talented and successful new generation of Australian batsmen, Bradman demonstrated that he was more than a freak product of a single era.

One critical area, which until now has resided more in the realm of anecdote than statistics, is Bradman's scoring speed. Modern players who read accounts of the 309 runs in one day (105 before lunch) on the way to 334 at Leeds in 1930 would be forgiven for thinking that such records are completely unassailable. But these feats should always be considered in the light of prevailing over-rates. On that day in Leeds, Bradman faced up to 50 per cent more balls (over 350) than any modern player could expect in a single day. This is not to denigrate the feat – the modern equivalent, about 220 runs, is still vanishingly rare. But players today can sometimes match Bradmanesque speeds. When Mark Taylor scored 103 before lunch during his 334 not out at Peshawar in 1998-99, it attracted little notice, mainly because the session lasted three hours. Surprisingly, though, Taylor actually required fewer balls (about 140) than Bradman's pre-lunch century (154 balls).

There is enough information available now to make a reliable estimate of scoring speeds for nearly all major Test batsmen; the fastest average speeds are listed in Table 2.

Table 2: Highest Test Career Scoring Speeds

	Runs/ 100 balls	Batting Average	Career Runs	Coverage
Kapil Dev (India)	79	31.1	5,248	75%
A. C. Gilchrist (Australia)	75	47.4	994	100%
M. W. Tate (England)	70	25.5	1,198	62%
I. V. A. Richards (West Indies)	69	50.0	8,542	84%
V. T. Trumper (Australia)	67	39.0	3,163	96%
S. M. Patil (India)	66	36.9	1,588	81%
J. M. Gregory (Australia)	65	37.0	1,146	99%
S. T. Jayasuriya (Sri Lanka)	64	39.2	3,604	97%
L. R. D. Mendis (Sri Lanka)	64	31.6	1,329	58%
K. Srikkanth (India)	62	29.9	2,062	69%
I. D. S. Smith (New Zealand)	62	25.6	1,815	99%
S. J. McCabe (Australia)	62	48.2	2,748	100%
D. G. Bradman (Australia)	61	99.9	6,996	100%
R. S. Kaluwitharana (Sri Lanka)	61	27.2	1,629	100%
B. C. Lara (West Indies)	61	47.7	6,533	100%
I. T. Botham (England)	60	33.5	5,200	96%
C. G. Macartney (Australia)	60	41.8	2,131	98%

Qualification: 990 career runs.
Coverage = percentage of career for which time information is available. Where information on the number of balls faced is not available, scoring speeds have been estimated using times and over-rates.

Table 2 is based on an analysis of about 400 major Test batsmen since 1894. This is one major statistic where Bradman does not dominate, but still there are only a handful of important specialist batsmen above him. Only Viv Richards has ever scored faster than Bradman while still achieving an average of 50.

There is evidence that Bradman developed a scoring speed which suited him best. His early innings, including his 118 on first-class debut, were not especially fast, and his breakthrough innings, 340 not out in 488 minutes (off about 500 balls) against Victoria in 1928-29, remained his longest innings. After this he quickly acquired a greater confidence in his ability to score rapidly but safely, culminating in his world record 452 not out in only 415 minutes the following season. All the time he maintained a determination to play within the limits of specific circumstances. The only sustained period where his sense of discipline deserted him was during the early part of the 1934 tour of England. In 19 innings he scored only one century, yet his scoring speed was 20 per cent faster than normal (the century was scored at Jessopian speed – 160 in 124 minutes), and he was out caught in 76 per cent of his dismissals. Once back on track, he controlled his hitting and was invulnerable once again, and scored a then record 625 runs in the last two Tests (304, 244 and 77 – a record since broken by Graham Gooch).

Bradman's scoring depended little on location; any preference or dislike for particular grounds, with the possible exception of Leeds, can be put down mainly to chance variability. He said he liked batting at the SCG, even though he averaged "only" 58 in Tests there: he had no problems in other first-class matches at the SCG, the site of his 452 not out. He was unfazed in any way by English conditions: his average and scoring rate there (96 and 42 runs an hour in all matches) was much the same as in Australia (95 and 43 runs an hour). Overall, his scoring rate was unaffected by the timeless nature of Tests in Australia, and although he did sometimes slow down in Ashes Tests at home, he made up for it in Tests against other countries.

In Australia, it was in Tests against South Africa (1931-32) and India (1947-48) that Bradman was at his most irresistible. His averages of 201.5 and 178.4 respectively in those series are, by far, the two highest ever recorded for series of four or more Tests. The South African bowlers, who otherwise were quite competitive against the Australians (as they had been the previous year against England), were at a loss against a Bradman at the peak of his powers: he scored almost as many runs as the next three best batsmen put together. Sixteen years later, the Indians were similarly overawed. After scoring 156 and 172 in lead-up games, Bradman scored 185 in the First Test at Brisbane, and in doing so achieved one of the rarest, and rarely recognised, feats in Tests, by scoring more runs in one innings than the entire opposing team in both (58 and 98).

Test cricket has grown and changed, bringing persistent questions as to how the greats of yesteryear would actually perform today. This is a major topic in itself. Usually the questions are regarded as unresolved, but it turns out that the stats do have something to say on the matter. It is possible to calculate a set of adjustment factors which allow for changes in standard of opposition, cricket practices and conditions (a detailed explanation of this, and a comparison with other sports, is given in my book *The Best of the Best*). The resulting averages bring down some players from the high-scoring 1930s and 1940s, and help those from the 1890s and 1900s, when pitches were worse, and current players, who on average face tougher opposition (Table 3).

Table 3: Test Batting Averages Adjusted for Strength of Opposition and Historical Changes

		Tests	Runs	Original Average	Standardised Average
D. G. Bradman (Aus)	1928–1948	52	6,996	99.9	84.5
R. G. Pollock (SAf)	1963–1970	23	2,256	61.0	58.9
G. A. Headley (WI)	1930–1954	22	2,190	60.8	58.2
S. R. Tendulkar (Ind)	*1989–*	*82*	*6,720*	*56.9*	*57.9*
G. S. Sobers (WI)	1954–1974	93	8,032	57.8	56.6
F. S. Jackson (Eng)	1893–1905	20	1,415	48.8	56.1
J. B. Hobbs (Eng)	1908–1930	61	5,410	57.6	55.5
K. F. Barrington (Eng) ...	1955–1968	82	6,806	58.7	55.5
R. S. Dravid (Ind)	*1996–*	*41*	*3,473*	*53.4*	*55.5*
C. L. Walcott (WI)	1948–1960	44	3,798	56.7	53.8
K. S. Ranjitsinhji (Eng) ..	1896–1902	15	989	45.0	53.3
E. D. Weekes (WI)	1948–1958	48	4,455	58.6	52.3
H. Sutcliffe (Eng)	1924–1935	54	4,555	60.7	52.1
L. Hutton (Eng)	1937–1955	79	6,971	56.7	51.8
F. A. Iredale (Aus)	1894–1899	14	807	36.7	51.7
G. S. Chappell (Aus)	1970–1984	88	7,110	53.9	51.7
A. Flower (Zim)	*1992–*	*50*	*3,721*	*51.0*	*51.2*
B. C. Lara (WI)	*1990–*	*80*	*6,533*	*47.7*	*50.5*
F. M. M. Worrell (WI) ...	1948–1963	51	3,860	49.5	50.3
S. R. Waugh (Aus)	*1985–*	*135*	*8,965*	*50.9*	*49.9*
Javed Miandad (Pak)	1976–1993	124	8,832	52.6	49.8

Qualification: batted in 10 Tests to May 2001.

Table 3 is by no means the final word on batting greatness, but it shows that whichever way you look at careers, there is an enormous gap between Bradman and everyone else. The Don loses 15 per cent of his average in this analysis but remains unrivalled. When the analysis is extended to other sports, the uniqueness of the Don takes on another dimension. No other major sport has ever had a figure equivalent to Don Bradman. Let that be testament enough.

	Tests	First-class
Matches	52	234
Runs	6,996	28,067
Innings	80	338
Not out	10	43
Average	99.9	95.1
300+	2	6
200+	12	37
100+	29	117
50–99	13	69
Ducks	6	16
Minutes batted	11,360	39,600
Runs per hour	37	43
Runs per 100 balls	61	n/a
Average minutes to 100	165	143

AUSTRALIA HOLDS ICC TEST CHAMPIONSHIP

Australia were officially confirmed as the best team in Test match cricket when their captain, Steve Waugh, was presented with the ICC Test Championship trophy at Edgbaston on July 4, 2001. The new trophy is awarded to the country at the head of the ICC Test Championship, which was introduced at the start of the England–Pakistan series in May. Australia tops the table with an average of 1.62 points from its 13 completed series, followed by South Africa (1.47 from 15 series) and England (1.14 from 14 series).

Waugh commented: "Since the game began people have debated which the best Test side is at any one time. The introduction of this league table, coupled with the ICC's ten-year tours programme, means we will now get a definitive answer to that question. It's great to see the traditional form of the game getting its due reward and I hope the Championship will help ensure Test cricket retains its status as the purest form of the game."

The table, updated at the conclusion of the drawn series between Zimbabwe and India in July 2001, shows:

	Test Matches	Series Played	Won	Lost	Drawn	Points Average
Australia	13	10	2	1	21	1.62
South Africa	15	10	3	2	22	1.47
England	14	7	5	2	16	1.14
Sri Lanka	13	5	5	3	13	1.00
New Zealand	15	6	7	2	14	0.93
West Indies	12	5	6	1	11	0.92
India	13	3	6	4	10	0.77
Pakistan	15	3	7	5	11	0.73
Zimbabwe	13	2	9	2	6	0.46
Bangladesh	1	0	1	0	0	–

SIR DONALD BRADMAN

Born: August 27, 1908, Cootamundra, New South Wales
Died: February 25, 2001, Kensington Park, South Australia

By PHILIP DERRIMAN

It was to be expected after Sir Donald Bradman's death that Australia's newspapers and television channels would outdo themselves with tributes, given his special place in the nation's life, but nobody could have foreseen the extraordinary response to his death in the rest of the cricket world. In England, where Bradman's supremacy as a batsman used to be acknowledged only grudgingly, the obituaries were long and effusive, and more than one writer was prepared to argue that Bradman was unique not merely in cricket but in world sport as a whole. *The Times*'s Simon Barnes, for instance, noting that nobody else had dominated his or her sport as Bradman had dominated cricket, wrote that there was a genuine case for declaring Bradman "the greatest player of any sport that ever plied his trade".

It was the *degree* of Bradman's superiority, of course, which made, and has kept, him so famous. For an individual to be acknowledged, almost universally, as the best-ever in a sport is rare enough. What sets Bradman apart, though, is not merely that he was the best but that he was so much better than everyone else – that, as the England bowler Bill Bowes once described it, he was "better from the ankles up". The scorebooks confirm that he was, and so do the first-hand accounts of those who played with and against him, virtually all of whom, it seems, regarded him as being in a class of his own. Unfortunately, those contemporaries never quite managed to identify the secret of his success. We still do not really know how this small, entirely self-taught cricketer from a country town managed to out-perform all others in the world by a staggering margin. Now that Bradman and most of his contemporaries are gone, perhaps we never will.

The figures prove the case. As well as averaging 99.94 in Tests, Bradman averaged 110.19 in Sheffield Shield matches and 95.14 in all first-class cricket. He scored 12 double- or triple-centuries in Tests, one per 6.7 innings, and he scored a Test century every 2.8 visits to the crease. Yet these statistics and others like them have

Glenn McGrath

PURA CUP CRICKETER OF THE YEAR

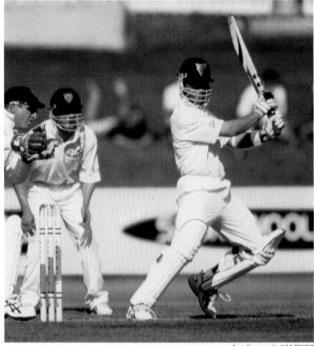

Sean Garnsworthy/ALLSPORT

Jamie Cox

QUEENSLAND'S CUP

Darren England/ALLSPORT

Queensland captain Stuart Law holds the Pura Cup aloft after his team's second successive final victory over Victoria on March 27 at The Gabba, Brisbane. Queensland's bowlers dominated the match, but with 87 to win on the final day they suffered a minor collapse to create a period of high tension. Law steadied the ship in his retirement match and the Bulls won by four wickets.

HAT TRICK

Sean Garnsworthy/ALLSPORT

Glenn McGrath is swamped by team-mates after taking a hat-trick and his 301st Test wicket in the Second Test against the West Indies at the WACA Ground, Perth on December 1, 2000. McGrath's 15,090th Test delivery was fended by West Indies captain Jimmy Adams to Justin Langer at short leg, and Adams followed Sherwin Campbell and Brian Lara to the pavilion.

BATTING HEROICS

Shaun Botterell/ALLSPORT

Matthew Hayden plays his signature sweep shot during his double-century innings in the Third Test against India at Chennai, from March 18, won by India. The powerfully built Queensland veteran renewed his career with a three-match series total of 542 runs at an average of 109.80.

Shaun Botterell/ALLSPORT

V. V. S. Laxman, India's saviour in the Second Test with his marathon score of 280 at Eden Gardens, Kolkata, from March 11. Laxman combined with Rahul Dravid (180) in a partnership of 364, which took the Indian score to 629 and led to a victory that evened the series.

GILCHRIST'S FIREWORKS

Hamish Blair/ALLSPORT

Australian wicket-keeper Adam Gilchrist's spectacular innings have made him the most feared late-order batsman in modern cricket. The vice-captain celebrates his century during his innings of 122 in the First Test against India at Mumbai, starting on February 27, won by Australia by 171 runs.

Shaun Botterell/ALLSPORT

Glenn McGrath and Jason Gillespie, spearheading the Australian attack against the West Indies, India and then England, have proved to be a pace combination on a level with the best Australia has produced. They discuss their craft during training on the tour of India.

Lyndon Howe

Australian captain Stephen Waugh and Prime Minister of Australia, John Howard, with a painting of the Aboriginal team that visited England in 1860, on display during the match in Canberra between the Prime Minister's XI and the ATSIC (Aboriginal and Torres Strait Islander Commission) Chairman's XI. An under-19 Aboriginal team toured England in 2001.

400 FOR WARNE

Hamish Blair/ALLSPORT

In the Fourth Test at the Oval in England on August 25, Australian leg spinner Shane Warne became the first Australian, and only the sixth player, to pass 400 Test wickets. At the start of his England Test campaign he takes the wicket of Ashley Giles in the First Test at Edgbaston, Birmingham.

been reproduced so often that they have ceased to convey to people how astonishing Bradman's record really is. An alternative is to browse through the first volume of Ray Webster's *First-Class Cricket in Australia Volume 1*, which contains scorecards and match reports of every first-class match in the country up to World War II. As you turn the pages, match by match, and read of one stupendous Bradman innings after another, hardly any of which rate the slightest mention in the various accounts of Bradman's career, you begin to grasp the scale of his accomplishments and to understand the fantastic appeal he had to spectators wherever he played.

Inevitably, Bradman's batting methods have come to be analysed in retrospect. Greg Chappell has taken a special interest in his unusual stance and backlift, believing they may have been the key to his marvellous balance, while in England a coach named Tony Shillinglaw has begun teaching Bradman's technique to young English batsmen. He is convinced that Bradman's "unorthodox" methods should be accepted as the model for all batsmen to follow. Behind all this is the quite reasonable belief that, to do what he did, Bradman must have tapped some special, hitherto unknown source of performance, both mental and mechanical.

Whatever the secret of Bradman's success may have been, Bowral was its origin. When Bradman arrived in Sydney, aged 18, to play grade cricket in 1926-27, he already had in him the makings of the world-beater he was to become, for otherwise he could hardly have made the Australian XI barely two years later. So Bowral must be the key. Bradman's parents, George and Emily, moved the family there in 1911 from Cootamundra, where Don had been born on August 27, 1908. Both parents were from farming stock, so although Don grew up in town his background was rural: the Bradmans were essentially "bushies". The Bowral-based historian Rodney Cavalier, now the SCG Trust's chairman, rejects the idea that young Bradman made it to the top against the odds. On the contrary, having made a close study of Bradman's childhood he believes that the Bradman home in Bowral – a stable, loving, disciplined, sports-oriented household in a country town mad on cricket – was an absolutely ideal place for the future batting star, cricket administrator and stockbroker to spend his formative years.

It seems everyone who played with or against Bradman or who got to know him outside cricket was fascinated by his personality. For good or ill, Bradman was a special character. All who came in contact with him felt he was different, and the essence of that difference was that he seemed to deal with things as they really were and did not allow emotion to affect his judgment of them. He was the supremely practical man. This wasn't a particularly endearing trait, for it could make Bradman seem blunt, inflexible and unfeeling, but it was undoubtedly an important part of the psychology that he applied to his cricket. If he abounded in confidence at the batting crease, it was because he *knew* he had every bowler's measure and was not distracted by baseless self-doubts. As the writer Evan Whitton concluded, he wasn't an enigma, as many have suggested, but actually quite a simple man with "a remarkable capacity to focus on essentials".

Bradman's singular personality revealed itself early on in the now famous boyhood pastime he devised for himself: hitting a golf ball against a brick tank-stand with a cricket stump. It was a game only an unusually self-contained boy, happy with his own company, would wish to play. It was also a game which only a boy with uncanny ball sense would attempt. Yet by far the most remarkable feature of Bradman's early development as a batsman is that he didn't play cricket regularly until he was 17 – that is, until the summer of 1925-26. Before that, he had played occasionally for Bowral, but tennis was the sport he concentrated on. Now, having at last devoted himself to cricket, Bradman was an immediate and spectacular success. His massive scoring for Bowral that summer, including the first triple-century ever made in the district, earned him a trial in the nets in Sydney at the start of the following summer, 1926-27, which in turn led to his recruitment as a first-grader by the St George club. A season later he was in the New South Wales side, and a season after that in the Australian.

The speed of Bradman's promotion was a credit to the selectors of the day, who recognised his potential some time before it was generally obvious. Bradman made the Test side in the 1928-29 Ashes series, aged 20, on the strength of good performances in first-class cricket (at this stage he had scored 976 first-class runs at an average of 69.71), but it cannot be said he had taken the cricket world by storm, which explains why, after he failed in the First Test, he was demoted to 12th man for the second. Reinstated for the Third Test, he scored a century – and he scored another century in the Fifth. The Bradman run machine was moving into top gear. Just before the season ended, he scored 340 not out against Victoria.

Then, half-way through the next season, he scored a world-record 452 not out against Queensland. Nobody now could doubt that a rare talent had appeared on the scene.

That innings of 452 not out in January 1930, followed by Bradman's fantastically successful tour of England the same year, where he scored 974 runs in the Tests at an average of 139.14, elevated him to superstar status. He became a national obsession, causing one English journalist to comment that the whole of Australia had gone Bradman mad. His mere presence at the crease, according to an analysis of 1930s attendances by the historian Richard Cashman, had the effect of almost doubling the crowd. He was the ideal hero: young, modest, clean-cut and prodigiously successful. Against the visiting South Africans in 1931-32 his average in the Tests actually topped 200. It was obvious no team could hope to beat Australia when Bradman was in the side – unless, of course, some novel means of stifling him could be found.

Bodyline was the means. Bradman's average in that infamous Ashes series of 1932-33 was reduced to 56.57 and England won. Bradman's high-risk method of trying to counter the bodyline attack, stepping back and trying to slam the ball to the largely vacant offside field, was apparently resented by others in the side, who felt that as Australia's premier batsman he ought to have given a lead to his less talented team-mates by batting in an orthodox manner. But Bradman may have had another reason for using the tactics he did. Lex Marinos, one of the directors of the *Bodyline* television series, suspected that, in Bradman's mind, to bat conventionally against bodyline was to legitimise it. Instead, by adopting an outlandish approach, he was declaring the England bowling to be outlandish too. However that may be, Bradman did play some astonishing strokes, one of which, a cross-bat smash of a Harold Larwood bumper, is possibly the most memorable of all Bradman newsreel clips.

Bodyline proved to be only a temporary setback. Cricket returned to normal and Bradman resumed his mammoth scoring. He had married his childhood sweetheart Jessie Menzies in 1932, which probably made him think harder about life outside cricket, and in 1934 he moved to Adelaide to join a stockbroking firm. It seems he would rather have stayed in Sydney, for after the Adelaide opportunity arose a friend approached New South Wales cricket officials on his behalf, asking if they couldn't do something to keep him, which meant finding him an equally attractive job in Sydney. In one of

Australian cricket's greatest administrative blunders, the New South Wales Cricket Association refused to do anything, and Bradman left. Two years later he became Australia's captain. In his first series in the job, 1936-37, Australia lost the first two Tests to England, after which Bradman peeled off a string of big scores and led his team to a 3-2 series win.

Nobody in Bradman's day considered him a graceful or stylish batsman, yet the newsreels show he was an exceptionally loose-limbed individual who possessed a wonderful freedom of movement, best exemplified by the ease with which he spun around while playing the pull shot, a favourite stroke, often ending up facing fine-leg. When you watch newsreel film of Bradman the overall impression he creates is one of well-oiled co-ordination – a "fluidity of movement", as Peter Roebuck described it after watching a television show on Bradman. He looks light, nimble, decisive, balanced, controlled. Then there is the extraordinary abandon with which he moved inside and outside the batting crease. In countless photos he can be seen a metre or more down the pitch, driving on the run. As Jack Fingleton noted, Bradman never hesitated to go down the pitch because he never, ever, counted on missing a ball. It is hard to think of a single photo of any modern batsman in a similar pose.

Bradman's appointment as captain in 1936 brought to a head a smouldering resentment against him within a section of the team. By all accounts, he had never been popular with fellow players, and no doubt jealousy had a lot to do with this. Among some players, most notably Bill O'Reilly and Fingleton, the hostility ran deeper. To some extent this can be explained by the fact that they were Catholics and that Bradman was a Mason at a time when Australian society as a whole – and cricket in particular – was afflicted by sectarian discord, but, certainly in O'Reilly's case, the ill-feeling probably had more to do with personalities. As O'Reilly once described it, he and Bradman were as compatible as a cat and a fox terrier.

Bradman was 31 when World War II began and, presumably, on the downside of his career. At this stage he had played 57 Test innings, scored 21 centuries and averaged 97.94. There seemed every chance later that this would remain his final Test record, for as the war dragged on and he grew older and less robust in health (he was invalided out of the Army with fibrositis in 1941 after serving briefly as a PT instructor) it became less likely he would play big cricket again. But, when the war finally ended, although he was now in his late thirties, he could not resist returning. He was to lead Australia in three more Test series, two against England and one against India.

The post-war Bradman was not nearly as dynamic a batsman as the Bradman of old. Bill O'Reilly wrote that he had lost his killer instinct. Yet he still scored Test centuries almost as often as before – eight of them in his 23 post-war Test innings for an average of 105.72. The difference now was that his centuries no longer tended to become double-centuries. The teams he led consisted largely of new, younger players, and it seems Bradman got on better with them than with the pre-war players of his own vintage. He finished his international career on a high note in 1948 by leading a powerful Australian team on a tour of England without losing a match. A few months later, in January 1949, he was knighted, and two months after that he bowed out as a player altogether.

He did not bow out of cricket, however. He was an Australian selector from 1936-37 to 1971-72, except for one season, 1952-53, when his son John was ill. He was a member of the Board of Control, later called the Australian Cricket Board, from 1945 to 1980, apart from two years in the late 1940s, and he was the board's chairman from 1960 to 1963 and from 1969 to 1972. Long after that, he remained a force in the game and was regularly consulted by the administrators in charge. Indeed, he is said to have remained, if reluctantly, influential in the game's affairs until the 1990s.

Lady Bradman died in 1997. They had three children – a son who died as an infant in 1936; John, born in 1939; and Shirley, born in 1941, who suffered from mild cerebral palsy. In 1972 John changed his name to Bradsen to escape the Bradman fame, but by the late 1990s he had been fully reconciled with his father and later changed his name back to Bradman. He played a leading role in his father's nationally televised memorial service.

To the end, Sir Donald guarded his privacy with as much determination as he had once guarded his wicket, invariably refusing requests for interviews and public appearances. On the other hand, he was an active correspondent who willingly exchanged letters even with people he knew only distantly, some of whom were surprised at the candour with which he expressed views on quite contentious matters.

After some initial reservations, Sir Donald supported and took a keen interest in the Bradman Museum at Bowral, whose opening he attended in 1989. It was his last trip to his home town. After he died on February 25, 2001, it was revealed he had chosen the museum's environs, close to the oval where he played as a boy for the Bowral XI, as the final resting place of his ashes.

HARBHAJAN JOINS AN ELITE GROUP

India's turbaned off-spinner Harbhajan Singh took 28 wickets in the last two Tests against Australia in March 2001. After capturing 7/123 (including a hat-trick) and 6/73 in the bewilderingly fluctuating Kolkata Test, he tightened the screws in the Chennai thriller by bagging 7/133 and 8/84.

How many bowlers have captured more than 28 wickets in two consecutive Tests?

Only one bowler, another off-spinner Jim Laker, had exceeded this number. For England against Australia in 1956, Laker took 5/58 and 6/55 in Leeds and in the next Test in Manchester had marvellous figures of 9/37 and all 10/53. Thus he had pouched 30 Australian scalps (including 19 on a trot) in two successive Tests, giving them a dose of 'Lakeritis'.

Two bowlers have taken 27 wickets in two consecutive Tests. They are: George Lohmann (England v South Africa in Port Elizabeth and Johannesburg in 1895-96) and Sydney Barnes (England v South Africa at Durban and Johannesburg in 1913-14).

In that Port Elizabeth Test, Lohmann bagged 7/38 and an incredible 8/7 (including a hat-trick) and followed up with hauls of 9/28 and 3/43 in the following Test in Johannesburg. Barnes was equally devastating against the same opponents 18 years later with figures of 5/57 and 5/48 in Durban and 8/56 and 9/103 in Johannesburg.

Thus out of four bowlers with 27 or more scalps in two consecutive Tests, Harbhajan is second on the list. – KERSI MEHER-HOMJI

THE DON

A EULOGY
DELIVERED AT THE MEMORIAL SERVICE FOR
SIR DONALD BRADMAN ON SUNDAY MARCH 25, 2001

By RICHIE BENAUD

It's not quite perfect outside, I guess. Rain coming down. A bit of a dodgy pitch. Wind blowing. But I reckon he would have handled it with all his consummate skill, no matter what it might provide out there.

There is a crowd out there filled with memories. The bowling changes here at the Cathedral end have been many and varied. We've now got an ageing leg-spinner, and I think the Don might have welcomed that.

He was the most famous of them all at a time when despair ruled Australia because of the Great Depression. Seventy years later 100 selectors from around the world nominated the five greatest players of the century. The Don received 100 votes. Not far away from him was that finest of all-rounders, Gary Sobers, who got 90. But 100 out of 100 is pretty good.

When I was six years old Bradman was captain of Australia in the concrete storeroom at Jugiong where I played Test matches. When I was ten he was still captain on the back verandah at Parramatta where he led and won and was absolutely brilliant in all those Test matches I used to play against England. I wasn't alone, in that thousands and thousands of other youngsters around Australia played their Test matches like that – Bradman and McCabe made all the runs and then O'Reilly and Grimmett bowled out England every time. Wondrous days.

It wasn't just cricket. It was family too, and I'm very conscious of John and Shirley with their memories of their father. In recent sad times I'm conscious of the way in which Greta and Tom have talked of their grandparents, and with all of them their love and respect for a great lady in Jessie.

When he first came under notice as a cricketer he was playing such good tennis that there was some thought that he would have to make a decision. When he was chosen in the combined country side to go to Sydney the decision was made for him. Percy Westbrook, his boss at the time, said he could have a week off to do one or the other, but not both.

And a year or so later, when he was thinking of coming up to Sydney to play club cricket, my own club, which was then known as Central Cumberland, had the opportunity of signing him. Not with the same sort of fat contract you might get these days: we had to pay his train fare from Bowral to Sydney and back to Bowral. It was around four and sixpence and quite correctly we decided that was far too expensive.

He was also a very good golfer. He shot his age for many years, but once he was dropped to B Grade at the club he played at in Adelaide. He made it known very quickly to the handicapper and to the chief executive of the club that he had never been B-grade at anything in his life. He won the silver medal the following week and was whizzed back up to A Grade.

I was lucky to be around as captain when that extraordinary series of Test matches was played against West Indies in 1960-61. One of the significant happenings in Australian cricket came about at the start of that series when, the night before the first day of the Tied Test, the Don came to me and asked if it would be all right if he came to speak to the team. Now this was a bit strange in those days. They called it protocol way back in 1960, and the players didn't know what it was all about. It was the first time it had ever happened. The gist of his short talk was that he and Jack Ryder and Dudley Seddon, the other two selectors, would be looking in kindly fashion on those cricketers in Australia who played the game in attractive and attacking fashion and thought of the game rather than themselves. The unspoken words were that anyone not wanting to fit in with those plans shouldn't think about giving up their day job.

It was that vision as a selector that I found so outstanding and interesting. A classic example was early in 1963. The phone rang, and it was Don on the other end. He said, "I have got a bit of news for you about your team for the last Test at the SCG. Neil Hawke is playing." I said, "What are you doing that for? Hawkey's quite a good prospect but has done nothing this year." He said, "I know that. And just in case he has an ordinary season next year we are giving him a Test under his belt because we have earmarked him to go to England in 1964." That is what I call vision.

Although he wrote very well on cricket, a variety of experiences over the years made him less than comfortable with journalists. He was certainly an unusual person in that regard, in that he guarded his privacy so much with the media. It was also unusual that he would be part of an Australian Cricket Board that chose a journalist to be their captain. In the early 1960s over a couple of glasses of red he expressed the thought that he and I seemed to be – "out of kilter" was his phrase – we were out of kilter in our relations with the press. That ideally he might have been better to have been more flexible in his time and I might have been better to have been slightly less so in my time.

His classic book *The Art of Cricket* managed to slice through the rhetoric of cricket coaching – no mean feat, I can tell you. It is also quite an achievement to have written a book which is just as good 40 years after it first rolled off the old-fashioned printing presses. When he was on tour in America with Arthur Mailey's team the photograph was taken that is on the front page of the book.

The more important tour was the one he undertook in 1948. That was the one where he was captain of the "Invincibles", and some of those great cricketers are here tonight. He was always of the opinion that it was close to impossible, because of changes in conditions, to judge which was the best-ever cricket team. One thing we can be sure of, though, is that those Invincibles would have given more than a reasonable account of themselves in any contest against any other combination in any era. Three of those – Miller and Morris and Lindwall – were wonderful mentors for me. They did a superb job of trying to get me to think about the game and people and to do the right thing, all in their completely different ways.

Miller underlined for me the fact that it's a good thing never to take oneself too seriously. Back in 1950-51 Freddie Brown had the MCC side out here, and New South Wales were playing South Australia in Adelaide in the Shield game just before the First Test in Brisbane. It was November and as a selector Don was watching the match just 20 yards along to the right where the visitors' dressing room was and still is. "Pancho" Ridings gave us a most awful hammering that day – thrashed us everywhere. We were a very weary bunch at the end of the day, resting in the leather chairs and looking over here to the Cathedral, not saying much. Except I was chirping away. You've got to bear in mind that I had just turned 20 and I knew most of what there was to be known about cricket, so I chirped. I didn't get much response at first but I chirped again. I said to Miller that because Bradman had retired the moment I came into the game it was one of the sorrows of my life that I had never been able to bowl my leg-spinners to him. It was still very hot, about 85 to 90 degrees at that time of the day, and South Australia had just belted their way to four for 374. Nugget never took his eyes off the Cathedral. He didn't turn to me but just looked straight ahead and ruminated for a full two seconds before murmuring: "We all have one lucky break in our lives, son, and that could have been yours."

In the images of the family funeral a few weeks ago there were some memorable moments, sad but memorable. Older people who had been touched by the Depression years and knew Bradman because of that. Younger ones who had seen Don as a sportsman, or might have seen him on Cinesound or Movietone news or in that splendid final interview on television with Ray Martin. I was particularly taken by three things, which to me had a bearing on the fact that he was regarded with affection by old and young.

There were older people standing silently and just looking. There was a youngster, a boy scout, who saluted and held his salute. And then there was what a few people had said to me they thought to be a little irreverent, and that was "Aussie, Aussie, Aussie, oi, oi, oi!" Because he was a sportsman with such vision and because he had a feel for young cricketers – no one ever had a better feel for them; of all the people I have known he wanted to see youngsters get on – I think he would have liked the blending of the modern with the old in that moment with the funeral procession going past. It all marries into something that he used to talk about, that cricket simply is a reflection of life.

In Don's time he only wrote two major articles for *Wisden*. One was in 1939, the other in 1986. They were on precisely the same theme but with different words and at different lengths. They were along the lines that cricket needed to adapt to the quickening tempo of modern life. In the 1986 article he expressed his love for the traditional game, and had he still been with us he would have seen and applauded the magnificent short series recently concluded in India. He added a list of the good things about limited-overs cricket. That it rids the game of the unutterable bore who thinks occupancy of the crease and his own personal aggrandisement are all that matter. He talked of the outstanding fielding and running between wickets of modern-day players in limited-overs cricket and now in Test cricket as well. He said it would seem logical in the future for cricket authorities to introduce arbitration from television cameras for some decisions. There was a lot of head-shaking about that. Some said it was absolute nonsense and would never happen. That was 15 years ago. It simply underlined the fact that he was still ahead of play. He had the most brilliant and incisive mind of anyone I have ever known in cricket.

Above all else he was very much an Aussie. He was an Aussie sportsman and a great sportsman – said by his critics never once to have questioned an umpire's decision. He was a sportsman, and it wasn't just for a few sessions or a few days, it was for all eras and for all sports followers.

Above all else he was a sportsman.

ALISTAIR CAMPBELL'S RECORD

In the Harare Test against Bangladesh in February 2001, Zimbabwean batsmen Alistair Campbell and Andy Flower became the only players to appear for a country in its first 50 Tests, in their case since Zimbabwe's initial Test against India at Harare in 1992-93. As at July 2001, the record is held by Campbell, who has played in all 53 Tests played by Zimbabwe, after Andy Flower (Zimbabwe's first 52 Tests) missed the First Test against West Indies at Bulawayo on July 19 due to an injury.

The record had been held for many years by Imtiaz Ahmed, who appeared in the first 39 Tests played by Pakistan from October 1952 in Delhi to Lord's in June 1962. Next on the list is Grant Flower, who played in Zimbabwe's first 30 Tests before he missed the Harare Test of 1998-99 against India due to a broken finger.

The best such sequence for Australia was by Jack Blackham, who kept wicket in the first 17 Tests played from March 1877 to December 1884. The sequence could have been longer, but all 11 players in the Sydney Test of December 1884, including Blackham, refused to play in the Melbourne Test the following month, demanding 50 per cent of the gate money.

The record for most consecutive Test appearances is held by Australia's Allan Border, 153 Tests from 1978-79 against Pakistan in Melbourne to 1993-94 against South Africa in Durban. He had been dropped after playing his first three Tests against England in 1978-79. – KERSI MEHER-HOMJI

THE AUSTRALIAN HERO

By BRETT HUTCHINS

The dramas played out on the cricket field, the ebb and flow of the action, the victories and defeats all manage to communicate something about the characters involved. Players speak directly to us through their style, demeanour and courage. By his dominance and success, Sir Donald Bradman is the apotheosis of this phenomenon in Australia. He not only allowed people to bask in his reflected glory; he also offered them the opportunity to express something remarkable about their nation.

Heroes and icons do not just reflect the character of a culture – they help to create it. Australians collectively adopt the outstanding talent of an athlete like Cathy Freeman and the wholesome reliability of a musician like Slim Dusty, and use them as defining characteristics of Australianness. In this way, these heroes give shape and form to what it means to be Australian. This is why Don Bradman remains a vital figure for the nation. He is a hero who has played a major role in defining Australia's past, and his continuing prominence and symbolism may also help to shape the future.

Bradman's death served as a reminder of his place in the Australian pantheon. A tidal wave of sentiment engulfed television, radio and newspapers. Headlines announced "Death of a Legend", "The Nation Loses its Hero", and "A Nation Mourns". A heady mixture of obituary, nationalism, nostalgia and history represented the life and times of the Don. Australian rugby captain John Eales believed Bradman's death was so momentous that Australians will always remember where they were the day he died. Prime Minister John Howard made the bold claim that the Don "was the most remarkable figure that Australia has produced in the last 100 years". Bradman appeared to possess more popular historical appeal than Ned Kelly, Simpson, the man with the donkey, and Ginger Meggs combined. The request of John Bradman not to enslave his father with worship had little impact. Sir Don may have been only a cricketer, but he had been entered into the register of sacred Australian history.

Plaudits for the Don were about far more than cricket. Many journalists and cricket writers largely abrogated their responsibility to explain in any depth why he had become a hero of such massive proportions. Instead, endless details of his playing career were recalled and his regard within the cricket community was made clear. The standard explanation for Bradman's stature – that he provided hope in the dark years of the Great Depression and World War II – was trotted out repeatedly. Most commentators offered the truism that the Don was far more than a cricketer, but there was little informed analysis as to why he was a pre-eminent national hero.

Writers attempting to situate Don Bradman within the wider context of Australian culture are all too rare. With varying degrees of success, Gideon Haigh, Irving Rosenwater and Charles Williams have laid some foundations. In seeking to build on their work, I must offer the qualifier: it is impossible to explain Bradman's heroism in the space of an essay. What I aim to do is provide some thought-provoking ideas and arguments as to why the Don captured the Australian imagination.

What does Bradman symbolise, and what does he mean in Australian history and culture? What is it about the Don that allowed him to tap into a vein of popular sentiment and appeal so overwhelmingly to the nation? In seeking to address these questions, I assure the reader that I am not trying to tear down an icon but, rather, trying to provide some balance to the mountain of nostalgic dedications. Bringing perspective to Bradman's place in Australian society and history does as much to honour his memory as any superficial tribute.

A short clarification is required. When I speak of the Bradman myth, I am not claiming that the Don has been fictionalised or that accounts of his career are falsified. The concept of myth signifies that a heroic and praiseworthy image of Bradman has been generally accepted as true that ignores more critical accounts of his life and career. For example, although criticisms of the Don by former Test team-mates such as Jack Fingleton and Bill O'Reilly are on the public record, their critique is more often than not discounted or rejected when an almost super-heroic Bradman is presented in biographies such as Michael Page's *Bradman: The Illustrated Biography* (1983) and Roland Perry's *The Don* (1996). My point is that Page and Perry may offer the preferred version of Bradman's story, but they are not the only accounts available.

Three general points foreground my arguments.

First, it was advantageous that Bradman excelled at cricket, which is regarded as a cornerstone of Australian culture. Unlike football with its various regional loyalties to particular codes, cricket has the largest possible following throughout the land. Furthermore, cricket's lengthy history, strong traditions and affinity for statistical documentation complement its popularity. Historically noteworthy performances and achievements are easily compared, validated and celebrated. The endless discussions of runs, averages and players that are the staple diet of cricket devotees help to give the game its peculiarly rich sense of history. And, of course, Australian people love honouring Australian heroes.

Second, the Don's longevity was another factor in the maintenance of his stature. Bill Brown is now the only surviving Test player who played alongside Bradman before World War II, and those players who were critical of him passed away before the Don. Also, the Bradman Foundation and Museum vigilantly protect his memory and reputation, while most of the articles, books and videos about him can be better described as hagiographical than biographical. Cumulatively, these factors build an almost impregnable line of consensus on who and what Bradman was – a seemingly flawless hero.

Third, the Don's reserved character and regard for privacy made it easy for journalists and others to continue bolstering the Bradman myth. He did not give much away. Bradman's autobiography, *Farewell to Cricket*, with its matter-of-fact prose and minimalist detail, posed more questions than answers. It was a writing style reminiscent of the laconic, no-nonsense manner that is seen as characteristic of many older Australian men. By shying away from the public domain Bradman left a blank space for others to fill with their own perceptions. As Peter Fitzsimons explained, the Don's profile was "low enough that we Australians are able to visit upon him pretty much any kind of personality traits we like – to best suit whatever we think the most admirable – for the most part unfettered by the reality of what he is actually like".

Without one or all of these things – cricket's popularity and traditions and Bradman's longevity and character – the Don may not have become the exemplary icon that he was and still is.

In sport, performances cannot be faked. It is easy to lose sight of the fact that without his incredible scores it would have been impossible for Bradman to transcend the game he played. His landmark Test batting average of 99.94 is the central pillar upon which the Bradman legend stands, and easily exceeds the averages of other batting champions such as Sir Garfield Sobers (57.78) and Graeme Pollock (60.97). Bradman's career statistics make his extraordinary achievements clear to everybody, even for those with no interest in the game, and have made him the reference point for measuring the merits of batsmen throughout history.

At a more fundamental social and cultural level, Bradman's statistical dominance captured the spirit of his age. Technology and productivity increasingly paved the way for national development during the interwar years. The Australian economy experienced a manufacturing production increase of 70 per cent from the start of World War I to the Great Depression, and in the 1930s it more than doubled despite the Depression. Technological and industrial innovations were unfurled with the opening of the Sydney Harbour Bridge and the growth of commercial air travel. It is also estimated that by 1934 there were over one million wireless receivers with the capacity to carry descriptions of Bradman's batting to ever-increasing audiences.

Given the emphasis on production and technology, Bradman's relentless run-getting celebrated the overall mood of social development. The chase for productivity during these years adds to the fascination that his Test average elicits, as he alone possessed the potential to reach the goal of perfection symbolised by the average of 100 runs per innings. Bradman's 99.94 average, falling so tantalisingly short of the target, is a captivating number not only for its unprecedented scale, but also for its imperfection and reflection of human fallibility.

As well as success in their chosen pursuit, heroes must appeal to ideals of national character. Bradman's background as "the boy from Bowral" does this by directly engaging with the Australian fascination for the bush. Rural life is regarded as typically or genuinely Australian in a way that city life can never be. In framing Bradman as a quintessential Australian hero, it is always stressed that the Don is not from the city, but from the country town of Bowral and, according to Geoffrey Blainey, from a time "when Australia was much more rural". He was a boy from the bush who took on the world and not only won, but also dominated. An editorial published in the Sydney *Daily Telegraph* after his death told us that the very sound of his name is "like a whiff of clean country air". Further to this, Phil Tresidder reminded us in an *Inside Edge* magazine special, Bradman: A Tribute, that the Don's story refreshes the egalitarian myth – if the son of a carpenter from "out bush" can make it then surely "the same opportunity exists for every Australian boy". Statements like this align Bradman with a mythical universal Australian experience, and give his heroism abundant cultural power.

With his "typically Australian" country childhood, Bradman takes on the appearance of being both ordinary in his experience – "one of us" – and extraordinary in his ability. He is a hero with the common touch. The image of a young Don hitting a golf ball against the base of a water tank with a cricket stump tells us that this was a champion made in the ubiquitous Australian backyard, not in the specialist scientific training programmes and academies of the present day that are accessible only to a lucky few. The homespun warmth of Bradman's story continued to grow after his death. The Don had planned a symbolic return to his roots by asking that his ashes be scattered at the Bradman Oval in his former home town.

The attraction of Bradman as the boy from Bowral also needs to be understood against the challenges to national identity and character in an era of globalisation. Bradman offers a distinctly comforting image in the face of often upsetting social change as he symbolises and harks back to a seemingly unified and triumphant Australian nation. As emphasised in the 1995 advertising campaign for the breakfast cereal Weet-Bix that used Bradman's image, the Don appeals to our national history and represents an Australian hero who is seen as more organic and healthy than the global idol many Australian children admire, American basketballer Michael Jordan.

The Don's magnetism is also underpinned by the appearance that he was above the common ruck of politics. Bradman rarely offered political opinions in public despite receiving invitations to join each side of Australian politics. Both the Liberal and Labor parties openly and warmly offered dedications to him after his death. This bridge across the political divide helped to construct Bradman's widespread appeal. His name was absent from political disputes, and he was never a lightning rod for activism or dissent.

Fair play and gentlemanly conduct are motifs in reminiscences on the days of amateur cricket, and Bradman is a personification of this bygone era. He said as much when he claimed that he and his counterparts in the 1930s and 1940s "were all amateurs … We played cricket because we loved it, for the fun of the game." This image is especially attractive in an era of professionalism and hyper-commercialisation when money is a driving force for many players, and sponsors and television networks increasingly call the tune. In this world, Bradman stands as a measure for sporting integrity precisely because he is rarely thought of in terms of financial calculation. It has not mattered that Bradman endorsed many products when he played, that he was a successful businessman or that as an administrator he eventually endorsed professionalism. The dominant perception is that the Don played for the "right" reason – love of the game – and that he never succumbed to the temptation of cashing in.

Integrity is thought to be synonymous with Bradman, especially against the background of the international cricket scandals of recent years. Betting scandals involving Hansie Cronje, Salim Malik, Mohammad Azharuddin and even the Australian pair of Shane Warne and Mark Waugh have sullied the reputation of international cricket. By contrast, the years in which Bradman played are depicted as a golden age where morals and respectability held sway and money was of little consequence. The by-product of this golden-age glow is the elevation of Bradman and an idealised cricketing past. As ethics commentator Simon Longstaff says, "Cricket has gone to the dogs. How that comparison must [have] hurt former greats such as Sir Donald Bradman, who helped develop a game that was, at one time, synonymous with the ideal of decency and fair play." Bradman represents the honesty of cricket in the past against the corruption and moral stain affecting cricket now. The more scandalous cricket becomes, the more heroic Bradman becomes.

How will Bradman's heroism be thought of in the future? Generalisations reaffirming that "he was a great man" and an "inspiration to a nation" fail to convey the nuances of Bradman's appeal or the deeper reasons explaining why so many Australians have embraced him. In acknowledging and even celebrating Bradman's valued part of the nation's cultural fabric, it is imperative to place the Don in some cultural and historical context. Hagiography and wallowing in nostalgia are detrimental to a proper understanding of the past, and to an appreciation of Bradman that is respectful without being sycophantic.

The coming challenge for the cricket fraternity and the nation is to justify why Bradman should continue to be thought of as more than just a cricketer. Without level-headed assessment of the Don and his part in defining Australia's national identity, he runs the risk of becoming just a symbol for an older sepia-toned Australia, one that is easily marginalised amid the irresistible promises and uncertainties of globalisation, the information super-highway, and the growing engagement with our neighbours in the Asia–Pacific. Those who write or speak publicly about Bradman need to apply this level-headed assessment to his memory. Another round of blindly worshipping tributes will not tell us anything we do not already know and will fail to demonstrate why the Don should remain a paramount emblem of the nation.

THE RISE AND RISE OF QUEENSLAND CRICKET

By MARTIN ROGERS

The rise and rise of Queensland to a position as the top Pura Cup team in Australia did not occur by accident. Once a familiar object of fond barracking and branded the perennial under-achievers of domestic cricket, they have become a model for the rest after successfully reinventing themselves. From 1995, when John Buchanan famously steered them to a long-awaited first Sheffield Shield in his debut coaching year, Queensland have contested five out of seven state finals, and four times Stuart Law has hoisted the trophy aloft. There are a couple of Mercantile Mutual Cup limited-overs victories in there, too, and by any test Queensland have established themselves as the most consistently successful outfit in the land.

The players, as well as the trappings, are those of an impressively professional organisation in every contemporary sense of the word. The once venerable Brisbane Cricket Ground is now an ultra-modern floodlit arena with a capacity of 37,500, home to arguably the most enduringly excellent playing conditions in Australia as well as a team comfortable at last with all the winning details. The Gabba greyhound track, the old hill, the ramshackle buildings have disappeared, and with them the country town ethos. The general manager, Graham Dixon, presides over an enthusiastic and motivated staff of 36 at Allan Border Field at Albion, developed as the association headquarters, a model of practicality dressed in a fashionably contemporary frock. Following initial reservations, the "Bulls" concept pioneered by Queensland's marketing manager Andrew Blucher has become widely admired and imitated, and the commercial and public face of Queensland cricket is far removed from the old boys' club of the past.

But the most visible revolution has expressed itself on the field – fashioned in committee and selection rooms, the script cut and edited in the video analysis rooms, the philosophies refined in the dressing room and the final product a testimony to the detail which made the seemingly impossible suddenly possible. These days things are so different that it now seems far longer than a decade since Queensland embarked on the most stunning makeover in modern cricket.

Buchanan's methods proved to be as challenging and ground-breaking as his credentials. Instead of the decorated playing career once considered *de rigueur* in any coaching appointment, the professorial Buchanan (seven Shield appearances when the Packer era briefly opened a window of opportunity) showed it was possible to succeed as an expert coach in an area previously considered the preserve of former star names. Even his departure to preside over the record-breaking fortunes of the national team passed almost unnoticed in Queensland as his successor, former rugby league player Bennett King, produced successive Pura Cup victories in his first two seasons. King, previously a Buchanan assistant, boasted playing credentials which went no further than the Australian Under-19s team. Outstanding people skills, sophisticated analysis, and lateral thinking by professional coaches helped bring consistent success where earlier generations of well-intentioned players and administrators had consistently failed.

For one who had followed Essex for most of his life, as I had, coming to Queensland had more than a sense of *déjà vu* about it. Essex, for all their bright and breezy cricket and catalogue of notables, entered the English county championship in 1895 and contrived to avoid winning it, or indeed any trophy, until 1979. Once they broke the curse, they could scarcely stop winning.

To learn on arrival in the Sunshine State that Queensland were still seeking their first Sheffield Shield a mere 60-odd years after they entered the competition, was akin to jumping out of the fire and into the frying pan. It did not take long to discover why they were such consistent under-achievers. Queensland's "maybe tomorrow, she'll be right" optimism could have been imported straight from the Emerald Isle: lovely people, shame about the inability to address tomorrow's challenges today. It's also an Australian and Queensland tradition to play hard and party harder, and while distance blurs accurate assessment of the good old bad old days, some critics believe too many of the principals involved were world-class at managing to drown their disappointments and disguise their shortcomings.

The Queensland cricket hierarchy meanwhile was stereotypical old school – government by big unwieldy committee, much internal strife, plenty of introspection but not a lot of imaginative thinking. History records the great and the good players came and went, indomitable home-grown worthies like Don Tallon, Peter Burge,

Ken 'Slasher' Mackay, Wally Grout, Greg Ritchie and Trevor Hohns and star imports including Bill Brown – even though he was born in the state – Ray Lindwall, Wes Hall, Greg Chappell, Jeff Thomson, Viv Richards, Allan Border and Ian Botham. But too often it seemed there was a distance between the stars and the non-internationals, a gulf between the haves and the have-nots which was by no means exclusive to Queensland. Nevertheless, Queensland perfected it, and a succession of teams composed of ingredients that should have turned out to be irresistible all too often went limp in the middle. Home form was almost invariably good in the opening months of the season, but tradition demanded it should fall away on interstate trips and stay away in the second half of summer after summer.

It needed the chairmanship of Allan Pettigrew, a former Bundaberg journalist and Ministry of Sport official, and the worldly wisdom of Barry Richards to open closed minds. Pettigrew pushed for the appointment as chief executive of the one-time South African great who was at the time coaching the South Australian team. For eight vibrant years Richards was a persuasive and stylish driving force, and it was a further tribute to Pettigrew, who died in 1993 after presiding over an overdue streamlining of the association's management and governing structure, that progress continued seamlessly. John Maclean then John McKnoulty led as chairmen should, and the fresh stewardship of Dr Cam Battersby and his youthful successor Damien Mullins maintained the emphasis on forward planning.

Directors of corporations and companies can remain faceless, but the consequences of their actions are widespread, and possibly the appointment from left field of Buchanan was the ultimate masterstroke of the reconstituted Queensland board. The new beginning also had its makings in the selection room where the bespectacled, studious-looking Max Walters, for eight years chairman of the panel, displayed the rare knack of identifying talent and then being bold enough to support and promote young players. No less importantly, the selectors were game to pension off established performers whose statistics at times belied their inability to give their best when it was most needed. Queensland twice had come achingly close in Shield finals in Sydney in the 1980s, and reached two more there (1990 and 1993) as the new decade dawned, but were thrashed each time. These were false dawns, the thrill of anticipation followed by the nausea of another disappointing failure, all felt as acutely in the press box as elsewhere.

John Benaud, a regular visitor when he was a national selector, regarded the Gabba press corps as the most parochial in the country, though undeniably the most fun. We all would have been able to retire rich if we had a dollar for every time Robert Craddock – who became Queensland's outstanding contribution to the international fourth estate – over-excitedly exclaimed, "We've won the Shield".

Those changes in philosophy and personnel were well overdue. The behind-the-scenes bounce of director of coaching Ashley ("Toot") Byron, identification of talent from around the vast state, and the sensitive touch of Queensland Academy of Sport coach Dave Gilbert did much to prepare a new crop of youngsters for first-class cricket and beyond. But it took the exceptional skills of Buchanan, aided by the computing wizardry of Jim Hunter, to make the mix come together and stay together. In his rookie year, Buchanan not only cosseted the developing talents of youngsters such as Martin Love, Jimmy Maher and Andy Bichel, he also drew the best out of venerable warhorses like Dirk Tazelaar and, impressively, coaxed unqualified support from Border, Carl Rackemann and Trevor Barsby, old soldiers who had done things their way for years.

That was a masterly achievement, given that Border, then the biggest name in Australian cricket, reportedly threw Buchanan's first dossiers of detailed information on an opposing team into the nearest rubbish bin without so much as a second glance. The team elders were not much into computer analysis, game plans, gym work or new-age philosophy. They came from the Jeff Thomson era, the "up boys and at 'em" school which produced spurts of emotion and sessions of splendour, but never the durability or nous to finish the job. Frequent changes of coach and captain and behind-the-scenes machinations of Machiavellian proportions also contributed to those desperate near-misses and other more spectacular failures, so from one standpoint at least, there was not much to lose by appointing Buchanan.

The fruits of the transition continued as Andrew Symonds and Michael Kasprowicz began to translate potential into achievement and emerge as players of international pedigree. One mandate which Australian states readily embrace is their role to produce and develop Australian players, though when you get to be too good at it, the drain to Test and one-day commitments becomes tough to manage. Border, Craig McDermott and Ian Healy were among Australia's outstanding stars in the state's "nearly" years but were all too often absent when the Shield was there to be won. Queensland have been fortunate in recent years in being able to rely upon the core presence of high-achievers such as Law, Matthew Hayden, Adam Dale and Wade Seccombe, players on the fringe of representative honours but more often than not available for domestic duties.

Even when a fast bowling dynasty ended, notable successors put up their hands, and when Dale, Kasprowicz or Bichel made their excursions into and out of the national picture, a ready queue formed to fill the breach – Scott Muller, Joe Dawes and this year's surprising Pura Cup final Man of the Match and even more surprising Australian Cricket Board contract beneficiary and Ashes tourist, Ashley Noffke. Kasprowicz and Bichel had been a while polishing their talents, but after Rackemann bowed out after helping secure the Shield at last – in his swansong summer he took 52 wickets, the most in the country – they quickly picked up the slack.

The importance of the ability to bowl out sides is forever associated with one of the game's oldest adages. Kasprowicz was the leading wicket-taker in Australia in the next two seasons, followed in the 1996-97 list by Dale, who translated his limited-overs economy into striking success in the four-day game. Dale, a clothing company representative, Muller, a sales representative for major sponsors XXXX, and Dawes, a drug squad detective, bucked the trend of full-time professionalism to maintain the astonishing supply line. Bichel (60 wickets in 1999-2000) and Dawes (49 in 2000-01) were also the season's top destroyers – to make it five Queenslanders out of seven years – as McDermott, a role model for them all, had been before them. An invaluable ally, following in the Tallon–Grout–Healy tradition, is Seccombe, probably the best technical glove man in Australia these days, as a record-breaking 339 dismissals in just 69 matches and an Ashes tour will attest.

If the ability to dismiss sides was essential and an imposing record in Queensland no less important – 25 outright wins in 39 home matches during the past seven summers – the batsmen have also played their part. Hayden, albeit belatedly in the light of his massive scoring in the 1990s, looks like becoming an Australian fixture – but Queensland did win the 1996-97, 1999-2000 and 2000-01 finals without him. New South Wales stopped being the team to beat in domestic cricket as the international programme increasingly robbed them of their brightest stars, but Queensland appear to have discovered the trick of how to keep on keeping on regardless.

Law has only half a dozen names ahead of him in the all-time appearances list and his swag of runs has propelled him past Barsby, heroic figure of the first two Shield victories, and within sight of the prolific Sam Trimble. Love, Maher and Symonds are only in their mid-20s, yet they too are up there with the best. Even unspectacular bits-and-pieces men like Geoff Foley and Paul Jackson made vital contributions to the team framework as the titles rolled in.

If there was another Achilles heel to be confronted before the honours materialised, it was the inability to travel well. Critics often declare that the true measure of players and teams is how they perform away from the comforts of home. Queensland traditionally faltered on their road trips. Once they started to turn that around, their self-belief blossomed.

Beating South Australia in front of a raucous Gabba hill and to the accompaniment of Rupert McCall's bush poetry in March 1995 had been the delivery of the Holy Grail, but victory in Perth two years later was a defining moment as well. Perth had been a graveyard for so many visiting teams, and history shows that most finals are just a confirmation of the superiority of the first-placed host side. If anybody had demonstrated how to organise themselves in domestic cricket in the preceding decade and a half it was Western Australia, but Queensland's victory at Perth in 1996-97 underscored the transfer of power. Ironically Tom Moody and his mates served the by now buoyant Queenslanders with their most stinging and unexpected jolt in 1998-99 when they came to Brisbane and repaid the favour. It was, as Paul Keating might have said, the kick up the backside Queensland had to have.

With King taking over shortly after the start of the 1999-2000 season when Buchanan succeeded Geoff Marsh as national coach, Queensland responded by taking a record 48 points from ten matches. A draw against Victoria at Albion delivered title number three, and back at the Gabba 12 months on, against Victoria again, a ferociously hard-fought four-wicket win laced with controversy made it four.

With the talent pool still producing, and the framework established so new players tend to fit in without too much soul-searching adjustment, there is no reason to suppose the King dynasty cannot be as successful as that of Buchanan. Five of the Cup-winning side in March were playing in a final for the first time. Yet it took the mid-season jolt of losing Shane Watson, one of the most promising young all-rounders in the country, to remind everyone that those in waiting need to be nurtured. Watson, an Under-19 international and Cricket Academy tyro, was wooed away by Tasmania – never having played for Queensland at senior level – and finished his first stint in the top flight with a batting average over 50 and a swag of performances with the ball. A player who almost certainly should have been part of the Queensland plan for the next decade will be plying his trade elsewhere. While not an original story, it provided its lessons. Queensland are unlikely to be so careless again, and they are not short of promising players to filter into the side.

Meanwhile the durable Law, who has confessed irritation at a widely held public belief that it was Border, not he, who was at the helm when the Shield drought was broken, has matured impressively. As a sometimes fractious young turk he was tipped for great things, yet like a few other talented players – David Hookes and Jamie Siddons spring to mind – destiny decided his biggest contribution would be away from the international arena. Rarely lacking belief in his own capabilities, it still took him years to come to terms with the apparent indifference of the Test selectors, but huge accomplishments with Queensland (and a fruitful English county career – with Essex) have dulled the disappointment. Having led Queensland to their dazzling run of successes, Law is a major contributor to this story. His leadership is not flashy but he regularly pulls the right rein and backs himself and his players.

As with all winning teams, success begets confidence, and confidence brings more success – provided of course management, coaching staff and players never take their eyes off the ball.

HALF A CENTURY OF TEST-WATCHING:
A PERSONAL SURVEY

by DAVID FRITH

There is no need for me to consult a book or refer to photographs. I have only to close my eyes to see again the inviting expanse of the old Hill and the solid, world-famous scoreboard structure at the Edwardian-flavoured Sydney Cricket Ground, and to marvel again at Alec Bedser's strength as he bowled and bowled in a depleted England attack while Keith Miller stroked his way to 96 not out. Who could ever fail to remember vividly his first day at a Test match?

The changes that have overtaken the beloved game this past half-century would take hours to enumerate. By contrast, little had changed between 1901 and 1951. The elderly gentleman who lived in our street had watched the likes of Trumper and Noble, Mac-Laren and Blythe play at the SCG 50 years earlier. Costume, manners and technique had changed only minimally since then, and by 1951 the game was substantially still played to the same rhythms. I was only 13, but I was watching a Test match that differed only in personnel and a few minor details from the one my septuagenarian escort had watched all those years previously.

Now it is my turn to look back, and in sharp contrast I find the range of changes wrought during this latest half-century to be quite staggering.

The SCG, in company with most major cricket grounds around the world, is less a charming village than a towering city. Spectators in the public enclosures now wear garish clothing rather than trilby hats and suits, the vocalising from the stands bespeaks aggressive patriotism, and the renowned good humour of the Hill and elsewhere has long since echoed into oblivion.

Out in the middle, the preponderance of fast, short-pitched bowling since the 1970s has forced batsmen to don protective helmets. This is completely understandable, and was a precaution endorsed by Sir Donald Bradman, though helmets should never have been permitted for fieldsmen, who now stand intimidatingly close at short leg. On that fateful January day in 1951 we in the Bob Stand could all see perfectly the faces of Lindsay Hassett, Neil Harvey and Miller as they batted. Nobody needed a number on his back.

By far the greatest change has come with the game's utter inundation with commercial insignia. We are told repeatedly that crick-et would have died had it not offered itself to sponsorship. Well, the absence of sponsorship in cricket did not stop me from wanting to be Ray Lindwall. Evenings on end I bowled tennis balls against the school wall. Like many thousands of boys, I wanted to be a Test cricketer and – like my hero – gave no thought to remuneration. Had other major sports not been caught up in the frenzy of finance, per-haps cricket would have been left as it was, with players' shirts and bats free of advertisements. The lovely cream-coloured picket fence which ringed the SCG would not have been obliterated by adver-tisement hoardings, nor the sacred turf – and even the sightscreens – desecrated by sponsors' giant logos. But humankind inevitably, it seems, is impelled to adopt new moods and attitudes as the years roll by, and in this Age of Mammon insecurity and greed are every-where. Cricket could not hope to escape infection.

Soon after that youthful baptism at the SCG in 1951, I bumped into Alec Bedser in Castlereagh Street, lured him into conversation, and, suitably inspired, wrote a school essay proclaiming that I wanted to become a cricket writer. The enlightened New South Wales Cricket Association gave all schoolboys free tickets for the big matches, so I came to regard the SCG as some sort of temple, and many of the players as gods. Next season the exotic West Indians came, followed by an unfancied young South African side under Jack Cheetham which shook Australia by squaring the series. I was lapping all this up, and was quite unprepared for a summer with-out international cricket. But in 1953-54 there was only Sheffield Shield cricket to be seen or listened to, and worse followed, because after the enthralling 1954-55 Ashes series, when another hero, Len Hutton, led an attractive England side to victory, with my interest now at boiling point, suddenly there was no Test cricket pro-grammed in Australia during the next three summers. Youngsters of today may find that difficult to believe.

Of course, there were nocturnal marathons of wireless (radio) listening when Australia played in England in 1953 and 1956, cour-tesy of the fading/booming/undulating voices of Messrs Arlott, Swanton, Alston, Gilligan, Charlton, McGilvray and my Hunter Street sports-shopkeeper friend Bert Oldfield (Australia's pre-war wicket-keeper), with occasional crackles of static interference. Much was left to the imagination, which was no bad thing. If any-body had been empowered to divulge that in distant years to come we would be watching an instantaneous full-colour television picture from the other side of the world, with vivid close-ups and slow-motion replays and computerised statistical analysis and interactive remote control, we would have responded with a sideways look and a somewhat doubting "Oh, really?" And to think that at Sydney in 1951 we had no idea that Sam Loxton should have been adjudged run out by Washbrook's throw until we saw a picture in the next morning's newspaper.

A new age dawned with the 1958-59 series. Richie Benaud was now Australia's captain, and television was the revolutionary new medium of comfortable, easy spectatorship. I estimate that I have watched close to 200 Test matches in person and just as many on television. This is the most fundamental change of all, considering that every Test in the ten Test-playing regions of the globe is now not only televised but available, by subscription if necessary, to people all over the world.

The 1960s were not the most inspiring passage in cricket's history. The game somehow seemed tired, and there were plenty of turgid stonewallers around, batsmen not simply prepared to fight for a draw but averse in any circumstances to making runs at a decent rate. Thus the limited-overs format was experimented with and found almost by accident to be of appeal to the masses. It is both a relief and a surprise today to find that Test cricket has endured the challenge and continues to be recognised by those who truly love cricket as the purest form of international competition.

My 1964 pilgrimage to England – land of my birth (only a mile from Lord's, as it happens) – was with the ulterior motive of finding work as a cricket writer. We'll leave aside the matter of fluctuating allegiances during Ashes series. Now it was the era of Boycott, Edrich, Dexter, Barrington and Cowdrey; Lawry, Simpson, Burge, McKenzie and Booth ... and Norm O'Neill, my former St George Under-16s captain. Then the New Zealanders and South Africans came, and the glorious Sobers with his 1966 West Indians, the one-eyed Indian genius Pataudi and the fascinating and fragile world record-holder Hanif Mohammad.

For those who could afford it, the 1968 Ashes series could be tele-viewed in colour, and for me the whole business was so much more gripping because I was on the fringe of journalism and getting to know the players. Such was my mania, in fact, that I was already trying to embrace the entire 20th century by seeking out old-time players such as Wilfred Rhodes, S. F. Barnes, Herbert Strudwick, Frank Woolley, George Geary, Arthur Gilligan (so popular in Australia in the halcyon days of the Anglo-Australian fraternity). I taped their voices and took their photographs, and as the years passed the passion drove me to find the likes of Harold Larwood and Jack Gregory and Alan Kippax and "Stork" Hendry, and to savour a cherished friendship with Sir Donald Bradman. This attempt to span the years and broaden the continuity, all the while building up a cricket library and memorabilia collection, enriched my current interest immeasurably.

Extensions to the great roll-call continued as brilliant players from all parts emerged: Kanhai, Pollock, Snow, Walters, Gavaskar, Zaheer, Turner. The bouncer fusillades of Lillee and Thomson were soon to be intensified by the West Indians as they embarked on a 15-year reign of terror which made Bodyline seem kids' play, the remorseless hostility and monotonous stroke-denial of the four-pronged pace attack often upstaging the phenomenal power of the West Indies batting line-up. By the late 1980s cricket-lovers who cherished the skills and subtleties of spin bowling were thinking of adopting black armbands, for this keenest of cricket's arts was all but dead.

Cricket had lost its innocence – or such innocence as we fondly used to believe it had by decree of birthright. The Centenary Test celebrations in March 1977 remain cricket's greatest party of all time. Over 200 cricketers who had played in Ashes Tests were there, and the teams led by Greg Chappell and Tony Greig played out a remarkable match before Her Majesty the Queen and teeming thousands in the Melbourne sunshine. High drama, thrills and chivalry marked each of the five days, and the uncontrived result was amazingly identical to that in the first Test match, 100 years previously. To add to all this, my 40th birthday fell during the match, an anniversary which was generously crowned by breakfast with the Bradmans.

Yet all this joy was to be short-lived. Hardly had the Centenary cheering died away than cricket experienced its greatest upheaval. The Kerry Packer commercial revolution flung the game into turmoil. The Money Age had truly dawned. For two uncomfortable and argumentative years international cricket staggered on until an agreement was suddenly reached in 1979. Both factions had suffered, but there were sighs of relief all round and a much-changed game continued on its way, more money-fixated, commercially minded and perhaps with the last remnants of gentility flushed out from its corpus.

The Ashes continued to change hands at intervals, which assisted the credibility of this oldest of contests, though the English cricket administrators brought shame upon their heads by declaring that the three-Test series of 1979-80 was a non-Ashes contest. They failed to appreciate that the little urn, far from being theirs to award or withhold, was an ancient concept – and, yes, sacred too – which belonged to the MCC but also in spirit to the cricket fraternities of both England and Australia. Good Englishmen knew that with the 3-0 victory Greg Chappell's Australians had won back the Ashes lost earlier in series which had been denuded of several of their Packer players.

In 1981, the swashbuckling Botham, with the assistance of a few team-mates, won the Ashes back for England in one of those rare series when – particularly after Headingley – we agreed that no previous Test could possibly have been more stirring. Or was Melbourne 1895, The Oval 1902, Adelaide 1925, or Brisbane 1950 more exciting? All but the last, I beg you to believe, were well before my time.

So what of the past 20 years? Being professionally involved – editorially – has rendered a different flavour into this era, sometimes palatable, sometimes less so. The players of 1951 would never have worn wristwatches on the field, though they would perhaps envy the now universally accepted sunglasses. And how Lindwall and Trueman would have appreciated being plied with fluid and cool towels between overs down at the third-man fence.

There have been betrayals of the game, none more distressing or costly than the widespread corruption recently exposed, and there have been commercial and political exploitation and abuse that cause deep dismay to those who recall the apparently pristine and flawless game that most of us discovered while still schoolboys. Among themselves, cricket-lovers bewail any debasement of the game, but the responsibility falls squarely upon the shoulders of those who chronicle cricket to speak out forcefully against these abuses, be they political, commercial or player-driven. If only one were able to assert that the press-boxes of today – and the committee-rooms too – were peopled exclusively by men who cared first and foremost about cricket's welfare.

Privileged to have seen Test cricket in eight countries, an odyssey that delightfully embraced Sri Lanka's maiden Test match, I am still left with acute reservations about plans to elevate further nations, a money-obsessed ambition which, if activated, would dilute the significance of Test cricket as well as its records. Why cannot minor countries continue to enjoy international competition among themselves through the ICC Trophy?

It surprised many who perceived me as ultra-conservative that I should campaign vigorously from 1983 to 1992 for the adoption of video replays to assist umpiring decisions. I was indeed someone who, on the whole, believed in the old order and tended to dwell in the past (but only in order to enhance the pleasure derived from today's action, which itself was shortly going to become history). But no, I did not believe that when a man was run out – and seen to be out by many millions watching television – he should go on batting just because the umpire, the most important person in this context, did not have access to the clear reality that the rest of us had seen on the small screen.

I returned to the crusade at every opportunity, each unnecessary miscarriage of justice in the meantime causing anguish. At last the South Africans tried the third-umpire/video system, and its benefits were demonstrable at once. Now all the doubters were saying what a good idea it was – apart from the dunderheads who continued to claim that human error was a cherished and time-honoured ingredient. There is nothing attractive about human error. Let cricketers go on making their errors with bat and ball, but the umpires should avail themselves of all the assistance they can get.

This, I suppose, is as much a key development in cricket's evolution over the past half-century as anything else. And in all probability it has a way to go yet, for there is little sense in discernible decisions on-screen being left there while the man in the middle does his best with his merely human faculties. With television having devised ways – or so we are told – of proving or disproving leg-before decisions with missile-tracking, computerised technology, is this the ultimate step? And if so, is there much point in sending the two umpires out into the field? Big Brother upstairs can spot and instantly klaxon a no-ball or call a wide, and count to six (or why don't we make it four, so that more commercials can be squeezed into a televised day's play?). A hatstand can accommodate bowlers' caps and sweaters. Microphones can pick up extreme sledging, and erring players can spend the night in cold cells under the stands.

It's a long, long way from that near run-out of Sam Loxton, when players smiled freely and played honestly, and never thought for a moment – well, perhaps apart from Sid Barnes – of charging money for appearances or for their autographs. Who today could get away with telling an opposing fast bowler to desist from bowling bouncers, as Freddie Brown, England's John Bull captain in 1950-51, told Ray Lindwall?

We have seen or read about some wondrous feats over the past two decades. Dozens of new heroes from the world's cricket cradles have taken their imperishable places in the record books: Lara, Tendulkar, Gooch, Waqar Younis, Viv Richards, Marshall, Border, Muralitharan, the Waughs, McGrath, Harbhajan Singh, Donald, Cairns, Andy Flower, Jayasuriya, and perhaps most of all, because he rescued the art of wrist-spin bowling, Shane Warne.

As the cavalcade proceeds, inevitably things change. But what if the next 50 years should embrace as much change as the last? Between 1901 and 1951 little altered, despite two world wars. Pitches improved greatly, but the game that Bradman and Hammond played was in essence the same as the game known by Trumper and Hobbs. It is my particular generation that has had the misfortune to see "progress" break into a gallop, a gallop which has sometimes been blind and crazy, knocking down a few ornaments. Might cricket be spared further manipulation and dumbing-down? Might it not deserve a prolonged period of consolidation? Or is the well-worn truism that this game faithfully reflects contemporary society so undeniable that we are left with no choice but to absorb the hard-edged and more repugnant characteristics of the outside world as the 21st century opens?

The best formula is to cherish the memories while appreciating the day now unfolding. For Keith Miller read Ricky Ponting; for Alec Bedser read Darren Gough.

AUSTRALIA HAS MELTED

By TONY WILSON

It must bemuse international sportspeople when they hear that by contracting their muscles in a certain fashion, or by a split-second reflex response, they fundamentally affect the day-to-day lives of people they will never meet.

Take the case of Adam Gilchrist and me. At 5 p.m. AEST on March 29, 2001, we were living our separate lives. I was in Melbourne visiting my mother, drinking tomato soup and talking about tar shampoos. Gilchrist meanwhile was in India, batting for Australia and on the verge of deciding that viciously turning Mumbai clay was best combated by a firm belief in the primary-school slog-sweep.

At some point in the tar shampoo conversation, the television was turned on (honestly, Mum, it was just good fortune that I arrived during the Test) and for just over two hours, couch, tomato soup and slog-sweep intersected. By the time Gilchrist had launched his fourth six into the terraces, he had changed the course of my year.

At 10 a.m. the next day I had booked a flight to India for the Second Test. A week later, I was at Kolkata airport watching police baton-charge about 200 laughing Bengalis who were attempting to spray the passengers of flight SQ416 with coloured food dye.

"Have you come here for our dye-throwing Holi festival, sir?" a smiling policeman asked, fending off a pink-faced youth who was coming at us with a fluorescent pump-action water pistol.

"No, I'm here for the Second Test. I'm Australian," I said.

Before I could mention Gilchrist, the First Test and the slog-sweeps that had pulled me across oceans, the policeman had taken guard, lunged forward and presented an impeccably straight baton.

"Sachin Tendulkar!" he roared.

Five minutes later the cordon was on the charge again, and the policeman rushed across to threaten a boy with a raised stick. Like Sachin, it looked as though he could play the cross-bat shots as well.

Zaheer Khan charges in, bowls to Slater, who shuffles across and allows a slanting delivery to pass through to the keeper.

There's something romantic about the first ball of a Test match. Not romantic in the sense that if things aren't going well in a relationship, you might use the first ball of a Test match to try and patch things up. It's more the sense that in that first delivery stride a five-day wheel of sporting possibility is set in motion.

When the first ball was bowled at Eden Gardens, I was at deep cover, and whatever spiritual connection I expected to have with the moment was at least partially offset by the fact that the deep cover I was at was not at Eden Gardens. Instead, it was on the Lindsay Street footpath, 50 metres away from a street cricket match between the Calcutta Gandhi Sports Club in green, and the Nibli Boys Sporting Club in white. All 22 players had numbers on their backs, and the pitch was carved into the parking bays that lined the centre of the road. The bays had been left vacant, giving the impression that the road was always set aside on Sunday mornings for street cricket, an impression that was only thrown into question by the alarmingly fast-moving traffic that would sometimes find gaps in the infield. Overall, the scene made me wonder what the street cricket matches of my childhood would have been like had they been organised better, and played on Lonsdale Street.

Khan bowls … Slater back, across … hit on the pads … huge appeal … not out.

I had the radio on listening to the Test, and nearly missed the first big appeal of the game because the Nibli boys were up for an appeal of their own. Stumps were splattered, and a batsman in green lay flat on the asphalt, having dived desperately in an attempt to make his ground. Amazingly, the scruffy kid in the grey pants umpiring at square leg signalled grandly for the third umpire, which had me glancing around for a side-on home video camera.

"That means he's not out," said Lalbatsam, the captain of the Calcutta Gandhi team. "If it's close enough to go to the third umpire, we call it not out," he explained.

Both sides seemed happy enough with that, and Grey Pants stepped forward to dig the stumps back into the road.

"How does he get the stumps through the asphalt?" I asked Lalbatsam.

"We've used a sledge-hammer there to make a gap in the road," he replied casually. "Nobody minds."

Prasad to Hayden … Hayden puts one foot down the pitch and smashes it past silly mid-off for four. Glorious shot. Australia 28 for no wicket.

I must confess that I've taken some liberties in recounting the radio commentary. The Internet records suggest they're right, but at the time there was the small problem of the game being broadcast in Bengali. So in reality "Prasad ... something something something ... Hayden ... something something ... silly mid-off" is maybe a more accurate transcript of what I was hearing, making it tough when the Calcutta Gandhi boys started asking for scores. Eventually my head-phones became communal property, and a solution was worked out.

"We play 16 a side, and the rules are the same as for one-day internationals," Lalbatsam said. An over or so later, the tennis ball cannoned into the side of a taxi flying in front of the Ruby's Saree's boundary, and the umpire signalled by punching one hand into the other. "It's one run extra if you hit a taxi," Lalbatsam said by way of explanation. "Also drives that are lofted into the Surana Mansion building or the Punjab National Bank are rated by which floor the ball hits – two runs for the first floor, four for the second, and six for the third. Into the market on the full is out." Apart from that, I could assume, the rules were the same as for one-day internationals.

Meanwhile, the news was coming through from Eden Gardens that the Aussie openers were doing well – "Australia 31 without loss after 12 overs," said Prem, who had seized control of the head-phones. "Calcutta Gandhi was 91 after 12 overs," he stated proudly, as though it was the sort of news that would make the Australians wonder whether wild tonking in the first 12 overs was maybe the way to go.

Prem was the Calcutta Gandhi opener, and he spent the innings fielding abuse from his team-mates about his name, which means "love" in Bengali. "The opposition players also sledge me about being called 'Love'," he shouted. (The problem of speaking while wearing headphones is an international one.) "But they do not ruffle me – just as you Australians can never ruffle Tendulkar."

This prompted howls of abuse, more sledging, and an observation from Lalbatsam that if Loverboy was so unrufflable, why hadn't he been able to manage any more than three runs in his time at the crease. Prem responded by burying himself in the sound of the Test match. "Australia is 35 without loss," he said a few minutes later.

Of the last 22 Sundays, the Calcutta Gandhi boys had won 20 matches, but with an over to go, they were in big trouble. Chasing 122, they needed 12 from the last over with just one wicket in hand, and pawing the asphalt at the top of his mark was a tearaway quick who the Nibli boys simply called Wasim Akram.

"What is strange is that our player facing right now we also call Wasim Akram," Lalbatsam said.

Sure enough, encouragement was coming from all directions for various Wasims, which shows either that India is crying out for a good left-arm quick, or that there are some Muslims in the heart of Kolkata who are looking further afield for heroes. In any event, with two balls to go, bowling Wasim pitched up to batting Wasim who smashed the ball into the Punjab National Bank building and was caught on the rebound. As sporting moments go, maybe it wasn't going to be one that changed lives, unless of course the Nibli boys were mown down by the autorickshaw that seemed on a collision course with their victory huddle.

"Does anyone ever get hit by cars?" I asked Lalbatsam, the defeated captain.

"Sometimes," he replied. "See Leng," he said, pointing to a younger kid with a prominent scar on his right temple. "He was hit by a white Ambassador under that Moustache shirts sign." Leng pointed to his scar and offered himself up for a photo.

"I was hit by a motorbike, playing soccer," added Prem.

With lunch fast approaching in the Test, I thanked the boys for their co-operation and said I was off to Eden Gardens to watch the Test match. "You mean you have a ticket to the game and you're not there?" batting Wasim said with a look of disgust.

"Well, if there was a choice between watching this game and that game, which one would you choose?" I asked.

"That game," about ten kids droned in chorus. The rest said something else, which Lalbatsam said meant "that game" in Bengali.

When you travel 8,000 kilometres to see a man slog-sweep, it's disappointing when he plods his pad nonchalantly down the line of the pitch and is knocked over first ball leg-before. It's doubly disappointing when the ball seems to have pitched about a foot outside leg stump, and devastating if two minutes later the side is seven for 252 and you've just witnessed the first ever Indian Test hat-trick.

I say that as an Australian supporter. As a lover of sport, Harbhajan's hat-trick and the response it generated in the stands were as remarkable as anything I've seen, and that's even taking into account the fact that my view of the Warne dismissal was partly obscured by about 35 dancing commerce students.

"We have taken a day off study to come and watch the match today," a student called Gourav had said to me earlier in the day, but now his face was about five centimetres from mine and it was screaming just "Ay! Ay! Ay! Ay!"

"Don't you guys have exams tomorrow?" I asked, backing away to find myself wrapped in Indian tricolours as they descended from the rows behind.

"Yes," Gourav said. "But how can we study when Harbajan is making history here at Eden Gardens?"

For the sake of watching the rest of the last session in peace, I tried to argue that they'd be better served getting home and hitting the books, but nobody seemed to be leaving.

"I don't care if I fail," Gourav said. "I just saw a hat-trick."

Over the next four days I walked past the hallowed Lindsay Street asphalt about eight times, but didn't see anything more spectacular than a few over-ambitious three-point turns. My mood walking past fluctuated with the ebbs and flows of what was happening at Eden Gardens. On Day Two, there was relief that Australia had Steve Waugh – the man who gave up hooking and smiling in the late 1980s to concentrate on the biomechanics of perfect batting. On Day Three, surprise that the game wasn't over, and that I hadn't got sick from any of the 30-cent samosas I'd been eating out of the fast-food dungeons in D section. On Day Four, horror that Australia had gone wicketless, that Laxman could possibly be averaging 30 in Test cricket, and that the song in my head was the Bengali tune "Bom bom bole, Australia gelo gale" (Hip hip hooray, Australia has melted). And on Day Five, despair that the Aussies could lose the unloseable, yet also a strange sense of accomplishment at having done what I'd set out to do, which was to travel a long way to sit very still on a very hot piece of concrete.

Maybe the whole experience was best summed up by Santosh, a stenographer and member of the Bengali Communist Party who was standing next to me through the whole of that last session. For ten minutes after the game, we stood there watching flaming newspapers dot the stands, and smoke drift across the playing surface to bathe the ground in a surreal haze.

"You must not be sad, Tony," Santosh said. "Be happy, cricket at the Eden is the winner."

We then joined the shouting masses pushing out of the ground and Santosh scrawled a goodbye message in my notebook: "Tin diner por, aaj shob shofol holo. Aaj shob deklain, shuk, dukho, bhalobasa" (After three days, today everything was successful. Today you saw everything, joy, sorrow, love).

Unfortunately, the next Test in Chennai did too. I had kind of been banking on a little less sorrow.

A STEPPING STONE TO FIRST-CLASS CRICKET

By JOHN POLACK

If anyone had cause to doubt the worth of the ACB Cup, then its contribution to the spectacular development of at least three careers during 2000-01 must surely have helped close the book on most skepticism about Australia's national second eleven competition.

Nathan Bracken had started the summer as one of New South Wales' fringe fast bowlers, yet an early ACB Cup appearance proved the springboard of a campaign which saw him included in the national one-day squad and anointed as the country's Young Cricketer of the Year.

Similarly, the sight of Ashley Noffke turning out for the Queensland Academy of Sport arrived at the beginning of a triumphant season which culminated in his call-up as an injured Bracken's replacement on Australia's stunningly successful 2001 Ashes tour.

That it should have been possible for 19-year-old Queenslander Shane Watson to move to Adelaide to embark on a stint at the Commonwealth Bank Cricket Academy, and then end the summer in Hobart as one of the nation's brightest first-class prospects in many years, was another stellar exemplar of its utility.

There were other heartening stories too. Having found himself almost perennially on the verge of Queensland's state team, paceman Joe Dawes finally reaped the rewards of persistence at grade and second eleven level. In 2000-01, there was no other bowler in the country who claimed as many Pura Cup wickets.

Michael Lewis was still by no means a permanent member of Victoria's first team by the end of the season yet, like Noffke, took a giant step forward when he snared five wickets in an innings in the Pura Cup Final on the back of a pair of impressive ACB Cup displays earlier in the summer.

Youngsters like Luke Williams, Paul Rofe, James Hopes, Phil Jaques and Nathan Hauritz were among a range of other impressive performers. They were four among a total of 82 ACB Cup players who each represented their respective states at senior level through the course of the season.

Amid an otherwise disappointing six months, the ACB Cup also served to provide heart to Western Australian cricket followers. The 2000-01 season was not the West's most memorable either on or off the field. Yet few among its rivals can match it in terms of depth of playing resources and, in the state's emergence as ACB Cup champion, there was possibly no greater demonstration that emerging talent is continuing to be appropriately identified and harnessed beyond the Nullarbor.

The picture wasn't entirely rosy, of course, for there remain notable difficulties in co-ordinating the schedules of eight modestly funded teams from a disparate set of locations.

The vast majority of the matches in the competition were staged before even more limited audiences than attend Pura Cup and Mercantile Mutual Cup fixtures these days.

As the quest continued for balance in the arrangement of venues and the numbers of matches contested by each of the sides, there were also still some problems in establishing exactly the right format for the series. It remains a dilemma to which administrators are likely to devote significant energy over the winter months.

The regular movement of players between the Academy's team and those of their home states – as many as 17 players appeared for more than one ACB Cup side during the summer – is arguably another facet of the competition which may need to be reassessed.

Yet the value of a comprehensively structured second eleven programme remains irrefutable. Just as one of the chief forces behind Australia's success in international cricket in recent years has been the strength of its first-class structure, so it seems reasonable to expect that myriad benefits will flow from the overhaul of the ad hoc system that has traditionally acted as the stepping stone between grade and state cricket. Exposure on a national stage for the players and regular competition against higher calibre opposition than they are likely to face at club level can surely only be positive.

As positive, perhaps, as the prospects of Bracken, Noffke and Watson and undoubtedly many others behind them.

WISDEN AUSTRALIA
TEST CRICKETER OF THE YEAR

GLENN McGRATH

By RICK SMITH

When Glenn McGrath arrived in Perth for the Second Test against West Indies, the pace bowler's Test wicket tally stood at 298. Asked about the coming game, he laughed and said, "Sherwin Campbell for 299 and Brian Lara for 300. That'd be nice!" It proved to be the prediction of the summer, but it did not go nearly far enough.

After Brett Lee had removed Daren Ganga early in the proceedings, McGrath came on for the ninth over of the innings in search of another wicket to keep up the momentum. He found it when Campbell could only fend a lifting delivery to Ponting in the slips. Enter Lara to receive a perfect out-swinger which he edged to fourth slip where, for a breathtaking moment, Stuart MacGill juggled, then held the catch. Campbell 299 and Lara 300 – as predicted, but there was more to come. Captain Jimmy Adams' first ball came searing in at his ribs and all he could do was push it into the air for Justin Langer to take a simple catch at short leg. A hat-trick, West Indies reeling at four for 19 and the game effectively over in the first hour of play. Langer leapt into the bowler's arms in sheer delight.

It was compelling cricket, even watching on television on the other side of the continent. In just three deliveries McGrath had given a master class in the art of fast bowling: a lifting delivery outside off stump to a right-hander, followed by an out-swinger to a left-hander, and then a wicked ball into the ribs of another left-hander. Each was in exactly the right spot to one of the opposition's three best batsmen.

McGrath's influence was pivotal, both in Perth and in the First Test in Brisbane, which the Australians also won by an innings. In that game McGrath took 6/17 and 4/10, 10/27 off 33 overs, as the West Indies collapsed for 82 and 124. It was the cheapest ten-plus wickets in the history of Test cricket, surpassing the old mark of 15/28 taken by Johnny Briggs against South Africa in 1888-89.

Of particular significance at the Gabba was McGrath's removal of Lara for nought and four. It had been clear before the series began that the performances of Lara, his team's one great batsman, would be vital. By winning those first three battles, McGrath laid the foundations for a triumphant Australian summer, and although he did not maintain his early unplayability for the rest of the series, he still captured 21 wickets at 17.09 in the five Tests. Lara struck a superb 182 in Adelaide, but far from dominating the series as he had appeared set to do, he played no other innings of substance.

During the winter there had been much concern about McGrath's decision to play a season of county cricket with Worcestershire. Would his body stand the strain of months of constant bowling and still leave him at his best for the tough Australian summer campaign? He took 80 wickets at 13.21 to lead the wicket-taking list, and insisted that the stint in England had prepared him for the summer. Other people's fears that he was exposing himself to the likelihood of injury, which had haunted the early part of his career, proved unfounded. It now seems that the more he bowls the better he gets.

After spearheading the attack to a series whitewash of West Indies and victory in the triangular limited-overs series, McGrath set off to face a completely different challenge – a series in India. Bowling on surfaces notorious for their lack of assistance to pace bowlers and against a strong home line-up of Sachin Tendulkar, Rahul Dravid, Saurav Ganguly and the emerging V. V. S. Laxman, McGrath remained a force to be reckoned with. No batsman could relax against him. In Australia's First Test victory he took 3/19 and 2/25 from a match total of 36.1 overs. He continued to bowl well throughout the remaining two Tests, in spite of the onslaught launched by the Indian batsmen in general and Laxman in particular. In those games he took 4/18, 3/103, 3/75 and 2/21, always providing a threat, regardless of the match situation. At the end of the series he had captured 17 wickets at the remarkably low average of 15.35. The second-placed Australian was Jason Gillespie, whose 13 wickets cost 30.30 runs each. In addition to a low average and a high strike-rate, McGrath was almost impossible to score from. Throughout the season's eight Tests he had given up less than two runs an over.

Where does McGrath rate in the pantheon of Australian fast bowlers? He is not as fast as Jeff Thomson, lacks the variety of Dennis Lillee, does not swing the ball like Alan Davidson, or possess the poetry-in-motion action of Ray Lindwall. What he does do is get batsmen out, and he does it with a regularity and at an average which places him at the very top of the list.

McGrath is the world's number-one fast bowler, the most potent in the game. What is it about the 200 cm pace man that makes him such a threat? The key word is pressure. His attack on a batsman is relentless, almost robotic. There are so few bad balls that the batsman must sometimes wonder where his next run is coming from. The pressure builds until the batsman makes a mistake and loses his wicket. The word "robotic" implies an unthinking, programmed response, but McGrath is a thinking bowler able to vary his response to any situation or batsman, and he is certainly not without emotion.

McGrath possesses an almost uncanny ability to spot a weakness in an opposing batsman, and then the skill to exploit what he has discovered. He ruthlessly exposes faults, leaving a batsman like a rabbit caught in a hunter's spotlight. In recent seasons he has made no secret about targeting the opposition's best batsman, and his successful assault on Lara in the summer's first two Tests was just the latest episode in a remarkable saga.

Fast bowlers, and McGrath is no exception, play their cricket with fire and passion. Occasionally, his aggression upsets the game's purists, but pace bowling is an aggressive pursuit. However, it would be wrong to see him as simply a fire-breathing quick. Off the field he is still the country boy, devoted to friends and family. His support of his wife Jane, during her battle with breast cancer, showed a side of his personality no batsman is ever likely to see. He does not take his compassion onto the field, or he would surely have given some to the shell-shocked West Indies batsmen.

Growing up on the family wheat and sheep farm in rural New South Wales, McGrath did not play the game seriously until he was 15, an age when many are already in state under-age teams and special coaching squads. He may have started a little late, but he soon caught up. When it was suggested he should move to Sydney and try to make the big time, he did so, living in the family caravan for 13 months.

He is nothing if not determined, and that determination is best shown in the worst aspect of his game, his batting. Early in his career McGrath was, without putting too fine a point on it, hopeless, even by No. 11 standards. He did not enjoy being a batting joke, and over the years he has worked on this area of his game. Now he is now capable of "hanging around" and even scoring a few runs. He even made a fifty for Worcestershire, something which would have been greeted with total disbelief a few seasons ago. His ambition is to repeat the feat in Test cricket and relieve some team-mates of a large amount of cash, the result of a long-standing bet.

Once again, during the summer he had his batting moments. In the Second Test against India he fought valiantly to save the game until given out leg-before. His front leg was a long way down the pitch and his disappointment as the umpire's finger went up was palpable. He believed, with some justification, that he could have saved the game. This rearguard action followed 21 not out in the first innings when he added 43 for the last wicket with his captain, Steve Waugh. In fact, with the courtesy of some not-outs, he averaged 47 with the bat in the three-game series.

While his batting may be improving, and his out-fielding remains secure, it will always be his bowling that he will be remembered for. Now, at 31 years of age, he seems at the peak of his powers, with a strike-rate that suggests only injury will stop the Narromine farm boy from becoming the first Australian to take 500 Test wickets.

WISDEN AUSTRALIA
PURA CUP CRICKETER OF THE YEAR

JAMIE COX

By RIC FINLAY

He seems destined never to reach that pinnacle to which any Aussie cricketer with half an ounce of ambition aspires: opening the batting for his country. Since 1993-94, when Jamie Cox might first have reasonably been considered as an opening batsman for Australia, the national selectors have selected for the position five players in six different combinations, but Cox has not figured in any of them. "Taylor and Cox" has a nice ring to it, and would have pleased the ear of many of his fans, particularly when Michael Slater was discarded early in the 1996-97 season, and a tour of England was in the offing. But "Taylor and Elliott" it was, and although this was not an enduring partnership, one cannot criticise the selectors' decision, given the Victorian's form and success in the previous summer and in the subsequent Ashes series.

Even the retirement of Mark Taylor in 1999 failed to present Cox with the opportunity that many felt he deserved, Matthew Elliott, Greg Blewett and Matthew Hayden being preferred in succession. The decision not to provide Hayden and Slater with specialist back-up on the 2001 tour of England proved to be a cruel blow for Cox, who had just completed his second 1,000-run domestic first-class competition season. If a different policy had been pursued, then Cox must surely have joined the team, because he was selected for Australia A in its four-day match against the West Indians during the season, and made 94 in the second innings.

So, Tasmania's captain and most prolific batsman after David Boon will have to be satisfied, it would seem, with top nomination in the popular game that is perennially played around the nation: name Australia's best team never to play Test cricket. It is a reputation that is well deserved, for only Darren Lehmann has scored more runs in domestic competition in the last ten summers.

Jamie Cox, like many a good cricketer before him, hails from the north-west coast of Tasmania, and went to school at Wynyard, a small town so little known that the first edition of *Wisden Australia* felt constrained to spell it "Wynward" in the Births and Deaths section. This was not under Cox's entry (he was born at Burnie in October 1969) but under that of his school friend and opening partner Dene Hills. In recent times, the citizens of Wynyard have been so emboldened by the success of its favourite sons that they have issued a challenge to the rest of the nation to come up with a town that has as many sporting stars over a wide spectrum of different pursuits. The only response, predictably, has come from another town at the other end of the coastal strip.

Making his Tasmanian debut at the age of 18, Cox became a permanent member of the team at 20, and was so well regarded nationally (in contrast to more recent times, it might be observed) that he was chosen to lead an Australian youth team to the West Indies in the second half of 1990. Containing such luminaries as Michael Bevan, Damien Martyn, Shane Warne and Damien Fleming, the team carried all before it, and Cox's moderate personal form proved inconsequential.

More serious for his development in the ensuing couple of years was an untimely virus attack, which clearly affected his output of runs, and even resulted in a temporary demotion from the team. The restoration of both his health and his self to the team has proved to be a tale of almost continuous success for the elegant right-hander, and since 1994-95 he has compiled at least 700 runs in each competition season except for 1995-96, when he had to be content with 617. Not the least significant part of his contribution has been his record-breaking opening liaison with Dene Hills, with whom he has now amassed 5,963 runs in 137 opening stands at an average of just a tick under 45 runs each. The sheer consistency over many seasons of this pair puts them clearly at the top of the pile in Sheffield Shield/Pura Cup history, with daylight second. Having said that, the pair did attract some notoriety by each scoring pairs against Victoria at the MCG last season.

A fine athlete who has made his close-in fielding on the off-side an art form, Cox possesses one of the sweetest cover drives in the country, and his form may be measured by how far the ball rebounds off the advertising boards through extra cover at Bellerive Oval. Not always a certain starter, he holds the record for the number of ducks (22) as well as the number of centuries (27) for Tasmania in domestic first-class competition, and 72 of his 226 trips to the crease have fallen short of double figures. For someone so well-regarded for his equanimity in the face of adversity, the gremlins sometimes invade his thinking, as when he shouldered arms in his initial first-class innings to a Merv Hughes thunderbolt which neatly removed his off stump. And even his long-time coach Greg Shipperd shakes his head in bewilderment when Cox inexplicably pads up to balls homing in on his stumps, with predictable consequences.

When Cox is in form, however, there is no better striker of the ball. Chasing a challenging fourth-innings target against New South Wales at Bellerive in January 1990, Cox bludgeoned 102 in a session to bring his team victory against an attack that included Test bowlers Geoff Lawson and Peter Taylor. The New South Wales bowlers have legitimate cause to fear Cox, for not only did he score 175 in the first innings of that match, but he has also scored twin centuries against their bowlers on two further occasions. The latest of these was at Bellerive last season, while the return match at Sydney produced innings of 160 and 81.

Cox was long groomed to be David Boon's successor as captain of Tasmania, and he has grown into the job with a flair that has impressed those around him. Articulate and intelligent, he communicates well not only with those in his charge, but also with those charged with the responsibility of bringing before the public the events of each day's play. He has made the transition from player to captain while maintaining his affable demeanour, as if he had been doing the job all his life.

Last season, Tasmania experienced a mid-season slump in which the team posted five successive innings totals of less than 200 in three heavy losses. Cox presided over a re-evaluation of the team goals whereby each member was instructed to concentrate on his own contribution instead, as he put it, of "hiding behind the team thing". He candidly admits to being responsible for the dumping of one team member who he felt was performing well below his capabilities. The chastened bowler returned to the team a different player later in the season and was instrumental in Tasmania's remarkable revival. Led by Cox himself, with scores of 160, 81, 41, 139 not out, 20, 30 not out and 102, Tasmania stormed home to win the last three matches on the trot, including the traditionally difficult Perth assignment.

His three seasons as captain of Somerset in the English county championship, putting a career in the banking industry on hold, have furthered his experience in the job, and created a cross-pollination of ideas that has benefited both teams. His refreshing approach to the Tasmanian job has been rewarded with the best ratio of wins to matches captained of any Tasmanian captain since the state's admittance to the first-class competition in 1977.

But his friends and supporters must harp on the fact that in matters national, Jamie Cox has just been plain unlucky. The cricketing gods ordained this early last season, when against Western Australia at Bellerive, he made identical scores in each innings. And what were they? 87 and 87.

FOUR CENTURIONS TOGETHER

An obscure but major landmark was reached in the First Test at Edgbaston on July 5, 2001. For the first time in the 124-year history of Test cricket, four players each with more than 100 Test appearances played in the same Test. They were Australia's Steve Waugh (playing his 136th Test) and Mark Waugh (his 112th) and England's Mike Atherton and Alec Stewart (each playing his 111th). – KERSI MEHER-HOMJI

PART TWO: THE PLAYERS

INDEX TO PLAYER PROFILES

MARTYN, Damien Richard	119	RUMMANS, Graeme Clifford	76
MASON, Scott	100	SAKER, David James	101
MEULEMAN, Scott William	119	SECCOMBE, Wade Anthony	87
MILLER, Colin Reid	109	SLATER, Michael Jonathon	77
MILLER, Michael Christian	93	SMITH, Michael John	94
MOODY, Thomas Masson	119	SPENCER, Duncan John	121
MOSS, Jonathan	110	STEWART, James	77
MOTT, Matthew Peter	110	SWAIN, Brett Andrew	94
MUNDAY, Kade Michael	100	SWAN, Gavin Graham	121
NASH, Brendan Paul	85	SYMONDS, Andrew	88
NASH, Don Anthony	75	TARGETT, Benjamin Stuart	102
NICHOLSON, Matthew James	120	THOMAS, Bradley John	102
NIKITARAS, Steven	120	THOMPSON, Scott Michael	78
NOFFKE, Ashley Allan	85	TUBB, Shannon Benjamin	102
NORTH, Marcus James	120	TURNER, Dale Andrew	88
O'LEARY, Scott James	86	VAN DEINSEN, Brett Paul	78
OLDROYD, Bradley John	121	VAUGHAN, Jeffrey Mark	95
OLIVER, Benjamin Carl	110	VIMPANI, Graeme Ronald	112
PASCOE, Matthew David	86	WALSH, Mark Jason	122
PEAKE, Clinton John	111	WARNE, Shane Keith	112
PERREN, Clinton Terrence	86	WATES, Darren Jude	122
PHELPS, Matthew James	95	WATSON, Shane Robert	102
PILON, Nathan Steven	76	WAUGH, Mark Edward	78
PINNINGTON, Todd Andrew	100	WAUGH, Stephen Rodger	79
POLKINGHORNE, Adam William	101	WHITE, Cameron Leon	113
PONTING, Ricky Thomas	101	WILLIAMS, Bradley Andrew	122
PRESTWIDGE, Scott Arthur	87	WILLIAMS, Luke	95
REIFFEL, Paul Ronald	111	WILSON, Paul	95
RICHARDS, Corey John	76	WRIGHT, Damien Geoffrey	103
ROACH, Peter John	112	YOUNG, Bradley Evan	95
ROFE, Paul Cameron	94	YOUNG, Shaun	103

The players listed in this section are those who participated in first-class and/or domestic limited-overs competitions during the 2000-01 season.

First-class cricket is defined in accordance with Regulations of International Cricket 2.1, 2.2 and 2.3. It includes Test matches, three or four-day matches played by Australia against first-class sides while on tour, four-day matches between touring international teams and the states, four-day matches between touring international teams and Australian Elevens, four-day matches between the states for the Sheffield Shield or the Pura Cup, and some games played by the AIS Cricket Academy that fulfil the ICC's definitions.

International limited-overs cricket is defined in accordance with the Regulations of the International Cricket Council.

Domestic first-class cricket refers to matches between the states for either the Sheffield Shield or the Pura Cup.

Domestic limited-overs cricket refers to matches between the states for the Mercantile Mutual Cup or any earlier equivalent competition.

PLAYER PROFILES

The players listed in this section are all Australian players who participated in the 2000-01 season.

Note: First-class statistics and limited-overs international statistics are current to June 30, 2001.

* *Denotes not out.*

NEW SOUTH WALES
By Phil Wilkins

BEVAN, Michael Gwyl
Born: May 8, 1970 Belconnen (Australian Capital Territory)
Left-handed batsman, left-arm slow 'chinaman' bowler

Test cricket has regrettably become a secondary issue for one of the greatest limited-overs batsman of the era. Bevan was prominent in first-class matches in 2000-01, averaging just over 50 from his nine appearances and hitting two centuries, but it is his failure to hit a Test century that must account for the selectors' disinclination to reward him with a baggy green cap since his last Test in 1997-98. Bevan was at the heart of the Mercantile Mutual Cup final success over Western Australia in Perth with his unbeaten 135 from 137 balls, just as he was body and soul of the team's qualification for the final with a strike-rate of 89.05 from his eight games. While years in the professional game have taken their toll on his once mighty throwing arm, he remains swift and sure in the field. Although disappointed to lose the state captaincy, he remained a sturdy team man, more and more influential as the Cup final drew near, and a worthy New South Wales Player of the Year.

	M	I	NO	R	HS	100s	50s	Avge	Ct	St	W	Avge	BB
First-class	189	316	56	14,420	203*	49	64	55.46	105	0	112	44.21	6/82
Dom. first-class	84	149	30	6,864	203*	26	29	57.68	38	0	21	60.62	3/40
Test	18	30	3	785	91	0	6	29.07	8	0	29	24.24	6/82
Int'l limited-overs	164	145	51	5,384	108*	5	36	57.28	54	0	36	45.22	3/36
Dom. limited-overs	45	45	17	1,862	135*	1	16	66.50	10	0	5	38.80	2/24

BRACKEN, Nathan Wayne
Born: September 12, 1977 Penrith (New South Wales)
Right-handed batsman, left-arm fast-medium bowler
International limited-overs debut 2000-01

An injury-restricted start to his career seemingly behind him, the tall, lean pace man from the Blue Mountains blossomed into the discovery of the season, not simply for New South Wales but also for Australia, eventually winning the Sir Donald Bradman Young Cricketer of the Year award. The national selectors rewarded Bracken for his pace, accuracy and wicket-taking skills with selection for the limited-overs series against West Indies and Zimbabwe. Beginning with a fine haul of 4/36 in the Mercantile Mutual Cup match against Victoria, he worked hard and was the most economical New South Wales bowler after Glenn McGrath. In the Pura Cup, Bracken's inspirational 5/22 from 15 overs contributed to his team's stunning defeat of Western Australia at North Sydney Oval and three times he took four or more wickets in an innings on an SCG pitch renowned for spin. His outstanding season earned him selection to India and then in the Ashes team to England, only for injury to force his premature return from the tour.

Bracken's durability and resilience will undoubtedly increase with maturity, restoring him to the path to Test selection.

	M	I	NO	R	HS	100s	50s	Avge	Ct	St	W	Avge	BB
First-class	14	19	10	102	30	0	0	11.33	7	0	45	25.51	5/22
Dom. first-class	13	17	8	92	30	0	0	10.22	6	0	40	27.18	5/22
Int'l limited-overs	9	0	0	0	–	0	0	–	2	0	10	30.30	2/21
Dom. limited-overs	14	3	0	10	9	0	0	3.33	4	0	16	27.13	4/36

BRADSTREET, Shawn David
Born: February 28, 1972 Wollongong (New South Wales)
Right-handed batsman, right-arm medium bowler

Captain in 1999-2000 when Michael Bevan was unavailable, the resolute Manly all-rounder continued to win admirers for his strength of character and dependability. Bradstreet is a tough late-order batsman capable of hitting out or defending, a shrewd medium-paced bowler and a superb fieldsman, especially in the gully. His best performance came in Adelaide with innings of 36 not out and 60 as the team crumbled on a fine pitch. Inevitably, he was omitted when the internationals returned, so it was encouraging to see his contribution to the Mercantile Mutual Cup final victory in Perth.

	M	I	NO	R	HS	100s	50s	Avge	Ct	St	W	Avge	BB
First-class	7	14	3	238	60	0	1	21.64	6	0	11	46.82	2/32
Dom. first-class	7	14	3	238	60	0	1	21.64	6	0	11	46.82	2/32
Dom. limited-overs	20	16	7	282	75*	0	1	31.33	5	0	17	34.00	4/53

CLARK, Anthony Michael
Born: March 23, 1977 St Leonards (New South Wales)
Right-handed batsman, right-arm off-spin bowler
First-class and domestic first-class debut 2000-01

With Gavin Robertson's representative career drawing to a close, the New South Wales selectors intensified their search for an off-spin bowling partner for Stuart MacGill, seeking to establish a slow bowling combination to capitalise on the SCG's turning pitches. Eventually, the selectors chose the thick-set spinner from Fairfield–Liverpool. Clark made quiet and reassuring progress in four first-class games, gradually slowing and varying his flight. His debut season was best exemplified by two wickets in each innings of New South Wales' eight-wicket defeat of Queensland, followed by demotion to 12th man as the team was eliminated from the Pura Cup on the usual green Gabba pitch. Clark proved a commendable late-order batsman and reliable fieldsman, and more will surely be heard of him.

	M	I	NO	R	HS	100s	50s	Avge	Ct	St	W	Avge	BB
First-class	4	4	0	53	24	0	0	13.25	2	0	6	47.67	2/19
Dom. first-class	4	4	0	53	24	0	0	13.25	2	0	6	47.67	2/19

CLARK, Stuart Rupert
Born: September 28, 1975 Caringbah (New South Wales)
Right-handed batsman, right-arm fast-medium bowler

Tall and strongly built, Clark has been a surprisingly peripheral figure in the New South Wales team since his first-class debut in 1997-98. He bowls well at the helpful WACA Ground, where he obtains lift and cut, although his Mercantile Mutual Cup final performance of 0/63 was an exception. He bowled frugally and thoughtfully throughout the limited-overs series, staking a claim for permanent inclusion in the New South Wales limited-overs team.

	M	I	NO	R	HS	100s	50s	Avge	Ct	St	W	Avge	BB
First-class	10	16	4	90	20*	0	0	7.50	4	0	14	68.14	2/36
Dom. first-class	10	16	4	90	20*	0	0	7.50	4	0	14	68.14	2/36
Dom. limited-overs	22	5	2	25	11	0	0	8.33	5	0	27	26.78	4/26

CLARKE, Michael John
Born: April 2, 1981 Liverpool (New South Wales)
Right-handed batsman, left-arm fast-medium bowler
Domestic limited-overs debut 2000-01

For two years, the selectors have impatiently awaited the emergence of the former Australian Under-19s captain to occupy a middle-order batting role for New South Wales, and by the end of the season, their expectations appeared to have been fulfilled. Clarke's batting was neat, assured and crisp, featuring shots all around the wicket. He had limited opportunities before the new year, returning as a middle-order batsman to the Mercantile Mutual Cup side and playing his way to the top of the order to make 57 from 84 balls opening in the final. Heartened by this success, Clarke hit his maiden first-class century against a Victorian attack including Paul Reiffel and Mathew Inness, making 106 from 211 balls, only to be spreadeagled along with his team-mates by the all-conquering Queensland attack at the Gabba. He needs to work on his fielding, but has the ambition and will to succeed. His talent is not in question.

	M	I	NO	R	HS	100s	50s	Avge	Ct	St	W	Avge	BB
First-class	12	22	1	582	106	1	4	27.71	9	0	1	76.00	1/55
Dom. first-class	11	20	1	562	106	1	4	29.58	9	0	1	76.00	1/55
Dom. limited-overs	5	5	1	104	57	0	1	26.00	2	0	–	–	

COOK, Simon Hewitt
Born: January 29, 1972 Hastings (Victoria)
Left-handed batsman, right-arm fast-medium bowler

Frustrated by his inability to force his way back into the Victorian team, Cook returned to the Balmain club in Sydney only to experience similar difficulties with New South Wales. He made an overnight trip from Sydney to replace the injured Nathan Bracken in mid-December in Perth (where he made his Test debut in 1997-98 against New Zealand for match figures of 7/75), but without any glorious *déjà vu*. Failing to take a wicket, he was omitted again, and while he was chosen for two Mercantile Mutual Cup games, the former Test pace man lacked the consistent speed and vigour that had won him his two Test caps.

	M	I	NO	R	HS	100s	50s	Avge	Ct	St	W	Avge	BB
First-class	32	35	15	174	27	0	0	8.70	5	0	84	30.82	5/39
Dom. first-class	26	31	12	145	27	0	0	7.63	4	0	63	33.79	5/114
Test	2	2	2	3	3*	0	0	–	0	0	7	20.29	5/39
Dom. limited-overs	11	6	3	17	11*	0	0	5.67	5	0	11	34.55	4/42

HADDIN, Bradley James
Born: October 23, 1977 Cowra (New South Wales)
Right-handed batsman, wicket-keeper
International limited-overs debut 2000-01

With Nathan Bracken and Don Nash, Brad Haddin has been the best of New South Wales' young representatives. Enormously talented and prepared to work for his rewards, Haddin impressed the national selectors sufficiently in his second first-class season after his move from Canberra to be picked as Adam Gilchrist's understudy during the Carlton Series against West Indies and Zimbabwe. He played in the match against Zimbabwe at Hobart, keeping tidily and hitting 13 off 12 balls. Early in the summer, Haddin struck 69 from 52 balls against Victoria, outshining even the dashing

Michael Slater. One of the most exciting batsmen in Australia, Haddin must overcome the slick Queenslander, Wade Seccombe, if he is to succeed Gilchrist as Test wicket-keeper. Haddin's maiden first-class century must be close, judging from his Pura Cup innings of 93 in Adelaide and 87 at North Sydney Oval.

	M	I	NO	R	HS	100s	50s	Avge	Ct	St	W	Avge	BB
First-class	21	38	2	1,072	93	0	9	29.78	50	6	0	–	–
Dom. first-class	18	33	2	920	93	0	8	29.68	44	5	0	–	–
Int'l limited-overs	1	1	0	13	13	0	0	13.00	0	1	0	–	–
Dom. limited-overs	25	25	0	792	133	1	7	31.68	28	10	0	–	–

HIGGS, Mark Anthony
Born: June 30, 1976 Queanbeyan (New South Wales)
Left-handed batsman, left-arm slow orthodox and 'chinaman' bowler

Few players have had such an astonishing elevation to national honours and fewer still to such an exotic destination – Higgs was selected for Australia's team for the ICC limited-overs tournament in Nairobi in October 2000, restricted though he was to two practice matches before Australia's elimination. Higgs represented the Canberra Comets in 1997-98 before transferring to New South Wales, and while he had shown flashes of outstanding skill, his inclusion in the Australian side came as a surprise. By the end of the 2000-01 season, Higgs had displayed sufficient all-round capabilities to vindicate the selectors' judgment. He appeared in all 11 of the Blues' Mercantile Mutual Cup games, getting starts such as his 33-ball innings of 29 in the final without soaring to great heights. After several useful Pura Cup scores without reaching 50 it was reassuring to see the composure, beautiful cover drive and discipline in his unbeaten 181 against Queensland at the SCG in March. Higgs bowled left-arm orthodox spin or chinaman deliveries at will, without quite the desirable accuracy, his best return being 4/15 in the defeat of the Western Warriors at North Sydney Oval. He will improve the more he works at his game, not least in his fielding.

	M	I	NO	R	HS	100s	50s	Avge	Ct	St	W	Avge	BB
First-class	12	18	1	484	181*	1	0	28.47	10	0	10	56.90	3/59
Dom. first-class	12	18	1	484	181*	1	0	28.47	10	0	10	56.90	3/59
Dom. limited-overs	24	21	4	564	77	0	2	33.18	14	0	21	22.71	4/15

HORSLEY, Daniel Anthony
Born: July 20, 1972 Sydney (New South Wales)
Right-handed batsman, right-arm fast-medium bowler
First-class and domestic first-class debuts 2000-01

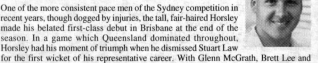

One of the more consistent pace men of the Sydney competition in recent years, though dogged by injuries, the tall, fair-haired Horsley made his belated first-class debut in Brisbane at the end of the season. In a game which Queensland dominated throughout, Horsley had his moment of triumph when he dismissed Stuart Law for the first wicket of his representative career. With Glenn McGrath, Brett Lee and Nathan Bracken required for international duty, Horsley, with his ability to swing the ball away, will undoubtedly be high on the selectors' list.

	M	I	NO	R	HS	100s	50s	Avge	Ct	St	W	Avge	BB
First-class	1	2	2	11	7*	0	0	–	2	0	1	107.00	1/93
Dom. first-class	1	2	2	11	7*	0	0	–	2	0	1	107.00	1/93

JAQUES, Philip Anthony
Born: May 3, 1979 Wollongong (New South Wales)
Left-handed batsman
First-class, domestic first-class and domestic limited-overs
debuts 2000-01

The Sutherland batsman broke into New South Wales' Mercantile
Mutual Cup side following Corey Richards' omission, making an
enterprising 40 from 41 balls against Western Australia in Perth
and receiving another opportunity against Western Australia later
in the summer. But it was Jaques' performance against Queensland
in the Brisbane Pura Cup game which attracted attention. Arriving at lunch as an
eleventh-hour replacement and batting at No. 10 after the top order collapsed, Jaques
made a spirited 40 from 55 balls. In the second innings he opened, making 23 from a
testing 75 balls. There was much to admire in his courage and his enthusiasm, qualities
which should help to assure him the continued attention of the selectors.

	M	I	NO	R	HS	100s	50s	Avge	Ct	St	W	Avge	BB
First-class	1	2	0	63	40	0	0	31.50	1	0	0	–	–
Dom. first-class	1	2	0	63	40	0	0	31.50	1	0	0	–	–
Dom. limited-overs	2	2	0	59	40	0	0	29.50	0	0	0	–	–

LEE, Brett
Born: November 8, 1976 Wollongong (New South Wales)
Right-handed batsman, right-arm fast bowler

The shooting star of Australian cricket, Brett Lee has joined Glenn McGrath and Jason
Gillespie to form one of the most fearsome Test attacks of recent years. Not tall by
today's fast bowling standards, Lee is a genuine speedster with a superb action and
impressive persona. Back injuries are the bane of the fast men, and he has modified his
action to be more square-on and remove some of the great stress on his body caused by
his explosive action. Nevertheless, after taking 11 wickets in the first two Tests against
West Indies, Lee was sidelined due to a fear that he would sustain stress fractures of the
back. Enjoying a return with Australia's limited-overs side, he damaged flexor ligaments
in his right elbow hurling in a return from the boundary in Perth, an injury which cost
him the tour of India. Lee played in five Mercantile Mutual Cup games before Christmas,
three of which New South Wales won, and two Pura Cup games including a win over
Victoria where he captured 5/42 in the second innings at Richmond. In just four first-
class games, Lee took 20 wickets at 20.55, finishing third in the national averages. He
also showed that he can be a combative tail-ender, making 151 runs at 50.33.

	M	I	NO	R	HS	100s	50s	Avge	Ct	St	W	Avge	BB
First-class	28	32	9	467	79	0	2	20.30	7	0	129	20.85	6/25
Dom. first-class	13	17	3	169	34	0	0	12.07	5	0	50	26.86	5/42
Test	7	7	3	150	62*	0	1	37.50	0	0	42	16.10	5/47
Int'l limited-overs	29	9	2	80	31	0	0	11.43	1	0	50	24.72	5/27
Dom. limited-overs	9	3	1	30	14*	0	0	15.00	2	0	15	24.53	3/41

LEE, Shane
Born: August 8, 1973 Wollongong (New South Wales)
Right-handed batsman, right-arm fast-medium bowler

Seeking a dynamic personality to lead New South Wales in Steve Waugh's absence, the
selectors turned to the dual World Cup all-rounder. Shane Lee did not immediately
answer the vote of confidence with the assured middle-order batting the selectors might
have expected, but as the season advanced his performances improved and his captaincy
gained in confidence. He played a 126-ball innings of 115 in the Mercantile Mutual
Cup match against the Western Warriors at North Sydney Oval and a month later, with

his team striving for a Pura Cup final berth, he hit 114 against subsequent winners Queensland at the SCG. But in a season without national call-up, an aggregate of 365 runs at 33.18 with one century and 17 wickets at 27.24 in nine first-class games, and a limited-overs return of 289 runs at 36.13 and eight wickets at 51.75 from the full quota of 11 Mercantile Mutual Cup games, were unsatisfactory to him and his team. There is no logical challenger for the state captaincy, and every reason to believe he will be a better captain and player in the seasons ahead. He took more responsibility with his vigorous pace bowling and his fielding remained at a high standard.

	M	I	NO	R	HS	100s	50s	Avge	Ct	St	W	Avge	BB
First-class	85	139	22	4,821	183*	12	24	41.21	64	0	145	39.70	4/20
Dom. first-class	61	103	16	3,221	183*	7	17	37.02	42	0	92	38.64	4/20
Int'l limited-overs	45	35	8	477	47	0	0	17.67	23	0	48	25.94	5/33
Dom. limited-overs	48	43	5	1,177	115	2	6	30.97	23	0	50	31.28	4/59

MacGILL, Stuart Charles Glyndwr
Born: February 25, 1971 Mount Lawley (Western Australia)
Right-handed batsman, right-arm leg-spin bowler

A season of splendid success and high frustration ended with MacGill failing to win selection for the tour of India, where he might well have displaced Shane Warne, and, less surprisingly, for the Ashes tour of England. But with Warne sidelined with a broken spinning finger, MacGill played a leading role in Australia's 5-0 defeat of West Indies with 16 wickets at 31.31 from four Test appearances. MacGill (30 wickets at 29.63) and Nathan Bracken (29 at 23.72) were the outstanding bowlers for New South Wales, each appearing in seven first-class games. MacGill was also the nation's leading Mercantile Mutual Cup wicket-taker with 18 at 27.78 in all 11 games. While his first-innings performance of 7/104 in the Sydney Test was the highlight of his season, MacGill was competitive, consistent and spirited throughout. Two highlights were the return to his native Perth for the Cup final in which he claimed a wicket, and the captaincy of the New South Wales team for the last game of the Pura Cup against Queensland.

	M	I	NO	R	HS	100s	50s	Avge	Ct	St	W	Avge	BB
First-class	60	83	17	552	43	0	0	8.36	34	0	254	27.68	7/29
Dom. first-class	34	50	12	264	16	0	0	6.95	19	0	122	33.34	6/64
Test	16	22	2	208	43	0	0	10.40	11	0	75	25.03	7/50
Int'l limited-overs	3	2	1	1	1	0	0	1.00	2	0	6	17.50	4/19
Dom. limited-overs	22	7	4	41	18	0	0	13.67	7	0	42	21.81	5/40

MAIL, Gregory John
Born: April 29, 1978 Penrith (New South Wales)
Right-handed batsman, wicket-keeper
Domestic limited-overs debut 2000-01

A tall, lean figure, Mail became one of the season's significant identities, proving obdurate and disciplined, an object lesson to a host of more talented, headstrong batsmen. There was no winkling Mail out – he had to be removed with bulldozer and forklift. He began with a Pura Cup innings of 92 from 255 balls against Western Australia at North Sydney Oval, but it was not until mid-February that his 176 against Tasmania earned him his maiden first-class hundred. Mail was generally content to allow the opposition bowlers to exhaust themselves after which, late in the day's play, he showed an excellent drive and pull shot. He also wears the gloves with aplomb, and acted as a capable back-up wicket-keeper. So valuable was he that New South Wales even resorted to using him at No. 9 in two limited-overs games. The longer his career has continued, the more Mail has thrived on responsibility. A gritty, valuable cricketer is emerging for New South Wales.

	M	I	NO	R	HS	100s	50s	Avge	Ct	St	W	Avge	BB
First-class	16	30	1	928	176	1	5	32.00	13	0	1	21.00	1/6
Dom. first-class	15	28	1	882	176	1	5	32.67	13	0	0	–	–
Dom. limited-overs	3	2	1	29	19*	0	0	29.00	2	1	0	–	–

McGRATH, Glenn Donald
Born: February 9, 1970 Dubbo (New South Wales)
Right-handed batsman, right-arm fast bowler

International cricket's first-choice strike bowler, McGrath is now the finest, most accurate and clever pace bowler Australia has produced since Dennis Lillee. Topping the wicket-takers in the five-Test series defeat of West Indies with 21 wickets to become Player of the Series, and reaching his 300th Test wicket in his 64th Test, McGrath performed equally well in the Carlton Series limited-overs tournament. His enormous international programme permitted McGrath only one appearance in the Pura Cup and four Mercantile Mutual Cup games, in which he proved the most economical of all New South Wales bowlers, conceding 3.65 runs an over. New South Wales won the Pura Cup game and two of the Mercantile Mutual Cup games and in each, McGrath bowled with all the pace and accuracy he brings to international cricket. He is one of the supreme cricketers of his generation.

	M	I	NO	R	HS	100s	50s	Avge	Ct	St	W	Avge	BB
First-class	126	133	42	654	55	0	1	7.19	34	0	566	20.57	8/38
Dom. first-class	19	18	7	71	18*	0	0	6.45	2	0	76	25.83	5/36
Test	70	85	27	388	39	0	0	6.69	21	0	326	21.71	8/38
Int'l limited-overs	140	41	24	70	11	0	0	4.12	17	0	212	23.59	5/14
Dom. limited-overs	15	0	0	0	–	0	0	–	4	0	18	25.72	4/17

NASH, Don Anthony
Born: March 29, 1978 Dubbo (New South Wales)
Right-handed batsman, right-arm fast-medium bowler

The thick-set all-rounder was so successful in the opening stages of the season that he won a position in the Australia A team, and he was on the short list to tour India with Steve Waugh's Australians before being nudged out by Michael Kasprowicz. Nash is genuinely fast, but it was his volcanic efforts with the bat which won him national attention. He plundered the Western Warriors for an unbeaten 61 at North Sydney Oval from just 28 balls in the Mercantile Mutual Cup, and scored his 255 first-class runs for the season from just 208 balls. However, Nash tore his hamstring muscle in the Pura Cup game against South Australia in Adelaide early in January and he never fully regained confidence thereafter to bowl at top pace. The selectors were compelled to drop him to 12th man for the Pura Cup game against Victoria at the SCG less than five weeks after his explosive innings, by which time he was bowling at barely half pace. Nash regained his place in the side for the last Pura Cup game against Queensland, but, for all his enormous talent, reservations remain about him until he completes a full season for New South Wales.

	M	I	NO	R	HS	100s	50s	Avge	Ct	St	W	Avge	BB
First-class	18	31	2	342	46	0	0	11.79	3	0	47	31.34	7/54
Dom. first-class	16	28	2	312	46	0	0	12.00	3	0	40	32.25	7/54
Dom. limited-overs	6	1	1	61	61*	0	1	–	1	0	7	27.14	3/31

PHELPS, Matthew James
Born: September 1, 1972 Lismore (New South Wales)
Right-handed batsman

A beefy personality from Sam Trimble territory on the far north coast of New South Wales, Phelps fought his way back into representative cricket yet again through sheer weight of runs for Manly in the Sydney grade competition. He shows some of the tenacity which made Trimble such a renowned run-scorer for Queensland. Phelps was recalled for the toughest of clashes against Queensland at the Gabba in the last game of the season, acquitting himself well in the crisis at No. 3 with innings of 40 and 30. Still not yet 30, Phelps has younger batsmen jostling around him, but he seems to have the necessary qualities to succeed even now at state level.

	M	I	NO	R	HS	100s	50s	Avge	Ct	St	W	Avge	BB
First-class	8	16	0	491	192	1	2	30.69	3	0	0	–	–
Dom. first-class	8	16	0	491	192	1	2	30.69	3	0	0	–	–
Dom. limited-overs	5	5	0	56	23	0	0	11.20	1	0	0	–	–

PILON, Nathan Steven
Born: October 27, 1976 Dubbo (New South Wales)
Right-handed batsman, wicket-keeper
First-class and domestic first-class debuts 2000-01

The thick-set son of a prominent country rugby league player and the product of a strong sporting family, Pilon broke into first-class cricket from the St George club in the absence of Brad Haddin in the Pura Cup game against Victoria at the SCG, making a favourable impression with five catches. Smart of foot and deft of hand, Pilon must hope that the national selectors continue to show interest in Haddin if he is not to spend too much time waiting in the New South Wales Second XI.

	M	I	NO	R	HS	100s	50s	Avge	Ct	St	W	Avge	BB
First-class	1	1	0	8	8	0	0	8.00	5	0	0	–	–
Dom. first-class	1	1	0	8	8	0	0	8.00	5	0	0	–	–

RICHARDS, Corey John
Born: August 25, 1975 Camden (New South Wales)
Right-handed batsman, right-arm medium bowler

Of all the painful decisions they made, omitting Richards from both the first-class and limited-over teams was probably the hardest of all for the selectors after persisting with him through thick and thin since his debut in 1995-96. In five years, often riding out barren patches, the smooth-stroking middle-order batsman made a century for Australia A against England in Hobart in 1998-99 as well as six other first-class hundreds and 109 in his Mercantile Mutual Cup debut against Western Australia in 1996-97. A lovely cover driver, smart in the field and conscientious, Richards had Australian representation written all over him, only for consistency to desert him. Four half-centuries in five innings including an unbeaten 73 from 60 balls against Queensland in Brisbane began 2000-01 well, but a horrific series of ducks, including four in succession in Pura Cup games, forced the issue and he was dropped early in the new year. At 26, Richards must become more fiercely tenacious or his career will end prematurely.

	M	I	NO	R	HS	100s	50s	Avge	Ct	St	W	Avge	BB
First-class	45	82	4	2,571	164	7	14	32.96	24	0	0	–	–
Dom. first-class	39	73	3	2,094	164	5	12	29.91	18	0	0	–	–
Dom. limited-overs	33	30	3	799	109	1	5	29.59	10	0	0	–	–

RUMMANS, Graeme Clifford
Born: December 13, 1976 Camperdown (New South Wales)
Left-handed batsman, left-arm medium

A stylish middle-order batsman from the renowned St George club, Rummans has followed a long line of batsmen tried and found wanting by New South Wales. But, like Corey Richards, he has always given the impression that a splendid representative career was awaiting him. Rummans was chosen in a full-strength New South Wales team for the first Mercantile Mutual Cup game, did not bat, was dropped, was recalled for a game in Brisbane two months later, dropped and recalled again five weeks later to become a regular member of the team, eventually scoring 30 not out from 27 balls in the Cup final in Perth. Consistent, if not high, scores earned Rummans a position in the last three games of the Pura Cup season, his season's top score of 46 against a rampant Queensland at the Gabba being an indication that better days lay ahead.

	M	I	NO	R	HS	100s	50s	Avge	Ct	St	W	Avge	BB
First-class	19	30	4	719	119	1	3	27.65	13	0	5	22.60	3/24
Dom. first-class	17	28	4	522	67	0	2	21.75	11	0	2	43.50	2/71
Dom. limited-overs	19	17	2	492	75	0	3	32.80	5	0	0	–	–

SLATER, Michael Jonathon
Born: February 21, 1970 Wagga Wagga (New South Wales)
Right-handed batsman, right-arm bowler

Recognised internationally as one of the most dynamic opening batsmen in the game and frustrated by his inability to break into Australia's limited-overs team, Slater has also encountered opposition to the New South Wales captaincy in Steve Waugh's absence. Three others have enjoyed the honour in the last two seasons. Slater appeared in nine of the team's 11 Mercantile Mutual Cup games, but with little joy, scoring just two half-centuries for an aggregate of 205 runs at 22.78, hardly enough to make the national selectors alter their stance. Perhaps at the instigation of the national selectors, Slater was dropped down the order to No. 3 and No. 4 while Brad Haddin and Michael Clarke opened the innings in later Mercantile Mutual Cup games. However, in one of his two Pura Cup appearances, he had the satisfaction of registering a century against Tasmania at Bellerive in November. Whatever the selectors' reservations about his limited-overs cricket, Slater's Test standing remains unchallenged, and he appeared in all five Tests against West Indies for 373 runs at 53.29. Slater, Mark Waugh and Glenn McGrath were the three players involved in every match of Australia's record run of 16 successive Test wins.

	M	I	NO	R	HS	100s	50s	Avge	Ct	St	W	Avge	BB
First-class	190	338	17	13,478	221	33	65	41.99	107	0	3	32.33	1/4
Dom. first-class	49	93	2	3,700	143	9	22	40.66	33	0	0	–	–
Test	70	124	7	5,142	219	14	20	43.95	32	0	1	10.00	1/4
Int'l limited-overs	42	42	1	987	73	0	9	24.07	9	0	0	–	–
Dom. limited-overs	34	34	0	837	96	0	7	24.62	10	0	0	–	–

STEWART, James
Born: August 22, 1970 East Fremantle (Western Australia)
Right-handed batsman, slow left-arm orthodox bowler

The leading wicket-taker in Sydney club cricket since his 1999 transfer from Western Australia, for whom he played 18 first-class games, Stewart's cagey, accurate bowling initially won him recognition in the New South Wales squads for the first two Mercantile Mutual Cup matches without making the playing team. Selected for the Pura Cup game against Western Australia, Stewart was called on to bowl just 13 overs at North Sydney Oval. He failed to take a wicket and was not summoned again, the selectors preferring Anthony Clark, a bowler with greater powers of flight and spin.

	M	I	NO	R	HS	100s	50s	Avge	Ct	St	W	Avge	BB
First-class	20	28	5	237	51	0	1	10.30	7	0	36	53.25	4/121
Dom. first-class	17	25	5	218	51	0	1	10.90	6	0	27	57.11	3/68
Dom. limited-overs	34	20	11	82	14	0	0	9.11	8	0	38	30.58	4/34

THOMPSON, Scott Michael
Born: May 4, 1972 Bankstown (New South Wales)
Right-handed batsman, right-arm fast-medium bowler

Having been one of the outstanding all-rounders of the 1990s in Sydney club cricket and a Bill O'Reilly Medallist as Sydney's leading cricketer, the paucity of Thompson's moments of representative satisfaction remains as perplexing to his admirers as to himself. Thompson's often volatile pace bowling and hard-hitting innings, his excellent fielding and competitiveness, for Bankstown–Canterbury and later St George, were first recognised in 1994-95, and while he has represented the state every season since, save for 1999-2000, his inability to make a half-century in 17 first-class games or take five wickets in an innings has prevented him from establishing himself in the team. But, as the Mercantile Mutual Cup neared its conclusion, the selectors again turned to Thompson, and he was part of the victorious Blues side for the final in Perth.

	M	I	NO	R	HS	100s	50s	Avge	Ct	St	W	Avge	BB
First-class	17	27	3	386	49*	0	0	16.08	9	0	42	43.67	4/56
Dom. first-class	16	26	3	376	49*	0	0	16.35	9	0	41	42.88	4/56
Dom. limited-overs	20	16	3	243	68*	0	1	18.69	5	0	15	42.40	2/29

VAN DEINSEN, Brett Paul
Born: December 28, 1977 Bankstown (New South Wales)
Right-handed batsman, right-arm fast-medium bowler

The selectors thought their opening problems without Michael Slater would be overcome when they made the tall, powerfully built Brett van Deinsen the partner of the slim, steely Greg Mail. They were half right. At club level for St George, van Deinsen was the most dominant of batsmen, yet he failed to reproduce innings of such authority at state level. He appeared in five successive Pura Cup games, with a top score of 29 against Western Australia at North Sydney Oval before he was omitted late in the competition. At 23 years of age, van Deinsen appears to have the talent and determination to play his way back into the side, and his Benaud Medal innings of 172 to help St George win the final did much to restore him to favour.

	M	I	NO	R	HS	100s	50s	Avge	Ct	St	W	Avge	BB
First-class	7	13	0	193	29	0	0	14.85	9	0	0	–	–
Dom. first-class	7	13	0	193	29	0	0	14.85	9	0	0	–	–

WAUGH, Mark Edward
Born: June 2, 1965 Canterbury (New South Wales)
Right-handed batsman, right-arm off-spin bowler

Champions can almost pick and choose their time and place, so it came as no surprise when Mark Waugh began his domestic season with an unbeaten 108 from 134 balls, opening the innings in the Mercantile Mutual Cup at his cricketing birthplace of Bankstown Oval. Waugh helped New South Wales to outright victory over Victoria with innings of 53 and 46 and punished Tasmania with an innings of 152 at Bellerive. Three forgettable Mercantile Mutual Cup innings followed, after which he was required for national duty, appearing in all five Tests against West Indies for 339 runs at 48.43, trailing only Steve Waugh and Michael Slater, and playing an even more distinguished role in the Carlton Series. Waugh made three centuries and two half-centuries in nine limited-overs internationals, including an all-time Australian record 173 from 148 balls in the Melbourne final, a feat all the more astonishing as he was subjected to an inquiry into alleged cricket corruption at the height of the play-offs. Mark finished one vote behind his brother, 62 to 63, in the Allan Border Medal count as the outstanding international cricketer for 2000-01.

	M	I	NO	R	HS	100s	50s	Avge	Ct	St	W	Avge	BB
First-class	324	521	64	24,074	229*	76	118	52.68	387	0	202	39.11	6/68
Dom. first-class	72	121	13	5,941	229*	22	23	55.01	85	0	51	36.78	4/130
Test	111	184	14	7,081	153*	18	42	41.65	152	0	54	38.98	5/40
Int'l limited-overs	237	229	19	8,374	173	18	49	39.88	105	0	83	34.84	5/24
Dom. limited-overs	41	40	4	1,269	112	2	8	35.25	23	0	19	31.26	3/23

WAUGH, Stephen Rodger
Born: June 2, 1965 Canterbury (New South Wales)
Right-handed batsman, right-arm medium bowler

Waugh senior joined the elite of his nation's cricketers when he was named Allan Border Medallist for 2000-01 after leading Australia to a 5-0 clean sweep in the Frank Worrell Trophy and, with Adam Gilchrist, captaining the side to an unprecedented ten-game winning streak in the Carlton Series. His summer was marred only by injury. Waugh sustained a groin strain early in the limited-overs tournament and missed three successive games. Prior to that setback, Waugh strained his buttock, forcing him out of the Adelaide Test against West Indies. Nevertheless, Waugh still topped Australia's Test averages with 349 runs at 69.80 including hundreds in the Boxing Day and New Year Tests. Waugh made his 25th Test hundred in Australia's first innings of 445 in the Second Test in Kolkata. His involvement with New South Wales was obviously restricted, with an innings of 75 not out from 73 balls against Tasmania in one of his five Mercantile Mutual Cup appearances his season's highest score domestically. He achieved little in his two Pura Cup games, which proved the man is only human. Waugh bowls rarely these days after back strains threatened his cricket, but there are few tougher and more secure fieldsmen in the game.

	M	I	NO	R	HS	100s	50s	Avge	Ct	St	W	Avge	BB
First-class	299	464	77	20,335	216*	64	86	52.55	239	0	243	32.03	6/51
Dom. first-class	70	119	13	5,390	216*	17	21	50.85	72	0	82	30.78	6/51
Test	135	215	39	8,965	200	25	42	50.94	96	0	89	35.74	5/28
Int'l limited-overs	317	281	57	7,382	120*	3	44	32.96	108	0	195	34.38	4/33
Dom. limited-overs	37	36	6	1,415	131	2	9	47.17	14	0	34	24.85	4/32

QUEENSLAND

By Stephen Gray

ANDERSON, Matthew Allen
Born: October 30, 1976 Darwin (Northern Territory)
Right-handed batsman, slow left-arm orthodox bowler

Patience is an integral aspect of spin bowling and, after tasting action in the first few matches of the summer, Matthew Anderson found himself calling upon all his reserves as Scott O'Leary was preferred for the second half of the season. His club cricket form for Sandgate–Redcliffe was solid, and he captured 29 wickets at 18.41 including a best of 7/67. With pace in the ascendancy in Queensland, the lot of the spinner continues to be a testing one. A rangy left-armer with a good temperament, Anderson travelled to England in the off-season to further his cricketing education, playing for Norwich in the East Anglia Premier League.

	M	I	NO	R	HS	100s	50s	Avge	Ct	St	W	Avge	BB
First-class	13	14	7	19	7*	0	0	2.71	5	0	25	37.16	4/50
Dom. first-class	11	12	7	15	7*	0	0	3.00	5	0	16	42.31	3/79
Dom. limited-overs	2	–	–	–	–	–	–	–	0	0	2	39.00	2/25

BICHEL, Andrew John
Born: August 27, 1970 Laidley (Queensland)
Right-handed batsman, right-arm fast-medium bowler

Andy Bichel thrives on a challenge, and his feats in both hemispheres during the past 12 months provide evidence of his steely determination to succeed. The strong man of the Queensland attack was involved in the first four Tests of 2000-01 against West Indies (playing in the first and fourth games) and enjoyed a career highlight with his first Test five-wicket haul in Melbourne. But the return of Jason Gillespie forced Bichel to shift his focus to state cricket, where he continued to take wickets at a strike-rate eclipsed by only a handful of other Queenslanders. He finished with 40 Pura Cup scalps at 21.80 from seven games, including key dismissals in the final, where he represents somewhat of a hoodoo for the Victorians. He made the pragmatic decision to join Worcestershire following hearty endorsements from their previous import Glenn McGrath and new coaching director Tom Moody. Bichel quickly showed their faith was not misplaced, scoring a cracking limited-overs century against Glamorgan and assuming the duty of strike bowler.

	M	I	NO	R	HS	100s	50s	Avge	Ct	St	W	Avge	BB
First-class	75	98	8	1,702	110	1	6	18.91	39	0	319	23.95	6/44
Dom. first-class	48	65	4	1,271	110	1	5	20.84	25	0	233	21.92	6/45
Test	5	7	0	58	18	0	0	8.29	2	0	9	46.78	5/60
Int'l limited-overs	17	11	4	99	27*	0	0	14.14	2	0	21	33.38	3/17
Dom. limited-overs	39	21	7	288	40*	0	0	20.57	14	0	40	36.23	4/45

CARSELDINE, Lee Andrew
Born: November 17, 1975 Nambour (Queensland)
Left-handed batsman, left-arm medium bowler
Domestic first-class debut 2000-01

An athletic talent in the purest sense, Carseldine is still searching for the alchemy that will turn his ability into results in the first-class and limited-overs arenas and win some long-term confidence from the selectors. He played five Pura Cup and ten Mercantile Mutual Cup matches, where he showed the development of his quickish left-arm bowling. Added to his ability as an attacking left-handed bat, his increased confidence in his ability with the ball should help him in the future. A personal fitness trainer, Carseldine played part of the off-season with Littleborough in the Central Lancashire League until a foot fracture ended his stint prematurely in July.

	M	I	NO	R	HS	100s	50s	Avge	Ct	St	W	Avge	BB
First-class	6	8	0	89	26	0	0	11.13	6	0	0	–	–
Dom. first-class	6	8	0	89	26	0	0	11.13	6	0	0	–	–
Dom. limited-overs	12	11	1	181	34	0	0	18.10	6	0	1	96.00	1/32

CASSELL, Jerry Lee
Born: January 12, 1975 Mona Vale (New South Wales)
Right-handed batsman, slow left-arm orthodox bowler
Domestic limited-overs debut 2000-01

The international splash created by Matthew Hayden has created some favourable ripples for Cassell, a dogged opening batsman. Cassell had been adrift since making his first-class debut against England A in 1996-97, but with his impressive youth career (Australian Under-19s and Cricket Academy) and some healthy scoring at grade and Second Eleven level in his favour, the selectors felt confident that he would swim rather than sink if called upon to fill the considerable gap left by Hayden. He largely confirmed that, with his 136 against Tasmania displaying a steely concentration and a strong array of shots. A former Australian youth volleyball player,

Cassell started as a left-arm pace bowler for the Wynnum–Manly club but found his home at the top of the order with the bat when he switched to bayside rivals Sandgate–Redcliffe. He has managed to mix first-class cricket with the demands of working as a crane operator on the Brisbane wharves.

	M	I	NO	R	HS	100s	50s	Avge	Ct	St	W	Avge	BB
First-class	9	14	1	374	136	1	1	28.77	6	0	0	–	–
Dom. first-class	8	13	1	352	136	1	1	29.33	5	0	0	–	–
Dom. limited-overs	1	1	0	13	13	0	0	13.00	0	0	0	–	–

CREEVEY, Brendan Neville
Born: February 18, 1970 Charleville (Queensland)
Right-handed batsman, right-arm fast-medium bowler

Creevey played three domestic limited-overs matches but without the success that had earned him selection for Australia A in 1999. He made his first appearance in first-class cricket since 1998-99 as a late replacement for Michael Kasprowicz, taking 3/42 against South Australia where he and the rest of the Queensland attack foundered on the rock that was Greg Blewett's double-century. Overlooked for a Queensland contract for 2001-02, Creevey, a primary school vice-principal, intends to play on with Sandgate–Redcliffe, where he captained the team last season.

	M	I	NO	R	HS	100s	50s	Avge	Ct	St	W	Avge	BB
First-class	12	18	5	241	52	0	1	18.54	4	0	31	30.00	6/70
Dom. first-class	11	17	5	241	52	0	1	20.08	4	0	25	33.08	5/32
Dom. limited-overs	25	18	8	215	32	0	0	21.50	2	0	28	31.89	3/26

DALE, Adam Craig
Born: December 30, 1968 Greensborough (Victoria)
Left-handed batsman, right-arm fast-medium bowler

As reliable as the day is long, Dale's value to Queensland will probably not be fully appreciated until he finally allows the sun to set on his career. His metronomic right-arm medium pace has produced a statistical record the envy of many of his peers. In 2000-01 he took 46 wickets at 23.39 for Queensland, his best season return, while assuming a heavy workload on occasions. This was highlighted by his effort in bowling 44 overs and taking 3/83 against New South Wales at the SCG in March. He bowled many more overs than any other bowler in the country, maintaining a miserly economy rate of only 1.88 runs per over, and never allowing batsmen a moment's rest.

	M	I	NO	R	HS	100s	50s	Avge	Ct	St	W	Avge	BB
First-class	54	64	11	783	55	0	1	14.77	11	0	226	20.69	7/24
Dom. first-class	39	48	7	644	48	0	0	15.71	9	0	165	22.15	7/40
Test	2	3	0	6	5	0	0	2.00	0	0	6	31.17	3/71
Int'l limited-overs	30	12	8	78	15*	0	0	19.50	11	0	32	30.59	3/18
Dom. limited-overs	27	11	6	55	14*	0	0	11.00	6	0	36	23.39	4/26

DAWES, Joseph Henry
Born: August 29, 1970 Herston (Queensland)
Right-handed batsman, right-arm fast-medium bowler

The 2000-01 season for Joe Dawes was the perfect instance of one player's misfortune being another's opportunity. Injuries to Scott Muller, Ashley Noffke and the late start by Michael Kasprowicz presented Dawes with an opening, and by the season's end he was the leading wicket-taker in the Pura Cup, where his 49 wickets at 20.46 played a key role in Queensland's victory. Having started the season with a solitary five-wicket haul in first-class cricket (for MCC in 1999) he finished it with three more, including career-best figures of 7/98 as part of his ten-wicket haul against South Australia in Adelaide. The robust plain-clothes policeman maintained a fine clean-up rate during an off-season stint in England, impressing again for MCC against the touring Australians at Arundel.

	M	I	NO	R	HS	100s	50s	Avge	Ct	St	W	Avge	BB
First-class	26	33	10	206	23*	0	0	8.96	6	0	113	21.89	7/98
Dom. first-class	24	30	9	194	23*	0	0	9.24	6	0	100	22.47	7/98
Dom. limited-overs	2	0	0	0	–	0	0	–	0	0	3	30.33	2/29

FOLEY, Geoffrey Ian
Born: October 11, 1967 Jandowie (Queensland)
Left-handed batsman, right-arm medium bowler

Geoff Foley announced his retirement from all cricket at the end of the 2000-01 season after a career that soared early, disappeared, and then re-emerged with a solid second wind. A regular in the Queensland line-up for the past four seasons, he missed selection early in the season due to illness and subsequently saw his opportunities for recall diminish as the selectors looked to the future. He played two Mercantile Mutual Cup matches, with a top score of 57, but acknowledged the end was nigh. His legacy as a hard-hitting left-hander and off-break bowler, who played 65 first-class games for Queensland, scoring 2,846 runs 30.60, taking 72 catches and 44 wickets, is more than noteworthy. A career highlight was his selection for Australia A in 1996-97, the same year he won the Mercantile Mutual Cup Player of the Year award. A popular team member, his reliability and good humour will be missed.

	M	I	NO	R	HS	100s	50s	Avge	Ct	St	W	Avge	BB
First-class	65	104	11	2,846	155	2	16	30.60	72	0	44	54.70	5/25
Dom. first-class	57	93	10	2,474	122	1	15	29.81	62	0	33	63.09	3/64
Dom. limited-overs	41	34	7	677	66	0	3	25.07	12	0	23	31.65	4/34

HAURITZ, Nathan Michael
Born: October 18, 1981 Wondai (Queensland)
Right-handed batsman, right-arm off-spin bowler
Domestic limited-overs debut 2000-01

A highly regarded young cricketer who could well emerge as Queensland's first-choice spinner in the next few seasons, Hauritz made his domestic limited-overs debut in 2000-01 and displayed enough to suggest that his impressive form in youth cricket could translate to a higher level. He captained the Australian Under-19s team against Sri Lanka, and the Cricket Academy on its tour of Bangladesh, before being recalled to Brisbane to make his debut against Victoria. He is a fine fielder and capable batsman whose coaches at youth and academy level believe he has the makings of a genuine all-rounder. Allan Border earmarked him for bigger things when he saw the then 16-year-old Nudgee College student perform as a net bowler. Hauritz is completing a Commerce degree at the Australian Catholic University.

	M	I	NO	R	HS	100s	50s	Avge	Ct	St	W	Avge	BB
Dom. limited-overs	5	2	0	1	1	0	0	0.50	1	0	4	33.50	2/13

Australia's Test Ball for over 50 years.

HAYDEN, Matthew Lawrence
Born: October 29, 1971 Kingaroy (Queensland)
Left-handed batsman, right-arm medium bowler

The cricketing gods elected to end Matthew Hayden's international purgatory in emphatic fashion, and his Indian tour provided both vindication for him and celebration for his many supporters. Hayden felt at home in India, where his Test return of 549 runs at 109.80, with a highest score of 203, revived the "Matt the Bat" sobriquet of his younger days. Naturally, Queensland saw less of him than ever before, with just three first-class and eight limited-overs matches for the state, although he added another century to give him 24 first-class hundreds for Queensland, equal with Sam Trimble and Peter Burge. A passionate angler, Hayden found time in a hectic Ashes schedule to indulge in a spot of fly-fishing, a hobby he had enjoyed greatly during his county stint with Northamptonshire.

	M	I	NO	R	HS	100s	50s	Avge	Ct	St	W	Avge	BB
First-class	188	327	33	15,370	235*	47	67	52.28	165	0	17	39.47	3/10
Dom. first-class	79	144	17	6,903	234	22	29	54.35	72	0	3	31.00	2/17
Test	16	28	1	1,085	203	3	4	40.19	19	0	0	–	–
Int'l limited-overs	27	25	2	788	111	1	7	34.26	10	0	0	–	–
Dom. limited-overs	46	46	9	2,162	152*	8	11	58.43	16	0	3	10.67	2/16

HOPES, James Redfern
Born: October 24, 1978 Townsville (Queensland)
Right-handed batsman, right-arm fast-medium bowler
Domestic limited-overs debut 2000-01

A pleasant surprise for Queensland, Hopes benefited from the Queensland limited-overs shake-up and took to his task with gusto. Although he played in only the last five limited-overs games, his 11 wickets at 17.18 made him the leading wicket-taker for the Queensland. His 5/29 against South Australia in Adelaide was the best bowling analysis in the competition, and the best by a Queensland bowler since Carl Rackemann in 1993-94. With his clever mixture of pace he neatly fills the role previously held by Scott Prestwidge. Although not tested greatly with the bat last season, he can point to a double of 96 and 102 for Queensland Colts in 1999-2000 as evidence that he has something to offer as an all-rounder. He toured Pakistan with the Australian youth team in 1997, went to the World Youth Cup in 1998 and attended the Cricket Academy in 1998-99.

	M	I	NO	R	HS	100s	50s	Avge	Ct	St	W	Avge	BB
Dom. limited-overs	5	5	0	33	24	0	0	6.60	1	0	11	17.18	5/29

KASPROWICZ, Michael Scott
Born: February 10, 1972 South Brisbane (Queensland)
Right-handed batsman, right-arm fast bowler

Fashionable for unfashionable tours – that was the tart observation passed by a supporter of the whole-hearted Queensland pace man following his omission from the 2001 Ashes squad a few months after returning from the tour of India. Kasprowicz was entitled to be disappointed after again finding himself quickly in and out of favour with the national selectors, especially after fighting back from major shoulder surgery after the tour of New Zealand. That injury kept him out of action for several months, including the first half of the season. He played just one first-class match for Queensland, grabbing 5/29 against Tasmania, but his past deeds stood him in good stead with a call-up for the Indian tour. He was not required to repeat the heroics of his previous Indian tour, playing just one Test this time, and younger bowlers were preferred for the Ashes squad. The

Australian Rugby Union made discreet inquiries as to whether the former Australian Schoolboys forward had considered trying his lot with another sport, but Kasprowicz elected not to trade in his flannels for the coming season.

	M	I	NO	R	HS	100s	50s	Avge	Ct	St	W	Avge	BB
First-class	144	188	39	2,684	92	0	8	18.01	52	0	550	26.89	7/36
Dom. first-class	65	86	15	1,147	52*	0	2	16.15	24	0	267	25.04	6/47
Test	17	23	5	234	25	0	0	13.00	6	0	47	37.00	7/36
Int'l limited-overs	16	8	6	60	28*	0	0	30.00	3	0	22	32.23	3/50
Dom. limited-overs	44	24	10	195	34	0	0	13.93	12	0	56	29.02	4/21

LAW, Stuart Grant
Born: October 18, 1968 Herston (Queensland)
Right-handed batsman, right-arm medium bowler

Law is destined to finish his career as one of the legends of the game in his home state, much in the manner of Jamie Siddons, Tom Moody and John Inverarity. Barring injury, Law is set to pass Sam Trimble's mark of 133 first-class matches as the most-capped Queensland player. He is already the state's most successful captain. Law has been in charge of all of Queensland's domestic four-day titles, and while his international aspirations have dropped away, he remains hungry for success. Law backs himself and his team, never more so than in the Pura Cup Final when he set up victory with his fearless strokeplay despite half a dozen lives. His batting remains potent, yielding 814 runs at 62.61. His love affair with the English game continues unabated. He produced a remarkable effort of three hundreds in four days for Essex in June, scoring unbeaten centuries in each innings against Lancashire and another century the next day in a limited-overs match against the same opponents.

	M	I	NO	R	HS	100s	50s	Avge	Ct	St	W	Avge	BB
First-class	229	381	41	17,138	263	53	82	50.41	263	0	80	48.54	5/39
Dom. first-class	114	188	22	7,532	216	22	38	45.37	103	0	50	44.68	5/39
Test	1	1	1	54	54*	0	1	–	1	0	0	–	–
Int'l limited-overs	54	51	5	1,237	110	1	9	26.89	12	0	12	52.92	2/22
Dom. limited-overs	64	59	6	1,830	159	5	5	34.53	24	0	20	28.95	4/33

LOVE, Martin Lloyd
Born: March 30, 1974 Mundubbera (Queensland)
Right-handed batsman

It was a case of physiotherapist heal thyself for Martin Love, with the languid right-hander finding himself at the centre of a classic "injury smokescreen" in the lead-up to the Pura Cup Final. Love, who works as a physiotherapist away from cricket, fractured his thumb against New South Wales and was expected to miss the final weeks of the season. Instead, it turned out to be thumbs up for Queensland and down for Victoria as Love, aided by a plastic splint, scored a timely 52 in the second innings as the match built to its thrilling climax. His excellent domestic season – including 910 first-class runs at 75.83 for Queensland and Australia A – earned him an array of rewards. The modest Love found attention heaped upon him as he collected the Ian Healy Trophy as Queensland's Player of the Year for the first time before setting off to make his county championship debut in England. Along the way he picked up an ACB contract as the national selectors continued their regime of succession planning. His run-scoring continued unabated with Durham, where he quickly found conditions to his liking.

	M	I	NO	R	HS	100s	50s	Avge	Ct	St	W	Avge	BB
First-class	98	168	13	7,057	228	18	32	45.53	117	0	1	5.00	1/5
Dom. first-class	72	122	8	5,093	228	13	21	44.68	84	0	1	5.00	1/5
Dom. limited-overs	47	44	6	1,321	124	1	7	34.76	18	0	0	–	–

MAHER, James Patrick
Born: February 27, 1974 Innisfail (Queensland)
Left-handed batsman, right-arm medium bowler

Maher finally broke through for the type of season that he and many others had believed was due by topping the run-scoring list for Queensland and passing 1,000 first-class runs in a season for the first time. Maher racked up 1,142 runs at 63.44 for Queensland and Australia A, and just missed 1,000 runs for Queensland (946 at 59.12). He was Queensland's leading limited-overs scorer as well, with 391 runs at 55.85. After celebrating back-to-back Pura Cup titles in customary fashion, the bubbly Maher broke out the champagne when he married Debbie Churchward. Their reception was held at the pavilion overlooking Allan Border Field. A stint with Glamorgan added further weight to his resume, and he scored his highest limited-overs score of 142 not out for the Welsh county. Australian cricket may yet benefit from his talents at the top of a national batting line-up.

	M	I	NO	R	HS	100s	50s	Avge	Ct	St	W	Avge	BB
First-class	99	173	24	5,979	208*	12	27	40.13	101	0	10	48.30	3/11
Dom. first-class	81	142	17	4,676	208*	7	23	37.41	86	0	10	30.20	3/11
Int'l limited-overs	2	2	0	21	13	0	0	10.50	0	0	0	–	–
Dom. limited-overs	50	50	8	2,035	128	4	12	48.45	18	0	2	43.50	2/43

NASH, Brendan Paul
Born: December 14, 1977 Bentley (Western Australia)
Left-handed batsman
First-class, domestic first-class and domestic limited-overs
debuts 2000-01

A diminutive left-hander and excellent fielder, Nash finished his season as a member of the Pura Cup championship team after playing four first-class and three domestic limited-overs matches in 2000-01. He impressed his team-mates with a composed limited-overs innings against South Australia and a knock of 44 in the second innings of the outright loss to New South Wales. Born in Perth and raised in Cairns before attending Nudgee College in Brisbane, Nash has a distinctly West Indian heritage. His parents grew up in Kingston, Jamaica, and his father represented Jamaica in swimming at the 1968 Olympics and the 1966 and 1970 Commonwealth Games. Since they settled in Brisbane, the Nash family home has been a regular stopping-off point for touring West Indian teams.

	M	I	NO	R	HS	100s	50s	Avge	Ct	St	W	Avge	BB
First-class	4	6	0	68	44	0	0	11.33	1	0	0	–	–
Dom. first-class	4	6	0	68	44	0	0	11.33	1	0	0	–	–
Dom. limited-overs	3	3	1	47	31	0	0	23.50	1	0	0	–	–

NOFFKE, Ashley Allan
Born: April 30, 1977 Nambour (Queensland)
Right-handed batsman, right-arm fast bowler
First-class, domestic first-class and domestic limited-overs debuts 2000-01

Noffke, who has been likened by some observers to Glenn McGrath, began the season highly regarded in Queensland cricket yet largely unheralded elsewhere, apart from Tasmania, who had already unsuccessfully sought him to lead their pace attack. Their loss was Queensland's gain. A foot injury traced back to bowling on the flint-hard WACA wicket took him out of circulation for almost a third of the season but his surprise elevation to the starting team for the Pura Cup Final proved a master-stroke. His first-innings 5/41 was a body blow to Victoria, who then had to endure his patient 43 as night-watchman and a further three second-innings wickets. His Player of the Match performance before the national selectors had its sequel a month later on his 24th birthday when he learned he had been granted an ACB contract after just six first-class matches. A few weeks later he was called up to replace Nathan Bracken on the Ashes tour. He made his first-class debut for the Cricket Academy in Zimbabwe in 1999 alongside Brett Lee.

	M	I	NO	R	HS	100s	50s	Avge	Ct	St	W	Avge	BB
First-class	6	5	2	63	43	0	0	21.00	2	0	24	26.96	5/41
Dom. first-class	5	5	2	63	43	0	0	21.00	2	0	21	30.10	5/41
Dom. limited-overs	10	1	0	1	1	0	0	1.00	2	0	8	46.50	3/32

O'LEARY, Scott James
Born: December 17, 1977 South Brisbane (Queensland)
Right-handed batsman, right-arm off-spin bowler
First-class, domestic first-class and domestic limited-overs debuts 2000-01

The overwhelming might of Queensland's pace bowlers on the first-class stage last season meant that O'Leary's initial foray at this level saw him largely consigned to a bit part rather than a starring role. He played three Mercantile Mutual Cup and seven Pura Cup matches, filling the 12th-man role in the final. His returns with the ball were modest – nine wickets at 63 with a best of 4/105 – but the experience could well be crucial in his future development. He was invited to the annual eight-day intensive camp at the MRF Pace Foundation in Chennai, where he worked on his spin technique with the likes of Bishen Bedi and Erapalli Prasanna.

	M	I	NO	R	HS	100s	50s	Avge	Ct	St	W	Avge	BB
First-class	7	7	3	42	19	0	0	10.50	5	0	9	63.11	4/105
Dom. first-class	7	7	3	42	19	0	0	10.50	5	0	9	63.11	4/105
Dom. limited-overs	3	0	0	–	–	0	0	–	1	0	0	–	–

PASCOE, Matthew David
Born: January 10, 1977 Camperdown (Queensland)
Right-handed batsman, right-arm fast bowler

Pascoe made a fleeting return to first-class cricket in 2000-01, going wicketless in his only match. Another strapping young pace man in Queensland's armoury, he kept his name before the selectors with his ACB Cup and grade performances (46 wickets at 21.26 for Toombul to be the competition's leading bowler), but his state contract was not renewed for 2001-02. His best options for an extended tilt at first-class cricket appear to lie interstate, and it was not surprising to see him agree to terms with Tasmania in June. A Queensland Under-15s and Under-16s basketball representative, he received a strong message about the sporting direction he should choose when judged player of the carnival at the Australian Under-17s cricket championships in Adelaide a few years ago.

	M	I	NO	R	HS	100s	50s	Avge	Ct	St	W	Avge	BB
First-class	2	3	1	120	62	0	1	60.00	1	0	4	34.75	3/67
Dom. first-class	2	3	1	120	62	0	1	60.00	1	0	4	34.75	3/67
Dom. limited-overs	2	–	–	–	–	–	–	–	0	0	4	20.00	3/43

PERREN, Clinton Terrence
Born: February 22, 1975 Herston (Queensland)
Right-handed batsman, right-arm fast-medium bowler

A confidence player who has been his own worst enemy in the past, Perren should embark on the next season with fewer doubts and more faith in his ability. It says a deal about the natural resources available to this compact right-hander that his 112 against

South Australia in Adelaide, his second first-class hundred, put a strokemaker such as Stuart Law in the shade. Not that his captain would have been miffed, as Law has been a major influence on Perren and a prominent supporter of his claims for a regular spot. Perren's stocks rose even higher in the final match of the summer, his doughty knocks of 56 and 41 in the Pura Cup Final vindicating the faith of his supporters. A regular off-season visitor to England, where he met his wife Cath, he was the professional at Rishton in the Lancashire League during the off-season.

	M	I	NO	R	HS	100s	50s	Avge	Ct	St	W	Avge	BB
First-class	13	19	1	560	153	2	1	31.11	12	0	0	–	–
Dom. first-class	13	19	1	560	153	2	1	31.11	12	0	0	–	–
Dom. limited-overs	15	11	1	289	86*	0	2	28.90	6	0	1	30.00	1/13

PRESTWIDGE, Scott Arthur
Born: May 15, 1968 Bankstown (New South Wales)
Right-handed batsman, right-arm fast-medium bowler

Swept away by the selectors' new broom as they cleaned house in the limited-overs outfit, Prestwidge elected to retire at season's end. It was clear that the Queensland brains trust felt that new blood was needed to reinvigorate the side, and perhaps the mid-season loss of Shane Watson to Tasmania acted as a warning that a more foresighted approach to selections was required. Prestwidge's four wickets in his five Mercantile Mutual Cup matches meant he finished as the second leading wicket-taker of all time behind Tom Moody, with 67 wickets at 26.19. Highlights in his nine-season career include a Man of the Match effort in the 1997-98 final and key contributions in the 1995-96 final win at the Gabba. As Gideon Haigh noted in his 1999 notes on the Mercantile Mutual Cup, whenever his television was turned to Channel Nine during summer, it seemed as if Scott Prestwidge was bowling to Geoff Parker. With both players now departed from the scene, there is a vacancy for another limited-overs stalwart to capture the cricket-loving public's attention.

	M	I	NO	R	HS	100s	50s	Avge	Ct	St	W	Avge	BB
First-class	3	5	2	118	48*	0	0	39.33	1	0	7	46.43	2/16
Dom. first-class	1	2	0	24	18	0	0	12.00	1	0	1	120.00	1/26
Dom. limited-overs	45	30	5	527	66	0	2	21.08	6	0	67	26.19	5/59

SECCOMBE, Wade Anthony
Born: October 30, 1971 Murgon (Queensland)
Right-handed batsman, wicket-keeper

Seccombe is poised to break a record with his first dismissal in the new season. His 58 first-class dismissals last season broke his own record for the most in a season by a Queensland keeper and brought him equal with John Maclean on 313 (289 catches, 24 stumpings) career dismissals in Sheffield Shield and Pura Cup. Maclean still has more first-class career dismissals for Queensland (375 – 346 caught, 29 stumped) but Seccombe (353 – 339 caught, 14 stumped) is set to overtake that record during the season. He joined Don Tallon, Wally Grout, Ian Healy and Ray Phillips as Queenslanders who have kept wicket on an Ashes tour. He represented Australia A in matches against the Zimbabweans and the West Indians and revealed afterwards that a spell keeping to Stuart MacGill was the first time he had kept to a leg-spinner in senior cricket.

	M	I	NO	R	HS	100s	50s	Avge	Ct	St	W	Avge	BB
First-class	70	102	17	2,126	151	2	5	25.01	326	14	0	–	–
Dom. first-class	63	92	15	1,930	151	2	5	25.06	303	10	0	–	–
Dom. limited-overs	38	31	9	466	64*	0	1	21.18	50	11	0	–	–

SYMONDS, Andrew
Born: June 9, 1975 Birmingham, West Midlands (England)
Right-handed batsman, right-arm medium-off spin bowler

Symonds is approaching a critical juncture in his career. He needs to extend his steady hold on a place in the Australian limited-overs team to Test cricket. He has played upwards of 40 limited-overs internationals, with a strike-rate of more than 100, although he has just two half-centuries to his credit. While his scything batting, brilliant fielding and developing all-round bowling skills are ideal for an international limited-overs career, the chemistry to produce Test honours may require more time in the lab. Former Australian spinner Greg Matthews has promised to make him a fully-fledged Test off-spinner if he agrees to ditch his medium-pacers and do some work with him. Symonds agreed to terms with Kent following the NatWest Series in England, replacing the injured Daryll Cullinan. It was his second county stint with Kent and third overall in England, having enjoyed some prolific seasons with Gloucestershire.

	M	I	NO	R	HS	100s	50s	Avge	Ct	St	W	Avge	BB
First-class	115	192	17	7,315	254*	22	29	41.80	65	0	81	40.41	4/39
Dom. first-class	54	88	6	3,087	163	9	10	37.65	29	0	51	33.33	4/39
Int'l limited-overs	44	31	6	693	68*	0	2	27.72	16	0	40	29.33	4/11
Dom. limited-overs	38	35	4	673	85	0	1	21.71	17	0	17	24.35	3/32

TURNER, Dale Andrew
Born: January 30, 1974 Bankstown (New South Wales)
Right-handed batsman, right-arm off-spin bowler
Domestic limited-overs debut 2000-01

After sound performances in the Queensland limited-overs side in 1999-2000, Turner lost his place just a month into the 2000-01 season, following Queensland's sluggish start, then had to look on as Scott O'Leary and Nathan Hauritz donned the coloured clothing ahead of him. Grade cricket provided him with an outlet, his all-round talents helping Souths to a premiership and netting him the individual reward of the Peter Burge Medal as the best and fairest grade player. His double-century for Souths included 31 fours, two sixes, and a gallop from 54 at tea to 210 not out at stumps. He returned to Sydney at the end of the season.

	M	I	NO	R	HS	100s	50s	Avge	Ct	St	W	Avge	BB
Dom. limited-overs	7	2	0	16	16	0	0	8.00	1	0	6	42.17	2/13

SOUTH AUSTRALIA

By Valkerie Mangnall

ADCOCK, Nathan Tennyson
Born: April 22, 1978 Campbelltown (South Australia)
Right-handed batsman, right-arm fast-medium bowler

After first playing for South Australia in 1997-98, Nathan Adcock made a comeback in the middle order late in 2000-01 after a successful switch from the Sturt club to the captaincy at University. He was recalled as the selectors made sweeping changes to the South Australian side still clinging to hopes of reaching the Mercantile Mutual Cup final. Adcock scored two runs and bowled five overs for a return of 0/38 as South Australia beat Victoria by five wickets on February 17. South Australia missed the limited-overs final but Adcock was then called upon to play against Queensland in the penultimate four-day match of the season. While he made just 14 in the first innings and bowled expensively for 0/80 from 18 overs, he made a commendable 48 from 78 balls in the second innings to retain his spot for the final Pura Cup game.

	M	I	NO	R	HS	100s	50s	Avge	Ct	St	W	Avge	BB
First-class	8	14	1	370	114	1	0	28.46	10	0	0	–	–
Dom. first-class	6	12	1	255	48	0	0	23.18	4	0	0	–	–
Dom. limited-overs	9	9	0	150	57	0	2	16.67	5	0	0	–	–

BLEWETT, Gregory Scott
Born: October 29, 1971 Adelaide (South Australia)
Right-handed batsman, right-arm medium bowler

Greg Blewett had a chance to strut his stuff on the international stage when selected in the ACB Chairman's XI to play the West Indians at Lilac Hill in early November, but heavy rain forced the match to be abandoned before the home side could bat. Overlooked for national duties, Blewett put aside any disappointment and set about representing his state with distinction, proving to be the linchpin of South Australia's four-day batting attack. His gritty 260 not out against Queensland at the Gabba in December salvaged a draw when his side appeared headed for defeat and was the first of a chain of eight consecutive scores over 50. He was by far South Australia's highest scorer for the season with 1,162 first-class runs at an average of 68.35. Blewett's ability to bowl well under pressure also proved useful, particularly when he snared four wickets in a nail-biting finish to the limited-overs match against Western Australia on December 9 to deliver South Australia a two-run victory.

	M	I	NO	R	HS	100s	50s	Avge	Ct	St	W	Avge	BB
First-class	171	303	21	13,029	268	33	64	46.20	141	0	110	42.91	5/29
Dom. first-class	73	138	6	6,507	268	16	33	49.30	51	0	64	41.86	4/39
Test	46	79	4	2,552	214	4	15	34.03	45	0	14	51.43	2/9
Int'l limited-overs	32	30	3	551	57*	0	2	20.41	7	0	14	46.14	2/6
Dom. limited-overs	50	48	5	1,597	101*	1	10	37.14	19	0	42	35.29	4/33

BORGAS, Cameron James
Born: September 1, 1983 Flinders (South Australia)
Right-handed batsman
First-class and domestic first-class debuts 2000-01

Rated by South Australian cricket manager Greg Chappell as the state's most exciting prospect for a decade, the Australian Under-17s and Under-19s squad member was among a number of young players blooded by South Australia's selectors towards the end of 2000-01. Having made his debut at the age of just 17 in the 36-run loss to Western Australia, Borgas made way for Nathan Adcock in the following match against Queensland but was recalled for South Australia's final Pura Cup match. Although his highest score in four innings was just 12, Borgas would have gained valuable experience and drawn confidence from having caught the selectors' attention.

	M	I	NO	R	HS	100s	50s	Avge	Ct	St	W	Avge	BB
First-class	2	4	0	28	12	0	0	7.00	0	0	0	–	–
Dom. first-class	2	4	0	28	12	0	0	7.00	0	0	0	–	–

DAVIES, Christopher James
Born: November 15, 1978 Bedford Park (South Australia)
Right-handed batsman

After a disappointing 1999-00, Chris Davies was impressive in limited-overs matches in 2000-01, scoring three half-centuries. He played only two Pura Cup matches, and injury ruled him out of the last three games of the season. His dogged performance in the five-wicket loss to Victoria at Adelaide Oval in February showed him to be a player with plenty of spirit. Having suffered what proved to be season-ending damage to his right knee as he lunged to make his ground while running between the wickets, Davies retired hurt on 52 when he had to be stretchered from the field. But he returned in the second innings and held out in obvious pain for nearly half an hour and nine runs. Surgery to repair the knee and to fix a niggling problem in his right shoulder should help ensure his fitness for the coming season.

	M	I	NO	R	HS	100s	50s	Avge	Ct	St	W	Avge	BB
First-class	15	29	2	687	69	0	5	25.44	4	0	0	–	–
Dom. first-class	13	26	2	600	69	0	5	25.00	4	0	0	–	–
Dom. limited-overs	25	24	0	728	125	1	5	30.33	10	0	0	–	–

DEITZ, Shane Alan
Born: May 4, 1975 Bankstown (New South Wales)
Left-handed batsman, wicket-keeper

Following his debut in 1999-00, Shane Deitz took another step in his development, establishing himself as a determined opening batsman. Originally recruited as a top-order batsman and wicket-keeper, Deitz concentrated heavily on his batting and fielding after it became evident that Graham Manou had secured the wicket-keeping position left vacant by the retirement of Tim Nielsen. Deitz seized the opportunity to bowl on a number of occasions, snatching 2/17 from four overs in the Pura Cup match against Queensland in Brisbane. He was the only South Australian batsman besides Greg Blewett and Darren Lehmann to make more than 400 runs in the four-day competition, his 608 at 33.77 including hard-fought centuries when his side was struggling against Queensland and Victoria.

	M	I	NO	R	HS	100s	50s	Avge	Ct	St	W	Avge	BB
First-class	13	26	0	897	114	2	4	34.50	10	0	2	46.50	2/17
Dom. first-class	13	26	0	897	114	2	4	34.50	10	0	2	46.50	2/17
Dom. limited-overs	6	6	0	134	44	0	0	22.33	3	0	0	–	–

FITZGERALD, David Andrew
Born: November 30, 1972 Osborne Park (Western Australia)
Right-handed batsman, right-arm medium bowler

After a highly successful season the previous year when he narrowly missed the 1,000 first-class-run mark, David Fitzgerald struggled for consistency. The opener managed just 356 Pura Cup runs at an average of 25.42. He scored his only four-day century for the season against New South Wales in January. But, having made the second of his two fifties for the year against Victoria at Adelaide Oval in February, he suffered a recurrence of a long-term back injury, which ruled him out of two matches. He returned for the final Pura Cup fixture of the year but had little impact, scoring 17 and 10 against Tasmania.

	M	I	NO	R	HS	100s	50s	Avge	Ct	St	W	Avge	BB
First-class	42	79	3	2,590	167	8	12	34.08	25	0	0	–	–
Dom. first-class	41	77	2	2,472	167	7	12	32.96	24	0	0	–	–
Dom. limited-overs	27	27	1	838	114	2	5	32.23	10	0	0	–	–

GILLESPIE, Jason Neil
Born: April 19, 1975 Sydney (New South Wales)
Right-handed batsman, right-arm fast-medium bowler

The man affectionately known as "Dizzy" spent the Australian winter of 2000 working on his fitness with Rishton in England's Lancashire League after surgeons removed a

40-centimetre rod from his right tibia. The pin had stabilised the shin he badly broke in that infamous fielding collision with Steve Waugh in Sri Lanka in 1999. After nearly a year on the sidelines, Gillespie made his comeback in Australia's limited-overs series against South Africa in August. He was fit for South Australia's first Pura Cup match of 2000-01. But injuries and international duties kept his appearances for the state to a minimum, and he played only five Mercantile Mutual Cup games. After missing the First Test against West Indies in Brisbane with a hamstring problem, Gillespie returned to peak form in the remaining four Tests, claiming 20 wickets for the series. He was sidelined with another hamstring complaint after the Sydney Test but recovered to be selected for the tour of India, where he took 13 Test wickets at 30.30. An injury to his left foot sent him home before the limited-overs series, but he returned to full fitness for the start of the Ashes tour.

	M	I	NO	R	HS	100s	50s	Avge	Ct	St	W	Avge	BB
First-class	60	80	15	882	58	0	3	13.57	24	0	220	23.45	7/34
Dom. first-class	22	35	3	379	58	0	2	11.84	11	0	81	24.35	6/68
Test	21	31	9	335	46	0	0	15.23	6	0	83	22.53	7/37
Int'l limited-overs	24	15	3	114	26	0	0	9.50	1	0	32	29.59	4/26
Dom. limited-overs	15	9	4	36	15	0	0	7.20	2	0	27	22.63	4/46

HARRIS, Ryan James
Born: October 11, 1979 Nowra (New South Wales)
Right-handed batsman, right-arm fast-medium bowler
Domestic limited-overs debut 2000-01

Recruited from the Northern Districts side which won the South Australian grade competition's limited-overs title in 1999-00, Harris made an impressive debut in the Mercantile Mutual Cup against Queensland, scoring 24 runs from 26 balls and taking 2/35. He played another six limited-overs matches, including one against a full-strength New South Wales side in November in which he scored a neat 31 not out. He showed promise with both bat and ball from his limited opportunities.

	M	I	NO	R	HS	100s	50s	Avge	Ct	St	W	Avge	BB
Dom. limited-overs	7	4	3	58	31*	0	0	58.00	3	0	5	43.20	2/29

HARRITY, Mark Andrew
Born: March 9, 1974 Semaphore (South Australia)
Right-handed batsman, left-arm fast-medium bowler

After a sluggish start, Mark Harrity took 29 wickets in Pura Cup and Mercantile Mutual Cup matches to be South Australia's third-highest wicket-taker behind Paul Wilson (32) and Peter McIntyre (31). After taking 0/38 from seven overs in South Australia's first limited-overs match of the season against Queensland in early October, it was not until late November that Harrity was called into the four-day team to replace Jason Gillespie, who was on international duties. His hauls of five and four wickets against Tasmania and New South Wales helped South Australia to victory, and another four wickets helped them take out first-innings points before losing to Victoria in February.

	M	I	NO	R	HS	100s	50s	Avge	Ct	St	W	Avge	BB
First-class	60	71	38	161	18	0	0	4.88	21	0	165	37.38	5/92
Dom. first-class	50	63	37	133	11*	0	0	5.12	19	0	136	37.90	5/92
Dom. limited-overs	23	3	2	7	4*	0	0	7.00	4	0	35	26.29	5/42

HIGGINS, Benjamin Hugh
Born: March 8, 1972 Adelaide (South Australia)
Left-handed batsman, left-arm bowler
First-class, domestic first-class and domestic limited-overs
debuts 2000-01

A talented player in the South Australian National Football League,
Ben Higgins was promoted to the state's 13-man squad for the Pura
Cup match against Victoria in late November after scoring 177 for
the South Australia Second XI. He did not play, however, and made
his first-class debut a week before his 29th birthday against Western
Australia in Perth. Higgins showed plenty of maturity in the middle order, scoring 29 and
51. He followed up with two more half-centuries less than a fortnight later in the final
Pura Cup match of the season batting at No. 4 in place of Darren Lehmann, who was
away with the Australian limited-overs team. As a result of his performances, Higgins
will press strongly for selection again in 2001-02.

	M	I	NO	R	HS	100s	50s	Avge	Ct	St	W	Avge	BB
First-class	3	6	0	222	65	0	3	37.00	0	0	0	–	–
Dom. first-class	3	6	0	222	65	0	3	37.00	0	0	0	–	–
Dom. limited-overs	1	1	0	0	0	0	0	0.00	0	0	0	–	–

JOHNSON, Benjamin Andrew
Born: August 1, 1973 Naracoorte (South Australia)
Left-handed batsman, right-arm medium bowler

For a player with as much talent as Ben Johnson, the year 2000-01 proved a frustrating
one. After being a productive member of the side for several seasons, Johnson battled
for form and was dropped after making 260 runs from five Pura Cup matches and 167
runs from nine limited-overs games. His medium-pace bowling also brought little
success.

	M	I	NO	R	HS	100s	50s	Avge	Ct	St	W	Avge	BB
First-class	53	99	10	2,949	168	5	14	33.13	21	0	41	41.73	3/16
Dom. first-class	49	92	10	2,795	168	5	13	34.09	21	0	39	41.13	3/16
Dom. limited-overs	33	32	6	654	83	0	2	25.15	14	0	15	30.60	3/46

LEHMANN, Darren Scott
Born: February 5, 1970 Gawler (South Australia)
Left-handed batsman, slow left-arm orthodox bowler

Named Domestic Cricketer of the Year for the second time in a row, Darren Lehmann
displayed stunning form with the bat in the short version of the game, becoming the most
prolific run-scorer in Australian domestic limited-overs cricket. He did it in style,
smashing 63 from just 44 balls against Western Australia at Adelaide Oval to pass Dean
Jones' total of 2,122 runs. His unbeaten 115 from 118 balls against a full-strength New
South Wales team on November 19 helped South Australia to a six-run win in Sydney
and caught the attention of the national selectors, who included him in the Australian
limited-overs squad. The highly respected South Australian captain was a regular match-
winner in the Mercantile Mutual Cup, scoring 524 runs in seven matches at the
remarkable average of 131. In the Pura Cup, he managed 645 runs at 46.07 to be South
Australia's second-highest run scorer. He was twice 12th man and played in six of
Australia's ten limited-overs internationals against West Indies and Zimbabwe.

	M	I	NO	R	HS	100s	50s	Avge	Ct	St	W	Avge	BB
First-class	184	314	21	16,183	255	51	76	55.23	100	0	40	46.13	4/42
Dom. first-class	112	203	13	10,164	255	33	43	53.49	71	0	16	56.25	2/15
Test	5	8	0	228	98	0	2	28.50	3	0	2	22.50	1/6
Int'l limited-overs	69	62	11	1,727	110*	2	10	33.86	14	0	12	40.83	2/4
Dom. limited-overs	59	58	7	2,249	142*	5	14	44.10	22	0	6	44.50	3/25

MANOU, Graham Allan
Born: April 23, 1979 Modbury (South Australia)
Right-handed batsman, wicket-keeper

Having settled into his role behind the stumps after being called upon to replace the retired Tim Nielsen, Manou continued to impress with his glove-work. He scored 200 runs in the Pura Cup with a top score of 53 and made a total of 106 runs with an unbeaten 42 his highest score in the Mercantile Mutual Cup. Manou shows talent as a batsman and will be looking to take this area of his game to another level.

	M	I	NO	R	HS	100s	50s	Avge	Ct	St	W	Avge	BB
First-class	22	38	8	506	78	0	2	16.87	55	10	0	–	–
Dom. first-class	19	33	6	461	78	0	2	17.07	48	10	0	–	–
Dom. limited-overs	15	11	4	131	42*	0	0	18.71	21	0	0	–	–

McINTYRE, Peter Edward
Born: April 27, 1966 Gisborne (Victoria)
Right-handed batsman, right-arm leg-spin bowler

The evergreen leg-spinner performed well for his state yet again, particularly on the spin-friendly Adelaide Oval wicket, to be South Australia's second-highest wicket-taker for the season. He showed his lasting reliability when he took six and five wickets respectively in the home wins against Tasmania and New South Wales and another six in the loss to Victoria in Adelaide.

	M	I	NO	R	HS	100s	50s	Avge	Ct	St	W	Avge	BB
First-class	91	122	33	677	43	0	0	7.61	33	0	304	39.58	6/43
Dom. first-class	69	97	29	550	43	0	0	8.09	26	0	227	42.68	6/64
Test	2	4	1	22	16	0	0	7.33	0	0	5	38.80	3/103
Dom. limited-overs	5	3	0	1	1	0	0	0.33	0	0	7	30.57	4/39

MILLER, Michael Christian
Born: May 30, 1979 Toowoomba (Queensland)
Left-handed batsman, right-arm fast-medium bowler

Mick Miller decided to try his luck in South Australia after moving in the off-season from his native Queensland, where he played two Sheffield Shield matches in 1998-99. The all-rounder proved to be a valuable acquisition. His unbeaten 82 off just 58 balls against New South Wales in Adelaide allowed his team to step ahead of New South Wales and into top spot briefly on the Mercantile Mutual Cup table. He played five limited-overs matches and two Pura Cup games for his adopted state before a shoulder injury ruled him out late in the season. Miller could well press for more permanent inclusion in the side for 2001-02, especially if he can improve the consistency of his batting.

	M	I	NO	R	HS	100s	50s	Avge	Ct	St	W	Avge	BB
First-class	4	6	0	88	33	0	0	14.67	4	0	5	49.00	2/30
Dom. first-class	4	6	0	88	33	0	0	14.67	4	0	5	49.00	2/30
Dom. limited-overs	7	7	4	105	82*	0	1	35.00	2	0	6	44.83	3/27

ROFE, Paul Cameron
Born: January 16, 1981 Adelaide (South Australia)
Right-handed batsman, right-arm fast bowler
First-class, domestic first-class and domestic limited-overs
debuts 2000-01

Among several inexperienced players brought into South
Australia's four-day side when injuries and poor form forced the
side out of contention for the final, Paul Rofe seized his
opportunity. Generating both lively pace and bounce from his lanky
frame, Rofe kept the batsmen under pressure in both Pura Cup and
Mercantile Mutual Cup competitions. If he can use the experience to increase his ability
to penetrate batsmen's defences, he will make a strong case to become a regular member
of the team, particularly with Jason Gillespie often away on national duties.

	M	I	NO	R	HS	100s	50s	Avge	Ct	St	W	Avge	BB
First-class	3	6	1	48	18	0	0	9.60	0	0	3	87.00	2/69
Dom. first-class	3	6	1	48	18	0	0	9.60	0	0	3	87.00	2/69
Dom. limited-overs	4	1	1	1	1*	0	0	–	0	0	3	61.00	2/47

SMITH, Mike John
Born: July 17, 1973 Rose Park (South Australia)
Right-handed batsman, right-arm medium bowler

Awarded the Sir Donald Bradman Medal as South Australia's best grade cricketer in
2000-01, Mike Smith returned to the state side for the last three games of the season after
making his first-class debut the previous year. Smith leapt at the chance to prove his
worth as a genuine all-rounder, scoring 76 against Queensland and taking four wickets
in South Australia's final match of the year. He will press hard for regular selection in
the side in 2001-02.

	M	I	NO	R	HS	100s	50s	Avge	Ct	St	W	Avge	BB
First-class	4	8	0	227	76	0	1	28.38	1	0	8	45.50	4/81
Dom. first-class	4	8	0	227	76	0	1	28.38	1	0	8	45.50	4/81
Dom. limited-overs	4	3	1	2	1*	0	0	1.00	0	0	2	76.00	1/30

SWAIN, Brett Andrew
Born: February 14, 1974 Stirling (South Australia)
Left-handed batsman, left-arm fast-medium bowler

Many years ago, Brett Swain's grandfather, Thomas (Tim) Wall, single-handedly
destroyed a star-studded batting line-up boasting names like Don Bradman when he
took 10/36 for South Australia in a Sheffield Shield match against New South Wales.
In 2000-01, Brett Swain's toil as part of South Australia's bowling attack was recognised
with selection in the Prime Minister's XI to play the West Indies in a limited-overs
match in early December after fellow South Australian Paul Wilson was ruled out with
an ankle injury. Swain was among three wicket-takers in that match, claiming 1/54 from
his ten overs. His ability to create genuine swing was a plus for South Australia as he
claimed 17 Pura Cup wickets at an average of 30.64 and six limited-overs wickets at
46.83. But Swain's season was curbed by a back complaint that caused him to miss the
last two Pura Cup matches.

	M	I	NO	R	HS	100s	50s	Avge	Ct	St	W	Avge	BB
First-class	23	35	7	264	36*	0	0	9.43	8	0	72	28.47	5/59
Dom. first-class	22	34	7	255	36*	0	0	9.44	8	0	71	27.99	5/59
Dom. limited-overs	18	7	2	84	35*	0	0	16.80	4	0	13	46.62	2/16

VAUGHAN, Jeffrey Mark
Born: March 26, 1974 Blacktown (New South Wales)
Right-handed batsman, right-arm fast-medium bowler

A season which started with so much promise had the gloss taken off it when Jeff Vaughan battled to find consistent touch. After scoring 131 not out in the opening Pura Cup match against Western Australia, Vaughan injured his thumb in the limited-overs game against Victoria a fortnight later. He missed the four-day match against Victoria in Melbourne and, apart from an unbeaten 85 in South Australia's win over Tasmania in December, Vaughan struggled for runs and was dropped for the last three Pura Cup matches.

	M	I	NO	R	HS	100s	50s	Avge	Ct	St	W	Avge	BB
First-class	24	45	4	1,334	157*	3	8	32.54	17	0	0	–	–
Dom. first-class	22	42	4	1,234	157*	3	7	32.47	17	0	0	–	–
Dom. limited-overs	16	15	1	205	57	0	2	14.64	7	0	0	–	–

WILLIAMS, Luke
Born: December 24, 1979 Henley Beach (South Australia)
Right-handed batsman
First-class and domestic first-class debuts 2000-01

Selected to replace injured opener David Fitzgerald, Luke Williams was among a number of youngsters blooded late in the season. While a total of 35 runs in the four innings he played against Western Australia and Queensland did not constitute an outstanding debut, the former Australian Under-19s representative gained a taste of what lies ahead, and that should inspire him to push his claims for a regular spot in the South Australian team.

	M	I	NO	R	HS	100s	50s	Avge	Ct	St	W	Avge	BB
First-class	2	4	0	35	16	0	0	8.75	1	0	0	–	–
Dom. first-class	2	4	0	35	16	0	0	8.75	0	0	0	–	–

WILSON, Paul
Born: January 12, 1972 Newcastle (New South Wales)
Right-handed batsman, right-arm fast-medium bowler

Despite foot and ankle problems restricting his season, Paul Wilson remained South Australia's leading wicket-taker in 2000-01 with 32 wickets in the Pura Cup and Mercantile Mutual Cup competitions combined. The hefty, hard-working bloke known as "Blocker" underwent surgery late in the season which revealed that a muscle leading to his left big toe had thickened to twice its normal size. The excess muscle was trimmed and the ankle joint cleaned out in an operation which was expected to restore Wilson to full fitness for the 2001-02 season.

	M	I	NO	R	HS	100s	50s	Avge	Ct	St	W	Avge	BB
First-class	39	52	16	330	32*	0	0	9.17	6	0	122	29.29	6/106
Dom. first-class	34	45	12	310	32*	0	0	9.39	6	0	109	28.91	5/68
Test	1	2	2	0	0*	0	0	–	0	0	0	–	–
Int'l limited-overs	11	5	2	4	2	0	0	1.33	1	0	13	34.62	3/39
Dom. limited-overs	40	20	5	127	16	0	0	8.47	1	0	62	24.02	4/23

YOUNG, Bradley Evan
Born: February 23, 1973 Semaphore (South Australia)
Right-handed batsman, slow left-arm orthodox bowler

A knee injury cruelly ended Brad Young's season before it really began. The talented all-rounder scored an unbeaten 71 to help South Australia draw the opening match against Western Australia. A fortnight later, Young damaged the anterior cruciate ligament in his left knee while training in Sydney after rain had forced the match against New South Wales to be abandoned. He underwent reconstructive surgery and an extensive rehabilitation program before heading to England to play for East Lancashire in the Lancashire League. He was the league's top wicket-taker when his injuries flared again and he was forced to return home in July.

	M	I	NO	R	HS	100s	50s	Avge	Ct	St	W	Avge	BB
First-class	41	69	16	1,572	114*	1	8	29.66	36	0	121	42.36	6/85
Dom. first-class	36	62	15	1,454	114*	1	8	30.94	32	0	111	43.43	6/85
Int'l limited-overs	6	3	1	31	18	0	0	15.50	2	0	1	251.00	1/26
Dom. limited-overs	27	25	5	285	31	0	0	14.25	15	0	23	41.74	4/24

TASMANIA

By David Stockdale

CLINGELEFFER, Sean Geoffrey
Born: May 9, 1980 Hobart (Tasmania)
Left-handed batsman, wicket-keeper
First-class, domestic first-class and domestic limited-overs
debuts 2000-01

Clingeleffer largely fulfilled the potential he had shown as Australia's Under-19s keeper with an impressive display behind the stumps in his first season, finishing with 21 catches and four stumpings. He is very agile for a tall man and has no problems taking medium-paced bowlers at the stumps. His batting (203 runs at 15.62) needs work, but two Australian Under-19s centuries suggest he will become more than handy down the order. He could be an Australian player of the future.

	M	I	NO	R	HS	100s	50s	Avge	Ct	St	W	Avge	BB
First-class	10	14	1	203	50	0	1	15.62	21	4	0	–	–
Dom. first-class	10	14	1	203	50	0	1	15.62	21	4	0	–	–
Dom. limited-overs	10	6	4	35	22*	0	0	17.50	11	1	0	–	–

COLEGRAVE, Mark David
Born: July 1, 1970 Hobart (Tasmania)
Right-handed batsman, right-arm medium bowler
First-class and domestic first-class debuts 2000-01

A prolific wicket-taker for Clarence in the TCA and a former premiership footballer with Hobart, the shaven-headed Colegrave was a breath of fresh air in his first-class debut against Western Australia. Bowling in his cap, he was initially economical if ultimately unsuccessful in his only appearance.

	M	I	NO	R	HS	100s	50s	Avge	Ct	St	W	Avge	BB
First-class	1	2	1	6	5	0	0	6.00	0	0	1	131.00	1/76
Dom. first-class	1	2	1	6	5	0	0	6.00	0	0	1	131.00	1/76

COX, Jamie
Born: October 15, 1969 Burnie (Tasmania)
Right-handed batsman – right-arm medium bowler

Had he lived in almost any other country, the Tasmanian captain would now be a regular Test opener. Despite another stellar season in which he scored 1,070 runs at 66.88 with five centuries – the third time he has topped 1,000 runs in a season at home and abroad – Cox was overlooked for the 2001 Ashes tour of England. He came as close as selection in the Australia A team against the West Indians on his home wicket at Bellerive, when he made 95 in the second innings. He also was the Tasmanian leading scorer in limited-overs games with 277 runs at 34.63 in a roving role in the top order. He returned to England for a third season as captain of Somerset.

	M	I	NO	R	HS	100s	50s	Avge	Ct	St	W	Avge	BB
First-class	177	313	21	13,166	245	40	56	45.09	78	0	4	80.75	3/46
Dom. first-class	123	226	15	8,941	245	27	38	42.37	58	0	0	–	–
Dom. limited-overs	53	52	2	1,412	99	0	12	28.24	13	0	0	–	–

CUNNINGHAM, Graeme Timothy
Born: January 25, 1975 Goulburn (New South Wales)
Right-handed batsman, right-arm off-spin bowler

Cunningham moved to Tasmania after the Australian Capital Territory were axed from the Mercantile Mutual Cup competition. A powerful striker of the ball who played some useful innings for New Town in the TCA competition, he succeeded only once in four innings by top-scoring with a barnstorming 68 off 46 balls with eight fours and two sixes in the away loss to Western Australia.

	M	I	NO	R	HS	100s	50s	Avge	Ct	St	W	Avge	BB
Dom. limited-overs	17	16	1	485	76	0	3	32.33	3	0	0	–	–

DENTON, Gerard John
Born: August 7, 1975 Mt Isa (Queensland)
Right-handed batsman, right-arm fast-medium bowler

Recurring back injuries continue to frustrate Tasmania's fastest bowler at a time when the team most needs reliable pace men following the retirement of Mark Ridgway. Denton was restricted to just one first-class match in 2000-01 after playing only three the previous season, and his absence was sorely felt. His great potential won him Australia A selection three seasons ago.

	M	I	NO	R	HS	100s	50s	Avge	Ct	St	W	Avge	BB
First-class	19	25	8	77	14	0	0	4.53	2	0	40	42.68	4/39
Dom. first-class	17	24	7	75	14	0	0	4.41	2	0	35	45.37	4/53
Dom. limited-overs	7	–	–	–	–	–	–	–	1	0	7	42.71	3/53

di VENUTO, Michael James
Born: December 12, 1973 Hobart (Tasmania)
Left-handed batsman

The richly talented but inconsistent Di Venuto had a poor season at No. 3, scoring only 466 first-class runs at 27.41, with four fifties and no centuries. He was not helped by the fact that opener Dene Hills was so often out cheaply. He needs to tighten his technique and be more discerning in his shot selection. His limited-overs form was also patchy, although his 124 off 130 balls against South Australia in Adelaide was vintage "Diva". He received offers from South Australia and Victoria before deciding to stay in Tasmania, and hoped to regain confidence during another season for English county Derbyshire.

	M	I	NO	R	HS	100s	50s	Avge	Ct	St	W	Avge	BB
First-class	128	220	10	8,046	189	14	54	38.31	108	0	5	65.20	1/0
Dom. first-class	80	141	5	5,525	189	9	40	40.63	64	0	2	94.00	1/0
Int'l limited-overs	9	9	0	241	89	0	2	26.78	1	0	0	–	–
Dom. limited-overs	49	48	7	1,261	129*	2	5	30.76	19	0	3	28.67	1/10

DOWNTON, Andrew Graham
Born: July 17, 1977 Auburn (New South Wales)
Right-handed batsman, left-arm fast-medium bowler

A mixture of injury and less responsive wickets, particularly at home, combined to blunt Downton's effectiveness, and he finished the season with 16 wickets at 34.25, after taking 24 wickets more cheaply in his debut season. He can swing and cut the ball, but is learning he must hit the deck harder when conditions do not provide movement. His batting form in club cricket, where he topped the TCA averages, suggests that he has the potential to become an all-rounder for the state, but his batting for Tasmania so far has produced little.

	M	I	NO	R	HS	100s	50s	Avge	Ct	St	W	Avge	BB
First-class	14	14	1	89	19	0	0	6.85	4	0	43	31.56	6/56
Dom. first-class	12	13	0	88	19	0	0	6.77	4	0	35	34.69	6/56
Dom. limited-overs	2	0	0	0	–	0	0	–	0	0	2	43.00	1/26

DYKES, James Andrew
Born: November 15, 1971 Hobart (Tasmania)
Right-handed batsman, right-arm medium bowler

This grandson of a Scottish soccer international had a horror season after looking as though he had finally arrived on the first-class scene the summer before. In four matches, Dykes could manage only 125 runs at 15.63. After a long wait for state representation, at nearly 30 years of age his career is at the crossroads.

	M	I	NO	R	HS	100s	50s	Avge	Ct	St	W	Avge	BB
First-class	18	29	0	811	153	2	1	27.97	10	0	2	172.50	1/23
Dom. first-class	17	28	0	750	153	2	0	26.79	10	0	2	171.00	1/23
Dom. limited-overs	16	9	5	89	20*	0	0	22.25	1	0	4	36.70	2/27

GEEVES, Brett
Born: June 13, 1982 Hobart (Tasmania)
Right-handed batsman, right-arm fast bowler
Domestic limited-overs debut 2000-01

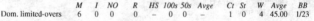

When the raw young pace man showed potential with his struggling TCA club Glenorchy, the state selectors took a punt on him. They were rewarded when Geeves tied down an end in four Mercantile Mutual Cup matches with his ability to bring the ball back in. He must learn to move the ball away if he is to graduate to first-class company. At the end of the season he won a full scholarship to the AIS Cricket Academy.

	M	I	NO	R	HS	100s	50s	Avge	Ct	St	W	Avge	BB
Dom. limited-overs	6	0	0	0	–	0	0	–	1	0	4	45.00	1/23

HILLS, Dene Fleetwood
Born: August 27, 1970 Wynyard (Tasmania)
Left-handed batsman

It was a nightmare season for this affable and experienced opening batsman, who with Jamie Cox has provided Tasmania with so many great starts. Hills, who won the national Sheffield Shield Player of the Year award with a 1,000-run-plus season in 1997-98, scored just 395 runs at 23.24 with three ducks. Again the cut shot was often his undoing. He needs to play more in the narrow "V" against the new ball. To his credit, Hills recaptured a glimpse of his old form with 120 against Victoria at Bellerive. He made useful scores in some Mercantile Mutual Cup matches. He would be hoping to return from a season in Scottish club cricket with his batting restored to its accustomed heights.

	M	I	NO	R	HS	100s	50s	Avge	Ct	St	W	Avge	BB
First-class	108	199	10	7,708	265	20	43	40.78	80	0	2	26.50	2/20
Dom. first-class	96	179	8	6,701	265	17	36	39.19	67	0	2	23.50	2/20
Dom. limited-overs	40	37	3	1,108	81	0	8	32.59	10	0	0	–	–

JURGENSEN, Shane John
Born: April 28, 1976 Redcliffe (Queensland)
Right-handed batsman, right-arm fast bowler

Recruited from Western Australia, where he played for the state team, the lanky pace man played two first-class games and took six wickets at 47.61 apiece. His best performance of 4/113 off 33.5 overs was typical of the willing if not overly penetrative workhorse he is. His selection was a reward for sharing the TCA Medal with fellow pace man Josh Marquet the previous season.

	M	I	NO	R	HS	100s	50s	Avge	Ct	St	W	Avge	BB
First-class	4	5	3	29	13*	0	0	14.50	1	0	8	59.13	4/113
Dom. first-class	3	4	2	16	13	0	0	8.00	0	0	7	55.00	4/113

KREMERSKOTHEN, Scott Paul
Born: January 5, 1979 Launceston (Tasmania)
Left-handed batsman, right-arm medium bowler

The lanky young all-rounder continued his improvement with both bat and ball. He showed good temperament at No. 7 with 402 runs at 44.67, his only shortcoming being a failure to build on his many good starts. He could have been given more work with the ball. He contributed some handy innings late in the order in the Mercantile Mutual Cup, where he was Tasmania's leading wicket-taker, with 14 wickets at a strike rate of a wicket every 16 balls, although he did concede more than six runs an over. He took some outstanding catches.

	M	I	NO	R	HS	100s	50s	Avge	Ct	St	W	Avge	BB
First-class	19	28	7	700	82*	0	3	33.33	10	0	17	50.12	3/64
Dom. first-class	18	27	6	699	82*	0	3	33.29	9	0	15	51.87	3/64
Dom. limited-overs	18	12	2	188	47	0	0	18.80	5	0	15	27.00	3/33

MARQUET, Joshua Phillip
Born: December 3, 1968 Melbourne (Victoria)
Right-handed batsman, right-arm fast-medium bowler

After sharing the TCA Medal the previous season for his lion-hearted performances for University, Marquet was recalled to the limited-overs side to replace the injured Damien Wright. The big pace man bowled with good control and at a lively pace to take nine wickets at 25.11 in six matches. His 3/29 off nine overs, including the prize scalp of Greg Blewett, was instrumental in the win over South Australia at Devonport.

	M	I	NO	R	HS	100s	50s	Avge	Ct	St	W	Avge	BB
First-class	22	18	9	28	10	0	0	3.11	9	0	60	42.48	5/94
Dom. first-class	21	18	9	28	10	0	0	3.11	9	0	59	41.46	5/94
Dom. limited-overs	14	5	2	7	6	0	0	2.33	4	0	21	26.86	5/23

MARSH, Daniel James
Born: June 14, 1973 Subiaco (Western Australia)
Right-handed batsman, slow left-arm orthodox bowler

After winning Tasmania's Player of the Year award the previous season, Marsh did not progress as he would have liked. Still, he had a solid, workmanlike season with 514 runs at 39.54 and 18 wickets at 40, but he needs to put more work on the ball to trouble top batsman. He caught well at first slip. In the Mercantile Mutual Cup he made some useful runs, with a top score of 57 not out in the home game against New South Wales. His selection in the Prime Minister's XI game against the West Indies showed that the national selectors still have him under notice. He played his first season of English county cricket for Leicestershire in 2001.

	M	I	NO	R	HS	100s	50s	Avge	Ct	St	W	Avge	BB
First-class	65	107	20	3,381	157	7	17	38.86	66	0	118	41.51	7/57
Dom. first-class	54	89	16	2,550	134	4	13	34.93	53	0	109	41.02	7/57
Dom. limited-overs	42	37	11	799	78*	0	4	30.73	21	0	19	56.47	3/47

MASON, Scott
Born: July 27, 1976 George Town (Tasmania)
Left-handed batsman

After previously filling the role of a back-up opener, the pugnacious Mason made little impression in the middle order in his only Pura Cup appearance against Victoria at Richmond, making a duck and nine. He will be looking to score heavily in club cricket in order to force his way back into the side.

	M	I	NO	R	HS	100s	50s	Avge	Ct	St	W	Avge	BB
First-class	4	7	0	100	28	0	0	14.29	0	0	0	–	–
Dom. first-class	3	5	0	61	23	0	0	12.20	0	0	0	–	–
Dom. limited-overs	5	4	0	31	14	0	0	7.75	3	0	0	–	–

MUNDAY, Kade Michael
Born: January 4, 1983 Burnie (Tasmania)
Right-handed batsman, right-arm medium bowler
Domestic limited-overs debut 2000-01

Munday made his Mercantile Mutual Cup debut in Tasmania's win over South Australia at Devonport as a late replacement for the injured David Saker. The Burnie youngster was unfortunate to be run out for one, but his fluent batting for Tasmania's Second XI and success in Under-19s and Under-17s carnivals mark him as a player to watch.

	M	I	NO	R	HS	100s	50s	Avge	Ct	St	W	Avge	BB
Dom. limited-overs	1	1	0	1	1	0	0	1.00	0	0	0	–	–

PINNINGTON, Todd Andrew
Born: March 21, 1971 Hobart (Tasmania)
Right-handed batsman, wicket-keeper

A heavy-scoring opener for his TCA club North Hobart, Pinnington struggled to take the step up. He failed with the bat in his only Pura Cup game against Queensland at Bellerive in which the pace and lift of Michael Kasprowicz found him wanting. The limited-overs arena was not much more productive for him, but he did bat well for his 38 to help Tasmania to a crushing nine-wicket win over Victoria at the MCG.

	M	I	NO	R	HS	100s	50s	Avge	Ct	St	W	Avge	BB
First-class	2	3	0	11	5	0	0	3.67	2	0	0	–	–
Dom. first-class	2	3	0	11	5	0	0	3.67	2	0	0	–	–
Dom. limited-overs	7	5	1	62	38	0	0	15.50	2	1	0	–	–

POLKINGHORNE, Adam William
Born: August 23, 1975 Karoonda (South Australia)
Left-handed batsman, right-arm medium and leg-spin bowler
Domestic limited-overs debut 2000-01

A former Bradman Medal winner in Adelaide district cricket, the
versatile Polkinghorne played two Mercantile Mutual Cup matches
late in the season. He made only 12 and 10, but if he can curb his
desire to thrash the bowling from the outset he could be a useful
addition to the side. His leg-spin bowling especially shows promise
and should help his cause when the selectors are choosing teams for the Pura Cup in the
forthcoming season. His outstanding all-round performances for South Hobart–Sandy
Bay (363 runs at 40.33 and 41 wickets at 15.61) made him joint winner of the TCA
Medal.

	M	I	NO	R	HS	100s	50s	Avge	Ct	St	W	Avge	BB
Dom. limited-overs	2	2	0	22	12	0	0	11.00	0	0	1	22.00	1/22

PONTING, Ricky Thomas
Born: December 19, 1974 Launceston (Tasmania)
Right-handed batsman, right-arm medium bowler

In his only two Pura Cup matches before the home Test series against West Indies,
Ponting began the season in spectacular fashion. He plundered a career-best 233 and 61
against Queensland in Brisbane and 187 not out in the first innings against New South
Wales at Bellerive to give him an average of 240.5. He was also in fine form in his four
Mercantile Mutual Cup appearances, making 153 runs at 51 with two fifties. Ponting
could not sustain his blazing early-season form and in the Test series had to be content
with 242 runs at 40.33 with a top score of 92. He was back in business for the triangular
limited-overs series with 393 at 49.13, including four fifties. But Ponting reached the
depths of despair on Australia's ill-fated tour of India, making just 17 runs in three Tests
as Harbhajan Singh ensnared him in a deadly web of spin. A match-winning 101 at
Visakhapatnam in the limited-overs series which followed gave him some solace.

	M	I	NO	R	HS	100s	50s	Avge	Ct	St	W	Avge	BB
First-class	123	208	30	9,403	233	31	43	52.83	114	0	12	51.42	2/10
Dom. first-class	45	83	13	4,382	233	18	13	62.60	30	0	4	85.50	1/7
Test	42	66	8	2,492	197	7	12	42.97	47	0	4	33.00	1/0
Int'l limited-overs	123	123	15	4,546	145	8	26	42.09	39	0	3	34.67	1/12
Dom. limited-overs	27	27	4	727	87*	0	5	31.61	12	0	5	23.80	3/34

SAKER, David James
Born: May 29, 1966 Oakleigh (Victoria)
Right-handed batsman, right-arm fast-medium bowler

Recruited from Victoria to replace the retired Mark Ridgway, the veteran Saker was
Tasmania's leading first-class wicket-taker with 26 at 41.54. A fierce competitor,
Saker's readiness to take batsmen on often meant his wickets did not come cheaply. He
went wicketless for three games in mid-season, and the fact that he bowled 350 overs –
134 more than the next hardest-working, spinner Dan Marsh – suggests that the heavy
workload for a pace man of his years may have blunted his effectiveness. His best
performance of 5/98 off 21 overs on a Bellerive "road" almost snatched victory against
Western Australia.

	M	I	NO	R	HS	100s	50s	Avge	Ct	St	W	Avge	BB
First-class	59	84	22	1,157	66*	0	3	18.66	14	0	208	30.22	7/32
Dom. first-class	55	78	20	1,051	66*	0	2	18.12	13	0	192	31.08	7/32
Dom. limited-overs	34	19	6	230	47*	0	0	17.69	3	0	35	32.20	4/35

TARGETT, Benjamin Stuart
Born: December 27, 1972 Paddington (New South Wales)
Right-handed batsman, right-arm fast-medium bowler

Again the giant pace man struggled to cement a place in the side, playing three first-class matches in which he captured seven wickets at 37.86. Easily Targett's best match was in the away loss to South Australia when he took 5/62 from 24 overs. While injuries have taken some toll on him, he needs to find an extra metre of pace and get the ball more into the zone of doubt in order to take full advantage of the bounce he gets from his height.

	M	I	NO	R	HS	100s	50s	Avge	Ct	St	W	Avge	BB
First-class	16	23	5	207	48*	0	0	11.50	5	0	40	34.83	5/62
Dom. first-class	16	23	5	207	48*	0	0	11.50	5	0	40	34.83	5/62
Dom. limited-overs	5	3	2	16	11	0	0	16.00	0	0	2	100.00	2/44

THOMAS, Bradley John
Born: January 18, 1972 Hobart (Tasmania)
Right-handed batsman, right-arm medium bowler
Domestic limited-overs debut 2000-01

Thomas decided to take his cricket more seriously and aim for higher achievement. The three-time TCA Medal winner played his way into two Mercantile Mutual Cup games, but had modest success. A broken finger in a state Second Eleven game prevented him from making his first-class debut against Western Australia at Bellerive.

	M	I	NO	R	HS	100s	50s	Avge	Ct	St	W	Avge	BB
Dom. limited-overs	2	2	0	32	16	0	0	16.00	0	0	1	15.00	1/15

TUBB, Shannon Benjamin
Born: May 11, 1980 Bracknell (Tasmania)
Right-handed batsman, left-arm slow 'chinaman' bowler

As Tubb is finding out, a chinaman bowler needs great determination and patience. He was used in only one game, when he took 0/70 from 14 overs against New South Wales on a Sydney wicket that was not its customary spin-friendly self. While control remains a problem – a couple of bad balls an over which can be spanked for four – so does gaining the confidence of his captain to bowl him, a traditional problem with this esoteric type of bowler.

	M	I	NO	R	HS	100s	50s	Avge	Ct	St	W	Avge	BB
First-class	2	4	0	60	42	0	0	15.00	0	0	0	–	–
Dom. first-class	2	4	0	60	42	0	0	15.00	0	0	0	–	–

WATSON, Shane Robert
Born: June 17, 1981 Ipswich (Queensland)
Right-handed batsman, right-arm medium bowler
First-class, domestic first-class and domestic limited-overs debut 2000-01

Many eyebrows were raised – especially in his home state of Queensland – when Tasmania signed the burly blond teenage all-rounder during the season from the AIS Cricket Academy. But such was Watson's rapid progress he finished third in both Tasmania's first-class batting averages (309 runs at 51.50) and bowling averages (11 wickets at 26.27), and scored a century in the victory over South Australia in Hobart. He also showed promise of being an asset in the limited-overs game, where he worked his way up the batting order. He has the potential to achieve higher honours.

	M	I	NO	R	HS	100s	50s	Avge	Ct	St	W	Avge	BB
First-class	5	8	2	309	105	1	2	51.50	1	0	11	26.27	2/22
Dom. first-class	5	8	2	309	105	1	2	51.50	1	0	11	26.27	2/22
Dom. limited-overs	6	6	2	103	28*	0	0	25.75	3	0	1	73.00	1/22

WRIGHT, Damien Geoffrey
Born: July 25, 1975 Casino (New South Wales)
Right-handed batsman, right-arm fast-medium bowler

Nagging injuries and a lapse in form restricted the blond-haired pace man to six first-class matches. Wright responded to captain Jamie Cox's call for him to lift by hitting the wicket harder, improving his line and getting movement away off the seam to be the Tasmania's second-highest first-class wicket-taker with 22 at 26.95. His formerly useful lower-order batting fell away, however. He again bowled well in limited-overs games with nine wickets at 24.89 and was one of only two Tasmanians to concede less than four runs an over. He spent the winter of 2001 playing club cricket in Scotland.

	M	I	NO	R	HS	100s	50s	Avge	Ct	St	W	Avge	BB
First-class	19	27	8	293	45	0	0	15.42	7	0	47	40.85	4/54
Dom. first-class	18	27	8	293	45	0	0	15.42	7	0	45	40.73	4/54
Dom. limited-overs	17	9	5	61	15*	0	0	15.25	4	0	24	22.08	3/16

YOUNG, Shaun
Born: June 13, 1970 Burnie (Tasmania)
Left-handed batsman, right-arm fast-medium bowler

It was a season of mixed blessings for this gifted if sometimes enigmatic all-rounder, who shed a lot of weight over the winter. Young finished the summer strongly after an indifferent start to make 433 first-class runs at 33.31, and was the third-highest wicket-taker with 21 at 25.33. In the final home game he led the Tasmanians to an innings win against South Australia when he hit an unbeaten 83 and combined penetration with extraordinary economy to take 3/24 over 23 overs and 4/33 off 11. "China", who became Tasmania's leading wicket-taker and joined its elite 100-game club, was a leading contributor to his side's limited-overs cause with 203 runs at 25.38 and 13 wickets at the impressive rate of only 3.18 an over. He spent the winter playing Lancashire League cricket as Bacup's professional.

	M	I	NO	R	HS	100s	50s	Avge	Ct	St	W	Avge	BB
First-class	133	219	37	6,953	237	14	41	38.20	81	0	273	35.38	7/64
Dom. first-class	99	168	29	5,306	175*	10	32	38.17	61	0	200	38.64	5/26
Test	1	2	1	4	4*	0	0	4.00	0	0	0	–	–
Dom. limited-overs	57	50	5	1,320	96	0	9	29.33	21	0	40	39.88	3/16

VICTORIA

By Ken Williams

ARNBERGER, Jason Lee
Born: November 18, 1972 Penrith (New South Wales)
Right-handed batsman

Arnberger was a model of consistency at the top of the order, having his best season to date with 1,006 runs at 47.90. Criticised in the past for being overweight, he commenced the season ten kilograms lighter and unlike 1999-00, when his form tapered off after an excellent start, he scored consistently throughout. His record was all the more meritorious considering that he was without his regular opening partner, Matthew Elliott, for the first half of the season. In addition to making centuries against Queensland and Tasmania, he made seven other scores over 50, including 99 (on his 28th birthday) against the West Indians. He maintained the more aggressive approach he had adopted in 1999-00, his batting being characterised by positive stroke selection, especially on the leg side. Surprisingly, he has yet to make an impact at limited-overs level, despite an innings of 75 against Queensland. In excellent form in premier cricket for Richmond, he finished second (to Elliott) in the competition's averages with 386 runs at 77.20.

	M	I	NO	R	HS	100s	50s	Avge	Ct	St	W	Avge	BB
First-class	47	89	5	3,137	214	5	20	37.35	37	0	0	–	–
Dom. first-class	44	84	5	2,995	214	5	19	37.91	34	0	0	–	–
Dom. limited-overs	19	18	1	293	75	0	2	17.24	0	0	0	–	–

BERRY, Darren Shane
Born: December 10, 1969 Melbourne (Victoria)
Right-handed batsman, wicket-keeper

Although his tally of 37 victims was his lowest for several seasons, partly the result of missing two Pura Cup games through injury late in the season, Berry maintained his excellent standard behind the stumps. Vice-captain to Paul Reiffel, his experience was of great value to the Victorian team and he took over the captaincy twice, against the West Indians and in one Mercantile Mutual Cup match. He had a lean year with the bat, beginning with just 39 runs in his first eight first-class hands, and although his form improved slightly thereafter, his record of 230 runs at 14.37 was disappointing for a No. 7 batsman. Not until the second innings of the Pura Cup Final against Queensland did he show his best form when, in a determined rearguard action, he compiled a combative 61. Berry has now dismissed 464 batsmen for the state, 199 ahead of the previous record holder, Richie Robinson, while his tally of 453 victims in Sheffield Shield/Pura Cup cricket is 105 ahead of second-placed Tim Zoehrer. After the season ended it was announced that he had been replaced as vice-captain of both Victoria's Pura Cup and limited-overs sides by Matthew Elliott and Brad Hodge.

	M	I	NO	R	HS	100s	50s	Avge	Ct	St	W	Avge	BB
First-class	128	194	28	3,453	166*	3	8	20.80	468	42	0	–	–
Dom. first-class	114	175	25	3,143	166*	3	7	20.95	415	38	0	–	–
Dom. limited-overs	63	47	13	575	64*	0	1	16.91	77	24	0	–	–

CRAIG, Shawn Andrew Jacob
Born: June 23, 1973 Carlton (Victoria)
Left-handed batsman, right-arm leg-spin bowler

Craig received an extended run in the Victorian team at the start of the season in the absence of Matthew Elliott. After being dismissed for a pair as a middle-order batsman in the opening match, he was called on to open the batting in Victoria's next four first-class matches. Despite his determination, he struggled to make an impact, with a highest score of just 35. Having batted in the middle order for most of his career for the state, it may have been asking too much of him to open the innings. Craig also played in Victoria's first three Mercantile Mutual Cup matches, but lost his place after taking 21 overs to make 28 against South Australia. His lean run for Victoria was in marked contrast to his record in Premier cricket, where he was a key member of St Kilda's premiership side and the competition's second-highest run-scorer with 818 runs at 62.92.

	M	I	NO	R	HS	100s	50s	Avge	Ct	St	W	Avge	BB
First-class	20	36	6	936	128*	1	4	31.20	20	0	8	83.00	2/89
Dom. first-class	17	31	5	807	128*	1	3	31.04	15	0	7	87.00	2/89
Dom. limited-overs	18	16	4	329	60	0	2	27.42	3	0	7	23.57	3/56

DART, Simon Paul
Born: February 3, 1978 Melbourne (Victoria)
Right-handed batsman, right-arm medium bowler
Domestic limited-overs debut 2000-01

An Australian Under-19s representative in 1995-96, Dart is a sound and stylish batsman who relies on good timing and placement and is a quick accumulator of runs once set. Following good scores in state Second Eleven matches he gained a regular place in Victoria's limited-overs side towards the end of the season, his best score being 38 against Queensland in Brisbane. However, although a useful slow-medium bowler at club level, he bowled only one over for the state. His brilliant diving catch at deep square leg to dismiss Queensland's Jimmy Maher at Melbourne was considered by some to be the best taken by a Victorian all season. Yet to make his first-class debut, Dart was 12th man in the Pura Cup match against South Australia in Adelaide, thereby emulating his father, Charlie, who was 12th man in a Shield game in Brisbane in 1968-69. He was in excellent form in Premier cricket for Hawthorn–Waverley, scoring 624 runs at 41.60 including three centuries, and topped the competition's bowling averages with 24 wickets at 12.20.

	M	I	NO	R	HS	100s	50s	Avge	Ct	St	W	Avge	BB
Dom. limited-overs	5	5	0	92	38	0	0	18.40	1	0	0	–	–

DAVISON, John Michael
Born: May 9, 1970 Campbell River, Vancouver Island, British Columbia, Canada
Right-handed batsman, right-arm off-spin bowler

The return of Colin Miller to Victoria's ranks suggested that Davison's days in the state team might be over, but after Miller's call-up to the Test team in December Davison played all but two of Victoria's last seven Pura Cup matches. As always he bowled tightly and economically for long spells, but penetration remained a problem. He finished with only ten wickets, his best performance coming against South Australia in Adelaide in February, when he captured 4/90. In good form in club cricket, he helped St Kilda to the premiership by capturing 33 wickets at 18.12. In July 2001 he represented Canada, the country of his birth, in the ICC Trophy competition, his all-round performances helping them to finish third and thus gain a place in the 2003 World Cup.

	M	I	NO	R	HS	100s	50s	Avge	Ct	St	W	Avge	BB
First-class	31	42	3	318	42	0	0	8.15	13	0	50	62.80	5/84
Dom. first-class	30	40	3	276	33	0	0	7.46	13	0	48	62.17	5/84
Dom. limited-overs	7	5	3	45	21	0	0	22.50	2	0	3	63.00	2/55

ELLIOTT, Matthew Thomas Gray
Born: September 28, 1971 Chelsea (Victoria)
Left-handed batsman, slow left-arm orthodox bowler

A chronic knee injury kept Elliott out of action until mid-December, and he never really got over his delayed start. His tally of 524 runs at 40.31 for Victoria, although respectable, was below his usual high standard. For the first time since his debut in 1992-93 he failed to make a first-class century for the state, though he came close in the Pura Cup Final, when he withstood Queensland's hostile pace attack for well over a day to compile a dogged 98. In the Mercantile Mutual Cup, a competition in which he had not previously excelled, he reeled off three speedy centuries in quick succession, while his four outings for Camberwell Magpies in Premier cricket produced scores of 133, 102, 58 and 128, which enabled him to head the competition's batting averages. At the end of the season his ACB contract was not renewed, but he received some consolation when he was named as Victoria's captain for the coming season's limited-overs side and vice-captain of the four-day side.

	M	I	NO	R	HS	100s	50s	Avge	Ct	St	W	Avge	BB
First-class	121	222	17	10,236	203	33	45	49.93	139	0	9	62.56	1/3
Dom. first-class	64	124	10	6,193	203	22	27	54.32	87	0	7	50.86	1/3
Test	20	34	1	1,171	199	3	4	35.48	13	0	0	–	–
Int'l limited-overs	1	1	0	1	1	0	0	1.00	0	0	0	–	–
Dom. limited-overs	42	40	3	1,156	112	4	4	31.24	20	0	0	–	–

FLEMING, Damien William
Born: April 24, 1970 Bentley (Western Australia)
Right-handed batsman, right-arm fast-medium bowler

After taking 30 wickets in six Tests at home in 1999-00, Fleming had a frustrating season. A broken finger, incurred while batting for South Melbourne in a club match in October, kept him out action for a month; and a stiff neck, later diagnosed as a bulging disc, which prevented him from bowling in the Pura Cup match against Queensland at Melbourne in late November, sidelined him for a further month. In January he returned to play three Mercantile Mutual Cup matches for Victoria and two limited-overs matches for Australia A and did well enough to be recalled to the Australian side during the Carlton Series. He performed usefully, capturing nine wickets, including two wickets in each of the two finals against West Indies. Selected for the tour of India, he met with little success, though he appeared in the First Test in what proved to be his only Test for the summer. Despite his disappointing season he was chosen for both Australia's limited-overs and Ashes tours of England.

	M	I	NO	R	HS	100s	50s	Avge	Ct	St	W	Avge	BB
First-class	104	126	36	1,334	71*	0	4	14.82	53	0	350	28.17	7/90
Dom. first-class	62	81	24	727	45*	0	2	12.75	28	0	208	30.21	7/90
Test	20	19	3	305	71*	0	2	19.06	9	0	75	25.89	5/30
Int'l limited-overs	88	31	18	152	29	0	0	11.69	14	0	134	25.39	5/36
Dom. limited-overs	39	20	10	140	21	0	0	14.00	10	0	42	31.74	3/25

HARPER, Peter Quinton
Born: December 11, 1977 Burwood (Victoria)
Right-handed batsman, right-arm medium bowler
Domestic limited-overs debut 2000-01

Harper made his only first-class appearance of the summer against the West Indians when, batting in the unaccustomed position of No. 6, he made 15. This was only his second first-class match for the state after scoring one and a duck on debut against Western Australia in 1997-98. He later opened the batting in three Mercantile Mutual Cup matches, scoring 51 runs in three innings. In 1998 Harper was the youngest-ever winner of the Ryder Medal and he maintained his good form in Premier cricket in 2000-01, compiling 743 runs at 46.43 for University, including the season's highest individual score of 195.

	M	I	NO	R	HS	100s	50s	Avge	Ct	St	W	Avge	BB
First-class	2	3	0	16	15	0	0	5.33	1	0	0	–	–
Dom. first-class	1	2	0	1	1	0	0	0.50	0	0	0	–	–
Dom. limited-overs	3	3	0	51	27	0	0	17.00	0	0	0	–	–

HARVEY, Ian Joseph
Born: April 10, 1972 Wonthaggi (Victoria)
Right-handed batsman, right-arm fast-medium bowler

Now established as a regular member of the national limited-overs team, the mercurial Harvey showed only patches of his best form for Victoria, with returns of 481 runs at 34.36 and 17 wickets at 27.88 at first-class level. His best efforts with the ball were both recorded against Queensland early in the season – an even hundred in the second innings at Brisbane and a breezy 93 in the return match in Melbourne. Troubled by a shoulder injury early on, the legacy of a successful season with Gloucestershire, his best contributions with the ball came later in the season, especially his 4/19 against South Australia in Adelaide. His greatest value to the Australian limited-overs team is as a bowler, where his accuracy and well-concealed variations of pace make him well-suited to bowl at the end of an innings. His 12 wickets in the Carlton Series against West Indies and Zimbabwe made him Australia's equal second-highest wicket-taker but he received limited opportunities with the bat. A broken finger incurred while batting against Tasmania in Hobart brought his season for Victoria to an early close, but he recovered in time to play in the limited-overs series in India. He performed usefully for Australia's limited-overs side in the NatWest series against England and Pakistan in June before rejoining Gloucestershire for his third season of county cricket.

	M	I	NO	R	HS	100s	50s	Avge	Ct	St	W	Avge	BB
First-class	85	144	9	3,979	136	5	23	29.47	63	0	221	28.82	7/44
Dom. first-class	55	97	8	2,920	136	4	19	32.81	41	0	128	33.00	7/44
Int'l limited-overs	35	25	8	363	47*	0	0	21.35	10	0	38	33.16	4/28
Dom. limited-overs	45	40	3	722	71	0	4	19.51	12	0	51	28.98	5/34

HEWETT, Ian Stephen Louis
Born: January 24, 1976 East Melbourne (Victoria)
Left-handed batsman, left-arm fast-medium bowler

Something of a forgotten man in Victorian cricket, Hewett has not played first-class cricket since appearing in two Shield games in 1995-96, and had not represented the state at limited-overs level since 1997-98. However, an excellent club season for Richmond in 1999-00 brought him back into contention for state selection, and a good all-round performance in a practice match for the Victorians against an Australian XI at St Kilda in early January brought about his recall to Victoria's limited-overs side. Appearing in the last five Mercantile Mutual Cup games, he captured three wickets in each of his first two matches and headed Victoria's limited-overs bowling averages with nine wickets at 19.66. He was a tearaway fast bowler with a long run-up when he first represented the state, but back problems have led him to shorten his run-up and he now relies more on control and movement.

	M	I	NO	R	HS	100s	50s	Avge	Ct	St	W	Avge	BB
First-class	2	2	2	38	34*	0	0	–	1	0	3	69.67	2/72
Dom. first-class	2	2	2	38	34*	0	0	–	1	0	3	69.67	2/72
Dom. limited-overs	8	7	1	34	9	0	0	5.67	1	0	11	24.00	3/38

HODGE, Bradley John
Born: December 29, 1974 Sandringham (Victoria)
Right-handed batsman, right-arm off-spin bowler

Hodge was Victoria's outstanding player in 2000-01 in both the Pura Cup and Mercantile Mutual Cup competitions. After a poor season in 1999-00 he finally fulfilled the high expectations he raised as an 18-year-old in 1993-94. His 1,107 first-class runs for Victoria at 61.50 in 2000-01 included one purple patch in November when, in consecutive innings, he scored 101 not out against Queensland, 134 retired hurt against the West Indians, 104 and 24 against South Australia in Melbourne and 111 in the return match against Queensland. He added a fifth century, 125 against New South Wales, later on. All through the season his batting was composed and confident and his strokeplay crisp and precise. In addition he snared useful wickets with his off-spin and fielded brilliantly. He was Victoria's leading run-scorer in the Mercantile Mutual Cup competition, including four attractive half-centuries in his 374 runs at 46.75. Still only 26, he may yet achieve higher honours.

	M	I	NO	R	HS	100s	50s	Avge	Ct	St	W	Avge	BB
First-class	76	141	14	4,788	134*	12	24	37.70	42	0	34	35.71	4/17
Dom. first-class	68	127	11	4,199	125	9	22	36.20	39	0	25	45.48	4/92
Dom. limited-overs	47	45	5	1,512	118*	2	11	37.80	19	0	5	38.40	2/25

INNESS, Mathew William Hunter
Born: January 13, 1978 East Melbourne (Victoria)
Left-handed batsman, left-arm fast-medium bowler

Inness was Paul Reiffel's regular opening bowling partner throughout the season and finished with the impressive return of 42 wickets at 23.40, in the process capturing his 100th wicket for the state. With a whippy action, he often took wickets in bursts, working up good pace and troubling batsmen with his ability to move the ball either way. In consecutive matches in November, against the West Indians and South Australia, he had identical figures of 6/26, and was rewarded with selection in the Australia A side that played the West Indians in Hobart. In fine form for Essendon in Premier cricket, he finished second in the competition's bowling averages with 27 wickets at 12.62. During the winter he returned to the AIS Cricket Academy in Adelaide as a scholarship coach.

	M	I	NO	R	HS	100s	50s	Avge	Ct	St	W	Avge	BB
First-class	34	34	11	66	27	0	0	2.87	9	0	117	25.97	6/26
Dom. first-class	31	33	11	63	27	0	0	2.86	8	0	106	25.98	6/26
Dom. limited-overs	5	0	0	–	–	0	0	–	2	0	0	–	–

KLINGER, Michael
Born: July 4, 1980 Kew (Victoria)
Right-handed batsman

Regarded as Victoria's best home-grown batting prospect in recent years, Klinger was given an extended trial. He was one of only two players to appear in all ten Mercantile Mutual Cup matches. After being omitted for two Pura Cup games in the middle of the season, his best form came straight after his return to the side. His calm 66 not out against South Australia in Adelaide, his maiden half-century for the state, was made under great pressure and took Victoria to a hard-earned victory; in his next knock, against Tasmania in Hobart, he was denied his maiden first-class century when the innings was declared with his score on 99. Low scores in the later games, including a double failure in the Pura Cup Final, suggest that he still has some way to go before establishing himself at first-class level. His fielding, especially square of the wicket on the off side, was brilliant and he proved an adequate stand-in keeper against Queensland, holding three catches when Darren Berry was off the field through illness. In Premier cricket for St Kilda he scored 494 runs at 61.75 and was a member of their premiership side.

	M	I	NO	R	HS	100s	50s	Avge	Ct	St	W	Avge	BB
First-class	13	20	2	510	99*	0	4	28.33	9	0	0	–	–
Dom. first-class	10	17	2	379	99*	0	3	25.27	8	0	0	–	–
Dom. limited-overs	11	11	2	262	80*	0	1	29.11	1	0	0	–	–

LEWIS, Michael Llewellyn
Born: June 29, 1974 Greensborough (Victoria)
Right-handed batsman, right-arm fast-medium bowler

At the start of the season it appeared that Lewis would be no more than a fringe member of the Victorian side. However, he appeared in seven Pura Cup matches and, along with Michael Klinger, was the only player to appear in all ten Mercantile Mutual Cup games. He worked hard to improve his control and develop more variety, and his persistence was rewarded in the Pura Cup Final when he bowled fast and straight to capture his career-best figures of 5/57, a noteworthy achievement for a player who three years previously was playing in a non-turf suburban competition. For Victoria he finished with 23 wickets at 33.57 while in Premier cricket for Northcote he captured 28 wickets at 15.57.

	M	I	NO	R	HS	100s	50s	Avge	Ct	St	W	Avge	BB
First-class	12	16	7	58	11*	0	0	6.44	2	0	38	31.55	5/57
Dom. first-class	12	16	7	58	11*	0	0	6.44	2	0	38	31.55	5/57
Dom. limited-overs	14	0	0	0	–	0	0	–	4	0	16	32.81	3/51

MILLER, Colin Reid
Born: February 6, 1964 Footscray (Victoria)
Right-handed batsman, right-arm medium-off spin bowler

Miller achieved another highlight in his remarkable Test career when in February he was named as Australia's Test Player of the Year. Overlooked for the first two Tests against West Indies, he made a huge impact with his off-spinners in the Third Test at Adelaide. He captured the last five wickets of the West Indies first innings, then brilliantly exploited a wearing pitch in the second to capture 5/32, including one spell of 5/8. Bowling at a pace quick enough to keep the West Indies batsmen pinned to the crease, he was able to make the ball turn and bounce alarmingly, and his match figures of 10/113, which enabled him to take his 50th Test wicket, enabled him to win his first Man of the Match award at Test level. In the Fifth Test at Sydney his appearance at the bowling crease on the second day with his hair dyed bright "Federation" blue caused great merriment. At state level his career turned full-circle when he played in Victoria's first five first-class matches, his first matches for the state since making his debut 14 seasons ago. Alternating between medium pace and off-spin, he took 20 wickets at 31.65 with best figures of 4/71 against New South Wales in the opening match. Subsequently he toured India, where he played in one Test, capturing six wickets, and was chosen for the Ashes tour of England.

	M	I	NO	R	HS	100s	50s	Avge	Ct	St	W	Avge	BB
First-class	119	144	29	1,496	62	0	3	13.01	38	0	432	30.13	7/49
Dom. first-class	80	101	21	1,110	60*	0	2	13.88	25	0	298	31.22	7/49
Test	18	24	3	174	43	0	0	8.29	6	0	69	26.16	5/32
Dom. limited-overs	45	27	6	232	32	0	0	11.05	9	0	46	36.46	4/36

MOSS, Jonathan
Born: May 4, 1975 Manly (New South Wales)
Right-handed batsman, right-arm fast-medium bowler
First-class, domestic first-class and domestic limited-overs debuts
2000-01

Moss began the season playing grade cricket in Sydney for
Manly–Warringah and ended it by representing Victoria in the Pura
Cup Final. Frustrated at his inability to gain selection for New South
Wales, he moved to Melbourne in November. He was all but
unknown to Victorian cricket followers when, in late January, he captured 5/47 on his
debut in a Mercantile Mutual Cup game against Queensland in Melbourne. He went on
to play in Victoria's last three Pura Cup matches, including the final. His best effort in
these games was an innings of 62 against Western Australia in Melbourne. Just over six
feet tall, he is a talented stroke-maker, particularly strong off his legs, a lively and
aggressive bowler who can move the ball both ways with good control, and an athletic
fielder. In Premier cricket he headed Prahran's batting and bowling averages with 423
runs at 32.53 and 35 wickets at 16.34.

	M	I	NO	R	HS	100s	50s	Avge	Ct	St	W	Avge	BB
First-class	3	5	0	136	62	0	1	27.20	0	0	4	41.00	1/17
Dom. first-class	3	5	0	136	62	0	1	27.20	0	0	4	41.00	1/17
Dom. limited-overs	3	2	0	35	19	0	0	17.50	1	0	5	24.20	5/47

MOTT, Matthew Peter
Born: October 3, 1973 Charleville (Queensland)
Left-handed batsman, right-arm medium bowler

Mott occupied the No. 3 batting position for Victoria throughout the season, scoring 695
runs at 33.09. A gritty batsman who sells his wicket dearly, he started the season
moderately, passing 50 only once in the first five matches, but played several good
innings later on, notably 154 against Western Australia in Melbourne. Perhaps his most
valuable contributions were 62 and 40 against South Australia in February which helped
Victoria to victory. At times he scored very slowly, notably in the second innings of the
Pura Cup Final when he batted three hours for 19, but his doggedness in the top order
was often of value to the team. He fielded excellently in the gully, holding 15 catches,
some of them brilliant, and put in some useful spells of medium-pace bowling. He was
less successful in the Mutual Mercantile Cup, where he lost his place after four matches.
He batted with more freedom in Premier cricket, scoring 520 runs at 74.28 for bottom-
placed Frankston Peninsula.

	M	I	NO	R	HS	100s	50s	Avge	Ct	St	W	Avge	BB
First-class	48	85	4	2,815	154	6	15	34.75	42	0	7	61.57	3/35
Dom. first-class	44	79	4	2,649	154	6	13	35.32	37	0	7	59.14	3/35
Dom. limited-overs	17	15	1	265	55*	0	2	18.93	7	0	4	21.50	2/2

OLIVER, Benjamin Carl
Born: October 24, 1979 Castlemaine (Victoria)
Right-handed batsman, right-arm fast-medium bowler
First-class debut 2000-01

Regarded as one of the Victoria's best young prospects, Oliver received an extended trial
in the Mercantile Mutual Cup side. His steady batting and accurate bowling just short
of a length made a good impression early in the season. Against New South Wales at
Richmond, he won the Man of the Match award after bowling tightly and making a
composed 29 to steer Victoria to victory. His bowling also impressed on his first-class
debut against the West Indians when he captured three cheap wickets including those of

Shivnarine Chanderpaul and Brian Lara. However, his form tapered off after Christmas, and when Ian Harvey was unavailable for Victoria's later Pura Cup matches, the selectors opted for Jonathan Moss as the team's all-rounder. Oliver had a good record with the ball in Premier cricket for Geelong, capturing 22 wickets at 17.40.

	M	I	NO	R	HS	100s	50s	Avge	Ct	St	W	Avge	BB
First-class	1	1	0	0	0	0	0	0.00	1	0	3	15.00	2/13
Dom. limited-overs	10	8	2	147	39*	0	0	24.50	4	0	5	49.40	2/36

PEAKE, Clinton John
Born: March 25, 1977 Geelong (Victoria)
Left-handed batsman, slow-left arm orthodox bowler

Peake briefly replaced Michael Klinger in the Pura Cup side, but scored only 53 runs in two matches and was dropped. He lost his place in the limited-overs side after making only 19 runs in three innings. After a promising start to his first-class career as an 18-year-old in 1995-96, Peake has received few opportunities, though many believe this talented strokemaker has the ability to succeed at first-class level. In fine form for Geelong in Premier cricket, he compiled 714 runs at 54.92, but was surprisingly left off Victoria's list of contracted players for the 2001-02 season.

	M	I	NO	R	HS	100s	50s	Avge	Ct	St	W	Avge	BB
First-class	9	17	2	303	46	0	0	20.20	7	0	2	53.00	1/11
Dom. first-class	8	15	1	274	46	0	0	19.57	6	0	1	86.00	1/11
Dom. limited-overs	5	5	1	24	14	0	0	6.00	2	0	0	–	–

REIFFEL, Paul Ronald
Born: April 19, 1966 Box Hill (Victoria)
Right-handed batsman, right-arm fast-medium bowler

In his second season as Victorian captain, Reiffel again led Victoria into the Pura Cup Final. Co-opted by Nottinghamshire to play county cricket during the previous winter, he scarcely had the ideal preparation for a 34-year-old fast bowler before an arduous Australian season. However, despite some niggling injuries and chronic soreness, he appeared in all Victoria's Pura Cup matches and missed only one Mercantile Mutual Cup game. Although his tally of victims dropped from 59 at 16.64 in 1999-00 to 30 at 27.47, his bowling always commanded respect though, understandably in the light of his heavy workload, his penetration tapered off in the later matches. During the season he became Victoria's highest wicket-taker in Sheffield Shield/Pura Cup matches and he is now only three wickets short of Alan Connolly's record tally of 330 wickets in all first-class matches for the state. Batting at No. 8, Reiffel made 337 runs at 24.07 and was the only reliable Victorian lower-order batsman. Despite attracting controversy by declaring when Michael Klinger was on 99 in the game against Tasmania, his captaincy again earned respect, and he will continue for a third season as Victoria's captain in 2001-02. However, he relinquished the captaincy of Victoria's limited-overs side and will be available for only occasional limited-overs games in the future.

	M	I	NO	R	HS	100s	50s	Avge	Ct	St	W	Avge	BB
First-class	163	202	57	3,568	86	0	17	24.61	74	0	535	26.38	6/57
Dom. first-class	82	110	28	1,697	86	0	5	20.70	39	0	308	25.85	6/57
Test	35	50	14	955	79*	0	6	26.53	15	0	104	26.96	6/71
Int'l limited-overs	92	57	21	503	58	0	1	13.97	25	0	106	29.20	4/13
Dom. limited-overs	40	26	10	251	44	0	0	15.69	12	0	37	32.46	4/14

ROACH, Peter John
Born: May 19, 1975 Kew (Victoria)
Right-handed batsman, wicket-keeper

Roach returned to the state side to keep wickets in two Pura Cup games late in the season when Darren Berry was injured. He kept tidily in both games and demonstrated his batting ability with a well-made half-century at a crucial stage against Western Australia. Highly regarded for his leadership and tactical skills, Roach captains Hawthorn–Waverley in Premier cricket, for whom he scored 662 runs at 41.37.

	M	I	NO	R	HS	100s	50s	Avge	Ct	St	W	Avge	BB
First-class	11	21	8	471	84	0	4	36.23	36	1	0	–	–
Dom. first-class	9	17	7	327	84	0	3	32.70	32	0	0	–	–
Dom. limited-overs	4	3	0	42	26	0	0	14.00	4	0	0	–	–

VIMPANI, Graeme Ronald
Born: January 27, 1972 Herston (Queensland)
Right-handed batsman, right-arm medium bowler

Vimpani lost his place in the Victorian side after disappointing performances in the opening Mercantile Mutual Cup and Pura Cup matches against New South Wales. Although a talented strokemaker, his record has been disappointing since he made 752 first-class runs in 1996-97, and he was not named in the 2001-02 state squad.

	M	I	NO	R	HS	100s	50s	Avge	Ct	St	W	Avge	BB
First-class	30	57	3	1,598	161	3	8	29.59	19	0	0	–	–
Dom. first-class	25	47	2	1,236	161	2	6	27.47	18	0	0	–	–
Dom. limited-overs	19	19	0	467	92	0	2	24.58	8	0	0	–	–

WARNE, Shane Keith
Born: September 13, 1969 Ferntree Gully (Victoria)
Right-handed batsman, right-arm leg-spin bowler

Warne's season could scarcely have got off to a worse start. He lost the Australian vice-captaincy in August, and after returning from his arduous season with Hampshire he had to undergo surgery to a troublesome knee. Then, on the opening day of Victoria's first Pura Cup fixture, against New South Wales at Richmond, he broke the top joint of the third finger of his right hand when he held a skied catch to dismiss Mark Waugh. He also suffered ligament damage to the finger, the same one on which he had undergone surgery four years earlier. He was out of action for two months, missing the entire Test series against West Indies. At the start of January he returned to the Victorian side for a limited-overs match against Western Australia in Perth, taking three wickets. In the following Pura Cup match against Western Australia his superb 4/53 and 5/49 led the Victorians to victory. The Australian selectors wasted no time in naming him in the Australian side for the Carlton Series. Although understandably not quite at his best, he captured 18 wickets at 20.94, easily the highest tally for any bowler in the series, and was picked for Australia's tour of India. However, as on his previous visit there in 1997-98, when he was troubled by a serious shoulder injury, his bowling came in for punishment, especially from V. V. S. Laxman and Sachin Tendulkar. Nevertheless his standing as Australia's leading spinner remained undiminished, and he produced some telling performances in the limited-overs NatWest series against England and Pakistan in June and commenced his third Ashes series in England needing 24 wickets to become the first Australian to capture 400 Test wickets.

	M	I	NO	R	HS	100s	50s	Avge	Ct	St	W	Avge	BB
First-class	174	234	32	3,476	86	0	11	17.21	133	0	716	26.59	8/71
Dom. first-class	31	40	6	584	69	0	2	17.18	23	0	106	36.24	6/42
Test	87	122	12	1,663	86	0	4	15.12	66	0	376	26.62	8/71
Int'l limited-overs	167	91	26	835	55	0	1	12.85	70	0	262	24.97	5/33
Dom. limited-overs	16	12	1	160	32	0	0	14.55	7	0	25	23.80	5/35

WHITE, Cameron Leon
Born: August 18, 1983 Bairnsdale (Victoria)
Right-handed batsman, right-arm leg-spin bowler
First-class and domestic first-class debut 2000-01

Aged just 17 years and 203 days when he played against New South
Wales at Sydney in March, White became the youngest player to
represent Victoria since World War II and the first 17-year-old to
appear for the state since Geoff Parker in 1985-86. Chosen
primarily for his leg-spin bowling, he displayed excellent
temperament on his debut, capturing 4/65, including the wickets of Michael Bevan and
Shane Lee, a performance which helped Victoria to first-innings points and a place in
the Pura Cup Final. Tall and well-built, he delivers his leg-breaks at a brisk pace, and
batsmen find it difficult to use their feet to him. Although not as yet a big turner of the
ball, he has good control, uses his height to obtain bounce and is developing his
wrong'un. He is also a capable batsman, strong off his legs and a powerful driver. A Year
12 student at Bairnsdale High School and the current vice-captain of the Victorian
Under-19s team, he burst into prominence with a string of outstanding performances in
Premier cricket with Dandenong, including 6/6 including a hat-trick against South
Melbourne and two centuries and two half-centuries in quick succession after Christmas.

	M	I	NO	R	HS	100s	50s	Avge	Ct	St	W	Avge	BB
First-class	2	3	2	12	11	0	0	12.00	0	0	4	34.00	4/65
Dom. first-class	2	3	2	12	11	0	0	12.00	0	0	4	34.00	4/65

WESTERN AUSTRALIA

By Ken Casellas

ANGEL, Jo
Born: April 22, 1968 Mt Lawley (Western Australia)
Left-handed batsman, right-arm fast bowler

Seemingly indestructible, the lion-hearted Angel was his state's leading wicket-taker (37
at 23.43) in Pura Cup matches in the 2000-01 season, and he moved past Dennis Lillee
into second place in the list of Western Australia's bowlers. After finishing his tenth first-
class season with a career tally of 343 wickets in Australian Domestic First-class cricket,
the burly Angel declared he was keen to saddle up for one or two more seasons. He is
on target to overhaul Terry Alderman's Western Australian record of 384 wickets. He
took five or more wickets in a first-class innings for the 14th time when he bowled with
tremendous spirit to finish with 5/78 off 32.4 overs against Tasmania at the WACA
Ground in March. Though no longer a fiery enforcer, Angel has developed into an
extremely capable into-the-wind new-ball bowler who invariably builds pressure on the
batsmen. He was also a dependable performer in Mercantile Mutual Cup matches, taking
12 wickets at 32.16.

	M	I	NO	R	HS	100s	50s	Avge	Ct	St	W	Avge	BB
First-class	98	124	36	1,119	84*	0	3	12.72	26	0	405	24.31	6/64
Dom. first-class	84	107	29	968	84*	0	3	12.41	18	0	343	24.11	6/64
Test	4	7	1	35	11	0	0	5.83	1	0	10	46.30	3/54
Int'l limited-overs	3	1	0	0	0	0	0	0.00	0	0	4	28.25	2/47
Dom. limited-overs	53	12	5	61	19*	0	0	8.71	5	0	59	29.17	3/37

ATKINSON, Mark Peter
Born: November 27, 1970 Bentley (Western Australia)
Right-handed batsman, right-arm medium bowler

For the second successive season Atkinson failed to make a first-class appearance. He was overlooked after playing in Western Australia's opening Mercantile Mutual Cup match, against South Australia in Perth, when he conceded 53 runs off eight overs and took one wicket, that of Greg Blewett. Once again, he was a sound performer in first-grade club ranks for Mount Lawley, taking 26 wickets at 18.30 and scoring 373 runs at 31.08. He has done valuable work coaching youngsters.

	M	I	NO	R	HS	100s	50s	Avge	Ct	St	W	Avge	BB
First-class	21	29	9	423	52*	0	1	21.15	13	0	54	35.61	5/92
Dom. first-class	19	27	9	349	52*	0	1	19.39	13	0	47	37.79	5/92
Dom. limited-overs	27	18	4	135	31	0	0	9.64	9	0	34	28.94	4/38

CAMPBELL, Ryan John
Born: February 7, 1972 Osborne Park (Western Australia)
Right-handed batsman, wicket-keeper

A major knee operation before the season did not help the flamboyant opening batsman and Campbell was involved in controversy for much of the season, mainly because of his outspoken comments. After the selectors decided to rest him from the opening Mercantile Mutual Cup match, he described his omission as a joke, and at the end of the season he said he had not been given a fair go and that the selectors had treated him and other players like pieces of meat. He then rejected a lucrative offer to sign with Victoria and declared he would make every effort to re-establish himself in the Western Australian side. In a miserable season for him, he was dropped from the Pura Cup side halfway through the season after scoring a mere 167 first-class runs at 18.55. He also failed to deliver the goods in Mercantile Mutual Cup matches, scoring only 135 runs at 15.00. However, he excelled behind the stumps in the limited-overs matches in the absence of Adam Gilchrist, taking 18 catches and making three stumpings in the seven matches he kept in. He had six victims (five catches and a stumping) against New South Wales and took six catches against Tasmania to equal the best performance by a wicket-keeper in the competition. Campbell also struggled in first-grade cricket for Scarborough, and has decided to switch to his third club, Joondalup, for the 2001-02 season.

	M	I	NO	R	HS	100s	50s	Avge	Ct	St	W	Avge	BB
First-class	52	92	2	3,283	203	7	19	36.48	118	3	0	–	–
Dom. first-class	47	83	1	2,954	203	6	18	36.02	105	1	0	–	–
Dom. limited-overs	42	41	0	852	108	1	5	20.78	50	5	0	–	–

CARY, Sean Ross
Born: March 10, 1971 Subiaco (Western Australia)
Right-handed batsman, right-arm fast-medium bowler

A hard-working into-the-wind swing bowler, Cary has suffered since Jo Angel relinquished his down-wind role and proved highly effective into the breeze. The willowy Cary was not required after appearing in the first Pura Cup match, against Queensland at the WACA Ground, when he failed to take a wicket. Now in his thirties, Cary appears to have limited opportunities. He is still a steady, patient bowler, however, who did not let the disappointment of being overlooked by the Western Australian selectors affect his performances for Willetton in first-grade cricket. With 52 at 17.76, he was the leading wicket-taker in the competition.

	M	I	NO	R	HS	100s	50s	Avge	Ct	St	W	Avge	BB
First-class	36	36	16	153	13	0	0	7.65	13	0	99	34.28	4/9
Dom. first-class	33	34	16	143	13	0	0	7.94	12	0	90	34.24	4/9
Dom. limited-overs	12	4	3	8	7*	0	0	8.00	2	0	7	56.14	2/55

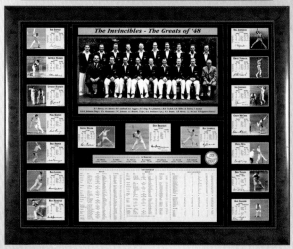

CULLEN, Geoffrey Ian
Born: March 16, 1977 Perth (Western Australia)
Left-handed batsman, right-arm off-spin bowler
First-class and domestic first-class debuts 2000-01

A bountiful season with Claremont–Nedlands in the first-grade competition, plus some encouraging form in the state Second Eleven, earned Geoff Cullen his first-class debut, against Victoria at the MCG in the final match of the season. He was out for five in his only first-class innings, but he shows promise and deserves further opportunities. A final-year student in politics and geography at the University of Western Australia, he finished the first-grade season with 852 runs at an average of 56.80.

	M	I	NO	R	HS	100s	50s	Avge	Ct	St	W	Avge	BB
First-class	1	1	0	5	5	0	0	5.00	0	0	0	–	–
Dom. first-class	1	1	0	5	5	0	0	5.00	0	0	0	–	–

GILCHRIST, Adam Craig
Born: November 14, 1971 Bellingen (New South Wales)
Left-handed batsman, wicket-keeper

Adam Gilchrist continued on his spectacular way in international cricket and became the only player in history to be a member of a winning Test side in his first 15 Test appearances. The end of this remarkable sequence coincided with a rare personal form slump when Australia lost to India in the Second and Third Tests in March. Gilchrist was out leg before wicket, sweeping, in his four innings in those two Test defeats, being dismissed for a pair in Calcutta and for one in each innings in Chennai. These failures followed his superb 122 in the First Test in Mumbai and came after a successful summer in Australia. In the five Tests against West Indies he scored 241 runs at 48.20, and he amassed 326 runs at 40.75 in the limited-overs triangular series against West Indies and Zimbabwe. International duties restricted Gilchrist to two Pura Cup matches (59 and 109 not out against Queensland in Perth and 102 against South Australia in Adelaide) and three Mercantile Mutual Cup matches (69 runs at 23.00).

	M	I	NO	R	HS	100s	50s	Avge	Ct	St	W	Avge	BB
First-class	99	152	28	5,164	203*	14	20	41.65	407	23	0	–	–
Dom. first-class	57	91	13	2,993	203*	8	10	38.37	246	8	0	–	–
Test	17	25	4	994	149*	2	7	47.33	70	5	0	–	–
Int'l limited-overs	119	115	5	3,848	154	6	22	34.98	153	29	0	–	–
Dom. limited-overs	32	29	3	871	115	1	6	33.50	51	5	0	–	–

GOODWIN, Murray William
Born: December 11, 1972 Salisbury (Rhodesia)
Right-handed batsman, right-arm leg-spin bowler

Citing a lack of financial assistance from the Zimbabwean Cricket Union, Murray Goodwin returned to Perth after a successful stint as a Test batsman with Zimbabwe. His season 2000-01 was one of marked contrasts. He failed miserably in Pura Cup matches and was dropped for the final match after managing a mere 145 runs at an average of 11.15. Yet he was an outstanding success in Mercantile Mutual Cup matches, amassing the record aggregate for a season, 534 runs at 76.28, including the highest-ever innings of 167 against New South Wales at the WACA Ground in January. He was looking forward to overcoming some technical deficiencies during a season with Sussex in the English county competition.

	M	I	NO	R	HS	100s	50s	Avge	Ct	St	W	Avge	BB
First-class	59	105	11	4,405	203*	12	22	46.86	47	0	7	41.86	2/23
Dom. first-class	20	36	4	903	127	1	5	28.22	21	0	0	–	–
Test	19	37	4	1,414	166*	3	8	42.85	11	0	0	–	–
Int'l limited-overs	71	70	3	1,818	112*	2	8	27.13	20	0	4	52.50	1/12
Dom. limited-overs	13	12	3	555	167	1	4	61.67	4	0	0	–	–

HARVEY, Kade Murray
Born: October 7, 1975 Subiaco (Western Australia)
Right-handed batsman, right-arm fast-medium bowler

Harvey continued to be a permanent member of Western Australia's limited-overs side, but for the second successive season he failed to make a first-class appearance. His wonderfully competitive bowling earned him 11 wickets at 32.90 in Mercantile Mutual Cup matches. He was also Western Australia's leading wicket-taker in the inaugural Champions Cup tournament against Mumbai, KwaZulu-Natal and New Zealand's Central Districts side at the WACA Ground, with six at 16.66. Again, Harvey excelled for Scarborough in the first-grade competition, finishing with 681 runs at 56.75 and 29 wickets at 17.79.

	M	I	NO	R	HS	100s	50s	Avge	Ct	St	W	Avge	BB
First-class	10	11	2	189	79	0	1	21.00	8	0	22	32.77	3/30
Dom. first-class	6	7	1	94	41	0	0	15.67	6	0	17	27.41	3/30
Dom. limited-overs	40	22	8	263	31	0	0	18.79	6	0	55	24.91	4/8

HOGG, George Bradley
Born: February 6, 1971 Narrogin (Western Australia)
Left-handed batsman, left-arm slow 'chinaman' bowler

A regular member of Western Australia's first-class side in the 1999-00 season, Brad Hogg made only three first-class appearances in 2000-01 (65 runs at 21.66 and five wickets at 41.00), opposition bowlers finding it too easy to tie him down. But he remained a vital member of the limited-overs side. In Mercantile Mutual Cup matches he batted down the order and made several important late contributions, finishing with 131 runs at 43.66, and he was the side's most successful bowler, with 13 wickets at 28.84. A brilliant run-saving fieldsman, he also took seven catches in this competition, including a magnificent right-handed catch off his own bowling to get rid of Brad Hodge and a remarkable catch at backward point when he flung himself low to his left to dismiss David Fitzgerald. He also performed well in the Champions Cup, with five wickets at 24.40. He continued to excel in club cricket, topping the first-grade aggregate with 875 runs at 72.91, with a top score of 285, a competition record.

	M	I	NO	R	HS	100s	50s	Avge	Ct	St	W	Avge	BB
First-class	54	81	17	1,626	111*	2	7	25.41	32	0	60	50.77	5/53
Dom. first-class	47	71	14	1,455	111*	1	7	25.53	31	0	54	48.39	5/53
Test	1	2	0	5	4	0	0	2.50	0	0	1	69.00	1/69
Int'l limited-overs	7	7	0	38	11*	0	0	12.67	2	0	3	72.67	1/23
Dom. limited-overs	44	35	15	633	59	0	2	31.65	25	0	26	27.50	3/37

HUSSEY, Michael Edward
Born: May 27, 1975 Morley (Western Australia)
Left-handed batsman, right-arm medium bowler

Mike Hussey's elevation to an ACB contract and the constant early-season speculation that he was competing with Matthew Hayden for the position as Michael Slater's opening partner in the Test side gravely affected his batting. Much of the fun went from his game and he became obsessive in his quest to be fitter and better prepared than ever before. He was too dedicated for his own good, had a nightmare of a season, and lost his ACB contract. He failed to reach a half-century in his first 17 first-class innings, before a five-hour innings of 90 against Tasmania at the WACA Ground and a second-innings 137 against Victoria at the MCG boosted his season's tally to 605 runs at 30.25, well below his splendid efforts in the previous five seasons. He enjoyed greater success in Mercantile Mutual Cup matches, finishing the season with 428 runs at 53.50. His fine limited-overs form carried over into the Champions Cup tournament in which he scored

117 runs for once out, off only 101 deliveries. He looked to a season with Northamptonshire in English county cricket to restore his game for the 2001-02 season.

	M	I	NO	R	HS	100s	50s	Avge	Ct	St	W	Avge	BB
First-class	80	145	8	6,051	187	14	28	44.17	58	0	4	48.75	2/21
Dom. first-class	65	119	6	4,771	187	11	20	42.22	49	0	3	54.33	2/21
Dom. limited-overs	35	32	3	1,098	100*	1	9	37.86	18	0	3	23.67	3/52

JULIAN, Brendon Paul
Born: August 10, 1970 Hamilton (New Zealand)
Right-handed batsman, left-arm fast-medium bowler

In June 2001, Brendon Julian announced his decision to retire from cricket. He was a fine contributor to Western Australia, and sometimes Australia, over 12 seasons, and always attractive to watch, but one of the world's most enigmatic cricketers. A gifted all-rounder, Julian had explosive qualities with bat and ball that could swing the course of any contest, but he seemed unable to harness his talent consistently. He had been troubled by injury in recent years, and made a late start to the 2000-01 season after recovering from knee surgery. He played some important Pura Cup innings without reaching his best standards, but he bowled with admirable spirit and his 32 wickets at 29.18 for the season took his aggregate for Western Australia past the 300 mark. He took 4/41 against South Australia in a Mercantile Mutual Cup match in Adelaide and finished the season with nine limited-overs wickets at 29.77.

	M	I	NO	R	HS	100s	50s	Avge	Ct	St	W	Avge	BB
First-class	138	192	34	4,074	124	4	20	25.46	88	0	435	30.56	7/39
Dom. first-class	87	128	19	2,507	124	2	11	23.00	58	0	292	29.36	7/39
Test	7	9	1	128	56*	0	1	16.00	4	0	15	39.93	4/36
Int'l limited-overs	25	17	0	224	35	0	0	13.18	8	0	22	45.32	3/40
Dom. limited-overs	54	44	5	524	48*	0	0	13.44	16	0	59	30.15	4/41

KARPPINEN, Stuart James
Born: June 13, 1973 Townsville (Queensland)
Right-handed batsman, right-arm fast-medium bowler
First-class and domestic first-class debuts 2000-01

A naturally athletic sportsman, Stuart Karppinen made only one Pura Cup appearance, against Victoria at the WACA Ground, and enjoyed a successful first-class debut with figures of 2/34 and 3/34. Matthew Nicholson was fit for the remainder of the season, which denied Karppinen further opportunities. He is over-fond of theory, but when he relaxes and exploits his natural ability he is a fine bowler who is well worth persevering with. For South Perth he took 31 wickets at 20.77 and scored 272 runs at 27.20.

	M	I	NO	R	HS	100s	50s	Avge	Ct	St	W	Avge	BB
First-class	1	2	0	18	17	0	0	9.00	0	0	5	13.60	3/34
Dom. first-class	1	2	0	18	17	0	0	9.00	0	0	5	13.60	3/34
Dom. limited-overs	11	7	3	48	15	0	0	12.00	4	0	11	37.45	2/35

KATICH, Simon Matthew
Born: August 21, 1975 Middle Swan (Western Australia)
Left-handed batsman, slow left-arm orthodox bowler
International limited-overs debut 2000-01

Almost fully recovered from a debilitating illness, Simon Katich enjoyed spectacular success in the 2000-01 season and was rewarded with the vice-captaincy of the Australia A side, an appearance in the Australian senior limited-overs side (when he did not get a bat) and selection for the Ashes tour of England. He became the first Western Australian to score a hundred against each of the states in one season, amassing 1,236 runs at 72.70, and his 1,145 runs in Pura Cup matches was a record for a Western

Australian player. His magnificent unbeaten 228 against South Australia at the WACA Ground made him only the 12th player to score a double-century for Western Australia in a Sheffield Shield or Pura Cup match. He started the season with a defiant, match-saving innings of 105 not out against Queensland at the WACA Ground, completing his century off 379 deliveries in 460 minutes to take the mantle as the scorer of the slowest first-class century for Western Australia. He took over as state captain for the final two Pura Cup matches after Tom Moody's retirement and continued to impress with his leadership qualities. In Mercantile Mutual Cup matches, Katich scored 300 runs at 42.85, and he shone in the Champions Cup tournament, scoring 170 runs at 85.00.

	M	I	NO	R	HS	100s	50s	Avge	Ct	St	W	Avge	BB
First-class	58	105	19	4,575	228*	15	19	53.20	61	0	11	70.00	3/46
Dom. first-class	36	66	10	2,913	228*	10	12	52.02	31	0	6	51.67	3/46
Int'l limited-overs	1	0	0	0	–	0	0	–	0	0	0	–	–
Dom. limited-overs	28	27	3	885	116	1	7	36.88	9	0	0	–	–

LANGER, Justin Lee
Born: November 21, 1970 Perth (Western Australia)
Left-handed batsman, right-arm medium bowler

Langer enjoyed only modest success after his bountiful summer the previous season, but retained his position as Australia's Test No. 3 batsman. Starting the season with a pair against Queensland at the WACA Ground in October, he was then out a few days later for a second-ball duck in a Mercantile Mutual Cup match against South Australia. Test duties restricted his first-class appearances for Western Australia to three matches (110 runs at 22.00) and he managed only one half-century in eight innings in the five-Test series against West Indies. He made a sound start in all of his five innings in the three Tests against India, but again made only one half-century. Langer enjoyed success for Western Australia in limited-overs matches, scoring 228 runs at 32.57 in the Mercantile Mutual Cup competition and scoring the only century (an unbeaten 119 against Mumbai) in the Champions Cup tournament in Perth. Langer was a member of the Australian side throughout its record-breaking sequence of 16 successive Test victories.

	M	I	NO	R	HS	100s	50s	Avge	Ct	St	W	Avge	BB
First-class	193	339	35	15,348	274*	47	59	50.49	168	0	5	38.80	2/17
Dom. first-class	67	123	10	6,093	274*	19	21	53.92	57	0	0	–	–
Test	41	68	2	2,577	223	7	12	39.05	28	0	–	–	–
Int'l limited-overs	8	7	2	160	36	0	0	32.00	2	1	0	–	–
Dom. limited-overs	55	53	5	1,866	146	1	16	38.88	20	0	0	–	–

MARSH, Shaun Edwards
Born: July 9, 1983 Subiaco (Western Australia)
Left-handed batsman
First-class and domestic first-class debuts 2000-01

The son of former Western Australian captain and Australian Test vice-captain Geoff Marsh, Shaun Marsh is a left-hander with enormous potential. He made his first-class debut at 17 years and 235 days when he looked the part in scoring 12 and 28 not out against South Australia at the WACA Ground. He played in Western Australia's final three Pura Cup matches of the season, scoring 102 runs at 25.50. He has an excellent technique and is a more adventurous strokemaker than his renowned father. He scored prolifically in minor cricket during 2000-01, hitting eight centuries, including 112 for the state Second Eleven against the Tasmanian Second XI, 123 for the Australians against Sri Lanka in an Under-19s Test and two hundreds on an Under-19s tour of Bangladesh. He also scored 440 first-grade runs at 55.00 for Willetton. He attended the AIS Cricket Academy in the winter of 2001.

	M	I	NO	R	HS	100s	50s	Avge	Ct	St	W	Avge	BB
First-class	3	5	1	102	46	0	0	25.50	2	0	0	–	–
Dom. first-class	3	5	1	102	46	0	0	25.50	2	0	0	–	–

MARTYN, Damien Richard
Born: October 21, 1971 Darwin (Northern Territory)
Right-handed batsman, right-arm medium bowler

Centuries against South Australia and Tasmania and two scores in the nineties were highlights of a successful season for Martyn that produced 571 first-class runs at 57.10 for Western Australia. He led the Australia A side against the West Indians in Hobart, and gave further proof that he is a batsman of the highest quality in his only Test appearance of the summer when he scored 46 not out and 34 not out in the Third Test against West Indies in Adelaide. Martyn excelled for Australia in limited-overs internationals, scoring 298 runs at an average of 149.00 and at a wonderful strike rate of 93.13 (the highest for Australia in the series) in the tournament against West Indies and Zimbabwe. He was given a chance to open the batting against Zimbabwe in Perth and delighted the fans with a sparkling, flawless 144 not out. He is at last making the most of every opportunity after squandering some wonderful chances in his younger days.

	M	I	NO	R	HS	100s	50s	Avge	Ct	St	W	Avge	BB
First-class	135	234	32	9,614	203*	27	51	47.59	112	2	34	40.35	4/30
Dom. first-class	90	159	16	6,416	203*	19	32	44.87	80	1	32	38.69	4/30
Test	11	20	5	638	89*	0	5	42.53	5	0	0	–	–
Int'l limited-overs	79	65	23	1,681	144*	2	9	40.02	29	0	10	54.80	2/21
Dom. limited-overs	48	45	7	1,655	140	2	12	43.55	14	0	18	16.33	3/3

MEULEMAN, Scott William
Born: July 17, 1980 Subiaco (Western Australia)
Right-handed batsman, right-arm leg-spin bowler
First-class and domestic first-class debuts 2000-01

This young opening batsman joined his grandfather Ken and father Bob as a Western Australian first-class cricketer when he opened the innings with Mike Hussey against Tasmania at the WACA Ground in March. He immediately looked at home as he batted with considerable aplomb in scoring 27 and 46 before failing against Victoria at the MCG. The only other family to provide three generations of players for Western Australia has been the MacGill family, Charlie, Terry and Stuart. Scott Meuleman is blessed with an excellent technique and nimble footwork, both forward and back. He appears to have all the attributes for a first-class opener. He suffered a disappointment in autumn when a dislocated shoulder forced him to curtail his stint at the Cricket Academy in Adelaide.

	M	I	NO	R	HS	100s	50s	Avge	Ct	St	W	Avge	BB
First-class	2	4	0	77	46	0	0	19.25	0	0	0	–	–
Dom. first-class	2	4	0	77	46	0	0	19.25	0	0	0	–	–

MOODY, Thomas Masson
Born: October 2, 1965 Adelaide (South Australia)
Right-handed batsman, right-arm medium bowler

Tom Moody returned to action after a back injury had prevented him from playing in the summer of 1999-00, and though his leadership greatly enhanced Western Australia, the side had a lean summer. Moody decided to retire when his side was out of contention for a place in the Pura Cup final, with two qualifying matches remaining. He struggled to regain his best form and managed only 324 runs at 27.00. To be fair, he frequently went in to bat when his side was in trouble. His bowling was not as damaging as in many previous seasons, yet he still managed 20 wickets at 22.75, including 4/14 off 12 overs against the West Indians, 5/26 against New South Wales at the WACA Ground and 4/38 against Queensland at the Gabba. It was fitting that his most delightful innings was his final knock, a wonderfully authoritative 67-ball innings of 55. That came a week after he had opened and scored 78 off 79 deliveries in the Mercantile Mutual Cup final against New South Wales. Moody has made a sustained and distinguished contribution to the game and will be sadly missed, having given unstinting service to his state since his debut in October 1985. In 2001 he spent the first season of a three-year contract as director of cricket operations with Worcestershire.

	M	I	NO	R	HS	100s	50s	Avge	Ct	St	W	Avge	BB
First-class	300	501	47	21,001	272	64	94	46.26	294	0	361	30.70	7/38
Dom. first-class	132	228	22	8,853	272	20	46	42.98	114	0	220	28.62	7/38
Test	8	14	0	456	106	2	3	32.57	9	0	2	73.50	1/17
Int'l limited-overs	76	64	12	1,211	89	0	10	23.29	21	0	52	38.73	3/25
Dom. limited-overs	75	71	12	2,004	102*	2	14	33.97	25	0	70	30.44	4/30

NICHOLSON, Matthew James
Born: October 2, 1974 St Leonards (New South Wales)
Right-handed batsman, right-arm fast-medium bowler

Again this tall, talented fast bowler had a season interrupted by injury. He broke down with a knee problem against Tasmania in a Pura Cup match at Bellerive Oval in November. After successful surgery he returned to the side and bowled with plenty of fire in the final four matches, to finish the first-class season with 25 wickets at 30.92, and a valuable 241 runs at 26.77. He did not play in any Mercantile Mutual Cup matches, but showed good form against Mumbai, Central Districts and KwaZulu-Natal in the Champions Cup tournament at the WACA Ground when he took five wickets at 29.40. He spent the 2001 winter playing for Todmorden in the Lancashire League.

	M	I	NO	R	HS	100s	50s	Avge	Ct	St	W	Avge	BB
First-class	26	37	8	694	58*	0	2	23.93	11	0	86	30.26	7/77
Dom. first-class	21	32	7	563	48	0	0	22.52	10	0	67	31.58	5/49
Test	1	2	0	14	9	0	0	7.00	0	0	4	28.75	3/56
Dom. limited-overs	1	1	0	5	5	0	0	5.00	0	0	0	–	–

NIKITARAS, Steven
Born: August 31, 1970 Port Kembla (New South Wales)
Right-handed batsman, left-arm fast-medium bowler

Affected during the season by a groin strain, Nikitaras made only one first-class appearance, when he took 2/91 against the West Indians. He did not flatter in three Mercantile Mutual Cup matches when he took 0/71 off 15 overs. At this stage in his career, he will need to show greater application to gain further opportunities.

	M	I	NO	R	HS	100s	50s	Avge	Ct	St	W	Avge	BB
First-class	4	6	2	24	12	0	0	6.00	2	0	7	49.71	3/76
Dom. first-class	3	5	2	24	12	0	0	8.00	2	0	5	51.40	3/76
Dom. limited-overs	12	3	0	6	6	0	0	2.00	4	0	7	55.14	3/30

NORTH, Marcus James
Born: July 28, 1979 Melbourne (Victoria)
Left-handed batsman, right-arm off-spin bowler

Although he has been tried as an opener, North appears to be best suited down the order. He has an excellent temperament, but needs further work on his technique, as at times he gets caught on the crease and is too open with his blade. He bowls his off-spin capably, and shows promise of developing into an all-rounder. He scored 277 first-class runs at 25.18 and took four wickets at 38.00. In first-grade matches for Bayswater-Morley he had a highest score of 192 and an aggregate of 623 at 62.30. He played some fine all-round cricket as Colne's professional in the Lancashire League in 2001.

	M	I	NO	R	HS	100s	50s	Avge	Ct	St	W	Avge	BB
First-class	12	19	1	457	60	0	4	25.39	6	0	10	31.50	3/23
Dom. first-class	10	16	1	394	60	0	3	26.27	6	0	9	31.22	3/23
Dom. limited-overs	6	5	1	30	14	0	0	7.50	1	0	0	–	–

OLDROYD, Bradley John
Born: November 5, 1973 Bentley (Western Australia)
Left-handed batsman, slow left-arm orthodox bowler

Brad Oldroyd is a complex individual who has not yet realised his potential, mainly because of discipline problems and a lack of focus. He was dropped from the state squad before the start of the 2000-01 season, but after knuckling down at South Perth he regained a spot in the Pura Cup side and played for Australia A against the West Indies in Hobart. With the fast WACA Ground pitches generally favouring new-ball bowlers, Brad Oldroyd has often been overlooked for home matches. He played in four Pura Cup matches during the season (three away from home), taking 13 wickets at 25.76. For South Perth he took 33 wickets at 17.66.

	M	I	NO	R	HS	100s	50s	Avge	Ct	St	W	Avge	BB
First-class	27	36	12	261	47	0	0	10.88	8	0	55	36.44	4/68
Dom. first-class	24	34	11	248	47	0	0	10.78	6	0	49	35.20	4/68
Dom. limited-overs	7	2	2	8	5*	0	0	–	1	0	5	45.80	2/36

SPENCER, Duncan John
Born: April 5, 1972 Burnley, Lancashire (England)
Right-handed batsman, right-arm fast bowler

This dynamic, pocket-sized express bowler made what seemed a fairytale return to interstate cricket after stress fractures in his spine had kept him out of the big time for seven years. He reappeared in the Mercantile Mutual Cup match against Victoria at the WACA Ground in the first week of January and bowled fast and straight, taking 4/43 off 9.5 overs to play a vital role in his side's seven-run victory. He took 11 wickets at 22.36 in limited-overs matches but did not force his way back into the side for Pura Cup matches. Off only 115.1 overs for Gosnells in first-grade ranks he had the impressive tally of 27 wickets at 12.37. However, it emerged that the drug he had been taking to treat his injuries was on the banned list, and in April he was disqualified from first-class cricket for 18 months.

	M	I	NO	R	HS	100s	50s	Avge	Ct	St	W	Avge	BB
First-class	14	16	2	200	75	0	1	14.29	9	0	34	36.97	4/31
Dom. first-class	8	8	1	75	38	0	0	10.71	7	0	20	37.50	4/85
Dom. limited-overs	10	5	1	19	10	0	0	4.75	3	0	15	27.47	4/35

SWAN, Gavin Graham
Born: October 30, 1970 Subiaco (Western Australia)
Right-handed batsman, right-arm fast-medium bowler

Swan grasped his opportunities and performed soundly when filling in while his better-known team-mates were injured. He played in Western Australia's first seven first-class matches before losing his place for the final four Pura Cup matches. A wholehearted performer who hit the pitch hard and got the ball to seam about, Gavin Swan had every right to feel pleased with his 18 first-class wickets at an average of 37.38. Now in his thirties, Swan's long-term future is not bright, but he lacks nothing in spirit and should continue to be a handy support bowler when required. Once again he was an outstanding competitor in club cricket, leading Subiaco–Floreat to an effortless victory over Wanneroo in the first-grade final, in which he took 5/24 off 18 overs, after his 7/52 against Scarborough in the semi-final.

	M	I	NO	R	HS	100s	50s	Avge	Ct	St	W	Avge	BB
First-class	8	9	5	8	8*	0	0	2.00	6	0	24	31.96	5/54
Dom. first-class	7	8	5	8	8*	0	0	2.67	6	0	20	33.90	5/54

WALSH, Mark Jason
Born: April 28, 1972 Townsville (Queensland)
Right-handed batsman, wicket-keeper

With Adam Gilchrist away on international duty and Ryan Campbell struggling with the bat, Mark Walsh received further opportunities to fill in behind the stumps. A fine team man with great determination, Walsh had some highly successful matches despite a few mediocre days, taking nine catches against South Australia in Perth and seven against New South Wales, also in Perth. He dropped a catch in each of those matches, and after scoring 50 against Tasmania his batting fell away and he finished with 195 runs at 15.00.

	M	I	NO	R	HS	100s	50s	Avge	Ct	St	W	Avge	BB
First-class	12	18	1	293	50	0	2	17.24	47	4	0	–	–
Dom. first-class	12	18	1	293	50	0	2	17.24	47	4	0	–	–

WATES, Darren Jude
Born: July 2, 1977 Subiaco (Western Australia)
Right-handed batsman, right-arm fast-medium bowler

Wates did not progress as swiftly as generally expected, mainly because of an early-season injury. However, he returned in mid-season and played five Mercantile Mutual Cup matches, taking five wickets at 27.60 but making little impact with the bat. He failed to break into the side for a first-class match. He is a fine swing bowler, well suited to Perth conditions, but he must improve his batting. In a good season with South Perth, he took 33 first-grade wickets at an average of 16.72.

	M	I	NO	R	HS	100s	50s	Avge	Ct	St	W	Avge	BB
First-class	2	4	1	104	62	0	1	34.67	1	0	2	50.00	1/31
Dom. first-class	2	4	1	104	62	0	1	34.67	1	0	2	50.00	1/31
Dom. limited-overs	12	5	2	28	11	0	0	9.33	1	0	15	28.80	3/45

WILLIAMS, Bradley Andrew
Born: November 20, 1974 Frankston (Victoria)
Right-handed batsman, right-arm fast bowler

After his spectacular first season with Western Australia in the summer of 1999-00 Williams crashed back to earth with a thud. The beefy blond speedster was beset with injuries – to his elbow, groin, back and hamstring – and he underwent arthroscopic surgery in January to remove debris from his right elbow. He played in only Western Australia's final three Pura Cup matches, taking nine wickets at 24.44, and took three expensive wickets in three Mercantile Mutual Cup matches. There is no doubting his ability to bowl at a ferocious pace and to take wickets, particularly at the WACA Ground. At the end of the season, after expressing doubts about his own motivation, he declared that he was prepared to work hard to be fit for the following season.

	M	I	NO	R	HS	100s	50s	Avge	Ct	St	W	Avge	BB
First-class	36	52	16	571	41*	0	0	15.86	12	0	124	31.04	6/74
Dom. first-class	28	42	14	439	41*	0	0	15.68	10	0	100	31.21	6/74
Dom. limited-overs	16	2	1	16	16	0	0	16.00	2	0	15	40.40	2/30

AUSTRALIAN TEST CRICKETERS

Note: The Third Test at the Melbourne Cricket Ground from December 31–January 5, 1971 has been sanctioned by the Australian Cricket Board as an official Test match. The Australian Cricket Board in consultation with the MCC tour management declared the Test a draw. This decision was determined as the two teams had been officially announced, including the 12th men, and the toss had been made. The umpires were walking out to the ground when rain began to fall and prevented any further play in the match.

FULL LIST FROM 1876-77 TO MAY 1, 2001

Abbreviations: *Eng* (England), *Ind* (India), *NZ* (New Zealand), *Pak* (Pakistan), *SAf* (South Africa), *SL* (Sri Lanka), *WI* (West Indies), *Zim* (Zimbabwe).

Number of Test Cricketers: 383

a'BECKETT, Edward Lambert (4)
Debut: 1928-29	Eng	Ind	NZ	Pak	SAf	SL	WI	Zim	Total
Tests at home	2	–	–	–	1	–	–	–	3
Tests abroad	1	–	–	–	–	–	–	–	1

ALDERMAN, Terence Michael (41)
Debut: 1981	Eng	Ind	NZ	Pak	SAf	SL	WI	Zim	Total
Tests at home	5	–	1	5	–	2	7	–	20
Tests abroad	12	–	4	1	–	–	4	–	21

ALEXANDER, George (2)
Debut: 1880	Eng	Ind	NZ	Pak	SAf	SL	WI	Zim	Total
Tests at home	1	–	–	–	–	–	–	–	1
Tests abroad	1	–	–	–	–	–	–	–	1

ALEXANDER, Harry Houston (1)
Debut: 1932-33	Eng	Ind	NZ	Pak	SAf	SL	WI	Zim	Total
Tests at home	1	–	–	–	–	–	–	–	1

ALLAN, Francis Erskine (1)
Debut: 1878-79	Eng	Ind	NZ	Pak	SAf	SL	WI	Zim	Total
Tests at home	1	–	–	–	–	–	–	–	1

ALLAN, Peter John (1)
Debut: 1965-66	Eng	Ind	NZ	Pak	SAf	SL	WI	Zim	Total
Tests at home	1	–	–	–	–	–	–	–	1

ALLEN, Reginald Charles (1)
Debut: 1886-87	Eng	Ind	NZ	Pak	SAf	SL	WI	Zim	Total
Tests at home	1	–	–	–	–	–	–	–	1

ANDREWS, Thomas James Edwin (16)
Debut: 1921	Eng	Ind	NZ	Pak	SAf	SL	WI	Zim	Total
Tests at home	3	–	–	–	–	–	–	–	3
Tests abroad	10	–	–	–	3	–	–	–	13

ANGEL, Jo (4)
Debut: 1992-93	Eng	Ind	NZ	Pak	SAf	SL	WI	Zim	Total
Tests at home	1	–	–	–	–	–	1	–	2
Tests abroad	–	–	–	2	–	–	–	–	2

ARCHER, Kenneth Alan (5)
Debut: 1950-51	Eng	Ind	NZ	Pak	SAf	SL	WI	Zim	Total
Tests at home	3	–	–	–	–	–	2	–	5

ARCHER, Ronald Graham (19)
Debut: 1952-53	Eng	Ind	NZ	Pak	SAf	SL	WI	Zim	Total
Tests at home	4	–	–	–	1	–	–	–	5
Tests abroad	8	–	–	1	–	–	5	–	14

ARMSTRONG, Warwick Windridge (50)

Debut: 1901-02	Eng	Ind	NZ	Pak	SAf	SL	WI	Zim	Total
Tests at home	22	–	–	–	5	–	–	–	27
Tests abroad	20	–	–	–	3	–	–	–	23

BADCOCK, Clayvel Lindsay (7)

Debut: 1936-37	Eng	Ind	NZ	Pak	SAf	SL	WI	Zim	Total
Tests at home	3	–	–	–	–	–	–	–	3
Tests abroad	4	–	–	–	–	–	–	–	4

BANNERMAN, Alexander Chalmers (28)

Debut: 1878-79	Eng	Ind	NZ	Pak	SAf	SL	WI	Zim	Total
Tests at home	17	–	–	–	–	–	–	–	17
Tests abroad	11	–	–	–	–	–	–	–	11

BANNERMAN, Charles (3)

Debut: 1876-77	Eng	Ind	NZ	Pak	SAf	SL	WI	Zim	Total
Tests at home	3	–	–	–	–	–	–	–	3

BARDSLEY, Warren (41)

Debut: 1909	Eng	Ind	NZ	Pak	SAf	SL	WI	Zim	Total
Tests at home	12	–	–	–	5	–	–	–	17
Tests abroad	18	–	–	–	6	–	–	–	24

BARNES, Sydney George (13)

Debut: 1938	Eng	Ind	NZ	Pak	SAf	SL	WI	Zim	Total
Tests at home	4	3	–	–	–	–	–	–	7
Tests abroad	5	–	1	–	–	–	–	–	6

BARNETT, Benjamin Arthur (4)

Debut: 1938	Eng	Ind	NZ	Pak	SAf	SL	WI	Zim	Total
Tests abroad	4	–	–	–	–	–	–	–	4

BARRETT, John Edward (2)

Debut: 1890	Eng	Ind	NZ	Pak	SAf	SL	WI	Zim	Total
Tests abroad	2	–	–	–	–	–	–	–	2

BEARD, Graeme Robert (3)

Debut: 1979-80	Eng	Ind	NZ	Pak	SAf	SL	WI	Zim	Total
Tests abroad	–	–	–	3	–	–	–	–	3

BENAUD, John (3)

Debut: 1972-73	Eng	Ind	NZ	Pak	SAf	SL	WI	Zim	Total
Tests at home	–	–	–	2	–	–	–	–	2
Tests abroad	–	–	–	–	–	–	1	–	1

BENAUD, Richard (63)

Debut: 1951-52	Eng	Ind	NZ	Pak	SAf	SL	WI	Zim	Total
Tests at home	15	–	–	–	8	–	6	–	29
Tests abroad	12	8	–	4	5	–	5	–	34

BENNETT, Murray John (3)

Debut: 1984-85	Eng	Ind	NZ	Pak	SAf	SL	WI	Zim	Total
Tests at home	–	–	–	–	–	–	2	–	2
Tests abroad	1	–	–	–	–	–	–	–	1

BEVAN, Michael Gwyl (18)

Debut: 1994-95	Eng	Ind	NZ	Pak	SAf	SL	WI	Zim	Total
Tests at home	3	–	–	–	1	–	4	–	8
Tests abroad	3	1	–	3	3	–	–	–	10

BICHEL, Andrew John (5)

Debut: 1996-97	Eng	Ind	NZ	Pak	SAf	SL	WI	Zim	Total
Tests at home	–	–	–	–	1	–	4	–	5

BLACKHAM, John McCarthy (35)

Debut: 1876-77	Eng	Ind	NZ	Pak	SAf	SL	WI	Zim	Total
Tests at home	19	–	–	–	–	–	–	–	19
Tests abroad	16	–	–	–	–	–	–	–	16

BLACKIE, Donald Dearness (3)

Debut: 1928-29	Eng	Ind	NZ	Pak	SAf	SL	WI	Zim	Total
Tests at home	3	–	–	–	–	–	–	–	3

BLEWETT, Gregory Scott (46)

Debut: 1994-95	Eng	Ind	NZ	Pak	SAf	SL	WI	Zim	Total
Tests at home	2	3	3	6	3	–	4	–	21
Tests abroad	6	3	2	–	3	3	7	1	25

BONNOR, George John (17)

Debut: 1880	Eng	Ind	NZ	Pak	SAf	SL	WI	Zim	Total
Tests at home	7	–	–	–					
Tests abroad	10	–			–		–	–	10

BOON, David Clarence (107)

Debut: 1984-85	Eng	Ind	NZ	Pak	SAf	SL	WI	Zim	Total
Tests at home	15	8	10	5	3	6	13	–	60
Tests abroad	16	3	7	6	3	3	9	–	47

BOOTH, Brian Charles (29)

Debut: 1961	Eng	Ind	NZ	Pak	SAf	SL	WI	Zim	Total
Tests at home	8	–	–	1	4	–	–	–	13
Tests abroad	7	3	–	1	–	–	5	–	16

BORDER, Allan Robert (156)

Debut: 1978-79	Eng	Ind	NZ	Pak	SAf	SL	WI	Zim	Total
Tests at home	22	11	13	13	3	3	21	–	86
Tests abroad	25	9	10	9	3	4	10	–	70

BOYLE, Henry Frederick (12)

Debut: 1878-79	Eng	Ind	NZ	Pak	SAf	SL	WI	Zim	Total
Tests at home	7	–	–	–	–	–	–	–	7
Tests abroad	5	–	–	–	–	–	–	–	5

BRADMAN, Donald George (52)

Debut: 1928-29	Eng	Ind	NZ	Pak	SAf	SL	WI	Zim	Total
Tests at home	18	5	–	–	5	–	5	–	33
Tests abroad	19	–	–	–	–	–	–	–	19

BRIGHT, Raymond James (25)

Debut: 1977	Eng	Ind	NZ	Pak	SAf	SL	WI	Zim	Total
Tests at home	1	3	1	–	–	–	1	–	6
Tests abroad	9	3	2	5	–	–	–	–	19

BROMLEY, Ernest Harvey (2)

Debut: 1932-33	Eng	Ind	NZ	Pak	SAf	SL	WI	Zim	Total
Tests at home	1	–	–	–	–	–	–	–	1
Tests abroad	1	–	–	–	–	–	–	–	1

BROWN, William Alfred (22)

Debut: 1934	Eng	Ind	NZ	Pak	SAf	SL	WI	Zim	Total
Tests at home	2	3	–	–	–	–	–	–	5
Tests abroad	11	–	1	–	5	–	–	–	17

BRUCE, William (14)

Debut: 1884-85	Eng	Ind	NZ	Pak	SAf	SL	WI	Zim	Total
Tests at home	9	–	–	–	–	–	–	–	9
Tests abroad	5	–	–	–	–	–	–	–	5

BURGE, Peter John Parnell (42)

Debut: 1954-55	Eng	Ind	NZ	Pak	SAf	SL	WI	Zim	Total
Tests at home	9	–	–	–	5	–	2	–	16
Tests abroad	13	8	–	3	1	–	1	–	26

BURKE, James Wallace (24)

Debut: 1950-51	Eng	Ind	NZ	Pak	SAf	SL	WI	Zim	Total
Tests at home	9	–	–	–	–	–	1	–	10
Tests abroad	5	3	–	1	5	–	–	–	14

BURN, Edwin James Kenneth (2)

Debut: 1890	Eng	Ind	NZ	Pak	SAf	SL	WI	Zim	Total
Tests abroad	2	–	–	–	–	–	–	–	2

BURTON, Frederick John (2)

Debut: 1886-87	Eng	Ind	NZ	Pak	SAf	SL	WI	Zim	Total
Tests at home	2	–	–	–	–	–	–	–	2

CALLAWAY, Sydney Thomas (3)

Debut: 1891-92	Eng	Ind	NZ	Pak	SAf	SL	WI	Zim	Total
Tests at home	3	–	–	–	–	–	–	–	3

CALLEN, Ian Wayne (1)

Debut: 1977-78	Eng	Ind	NZ	Pak	SAf	SL	WI	Zim	Total
Tests at home	–	1	–	–	–	–	–	–	1

CAMPBELL, Gregory Dale (4)

Debut: 1989	Eng	Ind	NZ	Pak	SAf	SL	WI	Zim	Total
Tests at home	–	–	–	1	–	1	–	–	2
Tests abroad	1	–	1	–	–	–	–	–	2

CARKEEK, William (6)

Debut: 1912	Eng	Ind	NZ	Pak	SAf	SL	WI	Zim	Total
Tests abroad	3	–	–	–	3	–	–	–	6

CARLSON, Phillip Henry (2)

Debut: 1978-79	Eng	Ind	NZ	Pak	SAf	SL	WI	Zim	Total
Tests at home	2	–	–	–	–	–	–	–	2

CARTER, Hanson (28)

Debut: 1907-08	Eng	Ind	NZ	Pak	SAf	SL	WI	Zim	Total
Tests at home	12	–	–	–	5	–	–	–	17
Tests abroad	9	–	–	–	2	–	–	–	11

CHAPPELL, Gregory Stephen (88)

Debut: 1970-71	Eng	Ind	NZ	Pak	SAf	SL	WI	Zim	Total
Tests at home	21	3	6	14	–	–	12	–	56
Tests abroad	15	–	8	3	–	1	5	–	32

CHAPPELL, Ian Michael (76)

Debut: 1964-65	Eng	Ind	NZ	Pak	SAf	SL	WI	Zim	Total
Tests at home	17	4	3	4	–	–	12	–	40
Tests abroad	14	5	3	–	9	–	5	–	36

CHAPPELL, Trevor Martin (3)

Debut: 1981	Eng	Ind	NZ	Pak	SAf	SL	WI	Zim	Total
Tests abroad	3	–	–	–	–	–	–	–	3

CHARLTON, Percie Chater (2)

Debut: 1890	Eng	Ind	NZ	Pak	SAf	SL	WI	Zim	Total
Tests abroad	2	–	–	–	–	–	–	–	2

CHIPPERFIELD, Arthur Gordon (14)

Debut: 1934	Eng	Ind	NZ	Pak	SAf	SL	WI	Zim	Total
Tests at home	3	–	–	–	–	–	–	–	3
Tests abroad	6	–	–	–	5	–	–	–	11

CLARK, Wayne Maxwell (10)

Debut: 1977-78	Eng	Ind	NZ	Pak	SAf	SL	WI	Zim	Total
Tests at home	–	5	–	1	–	–	–	–	6
Tests abroad	–	–	–	–	–	–	4	–	4

COLLEY, David John (3)

Debut: 1972	Eng	Ind	NZ	Pak	SAf	SL	WI	Zim	Total
Tests abroad	3	–	–	–	–	–	–	–	3

COLLINS, Herbert Leslie (19)

Debut: 1920-21	Eng	Ind	NZ	Pak	SAf	SL	WI	Zim	Total
Tests at home	10	–	–	–	–	–	–	–	10
Tests abroad	6	–	–	–	3	–	–	–	9

CONINGHAM, Arthur (1)

Debut: 1894-95	Eng	Ind	NZ	Pak	SAf	SL	WI	Zim	Total
Tests at home	1	–	–	–	–	–	–	–	1

CONNOLLY, Alan Norman (30)

Debut: 1963-64	Eng	Ind	NZ	Pak	SAf	SL	WI	Zim	Total
Tests at home	3	3	–	–	3	–	5	–	14
Tests abroad	5	7	–	–	4	–	–	–	16

COOK, Simon Hewitt (2)

Debut: 1997-98	Eng	Ind	NZ	Pak	SAf	SL	WI	Zim	Total
Tests at home	–	–	2	–	–	–	–	–	2

COOPER, Bransby Beauchamp (1)

Debut: 1876-77	Eng	Ind	NZ	Pak	SAf	SL	WI	Zim	Total
Tests at home	1	–	–	–	–	–	–	–	1

COOPER, William Henry (2)

Debut: 1881-82	Eng	Ind	NZ	Pak	SAf	SL	WI	Zim	Total
Tests at home	2	–	–	–	–	–	–	–	2

CORLING, Grahame Edward (5)

Debut: 1964	Eng	Ind	NZ	Pak	SAf	SL	WI	Zim	Total
Tests abroad	5	–	–	–	–	–	–	–	5

COSIER, Gary John (18)

Debut: 1975-76	Eng	Ind	NZ	Pak	SAf	SL	WI	Zim	Total
Tests at home	3	4	–	3	–	–	3	–	13
Tests abroad	–	–	2	–	–	–	3	–	5

COTTAM, John Thomas (1)

Debut: 1886-87	Eng	Ind	NZ	Pak	SAf	SL	WI	Zim	Total
Tests at home	1	–	–	–	–	–	–	–	1

COTTER, Albert (21)

Debut: 1903-04	Eng	Ind	NZ	Pak	SAf	SL	WI	Zim	Total
Tests at home	8	–	–	–	5	–	–	–	13
Tests abroad	8	–	–	–	–	–	–	–	8

COULTHARD, George (1)

Debut: 1881-82	Eng	Ind	NZ	Pak	SAf	SL	WI	Zim	Total
Tests at home	1	–	–	–	–	–	–	–	1

COWPER, Robert Maskew (27)

Debut: 1964	Eng	Ind	NZ	Pak	SAf	SL	WI	Zim	Total
Tests at home	4	4	–	1	–	–	–	–	9
Tests abroad	5	2	–	1	5	–	5	–	18

CRAIG, Ian David (11)

Debut: 1952-53	Eng	Ind	NZ	Pak	SAf	SL	WI	Zim	Total
Tests at home	–	–	–	–	1	–	–	–	1
Tests abroad	2	2	–	1	5	–	–	–	10

CRAWFORD, William Patrick Anthony (4)

Debut: 1956	Eng	Ind	NZ	Pak	SAf	SL	WI	Zim	Total
Tests abroad	1	3	–	–	–	–	–	–	4

DALE, Adam Craig (2)

Debut: 1997-98	Eng	Ind	NZ	Pak	SAf	SL	WI	Zim	Total
Tests abroad	–	1	–	–	–	–	1	–	2

DARLING, Joseph (34)

Debut: 1894-95	Eng	Ind	NZ	Pak	SAf	SL	WI	Zim	Total
Tests at home	13	–	–	–	–	–	–	–	13
Tests abroad	18	–	–	–	3	–	–	–	21

DARLING, Leonard Stuart (12)

Debut: 1932-33	Eng	Ind	NZ	Pak	SAf	SL	WI	Zim	Total
Tests at home	3	–	–	–	–	–	–	–	3
Tests abroad	4	–	–	–	5	–	–	–	9

DARLING, Warrick Maxwell (14)

Debut: 1977-78	Eng	Ind	NZ	Pak	SAf	SL	WI	Zim	Total
Tests at home	4	1	–	1	–	–	–	–	6
Tests abroad	–	5	–	–	–	–	3	–	8

DAVIDSON, Alan Keith (44)

Debut: 1953	Eng	Ind	NZ	Pak	SAf	SL	WI	Zim	Total
Tests at home	13	–	–	–	–	–	4	–	17
Tests abroad	12	6	–	4	5	–	–	–	27

DAVIS, Ian Charles (15)

Debut: 1973-74	Eng	Ind	NZ	Pak	SAf	SL	WI	Zim	Total
Tests at home	1	–	3	3	–	–	–	–	7
Tests abroad	3	–	5	–	–	–	–	–	8

DAVIS, Simon Peter (1)

Debut: 1985-86	Eng	Ind	NZ	Pak	SAf	SL	WI	Zim	Total
Tests abroad	–	–	1	–	–	–	–	–	1

DE COURCY, James Harry (3)

Debut: 1953	Eng	Ind	NZ	Pak	SAf	SL	WI	Zim	Total
Tests abroad	3	–	–	–	–	–	–	–	3

DELL, Anthony Ross (2)

Debut: 1970-71	Eng	Ind	NZ	Pak	SAf	SL	WI	Zim	Total
Tests at home	1	–	1	–	–	–	–	–	2

DODEMAIDE, Anthony Ian Christopher (10)

Debut: 1987-88	Eng	Ind	NZ	Pak	SAf	SL	WI	Zim	Total
Tests at home	1	–	1	–	–	1	2	–	5
Tests abroad	–	–	–	3	–	2	–	–	5

DONNAN, Harry (5)

Debut: 1891-92	Eng	Ind	NZ	Pak	SAf	SL	WI	Zim	Total
Tests at home	2	–	–	–	–	–	–	–	2
Tests abroad	3	–	–	–	–	–	–	–	3

DOOLAND, Bruce (3)

Debut: 1946-47	Eng	Ind	NZ	Pak	SAf	SL	WI	Zim	Total
Tests at home	2	1	–	–	–	–	–	–	3

DUFF, Reginald Alexander (22)

Debut: 1901-02	Eng	Ind	NZ	Pak	SAf	SL	WI	Zim	Total
Tests at home	9	–	–	–	–	–	–	–	9
Tests abroad	10	–	–	–	3	–	–	–	13

DUNCAN, John Ross Frederick (1)

Debut: 1970-71	Eng	Ind	NZ	Pak	SAf	SL	WI	Zim	Total
Tests at home	1	–	–	–	–	–	–	–	1

DYER, Gregory Charles (6)

Debut: 1986-87	Eng	Ind	NZ	Pak	SAf	SL	WI	Zim	Total
Tests at home	2	–	3	–	–	1	–	–	6

DYMOCK, Geoffrey (21)

Debut: 1973-74	Eng	Ind	NZ	Pak	SAf	SL	WI	Zim	Total
Tests at home	7	–	1	1	–	–	2	–	11
Tests abroad	–	5	2	3	–	–	–	–	10

DYSON, John (30)

Debut: 1977-78	Eng	Ind	NZ	Pak	SAf	SL	WI	Zim	Total
Tests at home	5	6	3	–	–	–	5	–	19
Tests abroad	5	–	3	3	–	–	–	–	11

EADY, Charles John (2)

Debut: 1896	Eng	Ind	NZ	Pak	SAf	SL	WI	Zim	Total
Tests at home	1	–	–	–	–	–	–	–	1
Tests abroad	1	–	–	–	–	–	–	–	1

EASTWOOD, Kenneth Humphrey (1)

Debut: 1970-71	Eng	Ind	NZ	Pak	SAf	SL	WI	Zim	Total
Tests at home	1	–	–	–	–	–	–	–	1

EBELING, Hans Irvine (1)

Debut: 1934	Eng	Ind	NZ	Pak	SAf	SL	WI	Zim	Total
Tests abroad	1	–	–	–	–	–	–	–	1

EDWARDS, John Dunlop (3)

Debut: 1888	Eng	Ind	NZ	Pak	SAf	SL	WI	Zim	Total
Tests abroad	3	–	–	–	–	–	–	–	3

EDWARDS, Ross (20)

Debut: 1972	Eng	Ind	NZ	Pak	SAf	SL	WI	Zim	Total
Tests at home	5	–	–	2	–	–	–	–	7
Tests abroad	8	–	–	–	–	–	5	–	13

EDWARDS, Walter John (3)

Debut: 1974-75	Eng	Ind	NZ	Pak	SAf	SL	WI	Zim	Total
Tests at home	3	–	–	–	–	–	–	–	3

ELLIOTT, Matthew Thomas Gray (20)

Debut: 1996-97	Eng	Ind	NZ	Pak	SAf	SL	WI	Zim	Total
Tests at home	–	–	3	–	3	–	2	–	8
Tests abroad	6	–	–	–	3	–	3	–	12

EMERY, Philip Allen (1)

Debut: 1994-95	Eng	Ind	NZ	Pak	SAf	SL	WI	Zim	Total
Tests abroad	–	–	–	1	–	–	–	–	1

EMERY, Sidney Hand (4)

Debut: 1912	Eng	Ind	NZ	Pak	SAf	SL	WI	Zim	Total
Tests abroad	2	–	–	–	2	–	–	–	4

EVANS, Edwin (6)

Debut: 1881-82	Eng	Ind	NZ	Pak	SAf	SL	WI	Zim	Total
Tests at home	4	–	–	–	–	–	–	–	4
Tests abroad	2	–	–	–	–	–	–	–	2

FAIRFAX, Alan George (10)

Debut: 1928-29	Eng	Ind	NZ	Pak	SAf	SL	WI	Zim	Total
Tests at home	1	–	–	–	–	–	5	–	6
Tests abroad	4	–	–	–	–	–	–	–	4

FAVELL, Leslie Ernest (19)

Debut: 1954-55	Eng	Ind	NZ	Pak	SAf	SL	WI	Zim	Total
Tests at home	6	–	–	–	–	–	4	–	10
Tests abroad	–	4	–	3	–	–	2	–	9

FERRIS, John James (8)

Debut: 1886-87	Eng	Ind	NZ	Pak	SAf	SL	WI	Zim	Total
Tests at home	3	–	–	–	–	–	–	–	3
Tests abroad	5	–	–	–	–	–	–	–	5

FINGLETON, John Henry Webb (18)

Debut: 1931-32	Eng	Ind	NZ	Pak	SAf	SL	WI	Zim	Total
Tests at home	8	–	–	–	1	–	–	–	9
Tests abroad	4	–	–	–	5	–	–	–	9

FLEETWOOD-SMITH, Leslie O'Brien (10)

Debut: 1935-36	Eng	Ind	NZ	Pak	SAf	SL	WI	Zim	Total
Tests at home	3	–	–	–	–	–	–	–	3
Tests abroad	4	–	–	–	3	–	–	–	7

FLEMING, Damien William (20)

Debut: 1994-95	Eng	Ind	NZ	Pak	SAf	SL	WI	Zim	Total
Tests at home	7	3	–	3	–	–	–	–	13
Tests abroad	–	1	–	3	–	2	–	1	7

FRANCIS, Bruce Colin (3)

Debut: 1972	Eng	Ind	NZ	Pak	SAf	SL	WI	Zim	Total
Tests abroad	3	–	–	–	–	–	–	–	3

FREEMAN, Eric Walter (11)

Debut: 1967-68	Eng	Ind	NZ	Pak	SAf	SL	WI	Zim	Total
Tests at home	–	2	–	–	–	–	4	–	6
Tests abroad	2	1	–	–	2	–	–	–	5

FREER, Frederick Alfred William (1)

Debut: 1946-47	Eng	Ind	NZ	Pak	SAf	SL	WI	Zim	Total
Tests at home	1	–	–	–	–	–	–	–	1

GANNON, John Bryant (3)

Debut: 1977-78	Eng	Ind	NZ	Pak	SAf	SL	WI	Zim	Total
Tests at home	–	3	–	–	–	–	–	–	3

GARRETT, Thomas William (19)

Debut: 1876-77	Eng	Ind	NZ	Pak	SAf	SL	WI	Zim	Total
Tests at home	15	–	–	–	–	–	–	–	15
Tests abroad	4	–	–	–	–	–	–	–	4

GAUNT, Ronald Arthur (3)

Debut: 1957-58	Eng	Ind	NZ	Pak	SAf	SL	WI	Zim	Total
Tests at home	–	–	–	–	1	–	–	–	1
Tests abroad	1	–	–	–	1	–	–	–	2

GEHRS, Donald Raeburn Algernon (6)

Debut: 1903-04	Eng	Ind	NZ	Pak	SAf	SL	WI	Zim	Total
Tests at home	1	–	–	–	4	–	–	–	5
Tests abroad	1	–	–	–	–	–	–	–	1

GIFFEN, George (31)

Debut: 1881-82	Eng	Ind	NZ	Pak	SAf	SL	WI	Zim	Total
Tests at home	18	–	–	–	–	–	–	–	18
Tests abroad	13	–	–	–	–	–	–	–	13

GIFFEN, Walter Frank (3)

Debut: 1886-87	Eng	Ind	NZ	Pak	SAf	SL	WI	Zim	Total
Tests at home	3	–	–	–	–	–	–	–	3

GILBERT, David Robert (9)

Debut: 1985	Eng	Ind	NZ	Pak	SAf	SL	WI	Zim	Total
Tests at home	–	2	3	–	–	–	–	–	5
Tests abroad	1	2	1	–	–	–	–	–	4

GILCHRIST, Adam Craig (17)

Debut: 1999-00	Eng	Ind	NZ	Pak	SAf	SL	WI	Zim	Total
Tests at home	–	3	–	3	–	–	5	–	11
Tests abroad	–	3	3	–	–	–	–	–	6

GILLESPIE, Jason Neil (21)

Debut: 1996-97	Eng	Ind	NZ	Pak	SAf	SL	WI	Zim	Total
Tests at home	1	–	–	–	–	–	6	–	7
Tests abroad	4	3	–	–	3	1	3	–	14

GILMOUR, Gary John (15)

Debut: 1973-74	Eng	Ind	NZ	Pak	SAf	SL	WI	Zim	Total
Tests at home	1	–	2	3	–	–	5	–	11
Tests abroad	1	–	3	–	–	–	–	–	4

GLEESON, John William (30)

Debut: 1967-68	Eng	Ind	NZ	Pak	SAf	SL	WI	Zim	Total
Tests at home	6	4	–	–	–	–	5	–	15
Tests abroad	8	3	–	–	4	–	–	–	15

GRAHAM, Henry (6)

Debut: 1893	Eng	Ind	NZ	Pak	SAf	SL	WI	Zim	Total
Tests at home	2	–	–	–	–	–	–	–	2
Tests abroad	4	–	–	–	–	–	–	–	4

GREGORY, David William (3)

Debut: 1876-77	Eng	Ind	NZ	Pak	SAf	SL	WI	Zim	Total
Tests at home	3	–	–	–	–	–	–	–	3

GREGORY, Edward James (1)

Debut: 1876-77	Eng	Ind	NZ	Pak	SAf	SL	WI	Zim	Total
Tests at home	1	–	–	–	–	–	–	–	1

GREGORY, Edward Sydney (58)

Debut: 1890	Eng	Ind	NZ	Pak	SAf	SL	WI	Zim	Total
Tests at home	23	–	–	–	–	–	–	–	23
Tests abroad	29	–	–	–	6	–	–	–	35

GREGORY, Jack Morrison (24)

Debut: 1920-21	Eng	Ind	NZ	Pak	SAf	SL	WI	Zim	Total
Tests at home	11	–	–	–	–	–	–	–	11
Tests abroad	10	–	–	–	3	–	–	–	13

GREGORY, Ross Gerald (2)

Debut: 1936-37	Eng	Ind	NZ	Pak	SAf	SL	WI	Zim	Total
Tests at home	2	–	–	–	–	–	–	–	2

GRIMMETT, Clarence Victor (37)

Debut: 1924-25	Eng	Ind	NZ	Pak	SAf	SL	WI	Zim	Total
Tests at home	9	–	–	–	5	–	5	–	19
Tests abroad	13	–	–	–	5	–	–	–	18

GROUBE, Thomas Underwood (1)

Debut: 1880	Eng	Ind	NZ	Pak	SAf	SL	WI	Zim	Total
Tests abroad	1	–	–	–	–	–	–	–	1

GROUT, Arthur Theodore Wallace (51)

Debut: 1957-58	Eng	Ind	NZ	Pak	SAf	SL	WI	Zim	Total
Tests at home	12	–	–	–	5	–	5	–	22
Tests abroad	10	5	–	4	5	–	5	–	29

GUEST, Colin Ernest James (1)

Debut: 1962-63	Eng	Ind	NZ	Pak	SAf	SL	WI	Zim	Total
Tests at home	1	–	–	–	–	–	–	–	1

HAMENCE, Ronald Arthur (3)

Debut: 1946-47	Eng	Ind	NZ	Pak	SAf	SL	WI	Zim	Total
Tests at home	1	2	–	–	–	–	–	–	3

HAMMOND, Jeffrey Roy (5)

Debut: 1972-73	Eng	Ind	NZ	Pak	SAf	SL	WI	Zim	Total
Tests abroad	–	–	–	–	–	5	–	–	5

HARRY, John (1)

Debut: 1894-95	Eng	Ind	NZ	Pak	SAf	SL	WI	Zim	Total
Tests at home	1	–	–	–	–	–	–	–	1

HARTIGAN, Michael Joseph (2)

Debut: 1907-08	Eng	Ind	NZ	Pak	SAf	SL	WI	Zim	Total
Tests at home	2	–	–	–	–	–	–	–	2

HARTKOPF, Albert Ernest Victor (1)

Debut: 1924-25	Eng	Ind	NZ	Pak	SAf	SL	WI	Zim	Total
Tests at home	1	–	–	–	–	–	–	–	1

HARVEY, Mervyn Roye (1)

Debut: 1946-47	Eng	Ind	NZ	Pak	SAf	SL	WI	Zim	Total
Tests at home	1	–	–	–	–	–	–	–	1

HARVEY, Robert Neil (79)

Debut: 1947-48	Eng	Ind	NZ	Pak	SAf	SL	WI	Zim	Total
Tests at home	20	2	–	–	5	–	9	–	36
Tests abroad	17	8	–	4	9	–	5	–	43

HASSETT, Arthur Lindsay (43)

Debut: 1938	Eng	Ind	NZ	Pak	SAf	SL	WI	Zim	Total
Tests at home	10	4	–	–	5	–	4	–	23
Tests abroad	14	–	1	–	5	–	–	–	20

HAWKE, Neil James Napier (27)

Debut: 1962-63	Eng	Ind	NZ	Pak	SAf	SL	WI	Zim	Total
Tests at home	5	1	–	1	4	–	–	–	11
Tests abroad	7	1	–	1	2	–	5	–	16

HAYDEN, Matthew Lawrence (16)

Debut: 1993-94	Eng	Ind	NZ	Pak	SAf	SL	WI	Zim	Total
Tests at home	–	–	–	–	–	–	6	–	6
Tests abroad	–	3	1	–	4	–	–	–	8

HAZLITT, Gervys Rignold (9)

Debut: 1907-08	Eng	Ind	NZ	Pak	SAf	SL	WI	Zim	Total
Tests at home	3	–	–	–	–	–	–	–	3
Tests abroad	3	–	–	–	3	–	–	–	6

HEALY, Ian Andrew (119)

Debut: 1988-89	Eng	Ind	NZ	Pak	SAf	SL	WI	Zim	Total
Tests at home	15	5	7	6	6	5	15	–	59
Tests abroad	18	4	4	8	6	6	13	1	60

HENDRY, Hunter Scott Thomas Laurie (11)

Debut: 1921	Eng	Ind	NZ	Pak	SAf	SL	WI	Zim	Total
Tests at home	5	–	–	–	–	–	–	–	5
Tests abroad	4	–	–	–	2	–	–	–	6

HIBBERT, Paul Anthony (1)

Debut: 1977-78	Eng	Ind	NZ	Pak	SAf	SL	WI	Zim	Total
Tests at home	–	1	–	–	–	–	–	–	1

HIGGS, James Donald (22)

Debut: 1977-78	Eng	Ind	NZ	Pak	SAf	SL	WI	Zim	Total
Tests at home	6	2	3	–	–	–	1	–	12
Tests abroad	–	6	–	–	–	–	4	–	10

HILDITCH, Andrew Mark Jefferson (18)

Debut: 1978-79	Eng	Ind	NZ	Pak	SAf	SL	WI	Zim	Total
Tests at home	1	–	1	2	–	–	2	–	6
Tests abroad	6	6	–	–	–	–	–	–	12

HILL, Clement (49)

Debut: 1896	Eng	Ind	NZ	Pak	SAf	SL	WI	Zim	Total
Tests at home	25	–	–	–	5	–	–	–	30
Tests abroad	16	–	–	–	3	–	–	–	19

HILL, John Charles (3)

Debut: 1953	Eng	Ind	NZ	Pak	SAf	SL	WI	Zim	Total
Tests abroad	2	–	–	–	–	–	1	–	3

HOARE, Desmond Edward (1)

Debut: 1960-61	Eng	Ind	NZ	Pak	SAf	SL	WI	Zim	Total
Tests at home	–	–	–	–	–	–	1	–	1

HODGES, John Robart (2)

Debut: 1876-77	Eng	Ind	NZ	Pak	SAf	SL	WI	Zim	Total
Tests at home	2	–	–	–	–	–	–	–	2

HOGAN, Tom George (7)

Debut: 1982-83	Eng	Ind	NZ	Pak	SAf	SL	WI	Zim	Total
Tests at home	–	–	–	1	–	–	–	–	1
Tests abroad	–	–	–	–	–	1	5	–	6

HOGG, George Bradley (1)

Debut: 1996-97	Eng	Ind	NZ	Pak	SAf	SL	WI	Zim	Total
Tests abroad	–	1	–	–	–	–	–	–	1

HOGG, Rodney Malcolm (38)

Debut: 1978-79	*Eng*	*Ind*	*NZ*	*Pak*	*SAf*	*SL*	*WI*	*Zim*	*Total*
Tests at home	9	2	2	6	–	–	6	–	25
Tests abroad	2	6	–	–	–	1	4	–	13

HOHNS, Trevor Victor (7)

Debut: 1988-89	*Eng*	*Ind*	*NZ*	*Pak*	*SAf*	*SL*	*WI*	*Zim*	*Total*
Tests at home	–	–	–	–	–	–	2	–	2
Tests abroad	5	–	–	–	–	–	–	–	5

HOLE, Graeme Blake (18)

Debut: 1950-51	*Eng*	*Ind*	*NZ*	*Pak*	*SAf*	*SL*	*WI*	*Zim*	*Total*
Tests at home	4	–	–	–	4	–	5	–	13
Tests abroad	5	–	–	–	–	–	–	–	5

HOLLAND, Robert George (11)

Debut: 1984-85	*Eng*	*Ind*	*NZ*	*Pak*	*SAf*	*SL*	*WI*	*Zim*	*Total*
Tests at home	–	1	3	–	–	–	3	–	7
Tests abroad	4	–	–	–	–	–	–	–	4

HOOKES, David William (23)

Debut: 1976-77	*Eng*	*Ind*	*NZ*	*Pak*	*SAf*	*SL*	*WI*	*Zim*	*Total*
Tests at home	6	2	2	–	–	–	1	–	11
Tests abroad	5	–	–	1	–	1	5	–	12

HOPKINS, Albert John Young (20)

Debut: 1901-02	*Eng*	*Ind*	*NZ*	*Pak*	*SAf*	*SL*	*WI*	*Zim*	*Total*
Tests at home	7	–	–	–	–	–	–	–	7
Tests abroad	10	–	–	–	3	–	–	–	13

HORAN, Thomas Patrick (15)

Debut: 1876-77	*Eng*	*Ind*	*NZ*	*Pak*	*SAf*	*SL*	*WI*	*Zim*	*Total*
Tests at home	14	–	–	–	–	–	–	–	14
Tests abroad	1	–	–	–	–	–	–	–	1

HORDERN, Herbert Vivian (7)

Debut: 1910-11	*Eng*	*Ind*	*NZ*	*Pak*	*SAf*	*SL*	*WI*	*Zim*	*Total*
Tests at home	5	–	–	–	2	–	–	–	7

HORNIBROOK, Percival Mitchell (6)

Debut: 1928-29	*Eng*	*Ind*	*NZ*	*Pak*	*SAf*	*SL*	*WI*	*Zim*	*Total*
Tests at home	1	–	–	–	–	–	–	–	1
Tests abroad	5	–	–	–	–	–	–	–	5

HOWELL, William Peter (18)

Debut: 1897-98	*Eng*	*Ind*	*NZ*	*Pak*	*SAf*	*SL*	*WI*	*Zim*	*Total*
Tests at home	10	–	–	–	–	–	–	–	10
Tests abroad	6	–	–	–	2	–	–	–	8

HUGHES, Kimberley John (70)

Debut: 1977	*Eng*	*Ind*	*NZ*	*Pak*	*SAf*	*SL*	*WI*	*Zim*	*Total*
Tests at home	14	5	3	10	–	–	10	–	42
Tests abroad	8	6	3	6	–	–	5	–	28

HUGHES, Mervyn Gregory (53)

Debut: 1985-86	*Eng*	*Ind*	*NZ*	*Pak*	*SAf*	*SL*	*WI*	*Zim*	*Total*
Tests at home	8	6	2	3	–	3	9	–	31
Tests abroad	12	–	3	–	2	–	5	–	22

HUNT, William Alfred (1)

Debut: 1931-32	*Eng*	*Ind*	*NZ*	*Pak*	*SAf*	*SL*	*WI*	*Zim*	*Total*
Tests at home	–	–	–	–	1	–	–	–	1

HURST, Alan George (12)

Debut: 1973-74	*Eng*	*Ind*	*NZ*	*Pak*	*SAf*	*SL*	*WI*	*Zim*	*Total*
Tests at home	6	1	1	2	–	–	–	–	10
Tests abroad	–	2	–	–	–	–	–	–	2

HURWOOD, Alexander (2)

Debut: 1930-31	Eng	Ind	NZ	Pak	SAf	SL	WI	Zim	Total
Tests at home	–	–	–	–	–	–	2	–	2

INVERARITY, Robert John (6)

Debut: 1968	Eng	Ind	NZ	Pak	SAf	SL	WI	Zim	Total
Tests at home	–	–	–	–	–	–	1	–	1
Tests abroad	5	–	–	–	–	–	–	–	5

IREDALE, Francis Adams (14)

Debut: 1894-95	Eng	Ind	NZ	Pak	SAf	SL	WI	Zim	Total
Tests at home	9	–	–	–	–	–	–	–	9
Tests abroad	5	–	–	–	–	–	–	–	5

IRONMONGER, Herbert (14)

Debut: 1928-29	Eng	Ind	NZ	Pak	SAf	SL	WI	Zim	Total
Tests at home	6	–	–	–	4	–	4	–	14

IVERSON, John Brian (5)

Debut: 1950-51	Eng	Ind	NZ	Pak	SAf	SL	WI	Zim	Total
Tests at home	5	–	–	–	–	–	–	–	5

JACKSON, Archibald (8)

Debut: 1928-29	Eng	Ind	NZ	Pak	SAf	SL	WI	Zim	Total
Tests at home	2	–	–	–	–	–	4	–	6
Tests abroad	2	–	–	–	–	–	–	–	2

JARMAN, Barrington Noel (19)

Debut: 1959-60	Eng	Ind	NZ	Pak	SAf	SL	WI	Zim	Total
Tests at home	3	4	–	1	–	–	4	–	12
Tests abroad	4	3	–	–	–	–	–	–	7

JARVIS, Arthur Harwood (11)

Debut: 1884-85	Eng	Ind	NZ	Pak	SAf	SL	WI	Zim	Total
Tests at home	7	–	–	–	–	–	–	–	7
Tests abroad	4	–	–	–	–	–	–	–	4

JENNER, Terrence James (9)

Debut: 1970-71	Eng	Ind	NZ	Pak	SAf	SL	WI	Zim	Total
Tests at home	4	–	–	–	–	–	1	–	5
Tests abroad	–	–	–	–	–	–	4	–	4

JENNINGS, Claude Burrows (6)

Debut: 1912	Eng	Ind	NZ	Pak	SAf	SL	WI	Zim	Total
Tests at home	3	–	–	–	3	–	–	–	6

JOHNSON, Ian William Geddes (45)

Debut: 1945-46	Eng	Ind	NZ	Pak	SAf	SL	WI	Zim	Total
Tests at home	13	4	–	–	1	–	4	–	22
Tests abroad	9	2	1	1	5	–	5	–	23

JOHNSON, Leonard Joseph (1)

Debut: 1947-48	Eng	Ind	NZ	Pak	SAf	SL	WI	Zim	Total
Tests at home	–	1	–	–	–	–	–	–	1

JOHNSTON, William Arras (40)

Debut: 1947-48	Eng	Ind	NZ	Pak	SAf	SL	WI	Zim	Total
Tests at home	9	4	–	–	5	–	5	–	23
Tests abroad	8	–	–	–	5	–	4	–	17

JONES, Dean Mervyn (52)

Debut: 1983-84	Eng	Ind	NZ	Pak	SAf	SL	WI	Zim	Total
Tests at home	11	5	4	3	–	3	3	–	29
Tests abroad	6	3	1	3	–	3	7	–	23

JONES, Ernest (19)

Debut: 1894-95	Eng	Ind	NZ	Pak	SAf	SL	WI	Zim	Total
Tests at home	8	–	–	–	–	–	–	–	8
Tests abroad	10	–	–	–	1	–	–	–	11

JONES, Samuel Percy (12)

Debut: 1881-82	Eng	Ind	NZ	Pak	SAf	SL	WI	Zim	Total
Tests at home	8	–	–	–	–	–	–	–	8
Tests abroad	4	–	–	–	–	–	–	–	4

JOSLIN, Leslie Ronald (1)

Debut: 1967-68	Eng	Ind	NZ	Pak	SAf	SL	WI	Zim	Total
Tests at home	–	1	–	–	–	–	–	–	1

JULIAN, Brendon Paul (7)

Debut: 1993	Eng	Ind	NZ	Pak	SAf	SL	WI	Zim	Total
Tests at home	–	–	–	–	–	1	–	–	1
Tests abroad	2	–	–	–	–	–	4	–	6

KASPROWICZ, Michael Scott (17)

Debut: 1996-97	Eng	Ind	NZ	Pak	SAf	SL	WI	Zim	Total
Tests at home	1	1	3	1	2	–	2	–	10
Tests abroad	3	4	–	–	–	–	–	–	7

KELLEWAY, Charles (26)

Debut: 1910-11	Eng	Ind	NZ	Pak	SAf	SL	WI	Zim	Total
Tests at home	15	–	–	–	5	–	–	–	20
Tests abroad	3	–	–	–	3	–	–	–	6

KELLY, James Joseph (36)

Debut: 1896	Eng	Ind	NZ	Pak	SAf	SL	WI	Zim	Total
Tests at home	15	–	–	–	–	–	–	–	15
Tests abroad	18	–	–	–	3	–	–	–	21

KELLY, Thomas Joseph Dart (2)

Debut: 1876-77	Eng	Ind	NZ	Pak	SAf	SL	WI	Zim	Total
Tests at home	2	–	–	–	–	–	–	–	2

KENDALL, Thomas Kingston (2)

Debut: 1876-77	Eng	Ind	NZ	Pak	SAf	SL	WI	Zim	Total
Tests at home	2	–	–	–	–	–	–	–	2

KENT, Martin Francis (3)

Debut: 1981	Eng	Ind	NZ	Pak	SAf	SL	WI	Zim	Total
Tests abroad	3	–	–	–	–	–	–	–	3

KERR, Robert Byers (2)

Debut: 1985-86	Eng	Ind	NZ	Pak	SAf	SL	WI	Zim	Total
Tests at home	–	–	2	–	–	–	–	–	2

KIPPAX, Alan Falconer (22)

Debut: 1924-25	Eng	Ind	NZ	Pak	SAf	SL	WI	Zim	Total
Tests at home	7	–	–	–	4	–	5	–	16
Tests abroad	6	–	–	–	–	–	–	–	6

KLINE, Lindsay Francis (13)

Debut: 1957-58	Eng	Ind	NZ	Pak	SAf	SL	WI	Zim	Total
Tests at home	2	–	–	–	–	–	2	–	4
Tests abroad	–	3	–	1	5	–	–	–	9

LAIRD, Bruce Malcolm (21)

Debut: 1979-80	Eng	Ind	NZ	Pak	SAf	SL	WI	Zim	Total
Tests at home	2	–	–	3	–	–	6	–	11
Tests abroad	1	–	3	6	–	–	–	–	10

LANGER, Justin Lee (41)

Debut: 1992-93	Eng	Ind	NZ	Pak	SAf	SL	WI	Zim	Total
Tests at home	5	3	–	3	–	–	9	–	20
Tests abroad	–	3	6	4	–	3	4	1	21

LANGLEY, Gilbert Roche Andrews (26)

Debut: 1951-52	Eng	Ind	NZ	Pak	SAf	SL	WI	Zim	Total
Tests at home	2	–	–	–	5	–	5	–	12
Tests abroad	7	2	–	1	–	–	4	–	14

LAUGHLIN, Trevor John (3)

Debut: 1977-78	Eng	Ind	NZ	Pak	SAf	SL	WI	Zim	Total
Tests at home	1	–	–	–	–	–	–	–	1
Tests abroad	–	–	–	–	–	–	2	–	2

LAVER, Frank (15)

Debut: 1899	Eng	Ind	NZ	Pak	SAf	SL	WI	Zim	Total
Tests at home	2	–	–	–	–	–	–	–	2
Tests abroad	13	–	–	–	–	–	–	–	13

LAW, Stuart Grant (1)

Debut: 1995-96	Eng	Ind	NZ	Pak	SAf	SL	WI	Zim	Total
Tests at home	–	–	–	–	–	1	–	–	1

LAWRY, William Morris (68)

Debut: 1961	Eng	Ind	NZ	Pak	SAf	SL	WI	Zim	Total
Tests at home	16	4	–	1	5	–	5	–	31
Tests abroad	14	8	–	1	9	–	5	–	37

LAWSON, Geoffrey Francis (46)

Debut: 1980-81	Eng	Ind	NZ	Pak	SAf	SL	WI	Zim	Total
Tests at home	6	–	4	5	–	1	7	–	23
Tests abroad	15	–	–	3	–	–	5	–	23

LEE, Brett (7)

Debut: 1999-00	Eng	Ind	NZ	Pak	SAf	SL	WI	Zim	Total
Tests at home	–	2	–	–	–	–	2	–	4
Tests abroad	–	–	3	–	–	–	–	–	3

LEE, Philip Keith (2)

Debut: 1931-32	Eng	Ind	NZ	Pak	SAf	SL	WI	Zim	Total
Tests at home	1	–	–	–	1	–	–	–	2

LEHMANN, Darren Scott (5)

Debut: 1997-98	Eng	Ind	NZ	Pak	SAf	SL	WI	Zim	Total
Tests at home	2	–	–	–	–	–	–	–	2
Tests abroad	–	1	–	2	–	–	–	–	3

LILLEE, Dennis Keith (70)

Debut: 1970-71	Eng	Ind	NZ	Pak	SAf	SL	WI	Zim	Total
Tests at home	13	3	3	14	–	–	11	–	44
Tests abroad	16	–	5	3	–	1	1	–	26

LINDWALL, Raymond Russell (61)

Debut: 1945-46	Eng	Ind	NZ	Pak	SAf	SL	WI	Zim	Total
Tests at home	15	5	–	–	4	–	5	–	29
Tests abroad	14	5	1	3	4	–	5	–	32

LOVE, Hampden Stanley Bray (1)

Debut: 1932-33	Eng	Ind	NZ	Pak	SAf	SL	WI	Zim	Total
Tests at home	1	–	–	–	–	–	–	–	1

LOXTON, Samuel John Everett (12)

Debut: 1947-48	Eng	Ind	NZ	Pak	SAf	SL	WI	Zim	Total
Tests at home	3	1	–	–	–	–	–	–	4
Tests abroad	3	–	–	–	5	–	–	–	8

LYONS, John James (14)

Debut: 1886-87	Eng	Ind	NZ	Pak	SAf	SL	WI	Zim	Total
Tests at home	8	–	–	–	–	–	–	–	8
Tests abroad	6	–	–	–	–	–	–	–	6

McALISTER, Peter Alexander (8)

Debut: 1903-04	Eng	Ind	NZ	Pak	SAf	SL	WI	Zim	Total
Tests at home	6	–	–	–	–	–	–	–	6
Tests abroad	2	–	–	–	–	–	–	–	2

MACARTNEY, Charles George (35)

Debut: 1907-08	Eng	Ind	NZ	Pak	SAf	SL	WI	Zim	Total
Tests at home	8	–	–	–	4	–	–	–	12
Tests abroad	18	–	–	–	5	–	–	–	23

McCABE, Stanley Joseph (39)

Debut: 1930	Eng	Ind	NZ	Pak	SAf	SL	WI	Zim	Total
Tests at home	10	–	–	–	5	–	5	–	20
Tests abroad	14	–	–	–	5	–	–	–	19

McCOOL, Colin Leslie (14)

Debut: 1945-46	Eng	Ind	NZ	Pak	SAf	SL	WI	Zim	Total
Tests at home	5	3	–	–	–	–	–	–	8
Tests abroad	–	–	1	–	5	–	–	–	6

McCORMICK, Ernest Leslie (12)

Debut: 1935-36	Eng	Ind	NZ	Pak	SAf	SL	WI	Zim	Total
Tests at home	4	–	–	–	–	–	–	–	4
Tests abroad	3	–	–	–	5	–	–	–	8

McCOSKER, Richard Bede (25)

Debut: 1974-75	Eng	Ind	NZ	Pak	SAf	SL	WI	Zim	Total
Tests at home	6	–	–	3	–	–	5	–	14
Tests abroad	9	–	2	–	–	–	–	–	11

McDERMOTT, Craig John (71)

Debut: 1984-85	Eng	Ind	NZ	Pak	SAf	SL	WI	Zim	Total
Tests at home	9	7	8	3	3	4	9	–	43
Tests abroad	8	2	5	2	3	3	5	–	28

McDONALD, Colin Campbell (47)

Debut: 1951-52	Eng	Ind	NZ	Pak	SAf	SL	WI	Zim	Total
Tests at home	7	–	–	–	5	–	6	–	18
Tests abroad	8	7	–	4	5	–	5	–	29

McDONALD, Edgar Arthur (11)

Debut: 1920-21	Eng	Ind	NZ	Pak	SAf	SL	WI	Zim	Total
Tests at home	3	–	–	–	–	–	–	–	3
Tests abroad	5	–	–	–	3	–	–	–	8

McDONNELL, Percy Stanislaus (19)

Debut: 1880	Eng	Ind	NZ	Pak	SAf	SL	WI	Zim	Total
Tests at home	12	–	–	–	–	–	–	–	12
Tests abroad	7	–	–	–	–	–	–	–	7

MacGILL, Stuart Charles Glyndwr (16)

Debut: 1997-98	Eng	Ind	NZ	Pak	SAf	SL	WI	Zim	Total
Tests at home	4	–	–	–	1	–	4	–	9
Tests abroad	–	–	–	3	–	–	4	–	7

McGRATH, Glenn Donald (70)

Debut: 1993-94	Eng	Ind	NZ	Pak	SAf	SL	WI	Zim	Total
Tests at home	7	3	3	6	3	3	10	–	35
Tests abroad	6	4	3	5	5	3	8	1	35

McILWRAITH, John (1)

Debut: 1886	Eng	Ind	NZ	Pak	SAf	SL	WI	Zim	Total
Tests abroad	1	–	–	–	–	–	–	–	1

McINTYRE, Peter Edward (2)

Debut: 1994-95	Eng	Ind	NZ	Pak	SAf	SL	WI	Zim	Total
Tests at home	1	–	–	–	–	–	–	–	1
Tests abroad	–	1	–	–	–	–	–	–	1

MACKAY, Kenneth Donald (37)

Debut: 1956	Eng	Ind	NZ	Pak	SAf	SL	WI	Zim	Total
Tests at home	8	–	–	–	–	–	5	–	13
Tests abroad	8	8	–	3	5	–	–	–	24

McKENZIE, Graham Douglas (61)

Debut: 1961	Eng	Ind	NZ	Pak	SAf	SL	WI	Zim	Total
Tests at home	13	2	–	1	5	–	5	–	26
Tests abroad	13	8	–	1	8	–	5	–	35

McKIBBIN, Thomas Robert (5)

Debut: 1894-95	Eng	Ind	NZ	Pak	SAf	SL	WI	Zim	Total
Tests at home	3	–	–	–	–	–	–	–	3
Tests abroad	2	–	–	–	–	–	–	–	2

McLAREN, John William (1)

Debut: 1911-12	Eng	Ind	NZ	Pak	SAf	SL	WI	Zim	Total
Tests at home	1	–	–	–	–	–	–	–	1

MACLEAN, John Alexander (4)

Debut: 1978-79	Eng	Ind	NZ	Pak	SAf	SL	WI	Zim	Total
Tests at home	4	–	–	–	–	–	–	–	4

McLEOD, Charles Edward (17)

Debut: 1894-95	Eng	Ind	NZ	Pak	SAf	SL	WI	Zim	Total
Tests at home	11	–	–	–	–	–	–	–	11
Tests abroad	6	–	–	–	–	–	–	–	6

McLEOD, Robert William (6)

Debut: 1891-92	Eng	Ind	NZ	Pak	SAf	SL	WI	Zim	Total
Tests at home	3	–	–	–	–	–	–	–	3
Tests abroad	3	–	–	–	–	–	–	–	3

McSHANE, Patrick George (3)

Debut: 1884-85	Eng	Ind	NZ	Pak	SAf	SL	WI	Zim	Total
Tests at home	3	–	–	–	–	–	–	–	3

MADDOCKS, Leonard Victor (7)

Debut: 1954-55	Eng	Ind	NZ	Pak	SAf	SL	WI	Zim	Total
Tests at home	3	–	–	–	–	–	–	–	3
Tests abroad	2	1	–	–	–	–	1	–	4

MAGUIRE, John Norman (3)

Debut: 1983-84	Eng	Ind	NZ	Pak	SAf	SL	WI	Zim	Total
Tests at home	–	–	–	1	–	–	–	–	1
Tests abroad	–	–	–	–	–	–	2	–	2

MAILEY, Arthur Alfred (21)

Debut: 1920-21	Eng	Ind	NZ	Pak	SAf	SL	WI	Zim	Total
Tests at home	10	–	–	–	–	–	–	–	10
Tests abroad	8	–	–	–	3	–	–	–	11

MALLETT, Ashley Alexander (39)

Debut: 1968	Eng	Ind	NZ	Pak	SAf	SL	WI	Zim	Total
Tests at home	9	–	3	2	–	–	8	–	22
Tests abroad	8	5	3	–	1	–	–	–	17

MALONE, Michael Francis (1)

Debut: 1977	Eng	Ind	NZ	Pak	SAf	SL	WI	Zim	Total
Tests abroad	1	–	–	–	–	–	–	–	1

MANN, Anthony Longford (4)

Debut: 1977-78	Eng	Ind	NZ	Pak	SAf	SL	WI	Zim	Total
Tests at home	–	4	–	–	–	–	–	–	4

MARR, Alfred Percy (1)

Debut: 1884-85	Eng	Ind	NZ	Pak	SAf	SL	WI	Zim	Total
Tests at home	1	–	–	–	–	–	–	–	1

MARSH, Geoffrey Robert (50)

Debut: 1985-86	Eng	Ind	NZ	Pak	SAf	SL	WI	Zim	Total
Tests at home	11	7	3	2	–	1	5	–	29
Tests abroad	6	3	4	3	–	–	5	–	21

MARSH, Rodney William (97)

Debut: 1970-71	Eng	Ind	NZ	Pak	SAf	SL	WI	Zim	Total
Tests at home	22	3	6	14	–	–	12	–	57
Tests abroad	21	–	8	6	–	–	5	–	40

MARTIN, John Wesley (8)

Debut: 1960-61	Eng	Ind	NZ	Pak	SAf	SL	WI	Zim	Total
Tests at home	–	–	–	–	1	–	3	–	4
Tests abroad	–	2	–	1	1	–	–	–	4

MARTYN, Damien Richard (11)

Debut: 1992-93	Eng	Ind	NZ	Pak	SAf	SL	WI	Zim	Total
Tests at home	–	–	–	–	2	–	5	–	7
Tests abroad	–	–	4	–	–	–	–	–	4

MASSIE, Hugh Hamon (9)

Debut: 1881-82	Eng	Ind	NZ	Pak	SAf	SL	WI	Zim	Total
Tests at home	8	–	–	–	–	–	–	–	8
Tests abroad	1	–	–	–	–	–	–	–	1

MASSIE, Robert Arnold Lockyer (6)

Debut: 1972	Eng	Ind	NZ	Pak	SAf	SL	WI	Zim	Total
Tests at home	–	–	–	2	–	–	–	–	2
Tests abroad	4	–	–	–	–	–	–	–	4

MATTHEWS, Christopher Darrell (3)

Debut: 1986-87	Eng	Ind	NZ	Pak	SAf	SL	WI	Zim	Total
Tests at home	2	–	–	–	–	–	1	–	3

MATTHEWS, Gregory Richard John (33)

Debut: 1983-84	Eng	Ind	NZ	Pak	SAf	SL	WI	Zim	Total
Tests at home	9	3	3	2	–	–	3	–	20
Tests abroad	1	3	3	–	–	3	3	–	13

MATTHEWS, Thomas James (8)

Debut: 1911-12	Eng	Ind	NZ	Pak	SAf	SL	WI	Zim	Total
Tests at home	2	–	–	–	–	–	–	–	2
Tests abroad	3	–	–	–	3	–	–	–	6

MAY, Timothy Brian Alexander (24)

Debut: 1987-88	Eng	Ind	NZ	Pak	SAf	SL	WI	Zim	Total
Tests at home	3	–	3	–	3	–	4	–	13
Tests abroad	5	–	–	5	1	–	–	–	11

MAYNE, Lawrence Charles (6)

Debut: 1964-65	Eng	Ind	NZ	Pak	SAf	SL	WI	Zim	Total
Tests abroad	–	1	–	–	2	–	3	–	6

MAYNE, Richard Edgar (4)

Debut: 1912	Eng	Ind	NZ	Pak	SAf	SL	WI	Zim	Total
Tests abroad	1	–	–	–	3	–	–	–	4

MECKIFF, Ian (18)

Debut: 1957-58	Eng	Ind	NZ	Pak	SAf	SL	WI	Zim	Total
Tests at home	4	–	–	–	1	–	2	–	7
Tests abroad	–	5	–	2	4	–	–	–	11

MEULEMAN, Kenneth Douglas (1)

Debut: 1945-46	Eng	Ind	NZ	Pak	SAf	SL	WI	Zim	Total
Tests abroad	–	–	1	–	–	–	–	–	1

MIDWINTER, William Evans (8)

Debut: 1876-77	Eng	Ind	NZ	Pak	SAf	SL	WI	Zim	Total
Tests at home	5	–	–	–	–	–	–	–	5
Tests abroad	3	–	–	–	–	–	–	–	3

MILLER, Colin Reid (18)

Debut: 1998-99	Eng	Ind	NZ	Pak	SAf	SL	WI	Zim	Total
Tests at home	3	–	–	–	–	–	3	–	6
Tests abroad	–	1	3	3	–	3	1	1	12

MILLER, Keith Ross (55)

Debut: 1945-46	Eng	Ind	NZ	Pak	SAf	SL	WI	Zim	Total
Tests at home	14	5	–	–	4	–	5	–	28
Tests abroad	15	–	1	1	5	–	5	–	27

MINNETT, Roy Baldwin (9)

Debut: 1911-12	Eng	Ind	NZ	Pak	SAf	SL	WI	Zim	Total
Tests at home	5	–	–	–	–	–	–	–	5
Tests abroad	1	–	–	–	3	–	–	–	4

MISSON, Francis Michael (5)

Debut: 1960-61	Eng	Ind	NZ	Pak	SAf	SL	WI	Zim	Total
Tests at home	–	–	–	–	–	–	3	–	3
Tests abroad	2	–	–	–	–	–	–	–	2

MOODY, Thomas Masson (8)

Debut: 1989-90	Eng	Ind	NZ	Pak	SAf	SL	WI	Zim	Total
Tests at home	–	1	1	1	–	2	–	–	5
Tests abroad	–	–	–	–	–	3	–	–	3

MORONEY, John (7)

Debut: 1949-50	Eng	Ind	NZ	Pak	SAf	SL	WI	Zim	Total
Tests at home	1	–	–	–	–	–	1	–	2
Tests abroad	–	–	–	–	5	–	–	–	5

MORRIS, Arthur Robert (46)

Debut: 1946-47	Eng	Ind	NZ	Pak	SAf	SL	WI	Zim	Total
Tests at home	14	4	–	–	5	–	4	–	27
Tests abroad	10	–	–	–	5	–	4	–	19

MORRIS, Samuel (1)

Debut: 1884-85	Eng	Ind	NZ	Pak	SAf	SL	WI	Zim	Total
Tests at home	1	–	–	–	–	–	–	–	1

MOSES, Henry (6)

Debut: 1886-87	Eng	Ind	NZ	Pak	SAf	SL	WI	Zim	Total
Tests at home	6	–	–	–	–	–	–	–	6

MOSS, Jeffrey Kenneth (1)

Debut: 1978-79	Eng	Ind	NZ	Pak	SAf	SL	WI	Zim	Total
Tests at home	–	–	–	1	–	–	–	–	1

MOULE, William Henry (1)

Debut: 1880	Eng	Ind	NZ	Pak	SAf	SL	WI	Zim	Total
Tests abroad	1	–	–	–	–	–	–	–	1

MULLER, Scott Andrew (2)

Debut: 1999-00	Eng	Ind	NZ	Pak	SAf	SL	WI	Zim	Total
Tests at home	–	–	–	2	–	–	–	–	2

MURDOCH, William Lloyd (18)

Debut: 1876-77	Eng	Ind	NZ	Pak	SAf	SL	WI	Zim	Total
Tests at home	11	–	–	–	–	–	–	–	11
Tests abroad	7	–	–	–	–	–	–	–	7

MUSGROVE, Henry Alfred (1)

Debut: 1884-85	Eng	Ind	NZ	Pak	SAf	SL	WI	Zim	Total
Tests at home	1	–	–	–	–	–	–	–	1

NAGEL, Lisle Ernest (1)

Debut: 1932-33	Eng	Ind	NZ	Pak	SAf	SL	WI	Zim	Total
Tests at home	1	–	–	–	–	–	–	–	1

NASH, Laurence John (2)

Debut: 1931-32	Eng	Ind	NZ	Pak	SAf	SL	WI	Zim	Total
Tests at home	1	–	–	–	1	–	–	–	2

NICHOLSON, Matthew James (1)

Debut: 1998-99	Eng	Ind	NZ	Pak	SAf	SL	WI	Zim	Total
Tests at home	1	–	–	–	–	–	–	–	1

NITSCHKE, Holmesdale Carl (2)

Debut: 1931-32	Eng	Ind	NZ	Pak	SAf	SL	WI	Zim	Total
Tests at home	–	–	–	2	–	–	–	–	2

NOBLE, Montague Alfred (42)

Debut: 1897-98	Eng	Ind	NZ	Pak	SAf	SL	WI	Zim	Total
Tests at home	19	–	–	–	–	–	–	–	19
Tests abroad	20	–	–	–	3	–	–	–	23

NOBLET, Geffery (3)

Debut: 1949-50	Eng	Ind	NZ	Pak	SAf	SL	WI	Zim	Total
Tests at home	–	–	–	–	1	–	1	–	2
Tests abroad	–	–	–	–	1	–	–	–	1

NOTHLING, Otto Ernest (1)

Debut: 1928-29	Eng	Ind	NZ	Pak	SAf	SL	WI	Zim	Total
Tests at home	1	–	–	–	–	–	–	–	1

O'BRIEN, Leo Patrick Joseph (5)

Debut: 1932-33	Eng	Ind	NZ	Pak	SAf	SL	WI	Zim	Total
Tests at home	3	–	–	–	–	–	–	–	3
Tests abroad	–	–	–	–	2	–	–	–	2

O'CONNOR, John Denis Alphonsus (4)

Debut: 1907-08	Eng	Ind	NZ	Pak	SAf	SL	WI	Zim	Total
Tests at home	3	–	–	–	–	–	–	–	3
Tests abroad	1	–	–	–	–	–	–	–	1

O'DONNELL, Simon Patrick (6)

Debut: 1985	Eng	Ind	NZ	Pak	SAf	SL	WI	Zim	Total
Tests at home	–	–	1	–	–	–	–	–	1
Tests abroad	5	–	–	–	–	–	–	–	5

OGILVIE, Alan David (5)

Debut: 1977-78	Eng	Ind	NZ	Pak	SAf	SL	WI	Zim	Total
Tests at home	–	3	–	–	–	–	–	–	3
Tests abroad	–	–	–	–	–	–	2	–	2

O'KEEFFE, Kerry James (24)

Debut: 1970-71	Eng	Ind	NZ	Pak	SAf	SL	WI	Zim	Total
Tests at home	3	–	3	5	–	–	–	–	11
Tests abroad	3	–	5	–	–	–	5	–	13

OLDFIELD, William Albert Stanley (54)

Debut: 1920-21	Eng	Ind	NZ	Pak	SAf	SL	WI	Zim	Total
Tests at home	22	–	–	–	5	–	5	–	32
Tests abroad	16	–	–	–	6	–	–	–	22

O'NEILL, Norman Clifford (42)

Debut: 1958-59	Eng	Ind	NZ	Pak	SAf	SL	WI	Zim	Total
Tests at home	10	–	–	–	4	–	5	–	19
Tests abroad	9	7	–	3	–	–	4	–	23

O'REILLY, William Joseph (27)

Debut: 1931-32	Eng	Ind	NZ	Pak	SAf	SL	WI	Zim	Total
Tests at home	10	–	–	–	2	–	–	–	12
Tests abroad	9	–	1	–	5	–	–	–	15

OXENHAM, Ronald Keven (7)

Debut: 1928-29	Eng	Ind	NZ	Pak	SAf	SL	WI	Zim	Total
Tests at home	3	–	–	–	1	–	3	–	7

PALMER, George Eugene (17)

Debut: 1880	Eng	Ind	NZ	Pak	SAf	SL	WI	Zim	Total
Tests at home	10	–	–	–	–	–	–	–	10
Tests abroad	7	–	–	–	–	–	–	–	7

PARK, Roy Lindsay (1)

Debut: 1920-21	Eng	Ind	NZ	Pak	SAf	SL	WI	Zim	Total
Tests at home	1	–	–	–	–	–	–	–	1

PASCOE, Len Stephen (14)

Debut: 1977	Eng	Ind	NZ	Pak	SAf	SL	WI	Zim	Total
Tests at home	2	3	3	–	–	–	2	–	10
Tests abroad	4	–	–	–	–	–	–	–	4

PELLEW, Clarence Everard (10)

Debut: 1920-21	Eng	Ind	NZ	Pak	SAf	SL	WI	Zim	Total
Tests at home	4	–	–	–	–	–	–	–	4
Tests abroad	5	–	–	–	1	–	–	–	6

PHILLIPS, Wayne Bentley (27)

Debut: 1983-84	Eng	Ind	NZ	Pak	SAf	SL	WI	Zim	Total
Tests at home	–	3	3	5	–	–	2	–	13
Tests abroad	6	–	3	–	–	–	5	–	14

PHILLIPS, Wayne Norman (1)

Debut: 1991-92	Eng	Ind	NZ	Pak	SAf	SL	WI	Zim	Total
Tests at home	–	1	–	–	–	–	–	–	1

PHILPOTT, Peter Ian (8)

Debut: 1964-65	Eng	Ind	NZ	Pak	SAf	SL	WI	Zim	Total
Tests at home	3	–	–	–	–	–	–	–	3
Tests abroad	–	–	–	–	–	–	5	–	5

PONSFORD, William Harold (29)

Debut: 1924-25	Eng	Ind	NZ	Pak	SAf	SL	WI	Zim	Total
Tests at home	10	–	–	–	4	–	5	–	19
Tests abroad	10	–	–	–	–	–	–	–	10

PONTING, Ricky Thomas (42)

Debut: 1995-96	Eng	Ind	NZ	Pak	SAf	SL	WI	Zim	Total
Tests at home	3	3	3	3	3	3	7	–	25
Tests abroad	3	7	–	1	–	3	2	1	17

POPE, Roland James (1)

Debut: 1884-85	Eng	Ind	NZ	Pak	SAf	SL	WI	Zim	Total
Tests at home	1	–	–	–	–	–	–	–	1

RACKEMANN, Carl Grey (12)

Debut: 1982-83	Eng	Ind	NZ	Pak	SAf	SL	WI	Zim	Total
Tests at home	2	–	1	5	–	1	1	–	10
Tests abroad	–	–	1	–	–	–	1	–	2

RANSFORD, Vernon Seymour (20)

Debut: 1907-08	Eng	Ind	NZ	Pak	SAf	SL	WI	Zim	Total
Tests at home	10	–	–	–	5	–	–	–	15
Tests abroad	5	–	–	–	–	–	–	–	5

REDPATH, Ian Ritchie (67)

Debut: 1963-64	Eng	Ind	NZ	Pak	SAf	SL	WI	Zim	Total
Tests at home	14	3	–	3	1	–	11	–	32
Tests abroad	10	7	3	1	9	–	5	–	35

REEDMAN, John Cole (1)

Debut: 1894-95	Eng	Ind	NZ	Pak	SAf	SL	WI	Zim	Total
Tests at home	1	–	–	–	–	–	–	–	1

REID, Bruce Anthony (27)

Debut: 1985-86	Eng	Ind	NZ	Pak	SAf	SL	WI	Zim	Total
Tests at home	9	5	2	–	–	–	1	–	17
Tests abroad	–	2	3	3	–	–	2	–	10

REIFFEL, Paul Ronald (35)

Debut: 1991-92	Eng	Ind	NZ	Pak	SAf	SL	WI	Zim	Total
Tests at home	–	1	5	3	4	2	3	–	18
Tests abroad	7	2	3	–	1	–	4	–	17

RENNEBERG, David Alexander (8)

Debut: 1966-67	Eng	Ind	NZ	Pak	SAf	SL	WI	Zim	Total
Tests at home	–	3	–	–	–	–	–	–	3
Tests abroad	–	–	–	–	5	–	–	–	5

RICHARDSON, Arthur John (9)

Debut: 1924-25	Eng	Ind	NZ	Pak	SAf	SL	WI	Zim	Total
Tests at home	4	–	–	–	–	–	–	–	4
Tests abroad	5	–	–	–	–	–	–	–	5

RICHARDSON, Victor York (19)

Debut: 1924-25	Eng	Ind	NZ	Pak	SAf	SL	WI	Zim	Total
Tests at home	10	–	–	–	–	–	–	–	10
Tests abroad	4	–	–	–	5	–	–	–	9

RIGG, Keith Edward (8)

Debut: 1930-31	Eng	Ind	NZ	Pak	SAf	SL	WI	Zim	Total
Tests at home	3	–	–	–	4	–	1	–	8

RING, Douglas Thomas (13)

Debut: 1947-48	Eng	Ind	NZ	Pak	SAf	SL	WI	Zim	Total
Tests at home	–	1	–	–	5	–	5	–	11
Tests abroad	2	–	–	–	–	–	–	–	2

RITCHIE, Gregory Michael (30)

Debut: 1982-83	Eng	Ind	NZ	Pak	SAf	SL	WI	Zim	Total
Tests at home	4	2	3	–	–	–	1	–	10
Tests abroad	6	3	3	3	–	–	5	–	20

RIXON, Stephen John (13)

Debut: 1977-78	Eng	Ind	NZ	Pak	SAf	SL	WI	Zim	Total
Tests at home	–	5	–	–	–	–	3	–	8
Tests abroad	–	–	–	–	–	–	5	–	5

ROBERTSON, Gavin Ron (4)

Debut: 1997-98	Eng	Ind	NZ	Pak	SAf	SL	WI	Zim	Total
Tests abroad	–	3	–	1	–	–	–	–	4

ROBERTSON, William Roderick (1)

Debut: 1884-85	Eng	Ind	NZ	Pak	SAf	SL	WI	Zim	Total
Tests at home	1	–	–	–	–	–	–	–	1

ROBINSON, Richard Daryl (3)

Debut: 1977	Eng	Ind	NZ	Pak	SAf	SL	WI	Zim	Total
Tests abroad	3	–	–	–	–	–	–	–	3

ROBINSON, Rayford Harold (1)

Debut: 1936-37	Eng	Ind	NZ	Pak	SAf	SL	WI	Zim	Total
Tests at home	1	–	–	–	–	–	–	–	1

RORKE, Gordon Frederick (4)

Debut: 1958-59	Eng	Ind	NZ	Pak	SAf	SL	WI	Zim	Total
Tests at home	2	–	–	–	–	–	–	–	2
Tests abroad	–	2	–	–	–	–	–	–	2

RUTHERFORD, John Walter (1)

Debut: 1956-57	Eng	Ind	NZ	Pak	SAf	SL	WI	Zim	Total
Tests abroad	–	1	–	–	–	–	–	–	1

RYDER, John (20)

Debut: 1920-21	Eng	Ind	NZ	Pak	SAf	SL	WI	Zim	Total
Tests at home	13	–	–	–	–	–	–	–	13
Tests abroad	4	–	–	–	3	–	–	–	7

SAGGERS, Ronald Arthur (6)

Debut: 1948	Eng	Ind	NZ	Pak	SAf	SL	WI	Zim	Total
Tests abroad	1	–	–	–	5	–	–	–	6

SAUNDERS, John Victor (14)

Debut: 1901-02	Eng	Ind	NZ	Pak	SAf	SL	WI	Zim	Total
Tests at home	8	–	–	–	–	–	–	–	8
Tests abroad	4	–	–	–	2	–	–	–	6

SCOTT, Henry James Herbert (8)

Debut: 1884	Eng	Ind	NZ	Pak	SAf	SL	WI	Zim	Total
Tests at home	2	–	–	–	–	–	–	–	2
Tests abroad	6	–	–	–	–	–	–	–	6

SELLERS, Reginald Hugh Durning (1)

Debut: 1964-65	Eng	Ind	NZ	Pak	SAf	SL	WI	Zim	Total
Tests abroad	–	1	–	–	–	–	–	–	1

SERJEANT, Craig Stanton (12)

Debut: 1977	Eng	Ind	NZ	Pak	SAf	SL	WI	Zim	Total
Tests at home	–	4	–	–	–	–	–	–	4
Tests abroad	3	–	–	–	–	–	5	–	8

SHEAHAN, Andrew Paul (31)

Debut: 1967-68	Eng	Ind	NZ	Pak	SAf	SL	WI	Zim	Total
Tests at home	2	4	2	2	–	–	5	–	15
Tests abroad	7	5	–	–	4	–	–	–	16

SHEPHERD, Barry Kenneth (9)

Debut: 1962-63	Eng	Ind	NZ	Pak	SAf	SL	WI	Zim	Total
Tests at home	2	–	–	1	4	–	–	–	7
Tests abroad	–	–	–	–	–	–	2	–	2

SIEVERS, Morris William (3)

Debut: 1936-37	Eng	Ind	NZ	Pak	SAf	SL	WI	Zim	Total
Tests at home	3	–	–	–	–	–	–	–	3

SIMPSON, Robert Baddeley (62)

Debut: 1957-58	Eng	Ind	NZ	Pak	SAf	SL	WI	Zim	Total
Tests at home	9	8	–	1	5	–	5	–	28
Tests abroad	10	3	–	1	10	–	10	–	34

SINCOCK, David John (3)

Debut: 1964-65	Eng	Ind	NZ	Pak	SAf	SL	WI	Zim	Total
Tests at home	1	–	–	1	–	–	–	–	2
Tests abroad	–	–	–	–	–	–	1	–	1

SLATER, Keith Nichol (1)

Debut: 1958-59	Eng	Ind	NZ	Pak	SAf	SL	WI	Zim	Total
Tests at home	1	–	–	–	–	–	–	–	1

SLATER, Michael Jonathon (70)

Debut: 1993	Eng	Ind	NZ	Pak	SAf	SL	WI	Zim	Total
Tests at home	10	3	3	6	3	3	5	–	33
Tests abroad	6	7	3	6	3	3	8	1	37

SLEEP, Peter Raymond (14)

Debut: 1978-79	Eng	Ind	NZ	Pak	SAf	SL	WI	Zim	Total
Tests at home	4	–	3	2	–	1	–	–	10
Tests abroad	–	2	–	2	–	–	–	–	4

SLIGHT, James (1)

Debut: 1880	Eng	Ind	NZ	Pak	SAf	SL	WI	Zim	Total
Tests abroad	1	–	–	–	–	–	–	–	1

SMITH, David Betram Miller (2)

Debut: 1912	Eng	Ind	NZ	Pak	SAf	SL	WI	Zim	Total
Tests abroad	2	–	–	–	–	–	–	–	2

SMITH, Stephen Barry (3)

Debut: 1983-84	Eng	Ind	NZ	Pak	SAf	SL	WI	Zim	Total
Tests abroad	–	–	–	–	–	–	3	–	3

SPOFFORTH, Frederick Robert (18)

Debut: 1876-77	Eng	Ind	NZ	Pak	SAf	SL	WI	Zim	Total
Tests at home	11	–	–	–	–	–	–	–	11
Tests abroad	7	–	–	–	–	–	–	–	7

STACKPOLE, Keith Raymond (44)

Debut: 1965-66	Eng	Ind	NZ	Pak	SAf	SL	WI	Zim	Total
Tests at home	9	–	3	1	–	–	5	–	18
Tests abroad	5	5	3	–	9	–	4	–	26

STEVENS, Gavin Byron (4)

Debut: 1959-60	Eng	Ind	NZ	Pak	SAf	SL	WI	Zim	Total
Tests abroad	–	2	–	2	–	–	–	–	4

TABER, Hedley Brian (16)

Debut: 1966-67	Eng	Ind	NZ	Pak	SAf	SL	WI	Zim	Total
Tests at home	–	–	–	–	–	–	1	–	1
Tests abroad	1	5	–	–	9	–	–	–	15

TALLON, Donald (21)

Debut: 1945-46	Eng	Ind	NZ	Pak	SAf	SL	WI	Zim	Total
Tests at home	10	5	–	–	–	–	–	–	15
Tests abroad	5	–	1	–	–	–	–	–	6

TAYLOR, John Morris (20)

Debut: 1920-21	Eng	Ind	NZ	Pak	SAf	SL	WI	Zim	Total
Tests at home	10	–	–	–	–	–	–	–	10
Tests abroad	8	–	–	–	2	–	–	–	10

TAYLOR, Mark Anthony (104)

Debut: 1988-89	Eng	Ind	NZ	Pak	SAf	SL	WI	Zim	Total
Tests at home	15	5	7	6	6	5	11	–	55
Tests abroad	18	4	4	6	5	3	9	–	49

TAYLOR, Peter Laurence (13)

Debut: 1986-87	Eng	Ind	NZ	Pak	SAf	SL	WI	Zim	Total
Tests at home	2	2	–	2	–	1	2	–	9
Tests abroad	–	–	1	2	–	–	1	–	4

THOMAS, Grahame (8)

Debut: 1964-65	Eng	Ind	NZ	Pak	SAf	SL	WI	Zim	Total
Tests at home	3	–	–	–	–	–	–	–	3
Tests abroad	–	–	–	–	–	–	5	–	5

THOMS, George Ronald (1)

Debut: 1951-52	Eng	Ind	NZ	Pak	SAf	SL	WI	Zim	Total
Tests at home	–	–	–	–	–	–	1	–	1

THOMSON, Alan Lloyd (4)

Debut: 1970-71	Eng	Ind	NZ	Pak	SAf	SL	WI	Zim	Total
Tests at home	4	–	–	–	–	–	–	–	4

THOMSON, Jeffrey Robert (51)

Debut: 1972-73	Eng	Ind	NZ	Pak	SAf	SL	WI	Zim	Total
Tests at home	10	5	–	5	–	–	9	–	29
Tests abroad	11	–	3	3	–	–	5	–	22

THOMSON, Nathaniel Frampton Davis (2)

Debut: 1876-77	Eng	Ind	NZ	Pak	SAf	SL	WI	Zim	Total
Tests at home	2	–	–	–	–	–	–	–	2

THURLOW, Hugh Motley (1)

Debut: 1931-32	Eng	Ind	NZ	Pak	SAf	SL	WI	Zim	Total
Tests at home	–	–	–	–	1	–	–	–	1

TOOHEY, Peter Michael (15)

Debut: 1977-78	Eng	Ind	NZ	Pak	SAf	SL	WI	Zim	Total
Tests at home	6	5	–	–	–	–	1	–	12
Tests abroad	–	–	–	–	–	–	3	–	3

TOSHACK, Ernest Raymond Herbert (12)

Debut: 1945-46	Eng	Ind	NZ	Pak	SAf	SL	WI	Zim	Total
Tests at home	5	2	–	–	–	–	–	–	7
Tests abroad	4	–	1	–	–	–	–	–	5

TRAVERS, Joseph Patrick Francis (1)

Debut: 1901-02	Eng	Ind	NZ	Pak	SAf	SL	WI	Zim	Total
Tests at home	1	–	–	–	–	–	–	–	1

TRIBE, George Edward (3)

Debut: 1946-47	Eng	Ind	NZ	Pak	SAf	SL	WI	Zim	Total
Tests at home	3	–	–	–	–	–	–	–	3

TROTT, Albert Edwin (3)

Debut: 1894-95	Eng	Ind	NZ	Pak	SAf	SL	WI	Zim	Total
Tests at home	3	–	–	–	–	–	–	–	3

TROTT, George Henry Stephens (24)

Debut: 1888	Eng	Ind	NZ	Pak	SAf	SL	WI	Zim	Total
Tests at home	13	–	–	–	–	–	–	–	13
Tests abroad	11	–	–	–	–	–	–	–	11

TRUMBLE, Hugh (32)

Debut: 1890	Eng	Ind	NZ	Pak	SAf	SL	WI	Zim	Total
Tests at home	15	–	–	–	–	–	–	–	15
Tests abroad	16	–	–	–	1	–	–	–	17

TRUMBLE, John William (7)

Debut: 1884-85	Eng	Ind	NZ	Pak	SAf	SL	WI	Zim	Total
Tests at home	4	–	–	–	–	–	–	–	4
Tests abroad	3	–	–	–	–	–	–	–	3

TRUMPER, Victor Thomas (48)

Debut: 1899	Eng	Ind	NZ	Pak	SAf	SL	WI	Zim	Total
Tests at home	20	–	–	–	5	–	–	–	25
Tests abroad	20	–	–	–	3	–	–	–	23

TURNER, Alan (14)

Debut: 1975	Eng	Ind	NZ	Pak	SAf	SL	WI	Zim	Total
Tests at home	–	–	–	3	–	–	6	–	9
Tests abroad	3	–	2	–	–	–	–	–	5

TURNER, Charles Thomas Byass (17)

Debut: 1886-87	Eng	Ind	NZ	Pak	SAf	SL	WI	Zim	Total
Tests at home	9	–	–	–	–	–	–	–	9
Tests abroad	8	–	–	–	–	–	–	–	8

VEIVERS, Thomas Robert (21)

Debut: 1963-64	Eng	Ind	NZ	Pak	SAf	SL	WI	Zim	Total
Tests at home	4	–	–	1	3	–	–	–	8
Tests abroad	5	3	–	1	4	–	–	–	13

VELETTA, Michael Robert John (8)

Debut: 1987-88	Eng	Ind	NZ	Pak	SAf	SL	WI	Zim	Total
Tests at home	1	–	3	1	–	1	2	–	8

WAITE, Mervyn George (2)

Debut: 1938	Eng	Ind	NZ	Pak	SAf	SL	WI	Zim	Total
Tests abroad	2	–	–	–	–	–	–	–	2

WALKER, Maxwell Henry Norman (34)

Debut: 1972-73	Eng	Ind	NZ	Pak	SAf	SL	WI	Zim	Total
Tests at home	7	–	1	4	–	–	3	–	15
Tests abroad	9	–	5	–	–	–	5	–	19

WALL, Thomas Welbourn (18)

Debut: 1928-29	Eng	Ind	NZ	Pak	SAf	SL	WI	Zim	Total
Tests at home	5	–	–	–	3	–	1	–	9
Tests abroad	9	–	–	–	–	–	–	–	9

WALTERS, Francis Henry (1)

Debut: 1884-85	*Eng*	*Ind*	*NZ*	*Pak*	*SAf*	*SL*	*WI*	*Zim*	*Total*
Tests at home	1	–	–	–	–	–	–	–	1

WALTERS, Kevin Douglas (75)

Debut: 1965-66	*Eng*	*Ind*	*NZ*	*Pak*	*SAf*	*SL*	*WI*	*Zim*	*Total*
Tests at home	19	5	6	4	–	–	4	–	38
Tests abroad	18	5	5	–	4	–	5	–	37

WARD, Francis Anthony (4)

Debut: 1936-37	*Eng*	*Ind*	*NZ*	*Pak*	*SAf*	*SL*	*WI*	*Zim*	*Total*
Tests at home	3	–	–	–	–	–	–	–	3
Tests abroad	1	–	–	–	–	–	–	–	1

WARNE, Shane Keith (87)

Debut: 1991-92	*Eng*	*Ind*	*NZ*	*Pak*	*SAf*	*SL*	*WI*	*Zim*	*Total*
Tests at home	6	5	6	6	6	3	9	–	41
Tests abroad	12	6	6	3	6	5	7	1	46

WATKINS, John Russell (1)

Debut: 1972-73	*Eng*	*Ind*	*NZ*	*Pak*	*SAf*	*SL*	*WI*	*Zim*	*Total*
Tests at home	–	–	–	1	–	–	–	–	1

WATSON, Graeme Donald (5)

Debut: 1966-67	*Eng*	*Ind*	*NZ*	*Pak*	*SAf*	*SL*	*WI*	*Zim*	*Total*
Tests abroad	2	–	–	–	3	–	–	–	5

WATSON, William James (4)

Debut: 1954-55	*Eng*	*Ind*	*NZ*	*Pak*	*SAf*	*SL*	*WI*	*Zim*	*Total*
Tests at home	1	–	–	–	–	–	–	–	1
Tests abroad	–	–	–	–	–	–	3	–	3

WAUGH, Mark Edward (111)

Debut: 1990-91	*Eng*	*Ind*	*NZ*	*Pak*	*SAf*	*SL*	*WI*	*Zim*	*Total*
Tests at home	12	7	6	6	6	3	15	–	55
Tests abroad	12	7	5	6	6	6	13	1	56

WAUGH, Stephen Rodger (135)

Debut: 1985-86	*Eng*	*Ind*	*NZ*	*Pak*	*SAf*	*SL*	*WI*	*Zim*	*Total*
Tests at home	19	5	10	9	4	5	18	–	70
Tests abroad	18	9	10	8	6	3	10	1	65

WELLHAM, Dirk Macdonald (6)

Debut: 1981	*Eng*	*Ind*	*NZ*	*Pak*	*SAf*	*SL*	*WI*	*Zim*	*Total*
Tests at home	1	–	–	2	–	–	1	–	4
Tests abroad	2	–	–	–	–	–	–	–	2

WESSELS, Kepler Christoffel (24)

Debut: 1982-83	*Eng*	*Ind*	*NZ*	*Pak*	*SAf*	*SL*	*WI*	*Zim*	*Total*
Tests at home	4	–	1	5	–	–	5	–	15
Tests abroad	6	–	–	–	–	1	2	–	9

WHATMORE, Davenell Frederick (7)

Debut: 1978-79	*Eng*	*Ind*	*NZ*	*Pak*	*SAf*	*SL*	*WI*	*Zim*	*Total*
Tests at home	–	–	–	2	–	–	–	–	2
Tests abroad	–	5	–	–	–	–	–	–	5

WHITNEY, Michael Roy (12)

Debut: 1981	*Eng*	*Ind*	*NZ*	*Pak*	*SAf*	*SL*	*WI*	*Zim*	*Total*
Tests at home	–	3	1	–	–	–	2	–	6
Tests abroad	2	–	–	–	–	2	2	–	6

WHITTY, William James (14)

Debut: 1909	*Eng*	*Ind*	*NZ*	*Pak*	*SAf*	*SL*	*WI*	*Zim*	*Total*
Tests at home	2	–	–	–	5	–	–	–	7
Tests abroad	4	–	–	–	3	–	–	–	7

WIENER, Julien Mark (6)

Debut: 1979-80	Eng	Ind	NZ	Pak	SAf	SL	WI	Zim	Total
Tests at home	2	–	–	–	–	–	2	–	4
Tests abroad	–	–	–	2	–	–	–	–	2

WILSON, John William (1)

Debut: 1956-57	Eng	Ind	NZ	Pak	SAf	SL	WI	Zim	Total
Tests abroad	–	1	–	–	–	–	–	–	1

WILSON, Paul (1)

Debut: 1997-98	Eng	Ind	NZ	Pak	SAf	SL	WI	Zim	Total
Tests abroad	–	1	–	–	–	–	–	–	1

WOOD, Graeme Malcolm (59)

Debut: 1977-78	Eng	Ind	NZ	Pak	SAf	SL	WI	Zim	Total
Tests at home	7	4	3	4	–	–	11	–	29
Tests abroad	12	2	3	6	–	1	6	–	30

WOODCOCK, Ashley James (1)

Debut: 1973-74	Eng	Ind	NZ	Pak	SAf	SL	WI	Zim	Total
Tests at home	–	–	1	–	–	–	–	–	1

WOODFULL, William Maldon (35)

Debut: 1926	Eng	Ind	NZ	Pak	SAf	SL	WI	Zim	Total
Tests at home	10	–	–	–	5	–	5	–	20
Tests abroad	15	–	–	–	–	–	–	–	15

WOODS, Samuel Moses James (3)

Debut: 1888	Eng	Ind	NZ	Pak	SAf	SL	WI	Zim	Total
Tests abroad	3	–	–	–	–	–	–	–	3

WOOLLEY, Roger Douglas (2)

Debut: 1982-83	Eng	Ind	NZ	Pak	SAf	SL	WI	Zim	Total
Tests abroad	–	–	–	–	–	1	1	–	2

WORRALL, John (11)

Debut: 1884-85	Eng	Ind	NZ	Pak	SAf	SL	WI	Zim	Total
Tests at home	4	–	–	–	–	–	–	–	4
Tests abroad	7	–	–	–	–	–	–	–	7

WRIGHT, Kevin John (10)

Debut: 1978-79	Eng	Ind	NZ	Pak	SAf	SL	WI	Zim	Total
Tests at home	2	–	–	2	–	–	–	–	4
Tests abroad	–	6	–	–	–	–	–	–	6

YALLOP, Graham Neil (39)

Debut: 1975-76	Eng	Ind	NZ	Pak	SAf	SL	WI	Zim	Total
Tests at home	6	1	–	7	–	–	4	–	18
Tests abroad	7	6	–	3	–	1	4	–	21

YARDLEY, Bruce (33)

Debut: 1977-78	Eng	Ind	NZ	Pak	SAf	SL	WI	Zim	Total
Tests at home	9	3	–	4	–	–	3	–	19
Tests abroad	–	3	3	2	–	1	5	–	14

YOUNG, Shaun (1)

Debut: 1997	Eng	Ind	NZ	Pak	SAf	SL	WI	Zim	Total
Tests abroad	1	–	–	–	–	–	–	–	1

ZOEHRER, Timothy Joseph (10)

Debut: 1985-86	Eng	Ind	NZ	Pak	SAf	SL	WI	Zim	Total
Tests at home	4	–	–	–	–	–	–	–	4
Tests abroad	–	3	3	–	–	–	–	–	6

BIRTHS AND DEATHS OF CRICKETERS

The following list details information on the 3,130 players to have represented an Australian first-class cricket team.

The compiler of this section welcomes any information from readers regarding the details contained therein.

Key to abbreviations

Australian states and territories: ACT – Australian Capital Territory, NSW – New South Wales, NT – Northern Territory, Qld – Queensland, SAust – South Australia, Tas – Tasmania, Vic – Victoria, WAust – Western Australia.

*Denotes Test player.

**Denotes Test player for two countries.

There is a full list of Australian Test players from page 123.

a'Beckett, Edward Clive (Vic) b Jan. 18, 1940 East Melbourne (Vic)

a'Beckett, Edward Fitzhayley (Vic) b April 16, 1836 Holborn, London, (England) d March 25, 1922 Upper Beaconsfield (Vic)

* a'Beckett, Edward Lambert (Vic) b Aug. 11, 1907 East St Kilda (Vic) d June 2, 1989 Terang (Vic)

a'Beckett, Malwyn (Vic) b Sept. 26, 1834 London, Middlesex (England) d June 25, 1906 Sale (Vic)

Abell, William (Qld) b c. 1874 d c. 1955 (Qld)

Achurch, Claude Septimus (NSW) b Aug. 16, 1896 Dubbo (NSW) d Aug. 15, 1979 Nambour (Qld)

Adams, Edward William (NSW) b July 10, 1896 Bathurst (NSW) d May 25, 1977 Bexley (NSW)

Adams, Francis (NSW) b c. 1836 Doohat, County Fermanagh (Ireland) d Feb. 10, 1911 North Sydney (NSW)

Adams, James William (Qld) b Feb. 22, 1904 Toowong (Qld) d Jan. 8, 1988 Willoughby (NSW)

Adamson, Charles Young (Qld) b April 18, 1875 Neville's Cross, Durham (England) d Sept. 17, 1918 Salonica (Greece)

Adcock, Nathan Tennyson (SAust) b April 22, 1978 Campbelltown (SAust)

Addison, Alexander Gollan (Tas) b Sept. 29, 1877 Adelaide (SAust) d Oct. 12, 1935 Double Bay (NSW)

Ainslie, James (Vic) b June 9, 1880 Elsternwick (Vic) d Dec. 31, 1953 St Kilda (Vic)

Albury, William Douglas (Qld) b Feb. 9, 1947 Herston (Qld)

* Alderman, Terence Michael (WAust) b June 12, 1956 Subiaco (WAust)

Aldridge, Keith John (Tas) b March 13, 1935 Evesham, Worcestershire (England)

Alexander, Francis James (WAust) b April 15, 1911 Perth (WAust)

* Alexander, George (Vic) b April 22, 1851 Oxfordshire (England) d Nov. 6, 1930 East Melbourne (Vic)

* Alexander, Harry Houston (Vic) b June 9, 1905 Ascot Vale (Vic) d April 15, 1993 East Melbourne (Vic)

Alexander, Leonard James (Tas) b Sept. 1, 1922 Hobart (Tas)

Alexander, William Colin (SAust) b Sept. 14, 1907 Gawler (SAust) d Feb. 8, 1993 Melbourne (Vic)

* Allan, Francis Erskine (Vic) b Dec. 2, 1849 Allansford (Vic) d Feb. 9, 1917 East Melbourne (Vic)

Allan, George Harold (Tas) b Feb. 18, 1887 Albury (NSW) d Nov. 2, 1932 Adelaide (SAust)

Allan, Henry Alexander (NSW) b Jan. 6, 1846 Westminster, London, Middlesex (England) d Apr. 26, 1926 East Melbourne (Vic)

* Allan, Peter John (Qld) b Dec. 31, 1935 Coorparoo (Qld)

Allanby, Nicholas John (Tas) b Aug. 24, 1957 Hobart (Tas)

Allanby, Richard Andrew (Tas) b July 26, 1971 Hobart (Tas)

Allanson, Noel Laurence (Vic) b Dec. 25, 1925 North Carlton (Vic)

Allardice, Geoffrey John (Vic) b May 7, 1967 Melbourne (Vic)

Allee, Charles George (Vic) b Feb. 10, 1848 Melbourne (Vic) d June 7, 1896 East Melbourne (Vic)

Allen, Donald John (Qld) b Feb. 26, 1947 Lismore (NSW)

Allen, Donald Radford (Vic) b Dec. 13, 1926 East St Kilda (Vic)

Allen, Harold Eric (Tas) b Oct. 13, 1886 Invercargill (New Zealand) d July 9, 1939 West Hobart (Tas)

Allen, Harold Hedley (Tas) b Nov. 15, 1940 Latrobe (Tas)

Allen, Jeremy Michael (WAust) b June 11, 1971 Subiaco (WAust)

Allen, Leslie Graham (Tas) b Sept. 13, 1954 Wynyard (Tas)

* Allen, Reginald Charles (NSW) b July 2, 1858 Glebe (NSW) d May 2, 1952 Sydney (NSW)

Allen, Ross Thomas (Qld) b Aug. 12, 1939 Toowoomba (Qld)

Allen, Thomas (Qld) b Sept. 5, 1912 Toowoomba (Qld) d March 18, 1954 Cambooya (Qld)

Allen, Thorpe (Qld) b March 7, 1870 Oxley (Qld) d Jan. 25, 1950 East Brisbane (Qld)

Allen, William Miller (Vic) b July 7, 1889 Ballarat (Vic) d Nov. 13, 1948 Ringwood (Vic)

Alley, Phillip John Sydney (SAust & NSW) b July 26, 1970 Orange (NSW)

Alley, William Edward (NSW) b Feb. 3, 1919 Hornsby (NSW)

Alleyne, John Placid (NSW) b Aug. 1, 1908 Glebe (NSW) d June 24, 1980 Glebe (NSW)

Allison, Henry (Tas) b July 14, 1828 Campbell Town (Tas)

Allsopp, Arthur Henry (NSW & Vic) b March 1, 1908 Lithgow (NSW) d Feb. 6, 1993 Chadstone (Vic)

Alsop, Charles James (Vic) b Nov. 24, 1868 Moonee Ponds (Vic) d Sept. 17, 1948 Melbourne (Vic)

Amalfi, Anthony John (Vic) b Jan. 19, 1967 East Melbourne (Vic)

Ambler, Albert Mark (SAust) b Sept. 27, 1892 Murray Bridge (SAust) d Nov. 27, 1970 Prospect (SAust)

Amos, Gordon Stanley (NSW & Qld) b April 4, 1905 Newtown (NSW) d April 7, 1995 Labrador (Qld)

Amos, William (SAust) b April 20, 1860 Glen Osmond (SAust) d May 14, 1935 North Adelaide (SAust)

Anderson, Allan David (NSW) b April 22, 1949 Greenwich (NSW)

Anderson, Dale Thomas (Tas) b June 10, 1931 Latrobe (Tas)

Anderson, David John (Vic) b Jan. 26, 1940 Warrnambool (Vic)

Anderson, James Clayton (Qld) b Feb. 27, 1895 (Qld) death details unknown

Anderson, John Gregory (Vic) b Feb. 15, 1955 East Melbourne (Vic)

Anderson, John Theodore (WAust) b Aug. 10, 1878 Warrnambool (Vic) d Aug. 29, 1926 South Yarra (Vic)

Anderson, Matthew Allen (Qld) b Oct. 30, 1976 Darwin (NT)

Anderson, Peter Gordon (NSW) b Oct. 4, 1933 Camberwell (Vic)

Anderson, Peter McKenzie (Vic) b Sept. 17, 1968 Geelong (Vic)

Anderson, Peter William (Qld & SAust) b May 22, 1961 South Brisbane (Qld)

Andrew-Street, Alfred Gordon (Vic) b April 8, 1914 Bondi (NSW) d Dec. 13, 1984 Concord (NSW)

* Andrews, Thomas James Edwin (NSW) b Aug. 26, 1890 Newtown (NSW) d Jan. 28, 1970 Croydon (NSW)

Andrews, Wayne Stewart (WAust) b Nov. 19, 1958 Melbourne (Vic)

Andrews, William Charles (NSW & Qld) b July 14, 1908 West Maitland (NSW) d June 9, 1962 Bombay (India)

* Angel, Jo (WAust) b April 22, 1968 Mt Lawley (WAust)

Antill, Thomas Wills (Vic) b Nov. 20, 1830 Jarvisfield (NSW) d May 11, 1865 Nelson (New Zealand)

Appleton, Leslie Joseph Francis (Tas) b Sept. 28, 1947 Hobart (Tas)

Archer, Daniel John Lancelot (Tas) b June 17, 1939 Launceston (Tas)

* Archer, Kenneth Alan (Qld) b Jan. 17, 1928 Yeerongpilly (Qld)

* Archer, Ronald Graham (Qld) b Oct. 25, 1933 Highgate Hill (Qld)

Armstrong, Edward Killeen (Qld) b Feb. 15, 1881 Milton (Qld) d April 29, 1963 Brisbane (Qld)

Armstrong, George Gort (Qld) b Dec. 29, 1882 Milton (Qld) d Jan. 12, 1956 Brisbane (Qld)

Armstrong, Glenarvon Huntley (SAust) b Nov. 17, 1969 Hobart (Tas)

Armstrong, Thomas Goldsmith (Vic) b Oct. 31, 1889 Caulfield (Vic) d April 15, 1963 Bairnsdale (Vic)

* Armstrong, Warwick Windridge (Vic) b May 22, 1879 Kyneton (Vic) d July 13, 1947 Darling Point (NSW)

Armstrong, William Anthony (Qld) b May 2, 1886 Milton (Qld) d May 29, 1955 Brisbane (Qld)

Arnberger, Jason Lee (NSW & Vic) b Nov. 18, 1972 Penrith (NSW)

Arnold, Colin Robert (Tas) b Aug. 19, 1957 Devonport (Tas)

Arnold, Evan Matthew Campbell (SAust) b Aug. 20, 1974 North Adelaide (SAust)

Arnold, Weller (Tas) b Sept. 23, 1882 North Hobart (Tas) d Oct. 28, 1957 Hobart (Tas)

Arnott, Percival Sinclair (NSW) b July 9, 1889 Newcastle (NSW) d Dec. 23, 1950 Camperdown (NSW)

Arthur, Charles (Tas) b Feb. 5, 1808 Plymouth, Devon (England) d July 29, 1884 Longford (Tas)

Arthur, George Henry (Tas) b March 10, 1849 Longford (Tas) d Nov. 13, 1932 Longford (Tas)

Arthur, Gerald Charles (WAust) b July 25, 1913 Yarloop (WAust)

Arthur, John Lake Allen (Tas) b April 7, 1847 Longford (Tas) d April 26, 1877 Longford (Tas)

Asher, Oswald Philip (NSW) b May 21, 1891 Paddington (NSW) d July 16, 1970 Waverton (NSW)

Ashley, Nathan William (Cricket Academy) b Oct. 3, 1973 St Leonards (NSW)

Astley, Graeme Patrick (Tas) b March 31, 1957 Sydney (NSW)

Atkins, Arthur Alfred (Qld & NSW) b April 22, 1874 (NSW) death details unknown

Atkinson, James Archibald (Vic & Tas) b April 4, 1896 North Fitzroy (Vic) d June 11, 1956 Beaconsfield (Vic)

Atkinson, Mark Neville (Tas) b Feb. 11, 1969 Sydney (NSW)

Atkinson, Mark Peter (WAust) b Nov. 27, 1970 Bentley (WAust)

Attenborough, Geoffrey Robert (SAust) b Jan. 17, 1951 Mile End (SAust)

Austen, Ernest Thomas (Vic) b Sept. 23, 1900 Hawthorn (Vic) d June 21, 1983 Melbourne (Vic)

Austen, Victor Cecil (SAust) b Nov. 30, 1918 Kew (Vic)

Austin, Harold MacPherson (Vic) b March 8, 1903 Skipton (Vic) d July 31, 1981 Timboon (Vic)

Austin, Sydney Walter (NSW & Qld) b Nov. 16, 1866 Sydney (NSW) d Sept. 9, 1932 Randwick (NSW)

Auty, Clinton (WAust) b Oct. 29, 1969 Auckland (New Zealand)

Aylett, Allen James (Vic) b April 24, 1934 Melbourne (Vic)

Ayres, Ryall Sydney (Qld) b Sept. 1, 1931 Clayfield (Qld) d Nov. 24, 1991 Sydney (NSW)

Ayres, Sydney William (Qld) b Aug. 7, 1889 Enmore (NSW) d Aug. 7, 1974 Castle Hill (NSW)

Ayres, Warren Geoffrey (Vic) b Oct. 25, 1965 Moorabbin (Vic)

Back, William (WAust) b c. 1856 Rottnest Island (WAust) d Feb. 15, 1911 Perth (WAust)

Backman, Charles James (SAust) b Dec. 14, 1890 Bowden (SAust) d April 25, 1915 Gallipoli (Turkey)

* Badcock, Clayvel Lindsay (Tas & SAust) b April 10, 1914 Exton (Tas) d Dec. 13, 1982 Exton (Tas)

Badcock, Kevin Bruce (Tas) b March 24, 1951 Launceston (Tas)

Bagshaw, Kenneth James (SAust) b Oct. 22, 1920 Kadina (SAust) d Oct. 8, 1985 Watson (ACT)

Bailey, Alfred John Thomas Slater (SAust) b March 3, 1932 North Adelaide (SAust)

Bailey, Bertram Theodore (SAust) b Dec. 5, 1874 Adelaide (SAust) d Oct. 3, 1964 Payneham (SAust)

Bailey, Ernest Albert (SAust) b Nov. 15, 1881 Adelaide (SAust) d Aug. 16, 1966 Northfield (SAust)

Bailey, George Herbert (Tas) b Oct. 29, 1853 Colombo (Ceylon) d Oct. 10, 1926 Hobart (Tas)

Bailey, George Keith Brooke (Tas) b Jan. 3, 1882 Hobart (Tas) d June 17, 1964 Hobart (Tas)

Bailey, Peter George (Vic) b Aug. 16, 1939 Glenhuntly (Vic)

Bailey, Rowland Herbert (Vic) b Oct. 5, 1876 Melbourne (Vic) d March 24, 1950 Ivanhoe (Vic)

Bailey, William Henry (Vic) b July 20, 1898 Condoblin (NSW) d Feb. 27, 1983 Geelong (Vic)

Baird, James George (Vic) b Nov. 9, 1920 Parkville (Vic)

Baird, Keith Hugh (WAust) b Dec. 27, 1911 Perth (WAust) d July 18, 1965 Peppermint Grove (WAust)

Baker, Charles Michael (Vic) b June 18, 1880 Ballarat East (Vic) d May 4, 1962 Ballarat (Vic)

Baker, Charles Ronald (NSW) b March 24, 1939 Islington (NSW)

Baker, Dennis James (WAust & Tas) b Dec. 29, 1947 Norseman (WAust)

Baker, Everard Audley (Vic) b Nov. 9, 1920 Parkville (Vic) d March 30, 1987 Melbourne (Vic)

Baker, Frederick (Vic) b c. 1851 (England) d c. 1925

Baker, Glen William (Qld) b Aug. 9, 1915 Townsville (Qld) d Dec. 15, 1943 Buna (Papua New Guinea) on active service

Baker, Leigh James (Vic) b Sept. 20, 1951 Oakleigh (Vic)

Baker, Robert Michael (WAust) b July 24, 1975 Osborne Park (WAust)

Bakker, Jason Richard (Vic) b Nov. 12, 1967 Geelong (Vic)

Balcam, Leonard Frank (Qld & Vic) b Aug. 20, 1957 Footscray (Vic)

Baldock, Darrel John (Tas) b Sept. 29, 1938 Devonport (Tas)

Baldry, Robert John (Vic) b Nov. 30, 1950 Warragul (Vic)

Ball, Thomas Edward (Qld) b Dec. 3, 1921 Atherton (Qld)

Ballans, David Murray (SAust) b June 30, 1868 at sea d June 26, 1957 Goodwood Park (SAust)

Bandy, Lawrence Henry (WAust) b Sept. 3, 1911 Perth (WAust) d July 18, 1984 Scarborough (WAust)

Banks, Albert James (WAust) b Dec. 10, 1883 Maryborough (Vic) d July 5, 1930 Toodyay (WAust)

* Bannerman, Alexander Chalmers (NSW) b March 21, 1854 Paddington (NSW) d Sept. 19, 1924 Paddington (NSW)

* Bannerman, Charles (NSW) b July 23, 1851 Woolwich, Kent (England) d Aug. 20, 1930 Surry Hills (NSW)

Barbour, Eric Pitty (NSW) b Jan. 27, 1891 Ashfield (NSW) d Dec. 7, 1934 Darlinghurst (NSW)

Barbour, Robert Roy (Qld) b March 29, 1899 Ashfield (NSW) d Dec. 29, 1994 Berwick (Vic)

Bardsley, Raymond (NSW) b Jan. 19, 1894 Glebe Point (NSW) d June 25, 1983 death place unknown

* Bardsley, Warren (NSW) b Dec. 6, 1882 Nevertire (NSW) d Jan. 20, 1954 Collaroy (NSW)

Baring, Frederick Albert (Vic) b Dec. 15, 1890 Hotham East (Vic) d Dec. 10, 1961 Doncaster (Vic)

Baring, Hugh Thomas (Vic) b Aug. 17, 1906 East Melbourne (Vic) d July 9, 1968 Fitzroy (Vic)

Barnard, Francis George Allman (Vic) b Dec. 26, 1857 Kew (Vic) d June 1, 1932 Melbourne (Vic)

Barnes, James Charles (NSW) b Oct. 16, 1882 Alexandria (NSW) death details unknown

Barnes, Jeffrey Robert (SAust) b Jan. 9, 1948 Glenelg (SAust)

Barnes, John Francis (Qld) b Sept. 27, 1916 Rockhampton (Qld)

Barnes, John Robert (Vic) b May 20, 1905 Williamstown (Vic) d Oct. 6, 1999 Williamstown (Vic)

Barnes, Richard Thomas Bygrove (Tas) b Sept. 5, 1852 Hobart (Tas) d April 30, 1902 Heidelberg (Vic)

* Barnes, Sydney George (NSW) b June 5, 1916 Annandale (NSW) d Dec. 16, 1973 Collaroy (NSW)

Barnett, Benjamin Arthur (Vic) b March 23, 1908 Auburn (Vic) d June 29, 1979 Newcastle (NSW)

Barras, Alexander Edward Owen (WAust) b Jan. 26, 1914 Auburn (Vic) d Aug. 15, 1986 Mt Lawley (WAust)

Barrett, Edgar Alfred (Vic) b June 26, 1869 Emerald Hill (Vic) d April 29, 1959 Kew (Vic)

Barrett, Henry (Tas) b Aug. 19, 1837 Launceston (Tas)

* Barrett, John Edward (Vic) b Oct. 15, 1866 Emerald Hill (Vic) d Feb. 6, 1916 Peak Hill (WAust)

Barsby, Trevor John (Qld) b Jan. 16, 1964 Herston (Qld)

Barstow, Charles Banks (Qld) b March 13, 1883 Brisbane (Qld) d July 12, 1935 Eagle Junction (Qld)

Bartlett, Albert James (SAust) b April 23, 1900 Parkside (SAust) d Oct. 6, 1968 Woodville South (SAust)

Bartlett, Robert Andrew (Vic) b Jan. 2, 1972 Melbourne (Vic)

Bateman, William Augustus (WAust) b Sept. 11, 1866 Fremantle (WAust) d July 27, 1935 South Perth (WAust)

Bates, Barry (NSW) b July 1, 1939 Mayfield (NSW)

Bayles, Robert Charles Alfred Vivian (Tas) b July 7, 1892 Ross (Tas) d May 16, 1959 Launceston (Tas)

Bayles, William Headlam (Tas) b Jan. 8, 1896 Ross (Tas) d Dec. 17, 1960 Launceston (Tas)

Bayliss, Trevor Harley (NSW) b Dec. 21, 1962 Goulburn (NSW)

Bayly, Henry Vincent (Tas) b Nov. 19, 1850 Dulcot (Tas) d Jan. 7, 1903 New Town (Tas)

Beacham, George (Vic) b Oct. 27, 1867 (Qld) d Jan. 11, 1925 South Fitzroy (Vic)

Beagley, John William (SAust) b March 23, 1933 Adelaide (SAust)

Beal, Charles William (Australians) b June 24, 1855 Sydney (NSW) d Feb. 5, 1921 Randwick (NSW)

Beal, James Charles (NSW) b May 26, 1830 Sydney (NSW) d Aug. 24, 1904 Milton (Qld)

Beames, Percy James (Vic) b July 27, 1911 Ballarat (Vic)

Bean, Ernest Edward (Vic) b April 17, 1866 Miner's Rest, near Ballarat (Vic) d March 22, 1939 Hampton (Vic)

Beard, Barry Allan (Tas) b Dec. 21, 1941 Bothwell (Tas) d June 9, 2001 Ulverstone (Tas)

* Beard, Graeme Robert (NSW) b Aug. 19, 1950 Auburn (NSW)

Beath, Neville Ray James (NSW) b Nov. 12, 1921 Goolagong (NSW) d Nov. 22, 1987 Richmond (NSW)

Beattie, Simon Guy (Qld) b Dec. 10, 1958 Junee (NSW)

Beatty, Christopher (NSW) b Oct. 21, 1952 Newcastle (NSW)

Beatty, Reginald George (NSW) b Dec. 24, 1913 Wickham (NSW) d May 27, 1957 Waratah (NSW)

Becker, Gordon Charles (WAust) b March 14, 1936 Katanning (WAust)

Bedford, Albert Austen (SAust) b Sept. 12, 1932 Rose Park (SAust) d March 25, 2001 Noarlunga (SAust)

Bedford, Peter Lawrence Anthony (Vic) b April 11, 1947 Melbourne (Vic)

Bednall, Philip Malcolm (SAust) b Jan. 27, 1931 Burra (SAust)

Beeston, Norman Charles (Qld) b Sept. 29, 1900 Brisbane (Qld) d Feb. 4, 1985 South Brisbane (Qld)

Beetson, John Lievesley (NSW) b c. 1830 Lancashire (England) d June 1, 1873 Newcastle (NSW)

Belcher, Samuel Harborne (NSW) b Nov. 1, 1834 (England) d Aug. 22, 1920 Garroorigang (NSW)

Bell, John Clifford (Qld) b Jan. 18, 1949 Ipswich (Qld)

* Benaud, John (NSW) b May 11, 1944 Auburn (NSW)

* Benaud, Richard (NSW) b Oct. 6, 1930 Penrith (NSW)

Benbow, Ernest Aldred (Qld) b March 14, 1888 Mt Walker (Qld) d Dec. 28, 1940 Springsure (Qld)

Bendixen, Hilton Fewtrell (Qld) b Feb. 21, 1910 Nambour (Qld) d April 15, 1962 Nambour (Qld)

Benjamin, Emmanuel (Tas) b Feb. 2, 1955 Jullundur City (India)

Bennett, Albert (NSW) b May 21, 1910 St Helens, Lancashire (England) d c. 1985 full death details unknown

Bennett, Floyd Chester (SAust & WAust) b April 12, 1919 North Perth (WAust) d Nov. 26, 1997 Stirling (SAust)

Bennett, George Henry (NSW) b Aug. 16, 1906 Brookvale (NSW) d c. 1983 full death details unknown

Bennett, Harry Francis (WAust) b June 22, 1859 Prahran (Vic) d Oct. 4, 1898 Guildford (WAust)

Bennett, Joseph (Vic) birth and death details unknown

* Bennett, Murray John (NSW) b Oct. 6, 1956 Brisbane (Qld)

Bennett, Rex Leland (SAust & Tas) b June 25, 1896 Snowtown (SAust) d Dec. 14, 1963 Collaroy (NSW)

Bennett, Richard John (Tas) b June 5, 1965 Launceston (Tas)

Bennett, Thomas (SAust) b Oct. 11, 1866 Littlehampton (SAust) d Dec. 26, 1942 Northfield (SAust)

Bennetts, Gordon Kissack (Vic) b March 26, 1909 Wellington (NSW) d April 4, 1987 Geelong (Vic)

Benneworth, Anthony John (Tas) b Dec. 12, 1949 Launceston (Tas)

Bennison, James Ernest (Tas) b Feb. 16, 1854 Hobart (Tas) d Nov. 14, 1916 Hobart (Tas)

Bensley, Gary Robert (NSW) b Oct. 17, 1958 Inverell (NSW)

Bensted, Eric Charles (Qld) b Feb. 11, 1901 Killarney (Qld) d March 24, 1980 Brisbane (Qld)

Benton, Jeffrey John (SAust) b Oct. 9, 1953 Mildura (Vic)

Bernard, Stephen Russell (NSW) b Dec. 28, 1949 Orange (NSW)

Berrie, Edward Bruce (NSW) b April 8, 1884 Tomenbil, near Forbes (NSW) d Dec. 8, 1963 Tamworth (NSW)

Berry, Darren Shane (Vic & SAust) b Dec. 10, 1969 Melbourne (Vic)

Berry, Walter Lyall (NSW) b April 9, 1893 Woolwich (NSW) d April 20, 1970 Ettalong Beach (NSW)

Bessen, Mervyn Oscar (WAust) b Aug. 29, 1913 Tambellup (WAust)

Best, Leslie (NSW) b Nov. 20, 1893 Seven Hills (NSW) d Aug. 27, 1925 Sydney (NSW)

Bettington, Brindley Cecil John (NSW) b Sept. 2, 1898 Parramatta (NSW) d Aug. 26, 1931 Merriwa (NSW)

Bettington, Reginald Henshall Brindley (NSW) b Feb. 24, 1900 Parramatta (NSW) d June 24, 1969 Gisborne (New Zealand)

Betts, Arthur John (Tas) b Feb. 26, 1880 Launceston (Tas) d c. 1954 Belgrave (Vic)

Bevan, Hubert George (WAust) b Dec. 21, 1932 Perth (WAust)

Bevan, John Lawrence (SAust) b May 10, 1846 Swansea, Glamorgan (Wales) d March 31, 1918 Portland Estate (SAust)

* Bevan, Michael Gwyl (SAust & NSW) b May 8, 1970 Belconnen (ACT)

Beven, Ian Robert (Tas) b Nov. 27, 1958 Hobart (Tas)

* Bichel, Andrew John (Qld) b Aug. 27, 1970 Laidley (Qld)

Bichel, Donald Alan (Qld) b May 4, 1935 Lowood (Qld)

Bidstrup, Trevor Allan (WAust) b Dec. 29, 1937 Midland (WAust)

Biffin, Raymond Leo (Tas) b May 6, 1949 Launceston (Tas)

Biggs, Malcolm (Qld) b July 7, 1904 Caboolture (Qld) d Aug. 1, 1972 Ipswich (Qld)

Bill, Oscar Wendell (NSW) b April 8, 1909 Waverley (NSW) d May 10, 1988 Sydney (NSW)

Bingham, John Edmund (Tas) b July 15, 1864 Forcett (Tas) d July 23, 1946 Hobart (Tas)

Binney, Edgar James (Vic) b May 31, 1885 Port Tremayne (SAust) d Sept. 9, 1978 Brighton (Vic)

Birch, William Thomas (Tas) b Oct. 26, 1849 Hobart (Tas) d Aug. 18, 1897 Hobart (Tas)

Birchall, James Thomas Wardlaw (SAust) b Nov. 23, 1962 North Adelaide (SAust)

Bird, Thomas Robert (Vic) b Aug. 31, 1904 Collingwood (Vic) d April 12, 1979 Thornbury (Vic)

Bishop, Edward George (WAust) b Aug. 4, 1872 birthplace unknown d Feb. 16, 1943 Nedlands (WAust)

Bishop, Glenn Andrew (SAust) b Feb. 25, 1960 North Adelaide (SAust)

Bishop, Henry Symons (Vic) b Dec. 15, 1849 Torrington, Devon (England) d July 18, 1891 Prahran (Vic)

Bitmead, Robert Clyde (Vic) b July 17, 1942 Fitzroy (Vic)

Bizzell, Graham Maurice (Qld) b Nov. 19, 1941 Beenleigh (Qld)

Black, Alfred A. (Vic) birth details unknown d c. 1859

Black, George Gordon (NSW) b Jan. 19, 1885 Darling Point (NSW) d Dec. 6, 1954 Orange (NSW)

Black, Graham Ash (SAust) b May 14, 1924 Unley (SAust)

* Blackham, John McCarthy (Vic) b May 11, 1854 North Fitzroy (Vic) d Dec. 28, 1932 Melbourne (Vic)

* Blackie, Donald Dearness (Vic) b April 5, 1882 Bendigo (Vic) d April 18, 1955 South Melbourne (Vic)

Blackman, Oswald Colin (NSW) b March 9, 1942 Griffith (NSW)

Blackstock, John MacDonald (Qld) b Jan. 16, 1871 Drum, Thornhill, Edinburgh (Scotland) d post-1945 Sydney (NSW)

Blair, Dennis John (Tas) b Sept. 27, 1934 birthplace unknown

Blair, Gregory David (Tas & Vic) b Dec. 15, 1947 Launceston (Tas)

Blanchard, C. O. (Surrey) b c. 1842 d c. 1919 Newtown (NSW)

Blaxland, Marcus Herbert (NSW & Qld) b April 29, 1884 Callan Park (NSW) d July 31, 1958 Clayfield (Qld)

* Blewett, Gregory Scott (SAust) b Oct. 29, 1971 Adelaide (SAust)

Blewett, Robert Kevin (SAust) b March 30, 1943 Prospect (SAust)

Blinman, Harry (SAust) b Dec. 30, 1861 Adelaide (SAust) d July 23, 1950 Adelaide (SAust)

Blizzard, Phillip Ashley (Tas & NSW) b Feb. 6, 1958 Burnie (Tas)

Bloomfield, George Thomas (SAust) b Feb. 5, 1882 Bowden (SAust) d Nov. 1, 1958 Adelaide (SAust)

Blundell, George Robert (WAust) b April 19, 1896 Perth (WAust) d Feb. 11, 1940 West Perth (WAust)

Blundell, Norman Charles (Vic) b Sept. 2, 1917 North Carlton (Vic)

Blundell, Rex Pole (SAust) b May 8, 1942 Adelaide (SAust)

Blundell, William Walter (Vic) b Dec. 30, 1866 Majorca (Vic) d Feb. 28, 1946 Kensington (Vic)

Boag, Kenneth John (Qld) b Sept. 6, 1914 Toowoomba (Qld) d July 10, 1984 Port Kembla (NSW)

Boddam, Edmund Tudor (Tas) b Nov. 23, 1879 Hobart (Tas) d Sept. 9, 1959 New Town (Tas)

Bogle, James (NSW) b Jan. 4, 1893 Mossgiel (NSW) d Oct. 19, 1963 Southport (Qld)

Bolton, John Turner (Qld) b Oct. 3, 1888 Riverstone (NSW)

* Bonnor, George John (Vic & NSW) b Feb. 25, 1855 Bathurst (NSW) d June 27, 1912 East Orange (NSW)

* Boon, David Clarence (Tas) b Dec. 29, 1960 Launceston (Tas)

* Booth, Brian Charles (NSW) b Oct. 19, 1933 Perthville (NSW)

Booth, Ernest Brian Nelson (Tas) b Sept. 30, 1924 Scottsdale (Tas)

* Border, Allan Robert (NSW & Qld) b July 27, 1955 Cremorne (NSW)

Borgas, Cameron James (SAust) b Sept. 1, 1983 Flinders (SAust)

Bosley, Marcus Williams (NSW) b Aug. 10, 1897 Liverpool (NSW) d June 12, 1982 Newport (NSW)

* Botham, Ian Terence (Qld) b Nov. 24, 1955 Heswall, Cheshire (England)

Botham, Leslie John (Vic) b May 5, 1930 Hawthorn (Vic) d April 17, 1999 Melbourne (Vic)

Bott, Leonidas Cecil (WAust) b July 14, 1889 Adelaide (SAust) d Aug. 21, 1968 Perth (WAust)

Botten, Robert Dyas (SAust) b Oct. 11, 1853 Lewisham, Kent (England) d April 26, 1935 Medindie (SAust)

Boulter, Edward Samuel (Vic) b March 23, 1886 North Fitzroy (Vic) d June 10, 1968 North Balwyn (Vic)

Bourne, Gordon Alister (Qld) b April 21, 1913 Tintenbar (NSW) d Sept. 13, 1993 Goomeri (Qld)

Bovell, Henry Edward Joseph (WAust) b March 15, 1936 East Fremantle (WAust)

Bowden, Albert John (NSW) b Sept. 28, 1874 Sydney (NSW) d Aug. 8, 1943 Northwood (NSW)

Bowden, Samuel Hedskis (Qld) b Sept. 29, 1867 Sydney (NSW) d Aug. 25, 1945 Manly (NSW)

Bowe, Ronald Doig (WAust) b Dec. 10, 1939 Beaconsfield (WAust)

Bower, Rodney John (NSW) b Nov. 30, 1959 Bankstown (NSW)

Bower, Timothy Donald (Tas) b Sept. 10, 1968 Devonport (Tas)

Bowler, Peter Duncan (Tas) b July 30, 1963 Plymouth, Devon (England)

Bowley, Bruce Leonard (SAust) b Jan. 1, 1922 Clare (SAust)

Bowley, Edwin Leonard (SAust) b Feb. 27, 1888 Clare (SAust) d April 22, 1963 Woodville (SAust)

Bowman, Alcon Ninus Ascot (Vic) b May 10, 1862 Ascot Vale (Vic) d June 30, 1938 Surrey Hills (Vic)

Box, Henry (Vic) b c. Sept. 1837 Walsall, London, Staffordshire (England) d June 3, 1916 death place unknown

Boyce, Raymond Charles Manning (NSW) b June 28, 1891 Taree (NSW) d Jan. 20, 1941 Northwood (NSW)

Boyd, David Laurence (WAust) b Nov. 21, 1955 Kalgoorlie (WAust)

Boyd, Trevor Joseph (NSW) b Oct. 22, 1944 Nyngan (NSW)

* Boyle, Henry Frederick (Vic) b Dec. 10, 1847 Sydney (NSW) d Nov. 21, 1907 Bendigo (Vic)

Brabon, George William (Qld) b Aug. 2, 1957 Ayr (Qld)

Bracher, Herbert Henry Gladstone (Vic) b Aug. 28, 1886 Footscray (Vic) d Feb. 25, 1974 Hawthorn (Vic)

Bracken, Nathan Wayne (NSW) b Sept. 12, 1977 Penrith (NSW)

Bradbridge, John Sidney (NSW) b Dec. 1, 1831 Sydney (NSW) d July 14, 1905 Dulwich Hill (NSW)

Bradley, Craig Edwin (SAust & Vic) b Oct. 23, 1964 Ashford (SAust)

Bradley, William Francis (Qld) b Oct. 8, 1867 Brisbane (Qld) d Sept. 7, 1948 Ipswich (Qld)

* Bradman, Donald George (NSW & SAust) b Aug. 27, 1908 Cootamundra (NSW) d Feb. 25, 2001 Kensington Park (SAust)

Bradshaw, Keith (Tas) b Oct. 2, 1963 Hobart (Tas)

Bradstreet, Shawn David (NSW) b Feb. 28, 1972 Wollongong (NSW)

Braid, Rupert Lee (Vic) b March 3, 1888 Talbot (Vic) d Nov. 11, 1963 Upper Ferntree Gully (Vic)

Brain, Desmond Morrah (Tas) b Dec. 16, 1909 Hobart (Tas) d March 1, 1990 Tumut (NSW)

Brain, John Heather (Tas) b Feb. 9, 1905 Hobart (Tas) d June 21, 1961 Hobart (Tas)

Brain, Roy Albert (Tas) b Sept. 2, 1926 Hobart (Tas)

Braithwaite, Arthur (Tas) b Sept. 2, 1880 Rushworth (Vic) d c. 1953 Cheltenham (Vic)

Brakey, Gary Leslie (Combined XI) b Oct. 8, 1942 Wynyard (Tas) d Feb. 3, 1987 Killarney Heights (NSW)

Braslin, Leon Anthony (Tas) b May 12, 1938 New Norfolk (Tas)

Bratchford, James Douglas (Qld) b Feb. 2, 1929 Cleveland (Qld) d Oct. 5, 1997 on flight from USA to Australia

Braybrook, Clive (SAust) b Sept. 27, 1901 Goodwood (SAust) d July 16, 1985 Swan Hill (Vic)

Brayshaw, Ian James (WAust) b Jan. 14, 1942 South Perth (WAust)

Brayshaw, James Antony (WAust & SAust) b May 11, 1967 Subiaco (WAust)

Breman, Todd George (WAust) b Oct. 28, 1965 Subiaco (WAust)

Bremner, Colin David (Services) b Jan. 29, 1920 Hawthorn (Vic)

Brew, Francis Malcolm (Qld) b Jan. 5, 1903 Petrie Terrace (Qld) d Jan. 13, 1974 Sandgate (Qld)

Brewster, Robert Colin (NSW) b Aug. 17, 1867 Sydney (NSW) d Nov. 8, 1962 Killara (NSW)

Briant, George William (Tas) b c. 1828 Hackney, London, Middlesex (England) d May 10, 1914 Hobart (Tas)

Brideson, John Holmes (SAust) b July 9, 1856 Rushworth (Vic) d Feb. 1, 1898 Belair (SAust)

Bridgman, Hugh Hossick Mackay (SAust) b Feb. 1, 1890 Findon (SAust) d Dec. 3, 1953 Torrensville (SAust)

Briggs, Ronald Edward (NSW) b Sept. 22, 1929 Belmore (NSW)

* Bright, Raymond James (Vic) b July 13, 1954 Footscray (Vic)

Britt, Harold James (Vic) b May 6, 1911 Doncaster (Vic)

Broad, David John (Vic) b Sept. 25, 1953 Kew (Vic)

Broad, Wayne Ronald (Qld) b June 20, 1956 Brisbane (Qld)

Broadby, Christopher Laurence (Tas) b March 17, 1959 Hobart (Tas)

Brodie, James Chalmers (Vic) b Sept. 28, 1820 Perth, Perthshire (Scotland) d Feb. 19, 1912 Balwyn (Vic)

Brodie, Richard Sinclair (Vic) b Sept. 9, 1813 County Caithness (Scotland) d Jan. 18, 1872 Bulla Bulla (Vic)

* Bromley, Ernest Harvey (WAust & Vic) b Sept. 3, 1912 Fremantle (WAust) d Feb. 1, 1967 Clayton (Vic)

Brooks, Gordon Victor (SAust) b May 30, 1938 Ceduna (SAust)

Brooks, Thomas Francis (NSW) b March 28, 1919 Paddington (NSW)

Broomby, Reginald Arthur (Tas) b Jan. 6, 1905 Launceston (Tas) d May 10, 1984 Southport (Qld)

Broster, Paul Alexander (Vic) b Jan. 31, 1973 Wangaratta (Vic)

Broughton, Donald Ean (Tas) b Feb. 4, 1931 Hobart (Tas) d Dec. 11, 1987 Hobart (Tas)

Brown, Albert Ernest (Vic) b Dec. 22, 1890 Clifton Hill (Vic) d Nov. 17, 1954 Northcote (Vic)

Brown, Anthony Norman (Qld) b March 30, 1961 Herston (Qld)

Brown, Craig Franklin Archer (Tas) b Jan. 25, 1954 Hobart (Tas)

Brown, Edward (NSW) b c. Jan. 1837 Uppingham, Rutland (England) d full death details unknown

Brown, Edward Keith Faulkner (NSW) b March 7, 1891 Newcastle (NSW) d March 12, 1949 Bowenfels (NSW)

Brown, Graham Campbell (Vic) b May 9, 1944 Burwood (Vic)

Brown, Guy Archibald Loeman (Qld) b July 31, 1884 Dalby (Qld) d March 21, 1958 New Farm (Qld)

Brown, John (Qld) b May 13, 1943 Mt Morgan (Qld)

Brown, Kevin Ronald (Tas) b July 1, 1941 Devonport (Tas)

Brown, Norman Eric (Vic) b April 1, 1889 North Fitzroy (Vic) d July 7, 1962 Carrum (Vic)

Brown, Raymond Kinnear (Tas) b Nov. 3, 1950 New Norfolk (Tas)

Brown, Roger Leedham (Tas) b Aug. 9, 1959 Launceston (Tas)

Brown, Vallancey Kennedy (Vic) b Dec. 7, 1912 Ashfield (NSW) d Oct. 24, 1987 Melbourne (Vic)

Brown, Walter Graham Fairfax (NSW) b April 12, 1899 Summer Hill (NSW) d May 21, 1931 Mosman (NSW)

Brown, Wilfred Martin (Qld) b March 21, 1930 Warwick (Qld)

Brown, William (Tas) b c. 1807 (England) d Aug. 28, 1859 Hobart (Tas)

* Brown, William Alfred (NSW & Qld) b July 31, 1912 Toowoomba (Qld)

Browne, William Creighton (Qld) b Nov. 6, 1898 Toowoomba (Qld) d Oct. 25, 1980 Southport (Qld)

Browning, George Richard (Vic) b Dec. 12, 1858 Hepburn (Vic) d Oct. 9, 1900 North Carlton (Vic)

Brownlow, Bertie (Tas) b May 22, 1920 Portland (NSW)

* Bruce, William (Vic) b May 22, 1864 South Yarra (Vic) d Aug. 3, 1925 Elwood (Vic)

Bryant, Francis Joseph (WAust) b Nov. 7, 1907 Perth (WAust) d March 11, 1984 Glendalough (WAust)

Bryant, James Mark (Vic) b 1826 birth day and month unknown Caterham, Surrey (England) d Dec. 10, 1881 Sale (Vic)

Bryant, Richard (NSW) b c. 1847 Maitland (NSW) d Oct. 27, 1931 Stockton (NSW)

Bryant, Richard John (WAust) b May 8, 1904 Perth (WAust) d Aug. 17, 1989 Mt Lawley (WAust)

Bryant, William James (WAust) b Jan. 15, 1906 Perth (WAust) d Jan. 1, 1995 Perth (WAust)

Bryce, William Cecil James (Qld) b Aug. 18, 1911 Maryborough (Qld) d Feb. 8, 1986 Spring Hill (Qld)

Bubb, Ernest Reinhard (NSW) b Dec. 6, 1884 Summer Hill (NSW) d Nov. 26, 1946 Neutral Bay (NSW)

Bubb, Roy Alfred Reinhard (NSW) b June 23, 1900 Darlinghurst (NSW) d April 4, 1965 Hamilton (NSW)

Buchanan, John Marshall (Qld) b April 5, 1953 Ipswich (Qld)

Buckingham, Danny James (Tas) b Dec. 2, 1964 Burnie (Tas)

Buckle, Frank (NSW) b Nov. 11, 1891 Pyrmont (NSW) d June 4, 1982 Sydney (NSW)

Buckle, William Harvey (Qld) b June 3, 1943 Wooloowin (Qld)

Buggins, Bruce Leonard (WAust) b Jan. 29, 1935 Perth (WAust)

Bull, Desmond Frederick Earl (Qld) b Aug. 13, 1935 Brisbane (Qld)

Bull, Eric Alister (NSW) b Sept. 28, 1886 Bourke (NSW) d May 14, 1954 Mt Kuring-Gai (NSW)

Bullough, Walter (SAust) b Oct. 21, 1855 Hunslet, Yorkshire (England) d Sept. 17, 1888 Hindmarsh (SAust)

Burchett, Alfred (Vic) b 1831 birth day and month unknown London (England) d Nov. 12, 1888 St Kilda (Vic)

Burchett, Frederick (Vic) b 1824 birth day and month unknown London (England) d July 16, 1861 Melbourne (Vic)

* Burge, Peter John Parnell (Qld) b May 17, 1932 Kangaroo Point (Qld)

* Burke, James Wallace (NSW) b June 12, 1930 Mosman (NSW) d Feb. 2, 1979 Manly (NSW)

* Burn, Edwin James Kenneth (Tas) b Sept. 17, 1862 Richmond (Tas) d July 20, 1956 Hobart (Tas)

Burn, James Henry (Tas) b July 31, 1849 Hobart (Tas), death details unknown

Burns, Harold Vincent (Qld) b May 20, 1908 Ebagoolah (Qld) d June 6, 1944 Cairns (Qld)

Burrows, Arthur Owen (Tas) b Oct. 17, 1903 Hobart (Tas) d Jan. 4, 1984 Sandy Bay (Tas)

Burrows, Ian Donald (Combined XI) b Nov. 20, 1944 Hobart (Tas)

Burrows, J. (NSW) b Dec. 12, 1903 Hillgrove (NSW), d Feb. 14, 1959 (NSW)

Burt, Selby John Wright (NSW) b Dec. 12, 1903 Hillgrove (NSW) d Feb. 14, 1959 Camperdown (NSW)

* Burton, Frederick John (NSW & Vic) b Nov. 2, 1865 Collingwood (Vic) d Aug. 25, 1929 Wanganui (New Zealand)

Burton, Garth (SAust) b Jan. 21, 1913 Black Forest (SAust) d Sept. 6, 1993 South Brighton (SAust)

Burton, Jack Richard (SAust) b Nov. 3, 1923 Cleve (SAust)

Bush, Giles Edmund Wreford (WAust) b Sept. 9, 1956 Subiaco (WAust)

* Butcher, Roland Orlando (Tas) b Oct. 14, 1953 East Point, St Philip (Barbados)

Butler, Charles William (Tas) b Sept. 18, 1854 Battery Point (Tas) d June 10, 1937 Sandy Bay (Tas)

Butler, Edward Henry (Tas & Vic) b March 15, 1851 Battery Point (Tas) d Jan. 5, 1928 Lower Sandy Bay (Tas)

Butler, Edward Lionel Austin (Tas) b April 10, 1883 Hobart (Tas) d Aug. 23, 1916 Puchevillers (France)

Butler, Frank (Tas) b Nov. 13, 1889 Brighton (Vic) d May 8, 1965 Kew (Vic)

Butler, Walter John (WAust) b May 30, 1882 Port Adelaide (SAust) d March 12, 1966 Bruce Rock (WAust)

Butterworth, Benjamin (Vic) b 1832 birth day and month unknown Rochdale, Lancashire (England) d Jan. 6, 1879 Chiswick, Middlesex (England)

Butterworth, Thomas (Vic) b Dec. 17, 1828 Rochdale, Lancashire (England) d July 15, 1877 Kensington, London, Middlesex (England)

Buttsworth, Frederick James (WAust) b May 29, 1927 North Perth (WAust)

Buttsworth, Frederick Richard (WAust) b April 28, 1880 Wilberforce (NSW) d Feb. 26, 1974 Perth (WAust)

Buttsworth, Wallace Francis (WAust) b Jan. 21, 1917 North Perth (WAust)

Byfield, Arnold Stanley (WAust) b Nov. 1, 1923 Northam (WAust)

Byrne, Thomas (Qld) b July 11, 1868 Paterson (NSW) d Dec. 19, 1951 Herston (Qld)

Caban, Timothy Kenneth (Qld) b Feb. 15, 1952 Cessnock (NSW)

Caffyn, William (NSW) b Feb. 2, 1828 Reigate, Surrey (England) d Aug. 28, 1919 Reigate, Surrey (England)

Cahill, Keyran William Jack (Tas) b Dec. 3, 1911 Hobart (Tas) d March 7, 1966 Launceston (Tas)

Cain, William (Qld) b Dec. 17, 1899 Paddington (Qld) d Dec. 24, 1981 Sherwood (Qld)

Calder, Henry (WAust) b July 3, 1906 Guildford (WAust) d Aug. 27, 1970 South Perth (WAust)

Caldwell, Tim Charles John (NSW) b Oct. 29, 1913 Clayfield (Qld) d June 17, 1994 Orange (NSW)

Callachor, John Joseph Casimir (NSW) b Nov. 10, 1857 Woolloomooloo (NSW) d Feb. 20, 1924 Lane Cove (NSW)

Callaway, Norman Frank (NSW) b April 5, 1896 Hay (NSW) d May 3, 1917 Bullecourt (France)

* Callaway, Sydney Thomas (NSW) b Feb. 6, 1868 Redfern (NSW) d Nov. 25, 1923 Christchurch (New Zealand)

* Callen, Ian Wayne (Vic) b May 2, 1955 Alexandra (Vic)

Calvert, Derreck (Tas) b Dec. 22, 1919 South Arm (Tas)

Cameron, Robert Alastair (SAust) b Sept. 6, 1938 North Adelaide (SAust)

Cameron, Verney Lovett (Vic) b c. 1842 Sorrento (Vic) d May 27, 1881 Richmond (Vic)

Campbell, Blair Maismore (Vic & Tas) b Aug. 20, 1946 Kew (Vic)

Campbell, Colin Mansfield (Tas) b Aug. 13, 1872 Cressy (Tas) d April 3, 1907 Winlaton, Northumberland (Eng)

Campbell, Donald (Vic) b Sept. 18, 1851 Loddon Plains (Vic) d Sept. 14, 1887 South Yarra (Vic)

Campbell, Francis Beresford (Tas) b April 20, 1867 Hobart (Tas) d c. 1929 Ryde (NSW)

Campbell, Gordon Cathcart (SAust) b June 4, 1885 Myrtle Bank (SAust) d Aug. 13, 1961 Woodville South (SAust)

* Campbell, Gregory Dale (Tas) b March 10, 1964 Launceston (Tas)

Campbell, Ivan James (WAust) b Oct. 29, 1908 Perth (WAust) d Jan. 22, 1962 Hollywood (WAust)

Campbell, James Norval (NSW) b Sept. 21, 1908 Chatswood (NSW) d Sept. 11, 1973 St Ives (NSW)

Campbell, Leslie Percy (NSW) b Oct. 14, 1902 Marrickville (NSW) d Aug. 19, 1970 Southport (Qld)

Campbell, Malcolm MacDonald (Qld) b Jan. 7, 1881 Ipswich (Qld) d Dec. 14, 1967 Ipswich (Qld)

Campbell, Ryan John (WAust) b Feb. 7, 1972 Osborne Park (WAust)

Campbell, Stoddart William Grylls (Vic) b Sept. 19, 1846 Melbourne (Vic) d Sept. 2, 1903 East Melbourne (Vic)

Camphin, William Joseph (NSW) b Nov. 13, 1867 Sydney (NSW) d Sept. 11, 1942 Quirindi (NSW)

Campling, Campbell Roy (NSW) b April 3, 1892 Burwood (NSW) d April 21, 1977 Greenwich (NSW)

Canning, Tamahau (Cricket Academy) b April 7, 1977 Adelaide (SAust)

Cannon, William Henry (Vic) b Sept. 11, 1871 Eaglehawk (Vic) d April 29, 1933 North Fitzroy (Vic)

Cantrell, Peter Edward (Qld) b Oct. 28, 1962 Gunnedah (NSW)

Cantwell, Hubert Richard (WAust) b Oct. 24, 1905 Warbleton, Sussex (England) d April 22, 1956 Esperance (WAust)

Capes, Peter Andrew (WAust) b Feb. 26, 1962 East Fremantle (WAust)

Carew, James (Qld) b Jan. 23, 1872 Pine Mountain (Qld) d Sept. 1, 1950 Kelvin Grove (Qld)

Carew, Patrick (Qld) b Sept. 8, 1875 Pine Mountain (Qld) d March 31, 1942 Queanbeyan (NSW)

Carew, Paul John (Qld & SAust) b July 9, 1967 South Brisbane (Qld)

* Carkeek, William (Vic) b Oct. 17, 1878 Walhalla (Vic) d Feb. 20, 1937 Prahran (Vic)
* Carlson, Phillip Henry (Qld) b Aug. 8, 1951 Nundah (Qld)
Carlson, Victor Charles (WAust) b July 16, 1893 Adelaide (SAust) d Feb. 23, 1974 Perth (WAust)
Carlton, Alfred Robert (Vic) b Nov. 13, 1867 Bacchus Marsh (Vic) d Sept. 10, 1941 Camberwell (Vic)
Carlton, John (Vic & Qld) b July 6, 1866 Bacchus Marsh (Vic) d Aug. 13, 1945 Parkville (Vic)
Carlton, Thomas Andrew (Vic & SAust) b Dec. 8, 1890 Footscray (Vic) d Dec. 17, 1973 Brunswick (Vic)
Carlton, William (Vic) b May 22, 1876 Fitzroy (Vic) d Dec. 23, 1959 Parkville (Vic)
Carlyon, Norman Murdoch (Vic) b May 5, 1938 East Melbourne (Vic)
Carmichael, Ian Robert (SAust) b Dec. 17, 1960 Hull, Yorkshire (England)
Carmody, Douglas Keith (NSW & WAust) b Feb. 16, 1919 Mosman (NSW) d Oct. 21, 1977 Concord (NSW)
Carney, Brian William (Tas) b June 2, 1931 Launceston (Tas)
Carr, Charles Seymour (Vic) b Nov. 22, 1849 (Jamaica) d March 30, 1921 East Melbourne (Vic)
Carracher, Arthur James (SAust) b July 7, 1867 Heywood (Vic) d Oct. 15, 1935 North Adelaide (SAust)
Carragher, Edward John (SAust) b May 24, 1891 Broken Hill (NSW) d Nov. 28, 1977 Broken Hill (NSW)
Carrigan, Aubrey Herbert (Qld) b Aug. 26, 1917 Zillmere (Qld)
Carroll, Edmund Louis (Vic) b Oct. 22, 1886 Albert Park (Vic) d June 6, 1959 Ormond (Vic)
Carroll, Eugene Vincent (Vic) b Jan. 17, 1885 South Melbourne (Vic) d Sept. 18, 1965 Elsternwick (Vic)
Carroll, Sidney Joseph (NSW) b Nov. 28, 1922 Willoughby (NSW) d Oct. 12, 1984 Willoughby (NSW)
Carroll, Thomas Davis (Tas) b Feb. 26, 1884 Hobart (Tas) d June 3, 1957 Hobart (Tas)
Carseldine, Lee Andrew (Qld) b Nov. 17, 1975 Nambour (Qld)
Carter, Alfred Snowden (Vic) b March 1, 1869 Kew (Vic) d June 7, 1920 Camberwell (Vic)
Carter, Edmund Sardinson (Vic) b Feb. 3, 1845 Malton, Yorkshire (England) d May 23, 1923 Scarborough, Yorkshire (England)
Carter, Edwin Lewis (Vic) b May 2, 1925 Caulfield (Vic)
* Carter, Hanson (NSW) b March 15, 1878 Halifax, Yorkshire (England) d June 8, 1948 Bellevue Hill (NSW)

Carter, Reginald Clarence (WAust) b March 1, 1888 Brunswick East (Vic) d July 16, 1970 Subiaco (WAust)
Carter, William Jack Sydney (NSW) b Dec. 7, 1907 Randwick (NSW) d Aug. 19, 1995 Penshurst (NSW)
Cartledge, Brian Lewis (Tas) b March 3, 1941 Smithton (Tas)
Cary, Sean Ross (WAust) b March 10, 1971 Subiaco (WAust)
Cass, George Rodney (Tas) b April 23, 1940 Overton, Yorkshire (Eng)
Cassell, Jerry Lee (Qld) b Jan. 12, 1975 Mona Vale (NSW)
Castle, David James (Tas) b May 25, 1972 Launceston (Tas)
Catchlove, Walter Evered (SAust) b Feb. 24, 1907 North Adelaide (SAust) d April 12, 1997 Glen Osmond (SAust)
Caterer, Thomas Ainslie (SAust) b May 16, 1858 Woodville (SAust) d Aug. 25, 1924 Walkerville (SAust)
Causby, Barry Leon (SAust) b Sept. 9, 1948 Adelaide (SAust)
Causby, John Phillip (SAust) b Oct. 27, 1942 Hindmarsh (SAust)
Cavenagh, George (Vic) b June 16, 1836 Sydney (NSW) d Nov. 23, 1922 Albert Park (Vic)
Chadwick, Derek (WAust) b March 21, 1941 Busselton (WAust)
Chamberlain, Cornelius Thomas (SAust) b c. 1882 (Ireland) d Nov. 14, 1943 Rose Park (SAust)
Chamberlain, John Aloysius (SAust) b Aug. 29, 1884 Glanville (SAust) d April 1, 1941 Leabrook (SAust)
Chamberlain, William Leonard (SAust) b Jan. 15, 1889 Port Adelaide (SAust) d March 21, 1956 Darlinghurst (NSW)
Chambers, John Lindsay (Vic) b Oct. 14, 1930 Geelong (Vic)
Chancellor, Frederick Edgar (Tas) b Aug. 28, 1878 Hobart (Tas) d June 16, 1939 Hobart (Tas)
Chapman, Frederick Douglas (Vic) b March 21, 1901 Clifton Hill (Vic) d June 27, 1964 Northcote (Vic)
Chapman, George Arthur Northcote (NSW) b April 21, 1904 Chatswood (NSW)
Chapman, Henry William (Qld) b Jan. 1, 1868 birthplace and death details unknown
Chapman, Lawrence Gordon (Qld) b June 25, 1928 Tingalpa (Qld)
Chapman, Ross Albert (NSW) b Oct. 22, 1952 New Lambton (NSW)
* Chappell, Gregory Stephen (SAust & Qld) b Aug. 7, 1948 Unley (SAust)
* Chappell, Ian Michael (SAust) b Sept. 26, 1943 Unley (SAust)
* Chappell, Trevor Martin (SAust, WAust & NSW) b Oct. 12, 1952 Glenelg (SAust)

Chardon, David Michael (NSW) b Dec. 12, 1951 Newtown (NSW)

Charlesworth, Lester (WAust) b Oct. 11, 1916 Kanowna (WAust) d Jan. 15, 1980 Perth (WAust)

Charlesworth, Richard Ian (WAust) b Dec. 6, 1952 Subiaco (WAust)

* Charlton, Percie Chater (NSW) b April 9, 1867 Surry Hills (NSW) d Sept. 30, 1954 Pymble (NSW)

Chee Quee, Richard (NSW) b Jan. 4, 1971 Camperdown (NSW)

Cheetham, Albert George (NSW) b Dec. 7, 1915 Ryde (NSW) d May 23, 1997 Sandringham (Vic)

Chegwyn, John William (NSW) b March 18, 1909 Botany (NSW) d May 26, 1992 Sydney (NSW)

Chillingworth, Garry Andrew (SAust) b Jan. 23, 1970 Sutherland (NSW)

Chilvers, Hugh Cecil (NSW) b Oct. 26, 1902 Sawbridgeworth, Hertfordshire (England) d Dec. 1, 1994 Sydney (NSW)

Chinner, Hubert George Williams (SAust) b Aug. 30, 1870 Brighton (SAust) d June 12, 1953 Unley Park (SAust)

* Chipperfield, Arthur Gordon (NSW) b Nov. 17, 1905 Ashfield (NSW) d July 29, 1987 Ryde (NSW)

Chittleborough, Henry Carew (SAust) b April 14, 1861 Wallaroo (SAust) d June 25, 1925 Malvern (SAust)

Chivers, Alfred Percy (Vic) b Aug. 15, 1908 Templestowe (Vic) d July 11, 1997 Templestowe (Vic)

Christ, Charles Percival (Qld) b June 10, 1911 Paddington (Qld) d Jan. 22, 1998 Redcliffe (Qld)

Christensen, Robert Thomas (SAust) b Oct. 31, 1959 Hindmarsh (SAust)

Christian, Arthur Hugh (Vic & WAust) b Jan. 22, 1877 Richmond (Vic) d Sept. 8, 1950 Claremont (WAust)

Christy, Frederick Collier (Surrey) b Sept. 9, 1822 birthplace and death details unknown

* Christy, James Alexander Joseph (Qld) b Dec. 12, 1904 Pretoria (South Africa) d Feb. 1, 1971 Durban (South Africa)

Chyer, Darren Scott (SAust) b July 28, 1966 Glenelg (SAust)

Clark, Anthony Michael (NSW) b March 23, 1977 St Leonards (NSW)

Clark, Donald Jack (Tas) b Jan. 19, 1914 Hobart (Tas) d Aug. 16, 1994 Hobart (Tas)

Clark, Henry Judge (WAust) b April 23, 1892 Sydney (NSW) d Feb. 8, 1973 Perth (WAust)

Clark, James Patrick (Qld) b March 14, 1871 (Qld) d June 6, 1941 Coolangatta (Qld)

Clark, John Lawrence (Qld & NSW) b Oct. 14, 1928 Paddington (NSW)

Clark, Stuart Rupert (NSW) b Sept. 28, 1975 Caringbah (NSW)

* Clark, Wayne Maxwell (WAust) b Sept. 19, 1953 Perth (WAust)

Clarke, Alfred Edward (NSW) b April 6, 1868 Surry Hills (NSW) d Sept. 16, 1940 Wellington (New Zealand)

Clarke, David Alexander (SAust) b Jan. 25, 1970 Adelaide (SAust)

Clarke, Gerard John (Vic) b Dec. 31, 1966 Malvern (Vic)

Clarke, Gother Robert Carlisle (NSW) b April 27, 1875 North Sydney (NSW) d Oct. 12, 1917 Zonnebeke (Belgium)

Clarke, Graham Cornelius (SAust) b July 10, 1939 Laura (SAust)

Clarke, John Turner (NSW) b c. 1829 d Feb. 29, 1872 Bourke (NSW)

Clarke, Michael John (NSW) b April 2, 1981 Liverpool (NSW)

Claxton, Norman (SAust) b Nov. 2, 1877 North Adelaide (SAust) d Dec. 5, 1951 North Adelaide (SAust)

Claxton, William David Hambridge (SAust) b June 2, 1857 Kensington (SAust) d March 12, 1937 Glenelg (SAust)

Clay, Ivor Thomas (Tas) b May 7, 1915 Bendigo (Vic) d Aug. 12, 1958 Essendon (Vic)

Clayton, Nicholas George (Tas) b March 11, 1826 Norfolk Plains (Tas) d c. 1865 Auckland (New Zealand)

Cleary, Edward Joseph (Vic) b April 18, 1913 Benalla (Vic) d April 6, 1985 Benalla (Vic)

Cleeve, John Oatley (NSW) b Feb. 14, 1864 Sydney (NSW) d Feb. 8, 1909 Moree (NSW)

Clem, Gordon Rex (Qld) b July 5, 1909 Milora (Qld) d March 3, 1970 Melbourne (Vic)

Clements, Peter John (SAust) b Jan. 23, 1953 Glenelg (SAust)

Clements, Shane Clifton (WAust) b June 28, 1958 Middle Swan (WAust) d April 22, 2001 Inglewood (WAust)

Clews, Mark Lindsay (NSW) b Jan. 13, 1952 Grange (SAust)

Clifford, Peter Stanley (NSW & Qld) b Nov. 4, 1959 Bellingen (NSW)

Clingeleffer, Sean Geoffrey (Tas) b May 9, 1980 Hobart (Tas)

Clingly, Michael Thomas (SAust) b April 18, 1932 Prospect (SAust)

Clough, Peter Michael (Tas & WAust) b Aug. 17, 1956 Sydney (NSW)

Clutterbuck, Stanley Herwin (SAust) b May 27, 1888 Kapunda (SAust) d Jan. 24, 1972 Adelaide (SAust)

Coates, Joseph (NSW) b Nov. 13, 1844 Huddersfield, Yorkshire (England) d Sept. 9, 1896 Sydney (NSW)

Coats, James (Qld) b Feb. 26, 1914 Annerley (Qld)

Cobcroft, Leslie Thomas (NSW) b Feb. 12, 1867 Muswellbrook (NSW) d March 9, 1938 Wellington (New Zealand)

Cockburn, James Sydney David (Qld) b May 20, 1916 Maryborough (Qld) d Nov. 13, 1990 Herston (Qld)

Cockburn, William Frederick (Vic) b Nov. 28, 1916 Richmond (Vic)

Cody, Leslie Alwyn (NSW & Vic) b Oct. 11, 1890 Paddington (NSW) d Aug. 10, 1969 Toorak (Vic)

Cohen, Bertram Louis (Vic) b Sept. 25, 1892 London (England) d June 30, 1955 North Caulfield (Vic)

Cohen, Morton Barnett (NSW) b Sept. 19, 1913 Paddington (NSW) d Jan. 14, 1968 Vaucluse (NSW)

Colegrave, Mark David (Tas) b July 1, 1970 Hobart (Tas)

Colgan, Gregory (WAust) b Nov. 5, 1953 Subiaco (WAust)

* Colley, David John (NSW) b March 15, 1947 Mosman (NSW)

Colley, Timothy Peter Michael (SAust) b July 10, 1935 Sydney (NSW)

Collins, Frank Henry Kenneth (SAust) b Dec. 16, 1910 Queenstown (SAust) d Jan 24, 2001 Penola (SAust)

Collins, Frederick Bisset (Vic) b Feb. 25, 1881 Richmond (Vic) d Oct. 4, 1917 Ypres (Belgium)

* Collins, Herbert Leslie (NSW) b Jan. 21, 1888 Randwick (NSW) d May 28, 1959 Little Bay (NSW)

Collins, Ross Phillip (NSW) b Dec. 9, 1945 Paddington (NSW)

Collins, Vincent A (NSW) b c. 1917 Newtown (NSW) d Oct. 30, 1989 Sunnybank (Qld)

Collins, William Anthony (Tas) b Dec. 9, 1837 Launceston (Tas) d Jan. 12, 1876 Launceston (Tas)

Colreavy, Bernard Xavier (NSW) b June 30, 1871 Dripstone (NSW) d Nov. 30, 1946 Dubbo (NSW)

Combes, Geoffrey Arthur (Tas) b May 19, 1913 Greymouth (New Zealand) d Feb. 4, 1997 Woodstock near Huonville (Tas)

Combes, Maxwell James (Tas) b July 29, 1911 Greymouth (New Zealand) d March 10, 1983 Longley (Tas)

* Coningham, Arthur (NSW & Qld) b July 14, 1863 South Melbourne (Vic) d June 13, 1939 Gladesville (NSW)

Connell, Thomas William Christopher (NSW) b March 4, 1869 Invercargill (New Zealand) d Aug. 5, 1916 Mascot (NSW)

* Connolly, Alan Norman (Vic) b June 29, 1939 Skipton (Vic)

Connor, Gerald O'Grady (WAust & Tas) b Sept. 15, 1932 Perth (WAust) d Sept. 5, 1993 Perth (WAust)

Considine, Bernard Thomas (Vic & Tas) b April 8, 1925 Ararat (Vic) d June 4, 1989 (Qld)

Conway, John (Vic) b Feb. 3, 1842 Fyansford (Vic) d Aug. 22, 1909 Frankston (Vic)

Cook, Bernard William (Qld) b March 15, 1879 Torquay, Devon (England) d March 15, 1944 Sherwood (Qld)

Cook, Bruce (NSW) b Oct. 24, 1914 Orange (NSW) d Jan. 2, 1981 Balgowlah (NSW)

Cook, Geoffrey Glover (Qld) b June 29, 1910 Chelmer (Qld) d Sept. 12, 1982 Chelmer (Qld)

Cook, Russell Frederick (Vic) b Sept. 23, 1947 South Melbourne (Vic)

* Cook, Simon Hewitt (Vic & NSW) b Jan. 29, 1972 Hastings (Vic)

Cooke, Colin John (Qld) b Nov. 21, 1947 Harrisville (Qld)

Cooley, Troy James (Tas) b Dec. 9, 1965 Launceston (Tas)

Coombe, Ephraim Henry (SAust) b Aug. 26, 1858 Gawler (SAust) d April 5, 1917 Semaphore (SAust)

Coombe, Percy Howard (SAust) b Jan. 7, 1880 Brompton (SAust) d July 28, 1947 Prospect (SAust)

Coombe, Thomas Melrose (WAust) b Dec. 3, 1873 Gladstone (SAust) d July 22, 1959 London (England)

Cooper, Allan Ferguson (NSW) b March 18, 1916 Sydney (NSW) d Sept. 7, 1970 Concord (NSW)

* Cooper, Bransby Beauchamp (Vic) b March 15, 1844 Dacca (India) d Aug. 7, 1914 Geelong (Vic)

Cooper, Bryce Arnott (NSW) b Dec. 19, 1905 Lewisham (NSW)

Cooper, Duncan Elphinstone (Vic) b c. 1813 (India) d Nov. 22, 1904 Paddington, London (England)

Cooper, George Henry (Qld) b Feb. 15, 1907 Gympie (Qld) d Jan. 3, 2000 Mudgeeraba (Qld)

Cooper, John Richard (Qld) b July 11, 1922 Lilydale (Vic)

Cooper, Lewis Dale (Qld) b May 14, 1937 Mackay (Qld)

* Cooper, William Henry (Vic) b Sept. 11, 1849 Maidstone, Kent (England) d April 5, 1939 Malvern (Vic)

Cooper, William Osborne (SAust) b Feb. 13, 1891 North Adelaide (SAust) d June 28, 1930 Glenelg (SAust)

Corbett, Troy Frederick (Vic) b Oct. 10, 1972 Ouyen (Vic)

Cordner, John Pruen (Vic) b March 20, 1929 Diamond Creek (Vic)

Cordner, Laurence Osmaston (Vic) b Feb. 7, 1911 Warrnambool (Vic) d July 11, 1992 Penshurst (Vic)

* Corling, Grahame Edward (NSW) b July 13, 1941 Newcastle (NSW)

Cormack, Geoffrey Fairhurst (Vic) b Feb. 26, 1929 Camberwell (Vic)

Cornelius, William John (Vic) b Feb. 17, 1915 Port Melbourne (Vic)

Corstorphin, Colin James (Vic) b July 20, 1954 Bairnsdale (Vic) d Sept. 4, 1998 Melbourne (Victoria)

Cosgrave, Bryan (Vic) b March 23, 1903 Clifton Hill (Vic) d Nov. 22, 1992 Melbourne (Vic)

Cosgrave, James (Vic) b March 16, 1932 Parkville (Vic)

* Cosier, Gary John (Vic, SAust & Qld) b April 25, 1953 Richmond (Vic)

Cossart, Charles Edward (Qld) b Sept. 2, 1885 Rosewood (Qld) d June 6, 1963 Boonah (Qld)

Cosstick, Samuel (Vic & NSW) b Jan. 1, 1836 Croydon, Surrey (England) d April 8, 1896 West Maitland (NSW)

* Cottam, John Thomas (NSW) b Sept. 5, 1867 Strawberry Hills (NSW) d Jan. 30, 1897 Coolgardie (WAust)

* Cotter, Albert (NSW) b Dec. 3, 1884 Sydney (NSW) d Oct. 31, 1917 Beersheba (Palestine)

Cotter, Denis Francis (Vic) b c. 1862 Fitzroy (Vic) d Nov. 18, 1905 North Fitzroy (Vic)

Cotton, Edward Kenneth (NSW) b Aug. 8, 1929 Paddington (NSW)

Cotton, Harold Norman Jack (SAust) b Dec. 3, 1914 Prospect (SAust) d April 6, 1966 Malvern (SAust)

Coulson, Craig Edward (WAust) b June 13, 1967 South Perth (WAust)

Coulstock, Richard (Vic) b c. 1823 Surrey (England) d Dec. 15, 1870 South Melbourne (Vic)

* Coulthard, George (Vic) b Aug. 1, 1856 Boroondara (Vic) d Oct. 22, 1883 Carlton (Vic)

Courtice, Brian Andrew (Qld) b March 30, 1961 South Brisbane (Qld)

Courtney, Nicholas Charles Palliser (Tas) b July 18, 1967 Launceston (Tas)

Coverdale, Miles Colquhoun (Tas) b Aug. 4, 1846 Richmond (Tas) d April 3, 1898 Hobart (Tas)

Cowan, Robert Francis (SAust) b May 3, 1880 Angaston (SAust) d Nov. 11, 1962 Neutral Bay (NSW)

Cowley, Ian Arthur (Tas) b March 20, 1937 Launceston (Tas)

Cowley, Owen William (NSW & Qld) b Dec. 14, 1868 Port Louis (Mauritius) d Feb. 27, 1922 Brisbane (Qld)

Cowley, Terence John (Tas) b July 17, 1928 Evandale (Tas)

Cowmeadow, Garry John (Tas) b Aug. 21, 1954 Huonville (Tas)

Cowper, David Raymond (Vic) b Jan. 25, 1939 Kew (Vic)

Cowper, George (NSW) b c. 1858 full birth and death details unknown

* Cowper, Robert Maskew (Vic & WAust) b Oct. 5, 1940 Kew (Vic)

Cox, Douglas Edward (Qld) b July 9, 1919 West End (Qld) d Jan. 9, 1982 Dakabin (Qld)

Cox, Jamie (Tas) b Oct. 15, 1969 Burnie (Tas)

Cox, John (Tas & Vic) b 1823 birth day and month unknown Norfolk Plains (Tas) full birth and death details unknown

Cox, Michael John (WAust) b April 26, 1957 Newcastle (NSW)

Cox, Peter John (Vic) b Jan. 13, 1954 Mildura (Vic)

Cox, Richard (Tas) b April 21, 1830 Hobart (Tas) d March 27, 1865 Fingal (Tas)

Coyle, Timothy Charles (Tas) b July 22, 1960 Launceston (Tas)

Coyne, Thomas Harold (WAust) b Oct. 12, 1873 Tornagullah (Vic) d April 8, 1955 Christchurch (New Zealand)

* Craig, Ian David (NSW) b June 12, 1935 Yass (NSW)

Craig, Reginald Jack (SAust) b Aug. 3, 1916 North Adelaide (SAust) d April 17, 1985 Walker Flat (SAust)

Craig, Shawn Andrew Jacob (Vic) b June 23, 1973 Carlton (Vic)

Craigie, John Edwin (SAust) b Aug. 25, 1866 Adelaide (SAust) d Oct. 13, 1948 Gilberton (SAust)

Crane, Frederick Robert (Qld) b July 10, 1942 Mullumbimby (NSW)

Cranney, Harold (NSW) b Oct. 23, 1886 Parramatta (NSW) d Jan. 29, 1971 North Rocks (NSW)

* Crawford, John Neville (SAust) b Dec. 1, 1886 Cane Hill, Surrey (England) d May 2, 1963 Epsom, Surrey (England)

* Crawford, William Patrick Anthony (NSW) b Aug. 3, 1933 Dubbo (NSW)

Creevey, Brendan Neville (Qld) b Feb. 18, 1970 Charleville (Qld)

Cresswick, Ernest Albert (Qld) b Oct. 16, 1867 Newcastle (NSW) d Sept. 23, 1939 Waverley (NSW)

Creswick, Henry (Vic) b April 13, 1824 Sheffield, Yorkshire (England) d Oct. 24, 1892 Hawthorn (Vic)

Crippin, Ronald James (NSW) b April 23, 1947 Darlinghurst (NSW)

Cripps, Alan Edward (WAust) b Aug. 11, 1930 Lakemba (NSW)

Cristofani, Desmond Robert (NSW) b Nov. 14, 1920 Waverley (NSW)

Crompton, Colin Neil (Vic) b Aug. 16, 1937 Dandenong (Vic)

Crook, Andrew Richard (SAust) b Oct. 14, 1980 Modbury (SAust)

Crossan, Ernest Eric (NSW) b Nov. 3, 1914 Footscray (Vic)

Crouch, Edward Robert (Qld) b Jan. 11, 1873 Holborn, London, (England) d Aug. 8, 1962 South Brisbane (Qld)

Crouch, George Stanton (Qld) b Aug. 20, 1878 Strand, London, Middlesex (England) d Aug. 21, 1952 Indooroopilly (Qld)

Crow, Thomas Leslie (Vic) b Aug. 23, 1931 Hawthorn (Vic)

Crowden, Ian Bruce (Tas) b Feb. 22, 1933 Deloraine (Tas)

Crowder, Arthur Beaumont (Tas) b July 4, 1892 Sorell (Tas) d Feb. 16, 1964 Hobart (Tas)

* Crowe, Jeffrey John (SAust) b Sept. 14, 1958 Cornwall Park, Auckland (New Zealand)

Cruse, Bruce Andrew (Tas) b April 26, 1967 Launceston (Tas)

Cuff, Alan Gordon (Tas) b June 7, 1908 Launceston (Tas) d April 23, 1995 Launceston (Tas)

Cuff, Leonard Albert (Tas) b March 28, 1866 Christchurch (New Zealand) d Oct. 9, 1954 Launceston (Tas)

Cuffe, John Alexander (NSW) b June 26, 1880 Dubbo (NSW) d April 16, 1931 Burton-on-Trent, Staffordshire (England)

Cullen, Daniel Robert (NSW) b April 27, 1889 Balmain (NSW) d July 21, 1971 Concord (NSW)

Cullen, Geoff Ian (WAust) b March 16, 1977 Perth (WAust)

Cullen, William (NSW) b c. 1887 Wellington (New Zealand) d May 7, 1945 Double Bay (NSW)

Cullinan, Thomas (WAust) b (SAust) full birth details unknown d July 31, 1907 Fremantle (WAust)

Cumberland, Charles Brownlow (Vic) b c. 1801 d Nov. 27, 1882 Leamington, Warwickshire (England)

Cumming, Kenneth Roy (WAust) b April 12, 1916 East Coolgardie (WAust) d Oct. 11, 1988 Perth (WAust)

Cummins, Frank Septimus (NSW) b Aug. 8, 1906 West Maitland (NSW) d April 27, 1966 North Sydney (NSW)

Cunningham, Kenneth George (SAust) b July 26, 1939 Adelaide (SAust)

Currie, Ernest William (Qld) b April 9, 1873 Dunedin (New Zealand) d Oct. 23, 1932 Randwick (NSW)

Curtin, Barry George (SAust) b June 30, 1951 Rose Park (SAust)

Curtin, Paul (SAust) b May 10, 1954 Rose Park (SAust)

Curtin, Pearce William Edward (WAust) b Sept. 27, 1907 Boulder (WAust) d May 17, 1997 Canberra (ACT)

Curtin, Peter Donald (SAust) b Sept. 22, 1949 Rose Park (SAust)

Curtis, George Thomas (NSW) b Aug. 17, 1837 Sydney (NSW) d April 2, 1885 Darlinghurst (NSW)

Curtis, Louis David (SAust) b Aug. 5, 1928 Loxton (SAust)

Cush, Norman Lloyd (NSW) b Oct. 4, 1911 Glebe Point (NSW) d Jan. 22, 1983 Maroubra (NSW)

Cuthbert, Daniel Charles (Tas) b Feb. 2, 1846 Franklin (Tas) d July 6, 1912 Hobart (Tas)

* Dale, Adam Craig (Qld) b Dec. 30, 1968 Greensborough (Vic)

Daly, Anthony John (Tas) b July 25, 1969 Newcastle (NSW)

Daly, Thomas (Tas) b c. 1847 d Sept. 23, 1887 Inveresk (Tas)

Daniel, Jack (Vic) b Dec. 9, 1923 Leeds, Yorkshire (England)

* Daniel, Wayne Wendell (WAust) b Jan. 16, 1956 Brereton Village, St Philip (Barbados)

Dansie, Hampton Neil (SAust) b July 2, 1928 Nuriootpa (SAust)

D'Arcy, D (NSW) birth and death details unknown

Darke, William Floyd (Vic) b July 24, 1846 Sydney (NSW) d Jan. 24, 1925 Elsternwick (Vic)

* Darling, Joseph (SAust) b Nov. 21, 1870 Glen Osmond (SAust) d Jan. 2, 1946 Hobart (Tas)

* Darling, Leonard Stuart (Vic) b Aug. 14, 1909 South Yarra (Vic) d June 24, 1992 Daw Park (SAust)

* Darling, Warrick Maxwell (SAust) b May 1, 1957 Waikerie (SAust)

Davey, John Richard (SAust) b Aug. 26, 1957 Bournemouth, Hampshire (England)

Davey, John Ryan (SAust) b Sept. 20, 1913 Broken Hill (NSW) d Sept. 6, 1992 Unley (SAust)

Davidson, Alan Andrew (Vic) b July 14, 1897 Brunswick (Vic) d Aug. 1, 1962 Ringwood (Vic)

* Davidson, Alan Keith (NSW) b June 14, 1929 Lisarow (NSW)

Davidson, Hugh Lavery (NSW) b May 17, 1907 South Yarra (Vic) d April 22, 1960 Wamberal (NSW)

Davidson, Thomas Rex (Tas) b July 30, 1927 Campbell Town (Tas)

Davie, Bert Joseph James (Tas & Vic) b May 2, 1899 Hobart (Tas) d June 3, 1979 Melbourne (Vic)

Davies, Christopher James (SAust) b Nov. 15, 1978 Bedford Park (SAust)

Davies, George Arthur (Vic) b March 19, 1892 Maindample (Vic) d Nov. 27, 1957 Essendon (Vic)

Davies, Geoffrey Robert (NSW) b July 22, 1946 Randwick (NSW)

Davies, Gerald Stanley (Tas) b Jan. 29, 1949 Cinderford, Gloucestershire (England)

Davies, John George (Tas) b Feb. 17, 1846 Melbourne (Vic) d Nov. 12, 1913 New Town (Tas)

Davies, Peter John (Vic) b Aug. 18, 1957 Melbourne (Vic)

Davis, Arthur Hugh (Tas) b Nov. 6, 1898 Launceston (Tas) d March 5, 1947 Camberwell (Vic)

Davis, Frank Alexander (Tas) b May 29, 1904 Launceston (Tas) d Sept. 12, 1973 Launceston (Tas)

Davis, Horace Hyman (NSW) b Feb. 1, 1889 Darlinghurst (NSW) d Feb. 4, 1960 Sydney (NSW)

* Davis, Ian Charles (NSW & Qld) b June 25, 1953 North Sydney (NSW)

Davis, Jonas J. (NSW) b May 12, 1859 Goulburn (NSW) d May 18, 1911 Waverley (NSW)

Davis, Neil Wilton (Tas) b Aug. 1, 1900 Launceston (Tas) d April 25, 1974 Evans Head (NSW)

Davis, Reginald Augur (Tas) b Oct. 22, 1892 Invermay (Tas) d July 11, 1957 Launceston (Tas)

* Davis, Simon Peter (Vic) b Nov. 8, 1959 Brighton (Vic)

* Davis, Winston Walter (Tas) b Sept. 18, 1958 Sion Hill, Kingstown (St Vincent)

Davison, Brian Fettes (Tas) b Dec. 21, 1946 Bulawayo (Southern Rhodesia)

Davison, John Michael (Vic) b May 9, 1970 Campbell River, Vancouver Island, British Columbia (Canada)

Davison, Lindsay John (Vic) b Oct. 11, 1941 Malvern (Vic)

Davison, Rodney John (NSW) b June 26, 1969 Kogarah (NSW)

Dawes, Joseph Henry (Qld) b Aug. 29, 1970 Herston (Qld)

Day, Arthur Charles (Vic) b Aug. 8, 1933 Sunshine (Vic)

Day, Herbert John (SAust) b April 1, 1868 Bowden (SAust) d Oct. 14, 1947 Hindmarsh (SAust)

* De Courcy, James Harry (NSW) b April 18, 1927 Newcastle (NSW) d June 20, 2000 Newcastle (NSW)

De Gruchy, Henry William (Vic) b May 15, 1898 Sydney (NSW) d May 2, 1952 Parkville (Vic)

De Jong, Howard Keith (Qld) b Feb. 12, 1956 Mt Lavinia, Colombo (Ceylon)

De Winter, Allister John (Tas) b March 12, 1968 Launceston (Tas)

Dean, Archibald Herbert (Vic) b Oct. 3, 1885 Hawthorn (Vic) d Sept. 3, 1939 Norfolk Island (NSW)

Dean, Arthur Edgar (Vic) b July 23, 1931 Williamstown (Vic)

Dean, Oscar Hessel (NSW) b April 30, 1886 Windsor (NSW) d May 11, 1962 Windsor (NSW)

Deane, Norman Younger (NSW) b Aug. 29, 1875 Neutral Bay (NSW) d Sept. 30, 1950 Lindfield (NSW)

Deane, Sidney (NSW) b March 1, 1867 Sydney (NSW) d March 20, 1934 New York (United States of America)

Deely, Patrick Joseph (Vic) b Feb. 18, 1864 North Melbourne (Vic) d Feb. 28, 1925 Brighton (Vic)

Deitz, Shane Alan (SAust) b May 4, 1975 Bankstown (NSW)

Delaney, William (SAust) b Jan. 17, 1866 Kapunda (SAust) d Dec. 16, 1921 Port Augusta (SAust)

* Dell, Anthony Ross (Qld) b Aug. 6, 1945 Lymington, Hampshire (England)

Dell, Christopher Ronald (Tas) b Oct. 27, 1960 Devonport (Tas)

Delves, Thomas Frederick (Vic) b Aug. 23, 1876 Carlton (Vic) d July 28, 1944 Heidelberg (Vic)

Delves, Walter Frederick (Vic) b Feb. 17, 1891 Brunswick (Vic) d May 27, 1955 Canterbury (Vic)

Dempster, Robert Alexander (Vic) b March 11, 1915 Hotham West (Vic) d April 2, 1974 Fitzroy (Vic)

Denton, Gerard John (Tas) b Aug. 7, 1975 Mt Isa (Qld)

Desmazeures, Pitre Cesar (Vic & SAust) b Aug. 17, 1880 Collingwood (Vic) d Oct. 7, 1942 New Norfolk (Tas)

Deveney, Frank Barclay (Vic) b Aug. 16, 1910 Berwick (Vic) d Oct. 30, 1998 Melbourne (Vic)

Devenish-Meares, Frank (WAust & NSW) b April 25, 1873 Surry Hills (NSW) d July 4, 1952 Petersham (NSW)

Deverson, Charles Sydney (SAust) b Nov. 2, 1905 Alberton (SAust) d Feb. 2, 1945 Port Adelaide (SAust)

Di Venuto, Michael James (Tas) b Dec. 12, 1973 Hobart (Tas)

Diamond, Austin (NSW) b July 10, 1874 Huddersfield, Yorkshire (England) d Aug. 5, 1966 Concord (NSW)

Dick, Alexander Williamson (WAust) b Nov. 30, 1922 Boulder (WAust)

Dick, Andrew M. (Vic) birth and death details unknown

Dick, Ian Robinson (WAust) b Aug. 30, 1926 Boulder (WAust)

Dick, William Allan (Vic) b Nov. 10, 1922 Newcastle (NSW)

Dickson, George D. (NSW) birth and death details unknown

Dighton, Michael Gray (WAust) b July 24, 1976 Toowoomba (Qld)

Births and Deaths of Cricketers

Dillon, Marshall (Vic) b July 22, 1925 Ballarat (Vic) d Oct. 11, 1979 Beaumaris (Vic)

Dimattina, Michael Gerard David (Vic) b May 11, 1965 Malvern (Vic)

Diprose, Noel Vertigan (Tas) b March 5, 1922 Glenorchy (Tas)

Ditchburn, Albert James (WAust) b Aug. 24, 1908 Boulder (WAust) d March 7, 1964 Perth (WAust)

Dive, Percy William (NSW) b July 10, 1881 Paddington (NSW) d Sept. 17, 1965 Roseville (NSW)

Dixon, Joseph Black (Tas) b Sept. 26, 1836 Hobart (Tas) d March 6, 1882 Battery Point (Tas)

Dixon, Patrick Leslie (Qld) b Jan. 13, 1916 Eagle Junction (Qld) d Nov. 5, 1996 Goulburn (NSW)

Dixon, Troy James (Qld) b Dec. 22, 1969 Geelong (Vic)

Doble, Alan William (Vic) b Dec. 27, 1942 Glenhuntly (Vic)

Docker, Arthur Robert (NSW) b June 3, 1848 Thornthwaite (NSW) d April 8, 1929 Enfield, Middlesex (England)

Docker, Cyril Talbot (NSW) b March 3, 1884 Ryde (NSW) d March 26, 1975 Double Bay (NSW)

Docker, Ernest Brougham (NSW) b April 1, 1842 Thornthwaite (NSW) d Aug. 12, 1923 Elizabeth Bay (NSW)

Docker, Keith Brougham (NSW) b Sept. 1, 1888 Ryde (NSW) d May 16, 1977 Ashfield (NSW)

Docker, Phillip Wybergh (NSW) b April 8, 1886 Ryde (NSW) d Oct. 29, 1978 Concord (NSW)

Docking, Trevor William (Tas) b Dec. 22, 1952 Burnie (Tas)

Dodds, Norman (Tas) b Aug. 30, 1876 Hobart (Tas) d Dec. 15, 1916 Hobart (Tas)

* Dodemaide, Anthony Ian Christopher (Vic) b Oct. 5, 1963 Williamstown (Vic)

Doig, Ronald Oldham (WAust) b July 10, 1909 Fremantle (WAust) d Sept. 17, 1932 Beaconsfield (WAust)

Dollery, Keith Robert (Qld & Tas) b Dec. 9, 1924 Cooroy (Qld)

Dolling, Charles Edward (SAust) b Sept. 4, 1886 Wokurna (SAust) d June 11, 1936 Adelaide (SAust)

Dolman, Michael Charles (SAust) b June 14, 1960 North Adelaide (SAust)

Donahoo, Sydney John (Vic & Qld) b April 14, 1871 St Kilda (Vic) d Jan. 14, 1946 St Kilda (Vic)

Donaldson, John Stuart (SAust) b April 14, 1950 Adelaide (SAust)

Donaldson, William Peter James (NSW) b Oct. 26, 1923 Lilyfield (NSW) d Aug. 8, 1999 Sydney (NSW)

Done, Richard Phillip (NSW) b Aug. 5, 1955 Ryde (NSW)

* Donnan, Harry (NSW) b Nov. 12, 1864 Liverpool (NSW) d Aug. 13, 1956 Bexley (NSW)

Donnelly, James Louis (NSW) b June 24, 1906 Merimbula (NSW) d March 2, 1978 Koorawatha (NSW)

Doolan, Bruce Richard (Tas) b Sept. 9, 1947 Launceston (Tas)

* Dooland, Bruce (SAust) b Nov. 1, 1923 Cowandilla (SAust) d Sept. 8, 1980 Bedford Park (SAust)

Douglas, Adye (Tas) b May 31, 1815 Thorpe-next-Norwich (England) d April 10, 1906 Hobart (Tas)

Douglas, Alfred Jamieson (Tas) b Feb. 4, 1872 Newstead (Tas) d June 9, 1938 Malvern (Vic)

Douglas, John Raymond (Vic) b Oct. 24, 1951 East Brunswick (Vic)

Douglas, Osborne Henry (Tas) b March 14, 1880 Launceston (Tas) d April 24, 1918 Dernancourt, near Albert (France)

Dowling, Gerard Patrick (Vic) b Nov. 10, 1964 Preston (Vic)

Down, Granville James Stuart (SAust) b May 24, 1883 Dubbo (NSW) d May 14, 1970 St Kilda (Vic)

Downes, Francis (NSW) b June 11, 1864 Redfern (NSW) d May 20, 1916 Little Bay (NSW)

Downey, Donnell Raymond (SAust) b April 12, 1907 Parkside (SAust) d Jan. 23, 1966 Adelaide (SAust)

Downey, Joseph Aloysius (Qld) b Feb. 4, 1895 (Qld) d April 18, 1934 Kangaroo Point (Qld)

Downton, Andrew Graham (Tas) b July 17, 1977 Auburn (NSW)

Dowsley, Harcourt (Vic) b July 15, 1919 Essendon (Vic)

Doyle, Bryan Bernard John (Vic) b Oct. 20, 1968 Carlton (Vic)

Draney, John Davis Rodney (Qld) b May 10, 1927 Indooroopilly (Qld)

Drape, Isaac Selby (Vic & Qld) b May 13, 1866 Hotham (Vic) d Feb. 7, 1916 St Kilda (Vic)

Drennan, John (SAust) b Nov. 13, 1932 West Croydon (SAust)

Drew, Albert David (WAust) b Oct. 30, 1906 West Leederville (WAust) d Feb. 20, 1984 Shenton Park (WAust)

Drew, Charles Francis (SAust) b April 24, 1888 Kooringa, now Burra (SAust) d Feb. 19, 1960 Adelaide (SAust)

Drew, James Leggat (Vic) b Jan. 20, 1872 Williamstown (Vic) d Jan. 22, 1944 Maryborough (Vic)

Drew, Thomas Mitchell (SAust) b June 9, 1875 Kooringa, now Burra (SAust) d Jan. 9, 1928 Toowoomba (Qld)

Drewer, Richard Harris (SAust) b June 12, 1946 Parkside (SAust)

Drinnen, Peter John (Qld) b Oct. 5, 1967 Bundaberg (Qld)

Driscoll, Clarence Rheuben (Tas) b Sept. 4, 1895 Glebe (Tas) d May 1, 1948 Hobart (Tas)

Driscoll, Vernon Reginald (Tas) b April 11, 1891 Glebe (Tas) d March 19, 1967 Bellerive (Tas)

Driver, Richard (NSW) b Sept. 16, 1829 Cabramatta (NSW) d July 8, 1880 Moore Park (NSW)

Driver, Walter George (Vic & WAust) b Sept. 25, 1922 Glenhuntly (Vic) d Jan. 11, 1994 Mooloolooba (Qld)

Druery, William Lance (Qld) b May 14, 1927 Townsville (Qld) d Aug. 10, 1993 Carina (Qld)

Drysdale, John (Vic) b c. 1862 Castlemaine (Vic) d Feb. 15, 1922 Kew (Vic)

Du Croz, Gervase Bedford (Tas & Vic) b c. 1830 (England) d Feb. 19, 1855 Launceston (Tas)

Ducker, John Robert (SAust) b June 12, 1934 Prospect (SAust)

Dudgeon, Keith Edward (Qld) b Sept. 5, 1946 Cairns (Qld)

Dudley, Walter John (Vic) b May 29, 1918 Carlton North (Vic) d April 5, 1978 Northcote (Vic)

* Duff, Reginald Alexander (NSW) b Aug. 17, 1878 Sydney (NSW) d Dec. 13, 1911 North Sydney (NSW)

Duff, Walter Scott (NSW) b April 22, 1876 Sydney (NSW) d Nov. 11, 1921 Sydney (NSW)

Duffy, Joseph Thomas (Vic) b c. 1860 Ballarat (Vic) d c. 1936 Ballarat (Vic)

Duffy, William Vincent (WAust) b July 8, 1866 Doutta Galla (Vic) d June 13, 1959 Subiaco (WAust)

Dufty, Ross (Tas) b Aug. 13, 1927 Bingara (NSW)

Dugan, Robert Wayne (SAust) b Aug. 10, 1959 Broken Hill (NSW)

Duldig, Lance Desmond (SAust) b Feb. 21, 1922 Eudunda (SAust) d Sept. 14, 1998 Beaumont (SA)

Dulling, Philip (Tas) b May 5, 1909 Launceston (Tas) d Sept. 1, 1974 Launceston (Tas)

Dumaresq, Henry Rowland Gascoigne (Tas) b Feb. 28, 1839 Longford (Tas) d Oct. 31, 1924 Ulverstone (Tas)

Dummett, Arthur William (Vic) b Nov. 18, 1900 Clifton Hill (Vic) d June 4, 1968 Ivanhoe (Vic)

Dummett, William (NSW) b July 18, 1840 Sydney (NSW) d c. 1906 (NSW)

* Duncan, John Ross Frederick (Qld & Vic) b March 25, 1944 Herston (Qld)

Duncan, William (Qld) b Oct. 19, 1912 Brisbane (Qld) d c. 1988 Brisbane (Qld) full death details unknown

Dunn, Martin Matthew Francis (Qld) b May 10, 1883 Maryborough (Qld) d Dec. 31, 1942 Woollahra (NSW)

Dunn, Wallace Peter (WAust) b Aug. 8, 1921 Westonia (WAust)

Dunstan, William John (WAust) b Dec. 4, 1878 Glen Osmond (SAust) d April 11, 1955 Perth (WAust)

Dupain, Francois Henri (NSW) b Aug. 11, 1889 Ashfield (NSW) d Sept. 29, 1959 Burradoo (NSW)

Duperouzel, Bruce (WAust) b April 21, 1950 Northam (WAust)

Dwyer, Christopher (Vic) b c. 1879 Albury (NSW) d July 21, 1961 Kew (Vic)

Dwyer, Edmund Alfred (NSW) b Oct. 19, 1894 Mosman (NSW) d Sept. 10, 1975 Mosman (NSW)

Dwyer, Eric William (Tas) b June 15, 1917 St Helen's (Tas) d May 15, 1997 Canberra (ACT)

* Dyer, Gregory Charles (NSW) b March 16, 1959 Parramatta (NSW)

Dyer, Robert Henry (SAust) b c. 1860 (England) d Aug. 31, 1950 Nailsworth (SAust)

Dykes, James Andrew (Tas) b Nov. 15, 1971 Hobart (Tas)

* Dymock, Geoffrey (Qld) b July 21, 1945 Maryborough (Qld)

* Dyson, John (NSW) b June 11, 1954 Kogarah (NSW)

* Eady, Charles John (Tas) b Oct. 29, 1870 Hobart (Tas) d Dec. 20, 1945 Hobart (Tas)

Easton, Frank Alexander (NSW) b Feb. 19, 1910 Waterloo (NSW) d May 5, 1989 Sydney (NSW)

Easton, Robert Peter (Qld) b Oct. 21, 1936 Windsor (Qld)

* Eastwood, Kenneth Humphrey (Vic) b Nov. 23, 1935 Chatswood (NSW)

Eaton, Anthony Mark (SAust) b June 11, 1953 Prospect (SAust)

Eaton, George Melville (Vic) b Oct. 23, 1904 Durban (South Africa) d May 28, 1938 East Melbourne (Vic)

Eaton, Harry Ronald (NSW) b c. 1909 St Leonards (NSW) d May 13, 1960 Castlecrag (NSW)

* Ebeling, Hans Irvine (Vic) b Jan. 1, 1905 Avoca (Vic) d Jan. 12, 1980 East Bentleigh (Vic)

Ebsworth, Norman (NSW) b Jan. 2, 1878 Sydney (NSW) d Nov. 19, 1949 Kirribilli (NSW)

Edmondson, Henry Pudsey Dawson (WAust) b Nov. 25, 1872 Hobart (Tas) d Aug. 18, 1946 Perth (WAust)

Edwards, Alan Robert (WAust) b Dec. 24, 1921 Perth (WAust)

Edwards, Allen Crisp (SAust) b Nov. 18, 1868 Brighton (SAust) d Jan. 1, 1961 Adelaide (SAust)

Edwards, Edmund Keane (WAust) b Jan. 6, 1910 Cottesloe (WAust) d Aug. 18, 1990 Cottesloe (WAust)

Edwards, Frederick Raymond (SAust) b Feb. 28, 1908 Sydney (NSW) d April 27, 1982 St Leonards (NSW)

* Edwards, John Dunlop (Vic) b June 12, 1860 Prahran (Vic) d July 31, 1911 Hawksburn (Vic)

Edwards, John Neild (Vic) b Aug. 16, 1928 Ormond (Vic)

* Edwards, Ross (WAust & NSW) b Dec. 1, 1942 Cottesloe (WAust)

* Edwards, Walter John (WAust) b Dec. 23, 1949 Subiaco (WAust)

Egan, Grahame Maxwell (Qld) b June 8, 1941 Armidale (NSW)

Egan, Thomas Charles Wills (NSW) b Oct. 5, 1906 Warren (NSW) d Nov. 29, 1979 Double Bay (NSW)

Egglestone, John Waterhouse (Vic) b July 7, 1847 Hobart (Tas) d Oct. 17, 1912 Malvern (Vic)

Eime, Andrew Barry (SAust) b July 3, 1971 North Adelaide (SAust)

Elliott, Edward Hudspith (Vic) b April 19, 1851 Sunderland, Durham (England) d March 19, 1885 North Carlton (Vic)

Elliott, Gideon (Vic) b April 17, 1828 Merstham, Surrey (England) d Feb. 15, 1869 Richmond (Vic)

* Elliott, Matthew Thomas Gray (Vic) b Sept. 28, 1971 Chelsea (Vic)

Elliott, Raymond Allister (Tas) b Jan. 1, 1917 New Norfolk (Tas) d Sept. 8, 1997 New Town (Tas)

Elliott, Thomas Henry (Tas) b March 22, 1879 Hobart (Tas) d Oct. 21, 1939 Launceston (Tas)

Ellis, David Leigh (Qld) b Jan. 2, 1951 Herston (Qld)

Ellis, Donald George (Tas) b Oct. 5, 1917 Launceston (Tas)

Ellis, John Albert (Qld) b June 10, 1914 Spring Hill (Qld) d Oct. 17, 1994 Greenslopes (Qld)

Ellis, John Leslie (Vic) b May 9, 1890 Malvern (Vic) d July 26, 1974 Glen Iris (Vic)

Ellis, Leslie George (NSW) b March 2, 1936 New Lambton (NSW)

Ellis, Matthew (Vic) b Feb. 3, 1870 Melbourne (Vic) d Nov. 19, 1940 Fitzroy (Vic)

Ellis, Percy Arthur (Vic) b May 10, 1906 Abbotsford (Vic) d April 25, 1992 Lilydale (Vic)

Ellis, Reginald Newnham (Vic) b Feb. 22, 1891 Randwick (NSW) d May 26, 1959 Cheltenham (Vic)

Ellis, Reginald Sidney (SAust) b Nov. 26, 1917 Angaston (SAust)

* Ellison, Richard Mark (Tas) b Sept. 21, 1959 Willesborough, Kent (England)

Eltham, William Keith (Tas) b Oct. 10, 1886 Hobart (Tas) d Dec. 31, 1916 Lesboeufs (France)

Emerson, David Alan (Vic) b March 10, 1961 Malvern (Vic)

Emerson, Norman Leonard (Vic) b Oct. 26, 1939 Ararat (Vic)

* Emery, Philip Allen (NSW) b June 25, 1964 St Ives (NSW)

* Emery, Sidney Hand (NSW) b Oct. 16, 1885 Macdonaldtown (NSW) d Jan. 7, 1967 Petersham (NSW)

Emery, Victor Rupert (NSW) b Dec. 20, 1920 Redfern (NSW)

Eneberg, Alfred (SAust) b Nov. 30, 1928 Birkenhead (SAust)

England, Ernest James (WAust & SAust) b May 26, 1927 Bunbury (WAust)

Englefield, William (SAust) b Oct. 6, 1917 Leichhardt (NSW) d June 3, 1988 Ryde (NSW)

Epstein, Jan (WAust) b Oct. 1, 1918 West Perth (WAust) d March 24, 1988 Melbourne (Vic)

Evan, Laurence William (SAust) b Oct. 27, 1864 Adelaide (SAust) d Aug. 12, 1894 North Adelaide (SAust)

Evans, Arthur Ernest (SAust) b July 12, 1871 East Adelaide (SAust) d March 26, 1950 Bordertown (SAust)

Evans, Charles F (Tas) birth and death details unknown

* Evans, Edwin (NSW) b March 26, 1849 Emu Plains (NSW) d July 2, 1921 Walgett (NSW)

Evans, George Nicholas (WAust) b Dec. 24, 1915 Boulder (WAust) d April 11, 1965 Hollywood (WAust)

Evans, Henry (Tas) b Aug. 6, 1846 Launceston (Tas) death details unknown

Evans, Richard (SAust) b Sept. 9, 1867 Hindmarsh (SAust) d Nov. 1, 1939 Hindmarsh (SAust)

Evans, Royston Macauley (WAust) b Jan. 13, 1884 Semaphore (SAust) d March 12, 1977 Perth (WAust)

Evans, Walter Allan (WAust) b Sept. 29, 1897 Gympie (Qld) d Jan. 15, 1955 Hollywood (WAust)

Evans, William Thomas (Qld) b April 9, 1876 Indooroopilly (Qld) d July 19, 1964 Woolloongabba (Qld)

Everett, Charles Samuel (NSW) b June 17, 1901 Marrickville (NSW) d Oct. 10, 1970 Concord (NSW)

Everett, Dudley Tabor (WAust) b March 9, 1912 Perth (WAust) d May 3, 1943 Ontario (Canada) on active service

Everett, James Seabrook (WAust) b July 20, 1884 Toodyay (WAust) d June 19, 1968 Nedlands (WAust)

Evers, Harold Albert (NSW & WAust) b Feb. 28, 1876 Newcastle (NSW) d Feb. 6, 1937 Perth (WAust)

Eyres, Gordon (WAust) b Dec. 20, 1912 Kalgoorlie (WAust)

Facy, Ashley Cooper (Tas & Vic) b Jan. 26, 1886 Bellerive (Tas) d Dec. 2, 1954 Hobart (Tas)

Fagan, Arthur Mervyn (NSW) b April 24, 1931 birthplace unknown

Fairbairn, Clive Lindsay (Vic) b Aug. 25, 1919 Geelong (Vic)

* Fairfax, Alan George (NSW) b June 16, 1906 Summer Hill (NSW) d May 17, 1955 Kensington, London (England)

Fairweather, Robert John (NSW) b July 24, 1845 Pyrmont (NSW) d May 31, 1925 Waverley (NSW)

Faithfull, Henry Montague (NSW) b June 16, 1847 Springfield (NSW) d Oct. 22, 1908 Elizabeth Bay (NSW)

Fallowfield, Leslie John (NSW) b March 12, 1914 North Sydney (NSW) d May 29, 1999 North Ryde (NSW)

Fanning, Edward (Vic) b March 16, 1848 Sydney (NSW) d Nov. 30, 1917 St Kilda (Vic)

Farnsworth, Andrew William (NSW) b Jan. 14, 1887 Sydney (NSW) d Oct. 30, 1966 Waterfall (NSW)

Farquhar, Barclay Wallace (NSW) b Feb. 22, 1875 West Maitland (NSW) d May 31, 1960 death place unknown

Farquhar, John Kennedy (Qld) b Jan. 30, 1887 Home Hill (Qld) d July 31, 1977 Chermside (Qld)

Farrar, Frank Martindale (NSW) b March 29, 1893 Rylstone (NSW) d May 30, 1973 Waverley (NSW)

Farrell, Graeme Ian (Tas) b Nov. 2, 1947 Launceston (Tas)

Farrell, Graeme Stanley (SAust) b Feb. 4, 1943 Norwood (SAust)

Farrell, Michael Graeme (Tas) b Sept. 24, 1968 Melbourne (Vic)

Faulkner, Peter Ian (Tas) b April 18, 1960 Launceston (Tas)

Faull, Martin Peter (SAust) b May 10, 1968 Darwin (NT)

Faunce, Thomas Bowman (Qld) b March 19, 1883 (Qld) d May 27, 1968 Greenslopes (Qld)

Favell, Alan Leslie (SAust) b June 6, 1960 North Adelaide (SAust)

* Favell, Leslie Ernest (SAust) b Oct. 6, 1929 Rockdale (NSW) d June 14, 1987 Magill (SAust)

Fennelly, Sidney James (Qld) b March 22, 1887 Sydney (NSW) d Aug. 25, 1964 Brighton (Qld)

Fenton, Arthur (Vic) b Feb. 27, 1870 Tarnagulla (Vic) d May 20, 1950 Melbourne (Vic)

Ferguson, James Alexander (Tas) b Feb. 19, 1848 Launceston (Tas) d May 10, 1913 Brisbane (Qld)

Ferguson, Leslie Drummond (Vic) b Dec. 8, 1892 North Brighton (Vic) d Jan. 30, 1957 East Melbourne (Vic)

Ferrall, Raymond Alfred (Tas) b May 27, 1906 Launceston (Tas) d June 1, 2000 Launceston (Tas)

Ferries, Kenneth Ian (WAust) b May 7, 1936 Wyalkatchem (WAust)

**Ferris, John James (NSW & SAust) b May 21, 1867 Sydney (NSW) d Nov. 21, 1900 Durban (South Africa)

Fett, Frederick (Qld) b May 2, 1886 Toowoomba (Qld) d Aug. 27, 1979 Woolloongabba (Qld)

Fewin, Henry (Qld) b Jan. 25, 1896 Townsville (Qld) d Aug. 25, 1980 Bongaree (Qld)

Fidock, Harold Edward (WAust) b Aug. 24, 1902 Adelaide (SAust) d Feb. 9, 1986 Nedlands (WAust)

Field, William (Tas) b March 17, 1816 Port Dalrymple (Tas) d June 22, 1890 Bishopsbourne (Tas)

Fielke, Noel Robert (SAust) b Dec. 23, 1966 Blackwood (SAust)

Findlay, Algernon Percy (Tas) b March 17, 1892 Launceston (Tas) d Jan. 9, 1956 Launceston (Tas)

* Fingleton, John Henry Webb (NSW) b April 28, 1908 Waverley (NSW) d Nov. 22, 1981 St Leonards (NSW)

Fisher, Alexander (Qld) b March 14, 1908 Gatton (Qld) d Oct. 6, 1968 Maryborough (Qld)

Fisher, Arthur Donnelly Wentworth (NSW) b Dec. 14, 1882 Lavender Bay (NSW) d July 9, 1968 Neutral Bay (NSW)

Fisher, Barry (Qld) b Jan. 20, 1934 Brisbane (Qld) d April 6, 1980 Inverell (NSW)

Fisher, Harry Medcalf (SAust) b May 28, 1899 North Adelaide (SAust) d Oct. 14, 1982 South Launceston (Tas)

Fisher, William Thornton (Qld) b Aug. 31, 1865 Brisbane (Qld) d June 1, 1945 Herston (Qld)

Fitchett, Michael King (Vic) b Nov. 30, 1927 Hawthorn (Vic)

Fitness, Gavin Arthur James (Qld) b June 4, 1968 Maryborough (Qld)

Fitzgerald, David Andrew (WAust & SAust) b Nov. 30, 1972 Osborne Park (WAust)

Fitzgerald, James (Qld) b Feb. 19, 1874 Surry Hills (NSW) d Aug. 20, 1950 Graceville (Qld)

Fitzmaurice, Desmond Michael John (Vic) b Oct. 16, 1917 Carlton (Vic) d Jan. 19, 1981 Prahran (Vic)

Fitzmaurice, Dudley James Anthony (Vic) b May 21, 1913 Carlton (Vic) d June 28, 2001 Melbourne (Vic)

Fitzpatrick, Jack Herbert (NSW) b Sept. 18, 1911 Bankstown (NSW) d Jan. 23, 1999 Bankstown (NSW)

Fitzpatrick, John Milling (Vic) b June 26, 1889 Waverley (NSW) d Aug. 16, 1952 Coogee (NSW)

Fleay, Clarence William Edward James (WAust) b Dec. 27, 1886 Gilgering (WAust) d Aug. 6, 1955 Katanning (WAust)

* Fleetwood-Smith, Leslie O'Brien (Vic) b March 30, 1908 Stawell (Vic) d March 16, 1971 Fitzroy (Vic)

Flegler, Shawn Leonard (Qld) b March 23, 1972 Darwin (NT)

* Fleming, Damien William (Vic) b April 24, 1970 Bentley (WAust)

Fletcher, John Henry (Qld) b Oct. 27, 1893 Brisbane (Qld)

Fletcher, John William (Qld) b Jan. 25, 1884 Woollahra (NSW) d March 13, 1965 South Brisbane (Qld)

Flint, Kerry Royce (Tas) b Sept. 17, 1946 Smithton (Tas)

Flockton, Raymond George (NSW) b March 14, 1930 Paddington (NSW)

Flynn, Brian James (Qld) b June 7, 1929 Darlinghurst (NSW) d Aug. 3, 1986 Vesty's Beach, Darwin (NT)

Flynn, John Paul (NSW) b June 29, 1890 Paddington (NSW) d May 28, 1952 Chatswood (NSW)

Foley, Geoffrey Ian (Qld) b Oct. 11, 1967 Jandowae (Qld)

Foley, Maurice Hinton (WAust) b Feb. 4, 1930 Perth (WAust)

Folkard, Bernard James (NSW) b May 17, 1878 Ryde (NSW) d Jan. 31, 1937 Leichhardt (NSW)

Fontaine, Frederick Ernest (Vic) b Dec. 14, 1912 Northcote (Vic) d Oct. 24, 1982 Greensborough (Vic)

Foot, Charles Francis (Vic) b Aug. 14, 1855 Brighton (Vic) d July 2, 1926 East Melbourne (Vic)

Foot, Henry Boorn (Vic) b Nov. 21, 1805 Romsey, Hampshire (England) d May 14, 1857 Brighton (Vic)

Ford, Douglas Allan (NSW) b Dec. 16, 1928 Maryville (NSW)

Forsaith, Geoffrey Milner (WAust) b Jan. 5, 1931 Perth (WAust)

Forssberg, Edward Ernest Brackley (NSW) b Dec. 10, 1894 Sydney (NSW) d May 23, 1953 Bondi (NSW)

Forster, William Robert (Tas) b March 1, 1884 Gateshead-on-Tyne, Durham (England) d Feb. 7, 1930 Richmond (Tas)

Foster, Michael Robert (Vic) b March 5, 1973 East Melbourne (Vic)

Foster, Norman Kelk (Qld) b Jan. 19, 1878 Brisbane (Qld) d March 15, 1960 Clayfield (Qld)

Foster, Thomas Henry (NSW) b Sept. 30, 1883 Glebe (NSW) d June 27, 1947 Leichhardt (NSW)

Fothergill, Desmond Hugh (Vic) b July 15, 1920 Northcote (Vic) d March 16, 1996 Melbourne (Vic)

Fowler, Edwin (Vic) b c. 1841 London (England) d May 31, 1909 St Kilda (Vic)

Fox, Albert Henry Newnham (Vic) b April 20, 1867 Battery Point (Tas) d Dec. 24, 1946 Brighton (Vic)

Fox, Norman Henry (NSW) b July 29, 1904 Longueville (NSW) d May 7, 1972 Castle Cove (NSW)

* Francis, Bruce Colin (NSW) b Feb. 18, 1948 Sydney (NSW)

Francis, Craig Lawrence (SAust) b Nov. 25, 1966 North Adelaide (SAust)

Francis, John Charles (Vic) b June 22, 1908 Hawthorn (Vic) d July 6, 2001 Camberwell (Vic)

Francis, Keith Raymond (NSW) b Nov. 14, 1933 Arncliffe (NSW)

Francis, Stanley George (WAust) b April 14, 1906 Geelong (Vic) d Jan. 25, 1994 Nedlands (WAust)

Francke, Fredrick Malcolm (Qld) b March 21, 1939 Mt Lavinia, Colombo (Ceylon)

Frankish, Ronald Richard (WAust) b Oct. 6, 1925 Perth (WAust)

Fraser, Neville Graham (Qld) b Sept. 28, 1930 Cleveland (Qld)

Fraser, Robert Alexander (SAust) b Feb. 13, 1954 Parkside (SAust)

Frazer, Ian Douglas (Vic) b Sept. 7, 1966 Lilydale (Vic)

Frederick, John (Vic) b Dec. 18, 1910 Armadale (Vic)

Free, Ernest Peardon (Tas) b Sept. 7, 1867 Rokeby (Tas) d July 5, 1946 Hobart (Tas)

Freedman, David Andrew (NSW) b June 19, 1964 Sydney (NSW)

Freeman, Edward John (Tas) b Nov. 7, 1848 Hobart (Tas) d Aug. 11, 1905 Hobart (Tas)

* Freeman, Eric Walter (SAust) b July 13, 1944 Largs Bay (SAust)

Freeman, Harry Septimus (Vic & Qld) b June 11, 1860 Carlton (Vic) d Nov. 7, 1933 Brunswick (Vic)

Freeman, John Edward (Qld) b June 28, 1935 Nundah (Qld)

Freeman, Thomas Daniel (Tas) b June 13, 1894 Hobart (Tas) d June 19, 1965 Heidelberg (Vic)

Freemantle, Leslie Francis (Vic & WAust) b May 11, 1898 Canterbury (Vic) d June 6, 1963 Kew (Vic)

* Freer, Frederick Alfred William (Vic) b Dec. 4, 1915 North Carlton (Vic) d Nov. 2, 1998 Frankston (Vic)

Frei, Harald (Qld) b May 1, 1951 Nuremberg (Germany)

Frick, John (SAust) b March 24, 1957 Medindie (SAust)

Friend, Raymond Grattan (Tas) b April 11, 1898 Prahran (Vic) death details unknown

Frost, Albert Edgar (Tas) b March 19, 1878 Launceston (Tas) d Oct. 25, 1951 Launceston (Tas)

Frost, Allan Russell (SAust) b Dec. 2, 1942 Adelaide (SAust)

Frost, Sydney Robert (Tas) b Jan. 21, 1881 Launceston (Tas) d Dec. 19, 1952 Middle Park (Vic)

Fry, Herbert James (Vic) b Oct. 28, 1870 Morphett Vale (SAust) d Jan. 19, 1953 Hawthorn (Vic)

Furlong, Ronald William (Vic) b May 16, 1936 Ballarat (Vic)

Furness, Arthur John (NSW) b Jan. 11, 1873 Sydney (NSW) d Oct. 31, 1948 Strathfield (NSW)

Gaggin, William Wakeham (Vic) b Nov. 23, 1847 County Cork (Ireland) d July 5, 1925 Elsternwick (Vic)

Gallagher, Ian Noel (Qld) b Nov. 20, 1950 Greenslopes (Qld)

Gallash, Ian (WAust) b June 17, 1936 Perth (WAust)

Galloway, Paul Warren (SAust) b Sept. 14, 1943 North Sydney (NSW) d Aug. 20, 1996 Loxton (SAust)

Gamble, Herbert Spencer (Vic & Qld) b March 2, 1903 Sunbury (Vic) d June 15, 1962 Shorncliffe (Qld)

Gandy, Michael George (Tas) b Aug. 28, 1944 Hobart (Tas)

* Gannon, John Bryant (WAust) b Feb. 8, 1947 Subiaco (WAust)

Gardiner, George Allan (WAust) b Nov. 27, 1914 Perth (WAust)

Gardiner, Grant Bruce (Vic) b Feb. 26, 1965 Melbourne (Vic)

Gardiner, Jack (Tas) b May 20, 1913 Hobart (Tas) d Sept. 11, 1976 Hobart (Tas)

Gardner, Charles Allan (Vic) b Oct. 28, 1908 Brighton East (Vic)

Gardner, Roy (Vic) b Jan. 18, 1914 Hotham West (Vic)

Garland, John George Morton (Vic) b Aug. 22, 1875 Hotham (Vic) d Feb. 23, 1938 Hawthorn (Vic)

Garlick, Paul Anthony (Vic) b Sept. 21, 1968 Sandringham (Vic)

Garnaut, Matthew Stuart (WAust) b Nov. 7, 1973 Subiaco (WAust)

* Garner, Joel (SAust) b Dec. 16, 1952 Enterprise, Christ Church (Barbados)

Garnsey, George Leonard (NSW) b Feb. 10, 1881 Sydney (NSW) d April 18, 1951 Canberra (ACT)

* Garrett, Thomas William (NSW) b July 26, 1858 Wollongong (NSW) d Aug. 6, 1943 Warrawee (NSW)

Gartrell, Kevin Boyd (WAust) b March 4, 1936 Midland (WAust)

Gartrell, Robert Boyd (WAust & Tas) b March 9, 1962 Middle Swan (WAust)

Garwood, Rex Elvyn (Tas) b May 15, 1930 Hobart (Tas)

Gaskell, Mark Andrew (Qld) b Oct. 17, 1956 Herston (Qld)

Gatehouse, George Henry (Tas) b June 20, 1864 Sorell (Tas) d Jan. 25, 1947 Toorak (Vic)

Gatenby, David John (Tas) b Feb. 12, 1952 Launceston (Tas)

Gatenby, Lawrence Frank (Tas) b April 10, 1889 Epping Forest (Tas) d Jan. 14, 1917 Armentieres (France)

Gatenby, Peter Robert (Tas) b May 26, 1949 Launceston (Tas)

* Gaunt, Ronald Arthur (WAust & Vic) b Feb. 26, 1934 Yarloop (WAust)

Geary, Alfred (NSW) b Aug. 8, 1849 birthplace unknown d Oct. 14, 1911 Brisbane (Qld)

Gee, Daniel Albert (NSW) b Sept. 30, 1875 Sydney (NSW) d Jan. 16, 1947 Adelaide (SAust)

Gehan, Rodney Arthur Howard (SAust) b Nov. 12, 1942 Werribee (Vic) d Feb. 8, 2001 Hope Island (Qld)

* Gehrs, Donald Raeburn Algernon (SAust) b Nov. 29, 1880 Port Victor (SAust) d June 25, 1953 Kings Park (SAust)

Geise, Gregory Gordon (NSW) b April 3, 1960 Wallsend (NSW)

Gentle, Steven Robert (SAust) b May 30, 1955 Rose Park (SAust)

George, Shane Peter (SAust) b Oct. 20, 1970 Adelaide (SAust)

Germaine, Lewis (Vic & WAust) b March 1, 1935 Glenhuntly (Vic) d April 8, 1992 Melbourne (Vic)

Geyer, Kevin James (NSW) b Oct. 11, 1973 Bathurst (NSW)

Gibaud, Henry Peter (Vic) b May 1, 1892 Carlton (Vic) d July 29, 1964 Fitzroy (Vic)

Gibbs, Charles H. (SAust) b c. 1841 full birth and death details unknown

* Gibbs, Lancelot Richard (SAust) b Sept. 29, 1934 Georgetown (British Guiana)

Giblin, Vincent Wanostrocht (Tas) b Nov. 13, 1817 Kingston upon Thames, Surrey (England) d May 15, 1884 Milsons Point (NSW)

Gibson, George (Tas) b 1827 birth day and month unknown Norfolk Plains (Tas) d Oct. 8, 1873 Sandy Bay (Tas)

Gibson, George Watson Hogg (Vic) b 1827 birth day and month unknown Thakambau (Jamaica) d Sept. 5, 1910 Carlton (Vic)

Gibson, Gordon Galloway (Tas) b Nov. 1, 1908 Hobart (Tas) d July 7, 1967 Melbourne (Vic)

Gibson, Vincent Roy (SAust) b May 14, 1916 Rose Park (SAust) d Nov. 28, 1983 Neutral Bay (NSW)

* Giffen, George (SAust) b March 27, 1859 Adelaide (SAust) d Nov. 29, 1927 Parkside (SAust)

* Giffen, Walter Frank (SAust) b Sept. 21, 1861 Adelaide (SAust) d June 28, 1949 North Unley (SAust)

Gilbert, Ashley Stephen (Vic) b Nov. 26, 1971 Melbourne (Vic)

* Gilbert, David Robert (NSW & Tas) b Dec. 19, 1960 Darlinghurst (NSW)

Gilbert, Eddie (Qld) b 1904 birth day and month unknown Woodford (Qld) d Jan. 9, 1978 Wacol (Qld)

Gilbert, George Henry Bailey (NSW) b Sept. 2, 1829 Cheltenham, Gloucestershire (England) d June 16, 1906 Summer Hill (NSW)

Gilbourne, Robert James (SAust) b July 16, 1943 Adelaide (SAust)

* Gilchrist, Adam Craig (NSW & WAust) b Nov. 14, 1971 Bellingen (NSW)

Giles, Leonard George (SAust) b June 17, 1921 Yorketown (SAust) d Aug. 23, 1994 Glandore (SAust)

Gill, Lynwood Laurence (Tas & Qld) b Nov. 19, 1891 Macquarie Plains (Tas) d Dec. 4, 1986 Pullenvale (Qld)

Giller, James Frederick (Vic) b May 1, 1870 Melbourne (Vic) d June 13, 1947 Albert Park (Vic)

* Gillespie, Jason Neil (SAust) b April 19, 1975 Sydney (NSW)

Gilmore, Francis Patrick John (NSW) b c. 1909 Yass (NSW) d April 26, 1955 Camperdown (NSW)

* Gilmour, Gary John (NSW) b June 26, 1951 Waratah (NSW)

Gladigau, Peter Wayne (SAust) b May 23, 1965 Whyalla (SAust)

Glassock, Craig Anthony (NSW) b Nov. 29, 1973 Mona Vale (NSW)

* Gleeson, John William (NSW) b March 14, 1938 Kyogle (NSW)

Glew, Steven Adam (Cricket Academy) b March 11, 1977 Perth (WAust)

Glynn, William Thomas (Tas) b c. 1846 d June 18, 1895 Fitzroy (Vic)

Goddard, Henry (NSW) b Nov. 16, 1885 Sydney (NSW) d May 13, 1925 Maroubra (NSW)

Godfrey, Charles George (SAust) b Nov. 17, 1860 Adelaide (SAust) d March 27, 1940 Rose Park (SAust)

Goffet, Gordon (NSW) b March 4, 1941 Speers Point (NSW)

Goggin, Peter John Thomas (Qld) b Oct. 30, 1965 Roma (Qld)

Gogler, Keith Geoffrey (SAust) b May 1, 1923 Port Augusta (SAust) d Aug. 24, 1983 Glenelg (SAust)

Goldman, Albert Edward Arms (Qld) b Oct. 4, 1868 Wee Waa (NSW) d Dec. 31, 1939 Sydney (NSW)

Goldsmith, Louis (Vic) b Sept. 14, 1846 Melbourne (Vic) d Sept. 15, 1911 East Melbourne (Vic)

Gonnella, Peter (WAust) b Jan. 14, 1963 Canberra (ACT)

Good, Robert Norman Scott (WAust) b March 29, 1885 East Melbourne (Vic) d June 16, 1962 Camberwell (Vic)

Goode, Benjamin Ryall (SAust) b Jan. 23, 1924 Port Lincoln (SAust)

Gooden, Henry Alfred (SAust) b Jan. 12, 1858 Adelaide (SAust) d March 30, 1904 North Fitzroy (Vic)

Gooden, James Edward (SAust) b Dec. 23, 1845 Brentford, Middlesex (England) d July 17, 1913 Norwood (SAust)

Gooden, Norman Leslie (SAust) b Dec. 27, 1889 Norwood (SAust) d July 5, 1966 Unley Park (SAust)

Goodfellow, James Edward (SAust) b Aug. 21, 1850 Surrey (England) d July 22, 1924 Malvern (SAust)

Goodman, Gary Weech (Tas & SAust) b Dec. 6, 1953 Sydney (NSW)

Goodrick, Garnet Gordon (Tas) b Feb. 19, 1895 Franklin (Tas) d Jan. 26, 1929 South Melbourne (Vic)

Goodwin, Charles Geoffrey (Tas) b Feb. 12, 1923 Hobart (Tas) d Sept. 20, 1981 Fitzroy (Vic)

* Goodwin, Murray William (WAust) b Dec. 11, 1972 Salisbury (Southern Rhodesia)

Goodwin, Victor Henry Vallance (Qld) b Oct. 26, 1906 Newtown (NSW) d Sept. 22, 1957 Leichhardt (NSW)

Gooma, George Arlington (Qld) b June 25, 1918 Fortitude Valley (Qld) d Oct. 1, 1985 Greenslopes (Qld)

Gooneseena, Gamini (NSW) b Feb. 16, 1931 Mt Lavinia, Colombo (Ceylon)

Gordon, Charles Steward (Vic) b Sept. 8, 1849 Oakleaze, Gloucestershire (England) d March 24, 1930 Nottington, Dorset (England)

Gordon, Evan Shawn (NSW) b Sept. 26, 1960 Pinelands, Cape Town (South Africa)

Gordon, George Birnie (Vic) b Aug. 12, 1860 South Melbourne (Vic) d March 5, 1946 Rose Bay (NSW)

Gordon, George Hollinworth (NSW) b Sept. 20, 1846 New England District (NSW) d May 18, 1923 Darling Point (NSW)

Gordon, Trevor Fairburn (Tas) b Feb. 18, 1915 Hobart (Tas)

Gorman, Frank O. (NSW) birth and death details unknown

Gorringe, Harrison Reginald (WAust) b March 7, 1928 Carlisle (WAust)

Gorry, Charles Richard (NSW) b Sept. 18, 1878 Auckland (New Zealand) d Sept. 13, 1950 Petersham (NSW)

Goss, Edward Alfred (Vic) b Nov. 28, 1875 Richmond (Vic) d Sept. 1, 1955 Camberwell (Vic)

Gostelow, Reginald Edwin Potter (NSW) b July 26, 1900 Darlinghurst (NSW) d Aug. 2, 1984 Darling Point (NSW)

Gott, Douglas Lawrence (Vic) b June 30, 1950 Melbourne (Vic)

Gough, Francis Joseph (Qld) b July 26, 1898 Sandgate (Qld) d Jan. 30, 1980 Sandgate (Qld)

Gould, Fred Keen (SAust) b Sept. 18, 1891 Hindmarsh (SAust) d Feb. 15, 1954 Kingswood (SAust)

Gould, John William (NSW) b Oct. 1, 1868 Sydney (NSW) d Dec. 4, 1908 Lewisham (NSW)

Gouly, Lionel (WAust) b Feb. 12, 1873 Woolloomooloo (NSW) d April 15, 1911 Perth (WAust)

Gourlay, Kenneth Garrett (Tas) b June 27, 1914 Hobart (Tas) d Jan. 28, 1999 Lenah Valley (Tas)

Govan, John Macmillan (Qld) b Dec. 30, 1914 Coorparoo (Qld) d July 20, 1996 South Brisbane (Qld)

Gow, Frederick Kingswood (NSW) b Dec. 18, 1882 Richmond (NSW) d Oct. 11, 1961 Randwick (NSW)

Grace, Brian James David (Qld) b Dec. 30, 1945 Herston (Qld)

Graf, Shaun Francis (Vic & WAust) b May 19, 1957 Somerville (Vic)

* Graham, Henry (Vic) b Nov. 22, 1870 Carlton (Vic) d Feb. 7, 1911 Dunedin (New Zealand)

Grangel, Horace Henry Eric (Vic) b Nov. 23, 1908 Burwood (NSW)

Grant, Bartholomew (Vic) b Aug. 13, 1876 St Kilda (Vic) death details unknown

Grant, Colin Spicer (SAust) b June 22, 1927 Alberton (SAust) d Sept. 3, 1998 Clare (SAust)

Grant, John William (Vic) b Feb. 9, 1941 Essendon (Vic)

Grant, Norman Frederic (Qld) b Jan. 15, 1891 Sydney (NSW) d Sept. 17, 1966 Coorparoo (Qld)

Grant, Thomas Christopher (Vic) b Dec. 20, 1879 St Kilda (Vic) d c. 1934 Kurri Kurri (NSW)

* Graveney, Thomas William (Qld) b June 16, 1927 Riding Mill, Northumberland (England)

Gray, Arthur Thomas (NSW) b June 12, 1892 Glebe (NSW) d July 19, 1977 Glebe (NSW)

Gray, Cecil Douglas (SAust) b April 28, 1902 Henley Beach (SAust) d c. 1976

Gray, Geoffrey Thomas (Qld) b Aug. 27, 1943 Ipswich (Qld)

Greaves, William Henry (Vic) b c. 1830 (England) d Aug. 6, 1869 Warrnambool (Vic)

Green, Albert (SAust) b Jan. 28, 1874 Medindie (SAust) d c. 1913

Green, Braddon Clive (Vic) b Jan. 18, 1958 Benalla (Vic)

Green, Donald William (Vic) b Nov. 22, 1933 Canterbury (Vic)

Green, Douglas Carling (Tas) b May 19, 1902 Hobart (Tas) d Nov. 28, 1990 Hobart (Tas)

Green, Jack Godfrey (Vic) b Oct. 4, 1921 Brighton (Vic)

Green, Randal James (NSW) b July 15, 1961 Hawthorn (Vic)

Gregg, Donald Malcolm (SAust) b Sept. 17, 1924 Tumby Bay (SAust)

Gregg, Norman McAlister (NSW) b March 7, 1892 Burwood (NSW) d July 27, 1966 Woollahra (NSW)

Gregory, Arthur Herbert (NSW) b July 7, 1861 Sydney (NSW) d Aug. 17, 1929 Chatswood (NSW)

Gregory, Charles Smith (NSW) b June 5, 1847 Wollongong (NSW) d April 5, 1935 Chatswood (NSW)

Gregory, Charles William (NSW) b Sept. 30, 1878 Randwick (NSW) d Nov. 14, 1910 Darlinghurst (NSW)

* Gregory, David William (NSW) b April 15, 1845 Fairy Meadow (NSW) d Aug. 4, 1919 Turramurra (NSW)

* Gregory, Edward James (NSW) b May 29, 1839 Waverley (NSW) d April 22, 1899 Randwick (NSW)

* Gregory, Edward Sydney (NSW) b April 14, 1870 Randwick (NSW) d Aug. 1, 1929 Randwick (NSW)

* Gregory, Jack Morrison (NSW) b Aug. 14, 1895 North Sydney (NSW) d Aug. 7, 1973 Bega (NSW)

* Gregory, Ross Gerald (Vic) b Feb. 28, 1916 Malvern (Vic) d June 10, 1942 in action over Ghafargon, Assam (India)

Grew, Ernest Sadler (Qld) b Aug. 11, 1867 Birmingham, Warwickshire (England) d Sept. 4, 1954 Brisbane (Qld)

Grieves, Kenneth John (NSW) b Aug. 27, 1925 Burwood (NSW) d Jan. 3, 1992 Rawtenstall, Lancashire (England)

Griffith, Harold Bickerton (Qld) b Oct. 10, 1879 Manly (NSW) d May 30, 1947 Herston (Qld)

Griffiths, Charles Samuel (Qld) b May 28, 1889 Townsville (Qld) d May 12, 1928 Rockhampton (Qld)

Griffiths, George Edward (NSW & SAust) b April 9, 1938 Glebe (NSW)

Grigg, Henry Tattersall (WAust) b May 24, 1906 Fremantle (WAust) d July 9, 1991 Inglewood (WAust)

* Grimmett, Clarence Victor (Vic & SAust) b Dec. 25, 1891 Caversham, Dunedin (New Zealand) d May 2, 1980 Kensington (SAust)

Grinrod, Barton (Vic) b April 25, 1834 Liverpool , Lancashire (England) d May 23, 1895 Great Crosby, Lancashire (England)

Grosser, John William (NSW) b Aug. 29, 1942 Gunnedah (NSW)

* Groube, Thomas Underwood (Vic) b Sept. 2, 1857 New Plymouth, Taranaki (New Zealand) d Aug. 5, 1927 Hawthorn (Vic)

Grounds, William Thomas (NSW) b Jan. 14, 1878 Surry Hills (NSW) d July 21, 1950 Mortdale (NSW)

* Grout, Arthur Theodore Wallace (Qld) b March 30, 1927 Mackay (Qld) d Nov. 9, 1968 Spring Hill (Qld)

Grove, Percival Brian (SAust) b Feb. 23, 1921 Adelaide (SAust)

* Guest, Colin Ernest John (Vic & WAust) b Oct. 7, 1937 Melbourne (Vic)

Gulliver, Kenneth Charles (NSW) b Aug. 14, 1913 East Maitland (NSW) d June 11, 2001 Collaroy (NSW)

Gumley, William Dudgeon (Qld) b June 28, 1923 Bangalow (NSW) d Aug. 14, 1988 Redcliffe (Qld)

Gun, Lancelot Townsend (SAust) b April 13, 1903 Port Adelaide (SAust) d May 25, 1958 North Adelaide (SAust)

Gunston, Edward Claude (Vic) b May 7, 1913 Brunswick (Vic) d Feb. 28, 1991 Melbourne (Vic)

Gunthorpe, Gilbert Dudley (Qld) b Aug. 9, 1910 Mt Morgan (Qld) d June 3, 1998 Casino (NSW)

Gurr, Gordon Caleb (SAust) b Dec. 22, 1881 Hyde Park (SAust) d Aug. 11, 1960 Loxton (SAust)

Guthrie, Herbert France (Vic) b Sept. 29, 1902 Brisbane (Qld) d Jan. 26, 1951 Bellevue Hill (NSW)

Guttormsen, Maurice Stewart (Qld) b July 29, 1916 Coorpooroo (Qld) d Aug. 8, 1998 Redcliffe (Qld)

Guy, Richard Henry (NSW) b April 4, 1937 St Leonards (NSW)

Gwynne, Leslie William (NSW) b Jan. 26, 1893 Sydney (NSW) d Oct. 25, 1962 Keith (SAust)

Hack, Alfred Thomas (SAust) b June 12, 1905 Glenelg (SAust) d Feb. 4, 1933 Adelaide (SAust)

Hack, Frederick Theodore (SAust) b Aug. 24, 1877 Aldinga (SAust) d April 10, 1939 Brisbane (Qld)

Hack, Norman Reginald (SAust) b Feb. 25, 1907 Glenelg (SAust) d Oct. 13, 1971 Keith (SAust)

Hackett, James Victor (Qld) b Oct. 8, 1917 Perth (WAust)

Haddin, Bradley James (NSW) b Oct. 23, 1977 Cowra (NSW)

Haddrick, Alfred Page (Vic) b July 14, 1868 Adelaide (SAust) d c. 1935 Adelaide (SAust)

Haddrick, Ronald Norman (SAust) b April 9, 1929 Glenelg (SAust)

* Hadlee, Richard John (Tas) b July 3, 1951 St Albans, Christchurch (New Zealand)

Hagdorn, Kim John (WAust) b April 8, 1955 Subiaco (WAust)

Halbert, John Arno (SAust) b Sept. 5, 1937 Hyde Park (SAust)

Halcombe, Ronald Andrewes (SAust & WAust) b March 19, 1906 Petersburg (SAust) d Aug. 1, 1993 Geelong (Vic)

Haldane, Harry (SAust) b July 13, 1865 Kent Town (SAust) d Aug. 12, 1951 Ararat (Vic)

Hale, David John (Qld) b Nov. 11, 1941 Ashgrove (Qld)

Hale, Harold (Tas) b March 27, 1867 Perth (WAust) d Aug. 2, 1947 Melbourne (Vic)

Hall, Melmoth (Vic) b April 26, 1811 Horringer, Suffolk (England) d Oct. 4, 1885 Ashfield (NSW)

Hall, Richard (NSW) birth and death details unknown

* Hall, Wesley Winfield (Qld) b Sept. 12, 1937 Glebe Land, Station Hill, St Michael (Barbados)

Hallebone, Jeffrey (Vic) b Aug. 3, 1929 East Coburg (Vic)

* Hamence, Ronald Arthur (SAust) b Nov. 25, 1915 Hindmarsh (SAust)

Hamilton, James (Tas) b May 16, 1843 birthplace unknown d July 28, 1881 Launceston (Tas)

Hamilton, Thomas Ferrier (Vic) b c. 1820 Cathlaw (Scotland) d Aug. 7, 1905 St Kilda (Vic)

Hammelmann, Andrew John (Qld) b May 9, 1966 Corinda (Qld)

Hammersley, William Josiah Sumner (Vic) b Sept. 26, 1828 Ash, Surrey (England) d Nov. 15, 1886 Fitzroy (Vic)

Hammond, Ashley James (SAust) b Sept. 27, 1969 Burnside (SAust)

Hammond, Charles Pitt (Tas) b Aug. 31, 1868 Hobart (Tas) d c. 1955 Hollywood, California (United States of America)

* Hammond, Jeffrey Roy (SAust) b April 19, 1950 North Adelaide (SAust)

* Hampshire, John Harry (Tas) b Feb. 10, 1941 Thurnscoe, Yorkshire (England)

Hand, Walter Charles (NSW) b July 22, 1847 Richmond, Surrey (England) death details unknown

Handrickan, Anthony John (SAust) b Jan. 6, 1959 Largs Bay (SAust)

Hanify, Cecil Page (Qld) b Aug. 1, 1887 Brisbane (Qld) d Oct. 28, 1964 Manly (Qld)

Hanlin, David Walter (NSW) b Dec. 8, 1928 Chester (England) d June 6, 2001 Chester (England)

Hanna, Brian Leslie (WAust) b Oct. 7, 1946 Katanning (WAust)

Hansen, Christopher Desmond Petrie (Qld) b May 20, 1912 Childers (Qld)

Hanson, Frederick James (Tas) b April 7, 1872 Hobart (Tas) d Sept. 24, 1917 Moonah (Tas)

Hanson, Leopole Harry (SAust) b Sept. 27, 1883 Woodville (SAust) d April 27, 1952 Kingscote (SAust)

Hantke, Theodore Charles Muncaster (WAust) b Aug. 1, 1875 Blinman (SAust) d May 22, 1931 South Perth (WAust)

Harburn, Colin Malcolm (WAust) b Sept. 3, 1938 Subiaco (WAust)

Hardcastle, Gilbert William (Qld) b Feb. 26, 1910 Bowen Hills (Qld) d Feb. 14, 2000 Currimundi (Qld)

Hardie, Archibald Edward (WAust) b April 14, 1892 Warrnambool (Vic) d March 31, 1976 Nedlands (WAust)

Hardie, J. (Australians) birth and death details unknown

Hargrave, Christopher George (Tas) b Aug. 31, 1951 Kiverton, Yorkshire (England)

Harms, Christopher Louis (SAust) b April 21, 1956 Albury (NSW)

Harper, Barry James (Tas) b Oct. 30, 1938 Launceston (Tas)

Harper, Charles Walter (WAust) b Jan. 27, 1880 Guildford (WAust) d July 1, 1956 South Perth (WAust)

Harper, Laurence Damien (Vic) b Dec. 10, 1970 Deniliquin (NSW)

Harper, Peter Quinton (Vic) b Dec. 11, 1977 Burwood (Vic)

Harris, Daniel Joseph (SAust) b Dec. 31, 1979 Adelaide (SAust)

Harris, David (SAust) b Dec. 19, 1930 Alberton (SAust)

Harris, David Andrew (Vic) b March 17, 1966 Newtown (Vic)

Harris, Douglas James (WAust) b Dec. 20, 1962 Subiaco (WAust)

Harris, Errol John (Tas) b May 2, 1963 Cairns (Qld)

Harris, Gordon William (SAust) b Dec. 11, 1897 Alberton (SAust) d June 30, 1974 Kensington Park (SAust)

Harris, Henry Vere Poulett (Tas & WAust) b April 22, 1865 Hobart (Tas) d March 7, 1933 Perth (WAust)

Harris, Kim Phillip (SAust) b Jan. 24, 1952 North Adelaide (SAust)

Harrison, Colin William (SAust) b May 10, 1928 West Croydon (SAust)

Harrison, Ernest Weedon (Tas) b July 22, 1874 Campbell Town (Tas) d Nov. 14, 1968 New Norfolk (Tas)

Harrity, Mark Andrew (SAust) b March 9, 1974 Semaphore (SAust)

Harrold, Hubert Walton (WAust) b March 9, 1898 East Perth (WAust) d April 14, 1968 Hollywood (WAust)

* Harry, John (Vic) b Aug. 1, 1857 Ballarat (Vic) d Oct. 27, 1919 Surrey Hills (Vic)

Harry, Rex Alexander (Vic) b Oct. 19, 1936 Melbourne (Vic)

Hart, Harold William (Vic) b Jan. 4, 1889 Fitzroy South (Vic) d Jan. 2, 1953 Yarraville (Vic)

Hart, Trevor Herbert (Vic) b Nov. 18, 1935 Morwell (Vic)

Harten, James Thomas (Qld) b Nov. 11, 1924 Brisbane (Qld)

* Hartigan, Michael Joseph (NSW & Qld) b Dec. 12, 1879 Chatswood (NSW) d June 7, 1958 Brisbane (Qld)

Hartigan, Thomas Joseph (NSW) b Dec. 8, 1877 Chatswood (NSW) d May 2, 1963 Mosman (NSW)

* Hartkopf, Albert Ernest Victor (Vic) b Dec. 28, 1889 South Fitzroy (Vic) d May 20, 1968 Kew (Vic)

Harvey, Clarence Edgar (Vic & Qld) b March 17, 1921 Newcastle (NSW)

Harvey, Ernest (WAust) b Dec. 14, 1880 Redfern (NSW) d Oct. 19, 1923 Perth (WAust)

Harvey, George Graham (NSW) b c. 1885 Mudgee (NSW) death details unknown

Harvey, Ian Joseph (Vic) b April 10, 1972 Wonthaggi (Vic)

Harvey, Kade Murray (WAust) b Oct. 7, 1975 Subiaco (WAust)

* Harvey, Mervyn Roye (Vic) b April 29, 1918 Broken Hill (NSW) d March 18, 1995 Footscray (Vic)

Harvey, Raymond (Vic) b Jan. 3, 1926 Sydney (NSW)

* Harvey, Robert Neil (Vic & NSW) b Oct. 8, 1928 Fitzroy (Vic)

Harvey, Ronald Mason (NSW) b Oct. 26, 1933 Newcastle (NSW)

* Hassett, Arthur Lindsay (Vic) b Aug. 28, 1913 Geelong (Vic) d June 16, 1993 Batehaven (NSW)

Hassett, Richard Joseph (Vic) b Sept. 7, 1909 Geelong (Vic)

Hastings, Edward Percival (Vic) b c. 1849 (England) d May 31, 1905 Brighton East (Vic)

Hastings, Thomas James (Vic) b Jan. 16, 1865 Melbourne (Vic) d June 14, 1938 North Brighton (Vic)

Hatton, Mark Aaron (Tas) b Jan. 24, 1974 Waverley (NSW)

* Hawke, Neil James Napier (WAust, SAust & Tas) b June 27, 1939 Cheltenham (SAust) d Dec. 25, 2000 Adelaide (SAust)

Hawkins, George William (Vic) b Dec. 7, 1908 Brunswick (Vic) d July 20, 1979 Chiltern (Vic)

Hawson, Edgar Stanley (Tas) b July 25, 1878 Hobart (Tas) d Sept. 29, 1946 Hobart (Tas)

Hawson, Reginald James (Tas) b Sept. 2, 1880 Hobart (Tas) d Feb. 20, 1928 Hobart (Tas)

Hay, Henry (SAust) b March 30, 1874 Adelaide (SAust) d May 16, 1960 Adelaide (SAust)

* Hayden, Matthew Lawrence (Qld) b Oct. 29, 1971 Kingaroy (Qld)

Hayes, William Bede (Qld) b Oct. 16, 1883 Surry Hills (NSW) d Nov. 5, 1926 Corinda (Qld)

Haymes, Frederick George (Tas) b April 5, 1849 Launceston (Tas) d March 12, 1928 Lakes Entrance (Vic)

Hayne, Greg John (NSW) b Oct. 2, 1971 Moree (NSW)

Haysman, Michael Donald (SAust) b April 22, 1961 North Adelaide (SAust)

Hayward, Charles Waterfield (SAust) b June 6, 1867 Norwood (SAust) d Feb. 2, 1934 North Adelaide (SAust)

Haywood, Martin Thomas (NSW) b Oct. 7, 1969 Tamworth (NSW)

* Hazlitt, Gervys Rignold (Vic & NSW) b Sept. 4, 1888 Enfield (NSW) d Oct. 30, 1915 Parramatta (NSW)

Head, Lindsay Hudson (SAust) b Sept. 16, 1935 North Adelaide (SAust)

Headlam, Eustace Slade (Tas) b May 20, 1892 Bothwell (Tas) d May 25, 1958 Launceston (Tas)

Headlam, Felix Emerson (Tas) b June 20, 1897 Bothwell (Tas) d Oct. 5, 1965 Bowral (NSW)

Heairfield, Herbert Venters (SAust) b Feb. 28, 1907 Adelaide (SAust)

Healy, Edwin Francis (Vic) b Sept. 26, 1909 Hawthorn (Vic) d June 14, 1995 Camberwell (Vic)

Healy, Eric Nicholas (WAust) b Nov. 5, 1888 Elizabeth Bay (NSW) d Oct. 9, 1954 Cottesloe (WAust)

Healy, Gerald Edward James (Vic) b March 26, 1885 Prahran (Vic) d July 12, 1946 Armadale (Vic)

* Healy, Ian Andrew (Qld) b April 30, 1964 Spring Hill (Qld)

Healy, John Joseph (Vic) b June 23, 1851 Burra (SAust) d May 17, 1916 East Melbourne (Vic)

Healy, Kenneth James (Qld) b Oct. 15, 1967 South Brisbane (Qld)

Heath, Henry Francis Trafford (SAust) b Dec. 19, 1885 Kadina (SAust) d July 9, 1967 Edinburgh (Scotland)

Heath, Jamie Matthew (NSW) b April 25, 1977 Belmont (NSW)

Heather, Edward Drinkall (Vic) b Oct. 6, 1848 Marylebone, London (England) d July 10, 1935 South Melbourne (Vic)

Heather, Percival Jackson (Vic) b Oct. 6, 1882 Emerald Hill (Vic) d June 29, 1956 Melbourne (Vic)

Hefferan, Francis Urban (Qld) b May 25, 1901 Bowen (Qld) d Sept. 21, 1974 Tweed Heads (NSW)

Heffernan, Ray Leslie (Tas) b Oct. 13, 1935 Hobart (Tas)

Heindrichs, Adolphos Heinrich Julius Carl (WAust) b April 28, 1883 (Germany) d June 24, 1967 Adelaide (SAust)

Henderson, Frank (NSW) b June 1, 1908 Wickham (NSW) d Dec. 6, 1954 Heidelberg (Vic)

Hendricks, Michael (NSW & SAust) b Dec. 12, 1942 Corrimal (NSW)

Hendrie, Charles Richard (Vic) b July 5, 1886 Richmond (Vic) death details unknown

* Hendry, Hunter Scott Thomas Laurie (NSW & Vic) b May 24, 1895 Woollahra (NSW) d Dec. 16, 1988 Rose Bay (NSW)

Hennah, Walter Henry (WAust) b March 16, 1880 Ballarat (Vic) d Aug. 13, 1946 Perth (WAust)

Henri, Harry James Tepapa (Tas) b July 27, 1865 Tauranga (New Zealand) d Feb. 5, 1947 Lindisfarne (Tas)

Henry, Albert (Qld) b c. 1880 Boonah (Qld) d March 13, 1909 Yarrabah (Qld)

Henry, Donald McKenzie (SAust) b June 24, 1885 Parkside (SAust) d July 31, 1973 Felixstow (SAust)

Henschell, Allan Brett (Qld) b June 6, 1961 Dalby (Qld)

Henty, Philip Guy (Tas) b Feb. 4, 1883 Pakenham (Vic) d Oct. 21, 1949 Hobart (Tas)

Henty, William (Tas) b Sept. 23, 1808 West Tarring, Sussex (England) d July 11, 1881 Hove, Sussex (England)

Hepburn, Thomas Robert (Vic) b Dec. 20, 1839 Collingwood (Vic) d April 22, 1921 St Kilda (Vic)

Herbert, Henry James (WAust) b April 24, 1895 Fremantle (WAust) d Nov. 21, 1957 Claremont (WAust)

Herbert, Morgan Uriah (WAust) b Aug. 4, 1918 Albany (WAust) d June 15, 2000 Duncraig (WAust)

Herbert, Peter Jeffrey (SAust) b Jan. 8, 1947 Adelaide (SAust)

Herman, Richard John (Vic) b July 31, 1967 Melbourne (Vic)

Herring, Llewellyn Lloyd (WAust) b April 3, 1871 Clunes (Vic) d Aug. 5, 1922 Fremantle (WAust)

Herring, Robert Wolseley (Vic) b June 8, 1898 Maryborough (Vic) d Oct. 8, 1964 Melbourne (Vic)

Hervey, Matthew (Vic) b Jan. 27, 1820 Glasgow, Lanarkshire (Scotland) d Dec. 1, 1874 Turnbull Plains (Vic)

Herzberg, Steven (WAust & Tas) b May 25, 1967 Carshalton, Surrey (England)

Hetherington, Henry Francisco (Vic) b Sept. 3, 1874 West Melbourne (Vic) d July 11, 1950 Malvern (Vic)

Hewer, William Albert (SAust) b May 7, 1877 Goodwood (SAust) d June 2, 1948 Wayville (SAust)

Hewett, Ian Stephen Louis (Vic) b Jan. 24, 1976 East Melbourne (Vic)

Hewitt, Albert Hedley Vickers (Qld) b Jan. 21, 1866 Nowra (NSW) d July 15, 1947 death place unknown

Hewitt, Richard Child (NSW) b Feb. 13, 1844 Beverley, Yorkshire (England) d c. 1920 Granville (NSW)

Hewson, Robert Henry (WAust) b Aug. 4, 1893 Carlton (Vic) d Oct. 21, 1972 Melbourne (Vic)

* Hibbert, Paul Anthony (Vic) b July 23, 1952 Brunswick (Vic)

* Hick, Graeme Ashley (Qld) b May 23, 1966 Salisbury (Rhodesia)

Hickey, Denis Jon (Vic & SAust) b Dec. 31, 1964 Mooroopna (Vic)

Hickson, Robert Newburgh (NSW) b May 2, 1884 Newcastle (NSW) d June 21, 1963 Armidale (NSW)

Hiddleston, Hugh Charles Stewart (NSW) b c. 1855 full birth details unknown d May 14, 1934 Coolgardie (WAust)

Hide, Jesse Bollard (SAust) b March 12, 1857 Eastbourne, Sussex (England) d March 19, 1924 Edinburgh (Scotland)

Hiern, Barry Neil (SAust) b Aug. 8, 1951 North Adelaide (SAust)

Hiern, Ross Noel (SAust) b Aug. 2, 1922 Parkside (SAust) d Aug. 21, 1999 Morphettville (SAust)

Higgins, Benjamin Hugh (SAust) b March 8, 1972 Adelaide (SAust)

Higgins, Henry James Roy (Qld) b Jan. 27, 1900 Rosalie (Qld) d Feb. 24, 1990 Chermside (Qld)

Higgins, James (Qld) b Nov. 14, 1874 Ormiston (Qld) d Nov. 24, 1957 Sandgate (Qld)

* Higgs, James Donald (Vic) b July 11, 1950 Kyabram (Vic)

Higgs, Mark Anthony (NSW) b June 30, 1976 Queanbeyan (NSW)

* Hilditch, Andrew Mark Jefferson (NSW & SAust) b May 20, 1956 North Adelaide (SAust)

Hill, Arthur (SAust) b May 28, 1871 Adelaide (SAust) d June 22, 1936 Glenelg (SAust)

* Hill, Clement (SAust) b March 18, 1877 Hindmarsh (SAust) d Sept. 5, 1945 Parkville (Vic)

Hill, Clement John (NSW) b July 2, 1904 Beryl (NSW) d May 21, 1988 Belmont (NSW)

Hill, Henry John (SAust) b July 7, 1878 Adelaide (SAust) d Oct. 30, 1906 Kensington Park (SAust)

* Hill, John Charles (Vic) b June 25, 1923 Murrumbeena (Vic) d Aug. 11, 1974 Caulfield (Vic)

Hill, John Gerard (Qld) b Nov. 11, 1956 Waratah (NSW)

Hill, Kenneth Michael (NSW) b Jan. 26, 1945 Merewether (NSW)

Hill, Leon Trevor (SAust & Qld) b Feb. 28, 1936 West Croydon (SAust)

Hill, Leslie Roy (SAust) b April 27, 1884 Adelaide (SAust) d Dec. 15, 1952 North Adelaide (SAust)

Hill, Mark Anthony (Tas) b July 27, 1964 Perth (WAust)

Hill, Percy (SAust) b July 4, 1868 Kent Town (SAust) d July 24, 1950 Adelaide (SAust)

Hill, Peter Distin (SAust) b Jan. 28, 1923 North Adelaide (SAust)

Hill, Roland James (SAust) b Oct. 18, 1868 Parkside (SAust) d Jan. 10, 1929 Glenelg (SAust)

Hill, Stanley (SAust & NSW) b Aug. 22, 1885 Adelaide (SAust) d May 10, 1970 Englefield Green, Surrey (England)

Hill, Wayne Douglas (WAust) b Dec. 5, 1953 Subiaco (WAust)

Hill-Smith, Wyndham (WAust) b Feb. 16, 1909 Angaston (SAust) d Oct. 25, 1990 Angaston (SAust)

Hilliard, Henry (NSW) b Nov. 7, 1826 Sydney (NSW) d March 19, 1914 Willoughby (NSW)

Hills, Dene Fleetwood (Tas) b Aug. 27, 1970 Wynyard (Tas)

Hird, Sydney Francis (NSW) b Jan. 7, 1910 Balmain (NSW) d Dec. 20, 1980 Bloemfontein (South Africa)

Hird, William (Tas) b Sept. 23, 1921 Stanley, Durham (England)

Hiscock, Ernest John (SAust) b April 9, 1868 Penrice (SAust) d Dec. 16, 1895 Alberton (SAust)

Hitchcock, Oswould Charles (Qld) b Sept. 9, 1859 Greenhill, Shoalhaven (NSW) death details unknown

Hitchcock, Robert Alan (SAust) b May 14, 1938 North Adelaide (SAust)

* Hoare, Desmond Edward (WAust) b Oct. 19, 1934 Perth (WAust)

Hoare, William (Qld) b Oct. 23, 1868 Brisbane (Qld) death details unknown

Hodge, Bradley John (Vic) b Dec. 29, 1974 Sandringham (Vic)

Hodge, Malcolm Gordon Fergurson (SAust) b Aug. 28, 1934 Adelaide (SAust)

* Hodges, John Robart (Vic) b Aug. 11, 1855 Knightsbridge (London) d Jan. 17, 1933 details unknown

Hodgetts, Bruce Frederick (Tas) b Jan. 25, 1947 Burnie (Tas)

Hodgkinson, John Ernest (NSW) b Feb. 7, 1873 Surry Hills (NSW) d Nov. 19, 1939 Burwood (NSW)

Hodgson, Robert William (Tas) b Feb. 22, 1973 Launceston (Tas)

* Hogan, Tom George (WAust) b Sept. 23, 1956 Merredin (WAust)

Hogg, Geoffrey Charles Huxtable (NSW) b Sept. 28, 1909 Goulburn (NSW) d Aug. 14, 1959 Coorparoo (Qld)

* Hogg, George Bradley (WAust) b Feb. 6, 1971 Narrogin (WAust)

Hogg, James Edgar Phipps (NSW & Qld) b Oct. 16, 1906 Goulburn (NSW) d Dec. 2, 1975 West Ryde (NSW)

* Hogg, Rodney Malcolm (SAust & Vic) b March 5, 1951 Richmond (Vic)

Hogg, Thomas (Combined XIII) b March 12, 1845 Hobart (Tas) d July 13, 1890 Trevallyn (Tas)

Hogue, Thomas Herbert (NSW & WAust) b Oct. 5, 1877 Wickham (NSW) d May 6, 1956 Nedlands (WAust)

Hogue, Wallace White (WAust) b Dec. 9, 1879 Wickham (NSW) d June 1, 1946 Cook's Hill (NSW)

* Hohns, Trevor Victor (Qld) b Jan. 23, 1954 Nundah (Qld)

* Holding, Michael Anthony (Tas) b Feb. 16, 1954 Half Way Tree, Kingston (Jamaica)

Holdsworth, Wayne John (NSW) b Oct. 5, 1968 Paddington (NSW)

* Hole, Graeme Blake (NSW & SAust) b Jan. 6, 1931 Concord West (NSW) d Feb. 14, 1990 Kensington Gardens (SAust)

* Holland, Robert George (NSW) b Oct. 19, 1946 Camperdown (NSW)

Holman, Raymond Sidney (SAust) b Sept. 17, 1919 Largs Bay (SAust) d Sept. 19, 1989 Woodville South (SAust)

Holten, Charles Valentine (Vic) b Sept. 15, 1927 Brighton (Vic)

Holton, Leslie George (SAust) b March 13, 1903 Carlton (Vic) d Feb. 1, 1956 Hawthorn (Vic)

Holyman, Josef Michael (Tas) b June 10, 1970 Launceston (Tas)

Homburg, Robert Otto (SAust) b Jan. 31, 1876 Norwood (SAust) d Oct. 21, 1948 Medindie (SAust)

Hone, Brian William (SAust) b July 1, 1907 Semaphore (SAust) d May 28, 1978 Paris (France)

Hone, Garton Maxwell (SAust) b Feb. 21, 1901 Morphett Vale (SAust) d May 28, 1991 Myrtle Bank (SAust)

Honeybone, George Alfred (Vic) b April 2, 1875 London (England) d Nov. 1, 1956 Ashburton (Vic)

Honour, Victor Gerald (Qld) b Oct. 25, 1910 Bierton, Buckinghamshire (England) d Jan. 3, 2001 Brookfield (Qld)

Hook, Benjamin James (SAust) b March 5, 1973 Kingswood (SAust)

Hooker, John Edward Halford (NSW) b March 6, 1898 Summer Hill (NSW) d Feb. 12, 1982 Winmalee (NSW)

* Hookes, David William (SAust) b May 3, 1955 Mile End (SAust)

Hookey, Scott Gregory (NSW & Tas) b Feb. 10, 1967 Sydney (NSW)

Hooper, Kerry (Tas) b June 9, 1942 Launceston (Tas)

Hooper, Victor Leonard (Tas) b April 23, 1905 Mt Stuart (Tas) d Sept. 3, 1990 New Town (Tas)

Hope, Adam (Vic) b c. 1834 (England) d Oct. 9, 1916 East Melbourne (Vic)

* Hopkins, Albert John Young (NSW) b May 3, 1874 Young (NSW) d April 25, 1931 North Sydney (NSW)

Hopkins, Isaac (Vic) b Nov. 9, 1870 Collingwood (Vic) d Oct. 25, 1913 Richmond (Vic)

Hopkinson, Samuel Goop (Vic) b Oct. 1, 1825 Thorne, Yorkshire (England) d June 26, 1887 South Melbourne (Vic)

Horan, James Francis (Vic) b June 8, 1880 Fitzroy (Vic) d Nov. 1, 1945 Malvern (Vic)

Horan, Thomas Ignatius Bernard (Vic) b April 7, 1886 Fitzroy (Vic) d May 26, 1952 East Camberwell (Vic)

* Horan, Thomas Patrick (Vic) b March 8, 1854 Midleton, County Cork (Ireland) d April 16, 1916 Malvern (Vic)

* Hordern, Herbert Vivian (NSW) b Feb. 10, 1883 North Sydney (NSW) d June 17, 1938 Darlinghurst (NSW)

Horley, John Rasalle (SAust) b Jan. 23, 1936 Medindie (SAust)

* Hornibrook, Percival Mitchell (Qld) b July 27, 1899 Obi Obi (Qld) d Aug. 25, 1976 Spring Hill (Qld)

Horrocks, William John (WAust) b June 18, 1905 Warrington, Lancashire (England) d Nov. 15, 1985 Parkdale (Vic)

Horsell, Jack Aymat James (SAust) b July 12, 1914 Stepney (SAust) d April 20, 1985 Sydney (NSW)

Horsfield, Gordon Cameron (NSW) b March 24, 1913 Balmain (NSW) d Aug. 25, 1982 Mosman (NSW)

Horsley, Daniel, Anthony (NSW) b July 20, 1972 Sydney (NSW)

Horsnell, Kenneth George (SAust) b Sept. 3, 1933 Joslin (SAust)

Horton, Arnell Stanley (Tas) b Sept. 21, 1892 Burnie (Tas) d Sept. 15, 1987 Newstead (Tas)

Hosie, Robert (Vic) b Sept. 8, 1858 Collingwood (Vic) d Sept. 29, 1932 Richmond (Vic)

Hosking, Peter Mowat (Vic) b Sept. 30, 1932 Fairfield (Vic)

Hoskings, Arthur G. W. (WAust) b c. 1872 d Sept. 2, 1919 Dunella, New Jersey (United States of America)

Hotchin, Mortimer Douglas (Vic) b May 20, 1889 Prahran (Vic) d June 21, 1958 East Melbourne (Vic)

Hotham, Augustus Thomas (Vic) b c. 1817 (christened Jan. 25) Dennington, Suffolk (England) d Dec. 24, 1896 Tunbridge Wells, Kent (England)

Hourn, David William (NSW) b Sept. 9, 1949 Bondi (NSW)

House, Graham Warwick Charles (WAust & SAust) b Sept. 4, 1950 Busselton (WAust)

Houston, Richard Shinnock (Vic) b June 30, 1863 Brighton (Vic) d Nov. 27, 1921 Williamstown (Vic)

Howard, Craig (Vic) b April 8, 1974 Lilydale (Vic)

Howard, Harry Cecil (WAust) b June 30, 1885 Adelaide (SAust) d Sept. 18, 1960 Perth (WAust)

Howard, Leonard Easther (SAust) b April 18, 1886 Adelaide (SAust) d Aug. 14, 1945 Prospect (SAust)

Howard, Roy (Vic) b Nov. 15, 1922 Terang (Vic)

Howard, Stephen John (Tas) b Feb. 7, 1949 Launceston (Tas)

Howard, Thomas Harris (NSW) b May 2, 1877 Sydney (NSW) d Oct. 6, 1965 Randwick (NSW)

Howe, John Sidney (Tas) b Dec. 27, 1868 Kotree (India) d July 29, 1939 Neutral Bay (NSW)

Howell, George (NSW) b June 9, 1822 Sydney (NSW) d Nov. 18, 1890 Sydney (NSW)

Howell, William Hunter (NSW) b Jan. 12, 1902 Penrith (NSW) d Jan. 23, 1987 Penrith (NSW)

* Howell, William Peter (NSW) b Dec. 29, 1869 Penrith (NSW) d July 14, 1940 Castlereagh (NSW)

Howlett, John Thomas (Vic) b April 8, 1868 North Melbourne (Vic) d June 15, 1931 East Melbourne (Vic)

Howson, Herbert (Vic) b Aug. 11, 1872 Newstead (Vic) d May 8, 1948 Murrumbeena (Vic)

Hubbard, Edward Francis (Qld) b June 27, 1906 Brisbane (Qld) d Oct. 1, 1969 Herston (Qld)

Hubble, James Merrick (WAust) b Aug. 12, 1942 Beaconsfield (WAust)

Huddleston, John (Vic) b Nov. 25, 1837 Nottingham, Nottinghamshire (England) d c. 1904 Brunswick (Vic)

Hudson, Graeme Charles (Tas) b June 16, 1930 Wynyard (Tas) d Sept. 23, 1974 Launceston (Tas)

Hudson, John Lambert (Tas) b July 23, 1882 Launceston (Tas) d March 16, 1961 Hobart (Tas)

Hughes, David Paul (Tas) b April 13, 1947 Newton-le-Willows, Lancashire (England)

Hughes, Glenn Arthur (Tas) b Nov. 23, 1959 Goomalling (WAust)

Hughes, Graeme Christopher (NSW) b Dec. 6, 1955 Stanmore (NSW)

* Hughes, Kimberley John (WAust) b Jan. 26, 1954 Margaret River (WAust)

* Hughes, Mervyn Gregory (Vic) b Nov. 23, 1961 Euroa (Vic)

Hughes, Walter Cecil (WAust) b Aug. 13, 1882 Adelaide (SAust) d Aug. 16, 1917 Perth (WAust)

Hughson, Desmond George (Qld) b May 27, 1941 Herston (Qld)

Hugo, Victor (SAust) b Nov. 25, 1877 Adelaide (SAust) d April 8, 1930 Malvern (SAust)

Hume, Andrew Ernest (NSW) b Feb. 5, 1869 Redfern (NSW) d June 22, 1912 London (England)

Humphreys, Anthony John Rolph (Tas) b June 9, 1971 Launceston (Tas)

Humphreys, John (NSW) birth and death details unknown

Hunt, Horace Charles (Vic) b July 15, 1907 Stawell (Vic) d Oct. 15, 1984 Melbourne (Vic)

* Hunt, William Alfred (NSW) b Aug. 26, 1908 Balmain (NSW) d Dec. 30, 1983 Balmain (NSW)

Huntington, Ian Ross (Vic) b Oct. 18, 1931 Coburg (Vic)

Hurburgh, Clifton Maurice (Tas) b Jan. 15, 1917 Hobart (Tas)

Hurn, Brian Morgan (SAust) b March 4, 1939 Angaston (SAust)

* Hurst, Alan George (Vic) b July 15, 1950 Altona (Vic)

* Hurwood, Alexander (Qld) b June 17, 1902 Kangaroo Point (Qld) d Sept. 26, 1982 Coffs Harbour (NSW)

Hussey, Michael Edward (WAust) b May 27, 1975 Morley (WAust)

Hussey, Percival Leitch (WAust) b June 23, 1869 Perth (WAust) d May 13, 1944 Adelaide (SAust)

Hutcheon, Ernest Henry (Qld) b June 17, 1889 Toowoomba (Qld) d June 9, 1937 Brisbane (Qld)

Hutcheon, John Silvester (Qld) b April 5, 1882 Warwick (Qld) d June 18, 1957 Albion Heights (Qld)

Hutchison, Paul James (SAust & Tas) b Feb. 17, 1968 Glen Innes (NSW)

Hutton, Ernest Hamilton (Vic & Qld) b March 29, 1867 Mt Rouse (Vic) d July 12, 1929 Ascot (Qld)

Hutton, Henry George (SAust) b Aug. 26, 1878 Masterton (New Zealand) d Aug. 13, 1968 Norwood (SAust)

Hutton, Maurice Percy (SAust) b March 21, 1903 Parkside (SAust) d Feb. 20, 1940 Mitcham (SAust)

Hutton, Mervyn Douglas (SAust) b Aug. 24, 1911 Port Augusta (SAust) d Sept. 28, 1988 Melbourne (Vic)

Hutton, Norman Harvey (SAust) b Aug. 10, 1911 Unley (SAust) d Aug. 27, 1965 Fullarton (SAust)

Hutton, William Frederick Percy (SAust) b Oct. 2, 1876 Mintaro (SAust) d Oct. 1, 1951 Millswood (SAust)

Hyatt, Roland Shane (Tas) b Dec. 30, 1961 Hobart (Tas)

Hyde, Phillip Andrew (Vic) b Oct. 22, 1958 Melbourne (Vic)

Hyett, Francis William (Vic) b Feb. 9, 1882 Bolwarra (Vic) d April 25, 1919 Fitzroy (Vic)

Hyland, Byron John (Tas) b Jan. 14, 1930 New Norfolk (Tas)

Hynes, Lincoln Carruthers (NSW) b April 12, 1912 Balmain (NSW) d Aug. 7, 1977 Killara (NSW)

Hyslop, Hector Henry (Australians) b Dec. 13, 1840 Southampton, Hampshire (England) d Sept. 11, 1920 Cosham, Hampshire (England)

* Ibadulla, Khalid (Tas) b Dec. 20, 1935 Lahore (Pakistan)

Iceton, Thomas Henry (NSW) b Oct. 12, 1849 Sydney (NSW) d May 19, 1908 Ashfield (NSW)

Illingworth, Edward Philip (Vic) b Nov. 27, 1938 Fairfield (Vic)

Illman, Brian Kevin (SAust) b Oct. 23, 1937 Unley Park (SAust)

* Imran Khan (NSW) b Nov. 25, 1952 Lahore (Pakistan)

Ingleton, Walter George (Vic) b Feb. 16, 1867 Collingwood (Vic) d Feb. 4, 1923 East Melbourne (Vic)

Inkster, Gordon Bradford (SAust) b June 30, 1893 Portland Estate (SAust) d March 22, 1957 Darlinghurst (NSW)

Inness, Mathew William Hunter (Vic) b Jan. 13, 1978 East Melbourne (Vic)

Inverarity, Mervyn (WAust) b Oct. 25, 1907 Claremont (WAust) d March 17, 1979 Cottesloe (WAust)

* Inverarity, Robert John (WAust & SAust) b Jan. 31, 1944 Subiaco (WAust)

Inwood, Bradley Phillip (Qld) b July 23, 1963 Gladstone (Qld)

* Iredale, Francis Adams (NSW) b June 19, 1867 Surry Hills (NSW) d April 15, 1926 Crows Nest (NSW)

Ireland, Gary John (WAust) b Oct. 3, 1961 Collie (WAust)

* Ironmonger, Herbert (Qld & Vic) b April 7, 1882 Pine Mountain (Qld) d June 1, 1971 St Kilda (Vic)

Irvine, John Taylor (WAust) b April 13, 1944 Subiaco (WAust)

* Iverson, John Brian (Vic) b July 27, 1915 Melbourne (Vic) d Oct. 23, 1973 Brighton (Vic)

Ives, William Francis (NSW) b Nov. 14, 1896 Glebe (NSW) d March 23, 1975 Newport Beach (NSW)

Ivory, Wilfred Charles (Rest of Australia) b Sept. 12, 1888 South Yarra (Vic) d Oct. 13, 1975 North Brighton (Vic)

Jack, Keith Mayall (Qld) b April 25, 1927 Tambo (Qld) d Nov. 22, 1982 Buderim (Qld)

Jackman, Darrell (Tas) b May 31, 1921 Hobart (Tas) d April 5, 1991 Cheltenham (Tas)

* Jackson, Archibald (NSW) b Sept. 5, 1909 Rutherglen, Lanarkshire (Scotland) d Feb. 16, 1933 Clayfield (Qld)

Jackson, Arthur Enderby (WAust) b Jan. 6, 1872 Kapunda (SAust) d June 29, 1935 Cottesloe (WAust)

Jackson, Paul William (Vic & Qld) b Nov. 1, 1961 East Melbourne (Vic)

Jackson, Victor Edward (NSW) b Oct. 25, 1916 Woollahra (NSW) d Jan. 30, 1965 Manildra (NSW)

Jacobson, Alan Melville (Tas) b Nov. 12, 1942 Sydney (NSW)

Jacomb, John Newton (Vic) b c. 1843 Melbourne (Vic) d Nov. 5, 1891 Walhalla (Vic)

Jakins, James Albert (Tas) b Oct. 1, 1886 Hawthorn (Vic) d Dec. 12, 1948 Wivenhoe (Tas)

James, Alec Pearce (SAust) b May 31, 1883 Neath (Wales) d c. 1961 Newton Abbot, Devon (England)

James, Eric Lisle (Tas) b Oct. 21, 1881 Low Head (Tas) d c. 1948 Malvern (Vic)

James, Eric Pearse (WAust) b Feb. 27, 1923 Albany (WAust) d March 28, 1999 Albany (WAust)

James, Gerald Thomas Henry (Tas) b March 22, 1908 New Norfolk (Tas) d Dec. 24, 1967 Hobart (Tas)

James, Ronald Victor (NSW & SAust) b May 23, 1920 Paddington (NSW) d April 28, 1983 Auburn (NSW)

James, Sidney Victor Austin (Tas) b Oct. 26, 1895 Adelaide (SAust) d Aug. 3, 1966 Canterbury (Vic)

Jamieson, Dudley Garfield (SAust) b July 4, 1912 Redruth (SAust) d Jan. 14, 1979 Burnside (SAust)

Jamieson, Walter Angus Bethune (Tas) b 1828 birth day and month unknown Plenty (Tas) d Dec. 28, 1881 Plenty (Tas)

Jansan, Ernest William (NSW) b Aug. 26, 1874 Gulgong (NSW) d May 31, 1945 Leichhardt (NSW)

Jaques, Philip Anthony (NSW) b May 3, 1979 Wollongong (NSW)

* Jarman, Barrington Noel (SAust) b Feb. 17, 1936 Hindmarsh (SAust)

Jarvis, Alfred (SAust) b Feb. 15, 1868 Hindmarsh (SAust) d Aug. 12, 1938 Semaphore (SAust)

* Jarvis, Arthur Harwood (SAust) b Oct. 19, 1860 Hindmarsh (SAust) d Nov. 15, 1933 Hindmarsh (SAust)

Jarvis, Carlisle Melrose Byron (WAust) b Dec. 10, 1906 East Fremantle (WAust) d Nov. 6, 1979 Mt Lawley (WAust)

Jarvis, Harwood Samuel Coombe (SAust) b Aug. 30, 1884 Brompton (SAust) d Oct. 10, 1936 Port Pirie (SAust)

Jeffrey, Clifton Linley (Tas) b Jan. 10, 1913 Hobart (Tas) d Feb. 11, 1987 Launceston (Tas)

Jeffrey, Robert Frederick (NSW & Tas) b Sept. 19, 1953 Goulburn (NSW)

Jeffreys, Arthur Frederick (NSW) b April 7, 1848 London (England) d Feb. 4, 1906 Lasham, Hampshire (England)

Jeffreys, John Alan (WAust) b April 17, 1913 Fremantle (WAust) d Nov. 3, 1943 Shipham, Somerset (England)

Jeffreys, Keith Stanley (WAust) b Jan. 18, 1921 Bridgetown (WAust) d May 16, 2000 Mandurah (WAust)

Jelich, Neville (Qld & Tas) b March 11, 1962 Orasje, near Belgrade (Yugoslavia)

* Jenner, Terrence James (WAust & SAust) b Sept. 8, 1944 Mt Lawley (WAust)

* Jennings, Claude Burrows (SAust & Qld) b June 5, 1884 East St Kilda (Vic) d June 20, 1950 Adelaide (SAust)

Jennings, Henry John (Vic) b April 9, 1849 Launceston (Tas) d June 6, 1925 St Kilda (Vic)

Jinks, Allan (Vic) b Dec. 29, 1913 Carlton North (Vic) d Nov. 7, 1997 Melbourne (Vic)

Jinks, Frederick (Vic) b May 6, 1909 Eaglehawk (Vic) d Aug. 16, 1996 Melbourne (Vic)

John, Bruce Duncanson (Tas) b July 20, 1937 Launceston (Tas)

Johns, Alfred Edward (Vic) b Jan. 22, 1868 Hawthorn (Vic) d Feb. 13, 1934 Melbourne (Vic)

Johnson, Benjamin Andrew (SAust) b Aug. 1, 1973 Naracoorte (SAust)

Johnson, Eric Alfred (SAust) b July 11, 1902 North Norwood (SAust) d Jan. 10, 1976 Adelaide (SAust)

Johnson, Francis Barry (NSW) b May 21, 1880 birthplace unknown d May 28, 1951 Longueville (NSW)

* Johnson, Ian William Geddes (Vic) b Dec. 8, 1917 Hotham West (Vic) d Oct. 9, 1998 Malvern (Vic)

Johnson, James William (Vic) b Sept. 22, 1884 Footscray (Vic) d Aug. 14, 1941 Middle Park (Vic)

* Johnson, Leonard Joseph (Qld) b March 18, 1919 Ipswich (Qld) d April 20, 1977 Silkstone (Qld)

Johnston, Aubrey Edmund (NSW) b Sept. 7, 1882 Canterbury (NSW) d June 16, 1960 Manly (NSW)

Johnston, Clive William (NSW) b Aug. 4, 1925 Petersham (NSW) d May 11, 1991 Petersham (NSW)

Johnston, David Alexander Hughes (NSW) b July 10, 1955 Maitland (NSW)

Johnston, David Allan (SAust) b Dec. 4, 1954 Melbourne (Vic)

Johnston, David Trent (NSW) b April 29, 1974 Wollongong (NSW)

Johnston, Frederick Bourke (NSW) b Sept. 10, 1915 Sydney (NSW) d Sept. 6, 1977 Hillsdale (NSW)

* Johnston, William Arras (Vic) b Feb. 26, 1922 Beeac (Vic)

Johnstone, Richard Gordon (Vic) b Feb. 9, 1885 Malvern (Vic) d Nov. 9, 1961 Geelong (Vic)

Jolly, Harvey Bruce (SAust) b Aug. 1, 1960 Naracoorte (SAust)

Jones, Alan (WAust) b Nov. 4, 1938 Velindre, Glamorgan (Wales)

Jones, Alan Robert (Qld) b June 11, 1948 Greenslopes (Qld)

Jones, Arthur Harold (Qld) b Dec. 17, 1874 Brisbane (Qld) d Dec. 2, 1917 Salisbury Plain, Wiltshire (England)

Jones, Charles Frederick (Vic) b Feb. 9, 1870 Williamstown (Vic) d March 25, 1957 Williamstown (Vic)

* Jones, Dean Mervyn (Vic) b March 24, 1961 Coburg (Vic)

* Jones, Ernest (SAust & WAust) b Sept. 30, 1869 East Auburn (SAust) d Nov. 23, 1943 Norwood (SAust)

Jones, John Raymond (WAust) b May 10, 1899 Clunes (Vic) d March 14, 1991 Hamilton Hill (WAust)

Jones, Neil Richard (NSW) b July 12, 1966 Stourport-on-Severn, Worcestershire (England)

Jones, Ronald Andrew (NSW) b March 28, 1964 Dubbo (NSW)

* Jones, Samuel Percy (NSW & Qld) b Aug. 1, 1861 Sydney (NSW) d July 14, 1951 Auckland (New Zealand)

Jones, Sidney (NSW) birth and death details unknown

Jones, Stephen Alexander (WAust) b July 1, 1949 Sydney (NSW)

Jones, Victor Clarence (WAust) b May 11, 1881 Ballarat (Vic) d July 20, 1923 Mt Lawley (WAust)

Jones, William George (SAust) b May 13, 1864 Hindmarsh (SAust) d July 16, 1924 Adelaide (SAust)

Jordan, Frank Slater (NSW) b Sept. 19, 1905 Darlington (NSW) d Oct. 22, 1995 Vaucluse (NSW)

Jordan, Grant Leigh (Vic) b March 18, 1965 Ivanhoe (Vic)

Jordon, Raymond Clarence (Vic) b Feb. 17, 1936 Melbourne (Vic)

Jose, Anthony Douglas (SAust) b Feb. 17, 1929 Knoxville (SAust) d Feb. 3, 1972 Los Angeles, California (United States of America)

Jose, Gilbert Edgar (SAust) b Nov. 1, 1898 Taichow (China) d March 27, 1942 Changi POW Camp (Singapore)

Joseph, Joel P. (NSW) b c. 1867 d c. 1942 Canterbury (NSW)

* Joslin, Leslie Ronald (Vic) b Dec. 13, 1947 Yarraville (Vic)

Joyce, Robert Eric (Qld) b Dec. 11, 1947 Auchenflower (Qld)

Joynt, Hartley Kelly (WAust) b June 14, 1938 Subiaco (WAust)

* Julian, Brendon Paul (WAust) b Aug. 10, 1970 Hamilton (New Zealand)

Junor, John Leonard (Vic) b April 27, 1914 Thornbury (Vic)

Junor, Robert Johnston (Vic) b Jan. 10, 1888 Marcus Hill (Vic) d July 26, 1957 Heidelberg (Vic)

Jurgensen, Shane John (WAust) b April 28, 1976 Redcliffe (Qld)

Kahler, Lance Warren (Qld) b June 27, 1977 Crows Nest (Qld)

* Kallicharran, Alvin Isaac (Qld) b March 21, 1949 Paidama (British Guiana)

* Kanhai, Rohan Bholal (WAust & Tas) b Dec. 26, 1935 Port Mourant, Berbice (British Guiana)

* Kasprowicz, Michael Scott (Qld) b Feb. 10, 1972 South Brisbane (Qld)

Katich, Simon Matthew (WAust) b Aug. 21, 1975 Middle Swan (WAust)

Kay, William Malcolm (Qld) b May 4, 1893 Gympie (Qld) d July 7, 1973 Taringa (Qld)

Keating, James Leslie (Vic) b Oct. 1, 1891 Brunswick East (Vic) d March 13, 1962 Fitzroy (Vic)

Kekwick, Edwin Huntley (SAust) b March 5, 1875 Port MacDonell (SAust) d Aug. 29, 1950 Adelaide (SAust)

* Kelleway, Charles (NSW) b April 25, 1886 Lismore (NSW) d Nov. 16, 1944 Lindfield (NSW)

Kellick, Charles Moore (NSW) b Nov. 21, 1842 Sydney (NSW) d March 27, 1918 Strathfield (NSW)

Kellick, James (NSW) b Aug. 24, 1840 Sydney (NSW) d Aug. 8, 1926 Sydney (NSW)

Kelly, David John (SAust) b Jan. 28, 1959 North Adelaide (SAust)

Kelly, Ian Donald Cameron (Qld) b May 5, 1959 Herston (Qld)

* Kelly, James Joseph (NSW) b May 10, 1867 Sandridge (Vic) d Aug. 14, 1938 Bellevue Hill (NSW)

Kelly, Otto Harvey (WAust) b May 15, 1880 Sandridge (Vic) d July 30, 1946 Mt Lawley (WAust)

Kelly, Peter Charles (NSW & WAust) b April 28, 1942 Mosman (NSW)

Kelly, Richard Terence Bonynge (Vic) b March 21, 1870 Ballan (Vic) d Dec. 27, 1941 St Kilda (Vic)

Kelly, Robert Charles (WAust) b May 18, 1969 Subiaco (WAust)

* Kelly, Thomas Joseph Dart (Vic) b May 3, 1844 County Waterford (Ireland) d July 20, 1893 Hawthorn (Vic)

Kelly, William Harvey (WAust) b March 24, 1883 St Kilda (Vic) d c. 1944 Croydon (Vic)

Kelly, William Lucius Usna (Vic) b Jan. 20, 1875 Rosedale (Vic) d Dec. 27, 1968 Bulla (Vic)

Kelton, Matthew David (SAust) b April 9, 1974 Woodville South (SAust)

Kemp, Benjamin Charles Ernest (SAust & Vic) b Jan. 30, 1864 Plymouth, Devon (England) d Dec. 3, 1940 Albert Park (Vic)

Kemp, Leonard Denton (Vic) b June 6, 1909 Malvern (Vic)

Kendall, Keith Harold Dudley (Vic) b March 16, 1929 South Melbourne (Vic)

* Kendall, Thomas Kingston (Vic & Tas) b Aug. 24, 1851 Bedford, Bedfordshire (England) d Aug. 17, 1924 Hobart (Tas)

Kenneally, Cornelius James (SAust) b July 28, 1926 Edwardstown (Vic) d Jan. 18, 1995 Ashford (SAust)

Kenny, Arthur (Vic) b Aug. 9, 1878 Emerald Hill (Vic) d Aug. 2, 1934 South Melbourne (Vic)

Kenny, Justin Dean (NSW) b Sept. 24, 1966 Camperdown (NSW)

* Kent, Martin Francis (Qld) b Nov. 23, 1953 Mossman (Qld)

Keogh, Ernest John (WAust) b c. 1869 South Melbourne (Vic) d c. 1951 South Yarra (Vic)

Kermode, Alexander (NSW) b May 15, 1876 Sydney (NSW) d July 17, 1934 Balmain (NSW)

Kerr, Eric Alan David (Vic) b June 28, 1923 Auburn (Vic) d Feb. 16, 1989 Melbourne (Vic)

* Kerr, Robert Byers (Qld) b June 16, 1961 Herston (Qld)

Kershler, Anthony John (NSW) b July 6, 1968 St Leonards (NSW)

Kessey, Gwilym Taf (WAust) b Jan. 13, 1919 Meekatharra (WAust) d June 25, 1986 Perth (WAust)

Kettle, John Louis (NSW) b Dec. 3, 1830 Sydney (NSW) d Oct. 30, 1891 Newtown (NSW)

Kiernan, Christopher (Vic) b March 23, 1878 Fitzroy (Vic) d Dec. 2, 1925 North Fitzroy (Vic)

Kierse, John Michael (SAust) b Jan. 11, 1918 Nhill (Vic)

Kildey, Edward Keith (Tas) b April 30, 1919 Leeton (NSW)

Killen, Christopher Michael (SAust) b Sept. 23, 1967 Dubbo (NSW)

Kimber, Adam Patrick (SAust) b Sept. 30, 1969 North Adelaide (SAust)

Kimpton, Robert Webb (WAust) b Jan. 5, 1914 Essendon (Vic)

King, Darryl James (Qld) b June 6, 1942 East Brisbane (Qld)

King, Ian Harold (Qld) b June 1, 1943 Herston (Qld)

King, James Francis (SAust) b May 23, 1851 Hindmarsh (SAust) d June 28, 1921 Hindmarsh (SAust)

King, Norman Reginald (SAust) b April 9, 1915 Mile End (SAust) d April 25, 1973 Linden Park (SAust)

King, Percy Macgregor (NSW) b Sept. 2, 1889 Richmond (Vic) d Dec. 9, 1967 Rose Bay (NSW)

King, Peter Denis (Vic) b May 24, 1959 Melbourne (Vic)

King, Stuart Patrick (Vic) b April 22, 1906 Ararat (Vic) d Feb. 28, 1943 in action on the Coral Sea

Kingdon, Darren Robert (Qld) b Sept. 24, 1969 Dubbo (NSW)

Kington, Philip Oliphant (Vic) b Dec. 17, 1832 Clifton, Gloucestershire (England) d July 2, 1892 Dachet, Buckinghamshire (England)

Kinloch, John (NSW) b c. 1833 Dublin (Ireland) d April 9, 1897 Camperdown (NSW)

Kinnear, Joseph David (Vic) b Feb. 12, 1912 West Brunswick (Vic) d Dec. 14, 1981 Moreland (Vic)

Kinnear, William George (Vic) b Aug. 19, 1914 West Brunswick (Vic) d Dec. 7, 1982 West Brunswick (Vic)

* Kippax, Alan Falconer (NSW) b May 25, 1897 Sydney (NSW) d Sept. 5, 1972 Bellevue Hill (NSW)

Kirby, Keith William (Vic) b Oct. 1, 1939 Essendon (Vic)

Kirby, Richard George (Tas) b Jan. 28, 1861 Hobart (Tas) d Aug. 26, 1947 Hobart (Tas)

Kirkman, William Stanley (Tas) b Feb. 14, 1961 Launceston (Tas)

Kirkwood, Harold Peter (SAust) b Sept. 15, 1882 Orroroo (SAust) d May 19, 1943 Unley (SAust)

Kissell, Ronald Keith (NSW) b Aug. 9, 1928 Camperdown (NSW)

Kitson, Eugene Henry (SAust) b Nov. 28, 1889 Adelaide (SAust) d Aug. 4, 1962 Heidelberg (Vic)

Kline, Lindsay Francis (Vic) b Sept. 29, 1934 Camberwell (Vic)

Klinger, Michael (Vic) b July 4, 1980 Kew (Vic)

Klose, Tom Elliott (SAust) b Jan. 22, 1918 North Adelaide (SAust) d June 13, 1986 Nailsworth (SAust)

* Knight, David Jeffrey (Vic) b Aug. 21, 1956 Coburg (Vic)

Knight, Gary William (Combined XI) b July 20, 1950 Launceston (Tas)

Knight, Robert Leonard (Tas) b Nov. 20, 1957 Launceston (Tas)

Knill, William (SAust) b Jan. 28, 1859 Prospect Village (SAust) d July 8, 1940 North Adelaide (SAust)

* Knott, Alan Philip Eric (Tas) b April 9, 1946 Belvedere, Kent (England)

Knowles, Eric Charles (Qld) b March 9, 1896 Toowoomba (Qld) d Sept. 15, 1978 Southport (Qld)

Kortlang, Henry Frederick Lorenz (Vic) b March 12, 1880 Carlton (Vic) d Feb. 15, 1961 Cottesloe (WAust)

Kowalick, Jeffrey Peter (SAust) b July 22, 1946 Maylands (SAust)

Kremerskothen, Scott Paul (Tas) b Jan. 5, 1979 Launceston (Tas)

Kroger, Henry Jack (Vic) b June 27, 1906 Caulfield (Vic) d July 16, 1987 Malvern (Vic)

Kyle, James Henderson (Vic) b May 29, 1880 Bacchus Marsh (Vic) d Jan. 11, 1919 Albert Park (Vic)

La Frantz, Errold Campbell (Qld) b May 25, 1919 Wooloowin (Qld)

* Laird, Bruce Malcolm (WAust) b Nov. 21, 1950 Mt Lawley (WAust)

Lambert, Daryl John (SAust) b Oct. 8, 1946 Prospect (SAust)

Lambert, Henry Francis (Vic) b July 8, 1918 Bairnsdale (Vic) d June 19, 1995 Grange (SAust)

Lambert, Oswald (NSW) b Aug. 23, 1926 New Lambton (NSW)

Lampard, Albert Wallis (Vic) b July 3, 1885 Richmond (Vic) d Jan. 11, 1984 Armadale (Vic)

Lampe, William Henry Warwick (NSW) b Aug. 29, 1902 Wagga Wagga (NSW) d Dec. 22, 1987 Wagga Wagga (NSW)

Lane, John Bayley (NSW) b Jan. 7, 1886 Petersham (NSW) d Aug. 30, 1937 Manly (NSW)

Lang, Harold King (WAust) b Aug. 23, 1905 Bangena (Vic) d April 23, 1991 Nedlands (WAust)

Langdon, Christopher Walter (WAust) b July 4, 1922 Boulder (WAust)

* Langer, Justin Lee (WAust) b Nov. 21, 1970 Perth (WAust)

Langer, Robert Samuel (WAust) b Oct. 3, 1948 Subiaco (WAust)

Langford, Ian Frederick (Vic) b June 2, 1936 Kew (Vic)

* Langley, Gilbert Roche Andrews (SAust) b Sept. 14, 1919 North Adelaide (SAust) d May 14, 2001 Fullarton (SAust)

Langley, Jeffrey Noel (SAust & Qld) b Oct. 28, 1948 Adelaide (SAust)

Lanigan, Emmet Robert (Vic) b Sept. 6, 1909 Maffra (Vic)

Lanigan, Joseph Patrick (WAust) b July 8, 1891 Mogumber (WAust) d Sept. 30, 1972 Glendalough (WAust)

Lansdown, Albert Joseph Walter (Vic) b March 10, 1897 Fitzroy South (Vic) d Jan. 7, 1979 Frankston (Vic)

Lansdown, Harold Charles (Vic) b Feb. 18, 1900 North Fitzroy (Vic) d April 18, 1957 Ivanhoe (Vic)

Larkin, Rohan Patrick (Vic) b Oct. 19, 1969 Seymour (Vic)

* Laughlin, Trevor John (Vic) b Jan. 30, 1951 Nyah West (Vic)

Lavender, Mark Philip (WAust) b Aug. 28, 1967 Madras (India)

* Laver, Frank (Vic) b Dec. 7, 1869 Castlemaine (Vic) d Sept. 24, 1919 East Melbourne (Vic)

Laver, John Francis Lee (Tas) b March 9, 1917 Malvern (Vic)

Law, Ian Kennon (Vic) b Sept. 27, 1938 Richmond (Vic)

Law, Rupert William (Qld) b Feb. 24, 1890 Sydney (NSW) d May 5, 1942 Randwick (NSW)

* Law, Stuart Grant (Qld) b Oct. 18, 1968 Herston (Qld)

Lawes, Charles Henry Wickham (NSW) b Dec. 9, 1899 Cobar (NSW) death details unknown

Lawlor, John (Vic) b Jan. 25, 1864 Castleisland, County Kerry (Ireland) d Jan. 29, 1908 Melbourne (Vic)

Lawrence, Charles (NSW) b Dec. 16, 1828 Hoxton, London (England) d Dec. 20, 1916 Canterbury (Vic)

Lawrence, Rodney John (Qld) b Aug. 8, 1954 Herston (Qld)

* Lawry, William Morris (Vic) b Feb. 11, 1937 Thornbury (Vic)

* Lawson, Geoffrey Francis (NSW) b Dec. 7, 1957 Wagga Wagga (NSW)

Lawson, Robert James (Vic) b March 23, 1901 South Melbourne (Vic) d Nov. 28, 1974 West Brunswick (Vic)

Laycock, Henry (SAust) b Oct. 31, 1901 Edwardstown (SAust) d Aug. 6, 1983 Port Noarlunga (SAust)

Le Couteur, Philip Ridgeway (Vic) b June 26, 1885 Kyneton (Vic) d June 30, 1958 Gunnedah (NSW)

Leabeater, Leonard Raymond (NSW) b July 10, 1906 Parramatta (NSW) d June 1, 1996 Port Macquarie (NSW)

Leak, Brian Headley (SAust) b May 5, 1917 Hawthorn (SAust)

Leak, Ernest Howard (SAust) b Oct. 28, 1872 Finniss Vale (SAust) d Aug. 22, 1945 Adelaide (SAust)

Leak, Stanley Garfield (SAust) b March 12, 1886 Goodwood (SAust) d Jan. 10, 1963 Millswood (SAust)

Leary, John Denis (Qld) b c. 1862 Picton (NSW) d Jan. 16, 1940 Herston (Qld)

Leather, Thomas William (Vic) b June 2, 1910 Rutherglen, Lanarkshire (Scotland) d May 10, 1991 Prahran (Vic)

Ledger, Scott Norman (Qld) b Sept. 1, 1952 Nambour (Qld)

Ledward, John Allan (Vic) b April 22, 1909 East Melbourne (Vic) d July 22, 1997 Box Hill (Vic)

* Lee, Brett (NSW) b Nov. 8, 1976 Wollongong (NSW)

Lee, Clarence Leslie (Tas) b Dec. 28, 1890 Cressy (Tas) d Feb. 5, 1959 Invermay (Tas)

Lee, Ian Somerville (Vic) b March 24, 1914 Brunswick North (Vic) d April 14, 1976 Port Melbourne (Vic)

* Lee, Philip Keith (SAust) b Sept. 15, 1904 Gladstone (SAust) d Aug. 8, 1980 Woodville South (SAust)

Lee, Robert William (SAust) b Jan. 31, 1927 Hindmarsh (SAust) d June 9, 2001 Adelaide (SAust)

Lee, Shane (NSW) b Aug. 8, 1973 Wollongong (NSW)

Lee, Terance Henry (NSW) b Aug. 31, 1940 Manly (NSW)

Leedham, Michael John (Tas) b Feb. 22, 1950 Campbell Town (Tas)

Leehane, John Francis (Vic) b Dec. 11, 1950 Coburg (Vic)

Leehane, John Thomas (Vic) b Oct. 20, 1921 Brunswick (Vic) d July 22, 1991 Caulfield (Vic)

Leeson, Henry Follie (Qld) b July 20, 1908 Mount Morgan (Qld) d June 25, 1950 Logan River (Qld)

Lehmann, Charles Albert (WAust) b Sept. 16, 1878 Caltowie (SAust) d April 27, 1940 Melbourne (Vic)

* Lehmann, Darren Scott (SAust & Vic) b Feb. 5, 1970 Gawler (SAust)

Leslie, Peter Glen (NSW) b Feb. 24, 1947 Bexley (NSW)

Letcher, Charles (Vic) b c. 1869 Collingwood (Vic) d Nov. 30, 1916 Perth (WAust)

Lethborg, Gordon John (Tas) b Nov. 23, 1907 Scottsdale (Tas) d Aug. 31, 1989 Launceston (Tas)

Lette, Henry Elms (Tas) b 1829 birth day and month unknown Curramore (Tas) d Aug. 15, 1892 Launceston (Tas)

* Lever, Peter (Tas) b Sept. 17, 1940 Todmorden, Yorkshire (England)

Levingston, Raydon Charles (Qld) b Jan. 17, 1946 Toowoomba (Qld)

Levy, Graham Bruce (SAust) b Feb. 10, 1938 North Adelaide (SAust)

Levy, Roy Mark (Qld) b April 20, 1906 Waverley (NSW) d Dec. 12, 1965 Clayfield (Qld)

Lewis, Arthur (Vic) b c. 1830 full birth details unknown d June 1, 1907 Alexandra (Vic)

Lewis, John William (Qld) b Nov. 21, 1867 St George (Qld) d Sept. 19, 1939 Brisbane (Qld)

Lewis, Keith (SAust) b Feb. 4, 1923 Prospect (SAust)

Lewis, Kevin John (SAust) b Nov. 27, 1947 Hindmarsh (SAust)

Lewis, Laurence Robert (SAust) b May 24, 1889 Cherry Gardens (SAust) d Sept. 2, 1947 Prospect (SAust)

Lewis, Michael Llewellyn (Vic) b June 29, 1974 Greensborough (Vic)

Lewis, Oswald Hoddle (NSW) b Feb. 28, 1833 Sydney (NSW) d April 28, 1895 Darlinghurst (NSW)

Lewis, Percy Markham (Vic) b March 13, 1864 Hamilton (Vic) d Nov. 24, 1922 St Kilda (Vic)

Lewis, Thomas Harvie (NSW) b c. 1828 London (England) d June 19, 1901 Darlinghurst (NSW)

Liddicut, Arthur Edward (Vic) b Oct. 17, 1891 Fitzroy (Vic) d April 8, 1983 Parkdale (Vic)

Lihou, Jack (Qld) b Sept. 9, 1930 Sandgate (Qld)

Lill, John Charles (SAust) b Dec. 7, 1933 Maylands (SAust)

* Lillee, Dennis Keith (WAust & Tas) b July 18, 1949 Subiaco (WAust)

Lillie, Dennis John (Qld) b Oct. 28, 1945 Auchenflower (Qld)

Lilly, Kenneth Edward (WAust) b Dec. 25, 1959 Perth (WAust)

Limb, Allen (Tas) b Sept. 29, 1886 Gawler (SAust) d July 1, 1975 Battery Point (Tas)

* Lindwall, Raymond Russell (NSW & Qld) b Oct. 3, 1921 Mascot (NSW) d June 22, 1996 Greenslopes (Qld)

Linney, George Frederick (Tas) b Nov. 18, 1869 Guildford, Surrey (England) d Nov. 5, 1927 Weston-super-Mare, Somerset (England)

Lister, Charles (Vic) b Nov. 7, 1811 Armitage Park, Staffordshire (England) d Aug. 18, 1873 Laverstock Asylum, Alderbury, Wiltshire (England)

Liston, George Grieve (SAust) b April 29, 1860 Tanunda (SAust) d June 6, 1929 Kent Town (SAust)

Litster, John Lewis (Qld) b Feb. 2, 1904 Townsville (Qld) d March 11, 1982 Railway Estate, Townsville (Qld)

Little, Raymond Cecil James (NSW) b Oct. 7, 1914 Armidale (NSW) d April 28, 1995 Burwood (NSW)

Living, Gary Francis (Vic) b Oct. 1, 1952 Dandenong (Vic)

Livingston, Bruce Arthur Lionel (NSW) b May 11, 1927 Marrickville (NSW)

Livingston, Leonard (NSW) b May 3, 1920 Hurlstone Park (NSW) d Jan. 16, 1998 Hurlstone Park (NSW)

Lloyd, Robert Grantley (SAust) b Oct. 24, 1940 Gladstone (SAust)

* Loader, Peter James (WAust) b Oct. 25, 1929 Wallington, Surrey (England)

Lochner, Augustus Meyer (Tas) b Oct. 1, 1827 Enfield, Middlesex (England) d Feb. 20, 1865 Plumstead Common, Kent (England)

* Lock, Graham Anthony Richard (WAust) b July 5, 1929 Limpsfield, Surrey (England) d March 29, 1995 Beechboro (WAust)

Lockie, George William (Qld) b Feb. 18, 1910 Mt Morgan (Qld) d Nov. 2, 1971 Northgate (Qld)

Lockwood, William Thomas (WAust) b June 26, 1868 Geelong (Vic) d Aug. 29, 1953 Tuart Hill (WAust)

Lodding, Brent Andrew (Vic) b March 20, 1973 Upper Ferntree Gully (Vic)

Loder, Robert Roy (NSW) b Dec. 17, 1896 East Maitland (NSW) d Feb. 13, 1964 French's Forest (NSW)

Lodge, Arthur Oliver (WAust) b April 7, 1933 Guildford (WAust)

Logan, William (Vic) birth and death details unknown

Lonergan, Albert Roy (SAust & NSW) b Dec. 6, 1909 Maylands (WAust) d Oct. 22, 1956 Adelaide (SAust)

Loney, Geoffrey Souter (Tas) b March 31, 1894 Campbelltown (NSW) d April 7, 1985 Hobart (Tas)

Long, Edmund James (NSW) b March 28, 1883 Darlinghurst (NSW) d Dec. 8, 1947 Leichhardt (NSW)

Long, Gordon Hillhouse (Combined XI) b May 6, 1934 Hobart (Tas)

Long, Thomas Tasman Thompson (Qld) b Sept. 11, 1875 at sea d Oct. 20, 1926 Spring Hill (Qld)

Longney, Geoffrey Wallace (Vic) b May 25, 1935 Oakleigh (Vic)

Lord, John Carr (Tas) b Aug. 17, 1844 Hobart (Tas) d May 25, 1911 Antill Ponds (Tas)

Lord, Sidney (Tas) b Oct. 20, 1886 birthplace and death details unknown

Loton, Cecil Vernon (WAust) b Jan. 5, 1906 Upper Swan (WAust) d June 8, 1986 Pinjarra (WAust)

Loton, Morris William (WAust) b March 18, 1905 Springhill (WAust) d March 2, 1976 Northam (WAust)

Lough, William David (NSW) b Oct. 31, 1886 Bourke (NSW) d c. 1939 Newtown (NSW)

Loughnan, Austin Robert (Vic) b June 15, 1851 Hobart (Tas) d Oct. 9, 1926 Cheltenham (Vic)

* Love, Hampden Stanley Bray (NSW & Vic) b Aug. 10, 1895 Lilyfield (NSW) d July 22, 1969 Sydney (NSW)

Love, Martin Lloyd (Qld) b March 30, 1974 Mundubbera (Qld)

Lovell, David Cameron (SAust) b Feb. 17, 1955 North Adelaide (SAust)

Lovelock, Oswald Ifould (WAust) b Aug. 28, 1911 Highgate (WAust) d Aug. 1, 1981 Subiaco (WAust)

Loveridge, Eustace Alfred (SAust) b April 14, 1891 Yongala (SAust) d July 29, 1959 Adelaide (SAust)

Loveridge, Walter David (NSW) b Sept. 13, 1867 Redfern (NSW) d Jan. 6, 1940 East Brisbane (Qld)

Lovett, Arthur Frederick (Tas & WAust) b June 1, 1920 St Kilda (Vic) d July 1, 1990 Coffs Harbour (NSW)

Lovett, Henry Charles (Tas) b March 3, 1856 Battery Point (Tas) d May 20, 1937 Hobart (Tas)

Lowe, Frederick (Vic) b Sept. 7, 1827 Holme Pierrepont, Nottinghamshire (England) d Oct. 15, 1887 Ararat (Vic)

Lowry, Jack Brown (Vic) b Nov. 25, 1916 Lambton (NSW)

Loxton, Colin Cameron (Qld) b Jan. 1, 1914 Beecroft (NSW) d Sept. 2, 2000 Greenslopes (Qld)

Loxton, John Frederick Cameron (Qld) b Nov. 26, 1945 Ashgrove (Qld)

* Loxton, Samuel John Everett (Vic) b March 29, 1921 Albert Park (Vic)

Lucas, Clyde Edward (Tas) b Aug. 11, 1898 Kingston (Tas) d Jan. 12, 1988 Palm Beach (Qld)

Lucas, Edward (Tas) b June 16, 1848 Kingston (Tas) d April 19, 1916 Kingston (Tas)

Lucas, Frank Russell (SAust) b Nov. 9, 1888 Port Pirie (SAust) d Aug. 31, 1941 Adelaide (SAust)

Lucas, Michael John (Qld) b April 14, 1944 Ashgrove (Qld)

Lucas, Thomas Turland (SAust) b Feb. 18, 1852 Eyres Flat (SAust) d March 13, 1945 Norwood (SAust)

Lugton, Frank Leslie (Vic) b Nov. 4, 1893 Northcote (Vic) d July 29, 1916 near Villers-Bretonneux (France)

Lukeman, Eric William (NSW) b March 11, 1923 Drummoyne (NSW) d April 18, 1993 Palm Beach (Qld)

Lush, John Grantley (NSW) b Oct. 14, 1913 Prahran (Vic) d Aug. 23, 1985 Sydney (NSW)

* Lyons, John James (SAust) b May 21, 1863 Gawler (SAust) d July 21, 1927 Magill (SAust)

Lyons, Rodney Bernard (Qld) b April 24, 1924 Cairns (Qld)

* McAlister, Peter Alexander (Vic) b July 11, 1869 Williamstown (Vic) d May 10, 1938 Richmond (Vic)

McAllen, Charles (Tas) b July 2, 1860 Hobart (Tas) d Jan. 15, 1924 Hobart (Tas)

McAllister, Donald Ernest (SAust) b Nov. 19, 1936 Hindmarsh (SAust)

McAndrew, John William (Qld) b Nov. 4, 1889 Berrima (NSW) d April 10, 1960 Ipswich (Qld)

McArdle, Brendan Joseph (Vic) b March 2, 1952 Preston (Vic)

* Macartney, Charles George (NSW) b June 27, 1886 West Maitland (NSW) d Sept. 9, 1958 Little Bay (NSW)

McAullay, Kenneth James (WAust) b Sept. 29, 1949 Subiaco (WAust)

McBeath, Arthur (NSW & SAust) b June 17, 1876 Mudgee (NSW) d March 17, 1945 Surry Hills (NSW)

* McCabe, Stanley Joseph (NSW) b July 16, 1910 Grenfell (NSW) d Aug. 25, 1968 Beauty Point (NSW)

McCaffrey, Michael Francis (Qld) b Feb. 18, 1878 Rockhampton (Qld) d Dec. 31, 1948 death place unknown

McCaffrey, Victor William (NSW) b Aug. 11, 1918 Goulburn (NSW)

* McCague, Martin John (WAust) b May 24, 1969 Larne (Northern Ireland)

McCarthy, John Edward (Qld) b Feb. 22, 1917 Maryborough (Qld) d Feb. 18, 1998 Gold Coast (Qld)

McCarthy, Kevin Joseph (SAust) b Oct. 11, 1945 Rose Park (SAust)

McCarthy, Patrick Covell Derrick (WAust) b Oct. 24, 1919 (Ceylon)

McCarthy, Richard Charles Arthur Marum (Vic) b Dec. 21, 1961 Geelong (Vic)

McCauley, Bede Vincent (NSW) b June 11, 1909 Coogee (NSW) d Oct. 14, 1994 Sydney (NSW)

McCloy, William Stanley Swain (Qld & NSW) b Nov. 10, 1886 Paddington (NSW) d Nov. 10, 1975 Young (NSW)

McCooke, Steven Milne (Vic) b Jan. 31, 1960 South Caulfield (Vic)

* McCool, Colin Leslie (NSW & Qld) b Dec. 9, 1916 Paddington (NSW) d April 5, 1986 Concord (NSW)

McCoombe, Clarence Arthur (Qld) b Feb. 23, 1904 Cooktown (Qld) d Sept. 6, 1955 Sydney (NSW)

McCormack, William Henry (Vic) b May 5, 1877 St Kilda (Vic) d April 26, 1946 Stawell (Vic)

* McCormick, Ernest Leslie (Vic) b May 16, 1906 North Carlton (Vic) d June 28, 1991 Tweed Heads (NSW)

McCormick, Raymond Vincent (SAust) b Jan. 30, 1931 Mile End (SAust)

* McCosker, Richard Bede (NSW) b Dec. 11, 1946 Inverell (NSW)

McCoy, Bernard Leslie (NSW) b March 26, 1896 Kangaroo Valley (NSW) d June 11, 1970 Sydney (NSW)

McCurdy, Rodney John (Tas, Vic & SAust) b Dec. 30, 1959 Melbourne (Vic)

* McDermott, Craig John (Qld) b April 14, 1965 Ipswich (Qld)

* McDonald, Colin Campbell (Vic) b Nov. 17, 1928 Glen Iris (Vic)

* McDonald, Edgar Arthur (Tas & Vic) b Jan. 6, 1891 Launceston (Tas) d July 22, 1937 Blackrod, near Bolton, Lancashire (England)

McDonald, Ian Hamilton (Vic) b July 28, 1923 Windsor (Vic)

Macdonald, Kenneth Locke (Tas) b Jan. 3, 1934 Premaydena (Tas) d July 1, 1999 Hobart (Tas)

Macdonald, Robert (Qld) b Feb. 14, 1870 Clunes (Vic) d March 7, 1946 Victoria, British Columbia (Canada)

McDonald, Walter Hugh (Vic, Qld & Tas) b March 24, 1884 Shepparton (Vic) d March 22, 1955 Kew (Vic)

* McDonnell, Percy Stanislaus (Vic, NSW & Qld) b Nov. 13, 1858 Kennington, Kent (England) d Sept. 24, 1896 South Brisbane (Qld)

McDowell, Robert Murray (Tas) b Sheffield, Yorkshire (England) full birth and death details unknown

Mace, Christopher (Vic) b Dec. 24, 1830 Bedale, Yorkshire (England) d Nov. 23, 1907 Sydenham (NSW)

Mace, John (Vic) b Dec. 28, 1828 Bedale, Yorkshire (England) d April 30, 1905 Te Aroha (New Zealand)

Mace, John Cruttenden (Tas) b May 7, 1839 Sydney (NSW) d April 18, 1906 Hawley-with-Minley, Hampshire (England)

McElhone, Frank Eric (NSW) b June 27, 1887 Waverley (NSW) d July 21, 1981 Darlinghurst (NSW)

McEvoy, Daniel Michael (WAust) b Aug. 19, 1946 Mount Lawley (WAust)

McEvoy, Frederick Aloysius (Vic) b July 4, 1856 Gundagai (NSW) d Nov. 5, 1913 Brighton (Vic)

McEvoy, William Joseph (Vic) b c. 1845 Sydney (NSW) d July 14, 1930 (England)

McEwan, Kenneth Scott (WAust) b July 16, 1952 Bedford, Cape Province (South Africa)

McEwan, W. (Tas) b 1815 birth day and month unknown Perth, Perthshire (Scotland) d c. 1862 (Vic)

McFarland, Robert (Vic) b July 9, 1847 birthplace unknown d c. 1876 Coleraine (Vic)

McFarlane, Clement Basil Patrick (Qld) b Aug. 20, 1900 New Farm (Qld) d March 2, 1946 Grange (Qld)

McFarlane, Robert Donald (WAust) b Feb. 7, 1955 Corrigin (WAust)

McGan, Bryan (Vic) b c. 1848 Melbourne (Vic) d July 9, 1894 South Melbourne (Vic)

McGhee, Robert William (Qld) b March 24, 1963 Richmond (Qld)

MacGill, Charles William Terry (WAust) b June 16, 1916 Perth (WAust) d Oct. 31, 1999 Perth (WAust)

* MacGill, Stuart Charles Glyndwr (WAust & NSW) b Feb. 25, 1971 Mt Lawley (WAust)

MacGill, Terry Mornington David (WAust) b Dec. 22, 1945 Moreland (Vic)

McGilvray, Alan David (NSW) b Dec. 6, 1909 Paddington (NSW) d July 17, 1996 Darlinghurst (NSW)

McGinn, Albert Howard (Qld) b Nov. 11, 1913 Upper Kedron (Qld)

McGinty, Adam David (Vic) b March 24, 1971 Melbourne (Vic)

McGlinchy, William Walter (NSW & Qld) b Jan. 31, 1864 Newcastle (NSW) d July 1, 1946 Sydney (NSW)

* McGrath, Glenn Donald (NSW) b Feb. 9, 1970 Dubbo (NSW)

McGregor, William (Australians) b Feb. 23, 1888 St Kilda (Vic) d Oct. 5, 1980 Benalla (Vic)

McGuire, David Victor (Tas) b Nov. 13, 1931 Hobart (Tas)

McGuirk, Harold Vincent (NSW) b Oct. 17, 1906 Crookwell (NSW) death details unknown

McGuirk, Leo Daniel (NSW) b May 3, 1908 Crookwell (NSW) d June 15, 1974 Sydney (NSW)

* McIlwraith, John (Vic) b Sept. 7, 1857 Collingwood (Vic) d July 5, 1938 Camberwell (Vic)

McInnes, Alan Roderick (Vic) b May 29, 1907 Kensington (Vic) d Sept. 16, 1991 Dandenong (Vic)

McInnes, Mark William (Cricket Academy) b April 16, 1977 Wagga Wagga (NSW)

McIntyre, Ernest John (Vic) b April 19, 1921 Albert Park (Vic)

* McIntyre, Peter Edward (Vic & SAust) b April 27, 1966 Gisborne (Vic)

McIntyre, William Robert (NSW) b April 10, 1877 Forbes (NSW) d c. 1943 Drummoyne (NSW)

Mack, Christopher David (WAust) b June 30, 1970 Subiaco (WAust)

McKay, Douglas Gordon (SAust) b July 2, 1904 North Adelaide (SAust) d April 9, 1994 North Adelaide (SAust)

Mackay, George (Vic) b July 6, 1860 Castlemaine (Vic) d May 22, 1948 Bendigo (Vic)

McKay, Henry James (SAust) b Jan. 1, 1883 Goodwood (SAust) d Feb. 12, 1926 Hawthorn (SAust)

Mackay, James Rainey Munro (NSW) b Sept. 9, 1880 Armidale (NSW) d June 13, 1953 Walcha (NSW)

Mackay, John Robert Edward (Qld) b Nov. 24, 1937 Rockhampton (Qld)

* Mackay, Kenneth Donald (Qld) b Oct. 24, 1925 Windsor (Qld) d June 13, 1982 Point Lookout, Stradbroke Island (Qld)

Mackay, Kerry (NSW) b May 7, 1949 Brighton-Le-Sands (NSW)

MacKenzie, Alexander Cecil Knox (NSW) b Aug. 7, 1870 Sydney (NSW) d April 11, 1947 Epping (NSW)

McKenzie, Colin (Vic) b Dec. 12, 1880 Trawool (Vic) d Aug. 31, 1930 Avenel (Vic)

McKenzie, Douglas Charles (WAust) b March 15, 1906 Kew (Vic) d July 1, 1979 Perth (WAust)

McKenzie, Eric Norman (WAust) b Dec. 9, 1910 Kalgoorlie (WAust) d April 28, 1994 Cottesloe (WAust)

* McKenzie, Graham Douglas (WAust) b June 24, 1941 Cottesloe (WAust)

McKenzie, John (SAust) b Oct. 11, 1862 Aldinga (SAust) d June 3, 1944 Hazelwood Park (SAust)

McKenzie, Matthew Stanley (Tas) b May 17, 1890 Launceston (Tas) d Dec. 8, 1915 Alexandria (Egypt)

McKew, Cecil George (NSW) b Aug. 12, 1887 Leichhardt (NSW) d Oct. 12, 1974 Lilli Pilli (NSW)

* McKibbin, Thomas Robert (NSW) b Dec. 10, 1870 Raglan (NSW) d Dec. 15, 1939 Bathurst (NSW)

McKone, John James (NSW) b Oct. 3, 1835 Sydney (NSW) d Aug. 7, 1882 Sydney (NSW)

McLachlan, Ian Murray (SAust) b Oct. 2, 1936 North Adelaide (SAust)

* McLaren, John William (Qld) b Dec. 22, 1886 Toowong (Qld) d Nov. 17, 1921 Highgate Hill (Qld)

McLaughlin, John Joseph (Qld) b Feb. 18, 1930 Corinda (Qld)

McLay, Gregory Francis (NSW) b May 7, 1969 Wagga Wagga (NSW)

McLean, Allan Robert Charles (SAust) b Feb. 1, 1914 Mile End (SAust) d Nov. 9, 1989 Christies Beach (SAust)

McLean, Hugh (Vic) b Nov. 26, 1864 Woodford (Vic) d Feb. 19, 1915 East Melbourne (Vic)

McLean, Ian Robert (SAust) b Jan. 30, 1954 Semaphore (SAust)

* MacLean, John Alexander (Qld) b April 27, 1946 Herston (Qld)

MacLeay, Kenneth Hervey (WAust) b April 2, 1959 Bradford-on-Avon, Wiltshire (England)

McLellan, Ross Malcolm (SAust) b Feb. 20, 1955 Glenhuntly (Vic)

* McLeod, Charles Edward (Vic) b Oct. 24, 1869 Sandridge (Vic) d Nov. 26, 1918 Armadale (Vic)

McLeod, Daniel Hutton (Vic) b March 29, 1872 Sandridge (Vic) d Nov. 25, 1901 Port Melbourne (Vic)

* McLeod, Robert William (Vic) b Jan. 19, 1868 Sandridge (Vic) d June 14, 1907 Middle Park (Vic)

McMahon, John Terrence (Qld) b May 18, 1932 Five Dock (NSW)

McMahon, Vincent Gerald (Qld) b Jan. 18, 1918 Chinchilla (Qld) d Jan. 23, 1988 Greenslopes (Qld)

McMichael, Samuel Albert (Vic) b July 18, 1869 Collingwood (Vic) d July 21, 1923 Elsternwick (Vic)

McNamara, Bradley Edward (NSW) b Dec. 30, 1965 Sydney (NSW)

McNamee, Raymond Leonard Alphonsus (NSW) b Aug. 26, 1895 Orange (NSW) d Sept. 18, 1949 Little Bay (NSW)

McNaughton, John Leonard (Vic) b Jan. 15, 1884 Richmond (Vic) d Dec. 26, 1970 Lower Kingswood, Surrey (England)

MacNish, William George (NSW) b Oct. 29, 1842 Paddington (NSW) d Nov. 29, 1873 Bundaberg (Qld)

McPetrie, William Martin (Vic) b Feb. 15, 1880 Emerald Hill (Vic) d June 30, 1951 Hawthorn (Vic)

McPhee, Mark William (WAust) b Jan. 25, 1964 Katanning (WAust) d Aug. 15, 1999 Gingin (WAust)

McPhee, Peter Thomas (Tas) b July 29, 1963 South Brisbane (Qld)

MacPherson, Herbert James Keele (NSW) b Feb. 20, 1869 Mudgee (NSW) d Nov. 12, 1953 Mudgee (NSW)

McPherson, James Philip (Vic) b Nov. 20, 1842 Moonee Ponds (Vic) d Aug. 23, 1891 Melbourne (Vic)

McPhillamy, Keith (NSW) b June 20, 1882 Bathurst (NSW) d May 3, 1937 Bowral (NSW)

McRae, Donald (SAust) b June 13, 1873 Aldinga (SAust) d Oct. 22, 1940 Prospect (SAust)

McRae, William Alexander (WAust) b June 18, 1904 Geelong (Vic) d July 25, 1973 Subiaco (WAust)

MacRow, William Reginald Fairbairn (Vic) b July 7, 1889 Kew (Vic) d May 19, 1970 Heidelberg (Vic)

* McShane, Patrick George (Vic) b April 18, 1858 Keilor (Vic) d Dec. 11, 1903 Kew (Vic)

Madden, Robert Harold (NSW) b Dec. 12, 1928 Camperdown (NSW)

Maddern, James Gregory (Qld) b March 22, 1914 Crows Nest (Qld) d March 27, 1987 Nambour (Qld)

Madders, Garry James (Qld) b Jan. 21, 1953 Maryborough (Qld)

Maddock, Charles Edward Rokeby (Qld) b Aug. 14, 1887 (Qld) d Feb. 14, 1957 Herston (Qld)

Maddocks, Ian Leonard (Vic) b April 12, 1951 Ashburton (Vic)

* Maddocks, Leonard Victor (Vic & Tas) b May 24, 1926 Beaconsfield (Vic)

Maddocks, Richard Ivor (Vic) b July 30, 1928 Carnegie (Vic) d Sept. 10, 1968 Blackburn (Vic)

Maddox, George (Tas) b c. 1811 (Ireland) d July 7, 1867 Melbourne (Vic)

Maddox, John Montgomery (Tas) b Dec. 30, 1930 St Mary's (Tas)

Magarey, William Ashley (SAust) b Jan. 30, 1868 North Adelaide (SAust) d Oct. 18, 1929 North Adelaide (SAust)

* Maguire, John Norman (Qld) b Sept. 15, 1956 Murwillumbah (NSW)

Maher, James Patrick (Qld) b Feb. 27, 1974 Innisfail (Qld)

Mahony, Hector James Henry (Qld) b Sept. 8, 1913 Maryborough (Qld) d Sept. 25, 1991 Maryborough (Qld)

Mail, Gregory John (NSW) b April 29, 1978 Penrith (NSW)

Mailer, David (Vic) b Aug. 18, 1874 Coburg (Vic) d Dec. 21, 1937 Shepparton (Vic)

* Mailey, Arthur Alfred (NSW) b Jan. 3, 1886 Zetland (NSW) d Dec. 31, 1967 Kirrawee (NSW)

Mainhardt, Michael Shane (Qld) b Jan. 6, 1960 Clermont (Qld)

Mair, Frederick (NSW) b April 15, 1901 Balmain (NSW) d Dec. 25, 1959 Sydney (NSW)

Majewski, Neil John (Tas) b May 27, 1954 Footscray (Vic)

* Majid Jahangir Khan (Qld) b Sept. 28, 1946 Ludhiana (India)

Major, Albert George (Vic) b March 20, 1851 Langport, Somerset (England) d Oct. 16, 1921 Caulfield (Vic)

Makin, James Charles (Vic) b Feb. 11, 1904 Collingwood (Vic) d Jan. 15, 1973 Heidelberg (Vic)

Makin, William Samuel (NSW) b Oct. 4, 1889 Mount Keira (NSW) d Jan. 11, 1962 West Kogarah (NSW)

Makinson, Charles (Vic) b c. 1831 Salford, Lancashire (England) d June 12, 1895 Rugeley, Staffordshire (England)

* Mallett, Ashley Alexander (SAust) b July 13, 1945 Chatswood (NSW)

* Malone, Michael Francis (WAust) b Oct. 9, 1950 Perth (WAust)

Maloney, Peter Ivan (NSW) b Nov. 5, 1950 Ballina (NSW)

Mancell, Peter John (Tas) b March 15, 1958 Goulburn (NSW)

* Mann, Anthony Longford (WAust) b Nov. 8, 1945 Middle Swan (WAust)

Mann, John Lewis (SAust) b April 26, 1919 Strathalbyn (SAust) d Sept. 24, 1969 Lockleys (SAust)

Manning, John Stephen (SAust) b June 11, 1923 Ethelton (SAust) d May 31, 1988 Belair (SAust)

Manou, Graham Allan (SAust) b April 23, 1979 Modbury (SAust)

Mansfield, Graeme Edward (Tas) b Dec. 27, 1942 Hobart (Tas)

Mansfield, J. (Tas) birth and death details unknown

Maplestone, Henry Carman (Vic) b Jan. 11, 1870 Parkville (Vic) d Dec. 10, 1949 Moonee Ponds (Vic)

Maranta, Michael Gerard (Qld) b March 20, 1961 South Brisbane (Qld)

Marjoribanks, Hugh Lynch (NSW) b Aug. 12, 1933 Mackay (Qld)

Marks, Alexander Edward (NSW) b Dec. 9, 1910 Toowong (Qld) d July 28, 1983 Wahroonga (NSW)

Marks, Lynn Alexander (NSW & SAust) b Aug. 15, 1942 Randwick (NSW) d Dec. 7, 1997 Mona Vale (NSW)

Marks, Neil Graham (NSW) b Sept. 13, 1938 Randwick (NSW)

Marks, Phillip Henry (NSW) b April 30, 1961 Salisbury (Southern Rhodesia)

* Marks, Victor James (WAust) b June 25, 1955 Middle Chinnock, Somerset (England)

Marquet, Joshua Phillip (Tas) b Dec. 3, 1968 Melbourne (Vic)

* Marr, Alfred Percy (NSW) b March 28, 1862 Pyrmont (NSW) d March 15, 1940 Arncliffe (NSW)

Marriott, Arthur John (Tas) b c.1821 (England) d March 31, 1866 Nice (France)

Marsden, Albert John (Qld) b June 13, 1887 Maryborough (Qld) d Dec. 17, 1971 Kallista (Vic)

Marsden, Frederick William (Vic) b c. 1819 Lewisham, London (England) d March 20, 1870 Fitzroy (Vic)

Marsh, Daniel James (SAust & Tas) b June 14, 1973 Subiaco (WAust)

* Marsh, Geoffrey Robert (WAust) b Dec. 31, 1958 Northam (WAust)

Marsh, Jack (NSW) b c. 1874 Yugilbar (NSW) d May 25, 1916 Orange (NSW)

* Marsh, Rodney William (WAust) b Nov. 4, 1947 Armadale (WAust)

Marsh, Shaun Edwards (WAust) b July 9, 1983 Subiaco (WAust)

Marshal, Alan (Qld) b June 12, 1883 Warwick (Qld) d July 23, 1915 Imtarfa Military Hospital (Malta)

Marshall, Angus Neil (Qld) b Jan. 27, 1906 Essequibo (British Guiana) d Aug. 29, 1969 Nundah (Qld)

Marshall, George (Tas) b 1832 birth day and month unknown Sorell (Tas) d July 13, 1905 Sorell (Tas)

Marshall, George (Vic) b Dec. 20, 1829 Nottingham, Nottinghamshire (England) d March 6, 1868 Melbourne (Vic)

Marshall, John (Tas) b c. 1796 (England) d Sept. 7, 1876 New Town (Tas)

Martin, Charles (Qld) b May 15, 1867 Ipswich (Qld) d c. 1942 Sydney (NSW)

Martin, Charles Albert (SAust) b March 29, 1863 Adelaide (SAust) d May 14, 1955 St Georges (SAust)

Martin, Charles William Beresford (Tas) b Oct. 6, 1888 Launceston (Tas) d Oct. 30, 1951 Camberwell (Vic)

Martin, Edmund John (WAust) b Sept. 30, 1902 Eaglehawk (Vic)

Martin, Geoffrey Bernard (Tas) b July 16, 1927 Launceston (Tas)

Martin, Geoffrey William (Tas) b March 7, 1896 Launceston (Tas) d March 7, 1968 Launceston (Tas)

Martin, Gordon Francis (Qld) b Jan. 14, 1885 Clunes (Vic) d Aug. 19, 1974 Canberra (ACT)

Martin, Hugh (NSW) b Aug. 3, 1947 Enkeldoorn (Southern Rhodesia)

Martin, James Macfie (Tas) b Feb. 25, 1851 Launceston (Tas) d Oct. 22, 1930 Launceston (Tas)

Martin, John Frank (NSW) b May 8, 1942 Alton, Hampshire (England)

* Martin, John Wesley (NSW & SAust) b July 28, 1931 Wingham (NSW) d July 15, 1992 Burrell Creek (NSW)

Martin, William (Tas) b June 21, 1856 Westbury (Tas) d July 10, 1938 Launceston (Tas)

* Martyn, Damien Richard (WAust) b Oct. 21, 1971 Darwin (NT)

Mason, Matthew Sean (WAust) b March 20, 1974 Claremont (WAust)

Mason, Scott Robert (Tas) b July 27, 1976 George Town (Tas)

Massey, Richard Eric Charles (SAust) b June 5, 1961 Tamworth (NSW)

* Massie, Hugh Hamon (NSW) b April 11, 1854 near Belfast (Vic) d Oct. 12, 1938 Point Piper (NSW)

* Massie, Robert Arnold Lockyer (WAust) b April 14, 1947 Subiaco (WAust)

Massie, Robert John Allwright (NSW) b July 8, 1890 North Sydney (NSW) d Feb. 14, 1966 Mosman (NSW)

Mateljan, Tony (WAust) b Feb. 18, 1934 Middle Swan (WAust)

Mather, Adam (NSW) b Nov. 26, 1860 Paterson (NSW) d Aug. 31, 1917 Singleton (NSW)

Mather, John Henry (Vic) b Nov. 19, 1822 Everton, Lancashire (England) d Aug. 4, 1870 Iquique (Chile)

Mathers, James (Vic) b June 30, 1894 Minmi (NSW) d March 28, 1977 Eastwood (NSW)

Mathieson, Donald Kenneth (Vic) b April 24, 1931 Nhill (Vic)

Matson, George (Tas) b Dec. 5, 1817 Rochester, Kent (England) d July 22, 1898 Brighton, Sussex (England)

* Matthews, Christopher Darrell (WAust & Tas) b Sept. 22, 1962 Cunderdin (WAust)

* Matthews, Gregory Richard John (NSW) b Dec. 15, 1959 Newcastle (NSW)

Matthews, James George Facey (SAust) b Sept. 27, 1876 Roseworthy (SAust) d Oct. 8, 1963 Prospect (SAust)

Matthews, Robert Graham (Vic) b April 17, 1953 Camberwell (Vic)

Matthews, Thomas Harold (Tas) b Feb. 9, 1905 Longley (Tas) d May 11, 1990 Longley (Tas)

* Matthews, Thomas James (Vic) b April 3, 1884 Mt Gambier (SAust) d Oct. 14, 1943 Caulfield (Vic)

Maxwell, Eustace (Tas) b Jan. 20, 1864 Hobart (Tas) d May 18, 1939 Hobart (Tas)

Maxwell, Neil Donald (Vic & NSW) b June 12, 1967 Lautoka (Fiji)

* May, Timothy Brian Alexander (SAust) b Jan. 26, 1962 North Adelaide (SAust)

Mayes, Alexander Dunbar Aitken (NSW & Qld) b July 24, 1901 Toowooma (Qld) d Feb. 8, 1983 Spring Hill (Qld)

* Mayne, Lawrence Charles (WAust) b Jan. 23, 1942 Westonia (WAust)
* Mayne, Richard Edgar (SAust & Vic) b July 2, 1882 Jamestown (SAust) d Oct. 26, 1961 Richmond (Vic)
* Meckiff, Ian (Vic) b Jan. 6, 1935 Mentone (Vic)
Meech, James Robert (Tas) b Dec. 16, 1884 Hobart (Tas) d Oct. 31, 1955 Hobart (Tas)
Meek, Andrew Bonar (WAust) b Dec. 7, 1889 Gulgong (NSW) d Feb. 13, 1957 Perth (WAust)
Meikle, George Stanley (Vic) b Oct. 22, 1916 Footscray (Vic) d July 25, 1991 Brighton (Vic)
Melville, Paul (Vic) b Dec. 27, 1956 South Shields, Durham (England) d Nov. 21, 1978 Vermont South (Vic)
Menegon, Lyndon John (Tas) b Feb. 11, 1948 Burnie (Tas)
Mengel, Douglas Charles (Qld) b March 2, 1933 Brisbane (Qld)
Metcalfe, Evelyn James (Qld) b Sept. 29, 1865 Kennington, Kent (England) d June 14, 1951 Cambridge, Cambridgeshire (England)
* Meuleman, Kenneth Douglas (Vic & WAust) b Sept. 5, 1923 Melbourne (Vic)
Meuleman, Robert Douglas (WAust) b Sept. 6, 1949 Melbourne (Vic)
Meuleman, Scott William (WAust) b July 17, 1980 Subiaco (WAust)
Michael, Constantine Anthony (WAust) b Jan. 12, 1953 Victoria Park (WAust)
Michael, Leonard (SAust) b June 3, 1921 Medindie (SAust) d March 16, 1996 Adelaide (SAust)
Middleton, Frederick Stewart (NSW) b May 28, 1883 Burrowa (now Booroowa) (NSW) d July 21, 1956 Auckland (New Zealand)
Middleton, Roy Foster (SAust) b Sept. 18, 1889 Kent Town (SAust) d March 19, 1975 Adelaide (SAust)
**Midwinter, William Evans (Vic) b June 19, 1851 St Briavel's, Gloucestershire (England) d Dec. 3, 1890 Kew Asylum (Vic)
Mihell, Robert William (Qld) b Jan. 8, 1937 Lismore (NSW)
* Milburn, Colin (WAust) b Oct. 23, 1941 Burnopfield, Durham (England) d Feb. 28, 1990 Newton Aycliffe, Durham (England)
Miles, Geoffrey John (Vic) b Aug. 7, 1957 Kew (Vic)
Millar, Geoffrey Alan (WAust) b Nov. 22, 1955 Subiaco (WAust)
Millar, Keith James (Vic) b Aug. 15, 1906 Richmond (Vic) d July 13, 1971 Camberwell (Vic)
* Miller, Colin Reid (Vic, SAust & Tas) b Feb. 6, 1964 Footscray (Vic)
Miller, David Lawson (NSW & Qld) b Jan. 30, 1870 Holytown, Lanarkshire (Scotland) d April 12, 1943 Clayfield (Qld)

Miller, Graeme Geoffrey (Combined XI) b Sept. 24, 1940 Launceston (Tas)
Miller, Ivan Derness (Vic) b Dec. 30, 1913 Ivanhoe (Vic) d May 6, 1966 Heidelberg (Vic)
* Miller, Keith Ross (Vic & NSW) b Nov. 28, 1919 Sunshine (Vic)
Miller, Kevin Roy (Tas) b Oct. 12, 1936 Launceston (Tas)
Miller, Leslie Percy Robert (Vic) b June 16, 1880 St Kilda (Vic) d July 2, 1963 death place unknown
Miller, Michael Christian (Qld & SAust) b May 30, 1979 Toowoomba (Qld)
Miller, Noel Keith (NSW) b July 1, 1913 Wyong (NSW)
Miller, William Edward (WAust) b March 9, 1905 East Perth (WAust) d July 24, 1974 Perth (WAust)
Milliken, Geoffrey Scott (NSW) b May 6, 1964 Hay (NSW)
Millns, David James (Tas) b Feb. 27, 1965 Clipstone, Nottinghamshire (England)
Mills, John (NSW) b June 3, 1836 Botley, Hampshire (England) d Feb. 24, 1899 Bisterne, Hampshire (England)
Mills, Rowland Leslie (WAust) b July 14, 1914 Leederville (WAust) d Feb. 27, 2000 Perth (WAust)
Milosz, Stephen Joseph (WAust & Tas) b Dec. 26, 1955 Northam (WAust)
Minagall, Matthew John Peter (SAust) b Nov. 13, 1971 Woodville (SAust)
Minchin, James Melbourne (Vic) b Aug. 15, 1859 Emerald Hill (Vic) d Feb. 13, 1919 Cheltenham (Vic)
Minnett, Leslie Alma (NSW) b May 19, 1883 St Leonards (NSW) d Aug. 8, 1934 Collaroy (NSW)
* Minnett, Roy Baldwin (NSW) b June 13, 1886 St Leonards (NSW) d Oct. 21, 1955 Manly (NSW)
Minnett, Rupert Villiers (NSW) b Sept. 2, 1884 St Leonards (NSW) d June 24, 1974 Cremorne (NSW)
Minter, Eric James (NSW) b Sept. 13, 1917 Kempsey (NSW) d July 1, 1985 Vincentia (NSW)
* Misson, Francis Michael (NSW) b Nov. 19, 1938 Darlinghurst (NSW)
Mitchell, Brian Gordon (SAust) b March 15, 1959 Glenelg (SAust)
Mitchell, Norman Frederick (Vic) b Feb. 19, 1900 Collingwood (Vic) d March 8, 1973 Melbourne (Vic)
Mitchell, Robert (Vic) b April 11, 1862 Campbellfield (Vic) d Sept. 17, 1926 West Preston (Vic)
Moffat, William (SAust) b July 22, 1858 Byethorne (SAust) d July 30, 1922 Jamestown (SAust)

Moffatt, Alfred Augustine (WAust) b March 15, 1870 Perth (WAust) d Dec. 8, 1956 Perth (WAust)

Moir, Bruce Graeme (Vic) b Nov. 10, 1960 Melbourne (Vic)

Monfries, John Elliott (Vic) b Dec. 25, 1873 Gumeracha (SAust) d Sept. 2, 1954 Hobart (Tas)

Monohan, Vincent Clifford (Vic) b April 22, 1896 Collingwood (Vic) d July 9, 1974 Linden Park (SAust)

Monty, Stephen (Qld) b March 3, 1963 Glenelg (SAust)

* Moody, Thomas Masson (WAust) b Oct. 2, 1965 Adelaide (SAust)

Moore, David John Arthur (NSW) b Oct. 16, 1964 Sydney (NSW)

Moore, George (NSW) b April 18, 1820 Ampthill, Bedfordshire (England) d Sept. 29, 1916 West Maitland (NSW)

Moore, George Stanley (NSW & Qld) b April 18, 1886 North Sydney (NSW) d March 22, 1948 Bundaberg (Qld)

Moore, Henry Thomas (SAust) b c.1860 Plomesgate (England) death details unknown

Moore, James (NSW) b c.1839 Ampthill, Bedfordshire (England) d April 19, 1890 West Maitland (NSW)

Moore, Leonard David (NSW) b Feb. 8, 1871 West Maitland (NSW) d Sept. 11, 1934 Maitland (NSW)

Moore, William Henry (NSW & WAust) b Oct. 16, 1863 West Maitland (NSW) d Feb. 25, 1956 Lane Cove (NSW)

Morcom, Samuel (Combined XIII) b c.1847 full birth details unknown d Jan. 15, 1888 Adelaide (SAust)

Morgan, Charles Edward (Vic) b Aug. 10, 1900 Collingwood (Vic) d Dec. 8, 1965 Preston (Vic)

Morgan, Charles William (Qld) b Jan. 10, 1877 Hotham (Vic) d April 15, 1937 death place unknown

Morgan, George (NSW) b July 7, 1844 Bathurst (NSW) d July 17, 1896 Sydney (NSW)

Morgan, John Gordon (NSW) b March 6, 1893 Camperdown (NSW) d May 7, 1967 Concord (NSW)

Morgan, Oliver John (Qld) b June 7, 1945 Herston (Qld)

Morgan, Walter Millard (Vic) b Nov. 1, 1871 Ballarat (Vic) d July 10, 1941 Ballarat (Vic)

Morgan, Wayne Geoffrey (Qld) b July 10, 1955 Greenslopes (Qld)

* Moroney, John (NSW) b July 24, 1917 Macksville (NSW) d July 1, 1999 Orange (NSW)

Moroney, Robert (SAust) b Jan. 23, 1885 Upper Sturt (SAust) d Aug. 4, 1958 Parkside (SAust)

Morres, Thomas Furley (Vic) b Sept. 12, 1829 Wokingham, Berkshire (England) d Sept. 28, 1884 East Melbourne (Vic)

* Morris, Arthur Robert (NSW) b Jan. 19, 1922 Bondi (NSW)

Morris, John Humphrey (NSW) b June 5, 1831 Sydney (NSW) d Dec. 9, 1921 Glebe Point (NSW)

Morris, Maesmore Alfred (Vic) b c.1868 Northcote (Vic) d Aug. 31, 1917 Heidelberg (Vic)

Morris, Norman O'Neil (NSW) b May 9, 1907 Camperdown (NSW) d July 15, 1982 Leichhardt (NSW)

* Morris, Samuel (Vic) b June 22, 1855 Hobart (Tas) d Sept. 20, 1931 South Melbourne (Vic)

Morris, William Wallace (Qld) b March 6, 1918 Thornleigh (NSW)

Morrisby, Ronald Orlando George (Tas) b Jan. 12, 1915 Hobart (Tas) d June 12, 1995 Hobart (Tas)

Morrissey, Charles Vincent (NSW) b April 26, 1903 Corowa (NSW) d Feb. 20, 1938 Quirindi (NSW)

Morse, Eric George Arnold (Tas) b Aug. 26, 1918 Sheffield (Tas)

Morton, Francis Lonsdale (SAust & Vic) b Dec. 21, 1901 Fullarton (SAust) d Oct. 14, 1971 Caulfield (Vic)

Morton, Hugh Gilbert Stuart (Qld) b Oct. 14, 1881 Maryborough (Qld) d Jan. 28, 1936 Herston (Qld)

* Moses, Henry (NSW) b Feb. 13, 1858 Windsor (NSW) d Dec. 7, 1938 Strathfield (NSW)

* Moss, Jeffrey Kenneth (Vic) b June 29, 1947 Melbourne (Vic)

Moss, Jonathan (Vic) b May 4, 1975 Manly (NSW)

Moss, Ronald Barbar (NSW) b June 13, 1922 Alexandria (NSW)

Mossop, Kenneth Leonard Mario (Qld) b Aug. 15, 1909 New Farm (Qld) d Sept. 18, 1975 Surfers Paradise (Qld)

Mott, Matthew Peter (Qld & Vic) b Oct. 3, 1973 Charleville (Qld)

* Moule, William Henry (Vic) b Jan. 31, 1858 Brighton (Vic) d Aug. 24, 1939 St Kilda (Vic)

Moyes, Alban George (SAust & Vic) b Jan. 2, 1893 Gladstone (SAust) d Jan. 18, 1963 Chatswood (NSW)

Moyle, Charles Rule (SAust) b April 16, 1884 Adelaide (SAust) d Aug. 2, 1952 Adelaide (SAust)

Moyle, Edward James Ross (SAust) b Oct. 15, 1913 Moonta Mines (SAust) d Oct. 24, 1942 Cairo (Egypt) on active service

Moysey, George Bickford (WAust) b May 14, 1874 Battery Point (Tas) d May 18, 1932 Canterbury (Vic)

Muddle, Donald Gordon (Qld) b July 26, 1937 The Grange (Qld)

Mudge, Harold (NSW) b Feb. 14, 1914 Stanmore (NSW)

Mueller, Mervyn Edward Christopher Edgar (SAust) b Oct. 3, 1914 Yatala (SAust)

Muggleton, Mervyn Brian (WAust) b Sept. 4, 1941 Unley (SAust)

Muhl, Arthur Henry (Qld) b Feb. 12, 1913 South Brisbane (Qld) d April 17, 1994 South Brisbane (Qld)

Muir, William Frederick (Vic) b Feb. 8, 1907 Prahran (Vic) d Nov. 27, 1964 Box Hill (Vic)

Mulder, Brett (WAust) b Feb. 6, 1964 Subiaco (WAust)

Mulherin, Wayne Michael (NSW) b June 17, 1957 Canterbury (NSW)

Mullagh, Johnny (Unaarrimin) (Vic) b Aug. 13, 1841 Harrow (Vic) d Aug. 14, 1891 Pine Hills Station (Vic)

* Mullally, Alan David (WAust) b July 12, 1969 Southend-on-Sea, Essex (England)

Mullarkey, Desmond Antony (NSW) b Sept. 19, 1899 Rockdale (NSW) d Sept. 1, 1975 death place unknown

* Muller, Scott Andrew (Qld) b July 11, 1971 Herston (Qld)

Mullett, David Anthony (Tas) b Aug. 18, 1958 Burnie (Tas)

Mullett, Leonard Thomas (Vic) b Nov. 27, 1894 Moonee Ponds (Vic) d April 22, 1944 Toorak (Vic)

Mullooly, Thomas Cade (WAust) b Jan. 30, 1954 Mt Lawley (WAust)

Mundy, David Lloyd (SAust) b June 30, 1947 Enfield (SAust)

Munn, Arthur Reginald (NSW) b Feb. 22, 1888 Paddington (NSW) d Sept. 15, 1975 Sydney (NSW)

Munro, Charles (WAust) b March 21, 1871 Wallan (Vic) d Feb. 7, 1969 North Fremantle (WAust)

Munro, John Knox Ewing (WAust) b Dec. 27, 1928 Perth (WAust)

Munro, William (Qld) b c. 1862 Manchester, Lancashire (England) d Feb. 18, 1896 Stanthorpe (Qld)

Murch, Stewart Nigel Clifford (Vic) b June 27, 1944 Warrnambool (Vic)

**Murdoch, William Lloyd (NSW) b Oct. 18, 1854 Sandhurst (Vic) d Feb. 18, 1911 Melbourne (Vic)

Murfett, Julian Ivor (Tas) b July 2, 1915 Dunorlan (Tas) d April 27, 1982 Hobart (Tas)

Murphy, James Joseph (NSW) b Sept. 29, 1911 Bega (NSW) d May 7, 1984 Glenfield (NSW)

Murphy, Michael Augustus (Vic) b June 12, 1854 Sydney (NSW) d Sept. 2, 1890 Richmond (Vic)

Murray, Alfred Wynyatt (Vic) b Feb. 4, 1868 Long Gully (Vic) d July 27, 1936 Regent (Vic)

Murray, George Ian (WAust) b Nov. 6, 1940 South Perth (WAust)

Murray, John Tinline (SAust) b Dec. 1, 1892 Norwood (SAust) d Sept. 19, 1974 Stirling (WAust)

Murray, Norman Eric (Tas) b Nov. 2, 1908 Perth (WAust) d Aug. 21, 1967 Manly (NSW)

Murray, Richard (NSW) b c. 1831 Sydney (NSW) d Nov. 21, 1861 Manly (NSW)

Murray, William Walter Bruce (Vic) b Sept. 4, 1929 Red Cliffs (Vic)

* Musgrave, Henry Alfred (Vic) b Nov. 27, 1860 Surbiton, Surrey (England) d Nov. 2, 1931 Darlinghurst (NSW)

Musgrove, John (SAust) b July 28, 1861 Adelaide (SAust) d June 9, 1940 death place unknown

Mutton, Howard James Charles (SAust) b Oct. 21, 1924 Angaston (SAust) d Nov. 20, 1992 Adelaide (SAust)

Myers, Hubert (Tas) b Jan. 2, 1875 Yeadon, Yorkshire (England) d June 12, 1944 Hobart (Tas)

* Nagel, Lisle Ernest (Vic) b March 26, 1905 Bendigo (Vic) d Nov. 23, 1971 Mornington (Vic)

Nagel, Vernon George (Vic) b March 26, 1905 Bendigo (Vic) d April 27, 1974 Sandringham (Vic)

Nash, Don Anthony (NSW) b March 29, 1978 Dubbo (NSW)

Nash, John Eric (SAust) b April 16, 1950 North Adelaide (SAust)

* Nash, Laurence John (Tas & Vic) b May 2, 1910 Fitzroy (Vic) d July 24, 1986 Heidelberg (Vic)

Neill, Bruce William (Tas) b Feb. 23, 1949 Cabramatta (NSW)

Nettleton, Robert Glanville (Vic) b Sept. 16, 1909 Newport (Vic) d April 6, 1972 Newport (Vic)

Neville, Kevin John (Vic) b March 24, 1968 Numurkah (Vic)

Neville, Warwick John (Qld) b Dec. 31, 1948 Melbourne (Vic)

Newcombe, Henry Charles Edwin (NSW) b c. 1835 Sydney (NSW) d Oct. 26, 1908 Randwick (NSW)

Newell, Andrew Livingstone (NSW) b Nov. 13, 1868 Dungog (NSW) d March 8, 1915 Heron's Creek (NSW)

Newland, Philip Mesmer (SAust) b Feb. 2, 1875 Kensington (SAust) d Aug. 11, 1916 Knightsbridge (SAust)

Newman, Charles Frederick (WAust) b Nov. 7, 1909 Fremantle (WAust) d March 28, 1977 Fremantle (WAust)

Newman, Henry Albert (WAust) b March 13, 1907 Fremantle (WAust) d April 23, 1988 Riverton (WAust)

Newman, Richard Nelson (Tas) b Aug. 9, 1924 Brunswick (Vic)

Newstead, George Holt (Vic) b Aug. 11, 1910 Brighton (Vic) d July 21, 2000 Deepdene (Vic)

Newton, Alan Colin (Tas) b April 6, 1894 Longford (Tas) d March 27, 1979 Narrabeen (NSW)

Newton, Percy Allen (NSW) b Dec. 21, 1880 Newtown (NSW) d April 25, 1946 Rose Bay (NSW)

Nichols, Arthur Joseph (NSW) b Sept. 3, 1881 Sydney (NSW) d Nov. 19, 1937 North Sydney (NSW)

Nicholls, Charles Omer (NSW) b Dec. 5, 1901 Freeman's Reach (NSW) d Jan. 14, 1983 Freeman's Reach (NSW)

Nicholls, Paul Allen (WAust) b Nov. 10, 1946 East Fremantle (WAust)

Nicholls, Ronald Charles (Vic) b Sept. 1, 1951 Footscray (Vic)

* Nicholson, Matthew James (WAust) b Oct. 2, 1974 St Leonards (NSW)

Nicolson, John Norman Walter (Tas) b April 14, 1917 Campbell Town (Tas) d Oct. 7, 1992 Launceston (Tas)

Niehuus, Richard Dudley (SAust) b July 6, 1917 St Peters (SAust)

Nielsen, Timothy John (SAust) b May 5, 1968 Forest Gate, London (England)

Nikitaras, Steven (NSW & WAust) b Aug. 31, 1970 Port Kembla (NSW)

* Nitschke, Holmesdale Carl (SAust) b April 14, 1905 Adelaide (SAust) d Sept. 29, 1982 North Adelaide (SAust)

Nobes, Paul Christopher (Vic & SAust) b April 20, 1964 West Heidelberg (Vic)

Noble, Edward George (NSW) b Jan. 16, 1865 Brickfield Hill (NSW) d May 4, 1941 Balmain (NSW)

* Noble, Montague Alfred (NSW) b Jan. 28, 1873 Sydney (NSW) d June 22, 1940 Randwick (NSW)

* Noblet, Geffery (SAust) b Sept. 14, 1916 Evandale (SAust)

Noel, John (SAust) b March 28, 1856 Hindmarsh (SAust) d Jan. 9, 1938 Largs Bay (SAust)

Noffke, Ashley Allan (Cricket Academy) b April 30, 1977 Nambour (Qld)

Nolan, Francis Edward (Qld) b June 27, 1920 Manly (Qld)

Noonan, Daniel Francis (Vic) b May 11, 1873 North Melbourne (Vic) d May 30, 1910 North Melbourne (Vic)

Noonan, David James (NSW) b Jan. 8, 1876 Newtown (NSW) d March 10, 1929 Sydney (NSW)

Norman, Michael John (Tas) b Aug. 17, 1952 Launceston (Tas)

Norman, Hercules Rex (NSW) b 1890 birthplace unknown d Dec. 30, 1961 Parramatta (NSW)

North, Frederic Dudley (WAust) b Nov. 9, 1866 Kensington, London, Middlesex (England) d Aug. 22, 1921 Cottesloe (WAust)

North, Marcus James (WAust) b July 28, 1979 Melbourne (Vic)

* Nothling, Otto Ernest (NSW & Qld) b Aug. 1, 1900 Teutoburg (Qld) d Sept. 26, 1965 Chelmer (Qld)

Noyes, Alfred William Finch (Vic) b c. 1835 Torquay, Devon (England) d Sept. 30, 1902 Deniliquin (NSW)

Noyes, Harold David (Qld) b Aug. 12, 1892 Warwick (Qld) d July 14, 1968 Brisbane (Qld)

Numa, Herbert Leslie (Vic) b June 22, 1925 Carlton (Vic) d April 17, 1984 Heidelberg (Vic)

Nunn, Thomas (NSW) b Jan. 21, 1846 Penshurst, Kent (England) d May 31, 1889 Bexley (NSW)

Nutt, Richard Nathaniel (NSW) b June 25, 1911 Balmain (NSW) d Feb. 5, 1985 Gladesville (NSW)

Oakes, Cecil James Grellis (Tas) b March 1, 1915 Hobart (Tas) d Oct. 10, 1994 Canberra (ACT)

Oakley, Hector Herbert (Vic) b Jan. 10, 1909 North Fitzroy (Vic) d Dec. 19, 1998 Sandringham (Vic)

Oatley, James Napoleon (NSW) b Aug. 12, 1845 Newtown (NSW) d Dec. 17, 1925 Cremorne (NSW)

O'Brien, Charles Joseph (NSW) b c. 1921 birthplace unknown d Dec. 15, 1980 Coal Point (NSW)

O'Brien, Ernest Francis (NSW) b Aug. 26, 1900 Paddington (NSW) d Nov. 2, 1935 Newcastle (NSW)

* O'Brien, Leo Patrick Joseph (Vic) b July 2, 1907 West Melbourne (Vic) d March 13, 1997 Mentone (Vic)

O'Brien, Leslie John (NSW) d c. 1968 full birth and death details unknown

O'Brien, M. Evanson (Anderson's XI) birth and death details unknown

O'Brien, Robert (Qld) b July 16, 1869 Redfern (NSW) d Oct. 2, 1922 Brisbane (Qld)

O'Connell, Thomas Reginald (SAust) b March 10, 1916 Parkside (SAust)

O'Connor, Brian Redmond Devereaux (Qld) b July 5, 1913 South Brisbane (Qld) d Dec. 20, 1963 Red Hill (Qld)

O'Connor, Donald Frederick Gregory (SAust & Tas) b July 20, 1958 Gilgandra (NSW)

* O'Connor, John Denis Alphonsus (NSW & SAust) b Sept. 9, 1875 Booroowa (NSW) d Aug. 23, 1941 Lewisham (NSW)

O'Connor, John William (Vic) b Aug. 19, 1868 Geelong (Vic) d Feb. 2, 1952 Windsor (Vic)

O'Connor, Leo Patrick Devereaux (Qld) b April 11, 1890 Murtoa (Vic) d Jan. 16, 1985 Melbourne (Vic)

* O'Donnell, Simon Patrick (Vic) b Jan. 26, 1963 Deniliquin (NSW)

O'Dwyer, Thomas Edmund (WAust) b Nov. 5, 1919 Bridgetown (WAust)

* Ogilvie, Alan David (Qld) b June 3, 1951 Southport (Qld)

Ogilvy, David Skene (NSW) b c.1859 Wollongong (NSW) d Aug. 6, 1917 Liverpool (NSW)

O'Halloran, Dale Francis (Tas) b Feb. 15, 1955 Smithton (Tas)

O'Halloran, James Patrick (Vic) b Jan. 12, 1872 Richmond (Vic) d April 28, 1943 East Melbourne (Vic)

O'Halloran, William Matthew (Vic) b June 18, 1934 Corowa (NSW) d Dec. 13, 1994 East Melbourne (Vic)

O'Hanlon, William James (NSW) b March 10, 1863 Carlton (Vic) d June 23, 1940 Randwick (NSW)

Ohlstrom, Patrick Andreas Paul (SAust) b Dec. 16, 1890 Warooka (SAust) d June 10, 1940 Adelaide (SAust)

O'Keeffe, Francis Aloysius (NSW & Vic) b May 11, 1896 Waverley (NSW) d March 26, 1924 Hampstead, London (England)

* O'Keeffe, Kerry James (NSW) b Nov. 25, 1949 Hurstville (NSW)

O'Leary, Scott James (Qld) b Dec. 17, 1977 South Brisbane (Qld)

* Oldfield, William Albert Stanley (NSW) b Sept. 9, 1894 Alexandria (NSW) d Aug. 10, 1976 Killara (NSW)

Oldroyd, Bradley John (WAust) b Nov. 5, 1973 Bentley (WAust)

Oliver, Benjamin Carl (Vic) b Oct. 24, 1979 Castlemaine (Vic)

Oliver, Charles Nicholson Jewel (NSW) b April 24, 1848 Hobart (Tas) d June 14, 1920 Manly (NSW)

Oliver, Stuart Bradley (Tas) b March 20, 1972 Launceston (Tas)

O'Meara, Phillip Anthony (WAust) b June 13, 1951 Kellerberrin (WAust)

O'Mullane, George Jeremiah Patrick (Vic) b Dec. 3, 1842 Melbourne (Vic) d Dec. 20, 1866 East Melbourne (Vic)

O'Neill, Kevin Ignatius (SAust) b Aug. 16, 1919 Hectorville (SAust)

O'Neill, Mark Dorian (WAust & NSW) b March 5, 1959 Sutherland (NSW)

* O'Neill, Norman Clifford (NSW) b Feb. 19, 1937 Carlton (NSW)

Onyons, Basil Austin (Vic) b March 14, 1887 Prahran (Vic) d May 31, 1967 Glen Iris (Vic)

O'Regan, James Bernard (NSW) b April 23, 1938 Ashfield (NSW) d May 15, 1998 Randwick (NSW)

O'Reilly, John William (NSW) b Nov. 16, 1930 Mosman (NSW)

* O'Reilly, William Joseph (NSW) b Dec. 20, 1905 White Cliffs (NSW) d Oct. 6, 1992 Sutherland (NSW)

Orr, Herbert Richard (WAust) b Feb. 3, 1865 Kensington, London (England) d May 22, 1940 Sevenoaks, Kent (England)

Osborn, Francis James (SAust) b Feb. 13, 1935 Alberton (SAust)

Osborne, Mark (Vic) b Oct. 8, 1961 Kogarah (NSW)

Osborne, Noton Michael (Vic) b c.1844 (England) d Dec. 10, 1878 Hobart (Tas)

Osborne, Robert Henry (NSW) b Feb. 4, 1897 Redfern (NSW) d Feb. 21, 1975 Long Jetty (NSW)

Osborne, Robert Moorhead (Vic) b Sept. 29, 1881 St Kilda (Vic) d Nov. 19, 1927 Wesburn (Vic)

O'Shannassy, Robert Martin (SAust) b March 7, 1949 Hindmarsh (SAust)

O'Shaughnessy, Barney (WAust) b Feb. 28, 1912 Wiluna (WAust)

Oswald, Norman Hamilton (SAust) b Oct. 31, 1916 Prospect (SAust) d June 22, 1970 Adelaide (SAust)

Outridge, Thomas Michael (WAust) b Sept. 8, 1927 Perth (WAust)

Over, Willie (Vic) b Jan. 20, 1862 Richmond (Vic) d Nov. 10, 1910 Krugersdorp, Transvaal (South Africa)

Owen, Christopher John (SAust) b Dec. 21, 1963 Henley Beach (SAust)

Owen, Kerry Alfred (NSW) b June 23, 1943 Bondi Beach (NSW)

Oxenford, Bruce Nicholas James (Qld) b March 5, 1960 Southport (Qld)

Oxenford, Ian Bruce (Qld) b Sept. 3, 1932 South Brisbane (Qld)

Oxenham, Lionel Emmanuel (Qld) b Jan. 27, 1888 Nundah (Qld) d Jan. 10, 1970 Clayfield (Qld)

* Oxenham, Ronald Keven (Qld) b July 28, 1891 Nundah (Qld) d Aug. 16, 1939 Nundah (Qld)

Packham, Leonard (WAust) b Sept. 15, 1891 Norwood (SAust) d Oct. 4, 1958 Swanbourne (WAust)

Page, Clive Basil (Qld) b May 25, 1894 Rockhampton (Qld) d July 1, 1967 Greenslopes (Qld)

Palfreyman, Brent Avis Hardcastle (Tas) b Jan. 20, 1945 Hobart (Tas)

* Palmer, George Eugene (Vic & Tas) b Feb. 22, 1859 Mulwala (NSW) d Aug. 22, 1910 Benalla (Vic)

Palmer, George Hamilton (SAust) b Aug. 2, 1903 Eastwood (SAust) d Aug. 24, 1986 Woodville South (SAust)

Palmer, Jack Stirling (SAust) b Oct. 20, 1903 East Adelaide (SAust) d Dec. 11, 1979 Glenelg (SAust)

Panitzki, Robert James (Tas) b April 29, 1948 Hobart (Tas)

Park, Alfred Leath (NSW) b April 15, 1840 Oatlands (Tas) d Jan. 16, 1924 Liverpool (NSW)

* Park, Roy Lindsay (Vic) b July 30, 1892 Charlton (Vic) d Jan. 23, 1947 Middle Park (Vic)

Parker, Alec David (Qld) b June 12, 1955 Dalby (Qld)

Parker, Ernest Frederick (WAust) b Nov. 5, 1883 Perth (WAust) d May 2, 1918 Caestre (France)

Parker, Geoffrey Ross (Vic & SAust) b March 31, 1968 Malvern (Vic)

Parker, John Francis (WAust) b March 13, 1936 South Perth (WAust)

Parker, Robert Ernest (Qld) b Sept. 18, 1942 Toowoomba (Qld)

Parker, Ronald Arthur (SAust) b Feb. 23, 1916 Goodwood (SAust) d Aug. 27, 1993 San Francisco, California (United States of America)

Parker, Russell John (SAust) b Aug. 3, 1952 Sudbury, Middlesex (England)

Parkin, George Thomas (SAust) b Oct. 11, 1864 Adelaide (SAust) d Aug. 6, 1933 Adelaide (SAust)

Parkinson, Henry (Tas) b June 10, 1882 Port Arthur (Tas) d c. 1962 death place unknown

Parkinson, Samuel David Haslam (SAust) b July 8, 1960 Adelaide (SAust)

Parry, Cyril Norman (SAust & Tas) b Oct. 14, 1900 Queenstown (SAust) d July 6, 1984 Kew (Vic)

Parsonage, Thomas Griffiths (NSW) b Nov. 13, 1910 Chatswood (NSW) d Feb. 3, 1951 Manly (NSW)

Parsons, Herbert Fulton (Vic) b May 21, 1875 Hawthorn (Vic) d Dec. 20, 1937 Canterbury (Vic)

* Pascoe, Len Stephen (NSW) b Feb. 13, 1950 Bridgetown (WAust)

Pascoe, Matthew David (Qld) b Jan. 10, 1977 Camperdown (NSW)

Pateman, Robert (Vic) b Aug. 28, 1856 Magpie (Vic) death details unknown

Patfield, Alfred Samuel (WAust) b Sept. 6, 1884 Paterson (NSW) d Nov. 9, 1961 Perth (WAust)

Paton, George Douglas (Tas) b March 1, 1879 Hobart (Tas) d Oct. 5, 1950 Hobart (Tas)

Patrick, Charles Wright (NSW & Qld) b Jan. 13, 1866 Sydney (NSW) d Nov. 29, 1919 Coogee (NSW)

* Patterson, Balfour Patrick (Tas) b Sept. 15, 1961 Portland (Jamaica)

Patterson, Brian Clifford (Tas) b June 28, 1937 Hobart (Tas)

Patterson, Mark Winston (NSW) b Nov. 15, 1966 Dubbo (NSW)

Patterson, Thomas Francis (Tas) b Sept. 16, 1839 Hobart (Tas)

Paulsen, Robert George (Qld & WAust) b Oct. 18, 1947 Herston (Qld)

Pavy, Leonard (WAust) b Aug. 21, 1936 Boulder (WAust)

Pawley, Michael Bernard (NSW) b March 10, 1944 Glen Innes (NSW)

Payne, Charles Percy (Tas) b July 31, 1876 Hobart (Tas) d Jan. 28, 1938 Lower Sandy Bay (Tas)

Peachey, Mark (Qld) b Oct. 31, 1900 Tannymorel (Qld) d Nov. 23, 1987 Ipswich (Qld)

Peake, Clinton John (Vic) b March 25, 1977 Geelong (Vic)

Pearce, Donald Rex (Tas) b Feb. 21, 1941 Ulverstone (Tas) d Feb. 13, 1999 Burnie (Tas)

Pearce, Kevin Dudley (Tas) b Feb. 29, 1960 Devonport (Tas)

Pearce, Reginald Manus (NSW) b April 20, 1918 Tumbarumba (NSW) d June 19, 1995 Sydney (NSW)

Pearsall, Alan Louden (Tas) b May 24, 1915 Hobart (Tas) d March 8, 1941 in action in English Channel

Pearson, Trevor John (SAust) b Oct. 13, 1943 Goodwood (SAust)

Pearson, William Ernest (Vic) b Nov. 10, 1912 Kerang (Vic) d Sept. 11, 1987 Melbourne (Vic)

Pegg, Harry Robert Edgar (Qld) b March 19, 1916 Moorooka (Qld)

Pellew, Arthur Howard (SAust) b Jan. 20, 1878 Riverton (SAust) d Aug. 21, 1948 Rose Park (SAust)

* Pellew, Clarence Everard (SAust) b Sept. 21, 1893 Port Pirie (SAust) d May 9, 1981 Adelaide (SAust)

Pellew, John Harold (SAust) b July 17, 1882 Truro (SAust) d Oct. 17, 1946 Unley (SAust)

Pellew, Lancelot Vivian (SAust) b Dec. 15, 1899 Port Elliott (SAust) d Dec. 8, 1970 Adelaide (SAust)

Penman, Arthur Percival (NSW) b Jan. 23, 1885 Ultimo (NSW) d Sept. 11, 1944 Rockley (NSW)

Pennefather, George Shirley (Tas) b Sept. 28, 1864 Launceston (Tas) d Oct. 16, 1945 Launceston (Tas)

Pennycuick, Rupert James (Tas) b April 11, 1893 Jericho (Tas) d Jan. 17, 1963 Concord (NSW)

Penter, Colin Edward (WAust) b July 20, 1955 Albany (WAust)

Pepper, Cecil George (NSW) b Sept. 15, 1916 Forbes (NSW) d March 24, 1993 Littleborough, Lancashire (England)

Perraton, Jack Oldfield (Vic) b Feb. 26, 1909 Prahran (Vic) d Oct. 1, 1950 Kings Cross (NSW)

Perraton, William Thomas Crooke (Vic) b Aug. 27, 1867 Collingwood (Vic) d Sept. 23, 1952 Elsternwick (Vic)

Perren, Clinton Terrence (Qld) b Feb. 22, 1975 Herston (Qld)

Perrin, Thomas Henry (Vic) b Oct. 27, 1928 Prahran (Vic)

Perrins, Keith Robinson (Qld) b Jan. 17, 1931 Rockhampton (Qld)

Perry, Cecil Thomas Henry (Tas) b March 3, 1846 Battery Point (Tas) d Aug. 4, 1917 Timaru (New Zealand)

Perryman, Charles Henry (Vic) b Jan. 20, 1872 Richmond (Vic) d Aug. 30, 1950 St Kilda (Vic)

Peters, Arthur Ernest (SAust) b March 8, 1872 Adelaide (SAust) d Sept. 24, 1903 Henley Beach (SAust)

Pettiford, Jack (NSW) b Nov. 29, 1919 Freshwater (NSW) d Oct. 11, 1964 North Sydney (NSW)

Pettinger, Aldam Murr (SAust) b July 30, 1859 Kent Town (SAust) d Aug. 18, 1950 Lower Mitcham (SAust)

Phelps, Leslie R. (Tas) birth and death details unknown

Phelps, Matthew James (Tas) b Sept. 1, 1972 Lismore (NSW)

Phillips, Edward George (SAust) b March 1, 1851 Port Adelaide (SAust) d Feb. 8, 1933 North Adelaide (SAust)

Phillips, Edward Lauriston (SAust) b Sept. 2, 1892 North Adelaide (SAust) d Jan. 8, 1971 Adelaide (SAust)

Phillips, James (Vic) b Sept. 1, 1860 Pleasant Creek (Vic) d April 21, 1930 Burnaby, Vancouver, British Columbia (Canada)

Phillips, Joseph (Vic) b April 22, 1840 Parramatta (NSW) d May 7, 1901 Heidelberg (Vic)

Phillips, Norbert Eugene (NSW) b July 9, 1896 Cowra (NSW) d Oct. 3, 1961 Sydney (NSW)

Phillips, Raymond Berry (NSW & Qld) b May 23, 1954 Paddington (NSW)

* Phillips, Wayne Bentley (SAust) b March 1, 1958 Adelaide (SAust)

* Phillips, Wayne Norman (Vic) b Nov. 7, 1962 Geelong (Vic)

Philpott, Albert John William (Vic) b March 14, 1873 Gaffneys Creek (Vic) d Nov. 25, 1950 Kew (Vic)

* Philpott, Peter Ian (NSW) b Nov. 21, 1934 Manly (NSW)

Philpott, Richard Stamper (Vic) b Feb. 7, 1813 West Farleigh, Kent (England) d June 8, 1888 Brenchley, Kent (England)

Philpott, William (Vic) b Jan. 24, 1819 West Farleigh, Kent (England) d Nov. 4, 1891 Linton, Kent (England)

Pickering, George Thomas (Vic) b c. 1832 Sydney (NSW) d Dec. 1, 1858 Sandridge (Vic)

Pickering, Kelby Sinclair (SAust) b Jan. 3, 1973 Lameroo (SAust)

Pickett, Alfred William (Tas) b c. 1871 Ulverstone (Tas) d March 19, 1953 Ulverstone (Tas)

Pickett, Edward Arthur (Tas) b April 2, 1909 Ulverstone (Tas)

Pictet, Francis Stewart (Tas) b June 4, 1866 Bath, Somerset (England) death details unknown

Pierce, Michael (NSW & Qld) b Sept. 3, 1869 Paddington (NSW) d Feb. 4, 1913 Sydney (NSW)

Pilon, Nathan Steven (NSW) b Oct. 27, 1976 Dubbo (NSW)

Pinch, Colin John (NSW & SAust) b June 23, 1921 Brownsville (NSW)

Pinkus, Harold William (Tas) b Sept. 27, 1934 Smithton (Tas)

Pinnington, Todd Andrew (Tas) b March 21, 1971 Hobart (Tas)

Pitcher, Franklyn Joseph (Vic) b June 24, 1879 Collingwood (Vic) d Jan. 23, 1921 Northcote (Vic)

Pite, Walter Edward (NSW) b Sept. 24, 1876 Sydney (NSW) d May 7, 1955 Waverley (NSW)

Pittman, Brian Harold (SAust) b June 17, 1930 Rose Park (SAust)

Plant, Hugh Joseph (Vic) b Oct. 12, 1907 Narrandera (NSW) d Aug. 30, 1993 Geelong (Vic)

* Playle, William Rodger (WAust) b Dec. 1, 1938 Palmerston North (New Zealand)

Plummer, Neil Robert (SAust) b July 6, 1955 Lobethal (SAust)

Pocock, William Johnstone (NSW) b c. 1848 Clifton, Gloucestershire (England) d Sept. 27, 1928 East Brighton (Vic)

Poeppel, George Augustus (Qld) b Nov. 6, 1893 Bundaberg (Qld) d Feb. 2, 1917 POW camp (Germany)

Poidevin, Leslie Oswald Sheridan (NSW) b Nov. 5, 1876 Merrilla (NSW) d Nov. 19, 1931 Waverley (NSW)

Polzin, Michael Allan (Qld) b June 23, 1964 Wondai (Qld)

* Ponsford, William Harold (Vic) b Oct. 19, 1900 North Fitzroy (Vic) d April 6, 1991 Kyneton (Vic)

* Ponting, Ricky Thomas (Tas) b Dec. 19, 1974 Launceston (Tas)

Poon, Hunter Robert George (Qld) b May 14, 1894 Pimlico (NSW) d Jan. 25, 1980 Greenslopes (Qld)

* Pope, Roland James (NSW) b Feb. 18, 1864 Ashfield (NSW) d July 27, 1952 Manly (NSW)

Porter, Brian Clifford (Vic) b Dec. 20, 1942 Carlton (Vic)

Porter, Graham David (WAust) b March 18, 1955 Middle Swan (WAust)

Potter, Jack (Vic) b April 13, 1938 Melbourne (Vic)

Powell, George (NSW) b April 12, 1918 Newtown (NSW)

Powell, Ronald Hartley (Tas) b Sept. 27, 1883 New Norfolk (Tas) d Aug. 22, 1922 (Qld)

Powell, Theodore (NSW) b July 10, 1852 Berrima (NSW) d Sept. 3, 1913 Sydney (NSW)

Power, John Francis (Vic) b March 23, 1932 Port Melbourne (Vic)

Power, Laurence James (SAust) b July 31, 1898 Ovingham (SAust) d March 20, 1963 Glenelg (SAust)

Power, Louis Bertrand (SAust) b Oct. 10, 1905 Ovingham (SAust) d Sept. 30, 1988 Bedford Park (SAust)

Power, Robert (Vic) b c.1833 Galway (Ireland) d Nov. 4, 1914 Toorak (Vic)

Powlett, Frederick Armand (Vic) b Jan. 6, 1811 Shrewsbury, Shropshire (England) d June 9, 1865 Kyneton (Vic)

Pratten, Herbert Graham (NSW) b April 22, 1892 Ashfield (NSW) d Sept. 11, 1979 Neutral Bay (NSW)

Preen, Alan Thomas (WAust) b July 4, 1935 Fremantle (WAust)

Prentice, Warden Selby (NSW) b July 30, 1886 Homebush (NSW) d Feb. 26, 1969 Rosebery (NSW)

Prescott, Shaun St Aubyn (Vic) b Sept. 7, 1966 Melbourne (Vic)

Prestwidge, Scott Arthur (Qld) b May 15, 1968 Bankstown (NSW)

Pretty, Alfred Henry (SAust) b Jan. 29, 1874 Willunga (SAust) d June 21, 1929 Mile End (SAust)

Price, Charles Frederick Thomas (Services) b Feb. 17, 1917 Sydney (NSW) d Jan. 19, 1997 Avalon (NSW)

Price, Henry Alexander (Qld) b March 31, 1913 Spring Hill (Qld) d May 3, 1999 Wavell Heights (Qld)

Price, Reuben Henry (WAust) b April 27, 1923 London (England) d Feb. 26, 1991 Perth (WAust)

Price, Walter Davies (SAust) b March 24, 1886 Hawthorn (Vic) d July 29, 1944 Adelaide (SAust)

Prindiville, Kevin Joseph (WAust) b Sept. 18, 1949 Subiaco (WAust)

Prindiville, Terence John (WAust) b Nov. 20, 1942 Subiaco (WAust)

Prior, Wayne (SAust) b Sept. 30, 1952 Salisbury (SAust)

Pritchard, David Edward (SAust) b Jan. 5, 1893 Queenstown (SAust) d July 4, 1983 Myrtle Bank (SAust)

Prout, James Alexander (Qld) b Aug. 12, 1889 Flemington (Vic) d Feb. 18, 1952 Double Bay (NSW)

Pryor, David Godfrey (NSW) b Feb. 3, 1870 Maitland (NSW) d Jan. 3, 1937 Gosford (NSW)

Puckett, Charles William (WAust) b Feb. 21, 1911 Beddington Corner, Surrey (England)

Puckett, Maxwell Charles (SAust) b June 3, 1935 Unley Park (SAust) d Aug. 25, 1991 North Adelaide (SAust)

Punch, Austin Thomas Eugene (NSW & Tas) b Aug. 16, 1894 North Sydney (NSW) d Aug. 25, 1985 Cremorne (NSW)

Punch, Keith Francis (WAust) b Oct. 19, 1940 Subiaco (WAust)

Putman, Sydney William Leslie (Tas) b March 25, 1912 Hobart (Tas) d Sept. 20, 1947 Hobart (Tas)

Pye, Leslie Walter (NSW) b July 6, 1871 Windsor (NSW) d March 9, 1949 Parramatta (NSW)

Pyke, James Kendrick (SAust) b June 7, 1966 Cottesloe (WAust)

Pyke, Richard Dimond (Qld) b Aug. 15, 1877 Collingwood (Vic) d Dec. 4, 1914 Gympie (Qld)

Pynor, Ernest Ivan (SAust) b April 23, 1920 Essendon (Vic) d Oct. 23, 1999 East Doncaster (Vic)

Quelch, Leslie Norman (Qld) b Feb. 26, 1918 Maryborough (Qld) d April 13, 1987 Paddington (Qld)

Quick, Ian William (Vic) b Nov. 5, 1933 Geelong (Vic)

Quigley, Brian Maxwell (SAust) b Dec. 27, 1935 Henley Beach (SAust)

Quilty, John (SAust) b c.1860 Adelaide (SAust) d May 9, 1942 Kent Town (SAust)

Quin, Stanley Oldfield (Vic) b April 17, 1908 Caulfield (Vic) d Nov. 27, 1967 Brighton (Vic)

Quinlan, Francis Patrick (WAust) b March 17, 1891 Perth (WAust) d Aug. 15, 1935 Perth (WAust)

Quinn, Michael Brian (Vic) b July 2, 1962 Adelaide (SAust)

Quist, Karl Hugo (NSW, WAust & SAust) b Aug. 18, 1875 Milson's Point (NSW) d March 31, 1957 Plympton (SAust)

* Rackemann, Carl Gray (Qld) b June 3, 1960 Wondai (Qld)

Rahmann, Herbert William (Qld) b Aug. 23, 1886 Maryborough (Qld) d Oct. 12, 1957 Nundah (Qld)

Rainey, Leslie Newburn (Vic) b Jan. 10, 1881 South Yarra (Vic) d Aug. 27, 1962 Melbourne (Vic)

Ramsay, John (Tas) b Dec. 26, 1872 Glasgow, Lanarkshire (Scotland) d Feb. 6, 1944 Launceston (Tas)

Ramsay, Marmaduke Francis (Qld) b Dec. 8, 1860 Cheltenham, Gloucestershire (England) d Dec. 31, 1947 Lee, Canterbury, Kent (England)

Ramshaw, Darrin Joseph (WAust & Vic) b Nov. 29, 1965 Subiaco (WAust)

Randell, Alfred Charles (WAust) b May 10, 1884 Perth (WAust) d Sept. 13, 1958 Sydney (NSW)

Randell, Ernest Arthur (WAust) b Jan. 25, 1873 Perth (WAust) d May 12, 1938 Perth (WAust)

Randell, James Arthur (NSW) b Aug. 4, 1880 birthplace unknown d . Dec. 7, 1952 Balgowlah (NSW)

* Ransford, Vernon Seymour (Vic) b March 20, 1885 South Yarra (Vic) d March 19, 1958 Brighton (Vic)

Ratcliffe, Andrew Thomas (NSW) b April 3, 1891 Leichhardt (NSW) d Aug. 31, 1974 Banksia (NSW)

Rathie, David Stewart (Qld) b May 29, 1951 Roma (Qld)

Rawle, Keith Trevillian (Vic) b Oct. 29, 1924 Essendon (Vic)

Ray, Mark (NSW & Tas) b Oct. 2, 1952 Surry Hills (NSW)

Raymer, Vincent Norman (Qld) b May 4, 1918 Toowoomba (Qld)

Raymond, Ralph Cossart (Qld) b Nov. 28, 1912 Boonah (Qld) d Oct. 11, 1982 Murgon (Qld)

Rayson, Maxwell William (Vic) b Aug. 26, 1912 Kew (Vic) d May 11, 1993 Heidelberg (Vic)

Rayson, Roger William (Vic) b Feb. 17, 1942 Windsor (Vic)

Rayson, William Jones (Vic) b Dec. 18, 1889 Malmsbury (Vic) d Sept. 8, 1957 Parkdale (Vic)

Read, Arthur Edwin (WAust) b May 26, 1908 Unley (SAust)

Rebbeck, Phillip Douglas (SAust) b July 31, 1948 North Adelaide (SAust)

Reddrop, Walter William (Vic) b Sept. 9, 1901 Kyneton (Vic) d March 31, 1983 Parkville (Vic)

Redfearn, James (Vic) b c. 1836 Yorkshire (England) d March 10, 1916 Glenhuntly (Vic)

Redgrave, John Sidney (NSW & Qld) b Aug. 5, 1878 North Sydney (NSW) d Aug. 3, 1958 West End (Qld)

* Redpath, Ian Ritchie (Vic) b May 11, 1941 Geelong (Vic)

* Reedman, John Cole (SAust) b Oct. 9, 1865 Taminda (SAust) d March 25, 1924 Gilberton (SAust)

Rees, John Newman Stace (SAust) b Sept. 2, 1880 Hindmarsh (SAust) d Jan. 17, 1959 St Peters (SAust)

Rees, Robert Blackie Colston (SAust) b April 15, 1882 Hindmarsh (SAust) d Sept. 20, 1966 Bowmans Green, Hertfordshire (England)

Rees, William Gilbert (NSW) b April 6, 1827 St Issell's, Pembrokeshire (Wales) d Oct. 31, 1898 Marlborough (New Zealand)

Rees, William Lee (Vic) b Dec. 16, 1836 Bristol, Gloucestershire (England) d May 13, 1912 Gisborne (New Zealand)

Reeves, Damion Albert (SAust) b July 12, 1971 Darwin (NT)

Reeves, William Henry (Vic) b c. 1881 Fitzroy (Vic) d Sept. 13, 1962 Kew (Vic)

Regeling, Donald Carl (Qld) b Aug. 13, 1955 Boonah (Qld)

Reid, Alan Walter (Qld) b June 30, 1931 Maryborough (Qld)

Reid, Basil Stanley (Tas) b May 17, 1924 Launceston (Tas) d July 16, 2000 Launceston (Tas)

* Reid, Bruce Anthony (WAust) b March 14, 1963 Osborne Park (WAust)

Reid, Curtis Alexander (Vic) b July 16, 1836 Inverary Park (NSW) d July 1, 1886 Hawthorn (Vic)

Reid, Douglas Clement (NSW) b Sept. 23, 1886 St Peters (NSW) d Aug. 21, 1959 Wahroonga (NSW)

Reid, Stanley John (Tas) b May 5, 1955 St Helen's (Tas)

Reid, W. (Tas) birth and death details unknown

Reid, William (SAust) b c. 1871 North Adelaide (SAust) full birth and death details unknown

* Reiffel, Paul Ronald (Vic) b April 19, 1966 Box Hill (Vic)

Renfrey, Leslie Cotswold (WAust) b Feb. 15, 1893 Wallaroo Mines (SAust) d Sept. 23, 1958 Mt Lawley (WAust)

* Renneberg, David Alexander (NSW) b Sept. 23, 1942 Rozelle (NSW)

Reynolds, George Raymond (Qld) b Aug. 24, 1936 Bundaberg (Qld)

Rhodes, Brian Leslie (NSW) b March 7, 1951 Paddington (NSW)

Ricci, Brendan Paul (Vic) b April 24, 1965 East Melbourne (Vic)

* Richards, Barry Anderson (SAust) b July 21, 1945 Morningside, Durban, Natal (South Africa)

Richards, Corey John (NSW) b Aug. 25, 1975 Camden (NSW)

Richards, Frank Hitchen (Vic) d Fremantle (WAust) full birth and death details unknown

* Richards, Isaac Vivian Alexander (Qld) b March 7, 1952 St John's (Antigua)

Richards, Thomas Oliver (SAust) b July 5, 1855 Norwood (SAust) d Dec. 14, 1923 Cottonville (Qld)

* Richardson, Arthur John (SAust & WAust) b July 24, 1888 Sevenhills (SAust) d Dec. 23, 1973 Semaphore (SAust)

Richardson, Brian Douglas (Tas) b May 15, 1932 Hobart (Tas)

Richardson, Charles Augustus (NSW) b Feb. 22, 1864 Sydney (NSW) d Aug. 17, 1949 Waipara, Canterbury (New Zealand)

Richardson, Colin George (Tas) b June 6, 1920 Hobart (Tas) d Dec. 22, 1993 Hobart (Tas)

Richardson, Edward Noel (Tas) b Dec. 8, 1929 Hobart (Tas)

Richardson, Frederick William (Tas) b March 29, 1878 Campbell Town (Tas) d March 7, 1955 Campbell Town (Tas)

Richardson, Geoffrey William (Vic) b Dec. 7, 1956 Koo Wee Rup (Vic)

Richardson, George Biggs (NSW) b May 28, 1834 Bathurst (NSW) d May 1, 1911 Dandaloo (NSW)

Richardson, Howard James (Vic) b Oct. 29, 1894 Berwick (Vic) d Dec. 21, 1959 Richmond (Vic)

Richardson, Joseph (SAust) b Feb. 28, 1878 Kooringa (SAust) d June 13, 1951 Glenelg (SAust)

Richardson, Leonard Martin (NSW & Qld) b May 5, 1950 Paddington (NSW)

Richardson, Leslie Lambert (Tas) b Jan. 9, 1887 Ralph's Bay (Tas) d Nov. 15, 1962 Hobart (Tas)

Richardson, Leslie Walter (Tas) b Sept. 5, 1911 New Town (Tas) d Nov. 1, 1981 Hobart (Tas)

Richardson, Reginald Maxwell (Tas) b Oct. 6, 1922 Hobart (Tas)

* Richardson, Victor York (SAust) b Sept. 7, 1894 Parkside (SAust) d Oct. 29, 1969 Fullarton (SAust)

Richardson, Walter Barrett (Tas) b Oct. 24, 1876 Ralph's Bay (Tas) d May 30, 1962 Hobart (Tas)

Richardson, William Alfred (NSW) b Aug. 22, 1866 Sydney (NSW) d Jan. 3, 1930 Mosman (NSW)

Richter, Arthur Frederick (SAust) b Sept. 1, 1908 Telowie (SAust) d Aug. 16, 1936 Adelaide (SAust)

Rickman, Wilfred (Vic) b c. 1856 South Yarra (Vic) d June 6, 1911 Frankston (Vic)

Ridge, Frank Macquarie (NSW) b Jan. 10, 1873 Dubbo (NSW) d May 25, 1959 Manly (NSW)

Ridgway, Mark William (Tas) b May 21, 1960 Warragul (Vic)

Ridings, Kenneth Lovett (SAust) b Feb. 7, 1920 Malvern (SAust) d May 17, 1943 in action over Bay of Biscay, France

Ridings, Phillip Lovett (SAust) b Oct. 2, 1917 Malvern (SAust) d Sept. 13, 1998 Adelaide (SAust)

Rigaud, Stephen (SAust) b Nov. 25, 1856 Kenton Valley, Talunga (SAust) d Nov. 13, 1922 Claremont (WAust)

Rigby, Albert (WAust) b c. 1901 Lancashire (England) d Oct. 10, 1963 Hollywood (WAust)

Rigg, Basil Augustus (WAust) b Aug. 12, 1926 Highgate (WAust)

Rigg, Herbert William Hardy (WAust) b Aug. 18, 1923 Highgate (WAust)

* Rigg, Keith Edward (Vic) b May 21, 1906 Malvern (Vic) d Feb. 28, 1995 Malvern (Vic)

Riley, William Norman (SAust) b April 9, 1894 Hyde Park (SAust) d Oct. 2, 1960 North Adelaide (SAust)

Rimington, Stanley Garnet (Vic) b Jan. 22, 1892 Kew (Vic) d Nov. 23, 1991 Kew (Vic)

* Ring, Douglas Thomas (Vic) b Oct. 14, 1918 Hobart (Tas)

* Ritchie, Gregory Michael (Qld) b Jan. 23, 1960 Stanthorpe (Qld)

Ritossa, David John (SAust) b Jan. 22, 1971 Rose Park (SAust)

* Rixon, Stephen John (NSW) b Feb. 25, 1954 Albury (NSW)

Roach, Peter John (Vic) b May 19, 1975 Kew (Vic)

Roach, William Alexander (WAust) b Dec. 12, 1914 South Fremantle (WAust) d June 8, 1944 in action over Friesian Islands (Netherlands)

* Roberts, Anderson Montgomery Everton (NSW) b Jan. 29, 1951 Urlings Village (Antigua)

Roberts, Kevin Joseph (NSW) b July 2, 1972 North Sydney (NSW)

Roberts, Peter Gerald (Tas) b Feb. 16, 1952 Hobart (Tas)

Roberts, William (NSW) birth and death details unknown

Roberts, William Maurice (SAust) b Aug. 26, 1916 Wallaroo Mines (SAust) d Jan. 21, 1989 Adelaide (SAust)

Robertson, Ashley Peter Scott (Vic) b March 9, 1972 Footscray (Vic)

Robertson, David Alexander (SAust) b March 4, 1959 North Adelaide (SAust)

* Robertson, Gavin Ron (NSW & Tas) b May 28, 1966 St Leonards (NSW)

Robertson, George Pringle (Vic) b Aug. 22, 1842 Hobart (Tas) d June 23, 1895 East Melbourne (Vic)

Robertson, Trevor John (SAust) b Nov. 20, 1947 Rose Park (SAust)

* Robertson, William Roderick (Vic) b Oct. 6, 1861 Deniliquin (NSW) d June 24, 1938 Brighton (Vic)

Robins, Donnell (SAust) b March 7, 1934 Blackwood (SAust)

Robinson, Alexander (WAust) b Aug. 19, 1886 Brighton (Vic) d Oct. 4, 1967 Perth (WAust)

Robinson, Alexander William (WAust) b Aug. 14, 1924 Boulder (WAust)

Robinson, Brian Anthony (Tas) b Nov. 22, 1967 Devonport (Tas)

Robinson, Charles Henry (Tas & WAust) b Feb. 18, 1879 Dubbo (NSW) d Sept. 23, 1951 Ashfield (NSW)

Robinson, David Brian (Tas & Vic) b March 20, 1958 Devonport (Tas)

Robinson, George David (WAust) b Jan. 21, 1921 Boulder (WAust) d March 12, 1999 Kew (Vic)

Robinson, Henry Joseph Wickham (NSW) b March 11, 1864 Watsons Bay (NSW) d March 24, 1931 Mascot (NSW)

* Robinson, Rayford Harold (NSW & SAust) b March 26, 1914 Stockton (NSW) d Aug. 10, 1965 Stockton (NSW)

* Robinson, Richard Daryl (Vic) b June 8, 1946 East Melbourne (Vic)

Robison, William Carr (NSW) b Dec. 14, 1874 Camden (NSW) d July 5, 1916 Darlinghurst (NSW)

Robran, Barrie Charles (SAust) b Sept. 25, 1947 Whyalla (SAust)

Roche, William (Vic) b July 20, 1871 Brunswick (Vic) d Jan. 2, 1950 East Brunswick (Vic)

Rocher, Thomas Walter (Tas) b June 17, 1930 Scottsdale (Tas)

Rock, Claude William (Tas) b June 9, 1863 Deloraine (Tas) d July 27, 1950 Longford (Tas)

Rock, Harry Owen (NSW) b Oct. 18, 1896 Scone (NSW) d March 9, 1978 Manly (NSW)

Rock, Norman Vosper (Tas) b Aug. 30, 1864 Deloraine (Tas) d Feb. 7, 1945 Brighton (Vic)

Rockliffe, Thornton Francis Edward (Tas) b July 5, 1887 Sassafras (Tas) d March 18, 1961 East Devonport (Tas)

Rodwell, Edwin Emerson (Tas) b April 12, 1921 Hobart (Tas)

Roe, Richard (WAust) b Jan. 22, 1913 Geraldton (WAust)

Rofe, Paul Cameron (SAust) b Jan. 16, 1981 Adelaide (SAust)

Rogers, Christopher John Llewellyn (WAust) b Aug. 31, 1977 Sydney (NSW)

Rogers, John Edward (Vic) b Feb. 8, 1858 Botany (NSW) d July 8, 1935 South Melbourne (Vic)

Rogers, Noel Thomas (Qld) b Dec. 28, 1923 Spring Hill (Qld) d May 27, 1982 Annerley (Qld)

Rogers, Rex Ernest (Qld) b Aug. 24, 1916 Cairns (Qld) d May 22, 1996 Coorparoo (Qld)

Rogers, William John (NSW) b May 7, 1943 Gosford (NSW)

Rolfe, Douglas John (Vic & SAust) b Feb. 26, 1953 Wheelers Hill (Vic)

Roper, Arthur William (NSW) b Feb. 20, 1917 Petersham (NSW) d Sept. 4, 1972 Woy Woy (NSW)

* Rorke, Gordon Frederick (NSW) b June 27, 1938 Neutral Bay (NSW)

Rose, Robert Peter (Vic) b Feb. 6, 1952 Eastern Hill (Vic) d May 12, 1999 Heidelberg (Vic)

Rosen, Marshall Frederick (NSW) b Sept. 17, 1948 Paddington (NSW)

Rosman, Arthur Victor (SAust) b Nov. 26, 1870 Barossa Goldfields (SAust) d Feb. 10, 1948 Kent Town (SAust)

Ross, Charles Howard (Vic) b May 10, 1863 St Kilda (Vic) d Feb. 5, 1935 Sydney (NSW)

Ross, Graeme Thomson (Vic) b Feb. 5, 1955 Geelong (Vic)

Ross, William A. (Vic) birth and death details unknown

Rosser, John (Vic) b April 22, 1862 Fremantle (WAust) d Dec. 25, 1925 Toowoomba (Qld)

Rothwell, Barry Alan (NSW) b Aug. 18, 1939 Ryde (NSW)

Rothwell, John Wilson (Tas) b Oct. 1, 1913 Hobart (Tas)

Rowan, Robert Keith (Vic) b Sept. 14, 1947 Coburg (Vic)

Rowe, Raymond Curtis (NSW) b Dec. 9, 1913 Harris Park (NSW) d May 14, 1995 Parramatta (NSW)

Rowe, Samuel Harold Drew (WAust) b Nov. 5, 1883 Perth (WAust) d Oct. 29, 1968 Perth (WAust)

Rowe, William Denis (Qld) b Jan. 10, 1892 East Brisbane (Qld) d Sept. 3, 1972 South Brisbane (Qld)

Rowell, Gregory John (NSW, Qld & Tas) b Sept. 1, 1966 Lindfield (NSW)

Rowland, Frank Walter (NSW) b March 1, 1893 Inverell (NSW) d Feb. 25, 1957 Mosman (NSW)

Rowlands, Edward Richard (Vic) b c. 1826 Claines, Worcestershire (England) d c. 1860

Rowlands, William Trevor (WAust) b May 7, 1904 Echuca (Vic) d May 18, 1984 Subiaco (WAust)

Rowley, Francis (NSW) b Sept. 27, 1835 Burwood (NSW) d June 23, 1862 Woolloomooloo (NSW)

Roxby, Robert Charles (NSW & SAust) b March 16, 1926 Newcastle (NSW)

Rummans, Graeme Clifford (NSW) b Dec. 13, 1976 Camperdown (NSW)

Rundell, Joshua Upcott (SAust) b May 6, 1858 Sandhurst (Vic) d Jan. 7, 1922 Alberton (SAust)

Rundell, Percy Davies (SAust) b Nov. 20, 1890 Alberton (SAust) d March 24, 1979 North Adelaide (SAust)

Rush, Edward Reynolds (Vic) b March 29, 1868 Flemington (Vic) d May 6, 1936 Malvern (Vic)

Rush, John (Vic) b April 5, 1910 Malvern (Vic)

Rush, Thomas Reynolds (Vic) b Dec. 7, 1874 Collingwood (Vic) d Oct. 29, 1926 Malvern (Vic)

Rushbrook, Roy Francis Kerr (Qld) b Sept. 29, 1911 Spring Hill (Qld) d March 31, 1987 Mackay (Qld)

Rushforth, Alfred William (Tas) b April 23, 1898 Hobart (Tas) d Dec. 30, 1985 Taroona (Tas)

Russell, Bernard L. (NSW) b Aug. 1, 1891 Leichhardt (NSW) d July 13, 1961 Belmore (NSW)

Russell, Richard Stevan (WAust) b Jan. 22, 1968 Helensville (New Zealand)

Russen, Charles Gordon (Tas) b May 9, 1886 Launceston (Tas) d Dec. 16, 1969 Newstead (Tas)

* Rutherford, John Walter (WAust) b Sept. 25, 1929 Bungulluping (WAust)

Ryan, Alfred James (SAust) b April 27, 1904 Adelaide (SAust) d July 10, 1990 Semaphore (SAust)

Ryan, Gregory William (NSW) b March 13, 1913 Wallsend (NSW) d May 10, 1986 Randwick (NSW)

Ryan, Peter Andrew (Qld) b Feb. 18, 1951 East Melbourne (Vic)

Ryan, Roderick Thomas (WAust) b Nov. 15, 1909 Cannington (WAust) d Oct. 23, 1979 Toronto, Ontario (Canada)

Ryan, Thomas Patrick (Tas) b May 4, 1865 Hobart (Tas) d April 20, 1921 Hobart (Tas)

* Ryder, John (Vic) b Aug. 8, 1889 Collingwood (Vic) d April 3, 1977 Fitzroy (Vic)

Rymill, Jack Westall (SAust) b March 20, 1901 North Adelaide (SAust) d Feb. 11, 1976 Adelaide (SAust)

Saballus, Andrew William (Tas) b June 1, 1969 Hobart (Tas)

Sacristani, Peter Geoffrey (Vic) b Sept. 5, 1957 Melbourne (Vic)

Saddler, Edward (NSW) d Oct. 28, 1874 full birth and death details unknown

* Sadiq Mohammad (Tas) b May 5, 1945 Junagadh (India)

* Saggers, Ronald Arthur (NSW) b May 15, 1917 Sydenham (NSW) d March 17, 1987 Harbord (NSW)

Sainsbury, Andrew John (NSW) b May 11, 1974 Gosford (NSW)

Saint, John Michael (Tas) b Jan. 31, 1969 Auburn (NSW)

Saker, David James (Vic) b May 29, 1966 Oakleigh (Vic)

Salmon, Benjamin Melville (NSW) b Jan. 9, 1906 Footscray (Vic) d Jan. 24, 1979 Mosman (NSW)

Salmon, John Lionel (Vic) b March 31, 1934 Canterbury (Vic)

Salvado, John Frederick (Vic) b Nov. 11, 1939 Carlton (Vic)

Salvana, Louis Charles (Vic) b Jan. 20, 1897 Hawthorn (Vic) d Dec. 8, 1974 Mitcham (Vic)

Sams, Louis Robert (Tas) b Sept. 26, 1863 Westbury (Tas) d July 6, 1941 Redcliffe (Qld)

Sams, Richard Horace (Tas) b c. 1864 Westbury (Tas) d March 5, 1933 Roseville (NSW)

Samuels, Edward (NSW) b May 25, 1833 Sydney (NSW)

Sanders, Leyland Arthur (Qld) b Oct. 17, 1927 Sandgate (Qld)

Sandford, Horace Charles Augustus (Vic) b Oct. 14, 1891 St Leonards (NSW) d Aug. 16, 1967 Heidelberg (Vic)

Sands, Ronald Francis (WAust) b Sept. 16, 1921 Perth (WAust) d Sept. 5, 1995 Nedlands (WAust)

Sangster, Christopher Bagot (SAust) b May 1, 1908 Kooringa (SAust) d Feb. 27, 1995 North Adelaide (SAust)

Sangster, John Fraser (SAust) b Jan. 21, 1942 Adelaide (SAust)

Sankey, Clarence Joseph (Tas) b Oct. 27, 1913 Northtown (Tas) d March 12, 1996 Launceston (Tas)

Sargent, Murray Alfred James (SAust) b Aug. 23, 1928 Adelaide (SAust)

Sarovich, Theodor Keith (Vic) b May 20, 1915 Port Melbourne (Vic) d Nov. 23, 1987 Atherton (Qld)

Sarre, Ronald Basil (WAust) b Jan. 20, 1932 Midland (WAust)

Sartori, Ronald Joseph (WAust) b March 23, 1915 Fremantle (WAust)

* Saunders, John Victor (Vic) b March 21, 1876 Melbourne (Vic) d Dec. 21, 1927 Toorak (Vic)

Saunders, Stuart Lucas (Tas) b June 27, 1960 Hobart (Tas)

Saunders, Warren Joseph (NSW) b July 18, 1934 Arncliffe (NSW)

Savage, Harold (NSW) b c. 1886 Woollahra (NSW) death details unknown

Savage, Keith Douglas (Qld) b Sept. 19, 1926 Brisbane (Qld) d Jan. 18, 1979 Mt Morgan (Qld)

Savigny, John Horatio (Tas) b Aug. 25, 1867 Bathurst (NSW) d Feb. 11, 1923 Carrick (Tas)

Savigny, William Henry (Tas) b Feb. 17, 1864 Sydney (NSW) d Aug. 6, 1922 Burwood (NSW)

Sawle, Lawrence Michael (WAust) b Aug. 19, 1925 East Fremantle (WAust)

Sayers, Dean Keith (SAust) b June 11, 1954 Hindmarsh (SAust)

Sayers, Mervyn Gerald (WAust) b March 5, 1958 Subiaco (WAust)

Scaife, John Willie (Vic) b Nov. 14, 1908 Haslingden, Lancashire (England) d Oct. 27, 1995 Melbourne (Vic)

Scanes, Albert Edward (NSW) b Aug. 6, 1900 Erskineville (NSW) d Nov. 1, 1969 death place unknown

Scanlan, Edmund (NSW) b c. 1848 Newcastle on Tyne, Northumberland (England) d Jan. 9, 1916 Erskineville (NSW)

Scannell, Timothy Francis (Vic) b Nov. 12, 1882 Hotham (Vic) d c. 1939 Royal Park (Vic)

Scarff, Clark Steven (WAust) b Nov. 19, 1948 Subiaco (WAust)

Schade, Matias Anderson (Vic) b March 25, 1887 Huntly (Vic) d June 9, 1959 Williamstown (Vic)

Schenscher, Peter Malcolm (SAust) b May 4, 1962 Murray Bridge (SAust)

Schmidt, Keith Ernest (Tas) b Dec. 19, 1921 Hobart (Tas)

Schneider, Karl Joseph (Vic & SAust) b Aug. 15, 1905 Hawthorn (Vic) d Sept. 5, 1928 Kensington Park (SAust)

Scholes, Mark Bradley (Tas) b July 1, 1957 Carlton (Vic)

Scholes, Walter John (Vic) b Jan. 5, 1950 East Brunswick (Vic)

Schrader, Heinrich Christian (Vic) b Dec. 5, 1893 East Prahran (Vic) d June 10, 1980 Kew (Vic)

Schreiber, Sidney Arthur (Qld) b April 7, 1873 birthplace and death details unknown

Schuller, Denis Clemenceau (Qld) b May 5, 1948 Herston (Qld)

Schultz, Bruce (SAust) b March 13, 1913 Royston Park (SAust) d Jan. 11, 1980 Modbury (SAust)

Schultz, Julius William Eugene (SAust) b Sept. 25, 1888 Summer Town (SAust) d Aug. 8, 1966 Berri (SAust)

Scott, Darryl Bryan (SAust) b March 9, 1961 Glenelg (SAust)

* Scott, Henry James Herbert (Vic) b Dec. 26, 1858 Prahran (Vic) d Sept. 23, 1910 Scone (NSW)

Scott, Jack A. (SAust) b Jan. 14, 1910 Sydney (NSW) d May 22, 1980 Collaroy Beach (NSW)

Scott, John Drake (NSW & SAust) b Jan. 31, 1888 Petersham (NSW) d April 7, 1964 Springbank (SAust)

Scott, Robert Barrington (Vic & NSW) b Oct. 9, 1916 South Melbourne (Vic) d April 6, 1984 Melbourne (Vic)

Scott, Walter Aubrey (Vic) b Feb. 19, 1907 Camberwell (Vic) d Oct. 23, 1989 death place unknown

Scott, William John (Vic) b June 14, 1882 Hotham (Vic) d Sept. 30, 1965 Ferntree Gully (Vic)

Scrymgour, Bernard Vincent (SAust) b July 31, 1864 Adelaide (SAust) d April 16, 1943 Medindie (SAust)

Scuderi, Joseph Charles (SAust) b Dec. 24, 1968 Ingham (Qld)

Seabrook, Wayne John Stephen (NSW) b Sept. 6, 1961 Ryde (NSW)

Seale, Joseph (NSW) b April 18, 1855 Grafton (NSW) d Aug. 19, 1941 Waratah (NSW)

Searle, James (NSW) b Aug. 8, 1861 Surry Hills (NSW) d Dec. 28, 1936 Manly (NSW)

Searle, Richard Henry (Qld) b Jan. 16, 1934 Red Hill (Qld)

Seccombe, Donald Harry (Qld) b April 3, 1942 Goomeri (Qld)

Seccombe, Wade Anthony (Qld) b Oct. 30, 1971 Murgon (Qld)

Seddon, Cecil Dudley (NSW) b July 3, 1902 Campbelltown (NSW) d April 18, 1978 Dulwich Hill (NSW)

Seib, Ian Martin (Qld) b Sept. 15, 1946 Herston (Qld)

Seitz, John Arnold (Vic) b Sept. 19, 1883 Carlton (Vic) d May 1, 1963 St Kilda (Vic)

Selk, Rudolph Albert (WAust) b Oct. 6, 1871 Omeo (Vic) d Jan. 31, 1940 Pickering Brook (WAust)

Sellers, Michael John (Tas) b July 5, 1952 Launceston (Tas)

* Sellers, Reginald Hugh Durning (SAust) b Aug. 20, 1940 Bulsar (India)

Selth, Victor Poole (SAust) b June 1, 1895 Parkside (SAust) d Sept. 2, 1967 Daw Park (SAust)

* Serjeant, Craig Stanton (WAust) b Nov. 1, 1951 Nedlands (WAust)

Serjeant, David Maurice (Vic) b Jan. 18, 1830 Ramsey, Huntingdonshire (England) d Jan. 12, 1929 Camberwell, London (England)

Sewart, William Isaac (Qld & Vic) b Nov. 12, 1881 Allendale East (SAust) d Dec. 13, 1928 Caulfield (Vic)

Shade, Eric (Vic) b Aug. 27, 1943 Brighton (Vic)

Sharman, Baden Eric (Tas) b Aug. 11, 1939 Beulah (Tas)

* Sharpe, Duncan Albert (SAust) b Aug. 3, 1937 Rawalpindi (India)

Shaw, John Hilary (Vic) b Oct. 18, 1932 Geelong (Vic)

Shaw, Noel Clyde (Vic) b May 10, 1937 Euroa (Vic)

Shawe, Patrick Henry (Tas) b c. 1889 full birth details unknown d Sept. 24, 1945 East Melbourne (Vic)

Shea, John Adrian (WAust) b May 8, 1913 Boulder (WAust) d Feb. 7, 1986 Claremont (WAust)

Shea, Morris (NSW) b c. 1869 Campbelltown (NSW) death details unknown

Shea, Patrick Augustus (Vic) b March 17, 1886 Clunes (Vic) d May 29, 1954 Northbridge (NSW)

* Sheahan, Andrew Paul (Vic) b Sept. 30, 1948 Werribee (Vic)

Sheen, Brian Lawrence (Tas) b Dec. 30, 1938 Hobart (Tas)

Shelton, Herbert John (Tas) b Jan. 21, 1924 Launceston (Tas)

Shepard, David John (Vic) b Dec. 30, 1970 Berwick (Vic)

Shepard, Athol Lennard (Tas) b Aug. 16, 1920 Burnie (Tas)

Shepherd, Alan Gordon (SAust) b Sept. 29, 1912 Kilkenny (SAust) d Oct. 9, 1998 Marion (SAust)

* Shepherd, Barry Kenneth (WAust) b April 23, 1937 Donnybrook (WAust)

Shepherd, David Stanmore (Vic) b Aug. 3, 1956 Melbourne (Vic)

Shepherd, James (NSW) b May 24, 1856 Steiglitz (Vic) death details unknown

Shepherdson, Hartley Robert (SAust) b Sept. 4, 1913 Mt Gambier (SAust) d Aug. 19, 1992 Fitzroy (Vic)

Shepley, Herbert Neil (SAust) b Oct. 7, 1899 Knightsbridge (SAust) d Nov. 14, 1953 Tranmere (SAust)

Sheppard, Benjamin Joseph (Vic) b June 23, 1892 Fitzroy (Vic) d Sept. 9, 1931 Fitzroy (Vic)

Sheppard, James Francis (Qld) b Jan. 16, 1888 Brisbane (Qld) d Dec. 10, 1944 Hendra (Qld)

Sheridan, Edward Orwell (NSW) b Jan. 3, 1842 Sydney (NSW) d Nov. 30, 1923 West End (Qld)

Sherriff, Rowan James (Tas) b July 7, 1951 Sheffield (Tas)

Shewan, Leslie James (Qld) b June 12, 1892 Rushworth (Vic) d Sept. 25, 1977 Windsor (Vic)

Shiell, Alan Bruce (SAust) b April 25, 1945 St Peters (SAust)

Shillinglaw, Harold Arthur Edward (Vic) b Dec. 2, 1927 Fitzroy (Vic)

Shipperd, Gregory (WAust & Tas) b Nov. 13, 1956 Subiaco (WAust)

Short, Henry William (SAust) b March 31, 1874 Morphett Vale (SAust) d May 11, 1916 Lower Mitcham (SAust)

Shortland, Herbert (NSW) b April 7, 1881 Sydney (NSW) d July 17, 1946 death place unknown

Shugg, Albert William (Tas) b July 5, 1894 Hawthorn (Vic) d July 20, 1941 Hobart (Tas)

Siddons, James Darren (Vic & SAust) b April 25, 1964 Robinvale (Vic)

Sidebottom, William Lemuel (Tas) b Sept. 24, 1862 Evandale (Tas) d April 11, 1948 Launceston (Tas)

Sides, Francis William (Qld & Vic) b Dec. 15, 1913 Mackay (Qld) d Aug. 25, 1943 Kunai Spur, Salamaua (Papua New Guinea) in action

Sieler, Alan John (Vic) b July 17, 1948 Arncliffe (NSW)

* Sievers, Morris William (Vic) b April 13, 1912 Powlett River (Vic) d May 10, 1968 Parkville (Vic)

Siggs, Douglas (Qld) b Aug. 11, 1920 Fortitude Valley (Qld)

Sim, Charles Wallace (Qld) b March 30, 1895 Brisbane (Qld) d July 3, 1971 Woodville South (SAust)

Simmonds, W. (Anderson's XI) birth and death details unknown

Simmons, Arthur Harry (NSW) b Nov. 13, 1909 Croydon (NSW) d Feb. 28, 1990 Mirrabooka (NSW)

Simmons, Jack (Tas) b March 28, 1941 Clayton-le-Moors, Lancashire (England)

Simpson, Charles Edward (Qld & NSW) b March 27, 1882 Parramatta (NSW) d June 26, 1956 Sydney (NSW)

* Simpson, Robert Baddeley (NSW & WAust) b Feb. 3, 1936 Marrickville (NSW)

Sims, Alfred Edward (Qld) b Nov. 8, 1875 birthplace and death details unknown

Sims, Arthur (Australians) b July 27, 1877 Spridlington, Lincolnshire (England) d April 27, 1969 East Hoathly, Sussex (England)

Simunsen, Robert Francis (SAust) b June 7, 1941 Adelaide (SAust)

Sinclair, Arthur (NSW) birth details unknown d Nov. 29, 1869 Sydney (NSW)

Sincock, Andrew Thomas (SAust) b June 7, 1951 Adelaide (SAust)

* Sincock, David John (SAust) b Feb. 1, 1942 North Adelaide (SAust)

Sincock, Harrold Keith (SAust) b Dec. 10, 1907 Eastwood (SAust) d Feb. 2, 1982 Plympton (SAust)

Sincock, Peter Damien (SAust) b July 8, 1948 North Adelaide (SAust)

Sincock, Russell John (Vic) b Dec. 28, 1947 Kew (Vic)

Sindrey, Clive Alexander Hazell (Vic) b Aug. 10, 1903 Richmond (Vic) d June 26, 1981 Vermont (Vic)

Single, Clive Vallack (NSW) b Sept. 17, 1888 Penrith (NSW) d July 10, 1931 Woollahra (NSW)

Sismey, Stanley George (NSW) b July 15, 1916 Junee (NSW)

Skilbeck, Andrew John (NSW) b July 21, 1958 St Leonards (NSW)

Skuse, Alan Raymond (Qld) b March 28, 1942 Herston (Qld)

Sladen, Charles (Vic) b Aug. 28, 1816 Walmer, Kent (England) d Feb. 22, 1884 Geelong (Vic)

* Slater, Keith Nichol (WAust) b March 12, 1935 Midland (WAust)

* Slater, Michael Jonathon (NSW) b Feb. 21, 1970 Wagga Wagga (NSW)

* Sleep, Peter Raymond (SAust) b May 4, 1957 Penola (SAust)

Slight, Alexander Frank (SAust) b March 13, 1861 Emerald Hill (Vic) d July 5, 1930 Maylands (SAust)

* Slight, James (Vic) b Oct. 20, 1855 Ashby, Geelong (Vic) d Dec. 9, 1930 Elsternwick (Vic)

Slight, William (Vic & SAust) b Sept. 19, 1858 Emerald Hill (Vic) d Dec. 22, 1941 Toorak Gardens (SAust)

Small, Gladstone Cleophas (SAust) b Oct. 18, 1961 Brighton, St George (Barbados)

Small, Stephen Mark (NSW & Tas) b March 2, 1955 Canterbury (NSW)

Smart, Christopher Boddington (Qld) b Oct. 17, 1958 Port Moresby (Papua New Guinea)

Smart, Hadyn Warren Gavin (SAust) b Nov. 26, 1958 Hobart (Tas)

Smart, Lawrence Maxwell (SAust) b Feb. 16, 1928 Narridy (SAust)

Smith, Adam Matthew (Vic) b April 6, 1976 Greensborough (Vic)

Smith, Alfred Edward Charles (WAust) b Oct. 4, 1908 Prahran (WAust) d Jan. 17, 1989 Fremantle (WAust)

Smith, Andrew (SAust) b Sept. 1, 1889 Port Adelaide (SAust) d May 18, 1983 Adelaide (SAust)

Smith, Carey Kenneth (Vic) b Oct. 16, 1960 Moreland (Vic)

Smith, Cyril Robert (Qld) b Nov. 1, 1926 South Brisbane (Qld)

Smith, Darryl Donald (WAust) b June 8, 1960 Adelaide (SAust)

Smith, David Anthony (Tas) b Sept. 1, 1957 Launceston (Tas)

* Smith, David Betram Miller (Vic) b Sept. 14, 1884 Richmond (Vic) d July 29, 1963 Hawthorn (Vic)

Smith, Douglas Roy (Tas) b Oct. 9, 1880 Fingal (Tas) d Feb. 27, 1933 Port Fairy (Vic)

Smith, Edward Henry (Tas) b July 30, 1911 Nook (Tas) d Dec. 26, 1999 Launceston (Tas)

Smith, George Elms (Vic) b July 22, 1855 Emerald Hill (Vic) d April 7, 1897 St Kilda (Vic)

Smith, Harry Oxley (Tas & Vic) b Oct. 27, 1887 Launceston (Tas) d Aug. 24, 1916 Pinewood, London (England)

Smith, Herbert George (Vic) b March 21, 1914 Richmond (Vic) d c. 1997 Melbourne (Vic)

Smith, Horace Clitheroe (Tas) b Oct. 31, 1892 Sandy Bay (Tas) d April 6, 1977 Hobart (Tas)

Smith, Hubert George Selwyn (Qld) b Oct. 9, 1891 Beaudesert (Qld) d June 7, 1917 Messines (France)

Smith, James (NSW) birth and death details unknown

Smith, John Phillips (Vic) b March 6, 1936 Ballarat (Vic)

Smith, Lavington Albert (SAust) b Oct. 9, 1904 Medindie (SAust) d May 9, 1953 Adelaide (SAust)

Smith, Leonard Angus (Vic) b c. 1882 Hotham (Vic) d c. 1943 Heidelberg (Vic)

Smith, Lloyd Harold James (Tas) b Aug. 5, 1928 Hobart (Tas)

Smith, Michael John (SAust) b July 17, 1973 Rose Park (SAust)

Smith, Peter Julian (Vic) b Feb. 8, 1968 Greensborough (Vic)

Smith, Robert Thomas (Vic) b May 27, 1868 Harrow (Vic) d Aug. 21, 1927 East Melbourne (Vic)

Smith, Stanley Arthur John (Vic) b Jan. 8, 1910 Footscray (Vic) d c. 1984 death place unknown

* Smith, Stephen Barry (NSW) b Oct. 18, 1961 Sydney (NSW)

Smith, Struan McKinley (Rest of Australia) b June 4, 1907 St Leonards (NSW)

Smith, Thomas Henry (Qld) b Sept. 19, 1898 Talgai (Qld) d March 6, 1926 Warwick (Qld)

Smith, Warren Robert (WAust) b Dec. 29, 1941 Guildford (WAust)

Smyth, Neil Weston (Vic) b June 6, 1928 South Yarra (Vic)

* Sobers, Garfield St Aubrun (SAust) b July 28, 1936 Chelsea Road, Bay Land, Bridgetown (Barbados)

Solomon, Cyril Moss (NSW) b March 11, 1911 Cootamundra (NSW) d July 15, 1995 Manly (NSW)

Soule, Richard Eric (Tas) b Sept. 5, 1966 Launceston (Tas)

Souter, Vernon John (Vic) b Feb. 26, 1894 Uranquinty (NSW) d July 17, 1915 Elsternwick (Vic)

Spalding, Earl George (WAust) b March 13, 1965 South Perth (WAust)

Speirs, Norman Lennox (Vic) b May 31, 1886 Caulfield (Vic) d Aug. 1, 1960 Noosa Heads (Qld)

Spencer, Duncan John (WAust) b April 5, 1972 Burnley, Lancashire (England)

Spencer, Ernest Lott (Vic) b May 1, 1888 Hotham West (Vic) d Nov. 4, 1953 Essendon (Vic)

* Spofforth, Frederick Robert (NSW & Vic) b Sept. 9, 1853 Balmain (NSW) d June 4, 1926 Ditton Hill, Surrey (England)

Spring, Graham Allan (NSW) b April 20, 1961 Sydney (NSW)

Spry, Richard (Qld) b July 18, 1862 Melbourne (Vic) d Nov. 10, 1920 Linville (Qld)

Squires, Philip Horley (SAust) b June 18, 1939 Marden (SAust)

Stacey, Bradley John (Vic) b June 11, 1972 Geelong (Vic)

Stack, George Bagot (NSW) b March 12, 1846 West Maitland (NSW) d Oct. 7, 1930 Orange (NSW)

Stack, Walter Jaques (NSW) b Oct. 31, 1884 Croydon (NSW) d March 26, 1972 Bathurst (NSW)

* Stackpole, Keith Raymond (Vic) b July 10, 1940 Collingwood (Vic)

Stackpole, Keith William (Vic) b July 31, 1916 Melbourne (Vic) d Sept. 19, 1992 Heidelberg (Vic)

Stackpoole, John (Qld) b Nov. 23, 1916 Jundah (Qld)

Stalker, Walter (Vic) b Oct. 29, 1909 Elaine (Vic) d Jan. 13, 1977 Ballarat (Vic)

Stanes, John Gladstone (Vic) b Dec. 15, 1910 South Melbourne (Vic) d Feb. 7, 1983 Ferntree Gully (Vic)

Stanford, Graham Edwin (SAust) b April 25, 1948 Adelaide (SAust)

Stanford, Ross Milton (SAust) b Sept. 25, 1917 Fulham (SAust)

Stapleton, Harold Vincent (NSW) b Jan. 7, 1915 Kyogle (NSW)

Starr, Cecil Leonard Berry (SAust) b July 20, 1907 Quorn (SAust)

Steele, Donald Macdonald (SAust) b Aug. 17, 1892 East Adelaide (SAust) d July 13, 1962 Adelaide (SAust)

Steele, Harry Cornwall (NSW) b April 22, 1901 East Sydney (NSW) d Nov. 9, 1985 Sydney (NSW)

Steele, John Anthony (NSW) b Nov. 13, 1942 Waverley (NSW)

Steele, Kenneth Nagent (SAust) b Dec. 17, 1889 East Adelaide (SAust) d Dec. 19, 1956 North Adelaide (SAust)

Stephens, Jack Lawson (Vic) b Aug. 31, 1913 Majorca (Vic) d Sept. 2, 1967 Daylesford (Vic)

Stephens, John Raymond (Vic) b Sept. 15, 1950 East Melbourne (Vic)

Stephens, Reginald Stanley (Vic) b April 16, 1883 Creswick (Vic) d Sept. 7, 1965 Malvern (Vic)

Stephenson, Franklyn Dacosta (Tas) b April 8, 1959 Halls, St James (Barbados)

Stepto, Paul Douglas (NSW) b Dec. 23, 1966 Sydney (NSW)

* Stevens, Gavin Byron (SAust) b Feb. 29, 1932 Glenelg (SAust)

Stevens, John Grenfell (NSW) b Feb. 22, 1948 Muswellbrook (NSW)

Stevens, John Whitehall (Vic) birth and death details unknown

Stevens, Robert Barry (Vic) b Nov. 5, 1929 Melbourne (Vic)

Stewart, Barry James (Tas) b May 6, 1940 Wynyard (Tas) d July 23, 1975 Wynyard (Tas)

Stewart, Gordon Lionel (NSW) b June 16, 1906 Petersham (NSW) d c. 1992 Melbourne (Vic)

Stewart, James (WAust & SAust) b Aug. 22, 1970 East Fremantle (WAust)

Stewart, James C. (Vic) birth and death details unknown

Stewart, Trevor George (Qld) b March 15, 1940 Mt Isa (Qld)

Stewart, William (Vic) b c. 1844 full birth and death details unknown

Stibe, Colin George Reinzi (Qld) b April 22, 1916 Bundaberg (Qld) d Jan. 6, 1970 Sydney (NSW)

Still, Robert Stuart (Tas) b March 15, 1822 Bathurst (NSW) d July 5, 1907 Launceston (Tas)

Still, William Cathcart (NSW) b c. 1820 (England) d July 5, 1910 Sydney (NSW)

Stillman, William Leslie (Vic & SAust) b Oct. 5, 1949 Alexandra (Vic)

Stirling, William Stuart (SAust) b March 19, 1891 Jamestown (SAust) d July 18, 1971 Adelaide (SAust)

Stobo, Richard Montagu (NSW) b June 20, 1965 Toowoomba (Qld)

Stokes, George William (Vic) b Dec. 11, 1857 South Yarra (Vic) d Aug. 16, 1929 Brighton (Vic)

Stokes, Raymond Gordon (Tas) b May 21, 1924 Longford (Tas)

Stokes, William (WAust) b July 28, 1886 Geraldton (WAust) d Oct. 4, 1954 Perth (WAust)

Storey, Stephen Craig (Qld) b Nov. 23, 1964 Mona Vale (NSW)

Stratford, H. E. (Vic) birth and death details unknown

Strauss, Raymond Bernard (WAust) b Nov. 4, 1927 Perth (WAust)

Strudwick, David Charles (SAust) b Jan. 11, 1934 Adelaide (SAust)

Stuart, Anthony Mark (NSW) b Jan. 2, 1970 Waratah (NSW)

Stuart, William Percy (SAust) b March 7, 1871 Goolwa (SAust) d Aug. 20, 1956 Unley Park (SAust)

Stubbs, John Robert Marshall (WAust) b Oct. 15, 1931 Collie (WAust)

Stuckey, George (Vic) b July 6, 1871 Walhalla (Vic) d March 15, 1932 North Melbourne (Vic)

Stuckey, John Henry (Vic) b July 3, 1869 Walhalla (Vic) d Aug. 10, 1952 Cheltenham (Vic)

Such, Bruce Vincent (Qld) b c. 1907 Sydney (NSW) d April 14, 1933 Townsville (Qld)

Sullivan, Alfred Ernest (NSW) b Dec. 10, 1872 Balmain (NSW) d Sept. 25, 1942 Balmain (NSW)

Sullivan, William (Qld) b Aug. 19, 1877 Hotham (Vic) d Aug. 29, 1924 Albury (NSW)

Suppel, James Thomas (NSW) b Oct. 19, 1914 Warren (NSW) d March 9, 1994 Lidcombe (NSW)

* Surti, Rusi Framroz (Qld) b May 25, 1936 Surat (India)

Sutherland, David (Vic) b June 4, 1873 Boroondara (Vic) d Oct. 6, 1971 Hawthorn (Vic)

Sutherland, Donald John (SAust) b Nov. 28, 1949 Adelaide (SAust)

Sutherland, James Alexander (Vic) b July 14, 1965 East Melbourne (Vic)

Swain, Brett Andrew (SAust) b Feb. 14, 1974 Stirling (SAust)

Swan, Gavin Graham (WAust) b Oct. 30, 1970 Subiaco (WAust)

Swanson, John David (Vic) b April 5, 1940 Brunswick (Vic)

Swendsen, Robert Charles (Qld) b Oct. 18, 1929 Charters Towers (Qld)

Swift, John Sheddon (Vic) b Feb. 3, 1852 birthplace unknown d Feb. 28, 1926 Kew (Vic)

Symonds, Andrew (Qld) b June 9, 1975 Birmingham, West Midlands (England)

Symonds, Crawford (SAust) b Feb. 15, 1915 North Adelaide (SAust) d uly 20, 2000 Bedford Park (SAust)

Taaffe, Frederick Herbert (WAust) b Jan. 7, 1899 Deolali (India) d April 2, 1964 Ulladulla (NSW)

Tabart, John Lewis Benjamin (Tas) b Nov. 30, 1827 St Pancras, London (England) d Sept. 9, 1894 Launceston (Tas)

Tabart, Thomas Alfred (Tas) b Aug. 10, 1877 Campbell Town (Tas) d Aug. 29, 1950 East Melbourne (Vic)

* Taber, Hedley Brian (NSW) b April 29, 1940 Wagga Wagga (NSW)

Tait, Alan Houston (Qld) b Feb. 17, 1908 Toowoomba (Qld) d July 27, 1988 Indooroopilly (Qld)

Tait, George (Parr's XI) b April 12, 1844 Parramatta (NSW) d Dec. 21, 1934 East Malvern (Vic)

* Tallon, Donald (Qld) b Feb. 17, 1916 Bundaberg (Qld) d Sept. 7, 1984 Bundaberg (Qld)

Tallon, Leslie William Thomas (Qld) b July 9, 1914 Bundaberg (Qld) d Sept. 18, 1972 Coopers Plains (Qld)

Tamblyn, Geoffrey Leonard (Vic) b April 8, 1949 Melbourne (Vic)

Tamblyn, Gordon Erle (Vic) b April 23, 1918 Wallaroo Mines (SAust)

Tame, Michael Philip (Tas) b Jan. 6, 1956 Hobart (Tas)

Tardif, Joseph Henry (SAust) b May 17, 1860 Gawler (SAust) d June 14, 1920 Prospect (SAust)

Targett, Benjamin Stuart (Tas) b Dec. 27, 1972 Paddington (NSW)

Tarrant, Francis Alfred (Vic) b Dec. 11, 1880 Fitzroy (Vic) d Jan. 29, 1951 Upper Hawthorn (Vic)

Tarrant, William Ambrose (Vic) b Sept. 22, 1866 Fitzroy (Vic) d Nov. 1, 1938 North Fitzroy (Vic)

Tatchell, Thomas (Vic) b June 13, 1867 Inglewood (Vic) d Oct. 18, 1936 East Melbourne (Vic)

Taylor, Bruce William (Qld) b June 14, 1924 Brisbane (Qld) d Oct. 16, 1984 New Farm (Qld)

Taylor, David (NSW) b May 2, 1881 Sydney (NSW) death details unknown

* Taylor, John Morris (NSW) b Oct. 10, 1895 Stanmore (NSW) d May 12, 1971 Turramurra (NSW)

Taylor, Joseph Stanley (NSW) b Nov. 1, 1887 Leichhardt (NSW) d Sept. 3, 1954 Waratah (NSW)

* Taylor, Mark Anthony (NSW) b Oct. 27, 1964 Leeton (NSW)

Taylor, Michael David (Vic & Tas) b June 9, 1955 Chelsea (Vic)

* Taylor, Peter Laurence (NSW & Qld) b Aug. 22, 1956 North Sydney (NSW)

Taylor, Ross Simeon (NSW) b May 8, 1938 Mudgee (NSW) d Dec. 7, 1996 Tamworth (NSW)

Taylor, Stuart Gifford (Tas) b April 13, 1900 Prahran (Vic) d Feb. 2, 1978 Mosman Park (WAust)

Tazelaar, Dirk (Qld) b Jan. 13, 1963 Ipswich (Qld)

Teagle, Reginald Crump (SAust) b Feb. 27, 1909 Parkside (SAust) d June 8, 1987 Adelaide (SAust)

Teece, Richard (Combined XIII) b April 29, 1847 Paihia (New Zealand) d Dec. 13, 1928 Point Piper (NSW)

Teisseire, Francis Lawrence (SAust) b July 8, 1917 Rose Park (SAust) d Nov. 23, 1998 Glenelg (SAust)

Templeton, Robert Ian (Vic) b March 15, 1957 Hamilton (Vic)

Tennent, Hector Norman (Australians) b April 6, 1843 Hobart (Tas) d April 16, 1904 Westminster, London (England)

Tennent, John Pattison (Vic) b July 31, 1846 Hobart (Tas) d Oct. 31, 1893 Clifton Hill (Vic)

Terry, Richard Benjamin (Vic) birth and death details unknown

Thamm, Carl Friedrich Wilhelm (SAust) b Nov. 1, 1874 Nuriootpa (SAust) d July 4, 1944 Subiaco (WAust)

Thatcher, Allen Norman (NSW) b April 17, 1899 Sydney (NSW) d Feb. 12, 1932 Dulwich Hill (NSW)

Theak, Henry John Thomas (NSW) b March 19, 1909 Pyrmont (NSW) d Sept. 14, 1979 Narwee (NSW)

Thollar, Douglas Hugh (Tas) b Feb. 13, 1919 George Town (Tas)

Thomas, Arthur Churchill (SAust) b May 4, 1869 Unley (SAust) d April 28, 1934 Unley (SAust)

Thomas, George Alexander (NSW) b April 22, 1881 Sydney (NSW)

* Thomas, Grahame (NSW) b March 21, 1938 Croydon Park (NSW)

Thomas, Jeffrey Mark (Qld) b Oct. 19, 1971 Toowoomba (Qld)

Thomas, John Oliver (Tas) b April 12, 1852 Merthyr Tydfil (Wales) d May 29, 1915 Carlton (Vic)

Thomas, Josiah (Vic) b Aug. 27, 1910 Golden Square, Bendigo (Vic) d May 28, 1960 Essendon (Vic)

Thomas, Kenneth Bruce (Vic) b Oct. 5, 1942 East Melbourne (Vic)

Thomas, Llewellyn (Tas) b April 1, 1883 Fitzroy (Vic) d Nov. 2, 1962 Evandale (Tas)

Thomas, Maxwell Raymond (Tas) b June 28, 1921 Launceston (Tas) d May 20, 2001 Lenah Valley (Tas)

Thomas, Ramon Cedric (SAust) b Nov. 18, 1932 Mile End (SAust)

Thomas, Ronald Vivian (Tas) b Sept. 21, 1915 Longford (Tas) d May 28, 1987 Launceston (Tas)

Thomlinson, Arthur (Tas) b c. 1887 full birth and death details unknown

Thompson, C.D. (NSW) birth and death details unknown

Thompson, Francis Cecil (Qld) b Aug. 17, 1890 Stanwell (Qld) d Sept. 24, 1963 Southport (Qld)

Thompson, Horace Malcolm (SAust) b Nov. 29, 1913 Malvern (SAust) d March 19, 1936 Kalgoorlie (WAust)

Thompson, James Bogne (Vic) b c. 1829 Yorkshire (England) d July 18, 1877 Melbourne (Vic)

Thompson, Kerry William (NSW) b Dec. 12, 1949 Wallsend (NSW)

Thompson, Scott Michael (NSW) b May 4, 1972 Bankstown (NSW)

Thompson, William James (Qld) b Jan. 2, 1891 (Qld)

* Thoms, George Ronald (Vic) b March 22, 1927 Footscray (Vic)

Thomsett, Harold King (Qld) b Oct. 23, 1913 Yarraman (Qld) d April 12, 1991 Spring Hill (Qld)

* Thomson, Alan Lloyd (Vic) b Dec. 2, 1945 Reservoir (Vic)

Thomson, Alan Ogilvie (Vic) b Sept. 1, 1899 Tibooburra (NSW) d c. 1938 Tibooburra (NSW)

Thomson, Alfred Taddy (Vic) b 1818 birth day and month unknown Paddington, London, Middlesex (England) d Oct. 12, 1895 London (England)

Thomson, Geoffrey David (WAust) b April 21, 1959 Subiaco (WAust)

* Thomson, Jeffrey Robert (NSW & Qld) b Aug. 16, 1950 Greenacre (NSW)

Thomson, Joseph (Qld) b May 27, 1877 South Brisbane (Qld) d Aug. 1, 1953 (Qld)

Thomson, Kenneth Stephen (Tas) b Jan. 5, 1947 Hobart (Tas)

* Thomson, Nathaniel Frampton Davis (NSW) b May 29, 1839 Surry Hills (NSW) d Sept. 2, 1896 Burwood (NSW)

Thorn, Frank Leslie Oliver (Vic) b Aug. 16, 1912 St Arnaud (Vic) d Feb. 11, 1942 Gasmata (New Britain) in action

Thornton, Barry Thomas (WAust) b June 3, 1941 South Perth (WAust)

Thornton, John (Vic) b Jan. 16, 1835 Huddersfield, Yorkshire (England) d Dec. 15, 1919 Camperdown (Vic)

Thorpe, Henry (Combined XI) b c. 1862 Parramatta (NSW) d c. 1937 Artarmon (NSW)

Thorpe, Linsley James (Qld) b Feb. 15, 1923 Alpha (Qld)

Thurgarland, Wilfred John (SAust) b March 11, 1892 Queenstown (SAust) d July 12, 1974 Campbelltown (SAust)

* Thurlow, Hugh Morley (Qld) b Jan. 10, 1903 Townsville (Qld) d Dec. 3, 1975 Rosalie (Qld)

Thwaites, Colin Geoffrey (Vic) b Jan. 23, 1955 Lang Lang (Vic)

Thwaites, Thomas Edwin (Qld) b July 1, 1910 Beaudesert (Qld)

Tilyard, Gregory Almeria Sydney (Tas) b March 19, 1932 Sandford (Tas)

Timbury, Fredrick Richard Vaughan (Qld) b July 12, 1885 Gladstone (Qld) d April 14, 1945 Sydney (NSW)

Tindall, Edwin (NSW) b March 31, 1851 Liverpool (NSW) d Jan. 16, 1926 Marrickville (NSW)

Tobin, Bertrandt Joseph (SAust) b Nov. 11, 1910 North Adelaide (SAust) d Oct. 19, 1969 Adelaide (SAust)

Tobin, William Andrew (Vic) b June 7, 1859 Kensington, London, Middlesex (England) d Feb. 17, 1904 South Melbourne (Vic)

Toby, Frederick James (Tas) b Dec. 9, 1888 Redfern (NSW) death details unknown

Tolhurst, Edward Keith (Vic) b Oct. 29, 1895 St Kilda (Vic) d May 24, 1982 East Prahran (Vic)

Tooher, John Andrew (NSW) b Nov. 18, 1846 Sydney (NSW) d May 23, 1941 Neutral Bay (NSW)

* Toohey, Peter Michael (NSW) b April 20, 1954 Blayney (NSW)

Tooley, Mark Victor (Qld) b April 29, 1965 Toowoomba (Qld)

Toovey, Ernest Albert (Qld) b May 16, 1922 Warwick (Qld)

* Toshack, Ernest Raymond Herbert (NSW) b Dec. 8, 1914 Cobar (NSW)

Tovey, Edward Richard (Qld) b Dec. 25, 1930 Kings Cross (NSW)

Townley, Reginald Colin (Tas) b April 15, 1904 Hobart (Tas) d May 3, 1982 Hobart (Tas)

Townsend, Richard James Bruce (SAust) b Aug. 12, 1886 Mt Torrens (SAust) d Jan. 17, 1960 Waikerie (SAust)

Tozer, Claude John (NSW) b Sept. 27, 1890 Sydney (NSW) d Dec. 21, 1920 Lindfield (NSW)

Tozer, George Bruce (Vic) b June 27, 1926 Hopetoun (Vic)

Trapp, Vincent Burney (Vic) b Jan. 26, 1861 Prahran (Vic) d Oct. 21, 1929 Armadale (Vic)

* Travers, Joseph Patrick Francis (SAust) b Jan. 10, 1871 Adelaide (SAust) d Sept. 15, 1942 Adelaide (SAust)

Traves, Roger Norman (Qld) b Oct. 15, 1961 Cairns (Qld)

Treanor, John Cassimar (NSW) b Aug. 17, 1922 Darlinghurst (NSW) d Nov. 7, 1993 East Ballina (NSW)

Trebilcock, Arthur Joseph (Tas) b Dec. 13, 1907 Zeehan (Tas) d May 2, 1972 Hobart (Tas)

Tregoning, Jack (SAust) b June 13, 1919 West Adelaide (SAust) d June 26, 1989 North Adelaide (SAust)

Trembath, Thomas James (Vic) b Jan. 16, 1912 Moonta (SAust) d April 2, 1978 West Brunswick (Vic)

Trenerry, Edwin (NSW) b Feb. 24, 1897 Queanbeyan (NSW) d July 8, 1983 Woollahra (NSW)

Trenerry, William Leo (NSW) b Nov. 29, 1892 Queanbeyan (NSW) d Sept. 4, 1975 Mosman (NSW)

Trethewey, Peter Grant (SAust & Qld) b May 12, 1935 Croydon (SAust)

* Tribe, George Edward (Vic) b Oct. 4, 1920 Footscray (Vic)

Triffitt, Arthur (Tas) birth and death details unknown

Trimble, Glenn Samuel (Qld) b Jan. 1, 1963 Herston (Qld)

Trimble, Samuel Christy (Qld) b Aug. 16, 1934 Lismore (NSW)

Tringrove, James (Tas) b Nov. 25, 1907 Blackmans Bay (Tas) d Sept. 11, 1979 Blackmans Bay (Tas)

Trinnick, James (Vic) b Dec. 13, 1853 Kingsbridge, Devon (England) d July 12, 1928 Northcote (Vic)

**Trott, Albert Edwin (Vic) b Feb. 6, 1873 Collingwood (Vic) d July 30, 1914 Willesden Green, London (England)

* Trott, George Henry Stephens (Vic) b Aug. 5, 1866 Collingwood (Vic) d Nov. 10, 1917 South Melbourne (Vic)

Trowse, Dean Frederick (SAust) b Oct. 18, 1931 Rose Park (SAust)

Trueman, Geoffrey Stanley (NSW) b Jan. 7, 1926 Double Bay (NSW) d June 28, 1981 Sydney (NSW)

Truman, Frederick George (Vic) b Dec. 6, 1886 Carlton (Vic) d June 17, 1955 Brighton (Vic)

* Trumble, Hugh (Vic) b May 12, 1867 Abbotsford (Vic) d Aug. 14, 1938 Hawthorn (Vic)

* Trumble, John William (Vic) b Sept. 16, 1863 Collingwood (Vic) d Aug. 17, 1944 Brighton (Vic)

Trumper, Victor (NSW) b Oct. 7, 1913 Chatswood (NSW) d Aug. 31, 1981 Sydney (NSW)

* Trumper, Victor Thomas (NSW) b Nov. 2, 1877 Sydney (NSW) d June 28, 1915 Darlinghurst (NSW)

Truscott, William John (WAust) b Oct. 9, 1886 Lithgow (NSW) d June 20, 1966 Bayswater (WAust)

Tubb, Shannon Benjamin (Tas) b May 11, 1980 Bracknell (Tas)

Tucker, Adrian Edward (NSW) b Sept. 19, 1969 Ryde (NSW)

Tucker, Rodney James (NSW & Tas) b Aug. 28, 1964 Auburn (NSW)

Tuckwell, Bertie Joseph (Vic) b Oct. 6, 1882 Carlton (Vic) d Jan. 2, 1943 Wellington (New Zealand)

Tumilty, Leonard Ross (Tas) b June 12, 1884 Launceston (Tas) d March 27, 1962 Launceston (Tas)

Tunks, William (NSW) b April 8, 1816 Castlereagh (NSW) d April 12, 1883 St Leonards (NSW)

* Turner, Alan (NSW) b July 23, 1950 Camperdown (NSW)

* Turner, Charles Thomas Byass (NSW) b Nov. 16, 1862 Bathurst (NSW) d Jan. 1, 1944 Manly (NSW)

Turner, Edward (Vic) b Aug. 8, 1858 Northcote (Vic) d Jan. 26, 1893 Prahran (Vic)

Turner, J. B. (Vic) birth and death details unknown

Turner, Thomas (SAust & Vic) b March 7, 1865 Nuriootpa (SAust) d Oct. 27, 1936 Prospect (SAust)

Turner, Wilfred Herbert (Vic) b July 6, 1921 Woodvale (Vic)

Tuttle, Roy Thomas (Vic) b Sept. 11, 1920 Carlton (Vic) d c. 1997 Canberra (ACT)

Tweeddale, Ernest Richard (NSW) b Aug. 23, 1895 Newtown (NSW) d April 28, 1956 Dover Heights (NSW)

Twible, Paul William (Qld) b Dec. 14, 1957 Herston (Qld)

Twopenny (Murrumgunarriman) (NSW) b c. 1845 Bathurst (NSW) d March 12, 1883 West Maitland (NSW)

Van Deinsen, Brett Paul (NSW) b Dec. 28, 1977 Bankstown (NSW)

Varis, Leslie (WAust) b May 13, 1947 Kalgoorlie (WAust)

Vaughan, Frederick (Vic) b Nov. 8, 1876 (England) d Sept. 30, 1926 Elsternwick (Vic)

Vaughan, Jeffrey Mark (SAust) b March 26, 1974 Blacktown (NSW)

Vaughan, Leonard J. (NSW) b March 16, 1908 Waverley (NSW) d c. 1960 full death details unknown

Vaughan, Robert (NSW) b c. 1834 d July 12, 1865 at sea between Australia and New Zealand

Vaughton, Roland William (SAust) b May 5, 1914 Ardrossan (SAust) d Jan. 5, 1979 Adelaide (SAust)

Vautin, Charles Edwin (Tas) b June 24, 1867 Sorell (Tas) d Dec. 11, 1942 Moonah (Tas)

Vautin, Douglas Maynard (Tas) b July 26, 1896 Hobart (Tas) d Jan. 11, 1976 Mt Martha (Vic)

Vautin, George James Phillips (Tas & Vic) b April 23, 1869 Orielton (Tas) d Jan. 9, 1949 West Preston (Vic)

Vawser, Bruce Forbes (Vic) b June 17, 1929 Mitcham (Vic)

* Veivers, Thomas Robert (Qld) b April 6, 1937 Beenleigh (Qld)

* Veletta, Michael Robert John (WAust) b Oct. 30, 1963 Subiaco (WAust)

Vernon, Edward Henry George (Vic) b Oct. 11, 1911 Northcote (Vic) d May 8, 1968 Kew (Vic)

Vernon, Leslie Phillip (Vic) b May 29, 1880 Melbourne (Vic) d May 11, 1957 Ashwood (Vic)

Vernon, Murray Trevor (WAust) b Feb. 9, 1937 Kondinin (WAust)

Vidler, Robert Trevor (NSW) b Feb. 5, 1957 Cronulla (NSW)

Vimpani, Graeme Ronald (Vic) b Jan. 27, 1972 Herston (Qld)

Vincent, Brian Alfred (SAust) b Feb. 16, 1960 Unley (SAust)

Vincent, Norman Hill (Tas) b Nov. 10, 1883 (England) d Feb. 12, 1958 Prahran (Vic)

Vincent, Russell George (SAust) b March 25, 1954 Jamestown (SAust)

Vint, William (Vic) b June 30, 1851 Belfast (Ireland) d March 28, 1897 Helens Bay (Ireland)

Waddy, Edgar Lloyd (NSW) b Dec. 3, 1879 Morpeth (NSW) d Aug. 2, 1963 Collaroy (NSW)

Waddy, Ernest Frederick (NSW) b Oct. 5, 1880 Morpeth (NSW) d Sept. 23, 1958 Evesham , Worcestershire (England)

Wade, Frank Hainsworth (NSW) b Sept. 1, 1871 Farsley, Yorkshire (England) d Oct. 4, 1940 Lindfield (NSW)

Wainwright, Edmund George Chalwin (SAust) b May 18, 1903 North Adelaide (SAust) d Aug. 8, 1995 North Geelong (Vic)

* Waite, Mervyn George (SAust) b Jan. 7, 1911 Kent Town (SAust) d Dec. 16, 1985 Georgetown (SAust)

Waldron, Alfred Edward (SAust) b Feb. 26, 1857 Moorooduc (Vic) d June 7, 1929 Adelaide (SAust)

Wales, Isaac F. (NSW) b Jan. 31, 1865 Auckland (New Zealand) d c. 1942 full death details unknown

Walford, Sydney Rundle (NSW) b Nov. 19, 1857 Darlinghurst (NSW) d July 2, 1949 Woollahra (NSW)

Walker, Alan Keith (NSW) b Oct. 4, 1925 Manly (NSW)

Walker, Charles William (SAust) b Feb. 19, 1909 Brompton Park (SAust) d Dec. 18, 1942 in action over Soltau (Germany)

Walker, Darren Kenneth (Vic) b June 8, 1966 Bendigo (Vic)

Walker, Jeffrey Milton (Qld) b Sept. 11, 1960 Beaudesert (Qld)

Walker, Kenneth Victor John (Vic) b June 25, 1941 Melbourne (Vic)

* Walker, Maxwell Henry Norman (Vic) b Sept. 12, 1948 West Hobart (Tas)

Walker, Ronald Radford (Vic) b Jan. 1, 1926 Collingwood (Vic)

Walker, William Holden (Tas) b Dec. 16, 1835 Islington, London (England) d June 14, 1886 Hobart (Tas)

Walkerden, Henry Ernest (WAust) b Nov. 20, 1885 Brunswick (Vic) d May 16, 1966 Richmond (Vic)

Walkley, Edwin (SAust) b May 10, 1876 Wallaroo (SAust) d April 18, 1950 Randwick (NSW)

Wall, John Craik Lyall Sydney (NSW) b Oct. 25, 1891 Balmain (NSW) d June 9, 1969 West Pymble (NSW)

* Wall, Thomas Welbourn (SAust) b May 13, 1904 Semaphore (SAust) d March 26, 1981 Adelaide (SAust)

Wallace, Percival Henry (Vic) b Oct. 6, 1891 Bendigo (Vic) d Oct. 3, 1959 Glen Iris (Vic)

Wallace, Richard Miscamble (Tas) b March 22, 1934 Melbourne (Vic)

Walmsley, Walter Thomas (NSW, Tas & Qld) b March 16, 1916 Homebush (NSW) d Feb. 25, 1978 Hamilton (New Zealand)

Walsh, James Michael (Tas) b May 28, 1913 Launceston (Tas) d July 5, 1986 Launceston (Tas)

Walsh, John Edward (NSW) b Dec. 4, 1912 Walcha (NSW) d May 20, 1980 Wallsend (NSW)

Walsh, Lawrence Stanley (SAust) b Feb. 8, 1902 North Adelaide (SAust) d Jan. 12, 1976 St Georges (SAust)

Walsh, Mark Jason (WAust) b April 28, 1972 Townsville (Qld)

Walsh, Norman Arthur (SAust) b Feb. 8, 1902 North Adelaide (SAust) d Dec. 7, 1969 Adelaide (SAust)

Walshe, John Hamilton (Tas) b c. 1841 (England) d April 17, 1893 Sandy Bay (Tas)

* Walters, Francis Henry (Vic & NSW) b Feb. 9, 1860 Richmond (Vic) d June 1, 1922 at sea near Bombay

* Walters, Kevin Douglas (NSW) b Dec. 21, 1945 Dungog (NSW)

Walters, Maxwell John (Qld) b July 28, 1953 Bundaberg (Qld)

Walton, Douglas John (Tas) b April 9, 1927 New Norfolk (Tas) d Feb. 18, 2001 Glenorchy (Tas)

Ward, Edward Wolstenholme (NSW) b Aug. 17, 1823 Calcutta (India) d Feb. 5, 1890 Cannes (France)

* Ward, Francis Anthony (SAust) b Feb. 23, 1906 Leichhardt (NSW) d May 25, 1974 Brooklyn (NSW)

Ward, Harry Alexander (Tas) b Dec. 8, 1924 Hobart (Tas) d Dec. 8, 1993 Sandy Bay (Tas)

Ward, John Charles (Vic) b Nov. 15, 1946 Melbourne (Vic)

Ward, Leonard Keith (Tas) b Feb. 17, 1879 South Kingston (SAust) d Sept. 30, 1964 Heathpool (SAust)

Ward, Maxwell John (NSW) b Feb. 3, 1907 Randwick (NSW) d Oct. 24, 1983 New Lambton Heights (NSW)

Ward, Ronald Egbert (Tas) b May 7, 1905 Adelaide (SAust) d Nov. 8, 2000 Launceston (Tas)

Ward, William George (Tas) b May 15, 1863 West Hobart (Tas) d June 22, 1948 East Malvern (Vic)

Warden, Lester Griffith (Qld) b April 14, 1940 Wooloowin (Qld) d April 3, 1989 Greenslopes (Qld)

Wardill, Benjamin Johnson (Vic) b Oct. 15, 1842 Everton, Lancashire (England) d Oct. 15, 1917 Sandringham (Vic)

Wardill, Richard Wilson (Vic) b Nov. 3, 1840 Everton, Lancashire (England) d Aug. 17, 1873 Melbourne (Vic)

Wardlaw, Douglas McLaren Searl (Tas) b July 19, 1904 Hobart (Tas) d May 20, 1968 St Marys (Tas)

Wardlaw, Robert Bruce Searl (Tas) b Jan. 9, 1914 Hobart (Tas) d Sept. 12, 1986 Launceston (Tas)

Ware, Joseph Maitland (Tas) b Sept. 8, 1822 London (England) d Sept. 21, 1868 Lausanne (Switzerland)

Warne, Frank Belmont (Vic) b Oct. 3, 1906 North Carlton (Vic) d May 29, 1994 Edenvale (South Africa)

* Warne, Shane Keith (Vic) b Sept. 13, 1969 Ferntree Gully (Vic)

Warne, Tom Summerhayes (Vic) b Jan. 13, 1870 North Melbourne (Vic) d July 7, 1944 Carlton (Vic)

Warr, Gerald Gerrard (Qld) b May 17, 1939 Casino (NSW)

Warren, Peter Charles (Tas) b May 13, 1953 Launceston (Tas)

Wasley, Mark Andrew (WAust & Tas) b Oct. 6, 1965 Subiaco (WAust)

Waterman, Leonard William (Qld) b Feb. 18, 1892 Brisbane (Qld) d Jan. 1, 1952 Kangaroo Point (Qld)

Waters, Glen Wayne (Tas) b May 3, 1943 Launceston (Tas)

Waters, Robert William (SAust) b April 29, 1874 Gravesend, Kent (England) d Feb. 20, 1912 Woodville (SAust)

Wates, Darren Jude (WAust) b July 2, 1977 Subiaco (WAust)

* Watkins, John Russell (NSW) b April 16, 1943 Hamilton (NSW)

Watling, Walter Herbert (SAust) b March 13, 1864 Unley (SAust) d Dec. 19, 1928 Randfontein (South Africa)

Watmuff, Frederick John (Vic) b Sept. 16, 1915 St Kilda (Vic) d Aug. 10, 1972 Castlemaine (Vic)

Watsford, Goulburn (SAust) b July 1, 1859 Goulburn (NSW) d May 16, 1951 Melbourne (Vic)

Watson, Alfred Edward (Tas) b Aug. 31, 1888 Carlton (Vic) d May 6, 1957 South Melbourne (Vic)

Watson, Andrew Simon (SAust) b Oct. 14, 1955 Woomera (SAust)

Watson, Bertie Francis (NSW) b March 13, 1898 Maclean (NSW) d Nov. 18, 1987 Canberra (ACT)

* Watson, Graeme Donald (Vic, WAust & NSW) b March 8, 1945 Kew (Vic)

Watson, Gregory George (NSW & WAust) b Jan. 29, 1955 Gulgong (NSW)

Watson, John Wentworth (Tas) b 1828 birth day and month unknown Sorell (Tas) d June 26, 1920 Scottsdale (Tas)

Watson, Roy Clarence William (WAust) b June 21, 1933 Fremantle (WAust)

Watson, Shane Robert (Tas) b June 17, 1981 Ipswich (Qld)

Watson, William (NSW) b Nov. 10, 1881 Lambton (NSW) d Feb. 12, 1926 North Sydney (NSW)

* Watson, William James (NSW) b Jan. 31, 1931 Randwick (NSW)

Watt, Arthur David (WAust) b Nov. 24, 1913 Edinburgh (Scotland)

Watt, Arthur Kenneth Elwyn (Tas) b Dec. 12, 1891 Hobart (Tas) d Oct. 8, 1973 Hobart (Tas)

Watt, Donald (Qld) b March 15, 1920 Southport (Qld)

Watt, John (Tas) b Feb. 16, 1858 Hobart (Tas) d Nov. 14, 1918 Glebe (Tas)

Watt, John Charles (Tas) b July 6, 1884 Hobart (Tas) d Aug. 4, 1961 Hobart (Tas)

Watters, John Charles (Vic) b Oct. 6, 1924 Footscray (Vic)

Watts, Colin Arthur (SAust) b Jan. 9, 1921 St Peters (SAust)

Watts, Gary Maxwell (Vic) b Oct. 22, 1958 Dunolly (Vic)

Waugh, Dean Parma (NSW) b Feb. 3, 1969 Campsie (NSW)

* Waugh, Mark Edward (NSW) b June 2, 1965 Canterbury (NSW)

Waugh, Russell Frederick (NSW & WAust) b Sept. 29, 1941 Sydney (NSW)

* Waugh, Stephen Rodger (NSW) b June 2, 1965 Canterbury (NSW)

Waye, Libby Sibly (SAust) b Jan. 14, 1885 Willunga (SAust) d June 10, 1951 Frewville (SAust)

Wearne, William Stewart (NSW) b Jan. 18, 1857 Campbelltown (NSW) death details unknown

Webb, Berrowes Littleton (Qld) b April 15, 1915 Brisbane (Qld) d Feb. 7, 1983 Greenslopes (Qld)

Webb, Colin Ralph (SAust) b Jan. 20, 1926 North Adelaide (SAust)

Webb, Kenneth Norman (SAust) b Feb. 27, 1921 Unley (SAust) d March 7, 1994 Daw Park (SAust)

Webber, Darren Scott (SAust) b Aug. 18, 1971 Burnside (SAust)

Webster, Alexander Miles Clifton (WAust) b Nov. 25, 1908 East Fremantle (WAust) d March 28, 1964 Shenton Park (WAust)

Webster, Harold Wynne (SAust) b Feb. 17, 1887 Randwick (NSW) d Oct. 7, 1949 Randwick (NSW)

Webster, Stuart Edward (NSW) b June 11, 1946 Orange (NSW)

Wedgwood, Walter Bernard (Vic) b Oct. 23, 1912 Clifton Hill (Vic) d Dec. 2, 1977 Mornington (Vic)

Weekley, Leonard Rex (SAust) b July 21, 1922 Port Wakefield (SAust)

Weeks, Albert Edmund (SAust) b July 23, 1864 Bowden (SAust) d April 21, 1948 Hollywood (WAust)

Weir, Alexander John (SAust) b March 5, 1921 Largs Bay (SAust)

Weir, Harold Stanley (Qld) b April 23, 1904 Croydon Junction (Qld)

Welch, Charles William (Vic) b June 9, 1907 birthplace unknown d April 11, 1983 Melbourne (Vic)

* Wellham, Dirk Macdonald (NSW, Tas & Qld) b March 13, 1959 Marrickville (NSW)

Wellham, Walter Arthur (NSW) b Sept. 17, 1932 Belmont (NSW)

Wellington, Clement Wellesley (WAust) b Aug. 17, 1880 Yongala (SAust) d July 26, 1956 Underdale (SAust)

Wellington, Stephen Leslie (Tas) b July 4, 1899 Beaconsfield (Tas) d June 11, 1974 Scotts Head (NSW)

Wells, Arthur Phillip (NSW) b Sept. 4, 1900 Paddington (NSW) d Dec. 27, 1964 South Coogee (NSW)

**Wessels, Kepler Christoffel (Qld) b Sept. 14, 1957 Bloemfontein, Orange Free State (South Africa)

West, Neville Leonard (Vic) b Nov. 9, 1933 Marysville (Vic) d c. August 1987 Sydney (NSW)

Westaway, Colin Edward (Qld) b Aug. 27, 1936 Indooroopilly (Qld)

Westbrook, Keith Raymond (Tas) b May 28, 1887 Scottsdale (Tas) d Jan. 20, 1982 Burnie (Tas)

Westbrook, Norman Russell (Tas) b June 25, 1868 Launceston (Tas) d May 29, 1931 Launceston (Tas)

Westbrook, Roy Austin (Tas) b Jan. 3, 1889 Ringarooma (Tas) d Aug. 7, 1961 Wellington (New Zealand)

Westbrook, Thomas (Tas) b 1827 birth day and month unknown Hobart (Tas) d Sept. 13, 1911 Sandy Bay (Tas)

Westbrook, Walter Horatio (Tas) b Nov. 21, 1827 Hobart (Tas) d Jan. 3, 1897 Launceston (Tas)

Whalley, John (Qld) b Nov. 27, 1872 Spring Hill (Qld) d Oct. 29, 1925 Brisbane (Qld)

* Whatmore, Davenell Frederick (Vic) b March 16, 1954 Colombo (Ceylon)

Whiddon, Henry (NSW) b Nov. 20, 1878 Sydney (NSW) d Dec. 19, 1935 Manly (NSW)

White, Alfred Becher Stewart (NSW) b Oct. 4, 1879 Mudgee (NSW) d Dec. 15, 1962 Karuah (NSW)

White, Alfred Henry Ebsworth (NSW) b Oct. 18, 1901 Scone (NSW) d March 6, 1964 Darling Point (NSW)

White, Cameron Leon (Vic) b Aug. 18, 1983 Bairnsdale (Vic)

* White, Craig (Vic) b Dec. 16, 1969 Morley, Yorkshire (England)

White, Edward Clive Stewart (NSW) b April 17, 1913 Mosman (NSW) d Oct. 10, 1999 Hornsby (NSW)

Whiteside, Warren Gregory (Vic) b Nov. 1, 1961 Box Hill (Vic)

Whitesides, Thomas (Tas) b 1836 birth day and month unknown Hobart (Tas) d Sept. 24, 1919 Hobart (Tas)

Whitfield, Henry Edward (SAust) b Feb. 25, 1903 Kent Town (SAust) d Jan. 14, 1937 Royston Park (SAust)

Whitfield, Stephen Bourke John (NSW) b Nov. 21, 1950 Ryde (NSW)

Whitford, Graham Sydney (Vic) b July 25, 1938 Ascot Vale (Vic)

Whiting, Albert William Harley (NSW) b May 31, 1866 Darlinghurst (NSW) death details unknown

Whitington, Richard Smallpeice (SAust) b June 30, 1912 Unley Park (SAust) d March 13, 1984 Sydney (NSW)

Whitlow, Edward Hardmond (Vic) b c. 1832 Manchester, Lancashire (England) d Nov. 29, 1870 South Melbourne (Vic)

Whitney, Gary Reginald (Tas) b March 19, 1951 Campbell Town (Tas)

* Whitney, Michael Roy (NSW) b Feb. 24, 1959 Surry Hills (NSW)

Whitting, William Charles (NSW) b July 9, 1884 Drummoyne (NSW) d Oct. 26, 1936 Bellevue Hill (NSW)

* Whitty, William James (NSW & SAust) b Aug. 15, 1886 Sydney (NSW) d Jan. 30, 1974 Tantanoola (SAust)

Whyte, Graham Keith (Qld) b March 29, 1952 Herston (Qld)

* Wiener, Julien Mark (Vic) b May 1, 1955 Melbourne (Vic)

Wigley, Robert Strangways (SAust) b March 15, 1864 Windsor (Vic) d April 20, 1926 Glenelg (SAust)

Wigney, Bradley Neil (SAust) b June 30, 1965 Leongatha (Vic)

Wilberforce, Robert James (WAust) b July 31, 1910 Subiaco (WAust)

Wildsmith, Andrew (Vic) b Jan. 9, 1958 East Melbourne (Vic)

Wildsmith, John (Vic) b July 1, 1939 Fitzroy (Vic)

Wilkes, Alfred Ernest (Tas) b Nov. 15, 1922 Launceston (Tas) d Aug. 27, 1998 Evandale (Tas)

Wilkie, Daniel (Vic) b Dec. 1, 1843 Melbourne (Vic) d May 11, 1917 St Kilda (Vic)

Wilkin, John Winstanley Symons (SAust) b April 28, 1924 North Adelaide (SAust)

Wilkins, Roy (Tas) b April 18, 1892 North Hobart (Tas) d July 17, 1965 Hobart (Tas)

Wilkinson, Alfred (SAust) b Jan. 2, 1863 Kooringa (SAust) d Jan. 22, 1922 Lower Mitcham (SAust)

Wilkinson, James Scott (Tas) b Dec. 4, 1951 Hobart (Tas)

Wilkinson, Robert B. (Vic) birth and death details unknown

Wilkinson, William Archer (Vic) b Sept. 1, 1899 Clifton Hill (Vic) d May 5, 1974 Mildura (Vic)

Willcocks, Robert James (Qld) b Dec. 23, 1891 Brisbane (Qld) d March 21, 1965 Toowoomba (Qld)

Williams, Bradley Andrew (Vic & WAust) b Nov. 20, 1974 Frankston (Vic)

Williams, Brett Douglas (SAust) b Dec. 15, 1967 Camden (NSW)

Williams, Douglas Samuel Thomas (WAust) b July 3, 1919 Elwood (Vic)

Williams, Edward Alexander (Vic) b Sept. 18, 1915 North Fitzroy (Vic)

Williams, Luke (SAust) b Dec. 24, 1979 Henley Beach (SAust)

* Williams, Neil Fitzgerald (Tas) b July 2, 1962 Hope Well (St Vincent)

Williams, Norman Leonard (SAust) b Sept. 23, 1899 Exeter (SAust) d May 31, 1947 Semaphore (SAust)

Williams, Owen Charles (Vic) b June 20, 1847 Impression Bay (Tas) d Nov. 18, 1917 Kandy (Ceylon)

Williams, Peter David (Vic) b Feb. 9, 1942 Brighton (Vic)

Williams, Robert Graham (SAust) b April 4, 1911 St Peters (SAust) d Aug. 31, 1978 Medindie (SAust)

Williams, Scott Bradley (Qld) b Feb. 1, 1971 Herston (Qld)

Williamson, Cameron John (SAust) b March 26, 1970 Ryde (NSW)

Willis, Carl Bleackley (Vic) b March 23, 1893 Daylesford (Vic) d May 12, 1930 Berrigan (NSW)

Wills, Thomas Wentworth (Vic) b Dec. 19, 1835 Molonglo Plains (NSW) d May 2, 1880 Heidelberg (Vic)

Willsmore, Hurtle Binks (SAust) b Dec. 26, 1889 Beverley (SAust) d Sept. 17, 1985 Kings Park (SAust)

Wilson, Charles Geldart (Vic) b Jan. 9, 1869 Carngham (Vic) d June 28, 1952 Rosenerth (New Zealand)

Wilson, George Lindsay (Vic) b April 27, 1868 Collingwood (Vic) d March 9, 1920 St Kilda (Vic)

Wilson, Gregory James (Tas) b Jan. 4, 1958 Launceston (Tas)

Wilson, Henry (Tas) b March 31, 1865 Westbury (Tas) d Aug. 18, 1914 Sydney (NSW)

Wilson, Horace (WAust) b June 28, 1864 Kadina (SAust) d May 15, 1925 West Perth (WAust)

Wilson, John Thomas (Tas) b Nov. 27, 1868 Westbury (Tas) d July 24, 1906 Launceston (Tas)

Wilson, John Warwick (NSW) b Sept. 1, 1947 Paddington (NSW)

* Wilson, John William (Vic & SAust) b Aug. 20, 1921 Albert Park (Vic) d Oct. 13, 1985 Bayswater (Vic)

Wilson, Joseph Cameron (NSW) b Feb. 11, 1869 Braidwood (NSW) d c. 1938 Wollongong (NSW)

* Wilson, Paul (SAust) b Jan. 12, 1972 Newcastle (NSW)

Wilson, Richard (Qld) b Jan. 14, 1869 Paddington (NSW) d c. 1937 Parramatta (NSW)

Wilson, Stanley Vincent (WAust & SAust) b Sept. 23, 1948 Midland (WAust)

Wilson, William John (Vic) b c. 1912 Mildura (Vic)

Wilson, William Young (Vic) b Dec. 13, 1909 Essendon (Vic) d Sept. 30, 1976 Ascot Vale (Vic)

Windsor, Edward Arthur Cartwright (Tas) b March 9, 1869 Launceston (Tas) d Dec. 23, 1953 Launceston (Tas)

Wingrove, Francis William (Combined XI) b April 20, 1863 Eltham (Vic) d May 27, 1892 Rupanyup (Vic)

Winning, Charles Samuel (AIF) b July 17, 1889 Paddington (NSW) d April 20, 1967 Newport (NSW)

Winser, Cyril Legh (SAust) b Nov. 27, 1884 High Legh, Staffordshire (England) d Dec. 20, 1983 Barwon Heads (Vic)

Winter, Graham John (SAust) b Nov. 6, 1955 Medindie (SAust)

Wishart, Peter William (WAust) b June 18, 1937 Perth (WAust)

Wishart, Warren Keith (WAust) b Feb. 17, 1971 Subiaco (WAust)

Wolfe, Malcolm Frederick (WAust) b July 28, 1952 Gnowangerup (WAust)

Wood, Cecil Clunas (Tas) b April 8, 1896 Erin Bay (Tas) death details unknown

* Wood, Graeme Malcolm (WAust) b Nov. 6, 1956 East Fremantle (WAust)

Wood, Hartley Lionel (SAust) b April 5, 1930 Flinders Park (SAust) d Dec. 16, 1988 Elizabeth Vale (SAust)

Wood, John Robert (NSW) b April 11, 1865 Newcastle (NSW) d Feb. 14, 1928 Putney, London (England)

Wood, Percy Barnes (WAust) b Dec. 22, 1901 Wellington (New Zealand) d June 9, 1941 Litani River (Syria) in action

* Wood, Reginald (Vic) b March 7, 1860 Woodchurch, Cheshire (England) d Jan. 6, 1915 Manly (NSW)

Wood, William (NSW) b Nov. 11, 1849 Forglen, Banffshire (Scotland) d April 12, 1924 Marrickville (NSW)

Woodbury, William Joseph George (Vic) b Dec. 6, 1892 Balmain (NSW) d Aug. 31, 1983 Moe (Vic)

* Woodcock, Ashley James (SAust) b Feb. 27, 1947 Adelaide (SAust)

Woodford, John Robert Herbert (Vic & SAust) b June 23, 1881 Camberwell (Vic) d May 1, 1949 North Fitzroy (Vic)

* Woodfull, William Maldon (Vic) b Aug. 22, 1897 Maldon (Vic) d Aug. 11, 1965 Tweed Heads (NSW)

Woodhead, Derek John (WAust) b Sept. 7, 1934 Subiaco (WAust)

Woods, Julian Augustus (Tas) b Sept. 4, 1887 Oatlands (Tas) d Oct. 11, 1975 Lindisfarne (Tas)

**Woods, Samuel Moses James (Australia) b April 13, 1867 Ashfield (NSW) d April 30, 1931 Taunton, Somerset (England)

Woolcock, Arthur Henry (SAust) b June 10, 1887 Port Pirie (SAust) d June 29, 1975 Adelaide (SAust)

Woolf, Louis Sydney (Vic) b July 28, 1855 Collingwood (Vic) d July 6, 1942 Richmond (Vic)

Woolley, H. (Tas) birth and death details unknown

* Woolley, Roger Douglas (Tas) b Sept. 16, 1954 Hobart (Tas)

Woolmer, Gordon Rae (NSW) b Feb. 24, 1917 Hamilton (NSW) d July 31, 1999 Fairfield (NSW)

Wootton, John Richard (Vic) b Jan. 18, 1906 Rushworth (Vic) d July 18, 1986 death place unknown

Wootton, Stanley Eli (Vic) b April 28, 1895 South Yarra (Vic) d March 20, 1962 Heidelberg (Vic)

Wordsworth, Charles William (NSW) b Sept. 9, 1877 Rotherham, Yorkshire (England) d June 10, 1960 Redfern (NSW)

Workman, James Allen (Services) b March 17, 1917 Peterhead (SAust) d Dec. 23, 1970 Westminster, London (England)

* Worrall, John (Vic) b June 21, 1861 Chinamans Flat, Maryborough (Vic) d Nov. 17, 1937 Fairfield Park (Vic)

Wray, Thomas Fawcett (Vic) b c. 1827 Cleasby, Yorkshire (England) d Sept. 6, 1877 Melbourne (Vic)

Wrigglesworth, Ian Alastair (Vic) b Nov. 29, 1967 Sale (Vic)

Wright, Albert William (SAust) b Sept. 24, 1875 Norwood (SAust) d Dec. 23, 1938 North Adelaide (SAust)

Wright, Bert Harold (Vic) b Dec. 2, 1926 Wonthaggi (Vic) d Nov. 20, 1994 Beaumaris (Vic)

Wright, Damien Geoffrey (Tas) b July 25, 1975 Casino (NSW)

Wright, Francis John (Vic) b March 13, 1874 Ballarat East (Vic) d c. 1899 Ballarat East (Vic)

Wright, Gary John (SAust) b Nov. 9, 1970 Henley Beach (SAust)

Wright, Harry Lovegrove (Vic) b April 13, 1870 Ballarat West (Vic) d March 19, 1950 West Melbourne (Vic)

* Wright, Kevin John (WAust & SAust) b Dec. 27, 1953 North Fremantle (WAust)

Wright, Robert Raymond (SAust) b Nov. 11, 1914 Marryatville (SAust) d Jan. 20, 1965 Springfield (SAust)

Wundke, Stephen Christopher (SAust) b July 2, 1961 North Adelaide (SAust)

Wyatt, Alan Edward (NSW) b April 4, 1935 Annandale (NSW)

Wyeth, Ezra Robert Harding (Qld) b March 13, 1910 Toowoomba (Qld) d Oct. 15, 1992 Northbridge, California (United States of America)

Wynne, Lester Alan (Vic) b Oct. 7, 1908 Carlton (Vic) d Nov. 29, 1980 Melbourne (Vic)

Yagmich, Dennis Brian (WAust & SAust) b Aug. 23, 1948 Victoria Park (WAust)

* Yallop, Graham Neil (Vic) b Oct. 7, 1952 Balwyn (Vic)

* Yardley, Bruce (WAust) b Sept. 5, 1947 Midland (WAust)

Yeates, George Walter Carrington (NSW) b May 5, 1918 Erskineville (NSW) d April 8, 1967 Kogarah Bay (NSW)

Yeates, Sydney Fergus Macrae (Qld) b Aug. 20, 1912 Toowoomba (Qld) d March 19, 1992 Auchenflower (Qld)

Yeomans, Frederick Caleb (Vic) b Nov. 11, 1888 Northcote (Vic) d Jan. 16, 1965 Brighton (Vic)

Youill, George Joseph (NSW) b Oct. 2, 1871 Sydney (NSW) d Dec. 21, 1936 Glebe (NSW)

Young, Allan Stanley (Qld) b July 7, 1920 Ipswich (Qld) d Dec. 23, 1974 Albion (Qld)

Young, Bradley Evan (SAust) b Feb. 23, 1973 Semaphore (SAust)

Young, Claye Michael (Tas) b Dec. 31, 1964 Hobart (Tas)

Young, George Albert (WAust) b Feb. 3, 1949 Caulfield (Vic)

Young, Jason Carl (NSW) b Feb. 17, 1971 Wagga Wagga (NSW)

Young, Peter William (Vic) b Dec. 31, 1961 Geelong (Vic)

* Young, Shaun (Tas) b June 13, 1970 Burnie (Tas)

* Younis Mohammad Ahmed (SAust) b Oct. 20, 1947 Jullundur (India)

Zachariah, Harry (Vic) b June 4, 1911 Stirling (SAust)

Zadow, Robert John (SAust) b Jan. 17, 1955 Mannum (SAust)

Zesers, Andris Karlis (SAust) b March 11, 1967 Medindie (SAust)

Ziebell, Keith Percy (Qld) b July 26, 1942 Rosewood (Qld)

Zimbulis, Anthony George (WAust) b Feb. 11, 1918 Perth (WAust) d May 17, 1963 Palm Beach (WAust)

* Zoehrer, Timothy Joseph (WAust) b Sept. 25, 1961 Armadale (WAust)

Zschorn, Paul William (SAust) b July 16, 1886 North Unley (SAust) d June 13, 1953 Glen Iris (Vic)

THE PRICEWATERHOUSECOOPERS RATINGS

Introduced in 1987 as the Deloitte Ratings, and known from 1990 to 1998 as the Coopers and Lybrand Ratings, the PricewaterhouseCoopers Ratings rank Test cricketers on a scale up to 1,000 according to their performances in Test matches. A rating of 900 points is outstanding and rarely achieved. The ratings take into account playing conditions, the quality of the opposition and the result of the matches. A player cannot get a full rating until he has played 30 innings or taken 70 wickets in Tests. The leading 10 batsmen and bowlers in the ratings after matches played up to September 11, 2001 were:

Batsmen	Rating	Bowlers	Rating
1. Andy Flower (Zim)	895	1. Glenn McGrath (Aust)	919
2. Steve Waugh (Aust)	877	2. Shaun Pollock (SAf)	894
3. S.R.Tendulkar (Ind)	866	3. M.Muralitharan (SL)	864
4. Inzamam-ul-Haq (Pak)	818	4. Allan Donald (SAf)	809
5. M.Jayawardene (SL)	805	5. Darren Gough (Eng)	746
6. Rahul Dravid (Ind)	798	6. Shane Warne (Aust	736)
7. Adam Gilchrist (Aust)	790	7. Waqar Younis (Pak)	686
8. Brian Lara (WI)	769	8. Saqlain Mushtaq (Pak)	678
9. Mark Waugh (Aust)	743	9. Chris Cairns (NZ)	663
10. Daryll Cullinan (SAf)	739	10. Heath Streak (Zim)	661
		Jason Gillespie (Aust)	661

PART THREE: RECORDS

Because of time constraints in production, all records in this section provided by Ross Dundas cover the period up to and including July 1, 2001. Thus, performances by Australians in England after this date are excluded from this edition.

* Denotes not out or an unbroken partnership.

Key to abbreviations
Australian States: NSW – New South Wales, Qld – Queensland, SAust – South Australia, Tas – Tasmania, Vic – Victoria, WAust – Western Australia.
Countries: Aust – Australia, Ban – Bangladesh, Can – Canada, Eng – England, Ind – India, Ire – Ireland, Kya – Kenya, N Amer – North America, NZ – New Zealand, Pak – Pakistan, SAf – South Africa, Sco – Scotland, SL – Sri Lanka, WI – West Indies, Zim – Zimbabwe.
Australian Grounds: Bel – Bellerive Oval, CS – Colonial Stadium, Ex – Exhibition Ground, LRG – Lower "Railway" Ground, TCA – Tasmanian Cricket Association Ground.
Other Grounds: BS – Brabourne Stadium (Bombay/Mumbai), Corp – Corporation Stadium (Madras/Chennai), EP – Ellis Park, OW – Old Wanderers, PIS – R. Premadasa (Khettarama) International Stadium, PSS – P.Saravanamuttu Stadium, SSC – Sinhalese Sports Club Ground, WS – Wanderers Stadium (Johannesburg), Wankhede Stadium (Bombay/Mumbai).

AUSTRALIAN FIRST-CLASS RECORDS

BATTING RECORDS

BOWLING RECORDS

ALL-ROUND RECORDS

WICKET-KEEPING RECORDS

FIELDING RECORDS

TEAM RECORDS

MISCELLANEOUS

AUSTRALIAN TEST MATCH RECORDS

BATTING RECORDS

BOWLING RECORDS

WICKET-KEEPING RECORDS

FIELDING RECORDS

TEAM RECORDS

APPEARANCES

CAPTAINCY

TEST SERIES

AUSTRALIAN LIMITED-OVERS INTERNATIONAL RECORDS

BATTING RECORDS

BOWLING RECORDS

WICKET-KEEPING RECORDS

FIELDING RECORDS

TEAM RECORDS

AUSTRALIAN FIRST-CLASS RECORDS

BATTING RECORDS

HIGHEST INDIVIDUAL SCORES

452*	D. G. Bradman	New South Wales v Queensland at Sydney	1929-30
437	W. H. Ponsford	Victoria v Queensland at Melbourne	1927-28
429	W. H. Ponsford	Victoria v Tasmania at Melbourne	1922-23
383	C. W. Gregory	New South Wales v Queensland at Brisbane	1906-07
369	D. G. Bradman	South Australia v Tasmania at Adelaide	1935-36
365*	C. Hill	South Australia v New South Wales at Adelaide	1900-01
364	L. Hutton	England v Australia at The Oval	1938
359	R. B. Simpson	New South Wales v Queensland at Brisbane	1963-64
357	D. G. Bradman	South Australia v Victoria at Melbourne	1935-36
356	B. A. Richards	South Australia v Western Australia at Perth	1970-71
355*	G. R. Marsh	Western Australia v South Australia at Perth	1989-90
352	W. H. Ponsford	Victoria v New South Wales at Melbourne	1926-27
345	C. G. Macartney	Australians v Nottinghamshire at Nottingham	1921
340*	D. G. Bradman	New South Wales v Victoria at Sydney	1928-29
336	W. H. Ponsford	Victoria v South Australia at Melbourne	1927-28
334	D. G. Bradman	Australia v England at Leeds	1930
334*	M. A. Taylor	Australia v Pakistan at Peshawar	1998-99
325*	H. S. T. L. Hendry	Victoria v New Zealanders at Melbourne	1925-26
325	C. L. Badcock	South Australia v Victoria at Adelaide	1935-36
324*	D. M. Jones	Victoria v South Australia at Melbourne	1994-95
321	W. L. Murdoch	New South Wales v Victoria at Sydney	1881-82
315*	A. F. Kippax	New South Wales v Queensland at Sydney	1927-28
311	R. B. Simpson	Australia v England at Manchester	1964
307	M. C. Cowdrey	MCC v South Australia at Adelaide	1962-63
307	R. M. Cowper	Australia v England at Melbourne	1965-66
306*	D. W. Hookes	South Australia v Tasmania at Adelaide	1986-87
305*	F. E. Woolley	MCC v Tasmania at Hobart (TCA)	1911-12
304	D. G. Bradman	Australia v England at Leeds	1934
303*	W. W. Armstrong	Australians v Somerset at Bath	1905
300*	V. T. Trumper	Australians v Sussex at Hove	1899

HUNDRED ON FIRST-CLASS DEBUT
FOR AUSTRALIAN TEAMS

121	C. S. Gordon	Victoria v New South Wales at Melbourne	1869-70
128*	J. P. O'Halloran	Victoria v South Australia at Melbourne	1896-97
166	L. W. Pye	New South Wales v Queensland at Brisbane (Ex)	1896-97
135*	H. G. S. Morton	Queensland v Victoria at Melbourne	1904-05
123	W. M. McPetrie	Victoria v Tasmania at Melbourne	1904-05
104	A. G. Moyes	South Australia v Western Australia at Adelaide	1912-13
102	N. L. Gooden	South Australia v Western Australia at Adelaide	1912-13
108*	F. W. Hyett	Victoria v Tasmania at Melbourne	1914-15
207	N. F. Callaway	New South Wales v Queensland at Sydney	1914-15
145	J. Bogle	New South Wales v Victoria at Sydney	1918-19
143	E. E. B. Forssberg	New South Wales v Queensland at Sydney	1920-21
130	D. A. Mullarkey	New South Wales v Queensland at Brisbane (Ex)	1923-24
105	S. E. Wootton	Victoria v Tasmania at Hobart (TCA)	1923-24
127	H. O. Rock	New South Wales v South Australia at Sydney	1924-25
136*	L. T. Gun	South Australia v New South Wales at Adelaide	1924-25
118	D. G. Bradman	New South Wales v South Australia at Adelaide	1927-28
100	R. N. Ellis	Victoria v Tasmania at Hobart (TCA)	1927-28
137	B. W. Hone	South Australia v Victoria at Adelaide	1928-29
129	R. M. Levy	Queensland v Victoria at Brisbane (Ex)	1928-29
117	A. H. Allsopp	New South Wales v MCC at Sydney	1929-30
115	O. W. Bill	New South Wales v Tasmania at Sydney	1929-30
128	L. R. Leabeater	New South Wales v Tasmania at Sydney	1929-30
118	F. E. Fontaine	Victoria v Tasmania at Hobart (TCA)	1930-31
119	R. J. Lawson	Victoria v Tasmania at Hobart (TCA)	1930-31
102	R. N. Nutt	New South Wales v South Australia at Adelaide	1931-32
135	J. C. Francis	Victoria v Tasmania at Launceston	1932-33
108	H. H. E. Grangel	Victoria v Tasmania at Melbourne	1935-36
121	R. A. Hamence	South Australia v Tasmania at Adelaide	1935-36
181	K. R. Miller	Victoria v Tasmania at Melbourne	1937-38
113	A. E. O. Barras	Western Australia v Victoria at Perth	1938-39
148	A. R. Morris	New South Wales v Queensland at Sydney	1940-41
164	M. R. Thomas	Tasmania v Australian Services at Hobart (TCA)	1945-46
232*	S. J. E. Loxton	Victoria v Queensland at Melbourne	1946-47
118	E. W. Lukeman	New South Wales v South Australia at Adelaide	1946-47
112	E. A. D. Kerr	Victoria v Tasmania at Launceston	1946-47
122	J. L. Chambers	Victoria v Tasmania at Melbourne	1949-50
164	L. E. Favell	South Australia v New South Wales at Adelaide	1951-52
202	J. Hallebone	Victoria v Tasmania at Melbourne	1951-52
121	R. E. Briggs	New South Wales v Western Australia at Perth	1952-53
103*	B. K. Shepherd	Western Australia v Queensland at Perth	1955-56
102	R. B. Lyons	Queensland v Victoria at Brisbane	1955-56
102*	H. W. Pinkus	Tasmania v South Australia at Hobart (TCA)	1956-57
180	N. G. Marks	New South Wales v South Australia at Sydney	1958-59
129	D. Chadwick	Western Australia v Queensland at Brisbane	1963-64
100	J. F. C. Loxton	Queensland v Western Australia at Perth	1966-67
107	M. J. Lucas	Queensland v New South Wales at Brisbane	1968-69
104	R. W. Marsh	Western Australia v West Indians at Perth	1968-69
122	G. J. Gilmour	New South Wales v South Australia at Sydney	1971-72
140	M. F. Kent	Queensland v New South Wales at Brisbane	1974-75
119	K. J. Hughes	Western Australia v New South Wales at Perth	1975-76
106	J. M. Wiener	Victoria v Queensland at Brisbane	1977-78
107	M. D. Taylor	Victoria v Queensland at Melbourne	1977-78
112	C. E. Penter	Western Australia v New South Wales at Sydney	1979-80
100	D. M. Wellham	New South Wales v Victoria at Melbourne	1980-81
126	M. D. Haysman	South Australia v Queensland at Adelaide	1982-83
130	S. P. O'Donnell	Victoria v South Australia at Melbourne	1983-84
165	W. J. S. Seabrook	New South Wales v Victoria at Melbourne	1984-85
118	E. J. Harris	Tasmania v South Australia at Adelaide	1985-86
111	W. N. Phillips	Victoria v West Indians at Melbourne	1988-89

114	M.G. Bevan	South Australia v Western Australia at Perth	1989-90
155	G.I. Foley	Queensland v Pakistanis at Brisbane	1989-90
118	M.P. Lavender	Western Australia v Victoria at St Kilda	1990-91
149	M.L. Hayden	Queensland v South Australia at Brisbane	1991-92
133*	R.J. Davison	New South Wales v Tasmania at Sydney	1993-94

Note: A.R. Morris scored a century (111) in the second innings of his debut match, thus becoming the first player in world cricket to achieve such a feat.

HUNDRED IN EACH INNINGS OF A MATCH FOR AUSTRALIAN TEAMS

C.J. Eady	116	112*	Tasmania v Victoria at Hobart (TCA)	1894-95
V.T. Trumper	109	119	Australians v Essex at Leyton	1902
J.R.M. Mackay	105	102*	New South Wales v South Australia at Sydney	1905-06
D.R.A. Gehrs	148*	100*	South Australia v Western Australia at Fremantle	1905-06
M.A. Noble	176	123	New South Wales v Victoria at Sydney	1907-08
V.S. Ransford	182	110	Victoria v New South Wales at Sydney	1908-09
W. Bardsley	136	130	Australia v England at The Oval	1909
A. Kenny	164	100*	Victoria v Queensland at Brisbane	1909-10
C.G. Macartney	119	126	New South Wales v South Africans at Sydney	1910-11
C.G. Macartney	142	121	Australians v Sussex at Hove	1912
R.S. Stephens	108	181	Victoria v Tasmania at Launceston	1913-14
J.M. Gregory	122	102	AIF Team v New South Wales at Sydney	1919-20
W.W. Armstrong	157*	245	Victoria v South Australia at Melbourne	1920-21
F.A. O'Keefe	177	141	The Rest v Australian XI at Sydney	1921-22
W.H. Ponsford	110	110*	Victoria v New South Wales at Sydney	1923-24
V.Y. Richardson	100	125	South Australia v New South Wales at Sydney	1924-25
A.F. Kippax	127	131	New South Wales v Queensland at Brisbane (Ex)	1926-27
L.P.D. O'Connor	103	143*	Queensland v New South Wales at Sydney	1926-27
A. Jackson	131	122	New South Wales v South Australia at Sydney	1927-28
D.G. Bradman	131	133*	New South Wales v Queensland at Brisbane (Ex)	1928-29
B.A. Onyons	105	127	Victoria v Queensland at Brisbane (Ex)	1928-29
D.G. Bradman	124	225	W.M. Woodfull's XI v J. Ryder's XI at Sydney	1929-30
A.F. Kippax	158	102*	Australians v Sussex at Hove	1930
S.J. McCabe	106	103*	New South Wales v Victoria at Sydney	1931-32
A.R. Lonergan	115	100	South Australia v Victoria at Melbourne	1933-34
K.E. Rigg	100	167*	Victoria v New South Wales at Melbourne	1936-37
D.G. Bradman	107	113	South Australia v Queensland at Brisbane	1937-38
A.L. Hassett	122	122	Victoria v New South Wales at Sydney	1939-40
C.L. Badcock	120	102	South Australia v Victoria at Melbourne	1940-41
R.A. Hamence	130	103*	South Australia v Victoria at Melbourne	1940-41
A.R. Morris	148	111	New South Wales v Queensland at Sydney	1940-41
A.L. Hassett	187	124*	Australian Services v Prince's XI at Delhi	1945-46
A.R. Morris	122	124*	Australia v England at Adelaide	1946-47
R.A. Hamence	132	101*	South Australia v New South Wales at Adelaide	1946-47
D.G. Bradman	132	127*	Australia v India at Melbourne	1947-48
J. Moroney	118	101*	Australia v South Africa at Johannesburg	1949-50
A.R. Edwards	103	105	Western Australia v Queensland at Perth	1950-51
K.R. Miller	100	101	A.L. Hassett's XI v A.R. Morris's XI at Melbourne	1953-54
J.W. Burke	138	125*	Australians v Somerset at Taunton	1956
L.E. Favell	112	114	South Australia v New South Wales at Sydney	1956-57
C.J. Pinch	110	100	South Australia v Western Australia at Perth	1956-57
C.J. Pinch	102	102	South Australia v Victoria at Melbourne	1957-58
G.B. Stevens	164	111	South Australia v New South Wales at Sydney	1957-58
L.E. Favell	104	145	South Australia v Western Australia at Adelaide	1958-59
S.C. Trimble	113	136*	Queensland v Victoria at Brisbane	1963-64
R.B. Simpson	153	115	Australia v Pakistan at Karachi	1964-65
R.B. Simpson	121	142*	New South Wales v South Australia at Sydney	1964-65
P.C. Kelly	119	108*	Western Australia v MCC at Perth	1965-66
K.G. Cunningham	107	101*	South Australia v Western Australia at Adelaide	1966-67
K.D. Walters	242	103	Australia v West Indies at Sydney	1968-69

G. S. Chappell	129	156*	South Australia v Queensland at Brisbane	1969-70
I. M. Chappell	145	106	Australians v World XI at Brisbane	1971-72
A. J. Sieler	157	105	Victoria v Queensland at Brisbane	1973-74
G. S. Chappell	180	101	Queensland v Victoria at Brisbane	1973-74
I. M. Chappell	141*	130	South Australia v Victoria at Adelaide	1973-74
I. M. Chappell	145	121	Australia v New Zealand at Wellington	1973-74
G. S. Chappell	247*	133	Australia v New Zealand at Wellington	1973-74
R. B. McCosker	138	136*	New South Wales v Western Australia at Sydney	1974-75
R. B. McCosker	111	115	Australians v Sussex at Hove	1975
G. S. Chappell	123	109*	Australia v West Indies at Brisbane	1975-76
D. W. Hookes	185	105	South Australia v Queensland at Adelaide	1976-77
D. W. Hookes	135	156	South Australia v New South Wales at Adelaide	1976-77
G. N. Yallop	105	114*	Victoria v New South Wales at Sydney	1977-78
A. R. Border	150*	153	Australia v Pakistan at Lahore	1979-80
R. B. McCosker	123*	118*	New South Wales v Victoria at Sydney	1981-82
R. B. Kerr	158	141	Queensland v Western Australia at Perth	1981-82
D. W. Hookes	137	107	South Australia v Victoria at Adelaide	1982-83
G. N. Yallop	113	145*	Victoria v Western Australia at Melbourne	1983-84
S. B. Smith	105	116	Australians v Guyana at Georgetown	1983-84
A. R. Border	140	114*	Australia v New Zealand at Christchurch	1985-86
K. C. Wessels	135	105*	Australians v South Africans at Port Elizabeth	1986-87
D. C. Boon	108	143	Tasmania v Queensland at Launceston	1987-88
M. A. Taylor	107	152*	New South Wales v Western Australia at Perth	1988-89
T. M. Moody	162	159	Western Australia v South Australia at Perth	1988-89
D. M. Jones	116	121*	Australia v Pakistan at Adelaide	1989-90
J. Cox	175	102	Tasmania v New South Wales at Hobart (Bel)	1989-90
M. A. Taylor	127	100	New South Wales v Queensland at Sydney	1989-90
S. M. Small	115	126	New South Wales v Wellington at North Sydney	1990-91
S. G. Law	142*	105	Queensland v Western Australia at Perth	1990-91
D. R. Martyn	132*	112	Western Australia v Queensland at Brisbane	1992-93
R. T. Ponting	107	100*	Tasmania v Western Australia at Hobart (Bel)	1992-93
D. C. Boon	108	106	Australians v Worcestershire at Worcester	1993
M. L. Hayden	165	116	Queensland v South Australia at Adelaide	1993-94
P. C. Nobes	140	106	South Australia v Queensland at Adelaide	1993-94
M. L. Hayden	126	155	Queensland v Victoria at Brisbane	1993-94
D. M. Jones	145	152*	Victoria v South Australia at Melbourne	1993-94
D. F. Hills	114	126	Tasmania v South Australia at Adelaide	1993-94
M. L. Love	187	116	Queensland v Tasmania at Brisbane	1994-95
S. G. Law	102	138	Queensland v Tasmania at Hobart (Bel)	1994-95
R. T. Ponting	118*	100*	Tasmania v Queensland at Brisbane	1995-96
M. T. G. Elliott	104*	135	Victoria v Western Australia at Perth	1995-96
R. T. Ponting	126	145*	Tasmania v Queensland at Hobart (Bel)	1996-97
J. Cox	143	125	Tasmania v New South Wales at Sydney	1996-97
S. R. Waugh	108	116	Australia v England at Manchester	1997
A. Symonds	163	100*	Queensland v South Australia at Adelaide	1997-98
D. S. Lehmann	103	100†	Australians v Rawalpindi Cricket Assn at Rawalpindi	1998-99
M. T. G. Elliott	108	103*	Victoria v New South Wales at Melbourne	1998-99
G. S. Blewett	169*	213*	Australian XI v England XI at Hobart (Bel)	1998-99
D. S. Lehmann	101*	113	South Australia v Tasmania at Hobart (Bel)	1999-00

† *Retired hurt.*

HUNDRED IN EACH INNINGS OF A MATCH
AGAINST AUSTRALIAN TEAMS

A. C. Maclaren	142	100	A. E. Stoddart's XI v New South Wales at Sydney	1897-98
W. Rhodes	119	109	MCC v New South Wales at Sydney	1911-12
A. Sandham	137	104	MCC v New South Wales at Sydney	1924-25
H. Sutcliffe	176	127	England v Australia at Melbourne	1924-25
C. C. R. Dacre	127*	101*	Auckland v Victoria at Auckland	1924-25
W. R. Hammond	119*	177	England v Australia at Adelaide	1928-29
W. R. Hammond	104	136	MCC v South Australia at Adelaide	1936-37

D.C.S. Compton..	147	103*	England v Australia at Adelaide	1946-47
V.S. Hazare......	116	145	India v Australia at Adelaide	1947-48
H.J. Keith	111	113*	South Africans v Victoria at Melbourne	1952-53
M.C. Cowdrey ...	110	103	MCC v New South Wales at Sydney	1954-55
C.L. Walcott	126	110	West Indies v Australia at Port-of-Spain	1954-55
C.L. Walcott	155	110	West Indies v Australia at Kingston	1954-55
P.B.H. May......	140	114	MCC v Australian XI at Sydney	1958-59
R.B. Kanhai	117	115	West Indies v Australia at Adelaide	1960-61
M.C. Cowdrey ...	149	121	Kent v Australians at Canterbury	1961
P.E. Richardson ..	111	115	Kent v Australians at Canterbury	1964
B.F. Butcher	115	172	West Indians v Combined XI at Perth	1968-69
R.C. Fredericks...	158	118	Guyana v Australians at Georgetown	1972-73
G.M. Turner	101	110*	New Zealand v Australia at Christchurch	1973-74
I.V.A. Richards...	160	107*	West Indians v Tasmania at Hobart (TCA)	1975-76
Mudassar Nazar...	103	123	Pakistanis v Victoria at Melbourne	1983-84
P.N. Kirsten	173	105*	South Africans v Australians at Cape Town	1986-87
A.J. Lamb	154	105	England XI v Australian XI at Hobart (Bel)	1990-91
Asif Mujtaba	102*	125*	Pakistanis v Queensland at Brisbane	1992-93
Basit Ali........	137	101*	Pakistanis v South Australia at Adelaide	1995-96

MOST HUNDREDS IN CONSECUTIVE INNINGS
FOR AUSTRALIAN TEAMS

Six

D.G. Bradman	118	dnb	D.G. Bradman's XI v K.E. Rigg's XI at Melbourne ...	1938-39
	143	dnb	South Australia v New South Wales at Adelaide	1938-39
	225	dnb	South Australia v Queensland at Adelaide	1938-39
	107	dnb	South Australia v Victoria at Melbourne	1938-39
	186	dnb	South Australia v Queensland at Brisbane	1938-39
	135*	dnb	South Australia v New South Wales at Sydney	1938-39

Four

C.G. Macartney	105	dnb	Australians v Hampshire at Southampton	1921
	193	dnb	Australians v Northamptonshire at Northampton	1921
	345	dnb	Australians v Nottinghamshire at Nottingham	1921
	115	30	Australia v England at Leeds	1921
D.G. Bradman	dnb	135	New South Wales v South Africans at Sydney	1931-32
	226	dnb	Australia v South Africa at Brisbane	1931-32
	219	dnb	New South Wales v South Africans at Sydney	1931-32
	112	dnb	Australia v South Africa at Sydney	1931-32
D.G. Bradman	150	dnb	Australians v Gentlemen of England at Lord's	1948
	143	dnb	Australians v South of England at Hastings	1948
	153	dnb	Australians v H.G.D. Leveson Gower's XI at Scarborough	1948
	123	10	D.G. Bradman's XI v A.L. Hassett's XI at Melbourne .	1948-49
D.W. Hookes	185	105	South Australia v Queensland at Adelaide	1976-77
	135	156	South Australia v New South Wales at Adelaide	1976-77
A.R. Border	106	dnb	Australians v Somerset at Taunton	1985
	135	dnb	Australians v Worcestershire at Worcester	1985
	125	dnb	Australians v MCC at Lord's	1985
	100	dnb	Australians v Derbyshire at Derby	1985
M.G. Bevan	20	104	New South Wales v South Australia at Adelaide	1990-91
	153*	dnb	New South Wales v Victoria at Sydney	1990-91
	121	dnb	New South Wales v Queensland at Sydney	1990-91
	136	3	New South Wales v Tasmania at Hobart (Bel)	1990-91

MOST HUNDREDS IN A CAREER
(30 or more)

	100s	I	400+	300+	200+
D. G. Bradman	117	338	1	6	37
M. E. Waugh	76	521	0	0	5
G. S. Chappell	74	542	0	0	4
A. R. Border	70	625	0	0	3
D. C. Boon	68	585	0	0	3
R. N. Harvey	67	461	0	0	7
K. C. Wessels	66	539	0	0	4
T. M. Moody	64	501	0	0	4
S. R. Waugh	64	464	0	0	4
R. B. Simpson	60	436	0	2	10
I. M. Chappell	59	448	0	0	3
A. L. Hassett	59	322	0	0	8
D. M. Jones	55	415	0	1	8
W. Bardsley	53	376	0	0	7
S. G. Law	53	381	0	0	2
D. S. Lehmann	51	314	0	0	5
W. M. Lawry	50	417	0	0	4
C. G. Macartney	49	360	0	1	3
W. M. Woodfull	49	245	0	0	7
M. G. Bevan	49	316	0	0	2
W. H. Ponsford	47	235	2	2	9
J. L. Langer	47	339	0	0	7
M. L. Hayden	47	327	0	0	4
A. R. Morris	46	250	0	0	4
C. Hill	45	416	0	1	3
W. W. Armstrong	45	406	0	1	1
N. C. O'Neill	45	306	0	0	2
K. D. Walters	45	426	0	0	4
A. F. Kippax	43	256	0	0	6
V. T. Trumper	42	401	0	1	7
K. R. Miller	41	326	0	0	7
M. A. Taylor	41	435	0	1	1
J. Cox	40	313	0	0	3
W. A. Brown	39	284	0	0	5
P. J. P. Burge	38	354	0	0	5
M. A. Noble	37	377	0	0	7
J. D. Siddons	35	280	0	0	3
G. M. Wood	35	375	0	0	0
L. Livingston	34	384	0	0	4
F. A. Tarrant	33	541	0	0	4
G. R. Marsh	33	323	0	1	2
M. J. Slater	33	338	0	0	3
M. T. G. Elliott	33	222	0	0	2
G. S. Blewett	33	303	0	0	5
H. L. Collins	32	258	0	0	3
I. R. Redpath	32	391	0	0	2
D. W. Hookes	32	304	0	1	1
W. E. Alley	31	682	0	0	3
P. D. Bowler	31	400	0	0	3
G. N. Yallop	30	283	0	0	3

MOST RUNS IN AN AUSTRALIAN SEASON

	Season	M	I	NO	R	HS	100s	50s	Avge
D. G. Bradman (New South Wales) ..	1928-29	13	24	6	1,690	340*	7	5	93.88
R. N. Harvey (Victoria)	1952-53	16	27	1	1,659	205	5	8	63.80
D. G. Bradman (New South Wales) ..	1929-30	11	16	2	1,586	452*	5	4	113.28

	Season	M	I	NO	R	HS	100s	50s	Avge
W. R. Hammond (MCC)	1928-29	13	18	1	1,553	251	7	1	91.35
D. G. Bradman (South Australia)	1936-37	12	19	1	1,552	270	6	2	86.22
G. S. Chappell (Queensland)	1975-76	15	26	8	1,547	182*	6	7	85.94
R. B. Simpson (Western Australia)	1960-61	15	26	2	1,541	221*	4	9	64.21
B. A. Richards (South Australia)	1970-71	10	16	2	1,538	356	6	3	109.85
G. Boycott (MCC)	1970-71	13	22	6	1,535	173	6	7	95.93
G. A. Faulkner (South Africans)	1910-11	14	27	1	1,534	204	3	13	59.00
R. B. Simpson (New South Wales)	1963-64	14	25	2	1,524	359	4	4	66.26
E. J. Barlow (South Africans)	1963-64	14	25	2	1,523	209	6	4	66.21
G. S. Chappell (Queensland)	1980-81	14	22	2	1,502	204	5	6	75.10

1,000 RUNS IN A SEASON

12 Times: D. G. Bradman 1928-29 (1,690), 1929-30 (1,586), 1930-31 (1,422), 1931-32 (1,403), 1932-33 (1,171), 1933-34 (1,192), 1935-36 (1,173), 1936-37 (1,552), 1937-38 (1,437), 1939-40 (1,475), 1946-47 (1,032), 1947-48 (1,296).

6 Times: I. M. Chappell 1965-66 (1,019), 1968-69 (1,476), 1970-71 (1,210), 1971-72 (1,140), 1973-74 (1,074), 1975-76 (1,310).

5 Times: G. S. Chappell 1973-74 (1,288), 1974-75 (1,484), 1975-76 (1,547), 1979-80 (1,066), 1980-81 (1,502); A. R. Border 1978-79 (1,220), 1982-83 (1,081), 1985-86 (1,247), 1986-87 (1,002), 1987-88 (1,164); D. S. Lehmann 1989-90 (1,142), 1993-94 (1,087), 1994-95 (1,104), 1995-96 (1,237), 1999-00 (1,142).

4 Times: R. B. Simpson 1960-61 (1,541), 1962-63 (1,337), 1963-64 (1,524), 1967-68 (1,082); W. M. Lawry 1960-61 (1,042), 1963-64 (1,340), 1965-66 (1,445), 1968-69 (1,140); M. T. G. Elliott 1994-95 (1,029), 1995-96 (1,233), 1998-99 (1,014), 1999-00 (1,028); G. S. Blewett 1993-94 (1,036), 1995-96 (1,173), 1998-99 (1,187), 2000-01 (1,162).

3 Times: A. R. Morris 1946-47 (1,234), 1948-49 (1,069), 1950-51 (1,332); D. W. Hookes 1982-83 (1,424), 1985-86 (1,001), 1987-88 (1,149); J. D. Siddons 1987-88 (1,077), 1990-91 (1,034), 1992-93 (1,190); M. L. Hayden 1991-92 (1,028), 1992-93 (1,249), 1993-94 (1,136); G. S. Blewett 1993-94 (1,036), 1995-96 (1,173), 1998-99 (1,187); J. L. Langer 1993-94 (1,198), 1997-98 (1,075), 1999-00 (1,108).

MOST RUNS ON AN AUSTRALIAN OVERSEAS TOUR

		Season	M	I	NO	R	HS	100s	50s	Avge
D. G. Bradman	England	1930	27	36	6	2,960	334	10	5	98.66
V. T. Trumper	England	1902	36	53	0	2,570	128	11	11	48.49
D. G. Bradman	England	1938	20	26	5	2,429	278	13	5	115.66
D. G. Bradman	England	1948	23	31	4	2,428	187	11	8	89.92
W. Bardsley	England	1912	36	52	6	2,365	184*	8	9	51.41
C. G. Macartney	England	1921	31	41	2	2,317	345	8	6	59.41
C. G. Macartney	England	1912	33	49	1	2,187	208	6	8	45.56
S. J. McCabe	England	1934	26	37	7	2,078	240	8	7	69.26
W. Bardsley	England	1909	33	49	4	2,072	219	6	7	46.04
M. A. Noble	England	1905	31	46	2	2,053	267	6	13	46.66
R. N. Harvey	England	1953	25	35	4	2,040	202*	10	5	65.80
D. G. Bradman	England	1934	22	27	3	2,020	304	7	6	84.16
W. M. Lawry	England	1961	23	39	6	2,019	165	9	7	61.18
W. Bardsley	England	1921	30	41	4	2,005	209	8	10	54.18

Most in countries other than England:

R. N. Harvey	South Africa	1949-50	19	25	5	1,526	178	8	4	76.30
A. R. Border	India	1979-80	18	28	3	1,423	178	5	4	56.92
G. S. Chappell	West Indies	1972-73	10	17	1	1,109	154	4	6	69.31
W. M. Woodfull	New Zealand	1927-28	6	9	3	781	284	3	2	130.16
A. R. Border	Pakistan	1979-80	5	9	3	674	178	3	1	112.33
W. Bardsley	North America	1913-14	5	6	2	437	142*	3	0	109.25
M. J. Slater	Sri Lanka	1999-00	5	8	1	370	119	1	3	52.86
S. R. Waugh	Zimbabwe	1999-00	2	3	1	339	161	2	0	169.50

LEADING BATSMEN IN EACH AUSTRALIAN SEASON
(Qualification for top of averages: 8 completed innings)

Season	Leading Scorer	Runs	Avge	Top of Averages	Runs	Avge
1850-51	T. F. Hamilton (Vic)	45	22.50	n/a		
1851-52	T. F. Hamilton (Vic)	84	42.00	n/a		
1853-54	G. Cavenagh (Vic)	45	22.50	n/a		
1854-55	no games played					
1855-56	{ J. J. McKone (NSW)	18	18.00	n/a		
	{ R. Driver (NSW)	18	9.00	n/a		
1856-57	G. H. B. Gilbert (NSW)	33	16.50	n/a		
1857-58	T. W. Wills (Vic)	94	23.50	n/a		
1858-59	O. W. Lewis (NSW)	53	26.50	n/a		
1859-60	T. W. Wills (Vic)	24	12.00	n/a		
1860-61	J. M. Bryant (Vic)	32	16.00	n/a		
1861-62	W. Caffyn (England)	88	88.00	n/a		
1862-63	D. D'Arcy (NSW)	51	51.00	n/a		
1863-64	T. Lockyer (England)	84	84.00	n/a		
1864-65	no games played					
1865-66	E. J. Gregory (NSW)	61	30.50	n/a		
1866-67	S. Cosstick (Vic)	29	14.50	n/a		
1867-68	R. W. Wardill (Vic)	155	155.00	n/a		
1868-69	J. Phillips (Vic)	133	44.33	n/a		
1869-70	C. S. Gordon (Vic)	143	71.50	n/a		
1870-71	A. R. Loughnan (Vic)	71	23.67	n/a		
1871-72	N. Thompson (NSW)	46	23.00	n/a		
1872-73	J. L. A. Arthur (Tas)	86	28.67	n/a		
1873-74	no games played					
1874-75	C. Bannerman (NSW)	113	113.00	n/a		
1875-76	D. W. Gregory (NSW)	116	38.67	n/a		
1876-77	C. Bannerman (NSW)	243	48.60	n/a		
1877-78	N. Thompson (NSW)	101	33.67	n/a		
1878-79	G. Ulyett (England)	306	34.00	G. Ulyett (England)	306	34.00
1879-80	A. C. Bannerman (NSW)	103	25.75	n/a		
1880-81	T. P. Horan (Vic)	318	35.33	H. H. Massie (NSW)	299	37.38
1881-82	W. L. Murdoch (NSW)	679	61.73	W. L. Murdoch (NSW)	679	61.73
1882-83	A. C. Bannerman (NSW)	434	54.25	A. C. Bannerman (NSW)	434	54.25
1883-84	W. L. Murdoch (NSW)	567	113.40	n/a		
1884-85	W. Barnes (England)	520	43.33	W. Barnes (England)	520	43.33
1885-86	J. McIlwraith (Vic)	315	78.75	n/a		
1886-87	A. Shrewsbury (England)	721	48.07	A. Shrewsbury (England)	721	48.07
1887-88	H. Moses (NSW)	815	62.69	H. Moses (NSW)	815	62.69
1888-89	G. H. S. Trott (Vic)	507	39.00	G. H. S. Trott (Vic)	507	39.00
1889-90	J. J. Lyons (SAust)	254	63.50	n/a		
1890-91	G. Giffen (SAust)	275	91.67	n/a		
1891-92	J. J. Lyons (SAust)	557	55.70	J. J. Lyons (SAust)	557	55.70
1892-93	G. Giffen (SAust)	468	58.50	G. Giffen (SAust)	468	58.50
1893-94	G. Giffen (SAust)	526	75.14	G. Giffen (SAust)	526	75.14
1894-95	A. Ward (England)	916	41.64	A. E. Stoddart (England)	870	51.18
1895-96	H. Donnan (NSW)	626	69.56	H. Donnan (NSW)	626	69.56
1896-97	J. J. Lyons (SAust)	404	57.71	G. H. S. Trott (Vic)	323	40.38
1897-98	C. Hill (SAust)	1,196	66.44	C. Hill (SAust)	1,196	66.44
1898-99	V. T. Trumper (NSW)	873	62.36	C. Hill (SAust)	841	64.69
1899-00	V. T. Trumper (NSW)	721	72.10	V. T. Trumper (NSW)	721	72.10
1900-01	C. Hill (SAust)	620	103.33	n/a		
1901-02	C. Hill (SAust)	1,035	51.75	A. C. MacLaren (England)	929	58.06
1902-03	R. A. Duff (NSW)	786	87.33	R. A. Duff (NSW)	786	87.33
1903-04	V. T. Trumper (NSW)	990	55.00	M. A. Noble (NSW)	961	56.33
1904-05	W. W. Armstrong (Vic)	460	57.50	W. W. Armstrong (Vic)	460	57.50
1905-06	J. R. M. Mackay (NSW)	902	112.75	J. R. M. Mackay (NSW)	902	112.75
1906-07	A. J. Y. Hopkins (NSW)	617	56.09	A. J. Y. Hopkins (NSW)	617	56.09

Season	Leading Scorer	Runs	Avge	Top of Averages	Runs	Avge
1907-08	J. Hardstaff sr (MCC)	1,360	76.20	F. A. Tarrant (Vic)	762	76.20
1908-09	V. S. Ransford (Vic)	825	103.13	V. S. Ransford (Vic)	825	103.13
1909-10	H. H. L. Kortlang (Vic)	656	131.20	C. McKenzie (Vic)	377	47.13
1910-11	G. A. Faulkner (SAf)	1,534	59.00	V. T. Trumper (NSW)	1,246	69.22
1911-12	W. Rhodes (MCC)	1,098	54.90	R. B. Minnett (NSW)	882	63.00
1912-13	V. T. Trumper (NSW)	843	84.30	V. T. Trumper (NSW)	843	84.30
1913-14	C. G. Macartney (NSW)	892	111.50	C. G. Macartney (NSW)	892	111.50
1914-15	J. Ryder (Vic)	445	74.17	C. E. Pellew (SAust)	287	35.88
1915-16	no games played					
1916-17	no games played					
1917-18	no games played					
1918-19	W. W. Armstrong (Vic)	249	83.00	n/a		
1919-20	R. L. Park (Vic)	648	72.00	R. L. Park (Vic)	648	72.00
1920-21	E. H. Hendren (MCC)	1,178	62.00	W. W. Armstrong (Vic)	1,069	89.08
1921-22	F. A. O'Keefe (Vic)	708	118.00	H. S. B. Love (NSW)	424	43.00
1922-23	A. P. F. Chapman (MCC)	782	65.17	A. J. Richardson (SAust)	758	75.80
1923-24	W. H. Ponsford (Vic)	777	111.00	F. C. Thompson (Qld)	397	49.63
1924-25	H. Sutcliffe (MCC)	1,250	69.44	A. F. Kippax (NSW)	853	77.55
1925-26	A. J. Richardson (SAust)	904	50.22	C. G. Macartney (NSW)	795	88.33
1926-27	W. H. Ponsford (Vic)	1,229	122.90	W. H. Ponsford (Vic)	1,229	122.90
1927-28	W. H. Ponsford (Vic)	1,217	152.12	W. H. Ponsford (Vic)	1,217	152.12
1928-29	D. G. Bradman (NSW)	1,690	93.88	D. G. Bradman (NSW)	1,690	93.88
1929-30	D. G. Bradman (NSW)	1,586	113.28	D. G. Bradman (NSW)	1,586	113.28
1930-31	D. G. Bradman (NSW)	1,422	79.00	D. G. Bradman (NSW)	1,422	79.00
1931-32	D. G. Bradman (NSW)	1,403	116.91	D. G. Bradman (NSW)	1,403	116.91
1932-33	H. Sutcliffe (MCC)	1,318	73.22	H. Sutcliffe (MCC)	1,318	73.22
1933-34	D. G. Bradman (NSW)	1,192	132.44	D. G. Bradman (NSW)	1,192	132.44
1934-35	J. H. W. Fingleton (NSW)	880	58.67	L. S. Darling (Vic)	634	70.44
1935-36	D. G. Bradman (SAust)	1,173	130.33	D. G. Bradman (SAust)	1,173	130.33
1936-37	D. G. Bradman (SAust)	1,552	86.22	D. G. Bradman (SAust)	1,552	86.22
1937-38	D. G. Bradman (SAust)	1,437	89.81	D. G. Bradman (SAust)	1,437	89.81
1938-39	W. A. Brown (Qld)	1,057	105.70	W. A. Brown (Qld)	1,057	105.70
1939-40	D. G. Bradman (SAust)	1,475	122.91	D. G. Bradman (SAust)	1,475	122.91
1940-41	S. G. Barnes (NSW)	1,050	75.00	S. G. Barnes (NSW)	1,050	75.00
1941-42	V. N. Raymer (Qld)	130	130.00	n/a		
1942-43	no games played					
1943-44	no games played					
1944-45	no games played					
1945-46	S. G. Barnes (NSW)	794	88.22	S. G. Barnes (NSW)	794	88.22
1946-47	D. C. S. Compton (MCC)	1,432	65.09	D. G. Bradman (SAust)	1,032	79.38
1947-48	D. G. Bradman (SAust)	1,296	129.60	D. G. Bradman (SAust)	1,296	129.60
1948-49	A. R. Morris (NSW)	1,069	66.81	J. Moroney (NSW)	897	81.55
1949-50	A. R. C. McLean (SAust)	660	50.77	A. R. C. McLean (SAust)	660	50.77
1950-51	A. L. Hassett (Vic)	1,423	64.68	K. R. Miller (NSW)	1,332	78.35
1951-52	A. L. Hassett (Vic)	855	61.07	A. L. Hassett (Vic)	855	61.07
1952-53	R. N. Harvey (Vic)	1,659	63.80	R. N. Harvey (Vic)	1,659	63.80
1953-54	C. C. McDonald (Vic)	857	57.13	K. D. Mackay (Qld)	723	72.30
1954-55	R. N. Harvey (Vic)	1,009	45.86	D. C. S. Compton (MCC)	799	57.07
1955-56	J. W. Burke (NSW)	979	61.19	K. R. Miller (NSW)	638	70.89
1956-57	C. J. Pinch (SAust)	840	52.50	R. N. Harvey (Vic)	836	104.50
1957-58	N. C. O'Neill (NSW)	1,005	83.75	N. C. O'Neill (NSW)	1,005	83.75
1958-59	P. B. H. May (MCC)	1,197	57.00	C. C. McDonald (Vic)	990	61.87
1959-60	R. B. Simpson (WAust)	902	300.66	R. G. Flockton (NSW)	617	77.12
1960-61	R. B. Simpson (WAust)	1,541	64.21	B. C. Booth (NSW)	981	65.40
1961-62	R. B. Simpson (NSW)	704	46.93	B. K. Shepherd (WAust)	808	62.15
1962-63	K. F. Barrington (MCC)	1,451	85.35	K. F. Barrington (MCC)	1,451	85.35
1963-64	R. B. Simpson (NSW)	1,524	66.26	B. C. Booth (NSW)	1,180	90.76
1964-65	S. C. Trimble (Qld)	984	57.87	W. M. Lawry (Vic)	848	84.80
1965-66	W. M. Lawry (Vic)	1,445	72.25	R. M. Cowper (Vic)	1,418	74.63
1966-67	L. E. Favell (SAust)	847	49.82	N. C. O'Neill (NSW)	815	67.91
1967-68	R. B. Simpson (NSW)	1,082	56.94	A. P. Sheahan (Vic)	973	64.86

Season	Leading Scorer	Runs	Avge	Top of Averages	Runs	Avge
1968-69	I. M. Chappell (SAust)	1,476	82.00	I. M. Chappell (SAust)	1,476	82.00
1969-70	G. S. Chappell (SAust)	856	65.84	J. A. Steele (NSW)	677	67.70
1970-71	B. A. Richards (SAust)	1,538	109.85	B. A. Richards (SAust)	1,538	109.85
1971-72	I. M. Chappell (SAust)	1,140	60.00	K. D. Walters (NSW)	895	68.84
1972-73	A. P. Sheahan (Vic)	1,002	83.50	A. P. Sheahan (Vic)	1,002	83.50
1973-74	G. S. Chappell (Qld)	1,288	85.86	G. S. Chappell (Qld)	1,288	85.86
1974-75	G. S. Chappell (Qld)	1,484	61.83	G. S. Chappell (Qld)	1,484	61.83
1975-76	G. S. Chappell (Qld)	1,547	85.94	G. S. Chappell (Qld)	1,547	85.94
1976-77	D. W. Hookes (SAust)	861	71.75	R. D. Robinson (Vic)	828	82.80
1977-78	A. D. Ogilvie (Qld)	1,215	50.62	G. M. Wood (WAust)	678	56.50
1978-79	A. R. Border (NSW)	1,220	55.45	J. K. Moss (Vic)	881	67.77
1979-80	G. S. Chappell (Qld)	1,066	71.06	G. S. Chappell (Qld)	1,066	71.06
1980-81	G. S. Chappell (Qld)	1,502	75.10	G. S. Chappell (Qld)	1,502	75.10
1981-82	K. C. Wessels (Qld)	1,094	60.77	H. A. Gomes (West Indians)	712	89.00
1982-83	D. W. Hookes (SAust)	1,424	64.72	G. N. Yallop (Vic)	1,418	67.52
1983-84	G. N. Yallop (Vic)	1,132	113.20	G. N. Yallop (Vic)	1,132	113.20
1984-85	K. C. Wessels (Qld)	1,020	53.68	G. Shipperd (WAust)	823	68.58
1985-86	A. R. Border (Qld)	1,247	73.35	A. R. Border (Qld)	1,247	73.35
1986-87	G. R. Marsh (WAust)	1,200	48.00	M. R. J. Veletta (WAust)	971	74.69
1987-88	D. C. Boon (Tas)	1,287	67.74	M. D. Crowe (NZ)	715	89.38
1988-89	M. A. Taylor (NSW)	1,241	49.64	I. V. A. Richards (WI)	683	68.30
1989-90	M. A. Taylor (NSW)	1,403	70.15	M. E. Waugh (NSW)	1,009	77.62
1990-91	S. G. Law (Qld)	1,204	75.25	S. G. Law (Qld)	1,204	75.25
1991-92	D. M. Jones (Vic)	1,248	96.00	D. M. Jones (Vic)	1,248	96.00
1992-93	M. L. Hayden (Qld)	1,249	52.04	J. D. Siddons (SAust)	1,190	66.11
1993-94	M. G. Bevan (NSW)	1,312	77.18	M. L. Hayden (Qld)	1,136	126.22
1994-95	D. M. Jones (Vic)	1,251	69.50	D. M. Jones (Vic)	1,251	69.50
1995-96	D. S. Lehmann (SAust)	1,237	56.22	M. T. G. Elliott (Vic)	1,233	68.50
1996-97	J. Cox (Tas)	1,349	67.45	J. L. Langer (WAust)	771	77.10
1997-98	D. F. Hills (Tas)	1,220	55.45	T. M. Moody (WAust)	702	78.00
1998-99	G. S. Blewett (SAust)	1,187	118.70	G. S. Blewett (SAust)	1,187	118.70
1999-00	D. S. Lehmann (SAust)	1,142	63.44	R. T. Ponting (Tas)	582	72.75
2000-01	S. M. Katich (WAust)	1,282	71.22	R. T. Ponting (Tas)	726	80.67

HIGHEST BATTING AVERAGE IN AN AUSTRALIAN SEASON
(Minimum 500 runs)

	Season	M	I	NO	R	HS	100s	50s	Avge
R. B. Simpson (Western Australia)	1959-60	5	6	3	902	236*	3	3	300.66
W. H. Ponsford (Victoria)	1922-23	3	4	0	616	429	2	1	154.00
D. G. Bradman (South Australia)	1938-39	7	7	1	919	225	6	0	153.17
C. Hill (South Australia)	1909-10	3	4	0	609	205	3	0	152.25
W. H. Ponsford (Victoria)	1927-28	6	8	0	1,217	437	4	1	152.13
D. G. Bradman (New South Wales)	1933-34	7	11	2	1,192	253	5	3	132.44
H. H. L. Kortlang (Victoria)	1909-10	5	9	4	656	197	2	3	131.20
D. G. Bradman (South Australia)	1935-36	8	9	0	1,173	369	4	1	130.33
D. G. Bradman (South Australia)	1947-48	9	12	2	1,296	201	8	1	129.60
W. M. Woodfull (Victoria)	1927-28	5	7	2	645	191*	2	3	129.00
M. L. Hayden (Queensland)	1993-94	6	12	3	1,136	173*	7	1	126.22
D. G. Bradman (South Australia)	1939-80	9	15	3	1,475	267	5	4	122.92
W. H. Ponsford (Victoria)	1926-27	6	10	0	1,229	352	6	2	122.90
G. S. Blewett (South Australia)	1998-99	7	12	2	1,187	213*	6	1	118.70
F. A. O'Keefe (Victoria)	1921-22	4	6	0	708	180	3	2	118.00
D. G. Bradman (New South Wales)	1931-32	10	13	1	1,403	299*	7	0	116.92
W. L. Murdoch (New South Wales)	1883-84	4	6	1	567	279*	2	1	113.40
D. G. Bradman (New South Wales)	1929-30	11	16	2	1,586	452*	5	4	113.29
G. N. Yallop (Victoria)	1983-84	8	11	1	1,132	268	5	2	113.20
J. R. M. Mackay (New South Wales)	1905-06	6	9	1	902	203	5	2	112.75
M. D. Crowe (New Zealanders)	1985-86	4	7	2	562	242*	2	1	112.40
C. G. Macartney (New South Wales)	1913-14	7	9	1	892	201	5	2	111.50
W. H. Ponsford (Victoria)	1923-24	5	8	1	777	248	4	1	111.00

	Season	M	I	NO	R	HS	100s	50s	Avge
B. A. Richards (South Australia)	1970-71	10	16	2	1,538	356	6	3	109.86
C. L. Badcock (South Australia)	1938-39	7	8	3	540	271*	2	2	108.00
C. G. Macartney (New South Wales) ..	1912-13	4	7	1	646	154	2	4	107.67
M. G. Bevan (New South Wales)	1998-99	6	10	4	636	202*	3	1	106.00
W. A. Brown (Queensland)..........	1938-39	7	11	1	1,057	215	3	6	105.70
R. N. Harvey (Victoria).............	1956-57	6	10	2	836	209	4	3	104.50
C. Hill (South Australia)............	1900-01	4	7	1	620	365*	1	2	103.33
V. S. Ransford (Victoria)............	1908-09	6	10	2	825	182	4	2	103.13
J. Ryder (Victoria).................	1921-22	4	8	2	609	242	1	4	101.50

AUSTRALIANS WITH 10,000 RUNS IN FIRST-CLASS CRICKET

	Career	M	I	NO	R	HS	100s	50s	Avge
D. G. Bradman	1927-28 – 1948-49	234	338	43	28,067	452*	117	69	95.14
A. R. Border	1976-77 – 1995-96	385	625	97	27,131	205	70	142	51.38
K. C. Wessels	1973-74 – 1999-00	316	539	50	24,738	254	66	132	50.59
G. S. Chappell	1966-67 – 1983-84	322	542	72	24,535	247*	74	111	52.20
M. E. Waugh	1985-86 – 2001	324	521	64	24,074	229*	76	118	52.68
D. C. Boon	1978-79 – 1999	350	585	53	23,413	227	68	114	44.01
K. J. Greives	1945-46 – 1964	490	746	79	22,454	224	29	136	33.66
R. N. Harvey	1946-47 – 1962-63	306	461	35	21,699	231*	67	94	50.93
R. B. Simpson	1952-53 – 1977-78	257	436	62	21,029	359	60	100	56.22
T. M. Moody	1985-86 – 2000-01	300	501	47	21,001	272	64	94	46.26
S. R. Waugh	1984-85 – 2001	299	464	77	20,335	216*	64	86	52.55
I. M. Chappell	1961-62 – 1979-80	263	448	41	19,680	209	59	96	48.35
W. E. Alley	1945-46 – 1968	400	682	67	19,612	221*	31	92	31.88
D. M. Jones	1981-82 – 1997-98	245	415	45	19,188	324*	55	88	51.86
W. M. Lawry	1955-56 – 1971-72	250	417	49	18,734	266	50	100	50.90
F. A. Tarrant	1898-99 – 1936-37	329	541	48	17,952	250*	33	93	36.41
M. A. Taylor	1985-86 – 1998-99	253	435	20	17,415	334*	41	97	41.96
C. Hill	1892-93 – 1924-25	252	416	21	17,213	365*	45	82	43.57
S. G. Law	1988-89 – 2001	229	381	41	17,138	263	53	82	50.41
W. Bardsley	1903-04 – 1926-27	250	376	35	17,025	264	53	74	49.92
W. L. Murdoch	1875-76 – 1904	391	679	48	16,953	321	19	85	26.86
V. T. Trumper	1894-95 – 1913-14	255	401	21	16,939	300*	42	87	44.57
A. L. Hassett	1932-33 – 1953-54	216	322	32	16,890	232	59	76	58.24
D. S. Lehmann	1987-88 – 2001	184	314	21	16,183	255	51	76	55.23
K. D. Walters	1962-63 – 1980-81	259	426	57	16,180	253	45	81	43.84
W. W. Armstrong ...	1898-99 – 1921-22	269	406	61	16,158	303*	45	57	46.83
V. E. Jackson	1936-37 – 1958	354	605	53	15,698	170	21	72	28.43
J. L. Langer	1991-92 – 2001	193	339	35	15,348	274*	47	59	50.49
S. M. J. Woods	1886 – 1910	401	690	35	15,345	215	19	62	23.42
M. L. Hayden	1991-92 – 2001	188	327	33	15,370	235*	47	67	52.28
L. Livingston	1941-42 – 1964	236	384	45	15,269	210	34	78	45.04
E. S. Gregory	1889-90 – 1912	368	587	55	15,192	201	25	65	28.55
C. G. Macartney	1905-06 – 1935-36	249	360	32	15,019	345	49	53	45.78
I. R. Redpath	1961-62 – 1975-76	226	391	34	14,993	261	32	84	41.99
P. J. P. Burge	1952-53 – 1966-67	233	354	46	14,640	283	38	66	47.53
M. G. Bevan	1989-90 – 2000-01	189	316	56	14,420	203*	49	64	55.46
K. R. Miller	1937-38 – 1959	226	326	36	14,183	281*	41	63	48.90
M. A. Noble	1893-94 – 1919-20	248	377	34	13,975	284	37	65	40.74
N. C. O'Neill	1955-56 – 1967-68	188	306	34	13,859	284	45	64	50.95
W. A. Brown	1932-33 – 1949-50	189	284	15	13,838	265*	39	65	51.44
W. H. Ponsford	1920-21 – 1934-35	162	235	23	13,819	437	47	42	65.18
M. J. Slater	1991-92 – 2001	190	338	17	13,478	221	33	65	41.99
W. M. Woodfull	1921-22 – 1934-35	174	245	39	13,388	284	49	58	64.99
G. M. Wood	1976-77 – 1991-92	227	375	42	13,353	186*	35	61	40.09
J. Cox	1987-98 – 2001	177	313	21	13,166	245	40	56	45.09
G. S. Blewett	1991-92 – 2001	171	303	21	13,029	268	33	64	46.20
A. F. Kippax	1918-19 – 1935-36	175	256	33	12,762	315*	43	45	57.22

	Career	M	I	NO	R	HS	100s	50s	Avge
K. J. Hughes	1975-76 – 1990-91	216	368	20	12,711	213	26	69	36.52
D. W. Hookes	1975-76 – 1991-92	178	304	16	12,671	306*	32	65	43.39
A. R. Morris	1940-41 – 1963-64	162	250	15	12,614	290	46	46	53.67
C. L. McCool	1939-40 – 1960	251	412	34	12,420	172	18	66	32.85
L. E. Favell	1951-52 – 1969-70	202	347	9	12,379	190	27	68	36.62
S. J. McCabe	1928-29 – 1941-42	182	262	20	11,951	240	29	68	49.38
R. J. Inverarity	1962-63 – 1984-85	223	377	49	11,777	187	26	60	35.90
G. R. Marsh	1977-78 – 1993-94	184	323	25	11,760	355*	33	46	39.46
G. Giffen	1877-78 – 1903-04	251	421	23	11,758	271	18	51	29.54
R. Benaud	1948-49 – 1967-68	259	365	44	11,719	187	23	61	36.50
G. N. Yallop	1972-73 – 1986-87	164	280	30	11,615	268	30	57	45.90
J. D. Siddons	1984-85 – 1999-00	160	280	22	11,587	245	35	53	44.91
C. C. McDonald	1947-48 – 1962-63	192	307	26	11,376	229	24	57	40.48
B. C. Booth	1954-55 – 1968-69	183	283	35	11,265	214*	26	60	45.42
R. W. Marsh	1968-69 – 1983-84	258	396	41	11,067	236	12	54	31.17
K. D. Mackay	1946-47 – 1962-63	201	294	46	10,823	223	23	58	43.64
V. Y. Richardson	1918-19 – 1937-38	184	297	12	10,727	231	27	46	37.63
A. E. Trott	1892-93 – 1911	375	602	53	10,696	164	8	43	19.48
J. Darling	1893-94 – 1907-08	202	333	25	10,635	210	19	55	34.52
R. M. Cowper	1959-60 – 1969-70	147	228	31	10,595	307	26	53	53.78
J. Ryder	1912-13 – 1935-36	177	274	37	10,499	295	24	55	44.29
S. C. Trimble	1959-60 – 1975-76	144	262	16	10,282	252*	26	48	41.79
M. T. G. Elliott	1992-93 – 2000-01	121	222	17	10,236	203	33	45	49.93
G. E. Tribe	1945-46 – 1959	308	454	82	10,177	136*	7	48	27.34
G. M. Ritchie	1980-81 – 1991-92	159	255	24	10,171	213*	24	54	44.03
K. R. Stackpole	1959-60 – 1973-74	167	279	22	10,100	207	22	50	39.29

HIGHEST PARTNERSHIPS FOR EACH WICKET

First wicket

456	W. H. Ponsford and R. E. Mayne, Victoria v Queensland at Melbourne	1923-24
431	M. R. J. Veletta and G. R. Marsh, Western Australia v South Australia at Perth	1989-90
388	K. C. Wessels and R. B. Kerr, Queensland v Victoria at St Kilda	1982-83
382	W. M. Lawry and R. B. Simpson, Australia v West Indies at Bridgetown	1964-65
375	W. M. Woodfull and W. H. Ponsford, Victoria v New South Wales at Melbourne	1926-27
374	G. R. Marsh and M. R. J. Veletta, Western Australia v Tamil Nadu at Perth	1988-89
353	M. T. G. Elliott and J. L. Arnberger, Victoria v Tasmania at Richmond	1999-00
337	C. C. McDonald and K. D. Meuleman, Victoria v South Australia at Adelaide	1949-50
331	B. A. Courtice and R. B. Kerr, Queensland v Tasmania at Brisbane	1984-85
329	G. R. Marsh and M. A. Taylor, Australia v England at Nottingham	1989
328	C. Milburn and D. Chadwick, Western Australia v Queensland at Brisbane	1968-69
323	J. B. Hobbs and W. Rhodes, England v Australia at Melbourne	1911-12
323	M. L. Hayden and M. T. G. Elliott, Australian XI v West Indians at Hobart (Bel)	1996-97
319	J. Dyson and R. B. McCosker, New South Wales v Western Australia at Sydney	1980-81
314	A. C. MacLaren and T. W. Hayward, A. C. MacLaren's XI v NSW at Sydney	1901-02
313	A. J. Richardson and L. T. Gun, South Australia v Western Australia at Adelaide	1925-26
310	G. R. Marsh and M. R. J. Veletta, Western Australia v Tasmania at Hobart (Bel)	1988-89
308	R. B. Simpson and G. Thomas, New South Wales v Western Australia at Sydney	1963-64
301	K. R. Stackpole and G. D. Watson, Australians v Hampshire at Southampton	1972

Second wicket

451	W. H. Ponsford and D. G. Bradman, Australia v England at The Oval	1934
382	L. Hutton and M. Leyland, England v Australia at The Oval	1938
378	L. A. Marks and K. D. Walters, New South Wales v South Australia at Adelaide	1964-65
374	R. B. Simpson and R. M. Cowper, Australians v N. E. Transvaal at Pretoria	1966-67
368	W. Rhodes and C. A. G. Russell, MCC v South Australia at Adelaide	1920-21
368*	M. L. Hayden and M. L. Love, Queensland v Tasmania at Hobart (Bel)	1995-96
365	M. L. Hayden and M. L. Love, Queensland v Tasmania at Brisbane	1995-96

358 C. McKenzie and H. H. L. Kortlang, Victoria v Western Australia at Perth 1909-10
351 G. A. Gooch and D. I. Gower, England v Australia at The Oval 1985
345* G. S. Blewett and C. J. Richards, Australian XI v England XI at Hobart (Bel) 1998-99
334 A. Jackson and D. G. Bradman, New South Wales v South Australia at Adelaide 1930-31
331 R. T. Robinson and D. I. Gower, England v Australia at Birmingham 1985
323 I. D. Craig and R. N. Harvey, New South Wales v Queensland at Sydney 1960-61
314 W. H. Ponsford and H. S. T. L. Hendry, Victoria v Queensland at Melbourne 1927-28
311* W. N. Phillips and D. M. Jones, Victoria v South Australia at Melbourne 1993-94
308 B. A. Richards and I. M. Chappell, South Australia v Western Australia at Perth 1970-71
306 C. L. Badcock and W. J. Horrocks, Combined XI v MCC at Perth 1936-37
304 W. Bardsley and M. A. Noble, New South Wales v Victoria at Sydney 1908-09
302 W. N. Phillips and D. M. Jones, Victoria v South Australia at Melbourne 1991-92
301 A. R. Morris and D. G. Bradman, Australia v England at Leeds 1948

Third wicket

390* J. M. Wiener and J. K. Moss, Victoria v Western Australia at St Kilda 1981-82
389 W. H. Ponsford and S. J. McCabe, Australians v MCC at Lord's 1934
363 D. G. Bradman and A. F. Kippax, New South Wales v Queensland at Sydney 1933-34
362 W. Bardsley and C. G. Macartney, Australians v Essex at Leyton 1912
356 D. G. Bradman and R. A. Hamence, South Australia v Tasmania at Adelaide 1935-36
355 W. Bardsley and V. S. Ransford, Australians v Essex at Leyton 1909
349 D. M. Jones and T. M. Moody, Australians v Warwickshire at Birmingham 1989
345 W. Bardsley and J. M. Taylor, New South Wales v South Australia at Adelaide 1920-21
341 E. J. Barlow and R. G. Pollock, South Africa v Australia at Adelaide 1963-64
330 G. M. Wood and G. R. Marsh, Western Australia v New South Wales at Sydney 1983-84
326 M. L. Love and S. G. Law, Queensland v Tasmania at Brisbane 1994-95
320 W. W. Armstrong and M. A. Noble, Australians v Somerset at Bath 1905
318 G. A. Faulkner and A. W. Nourse, South Africans v New South Wales at Sydney ... 1910-11
315 C. J. Badcock and A. L. Hassett, Australians v Leicestershire at Leicester 1938
310 A. Shrewsbury and W. Gunn, Non Smokers v Smokers at East Melbourne 1886-87
308 R. B. Richardson and I. V. A. Richards, West Indies v Australia at St John's 1983-84
304 K. C. Wessels and G. M. Ritchie, Queensland v Tasmania at Devonport 1981-82
303 M. T. G. Elliott and L. D. Harper, Victoria v New South Wales at North Sydney 1997-98
300 I. M. Chappell and G. S. Chappell, Australians v Barbados at Bridgetown 1972-73

Fourth wicket

462* D. W. Hookes and W. B. Phillips, South Australia v Tasmania at Adelaide 1986-87
424 I. S. Lee and S. O. Quin, Victoria v Tasmania at Melbourne 1933-34
388 W. H. Ponsford and D. G. Bradman, Australia v England at Leeds 1934
377 K. R. Miller and J. H. de Courcy, Australians v Comb. Services at Kingston-on-Thames .. 1953
336 W. M. Lawry and K. D. Walters, Australia v West Indies at Sydney 1968-69
333 E. H. Hendren and W. R. Hammond, MCC v New South Wales at Sydney 1928-29
325 N. C. O'Neill and B. C. Booth, New South Wales v Victoria at Sydney 1957-58
318 J. A. Brayshaw and D. S. Lehmann, South Australia v Western Australia at Adelaide . 1993-94
315 M. A. Noble and E. S. Gregory, New South Wales v Victoria at Sydney 1907-08
306* Javed Miandad and Younis Ahmed, Glamorgan v Australians at Neath 1985
301 L. P. J. O'Brien and L. S. Darling, Victoria v Queensland at Brisbane 1932-33

Fifth wicket

464* M. E. Waugh and S. R. Waugh, New South Wales v Western Australia at Perth 1990-91
405 S. G. Barnes and D. G. Bradman, Australia v England at Sydney 1946-47
397 W. Bardsley and C. Kelleway, New South Wales v South Australia at Sydney 1920-21
385 S. R. Waugh and G. S. Blewett, Australia v South Africa at Johannesburg 1996-97
377* G. P. Thorpe and M. R. Ramprakash, England XI v South Australia at Adelaide 1998-99
376 V. V. S. Laxman and R. S. Dravid, India v Australia at Kolkata 2000-01
344 M. C. Cowdrey and T. W. Graveney, MCC v South Australia at Adelaide 1962-63
344 B. C. Lara, †P. T. Collins and J. C. Adams, West Indies v Australia at Kingston 1998-99
343 R. I. Maddocks and J. Hallebone, Victoria v Tasmania at Melbourne 1951-52
336 W. H. Ponsford and H. S. B. Love, Victoria v Tasmania at Melbourne 1922-23
327 J. L. Langer and R. T. Ponting, Australia v Pakistan at Perth 1999-00
322* A. R. Border and S. R. Waugh, Australia v England at Leeds 1993

319 R. T. Ponting and R. J. Tucker, Tasmania v Westralia Australia at Hobart (Bel) 1994-95
316* L. D. Harper and G. B. Gardiner, Victoria v South Australia at Carlton 1997-98
301* C. E. Pellew and C. B. Willis, AIF Team v Worcestershire at Worcester 1919
301* R. B. Simpson and K. D. Meuleman, Western Australia v New South Wales at Perth ... 1959-60

   † *Retired hurt*

Sixth wicket

428 M. A. Noble and W. W. Armstrong, Australians v Sussex at Hove 1902
365 R. D. Jacobs and B. C. Lara, West Indians v Australia A at Hobart (Bel) 2000-01
346 J. H. W. Fingleton and D. G. Bradman, Australia v England at Melbourne 1936-37
332 N. G. Marks and N. C. O'Neill, New South Wales v South Australia at Sydney 1958-59
323 E. H. Hendren and J. W. H. T. Douglas, MCC v Victoria at Melbourne 1920-21
298* D. B. Vengsarkar and R. J. Shastri, India v Australia at Bombay 1986-87
290 M. T. G. Elliott and D. S. Berry, Victoria v New South Wales at Sydney 1996-97
289 S. J. E. Loxton and D. T. Ring, Victoria v Queensland at Melbourne 1946-47
279 A. L. Hassett and E. A. Williams, Australian Services v Prince's XI at Delhi .. 1945-46
277 O. G. Smith and A. P. Binns, Jamaica v Australians at Kingston 1954-55
271 S. R. Waugh and G. R. J. Matthews, New South Wales v Tasmania at Hobart (Bel) .. 1989-90
269 V. T. Trumper and C. Hill, Australians v New Zealanders at Wellington 1904-05
262 A. Kenny and H. H. I. Kortlang, Victoria v Queensland at Brisbane 1909-10
260* D. M. Jones and S. R. Waugh, Australia v Sri Lanka at Hobart (Bel) 1989-90
260 D. S. Lehmann and T. J. Nielsen, South Australia v Queensland at Adelaide 1996-97
258 V. T. Trumper and F. A. Iredale, New South Wales v Tasmania at Sydney 1898-99
255 G. S. Sobers and B. N. Jarman, South Australia v Western Australia at Perth 1963-64
254 G. N. Yallop and R. D. Robinson, Victoria v Western Australia at Melbourne 1976-77
253 A. F. Kippax and J. G. Morgan, New South Wales v Queensland at Sydney 1927-28

Seventh wicket

347 D. S. Atkinson and C. C. Depeiza, West Indies v Australia at Bridgetown 1954-55
335 C. W. Andrews and E. C. Bensted, Queensland v New South Wales at Sydney 1934-35
273* W. W. Armstrong and J. Darling, Australians v Gentlemen of England at Lord's 1905
268 A. H. Kardar and Imtiaz Ahmed, North Zone v Australian Services at Lahore 1945-46
255 G. Thomas and R. Benaud, New South Wales v Victoria at Melbourne 1961-62
244 W. R. Patrick and C. F. W. Allcott, New Zealanders v New South Wales at Sydney .. 1925-26
232 W. Bruce and H. Trumble, Australians v Oxford and Cambridge Univ. at Portsmouth .. 1893
229 K. J. Schneider and W. A. S. Oldfield, Australians v Canterbury at Christchurch 1927-28
221 D. T. Lindsay and P. L. van der Merwe, South Africa v Australia at Johannesburg .. 1966-67
217 K. D. Walters and G. J. Gilmour, Australia v New Zealand at Christchurch 1976-77
208 C. G. Macartney and A. J. Y. Hopkins, New South Wales v Queensland at Sydney 1906-07
204 G. Shipperd and T. J. Zoehrer, Western Australia v New South Wales at Perth 1982-83
203* B. F. Davison and P. I. Faulkner, Tasmania v Western Australia at Perth 1983-84
202 S. J. E. Loxton and B. A. Barnett, Commonwealth XI v Bombay at Bombay 1953-54
200 Kapil Dev and C. S. Pandit, Indians v Queensland at Brisbane 1991-92

Eighth wicket

433 V. T. Trumper and A. Sims, Australians v Canterbury at Christchurch 1913-14
270 V. T. Trumper and E. P. Barbour, New South Wales v Victoria at Sydney 1912-13
243 M. J. Hartigan and C. Hill, Australia v England at Adelaide 1907-08
242* T. J. Zoehrer and K. H. MacLeay, Western Australia v New South Wales at Perth ... 1990-91
236 R. A. Duff and A. J. Y. Hopkins, New South Wales v Lord Hawke's XI at Sydney 1902-03
218 C. G. Macartney and J. D. Scott, New South Wales v Queensland at Sydney 1913-14
215 W. W. Armstrong and R. L. Park, Victoria v South Australia at Melbourne 1919-20
204 W. A. S. Oldfield and C. O. Nicholls, New South Wales v Victoria at Sydney 1927-28

Ninth wicket

232 C. Hill and E. Walkley, South Australia v New South Wales at Adelaide 1900-01
226 C. Kelleway and W. A. S. Oldfield, New South Wales v Victoria at Melbourne 1925-26
225 W. W. Armstrong and E. A. C. Windsor, Australian XI v The Rest at Sydney 1907-08
221 E. F. Waddy and W. P. Howell, New South Wales v South Australia at Adelaide 1904-05
201 E. E. B. Forssberg and H. S. B. Love, New South Wales v Queensland at Sydney 1920-21

Tenth wicket

307	A. F. Kippax and J. E. H. Hooker, New South Wales v Victoria at Melbourne	1928-29
211	M. Ellis and T. J. Hastings, Victoria v South Australia at Melbourne	1902-03
169	R. B. Minnett and C. G. McKew, New South Wales v Victoria at Sydney	1911-12
154	F. R. Buttsworth and J. P. Lanigan, Western Australia v Victoria at Perth	1921-22
147	C. G. Macartney and S. C. Everett, Australian XI v Tasmania at Hobart (TCA)	1925-26
145	G. A. Rotherham and J. H. Naumann, Cambridge Univ. v AIF Team at Cambridge	1919
138*	B. E. McNamara and P. J. S. Alley, New South Wales v Tasmania at Hobart (Bel)	1996-97
136	J. P. O'Halloran and A. E. Johns, Victoria v South Australia at Melbourne	1896-97
135	W. A. S. Oldfield and A. A. Mailey, New South Wales v South Australia at Adelaide	1923-24
132	R. W. McLeod and C. H. Ross, Victoria v South Australia at Adelaide	1899-00
130	R. E. Foster and W. Rhodes, England v Australia at Sydney	1903-04
127	J. M. Taylor and A. A. Mailey, Australia v England at Sydney	1924-25
124	W. A. S. Oldfield and A. A. Mailey, Australians v Warwickshire at Birmingham	1921
124	J. G. Bracewell and S. L. Boock, New Zealand v Australia at Sydney	1985-86
122	W. G. Ward and N. Dodds, Tasmania v Victoria at Hobart (TCA)	1898-99
120	R. A. Duff and W. W. Armstrong, Australia v England at Melbourne	1901-02
120	A. J. Y. Hopkins and W. H. McIntyre, New South Wales v Queensland at Sydney	1906-07
120	S. L. Saunders and P. M. Clough, Tasmania v Western Australia at Perth	1981-82
119*	W. H. Ponsford and A. J. Richardson, Australians v MCC at Lord's	1926
118	A. Hurwood and P. M. Hornibrook, Australians v Sussex at Hove	1930
118	D. S. Berry and M. W. H. Inness, Victoria v New South Wales at Melbourne	1997-98
116	R. E. Soule and G. D. Campbell, Tasmania v Queensland at Brisbane	1988-89
112	J. J. Kelly and F. J. Laver, Australians v Gloucestershire at Bristol	1905
112	C. Kelleway and H. Carter, New South Wales v South Australia at Adelaide	1920-21
112*	E. E. Hemmings and R. D. Jackman, England XI v South Australia at Adelaide	1982-83
111	M. A. Noble and W. P. Howell, New South Wales v Victoria at Sydney	1896-97
109	A. L. Newell and W. P. Howell, New South Wales v A. E. Stoddart's XI at Sydney	1897-98
105	L. W. Pye and A. J. Bowden, New South Wales v Queensland at Sydney	1899-00
105*	W. T. Walmsley and J. E. Freeman, Queensland v NSW at Brisbane	1957-58
104	K. C. James and H. B. Massey, Wellington v Australians at Wellington	1927-28
104	L. Michael and E. I. Pynor, South Australia v Victoria at Adelaide	1949-50
103	P. A. McAlister and F. A. Tarrant, Victoria v New Zealanders at Melbourne	1898-99
101	G. Giffen and J. P. F. Travers, South Australia v Victoria at Adelaide	1902-03
101	W. W. Armstrong and F. G. Trueman, Victoria v South Australia at Melbourne	1918-19
100	G. E. Palmer and W. H. Cooper, Victoria v New South Wales at Sydney	1881-82
100*	D. Tallon and G. Noblet, D. G. Bradman's XI v A. L. Hassett's XI at Melbourne	1948-49

BOWLING RECORDS

TEN WICKETS IN AN INNINGS

10/43	E. Barrett	The Bowlers v Australians at The Oval	1878
10/66	G. Giffen	Australian XI v The Rest at Sydney	1883-84
10/28	W. P. Howell	Australians v Surrey at The Oval	1899
10/66	A. A. Mailey	Australians v Gloucestershire at Cheltenham	1921
10/37	C. V. Grimmett	Australians v Yorkshire at Sheffield	1930
10/36	T. W. Wall	South Australia v New South Wales at Sydney	1932-33
10/53	J. C. Laker	England v Australia at Manchester	1956
10/88	J. C. Laker	Surrey v Australians at The Oval	1956
10/61	P. J. Allan	Queensland v Victoria at Melbourne	1965-66
10/44	I. J. Brayshaw	Western Australia v Victoria at Perth	1967-68

BEST BOWLING IN AN INNINGS ON FIRST-CLASS DEBUT

9/55	J. Quilty	South Australia v Victoria at Adelaide	1881-82
9/67	H. P. Hay	South Australia v Lord Hawke's XI at Unley	1902-03
8/31	W. Brown	Tasmania v Victoria at Hobart (LRG)	1857-58

8/35	R. Wilson	Queensland v Auckland at Auckland	1896-97
8/36	J. L. Bevan	South Australia v Tasmania at Adelaide	1877-78
8/81	H. V. Hordern	New South Wales v Queensland at Sydney	1905-06
8/111	M. Pierce	New South Wales v South Australia at Adelaide	1892-93

BEST BOWLING IN A MATCH ON FIRST-CLASS DEBUT

15/73	W. Brown	Tasmania v Victoria at Hobart (LRG)	1857-58
14/59	J. L. Bevan	South Australia v Tasmania at Adelaide	1877-78
13/61	T. W. Antill	Victoria v Tasmania at Launceston	1850-51
13/265	M. Pierce	New South Wales v South Australia at Adelaide	1892-93
11/48	S. Cosstick	Victoria v New South Wales at Sydney	1860-61
11/80	J. E. Barrett	Victoria v South Australia at Melbourne	1884-85
11/97	R. Wilson	Queensland v Auckland at Auckland	1896-97
11/103	M. A. Polzin	Queensland v South Australia at Brisbane	1986-87
11/126	D. J. Noonan	New South Wales v Canterbury at Christchurch	1895-96
10/34	G. Elliott	Victoria v New South Wales at Melbourne	1855-56
10/36	J. J. McKone	New South Wales v Victoria at Melbourne	1855-56
10/46	F. D. Stephenson	Tasmania v Victoria at Melbourne	1981-82
10/97	J. Quilty	South Australia v Victoria at Adelaide	1881-82
10/141	R. B. C. Rees	South Australia v Victoria at Melbourne	1903-04
10/145	L. O'B. Fleetwood-Smith	Victoria v Tasmania at Hobart (TCA)	1931-32
10/226	A. C. Facy	Tasmania v Victoria at Hobart (TCA)	1908-09

MOST WICKETS IN A MATCH FOR AUSTRALIAN TEAMS

17/50	C. T. B. Turner	Australians v England XI at Hastings	1888
17/54	W. P. Howell	Australians v Western Province at Cape Town	1902-03
17/201	G. Giffen	South Australia v Victoria at Adelaide	1885-86
16/65	G. Giffen	Australians v Lancashire at Manchester	1886
16/79	C. T. B. Turner	New South Wales v A. Shrewsbury's XI at Sydney	1887-88
16/101	G. Giffen	Australians v Derbyshire at Derby	1886
16/137	R. A. L. Massie	Australia v England at Lord's	1972
16/166	G. Giffen	South Australia v Victoria at Adelaide	1891-92
16/186	G. Giffen	South Australia v New South Wales at Adelaide	1894-95
16/201	G. Giffen	Australians v Derbyshire at Derby	1886
16/289	C. V. Grimmett	South Australia v Queensland at Adelaide	1934-35

HAT-TRICKS

G. H. B. Gilbert	New South Wales v Victoria at Melbourne	1857-58
F. R. Spofforth	Australians v MCC at Lord's	1878
J. Robertson	Middlesex v Australians at Lord's	1878
F. R. Spofforth	Australians v Players of England at The Oval	1878
F. R. Spofforth	Australia v England at Melbourne	1878-79
G. Ulyett (4 in 4)	Lord Hawke's XI v New South Wales at Sydney	1878-79
W. A. Humphreys	Sussex v Australians at Hove	1880
G. E. Palmer	Australians v Sussex at Hove	1882
W. Bates	England v Australia at Melbourne	1882-83
W. A. Humphreys	Sussex v Australians at Hove	1884
G. Giffen	Australians v Lancashire at Manchester	1884
F. R. Spofforth	Australians v South of England at The Oval	1884
C. T. B. Turner	New South Wales v Victoria at Melbourne	1886-87
G. Giffen	South Australia v G. F. Vernon's XI at Adelaide	1887-88
J. Briggs	England v Australia at Sydney	1891-92
H. Trumble	Australians v Gloucestershire at Cheltenham	1896
G. Giffen	Australians v Wembley Park XI at Wembley Park	1896
A. D. Pougher	MCC v Australians at Lord's	1896
T. R. McKibbin	Australians v Lancashire at Liverpool	1896
M. A. Noble	New South Wales v Tasmania at Sydney	1898-99

J. T. Hearne	England v Australia at Leeds	1899
H. Trumble	Australia v England at Melbourne	1901-02
A. J. Y. Hopkins	Australians v Cambridge University at Cambridge	1902
W. P. Howell (4 in 5)	Australians v Western Province at Cape Town	1902-03
W. W. Armstrong	Victoria v New South Wales at Melbourne	1902-03
T. H. Howard (4 in 5)	New South Wales v Queensland at Sydney	1902-03
H. Hay	South Australia v Lord Hawke's XI at Unley	1902-03
A. J. Y. Hopkins	New South Wales v South Australia at Sydney	1903-04
H. Trumble	Australia v England at Melbourne	1903-04
W. P. Howell	Australians v New Zealand XI at Wellington	1904-05
G. A. Wilson	Worcestershire v Australians at Worcester	1905
T. J. Matthews	Victoria v Tasmania at Launceston	1908-09
J. A. Newman	Hampshire v Australians at Southampton	1909
T. J. Matthews (1st inns)	Australia v South Africa at Manchester	1912
T. J. Matthews (2nd inns)	Australia v South Africa at Manchester	1912
T. J. Matthews	Australians v Philadelphia at Philadelphia	1912-13
J. N. Crawford	South Australia v Western Australia at Adelaide	1912-13
C. Kelleway	New South Wales v Queensland at Brisbane	1913-14
J. Horsley	Derbyshire v AIF Team at Derby	1919
J. W. H. T. Douglas	MCC v New South Wales at Sydney	1920-21
A. P. Freeman	MCC v South Australia at Adelaide	1922-23
H. Ironmonger	Victoria v MCC at Melbourne	1924-25
H. I. Ebeling	Victoria v Queensland at Melbourne	1928-29
J. E. H. Hooker (4 in 4)	New South Wales v Victoria at Sydney	1928-29
C. V. Grimmett	South Australia v Queensland at Brisbane (Ex)	1928-29
F. L. Morton	Victoria v Tasmania at Melbourne	1931-32
H. J. Enthoven	Middlesex v Australians at Lord's	1934
R. K. Oxenham	Australians v All Ceylon at Colombo (PSS)	1935-36
M. G. Waite	South Australia v MCC at Adelaide	1935-36
B. Dooland	South Australia v Victoria at Melbourne	1945-46
C. R. Rangachari	Indians v Tasmania at Hobart (TCA)	1947-48
A. K. Walker	New South Wales v Queensland at Sydney	1948-49
H. J. Tayfield	South Africans v Victoria at Melbourne	1952-53
J. C. Treanor	New South Wales v Queensland at Brisbane	1954-55
L. F. Kline	Australia v South Africa at Cape Town	1957-58
G. F. Rorke	New South Wales v Queensland at Sydney	1958-59
L. R. Gibbs	West Indies v Australia at Adelaide	1960-61
A. K. Davidson	New South Wales v Western Australia at Perth	1962-63
D. Robins (4 in 4)	South Australia v New South Wales at Adelaide	1965-66
R. F. Surti	Queensland v Western Australia at Perth	1968-69
R. A. Woolmer	MCC v Australians at Lord's	1975
W. Prior	South Australia v New South Wales at Adelaide	1975-76
A. T. Sincock	South Australia v Indians at Adelaide	1977-78
L. S. Pascoe	New South Wales v South Australia at Adelaide	1980-81
P. M. Clough	Tasmania v New South Wales at Hobart (TCA)	1982-83
J. R. Thomson	Queensland v Western Australia at Brisbane	1984-85
D. R. Gilbert	New South Wales v Victoria at Sydney	1984-85
G. S. Le Roux	South Africans v Australian XI at Johannesburg	1985-86
C. E. B. Rice	South Africans v Australian XI at Johannesburg	1985-86
J. N. Maguire	Australians v Eastern Province at Port Elizabeth	1986-87
C. A. Walsh	West Indies v Australia at Brisbane	1988-89
M. G. Hughes	Australia v West Indies at Perth	1988-89
W. K. M. Benjamin	Leicestershire v Australians at Leicester	1989
W. J. Holdsworth	Australians v Derbyshire at Derby	1993
D. W. Fleming	Australia v Pakistan at Rawalpindi	1994-95
S. K. Warne	Australia v England at Melbourne	1994-95
S. C. G. MacGill	New South Wales v New Zealanders at Newcastle	1997-98
D. Gough	England v Australia at Sydney	1998-99
M. S. Kasprowicz	Queensland v Victoria at Brisbane	1998-99
M. W. H. Inness	Victoria v New South Wales at Melbourne	1999-00
G. D. McGrath	Australia v West Indies at Perth	2000-01
Harbhajan Singh	India v Australia at Kolkata	2000-01

MOST WICKETS IN AN AUSTRALIAN SEASON

	Season	M	B	Mdns	R	W	BB	5Wi	10Wm	Avge
C. T. B Turner (NSW)	1887-88	12	4,267	473	1,441	106	8/39	13	5	13.59
G. Giffen (SAust)	1894-95	11	4,787	196	2,097	93	8/77	12	4	22.54
C. V. Grimmett (SAust) ...	1929-30	11	3,795	51	1,943	82	7/136	9	3	23.69
R. Benaud (NSW)	1958-59	13	4,467	142	1,579	82	7/32	6	1	19.25
A. A. Mailey (NSW)	1920-21	10	2,993	45	1,825	81	9/121	8	3	22.53
M. W. Tate (MCC)	1924-25	14	4,018	93	1,464	77	7/74	7	2	19.01
C. V. Grimmett (SAust) ...	1931-32	12	4,096	166	1,535	77	7/83	7	1	19.93
E. Jones (SAust)	1897-98	11	3,529	121	1,653	76	7/80	9	3	21.75
R. M. Hogg (SAust)	1978-79	14	3,483	97	1,249	76	6/74	6	2	16.43
C. V. Grimmett (SAust) ...	1930-31	11	3,524	99	1,417	74	7/87	7	1	19.14
C. V. Grimmett (SAust) ...	1939-40	9	3,543	57	1,654	73	6/118	10	3	22.65
C. V. Grimmett (SAust) ...	1928-29	10	5,152	135	2,432	71	6/109	5	0	34.25
C. T. B. Turner (NSW) ...	1886-87	7	2,145	273	538	70	8/32	8	3	7.68
W. J. Whitty (SAust)	1910-11	11	2,957	109	1,419	70	6/17	4	0	20.27
H. J. Tayfield (SAf)	1952-53	14	4,836	123	1,954	70	7/71	5	1	27.91
D. K. Lillee (WAust)	1976-77	11	2,832	59	1,368	70	6/26	8	4	19.54
C. R. Miller (Tas)	1997-98	12	3,896	172	1,749	70	7/49	5	2	24.99

50 WICKETS IN AN AUSTRALIAN SEASON

10 Times: C. V. Grimmett 59 (1924-25), 59 (1925-26), 71 (1928-29), 82 (1929-30), 74 (1930-31), 77 (1931-32), 55 (1932-33), 66 (1934-35), 73 (1939-40).

6 Times: D. K. Lillee 56 (1972-73), 62 (1973-74), 62 (1975-76), 70 (1976-77), 69 (1980-81), 59 (1983-84).

5 Times: L. O'B. Fleetwood-Smith 50 (1932-33), 53 (1933-34), 63 (1934-35), 53 (1936-37), 64 (1937-38); A. A. Mallett 54 (1971-72), 62 (1972-73), 57 (1974-75), 56 (1975-76), 53 (1979-80); W. J. O'Reilly 62 (1932-33), 51 (1936-37), 64 (1937-38), 55 (1939-40), 55 (1940-41).

4 Times: C. J. McDermott 58 (1986-87), 54 (1989-90), 67 (1990-91), 66 (1991-92).

3 Times: G. D. McKenzie 51 (1962-63), 53 (1967-68), 60 (1968-69); A. A. Mailey 81 (1920-21), 55 (1922-23), 59 (1924-25); C. D. Matthews 57 (1986-87), 57 (1987-88), 53 (1991-92); J. R. Thomson 62 (1974-75), 62 (1975-76), 57 (1977-78).

MOST WICKETS ON AN AUSTRALIAN OVERSEAS TOUR

			M	O	Mdns	R	W	BB	5Wi	10Wm	Avge
C. T. B. Turner	England	1888	36	2,427.2	1,127	3,307	283	9/15	31	12	11.69
F. R. Spofforth	England	1884	31	1,538.2	646	2,564	201	8/62	24	11	12.75
J. J. Ferris	England	1888	37	2,080.1	937	2,934	199	8/41	17	3	14.74
J. J. Ferris	England	1890	30	1,545.2	628	2,657	186	7/16	15	5	14.28
C. T. B. Turner	England	1890	31	1,500.1	652	2,526	178	7/23	16	4	14.19
F. R. Spofforth	England	1882	30	1,470	646	2,079	157	9/51	16	6	13.24
G. Giffen	England	1886	35	1,673.2	710	2,674	154	9/60	13	5	17.36
C. T. B. Turner	England	1893	26	1,079	413	2,018	148	8/95	16	5	13.64
H. Trumble	England	1896	30	1,140.1	380	2,340	148	7/67	11	5	15.81
C. V. Grimmett	England	1930	26	1,015.1	262	2,427	144	10/37	15	5	16.85
H. Trumble	England	1899	32	1,246.3	432	2,618	142	8/35	10	3	18.44
E. A. McDonald	England	1921	26	809.2	158	2,284	138	8/41	9	3	16.55
H. Trumble	England	1902	20	912	292	1,921	137	9/39	13	7	14.02
E. Jones	England	1899	28	1,163.2	331	2,849	135	7/31	10	4	21.10
A. A. Mailey	England	1921	28	800	103	2,595	133	10/66	7	1	19.51
G. E. Palmer	England	1884	30	1,214.3	446	2,099	130	7/74	13	5	16.14
A. A. Mailey	England	1926	27	816	162	2,437	126	9/86	12	4	19.34
H. F. Boyle	England	1882	27	1,101.2	488	1,523	125	7/32	13	3	12.18
T. W. Garrett	England	1886	34	1,654.1	778	2,221	123	6/22	5	1	18.06
J. V. Saunders	England	1902	25	710	160	2,085	123	6/9	10	3	16.95
W. W. Armstrong	England	1905	30	990.4	298	2,221	122	8/50	9	2	18.20

			M	O	Mdns	R	W	BB	5W/i	10W/m	Avge
E. Jones	England	1896	29	868.3	282	1,940	121	8/39	7	1	16.03
A. Cotter	England	1905	28	735.1	121	2,429	119	7/15	9	2	20.41
T. W. Garrett	England	1882	30	1,167.3	474	1,694	118	7/49	10	1	14.36
G. Giffen	England	1893	29	906.4	257	2,247	118	8/98	12	2	19.04
G. Giffen	England	1896	32	865.2	219	2,257	117	8/30	7	1	19.29
W. P. Howell	England	1899	32	1,119.4	426	2,381	117	10/28	6	2	20.35
J. M. Gregory	England	1921	27	655.4	126	1,924	116	7/52	8	2	16.39
F. J. Laver	England	1905	27	848.1	245	2,092	115	8/75	8	3	18.19
W. W. Armstrong	England	1909	29	857	263	1,852	113	6/35	9	0	16.39
C. V. Grimmett	England	1926	24	857.3	257	1,908	112	7/67	7	1	17.04
W. J. Whitty	England	1912	30	866.3	281	1,971	109	7/40	5	1	18.08
W. J. O'Reilly	England	1934	19	870	320	1,858	109	9/38	7	3	17.04
C. V. Grimmett	England	1934	21	985.4	308	2,159	109	7/109	9	1	19.80
H. Trumble	England	1893	29	834.1	274	1,794	108	7/31	9	3	16.61
L. O'B. Fleetwood-Smith	England	1934	20	713.5	160	2,036	106	7/40	12	3	19.20
W. J. O'Reilly	England	1938	20	709.4	213	1,726	104	8/104	9	2	16.59
W. A. Johnston	England	1948	21	850.1	278	1,675	102	7/81	6	2	16.42
G. E. Palmer	England	1886	33	1,393	552	2,306	101	7/84	6	1	22.83
T. R. McKibbin	England	1896	22	647.1	198	1,441	101	7/11	7	3	14.27
G. E. Palmer	England	1882	21	1,032.3	440	1,535	100	8/84	7	1	15.35
W. W. Armstrong	England	1921	30	733.1	271	1,444	100	7/55	8	1	14.44

Most in countries other than England:

			M	O	Mdns	R	W	BB	5W/i	10W/m	Avge
R. Benaud	SAf	1957-58	18	743.6	187	2,057	106	7/46	11	2	19.40
R. K. Oxenham	India	1935-36	11	303.3	89	555	75	7/13	8	4	7.40
W. W. Armstrong	NZ	1913-14	8	312	81	789	52	7/17	7	1	15.17
S. W. Austin	NZ	1893-94	7	1,747	85	612	52	8/14	6	1	11.77
P. I. Philpott	WI	1964-65	9	449	99	1,207	49	6/86	2	0	24.63
R. J. Bright	Pak	1979-80	5	230.2	72	558	29	7/87	4	2	19.24
J. N. Crawford	NAmer	1913-14	5	116.2	21	359	33	6/40	3	0	10.88
C. J. McDermott	SL	1992-93	5	182	43	514	16	4/53	0	0	32.13
C. R. Miller	SL	1999-00	5	122.3	25	363	16	6/57	1	0	22.69
D. R. Gilbert	Zim	1985-86	2	68	14	215	15	7/43	2	1	14.33

LEADING BOWLERS IN EACH AUSTRALIAN SEASON

(Qualification for top of averages: 20 wickets)

Season	Leading Wicket-Taker	W	Avge	Top of Averages	W	Avge
1850-51	T. W. Antill (Vic)	13	4.00	n/a		
1851-52	W. Henty (Tas)	10	10.00	n/a		
1852-53	no games played					
1853-54	R. M. McDowall (Tas)	8	6.25	n/a		
1854-55	no games played					
1855-56	J. J. McKone (NSW)	10	3.60	n/a		
1855-56	G. Elliott (Vic)	10	3.20	n/a		
1856-57	T. W. Wills (Vic)	10	6.50	n/a		
1857-58	T. W. Wills (Vic)	26	5.03	T. W. Wills (Vic)	26	5.03
1858-59	T. W. Wills (Vic)	11	4.45	n/a		
1859-60	T. W. Wills (Vic)	9	4.33	n/a		
1859-60	G. D. Richardson (NSW)	9	6.00	n/a		
1860-61	S. Cosstick (Vic)	11	4.36	n/a		
1861-62	G. Bennett (The World)	14	8.21	n/a		
1862-63	C. Lawrence (NSW)	14	5.21	n/a		
1863-64	E. M. Grace (Anderson's XI)	9	7.67	n/a		
1864-65	no games played					
1865-66	S. Cosstick (NSW)	8	13.63	n/a		
1865-66	J. Conway (Vic)	8	15.25	n/a		

Season	Leading Wicket-Taker	W	Avge	Top of Averages	W	Avge
1866-67	D. W. Gregory (NSW)	7	9.57	n/a		
1867-68	T. W. Wills (Vic)	9	16.56	n/a		
1868-69	S. Cosstick (Vic)	23	5.42	S. Cosstick (Vic)	23	5.42
1869-70	S. Cosstick (Vic)	10	7.70	n/a		
1870-71	C. A. Reid (Vic)	16	9.50	n/a		
1871-72	F. E. Allan (Vic)	13	4.62	n/a		
1872-73	S. Cosstick (Vic)	23	6.52	S. Cosstick (Vic)	23	6.52
1873-74	no games played					
1874-75	J. Coates (NSW)	15	10.67	n/a		
1875-76	E. Evans (NSW)	21	5.62	E. Evans (NSW)	21	5.62
1876-77	A. Shaw (Lillywhite's XI) ..	17	11.76	n/a		
1877-78	E. Evans (NSW)	18	10.72	n/a		
1878-79	T. Emmett (Eng)	44	11.84	T. Emmett (Eng)	44	11.84
1879-80	W. H. Cooper (Vic)	12	10.75	n/a		
1880-81	E. Evans (NSW)	32	11.25	E. Evans (NSW)	32	11.25
1881-82	G. E. Palmer (Vic)	47	21.55	W. Bates (Eng)	30	17.33
1882-83	G. E. Palmer (Vic)	51	11.53	H. F. Boyle (Vic)	24	11.00
1883-84	G. E. Palmer (Vic)	29	17.51	G. E. Palmer (Vic)	29	17.51
1884-85	R. Peel (England)	35	19.22	W. Barnes (England)	26	13.23
1885-86	F. R. Spofforth (NSW)	18	15.22	n/a		
1886-87	C. T. B. Turner (NSW)	70	7.68	C. T. B. Turner (NSW) ...	70	7.68
1887-88	C. T. B. Turner (NSW)	106	13.59	W. Attewell (Eng)	55	10.72
1888-89	J. J. Ferris (NSW)	36	15.83	G. Giffen (SAust)	22	12.95
1889-90	H. Trumble (Vic)	29	14.21	H. Trumble (Vic)	29	14.21
1890-91	J. Phillips (Vic)	25	10.00	J. Phillips (Vic)	25	10.00
1891-92	G. Giffen (SAust)	50	17.30	W. Attewell (Eng)	44	13.02
1892-93	G. Giffen (SAust)	33	23.00	H. Trumble (Vic)	22	13.55
1893-94	C. T. B. Turner (NSW)	30	12.30	C. T. B. Turner (NSW) ...	30	12.30
1894-95	G. Giffen (SAust)	93	22.54	T. R. McKibbin (NSW) ...	44	16.66
1895-96	T. R. McKibbin (NSW) ...	46	23.87	E. Jones (SAust)	31	17.67
1896-97	T. R. McKibbin (NSW)	44	14.89	T. R. McKibbin (NSW) ...	44	14.89
1897-98	E. Jones (SAust)	76	21.75	W. Roche (Vic)	33	20.73
1898-99	E. Jones (SAust)	45	27.53	C. E. McLeod (Vic)	36	17.86
1899-00	M. A. Noble (NSW)	37	20.65	M. A. Noble (NSW)	37	20.65
1900-01	{J. V. Saunders (Vic)	29	17.14	J. V. Saunders (Vic)	29	17.14
	{J. P. F. Travers (SAust)	29	20.76			
1901-02	L. C. Braund (Eng)	62	28.69	S. F. Barnes (Eng)	41	16.49
1902-03	J. V. Saunders (Vic)	32	20.81	L. W. Pye (NSW)	23	19.30
1903-04	W. Rhodes (MCC)	65	16.23	A. Cotter (NSW)	30	13.47
1904-05	F. B. Collins (Vic)	27	23.37	F. B. Collins (Vic)	27	23.37
1905-06	G. L. Garnsey (NSW)	36	21.03	J. D. A. O'Connor (NSW) .	32	21.70
1906-07	G. L. Garnsey (NSW)	32	21.94	M. A. Noble (NSW)	24	13.92
1907-08	{J. V. Saunders (Vic)	66	24.04	S. F. Barnes (Eng)	54	21.94
	{J. N. Crawford (MCC)	66	25.19			
1908-09	J. D. A. O'Connor (SAust) ..	40	23.00	A. H. Christian (WAust) ..	25	17.28
1909-10	J. V. Saunders (Vic)	49	17.33	J. D. Scott (NSW)	25	12.56
1910-11	W. J. Whitty (SAust)	70	20.27	H. V. Hordern (NSW)	58	14.83
1911-12	F. R. Foster (MCC)	62	20.19	F. R. Foster (MCC)	62	20.19
1912-13	R. J. A. Massie (NSW)	59	18.66	A. A. Mailey (NSW)	21	16.05
1913-14	C. Kelleway (NSW)	45	12.69	C. Kelleway (NSW)	45	12.69
1914-15	H. Ironmonger (Vic)	36	17.53	H. Ironmonger (Vic)	36	17.53
1915-16	no games played					
1916-17	no games played					
1917-18	no games played					
1918-19	E. A. McDonald (Vic)	25	15.72	E. A. McDonald (Vic)	25	15.72
1919-20	H. S. T. L. Hendry (NSW) ...	29	18.14	H. S. T. L. Hendry (NSW) .	29	18.14
1920-21	A. A. Mailey (NSW)	81	22.53	J. M. Gregory (NSW)	43	22.37
1921-22	E. A. McDonald (Vic)	28	21.50	P. H. Wallace (Vic)	20	17.85
1922-23	A. A. Mailey (NSW)	55	21.64	A. E. Liddicut (Vic)	20	21.05
1923-24	{A. E. V. Hartkopf (Vic)	26	24.58	A. E. V. Hartkopf (Vic) ...	26	24.58
	{N. L. Williams (SAust)	26	26.88			

Season	Leading Wicket-Taker	W	Avge	Top of Averages	W	Avge
1924-25	M. W. Tate (MCC)	77	19.01	R. K. Oxenham (Qld)	22	14.50
1925-26	C. V. Grimmett (SAust)	59	30.41	C. G. Macartney (NSW)	24	18.88
1926-27	N. L. Williams (SAust)	35	32.03	D. D. Blackie (Vic)	33	24.64
1927-28	C. V. Grimmett (SAust)	42	27.40	D. D. Blackie (Vic)	31	22.23
1928-29	C. V. Grimmett (SAust)	71	34.25	J. C. White (MCC)	65	22.63
1929-30	C. V. Grimmett (SAust)	82	23.69	E. L. A'Beckett (Vic)	27	15.22
1930-31	C. V. Grimmett (SAust)	74	19.14	H. Ironmonger (Vic)	68	14.29
1931-32	C. V. Grimmett (SAust)	77	19.93	L. O'B. Fleetwood-Smith (Vic)	37	16.27
1932-33	W. J. O'Reilly (NSW)	62	19.95	C. J. Hill (NSW)	22	15.27
1933-34	C. V. Grimmett (SAust)	66	21.83	S. A. J. Smith (Vic)	20	17.90
1934-35	L. O'B. Fleetwood-Smith (Vic)	63	20.34	H. C. Chilvers (NSW)	46	18.63
1935-36	F. A. Ward (SAust)	50	20.94	T. W. Wall (SAust)	22	17.09
1936-37	{ L. O'B. Fleetwood-Smith (Vic)	53	20.25	J. G. Lush (NSW)	27	17.89
	F. A. Ward (SAust) }	53	28.41			
1937-38	{ W. J. O'Reilly (NSW)	64	12.25	W. J. O'Reilly (NSW)	64	12.25
	L. O'B. Fleetwood-Smith (Vic) }	64	22.43			
1938-39	L. O'B. Fleetwood-Smith (Vic)	30	39.73	C. V. Grimmett (SAust)	27	20.85
1939-40	C. V. Grimmett (SAust)	73	22.65	W. J. O'Reilly (NSW)	55	15.13
1940-41	W. J. O'Reilly (NSW)	55	12.43	W. J. O'Reilly (NSW)	55	12.43
1941-42	W. J. O'Reilly (NSW)	9	13.78	n/a		
1942-43	no games played					
1943-44	no games played					
1944-45	no games played					
1945-46	G. E. Tribe (Vic)	40	19.03	W. J. O'Reilly (NSW)	33	14.36
1946-47	D. V. P. Wright (MCC)	51	33.31	R. R. Lindwall (NSW)	39	22.08
1947-48	M. H. Mankad (Ind)	61	26.14	G. Noblet (SAust)	40	19.43
1948-49	I. W. G. Johnson (Vic)	43	24.12	A. K. Walker (NSW)	39	15.31
1949-50	J. B. Iverson (Vic)	46	16.52	J. B. Iverson (Vic)	46	16.52
1950-51	A. E. Bedser (MCC)	51	19.80	R. H. Price (WAust)	24	18.42
1951-52	W. A. Johnston (Vic)	54	20.63	R. R. Lindwall (NSW)	42	17.33
1952-53	H. J. Tayfield (SAf)	70	27.91	G. Noblet (SAust)	55	17.84
1953-54	I. W. G. Johnson (Vic)	45	22.76	R. R. Lindwall (Qld)	22	20.14
1954-55	F. H. Tyson (MCC)	51	19.64	W. P. A. Crawford (NSW)	34	16.03
1955-56	R. Benaud (NSW)	44	21.61	W. P. A. Crawford (NSW)	35	19.80
1956-57	L. F. Kline (Vic)	39	28.21	I. W. Meckiff (Vic)	27	23.67
1957-58	I. W. Quick (Vic)	32	27.25	N. C. O'Neill (NSW)	26	20.42
1958-59	R. Benaud (NSW)	82	19.25	J. C. Laker (MCC)	38	17.23
1959-60	J. W. Martin (NSW)	45	23.64	R. A. Gaunt (WAust)	24	16.75
1960-61	A. K. Davidson (NSW)	47	20.87	A. K. Davidson (NSW)	47	20.87
1961-62	R. Benaud (NSW)	47	17.97	A. K. Davidson (NSW)	42	13.61
1962-63	I. W. Meckiff (Vic)	58	19.86	I. W. Meckiff (Vic)	58	19.86
1963-64	R. H. D. Sellers (SAust)	54	26.57	P. I. Philpott (NSW)	30	25.73
1964-65	N. J. N. Hawke (SAust)	41	26.29	D. E. Hoare (WAust)	29	22.86
1965-66	N. J. N. Hawke (SAust)	49	25.73	O. J. Morgan (Qld)	25	19.20
1966-67	G. A. R. Lock (WAust)	51	21.29	R. C. Bitmead (Vic)	33	19.66
1967-68	A. N. Connolly (Vic)	60	20.18	L. C. Mayne (WAust)	20	15.10
1968-69	G. D. McKenzie (WAust)	60	27.66	P. J. Allan (Qld)	46	16.37
1969-70	A. L. Thomson (Vic)	55	18.74	A. L. Thomson (Vic)	55	18.74
1970-71	A. L. Thomson (Vic)	51	30.09	J. R. Hammond (SAust)	34	20.26
1971-72	A. A. Mallett (SAust)	54	19.64	A. A. Mallett (SAust)	54	19.64
1972-73	A. A. Mallett (SAust)	62	19.09	G. D. Watson (WAust)	20	18.40
1973-74	G. Dymock (Qld)	51	19.88	R. J. Bright (Vic)	32	19.66
1974-75	{ J. R. Thomson (Qld)	62	19.37	J. R. Thomson (Qld)	62	19.37
	D. K. Lillee (WAust) }	62	25.14			
1975-76	{ J. R. Thomson (Qld)	62	23.75	W. Prior (SAust)	43	19.67
	D. K. Lillee (WAust) }	62	24.03			
1976-77	D. K. Lillee (WAust)	70	19.54	J. R. Thomson (Qld)	27	14.00
1977-78	J. R. Thomson (Qld)	57	21.86	I. J. Brayshaw (WAust)	35	18.03
1978-79	R. M. Hogg (SAust)	76	16.43	P. H. Carlson (Qld)	31	15.90
1979-80	A. A. Mallett (SAust)	53	28.30	J. Garner (WI)	32	20.03
1980-81	D. K. Lillee (WAust)	69	21.18	L. S. Pascoe (NSW)	63	19.52

Season	Leading Wicket-Taker	W	Avge	Top of Averages	W	Avge
1981-82	B. Yardley (WAust)	49	22.55	J. Garner (WI)	23	16.17
1982-83	G. F. Lawson (NSW)	65	21.04	C. G. Rackemann (Qld) ...	35	15.80
1983-84	D. K. Lillee (WAust)	59	25.64	C. G. Rackemann (Qld) ...	28	18.68
1984-85	R. G. Holland (NSW)	59	25.80	Imran Khan (Pak)	28	19.14
1985-86	R. G. Holland (NSW)	48	32.40	R. J. Hadlee (NZ)	37	14.51
1986-87	C. J. McDermott (Qld)	58	22.34	G. C. Small (England) ...	33	18.97
1987-88	C. D. Matthews (WAust) ...	57	22.40	G. F. Lawson (NSW)	42	18.86
1988-89	M. R. Whitney (NSW)	58	23.62	T. M. Alderman (WAust) ..	48	20.94
1989-90	C. G. Rackemann (Qld)	50	21.48	C. D. Matthews (WAust) ..	42	19.19
1990-91	C. J. McDermott (Qld)	67	19.46	A. I. C. Dodemaide (Vic) ..	20	12.25
1991-92	C. J. McDermott (Qld)	60	20.80	D. A. Freedman (NSW) ...	22	18.59
1992-93	W. J. Holdsworth (NSW) ...	53	25.96	C. E. L. Ambrose (WI)	38	18.13
1993-94	S. K. Warne (Vic)	63	19.92	S. K. Warne (Vic)	63	19.92
1994-95	C. G. Rackemann (Qld)	52	23.60	S. K. Warne (Vic)	40	20.35
1995-96	M. S. Kasprowicz (Qld)	64	20.47	A. M. Stuart (NSW)	25	13.40
1996-97	M. S. Kasprowicz (Qld)	48	25.54	J. C. Scuderi (SAust)	23	17.34
1997-98	C. R. Miller (Tas)	70	24.99	D. W. Fleming (Vic)	39	18.08
1998-99	D. J. Saker (Vic)	45	23.31	A. C. Dale (Qld)	31	17.10
1999-00	A. J. Bichel (Qld)	60	20.12	M. S. Kasprowicz (Qld) ...	49	14.41
2000-01	{ A. J. Bichel (Qld)	49	23.35	J. H. Dawes (Qld)	49	20.47
	{ J. H. Dawes (Qld)	49	20.47			

BEST BOWLING AVERAGE IN AN AUSTRALIAN SEASON
(Minimum 30 wickets)

		M	B	Mdns	R	W	BB	5Wi	10Wm	Avge
C. T. B. Turner (NSW)	1886-87	7	2,145	273	538	70	8/32	8	3	7.68
W. Attewell (Eng)	1887-88	9	3,086	425	590	54	7/15	4	2	10.92
E. Evans (NSW)	1880-81	4	1,749	251	360	32	5/34	5	1	11.25
G. E. Palmer (Vic)	1882-83	7	1,772	201	588	51	7/65	5	2	11.53
T. Emmett (Eng)	1878-79	5	1,933	255	521	44	8/47	6	2	11.84
G. A. Lohmann (Eng)	1887-88	8	2,667	364	755	63	7/43	7	2	11.98
W. J. O'Reilly (NSW)	1937-38	11	2,487	91	784	64	9/41	6	2	12.25
C. T. B. Turner (NSW)	1893-94	3	940	35	369	30	6/51	5	2	12.30
W. J. O'Reilly (NSW)	1940-41	8	1,838	448	684	55	6/60	5	0	12.43
C. Kelleway (NSW)	1913-14	7	1,498	76	571	45	7/35	3	1	12.69
W. Attewell (Eng)	1891-92	8	2,858	241	573	44	6/34	4	1	13.02
J. Briggs (Eng))	1891-92	8	1,212	71	420	32	6/49	4	1	13.13
A. Cotter (NSW)	1903-04	5	740	18	404	30	6/40	2	0	13.47
C. T. B. Turner (NSW)	1887-88	12	4,267	473	1,441	106	8/39	12	5	13.59
A. K. Davidson (NSW)	1961-62	9	1,696	52	572	42	7/31	2	0	13.61
H. Ironmonger (Vic)	1930-31	10	3,037	112	972	68	8/31	7	4	14.29
W. J. O'Reilly (NSW)	1945-46	6	1,257	20	474	33	6/43	1	0	14.36
M. S. Kasprowicz (Qld)	1999-00	8	1,485	69	706	49	5/32	4	1	14.41
R. J. Hadlee (NZ)	1985-86	5	1,449	65	537	37	9/52	5	2	14.51
J. Briggs (Eng)	1887-88	8	2,263	215	436	30	6/40	2	1	14.53
J. J. Ferris (NSW)	1886-87	7	1,967	224	689	47	5/28	3	0	14.66
H. V. Hordern (NSW)	1910-11	8	1,448	29	860	58	7/31	6	2	14.83
T. R. McKibbin (NSW)	1896-97	4	1,381	46	655	44	8/74	5	2	14.89

AUSTRALIANS WITH 400 WICKETS IN FIRST-CLASS CAREER

		M	R	W	BB	5Wi	10Wm	Avge
A. E. Trott	1892-93 – 1911	375	35,317	1,674	10/42	131	41	21.09
F. A. Tarrant	1898-99 – 1936-37	329	26,391	1,506	10/90	133	38	17.52
C. V. Grimmett	1911-12 – 1940-41	248	31,740	1,424	10/37	127	33	22.28
E. A. McDonald	1909-10 – 1935	281	28,966	1,395	8/41	119	31	20.76
G. E. Tribe	1945-46 – 1959	308	28,321	1,378	9/43	93	23	20.55
G. D. McKenzie	1959-60 – 1975	383	32,868	1,219	8/71	49	5	26.96
J. E. Walsh	1936-37 – 1956	296	29,226	1,190	9/101	98	26	24.56
S. M. J. Woods	1886 – 1910	401	21,653	1,040	10/69	77	21	20.82

		M	R	W	BB	5Wi	10W/m	Avge
G. Giffen	1877-78 – 1903-04	251	21,782	1,023	10/66	95	30	21.29
B. Dooland	1945-46 – 1957-58	214	22,332	1,016	8/20	84	23	21.98
C. T. B. Turner	1882-83 – 1909-10	155	14,147	993	9/15	102	35	14.24
V. E. Jackson	1936-37 – 1958	354	23,874	965	8/43	43	6	24.73
T. M. Alderman	1974-75 – 1992-93	245	22,701	956	8/46	53	8	23.74
R. Benaud	1948-49 – 1967-68	259	23,370	945	7/18	56	9	24.73
H. Trumble	1887-88 – 1903-04	344	17,134	929	9/39	69	25	18.44
D. K. Lillee	1969-70 – 1988	198	20,696	882	8/29	50	13	23.46
F. R. Spofforth	1874-75 – 1897	155	12,759	853	9/18	84	32	14.95
W. W. Armstrong	1898-99 – 1921-22	269	16,406	832	8/47	50	5	19.71
J. J. Ferris	1886-87 – 1897-98	198	14,260	813	8/41	63	11	17.53
R. R. Lindwall	1941-42 – 1961-62	228	16,956	794	7/20	34	2	21.35
A. A. Mailey	1912-13 – 1930-31	158	18,778	779	10/66	61	16	24.10
W. J. O'Reilly	1927-28 – 1945-46	135	12,850	774	9/38	63	17	16.60
W. E. Alley	1945-46 – 1968	400	17,421	768	8/65	30	1	22.68
J. A. Cuffe	1902-03 – 1914	221	18,798	738	9/38	33	7	25.47
S. K. Warne	1990-91 – 2001	174	19,039	716	8/71	33	4	26.59
A. A. Mallett	1967-68 – 1980-81	183	18,208	693	8/59	33	5	26.27
C. J. McDermott	1983-84 – 1995-96	174	19,025	677	8/44	37	4	28.10
A. N. Connolly	1959-60 – 1970-71	201	17,974	676	9/67	25	4	26.58
J. R. Thomson	1972-73 – 1985-86	187	17,864	675	7/27	28	3	26.46
A. K. Davidson	1949-50 – 1962-63	193	14,048	672	7/31	33	2	20.90
G. F. Lawson	1977-78 – 1991-92	191	16,564	666	8/112	28	2	24.87
E. Jones	1892-93 – 1907-08	144	14,638	641	8/39	47	9	22.83
M. A. Noble	1893-94 – 1919-20	248	14,445	625	8/48	33	7	23.11
I. W. G. Johnson	1935-36 – 1956-57	189	14,423	619	7/42	27	4	23.30
C. G. Rackemann	1979-80 – 1995-96	167	16,629	616	8/84	22	3	26.99
C. L. McCool	1939-40 – 1960	251	16,542	602	8/74	34	2	27.47
L. O. Fleetwood-Smith	1931-32 – 1939-40	112	13,519	597	9/36	57	18	22.64
G. E. Palmer	1878-79 – 1896-97	133	10,520	594	8/48	54	16	17.71
M. G. Hughes	1981-82 – 1994-95	165	17,249	593	8/87	21	3	29.09
G. D. McGrath	1992-93 – 2001	126	11,642	566	8/38	30	7	20.57
W. A. Johnston	1945-46 – 1954-55	142	12,936	554	8/52	29	6	23.35
J. V. Saunders	1899-00 – 1913-14	107	12,064	553	8/106	48	9	21.81
M. S. Kasprowicz	1989-90 – 2000-01	144	14,787	550	7/36	31	3	26.89
P. R. Reiffel	1987-88 – 2000-01	163	14,112	535	6/57	16	2	26.38
A. I. C. Dodemaide	1983-84 – 1997-98	184	17,096	534	6/58	17	0	32.01
W. P. Howell	1894-95 – 1905-06	141	11,157	520	10/28	30	5	21.45
G. R. J. Matthews	1982-83 – 1997-98	190	16,413	516	8/52	22	5	31.81
J. S. Manning	1951-52 – 1960	144	11,662	513	8/43	25	4	22.73
J. M. Gregory	1919 – 1928-29	129	10,580	504	9/32	33	8	20.99
M. H. N. Walker	1968-69 – 1981-82	135	13,209	499	8/143	21	0	26.47
K. R. Miller	1937-38 – 1959	226	11,087	497	7/12	16	1	22.30
W. J. Whitty	1907-08 – 1925-26	119	11,488	491	8/27	26	4	23.39
K. J. O'Keeffe	1968-69 – 1979-80	169	13,382	476	7/38	24	5	28.11
R. J. Bright	1972-73 – 1987-88	184	15,114	471	7/87	24	2	32.08
H. Ironmonger	1909-10 – 1935-36	96	9,980	464	8/31	36	10	21.50
N. J. N. Hawke	1959-60 – 1970-71	145	12,088	458	8/61	23	5	26.39
D. T. Ring	1938-39 – 1953	129	12,847	451	7/88	21	2	28.48
T. W. Garrett	1876-77 – 1897-98	160	8,353	445	7/38	29	5	18.77
J. W. Martin	1956-57 – 1967-68	135	13,872	445	8/97	17	1	31.17
A. Cotter	1901-02 – 1913-14	113	10,730	442	7/15	31	4	24.27
T. B. A. May	1984-85 – 1995-96	142	15,721	439	7/93	19	2	35.81
B. P. Julian	1989-90 – 2000-01	138	13,295	435	7/39	21	2	30.56
C. R. Miller	1985-86 – 2001	119	13,015	432	7/49	16	3	30.13
J. W. Gleeson	1966-67 – 1974-75	116	10,729	430	7/52	22	2	24.95
G. Dymock	1971-72 – 1981-82	126	11,438	425	7/67	13	1	26.91
W. E. Midwinter	1874-75 – 1886-87	160	7,298	419	7/27	27	3	17.41
C. G. Macartney	1905-06 – 1935-36	249	8,781	419	7/58	17	1	20.95
M. R. Whitney	1980-81 – 1994-95	118	11,023	412	7/27	19	1	26.75
J. Angel	1991-92 – 2000-01	98	9,846	405	6/64	14	1	24.31
F. J. Laver	1891-92 – 1913-14	163	9,989	404	8/31	19	5	24.72

MOST BALLS BOWLED IN AN INNINGS

Balls	M	R	W		
571	36	155	3	T. R. Veivers, Australia v England at Manchester	1964
522	12	309	5	G. Giffen, South Australia v A. E. Stoddart's XI at Adelaide	1894-95
522	11	298	1	L. O'B. Fleetwood-Smith, Australia v England at The Oval ..	1938
512	0	362	4	A. A. Mailey, New South Wales v Victoria at Melbourne	1926-27
510	26	178	3	W. J. O'Reilly, Australia v England at The Oval	1938
501	35	150	6	G. Giffen, South Australia v New South Wales at Adelaide ..	1890-91

MOST BALLS BOWLED IN A MATCH

Balls	M	R	W		
848	14	394	10	C. V. Grimmett, South Australia v New South Wales at Sydney .	1925-26
749	37	256	13	J. C. White, England v Australia at Adelaide	1928-29
748	22	255	10	D. D. Blackie, Victoria v South Australia at Adelaide	1926-27
736	16	267	9	C. V. Grimmett, South Australia v Victoria at Adelaide	1924-25
725	58	152	11	R. W. McLeod, Victoria v New South Wales at Melbourne ..	1892-93
712	19	228	11	M. W. Tate, England v Australia at Sydney	1924-25
708	42	239	8	G. Giffen, Australia v England at Sydney	1894-95

MOST RUNS CONCEDED IN A MATCH

Runs		
394 (4/192, 6/202)	C. V. Grimmett, South Australia v New South Wales at Sydney ...	1925-26
362 (4/362)	A. A. Mailey, New South Wales v Victoria at Melbourne	1926-27
345 (3/190, 0/155)	J. D. Scott, South Australia v New South Wales at Sydney	1925-26
326 (6/134, 5/192)	N. L. Williams, South Australia v Victoria at Adelaide	1928-29
322 (5/309, 0/13)	G. Giffen, South Australia v A. E. Stoddart's XI at Adelaide	1894-95
308 (4/129, 3/179)	A. A. Mailey, Australia v England at Sydney	1924-25
302 (5/160, 5/142)	A. A. Mailey, Australia v England at Adelaide	1920-21

ALL-ROUND RECORDS

100 RUNS IN AN INNINGS AND TEN WICKETS IN A MATCH

R. G. Barlow	101	10/48	North of England v Australians at Nottingham	1884
G. Giffen	166	14/125	South Australia v Victoria at Adelaide	1887-88
G. Giffen	135	13/159	South Australia v Victoria at Melbourne	1888-89
G. Giffen	237	12/192	South Australia v Victoria at Melbourne	1890-91
G. Giffen	271	16/165	South Australia v Victoria at Adelaide	1891-92
G. Giffen	120	12/150	South Australia v New South Wales at Sydney	1891-92
G. Giffen	181	11/235	South Australia v Victoria at Adelaide	1892-93
W. W. Armstrong .	126*	10/52	Australians v New Zealanders at Christchurch	1904-05
P. H. Carlson	102*	10/73	Queensland v New South Wales at Brisbane	1978-79
J. C. Scuderi.....	110	10/165	South Australia v New South Wales at Adelaide	1991-92

500 RUNS AND 50 WICKETS IN AN AUSTRALIAN SEASON

		M	R	Avge	W	Avge
G. Giffen (South Australia)	1891-92	6	509	50.90	50	17.30
G. Giffen (South Australia)	1894-95	11	902	50.11	93	22.55
L. C. Braund (MCC).	1907-08	16	783	35.59	50	32.88
J. N. Crawford (MCC)	1907-08	16	610	26.52	66	25.20
F. R. Foster (MCC).	1911-12	13	641	35.61	62	20.19
M. H. Mankad (Indians)	1947-48	13	889	38.65	61	26.15
G. S. Sobers (South Australia) ...	1962-63	10	1,001	52.68	51	26.56
G. S. Sobers (South Australia) ...	1963-64	9	1,128	80.57	51	28.25
G. R. J. Matthews (NSW).	1991-92	12	603	40.20	52	21.46
G. R. J. Matthews (NSW).	1992-93	13	625	36.76	51	28.92

10,000 RUNS AND 500 WICKETS IN A CAREER

	M	R	Avge	W	Avge
W. E. Alley	400	19,612	31.88	768	22.68
W. W. Armstrong	269	16,158	46.83	832	19.71
R. Benaud	259	11,719	36.50	945	23.74
G. Giffen	251	11,758	29.54	1,023	21.29
V. E. Jackson	354	15,698	28.43	965	24.73
C. L. McCool	251	12,420	32.85	602	27.47
M. A. Noble	248	13,975	40.74	625	23.11
F. A. Tarrant	326	17,857	36.37	1,489	17.66
G. E. Tribe	308	10,177	27.34	1,378	20.55
A. E. Trott	375	10,696	19.48	1,674	21.09

WICKET-KEEPING RECORDS

MOST DISMISSALS IN AN INNINGS

8	(all ct)	A. T. W. Grout, Queensland v Western Australia at Brisbane	1959-60
8	(6ct, 2st)	T. J. Zoehrer, Australians v Surrey at The Oval	1993
8	(7ct, 1st)	D. S. Berry, Victoria v South Australia at Melbourne	1996-97
7	(3ct, 4st)	D. Tallon, Queensland v Victoria at Brisbane	1938-39
7	(all ct)	R. A. Saggers, New South Wales v Combined XI at Brisbane	1940-41
7	(6ct, 1st)	H. B. Taber, New South Wales v South Australia at Adelaide	1968-69
7	(all ct)	J. A. Maclean, Queensland v Victoria at Melbourne	1977-78
7	(6ct, 1st)	R. B. Phillips, Queensland v New Zealanders at Brisbane	1982-83
7	(all ct)	J. M. Holyman, Tasmania v Western Australia at Hobart (Bel)	1990-91
7	(all ct)	A. C. Gilchrist, Western Australia v South Australia at Perth	1995-96

MOST DISMISSALS IN A MATCH

12	(9ct, 3st)	D. Tallon, Queensland v New South Wales at Sydney	1938-39
12	(9ct, 3st)	H. B. Taber, New South Wales v South Australia at Adelaide	1968-69
11	(all ct)	R. W. Marsh, Western Australia v Victoria at Perth	1975-76
11	(all ct)	T. J. Nielsen, South Australia v Western Australia at Perth	1990-91
11	(10ct, 1st)	I. A. Healy, Australians v N. Transvaal at Verwoerdburg	1993-94
11	(all ct)	D. S. Berry, Victoria v Pakistanis at Melbourne	1995-96
11	(10ct, 1st)	W. A. Seccombe, Queensland v Western Australia at Brisbane	1995-96
11	(10ct, 1st)	D. S. Berry, Victoria v South Australia at Melbourne	1996-97
10	(all ct)	A. C. Gilchrist, Australia v New Zealand at Hamilton	1999-00
10	(9ct, 1st)	R. A. Saggers, New South Wales v Combined XI at Brisbane	1940-41
10	(7ct, 3st)	B. N. Jarman, South Australia v New South Wales at Adelaide	1961-62
10	(9ct, 1st)	R. C. Jordon, Victoria v South Australia at Melbourne	1970-71
10	(all ct)	R. W. Marsh, Western Australia v South Australia at Perth	1976-77
10	(all ct)	S. J. Rixon, Australian XI v South Africa at Johannesburg	1985-86
10	(all ct)	S. J. Rixon, Australian XI v South Africa at Johannesburg	1986-87
10	(7ct, 3st)	A. C. Gilchrist, Young Australia v TCCB XI at Birmingham	1995
10	(all ct)	P. J. Roach, Victoria v South Australia at Melbourne	1995-96
10	(all ct)	A. C. Gilchrist, Western Australia v Victoria at Perth	1997-98
10	(all ct)	A. C. Gilchrist, Australia v New Zealand at Hamilton	1999-00

MOST DISMISSALS IN AN AUSTRALIAN SEASON

Total	Ct	St	M		
67	63	4	15	R. W. Marsh (Western Australia)	1975-76
67	64	3	13	W. A. Seccombe (Queensland)	1999-00
64	58	6	14	R. W. Marsh (Western Australia)	1974-75
62	58	4	12	A. C. Gilchrist (Western Australia)	1995-96
62	60	2	12	A. C. Gilchrist (Western Australia)	1996-97
61	59	2	14	R. W. Marsh (Western Australia)	1980-81
61	61	0	13	R. W. Marsh (Western Australia)	1982-83
59	54	5	13	R. W. Marsh (Western Australia)	1983-84
59	57	2	9	W. A. Seccombe (Queensland)	1995-96

Total	Ct	St	M		
58	57	1	11	W. A. Seccombe (Queensland)	2000-01
57	53	4	13	K. J. Wright (Western Australia)	1978-79
56	55	1	12	R. B. Phillips (Queensland)	1984-85
55	55	0	11	A. C. Gilchrist (Western Australia)	1994-95
54	52	2	13	P. A. Emery (New South Wales)	1992-93
54	52	2	11	D. S. Berry (Victoria)	1999-00
53	53	0	11	R. W. Marsh (Western Australia)	1976-77

AUSTRALIANS WITH 300 DISMISSALS IN A CAREER

	Career	M	Ct	St	Total
R. W. Marsh	1968-69 – 1983-84	241	788	66	854
I. A. Healy	1986-87 – 1999-00	231	698	69	767
W. A. S. Oldfield	1919 – 1937-38	238	396	262	658
A. T. W. Grout	1946-47 – 1965-55	178	471	114	585
B. N. Jarman	1955-56 – 1968-69	186	426	129	555
D. S. Berry	1989-90 – 2000-01	128	468	42	510
S. J. Rixon	1974-75 – 1987-88	150	395	64	459
T. J. Zoehrer	1980-81 – 1993-94	144	411	38	449
J. M. Blackham	1874-75 – 1894-95	250	259	181	440
D. Tallon	1933-34 – 1953-54	150	302	131	433
A. C. Gilchrist	1992-93 – 2001	99	407	23	430
H. B. Taber	1964-65 – 1973-74	125	341	50	391
P. A. Emery	1987-88 – 1998-99	121	337	47	384
J. A. Maclean	1968-69 – 1978-79	106	352	29	381
G. R. A. Langley	1945-46 – 1956-57	120	291	77	368
B. A. Barnett	1929-30 – 1961	173	216	142	358
J. J. Kelly	1894-95 – 1906-07	180	243	112	355
W. A. Seccombe	1992-93 – 2001	70	326	14	340
R. D. Robinson	1971-72 – 1981-82	97	289	40	329
C. W. Walker	1928-29 – 1940-41	109	171	149	320
T. J. Nielsen	1990-91 – 1998-99	101	284	32	315

FIELDING RECORDS

MOST CATCHES IN AN INNINGS

6	J. F. Sheppard	Queensland v New South Wales at Brisbane	1914-15

Note: There are 13 instances of 5 catches in an innings.

MOST CATCHES IN A MATCH

7	J. A. Atkinson	Tasmania v Victoria at Melbourne	1928-29
7	E. W. Freeman	South Australia v Western Australia at Adelaide	1971-72
7	G. S. Chappell	Australia v England at Perth	1974-75
7	M. A. Taylor	New South Wales v Victoria at Melbourne	1995-96

Note: There are 15 instances of 6 catches in a match.

MOST CATCHES IN AN AUSTRALIAN SEASON

Ct	M		
27	14	I. M. Chappell (South Australia)	1968-69
26	13	G. B. Hole (South Australia)	1952-53
26	13	M. A. Taylor (New South Wales)	1997-98
25	16	L. C. Braund (MCC)	1907-08
25	14	M. A. Taylor (New South Wales)	1991-92
24	11	L. C. Braund (A. C. MacLaren's XI)	1901-02
24	12	J. M. Gregory (New South Wales)	1920-21
24	15	R. B. Simpson (Western Australia)	1960-61
24	11	R. B. Simpson (New South Wales)	1967-68
24	14	I. M. Chappell (South Australia)	1974-75

Ct	M		
24	14	G. S. Chappell (Queensland)	1974-75
24	14	G. S. Chappell (Queensland)	1980-81
24	13	S. R. Waugh (New South Wales)	1986-87
24	13	M. R. J. Veletta (Western Australia)	1987-88
24	11	M. A. Taylor (New South Wales)	1995-96

AUSTRALIANS WITH 200 CATCHES IN A CAREER

	Career	M	Ct
K. J. Grieves	1945-46 – 1964	490	610
A. E. Trott	1892-93 – 1911	375	452
M. E. Waugh	1985-86 – 2001	324	387
R. B. Simpson	1952-53 – 1977-78	257	383
A. R. Border	1976-77 – 1995-96	385	379
G. S. Chappell	1966-67 – 1983-84	322	376
M. A. Taylor	1985-86 – 1998-99	253	350
H. Trumble	1887-88 – 1903-04	213	328
I. M. Chappell	1961-62 – 1979-80	263	312
F. A. Tarrant	1898-99 – 1936-37	329	304
T. M. Moody	1985-86 – 2000-01	300	294
W. E. Alley	1945-46 – 1968	400	293
D. C. Boon	1978-79 – 1999	350	283
S. M. J. Woods	1886 – 1910	401	279
W. W. Armstrong	1898-99 – 1921-22	269	274
K. C. Wessels	1973-74 – 1999-00	316	268
S. G. Law	1988-89 – 2001	229	263
C. L. McCool	1939-40 – 1960	251	262
R. Benaud	1948-49 – 1967-68	259	255
V. E. Jackson	1936-37 – 1958	354	250
R. J. Inverarity	1962-63 – 1984-85	223	250
G. E. Tribe	1945-46 – 1959	308	242
S. R. Waugh	1984-85 – 2001	299	239
R. N. Harvey	1946-47 – 1962-63	306	228
V. Y. Richardson	1918-19 – 1937-38	184	213
I. R. Redpath	1961-62 – 1975-76	226	211
J. E. Walsh	1936-37 – 1956	296	209
J. D. Siddons	1984-85 – 1999-00	160	206
G. D. McKenzie	1959-60 – 1975	383	201

TEAM RECORDS

HIGHEST INNINGS TOTALS

1,107	Victoria v New South Wales at Melbourne	1926-27
1,059	Victoria v Tasmania at Melbourne	1922-23
918	New South Wales v South Australia at Sydney	1900-01
7-903 dec.	England v Australia at The Oval	1938
843	Australians v Oxford and Cambridge Universities at Portsmouth	1893
839	New South Wales v Tasmania at Sydney	1898-99
7-821 dec.	South Australia v Queensland at Adelaide	1939-40
815	New South Wales v Victoria at Sydney	1908-09
807	New South Wales v South Australia at Adelaide	1899-00
805	New South Wales v Victoria at Melbourne	1905-06
803	Non Smokers v Smokers at East Melbourne	1886-87
802	New South Wales v South Australia at Sydney	1920-21
793	Victoria v Queensland at Melbourne	1927-28
786	New South Wales v South Australia at Adelaide	1922-23
775	New South Wales v Victoria at Sydney	1881-82
7-774 dec.	Australians v Gloucestershire at Bristol	1948

770	New South Wales v South Australia at Adelaide	1920-21
769	A. C. MacLaren's XI v New South Wales at Sydney	1901-02
763	New South Wales v Queensland at Brisbane	1906-07
8-761 dec.	New South Wales v Queensland at Sydney	1929-30
8-758 dec.	Australia v West Indies at Kingston	1954-55
8-752 dec.	New South Wales v Otago at Dunedin	1923-24
7-734 dec.	MCC v New South Wales at Sydney	1928-29
6-729 dec.	Australia v England at Lord's	1930
724	Victoria v South Australia at Melbourne	1920-21
721	Australians v Essex at Southend	1948
713	New South Wales v South Australia at Adelaide	1908-09
6-713 dec.	New South Wales v Victoria at Sydney	1928-29
5-708 dec.	Australians v Cambridge University at Cambridge	1921
7-708 dec.	Australians v Hampshire at Southampton	1938
708	New South Wales v Victoria at Sydney	1925-26
705	New South Wales v Victoria at Melbourne	1925-26
701	Australia v England at The Oval	1934

HIGHEST FOURTH-INNINGS TOTALS

To Win

6-506	South Australia v Queensland at Adelaide	1991-92
6-446	New South Wales v South Australia at Adelaide	1926-27
7-435	Victoria v New South Wales at Melbourne	1931-32
7-409	Victoria v South Australia at Adelaide	1924-25
8-409	The Rest v New South Wales at Sydney	1933-34
3-404	Australia v England at Leeds	1948
6-402	Tasmania v Western Australia at Perth	1995-96
4-401	New South Wales v Queensland at Brisbane (Ex)	1928-29
3-401	Tasmania v Victoria at Hobart (Bel)	1997-98
7-392	Western Australia v South Australia at Perth	1992-93
8-391	Victoria v New South Wales at Melbourne	1996-97
4-387	New South Wales v Victoria at Sydney	1918-19
7-387	Victoria v Queensland at Melbourne	1965-66
7-386	South Australia v New Zealanders at Adelaide	1987-88
3-376	Australian XI v England XI at Hobart (Bel)	1998-99
6-373	Queensland v Tasmania at Albion	2000-01
9-371	Derbyshire v Australians at Derby	1997
6-370	Western Australia v New South Wales at Perth	1977-78
5-370	Queensland v South Australia at Brisbane	1984-85
6-369	Victoria v South Australia at Adelaide	1883-84
6-369	Australia v Pakistan at Hobart (Bel)	1999-00
4-367	Western Australia v Tasmania at Hobart (Bel)	1997-98
6-366	Tasmania v South Australia at Adelaide	1993-94

To Tie

9-402 (set 403)	D. G. Bradman's XI v A. L. Hassett's XI at Melbourne	1948-49

To Draw

9-529 (set 579)	Combined XI v South Africans at Perth	1963-64
3-430 (set 447)	New South Wales v South Australia at Sydney	1931-32
9-422 (set 499)	MCC v Victoria at Melbourne	1907-08
9-388 (set 419)	South Australia v Victoria at Melbourne	1977-78
6-385 (set 473)	South Australia v Victoria at Adelaide	1987-88
8-384 (set 435)	Australian XI v West Indians at Perth	1960-61
7-383 (set 461)	Victoria v Queensland at Melbourne	1984-85
9-375 (set 389)	New South Wales v MCC at Sydney	1907-08
9-373 (set 387)	Western Australia v Tasmania at Perth	2000-01
5-358 (set 401)	South Australia v New South Wales at Adelaide	1948-49
7-358 (set 419)	Queensland v Western Australia at Perth	1974-75

To Lose

572 (set 593)	New South Wales v South Australia at Sydney	1907-08
518 (set 753)	Victoria v Queensland at Brisbane (Ex)	1926-27
472 (set 552)	New South Wales v Australian XI at Sydney	1905-06
466 (set 553)	New South Wales v West Indians at Sydney	1930-31
456 (set 507)	Queensland v Victoria at Melbourne	1928-29
445 (set 493)	India v Australia at Adelaide	1977-78
442 (set 487)	South Africans v New South Wales at Sydney	1910-11
430 (set 461)	Somerset v Young Australia at Taunton	1995
425 (set 547)	A. L. Hassett's XI v A. R. Morris's XI at Melbourne	1953-54
417 (set 463)	England v Australia at Melbourne	1976-77

LOWEST INNINGS TOTALS

15	Victoria v MCC at Melbourne	1903-04
17	Gloucestershire v Australians at Cheltenham	1896
18	Tasmania v Victoria at Melbourne	1868-69
18	Australians v MCC at Lord's	1896
19	MCC v Australians at Lord's	1878
23	South Australia v Victoria at East Melbourne	1882-83
23	Australians v Yorkshire at Leeds	1902
25	Tasmania v Victoria at Hobart (LRG)	1857-58
26	England XI v Australians at Birmingham	1884
27	Lord Sheffield's XI v Australians at Sheffield Park	1890
27	South Australia v New South Wales at Sydney	1955-56
28	Victoria v New South Wales at Melbourne	1855-56
28	England XI v Australians at Stoke-on-Trent	1888
28	Lancashire v Australians at Liverpool	1896
28	Leicestershire v Australians at Leicester	1899

HIGHEST MATCH AGGREGATES

R	W	Avge		
1,929	39	49.46	New South Wales v South Australia at Sydney	1925-26
1,911	34	56.20	New South Wales v Victoria at Sydney	1908-09
1,801	40	45.02	A. L. Hassett's XI v A. R. Morris's XI at Melbourne	1953-54
1,764	39	45.23	Australia v West Indies at Adelaide	1968-69
1,753	40	43.82	Australia v England at Adelaide	1920-21
1,752	34	51.52	New South Wales v Queensland at Sydney	1926-27
1,744	30	58.13	New South Wales v South Africans at Sydney	1910-11
1,739	40	43.47	New South Wales v A. E. Stoddart's XI at Sydney	1897-98
1,723	31	55.58	England v Australia at Leeds	1948
1,716	40	42.90	New South Wales v South Australia at Sydney	1907-08
1,704	39	43.69	J. Ryder's XI v W. M. Woodfull's XI at Sydney	1929-30

LOWEST MATCH AGGREGATE

(For a completed match)

R	W	Avge		
105	31	3.38	MCC v Australians at Lord's	1878

LARGEST VICTORIES

Largest Victories by Innings and Runs Margin

Inns and 666	Victoria v Tasmania at Melbourne	1922-23
Inns and 656	Victoria v New South Wales at Melbourne	1926-27
Inns and 605	New South Wales v South Australia at Sydney	1900-01
Inns and 579	England v Australia at The Oval	1938
Inns and 572	New South Wales v South Australia at Adelaide	1908-09
Inns and 517	Australians v Nottinghamshire at Nottingham	1921

Largest Victories by Runs Margin

685 runs	New South Wales v Queensland at Sydney	1929-30
675 runs	England v Australia at Brisbane (Ex)	1928-29
638 runs	New South Wales v South Australia at Adelaide	1920-21
571 runs	Victoria v South Australia at Melbourne	1926-27
562 runs	Australia v England at The Oval	1934
550 runs	Victoria v Tasmania at Launceston	1913-14
541 runs	New South Wales v South Australia at Sydney	1925-26
530 runs	Australia v South Africa at Melbourne	1910-11

NARROW VICTORIES

Victory by One Wicket

New South Wales def Victoria at Sydney (*Last Wkt:* 16)	1877-78
Nottinghamshire def Australians at Nottingham (*Last Wkt:* 2)	1880
Canterbury def Tasmania at Christchurch (*Last Wkt:* 8)	1883-84
Australians def Liverpool and Districts at Liverpool (*Last Wkt:* 4) ...	1884
Australians def Middlesex at Lord's (*Last Wkt:* 8)	1886
Victoria def New South Wales at Sydney (*Last Wkt:* 10)	1900-01
England def Australia at The Oval (*Last Wkt:* 15)	1902
Australians def England XI at Bournemouth (*Last Wkt:* 1)	1905
England def Australia at Melbourne (*Last Wkt:* 54)	1907-08
Australians def Sussex at Hove (*Last Wkt:* 22)	1909
AIF Team def Yorkshire at Sheffield (*Last Wkt:* 54)	1919
South Australia def New South Wales at Adelaide (*Last Wkt:* 5)	1927-28
Queensland def South Australia at Brisbane (Ex) (*Last Wkt:* 3)	1928-29
J. Ryder's XI def W. M. Woodfull's XI at Sydney (*Last Wkt:* 8)	1929-30
South Australia def West Indians at Adelaide (*Last Wkt:* 22)	1930-31
Tasmania def Victoria at Hobart (TCA) (*Last Wkt:* 11)	1935-36
Australians def Madras Presidency at Madras (*Last Wkt:* 77)	1935-36
New South Wales def Queensland at Brisbane (*Last Wkt:* 7)	1936-37
New South Wales def Qld and Victorian XI at Brisbane (*Last Wkt:* 10)	1940-41
New South Wales def Queensland at Sydney (*Last Wkt:* 17)	1949-50
Western Australia def West Indians at Perth (*Last Wkt:* 48)	1951-52
Australia def West Indies at Melbourne (*Last Wkt:* 38)	1951-52
Western Australia def South Australia at Adelaide (*Last Wkt:* 36) ..	1961-62
Queensland def Victoria at Melbourne (*Last Wkt:* 11)	1968-69
Queensland def Western Australia at Perth (*Last Wkt:* 2)	1968-69
Victoria def New South Wales at Melbourne (*Last Wkt:* 4)	1969-70
South Australia def New South Wales at Sydney (*Last Wkt:* 51)	1971-72
South Australia def Victoria at Adelaide (*Last Wkt:* 12)	1977-78
Victoria def New South Wales at Melbourne (*Last Wkt:* 6)	1979-80
England XI def Western Australia at Perth (*Last Wkt:* 5)	1982-83
New South Wales def Queensland at Sydney (*Last Wkt:* 14)	1984-85
New South Wales def Victoria at Sydney (*Last Wkt:* 2)	1986-87
Victoria def New South Wales at Melbourne (*Last Wkt:* 2)	1993-94
Pakistan def Australia at Karachi (*Last Wkt:* 57)	1994-95
Victoria def Tasmania at Melbourne (*Last Wkt:* 17)	1996-97
Derbyshire def Australians at Derby (*Last Wkt:* 11)	1997

England XI def Queensland at Cairns (*Last Wkt:* 36) 1998-99
West Indies def Australia at Bridgetown (*Last Wkt:* 9) 1998-99

Victory by Five Runs or Less

1	West Indies def Australia at Adelaide	1992-93
2	New South Wales def Queensland at Sydney	1903-04
2	Tasmania def Victoria at Launceston	1911-12
2	Philadelphia def Australians at Mannheim	1912-13
2	Western Australia def Victoria at Perth	1998-99
2	South Australia def Western Australia at Adelaide	1999-00
3	Australia def England at Manchester	1902
3	England def Australia at Melbourne	1982-83
3	Victoria def Queensland at Melbourne	1993-94
5	Western Australia def New South Wales at Fremantle	1906-07
5	Surrey def Australians at The Oval	1909
5	South Africa def Australia at Sydney	1993-94

OTHER VICTORIES

Victory after Following On

A. Shaw's XI (146 and 198) def Victoria (251 and 75) at Melbourne 1881-82
A. Shaw's XI (201 and 264) def Australian XI (294 and 114) at Melbourne 1886-87
Victoria (137 and 178) def New South Wales (240 and 63) at Sydney 1888-89
South Australia (212 and 330) def New South Wales (337 and 148) at Adelaide 1892-93
Kent (127 and 198) def Australians (229 and 60) at Canterbury 1893
Australians (196 and 319) def Cambridge University (290 and 108) at Cambridge 1893
England (325 and 437) def Australia (586 and 166) at Sydney 1894-95
South Australia (304 and 454) def Lord Hawke's XI (553 and 108) at Unley 1902-03
New South Wales (108 and 450) def Queensland (307 and 224) at Brisbane 1965-66
England (174 and 356) def Australia (9 for 401 dec. and 111) at Leeds 1981
India (171 and 7 for 657 dec.) def Australia (445 and 212) at Kolkata 2000-01

TIED MATCHES

Gloucestershire tied with Australians at Bristol 1930
MCC tied with Victoria at Melbourne 1932-33
A.L. Hassett's XI tied with D.G. Bradman's XI at Melbourne 1948-49
Victoria tied with New South Wales at St Kilda 1956-57
West Indies tied with Australia at Brisbane 1960-61
South Australia tied with Queensland at Adelaide 1976-77
New Zealanders tied with Victoria at Melbourne 1982-83
Australia tied with India at Madras 1986-87

MATCHES COMPLETED IN ONE DAY

Australians (41 and 1-12) def MCC (33 and 19) at Lord's .... May 27, 1878
Australia (76 and 6-33) def England XI (82 and 26) at Birmingham .... May 26, 1884
New South Wales (185 and 1-14) def Auckland (93 and 102) at Auckland .... Jan 20, 1894

MOST RUNS BY ONE SIDE IN A MATCH

R	W	Avge		
1,235	20	61.75	New South Wales v South Australia at Sydney	1925-26
1,107	10	110.70	Victoria v New South Wales at Melbourne	1926-27
1,074	20	53.70	New South Wales v South Australia at Adelaide	1920-21
1,059	10	105.90	Victoria v Tasmania at Melbourne	1922-23
1,034	20	51.70	Victoria v South Australia at Melbourne	1920-21
1,028	20	51.50	Australia v England at The Oval	1934
1,013	18	56.27	Australia v West Indies at Sydney	1968-69

LONGEST MATCHES

Nine days
New South Wales v Victoria at Redfern 1872-73
Eight days
Victoria v South Australia at Melbourne 1925-26
Australia v England at Melbourne 1928-29
Seven days
New South Wales v Victoria at Sydney 1907-08
Australia v England at Sydney 1911-12
Australia v England at Sydney 1924-25
Australia v England at Melbourne 1924-25
Australia v England at Adelaide 1924-25
Australia v England at Melbourne 1928-29
Australia v England at Adelaide 1928-29

MISCELLANEOUS

FIRST-CLASS TEAMS IN AUSTRALIA

	First Game	M	W	L	D	T
Tasmania	Feb 11 1851	394	57	177	160	0
Victoria	Feb 11 1851	963	371	286	303	3
New South Wales	Mar 26 1856	932	412	266	253	1
English Teams	Mar 1 1862	463	189	120	153	1
Combined Teams/Australian XIs	Dec 26 1872	143	41	44	58	0
Australia	Mar 15 1877	318	168	85	64	1
South Australia	Nov 10 1877	824	237	348	238	1
Western Australia	Mar 17 1893	567	174	175	218	0
Queensland	Apr 3 1893	699	180	265	253	1
New Zealanders	Feb 17 1899	76	11	32	32	1
South Africans	Nov 5 1910	74	20	24	30	0
West Indians	Nov 21 1930	133	43	51	38	1
Indians	Oct 17 1947	61	13	29	19	0
Pakistanis	Nov 27 1964	62	12	24	26	0
World XI	Nov 5 1971	12	5	2	5	0
Sri Lankans	Feb 10 1983	17	1	7	9	0
Zimbweans	Dec 18 1994	2	0	1	1	0
Others		46	14	14	16	2

TOURING TEAMS IN AUSTRALIA

		First-Class					All Matches				
	Captain	M	W	L	D	T	M	W	L	D	T
1861-62 H. H. Stephenson's Team	H. H. Stephenson	1	0	1	0	0	14	6	3	5	0
1863-64 G. Parr's Team	G. Parr	1	0	1	0	0	14	7	2	5	0
1873-74 W. G. Grace's Team	W. G. Grace	0	0	0	0	0	15	10	3	2	0
1876-77 J. Lillywhite's Team	J. Lillywhite	3	1	1	1	0	15	5	4	6	0
1878-79 Lord Harris's Team	Lord Harris	5	2	3	0	0	13	5	3	5	0
1881-82 A. Shaw's Team	A. Shaw	7	3	2	2	0	18	8	3	7	0
1882-83 Hon I. F. W. Bligh's Team	Hon I. F. W. Bligh	7	4	3	0	0	17	9	3	5	0
1884-85 A. Shaw's Team	A. Shrewsbury	8	6	2	0	0	33	16	2	15	0
1886-87 A. Shaw's Team	A. Shrewsbury	10	6	2	2	0	30	12	2	16	0
1887-88 G. F. Vernon's Team	G. F. Vernon	8	6	1	1	0	26	11	1	14	0
	A. Shrewsbury's Team	A. Shrewsbury	7	5	2	0	0	22	14	2	6	0
	Combined England	W. W. Read	1	1	0	0	0	1	1	0	0	0
1891-92 Lord Sheffield's Team	W. G. Grace	8	6	2	0	0	27	12	2	13	0
1894-95 A. E. Stoddart's Team	A. E. Stoddart	12	8	4	0	0	23	9	4	10	0
1897-98 A. E. Stoddart's Team	A. E. Stoddart	12	4	5	3	0	22	6	5	11	0
1898-99 New Zealanders	L. T. Cobcroft	2	0	2	0	0	4	1	2	1	0
1901-02 A. C. MacLaren's Team	A. C. MacLaren	11	5	6	0	0	22	8	6	8	0
1902-03 Lord Hawke's Team	P. F. Warner	3	0	2	1	0	3	0	2	1	0

			First-Class					All Matches				
	Captain	M	W	L	D	T	M	W	L	D	T	
1903-04 MCC	P.F. Warner	14	9	2	3	0	20	10	2	8	0	
1907-08 MCC	A.O. Jones	18	7	4	7	0	19	7	4	8	0	
1910-11 South Africans	P.W. Sherwell	15	6	7	2	0	22	12	7	3	0	
1911-12 MCC	J.W.H.T. Douglas	14	11	1	2	0	18	12	1	5	0	
1913-14 New Zealanders	D. Reese	4	1	2	1	0	9	5	2	2	0	
1920-21 MCC	J.W.H.T. Douglas	13	5	6	2	0	22	9	6	7	0	
1922-23 MCC	A.C. MacLaren	7	0	3	4	0	8	0	3	5	0	
1924-25 MCC	A.E.R. Gilligan	17	7	6	4	0	23	8	6	9	0	
1925-26 New Zealanders	W.R. Patrick	4	0	1	3	0	9	3	1	5	0	
1927-28 New Zealanders	T.C. Lowry	1	0	1	0	0	1	0	1	0	0	
1928-29 MCC	A.P.F. Chapman	17	8	1	8	0	24	10	1	13	0	
1929-30 MCC	A.H.H. Gilligan	5	2	2	1	0	5	2	2	1	0	
1930-31 West Indians	G.C. Grant	14	4	8	2	0	16	5	8	3	0	
1931-32 South Africans	H.B. Cameron	16	4	6	6	0	18	6	6	6	0	
1932-33 MCC	D.R. Jardine	17	10	1	5	1	22	10	1	10	1	
1935-36 MCC	E.R.T. Holmes	6	3	1	2	0	6	3	1	2	0	
1936-37 MCC	G.O.B. Allen	17	5	5	7	0	25	7	5	13	0	
1937-38 New Zealanders	M.L. Page	3	0	3	0	0	3	0	3	0	0	
1946-47 MCC	W.R. Hammond	17	1	3	13	0	25	4	3	18	0	
1947-48 Indians	L. Amarnath	14	2	7	5	0	20	5	7	8	0	
1950-51 MCC	F.R. Brown	16	5	4	7	0	25	7	4	14	0	
1951-52 West Indians	J.D.C. Goddard	13	4	8	1	0	15	5	8	2	0	
1952-53 South Africans	J.E. Cheetham	16	4	3	9	0	23	7	3	13	0	
1953-54 New Zealanders	B. Sutcliffe	3	2	0	1	0	3	2	0	1	0	
1954-55 MCC	L. Hutton	17	8	2	7	0	23	13	2	8	0	
1958-59 MCC	P.B.H. May	17	4	4	9	0	20	7	4	9	0	
1960-61 West Indians	F.M.M. Worrell	14	4	5	4	1	22	10	5	5	2	
1961-62 New Zealanders	J.R. Reid	3	0	2	1	0	3	0	2	1	0	
1962-63 MCC	E.R. Dexter	15	4	3	8	0	26	12	3	11	0	
1963-64 South Africans	T.L. Goddard	14	5	3	6	0	28	16	4	8	0	
1964-65 Pakistanis	Hanif Mohammad	4	0	0	4	0	4	0	0	4	0	
1965-66 MCC	M.J.K. Smith	15	5	2	8	0	23	13	2	8	0	
1967-68 New Zealanders	B.W. Sinclair	4	0	2	2	0	7	2	2	3	0	
Indians	Nawab of Pataudi jr	9	0	6	3	0	15	4	6	5	0	
1968-69 West Indians	G.S. Sobers	15	4	5	6	0	23	9	5	9	0	
1969-70 New Zealanders	G.T. Dowling	3	0	0	3	0	8	3	0	5	0	
1970-71 MCC	R. Illingworth	15	3	1	11	0	25	10	2	13	0	
New Zealanders	G.T. Dowling	1	0	0	1	0	2	0	1	1	0	
1971-72 World XI	G.S. Sobers	12	5	2	5	0	16	5	3	8	0	
New Zealanders	G.T. Dowling	0	0	0	0	0	2	1	1	0	0	
1972-73 Pakistanis	Intikhab Alam	8	2	5	1	0	13	5	6	2	0	
New Zealanders	B.E. Congdon	1	0	0	1	0	3	2	0	1	0	
1973-74 New Zealanders	B.E. Congdon	9	2	5	2	0	13	5	6	2	0	
1974-75 MCC	M.H. Denness	15	5	5	5	0	23	8	9	6	0	
New Zealanders	B.E. Congdon	0	0	0	0	0	3	3	0	0	0	
1975-76 West Indians	C.H. Lloyd	13	3	6	4	0	21	8	7	6	0	
1976-77 Pakistanis	Mushtaq Mohammad	5	1	2	2	0	5	1	2	2	0	
MCC	A.W. Greig	2	0	1	1	0	2	0	1	1	0	
1977-78 Indians	B.S. Bedi	11	6	5	0	0	20	12	6	2	0	
1978-79 England XI	J.M. Brearley	13	8	2	3	0	26	17	4	5	0	
Pakistanis	Mushtaq Mohammad	4	1	1	2	0	5	2	1	2	0	
1979-80 England XI	J.M. Brearley	8	3	3	2	0	21	13	5	3	0	
West Indians	C.H. Lloyd	7	5	1	1	0	20	10	7	3	0	
1980-81 New Zealanders	G.P. Howarth	7	1	2	4	0	29	14	9	6	0	
Indians	S.M. Gavaskar	8	2	2	4	0	25	8	11	6	0	
1981-82 Pakistanis	Javed Miandad	8	2	2	4	0	21	8	8	5	0	
West Indians	C.H. Lloyd	7	4	1	2	0	24	16	5	3	0	
1982-83 England XI	R.G.D. Willis	11	4	3	4	0	23	10	9	4	0	
New Zealanders	G.P. Howarth	2	0	0	1	1	22	13	7	1	1	
Sri Lankans	L.R.D. Mendis	2	0	0	2	0	5	1	1	3	0	
1983-84 Pakistanis	Imran Khan	11	3	3	5	0	24	7	11	6	0	
West Indians	C.H. Lloyd	0	0	0	0	0	13	10	2	0	1	

			First-Class					All Matches				
		Captain	M	W	L	D	T	M	W	L	D	T
1984-85	West Indians	C. H. Lloyd	11	4	2	5	0	33	24	4	5	0
	Sri Lankans	L. R. D. Mendis	1	1	0	0	0	22	11	11	0	0
	England XI	D. I. Gower	0	0	0	0	0	3	0	3	0	0
	Indians	S. M. Gavaskar	0	0	0	0	0	5	5	0	0	0
	Pakistanis	Javed Miandad	0	0	0	0	0	5	3	2	0	0
	New Zealanders	G. P. Howarth	0	0	0	0	0	4	1	2	1	0
1985-86	New Zealanders	J. V. Coney	6	2	1	3	0	19	5	7	7	0
	Indians	Kapil Dev	5	1	0	4	0	19	8	7	4	0
1986-87	England XI	M. W. Gatting	11	5	3	3	0	30	19	7	4	0
	Pakistanis	Imran Khan	0	0	0	0	0	4	2	2	0	0
	West Indians	I. V. A. Richards	1	0	0	1	0	13	4	8	1	0
1987-88	New Zealanders	J. J. Crowe	6	1	2	3	0	19	8	8	3	0
	Sri Lankans	R. S. Madugalle	3	0	1	2	0	18	6	9	3	0
	England XI	M. W. Gatting	1	0	0	1	0	2	0	1	1	0
1988-89	West Indians	I. V. A. Richards	11	4	2	5	0	23	11	7	5	0
	Tamil Nadu	S. Vasudevan	1	0	1	0	0	3	0	3	0	0
	Pakistanis	Imran Khan	1	0	0	1	0	14	6	7	1	0
	New Zealanders	J. G. Wright	0	0	0	0	0	1	0	1	0	0
	Worcestershire	P. A. Neale	0	0	0	0	0	2	0	2	0	0
1989-90	New Zealanders	J. G. Wright	3	0	0	3	0	4	0	1	3	0
	Sri Lankans	A. Ranatunga	6	0	2	4	0	17	5	9	3	0
	Pakistanis	Imran Khan	6	0	3	3	0	27	6	14	7	0
	Lancashire	D. P. Hughes	0	0	0	0	0	8	3	5	0	0
1990-91	England XI	G. A. Gooch	11	1	5	5	0	28	8	14	6	0
	Wellington	E. B. McSweeney	1	0	1	0	0	4	1	1	2	0
	New Zealanders	M. D. Crowe	0	0	0	0	0	11	4	7	0	0
	Lancashire	G. Fowler	0	0	0	0	0	6	4	2	0	0
1991-92	New Zealanders	M. D. Crowe	0	0	0	0	0	6	4	2	0	0
	Indians	M. Azharuddin	7	1	5	1	0	29	7	19	2	1
	West Indians	R. B. Richardson	1	0	0	1	0	22	12	8	1	1
	Pakistanis	Imran Khan	2	0	0	2	0	14	5	6	3	0
	South Africans	K. C. Wessels	0	0	0	0	0	12	7	3	2	0
	Zimbabweans	D. L. Houghton	0	0	0	0	0	6	1	5	0	0
	Sri Lankans	P. A. de Silva	0	0	0	0	0	7	2	4	1	0
	England XI	G. A. Gooch	0	0	0	0	0	9	6	2	1	0
1992-93	West Indians	R. B. Richardson	8	3	1	4	0	22	13	5	4	0
	Pakistanis	Javed Miandad	1	1	0	0	0	12	5	6	0	1
	England A	M. D. Moxon	4	0	2	2	0	11	4	4	3	0
1993-94	New Zealanders	M. D. Crowe	7	2	3	2	0	16	5	9	2	0
	South Africans	K. C. Wessels	5	1	2	2	0	17	6	9	2	0
	Indians	S. R. Tendulkar	0	0	0	0	0	3	0	3	0	0
1994-95	England XI	M. A. Atherton	11	3	4	4	0	24	9	11	4	0
	Zimbabweans	A. Flower	2	0	1	1	0	19	8	10	1	0
1995-96	Western Province	E. O. Simons	2	0	2	0	0	5	1	3	1	0
	Pakistanis	Rameez Raja	6	1	3	2	0	7	2	3	2	0
	Sri Lankans	A. Ranatunga	5	0	4	1	0	17	5	11	1	0
	West Indians	R. B. Richardson	2	0	0	2	0	14	4	8	2	0
1996-97	England A	A. J. Hollioake	3	2	0	1	0	6	3	1	2	0
	West Indians	C. A. Walsh	8	4	4	0	0	25	12	13	0	0
	Pakistanis	Wasim Akram	1	0	1	0	0	10	6	4	0	0
1997-98	Transvaal	K. R. Rutherford	0	0	0	0	0	7	1	6	0	0
	New Zealanders	S. P. Fleming	6	0	5	1	0	21	5	13	2	1
	South Africans	W. J. Cronje	6	0	1	5	0	20	11	4	5	0
1998-99	England XI	A. J. Stewart	10	2	4	4	0	27	10	13	4	0
	Sri Lankans	A. Ranatunga	0	0	0	0	0	15	5	10	0	0
1999-00	Pakistanis	Wasim Akram	5	1	4	0	0	21	6	15	0	0
	Indians	S. R. Tendulkar	6	1	4	1	0	15	2	12	1	0
2000	South Africans	S. M. Pollock	0	0	0	0	0	3	1	1	0	1
2000-01	South Africans	S. M. Pollock	0	0	0	0	0	3	1	1	0	1
	West Indians	J. C. Adams	8	0	7	1	0	18	2	14	2	0
	Zimbabweans	H. H. Streak	0	0	0	0	0	9	1	8	0	0

AUSTRALIANS ON TOUR

				First-Class					All Matches				
		Country	Captain	M	W	L	D	T	M	W	L	D	T
1868	Aboriginals	England	C. Lawrence	0	0	0	0	0	47	14	14	19	0
1877-78	Australians	New Zealand	D. W. Gregory	0	0	0	0	0	7	5	1	1	0
1878	Australians	England	D. W. Gregory	15	7	4	4	0	37	18	7	12	0
1878-79	Australians	North America	D. W. Gregory	1	0	0	1	0	6	4	0	2	0
1880	Australians	England	W. L. Murdoch	9	4	2	3	0	37	21	4	12	0
1880-81	Australians	New Zealand	W. L. Murdoch	0	0	0	0	0	10	6	1	3	0
1882	Australians	England	W. L. Murdoch	33	18	4	11	0	38	23	4	11	0
1882-83	Australians	North America	W. L. Murdoch	0	0	0	0	0	2	2	0	0	0
1883-84	Tasmania	New Zealand	J. G. Davies	4	0	3	1	0	7	2	3	2	0
1884	Australians	England	W. L. Murdoch	31	17	7	7	0	32	18	7	7	0
1886	Australians	England	H. J. H. Scott	37	9	7	21	0	39	9	8	22	0
1886-87	Australians	New Zealand	H. J. H. Scott	0	0	0	0	0	5	2	0	3	0
1888	Australians	England	P. S. McDonnell	37	17	13	7	0	40	19	14	7	0
1889-90	NSW	New Zealand	J. Davis	5	4	0	1	0	7	6	0	1	0
1890	Australians	England	W. L. Murdoch	34	10	16	8	0	38	13	16	9	0
1893	Australians	England	J. M. Blackham	31	14	10	7	0	36	18	10	8	0
1893-94	Australians	North America	J. M. Blackham	2	1	1	0	0	6	4	1	1	0
	NSW	New Zealand	J. Davis	7	4	1	2	0	8	4	1	3	0
1895-96	NSW	New Zealand	L. T. Cobcroft	5	3	1	1	0	5	3	1	1	0
1896	Australians	England	G. H. S. Trott	34	20	6	8	0	34	20	6	8	0
1896-97	Australians	North America	G. H. S. Trott	3	2	1	0	0	6	4	1	1	0
	Australians	New Zealand	G. H. S. Trott	0	0	0	0	0	5	3	0	2	0
	Queensland	New Zealand	O. C. Hitchcock	5	3	1	1	0	8	4	1	3	0
1899	Australians	England	J. Darling	35	16	3	16	0	35	16	3	16	0
1902	Australians	England	J. Darling	37	21	2	14	0	39	23	2	14	0
1902-03	Australians	South Africa	J. Darling	4	3	0	1	0	6	3	0	3	0
1904-05	Australians	New Zealand	M. A. Noble	4	3	0	1	0	6	4	0	2	0
1905	Australians	England	J. Darling	35	15	3	17	0	38	16	3	19	0
1909	Australians	England	M. A. Noble	37	11	4	22	0	39	13	4	22	0
1909-10	Australians	New Zealand	W. W. Armstrong	6	5	0	1	0	9	7	0	2	0
1912	Australians	England	E. S. Gregory	36	9	8	19	0	37	9	8	20	0
1912-13	Australians	North America	E. S. Gregory	2	1	1	0	0	7	5	1	1	0
1913-14	NSW	Ceylon	E. F. Waddy	0	0	0	0	0	9	8	1	0	0
	Australians	North America	A. Diamond	5	4	0	1	0	53	49	1	3	0
	Australians	New Zealand	A. Sims	8	6	0	2	0	16	8	0	8	0
1919	AIF Team	England	H. L. Collins	28	12	4	12	0	32	13	4	15	0
1919-20	AIF Team	South Africa	H. L. Collins	8	6	0	2	0	10	8	0	2	0
1920-21	Australians	New Zealand	V. S. Ransford	9	6	0	3	0	15	12	0	3	0
1921	Australians	England	W. W. Armstrong	34	21	2	11	0	39	23	2	14	0
1921-22	Australians	South Africa	H. L. Collins	6	4	0	2	0	6	4	0	2	0
1923-24	NSW	New Zealand	C. G. Macartney	6	5	0	1	0	12	8	0	4	0
1924-25	Victoria	New Zealand	R. E. Mayne	6	1	1	4	0	12	4	1	7	0
1926	Australians	England	H. L. Collins	33	9	1	23	0	40	12	1	27	0
1927-28	Australians	New Zealand	V. Y. Richardson	6	4	0	2	0	13	6	0	7	0
1930	Australians	England	W. M. Woodfull	31	11	1	18	1	33	12	1	19	1
1932-33	Australians	North America	V. Y. Richardson	0	0	0	0	0	51	46	1	4	0
1934	Australians	England	W. M. Woodfull	30	13	1	16	0	34	15	1	18	0
1935-36	Australians	Ceylon	J. Ryder	1	1	0	0	0	1	1	0	0	0
	Australians	India	J. Ryder	16	9	3	4	0	22	10	3	9	0
	Australians	South Africa	V. Y. Richardson	16	13	0	3	0	16	13	0	3	0
1938	Australians	England	D. G. Bradman	29	15	2	12	0	35	20	2	13	0
1945	Aus. Services	England	A. L. Hassett	6	3	2	1	0	48	24	9	15	0
1945-46	Australians	India	A. L. Hassett	8	1	2	5	0	9	1	2	6	0
	Australians	Ceylon	A. L. Hassett	1	1	0	0	0	1	1	0	0	0
	Australians	New Zealand	W. A. Brown	5	5	0	0	0	5	5	0	0	0
1948	Australians	England	D. G. Bradman	31	23	0	8	0	34	25	0	9	0
1949-50	Australians	South Africa	A. L. Hassett	21	14	0	7	0	25	18	0	7	0
	Australians	New Zealand	W. A. Brown	5	3	0	2	0	14	9	0	5	0

					First-Class					All Matches		
		Country	Captain	M	W	L	D	T	M	W	L	D	T
1953	Australians	England	A. L. Hassett	33	16	1	16	0	35	16	1	18	0
1954-55	Australians	West Indies	I. W. G. Johnson	9	5	0	4	0	11	5	0	6	0
1956	Australians	England	I. W. G. Johnson	31	9	3	19	0	35	12	3	20	0
1956-57	Australians	Pakistan	I. W. G. Johnson	1	0	1	0	0	1	0	1	0	0
	Australians	India	I. W. G. Johnson	3	2	0	1	0	3	2	0	1	0
	Australians	New Zealand	I. D. Craig	7	5	0	2	0	12	7	0	5	0
1957-58	Australians	South Africa	I. D. Craig	20	11	0	9	0	22	11	0	11	0
1959-60	Australians	Pakistan	R. Benaud	4	3	0	1	0	4	3	0	1	0
	Australians	India	R. Benaud	7	2	1	4	0	7	2	1	4	0
	Australians	New Zealand	I. D. Craig	6	2	0	4	0	9	4	0	5	0
1961	Australians	England	R. Benaud	32	13	1	18	0	37	14	2	21	0
1964	Australians	England	R. B. Simpson	30	11	3	16	0	36	14	4	18	0
1964-65	Australians	India	R. B. Simpson	3	1	1	1	0	3	1	1	1	0
	Australians	Pakistan	R. B. Simpson	1	0	0	1	0	1	0	0	1	0
	Australians	West Indies	R. B. Simpson	11	3	2	6	0	16	4	3	9	0
1966-67	Australians	South Africa	R. B. Simpson	17	7	5	5	0	24	11	6	7	0
	Australians	New Zealand	L. E. Favell	9	1	2	6	0	10	2	2	6	0
1968	Australians	England	W. M. Lawry	25	8	3	14	0	29	10	3	16	0
1969-70	Australians	Ceylon	W. M. Lawry	1	0	0	1	0	4	1	0	3	0
	Australians	India	W. M. Lawry	10	5	1	4	0	10	5	1	4	0
	Australians	South Africa	W. M. Lawry	12	4	4	4	0	12	4	4	4	0
	Australians	New Zealand	S. C. Trimble	8	2	0	6	0	8	2	0	6	0
1972	Australians	England	I. M. Chappell	26	11	5	10	0	37	14	10	13	0
1972-73	Australians	West Indies	I. M. Chappell	12	7	0	5	0	15	10	0	5	0
1973-74	Australians	New Zealand	I. M. Chappell	7	2	1	4	0	11	6	1	4	0
1974-75	Australians	North America	I. M. Chappell	0	0	0	0	0	5	2	1	2	0
1975	Australians	England	I. M. Chappell	15	8	2	5	0	21	12	4	5	0
1976-77	Australians	New Zealand	G. S. Chappell	6	5	0	1	0	8	5	2	1	0
1977	Australians	England	G. S. Chappell	22	5	4	13	0	31	8	8	15	0
1977-78	Australians	West Indies	R. B. Simpson	11	5	3	3	0	13	6	4	3	0
1979	Australians	England	K. J. Hughes	0	0	0	0	0	6	2	3	1	0
1979-80	Australians	India	K. J. Hughes	11	0	3	8	0	11	0	3	8	0
	Australians	Pakistan	G. S. Chappell	5	0	1	4	0	5	0	1	4	0
1980	Australians	England	G. S. Chappell	5	1	2	2	0	8	1	4	3	0
1980-81	Australians	Sri Lanka	K. J. Hughes	1	0	0	1	0	4	2	1	1	0
1981	Australians	England	K. J. Hughes	17	3	3	11	0	26	7	7	12	0
1981-82	Australians	New Zealand	G. S. Chappell	5	1	1	3	0	11	4	4	3	0
1982-83	Australians	Pakistan	K. J. Hughes	6	0	3	3	0	9	0	5	4	0
	Australians	Zimbabwe	D. M. Wellham	2	1	1	0	0	8	7	1	0	0
	Australians	Sri Lanka	G. S. Chappell	2	1	0	1	0	6	1	2	3	0
1983	Australians	England	K. J. Hughes	0	0	0	0	0	9	3	5	1	0
1983-84	Australians	West Indies	K. J. Hughes	10	1	3	6	0	15	2	6	7	0
1984-85	Australians	India	K. J. Hughes	0	0	0	0	0	6	4	0	2	0
	NSW	New Zealand	D. M. Wellham	0	0	0	0	0	1	1	0	0	0
	Australians	Sharjah	A. R. Border	0	0	0	0	0	2	1	1	0	0
1985	Australians	England	A. R. Border	20	4	3	13	0	29	9	5	15	0
1985-86	Australians	Zimbabwe	R. B. Kerr	2	1	0	1	0	9	3	5	1	0
	Australians	South Africa	K. J. Hughes	10	2	2	6	0	25	10	9	6	0
	Australians	New Zealand	A. R. Border	5	1	1	3	0	11	5	3	3	0
	Australians	Sharjah	R. J. Bright	0	0	0	0	0	1	0	1	0	0
1985-86	NSW	Zimbabwe	G. C. Dyer	2	1	0	1	0	8	5	2	1	0
1986-87	Australians	India	A. R. Border	7	0	0	6	1	13	2	3	7	1
	NSW	New Zealand	D. M. Wellham	0	0	0	0	0	2	1	1	0	0
	Australians	South Africa	K. J. Hughes	12	2	3	7	0	25	8	9	8	0
	SAust	New Zealand	D. W. Hookes	0	0	0	0	0	4	4	0	0	0
	Australians	Sharjah	A. R. Border	0	0	0	0	0	3	0	3	0	0
1987-88	NSW	Zimbabwe	D. M. Wellham	2	0	0	2	0	8	5	1	2	0
	Australians	India	A. R. Border	0	0	0	0	0	7	6	1	0	0
	Australians	Pakistan	A. R. Border	0	0	0	0	0	1	1	0	0	0
	Victoria	New Zealand	D. F. Whatmore	0	0	0	0	0	2	0	2	0	0

		Country	Captain	First-Class					All Matches				
				M	W	L	D	T	M	W	L	D	T
	Queensland	New Zealand	R. B. Kerr	0	0	0	0	0	3	3	0	0	0
1988	Aboriginals	England	J. MacGuire	0	0	0	0	0	27	15	11	1	0
1988-89	Australians	Pakistan	A. R. Border	6	0	1	5	0	7	0	2	5	0
1989	Australians	England	A. R. Border	20	12	1	7	0	31	20	3	7	1
1989-90	W Aust	India	G. M. Wood	1	0	0	1	0	4	1	2	1	0
	Australians	India	A. R. Border	0	0	0	0	0	5	2	3	0	0
	Australians	New Zealand	A. R. Border	1	0	1	0	0	6	5	0	1	0
	Australians	Sharjah	A. R. Border	0	0	0	0	0	4	3	1	0	0
1990-91	Australians	West Indies	A. R. Border	10	2	2	6	0	19	10	3	6	0
1991	Victoria	England	S. P. O'Donnell	1	0	0	1	0	4	1	1	2	0
1991-92	Australians	Zimbabwe	M. A. Taylor	2	2	0	0	0	6	5	1	0	0
	Australians	New Zealand	M. A. Taylor	0	0	0	0	0	2	1	1	0	0
1992-93	Australians	Sri Lanka	A. R. Border	5	1	0	4	0	8	2	2	4	0
	Australians	New Zealand	A. R. Border	4	2	1	1	0	10	5	4	1	0
1993	Australians	England	A. R. Border	21	10	2	9	0	30	18	3	9	0
1993-94	Australians	South Africa	A. R. Border	6	3	1	2	0	16	7	5	4	0
	NSW	New Zealand	P. A. Emery	0	0	0	0	0	1	1	0	0	0
	Australians	Sharjah	M. A. Taylor	0	0	0	0	0	3	2	1	0	0
1994-95	Australians	Sri Lanka	M. A. Taylor	0	0	0	0	0	3	1	2	0	0
	Australians	Pakistan	M. A. Taylor	4	0	1	3	0	10	5	2	3	0
	Australians	New Zealand	M. A. Taylor	0	0	0	0	0	4	3	1	0	0
	Cricket Academy	New Zealand	N. W. Ashley	1	1	0	0	0	6	6	0	0	0
	Australians	West Indies	M. A. Taylor	7	3	1	3	0	16	8	5	3	0
1995	Young Australia	England	S. G. Law	8	5	1	2	0	16	11	3	2	0
	NSW	England	M. A. Taylor	1	0	0	1	0	2	1	0	1	0
1995-96	Tasmania	Zimbabwe	D. C. Boon	2	0	2	0	0	5	3	0	2	0
	Australians	India	M. A. Taylor	0	0	0	0	0	6	5	1	0	0
	Australians	Pakistan	M. A. Taylor	0	0	0	0	0	1	0	1	0	0
1996-97	Australians	Sri Lanka	I. A. Healy	0	0	0	0	0	6	4	2	0	0
	Australians	India	M. A. Taylor	2	0	1	1	0	7	0	6	1	0
	Australians	South Africa	M. A. Taylor	6	5	1	0	0	17	13	4	0	0
1997	Australians	England	M. A. Taylor	16	6	3	6	1	27	11	7	7	2
1997-98	Australians	New Zealand	S. R. Waugh	0	0	0	0	0	4	2	2	0	0
	Australians	India	M. A. Taylor	6	1	2	3	0	6	1	2	3	0
	Australians	Sharjah	S. R. Waugh	0	0	0	0	0	5	4	1	0	0
1998	Australians	Scotland	M. J. Di Venuto	2	0	0	2	0	5	2	0	3	0
	Australians	Ireland	M. J. Di Venuto	1	1	0	0	0	6	5	0	1	0
1998-99	Australians	Pakistan	M. A. Taylor	5	2	0	3	0	9	6	0	3	0
	Australians	Bangladesh	M. A. Taylor	0	0	0	0	0	1	0	1	0	0
	Australians	West Indies	S. R. Waugh	7	4	2	1	0	14	7	5	1	1
	Cricket Academy	Zimbabwe	B. J. Hodge	2	2	0	0	0	7	5	2	0	0
1999	Australians	England	A. R. Waugh	0	0	0	0	0	10	7	2	0	1
1999-00	Australians	North America	A. C. Gilchrist	0	0	0	0	0	5	4	1	0	0
	Australians	Sri Lanka	S. R. Waugh	5	2	1	2	0	10	6	2	2	0
	Australians	Zimbabwe	S. R. Waugh	2	2	0	0	0	5	5	0	0	0
	Australians	New Zealand	S. R. Waugh	5	4	1	0	0	11	8	1	2	0
	Australians	South Africa	S. R. Waugh	0	0	0	0	0	3	2	1	0	0
2000-01	Australians	Kenya	S. R. Waugh	0	0	0	0	0	2	1	1	0	0
	Australians	India	S. R. Waugh	6	1	2	3	0	12	4	5	3	0
2001	Australians	England	S. R. Waugh	3	3	0	0	0	11	8	2	0	1

FIRST-CLASS GROUNDS

	First Game	Last Game	Games
NTCA Ground, Launceston, Tasmania	1850-51	1995-96	81
Emerald Hill Cricket Ground, Emerald Hill, Victoria	*1851-52		1
Melbourne Cricket Ground (MCG), Victoria	1855-56	2000-01	594

	First Game	Last Game	Games
The Domain, Sydney, New South Wales	*1856-57	1868-69	6
Lower Domain Ground, Hobart, Tasmania	*1857-58		1
Albert Ground, Redfern, New South Wales	*1870-71	1876-77	5
Adelaide Oval, South Australia	1877-78	2000-01	521
Sydney Cricket Ground (SCG), New South Wales	1877-78	2000-01	597
East Melbourne Cricket Ground, Victoria	*1880-81		4
Tasmanian Cricket Association Ground, Hobart, Tasmania	*1892-93	1930-31	28
Exhibition Ground, Brisbane, Queensland	**1892-93	1930-31	28
Brisbane Cricket Ground (The Gabba), Queensland	1897-98	2000-01	399
Western Australian Cricket Association Ground, Perth, WA	1898-99	2000-01	360
Unley Oval, South Australia	1902-03		1
Fremantle Oval, Western Australia	**1905-06	1909-10	5
South Melbourne Cricket Ground (Lakeside Oval), Victoria	*1907-08	1931-32	2
Fitzroy Cricket Ground (Brunswick Street Oval), Victoria	**1925-26		1
Richmond Cricket Ground (Punt Road Oval), Victoria	1932-33	2000-01	4
Carlton Recreation Ground (Princes Park), Victoria	1945-46	1997-98	7
St Kilda Cricket Ground (Junction Oval), Victoria	1945-46	1992-93	28
Kardinia Park, Geelong, Victoria	**1961-62	1981-92	6
Sydney Cricket Ground No 2, New South Wales	*1966-67		1
Devonport Oval, Tasmania	1977-78	1997-98	27
Manuka Oval, Canberra, Australian Capital Territory	1978-79	1998-99	5
Oakes Oval, Lismore, New South Wales	1979-80	1991-92	2
No 1 Sports Ground, Newcastle, New South Wales	1981-82	1997-98	16
Salter Oval, Bundaberg, Queensland	1982-83		1
Showgrounds Oval, Wangaratta, Victoria	1986-87	1996-97	2
Endeavour Park, Townsville, Queensland	1986-87		1
Bellerive Oval, Tasmania	1987-88	2000-01	76
Sale Oval, Victoria	1989-90		1
Lavington Sports Ground, Albury, New South Wales	1989-90	1990-91	2
North Sydney Oval, New South Wales	1990-91	2000-01	3
Eastern Oval, Ballarat, Victoria	1990-91		1
Carrara Sports Ground, Queensland	**1990-91		1
Queen Elizabeth Oval, Bendigo, Victoria	1991-92	1994-95	2
Henzell Park, Caloundra, Queensland	1992-93		1
Southern Cross Reserve, Toowoomba, Queensland	1994-95		1
Newtown Oval, Maryborough, Queensland	1994-95		1
Hurstville Oval, New South Wales	1995-96		1
Harrup Park, Mackay, Queensland	1995-96		1
Bankstown Memorial Oval, New South Wales	1996-97		1
Cazaly's Australian Football Park, Cairns, Queensland	1997-98	1998-99	2
Allan Border Field, Albion, Queensland	1999-00	2000-01	6

* Denotes the ground no longer exists; ** Denotes that the ground is no longer used for cricket.

AUSTRALIAN TEST MATCH RECORDS

BATTING RECORDS

HIGHEST INDIVIDUAL INNINGS

334	D. G. Bradman	v England at Leeds	1930
334*	M. A. Taylor	v Pakistan at Peshawar	1998-99
311	R. B. Simpson	v England at Manchester	1964
307	R. M. Cowper	v England at Melbourne	1965-66
304	D. G. Bradman	v England at Leeds	1934
299*	D. G. Bradman	v South Africa at Adelaide	1931-32
270	D. G. Bradman	v England at Melbourne	1936-37
268	G. N. Yallop	v Pakistan at Melbourne	1983-84

266	W. H. Ponsford	v England at The Oval	1934
254	D. G. Bradman	v England at Lord's	1930
250	K. D. Walters	v New Zealand at Christchurch	1976-77
247*	G. S. Chappell	v New Zealand at Wellington	1973-74
244	D. G. Bradman	v England at The Oval	1934
242	K. D. Walters	v West Indies at Sydney	1968-69
235	G. S. Chappell	v Pakistan at Faisalabad	1979-80
234	D. G. Bradman	v England at Sydney	1946-47
234	S. G. Barnes	v England at Sydney	1946-47
232	D. G. Bradman	v England at The Oval	1930
232	S. J. McCabe	v England at Nottingham	1938
226	D. G. Bradman	v South Africa at Brisbane	1931-32
225	R. B. Simpson	v England at Adelaide	1965-66
223	D. G. Bradman	v West Indies at Brisbane (Ex)	1930-31
223	J. L. Langer	v India at Sydney	1999-00
219	M. A. Taylor	v England at Nottingham	1989
219	M. J. Slater	v Sri Lanka at Perth	1995-96
216	D. M. Jones	v West Indies at Adelaide	1988-89
214*	V. T. Trumper	v South Africa at Adelaide	1910-11
214	G. S. Blewett	v South Africa at Johannesburg (WS)	1996-97
213	K. J. Hughes	v India at Adelaide	1980-81
212	D. G. Bradman	v England at Adelaide	1936-37
211	W. L. Murdoch	v England at The Oval	1884
210	W. M. Lawry	v West Indies at Bridgetown	1964-65
210	D. M. Jones	v India at Chennai (Chepauk)	1986-87
207	K. R. Stackpole	v England at Brisbane	1970-71
206*	W. A. Brown	v England at Lord's	1938
206	A. R. Morris	v England at Adelaide	1950-51
205	R. N. Harvey	v West Indies at Melbourne	1952-53
205	W. M. Lawry	v West Indies at Melbourne	1968-69
205	A. R. Border	v New Zealand at Adelaide	1987-88
204	R. N. Harvey	v West Indies at Kingston	1954-55
204	G. S. Chappell	v India at Sydney	1980-81
203	H. L. Collins	v South Africa at Johannesburg (OW)	1921-22
201	E. S. Gregory	v England at Sydney	1894-95
201*	J. Ryder	v England at Adelaide	1924-25
201	D. G. Bradman	v India at Adelaide	1947-48
201	R. B. Simpson	v West Indies at Bridgetown	1964-65
201	G. S. Chappell	v Pakistan at Brisbane	1981-82
200	D. C. Boon	v New Zealand at Perth	1989-90
200*	A. R. Border	v England at Leeds	1993
200	S. R. Waugh	v West Indies at Kingston	1994-95

HUNDRED ON DEBUT

C. Bannerman (165*)	v England at Melbourne	1876-77
H. Graham (107)	v England at Lord's	1893
R. A. Duff (104)	v England at Melbourne	1901-02
M. J. Hartigan (116)	v England at Adelaide	1907-08
H. L. Collins (104)	v England at Sydney	1920-21
W. H. Ponsford (110)	v England at Sydney	1924-25
A. Jackson (164)	v England at Adelaide	1928-29
J. W. Burke (101*)	v England at Adelaide	1950-51
K. D. Walters (155)	v England at Brisbane	1965-66
G. S. Chappell (108)	v England at Perth	1970-71
G. J. Cosier (109)	v West Indies at Melbourne	1975-76
D. M. Wellham (103)	v England at The Oval	1981
K. C. Wessels (162)	v England at Brisbane	1982-83
W. B. Phillips (159)	v Pakistan at Perth	1983-84
M. E. Waugh (138)	v England at Adelaide	1990-91
G. S. Blewett (102*)	v England at Adelaide	1994-95

HUNDRED IN EACH INNINGS OF A MATCH

	1st	*2nd*		
W. Bardsley	136	130	v England at The Oval	1909
A. R. Morris	122	124*	v England at Adelaide	1946-47
D. G. Bradman	132	127*	v India at Melbourne	1947-48
J. Moroney	118	101*	v South Africa at Johannesburg (EP)	1949-50
R. B. Simpson	153	115	v Pakistan at Karachi	1964-65
K. D. Walters	242	103	v West Indies at Sydney	1968-69
I. M. Chappell	145	121	v New Zealand at Wellington	1973-74
G. S. Chappell	247*	133	v New Zealand at Wellington	1973-74
G. S. Chappell	123	109*	v West Indies at Brisbane	1975-76
A. R. Border	150*	153	v Pakistan at Lahore	1979-80
A. R. Border	140	114*	v New Zealand at Christchurch	1985-86
D. M. Jones	116	121*	v Pakistan at Adelaide	1989-90
S. R. Waugh	108	116	v England at Manchester	1997

MOST RUNS IN A SERIES

	T	*I*	*NO*	*R*	*HS*	*100s*	*Avge*	*Series*
D. G. Bradman	5	7	0	974	334	4	139.14	1930 v England in England
M. A. Taylor	6	11	1	839	219	2	83.90	1989 v England in England
R. N. Harvey	5	9	0	834	205	4	92.66	1952-53 v South Africa in Australia
D. G. Bradman	5	9	0	810	270	3	90.00	1936-37 v England in Australia
D. G. Bradman	5	5	1	806	299*	4	201.50	1931-32 v South Africa in Australia
D. G. Bradman	5	8	0	758	304	2	94.75	1934 v England in England
D. G. Bradman	5	6	2	715	201	4	178.75	1947-48 v India in Australia
G. S. Chappell	6	11	5	702	182*	3	117.00	1975-76 v West Indies in Australia
K. D. Walters	4	6	0	699	242	4	116.50	1968-69 v West Indies in Australia
A. R. Morris	5	9	1	696	196	3	87.00	1948 v England in England
D. G. Bradman	5	8	1	680	234	2	97.14	1946-47 v England in Australia
W. M. Lawry	5	8	0	667	205	3	83.38	1968-69 v West Indies in Australia
V. T. Trumper	5	9	2	661	214*	2	94.43	1910-11 v South Africa in Australia
R. N. Harvey	5	8	3	660	178	4	132.00	1949-50 v South Africa in S. Africa
R. N. Harvey	5	7	1	650	204	3	108.33	1954-55 v West Indies in West Indies
K. R. Stackpole	7	12	0	627	207	2	52.25	1970-71 v England in Australia
M. J. Slater	5	10	0	623	176	3	62.30	1994-95 v England in Australia
G. S. Chappell	6	11	0	608	144	2	55.27	1974-75 v England in Australia
A. R. Border	6	11	2	597	196	2	66.33	1985 v England in England
K. J. Hughes	6	12	2	594	100	1	59.40	1979-80 v India in India
W. M. Lawry	5	7	0	592	166	3	84.57	1965-66 v England in Australia
I. R. Redpath	6	11	0	575	103	3	52.27	1975-76 v West Indies in Australia
V. T. Trumper	5	10	1	574	185*	2	63.77	1903-04 v England in Australia
W. Bardsley	5	9	0	573	132	1	63.67	1910-11 v South Africa in Australia
W. H. Ponsford	4	7	1	569	266	2	94.83	1934 v England in England
D. M. Jones	6	9	1	566	157	2	70.75	1989 v England in England
H. L. Collins	5	9	0	557	162	2	61.89	1920-21 v England in Australia
D. C. Boon	5	9	2	556	135	3	79.43	1991-92 v India in Australia
M. T. G. Elliott	6	10	0	556	199	2	55.60	1997 v England in England
D. C. Boon	6	10	2	555	164*	3	69.38	1993 v England in England
G. N. Yallop	5	6	0	554	268	2	92.33	1983-84 v Pakistan in Australia
M. E. Waugh	6	10	1	550	137	1	61.11	1993 v England in England
I. M. Chappell	5	8	0	548	165	2	68.50	1968-69 v West Indies in Australia
I. M. Chappell	5	9	2	542	109	2	77.43	1972-73 v West Indies in West Indies
J. M. Taylor	5	10	0	541	108	1	54.10	1924-25 v England in Australia
R. B. Simpson	5	10	0	539	176	2	53.90	1977-78 v India in Australia
J. Darling	5	8	0	537	178	3	67.13	1897-98 v England in Australia
A. R. Border	6	12	3	533	123*	2	59.22	1981 v England in England
B. C. Booth	4	7	1	531	169	2	88.50	1963-64 v South Africa in Australia
D. C. Boon	5	9	2	530	121	1	75.71	1990-91 v England in Australia
N. C. O'Neill	5	10	0	522	181	1	52.20	1960-61 v West Indies in Australia

	T	I	NO	R	HS	100s	Avge	Series
C. Hill	5	10	0	521	99	0	52.10	1901-02 v England in Australia
A. R. Border	6	12	0	521	162	1	43.42	1979-80 v India in India
A. R. Border	5	10	3	521	100*	1	74.43	1983-84 v West Indies in West Indies
C. C. McDonald ..	5	9	1	519	170	2	64.88	1958-59 v England in Australia
M. A. Taylor	3	5	1	513	334*	1	128.25	1998-99 v Pakistan in Pakistan
W. A. Brown	4	8	1	512	206*	1	73.14	1938 v England in England
D. M. Jones	5	10	1	511	184*	2	56.78	1986-87 v England in Australia
D. G. Bradman ..	5	9	2	508	173*	2	72.57	1948 v England in England
S. R. Waugh	6	8	4	506	177*	2	126.50	1989 v England in England
K. C. Wessels	5	9	0	505	173	1	56.11	1984-85 v West Indies in Australia
A. R. Morris	5	8	1	503	155	3	71.86	1946-47 v England in Australia

Most runs in a series against opponents not mentioned above:

	T	I	NO	R	HS	100s	Avge	Series
S. R. Waugh	2	3	2	362	170	2	362.00	1995-96 v Sri Lanka in Australia
G. S. Chappell ...	3	6	1	449	247*	2	89.30	1973-74 v New Zealand in N. Zealand
S. R. Waugh	1	1	1	151	151*	1	–	1999-00 v Zimbabwe in Zimbabwe

MOST RUNS IN A CALENDAR YEAR

	M	I	NO	R	HS	100s	Avge	Year
R. B. Simpson	14	26	3	1,381	311	3	60.04	1964
D. C. Boon	16	25	5	1,241	164*	4	62.05	1993
M. A. Taylor	11	20	1	1,219	219	4	64.16	1989
K. J. Hughes	15	28	4	1,163	130*	2	48.45	1979
M. A. Taylor	12	22	3	1,112	334*	1	58.53	1998
M. A. Taylor	15	23	2	1,106	170	4	52.67	1993
A. R. Border	11	20	3	1,099	196	4	64.65	1985
D. M. Jones	11	18	3	1,099	216	4	73.27	1989
A. R. Border	14	27	3	1,073	162	3	44.70	1979
G. S. Blewett	15	25	0	1,067	214	2	42.68	1997
C. Hill	12	21	2	1,060	142	2	55.79	1902
W. M. Lawry	14	27	2	1,056	157	2	42.24	1964
M. J. Slater	14	25	2	1,051	169	3	45.70	1999
M. E. Waugh	12	22	6	1,034	153	4	64.63	1998
D. G. Bradman	8	13	4	1,025	201	5	113.89	1948
A. R. Border	11	19	3	1,000	140	5	62.50	1986

MOST RUNS IN A CAREER

		M	I	NO	R	HS	100s	Avge
1	A. R. Border	156	265	44	11,174	205	27	50.56
2	S. R. Waugh	135	215	39	8,965	200	25	50.94
3	M. A. Taylor	104	186	13	7,525	334*	19	43.50
4	D. C. Boon	107	190	20	7,422	200	21	43.66
5	G. S. Chappell	88	151	19	7,110	247*	24	53.86
6	M. E. Waugh	111	184	14	7,081	153*	18	41.65
7	D. G. Bradman	52	80	10	6,996	334	29	99.94
8	R. N. Harvey	79	137	10	6,149	205	21	48.42
9	K. D. Walters	75	125	14	5,357	250	15	48.26
10	I. M. Chappell	76	136	10	5,345	196	14	42.42
11	W. M. Lawry	68	123	12	5,234	210	13	47.15
12	M. J. Slater	70	124	7	5,142	219	14	43.95
13	R. B. Simpson	62	111	7	4,869	311	10	46.82
14	I. R. Redpath	67	120	11	4,737	171	8	43.46
15	K. J. Hughes	70	124	6	4,415	213	9	37.42
16	I. A. Healy	119	182	23	4,356	161*	4	27.40
17	R. W. Marsh	97	150	13	3,633	132	3	26.52
18	D. M. Jones	52	89	11	3,631	216	11	46.55
19	A. R. Morris	46	79	3	3,533	206	12	46.49

		M	I	NO	R	HS	100s	Avge
20	C. Hill	49	89	2	3,412	191	7	39.22
21	G. M. Wood	59	112	6	3,374	172	9	31.83
22	V. T. Trumper	48	89	8	3,163	214*	8	39.05
23	C. C. McDonald	47	83	4	3,107	170	5	39.33
24	A. L. Hassett	43	69	3	3,073	198*	10	46.56
25	K. R. Miller	55	87	7	2,958	147	7	36.98
26	W. W. Armstrong	50	84	10	2,863	159*	6	38.69
27	G. R. Marsh	50	93	7	2,854	138	4	33.19
28	K. R. Stackpole	44	80	5	2,807	207	7	37.43
29	N. C. O'Neill	42	69	8	2,779	181	6	45.56
30	G. N. Yallop	39	70	3	2,756	268	8	41.13
31	S. J. McCabe	39	62	5	2,748	232	6	48.21
32	G. S. Blewett	46	79	4	2,552	214	4	34.03
33	J. L. Langer	41	68	2	2,577	223	7	39.05
34	R. T. Ponting	42	66	8	2,492	197	7	42.97
35	W. Bardsley	41	66	5	2,469	193*	6	40.48
36	W. M. Woodfull	35	54	4	2,300	161	7	46.00
37	P. J. P. Burge	42	68	8	2,290	181	4	38.17
38	E. S. Gregory	58	100	7	2,282	201	4	24.54
39	R. Benaud	63	97	7	2,201	122	3	24.46
40	C. G. Macartney	35	55	4	2,131	170	7	41.78
41	W. H. Ponsford	29	48	4	2,122	266	7	48.23
42	R. M. Cowper	27	46	2	2,061	307	5	46.84
43	M. A. Noble	42	73	7	1,997	133	1	30.26
44	G. R. J. Matthews	33	53	8	1,849	130	4	41.09
45	B. C. Booth	29	48	6	1,773	169	5	42.21
46	K. C. Wessels	24	42	1	1,761	179	4	42.95
47	G. M. Ritchie	30	53	5	1,690	146	3	35.21
48	S. K. Warne	87	122	12	1,663	86	0	15.12
49	J. Darling	34	60	2	1,657	178	3	28.57
50	R. B. McCosker	25	46	5	1,622	127	4	39.56

HIGHEST CAREER AVERAGES

	T	I	NO	R	HS	100s	Avge
A. E. Trott	3	5	3	205	85*	0	102.50
D. G. Bradman	52	80	10	6,996	334	29	99.94
S. G. Barnes	13	19	2	1,072	234	3	63.06
J. K. Moss	1	2	1	60	38*	0	60.00
C. Bannerman	3	6	2	239	165†	1	59.75
A. C. Gilchrist	9	14	3	629	149*	1	57.18
G. S. Chappell	88	151	19	7,110	247*	24	53.86
J. Ryder	20	32	5	1,394	201*	3	51.63
A. G. Fairfax	10	12	4	410	65	0	51.25
R. G. Gregory	2	3	0	153	80	0	51.00
S. R. Waugh	135	215	39	8,965	200	25	50.94
A. R. Border	156	265	44	11,174	205	27	50.56
R. N. Harvey	79	137	10	6,149	205	21	48.42
K. D. Walters	75	125	14	5,357	250	15	48.26
W. H. Ponsford	29	48	4	2,122	266	7	48.23
S. J. McCabe	39	62	5	2,748	232	6	48.21
A. Jackson	8	11	1	474	164	1	47.40
A. C. Gilchrist	17	25	4	994	149*	2	47.33
W. M. Lawry	68	123	12	5,234	210	13	47.15
R. M. Cowper	27	46	2	2,061	307	5	46.84

† *Bannerman retired hurt*

MOST HUNDREDS

	T	I	100s	Eng	SAf	WI	NZ	Ind	Pak	SL	Zim
D. G. Bradman ...	52	80	29	19	4	2	0	4	0	0	0
A. R. Border	156	265	27	8	0	3	5	4	6	1	0
S. R. Waugh	135	215	25	7	2	6	2	2	2	3	1
G. S. Chappell ...	88	151	24	9	0	5	3	1	6	0	0
R. N. Harvey	79	137	21	6	8	3	0	4	0	0	0
D. C. Boon	107	190	21	7	0	3	3	6	1	1	0
M. A. Taylor	104	186	19	6	2	1	2	2	4	2	0
M. E. Waugh	111	184	18	4	4	4	1	1	3	1	0
K. D. Walters ...	75	125	15	4	0	6	3	1	1	0	0
I. M. Chappell ...	76	136	14	4	0	5	2	2	1	0	0
M. J. Slater	70	124	14	7	0	1	2	0	3	1	0
W. M. Lawry	68	123	13	7	1	4	0	1	0	0	0
A. R. Morris	46	79	12	8	2	1	0	1	0	0	0
D. M. Jones	52	89	11	3	0	1	0	2	2	3	0
A. L. Hassett ...	43	69	10	4	3	2	0	1	0	0	0
R. B. Simpson ...	62	111	10	2	1	1	0	4	2	0	0

CARRYING BAT THROUGH AN INNINGS

(Figures in brackets show side's total)

J. E. Barrett	67*	(176)	v England at Lord's	1890
W. Bardsley.........	193*	(383)	v England at Lord's	1926
W. A. Brown	206*	(422)	v England at Lord's	1938
W. W. Armstrong ...	159*	(309)	v South Africa at Johannesburg (OW)	1902-03
W. M. Woodfull.....	30*	(66)†	v England at Brisbane (Ex)	1928-29
W. M. Woodfull.....	73*	(193)†	v England at Adelaide	1932-33
W. M. Lawry	49*	(107)	v India at Delhi	1969-70
W. M. Lawry	60*	(116)†	v England at Sydney	1970-71
I. R. Redpath	159*	(346)	v New Zealand at Auckland	1973-74
D. C. Boon..........	58*	(103)	v New Zealand at Auckland	1985-86
M. A. Taylor	169*	(350)	v South Africa at Adelaide	1997-98

† *Denotes one or more batsmen absent or retired.*

HIGHEST PARTNERSHIP FOR EACH WICKET

382 for 1st	W. M. Lawry (210)/R. B. Simpson (201)	v West Indies at Bridgetown ...	1964-65
451 for 2nd	W. H. Ponsford (266)/D. G. Bradman (244)	v England at The Oval	1934
295 for 3rd	C. C. McDonald (127)/R. N. Harvey (204)	v West Indies at Kingston	1954-55
388 for 4th	W. H. Ponsford (181)/D. G. Bradman (304)	v England at Leeds	1934
405 for 5th	S. G. Barnes(234)/D. G. Bradman (234)	v England at Sydney	1946-47
346 for 6th	J. H. W. Fingleton (136) /D. G. Bradman (270)	v England at Melbourne	1936-37
217 for 7th	K. D. Walters (250)/G. J. Gilmour (101)	v New Zealand at Christchurch ..	1976-77
243 for 8th	R. J. Hartigan (116) /C. Hill (160)	v England at Adelaide	1907-08
154 for 9th	E. S. Gregory (201)/J. M. Blackham (74)	v England at Sydney	1894-95
127 for 10th	J. M. Taylor (108)/A. A. Mailey (46*)	v England at Sydney	1924-25

PARTNERSHIP RECORDS

451 for 2nd	W. H. Ponsford (266)/D. G. Bradman (244)	v England at The Oval	1934
405 for 5th	S. G. Barnes (234)/D. G. Bradman (234)	v England at Sydney	1946-47
388 for 4th	W. H. Ponsford (181)/D. G. Bradman (304)	v England at Leeds	1934

385 for 5th	G. S. Blewett (214)/S. R. Waugh (160)	v SAf at Johannesburg (WS) .. 1996-97
382 for 1st	W. M. Lawry (210)/R. B. Simpson (201)	v West Indies at Bridgetown .. 1964-65
346 for 6th	J. H. W. Fingleton (136)/D. G. Bradman (270)	v England at Melbourne 1936-37
336 for 4th	W. M. Lawry (151)/K. D. Walters (242)	v West Indies at Sydney 1968-69
332* for 5th	A. R. Border (200*)/S. R. Waugh (157*)	v England at Leeds 1993
329 for 1st	G. R. Marsh (138)/M. A. Taylor (219)	v England at Nottingham 1989
327 for 5th	J. L. Langer (144)/R. T. Ponting (197)	v Pakistan at Perth 1999-00
301 for 2nd	A. R. Morris (182)/D. G. Bradman (173*)	v England at Leeds 1948
298 for 2nd	W. M. Lawry (205)/I. M. Chappell (165)	v West Indies at Melbourne ... 1968-69
295 for 3rd	C. C. McDonald (127)/R. N. Harvey (204)	v West Indies at Kingston 1954-55
279 for 2nd	M. A. Taylor (334*)/J. L. Langer (116)	v Pakistan at Peshawar 1998-99
277 for 2nd	R. B. McCosker (127)/I. M. Chappell (192)	v England at The Oval 1975
276 for 3rd	D. G. Bradman (187)/A. L. Hassett (128)	v England at Brisbane 1946-47
275 for 2nd	C. C. McDonald (154)/A. L. Hassett (163)	v South Africa at Adelaide 1952-53
274 for 2nd	W. M. Woodfull (161)/D. G. Bradman (167)	v South Africa at Melbourne .. 1931-32
269 for 1st	M. J. Slater (169)/G. S. Blewett (89)	v Pakistan at Brisbane 1999-00
268 for 5th	M. T. G. Elliott (199)/R. T. Ponting (127)	v England at Leeds 1997
264 for 3rd	I. M. Chappell (145)/G. S. Chappell (247*)	v New Zealand at Wellington .. 1973-74
260* for 6th	D. M. Jones (118*)/S. R. Waugh (134*)	v Sri Lanka at Hobart 1989-90
260 for 1st	M. A. Taylor (111)/M. J. Slater (152)	v England at Lord's 1993
259 for 2nd	W. B. Phillips (159)/G. N. Yallop (141)	v Pakistan at Perth 1983-84
251 for 4th	G. M. Wood (126)/C. S. Serjeant (124)	v West Indies at Georgetown .. 1977-78

BOWLING RECORDS

MOST WICKETS IN AN INNINGS

9/121	A. A. Mailey	v England at Melbourne	1920-21
8/31	F. Laver	v England at Manchester	1909
8/38	G. D. McGrath	v England at Lord's	1997
8/43	A. E. Trott	v England at Adelaide	1894-95
8/53	R. A. L. Massie	v England at Lord's	1972
8/59	A. A. Mallett	v Pakistan at Adelaide	1972-73
8/65	H. Trumble	v England at The Oval	1902
8/71	G. D. McKenzie	v West Indies at Melbourne	1968-69
8/71	S. K. Warne	v England at Brisbane	1994-95
8/84	R. A. L. Massie	v England at Lord's	1972
8/87	M. G. Hughes	v West Indies at Perth	1988-89
8/97	C. J. McDermott	v England at Perth	1990-91
8/112	G. F. Lawson	v West Indies at Adelaide	1984-85
8/141	C. J. McDermott	v England at Manchester	1985
8/143	M. H. N. Walker	v England at Melbourne	1974-75

MOST WICKETS IN AN INNINGS ON DEBUT

8/43	A. E. Trott	v England at Adelaide	1894-95
8/53	R. A. L. Massie	v England at Lord's	1972
8/84	R. A. L. Massie	v England at Lord's	1972
7/55	T. K. Kendall	v England at Melbourne	1876-77
6/15	C. T. B. Turner	v England at Sydney	1886-87
6/37	C. V. Grimmett	v England at Sydney	1924-25
6/49	M. A. Noble	v England at Melbourne	1897-98
6/58	A. I. C. Dodemaide	v New Zealand at Melbourne	1987-88
6/74	R. M. Hogg	v England at Brisbane	1978-79
6/78	P. L. Taylor	v England at Sydney	1986-87
6/102	F. A. Ward	v England at Brisbane	1936-37
6/120	W. H. Cooper	v England at Melbourne	1881-82

MOST WICKETS IN A MATCH

16/137	R. A. L. Massie	v England at Lord's	1972
14/90	F. R. Spofforth	v England at The Oval	1882
14/199	C. V. Grimmett	v South Africa at Adelaide	1931-32
13/77	M. A. Noble	v England at Melbourne	1901-02
13/110	F. R. Spofforth	v England at Melbourne	1878-79
13/148	B. A. Reid	v England at Melbourne	1990-91
13/173	C. V. Grimmett	v South Africa at Durban (Kingsmead)	1935-36
13/217	M. G. Hughes	v West Indies at Perth	1988-89
13/236	A. A. Mailey	v England at Melbourne	1920-21
12/87	C. T. B. Turner	v England at Sydney	1887-88

MOST WICKETS IN A MATCH ON DEBUT

16/137	R. A. L. Massie	v England at Lord's	1972
11/82	C. V. Grimmett	v England at Sydney	1924-25
9/103	J. J. Ferris	v England at Sydney	1886-87
9/130	T. M. Alderman	v England at Nottingham	1981
9/162	J. V. Saunders	v England at Sydney	1901-02
9/200	W. H. Cooper	v England at Melbourne	1881-82
8/52	A. E. Trott	v England at Adelaide	1894-95
8/68	C. T. B. Turner	v England at Sydney	1886-87
8/99	L. C. Mayne	v West Indies at Kingston	1964-65
8/105	H. V. Hordern	v South Africa at Melbourne	1910-11

HAT-TRICKS

F. R. Spofforth	v England at Melbourne	1878-79
H. Trumble	v England at Melbourne	1901-02
H. Trumble	v England at Melbourne	1903-04
T. J. Matthews*	v South Africa at Manchester	1912
T. J. Matthews†	v South Africa at Manchester	1912
L. F. Kline	v South Africa at Cape Town	1957-58
M. G. Hughes	v West Indies at Perth	1988-89
D. W. Fleming	v Pakistan at Rawalpindi	1994-95
S. K. Warne	v England at Melbourne	1994-95
G. D. McGrath	v West Indies at Perth	2000-01

* 1st Innings, † 2nd Innings

MOST WICKETS IN A SERIES

	T	O	Mdns	R	W	BB	5 W/i	10 W/m	Avge	
C. V. Grimmett	5	346.1	140	642	44	7/40	5	3	14.59	1935-36 v SAf in South Africa
T. M. Alderman	6	325	76	893	42	6/135	4	0	21.26	1981 v England in England
R. M. Hogg	6	217.4	60	527	41	6/74	5	2	12.85	1978-79 v England in Australia
T. M. Alderman	6	269.2	68	712	41	6/128	6	1	17.37	1989 v England in England
D. K. Lillee	6	311.4	81	870	39	7/89	2	1	22.31	1981 v England in England
W. J. Whitty	5	232.3	55	632	37	6/17	2	0	17.08	1910-11 v SAf in Australia
A. A. Mailey	5	244.1	27	946	36	9/121	4	2	26.28	1920-21 v England in Australia
G. D. McGrath	6	249.5	67	701	36	8/38	2	0	19.47	1997 v England in England
G. Giffen	5	343.2	111	820	34	6/155	3	0	24.12	1894-95 v England in Australia
G. F. Lawson	5	230.4	51	687	34	6/47	4	1	20.21	1982-83 v England in Australia
S. K. Warne	6	439.5	178	877	34	5/82	1	0	25.79	1993 v England in England
C. V. Grimmett	5	239.2	61	593	33	7/87	2	1	17.97	1930-31 v WI in Australia
C. V. Grimmett	5	306	108	557	33	7/83	3	1	16.88	1931-32 v SAf in Australia
A. K. Davidson	4	173.7	25	612	33	6/53	5	1	18.55	1960-61 v WI in Australia
J. R. Thomson	5	175.1	34	592	33	6/46	2	0	17.94	1974-75 v England in Australia
M. A. Noble	5	230	68	608	32	7/17	4	1	19.00	1901-02 v England in Australia
H. V. Hordern	5	277.3	43	780	32	7/90	4	2	24.38	1911-12 v England in Australia

	T	O	Mdns	R	W	BB	5 W/i	10 W/m	Avge	
C. J. McDermott	5	232.5	56	675	32	6/38	4	0	21.09	1994-95 v England in Australia
J. V. Saunders	5	267.1	52	716	31	5/28	3	0	23.10	1907-08 v England in Australia
H. Ironmonger	4	221.5	112	296	31	6/18	3	1	9.55	1931-32 v SAf in Australia
R. Benaud	5	233.2	65	584	31	5/83	2	0	18.84	1958-59 v England in Australia
D. K. Lillee	5	249.5	83	548	31	6/66	3	1	17.68	1972 v England in England
C. J. McDermott	5	264.2	75	670	31	5/54	3	1	21.61	1991-92 v India in Australia
M. G. Hughes	6	296.2	78	845	31	5/92	1	0	27.26	1993 v England in England
R. Benaud	5	242.1	56	658	30	5/49	4	0	21.93	1957-58 v SAf in South Africa
G. D. McKenzie	5	206.1	27	758	30	8/71	1	1	25.27	1968-69 v WI in Australia
C. J. McDermott	6	234.2	21	901	30	8/141	2	0	30.03	1985 v England in England
G. D. McGrath	4	199.4	59	508	30	5/28	4	1	16.93	1998-99 v WI in West Indies

Most wickets in a series against opponents not mentioned above:

G. F. Lawson	5	188.3	40	580	24	5/49	2	0	24.17	1983-84 v Pakistan in Australia
G. D. McGrath	3	154.5	35	438	21	5/40	1	0	20.86	1995-96 v SL in Australia
S. K. Warne	3	170.4	36	476	19	5/88	1	0	25.05	1997-98 v NZ in Australia
G. D. McGrath	1	54	19	90	6	3/44	0	0	15.00	1999-00 v Zim in Zimbabwe
S. K. Warne	1	53.1	13	137	6	3/68	0	0	22.83	1999-00 v Zim in Zimbabwe

MOST WICKETS IN A CAREER

		T	Balls	Mdns	R	W	BB	5W/i	10W/m	Avge
1	S. K. Warne	87	24,415	1,226	10,010	376	8/71	16	4	26.62
2	D. K. Lillee	70	18,467	652	8,493	355	7/83	23	7	23.92
3	G. D. McGrath	70	16,784	820	7,078	326	8/38	18	3	21.71
4	C. J. McDermott	71	16,586	581	8,332	291	8/97	14	2	28.63
5	R. Benaud	63	19,108	805	6,704	248	7/72	16	1	27.03
6	G. D. McKenzie	61	17,684	547	7,328	246	8/71	16	3	29.79
7	R. R. Lindwall	61	13,650	419	5,251	228	7/38	12	0	23.03
8	C. V. Grimmett	37	14,513	736	5,231	216	7/40	21	7	24.22
9	M. G. Hughes	53	12,285	499	6,017	212	8/87	7	1	28.38
10	J. R. Thomson	51	10,535	300	5,602	200	6/46	8	0	28.01
11	A. K. Davidson	44	11,587	431	3,819	186	7/93	14	2	20.53
12	G. F. Lawson	46	11,118	386	5,501	180	8/112	11	2	30.56
13	K. R. Miller	55	10,389	337	3,906	170	7/60	7	1	22.98
	T. M. Alderman	41	10,181	432	4,616	170	6/47	14	1	27.15
14	W. A. Johnston	40	11,048	372	3,826	160	6/44	7	0	23.91
15	W. J. O'Reilly	27	10,024	585	3,254	144	7/54	11	3	22.60
16	H. Trumble	32	8,099	452	3,072	141	8/65	9	3	21.79
17	M. H. N. Walker	34	10,094	380	3,792	138	8/143	6	0	27.48
18	A. A. Mallett	39	9,990	449	3,940	132	8/59	6	1	29.85
19	B. Yardley	33	8,909	379	3,986	126	7/98	6	1	31.63
20	R. M. Hogg	38	7,633	230	3,503	123	6/74	6	2	28.48
21	M. A. Noble	42	7,159	361	3,025	121	7/17	9	2	25.00
22	B. A. Reid	27	6,244	245	2,784	113	7/51	5	2	24.64
23	I. W. G. Johnson	45	8,780	330	3,182	109	7/44	3	0	29.19
24	P. R. Reiffel	35	6,403	279	2,804	104	6/71	5	0	26.96
25	G. Giffen	31	6,391	434	2,791	103	7/117	7	1	27.10
26	A. N. Connolly	30	7,818	289	2,981	102	6/47	4	0	29.23
27	C. T. B. Turner	17	5,179	457	1,670	101	7/43	11	2	16.53
28	A. A. Mailey	21	6,119	115	3,358	99	9/121	6	2	33.92
29	F. R. Spofforth	18	4,185	416	1,731	94	7/44	7	4	18.41
30	J. W. Gleeson	30	8,857	378	3,367	93	5/61	3	0	36.20
31	N. J. N. Hawke	27	6,974	238	2,677	91	7/105	6	1	29.42
32	A. Cotter	21	4,639	86	2,549	89	7/148	7	0	28.64
33	S. R. Waugh	135	7,175	309	3,181	89	5/28	3	0	35.74
35	W. W. Armstrong	50	8,022	407	2,923	87	6/35	3	0	33.60
36	J. M. Gregory	24	5,582	138	2,648	85	7/69	4	0	31.15
37	J. N. Gillespie	21	3,831	177	1,870	83	7/37	5	0	22.53

		T	Balls	Mdns	R	W	BB	5Wi	10W/m	Avge
38	J. V. Saunders	14	3,565	116	1,796	79	7/34	6	0	22.73
39	{ G. E. Palmer	17	4,517	452	1,678	78	7/65	6	2	21.51
	{ G. Dymock	21	5,545	179	2,116	78	7/67	5	1	27.13
	{ T. B. A. May	24	6,577	322	2,606	75	5/9	3	0	34.75
41	{ S. C. G. MacGill	16	3,747	134	1,877	75	7/50	4	1	25.03
	{ D. W. Fleming	20	4,129	153	1,942	75	5/30	3	0	25.89
44	H. Ironmonger	14	4,695	328	1,330	74	7/23	4	2	17.97
45	R. B. Simpson	62	6,881	253	3,001	71	5/57	2	0	42.27
46	C. R. Miller	18	4,091	163	1,805	69	5/32	3	1	26.16
47	J. D. Higgs	22	4,752	176	2,057	66	7/143	2	0	31.17
48	W. J. Whitty	14	3,357	163	1,373	65	6/17	3	0	21.12
49	{ E. Jones	19	3,754	161	1,857	64	7/88	3	1	29.02
	{ L. S. Pascoe	14	3,403	112	1,668	64	5/59	1	0	26.06
51	G. R. J. Matthews	33	6,271	256	2,942	61	5/103	2	1	48.23
52	T. W. Wall	18	4,812	154	2,010	56	5/14	3	0	35.89
53	{ G. J. Gilmour	15	2,661	51	1,406	54	6/85	3	0	26.04
	{ M. E. Waugh	111	4,344	157	2,105	54	5/40	1	0	38.98
55	{ K. J. O'Keeffe	24	5,384	189	2,018	53	5/101	1	0	38.08
	{ R. J. Bright	25	5,541	298	2,180	53	7/87	4	1	41.13
57	C. Kelleway	26	4,363	146	1,683	52	5/33	1	0	32.37
58	K. D. Mackay	37	5,792	267	1,721	50	6/42	2	0	34.42

LOWEST CAREER AVERAGES

	T	Balls	Mdns	R	W	BB	5Wi	10W/m	Avge
J. Benaud	3	24	1	12	2	2/12	0	0	6.00
W. H. Moule	1	51	4	23	3	3/23	0	0	7.67
P. C. Charlton	2	45	1	24	3	3/18	0	0	8.00
M. J. Slater	70	25	1	10	1	1/4	0	0	10.00
L. J. Johnson	1	282	10	74	6	3/8	0	0	12.33
L. J. Nash	2	311	12	126	10	4/18	0	0	12.60
M. F. Malone	1	342	24	77	6	5/63	1	0	12.83
T. P. Horan	15	373	45	143	11	6/40	1	0	13.00
J. P. F. Travers	1	48	2	14	1	1/14	0	0	14.00
J. H. Hodges	2	136	9	84	6	2/7	0	0	14.00
J. J. Ferris	8	2,030	224	684	48	5/26	4	0	14.25
A. E. Trott	5	948	54	390	26	8/43	2	0	15.00
J. W. Rutherford	1	36	2	15	1	1/11	0	0	15.00

WICKET-KEEPING RECORDS

MOST DISMISSALS IN AN INNINGS

6	(all ct)	A. T. W. Grout	v South Africa at Johannesburg	1957-58
6	(all ct)	R. W. Marsh	v England at Brisbane	1982-83
6	(all ct)	I. A. Healy	v England at Birmingham	1997

Note: There are 40 instances of 5 dismissals in an innings.

MOST DISMISSALS IN A MATCH

10	(all ct)	A. C. Gilchrist	v New Zealand at Hamilton	1999-00
9	(8ct, 1st)	G. R. A. Langley	v England at Lord's	1956
9	(all ct)	R. W. Marsh	v England at Brisbane	1982-83
9	(all ct)	I. A. Healy	v England at Brisbane	1994-95

Note: There are 13 instances of eight dismissals in a match.

MOST DISMISSALS IN A SERIES

28	(all ct)	R. W. Marsh	v England in Australia	1982-83
27	(25ct, 2st)	I. A. Healy	v England in England	1997
26	(all ct)	R. W. Marsh	v West Indies in Australia	1975-76
26	(21ct, 5st)	I. A. Healy	v England in England	1993
25	(23ct, 2st)	I. A. Healy	v England in Australia	1994-95
24	(all ct)	I. A. Healy	v England in Australia	1990-91
23	(20ct, 3st)	A. T. W. Grout	v West Indies in Australia	1960-61
23	(21ct, 2st)	R. W. Marsh	v England in England	1972
23	(all ct)	R. W. Marsh	v England in England	1981
23	(19ct, 4st)	I. A. Healy	v West Indies in Australia	1992-93
22	(all ct)	S. J. Rixon	v India in Australia	1977-78
21	(13ct, 8st)	R. A. Saggers	v South Africa in South Africa	1949-50
21	(16ct, 5st)	G. R. A. Langley	v West Indies in Australia	1951-52
21	(20ct, 1st)	A. T. W. Grout	v England in England	1961
21	(all ct)	R. W. Marsh	v Pakistan in Australia	1983-84
21	(19ct, 2st)	A. C. Gilchrist	v West Indies in Australia	2000-01
20	(16ct, 4st)	D. Tallon	v England in Australia	1946-47
20	(16ct, 4st)	G. R. A. Langley	v West Indies in West Indies	1954-55
20	(17ct, 3st)	A. T. W. Grout	v England in Australia	1958-59
20	(19ct, 1st)	H. B. Taber	v South Africa in South Africa	1966-67

MOST DISMISSALS IN A CAREER

		M	Ct	St	Total
1	I. A. Healy	119	366	29	395
2	R. W. Marsh	97	343	12	355
3	A. T. W. Grout	51	163	24	187
4	W. A. S. Oldfield	54	78	52	130
5	G. R. A. Langley	26	83	15	98
6.	A. C. Gilchrist	17	70	5	75
7.	H. Carter	28	44	21	65
8.	J. J. Kelly	36	43	20	63
9.	J. M. Blackham	35	36	24	60
10.	H. B. Taber	16	56	4	60
11.	D. Tallon	21	50	8	58
12.	B. N. Jarman	19	50	4	54
13.	S. J. Rixon	13	42	5	47
14.	W. B. Phillips	27	43	0	43
15.	K. J. Wright	10	31	4	35
16 {	R. A. Saggers	6	16	8	24
	G. C. Dyer	6	22	2	24
18	T. J. Zoehrer	10	18	1	19
19	L. V. Maddocks	7	18	1	19
20	A. H. Jarvis	11	9	9	18
21 {	J. A. Maclean	4	18	0	18
	R. D. Woolley	2	7	0	7
23 {	W. Carkeek	6	6	0	6
	P. A. Emery	1	5	1	6
25	B. A. Barnett	4	3	2	5
26	H. S. B. Love	1	3	0	3
27 {	W. L. Murdoch	18	1	1	2
	F. J. Burton	2	1	1	2

FIELDING RECORDS

MOST CATCHES IN AN INNINGS

5   V. Y. Richardson . . . . v South Africa at Durban 1935-36

Note: There are 17 instances of four catches in an innings.

MOST CATCHES IN A MATCH

7	G. S. Chappell	v England at Perth	1974-75
6	J. M. Gregory	v England at Sydney	1920-21
6	V. Y. Richardson	v South Africa at Durban	1935-36
6	R. N. Harvey	v England at Sydney	1962-63
6	I. M. Chappell	v New Zealand at Adelaide	1973-74
6	D. F. Whatmore	v India at Kanpur	1979-80
6	M. E. Waugh	v India at Chennai (Chepauk)	2000-01

Note: There are ten instances of five catches in a match.

MOST CATCHES IN A SERIES

15	J. M. Gregory	v England in Australia	1920-21
14	G. S. Chappell	v England in Australia	1974-75
13	R. B. Simpson	v South Africa in South Africa	1957-58
13	R. B. Simpson	v West Indies in Australia	1960-61
12	D. F. Whatmore	v India in India	1979-80
12	A. R. Border	v England in England	1981
11	R. B. Simpson	v West Indies in West Indies	1964-65
11	I. M. Chappell	v England in Australia	1974-75
11	I. R. Redpath	v England in Australia	1974-75
11	A. R. Border	v England in England	1985
11	M. A. Taylor	v England in England	1993
11	M. E. Waugh	v India in India	2000-01

Note: There are 14 instances of 10 catches in a series.

MOST CATCHES IN A CAREER

1	M. A. Taylor	157 in 104 matches
2	A. R. Border	156 in 156 matches
3	M. E. Waugh	152 in 111 matches
4	G. S. Chappell	122 in 88 matches
5	R. B. Simpson	110 in 62 matches
6	I. M. Chappell	105 in 76 matches
7	D. C. Boon	99 in 107 matches
8	S. R. Waugh	96 in 135 matches
9	I. R. Redpath	83 in 67 matches
10	S. K. Warne	66 in 87 matches

TEAM RECORDS

HIGHEST INNINGS TOTALS

8-758 dec.	v West Indies at Kingston	1954-55
6-729 dec.	v England at Lord's	1930
701	v England at The Oval	1934
695	v England at The Oval	1930
674	v India at Adelaide	1947-48
668	v West Indies at Bridgetown	1954-55
8-659 dec.	v England at Sydney	1946-47
8-656 dec.	v England at Manchester	1964

4-653 dec.	v England at Leeds	1993
6-650 dec.	v West Indies at Bridgetown	1964-65
645	v England at Brisbane	1946-47
4-632 dec.	v England at Lord's	1993
8-628 dec.	v South Africa at Johannesburg (WS)	1996-97
619	v West Indies at Sydney	1968-69
617	v Pakistan at Faisalabad	1979-80
5-617 dec.	v Sri Lanka at Perth	1995-96
6-607 dec.	v New Zealand at Brisbane	1993-94
604	v England at Melbourne	1936-37
6-602 dec.	v England at Nottingham	1989
8-601 dec.	v England at Brisbane	1954-55
7-601 dec.	v England at Leeds	1989
600	v England at Melbourne	1924-25
9-600 dec.	v West Indies at Port-of-Spain	1954-55

HIGHEST FOURTH-INNINGS TOTALS

To Win

3-404	v England at Leeds	1948
6-369	v Pakistan at Hobart (Bellerive)	1999-00
7-362	v West Indies at Georgetown	1977-78
8-342	v India at Perth	1977-78
5-336	v South Africa at Durban (Kingsmead)	1949-50

To Tie

232	(set 233)	v West Indies at Brisbane	1960-61

To Draw

7-344	(set 448)	v England at Sydney	1994-95
9-339	(set 359)	v West Indies at Adelaide	1968-69
3-329	(set 483)	v England at Lord's	1975
3-328	(set 468)	v England at Adelaide	1970-71
2-274	(set 398)	v South Africa at Johannesburg (OW)	1935-36

To Lose

402	(set 505)	v England at Manchester	1981
339	(set 377)	v South Africa at Adelaide	1910-11
336	(set 348)	v England at Adelaide	1928-29
335	(set 428)	v England at Nottingham	1930
333	(set 427)	v England at Melbourne	1894-95

LOWEST INNINGS TOTALS

36	v England at Birmingham	1902
42	v England at Sydney	1887-88
44	v England at The Oval	1896
53	v England at Lord's	1896
58	v England at Brisbane	1936-37
60	v England at Lord's	1888
63	v England at The Oval	1882
65	v England at The Oval	1912
66	v England at Brisbane	1928-29
68	v England at The Oval	1886
70	v England at Manchester	1888
74	v England at Birmingham	1909
75	v South Africa at Durban (Kingsmead)	1949-50
76	v West Indies at Perth	1984-85
78	v England at Lord's	1968
80	v England at The Oval	1888
80	v England at Sydney	1936-37

80	v Pakistan at Karachi	1956-57
81	v England at Manchester	1888
82	v England at Sydney	1887-88
82	v West Indies at Adelaide	1951-52
83	v England at Sydney	1882-83
83	v India at Melbourne	1980-81
84	v England at Sydney	1886-87
84	v England at Manchester	1956
86	v England at Manchester	1902
90	v West Indies at Port-of-Spain	1977-78
91	v England at The Oval	1893
92	v England at The Oval	1890
94	v West Indies at Port-of-Spain	1977-78
97	v England at Sydney	1886-87
97	v West Indies at Bridgetown	1983-84
100	v England at The Oval	1888
100	v England at Adelaide	1891-92

Lowest completed innings totals for opponents not mentioned above:

103	v New Zealand at Auckland	1985-86
188	v Sri Lanka at Kandy	1999-00
422	v Zimbabwe at Harare	1999-00

LARGEST VICTORIES

Largest Victories by Innings and Runs Margin

Innings and 332	v England at Brisbane	1946-47
Innings and 259	v South Africa at Port Elizabeth	1949-50
Innings and 226	v India at Brisbane	1947-48
Innings and 222	v New Zealand at Hobart	1993-94
Innings and 217	v West Indies at Brisbane (Ex)	1930-31
Innings and 200	v England at Melbourne	1936-37

Largest Victories by Runs Margin

562 runs	v England at The Oval	1934
530 runs	v South Africa at Melbourne	1910-11
409 runs	v England at Lord's	1948
382 runs	v England at Adelaide	1894-95
382 runs	v West Indies at Sydney	1968-69
377 runs	v England at Sydney	1920-21
365 runs	v England at Melbourne	1936-37
352 runs	v West Indies at Melbourne	2000-01
348 runs	v Pakistan at Melbourne	1976-77
329 runs	v England at Perth	1994-95

NARROW VICTORIES

Victory by One Wicket

v West Indies at Melbourne (*Last Wkt*: 38 D. T. Ring 32* and W. A. Johnston 7*) 1951-52

Victory by 20 Runs or Less

3	v England at Manchester	1902
6	v England at Sydney	1884-85
7	v England at The Oval	1882
11	v England at Adelaide	1924-25
16	v India at Brisbane	1977-78
16	v Sri Lanka at Colombo (SSC)	1992-93

HEAVIEST DEFEATS

Heaviest Defeat by an Innings and Runs Margin

Innings and 579	by England at The Oval	1938
Innings and 230	by England at Adelaide	1891-92
Innings and 225	by England at Melbourne	1911-12
Innings and 219	by India at Calcutta	1997-98
Innings and 217	by England at The Oval	1886

Heaviest Defeat by Runs Margin

675 runs	by England at Brisbane (Ex)	1928-29
408 runs	by West Indies at Adelaide	1979-80
343 runs	by West Indies at Bridgetown	1990-91
338 runs	by England at Adelaide	1932-33
323 runs	by South Africa at Port Elizabeth	1969-70
322 runs	by England at Brisbane	1936-37
307 runs	by South Africa at Johannesburg (WS)	1969-70
299 runs	by England at Sydney	1970-71
289 runs	by England at The Oval	1926
285 runs	by West Indies at Melbourne	1988-89

NARROW DEFEATS

Defeat by One Wicket

England at The Oval (*Last Wkt*:15 – G. H. Hirst 58* and W. Rhodes 6*)	1902
England at Melbourne (*Last Wkt*:39 – S. F. Barnes 38* and A. Fielder 18*)	1907-08
Pakistan at Karachi (*Last Wkt*: 57 – Inzamam-ul-Haq 58* and Mushtaq Ahmed 20*)	1994-95
West Indies at Bridgetown (*Last Wkt*: 9 – B. C. Lara 153* and C. A. Walsh 0*)	1998-99

Defeat by 20 Runs or Less

1	by West Indies at Adelaide	1992-93
3	by England at Melbourne	1982-83
5	by South Africa at Sydney	1993-94
10	by England at Sydney	1894-95
12	by England at Adelaide	1928-29
12	by England at Melbourne	1998-99
13	by England at Sydney	1886-87
18	by England at Leeds	1981
19	by England at The Oval	1997

APPEARANCES

MOST TEST APPEARANCES

	T	Eng	SAf	WI	NZ	Ind	Pak	SL	Zim
A. R. Border	156	47	6	31	23	20	22	7	–
S. R. Waugh	135	37	10	28	20	14	17	8	1
I. A. Healy	119	33	12	28	11	9	14	11	1
M. E. Waugh	111	24	12	28	11	14	12	9	1
D. C. Boon	107	31	6	22	17	11	11	9	–
M. A. Taylor	104	33	11	20	11	9	12	8	–
R. W. Marsh	97	43	–	17	14	3	20	–	–
G. S. Chappell	88	36	–	17	14	3	17	1	–
S. K. Warne	87	18	12	16	12	11	9	8	1
R. N. Harvey	79	37	14	14	–	10	4	–	–

YOUNGEST AUSTRALIAN PLAYERS ON DEBUT

Years	Days			
17	239	I. D. Craig	v South Africa at Sydney	1952-53
18	232	T. W. Garrett	v England at Melbourne	1876-77
19	54	A. Cotter	v England at Sydney	1903-04
19	96	C. Hill	v England at Lord's	1896
19	100	G. R. Hazlitt	v England at Sydney	1907-08
19	104	R. G. Archer	v South Africa at Melbourne	1952-53
19	107	R. N. Harvey	v India at Adelaide	1947-48
19	149	A. Jackson	v England at Adelaide	1928-29
19	173	J. T. Cottam	v England at Sydney	1886-87
19	252	J. J. Ferris	v England at Sydney	1886-87
19	252	C. J. McDermott	v West Indies at Melbourne	1984-85
19	331	S. J. McCabe	v England at Nottingham	1930
19	354	K. D. Walters	v England at Brisbane	1965-66
19	363	G. D. McKenzie	v England at Lord's	1961

OLDEST AUSTRALIAN PLAYERS ON DEBUT

Years	Days			
46	253	D. D. Blackie	v England at Sydney	1928-29
46	237	H. Ironmonger	v England at Brisbane (Ex)	1928-29
38	328	N. Thompson	v England at Melbourne	1876-77
38	35	R. G. Holland	v West Indies at Brisbane	1984-85
37	290	E. J. Gregory	v England at Melbourne	1876-77
37	184	H. S. B. Love	v England at Brisbane	1932-33
37	163	J. Harry	v England at Adelaide	1894-95
37	154	R. K. Oxenham	v England at Melbourne	1928-29
36	148	A. J. Richardson	v England at Sydney	1924-25
35	127	J. B. Iverson	v England at Brisbane	1950-51
35	81	K. H. Eastwood	v England at Sydney	1970-71
35	67	J. W. Wilson	v India at Bombay	1956-57
35	4	A. E. V. Hartkopf	v England at Melbourne	1924-25
35	3	T. V. Hohns	v West Indies at Sydney	1988-89

CAPTAINCY

CAPTAINS

		T	W	L	D	T	% Won
1	D. W. Gregory	3	2	1	0	0	66.66
2	W. L. Murdoch	16	5	7	4	0	31.25
3	T. P. Horan	2	0	2	0	0	0.00
4	H. H. Massie	1	1	0	0	0	100.00
5	J. M. Blackham	8	3	3	2	0	37.50
6	H. J. H. Scott	3	0	3	0	0	0.00
7	P. S. McDonnell	6	1	5	0	0	16.66
8	G. Giffen	4	2	2	0	0	50.00
9	G. H. S. Trott	8	5	3	0	0	62.50
10	J. Darling	21	7	4	10	0	33.33
11	H. Trumble	2	2	0	0	0	100.00
12	M. A. Noble	15	8	5	2	0	53.33
13	C. Hill	10	5	5	0	0	50.00
14	E. S. Gregory	6	2	1	3	0	33.33
15	W. W. Armstrong	10	8	0	2	0	80.00
16	H. L. Collins	11	5	2	4	0	45.45
17	W. Bardsley	2	0	0	2	0	0.00
18	J. Ryder	5	1	4	0	0	20.00

		T	W	L	D	T	% Won
19	W. M. Woodfull	25	14	7	4	0	56.00
20	V. Y. Richardson	5	4	0	1	0	80.00
21	D. G. Bradman	24	15	3	6	0	62.50
22	W. A. Brown	1	1	0	0	0	100.00
23	A. L. Hassett	24	14	4	6	0	58.33
24	A. R. Morris	2	0	2	0	0	0.00
25	I. W. G. Johnson	17	7	5	5	0	41.17
26	R. R. Lindwall	1	0	0	1	0	0.00
27	I. D. Craig	5	3	0	2	0	60.00
28	R. Benaud	28	12	4	11	1	42.85
29	R. N. Harvey	1	1	0	0	0	100.00
30	R. B. Simpson	39	12	12	15	0	30.76
31	B. C. Booth	2	0	1	1	0	0.00
32	W. M. Lawry	26	9	8	9	0	34.61
33	B. N. Jarman	1	0	0	1	0	0.00
34	I. M. Chappell	30	15	5	10	0	50.00
35	G. S. Chappell	48	21	13	14	0	43.75
36	G. N. Yallop	7	1	6	0	0	14.28
37	K. J. Hughes	28	4	13	11	0	14.28
38	A. R. Border	93	32	22	38	1	34.40
39	M. A. Taylor	50	26	13	11	0	52.00
40	S. R. Waugh	24	17	5	2	0	70.83
41	A. C. Gilchrist	1	1	0	0	0	100.00

MOST CONSECUTIVE TESTS AS CAPTAIN

93	A. R. Border	December 1984 to March 1994
50	M. A. Taylor	September 1994 to January 1999
30	I. M. Chappell	February 1972 to August 1975
25	W. M. Woodfull	June 1930 to August 1934
21	W. M. Lawry	August 1968 to January 1971
21	S. R. Waugh	March 1999 to December 2000
19	R. Benaud	December 1958 to June 1961
19	R. B. Simpson	January 1964 to May 1965
17	G. S. Chappell	November 1975 to August 1977
16	G. S. Chappell	December 1979 to February 1981
15	I. W. G. Johnson	December 1954 to October 1956

TEST SERIES

Note: The Third Test at the Melbourne Cricket Ground from December 31, 1970-January 5, 1971 has been sanctioned by the Australian Cricket Board as an official Test match. The Australian Cricket Board in consultation with the MCC tour management declared the Test as a 'DRAW'. This decision was determined as the two teams had been officially announced, including the 12th men and the toss having been made. The Umpires were walking out to the ground when rain began to fall and thus preventing any further play in the match.

Opponent	Date of First Test	Tests	Won	Lost	Drawn	Tied
England	Mar, 15, 1877	297	117	93	87	0
South Africa	Oct, 11, 1902	65	34	14	17	0
West Indies	Dec, 12, 1930	95	42	31	21	1
New Zealand	Mar, 29, 1946	38	18	7	13	0
India	Nov, 28, 1947	60	29	13	17	1
Pakistan	Oct, 11, 1956	46	18	11	17	0
Sri Lanka	Apr, 22, 1983	13	7	1	5	0
Zimbabwe	Oct 14, 1999	1	1	0	0	0
Total		615	266	170	177	2

AUSTRALIAN TEST MATCHES

Venue	Opponent	Result for Australia	Captain	Test/Opp
1876-77 in Australia				
Melbourne	England	Won by 45 runs	D. W. Gregory	1/1
Melbourne	England	Lost by four wickets	D. W. Gregory	2/2
1878-79 in Australia				
Melbourne	England	Won by ten wickets	D. W. Gregory	3/3
1880 in England				
The Oval	England	Lost by five wickets	W. L. Murdoch	4/4
1881-82 in Australia				
Melbourne	England	Drawn	W. L. Murdoch	5/5
Sydney	England	Won by five wickets	W. L. Murdoch	6/6
Sydney	England	Won by six wickets	W. L. Murdoch	7/7
Melbourne	England	Drawn	W. L. Murdoch	8/8
1882 in England				
The Oval	England	Won by seven runs	W. L. Murdoch	9/9
1882-83 in Australia				
Melbourne	England	Won by nine wickets	W. L. Murdoch	10/10
Melbourne	England	Lost by an innings and 27 runs	W. L. Murdoch	11/11
Sydney	England	Lost by 69 runs	W. L. Murdoch	12/12
Sydney	England	Won by four wickets	W. L. Murdoch	13/13
1884 in England				
Manchester	England	Drawn	W. L. Murdoch	14/14
Lord's	England	Lost by an innings and five runs	W. L. Murdoch	15/15
The Oval	England	Drawn	W. L. Murdoch	16/16
1884-85 in Australia				
Adelaide	England	Lost by eight wickets	W. L. Murdoch	17/17
Melbourne	England	Lost by ten wickets	T. P. Horan	18/18
Sydney	England	Won by six runs	H. H. Massie	19/19
Sydney	England	Won by eight wickets	J. M. Blackham	20/20
Melbourne	England	Lost by an innings and 98 runs	T. P. Horan	21/21
1886 in England				
Manchester	England	Lost by four wickets	H. J. H. Scott	22/22
Lord's	England	Lost by an innings and 106 runs	H. J. H. Scott	23/23
The Oval	England	Lost by an innings and 217 runs	H. J. H. Scott	24/24
1886-87 in Australia				
Sydney	England	Lost by 13 runs	P. S. McDonnell	25/25
Sydney	England	Lost by 71 runs	P. S. McDonnell	26/26
1887-88 in Australia				
Sydney	England	Lost by 126 runs	P. S. McDonnell	27/27
1888 in England				
Lord's	England	Won by 61 runs	P. S. McDonnell	28/28
The Oval	England	Lost by an innings and 137 runs	P. S. McDonnell	29/29
Manchester	England	Lost by an innings and 21 runs	P. S. McDonnell	30/30
1890 in England				
Lord's	England	Lost by seven wickets	W. L. Murdoch	31/31
The Oval	England	Lost by two wickets	W. L. Murdoch	32/32
1891-92 in Australia				
Melbourne	England	Won by 54 runs	J. M. Blackham	33/33
Sydney	England	Won by 72 runs	J. M. Blackham	34/34
Adelaide	England	Lost by an innings and 230 runs	J. M. Blackham	35/35

Venue	Opponent	Result for Australia	Captain	Test/Opp
1893 in England				
Lord's	England	Drawn	J. M. Blackham	36/36
The Oval	England	Lost by an innings and 43 runs	J. M. Blackham	37/37
Manchester	England	Drawn	J. M. Blackham	38/38
1894-95 in Australia				
Sydney	England	Lost by ten runs	J. M. Blackham	39/39
Melbourne	England	Lost by 94 runs	G. Giffen	40/40
Adelaide	England	Won by 382 runs	G. Giffen	41/41
Sydney	England	Won by an innings and 147 runs	G. Giffen	42/42
Melbourne	England	Lost by six wickets	G. Giffen	43/43
1896 in England				
Lord's	England	Lost by six wickets	G. H. S. Trott	44/44
Manchester	England	Won by three wickets	G. H. S. Trott	45/45
The Oval	England	Lost by 66 runs	G. H. S. Trott	46/46
1897-98 in Australia				
Sydney	England	Lost by nine wickets	G. H. S. Trott	47/47
Melbourne	England	Won by an innings and 55 runs	G. H. S. Trott	48/48
Adelaide	England	Won by an innings and 13 runs	G. H. S. Trott	49/49
Melbourne	England	Won by eight wickets	G. H. S. Trott	50/50
Sydney	England	Won by six wickets	G. H. S. Trott	51/51
1899 in England				
Nottingham	England	Drawn	J. Darling	52/52
Lord's	England	Won by ten wickets	J. Darling	53/53
Leeds	England	Drawn	J. Darling	54/54
Manchester	England	Drawn	J. Darling	55/55
The Oval	England	Drawn	J. Darling	56/56
1901-02 in Australia				
Sydney	England	Lost by an innings and 124 runs	J. Darling	57/57
Melbourne	England	Won by 229 runs	J. Darling	58/58
Adelaide	England	Won by four wickets	J. Darling	59/59
Sydney	England	Won by seven wickets	H. Trumble	60/60
Melbourne	England	Won by 32 runs	H. Trumble	61/61
1902 in England				
Birmingham	England	Drawn	J. Darling	62/62
Lord's	England	Drawn	J. Darling	63/63
Sheffield	England	Won by 143 runs	J. Darling	64/64
Manchester	England	Won by three runs	J. Darling	65/65
The Oval	England	Lost by one wicket	J. Darling	66/66
1902-03 in South Africa				
Johannesburg (OW)	South Africa	Drawn	J. Darling	67/1
Johannesburg (OW)	South Africa	Won by 159 runs	J. Darling	68/2
Cape Town	South Africa	Won by ten wickets	J. Darling	69/3
1903-04 in Australia				
Sydney	England	Lost by five wickets	M. A. Noble	70/67
Melbourne	England	Lost by 185 runs	M. A. Noble	71/68
Adelaide	England	Won by 216 runs	M. A. Noble	72/69
Sydney	England	Lost by 157 runs	M. A. Noble	73/70
Melbourne	England	Won by 218 runs	M. A. Noble	74/71
1905 in England				
Nottingham	England	Lost by 213 runs	J. Darling	75/72
Lord's	England	Drawn	J. Darling	76/73
Leeds	England	Drawn	J. Darling	77/74
Manchester	England	Lost by an innings and 80 runs	J. Darling	78/75
The Oval	England	Drawn	J. Darling	79/76

Venue	Opponent	Result for Australia	Captain	Test/Opp
1907-08 in Australia				
Sydney	England	Won by two wickets	M. A. Noble	80/77
Melbourne	England	Lost by one wicket	M. A. Noble	81/78
Adelaide	England	Won by 245 runs	M. A. Noble	82/79
Melbourne	England	Won by 308 runs	M. A. Noble	83/80
Sydney	England	Won by 49 runs	M. A. Noble	84/81
1909 in England				
Birmingham	England	Lost by ten wickets	M. A. Noble	85/82
Lord's	England	Won by nine wickets	M. A. Noble	86/83
Leeds	England	Won by 126 runs	M. A. Noble	87/84
Manchester	England	Drawn	M. A. Noble	88/85
The Oval	England	Drawn	M. A. Noble	89/86
1910-11 in Australia				
Sydney	South Africa	Won by an innings and 114 runs	C. Hill	90/4
Melbourne	South Africa	Won by 89 runs	C. Hill	91/5
Adelaide	South Africa	Lost by 38 runs	C. Hill	92/6
Melbourne	South Africa	Won by 530 runs	C. Hill	93/7
Sydney	South Africa	Won by seven wickets	C. Hill	94/8
1911-12 in Australia				
Sydney	England	Won by 146 runs	C. Hill	95/87
Melbourne	England	Lost by eight wickets	C. Hill	96/88
Adelaide	England	Lost by seven wickets	C. Hill	97/89
Melbourne	England	Lost by an innings and 225 runs	C. Hill	98/90
Sydney	England	Lost by 70 runs	C. Hill	99/91
1912 in England				
Manchester	South Africa	Won by an innings and 88 runs	E. S. Gregory	100/9
Lord's	England	Drawn	E. S. Gregory	101/92
Lord's	South Africa	Won by ten wickets	E. S. Gregory	102/10
Manchester	England	Drawn	E. S. Gregory	103/93
Nottingham	South Africa	Drawn	E. S. Gregory	104/11
The Oval	England	Lost by 244 runs	E. S. Gregory	105/94
1920-21 in Australia				
Sydney	England	Won by 377 runs	W. W. Armstrong	106/95
Melbourne	England	Won by an innings and 91 runs	W. W. Armstrong	107/96
Adelaide	England	Won by 119 runs	W. W. Armstrong	108/97
Melbourne	England	Won by eight wickets	W. W. Armstrong	109/98
Sydney	England	Won by nine wickets	W. W. Armstrong	110/99
1921 in England				
Nottingham	England	Won by ten wickets	W. W. Armstrong	111/100
Lord's	England	Won by eight wickets	W. W. Armstrong	112/101
Leeds	England	Won by 219 runs	W. W. Armstrong	113/102
Manchester	England	Drawn	W. W. Armstrong	114/103
The Oval	England	Drawn	W. W. Armstrong	115/104
1921-22 in South Africa				
Durban (Lord's)	South Africa	Drawn	H. L. Collins	116/12
Johannesburg (OW)	South Africa	Drawn	H. L. Collins	117/13
Cape Town	South Africa	Won by ten wickets	H. L. Collins	118/14
1924-25 in Australia				
Sydney	England	Won by 193 runs	H. L. Collins	119/105
Melbourne	England	Won by 81 runs	H. L. Collins	120/106
Adelaide	England	Won by 11 runs	H. L. Collins	121/107
Melbourne	England	Lost by an innings and 29 runs	H. L. Collins	122/108
Sydney	England	Won by 307 runs	H. L. Collins	123/109

Venue	Opponent	Result for Australia	Captain	Test/Opp
1926 in England				
Nottingham	England	Drawn	H. L. Collins	124/110
Lord's	England	Drawn	H. L. Collins	125/111
Leeds	England	Drawn	W. Bardsley	126/112
Manchester	England	Drawn	W. Bardsley	127/113
The Oval	England	Lost by 289 runs	H. L. Collins	128/114
1928-29 in Australia				
Brisbane (Ex)	England	Lost by 675 runs	J. Ryder	129/115
Sydney	England	Lost by eight wickets	J. Ryder	130/116
Melbourne	England	Lost by three wickets	J. Ryder	131/117
Adelaide	England	Lost by 12 runs	J. Ryder	132/118
Melbourne	England	Won by five wickets	J. Ryder	133/119
1930 in England				
Nottingham	England	Lost by 93 runs	W. M. Woodfull	134/120
Lord's	England	Won by seven wickets	W. M. Woodfull	135/121
Leeds	England	Drawn	W. M. Woodfull	136/122
Manchester	England	Drawn	W. M. Woodfull	137/123
The Oval	England	Won by an innings and 39 runs	W. M. Woodfull	138/124
1930-31 in Australia				
Adelaide	West Indies	Won by ten wickets	W. M. Woodfull	139/1
Sydney	West Indies	Won by an innings and 172 runs	W. M. Woodfull	140/2
Brisbane (Ex)	West Indies	Won by an innings and 217 runs	W. M. Woodfull	141/3
Melbourne	West Indies	Won by an innings and 122 runs	W. M. Woodfull	142/4
Sydney	West Indies	Lost by 30 runs	W. M. Woodfull	143/5
1931-32 in Australia				
Brisbane	South Africa	Won by an innings and 163 runs	W. M. Woodfull	144/15
Sydney	South Africa	Won by an innings and 155 runs	W. M. Woodfull	145/16
Melbourne	South Africa	Won by 169 runs	W. M. Woodfull	146/17
Adelaide	South Africa	Won by ten wickets	W. M. Woodfull	147/18
Melbourne	South Africa	Won by an innings and 72 runs	W. M. Woodfull	148/19
1932-33 in Australia				
Sydney	England	Lost by ten wickets	W. M. Woodfull	149/125
Melbourne	England	Won by 111 runs	W. M. Woodfull	150/126
Adelaide	England	Lost by 338 runs	W. M. Woodfull	151/127
Brisbane	England	Lost by six wickets	W. M. Woodfull	152/128
Sydney	England	Lost by eight wickets	W. M. Woodfull	153/129
1934 in England				
Nottingham	England	Won by 238 runs	W. M. Woodfull	154/130
Lord's	England	Lost by an innings and 38 runs	W. M. Woodfull	155/131
Manchester	England	Drawn	W. M. Woodfull	156/132
Leeds	England	Drawn	W. M. Woodfull	157/133
The Oval	England	Won by 562 runs	W. M. Woodfull	158/134
1935-36 in South Africa				
Durban (Kingsmead)	South Africa	Won by nine wickets	V. Y. Richardson	159/20
Johannesburg (OW)	South Africa	Drawn	V. Y. Richardson	160/21
Cape Town	South Africa	Won by an innings and 78 runs	V. Y. Richardson	161/22
Johannesburg (OW)	South Africa	Won by an innings and 184 runs	V. Y. Richardson	162/23
Durban (Kingsmead)	South Africa	Won by an innings and six runs	V. Y. Richardson	163/24
1936-37 in Australia				
Brisbane	England	Lost by 322 runs	D. G. Bradman	164/135
Sydney	England	Lost by an innings and 22 runs	D. G. Bradman	165/136
Melbourne	England	Won by 365 runs	D. G. Bradman	166/137
Adelaide	England	Won by 148 runs	D. G. Bradman	167/138
Melbourne	England	Won by an innings and 200 runs	D. G. Bradman	168/139

Venue	Opponent	Result for Australia	Captain	Test/Opp
1938 in England				
Nottingham	England	Drawn	D. G. Bradman	169/140
Lord's	England	Drawn	D. G. Bradman	170/141
Leeds	England	Won by five wickets	D. G. Bradman	171/142
The Oval	England	Lost by an innings and 579 runs	D. G. Bradman	172/143
1945-46 in New Zealand				
Wellington	New Zealand	Won by an innings and 103 runs	W. A. Brown	173/1
1946-47 in Australia				
Brisbane	England	Won by an innings and 332 runs	D. G. Bradman	174/144
Sydney	England	Won by an innings and 33 runs	D. G. Bradman	175/145
Melbourne	England	Drawn	D. G. Bradman	176/146
Adelaide	England	Drawn	D. G. Bradman	177/147
Sydney	England	Won by five wickets	D. G. Bradman	178/148
1947-48 in Australia				
Brisbane	India	Won by an innings and 226 runs	D. G. Bradman	179/1
Sydney	India	Drawn	D. G. Bradman	180/2
Melbourne	India	Won by 233 runs	D. G. Bradman	181/3
Adelaide	India	Won by an innings and 16 runs	D. G. Bradman	182/4
Melbourne	India	Won by an innings and 177 runs	D. G. Bradman	183/5
1948 in England				
Nottingham	England	Won by eight wickets	D. G. Bradman	184/149
Lord's	England	Won by 409 runs	D. G. Bradman	185/150
Manchester	England	Drawn	D. G. Bradman	186/151
Leeds	England	Won by seven wickets	D. G. Bradman	187/152
The Oval	England	Won by an innings and 149 runs	D. G. Bradman	188/153
1949-50 in South Africa				
Johannesburg (EP)	South Africa	Won by an innings and 85 runs	A. L. Hassett	189/25
Cape Town	South Africa	Won by eight wickets	A. L. Hassett	190/26
Durban (Kingsmead)	South Africa	Won by five wickets	A. L. Hassett	191/27
Johannesburg (EP)	South Africa	Drawn	A. L. Hassett	192/28
Port Elizabeth	South Africa	Won by an innings and 259 runs	A. L. Hassett	193/29
1950-51 in Australia				
Brisbane	England	Won by 70 runs	A. L. Hassett	194/154
Melbourne	England	Won by 28 runs	A. L. Hassett	195/155
Sydney	England	Won by an innings and 13 runs	A. L. Hassett	196/156
Adelaide	England	Won by 274 runs	A. L. Hassett	197/157
Melbourne	England	Lost by eight wickets	A. L. Hassett	198/158
1951-52 in Australia				
Brisbane	West Indies	Won by three wickets	A. L. Hassett	199/6
Sydney	West Indies	Won by seven wickets	A. L. Hassett	200/7
Adelaide	West Indies	Lost by six wickets	A. R. Morris	201/8
Melbourne	West Indies	Won by one wicket	A. L. Hassett	202/9
Sydney	West Indies	Won by 202 runs	A. L. Hassett	203/10
1952-53 in Australia				
Brisbane	South Africa	Won by 96 runs	A. L. Hassett	204/30
Melbourne	South Africa	Lost by 82 runs	A. L. Hassett	205/31
Sydney	South Africa	Won by an innings and 38 runs	A. L. Hassett	206/32
Adelaide	South Africa	Drawn	A. L. Hassett	207/33
Melbourne	South Africa	Lost by six wickets	A. L. Hassett	208/34
1953 in England				
Nottingham	England	Drawn	A. L. Hassett	209/159
Lord's	England	Drawn	A. L. Hassett	210/160
Manchester	England	Drawn	A. L. Hassett	211/161
Leeds	England	Drawn	A. L. Hassett	212/162
The Oval	England	Lost by eight wickets	A. L. Hassett	213/163

Venue	Opponent	Result for Australia	Captain	Test/Opp
1954-55 in Australia				
Brisbane	England	Won by an innings and 154 runs	I. W. G. Johnson	214/164
Sydney	England	Lost by 38 runs	A. R. Morris	215/165
Melbourne	England	Lost by 128 runs	I. W. G. Johnson	216/166
Adelaide	England	Lost by five wickets	I. W. G. Johnson	217/167
Sydney	England	Drawn	I. W. G. Johnson	218/168
1954-55 in West Indies				
Kingston	West Indies	Won by nine wickets	I. W. G. Johnson	219/11
Port-of-Spain	West Indies	Drawn	I. W. G. Johnson	220/12
Georgetown	West Indies	Won by eight wickets	I. W. G. Johnson	221/13
Bridgetown	West Indies	Drawn	I. W. G. Johnson	222/14
Kingston	West Indies	Won by an innings and 82 runs	I. W. G. Johnson	223/15
1956 in England				
Nottingham	England	Drawn	I. W. G. Johnson	224/169
Lord's	England	Won by 185 runs	I. W. G. Johnson	225/170
Leeds	England	Lost by an innings and 42 runs	I. W. G. Johnson	226/171
Manchester	England	Lost by an innings and 170 runs	I. W. G. Johnson	227/172
The Oval	England	Drawn	I. W. G. Johnson	228/173
1956-57 in Pakistan				
Karachi	Pakistan	Lost by nine wickets	I. W. G. Johnson	229/1
1956-57 in India				
Madras (Corp)	India	Won by an innings and five runs	I. W. G. Johnson	230/6
Bombay (BS)	India	Drawn	R. R. Lindwall	231/7
Calcutta	India	Won by 94 runs	I. W. G. Johnson	232/8
1957-58 in South Africa				
Johannesburg (WS)	South Africa	Drawn	I. D. Craig	233/35
Cape Town	South Africa	Won by an innings and 141 runs	I. D. Craig	234/36
Durban (Kingsmead)	South Africa	Drawn	I. D. Craig	235/37
Johannesburg (WS)	South Africa	Won by ten wickets	I. D. Craig	236/38
Port Elizabeth	South Africa	Won by eight wickets	I. D. Craig	237/39
1958-59 in Australia				
Brisbane	England	Won by eight wickets	R. Benaud	238/174
Melbourne	England	Won by eight wickets	R. Benaud	239/175
Sydney	England	Drawn	R. Benaud	240/176
Adelaide	England	Won by ten wickets	R. Benaud	241/177
Melbourne	England	Won by nine wickets	R. Benaud	242/178
1959-60 in Pakistan				
Dacca	Pakistan	Won by eight wickets	R. Benaud	243/2
Lahore	Pakistan	Won by seven wickets	R. Benaud	244/3
Karachi	Pakistan	Drawn	R. Benaud	245/4
1959-60 in India				
Delhi	India	Won by an innings and 127 runs	R. Benaud	246/9
Kanpur	India	Lost by 119 runs	R. Benaud	247/10
Bombay (BS)	India	Drawn	R. Benaud	248/11
Madras (Corp)	India	Won by an innings and 55 runs	R. Benaud	249/12
Calcutta	India	Drawn	R. Benaud	250/13
1960-61 in Australia				
Brisbane	West Indies	Tied	R. Benaud	251/16
Melbourne	West Indies	Won by seven wickets	R. Benaud	252/17
Sydney	West Indies	Lost by 222 runs	R. Benaud	253/18
Adelaide	West Indies	Drawn	R. Benaud	254/19
Melbourne	West Indies	Won by two wickets	R. Benaud	255/20

Venue	Opponent	Result for Australia	Captain	Test/Opp
1961 in England				
Birmingham	England	Drawn	R. Benaud	256/179
Lord's	England	Won by five wickets	R. N. Harvey	257/180
Leeds	England	Lost by eight wickets	R. Benaud	258/181
Manchester	England	Won by 54 runs	R. Benaud	259/182
The Oval	England	Drawn	R. Benaud	260/183
1962-63 in Australia				
Brisbane	England	Drawn	R. Benaud	261/184
Melbourne	England	Lost by seven wickets	R. Benaud	262/185
Sydney	England	Won by eight wickets	R. Benaud	263/186
Adelaide	England	Drawn	R. Benaud	264/187
Sydney	England	Drawn	R. Benaud	265/188
1963-64 in Australia				
Brisbane	South Africa	Drawn	R. Benaud	266/40
Melbourne	South Africa	Won by eight wickets	R. B. Simpson	267/41
Sydney	South Africa	Drawn	R. B. Simpson	268/42
Adelaide	South Africa	Lost by ten wickets	R. B. Simpson	269/43
Sydney	South Africa	Drawn	R. B. Simpson	270/44
1964 in England				
Nottingham	England	Drawn	R. B. Simpson	271/189
Lord's	England	Drawn	R. B. Simpson	272/190
Leeds	England	Won by seven wickets	R. B. Simpson	273/191
Manchester	England	Drawn	R. B. Simpson	274/192
The Oval	England	Drawn	R. B. Simpson	275/193
1964-65 in India				
Madras (Corp)	India	Won by 139 runs	R. B. Simpson	276/14
Bombay (BS)	India	Lost by two wickets	R. B. Simpson	277/15
Calcutta	India	Drawn	R. B. Simpson	278/16
1964-65 in Pakistan				
Karachi	Pakistan	Drawn	R. B. Simpson	279/5
1964-65 in Australia				
Melbourne	Pakistan	Drawn	R. B. Simpson	280/6
1964-65 in West Indies				
Kingston	West Indies	Lost by 179 runs	R. B. Simpson	281/21
Port-of-Spain	West Indies	Drawn	R. B. Simpson	282/22
Georgetown	West Indies	Lost by 212 runs	R. B. Simpson	283/23
Bridgetown	West Indies	Drawn	R. B. Simpson	284/24
Port-of-Spain	West Indies	Won by ten wickets	R. B. Simpson	285/25
1965-66 in Australia				
Brisbane	England	Drawn	B. C. Booth	286/194
Melbourne	England	Drawn	R. B. Simpson	287/195
Sydney	England	Lost by an innings and 93 runs	B. C. Booth	288/196
Adelaide	England	Won by an innings and nine runs	R. B. Simpson	289/197
Melbourne	England	Drawn	R. B. Simpson	290/198
1966-67 in South Africa				
Johannesburg (WS)	South Africa	Lost by 233 runs	R. B. Simpson	291/45
Cape Town	South Africa	Won by six wickets	R. B. Simpson	292/46
Durban (Kingsmead)	South Africa	Lost by eight wickets	R. B. Simpson	293/47
Johannesburg (WS)	South Africa	Drawn	R. B. Simpson	294/48
Port Elizabeth	South Africa	Lost by seven wickets	R. B. Simpson	295/49

Venue	Opponent	Result for Australia	Captain	Test/Opp
1967-68 in Australia				
Adelaide	India	Won by 146 runs	R. B. Simpson	296/17
Melbourne	India	Won by an innings and four runs	R. B. Simpson	297/18
Brisbane	India	Won by 39 runs	W. M. Lawry	298/19
Sydney	India	Won by 144 runs	W. M. Lawry	299/20
1968 in England				
Manchester	England	Won by 159 runs	W. M. Lawry	300/199
Lord's	England	Drawn	W. M. Lawry	301/200
Birmingham	England	Drawn	W. M. Lawry	302/201
Leeds	England	Drawn	B. N. Jarman	303/202
The Oval	England	Lost by 226 runs	W. M. Lawry	304/203
1968-69 in Australia				
Brisbane	West Indies	Lost by 125 runs	W. M. Lawry	305/26
Melbourne	West Indies	Won by an innings and 30 runs	W. M. Lawry	306/27
Sydney	West Indies	Won by ten wickets	W. M. Lawry	307/28
Adelaide	West Indies	Drawn	W. M. Lawry	308/29
Sydney	West Indies	Won by 382 runs	W. M. Lawry	309/30
1969-70 in India				
Bombay (BS)	India	Won by eight wickets	W. M. Lawry	310/21
Kanpur	India	Drawn	W. M. Lawry	311/22
Delhi	India	Lost by seven wickets	W. M. Lawry	312/23
Calcutta	India	Won by ten wickets	W. M. Lawry	313/24
Madras (Chepauk)	India	Won by 77 runs	W. M. Lawry	314/25
1969-70 in South Africa				
Cape Town	South Africa	Lost by 170 runs	W. M. Lawry	315/50
Durban (Kingsmead)	South Africa	Lost by an innings and 129 runs	W. M. Lawry	316/51
Johannesburg (WS)	South Africa	Lost by 307 runs	W. M. Lawry	317/52
Port Elizabeth	South Africa	Lost by 323 runs	W. M. Lawry	318/53
1970-71 in Australia				
Brisbane	England	Drawn	W. M. Lawry	319/204
Perth	England	Drawn	W. M. Lawry	320/205
Melbourne	England	Drawn	W. M. Lawry	321/206
Sydney	England	Lost by 299 runs	W. M. Lawry	322/207
Melbourne	England	Drawn	W. M. Lawry	323/208
Adelaide	England	Drawn	W. M. Lawry	324/209
Sydney	England	Lost by 62 runs	I. M. Chappell	325/210
1972 in England				
Manchester	England	Lost by 89 runs	I. M. Chappell	326/211
Lord's	England	Won by eight wickets	I. M. Chappell	327/212
Nottingham	England	Drawn	I. M. Chappell	328/213
Leeds	England	Lost by nine wickets	I. M. Chappell	329/214
The Oval	England	Won by five wickets	I. M. Chappell	330/215
1972-73 in Australia				
Adelaide	Pakistan	Won by an innings and 114 runs	I. M. Chappell	331/7
Melbourne	Pakistan	Won by 92 runs	I. M. Chappell	332/8
Sydney	Pakistan	Won by 52 runs	I. M. Chappell	333/9
1972-73 in West Indies				
Kingston	West Indies	Drawn	I. M. Chappell	334/31
Bridgetown	West Indies	Drawn	I. M. Chappell	335/32
Port-of-Spain	West Indies	Won by 44 runs	I. M. Chappell	336/33
Georgetown	West Indies	Won by ten wickets	I. M. Chappell	337/34
Port-of-Spain	West Indies	Drawn	I. M. Chappell	338/35

Venue	Opponent	Result for Australia	Captain	Test/Opp
1973-74 in Australia				
Melbourne	New Zealand	Won by an innings and 25 runs	I. M. Chappell	339/2
Sydney	New Zealand	Drawn	I. M. Chappell	340/3
Adelaide	New Zealand	Won by an innings and 57 runs	I. M. Chappell	341/4
1973-74 in New Zealand				
Wellington	New Zealand	Drawn	I. M. Chappell	342/5
Christchurch	New Zealand	Lost by five wickets	I. M. Chappell	343/6
Auckland	New Zealand	Won by 297 runs	I. M. Chappell	344/7
1974-75 in Australia				
Brisbane	England	Won by 166 runs	I. M. Chappell	345/216
Perth	England	Won by nine wickets	I. M. Chappell	346/217
Melbourne	England	Drawn	I. M. Chappell	347/218
Sydney	England	Won by 171 runs	I. M. Chappell	348/219
Adelaide	England	Won by 163 runs	I. M. Chappell	349/220
Melbourne	England	Lost by an innings and four runs	I. M. Chappell	350/221
1975 in England				
Birmingham	England	Won by an innings and 85 runs	I. M. Chappell	351/222
Lord's	England	Drawn	I. M. Chappell	352/223
Leeds	England	Drawn	I. M. Chappell	353/224
The Oval	England	Drawn	I. M. Chappell	354/225
1975-76 in Australia				
Brisbane	West Indies	Won by eight wickets	G. S. Chappell	355/36
Perth	West Indies	Lost by an innings and 87 runs	G. S. Chappell	356/37
Melbourne	West Indies	Won by eight wickets	G. S. Chappell	357/38
Sydney	West Indies	Won by seven wickets	G. S. Chappell	358/39
Adelaide	West Indies	Won by 190 runs	G. S. Chappell	359/40
Melbourne	West Indies	Won by 165 runs	G. S. Chappell	360/41
1976-77 in Australia				
Adelaide	Pakistan	Drawn	G. S. Chappell	361/10
Melbourne	Pakistan	Won by 348 runs	G. S. Chappell	362/11
Sydney	Pakistan	Lost by eight wickets	G. S. Chappell	363/12
1976-77 in New Zealand				
Christchurch	New Zealand	Drawn	G. S. Chappell	364/8
Auckland	New Zealand	Won by ten wickets	G. S. Chappell	365/9
1976-77 in Australia				
Melbourne	England	Won by 45 runs	G. S. Chappell	366/226
1977 in England				
Lord's	England	Drawn	G. S. Chappell	367/227
Manchester	England	Lost by nine wickets	G. S. Chappell	368/228
Nottingham	England	Lost by seven wickets	G. S. Chappell	369/229
Leeds	England	Lost by an innings and 85 runs	G. S. Chappell	370/230
The Oval	England	Drawn	G. S. Chappell	371/231
1977-78 in Australia				
Brisbane	India	Won by 16 runs	R. B. Simpson	372/26
Perth	India	Won by two wickets	R. B. Simpson	373/27
Melbourne	India	Lost by 222 runs	R. B. Simpson	374/28
Sydney	India	Lost by an innings and two runs	R. B. Simpson	375/29
Adelaide	India	Won by 47 runs	R. B. Simpson	376/30
1977-78 in West Indies				
Port-of-Spain	West Indies	Lost by an innings and 106 runs	R. B. Simpson	377/42
Bridgetown	West Indies	Lost by nine wickets	R. B. Simpson	378/43
Georgetown	West Indies	Won by three wickets	R. B. Simpson	379/44
Port-of-Spain	West Indies	Lost by 198 runs	R. B. Simpson	380/45
Kingston	West Indies	Drawn	R. B. Simpson	381/46

Venue	Opponent	Result for Australia	Captain	Test/Opp
1978-79 in Australia				
Brisbane	England	Lost by seven wickets	G. N. Yallop	382/232
Perth	England	Lost by 166 runs	G. N. Yallop	383/233
Melbourne	England	Won by 103 runs	G. N. Yallop	384/234
Sydney	England	Lost by 93 runs	G. N. Yallop	385/235
Adelaide	England	Lost by 205 runs	G. N. Yallop	386/236
Sydney	England	Lost by nine wickets	G. N. Yallop	387/237
Melbourne	Pakistan	Lost by 71 runs	G. N. Yallop	388/13
Perth	Pakistan	Won by seven wickets	K. J. Hughes	389/14
1979-80 in India				
Madras (Chepauk)	India	Drawn	K. J. Hughes	390/31
Bangalore	India	Drawn	K. J. Hughes	391/32
Kanpur	India	Lost by 153 runs	K. J. Hughes	392/33
Delhi	India	Drawn	K. J. Hughes	393/34
Calcutta	India	Drawn	K. J. Hughes	394/35
Bombay (WS)	India	Lost by an innings and 100 runs	K. J. Hughes	395/36
1979-80 in Australia				
Brisbane	West Indies	Drawn	G. S. Chappell	396/47
Perth	England	Won by 138 runs	G. S. Chappell	397/238
Melbourne	West Indies	Lost by ten wickets	G. S. Chappell	398/48
Sydney	England	Won by six wickets	G. S. Chappell	399/239
Adelaide	West Indies	Lost by 408 runs	G. S. Chappell	400/49
Melbourne	England	Won by eight wickets	G. S. Chappell	401/240
1979-80 in Pakistan				
Karachi	Pakistan	Lost by seven wickets	G. S. Chappell	402/15
Faisalabad	Pakistan	Drawn	G. S. Chappell	403/16
Lahore	Pakistan	Drawn	G. S. Chappell	404/17
1980 in England				
Lord's	England	Drawn	G. S. Chappell	405/241
1980-81 in Australia				
Brisbane	New Zealand	Won by ten wickets	G. S. Chappell	406/10
Perth	New Zealand	Won by eight wickets	G. S. Chappell	407/11
Melbourne	New Zealand	Drawn	G. S. Chappell	408/12
Sydney	India	Won by an innings and four runs	G. S. Chappell	409/37
Adelaide	India	Drawn	G. S. Chappell	410/38
Melbourne	India	Lost by 59 runs	G. S. Chappell	411/39
1981 in England				
Nottingham	England	Won by four wickets	K. J. Hughes	412/242
Lord's	England	Drawn	K. J. Hughes	413/243
Leeds	England	Lost by 18 runs	K. J. Hughes	414/244
Birmingham	England	Lost by 29 runs	K. J. Hughes	415/245
Manchester	England	Lost by 103 runs	K. J. Hughes	416/246
The Oval	England	Drawn	K. J. Hughes	417/247
1981-82 in Australia				
Perth	Pakistan	Won by 286 runs	G. S. Chappell	418/18
Brisbane	Pakistan	Won by ten wickets	G. S. Chappell	419/19
Melbourne	Pakistan	Lost by an innings and 82 runs	G. S. Chappell	420/20
Melbourne	West Indies	Won by 58 runs	G. S. Chappell	421/50
Sydney	West Indies	Drawn	G. S. Chappell	422/51
Adelaide	West Indies	Lost by five wickets	G. S. Chappell	423/52

Venue	Opponent	Result for Australia	Captain	Test/Opp
1981-82 in New Zealand				
Wellington	New Zealand	Drawn	G. S. Chappell	424/13
Auckland	New Zealand	Lost by five wickets	G. S. Chappell	425/14
Christchurch	New Zealand	Won by eight wickets	G. S. Chappell	426/15
1982-83 in Pakistan				
Karachi	Pakistan	Lost by nine wickets	K. J. Hughes	427/21
Faisalabad	Pakistan	Lost by an innings and three runs	K. J. Hughes	428/22
Lahore	Pakistan	Lost by nine wickets	K. J. Hughes	429/23
1982-83 in Australia				
Perth	England	Drawn	G. S. Chappell	430/248
Brisbane	England	Won by seven wickets	G. S. Chappell	431/249
Adelaide	England	Won by eight wickets	G. S. Chappell	432/250
Melbourne	England	Lost by three runs	G. S. Chappell	433/251
Sydney	England	Drawn	G. S. Chappell	434/252
1982-83 in Sri Lanka				
Kandy	Sri Lanka	Won by an innings and 38 runs	G. S. Chappell	435/1
1983-84 in Australia				
Perth	Pakistan	Won by an innings and nine runs	K. J. Hughes	436/24
Brisbane	Pakistan	Drawn	K. J. Hughes	437/25
Adelaide	Pakistan	Drawn	K. J. Hughes	438/26
Melbourne	Pakistan	Drawn	K. J. Hughes	439/27
Sydney	Pakistan	Won by ten wickets	K. J. Hughes	440/28
1983-84 in West Indies				
Georgetown	West Indies	Drawn	K. J. Hughes	441/53
Port-of-Spain	West Indies	Drawn	K. J. Hughes	442/54
Bridgetown	West Indies	Lost by ten wickets	K. J. Hughes	443/55
St John's	West Indies	Lost by an innings and 36 runs	K. J. Hughes	444/56
Kingston	West Indies	Lost by ten wickets	K. J. Hughes	445/57
1984-85 in Australia				
Perth	West Indies	Lost by an innings and 112 runs	K. J. Hughes	446/58
Brisbane	West Indies	Lost by eight wickets	K. J. Hughes	447/59
Adelaide	West Indies	Lost by 191 runs	A. R. Border	448/60
Melbourne	West Indies	Drawn	A. R. Border	449/61
Sydney	West Indies	Won by an innings and 55 runs	A. R. Border	450/62
1985 in England				
Leeds	England	Lost by five wickets	A. R. Border	451/253
Lord's	England	Won by four wickets	A. R. Border	452/254
Nottingham	England	Drawn	A. R. Border	453/255
Manchester	England	Drawn	A. R. Border	454/256
Birmingham	England	Lost by an innings and 118 runs	A. R. Border	455/257
The Oval	England	Lost by an innings and 94 runs	A. R. Border	456/258
1985-86 in Australia				
Brisbane	New Zealand	Lost by an innings and 41 runs	A. R. Border	457/16
Sydney	New Zealand	Won by four wickets	A. R. Border	458/17
Perth	New Zealand	Lost by six wickets	A. R. Border	459/18
Adelaide	India	Drawn	A. R. Border	460/40
Melbourne	India	Drawn	A. R. Border	461/41
Sydney	India	Drawn	A. R. Border	462/42
1985-86 in New Zealand				
Wellington	New Zealand	Drawn	A. R. Border	463/19
Christchurch	New Zealand	Drawn	A. R. Border	464/20
Auckland	New Zealand	Lost by eight wickets	A. R. Border	465/21

Venue	Opponent	Result for Australia	Captain	Test/Opp
1986-87 in India				
Madras (Chepauk)	India	Tied	A.R. Border	466/43
Delhi	India	Drawn	A.R. Border	467/44
Bombay (WS)	India	Drawn	A.R. Border	468/45
1986-87 in Australia				
Brisbane	England	Lost by seven wickets	A.R. Border	469/259
Perth	England	Drawn	A.R. Border	470/260
Adelaide	England	Drawn	A.R. Border	471/261
Melbourne	England	Lost by an innings and 14 runs	A.R. Border	472/262
Sydney	England	Won by 55 runs	A.R. Border	473/263
1987-88 in Australia				
Brisbane	New Zealand	Won by nine wickets	A.R. Border	474/22
Adelaide	New Zealand	Drawn	A.R. Border	475/23
Melbourne	New Zealand	Drawn	A.R. Border	476/24
Sydney	England	Drawn	A.R. Border	477/264
Perth	Sri Lanka	Won by an innings and 108 runs	A.R. Border	478/2
1988-89 in Pakistan				
Karachi	Pakistan	Lost by an innings and 188 runs	A.R. Border	479/29
Faisalabad	Pakistan	Drawn	A.R. Border	480/30
Lahore	Pakistan	Drawn	A.R. Border	481/31
1988-89 in Australia				
Brisbane	West Indies	Lost by eight wickets	A.R. Border	482/63
Perth	West Indies	Lost by 169 runs	A.R. Border	483/64
Melbourne	West Indies	Lost by 285 runs	A.R. Border	484/65
Sydney	West Indies	Won by seven wickets	A.R. Border	485/66
Adelaide	West Indies	Drawn	A.R. Border	486/67
1989 in England				
Leeds	England	Won by 210 runs	A.R. Border	487/265
Lord's	England	Won by six wickets	A.R. Border	488/266
Birmingham	England	Drawn	A.R. Border	489/267
Manchester	England	Won by nine wickets	A.R. Border	490/268
Nottingham	England	Won by an innings and 180 runs	A.R. Border	491/269
The Oval	England	Drawn	A.R. Border	492/270
1989-90 in Australia				
Perth	New Zealand	Drawn	A.R. Border	493/25
Brisbane	Sri Lanka	Drawn	A.R. Border	494/3
Hobart	Sri Lanka	Won by 173 runs	A.R. Border	495/4
Melbourne	Pakistan	Won by 92 runs	A.R. Border	496/32
Adelaide	Pakistan	Drawn	A.R. Border	497/33
Sydney	Pakistan	Drawn	A.R. Border	498/34
1989-90 in New Zealand				
Wellington	New Zealand	Lost by nine wickets	A.R. Border	499/26
1990-91 in Australia				
Brisbane	England	Won by ten wickets	A.R. Border	500/271
Melbourne	England	Won by eight wickets	A.R. Border	501/272
Sydney	England	Drawn	A.R. Border	502/273
Adelaide	England	Drawn	A.R. Border	503/274
Perth	England	Won by nine wickets	A.R. Border	504/275

Venue	Opponent	Result for Australia	Captain	Test/Opp
1990-91 in West Indies				
Kingston	West Indies	Drawn	A.R. Border	505/68
Georgetown	West Indies	Lost by ten wickets	A.R. Border	506/69
Port-of-Spain	West Indies	Drawn	A.R. Border	507/70
Bridgetown	West Indies	Lost by 343 runs	A.R. Border	508/71
St John's	West Indies	Won by 157 runs	A.R. Border	509/72
1991-92 in Australia				
Brisbane	India	Won by ten wickets	A.R. Border	510/46
Melbourne	India	Won by eight wickets	A.R. Border	511/47
Sydney	India	Drawn	A.R. Border	512/48
Adelaide	India	Won by 38 runs	A.R. Border	513/49
Perth	India	Won by 300 runs	A.R. Border	514/50
1992-93 in Sri Lanka				
Colombo (SSC)	Sri Lanka	Won by 16 runs	A.R. Border	515/5
Colombo (PIS)	Sri Lanka	Drawn	A.R. Border	516/6
Moratuwa	Sri Lanka	Drawn	A.R. Border	517/7
1992-93 in Australia				
Brisbane	West Indies	Drawn	A.R. Border	518/73
Melbourne	West Indies	Won by 139 runs	A.R. Border	519/74
Sydney	West Indies	Drawn	A.R. Border	520/75
Adelaide	West Indies	Lost by one run	A.R. Border	521/76
Perth	West Indies	Lost by an innings and 25 runs	A.R. Border	522/77
1992-93 in New Zealand				
Christchurch	New Zealand	Won by an innings and 60 runs	A.R. Border	523/27
Wellington	New Zealand	Drawn	A.R. Border	524/28
Auckland	New Zealand	Lost by five wickets	A.R. Border	525/29
1993 in England				
Manchester	England	Won by 179 runs	A.R. Border	526/276
Lord's	England	Won by an innings and 62 runs	A.R. Border	527/277
Nottingham	England	Drawn	A.R. Border	528/278
Leeds	England	Won by an innings and 148 runs	A.R. Border	529/279
Birmingham	England	Won by eight wickets	A.R. Border	530/280
The Oval	England	Lost by 161 runs	A.R. Border	531/281
1993-94 in Australia				
Perth	New Zealand	Drawn	A.R. Border	532/30
Hobart	New Zealand	Won by an innings and 222 runs	A.R. Border	533/31
Brisbane	New Zealand	Won by an innings and 96 runs	A.R. Border	534/32
Melbourne	South Africa	Drawn	A.R. Border	535/54
Sydney	South Africa	Lost by five runs	A.R. Border	536/55
Adelaide	South Africa	Won by 191 runs	A.R. Border	537/56
1993-94 in South Africa				
Johannesburg (WS)	South Africa	Lost by 197 runs	A.R. Border	538/57
Cape Town	South Africa	Won by nine wickets	A.R. Border	539/58
Durban (Kingsmead)	South Africa	Drawn	A.R. Border	540/59
1994-95 in Pakistan				
Karachi	Pakistan	Lost by one wicket	M.A. Taylor	541/35
Rawalpindi	Pakistan	Drawn	M.A. Taylor	542/36
Lahore	Pakistan	Drawn	M.A. Taylor	543/37

Venue	Opponent	Result for Australia	Captain	Test/Opp
1994-95 in Australia				
Brisbane	England	Won by 184 runs	M. A. Taylor	544/282
Melbourne	England	Won by 295 runs	M. A. Taylor	545/283
Sydney	England	Drawn	M. A. Taylor	546/284
Adelaide	England	Lost by 106 runs	M. A. Taylor	547/285
Perth	England	Won by 329 runs	M. A. Taylor	548/286
1994-95 in West Indies				
Bridgetown	West Indies	Won by ten wickets	M. A. Taylor	549/78
St John's	West Indies	Drawn	M. A. Taylor	550/79
Port-of-Spain	West Indies	Lost by nine wickets	M. A. Taylor	551/80
Kingston	West Indies	Won by an innings and 53 runs	M. A. Taylor	552/81
1995-96 in Australia				
Brisbane	Pakistan	Won by an innings and 126 runs	M. A. Taylor	553/38
Hobart	Pakistan	Won by 155 runs	M. A. Taylor	554/39
Sydney	Pakistan	Lost by 74 runs	M. A. Taylor	555/40
Perth	Sri Lanka	Won by an innings and 36 runs	M. A. Taylor	556/8
Melbourne	Sri Lanka	Won by ten wickets	M. A. Taylor	557/9
Adelaide	Sri Lanka	Won by 148 runs	M. A. Taylor	558/10
1996-97 in India				
Delhi	India	Lost by seven wickets	M. A. Taylor	559/51
1996-97 in Australia				
Brisbane	West Indies	Won by 123 runs	M. A. Taylor	560/82
Sydney	West Indies	Won by 124 runs	M. A. Taylor	561/83
Melbourne	West Indies	Lost by six wickets	M. A. Taylor	562/84
Adelaide	West Indies	Won by an innings and 183 runs	M. A. Taylor	563/85
Perth	West Indies	Lost by ten wickets	M. A. Taylor	564/86
1996-97 in South Africa				
Johannesburg (WS)	South Africa	Won by an innings and 196 runs	M. A. Taylor	565/60
Port Elizabeth	South Africa	Won by two wickets	M. A. Taylor	566/61
Centurion	South Africa	Lost by eight wickets	M. A. Taylor	567/62
1997 in England				
Birmingham	England	Lost by nine wickets	M. A. Taylor	568/287
Lord's	England	Drawn	M. A. Taylor	569/288
Manchester	England	Won by 268 runs	M. A. Taylor	570/289
Leeds	England	Won by an innings and 61 runs	M. A. Taylor	571/290
Nottingham	England	Won by 264 runs	M. A. Taylor	572/291
The Oval	England	Lost by 19 runs	M. A. Taylor	573/292
1997-98 in Australia				
Brisbane	New Zealand	Won by 186 runs	M. A. Taylor	574/33
Perth	New Zealand	Won by an innings and 70 runs	M. A. Taylor	575/34
Hobart	New Zealand	Drawn	M. A. Taylor	576/35
Melbourne	South Africa	Drawn	M. A. Taylor	577/63
Sydney	South Africa	Won by an innings and 21 runs	M. A. Taylor	578/64
Adelaide	South Africa	Drawn	M. A. Taylor	579/65
1997-98 in India				
Chennai (Chepauk)	India	Lost by 179 runs	M. A. Taylor	580/52
Calcutta	India	Lost by an innings and 219 runs	M. A. Taylor	581/53
Bangalore	India	Won by eight wickets	M. A. Taylor	582/54

Venue	Opponent	Result for Australia	Captain	Test/Opp
1998-99 in Pakistan				
Rawalpindi	Pakistan	Won by an innings and 99 runs	M. A. Taylor	583/40
Peshawar	Pakistan	Drawn	M. A. Taylor	584/41
Karachi	Pakistan	Drawn	M. A. Taylor	585/42
1998-99 in Australia				
Brisbane	England	Drawn	M. A. Taylor	586/293
Perth	England	Won by seven wickets	M. A. Taylor	587/294
Adelaide	England	Won by 205 runs	M. A. Taylor	588/295
Melbourne	England	Lost by 12 runs	M. A. Taylor	589/296
Sydney	England	Won by 98 runs	M. A. Taylor	590/297
1998-99 in West Indies				
Port-of-Spain	West Indies	Won by 312 runs	S. R. Waugh	591/87
Kingston	West Indies	Lost by ten wickets	S. R. Waugh	592/88
Bridgetown	West Indies	Lost by one wicket	S. R. Waugh	593/89
St John's	West Indies	Won by 176 runs	S. R. Waugh	594/90
1999-00 in Sri Lanka				
Kandy	Sri Lanka	Lost by six wickets	S. R. Waugh	595/11
Galle	Sri Lanka	Drawn	S. R. Waugh	596/12
Colombo (SSC)	Sri Lanka	Drawn	S. R. Waugh	597/13
1999-00 in Zimbabwe				
Harare	Zimbabwe	Won by ten wickets	S. R. Waugh	598/1
1999-00 in Australia				
Brisbane	Pakistan	Won by ten wickets	S. R. Waugh	599/44
Hobart (Bel)	Pakistan	Won by four wickets	S. R. Waugh	600/45
Perth	Pakistan	Won by an innings and 20 runs	S. R. Waugh	601/46
Adelaide	India	Won by 285 runs	S. R. Waugh	602/55
Melbourne	India	Won by 180 runs	S. R. Waugh	503/56
Sydney	India	Won by an innings and 141 runs	S. R. Waugh	604/57
1999-00 in New Zealand				
Auckland	New Zealand	Won by 62 runs	S. R. Waugh	605/36
Wellington	New Zealand	Won by six wickets	S. R. Waugh	606/37
Hamilton	New Zealand	Won by six wickets	S. R. Waugh	607/38
2000-01 in Australia				
Brisbane	West Indies	Won by an innings and 126 runs	S. R. Waugh	608/91
Perth	West Indies	Won by an innings and 27 runs	S. R. Waugh	609/92
Adelaide	West Indies	Won by five wickets	A. C. Gilchrist	610/93
Melbourne	West Indies	Won by 352 runs	S. R. Waugh	611/94
Sydney	West Indies	Won by six wickets	S. R. Waugh	612/95
2000-01 in India				
Mumbai (WS)	India	Won by ten wickets	S. R. Waugh	613/58
Kolkata	India	Lost by 171 runs	S. R. Waugh	614/59
Chennai (Chepauk)	India	Lost by two wickets	S. R. Waugh	615/60

SERIES RESULTS FOR AUSTRALIA

Season	Opponent	Venue	Tests	Won	Lost	Drawn	Tied	Result of series
1876-77	England	Australia	2	1	1	0	0	Drawn 1-1
1878-79	England	Australia	1	1	0	0	0	Won 1-0
1880	England	England	1	0	1	0	0	Lost 1-0
1881-82	England	Australia	4	2	0	2	0	Won 2-0
1882	England	England	1	1	0	0	0	Won 1-0

Season	Opponent	Venue	Tests	Won	Lost	Drawn	Tied	Result of series
1882-83	England	Australia	4	2	2	0	0	Drawn 2-2
1884	England	England	3	0	1	2	0	Lost 1-0
1884-85	England	Australia	5	2	3	0	0	Lost 3-2
1886	England	England	3	0	3	0	0	Lost 3-0
1886-87	England	Australia	2	0	2	0	0	Lost 2-0
1887-88	England	Australia	1	0	1	0	0	Lost 1-0
1888	England	England	3	1	2	0	0	Lost 2-1
1890	England	England	2	0	2	0	0	Lost 2-0
1891-92	England	Australia	3	2	1	0	0	Won 2-1
1893	England	England	3	0	1	2	0	Lost 1-0
1894-95	England	Australia	5	2	3	0	0	Lost 3-2
1896	England	England	3	1	2	0	0	Lost 2-1
1897-98	England	Australia	5	4	1	0	0	Won 4-1
1899	England	England	5	1	0	4	0	Won 1-0
1901-02	England	Australia	5	4	1	0	0	Won 4-1
1902	England	England	5	2	1	2	0	Won 2-1
1902-03	South Africa	South Africa	3	2	0	1	0	Won 2-0
1903-04	England	Australia	5	2	3	0	0	Lost 3-2
1905	England	England	5	0	2	3	0	Lost 2-0
1907-08	England	Australia	5	4	1	0	0	Won 4-1
1909	England	England	5	2	1	2	0	Won 2-1
1910-11	South Africa	Australia	5	4	1	0	0	Won 4-1
1911-12	England	Australia	5	1	4	0	0	Lost 4-1
1912	South Africa	England	3	2	0	1	0	Won 2-0
1912	England	England	3	0	1	2	0	Lost 1-0
1920-21	England	Australia	5	5	0	0	0	Won 5-0
1921	England	England	5	3	0	2	0	Won 3-0
1921-22	South Africa	South Africa	3	1	0	2	0	Won 1-0
1924-25	England	Australia	5	4	1	0	0	Won 4-1
1926	England	England	5	0	1	4	0	Lost 1-0
1928-29	England	Australia	5	1	4	0	0	Lost 4-1
1930	England	England	5	2	1	2	0	Won 2-1
1930-31	West Indies	Australia	5	4	1	0	0	Won 4-1
1931-32	South Africa	Australia	5	5	0	0	0	Won 5-0
1932-33	England	Australia	5	1	4	0	0	Lost 4-1
1934	England	England	5	2	1	2	0	Won 2-1
1935-36	South Africa	South Africa	5	4	0	1	0	Won 4-0
1936-37	England	Australia	5	3	2	0	0	Won 3-2
1938	England	England	4	1	1	2	0	Drawn 1-1
1945-46	New Zealand	New Zealand	1	1	0	0	0	Won 1-0
1946-47	England	Australia	5	3	0	2	0	Won 3-0
1947-48	India	Australia	5	4	0	1	0	Won 4-0
1948	England	England	5	4	0	1	0	Won 4-0
1949-50	South Africa	South Africa	5	4	0	1	0	Won 4-0
1950-51	England	Australia	5	4	1	0	0	Won 4-1
1951-52	West Indies	Australia	5	4	1	0	0	Won 4-1
1952-53	South Africa	Australia	5	2	2	1	0	Drawn 2-2
1953	England	England	5	0	1	4	0	Lost 1-0
1954-55	England	Australia	5	1	3	1	0	Lost 3-1
	West Indies	West Indies	5	3	0	2	0	Won 3-0
1956	England	England	5	1	2	2	0	Lost 2-1
1956-57	Pakistan	Pakistan	1	0	1	0	0	Lost 1-0
	India	India	3	2	0	1	0	Won 2-0
1957-58	South Africa	South Africa	5	3	0	2	0	Won 3-0
1958-59	England	Australia	5	4	0	1	0	Won 4-0
1959-60	Pakistan	Pakistan	3	2	0	1	0	Won 2-0
	India	India	5	2	1	2	0	Won 2-1
1960-61	West Indies	Australia	5	2	1	1	1	Won 2-1
1961	England	England	5	2	1	2	0	Won 2-1
1962-63	England	Australia	5	1	1	3	0	Drawn 1-1
1963-64	South Africa	Australia	5	1	1	3	0	Drawn 1-1

Season	Opponent	Venue	Tests	Won	Lost	Drawn	Tied	Result of series
1964	England	England	5	1	0	4	0	Won 1-0
1964-65	India	India	3	1	1	1	0	Drawn 1-1
	Pakistan	Pakistan	1	0	0	1	0	Drawn 0-0
	Pakistan	Australia	1	0	0	1	0	Drawn 0-0
	West Indies	West Indies	5	1	2	2	0	Lost 2-1
1965-66	England	Australia	5	1	1	3	0	Drawn 1-1
1966-67	South Africa	South Africa	5	1	3	1	0	Lost 3-1
1967-68	India	Australia	4	4	0	0	0	Won 4-0
1968	England	England	5	1	1	3	0	Drawn 1-1
1968-69	West Indies	Australia	5	3	1	1	0	Won 3-1
1969-70	India	India	5	3	1	1	0	Won 3-1
	South Africa	South Africa	4	0	4	0	0	Lost 4-0
1970-71	England	Australia	7	0	2	5	0	Lost 2-0
1972	England	England	5	2	2	1	0	Drawn 2-2
1972-73	Pakistan	Australia	3	3	0	0	0	Won 3-0
	West Indies	West Indies	5	2	0	3	0	Won 2-0
1973-74	New Zealand	Australia	3	2	0	1	0	Won 2-0
	New Zealand	New Zealand	3	1	1	1	0	Drawn 1-1
1974-75	England	Australia	6	4	1	1	0	Won 4-1
1975	England	England	4	1	0	3	0	Won 1-0
1975-76	West Indies	Australia	6	5	1	0	0	Won 5-1
1976-77	Pakistan	Australia	3	1	1	1	0	Drawn 1-1
	New Zealand	New Zealand	2	1	0	1	0	Won 1-0
	England	Australia	1	1	0	0	0	Won 1-0
1977	England	England	5	0	3	2	0	Lost 3-0
1977-78	India	Australia	5	3	2	0	0	Won 3-2
	West Indies	West Indies	5	1	3	1	0	Lost 3-1
1978-79	England	Australia	6	1	5	0	0	Lost 5-1
	Pakistan	Australia	2	1	1	0	0	Drawn 1-1
1979-80	India	India	6	0	2	4	0	Lost 2-0
	West Indies	Australia	3	0	2	1	0	Lost 2-0
	England	Australia	3	3	0	0	0	Won 3-0
	Pakistan	Pakistan	3	0	1	2	0	Lost 1-0
1980	England	England	1	0	0	1	0	Drawn 0-0
1980-81	New Zealand	Australia	3	2	0	1	0	Won 2-0
	India	Australia	3	1	1	1	0	Drawn 1-1
1981	England	England	6	1	3	2	0	Lost 3-1
1981-82	Pakistan	Australia	3	2	1	0	0	Won 2-1
	West Indies	Australia	3	1	1	1	0	Drawn 1-1
	New Zealand	New Zealand	3	1	1	1	0	Drawn 1-1
1982-83	Pakistan	Pakistan	3	0	3	0	0	Lost 3-0
	England	Australia	5	2	1	2	0	Won 2-1
	Sri Lanka	Sri Lanka	1	1	0	0	0	Won 1-0
1983-84	Pakistan	Australia	5	2	0	3	0	Won 2-0
	West Indies	West Indies	5	0	3	2	0	Lost 3-0
1984-85	West Indies	Australia	5	1	3	1	0	Lost 3-1
1985	England	England	6	1	3	2	0	Lost 3-1
1985-86	New Zealand	Australia	3	1	2	0	0	Lost 2-1
	India	Australia	3	0	0	3	0	Drawn 0-0
	New Zealand	New Zealand	3	0	1	2	0	Lost 1-0
1986-87	India	India	3	0	0	2	1	Drawn 0-0
	England	Australia	5	1	2	2	0	Lost 2-1
1987-88	New Zealand	Australia	3	1	0	2	0	Won 1-0
	England	Australia	1	0	0	1	0	Drawn 0-0
	Sri Lanka	Australia	1	1	0	0	0	Won 1-0
1988-89	Pakistan	Pakistan	3	0	1	2	0	Lost 1-0
	West Indies	Australia	5	1	3	1	0	Lost 3-1
1989	England	England	6	4	0	2	0	Won 4-0

Season	Opponent	Venue	Tests	Won	Lost	Drawn	Tied	Result of series
1989-90	New Zealand	Australia	1	0	0	1	0	Drawn 0-0
	Sri Lanka	Australia	2	1	0	1	0	Won 1-0
	Pakistan	Australia	3	1	0	2	0	Won 1-0
	New Zealand	New Zealand	1	0	1	0	0	Lost 1-0
1990-91	England	Australia	5	3	0	2	0	Won 3-0
	West Indies	West Indies	5	1	2	2	0	Lost 2-1
1991-92	India	Australia	5	4	0	1	0	Won 4-0
	Sri Lanka	Sri Lanka	3	1	0	2	0	Won 1-0
1992-93	West Indies	Australia	5	1	2	2	0	Lost 2-1
	New Zealand	New Zealand	3	1	1	1	0	Drawn 1-1
1993	England	England	6	4	1	1	0	Won 4-1
1993-94	New Zealand	Australia	3	2	0	1	0	Won 2-0
	South Africa	Australia	3	1	1	1	0	Drawn 1-1
	South Africa	South Africa	3	1	1	1	0	Drawn 1-1
1994-95	Pakistan	Pakistan	3	0	1	2	0	Lost 1-0
	England	Australia	5	3	1	1	0	Won 3-1
	West Indies	West Indies	4	2	1	1	0	Won 2-1
1995-96	Pakistan	Australia	3	2	1	0	0	Won 2-1
	Sri Lanka	Australia	3	3	0	0	0	Won 3-0
1996-97	India	India	1	1	0	0	0	Lost 1-0
	West Indies	Australia	5	3	2	0	0	Won 3-2
	South Africa	South Africa	3	2	1	0	0	Won 2-1
1997	England	England	6	3	2	1	0	Won 3-2
1997-98	New Zealand	Australia	3	2	0	1	0	Won 2-0
	South Africa	Australia	3	1	0	2	0	Won 1-0
	India	India	3	1	2	0	0	Lost 2-1
1998-99	Pakistan	Pakistan	3	1	0	2	0	Won 1-0
	England	Australia	5	3	1	1	0	Won 3-1
	West Indies	West Indies	4	2	2	0	0	Drawn 2-2
1999-00	Sri Lanka	Sri Lanka	3	0	1	2	0	Lost 1-0
	Zimbabwe	Zimbabwe	1	1	0	0	0	Won 1-0
	Pakistan	Australia	3	3	0	0	0	Won 3-0
	India	Australia	3	3	0	0	0	Won 3-0
	New Zealand	New Zealand	3	3	0	0	0	Won 3-0
2000-01	West Indies	Australia	5	5	0	0	0	Won 5-0
	India	India	3	1	2	0	0	Lost 1-2

Tests in Australia			318	169	85	63	1	
Tests abroad			297	97	85	114	1	
Total			615	266	170	177	2	

AUSTRALIAN LIMITED-OVERS INTERNATIONAL RECORDS

AUSTRALIAN LIMITED-OVERS INTERNATIONAL MATCHES

Date	Venue	Opponent	Result for Australia	Captain	Team/Opp
1970-71 in Australia					
Jan 5	Melbourne	England	Won by five wickets	W. M. Lawry	1/1
1972 in England					
Aug 24	Manchester	England	Lost by six wickets	I. M. Chappell	2/2
Aug 26	Lord's	England	Won by five wickets	I. M. Chappell	3/3
Aug 28	Birmingham	England	Lost by two wickets	I. M. Chappell	4/4
1973-74 in New Zealand					
Mar 30	Dunedin	New Zealand	Won by seven wickets	I. M. Chappell	5/1
Mar 31	Christchurch	New Zealand	Won by 31 runs	I. M. Chappell	6/2

Date	Venue	Opponent	Result for Australia	Captain	Team/Opp
1974-75 in Australia					
Jan 1	Melbourne	England	Lost by three wickets	I. M. Chappell	7/5
1975 World Cup in England					
Jun 7	Leeds	Pakistan	Won by 73 runs	I. M. Chappell	8/1
Jun 11	The Oval	Sri Lanka	Won by 52 runs	I. M. Chappell	9/1
Jun 14	The Oval	West Indies	Lost by seven wickets	I. M. Chappell	10/1
Jun 18	Leeds	England	Won by four wickets	I. M. Chappell	11/6
Jun 21	Lord's	West Indies	Lost by 17 runs	I. M. Chappell	12/2
1975-76 in Australia					
Dec 20	Adelaide	West Indies	Won by five wickets	G. S. Chappell	13/3
1977 in England					
Jun 2	Manchester	England	Lost by two wickets	G. S. Chappell	14/7
Jun 4	Birmingham	England	Lost by 99 runs	G. S. Chappell	15/8
Jun 6	The Oval	England	Won by two wickets	G. S. Chappell	16/9
1977-78 in West Indies					
Feb 22	St John's	West Indies	Lost on run-rate	R. B. Simpson	17/4
Apr 12	Castries	West Indies	Won by two wickets	R. B. Simpson	18/5
1978-79 in Australia					
Jan 13	Sydney	England	No result	G. N. Yallop	19/10
Jan 24	Melbourne	England	Lost by seven wickets	G. N. Yallop	20/11
Feb 4	Melbourne	England	Won by four wickets	G. N. Yallop	21/12
Feb 7	Melbourne	England	Won by six wickets	G. N. Yallop	22/13
1979 World Cup in England					
Jun 9	Lord's	England	Lost by six wickets	K. J. Hughes	23/14
Jun 13–14	Nottingham	Pakistan	Lost by 89 runs	K. J. Hughes	24/2
Jun 16	Birmingham	Canada	Won by seven wickets	K. J. Hughes	25/1
1979-80 World Series Cup in Australia					
Nov 27	Sydney	West Indies	Won by five wickets	G. S. Chappell	26/6
Dec 8	Melbourne	England	Lost by three wickets	G. S. Chappell	27/15
Dec 9	Melbourne	West Indies	Lost by 80 runs	G. S. Chappell	28/7
Dec 11	Sydney	England	Lost by 72 runs	G. S. Chappell	29/16
Dec 21	Sydney	West Indies	Won by seven runs	G. S. Chappell	30/8
Dec 26	Sydney	England	Lost by four wickets	G. S. Chappell	31/17
Jan 14	Sydney	England	Lost by two wickets	G. S. Chappell	32/18
Jan 18	Sydney	West Indies	Won by nine runs	G. S. Chappell	33/9
1980 in England					
Aug 20	The Oval	England	Lost by 23 runs	G. S. Chappell	34/19
Aug 22	Birmingham	England	Lost by 47 runs	G. S. Chappell	35/20
1980-81 World Series Cup in Australia					
Nov 23	Adelaide	New Zealand	Lost by three wickets	G. S. Chappell	36/3
Nov 25	Sydney	New Zealand	Won by 94 runs	G. S. Chappell	37/4
Dec 6	Melbourne	India	Lost by 66 runs	G. S. Chappell	38/1
Dec 7	Melbourne	New Zealand	Won by four wickets	G. S. Chappell	39/5
Dec 18	Sydney	India	Won by nine wickets	G. S. Chappell	40/2
Jan 8	Sydney	India	Won by nine wickets	G. S. Chappell	41/3
Jan 11	Melbourne	India	Won by seven wickets	G. S. Chappell	42/4
Jan 13	Sydney	New Zealand	Lost by one run	G. S. Chappell	43/6
Jan 15	Sydney	India	Won by 27 runs	G. S. Chappell	44/5
Jan 21	Sydney	New Zealand	No result	G. S. Chappell	45/7
Jan 29	Sydney	New Zealand	Lost by 78 runs	G. S. Chappell	46/8

Date	Venue	Opponent	Result for Australia	Captain	Team/Opp
Jan 31	Melbourne	New Zealand	Won by seven wickets	G. S. Chappell	47/9
Feb 1	Melbourne	New Zealand	Won by six runs	G. S. Chappell	48/10
Feb 3	Sydney	New Zealand	Won by six wickets	G. S. Chappell	49/11

1981 in England

Jun 4	Lord's	England	Lost by six wickets	K. J. Hughes	50/21
Jun 6	Birmingham	England	Won by two runs	K. J. Hughes	51/22
Jun 8	Leeds	England	Won by 71 runs	K. J. Hughes	52/23

1981-82 World Series Cup in Australia

Nov 21	Melbourne	Pakistan	Lost by four wickets	G. S. Chappell	53/3
Nov 24	Sydney	West Indies	Won by seven wickets	G. S. Chappell	54/10
Dec 6	Adelaide	Pakistan	Won by 38 runs	G. S. Chappell	55/4
Dec 17	Sydney	Pakistan	Lost by six wickets	G. S. Chappell	56/5
Dec 20	Perth	West Indies	Lost by eight wickets	G. S. Chappell	57/11
Jan 20	Melbourne	Pakistan	Lost by 25 runs	G. S. Chappell	58/6
Jan 10	Melbourne	West Indies	Lost by five wickets	G. S. Chappell	59/12
Jan 14	Sydney	Pakistan	Won by 76 runs	G. S. Chappell	60/7
Jan 17	Brisbane	West Indies	Lost by five wickets	G. S. Chappell	61/13
Jan 19	Sydney	West Indies	Won on run-rate	G. S. Chappell	62/14
Jan 23	Melbourne	West Indies	Lost by 86 runs	G. S. Chappell	63/15
Jan 24	Melbourne	West Indies	Lost by 128 runs	G. S. Chappell	64/16
Jan 26	Sydney	West Indies	Won by 46 runs	G. S. Chappell	65/17
Jan 27	Sydney	West Indies	Lost by 18 runs	G. S. Chappell	66/18

1981-82 in New Zealand

Feb 13	Auckland	New Zealand	Lost by 46 runs	G. S. Chappell	67/12
Feb 17	Dunedin	New Zealand	Won by six wickets	G. S. Chappell	68/13
Feb 9	Wellington	New Zealand	Won by eight wickets	G. S. Chappell	69/14

1982-83 in Pakistan

Sep 20	Hyderabad	Pakistan	Lost by 59 runs	K. J. Hughes	70/8
Oct 8	Lahore	Pakistan	Lost by 28 runs	K. J. Hughes	71/9
Oct 22	Karachi	Pakistan	No result	K. J. Hughes	72/10

1982-83 World Series Cup in Australia

Jan 9	Melbourne	New Zealand	Won by eight wickets	K. J. Hughes	73/15
Jan 11	Sydney	England	Won by 31 runs	K. J. Hughes	74/24
Jan 16	Brisbane	England	Won by seven wickets	K. J. Hughes	75/25
Jan 18	Sydney	New Zealand	Lost by 47 runs	K. J. Hughes	76/16
Jan 22	Melbourne	New Zealand	Lost by 58 runs	K. J. Hughes	77/17
Jan 23	Melbourne	England	Won by five wickets	K. J. Hughes	78/26
Jan 26	Sydney	England	Lost by 98 runs	K. J. Hughes	79/27
Jan 30	Adelaide	England	Lost by 14 runs	K. J. Hughes	80/28
Jan 31	Adelaide	New Zealand	Lost by 46 runs	K. J. Hughes	81/18
Feb 6	Perth	New Zealand	Won by 27 runs	K. J. Hughes	82/19
Feb 9	Sydney	New Zealand	Won by six wickets	K. J. Hughes	83/20
Feb 13	Melbourne	New Zealand	Won by 149 runs	K. J. Hughes	84/21

1982-83 in Australia

Mar 17	Sydney	New Zealand	Lost by 14 runs	K. J. Hughes	85/22

1982-83 in Sri Lanka

Apr 13	Colombo (PSS)	Sri Lanka	Lost by two wickets	G. S. Chappell	86/2
Apr 16	Colombo (PSS)	Sri Lanka	Lost by four wickets	G. S. Chappell	87/3
Apr 20	Colombo (SSC)	Sri Lanka	No result	G. S. Chappell	88/4
Apr 30	Colombo (SSC)	Sri Lanka	No result	G. S. Chappell	89/5

Date	Venue	Opponent	Result for Australia	Captain	Team/Opp
1983 World Cup in England					
Jun 9	Nottingham	Zimbabwe	Lost by 13 runs	K. J. Hughes	90/1
Jun 11–12	Leeds	West Indies	Lost by 101 runs	K. J. Hughes	91/19
Jun 13	Nottingham	India	Won by 162 runs	K. J. Hughes	92/6
Jun 16	Southampton	Zimbabwe	Won by 32 runs	K. J. Hughes	93/2
Jun 18	Lord's	West Indies	Lost by seven wickets	K. J. Hughes	94/20
Jun 20	Chelmsford	India	Lost by 118 runs	D. W. Hookes	95/7
1983-84 World Series Cup in Australia					
Jan 8	Melbourne	West Indies	Lost by 27 runs	K. J. Hughes	96/21
Jan 10	Sydney	Pakistan	Won by 34 runs	K. J. Hughes	97/11
Jan 15	Brisbane	Pakistan	No result	K. J. Hughes	98/12
Jan 17	Sydney	West Indies	Lost by 28 runs	K. J. Hughes	99/22
Jan 21	Melbourne	Pakistan	Won by 45 runs	K. J. Hughes	100/13
Jan 22	Melbourne	West Indies	Lost by 26 runs	K. J. Hughes	101/23
Jan 25	Sydney	Pakistan	Won by 87 runs	K. J. Hughes	102/14
Jan 29	Adelaide	West Indies	Lost by six wickets	K. J. Hughes	103/24
Jan 30	Adelaide	Pakistan	Won by 70 runs	K. J. Hughes	104/15
Feb 5	Perth	West Indies	Won by 14 runs	K. J. Hughes	105/25
Feb 8	Sydney	West Indies	Lost by nine wickets	K. J. Hughes	106/26
Feb 11	Melbourne	West Indies	Tied	K. J. Hughes	107/27
Feb 12	Melbourne	West Indies	Lost by six wickets	K. J. Hughes	108/28
1983-84 in West Indies					
Feb 29	Berbice	West Indies	Lost by eight wickets	K. J. Hughes	109/29
Mar 14	Port-of-Spain	West Indies	Won by four wickets	K. J. Hughes	110/30
Apr 19	Castries	West Indies	Lost by seven wickets	K. J. Hughes	111/31
Apr 26	Kingston	West Indies	Lost by nine wickets	K. J. Hughes	112/32
1984-85 in India					
Sep 28	New Delhi	India	Won by 48 runs	K. J. Hughes	113/8
Oct 1	Trivandrum	India	No result	K. J. Hughes	114/9
Oct 3	Jamshedpur	India	No result	K. J. Hughes	115/10
Oct 5	Ahmedabad	India	Won by seven wickets	K. J. Hughes	116/11
Oct 6	Indore	India	Won by six wickets	K. J. Hughes	117/12
1984-85 World Series Cup in Australia					
Jan 6	Melbourne	West Indies	Lost by seven wickets	A. R. Border	118/33
Jan 8	Sydney	Sri Lanka	Won by six wickets	A. R. Border	119/6
Jan 13	Brisbane	West Indies	Lost by five wickets	A. R. Border	120/34
Jan 15	Sydney	West Indies	Lost by five wickets	A. R. Border	121/35
Jan 19	Melbourne	Sri Lanka	Lost by four wickets	A. R. Border	122/7
Jan 20	Melbourne	West Indies	Lost by 65 runs	A. R. Border	123/36
Jan 23	Sydney	Sri Lanka	Won by three wickets	A. R. Border	124/8
Jan 27	Adelaide	West Indies	Lost by six wickets	A. R. Border	125/37
Jan 28	Adelaide	Sri Lanka	Won by 232 runs	A. R. Border	126/9
Feb 3	Perth	Sri Lanka	Won by nine wickets	A. R. Border	127/10
Feb 6	Sydney	West Indies	Won by 26 runs	A. R. Border	128/38
Feb 10	Melbourne	West Indies	Lost by four wickets	A. R. Border	129/39
Feb 12	Sydney	West Indies	Lost by seven wickets	A. R. Border	130/40
1984-85 World Championship in Australia					
Feb 17	Melbourne	England	Won by seven wickets	A. R. Border	131/29
Feb 24	Melbourne	Pakistan	Lost by 62 runs	A. R. Border	132/16
Mar 3	Melbourne	India	Lost by eight wickets	A. R. Border	133/13
1984-85 in United Arab Emirates					
Mar 24	Sharjah	England	Won by two wickets	A. R. Border	134/30
Mar 29	Sharjah	India	Lost by three wickets	A. R. Border	135/14

Date	Venue	Opponent	Result for Australia	Captain	Team/Opp
1985 in England					
May 30	Manchester	England	Won by three wickets	A. R. Border	136/31
Jun 1	Birmingham	England	Won by four wickets	A. R. Border	137/32
Jun 3	Lord's	England	Lost by eight wickets	A. R. Border	138/33
1985-86 World Series Cup in Australia					
Jan 9	Melbourne	New Zealand	No result	A. R. Border	139/23
Jan 12	Brisbane	India	Won by four wickets	A. R. Border	140/15
Jan 14	Sydney	New Zealand	Won by four wickets	A. R. Border	141/24
Jan 16	Melbourne	India	Lost by eight wickets	A. R. Border	142/16
Jan 19	Perth	New Zealand	Won by four wickets	A. R. Border	143/25
Jan 21	Sydney	India	Won by 100 runs	A. R. Border	144/17
Jan 26	Adelaide	India	Won by 36 runs	A. R. Border	145/18
Jan 27	Adelaide	New Zealand	Lost by 206 runs	A. R. Border	146/26
Jan 29	Sydney	New Zealand	Won by 99 runs	A. R. Border	147/27
Jan 31	Melbourne	India	Lost by six wickets	A. R. Border	148/19
Feb 5	Sydney	India	Won by 11 runs	A. R. Border	149/20
Feb 9	Melbourne	India	Won by seven wickets	A. R. Border	150/21
1985-86 in New Zealand					
Mar 19	Dunedin	New Zealand	Lost by 30 runs	A. R. Border	151/28
Mar 22	Christchurch	New Zealand	Lost by 53 runs	A. R. Border	152/29
Mar 26	Wellington	New Zealand	Won by three wickets	A. R. Border	153/30
Mar 29	Auckland	New Zealand	Won by 44 runs	A. R. Border	154/31
1985-86 in United Arab Emirates					
Apr 11	Sharjah	Pakistan	Lost by eight wickets	R. J. Bright	155/17
1986-87 in India					
Sep 7	Jaipur	India	Lost by seven wickets	A. R. Border	156/22
Sep 9	Srinagar	India	Won by three wickets	A. R. Border	157/23
Sep 24	Hyderabad	India	No result	A. R. Border	158/24
Oct 2	Delhi	India	Lost by three wickets	A. R. Border	159/25
Oct 5	Ahmedabad	India	Lost by 52 runs	A. R. Border	160/26
Oct 7	Rajkot	India	Won by seven wickets	A. R. Border	161/27
1986-87 World Challenge in Australia					
Jan 1	Perth	England	Lost by 37 runs	A. R. Border	162/34
Jan 2	Perth	Pakistan	Lost by one wicket	A. R. Border	163/18
Jan 4	Perth	West Indies	Lost by 164 runs	A. R. Border	164/41
1986-87 World Series Cup in Australia					
Jan 18	Brisbane	England	Won by 11 runs	A. R. Border	165/35
Jan 20	Melbourne	West Indies	Lost by seven wickets	A. R. Border	166/42
Jan 22	Sydney	England	Lost by three wickets	A. R. Border	167/36
Jan 25	Adelaide	West Indies	Lost by 16 runs	A. R. Border	168/43
Jan 26	Adelaide	England	Won by 33 runs	A. R. Border	169/37
Jan 28	Sydney	West Indies	Won by 36 runs	A. R. Border	170/44
Feb 1	Melbourne	England	Won by 109 runs	A. R. Border	171/38
Feb 6	Sydney	West Indies	Won by two wickets	A. R. Border	172/45
Feb 8	Melbourne	England	Lost by six wickets	A. R. Border	173/39
Feb 11	Sydney	England	Lost by eight runs	A. R. Border	174/40
1986-87 in United Arab Emirates					
Apr 3	Sharjah	Pakistan	Lost by six wickets	A. R. Border	175/19
Apr 6	Sharjah	India	Lost by seven wickets	G. R. Marsh	176/28
Apr 9	Sharjah	England	Lost by 11 runs	A. R. Border	177/41

Date	Venue	Opponent	Result for Australia	Captain	Team/Opp
1987-88 World Cup in India and Pakistan					
Oct 9	Madras	India	Won by one run	A.R. Border	178/29
Oct 13	Madras	Zimbabwe	Won by 96 runs	A.R. Border	179/3
Oct 19	Indore	New Zealand	Won by three runs	A.R. Border	180/32
Oct 22	New Delhi	India	Lost by 56 runs	A.R. Border	181/30
Oct 27	Chandigarh	New Zealand	Won by 17 runs	A.R. Border	182/33
Oct 30	Cuttack	Zimbabwe	Won by 70 runs	A.R. Border	183/4
Nov 4	Lahore	Pakistan	Won by 18 runs	A.R. Border	184/20
Nov 8	Calcutta	England	Won by seven runs	A.R. Border	185/42
1987-88 World Series Cup in Australia					
Jan 2	Perth	Sri Lanka	Won by 81 runs	A.R. Border	186/11
Jan 3	Perth	New Zealand	Lost by one run	A.R. Border	187/34
Jan 7	Melbourne	New Zealand	Won by six runs	A.R. Border	188/35
Jan 10	Adelaide	Sri Lanka	Won by 81 runs	A.R. Border	189/12
Jan 14	Melbourne	Sri Lanka	Won by 38 runs	A.R. Border	190/13
Jan 17	Brisbane	New Zealand	Won by five wickets	A.R. Border	191/36
Jan 19	Sydney	Sri Lanka	Won by three wickets	A.R. Border	192/14
Jan 20	Sydney	New Zealand	Won by 78 runs	A.R. Border	193/37
Jan 22	Melbourne	New Zealand	Won by eight wickets	A.R. Border	194/38
Jan 24	Sydney	New Zealand	Won by six wickets	A.R. Border	195/39
1987-88 in Australia					
Feb 4	Melbourne	England	Won by 22 runs	A.R. Border	196/43
1988-89 in Pakistan					
Oct 14	Lahore	Pakistan	Lost on fewer wickets	A.R. Border	197/21
1988-89 World Series in Australia					
Dec 11	Adelaide	Pakistan	Won by nine wickets	A.R. Border	198/22
Dec 13	Sydney	West Indies	Lost by one run	A.R. Border	199/46
Dec 15	Melbourne	West Indies	Lost by 34 runs	A.R. Border	200/47
Jan 2	Perth	Pakistan	Lost by 38 runs	A.R. Border	201/23
Jan 5	Melbourne	West Indies	Won by eight runs	A.R. Border	202/48
Jan 8	Brisbane	Pakistan	Won by five wickets	A.R. Border	203/24
Jan 10	Melbourne	Pakistan	Won on run-rate	A.R. Border	204/25
Jan 12	Sydney	West Indies	Won by 61 runs	A.R. Border	205/49
Jan 14	Melbourne	West Indies	Won by two runs	A.R. Border	206/50
Jan 16	Sydney	West Indies	Lost by 92 runs	A.R. Border	207/51
Jan 18	Sydney	West Indies	Lost on run-rate	A.R. Border	208/52
1989 in England					
May 25	Manchester	England	Lost by 95 runs	A.R. Border	209/44
May 27	Nottingham	England	Tied	A.R. Border	210/45
May 29	Lord's	England	Won by six wickets	A.R. Border	211/46
1989-90 in India					
Oct 19	Hyderabad	England	Lost by seven wickets	A.R. Border	212/47
Oct 21	Madras	West Indies	Won by 99 runs	A.R. Border	213/53
Oct 23	Bombay	Pakistan	Lost by 66 runs	A.R. Border	214/26
Oct 25	Goa	Sri Lanka	Won by 28 runs	A.R. Border	215/15
Oct 27	Bangalore	India	Lost by three wickets	A.R. Border	216/31
1989-90 World Series in Australia					
Dec 26	Melbourne	Sri Lanka	Won by 30 runs	A.R. Border	217/16
Dec 30	Perth	Sri Lanka	Won by nine wickets	A.R. Border	218/17
Jan 3	Melbourne	Pakistan	Won by seven wickets	A.R. Border	219/27
Jan 4	Melbourne	Sri Lanka	Won by 73 runs	A.R. Border	220/18
Feb 11	Brisbane	Pakistan	Won by 67 runs	A.R. Border	221/28
Feb 13	Sydney	Pakistan	Lost by five wickets	A.R. Border	222/29
Feb 18	Adelaide	Sri Lanka	Won by seven wickets	A.R. Border	223/19

Date	Venue	Opponent	Result for Australia	Captain	Team/Opp
Feb 20	Sydney	Pakistan	Lost by two runs	A.R. Border	224/30
Feb 23	Melbourne	Pakistan	Won by seven wickets	A.R. Border	225/31
Feb 25	Sydney	Pakistan	Won by 69 runs	A.R. Border	226/32

1989-90 in New Zealand

Mar 3	Christchurch	India	Won by 18 runs	A.R. Border	227/32
Mar 4	Christchurch	New Zealand	Won by 150 runs	A.R. Border	228/40
Mar 8	Hamilton	India	Won by seven wickets	A.R. Border	229/33
Mar 10	Auckland	New Zealand	Won on run-rate	G.R. Marsh	230/41
Mar 11	Auckland	New Zealand	Won by eight wickets	A.R. Border	231/42

1989-90 in United Arab Emirates

Apr 26	Sharjah	New Zealand	Won by 63 runs	A.R. Border	232/43
Apr 30	Sharjah	Bangladesh	Won by seven wickets	A.R. Border	233/1
May 2	Sharjah	Sri Lanka	Won by 114 runs	A.R. Border	234/20
May 4	Sharjah	Pakistan	Lost by 36 runs	A.R. Border	235/33

1990-91 World Series in Australia

Nov 29	Sydney	New Zealand	Won by 61 runs	A.R. Border	236/44
Dec 2	Adelaide	New Zealand	Won by six wickets	A.R. Border	237/45
Dec 9	Perth	England	Won by six wickets	A.R. Border	238/48
Dec 11	Melbourne	New Zealand	Won by 39 runs	A.R. Border	239/46
Dec 16	Brisbane	England	Won by 37 runs	A.R. Border	240/49
Dec 18	Hobart	New Zealand	Lost by one run	A.R. Border	241/47
Jan 1	Sydney	England	Won by 68 runs	A.R. Border	242/50
Jan 10	Melbourne	England	Won by three runs	A.R. Border	243/51
Jan 13	Sydney	New Zealand	Won by six wickets	G.R. Marsh	244/48
Jan 15	Melbourne	New Zealand	Won by seven wickets	G.R. Marsh	245/49

1990-91 in West Indies

Feb 26	Kingston	West Indies	Won by 35 runs	A.R. Border	246/54
Mar 9	Port-of-Spain	West Indies	Won by 45 runs	A.R. Border	247/55
Mar 10	Port-of-Spain	West Indies	Lost on run-rate	A.R. Border	248/56
Mar 13	Bridgetown	West Indies	Won by 46 runs	A.R. Border	249/57
Mar 20	Georgetown	West Indies	Won by six wickets	A.R. Border	250/58

1991-92 World Series in Australia

Dec 8	Perth	India	Lost by 107 runs	A.R. Border	251/34
Dec 10	Hobart	India	Won by eight wickets	A.R. Border	252/35
Dec 12	Melbourne	West Indies	Won by nine runs	A.R. Border	253/59
Dec 15	Adelaide	India	Won by six wickets	A.R. Border	254/36
Dec 18	Sydney	West Indies	Won by 51 runs	A.R. Border	255/60
Jan 9	Melbourne	West Indies	No result	A.R. Border	256/61
Jan 12	Brisbane	West Indies	Lost by 12 runs	A.R. Border	257/62
Jan 14	Sydney	India	Won by nine wickets	A.R. Border	258/37
Jan 18	Melbourne	India	Won by 88 runs	A.R. Border	259/38
Jan 20	Sydney	India	Won by six runs	A.R. Border	260/39

1991-92 World Cup in Australia and New Zealand

Feb 22	Auckland	New Zealand	Lost by 37 runs	A.R. Border	261/50
Feb 26	Sydney	South Africa	Lost by nine wickets	A.R. Border	262/1
Mar 1	Brisbane	India	Won by one run	A.R. Border	263/40
Mar 5	Sydney	England	Lost by eight wickets	A.R. Border	264/52
Mar 7	Adelaide	Sri Lanka	Won by seven wickets	A.R. Border	265/21
Mar 11	Perth	Pakistan	Lost by 48 runs	A.R. Border	266/34
Mar 14	Hobart	Zimbabwe	Won by 128 runs	A.R. Border	267/5
Mar 18	Melbourne	West Indies	Won by 57 runs	A.R. Border	268/63

Date	Venue	Opponent	Result for Australia	Captain	Team/Opp
1992-93 in Sri Lanka					
Aug 15	Colombo (PSS)	Sri Lanka	Lost by four wickets	A. R. Border	269/22
Sep 4	Colombo (PIS)	Sri Lanka	Lost on run-rate	A. R. Border	270/23
Sep 5	Colombo (PIS)	Sri Lanka	Won by five wickets	A. R. Border	271/24
1992-93 World Series in Australia					
Dec 6	Perth	West Indies	Lost by nine wickets	A. R. Border	272/64
Dec 8	Sydney	West Indies	Won by 14 runs	M. A. Taylor	273/65
Dec 10	Hobart	Pakistan	Tied	M. A. Taylor	274/35
Dec 13	Adelaide	Pakistan	Won by eight wickets	M. A. Taylor	275/36
Dec 15	Melbourne	West Indies	Won by four runs	M. A. Taylor	276/66
Jan 10	Brisbane	West Indies	Lost by seven runs	A. R. Border	277/67
Jan 12	Melbourne	Pakistan	Won by 32 runs	A. R. Border	278/37
Jan 14	Sydney	Pakistan	Won by 23 runs	A. R. Border	279/38
Jan 16	Sydney	West Indies	Lost by 25 runs	A. R. Border	280/69
Jan 18	Melbourne	West Indies	Lost by four wickets	A. R. Border	281/69
1992-93 in New Zealand					
Mar 19	Dunedin	New Zealand	Won by 129 runs	A. R. Border	282/51
Mar 21–22	Christchurch	New Zealand	Won by one wicket	M. A. Taylor	283/52
Mar 24	Wellington	New Zealand	Lost by 88 runs	A. R. Border	284/53
Mar 27	Hamilton	New Zealand	Lost by three wickets	M. A. Taylor	285/54
Mar 28	Auckland	New Zealand	Won by three runs	A. R. Border	286/55
1993 in England					
May 19	Manchester	England	Won by four runs	A. R. Border	287/53
May 21	Birmingham	England	Won by six wickets	A. R. Border	288/54
May 23	Lord's	England	Won by 19 runs	M. A. Taylor	289/55
1993-94 World Series in Australia					
Dec 9	Melbourne	South Africa	Lost by seven wickets	A. R. Border	290/2
Dec 12	Adelaide	New Zealand	Won by eight wickets	A. R. Border	291/56
Dec 14	Sydney	South Africa	Won by 103 runs	A. R. Border	292/3
Dec 16	Melbourne	New Zealand	Won by three runs	A. R. Border	293/57
Jan 9	Brisbane	South Africa	Won by 48 runs	A. R. Border	294/4
Jan 11	Sydney	New Zealand	Lost by 13 runs	A. R. Border	295/58
Jan 16	Perth	South Africa	Lost by 82 runs	M. A. Taylor	296/5
Jan 19	Melbourne	New Zealand	Won by 51 runs	A. R. Border	297/59
Jan 21	Melbourne	South Africa	Lost by 28 runs	A. R. Border	298/6
Jan 23	Sydney	South Africa	Won by 69 runs	A. R. Border	299/7
Jan 25	Sydney	South Africa	Won by 35 runs	A. R. Border	300/8
1993-94 in South Africa					
Feb 19	Johannesburg	South Africa	Lost by five runs	A. R. Border	301/9
Feb 20	Pretoria	South Africa	Lost by 56 runs	A. R. Border	302/10
Feb 22	Port Elizabeth	South Africa	Won by 88 runs	A. R. Border	303/11
Feb 24	Durban	South Africa	Lost by seven wickets	A. R. Border	304/12
Apr 2	East London	South Africa	Won by seven wickets	A. R. Border	305/13
Apr 4	Port Elizabeth	South Africa	Lost by 26 runs	A. R. Border	306/14
Apr 6	Cape Town	South Africa	Won by 36 runs	A. R. Border	307/15
Apr 8	Bloemfontein	South Africa	Won by one run	A. R. Border	308/16
1993-94 in United Arab Emirates					
Apr 14	Sharjah	Sri Lanka	Won by nine wickets	M. A. Taylor	309/25
Apr 16	Sharjah	New Zealand	Won by seven wickets	M. A. Taylor	310/60
Apr 19	Sharjah	India	Lost by seven wickets	M. A. Taylor	311/41

Date	Venue	Opponent	Result for Australia	Captain	Team/Opp
1994-95 in Sri Lanka					
Sep 7	Colombo (SSC)	Pakistan	Won by 28 runs	M. A. Taylor	312/39
Sep 9	Colombo (PIS)	India	Lost by 31 runs	M. A. Taylor	313/42
Sep 13	Colombo (SSC)	Sri Lanka	Lost on run-rate	M. A. Taylor	314/26
1994-95 in Pakistan					
Oct 12	Lahore	South Africa	Won by six wickets	M. A. Taylor	315/17
Oct 14	Multan	Pakistan	Won by seven wickets	M. A. Taylor	316/40
Oct 18	Faisalabad	South Africa	Won by 22 runs	M. A. Taylor	317/18
Oct 22	Rawalpindi	Pakistan	Lost by nine wickets	M. A. Taylor	318/41
Oct 24	Peshawar	South Africa	Won by three wickets	M. A. Taylor	319/19
Oct 30	Lahore	Pakistan	Won by 64 runs	M. A. Taylor	320/42
1994-95 World Series in Australia					
Dec 2	Perth	Zimbabwe	Won by two wickets	M. A. Taylor	321/6
Dec 6	Sydney	England	Won by 28 runs	M. A. Taylor	322/56
Dec 8	Hobart	Zimbabwe	Won by 85 runs	M. A. Taylor	323/7
Jan 10	Melbourne	England	Lost by 37 runs	M. A. Taylor	324/57
1994-95 in New Zealand					
Feb 15	Wellington	South Africa	Won by three wickets	M. A. Taylor	325/20
Feb 19	Auckland	New Zealand	Won by 27 runs	M. A. Taylor	326/61
Feb 22	Dunedin	India	Lost by five wickets	M. A. Taylor	327/43
Feb 26	Auckland	New Zealand	Won by six wickets	M. A. Taylor	326/62
1994-95 in West Indies					
Mar 8	Bridgetown	West Indies	Lost by six runs	M. A. Taylor	329/70
Mar 11	Port-of-Spain	West Indies	Won by 26 runs	M. A. Taylor	330/71
Mar 12	Port-of-Spain	West Indies	Lost by 133 runs	M. A. Taylor	331/72
Mar 15	Kingstown	West Indies	Lost on run-rate	M. A. Taylor	332/73
Mar 18	Georgetown	West Indies	Lost by five wickets	M. A. Taylor	333/74
1995-96 World Series in Australia					
Dec 17	Adelaide	West Indies	Won by 121 runs	M. A. Taylor	334/75
Dec 19	Melbourne	West Indies	Won by 24 runs	M. A. Taylor	335/76
Dec 21	Sydney	Sri Lanka	Won by five wickets	M. A. Taylor	336/27
Jan 1	Sydney	West Indies	Won by one wicket	M. A. Taylor	337/77
Jan 7	Brisbane	West Indies	Lost by 14 runs	M. A. Taylor	338/78
Jan 9	Melbourne	Sri Lanka	Lost by three wickets	M. A. Taylor	339/28
Jan 12	Perth	Sri Lanka	Won by 83 runs	M. A. Taylor	340/29
Jan 16	Melbourne	Sri Lanka	Lost by three wickets	M. A. Taylor	341/30
Jan 18	Melbourne	Sri Lanka	Won by 18 runs	M. A. Taylor	342/31
Jan 20	Sydney	Sri Lanka	Won on run-rate	M. A. Taylor	343/32
1995-96 World Cup in India, Pakistan and Sri Lanka					
Feb 23	Vishakhapatnam	Kenya	Won by 97 runs	M. A. Taylor	344/1
Feb 27	Bombay	India	Won by 16 runs	M. A. Taylor	345/44
Mar 1	Nagpur	Zimbabwe	Won by eight wickets	M. A. Taylor	346/8
Mar 4	Jaipur	West Indies	Lost by four wickets	M. A. Taylor	347/79
Mar 11	Chennai	New Zealand	Won by six wickets	M. A. Taylor	348/63
Mar 14	Chandigarh	West Indies	Won by five runs	M. A. Taylor	349/80
Mar 17	Lahore	Sri Lanka	Lost by seven wickets	M. A. Taylor	350/33
1996-97 in Sri Lanka					
Aug 26	Colombo (PIS)	Zimbabwe	Won by 125 runs	I. A. Healy	351/9
Aug 30	Colombo (PIS)	Sri Lanka	Lost by four wickets	I. A. Healy	352/34
Sep 6	Colombo (SSC)	India	Won by three wickets	I. A. Healy	353/45
Sep 7	Colombo (SSC)	Sri Lanka	Lost by 50 runs	I. A. Healy	354/35

Date	Venue	Opponent	Result for Australia	Captain	Team/Opp
1996-97 in India					
Oct 19	Indore	South Africa	Lost by seven wickets	M. A. Taylor	355/21
Oct 21	Bangalore	India	Lost by two wickets	M. A. Taylor	356/46
Oct 25	Faridabad	South Africa	Lost by two wickets	M. A. Taylor	357/22
Nov 1	Guwahati	South Africa	Lost by eight wickets	M. A. Taylor	358/23
Nov 3	Chandigarh	India	Lost by five runs	M. A. Taylor	359/47
1996-97 Carlton & United Series in Australia					
Dec 6	Melbourne	West Indies	Won by five wickets	M. A. Taylor	360/81
Dec 8	Sydney	West Indies	Won by eight wickets	M. A. Taylor	361/82
Dec 15	Adelaide	Pakistan	Lost by 12 runs	M. A. Taylor	362/43
Jan 1	Sydney	Pakistan	Lost by four wickets	M. A. Taylor	363/44
Jan 5	Brisbane	West Indies	Lost by seven wickets	M. A. Taylor	364/83
Jan 7	Hobart	Pakistan	Lost by 29 runs	M. A. Taylor	365/45
Jan 12	Perth	West Indies	Lost by four wickets	M. A. Taylor	366/84
Jan 16	Melbourne	Pakistan	Won by three wickets	M. A. Taylor	367/46
1996-97 in South Africa					
Mar 29	East London	South Africa	Lost by six wickets	M. A. Taylor	368/24
Mar 31	Port Elizabeth	South Africa	Won by seven wickets	M. A. Taylor	369/25
Apr 3	Cape Town	South Africa	Lost by 46 runs	I. A. Healy	370/26
Apr 5	Durban	South Africa	Won by 15 runs	I. A. Healy	371/27
Apr 8	Johannesburg	South Africa	Won by eight runs	I. A. Healy	372/28
Apr 10	Centurion	South Africa	Won by five wickets	I. A. Healy	373/29
Apr 13	Bloemfontein	South Africa	Lost by 109 runs	S. R. Waugh	374/30
1997 in England					
May 22	Leeds	England	Lost by six wickets	M. A. Taylor	375/58
May 24	The Oval	England	Lost by six wickets	M. A. Taylor	376/59
May 25	Lord's	England	Lost by six wickets	S. R. Waugh	377/60
1997-98 Carlton & United Series in Australia					
Dec 4	Sydney	South Africa	Lost by 67 runs	S. R. Waugh	378/31
Dec 7	Adelaide	New Zealand	Won by three wickets	S. R. Waugh	379/64
Dec 9	Melbourne	South Africa	Lost by 45 runs	S. R. Waugh	380/32
Dec 17	Melbourne	New Zealand	Won by six wickets	S. R. Waugh	381/65
Jan 11	Brisbane	South Africa	Lost by five wickets	S. R. Waugh	382/33
Jan 14	Sydney	New Zealand	Won by 131 runs	S. K. Warne	383/66
Jan 18	Perth	South Africa	Lost by seven wickets	S. R. Waugh	384/34
Jan 21	Melbourne	New Zealand	Lost by four wickets	S. R. Waugh	385/67
Jan 23	Melbourne	South Africa	Lost by six runs	S. R. Waugh	386/35
Jan 26	Sydney	South Africa	Won by seven wickets	S. R. Waugh	387/36
Jan 27	Sydney	South Africa	Won by 14 runs	S. R. Waugh	388/37
1997-98 in New Zealand					
Feb 8	Christchurch	New Zealand	Won by seven wickets	S. R. Waugh	389/68
Feb 10	Wellington	New Zealand	Won by 66 runs	S. R. Waugh	390/69
Feb 12	Napier	New Zealand	Lost by seven wickets	S. R. Waugh	391/70
Feb 14	Auckland	New Zealand	Lost by 30 runs	S. R. Waugh	392/71
1997-98 in India					
Apr 1	Kochi	India	Lost by 41 runs	S. R. Waugh	393/48
Apr 3	Ahmedabad	Zimbabwe	Won by 13 runs	S. R. Waugh	394/10
Apr 7	Kanpur	India	Lost by six wickets	S. R. Waugh	395/49
Apr 11	Delhi	Zimbabwe	Won by 16 runs	S. R. Waugh	396/11
Apr 14	Delhi	India	Won by four wickets	S. R. Waugh	397/50
1997-98 in United Arab Emirates					
Apr 18	Sharjah	New Zealand	Won by six wickets	S. R. Waugh	398/72
Apr 19	Sharjah	India	Won by 58 runs	S. R. Waugh	399/51
Apr 21	Sharjah	New Zealand	Won by five wickets	S. R. Waugh	400/73
Apr 22	Sharjah	India	Won on run-rate	S. R. Waugh	401/52
Apr 24	Sharjah	India	Lost by six wickets	S. R. Waugh	402/53

Date	Venue	Opponent	Result for Australia	Captain	Team/Opp
1998-99 in Bangladesh					
Oct 28	Dhaka	India	Lost by 44 runs	S. R. Waugh	403/54
1998-99 in Pakistan					
Nov 6	Karachi	Pakistan	Won by 86 runs	S. R. Waugh	404/47
Nov 8	Peshawar	Pakistan	Won by five wickets	S. R. Waugh	405/48
Nov 10	Lahore	Pakistan	Won by six wickets	S. R. Waugh	406/49
1998-99 Carlton & United Series in Australia					
Jan 10	Brisbane	England	Won on run-rate	S. K. Warne	407/61
Jan 13	Sydney	Sri Lanka	Won by eight wickets	S. K. Warne	408/36
Jan 15	Melbourne	England	Won by nine wickets	S. K. Warne	409/62
Jan 17	Sydney	England	Lost by seven runs	S. R. Waugh	410/63
Jan 21	Hobart	Sri Lanka	Lost by three wickets	S. R. Waugh	411/37
Jan 24	Adelaide	Sri Lanka	Won by 80 runs	S. K. Warne	412/38
Jan 26	Adelaide	England	Won by 16 runs	S. K. Warne	413/64
Jan 31	Perth	Sri Lanka	Won by 45 runs	S. K. Warne	414/39
Feb 5	Sydney	England	Won by four wickets	S. K. Warne	415/65
Feb 7	Melbourne	Sri Lanka	Won by 43 runs	S. K. Warne	416/40
Feb 10	Sydney	England	Won by ten runs	S. K. Warne	417/66
Feb 13	Melbourne	England	Won by 162 runs	S. K. Warne	418/67
1998-99 in West Indies					
Apr 11	Kingstown	West Indies	Lost by 44 runs	S. R. Waugh	419/85
Apr 14	St George's	West Indies	Won by 46 runs	S. R. Waugh	420/86
Apr 17	Port-of-Spain	West Indies	Lost by five wickets	S. R. Waugh	421/87
Apr 18	Port-of-Spain	West Indies	Won by 20 runs	S. R. Waugh	422/88
Apr 21	Georgetown	West Indies	Match tied	S. R. Waugh	423/89
Apr 24	Bridgetown	West Indies	Won by four wickets	S. R. Waugh	424/90
Apr 25	Bridgetown	West Indies	Lost on run-rate	S. R. Waugh	425/91
1999 World Cup in England					
May 16	Worcester	Scotland	Won by six wickets	S. R. Waugh	426/1
May 20	Cardiff	New Zealand	Lost by five wickets	S. R. Waugh	427/74
May 23	Leeds	Pakistan	Lost by ten runs	S. R. Waugh	428/50
May 27	Chester-le-Street	Bangladesh	Won by seven wickets	S. R. Waugh	429/2
May 30	Manchester	West Indies	Won by six wickets	S. R. Waugh	430/92
Jun 4	The Oval	India	Won by 77 runs	S. R. Waugh	431/55
Jun 9	Lord's	Zimbabwe	Won by 44 runs	S. R. Waugh	432/12
Jun 13	Leeds	South Africa	Won by five wickets	S. R. Waugh	433/38
Jun 17	Birmingham	South Africa	Match tied	S. R. Waugh	434/39
Jun 20	Lord's	Pakistan	Won by eight wickets	S. R. Waugh	435/51
1999-2000 in Sri Lanka					
Aug 22	Galle	Sri Lanka	Won on run rate	S. R. Waugh	436/41
Aug 23	Galle	India	Won on run rate	S. R. Waugh	437/56
Aug 26	Colombo (PIS)	Sri Lanka	Won by 27 runs	S. R. Waugh	438/42
Aug 28	Colombo (SSC)	India	Won by 41 runs	S. R. Waugh	439/57
Aug 31	Colombo (PIS)	Sri Lanka	Lost by eight wickets	S. R. Waugh	440/43
1999-2000 in Zimbabwe					
Oct 21	Bulawayo	Zimbabwe	Won by 83 runs	S. R. Waugh	441/13
Oct 23	Harare	Zimbabwe	Won by nine wickets	S. R. Waugh	442/14
Oct 24	Harare	Zimbabwe	Won by nine wickets	S. R. Waugh	443/15
1999-2000 Carlton & United Series in Australia					
Jan 9	Brisbane	Pakistan	Lost by 45 runs	S. R. Waugh	444/52
Jan 12	Melbourne	India	Won by 28 runs	S. R. Waugh	445/58
Jan 14	Sydney	India	Won by five wickets	S. R. Waugh	446/59
Jan 16	Melbourne	Pakistan	Won by six wickets	S. R. Waugh	447/53
Jan 19	Sydney	Pakistan	Won by 81 runs	S. R. Waugh	448/54

Date	Venue	Opponent	Result for Australia	Captain	Team/Opp
Jan 23	Melbourne	Pakistan	Won by 15 runs	S. R. Waugh	449/55
Jan 26	Adelaide	India	Won by 152 runs	S. R. Waugh	450/60
Jan 30	Perth	India	Won by four wickets	S. R. Waugh	451/61
Feb 2	Melbourne	Pakistan	Won by six wickets	S. R. Waugh	452/56
Feb 4	Sydney	Pakistan	Won by 152 runs	S. R. Waugh	453/57

1999-2000 in New Zealand
Feb 17	Wellington	New Zealand	No result	S. R. Waugh	454/75
Feb 19	Auckland	New Zealand	Won by five wickets	S. R. Waugh	455/76
Feb 23	Dunedin	New Zealand	Won by 50 runs	S. R. Waugh	456/77
Feb 26	Christchurch	New Zealand	Won by 48 runs	S. R. Waugh	457/78
Mar 1	Napier	New Zealand	Won by five wickets	S. R. Waugh	458/79
Mar 3	Auckland	New Zealand	Lost by seven wickets	S. R. Waugh	459/80

1999-2000 in South Africa
Apr 12	Durban	South Africa	Lost by six wickets	S. R. Waugh	460/40
Apr 14	Cape Town	South Africa	Won by five wickets	S. R. Waugh	461/41
Apr 16	Johannesburg	South Africa	Lost by four wickets	S. R. Waugh	462/42

2000 Super Challenge in Australia
Aug 12	Melbourne (CS)	South Africa	Won by 94 runs	S. R. Waugh	463/43
Aug 14	Melbourne (CS)	South Africa	Match tied	S. R. Waugh	464/44
Aug 16	Melbourne (CS)	South Africa	Lost by eight runs	S. R. Waugh	465/45

2000-01 in Kenya
Oct 7	Nairobi	India	Lost by 20 runs	S. R. Waugh	466/62

2000-01 in Australia
Jan 11	Melbourne	West Indies	Won by 74 runs	S. R. Waugh	467/93
Jan 14	Brisbane	West Indies	Won by nine wickets	A. C. Gilchrist	468/94
Jan 17	Sydney	West Indies	Won on run rate	A. C. Gilchrist	469/95
Jan 21	Melbourne	Zimbabwe	Won by eight wickets	A. C. Gilchrist	470/16
Jan 26	Adelaide	West Indies	Won by ten wickets	S. R. Waugh	471/96
Jan 28	Sydney	Zimbabwe	Won by 86 runs	S. R. Waugh	472/17
Jan 30	Hobart	Zimbabwe	Won by six wickets	S. R. Waugh	473/18
Feb 4	Perth	Zimbabwe	Won by one run	S. R. Waugh	474/19
Feb 7	Sydney	West Indies	Won by 134 runs	S. R. Waugh	475/97
Feb 9	Melbourne	West Indies	Won by 39 runs	S. R. Waugh	476/98

2000-01 in India
Mar 23	Bangalore	India	Lost by 60 runs	S. R. Waugh	477/63
Mar 28	Pune	India	Won by eight wickets	S. R. Waugh	478/64
Mar 31	Indore	India	Lost by 118 runs	S. R. Waugh	479/65
Apr 3	Visakhapatnam	India	Won by 93 runs	S. R. Waugh	480/66
Apr 6	Goa	India	Won by four wickets	S. R. Waugh	481/67

2001 in England
Jun 9	Cardiff	Pakistan	Won by seven wickets	S. R. Waugh	482/58
Jun 10	Bristol	England	Won by five wickets	S. R. Waugh	483/68
Jun 14	Manchester	England	Won on run rate	S. R. Waugh	484/69
Jun 19	Nottingham	Pakistan	Lost by 36 runs	S. R. Waugh	485/59
Jun 21	The Oval	England	Won by eight wickets	S. R. Waugh	486/70
Jun 23	Lord's	Pakistan	Won by nine wickets	S. R. Waugh	487/60

SUMMARY OF AUSTRALIAN LIMITED-OVERS INTERNATIONALS

	M	W	L	NR	T	% Won
England	70	38	30	1	1	54.29
New Zealand	80	55	22	2	0	68.75
Pakistan	60	33	24	2	1	55.00
Sri Lanka	43	28	13	2	0	65.12
West Indies	98	43	52	1	2	43.88
Canada	1	1	0	0	0	100.00
India	67	39	25	3	0	58.21
Zimbabwe	19	18	1	0	0	94.74
South Africa	42	20	21	0	1	47.62
Bangladesh	2	2	0	0	0	100.00
Kenya	1	1	0	0	0	100.00
Scotland	1	1	0	0	0	100.00
Total	487	280	189	12	6	57.49

CAPTAINS

	M	W	L	NR	T	% Won
W. M. Lawry	1	1	0	0	0	100.00
I. M. Chappell	11	6	5	0	0	54.54
G. S. Chappell	49	21	25	3	0	42.85
R. B. Simpson	2	1	1	0	0	50.00
G. N. Yallop	4	2	1	1	0	50.00
K. J. Hughes	49	21	23	4	1	42.85
D. W. Hookes	1	0	1	0	0	0.00
A. R. Border	178	107	67	3	1	60.11
R. J. Bright	1	0	1	0	0	0.00
G. R. Marsh	4	3	1	0	0	75.00
M. A. Taylor	67	37	29	0	1	55.22
I. A. Healy	8	5	3	0	0	62.50
S. R. Waugh	98	63	31	1	3	64.29
S. K. Warne	11	10	1	0	0	90.91
A. C. Gilchrist	3	3	0	0	0	100.00

MOST APPEARANCES

	M	Eng	NZ	Pak	SL	WI	Can	Ind	Zim	SAf	Ban	Kya	Sco
S. R. Waugh	317	30	56	43	24	50	–	53	14	43	2	1	1
A. R. Border	273	43	52	34	23	61	1	38	5	15	1	–	–
M. E. Waugh	237	21	35	29	23	47	–	27	13	39	1	1	1
D. C. Boon	181	21	39	19	16	32	–	29	5	19	1	–	–
I. A. Healy	168	16	23	25	20	39	–	15	5	23	1	1	–
S. K. Warne	167	14	22	16	17	27	–	18	12	38	1	1	1
D. M. Jones	164	20	27	21	17	41	–	21	3	13	1	–	–
M. G. Bevan	164	11	19	22	18	24	–	26	13	28	1	1	1
G. D. McGrath	140	14	14	19	15	18	–	19	10	28	1	1	1
C. J. McDermott	138	10	20	17	15	35	–	22	4	14	–	1	–

BATTING RECORDS

CENTURY-MAKERS

M. G. Bevan (5)	103	v South Africa at Centurion	1996-97
	108*	v England at The Oval	1997
	101*	v India at Sharjah	1997-98
	107	v New Zealand at Napier	1999-00
	106	v South Africa at Melbourne CS	2000-01
D. C. Boon (5)	111	v India at Jaipur	1986-87
	122	v Sri Lanka at Adelaide	1987-88
	102*	v India at Hobart	1991-92
	100	v New Zealand at Auckland	1991-92
	100	v West Indies at Melbourne	1991-92
A. R. Border (3)	105*	v India at Sydney	1980-81
	118*	v Sri Lanka at Adelaide	1984-85
	127*	v West Indies at Sydney	1984-85
G. S. Chappell (3)	125*	v England at The Oval	1977
	138*	v New Zealand at Sydney	1980-81
	108	v New Zealand at Auckland	1981-82
T. M. Chappell	110	v India at Nottingham	1983
A. C. Gilchrist (6)	100	v South Africa at Sydney	1997-98
	118	v New Zealand at Christchurch	1997-98
	103	v Pakistan at Lahore	1998-99
	131	v Sri Lanka at Sydney	1998-99
	154	v Sri Lanka at Melbourne	1998-99
	128	v New Zealand at Christchurch	1999-00
D. M. Jones (7)	104	v England at Perth	1986-87
	121	v Pakistan at Perth	1986-87
	101	v England at Brisbane	1986-87
	107	v New Zealand at Christchurch	1989-90
	102*	v New Zealand at Auckland	1989-90
	117*	v Sri Lanka at Sharjah	1989-90
	145	v England at Brisbane	1990-91
M. L. Hayden	111	v India at Visakhapatnam	2000-01
B. M. Laird	117*	v West Indies at Sydney	1981-82
S. G. Law	110	v Zimbabwe at Hobart	1994-95
D. S. Lehmann (2)	103*	v Pakistan at Karachi	1998-99
	110*	v West Indies at St George's	1998-99
G. R. Marsh (9)	125	v India at Sydney	1985-86
	104	v India at Jaipur	1986-87
	110	v India at Chennai	1987-88
	126*	v New Zealand at Chandigarh	1987-88
	101	v New Zealand at Sydney	1987-88
	125*	v Pakistan at Melbourne	1988-89
	111*	v England at Lord's	1989
	113	v West Indies at Bridgetown	1990-91
	106*	v West Indies at Georgetown	1990-91
D. R. Martyn (2)	116*	v New Zealand at Auckland	1999-00
	144*	v Zimbabwe at Perth	2000-01
R. T. Ponting (8)	123	v Sri Lanka at Melbourne	1995-96
	102	v West Indies at Jaipur	1995-96
	100	v New Zealand at Melbourne	1997-98
	145	v Zimbabwe at Delhi	1997-98
	124*	v Pakistan at Lahore	1998-99
	115	v India at Melbourne	1999-00
	101	v India at Visakhapatnam	2000-01
	102	v England at Bristol	2001
S. B. Smith (2)	117	v New Zealand at Melbourne	1982-83
	106	v Pakistan at Sydney	1983-84
M. A. Taylor	105	v India at Bangalore	1996-97

A. Turner	101	v Sri Lanka at The Oval	1975
M. E. Waugh (18)	108	v New Zealand at Hamilton	1992-93
	113	v England at Birmingham	1993
	107	v South Africa at Sydney	1993-94
	121*	v South Africa at Rawalpindi	1994-95
	130	v Sri Lanka at Perth	1995-96
	130	v Kenya at Vishakhapatnam	1995-96
	126	v India at Mumbai	1995-96
	110	v New Zealand at Chennai	1995-96
	102	v West Indies at Brisbane	1996-97
	115*	v South Africa at Port Elizabeth	1996-97
	104	v New Zealand at Adelaide	1996-97
	104	v Zimbabwe at Lord's	1999
	106	v Zimbabwe at Bulawayo	1999-00
	116	v India at Adelaide	1999-00
	112*	v West Indies at Brisbane	2000-01
	102*	v Zimbabwe at Hobart	2000-01
	173	v West Indies at Melbourne	2000-01
	133*	v India at Pune	2000-01
S. R. Waugh (3)	102*	v Sri Lanka at Melbourne	1995-96
	120*	v South Africa at Birmingham	1999
	114*	v South Africa at Melbourne CS	2000-01
K. C. Wessels	107	v India at New Delhi	1984-85
G. M. Wood (3)	108	v England at Leeds	1981
	104*	v West Indies at Adelaide	1984-85
	114*	v England at Lord's	1985

HIGHEST PARTNERSHIPS FOR EACH WICKET

212	for 1st	G. R. Marsh and D. C. Boon	v India at Jaipur	1986-87
219	for 2nd {	M. E. Waugh and R. T. Ponting	v Zimbabwe at Delhi	1997-98
		M. L. Hayden and R. T. Ponting	v India at Visakhapatnam	2000-01
224*	for 3rd	D. M. Jones and A. R. Border	v Sri Lanka at Adelaide	1984-85
222	for 4th	M. G. Bevan and S. R. Waugh	v South Africa at Melbourne (CS)	2000
172*	for 5th	D. S. Lehmann and M. G. Bevan	v West Indies at Kingston	1998-99
112	for 6th	M. E. Waugh and S. P. O'Donnell	v England at Sydney	1990-91
102*	for 7th	S. R. Waugh and G. C. Dyer	v India at Delhi	1986-87
119	for 8th	P. R. Reiffel and S. K. Warne	v South Africa at Port Elizabeth	1993-94
77	for 9th	M. G. Bevan and S. K. Warne	v West Indies at Port-of-Spain	1998-99
45	for 10th {	T. J. Laughlin and M. H. N. Walker	v England at Sydney	1979-80
		M. G. Bevan and A. C. Dale	v South Africa at East London	1996-97

MOST RUNS IN A CAREER

	M	I	NO	R	HS	100s	Avge	Stk/Rt
M. E. Waugh	237	229	19	8,374	173	18	39.88	76.63
S. R. Waugh	317	281	57	7,382	120*	3	32.96	75.96
A. R. Border	273	252	39	6,524	127*	3	30.63	71.14
D. M. Jones	164	161	25	6,068	145	7	44.62	72.49
D. C. Boon	181	177	16	5,964	122	5	37.04	64.95
M. G. Bevan	164	145	51	5,384	108*	5	57.28	75.13
R. T. Ponting	123	123	15	4,546	145	8	42.09	75.07
G. R. Marsh	117	115	6	4,357	126*	9	39.97	55.37
A. C. Gilchrist	119	115	5	3,848	154	6	34.98	89.43
M. A. Taylor	113	110	1	3,514	105	1	32.24	59.42
G. S. Chappell	74	72	14	2,331	138*	3	40.19	74.62
G. M. Wood	83	77	11	2,219	114*	3	33.62	59.43

	M	I	NO	R	HS	100s	Avge	Stk/Rt
K. J. Hughes	97	88	6	1,968	98	0	24.00	66.98
I. A. Healy	168	120	36	1,764	56	0	21.00	83.64
K. C. Wessels	54	51	3	1,740	107	1	36.25	62.08
D. S. Lehmann	69	62	11	1,727	110*	2	33.86	81.27
D. R. Martyn	79	65	23	1,681	144*	2	40.02	82.69
S. P. O'Donnell	87	64	15	1,242	74*	0	25.35	80.54
S. G. Law	54	51	5	1,237	110	1	26.89	74.74
R. W. Marsh	92	76	15	1,225	66	0	20.08	80.06

BOWLING RECORDS

BEST ANALYSES

T. M. Alderman (2)	5/17	v New Zealand at Wellington	1981-82
	5/32	v India at Christchurch	1989-90
G. S. Chappell (2)	5/20	v England at Birmingham	1977
	5/15	v India at Sydney	1980-81
G. J. Cosier	5/18	v England at Birmingham	1977
A. I. C. Dodemaide	5/21	v Sri Lanka at Perth	1989-90
D. W. Fleming	5/36	v India at Mumbai	1995-96
D. R. Gilbert	5/46	v New Zealand at Sydney	1985-86
G. J. Gilmour (2)	6/14	v England at Leeds	1975
	5/48	v West Indies at Lord's	1975
A. G. Hurst	5/21	v Canada at Birmingham	1979
B. Lee	5/27	v India at Adelaide	1999-00
S. Lee	5/33	v Sri Lanka at Melbourne	1998-99
D. K. Lillee	5/34	v Pakistan at Leeds	1975
K. H. MacLeay	6/39	v India at Nottingham	1983
C. J. McDermott	5/44	v Pakistan at Lahore	1987-88
G. D. McGrath (4)	5/52	v Pakistan at Lahore	1994-95
	5/40	v Sri Lanka at Adelaide	1998-99
	5/14	v West Indies at Manchester	1999
	5/49	v Pakistan at Sydney	1999-00
S. P. O'Donnell	5/13	v New Zealand at Christchurch	1989-90
L. S. Pascoe	5/30	v New Zealand at Sydney	1980-81
C. G. Rackemann	5/16	v Pakistan at Adelaide	1983-84
B. A. Reid	5/53	v India at Adelaide	1985-86
A. M. Stuart	5/26	v Pakistan at Melbourne	1996-97
S. K. Warne	5/23	v West Indies at Sydney	1996-97
M. E. Waugh	5/24	v West Indies at Melbourne	1992-93

HAT-TRICKS

B. A. Reid	v New Zealand at Sydney	1985-86
A. M. Stuart	v Pakistan at Melbourne	1996-97

MOST WICKETS IN A CAREER

	M	Balls	Mds	R	W	BB	5W/i	Avge
S. K. Warne	167	9,237	96	6,541	262	5/33	1	24.97
G. D. McGrath	140	7,512	151	5,002	212	5/14	4	23.59
C. J. McDermott	138	7,460	99	5,020	203	5/44	1	24.73
S. R. Waugh	317	8,823	54	6,705	195	4/33	0	34.38
D. W. Fleming	88	4,619	62	3,402	134	5/36	1	25.39
S. P. O'Donnell	87	4,350	49	3,102	108	5/13	1	28.72
P. R. Reiffel	92	4,732	84	3,095	106	4/13	0	29.20
D. K. Lillee	63	3,593	80	2,145	103	5/34	1	20.83

P.L. Taylor	83	3,937	32	2,740	97	4/38	0	28.25
T.M. Alderman	65	3,371	75	2,056	88	5/17	2	23.36
G.F. Lawson	79	4,259	94	2,592	88	4/26	0	29.45
R.M. Hogg	71	3,677	57	2,418	85	4/29	0	28.45
M.E. Waugh	237	3,621	10	2,892	83	5/24	1	34.84
C.G. Rackemann	52	2,791	51	1,833	82	5/16	1	22.35
A.R. Border	273	2,661	11	2,071	73	3/20	0	28.37
G.S. Chappell	74	3,108	41	2,096	72	5/15	2	29.11
B.A. Reid	61	3,250	53	2,201	63	5/53	1	34.94
G.R.J. Matthews	59	2,808	21	1,999	57	3/27	0	35.07
J.R. Thomson	50	2,696	37	1,942	55	4/67	0	35.31
L.S. Pascoe	29	1,568	21	1,066	53	5/30	1	20.11
B. Lee	29	1,531	17	1,236	50	5/27	1	24.72

WICKET-KEEPING RECORDS

MOST DISMISSALS IN AN INNINGS

6	(all ct)	A.C. Gilchrist v South Africa at Cape Town	1999-00
5	(all ct)	R.W. Marsh v England at Leeds	1981

Note: There are 21 instances of four dismissals in an innings.

MOST DISMISSALS IN A CAREER

	M	Ct	St	Total
I.A. Healy	168	194	39	233
A.C. Gilchrist	119	153	29	182
R.W. Marsh	92	120	4	124
W.B. Phillips	48	42	7	49
G.C. Dyer	23	24	4	28

FIELDING RECORDS

MOST CATCHES IN AN INNINGS

4   M.A. Taylor   v West Indies at Sydney 1992-93

Note: There are 18 instances of three catches in an innings.

MOST CATCHES IN A CAREER

A.R. Border	127 in 273 matches		M.A. Taylor	56 in 113 matches
S.R. Waugh	108 in 317 matches		M.G. Bevan	54 in 164 matches
M.E. Waugh	105 in 237 matches		D.M. Jones	54 in 164 matches
S.K. Warne	70 in 167 matches		D.C. Boon	45 in 180 matches

TEAM RECORDS

HIGHEST INNINGS TOTALS

Batting first

6-349	v New Zealand at Christchurch	1999-00
6-338	v West Indies at Melbourne	2000-01
4-338	v India at Visakhapatnam	2000-01
7-337	v Pakistan at Sydney	1999-00
3-332	v Sri Lanka at Sharjah	1989-90
5-329	v India at Adelaide	1999-00

5-328	v Sri Lanka at The Oval	1975
8-324	v Pakistan at Karachi	1998-99
2-323	v Sri Lanka at Adelaide	1984-85
9-320	v India at Nottingham	1983
8-310	v Sri Lanka at Melbourne	1998-99
4-310	v New Zealand at Napier	1999-00
7-304	v Kenya at Visakhapatnam	1995-96
4-303	v Zimbabwe at Lord's	1999
6-303	v Zimbabwe at Bulawayo	1999-00
8-302	v New Zealand at Melbourne	1982-83
5-302	v Zimbabwe at Perth	2000-01
5-300	v Pakistan at Brisbane	1989-90

Batting Second

4-316	v Pakistan at Lahore	1998-99
4-289	v New Zealand at Madras	1995-96
5-287	v South Africa at Centurion	1996-97
284	v India at Chandigarh	1996-97
4-282	v Zimbabwe at Hobart	2000-01
4-280	v England at Birmingham	199
4-279	v England at Lord's	1989
6-275	v England at Sydney	1998-99
274	v West Indies at Lord's	1975
5273	v England at Birmingham	1980
5-272	v South Africa at Leeds	1999
5-272	v England at Bristol	2001

PART FOUR: AUSTRALIAN CRICKET IN 2000-01

THE WEST INDIANS IN AUSTRALIA, 2000-01

Review by WARWICK FRANKS

In 1930-31, the first West Indies team to Australia arrived on a learning mission. Although they won only three of their 14 first-class matches, the tour concluded with wins over a New South Wales side which included Bradman, Kippax and McCabe and an initial Test victory in the final encounter of the series. Seventy years later, their successors managed to draw one of their eight first-class matches and lose the rest, including all five Tests, with varying degrees of comprehensiveness. Following the wretched tours of South Africa and England, and bearing in mind the intimidating success of the Lloyd–Richards era, the poverty of these results forces one to ask if the manifold achievements of West Indian cricket have been squandered. Poor management of generational change appears to have led to a plethora of recent Caribbean players who seem unable or unwilling to meet the challenges of Test cricket.

While statistics can be used to advance dubious cases, there is simply no refuge from the unrelenting misery of the figures for the West Indians on this tour. All five Tests were lost, the first two by an innings, and both state games were surrendered without a whimper. The batting was feeble in the extreme, with too many players too much out of form or too far out of their depth. In the seven first-class matches where the visitors completed both innings, they managed a combined total in excess of 500 only twice. Their paltry average of 21 per wicket for the tour contrasted with their opposition's 41. The bowlers never looked consistently menacing beyond the odd session and, revealingly, none of them took more than four wickets in an innings. Another symptom of the malaise affecting the team was that much of the fielding was sloppily amateurish.

As is so often the way with a team in this condition, Murphy's Law came savagely into effect. Kerry Jeremy had his jaw broken in the first match of the tour, while Shivnarine Chanderpaul's tour ended after his determined second innings in the First Test, when he was diagnosed with a stress fracture of the foot. By the time of the match against Australia A after the Second Test, a combination of sprains and influenza had reduced the tourists to awaiting the arrival of replacement batsman Marlon Samuels in Australia in order to field eleven fit men.

There was genuine sympathy for the invidious position of the captain, Jimmy Adams. His team was disintegrating, and he appeared to receive little assistance from a number of his senior players. The dire situation exposed his shortcomings as a captain; when initiative and inspiration were most needed he appeared to be stuck in a defensive rut, captaining by numbers. Previously a doughty fighter as a batsman, he lost form so markedly that his contributions were negligible. Nevertheless, he was unfailingly courteous and maintained a natural dignity despite being surrounded by so much that was ignominious.

Far too much depended on the ability of Brian Lara to stamp himself on proceedings. Despite a regal double-century against Australia A in Hobart which was immediately followed by 182 toughly fought runs in the Adelaide Test, the rest of his tour was barren. Only 178 runs came from his other 11 innings, which contained a mixture of the over-impetuous and the lackadaisical. His two failures in the First Test summarised both the lack of substance in his approach and the way in which it prompted the other batting to resemble a house of cards. The situation was exacerbated by Lara's apparent absorption in extra-curricular matters and the impression he gave of being uninterested in contributing to team morale.

The folly of picking only two specialist openers was swiftly exposed. Sherwin Campbell's batting slumped as his footwork deteriorated; his shuffling, fidgety presence at the crease showed the shattered state of his confidence which, however, made a belated reappearance in the final Test. Daren Ganga was almost strokeless; with his approach he needed to be able to occupy the crease for two days rather than two hours. Campbell and Ganga managed to average just 13 in their eight Test partnerships, and it was only when Campbell was joined by Wavell Hinds in the Fifth Test that the tourists had some respite. On that occasion, Hinds showed a welcome seriousness of purpose after having too often appeared irresolute and feckless.

Ramnaresh Sarwan, from whom much was expected, looked totally out of his depth and quickly became a woebegone figure whose main exercise was walking to and from the wicket. Having made just 37 runs in nine innings, he did show a glimpse of his quality in his last innings of the series. Amid the gloom, Marlon Samuels looked a picture of composure and confidence, blessedly free from the air of impending disaster which seemed to afflict most of his colleagues. At Melbourne, in only his second Test and eighth first-class match, he scored 106 in the match out of his side's total of 274; he made his runs under pressure with both elegance and combative steel.

The bowling was, in general, as limited as the batting. Total reliance on pace can be brutally effective if a side has the venom and skill of the West Indian sides of previous years. These pace men, however, were but distant echoes of those times. Courtney Walsh was unfailingly accurate and never allowed batsmen undue liberties but, shorn of the support of Curtly Ambrose, he never looked likely to run through a side. Marlon Black, Mervyn Dillon, Nixon McLean and Colin Stuart all bowled respectably most of the time and each had good spells but they never looked consistently dangerous. Too often, their ragged line and length dissipated any pressure they had exerted on the Australian batsmen. Mahendra Nagamootoo played with real commitment in his only Test and showed many of his batting betters what determination and counter-attack could do, but he does too little with his leg-spinners to trouble Test batsmen consistently.

The major beacon in the midst of so much cricketing gloom was the wicket-keeper/batsman Ridley Jacobs. Mature in both years and attitude, he played uncomplicated, productive cricket and, above all, with total commitment. He kept wicket safely and without ostentation and batted robustly; moreover, his presence on the field had an aura of the positive about it that was a welcome relief in the midst of so much passivity.

West Indies returned home to contemplate a visit by the South Africans. The interests of world cricket are not well served by one of its important members being reduced to a state of sustained weakness. Only a fundamental reshaping of the team, with players who appreciate the honour of being picked in a Test side, can start the process of reconstruction.

WEST INDIAN TOURING PARTY

J.C. Adams (Jamaica) (*captain*), S.L. Campbell (Barbados) (*vice-captain*), M.I. Black (Trinidad and Tobago), C.O. Browne (Barbados), S. Chanderpaul (Guyana), M. Dillon (Trinidad and Tobago), D. Ganga (Trinidad and Tobago), W.W. Hinds (Jamaica), R.D. Jacobs (Leeward Islands), K.C.B. Jeremy (Leeward Islands), B.C. Lara (Trinidad and Tobago), N.A.M. McLean (Windward Islands), M.V. Nagamootoo (Guyana), R.R. Sarwan (Guyana), C.E.L. Stuart (Guyana, C.A. Walsh (Jamaica).

M.N. Samuels (Jamaica) called as a replacement for S. Chanderpaul and C.E. Cuffy (Windward Islands) called as a replacement for M. Dillon. Cuffy arrived for the Carlton Series.

The West Indian touring party for the Carlton Series was as follows: J.C. Adams (Jamaica) (*captain*), S.L. Campbell (Barbados) (*vice-captain*), M.I. Black (Trinidad and Tobago), C.E. Cuffy (Windward Islands), D. Ganga (Trinidad and Tobago), W.W. Hinds (Jamaica), R.D. Jacobs (Leeward Islands), S.C. Joseph (Leeward Islands), B.C. Lara (Trinidad and Tobago), N.A.M. McLean (Windward Islands), M.V. Nagamootoo (Guyana), R.L. Powell (Jamaica), M.N. Samuels (Jamaica), C.E.L. Stuart (Guyana), L.R. Williams (Jamaica).

Manager: R. Skerritt. *Coach:* R.A. Harper. *Assistant coach:* P.J.L. Dujon. *Fielding coach:* J. Fontain. *Sports therapist:* R. Rogers. *Scorer:* G. Smith.

WEST INDIAN TOUR RESULTS

Test matches – Played 5: Lost 5.
First-class matches – Played 3: Lost 2, Drawn 1.
Losses – Western Australia and Victoria.
Draws – Australia A.
Limited-overs internationals – Played 10: Won 3, Lost 7. *Wins* – Zimbabwe (3).
Losses – Australia (6), Zimbabwe (1).
Other non-first-class matches – Played 4. Won 2, Lost 1, No Result 1. *Wins* – Northern Territory Invitational XI, Australia A; *Losses* – Prime Minister's XI, *No result* – ACB Chairman's XI

WEST INDIAN TOURING PARTY, 2000-01

Back row: J. Fontain (*fielding coach*), M.V. Nagamootoo, D. Ganga, K.C.B. Jeremy, W.W. Hinds, M. Dillon, N.A.M. McLean, M.I. Black, C.O. Browne, C.E.L. Stuart, R.R. Sarwan, R. Rogers (*sports therapist*), G. Smith (*scorer*). *Front Row*: R.A. Harper (*coach*), R.D. Jacobs, C.A. Walsh, J.C. Adams (*captain*), R. Skerritt (*team manager*), S.L. Campbell (*vice-captain*), B.C. Lara, S. Chanderpaul, P.J.L. Dujon (*assistant coach*). *Absent*: M.N. Samuels, C.E. Cuffy, R.L. Powell, L.R. Williams.

TEST MATCH AVERAGES

AUSTRALIA – BATTING

	M	I	NO	R	HS	100s	50s	Avge	Ct/St
S.R. Waugh	4	6	1	349	121*	2	0	69.80	0
M.J. Slater	5	8	1	373	96	0	4	53.29	3
M.E. Waugh	5	8	1	339	119	1	2	48.43	11
A.C. Gilchrist	5	6	1	241	87	0	2	48.20	19/2
R.T. Ponting	5	8	2	242	92	0	2	40.33	5
M.L. Hayden	5	8	0	236	69	0	2	29.50	8
C.R. Miller	3	4	1	78	37*	0	0	26.00	0
J.L. Langer	5	8	0	203	80	0	1	25.38	5
S.C.G. MacGill	4	4	1	44	19	0	0	14.67	3
J.N. Gillespie	4	4	0	48	23	0	0	12.00	2
G.D. McGrath	5	4	0	25	13	0	0	6.25	1
A.J. Bichel	2	2	0	11	8	0	0	5.50	1
B. Lee	2	2	2	103	62*	0	1	–	0
D.R. Martyn	1	2	2	80	46*	0	0	–	2

* Denotes not out.

BOWLING

	O	M	R	W	BB	5W/i	Avge
M.E. Waugh	11	4	15	1	1/10	0	15.00
B. Lee	59.1	21	177	11	5/61	1	16.09
G.D. McGrath	183.5	69	359	21	6/17	1	17.10
A.J. Bichel	43.3	9	124	7	5/60	1	17.71
C.R. Miller	143.2	37	365	20	5/32	2	18.25
J.N. Gillespie	141	40	368	20	6/40	2	18.40
S.C.G. MacGill	156	39	501	16	7/104	1	31.31
M.L. Hayden	2	0	9	0	–	0	–
R.T. Ponting	1	1	0	0	–	0	–

WEST INDIES – BATTING

	M	I	NO	R	HS	100s	50s	Avge	Ct/St
S. Chanderpaul	1	2	1	80	62*	0	1	80.00	0
M.V. Nagamootoo	1	2	0	80	68	0	1	40.00	0
M.N. Samuels	3	6	1	172	60*	0	1	34.40	1
B.C. Lara	5	10	0	321	182	1	0	32.10	5
R.D. Jacobs	5	10	1	288	96*	0	2	32.00	20/1
W.W. Hinds	4	8	0	247	70	0	2	30.88	4
J.C. Adams	5	10	2	151	49	0	0	18.88	3
S.L. Campbell	5	10	0	187	79	0	2	18.70	6
D. Ganga	4	8	0	107	32	0	0	13.38	1
M. Dillon	4	8	0	73	27	0	0	9.13	1
R.R. Sarwan	3	6	0	54	51	0	1	9.00	1
C.E.L. Stuart	2	4	1	21	12*	0	0	7.00	0
N.A.M. McLean	5	10	0	64	17	0	0	6.40	1
C.A. Walsh	5	10	2	19	9	0	0	2.38	0
M.I. Black	3	6	2	6	3*	0	0	1.50	0

* Denotes not out.

BOWLING

	O	M	R	W	BB	5W/i	Avge
M. Dillon	128.4	20	479	16	4/76	0	29.94
C.E.L. Stuart	60	10	239	6	2/52	0	39.83
M.I. Black	67	8	257	6	4/83	0	42.83
C.A. Walsh	199.4	46	481	11	2/39	0	43.73
M.V. Nagamootoo	44	4	147	3	3/119	0	49.00
N.A.M. McLean	137	19	476	9	2/69	0	52.89
M.N. Samuels	60.5	12	185	3	2/49	0	61.67
J.C. Adams	67.4	17	181	2	2/43	0	90.50

WEST INDIAN TOUR AVERAGES
FIRST-CLASS MATCHES

BATTING

	M	I	NO	R	HS	100s	50s	Avge	Ct/St
B.C. Lara	7	13	0	591	231	2	0	45.46	7
R.D. Jacobs	7	13	1	472	131	1	2	39.33	20/1
S. Chanderpaul	3	6	1	177	62*	0	1	35.40	3
M.V. Nagamootoo	2	4	0	128	68	0	1	32.00	0
M.N. Samuels	4	7	1	181	60*	0	1	30.17	2
W.W. Hinds	6	11	0	322	70	0	2	29.27	4
S.L. Campbell	8	15	0	372	119	1	2	24.80	7
C.O. Browne	2	3	1	43	21	0	0	21.50	8
J.C. Adams	8	15	2	213	49	0	0	16.38	7
K.C.B. Jeremy	2	2	1	16	9	0	0	16.00	1
C.E.L. Stuart	4	7	3	50	15*	0	0	12.50	1
D. Ganga	7	13	0	145	32	0	0	11.15	2
R.R. Sarwan	5	10	0	88	51	0	1	8.80	2
N.A.M. McLean	6	12	0	79	17	0	0	6.58	1
M. Dillon	6	12	0	76	27	0	0	6.33	2
C.A. Walsh	6	12	4	23	9	0	0	2.88	0
M.I. Black	5	9	2	20	11	0	0	2.86	1

* Denotes not out.

BOWLING

	O	M	R	W	BB	5W/i	Avge
M. Dillon	195.4	33	683	20	4/76	0	34.15
C.A. Walsh	232.4	61	547	15	4/66	0	36.47
C.E.L. Stuart	129.3	19	499	13	3/84	0	38.38
M.I. Black	142.2	26	494	12	4/83	0	41.17
W.W. Hinds	11	3	42	1	1/18	0	42.00
K.C.B. Jeremy	41	8	127	3	2/42	0	42.33
N.A.M. McLean	164	27	566	11	2/69	0	51.45
M.N. Samuels	102.2	18	319	6	3/100	0	53.17
M.V. Nagamootoo	58	6	208	3	3/119	0	69.33
J.C. Adams	117.4	24	331	3	2/43	0	110.33
R.D. Jacobs	2	2	0	0	–	0	–
D. Ganga	1	0	2	0	–	0	–

Note: Matches in this section that were not first-class are signified by a dagger.

†ACB CHAIRMAN'S XI v WEST INDIANS

At Lilac Hill Park, Guildford, November 11, 2000. No result. Toss: ACB Chairman's XI.

In the traditional first fixture for touring parties the "Battle of Lilac Hill" is more beer and skittles than serious combat. The top-order West Indian batsmen made the most of a chance to get their feet on Australian ground. The man on which their series seemed to rest, Brian Lara, thrilled the picnic crowd with an elegant 108, while opener Sherwin Campbell made 111. The tourists reached two for 276 in their 50 overs before rain ended the match.

Man of the Match: B. C. Lara. *Attendance:* 10,000 (approx).

West Indians

S. L. Campbell not out	111 (139)	B 3, l-b 4, w 4, n-b 1 12
D. Ganga b Nikitaras	43 (52)	
B. C. Lara c Hogg b Angel	108 (105)	(50 overs, 196 mins) (2 wkts) 276
W. W. Hinds not out	2	Fall: 87 250

*J. C. Adams, R. R. Sarwan, †R. D. Jacobs, M. V. Nagamootoo, N. A. M. McLean, M. Dillon, K. D. B. Jeremy and M. I. Black did not bat.

Bowling: Whitney 7–2–34–0; Angel 8–0–42–1; Nikitaras 9–1–42–1; Karppinen 10–0–55–0; Hogg 10–0–55–0; Moody 3–0–26–0; Katich 3–0–15–0.

ACB Chairman's XII

†A. C. Gilchrist, G. S. Blewett, J. L. Langer, D. C. Boon, *T. M. Moody, S. M. Katich, D. R. Martyn, G. B. Hogg, S. J. Karppinen, J. Angel, M. R. Whitney, S. Nikitaras.

Umpires: A. R. Craig and K. J. Rinaldi.

WESTERN AUSTRALIA v WEST INDIANS

At WACA Ground, Perth, November 9, 10, 11, 12, 2000. Western Australia won by seven wickets. Toss: Western Australia.

This match was finished as a contest and largely as a spectacle in the first few hours, as the West Indian batsmen succumbed to a less than deadly attack and were all out by tea. Facing the extravagant bowling of Matthew Nicholson and Brendon Julian, they watched numerous wides and bouncers go by, but to balls near a length they were inclined to aim big off-drives and feed catches to the keeper and the slips. Nicholson and his more sedate colleague Gavin Swan each gathered three wickets. The innings ended unhappily when Kenny Jeremy, after resisting for 85 minutes, was felled by a Nicholson bouncer, suffering two breaks to his jaw. The West Indian opening bowlers Mervyn Dillon and Marlon Black generated some early pace, but the Western Australian innings gathered strength and ended with a lead of 226. Its most notable features were a duck by Test aspirant Damien Martyn, 73 by young hope Simon Katich, and a brisk 54 from Nicholson, batting as nightwatchman. With the match long out of their reach, the West Indians took some comfort in their second innings from a marathon 119 in seven hours by Sherwin Campbell.

Attendance: 6,785.

Close of play: First day, Western Australia (1) 2-110 (Langer 40, Nicholson 0); Second day, West Indians (2) 1-31 (Campbell 19, Black 0); Third day, West Indians (2) 6-266 (Adams 41).

West Indians

S.L. Campbell c Gilchrist b Nicholson	8	– lbw b Moody	119
D. Ganga c Gilchrist b Julian	0	– c Gilchrist b Julian	8
W.W. Hinds c Gilchrist b Swan	8	– (4) c Gilchrist b Nikitaras	27
S. Chanderpaul c Gilchrist b Nicholson	21	– (5) c Katich b Swan	43
*J.C. Adams c Gilchrist b Swan	1	– (6) c Martyn b Moody	44
R.R. Sarwan c Martyn b Nicholson	22	– (8) lbw b Moody	12
†C.O. Browne c Moody b Nikitaras	20	– (9) not out	2
M. Dillon c Moody b Swan	0	– (7) c Langer b Moody	3
K.C.B. Jeremy retired hurt	7		
M.I. Black c Hussey b Julian	11	– (3) c Martyn b Nicholson	3
C.E.L. Stuart not out	15	– (10) c Katich b Julian	6
B 4, l-b 5, w 8, n-b 2	19	L-b 12, w 5, n-b 9	26

(58.5 overs, 262 mins)	132	(118 overs, 486 mins)	293
Fall: 11 12 26 29 64 82 89		Fall: 27 42 84 170 254 266 282	
94 113		285 293	

Bowling: First Innings—Nicholson 15.5–6–32–3; Julian 16–3–34–2; Swan 14–4–31–3; Nikitaras 10–4–25–1; Hussey 1–0–1–0; Hogg 2–2–0–0. *Second Innings*—Nicholson 21–6–43–1; Swan 24–9–58–1; Julian 22–5–58–2; Nikitaras 21–4–66–1; Hogg 14–6–28–0; Hussey 1–0–6–0; Martyn 3–1–8–0; Moody 12–7–14–4.

Western Australia

M.E. Hussey c Browne b Black	41	– (2) c Browne b Dillon	11
†A.C. Gilchrist c Browne b Dillon	14	– (1) c Hinds b Dillon	6
J.L. Langer run out (Ganga)	45	– c Browne b Black	5
M.J. Nicholson c Browne b Stuart	54		
D.R. Martyn c Chanderpaul b Stuart	0	– (4) not out	25
S.M. Katich c Adams b Stuart	73	– (5) not out	18
*T.M. Moody lbw b Adams	36		
G.B. Hogg not out	35		
B.P. Julian c Sarwan b Black	32		
S. Nikitaras c Chanderpaul b Black	0		
G.G. Swan b Black	0		
B 8, l-b 10, w 5, n-b 5	28	B 1, l-b 1, w 1, n-b 2	5

(102.2 overs, 451 mins)	358	(19.3 overs, 93 mins)	(3 wkts)	70
Fall: 30 106 120 124 191 276 298 343 347 358		Fall: 6 13 34		

Bowling: First Innings—Dillon 29–7–91–1; Black 31.2–7–100–4; Stuart 21–4–84–3; Hinds 8–3–24–0; Adams 13–1–41–1. *Second Innings*—Dillon 10–1–37–2; Black 6–3–17–1; Stuart 3.3–0–14–0.

Umpires: B. Bennett and R.J.U. Woolridge.
TV Umpire: A.R. Craig.

†NORTHERN TERRITORY INVITATIONAL XI v WEST INDIANS

At Traeger Park, Alice Springs, November 14, 2000. West Indians won by 57 runs. Toss: Northern Territory Invitational XI.

The pretty Alice Springs ground, with the MacDonnell Ranges glowing pink in the background, enhanced a new fixture that may become a regular part of touring teams' programmes in the future. Brian Lara showed again what he can do when neither team success nor reputation depends on him. After missing the important match against Western Australia with what he described as a "chronic" hamstring injury, he thrilled a crowd of 4,000 with 106 runs, including two sixes. Although the visitors cruised to victory, their attack was not convincing against the Invitational XI, with two run-outs and the mild spin of Jimmy Adams accounting for five of the nine wickets.

Attendance: 4,000.

West Indians

D. Ganga c Johnstone b Wapper 53	†R. D. Jacobs c Rothall b Senior 9
W. W. Hinds c Johnstone b Senior 9	M. V. Nagamootoo not out 21
B. C. Lara c Hodge b Miller 106	B 2, l-b 3, w 13, n-b 3 21
R. R. Sarwan b Miller 6	
S. Chanderpaul not out 31	(50 overs, 196 mins) (6 wkts) 259
*J. C. Adams c Wapper b Miller 3	Fall: 26 134 153 199 202 215

M. I. Black, C. E. L. Stuart, N. A. M. McLean and C. A. Walsh did not bat.

Bowling: Miller 10–2–40–3; Wilson 9–1–64–0; Senior 8–0–47–2; Wapper 10–1–46–1; Marsh 10–1–42–0; Hodge 3–0–15–0.

Northern Territory Invitational XI

M. J. Di Venuto c Chanderpaul b Adams ... 52	J. Wapper b Stuart 0
S. Williams st Jacobs b Adams 40	B. T. Wilson b Stuart 0
K. E. Vowles lbw b Black 31	C. R. Miller not out 3
*R. T. Ponting run out 26	
B. J. Hodge c McLean b Adams 6	L-b 13, w 4 17
D. J. Marsh lbw b McLean 20	
S. Johnstone run out 5	(50 overs, 207 mins) (9 wkts) 202
†J. Rothall not out 2	Fall: 89 113 146 157 167 192 192 195 195

D. K. Senior did not bat.

Bowling: Walsh 6–3–4–0; Black 8–0–42–1; McLean 8–1–40–1; Stuart 7–0–28–2; Nagamootoo 10–0–39–0; Adams 10–0–32–3; Sarwan 1–0–4–0.

Umpires: S. A. Davis and S. J. Davis.

†VICTORIA v WEST INDIANS

At Melbourne Cricket Ground, Melbourne, November 17, 18, 19, 2000. Victoria won by an innings and 63 runs. Toss: Victoria. First-class debut: B. C. Oliver.

With Test cricket in the offing this second thrashing by a state team augured ill for the West Indians. Their batting showed little spine against the Victorian pace attack, and their bowling was unable to extract the movement and bounce that the Victorians had found in the MCG pitch. The die was cast on the muggy first day when the varied medium-pacers of Test candidate Colin Miller cracked the tourists open with the wickets of Daren Ganga and Brian Lara. Mathew Inness did the rest, the West Indians, apart from Ridley Jacobs and Mahendra Nagamootoo, having no answer to his left-arm pace. Jason Arnberger (177 balls, ten fours and a six) and Brad Hodge (204 balls, 15 fours and two sixes) took Victoria to a declaration with a commanding lead of 177, only the indefatigable Courtney Walsh slowing their progress. The West Indians' threadbare batting line-up slumped to new depths in their second innings, their unwillingness to get behind the line again illustrated by another picnic of catches behind the wicket. This time the Victorian bowlers shared the wickets, Mathew Inness finishing with match figures of 9/73 as the match finished well inside three days.

Attendance: 8,531.

Close of play: First day, Victoria (1) 0-2 (Arnberger 1, Craig 0); Second day, Victoria (1) 3-304 (Hodge 134, Klinger 38).

West Indians

S. L. Campbell c Berry b Inness	29	–	c Berry b Fleming	20
D. Ganga c Berry b Miller	12	–	c Mott b Inness	0
B. C. Lara c Berry b Miller	19	–	c Miller b Oliver	20
S. Chanderpaul c Berry b Oliver	12	–	c Oliver b Miller	21
R. R. Sarwan lbw b Inness	0	–	c Craig b Oliver	0
*J. C. Adams c Mott b Inness	9	–	c Arnberger b Inness	8
†R. D. Jacobs run out (Inness/Berry)	28	–	c Craig b Miller	25
M. V. Nagamootoo c Miller b Inness	48	–	c Harper b Inness	0
N. A. M. McLean b Inness	6	–	c Craig b Miller	9
M. Dillon c Mott b Inness	0	–	c Mott b Fleming	0
C. A. Walsh not out	0	–	not out	4
L-b 3, n-b 1	4		B 1, w 6	7

(86.2 overs, 336 mins)	167	(46.3 overs, 188 mins)	114

Fall: 16 58 71 71 75 92 130 144 144 167

Fall: 2 33 58 62 72 78 78 97 106 114

Bowling: *First Innings*—Fleming 20–8–38–0; Inness 20.2–9–26–6; Oliver 19–8–32–1; Miller 26–6–68–2; Hodge 1–1–0–0. *Second Innings*—Fleming 10–3–27–2; Inness 15–7–47–3; Miller 15.3–9–26–3; Oliver 6–2–13–2.

Victoria

J. L. Arnberger c Lara b Dillon	99	*†D. S. Berry c Chanderpaul b Walsh		0
S. A. J. Craig c Lara b McLean	1	D. W. Fleming not out		6
M. P. Mott c Adams b Walsh	18	C. R. Miller not out		6
B. J. Hodge retired hurt	134	L-b 12, n-b 10		22
M. Klinger lbw b Walsh	43			
P. Q. Harper c Campbell b McLean	15	(115 overs, 479 mins)	(7 wkts dec)	344
B. C. Oliver c Dillon b Walsh	0	Fall: 4 61 182 329 331 331 331		

M. W. H. Inness did not bat.

Bowling: *First Innings*—Walsh 33–15–66–4; McLean 27–8–90–2; Dillon 28–5–76–1; Nagamootoo 14–2–61–0; Adams 13–2–39–0.

Umpires: R. L. Parry and R. G. Patterson.
TV Umpire: G. T. D. Morrow.

AUSTRALIA v WEST INDIES

First Test Match

At Brisbane Cricket Ground, Brisbane, November 23, 24, 25, 2000. Australia won by an innings and 126 runs. Toss: Australia. Test debut: M. I. Black.

As a meaningful contest, this game was over before stumps on the opening day as the home side passed its opponents' paltry total without losing a wicket. Australia went on to equal the West Indies record of 11 successive Test victories and, in so doing, underscored the barrenness of contemporary Caribbean cricket. The mortally fragile batting and the indolent ground fielding placed too great a burden on a bowling attack whose respectable competence could not intimidate batsmen in the manner of the West Indian speed barrage of the eighties. In contrast, Australia played with such all-round confidence and purpose that a minor crisis in the middle order seemed merely to act as a signal for a swift and telling counter-attack from the tail.

Steve Waugh had little hesitation in giving the visitors first use of a new pitch which, bleached of colour, remained generally benign during the match. In front of a crowd which grew to be the largest for the opening day of a Brisbane Test since 1932-33, West Indies struggled to make runs convincingly. In a decisive move, Stuart MacGill was swung into the attack after only 40 minutes and soon succeeded in surprising Sherwin Campbell with a bouncing leg-spinner. Predictably, Waugh immediately recalled Glenn McGrath when Brian Lara came in; equally predictably, perhaps, Lara pushed limply outside the off stump at the first ball and gave Adam Gilchrist an uncomplicated catch. In a calamitous period just after lunch, West Indies slid from three for 53 to nine for 67, a passage which included ten balls from McGrath during which he took four wickets without conceding a run. Although his final figures were a tribute to his unrelenting attention to the fundamentals of line and length, even he seemed surprised at the completeness of his dominance.

A symptom of the bizarre paralysis which took hold of the visitors was the way in which Ramnaresh Sarwan, who desperately needed a substantial occupation of the crease in order to stamp his claims as a batsman of Test class, ran himself out by calling for a superfluous and suicidal second leg-bye. As if to underline the feebleness of what had gone before, Courtney Walsh managed to stay for half an hour and join his captain in the third-highest partnership of the innings. The members of the 1960-61 West Indian team who had gathered in Brisbane to celebrate the 40th anniversary of the Tied Test would doubtless have ruminated on the fact that their team had reached seven for 359 on the corresponding day of that encounter.

The batting of Michael Slater and Matthew Hayden was forthright, if not flawless, Hayden in particular beginning to resemble the redoubtable figure he had so often looked in domestic cricket. Having created a new Brisbane record opening stand against West Indies, Hayden was the victim of Slater's skittish running between the wickets. Even so, Australia ended the day 25 runs ahead with nine wickets in hand.

For most of the first two sessions on the second day, the West Indian bowlers held the home batting in check. Walsh allowed no liberties but was palpably less effective without Curtly Ambrose as a partner, while Mervyn Dillon and Marlon Black had enough vim and perseverance to make Australia's progress uncertain. Slater's innings took five minutes under three hours; Mark Waugh inched his way to 24 in 149 minutes and 104 balls, while his brother was marginally more positive in reaching 41 in 134 minutes from 94 balls. From seven for 220, however, the innings flourished, thanks to the audacity of Gilchrist (98 minutes, 66 balls and eight fours) and the unexpectedly correct and clean strokeplay of Brett Lee, who hit an undefeated 62 (105 minutes, 80 balls, one superbly off-driven six from Black and seven fours). Their eighth-wicket partnership of 61 took only 44 minutes and opened the way for MacGill to offer unorthodox support to Lee in a partnership of 50 in 53 minutes, so that Australia were able to finish with a crushing lead of 250.

Again the West Indian innings began with a whimper rather than a bang. Campbell seemed a meek, predestined victim as he nudged the fourth ball of the innings to the keeper, while Lara top-edged a furious pull shot to give Gilchrist some sprinting practice. Four runs in two innings from 26 balls from the side's premier batsman could hardly engender team confidence. After West Indies started the third day at two for 25, Daren Ganga soon fell to a classic mixture of flight and turn; he had battled hard for a total of 214 minutes for his combined total of 28 runs, but he seemed too shackled to be effective. Shivnarine Chanderpaul (229 minutes, 157 balls, five fours) showed welcome application and a willingness to try to score runs responsibly. He looked to be the only batsman capable of holding out against an Australian attack in which McGrath again asserted his dominance to return the remarkable match figures of 10/27 from 33 overs. The Australian victory came at 1.53 p.m. on the third day after barely half the allotted time for play in the Test, leaving West Indies with few scraps of comfort from the game to take into the ensuing Tests. – WARWICK FRANKS.

Man of the Match: G. D. McGrath. *Attendance:* 48,441.

Close of play: First day, Australia (1) 1-107 (Slater 54, Bichel 4); Second day, West Indies (2) 2-25 (Ganga 8, Chanderpaul 7).

West Indies

S. L. Campbell c M. E. Waugh b MacGill	10	– c Gilchrist b McGrath	0
D. Ganga c Ponting b Bichel	20	– st Gilchrist b MacGill	8
B. C. Lara c Gilchrist b McGrath	0	– c Gilchrist b McGrath	4
S. Chanderpaul c Gilchrist b McGrath	18	– not out	62
*J. C. Adams not out	16	– c Gilchrist b Lee	16
R. R. Sarwan run out (Ponting/Gilchrist)	0	– b Lee	0
†R. D. Jacobs c M. E. Waugh b McGrath	2	– c M. E. Waugh b Bichel	4
N. A. M. McLean lbw b McGrath	0	– lbw b Lee	13
M. Dillon c Gilchrist b McGrath	0	– b McGrath	0
M. I. Black c MacGill b McGrath	0	– c Gilchrist b McGrath	2
C. A. Walsh c Langer b Lee	9	– c McGrath b MacGill	0
L-b 6, n-b 1	7	B 8, l-b 3, n-b 4	15

(49.1 overs, 208 mins)   82   (58 overs, 249 mins)   124
Fall: 21 25 53 59 60 63 63 67 67 82   Fall: 0 10 29 62 66 81 98 117 119 124

Bowling: *First Innings*—McGrath 20–12–17–6; Lee 11.1–5–24–1; MacGill 5–1–10–1; Bichel 13–3–25–1. *Second Innings*—McGrath 13–9–10–4; Lee 18–9–40–3; MacGill 16–5–42–2; Bichel 11–4–21–1.

Australia

M. J. Slater c Campbell b Black	54	B. Lee not out	62
M. L. Hayden run out (Sarwan/Jacobs)	44	S. C. G. MacGill run out (Campbell)	19
A. J. Bichel c Jacobs b Black	8	G. D. McGrath b Walsh	0
J. L. Langer c Jacobs b Black	3	L-b 5, n-b 4	9
M. E. Waugh c and b Dillon	24		
*S. R. Waugh c Campbell b Dillon	41	(114.4 overs, 498 mins)	332
R. T. Ponting c Jacobs b Black	20	Fall: 101 111 112 117 179 186 220 281	
†A. C. Gilchrist c Jacobs b Dillon	48	331 332	

Bowling: Walsh 31.4–7–78–1; Black 28–5–83–4; Dillon 25–8–79–3; McLean 25–5–79–0; Adams 5–2–8–0.

Umpires: D. B. Cowie (New Zealand) and D. J. Harper.
TV Umpire: P. D. Parker.
Referee: A. C. Smith (England).

AUSTRALIA v WEST INDIES

Second Test Match

At WACA Ground, Perth, December 1, 2, 3, 2000. Australia won by an innings and 27 runs. Toss: Australia.

It is a dangerous ploy for sportsmen to make bold predictions, as they are often left looking foolish. Glenn McGrath, however, had no misgivings when he publicly declared Brian Lara to be his bunny and prophesied before this match that he would dismiss opener Sherwin Campbell and then Lara to reach 300 Test wickets. Almost miraculously, he was spot on, but he went one better by also dismissing West Indian captain Jimmy Adams to become the eighth Australian in 123 years to take a Test hat-trick. All this dramatic action exploded in six minutes of mayhem in the ninth over of the Test after Steve Waugh had won the toss and sent the tourists in to bat on a typically fast, bouncy WACA pitch, and while many thousands of the crowd were held up in slow-moving queues outside the ground.

Lara dominated the build-up to the match, suffering hamstring problems and barely bothering to train. He was also embroiled in controversy for being allowed a female companion on tour, and there were reports that he was at a nightclub in the early hours of the morning two nights before the start of the Test. In contrast, secrecy surrounded the fitness of McGrath, who was in doubt until the last moment, suffering from damage to his bowling shoulder. Australia resisted the option of playing four fast bowlers, retaining leg-spinner Stuart MacGill and bringing in Jason Gillespie in place of Andy Bichel, to give Gillespie his first taste of Test cricket since breaking his leg and wrist in a fielding collision with Steve Waugh in Kandy 15 months earlier. A stress fracture of the left foot forced Shivnarine Chanderpaul out of the West Indian side, which gave Ramnaresh Sarwan a reprieve after he had initially been replaced by left-hander Wavell Hinds.

Apart from McGrath's hat-trick and his 300th Test wicket, this contest was notable for Australia setting a record of 12 successive Test wins, for Australia winning for the first time in their six Tests against West Indies in Perth, and for Mark Waugh's 18th Test century, a majestic masterpiece that rescued Australia from early trouble and was a crucial factor in the triumph. Perth maintained its tradition of early finishes, with this match ending at 3.48 p.m. on the third day. Only one of the past 11 Tests in Perth has ended in a draw, and only two have entered the fifth day. Of the past six Tests at the WACA Ground, four have ended on the third day and two on the fourth day.

West Indies' misery started in the second over when Lee struck a shuffling Daren Ganga on the pad for the first of the side's six ducks in the match. Umpire John Hampshire adjudged Ganga leg before wicket, although the ball appeared to be spearing wide of leg stump. In the ninth over Campbell, forced onto the back foot, edged to Ponting at first slip, and the atmosphere was electric as Lara came to the crease. To McGrath's 15,089th Test delivery the left-hander went back defensively to one that cut away, and the ball flew to fourth slip where MacGill fumbled it before grasping it to his chest. Adams then fended a lifting delivery into the safe hands of Justin Langer at short leg to give McGrath his hat-trick. McGrath made no attempt to become the first man in Test history to take four wickets in consecutive deliveries. His next ball, to the nervous Sarwan (who had not scored in his four previous first-class innings), was a bouncer that the right-hander ducked. But he departed for two in the following over, scooping a drive at Lee to Slater at cover, the only fieldsman in front of the wicket.

West Indies would have been six for 22 in the 11th over had Ponting, at first slip, not spilt a simple waist-high catch offered by Hinds. Hinds would have departed for 16, McGrath would have had 4/10, and there was the real prospect of the side being bundled out for a total of around 30. Then at five for 36 and with Hinds on 19, the left-hander drove at Gillespie and was brilliantly caught by a diving Michael Slater in the covers. But umpire Hampshire had called Gillespie for overstepping, fractionally. Hinds had further good fortune when on 33 he edged a ball from Brett Lee and was dropped by wicket-keeper Adam Gilchrist, diving left-handed in front of Ponting. Hinds went on to make 50 before he drove at MacGill and was snapped up at slip by Mark Waugh. He and the resolute Ridley Jacobs had taken the score to six for 97, and West Indies were eventually able to reach a total of 196, thanks to Jacobs and Mervyn Dillon. When Courtney Walsh dabbled outside off stump at Gillespie and was caught behind, the left-handed Jacobs was cruelly robbed of his first Test century, stranded on 96 after courageously taking up the fight against the rampant Australians. The only blemish in his 220-minute, 151-ball innings came when he was 82 and Ponting dropped him at first slip off Gillespie.

Australia were in early trouble at four for 123, of which opener Matthew Hayden had contributed a robust 69, before Mark Waugh took charge with his graceful century and Gilchrist (50 off 77 deliveries) and Lee (an unbeaten 41 off 58 balls) helped the side to reach a satisfactory eight for 396 before Steve Waugh declared. Each of the four West Indian fast bowlers battled determinedly to take two wickets. Then West Indies provided little more than token resistance as they were dismissed for 173. MacGill took the prized wicket of Lara when the left-hander missed with an adventurous pull and was bowled. The intimidating Lee's five wickets included 3/0 with the final six balls of the match. Subsequently, the Australians locked arms in a tight embrace and sang the team victory song on the field, signalling the end of three days of relentless, ruthless cricket. Steve

Waugh underlined the obvious by declaring that his team was both special and destined for even greater things. – KEN CASELLAS.

Man of the Match: M.E. Waugh. *Attendance:* 44,044.

Close of play: First day, Australia (1) 2-72 (Hayden 46, Gillespie 1); Second day, West Indies (2) 2-16 (Ganga 9).

West Indies

S.L. Campbell c Ponting b McGrath	3	– c Gillespie b Lee	4
D. Ganga lbw b Lee	0	– c Hayden b Gillespie	20
W.W. Hinds c M.E. Waugh b MacGill	50	– (4) b MacGill	41
B.C. Lara c MacGill b McGrath	0	– (5) b MacGill	17
*J.C. Adams c Langer b McGrath	0	– (6) not out	40
R.R. Sarwan c Slater b Lee	2	– (7) c Gilchrist b Lee	1
†R.D. Jacobs not out	96	– (8) run out (MacGill/Gilchrist)	24
N.A.M. McLean b MacGill	7	– (9) b Lee	11
M. Dillon c Hayden b Gillespie	27	– (3) c Gilchrist b McGrath	3
M.I. Black c Hayden b Gillespie	0	– b Lee	0
C.A. Walsh c Gilchrist b Gillespie	1	– lbw b Lee	0
L-b 3, n-b 7	10	B 1, l-b 8, n-b 3	12

(61 overs, 276 mins)   196 (66 overs, 288 mins)   173
Fall: 1 19 19 19 22 97 117 172 178 196   Fall: 7 16 42 78 95 96 150 173 173 173

Bowling: *First Innings*—McGrath 19–2–48–3; Lee 15–5–52–2; Gillespie 12–2–46–3; MacGill 15–2–47–2. *Second Innings*—McGrath 18–7–26–1; Lee 15–2–61–5; MacGill 17–6–37–2; Gillespie 12–4–26–1; Hayden 2–0–9–0; M.E. Waugh 2–1–5–0.

Australia

M.L. Hayden b Black	69	†A.C. Gilchrist c McLean b Walsh	50
M.J. Slater c Campbell b Dillon	19	B. Lee not out	41
J.L. Langer c Sarwan b McLean	5	S.C.G. MacGill not out	18
J.N. Gillespie c Lara b McLean	23	B 2, l-b 10, w 2, n-b 7	21
M.E. Waugh c Adams b Dillon	119		
*S.R. Waugh c Campbell b Walsh	26	(108 overs, 499 mins) (8 wkts dec)	396
R.T. Ponting b Black	5	Fall: 52 62 111 123 188 208 303 348	

G.D. McGrath did not bat.

Bowling: Walsh 31–10–74–2; Black 18–2–87–2; Dillon 29–4–130–2; McLean 22–3–78–2; Adams 8–3–15–0.

Umpires: J.H. Hampshire (England) and P.D. Parker.
TV Umpire: R.J.U. Woolridge.
Referee: A.C. Smith (England).

†PRIME MINISTER'S XI v WEST INDIANS

At Manuka Oval, Canberra, December 7, 2000. Prime Minister's XI won by four wickets. Toss: West Indians.

The hapless West Indians had become so accustomed to defeat that they let even this social fixture slip from their grasp, despite a 97 from their desperately under-performed opener Daren Ganga and a comforting contribution of 59 from 59 balls by beleaguered captain Jimmy Adams. They reached a creditable three for 230, but the spoilsport Australians knocked the target off with four wickets and nine balls to spare, the local pair of Anthony McQuire and Mark Higgs leading the way.

Attendance: 10,435.

West Indians

S.L. Campbell lbw b Swain	26	(43)
D. Ganga c Clingeleffer b Nash	97	(140)
W.W. Hinds c Love b Hodge	15	(43)
*J.C. Adams not out	59	(59)
R.D. Jacobs not out	22	(21)

L-b 4, w 5, n-b 2 11

(50 overs, 189 mins)   (3 wkts) 230

Fall: 62 112 179

†C.O. Browne, N.A.M. McLean, M.I. Black, C.E.L. Stuart, C.A. Walsh and K.C.B. Jeremy did not bat.

Bowling: Nash 10–2–32–1; Inness 8–0–52–0; Swain 10–0–54–1; Higgs 10–0–30–0; Marsh 2.5–1–8–0; Gilchrist 2.1–0–14–0; Hodge 7–0–36–1.

Prime Minister's XI

*A.C. Gilchrist c Hinds b Stuart	31	(47)
J.P. Maher c Browne b Black	4	(21)
B.J. Hodge b Black	7	(14)
M.L. Love c Hinds b Stuart	56	(98)
A.D. McQuire run out		
((sub)J Fontain/Browne)	57	(64)
M.A. Higgs not out	49	(40)

†S.G. Clingeleffer c and b Walsh ... 3 (9)

D.A. Nash not out 5 (3)

B 1, l-b 5, w 10, n-b 5 21

(48.3 overs, 205 mins)   (6 wkts) 233

Fall: 12 35 54 158 184 205

D.J. Marsh, B.A. Swain and M.W.H. Inness did not bat.

Bowling: Walsh 9.3–3–36–1; Black 9–1–52–2; McLean 4–0–19–0; Stuart 10–2–53–2; Jeremy 8–0–27–0; Adams 8–0–40–0.

Umpires: W.F. Ruse and R.J. Wooldridge.
TV Umpire: D.B. Harris.

AUSTRALIA A v WEST INDIANS

At Bellerive Oval, Hobart, December 9, 10, 11, 12, 2000. Match drawn. Toss: West Indians.

This match was dominated by the innings of Brian Lara. Troubled by injury and out of form, he came in late on the second day with the West Indians in accustomed bother at five for 80. He then unleashed the glorious range of his shots, flaying an attack of Test aspirants around Bellerive Oval, scoring his 231 off only 260 balls, with 40 fours and two sixes. He hit every ball of one over from Andy Bichel to the boundary as he raced to his second century off 82 balls. His partnership of 365 with Ridley Jacobs (373 minutes, 285 balls, 16 fours, one six) set a first-class record for the sixth wicket in Australia. It also gave the West Indians a first-innings lead for the first time on the tour, and raised the team's spirits after two heavy Test defeats. To underline their state of crisis, it had needed the arrival of Marlon Samuels to give the side 11 fit men to take the field. After Lara's dismissal, the game petered out tamely, and was called off an hour before the scheduled close, although not before Jamie Cox (282 minutes, 218 balls, seven fours, one six) had given a calm reminder of his mature skill. Earlier, Jimmy Maher had demonstrated a full array of strokes in his chanceless 150 (339 minutes, 262 balls, 14 fours, one six), and Don Nash had rounded off the Australia A innings with three sixes before taking three West Indian wickets with some lively pace bowling.

Close of play: First day, Australia A (1) 4-306 (Katich 25, Hodge 2); Second day, West Indians 5-172 (Jacobs 30, Lara 62); Third day, West Indians 492 all out.

Australia A

J. Cox b Stuart	6	–	(2) c Adams b Jeremy	94
J. P. Maher b Stuart	150	–	(1) c Browne b Jeremy	46
M. L. Love b Stuart	76			
*D. R. Martyn c Adams b Hinds	37	–	not out	58
S. M. Katich c Black b Jeremy	45	–	not out	0
B. J. Hodge c Samuels b Black	14	–	(3) c Browne b Stuart	8
†B. J. Haddin c Ganga b Samuels	37			
A. J. Bichel c Browne b Samuels	20			
D. A. Nash c Stuart b Samuels	30			
B. J. Oldroyd not out	4			
L-b 14, w 2, n-b 3	19		L-b 2, n-b 2	4

(117.3 overs, 480 mins)   (9 wkts dec) 439   (78 overs, 300 mins)   (3 wkts) 210
Fall: 16 172 262 289 341 343 405 406 439   Fall: 70 87 208

M. W. H. Inness did not bat.

Bowling: *First Innings*—Black 23–4–71–1; Stuart 28–1–110–3; Jeremy 23–3–85–1; Adams 13–2–41–0; Samuels 27.3–4–100–3; Hinds 3–0–18–1. *Second Innings*—Black 15–4–49–0; Stuart 17–4–52–1; Jeremy 18–5–42–2; Samuels 14–2–34–0; Adams 11–2–29–0; Ganga 1–0–2–0; Jacobs 2–2–0–0.

West Indians

S. L. Campbell c Oldroyd b Nash	9	M. I. Black st Haddin b Hodge	0
D. Ganga c Oldroyd b Bichel	18	C. E. L. Stuart not out	8
W. W. Hinds c Bichel b Nash	40	K. C. B. Jeremy lbw b Bichel	9
*J. C. Adams c Love b Inness	0		
M. N. Samuels c Haddin b Nash	9	B 1, l-b 8, n-b 7	16
R. D. Jacobs b Hodge	131		
B. C. Lara c Love b Hodge	231	(154.4 overs, 607 mins)	492
†C. O. Browne c Martyn b Hodge	21	Fall: 14 50 50 73 80 445 452 452 479 492	

Bowling: *First Innings*—Bichel 38.4–10–148–2; Nash 28–3–81–3; Inness 27–11–94–1; Oldroyd 33–13–75–0; Katich 16–3–62–0; Martyn 1–0–6–0; Hodge 11–5–17–4.

Umpires: D. J. Harper and J. H. Smeaton.

AUSTRALIA v WEST INDIES

Third Test Match

At Adelaide Oval, Adelaide, December 15, 16, 17, 18, 19, 2000. Australia won by five wickets. Toss: West Indies. Test debut: M. N. Samuels.

Brian Lara's engine finally kicked into life in the Adelaide sunshine. By the second afternoon, he had roared to 182, placing West Indies in control for the first time in the series. The wheels, however, were loosely attached, and when Lara was taken at slip, and none of his team-mates was able to score a half-century, they simply fell off. Adam Gilchrist, deputising ably for the injured Steve Waugh, oversaw a steady fightback that left Australia chasing 130 for victory. Despite early scares at three for 27 and four for

48, a 63-run stand between Justin Langer and Damien Martyn effectively settled the issue. And when Langer fell to a catch at the wicket, Gilchrist joined Martyn to steer Australia home.

In the end, Lara even forfeited the satisfaction of the Man of the Match award. Channel Nine's commentators surprisingly handed the $3,000 prize to Colin Miller, the 36-year-old off-spinner, who marked his return to the side with five wickets in each innings. The truth is that while Miller's fizzing off-breaks may have won the match, Lara's fireworks had made it a contest worth watching.

Lara had entered gingerly on the first morning, 25 overs after Jimmy Adams's first successful toss of the summer. Already suffering from a recurrence of his hamstring trouble, he also endured a blow on the helmet from a guided missile from Glenn McGrath, and a first hour that produced only 11 runs. Then, in the 49th over, he shifted gears, creaming Jason Gillespie for three successive boundaries. McGrath was next, speechless for once as consecutive length balls sped past cover, mid-wicket and backward point. But it was the spinners, particularly Stuart MacGill, who really felt the lash. Lara drove them ferociously on the up, making little effort to get to the pitch of the ball but simply guessing how much it would turn. He survived one chance, on 73, when an edged cut off MacGill eluded both Mark Waugh and Gilchrist. But eventually one of those flamboyant drives slewed into first slip's hands. Lara's 182 had used up just 234 balls, and he dominated a stand of 183 with his minder, Jimmy Adams. West Indies racked up 391, all but doubling their previous best effort of the series.

Australia's reply – like Michael Slater's running – was a stop-start affair. The openers had made 156 in 38 overs when Slater shot Matthew Hayden down with friendly fire, just as he had at Brisbane. He then became a first Test victim for Marlon Samuels, a promising debutant batsman and part-time off-spinner. In Steve Waugh's absence, Australia needed someone to play the middle-order hard man. And that is exactly what Ricky Ponting did, surviving a critical miss at slip on 41 and eventually finishing with 92, one of his ugliest but most telling innings for his country. Australia rebounded from four for 187 to five for 369, and then fell away again, losing the rest for just 34 runs.

MacGill, who had first-innings figures of 24–5–118–0, reacted badly to a dubious caught-behind decision. Storming up the players' race, MacGill barged into Ramnaresh Sarwan, West Indies' 12th man, who was coming the other way with drinks. A. C. Smith, the English match referee, let him off with a verbal warning. There was more unpleasantness the next morning, when Australia were convinced they had broken the pivotal stand by dismissing Daren Ganga caught behind. The lead was then 70, with the pitch deteriorating fast enough to give the home side jitters. But umpire Venkataraghavan rejected the appeal, prompting some curt remarks from the close fielders and a bodyline throw-in from Ponting. Lara, reverting to what Mark Taylor called his "antagonist" mode, stalked down the pitch to accuse Gilchrist of sledging.

Lara's strategy succeeded only in deflecting the heat back onto himself. And although West Indies survived to go to lunch on two for 82, an embattled Lara was taken at short-leg just two overs later. His demise triggered an avalanche of six wickets for 19, hastened by Miller's speed through the air. His slingy action pinned batsmen to their creases, throwing up ballooning bat-pad chances that reliably went to hand.

"We mucked up in the second innings," Adams admitted afterwards. His chance of grabbing a shock win had evaporated in just over an hour. Instead, Australia claimed the series and the Frank Worrell Trophy – though hardly anyone seemed to notice. The chase was on for an unprecedented whitewash of West Indies. – SIMON BRIGGS.

Man of the Match: C. R. Miller. *Attendance:* 61,486.

Close of play: First day, West Indies (1) 4-274 (Lara 136, Dillon 3); Second day, Australia (1) 3-180 (Waugh 10, Gillespie 2); Third day, Australia (1) 9-403 (Martyn 46, McGrath 1); Fourth day, Australia (2) 4-98 (Langer 43, Martyn 18).

West Indies

S. L. Campbell lbw b Gillespie	18	– c Gilchrist b McGrath	8
D. Ganga b Gillespie	23	– lbw b Miller	32
W. W. Hinds c Ponting b Gillespie	27	– c Martyn b MacGill	9
B. C. Lara c Waugh b Miller	182	– c Langer b Miller	39
*J.C. Adams c Gilchrist b Gillespie	49	– c Martyn b Miller	15
M. Dillon c Waugh b Gillespie	9	– (9) lbw b McGrath	19
M. N. Samuels lbw b Miller	35	– (6) c Hayden b MacGill	3
†R. D. Jacobs c Langer b Miller	21	– (7) c Ponting b Miller	2
N. A. M. McLean lbw b Miller	0	– (8) c Hayden b Miller	0
M. I. Black not out	1	– not out	3
C. A. Walsh b Miller	0	– c Gilchrist b McGrath	0
B 8, l-b 12, n-b 6	26	B 6, l-b 3, w 1, n-b 1	11

(128.5 overs, 520 mins)   391   (51.5 overs, 211 mins)   141
Fall: 45 52 86 269 280 354 376 382   Fall: 26 36 87 96 109 109 109 116
391 391   137 141

Bowling: *First Innings*—McGrath 36–14–83–0; Gillespie 32–9–89–5; Miller 35.5–13–81–5; MacGill 24–5–118–0; Ponting 1–1–0–0. *Second Innings*—McGrath 9.5–1–27–3; Gillespie 13–5–18–0; MacGill 12–2–55–2; Miller 17–6–32–5.

Australia

M. J. Slater c (sub) Sarwan b Samuels	83	– (2) c Jacobs b Dillon	1
M. L. Hayden run out (Campbell/Jacobs)	58	– (1) c Jacobs b Walsh	14
J. L. Langer c Lara b Samuels	6	– c Jacobs b Dillon	48
M. E. Waugh lbw b Dillon	63	– c Jacobs b Dillon	5
J. N. Gillespie lbw b Walsh	4		
R. T. Ponting c Jacobs b Walsh	92	– (5) lbw b Walsh	11
D. R. Martyn not out	46	– (6) not out	34
*†A. C. Gilchrist c Jacobs b McLean	9	– (7) not out	10
S. C. G. MacGill c Jacobs b Dillon	6		
C. R. Miller c Campbell b McLean	1		
G. D. McGrath b Dillon	1		
B 5, l-b 13, w 5, n-b 11	34	B 3, l-b 1, n-b 3	7

(127.4 overs, 537 mins)   403   (43 overs, 195 mins)   (5 wkts) 130
Fall: 156 160 169 187 310 369 386 397 398 403   Fall: 8 22 27 48 111

Bowling: *First Innings*—Walsh 32–7–73–2; Black 18–1–75–0; Dillon 24.4–2–84–3; McLean 21–1–69–2; Adams 13–2–35–0; Samuels 19–6–49–2. *Second Innings*—Walsh 14–4–39–2; Dillon 12–3–42–3; Samuels 6–1–17–0; McLean 5–1–9–0; Adams 3–0–7–0; Black 3–0–12–0.

Umpires: S. Venkataraghavan (India) and S. J. Davis.
TV Umpire: D. J. Harper.
Referee: A. C. Smith (England).

AUSTRALIA v WEST INDIES

Fourth Test Match

At Melbourne Cricket Ground, Melbourne, December 26, 27, 28, 29, 2000. Australia won by 352 runs. Toss: West Indies. Test debut: C.E.L. Stuart.

Had this Test been a movie, you'd have canned it: "Some good action sequences, but we've seen it all before. And are we really meant to believe that one cricket team can be so good, and its opponents so bad?" Yet that was the way of it. Australia extended their winning run to 14, West Indies endured their fourth consecutive rout in the series and incurred their 15th Test defeat in their last 17 starts. Steve Waugh became Test cricket's fifth-highest run-scorer and posted his 23rd century. Jimmy Adams collected a wretched pair. Coincidentally, Frank Worrell did the same in the corresponding Test 40 years ago; perhaps the only parallel between them as leaders on their respective journeys.

Adams inserted Australia on Boxing Day, ostensibly because the pitch seemed likely to assist the bowlers, although West Indies appeared to have no plan more elaborate than simply boring the home team out with the sheer monotony of their pace attack. The Australians almost fell into the trap, such as it was, essaying some rather casual strokes. But their unflappable captain atoned for the indiscretions of others with a 260-minute hundred, abetted by the tail; the last three wickets added 139 against increasingly innocuous bowling and ham-handed fielding. Only wicket-keeper Ridley Jacobs escaped censure, his seven catches equalling the Test record.

West Indies did not so much chase Australia's 364 as refuse at the first hurdle. The first scoring stroke, a despairing slash from Daren Ganga, did not eventuate until the third delivery of the eighth over. He fell next ball. Wavell Hinds was dropped from consecutive deliveries, but still collected a duck when athletically snared in the gully by Michael Slater. Sherwin Campbell agonised 52 interminable minutes over his first run, and managed only one further scoring shot in 41 minutes before falling to a trapeze-artist catch at silly point by Matthew Hayden. Brian Lara, off balance, was adeptly caught at second slip by Mark Waugh; Adams, trying not to offer, was adroitly caught at the wicket by Adam Gilchrist, changing direction. The bowling was expert, the catching breathtaking; the time may have come for Marylebone to consider a prohibition on intimidatory fielding.

After Jacobs had played some rousing strokes and Marlon Samuels some elegant ones, the tail was swiftly amputated. Courtney Walsh saved the follow-on, but was run out by Glenn McGrath from the same ball trying to turn two into three, leaving the willowy 19-year-old Samuels unconquered after 159 minutes of poised resistance. Andy Bichel, substituting for the injured Brett Lee, will bowl better for figures less eye-catching than his first five-wicket Test bag.

The Test drifted on the third day as Australia sought a suitable declaration target, with Justin Langer banking an overdue 80, Mark Waugh unbeaten 78. Old heads recalled the 735 that Bill Lawry set Garry Sobers' West Indies in Sydney in February 1969, but Steve Waugh was content to fix the target at 462 and loose his bowlers for 11 overs before the close. As if transfixed the visitors promptly slumped to three for 10, with Lara among the casualties after leaving a ball from Jason Gillespie that did no more than hold its line. The last ball of the day was bowled by Colin Miller with two slips, two leg slips and five more clustered around the bat. Campbell was yet to score at the close, apparently intent on being the first batsman to carry his bat without scoring a run.

Campbell's ungainly vigil ended after half an hour of the fourth day at the hands of Gillespie, who at one point had 6/18 out of six for 23, and whose claims to the match award must have been difficult to overlook. Another perky stand between Samuels and Jacobs of 54 from 97 balls delayed the end, but no later than 2.25 p.m. One left the ground with another sinking feeling common after a bad movie: that there was a sequel just around the corner. – GIDEON HAIGH.

Man of the Match: S.R. Waugh. *Attendance:* 133,299.

Close of play: First day, Australia (1) 7-295 (S.R. Waugh 98, Gillespie 14); Second day, West Indies (1) 165 all out; Third day, West Indies (2) 3-10 (Campbell 0, Stuart 3).

Australia

M.J. Slater c Jacobs b McLean	30	– (2) c Lara b Dillon	4
M.L. Hayden c Jacobs b Walsh	13	– (1) c Hinds b McLean	30
J.L. Langer c Jacobs b Stuart	31	– c Ganga b Adams	80
M.E. Waugh c Adams b Dillon	25	– not out	78
*S.R. Waugh not out	121	– c Jacobs b Stuart	20
R.T. Ponting c Hinds b McLean	23	– (7) not out	26
†A.C. Gilchrist c Campbell b Stuart	37	–	
A.J. Bichel c Jacobs b Dillon	3		
J.N. Gillespie c Jacobs b Walsh	19		
C.R. Miller c Jacobs b Dillon	29	– (6) st Jacobs b Adams	11
G.D. McGrath c Jacobs b Dillon	11		
L-b 4, w 1, n-b 17	22	B 5, l-b 4, w 1, n-b 3	13

(114 overs, 502 mins)	364	(77 overs, 325 mins) (5 wkts dec)	262
Fall: 41 47 101 105 149 210 225 306 347 364		Fall: 8 49 165 212 228	

Bowling: *First Innings*—Walsh 33–6–62–2; Dillon 21–2–76–4; McLean 27–5–95–2; Stuart 15–4–52–2; Samuels 14–0–56–0; Adams 4–0–19–0. *Second Innings*—Walsh 18–3–46–0; Dillon 17–1–68–1; McLean 9–1–30–1; Stuart 15–2–66–1; Adams 18–8–43–2.

West Indies

S.L. Campbell c Hayden b Miller	5	– c Ponting b Gillespie	6
D. Ganga c Gilchrist b Gillespie	4	– lbw b Gillespie	0
W.W. Hinds c Slater b Gillespie	0	– c Bichel b Gillespie	4
B.C. Lara c M.E. Waugh b Bichel	16	– b Gillespie	0
*J.C. Adams c Gilchrist b Bichel	0	– (6) c M.E. Waugh b Gillespie	0
M.N. Samuels not out	60	– (7) c Gillespie b Miller	46
†R.D. Jacobs c M.E. Waugh b Bichel	42	– (8) c Gilchrist b Miller	23
N.A.M. McLean b Bichel	17	– (9) run out (Bichel)	1
M. Dillon b Gillespie	0	– (10) b Miller	15
C.E.L. Stuart b Bichel	1	– (5) lbw b Gillespie	4
C.A. Walsh run out (McGrath/Bichel)	4	– not out	0
L-b 5, n-b 11	16	L-b 1, n-b 9	10

(57.3 overs, 249 mins)	165	(49.3 overs, 209 mins)	109
Fall: 5 6 28 28 103 144 150 157 165		Fall: 1 6 7 17 17 23 77 78 108 109	

Bowling: *First Innings*—McGrath 13–7–15–0; Gillespie 18–6–48–3; Bichel 13.3–2–60–5; Miller 13–5–37–1. *Second Innings*—McGrath 12–6–10–0; Gillespie 17–5–40–6; Miller 14.3–2–40–3; Bichel 6–0–18–0.

Umpires: S. Venkataraghavan (India) and S.J.A. Taufel.
TV Umpire: R.G. Patterson.
Referee: A.C. Smith (England).

AUSTRALIA v WEST INDIES

Fifth Test Match

At Sydney Cricket Ground, Sydney, January 2, 3, 4, 5, 6, 2001. Australia won by six wickets. Toss: West Indies.

The completion of Australia's first five-nil whitewash against West Indies in 70 years of Test combat took more effort than expected. The visitors mounted such effective resistance that, on the fifth morning, with Australia still needing 127 when the third wicket fell, a surprise consolation victory for Jimmy Adams and his battered unit was a clear possibility.

The Centenary of Federation Test began with ceremony, with the Prime Minister, John Howard, to the fore, and the Australian players sported special baggy green caps embellished with gold ribbing. West Indies of necessity took first use of a brand new straw-coloured pitch that bespoke encouragement to spin bowling, and Stuart MacGill was in action within half an hour. This, though, was where the pattern of predictability faded. Over 40,000 people – including the ten-millionth spectator in the history of international cricket at the Sydney Cricket Ground – watched as Sherwin Campbell passed 18 for the first time in the series, and his affluent stand with Wavell Hinds (his 11th opening partner in Tests) grew to 147, setting a new mark for West Indies' first wicket in Australia. It was the first time in 30 Tests that Australia's bowlers had conceded a century opening stand.

Mid-afternoon saw the old pattern restored. MacGill, bowling his leg-spin from the Randwick end and using the breeze from third man, dismissed both openers, Glenn McGrath trapped Jimmy Adams after he had made his 3,000th run in Tests, and after tea Brian Lara's flourishing 35 ended with a brilliant fingertip catch at slip by Mark Waugh. Ramnaresh Sarwan, replacing the injured Daren Ganga, added a duck to his previous miserable three runs from four innings, a victim of MacGill's "back-spinner". Marlon Samuels, possessed of the poise and strut of the young Cassius Clay, seemed unlucky to be given out as he swung to leg, and in his next over the rampant MacGill had the chance of a hat-trick when he dismissed Ridley Jacobs and Nixon McLean in two balls. McLean's duck was West Indies' 27th of the series, another unwelcome record. Colin Miller chipped in with a late wicket, leaving the visitors nine for 256. MacGill's overnight figures were a well-earned 7/92.

Australia took a firm grip on the second day, which began stunningly as Miller removed his cap to reveal a head of hair dyed "Federation blue". It provoked more laughter than condemnation, though some wondered if this was the ultimate endorsement of a Test series which had sometimes itself seemed a poor joke. Miller wrapped up the innings by taking the first Test wicket ever credited to a blue-haired bowler.

Australia soon lost Matthew Hayden and then Justin Langer, who had survived a referral to the third umpire after edging to Lara. Michael Slater, however, stormed to a 56-ball fifty, only to be involved in another run-out after lunch when he misread striker Mark Waugh's "body language" and sent him back. A further madcap moment came when Slater, on 96, and having survived two chances, charged at Mahendra Nagamootoo and spooned a catch to cover. It was the ninth time Australia's cavalier had fallen in the 90s in Tests, an unwanted record that he later characteristically turned to positive effect. The rest of the day belonged to Steve Waugh, playing his 132nd Test (now second only to Allan Border's 156), and Ricky Ponting, whose fifty was vigorously applauded. They took control and saw their side to 284 at stumps, 12 ahead with six wickets in hand. Waugh's 92 had included a six into the old Hill area off Nagamootoo, whose leg-spin was rather too brisk and lacking in imagination.

The persevering Colin Stuart quickly accounted for Ponting on the third morning and should then have claimed Adam Gilchrist first ball, when Adams turfed a high chance at gully. Gilchrist proceeded to slam boundaries, and Waugh strolled his 100th run after 280 minutes at the crease to become joint fifth in the Test centuries list with 24. After Gilchrist reached his fifty off 56 balls, the captain tried to kick away a spinner that landed in the footmarks and was mortified to see the ball bounce onto his stumps. The tail, particularly the free-swinging Miller, made useful contributions on a placid pitch after Gilchrist's blitz ended with a slip catch, and the lead was increased to 180.

McGrath then shared the new ball with Miller and his off-spin, and everyone sat back to await a final bout of West Indian embarrassment. For 38 overs Australia were frustrated, but just as the second century opening stand beckoned, in the last over Hinds misjudged a ball from McGrath, bowling around the wicket, and lost his off stump.

A familiar wobble on the fourth day left West Indies five down, including the key wicket of Lara, and still 26 behind. Adams, Campbell (to a glorious low catch by Gilchrist) and Samuels (first ball) all fell to pace, and Lara, having escaped when Miller spilt a sitter off MacGill, was caught behind off the errant fielder's bowling two runs later. For once, however, the late middle order prospered. Batting alongside the reliable Jacobs, young Sarwan now showed Australia that he could play. In a stand of 85 he displayed some deft touches during his two and a half hours. Nagamootoo then batted freely for 68, the top score of the innings, his fifty coming off only 51 balls. His stand with Jacobs set a West Indies seventh-wicket record for Sydney.

Australia's frustration showed, not least in the over-aggressive firing of the ball at the wicket-keeper, sometimes causing the batsman to take evasive action. Mark Waugh captured Jacobs' wicket; Nagamootoo was extremely annoyed at himself for lofting Miller to mid-off; McLean was caught at slip; Walsh was greeted by a guard of honour as his opponents acknowledged his final Test appearance in Australia; and at 5.05 p.m., with the floodlights on, the innings ended. Australia needed 173 to seal the whitewash.

Hayden again fell cheaply, bat raised, padding away, and when Langer was helplessly leg before wicket Walsh had his 494th Test wicket. While connoisseurs relished the restoration of some real tension, local nerves, unaccustomed to this sort of situation, were beginning to jangle. Slater was forced to duck and weave during one of the most fascinating spells of a one-sided series.

Then, on the final day, Mark Waugh was soon out, feeding a catch to slip, and if his brother could have been ejected quickly then Australia's haunting fourth-innings fallibility might have rematerialised. But the captain was stubborn as usual, while Slater simply ran amok. When Waugh was leg before wicket near lunch the job was almost done. Ponting soon hit the winning run, and Australia's 15th consecutive victory was in the bag.

For the once-supreme West Indies it was their first barren tour of Australia, and they had now suffered 18 defeats in their last 20 overseas Tests. Any hopes generated by their younger players shone from the wreckage like sapphires, gleaming blue as Colin Miller's hair but far more desperately needed. – DAVID FRITH.

Man of the Match: M.J. Slater. *Player of the Series:* G.D. McGrath. *Attendance:* 126,874.

Close of play: First day, West Indies (1) 9-256 (Stuart 0, Walsh 0); Second day, Australia (1) 4-284 (S.R. Waugh 82, Ponting 51); Third day, West Indies (2) 1-98 (Campbell 45); Fourth day, Australia (2) 2-44 (Slater 18, M.E. Waugh 3).

West Indies

S.L. Campbell	c and b MacGill	79	–	c Gilchrist b Gillespie	54
W.W. Hinds	b MacGill	70	–	b McGrath	46
*J.C. Adams	lbw b McGrath	10	–	lbw b McGrath	5
B.C. Lara	c M.E. Waugh b MacGill	35	–	c Gilchrist b Miller	28
M.N. Samuels	c Langer b MacGill	28	–	lbw b Gillespie	0
R.R. Sarwan	lbw b MacGill	0	–	c Gilchrist b McGrath	51
†R.D. Jacobs	st Gilchrist b MacGill	12	–	lbw b M.E. Waugh	62
M.V. Nagamootoo	c Slater b Miller	12	–	c Hayden b Miller	68
N.A.M. McLean	lbw b MacGill	0	–	c M.E. Waugh b Miller	15
C.E.L. Stuart	not out	12	–	lbw b Miller	4
C.A. Walsh	c Hayden b Miller	4	–	not out	1
	B 4, l-b 4, n-b 2	10		B 5, l-b 10, n-b 3	18

(102.1 overs, 363 mins)   272   (116.5 overs, 434 mins)   352
Fall: 147 152 174 210 210 235 240   Fall: 98 112 112 112 154 239 317
    240 252 272   347 351 352

Bowling: *First Innings*—McGrath 19–7–43–1; Gillespie 16–4–44–0; MacGill 37–11–104–7; Miller 30.1–8–73–2. *Second Innings*—McGrath 24–4–80–3; Miller 32.5–3–102–4; MacGill 30–7–88–0; Gillespie 21–5–57–2; M.E. Waugh 9–3–10–1.

Australia

M.J. Slater c Samuels b Nagamootoo	96	– (2) not out	86
M.L. Hayden c Lara b Walsh	3	– (1) lbw b Stuart	5
J.L. Langer c Jacobs b McLean	20	– lbw b Walsh	10
M.E. Waugh run out (Campbell/Jacobs)	22	– c Adams b McLean	3
*S.R. Waugh b Nagamootoo	103	– lbw b Samuels	38
R.T. Ponting lbw b Stuart	51	– not out	14
†A.C. Gilchrist c Lara b Stuart	87		
J.N. Gillespie c Hinds b Nagamootoo	2		
C.R. Miller not out	37		
S.C.G. MacGill run out ((sub) Jeremy/Nagamootoo)	1		
G.D. McGrath run out (Stuart/Adams)	13		
B 1, l-b 5, n-b 11	17	B 3, l-b 7, W 1, n-b 7	18

(135.4 overs, 520 mins)   452   (44.5 overs, 189 mins)   (4 wkts) 174
Fall: 17 55 109 157 289 360 374 408 410 452   Fall: 5 38 46 148

Bowling: *First Innings*—Walsh 25–4–74–1; Stuart 23–4–81–2; Nagamootoo 35–3–119–3; McLean 20–2–81–1; Adams 16.4–2–54–0; Samuels 16–5–37–0. *Second Innings*—Walsh 15–5–35–1; Stuart 7–0–40–1; McLean 8–1–35–1; Nagamootoo 9–1–28–0; Samuels 5.5–0–26–1.

Umpires: R.E. Koertzen (South Africa) and D.B. Hair.
TV Umpire: S.J.A. Taufel.
Referee: A.C. Smith (England).

†AUSTRALIA A v WEST INDIANS

At Adelaide Oval, Adelaide, January 9, 2001. West Indians won by four wickets. Toss: Austrlaia A.

After two miserable months the West Indians broke through for their first tour win in this lead-up match to the limited-overs series. Despite Australia A's line-up of aspirants for the national limited-overs side, they failed to knuckle down and the team fell for a lowly 145. The West Indians were cruising at two for 94, but the game flickered to fitful life when they slumped to six for 118. Their doughty wicket-keeper Ridley Jacobs and Laurie Williams then saw the tourists safely home.

Australia A

M.L. Hayden c Campbell b Cuffy	7	(21)	D.W. Fleming c Lara b Samuels	5	(7)
G.S. Blewett c Campbell b Black	15	(28)	S.C.G. MacGill b Nagamootoo	1	(5)
*S.M. Katich c Powell b Williams	4	(15)	P. Wilson not out	1	(9)
M.J. Slater c Campbell b Williams	19	(28)			
B.J. Hodge run out (Joseph/Jacobs)	18	(31)	L-b 4, w 5, n-b 4	13	
S. Lee st Jacobs b Nagamootoo	30	(42)			
†W.A. Seccombe b Nagamootoo	2	(18)	(42.3 overs, 156 mins)	145	
A.J. Bichel c Powell b Samuels	30	(55)	Fall: 26 26 35 64 95 100 111 118 120 145		

Bowling: Black 7–0–31–1; Cuffy 9–1–27–1; Williams 7–0–28–2; Nagamootoo 10–2–28–3; Samuels 9.3–0–27–2.

West Indians

*S.L. Campbell c Slater b Wilson	....	8	(13)	
W.W. Hinds c Blewett b MacGill	....	29	(79)	
B.C. Lara c Lee b Fleming	....	9	(20)	
M.N. Samuels st Seccombe b MacGill		45	(68)	
†S.C. Joseph c Seccombe b Fleming	.	13	(23)	
R.L. Powell b Fleming	....	0	(6)	

†R.D. Jacobs not out	....	15	(20)
L.R. Williams not out	....	11	(24)
B 3, l-b 5, w 6, n-b 2	....	16	
		—	
(41.5 overs, 170 mins)		(6 wkts) 146	
Fall: 14 23 94 113 118 118			

M.I. Black, M.V. Nagamootoo and C.E. Cuffy did not bat.

Bowling: Fleming 10–2–18–3; Wilson 8–0–29–1; Bichel 7–1–30–0; MacGill 10–2–37–2; Lee 6.5–0–24–0.

Umpires: R.G. Patterson and R.J. Woolridge.
TV Umpire: P.M. Angley.

THE ZIMBABWEANS IN AUSTRALIA, 2000-01

Review by KEN PIESSE

Despite the absence of three of their best players – Paul Strang, Murray Goodwin and Neil Johnson – Zimbabwe entered their second tour of Australia full of hope, especially with the recruiting of their new coach, Carl Rackemann, the former Australian Test fast bowler. On arrival, their captain Heath Streak said his team was passionate about winning the respect of the world champions and remained fully focused despite the political unrest and parlous economic conditions at home.

The four consecutive losses at the start of the tour, including an embarrassing defeat by an Australian Country team in Bowral, did little for the morale of the team, which was deficient in almost every area, except when the Flower brothers, Andy and Grant, were at the crease. Andy Flower, in particular, had enjoyed an outstanding 18 months leading up to the Australian tour. A busy left-hander, he made several half-centuries without reaching the heights of his form in New Zealand on the eve of the Australian visit. Grant Flower's preparation was interrupted by a broken finger, but he too played with assurance, even if lacking the shots of his older brother. His 85 in the final qualifying match in Perth helped set up the most exciting game of a lop-sided season, when with Stuart Carlisle he added 187 for the fourth wicket in the most enterprising assault on the Australian bowlers in many months.

The Flowers, Streak, Alistair Campbell and Guy Whittall were the only team members to have toured Australia previously, in 1994-95, when the side lost five of its six limited-overs internationals. This time Zimbabwe again won only once, but two of their losses were by only one run, and had they won these matches they would have displaced West Indies from the series finals.

Streak proved himself to be one of the leading all-rounders in the world in the limited-overs game, bowling an off-stump line and moving the ball away from the right-handers at a lively pace. He also batted bravely in the lower order, his 45 against West Indies at the Sydney Cricket Ground triggering his team's only victory.

Without the team's fastest bowler, Henry Olonga, who was considered too wayward to play a major role, the attack was generally mediocre apart from Streak, although Bryan Strang at times caused problems swinging the new ball back in late. Of the others, the 19-year-old medium-pacer Mluleki Nkala was the most promising. His eight wickets cost more than five runs an over, but he will gain from the experience.

ZIMBABWEAN TOURING PARTY

H. H. Streak (*captain*), G. J. Whittall (*vice-captain*), A. D. R. Campbell, S. V. Carlisle, A. Flower, G. W. Flower, T. J. Friend, A. J. Mackay, T. N. Madondo, D. A. Marillier, B. A. Murphy, M. L. Nkala, G. J. Rennie, B. C. Strang, D. P. Viljoen.

Manager: B. Meman. *Coach:* C. G. Rackemann. *Physiotherapist:* A. Machikicho. *Fitness trainer/analyst:* M. P. Jarvis

Stuart Carlisle of Zimbabwe hits out during his innings of 119 as wicket-keeper Adam Gilchrist of Australia looks on during the Carlton Series One Day International between Australia and Zimbabwe at the WACA Cricket Ground in Perth on February 4, 2001. Australia won the game by one run.

ZIMBABWEAN TOUR RESULTS

International limited-overs – Played 8: Won 1, Lost 7. *Won* – West Indies (1).
Losses – Australia (4), West Indies (3).
Other non-first-class matches – Played 2: Lost 2. *Losses* – Australia A, Australian Country XI.

AUSTRALIA A v ZIMBABWEANS

At Brisbane Cricket Ground, Brisbane, January 12, 2001. Day/night game. Australia A won by 216 runs. Toss: Zimbabweans.

A 167-run stand from 152 balls in just over an hour and a half between Greg Blewett and captain Simon Katich included a savage assault by Blewett on new-ball bowler Bryan Strang, three of his six sixes for the innings coming from five Strang deliveries. Michael Slater, batting at No. 4, helped himself to a half-century, pressing his claims for selection in the Australian one-day team. Despite fielding nine players with Test experience, the Zimbabweans in reply failed to bat out 30 overs, losing their last eight wickets for just 29.

Attendance: 15,571.

Australia A

G. S. Blewett c Mackay b Nkala 131 (122)	S. Lee not out 0	(1)
M. L. Hayden c and b Friend 18 (25)	B 1, l-b 4, w 10, n-b 1 16	
*S. M. Katich c Marillier b Viljoen ... 80 (84)		
M.J. Slater b Mackay 52 (48)	(50 overs, 191 mins) (4 wkts) 321	
B.J. Hodge not out 24 (21)	Fall: 57 224 260 320	

† W. A. Seccombe, D. W. Fleming, A. C. Dale, S. C. G. MacGill and P. Wilson did not bat.

Bowling: Friend 6–0–25–1; Strang 7–0–61–0; Mackay 8–0–48–1; Nkala 10–0–76–1; Viljoen 10–1–39–1; Marillier 5–0–39–0; Rennie 4–0–28–0.

Zimbabweans

A.D.R. Campbell c Hayden b Wilson . 31 (41)	T.J. Friend c Seccombe b MacGill .. 5 (15)	
† T. N. Madondo c Hodge b Fleming . 8 (14)	A. J. Mackay c Katich b MacGill 4 (8)	
S. V. Carlisle lbw b Dale 29 (38)	B.C. Strang not out 1 (1)	
G. J. Rennie st Seccombe b Dale 6 (16)		
*G.J. Whittall c Seccombe b Wilson . 1 (7)	L-b 1, w 2, n-b 4 7	
D.P. Viljoen c Hayden b Dale 7 (26)		
D. A. Marillier c Katich b MacGill ... 6 (14)	(30 overs, 122 mins) 105	
M.L. Nkala lbw b Dale 0 (4)	Fall: 23 63 76 78 80 93 93 94 103 105	

Bowling: Fleming 5–1–17–1; Wilson 10–1–49–2; Dale 10–1–31–4; MacGill 5–2–7–3.

Umpires: R. L. Parry and J. H. Smeaton.

AUSTRALIAN COUNTRY v ZIMBABWEANS

At Bradman Oval, Bowral, January 19, 2001. Australian Country won by 51 runs. Toss: Zimbabweans.

This was the fourth and the most decisive victory gained by the Australian Country team since they first played a match at Adelaide in 1986.

After the quick departure of Brian May, who has experienced such a grand season, the ACT pair of Cade Brown and Anthony McQuire added 76 runs in even time. David Todd, a former Queensland Colt and Gold Coast first grade player batted in his natural style and saw 96 runs added to the total. Only the veteran John Robson of the remaining batsmen withstood the wiles of Dirk Viljoen who baffled the inexperienced Country batsmen. The promising Newcastle Colt Mark Cameron removed Alastair Campbell in the opening over and then added the scalp of Stuart Carlisle. Guy Whittall batted steadily while Grant Flower set about the bowling when both had gone with the total on 84 the innings collapsed to nine for 111. Angus Mackay then joined his captain, Heath Streak, and made some lusty blows to help add 35 for the tenth wicket. Left-arm pace man Andrew Starr of the Armidale Cricket Club removed Whittall and then completely destroyed the middle order to return the best yet bowling figures for Australia Country in all matches played.

Australian Country XI

B. K. D. May c A. Flower b Streak	2	(4)	
C. Brown c Friend b Mackay	54	(83)	
A. D. McQuire c Marillier b Nkala	42	(59)	
D. A. Todd c A. Flower b Viljoen	53	(78)	
*C. J. Haworth c A. Flower b Mackay	7	(9)	
B. L. Campbell lbw b Viljoen	6	(16)	
G. P. Smith c Carlisle b Viljoen	0	(4)	
J. D. Robson not out	15	(25)	

† B. J. Glenn lbw b Viljoen	0	(4)	
A. J. Starr c A. Flower b Mackay	7	(14)	
M. A. Cameron run out	1	(1)	
L-b 3, w 5, n-b 2	10		
(49.1 overs, 198 mins)	197		
Fall: 3 78 129 140 171 174 174			
176 195 197			

D. Ellis did not bat.

Bowling: Streak 7–0–17–1; Friend 6–0–37–0; Whittall 3–0–16–0; Nkala 6.1–0–32–1; Viljoen 10–4–15–4; Mackay 9–0–39–3; G. W. Flower 8–0–38–0.

Zimbabweans

A. D. R. Campbell c Glenn b Mameron	4	(4)	
G. J. Whittall c Haworth b Starr	37	(85)	
S. V. Carlisle c Glenn b Cameron	2	(15)	
G. W. Flower b Ellis	23	(36)	
†A. Flower lbw b Starr	13	(27)	
G. J. Rennie c May b Smith	9	(14)	
D. A. Marillier c Brown b Starr	9	(9)	
D. P. Viljoen c Glenn b Starr	0	(2)	

*H. H. Streak not out	15	(27)	
M. L. Nkala lbw b Campbell	0	(2)	
A. J. Mackay c Haworth b Starr	21	(15)	
L-b 4, w 8, n-b 1	13		
(39.1 overs, 157 mins)	146		
Fall: 6 22 55 84 99 105 109 109 111 146			

T. J. Friend did not bat.

Bowling: Cameron 6–1–29–2; Ellis 10–1–23–1; Smith 10–0–36–1; Starr 9.1–1–37–5; Campbell 4–0–17–1.

Umpires: K. Burke and J. Mann.

Zimbabwe's matches v Australia and West Indies in the Carlton Series (January 11–February 9) may be found in that section.

CARLTON SERIES, 2000-01

By IAN JESSUP

It says much about the depth of talent in Australian cricket – and the lack of depth in Zimbabwe and the West Indies – that the home side cantered through the triangular limited-overs series. Whereas there were sessions of doubt and tension in their 5-0 Test series victory over West Indies, Australia had only four hairy minutes in achieving a perfect ten wins out of ten to complete the first-ever whitewash of a home summer. That was when Zimbabwe, chasing 303, scored 13 of the 15 runs they needed from Glenn McGrath's final over in the last preliminary match in Perth. Otherwise it was the most lopsided triangular series in the 22 years of the competition's history.

Steve Waugh admirably urges his World Cup champion team to play for victory at all times – a creed that other captains might profitably follow – but the consequent intensity with which the side plays inevitably also brings out the occasional Mr Hyde. Ricky Ponting refused to walk when caught low down at the MCG – a criticism that can never be made of Brian Lara. And Shane Warne had his cameo of controversy at the SCG when television viewers clearly heard the multiple obscenity he hurled at Zimbabwean batsman Stuart Carlisle after being hit powerfully. Viewers did not hear Lara and Michael Bevan exchanging unpleasantries in the first final at the SCG, but the picture told the story and had the rest of the world thinking again of ugly, sledging Aussies.

All the while Mark Waugh was under fire for refusing for the umpteenth time to speak to authorities about the illegal bookmaker affair. To an extent he had a point, but from a public-relations angle he scored poorly. That the younger of the immensely gifted twins managed such a brilliant summer with the bat and in the field suggested a far tougher hide than many had assumed, this author included. His record 173 in the second final should have been the crowning achievement of the summer and rewarded with a ride around the MCG on a $25,000 motorbike for Player of the Series. Instead the award went to Lara, who was visibly embarrassed, and pleaded that he did not deserve it. "I'm not sure how the points system works," he said. "And I can't ride a motorbike."

The system awards points for each game, 3–2–1, rather than assessing play in the series as a whole. Mark Waugh was rested three times under Australia's policy of rotation but still racked up 542 runs at 108.40, including three centuries, compared to Ponting's 393 at 49.13 and Lara's 372 runs at 46.50. The announcement was greeted with a chorus of boos from the MCG crowd. Steve Waugh was bemused. "It's crazy when you win every game and you don't get the Player of the Series," he said. "But good luck to Brian. He was pretty humble about it and in the overall scheme of things, it's not a big deal."

Australia started the series having won only two of their previous eight limited-overs games. Zimbabwe were coming off their first limited-overs series win overseas, against New Zealand, and West Indies, after losing the Test series so dismally, must have thought things could only get better. Steve

Waugh warned of a tight series, but the opening match was a reminder that beating Australia on Australian soil in front of packed houses is a rarity these days.

The West Indian attack worked hard during the series but, with the batsmen producing so few runs, it was not strong enough to challenge Australia's all-round consistency. Zimbabwe's captain Heath Streak showed he is a world-class all-rounder, but he lacked reliable support with bat or ball. Few of Australia's individual opponents put together two good games in a row, and after the preliminary rounds it surprised no one when Australia defeated West Indies in the finals with ridiculous ease. One indicator of Australia's dominance throughout the series was the fact that 12 of their 14 batsmen scored at a rate of 84 runs per 100 balls or better, while of their opponents on both sides, only Douglas Marillier, who hit 12 off the five balls he faced, could do the same.

Note: Matches in this section were not first-class.

AUSTRALIA – BATTING

	M	I	NO	R	HS	100s	50s	Avge	Ct/St	S-R
D.S. Lehmann	6	4	3	197	92*	0	2	197.00	3	101.55
D.R. Martyn	9	6	4	298	144*	1	1	149.00	7	93.13
M.E. Waugh	9	7	2	542	173	3	2	108.40	4	83.00
M.G. Bevan	9	7	2	261	74*	0	2	52.20	3	83.12
I.J. Harvey	8	4	2	99	47*	0	0	49.50	2	135.62
R.T. Ponting.......	9	9	1	393	93	0	4	49.13	3	89.52
S.R. Waugh	7	5	1	192	79	0	1	48.00	3	95.05
A.C. Gilchrist......	9	8	0	326	98	0	2	40.75	13/4	84.90
A. Symonds	9	5	1	135	60	0	1	33.75	5	127.36
D.W. Fleming	6	2	1	20	14	0	0	20.00	1	117.65
B.J. Haddin	1	1	0	13	13	0	0	13.00	0/1	118.18
S.K. Warne........	9	1	0	7	7	0	0	7.00	8	53.85
B. Lee	4	1	0	2	2	0	0	2.00	0	40.00
G.D. McGrath	8	1	1	1	1*	0	0	–	0	100.00
N.W. Bracken	6	0	0	0	–	0	0	–	1	–
S.M. Katich	1	0	0	0	–	0	0	–	0	–

* Denotes not out.

BOWLING

	O	M	R	W	BB	5W/i	Avge
R.T. Ponting.............	10	0	40	2	1/12	0	20.00
S.K. Warne..............	84.5	5	377	18	4/48	0	20.94
I.J. Harvey	67.1	7	277	12	4/28	0	23.08
G.D. McGrath	70.3	13	274	11	2/25	0	24.91
D.W. Fleming	50	6	235	9	3/32	0	26.11
A. Symonds	67	3	323	12	4/35	0	26.92
B. Lee	33	3	215	6	4/33	0	35.83
D.S. Lehmann	7	0	36	1	1/36	0	36.00
M.G. Bevan	15	0	75	2	1/20	0	37.50
N.W. Bracken	44	5	191	5	2/21	0	38.20
D.R. Martyn............	14	1	74	1	1/28	0	74.00

WEST INDIES – BATTING

	M	I	NO	R	HS	100s	50s	Avge	Ct/St	S-R
B.C. Lara	10	10	2	372	116*	1	2	46.50	4	80.35
M.N. Samuels	10	10	0	282	68	0	3	28.20	2	66.51
R.L. Powell	10	10	1	252	83*	0	1	28.00	7	83.44
J.C. Adams	10	10	2	176	44	0	0	22.00	2	58.86
W.W. Hinds	6	6	0	124	60	0	2	20.67	4	69.66
R.D. Jacobs	10	10	1	176	59	0	1	19.56	14	69.02
N.A.M. McLean	10	8	3	87	40*	0	0	17.40	3	79.82
S.C. Joseph	2	2	0	29	18	0	0	14.50	1	40.28
S.L. Campbell	7	7	0	74	42	0	0	10.57	5	47.44
L.R. Williams	8	8	2	62	26*	0	0	10.33	3	65.89
D. Ganga	5	5	0	46	22	0	0	9.20	1	45.54
M.V. Nagamootoo	9	9	1	73	22*	0	0	9.13	4	52.90
C.E. Cuffy	8	6	2	21	13	0	0	5.25	0	41.18
M.I. Black	4	1	0	4	4	0	0	4.00	0	50.00
C.E.L. Stuart	1	1	1	3	3*	0	0	–	0	23.08

* Denotes not out.

BOWLING

	O	M	R	W	BB	5W/i	Avge
C.E. Cuffy	73	8	308	12	4/24	0	25.67
M.N. Samuels	80.5	2	389	14	3/25	0	27.79
N.A.M. McLean	90.4	7	401	13	3/21	0	30.85
L.R. Williams	66	2	324	10	3/24	0	32.40
R.L. Powell	5	1	37	1	1/15	0	37.00
M.V. Nagamootoo	78.1	2	358	8	4/32	0	44.75
J.C. Adams	16	0	102	0	–	0	–
M.I. Black	29	0	153	0	–	0	–
C.E.L. Stuart	8	0	57	0	–	0	–

ZIMBABWE – BATTING

	M	I	NO	R	HS	100s	50s	Avge	Ct/St	S-R
A.D.R. Campbell	8	8	0	290	124	1	1	36.25	7	74.74
S.V. Carlisle	8	8	0	278	119	1	0	34.75	4	70.56
H.H. Streak	8	8	3	166	45	0	0	33.20	0	79.05
G.W. Flower	7	7	0	218	85	0	2	31.14	0	71.24
A. Flower	8	8	0	227	51	0	2	28.38	8	76.69
G.J. Whittall	7	7	0	133	36	0	0	19.00	2	53.41
G.J. Rennie	6	6	1	84	29	0	0	16.80	0	66.67
D.P. Viljoen	8	8	1	80	31	0	0	11.43	4	54.05
T.N. Madondo	2	2	0	16	10	0	0	8.00	0	44.44
B.A. Murphy	8	5	3	13	7*	0	0	6.50	1	27.08
M.L. Nkala	8	6	0	36	16	0	0	6.00	1	58.06
B.C. Strang	5	4	0	7	4	0	0	1.75	0	19.44
T.J. Friend	2	2	1	0	0*	0	0	0.00	0	0.00
D.A. Marillier	1	1	1	12	12*	0	0	–	0	240.00
A.J. Mackay	2	0	0	0	–	0	0	–	1	–

* Denotes not out.

BOWLING

	O	M	R	W	BB	5W/i	Avge
H. H. Streak	70	10	301	11	4/8	0	27.36
T. J. Friend	16.5	1	89	3	2/37	0	29.67
M. L. Nkala.	56.5	1	303	8	3/12	0	37.88
D. P. Viljoen	52.2	0	307	8	3/62	0	38.38
B. C. Strang.	44	6	181	4	3/15	0	45.25
B. A. Murphy	65	1	314	6	3/52	0	52.33
G. J. Whittall.	28.4	0	183	2	2/16	0	91.50
G. W. Flower	8	0	49	0	–	0	–
A. J. Mackay.	14	0	81	0	–	0	–

AUSTRALIA v WEST INDIES

At Melbourne Cricket Ground, Melbourne, January 11, 2001. Day/night game. Australia won by 74 runs. Toss: Australia. Australia 2 pts. Limited-overs international debut: N. W. Bracken.

Steve Waugh joined Mohammad Azharuddin and Wasim Akram in the 300-game club, but neither he nor anybody else is likely to remember this match. Australia had lost the opening match of the triangular series in each of the three previous seasons, but not this one against a West Indies side even weaker than the hapless Test version. The visitors displayed some dreadful fielding as Ricky Ponting and Mark Waugh added 111 at five an over for the second wicket, and Damien Martyn and Andrew Symonds plundered 74 off the last 8.4 overs. With Brett Lee and Jason Gillespie on the sidelines and Shane Warne making his comeback from a broken finger, West Indies had a chance to take the game to Australia. But 16 runs from a soporific first 11 overs meant Brian Lara had to produce a miracle. Instead Ian Harvey bowled an unplayable delivery that caught the edge of Lara's bat on its way through to the wicket-keeper. Part time off-spinner Andrew Symonds took three wickets in one over to destroy the middle order, and after West Indies slumped to seven for 139 in the 41st over the crowd began to thin out. "Last night looked really bad," conceded captain Jimmy Adams the next day. If only he had known what was to come.

Man of the Match: R. T. Ponting. *Attendance: 56,732.*

Australia

M. E. Waugh c Hinds b Williams	.... 51 (67)	A. Symonds not out 38 (26)
†A. C. Gilchrist c McLean b Cuffy	... 7 (9)	
R. T. Ponting c Powell b Cuffy	...... 73 (100)	L-b 6, w 4 10
M. G. Bevan c Lara b Williams	...... 17 (22)	
*S. R. Waugh c Nagamootoo b Samuels 29 (33)		(50 overs, 202 mins) (6 wkts) 267
D. R. Martyn run out (Jacobs)	.... 42 (43)	Fall: 7 118 144 174 193 267

I. J. Harvey, S. K. Warne, N. W. Bracken and G. D. McGrath did not bat.

Bowling: Cuffy 9–1–45–2; McLean 10–1–54–0; Williams 8–0–39–2; Nagamootoo 10–0–50–0; Adams 3–0–19–0; Samuels 10–0–54–1.

West Indies

S.L. Campbell c Bevan b Bracken	...	4 (17)
W.W. Hinds c Ponting b McGrath	...	1 (4)
B.C. Lara c Gilchrist b Harvey	.....	28 (48)
M.N. Samuels c and b Symonds	.....	57 (96)
R.L. Powell c S.R. Waugh b Symonds		12 (27)
†R.D. Jacobs c and b Symonds	......	24 (51)
M.V. Nagamootoo lbw b Symonds	...	3 (2)

*J.C. Adams not out 25 (33)
L.R. Williams not out 26 (22)

L–b 9, w 4 13

(50 overs, 190 mins)   (7 wkts) 193
Fall: 3 9 57 84 132 139 139

N.A.M. McLean and C.E. Cuffy did not bat.

Bowling: McGrath 6–2–7–1; Bracken 9–3–30–1; Harvey 9–0–55–1; Martyn 6–1–19–0; Warne 10–1–38–0; Symonds 10–1–35–4.

Umpires: D.J. Harper and S.J.A. Taufel.
TV Umpire: R.G. Patterson.
Referee: D.T. Lindsay (South Africa).

WEST INDIES v ZIMBABWE

At Brisbane Cricket Ground, Brisbane, January 13, 2001. Day/night game. West Indies won by one wicket. Toss: Zimbabwe. West Indies 2 pts.

West Indies achieved the first international victory of their wretched summer, but only after fighting to the death against lowly Zimbabwe who, in turn, had been thrashed two days before by 216 runs by Australia A. Nevertheless it seemed to be a crucial win for West Indies, who had won only one festival match and a limited-overs clash with Australia A since arriving in the country 10 weeks earlier. Ricardo Powell's 83 not out off 90 balls just managed to hold the later stages of the innings together, and there were eight balls to spare when he hit the winning runs off Guy Whittall. West Indies were in trouble at seven for 183, and soon after Powell should have been run out for 47, but he made the most of his reprieve to engineer the most exciting finish of the summer so far. Zimbabwe's competitive total was based on a fine innings by opener Alistair Campbell and a late flurry from Heath Streak. Marlon Samuels bowled economically before playing a brief innings that helped to set the stage for Powell's match-winning hand.

Man of the Match: R.L. Powell. *Attendance:* 12,034.

Zimbabwe

A.D.R. Campbell c and b Samuels	...	81 (105)
T.N. Madondo c Campbell b McLean		6 (21)
S.V. Carlisle c Jacobs b Williams	....	29 (42)
†A. Flower c Jacobs b Samuels	......	33 (42)
G.J. Rennie b McLean	. . . .	29 (39)
G.J. Whittall b Nagamootoo	. . . .	1 (8)
D.P. Viljoen run out (Lara)	. . . .	2 (9)
*H.H. Streak not out	. . . .	34 (28)

M.L. Nkala c Hinds b Cuffy 9 (6)
T.J. Friend b McLean 0 (2)
B.A. Murphy not out 1 (1)

L–b 3, w 9, n–b 3 15

(50 overs, 188 mins)   (9 wkts) 240
Fall: 14 68 154 161 167 174 214 231 231

Bowling: Cuffy 9–0–52–1; McLean 10–1–48–3; Williams 8–1–38–1; Nagamootoo 10–0–45–1; Samuels 10–0–41–2; Adams 3–0–13–0.

West Indies

S.L. Campbell c Flower b Whittall	... 42	(52)
W.W. Hinds b Friend	0	(5)
B.C. Lara c Viljoen b Nkala	21	(34)
M.N. Samuels b Viljoen	34	(33)
*J.C. Adams c Flower b Nkala	24	(24)
R.L. Powell not out	83	(90)
†R.D. Jacobs hit wicket b Murphy	... 4	(9)
L.R. Williams b Friend	9	(15)

M.V. Nagamootoo c Flower b Streak	8	(17)
N.A.M. McLean c Flower b Whittall	1	(12)
C.E. Cuffy not out	1	(2)
L–b 6, w 7, n–b 1	14	
(48.4 overs, 207 mins) (9 wkts)	241	
Fall: 6 52 72 119 137 155 183 229 239		

Bowling: Streak 10–1–41–1; Friend 10–1–37–2; Nkala 7–0–50–2; Whittall 3.4–0–16–2; Murphy 10–0–52–1; Viljoen 8–0–39–1.

Umpires: P.D. Parker and S.J.A. Taufel.
TV Umpire: S.J. Davis.
Referee: D.T. Lindsay (South Africa).

AUSTRALIA v WEST INDIES

At Brisbane Cricket Ground, Brisbane, January 14, 2001. Day/night game. Australia won by nine wickets. Toss: West Indies. Australia 2 pts. Limited-overs international debut: M.I. Black.

Four weeks after becoming Australia's 41st Test captain, wicket-keeper Adam Gilchrist took charge of the limited-overs team for the first time and led Australia to a demolition of West Indies. Chasing West Indies' modest total on an easy Gabba pitch, Gilchrist and Mark Waugh's opening stand of 206 – their eighth century partnership – set several new limited-overs marks. It was the best opening stand in Australia, the highest Australian partnership against West Indies, and only 18 runs shy of the highest Australian stand of all time. Waugh (seven fours) was effortless and Gilchrist (six fours and a six) brutal, and Australia reached the target with more than six overs to spare under balmy Brisbane skies. Wavell Hinds, who had earlier hit two sixes in top-scoring for West Indies, dropped a simple catch from Gilchrist in the opening overs. But the embarrassments that had started much earlier for West Indies, when Ricky Ponting's gentle part-time medium pace found the edge of Lara's bat.

Man of the Match: M.E. Waugh. *Attendance:* 35,168.

West Indies

S.L. Campbell c Gilchrist b McGrath	0	(5)
W.W. Hinds c and b Warne	54	(72)
B.C. Lara c Gilchrist b Ponting	19	(29)
M.N. Samuels c Waugh b Warne	20	(27)
*J.C. Adams c Martyn b Lee	44	(65)
R.L. Powell c Waugh b Warne	19	(26)
†R.D. Jacobs not out	44	(50)

L.R. Williams run out (Symonds)	... 15	(17)
M.V. Nagamootoo c Symonds b Bracken	0	(7)
N.A.M. McLean not out	6	(9)
L–b 1, w 5, n–b 7	13	
(50 overs, 202 mins) (8 wkts)	234	
Fall: 0 36 86 103 145 174 203 207		

M.I. Black did not bat.

Bowling: McGrath 10–2–42–1; Lee 7–0–40–1; Bracken 8–0–46–1; Ponting 5–0–28–1; Warne 10–0–41–3; Symonds 10–0–36–0.

Australia

*†A.C. Gilchrist c Williams b Powell	98	(122)
M.E. Waugh not out	112	(128)
R.T. Ponting not out	10	(19)
B 4, l–b 2, w 3, n–b 7	16	

(43.4 overs, 179 mins) (1 wkt) 236
Fall: 206

M.G. Bevan, D.S. Lehmann, D.R. Martyn, A. Symonds, S.K. Warne, B. Lee, N.W. Bracken and G.D. McGrath did not bat.

Bowling: McLean 9.4–0–38–0; Black 10–0–55–0; Williams 5–0–22–0; Samuels 5–0–38–0; Nagamootoo 8–0–43–0; Adams 3–0–19–0; Powell 3–1–15–1.

Umpires: S.J. Davis and D.B. Hair.
TV Umpire: P.D. Parker.
Referee: D.T. Lindsay (South Africa).

AUSTRALIA v WEST INDIES

At Sydney Cricket Ground, Sydney, January 17, 2001. Day/night game. Australia won on run rate. Toss: West Indies. Australia 2 pts. Limited-overs international debut: C.E.L. Stuart.

West Indies captain Jimmy Adams warned before this match that Brian Lara was ready to explode after his recent run of outs. And he did, belting the spin of Andrew Symonds and Shane Warne around the SCG, and hitting ten fours and two sixes (one of which brought up his hundred) in a forlorn effort to salvage this game for his side. Chasing 278 to win, West Indies were eight for 211 after 42.4 overs when the heavens opened at 9.53 p.m. and saturated the outfield. At that stage Lara and Colin Stuart had put on 45 in 6.2 overs, and West Indies needed another 67 from the last 7.2 overs, but the rain denied the capacity crowd any further pyrotechnics from Lara. Australia, who might have won much earlier if Steve Waugh had gone for the jugular, were awarded victory by 28 runs under the Duckworth/Lewis system. Earlier, Mark Waugh and Adam Gilchrist's 98-run opening stand merely served as an entree to Ricky Ponting's blazing innings (ten fours) in an imposing Australian total. West Indies were soon in trouble against Nathan Bracken and Ian Harvey, but Ricardo Powell hung around long enough for Lara to find his groove.

Man of the Match: B.C. Lara. *Attendance:* 39,540.

Australia

M.E. Waugh c Powell b Samuels	....	58 (94)
*†A.C. Gilchrist c Powell b Williams	.	40 (46)
R.T. Ponting c Adams b McLean	....	93 (74)
M.G. Bevan c Campbell b McLean	..	31 (55)
D.R. Martyn not out	....	21 (21)

D.S. Lehmann not out	....	19 (11)
L–b 9, w 5, n–b 1	....	15
(50 overs, 205 mins)	(4 wkts)	277
Fall: 98 109 187 246		

A. Symonds, I.J. Harvey, S.K. Warne, N.W. Bracken and G.D. McGrath did not bat.

Bowling: McLean 10–0–45–2; Black 8–0–49–0; Stuart 8–0–57–0; Williams 10–0–43–1; Samuels 10–1–39–1; Powell 2–0–22–0; Adams 2–0–13–0.

West Indies

W.W. Hinds c Warne b Bracken	.....	1 (9)
†R.D. Jacobs c Warne b Bracken	....	21 (23)
S.L. Campbell c Martyn b Harvey	...	23 (51)
B.C. Lara not out	....	116(106)
M.N. Samuels c Gilchrist b Harvey	..	1 (3)
*J.C. Adams b Warne	....	9 (12)
R.L. Powell c Bracken b Warne	.....	28 (37)

L.R. Williams st Gilchrist b Warne	..	1 (2)
N.A.M. McLean lbw b Symonds	...	0 (2)
C.E.L. Stuart not out	....	3 (13)
B 2, l–b 1, w 3, n–b 2	....	8
(42.4 overs, 182 mins)	(8 wkts)	211
Fall: 3 31 67 69 94 161 164 166		

M.I. Black did not bat.

Bowling: McGrath 7.4–1–37–0; Bracken 7–1–21–2; Harvey 7–1–16–2; Symonds 9–0–55–1; Warne 10–0–62–3; Martyn 2–0–17–0.

Umpires: D.B. Hair and S.J.A. Taufel.
TV Umpire: S.J. Davis.
Referee: D.T. Lindsay (South Africa).

AUSTRALIA v ZIMBABWE

At Melbourne Cricket Ground, Melbourne, January 21, 2001. Australia won by eight wickets. Toss: Zimbabwe. Australia 2 pts. Limited-overs international debut: S. M. Katich.

Australia entered a match without either of the Waugh twins for only the second time in the last 331 limited-overs matches, but there was no let-up for Zimbabwe, who had just been humbled by an Australian Country XI at Bowral. In an ebullient opening, Zimbabwe feasted on the wayward bowling of Brett Lee to reach 50 in the first eight overs. Then Ian Harvey applied the handbrake with his first ball to highlight his growing maturity, and after that only Grant Flower troubled the bowlers for long. On a good batting wicket the total was well short of a testing target. With Adam Gilchrist hitting six fours and a six, Australia started even faster than the Zimbabweans, and Darren Lehmann made the most of his recall, hitting nine fours as Australia coasted to victory. Ricky Ponting continued his strong form but exposed a side to the Australians' play that would come under scrutiny in India. On 12 he drove medium pacer Mluleki Nkala to short cover, where Stuart Carlisle appeared to catch the ball low in his left hand. Ponting stood his ground while the Zimbabweans celebrated; the third umpire gave him the benefit of the doubt.

Man of the Match: D. S. Lehmann. *Attendance:* 43,033.

Zimbabwe

A. D. R. Campbell c Bevan b Harvey	. 30	(54)
G. J. Whittall c Gilchrist b Harvey	 25	(28)
S. V. Carlisle c Harvey b Warne	 12	(26)
†A. Flower c Lehmann b Symonds	.. 23	(33)
G. W. Flower c and b Warne	 51	(78)
G. J. Rennie st Gilchrist b Symonds	.. 13	(16)
D. P. Viljoen c and b Lehmann	 7	(20)

*H. H. Streak c Lehmann b Harvey	.. 23	(30)
M. L. Nkala b Harvey	 16	(22)
T. J. Friend not out	 0	(0)
L–b 7, w 9, n–b 7	 23	

B. A. Murphy did not bat.

(50 overs, 208 mins)　　　　(9 wkts) 223
Fall: 50 67 78 117 145 160 187 219 223

Bowling: Lee 8–0–70–0; Bracken 6–0–23–0; Harvey 9–0–28–4; Warne 10–2–21–2; Symonds 10–2–38–2; Lehmann 7–0–36–1.

Australia

*†A. C. Gilchrist c Murphy b Friend	.. 39	(29)
D. S. Lehmann not out	 92	(104)
R. T. Ponting run out (Friend/A. Flower)	68	(73)
M. G. Bevan not out	 14	(16)

B 1, l–b 5, w 6, n–b 1 13

(36.5 overs, 158 mins)　　　(2 wkts) 226
Fall: 54 198

S. M. Katich, D. R. Martyn, A. Symonds, I. J. Harvey, S. K. Warne, B. Lee and N. W. Bracken did not bat.

Bowling: Streak 5–1–37–0; Friend 6.5–0–52–1; Murphy 10–0–47–0; Nkala 7–0–30–0; Viljoen 6–0–37–0; Whittall 2–0–17–0.

Umpires: S. J. Davis and P. D. Parker.
TV Umpire: R. G. Patterson.
Referee: D. T. Lindsay (South Africa).

WEST INDIES v ZIMBABWE

At Sydney Cricket Ground, Sydney, January 23, 2001. Day/night game. Zimbabwe won by 47 runs. Toss: West Indies. Zimbabwe 2 pts.

"We're still not happy with some aspects of our cricket," West Indies captain Jimmy Adams said on the eve of this scarcely believable match. How he felt afterwards is not recorded. Sent in, Zimbabwe dissolved before the bowling of Cameron Cuffy and Laurie

Williams, but at eight for 88 Heath Streak stood firm and managed to coax his partners into adding a vital 50 runs for the last two wickets. What happened next was surely even more humiliating for West Indies than being dismissed for 93 by Kenya at the 1995–96 World Cup. Streak was unplayable, achieving a kind of poetry with his figures of 8–4–8–4, while at the other end Bryan Strang removed Sherwin Campbell, Brian Lara and Marlon Samuels in successive overs for one run. At eight for 31 West Indies were staring at Pakistan's world record low score of 43 in 1993. To this point only seven fours had been struck in the match. Nixon McLean then struck six fours himself and with his captain gave West Indies a glimmer of hope, but Mluleki Nkala returned to the attack and polished off the innings. West Indies had slumped to their second-lowest score in limited-overs internationals, after their 87 at the same ground in 1993. At a time when limited-overs matches are devalued by their relentless frequency and the haze of match-fixing, this win actually meant something. Streak said his team felt responsible for bringing some good news to the people of their strife-torn nation.

Man of the Match: H. H. Streak. *Attendance:* 8,474.

Zimbabwe

A. D. R. Campbell c Jacobs b Cuffy	4	(10)	M. L. Nkala c Lara b Williams	0	(5)
G. J. Whittall c Campbell b Cuffy	11	(25)	B. C. Strang c Jacobs b Samuels	1	(17)
S. V. Carlisle c Powell b Williams	29	(54)	B. A. Murphy not out	7	(30)
†A. Flower c Jacobs b Cuffy	3	(11)			
G. W. Flower c Jacobs b Cuffy	7	(20)	L–b 5, w 4, n–b 1, penalties 5	15	
G. J. Rennie c Powell b Williams	4	(30)			
D. P. Viljoen c Jacobs b McLean	2	(13)	(47.2 overs, 177 mins)	138	
*H. H. Streak c (sub) Joseph b Samuels	45	(70)	Fall: 9 30 45 62 62 66 88 88 104 138		

Bowling: McLean 9–1–28–1; Cuffy 10–1–24–4; Williams 10–1–24–3; Samuels 8.2–0–28–2; Nagamootoo 8–0–19–0; Adams 2–0–5–0.

West Indies

W. W. Hinds c Campbell b Streak	8	(30)	M. V. Nagamootoo c Viljoen b Nkala	3	(11)
†R. D. Jacobs lbw b Streak	6	(21)	N. A. M. McLean not out	40	(32)
S. L. Campbell c Campbell b Strang	0	(2)	C. E. Cuffy c Carlisle b Nkala	0	(2)
B. C. Lara lbw b Strang	0	(7)			
M. N. Samuels c Carlisle b Strang	1	(6)	L–b 7, w 3, n–b 1	11	
*J. C. Adams c and b Nkala	22	(76)			
R. L. Powell lbw b Streak	0	(4)	(31.5 overs, 141 mins)	91	
L. R. Williams c Carlisle b Streak	0	(1)	Fall: 16 22 22 22 24 25 25 31 91 91		

Bowling: Streak 8–4–8–4; Strang 8–4–15–3; Nkala 5.5–1–12–3; Whittall 7–0–42–0; Murphy 3–1–7–0.

Umpires: P. D. Parker and S. J. A. Taufel.
TV Umpire: D. B. Hair.
Referee: D. T. Lindsay (South Africa).

WEST INDIES v ZIMBABWE

At Adelaide Oval, Adelaide, January 25, 2001. Day/night game. West Indies won on run rate. Toss: West Indies. West Indies 2 pts.

West Indies restored some pride after another typically dismal start. Brian Lara and Marlon Samuels added 133 in 29 overs, Ricardo Powell hit two sixes, and when heavy rain ended the innings after 47 overs West Indies had set a competitive target. Heath Streak's bowling enhanced his growing reputation in this country but he received little support. A two-hour delay meant a revised target under the Duckworth/Lewis method of 253 from 47 overs. In reply the Flowers were blossoming nicely, if slowly, and when Jimmy Adams tossed the ball to leg-spinner Mahendra Nagamootoo the asking rate was eight an over. Nagamootoo promptly took a brilliant return catch to get rid of Andy Flower and shatter Zimbabwe's hopes, and Adams almost knocked himself out crashing to the ground to dismiss Dirk Viljoen. Nagamootoo's bowling and some overdue fine fielding dismissed Zimbabwe and put West Indies in the box seat to make the finals.

Man of the Match: M.N. Samuels. *Attendance:* 6,878.

West Indies

D. Ganga run out (G.W. Flower/Strang)	6	(15)	*J.C. Adams not out	13	(13)
S.L. Campbell c Campbell b Streak . .	5	(17)	M.V. Nagamootoo not out	22	(12)
M.N. Samuels c A. Flower b Viljoen .	68	(98)	L–b 3, w 5, n–b 3	11
B.C. Lara c Campbell b Streak	70	(96)		
R.L. Powell b Streak	33	(26)	(47 overs, 202 mins) (6 wkts) 235
†R.D. Jacobs run out (Murphy/A. Flower)	7	(8)	Fall: 11 16 149 183 199 203

N.A.M. McLean, C.E. Cuffy and M.I. Black did not bat.

Bowling: Streak 8–1–27–3; Strang 10–1–44–0; Whittall 3–0–16–0; Nkala 8–0–43–0; Murphy 5–0–33–0; Viljoen 10–0–47–1; G.W. Flower 3–0–22–0.

Zimbabwe

A.D.R. Campbell c Powell b McLean	20	(31)	M.L. Nkala b Nagamootoo	0	(2)
G.J. Whittall c Samuels b McLean . . .	17	(27)	B.C. Strang run out (Campbell)	0	(3)
S.V. Carlisle b Cuffy	4	(11)	B.A. Murphy run out (Campbell/
†A. Flower c and b Nagamootoo	50	(73)	Nagamootoo) . .	1	(4)
G.W. Flower c Ganga b Samuels	41	(64)	L–b 7, w 5, n–b 3	15
G.J. Rennie not out	17	(17)		
*H.H. Streak lbw b Nagamootoo	3	(6)	(40.2 overs, 182 mins) 175
D.P. Viljoen c Adams b Nagamootoo .	7	(7)	Fall: 38 45 47 137 149 157 167 169 170 175

Bowling: McLean 8–1–31–2; Cuffy 10–1–37–1; Black 7–0–30–0; Samuels 8–0–38–1; Nagamootoo 7.2–0–32–4.

Umpires: D.B. Hair and P.D. Parker.
TV Umpire: S.J. Davis.
Referee: D.T. Lindsay (South Africa).

AUSTRALIA v WEST INDIES

At Adelaide Oval, Adelaide, January 26, 2001. Day/night game. Australia won by ten wickets. Toss: West Indies. Australia 2 pts.

This disappointing match lasted only 58 overs, and gave Australia its first ten-wicket win in limited-overs internationals. The main wrecker this time was Brett Lee, whose four wickets included Brian Lara for a first-ball duck. The rot set in from Damien Fleming's second ball when Daren Ganga edged to Mark Waugh at second slip. The ball struck Waugh on the shoulder and Shane Warne caught the easiest of rebounds. Only a last-wicket stand of 41 prevented West Indies being dismissed for their lowest score in limited-overs internationals and extended the game past the dinner break. The Australians bowled nine maidens, and the top-scorer for West Indies was sundries. Damien Martyn (nine fours) and Darren Lehmann were untroubled in scoring the winning runs with more than half the allotted overs to spare.

Man of the Match: B. Lee. *Attendance:* 27,640.

West Indies

†R. D. Jacobs b Lee	2	(13)		N. A. M. McLean not out	24	(39)
D. Ganga c Warne b Fleming	0	(2)		M. I. Black lbw b Fleming	4	(8)
M. N. Samuels c Gilchrist b Fleming	4	(20)		C. E. Cuffy lbw b Harvey	13	(29)
B. C. Lara lbw b Lee	0	(1)				
*J. C. Adams lbw b Lee	4	(11)		B 2, l-b 9, w 8, n-b 6	25	
R. L. Powell b Harvey	16	(21)				
S. C. Joseph lbw b Warne	11	(25)		(35.1 overs, 158 mins)	123	
M. V. Nagamootoo c Gilchrist b Lee	20	(48)		Fall: 0 6 6 10 32 41 65 75 82 123		

Bowling: Lee 10–3–33–4; Fleming 10–2–32–3; Harvey 7.1–3–11–2; Warne 8–1–36–1.

Australia

D. S. Lehmann not out	50	(58)
D. R. Martyn not out	69	(80)
B 1, w 3, n-b 1	5	

(22.5 overs, 91 mins)   (0 wkts) 124

M. E. Waugh, M. G. Bevan, *S. R. Waugh, †A. C. Gilchrist, A. Symonds, I. J. Harvey, S. K. Warne, B. Lee and D. W. Fleming did not bat.

Bowling: McLean 5–0–31–0; Cuffy 7–0–35–0; Black 4–0–19–0; Samuels 2–0–9–0; Nagamootoo 4.5–0–29–0.

Umpires: S. J. Davis and S. J. A. Taufel.
TV Umpire: P. D. Parker.
Referee: D. T. Lindsay (South Africa).

AUSTRALIA v ZIMBABWE

At Sydney Cricket Ground, Sydney, January 28, 2001. Day/night game. Australia won by 86 runs. Toss: Australia. Australia 2 pts.

Australia dominated this match from the start. After solid batting by Adam Gilchrist and the Waugh brothers had taken the score to four for 187, Michael Bevan, Andrew Symonds and Darren Lehmann belted 104 from the last 10.1 overs. Zimbabwe recovered somewhat after losing two wickets early, but once Andy Flower and Stuart Carlisle were parted the innings lost momentum. When Carlisle hit Shane Warne for two sixes as the Zimbabweans reached 100 in the 22nd over, Warne responded with an obscenity which the television microphones inadvertently broadcast live around the world. Channel Nine later apologised for the incident.

Man of the Match: M. G. Bevan. *Attendance:* 33,748.

Australia

†A. C. Gilchrist c Campbell b Strang	63	(76)		D. S. Lehmann b Streak	36	(21)
M. E. Waugh run out (Murphy)	36	(85)				
*S. R. Waugh c A. Flower b Viljoen	36	(40)		L-b 4, w 1, n-b 4	9	
M. G. Bevan not out	74	(80)				
R. T. Ponting c Whittall b Viljoen	15	(21)		(50 overs, 201 mins) (6 wkts) 291		
A. Symonds b Viljoen	22	(13)		Fall: 98 111 159 187 241 291		

S. K. Warne, D. W. Fleming, N. W. Bracken and G. D. McGrath did not bat.

Bowling: Streak 10–0–56–1; Strang 10–0–50–1; Nkala 8–0–56–0; Whittall 4–0–25–0; Murphy 8–0–38–0; Viljoen 10–0–62–3.

Zimbabwe

A.D.R. Campbell lbw b Fleming	3	(10)	M.L. Nkala c Gilchrist b Fleming	4	(11)
G.J. Whittall c Warne b McGrath	10	(12)	B.C. Strang run out (Fleming/McGrath)	2	(11)
S.V. Carlisle lbw b Warne	44	(69)	B.A. Murphy not out	2	(3)
†A. Flower c Symonds b Bevan	39	(55)	B 3, l-b 6, w 5, n-b 6	20	
G.W. Flower st Gilchrist b Symonds	30	(40)			
G.J. Rennie st Gilchrist b Symonds	11	(20)	(47.5 overs, 188 mins)	205	
D.P. Viljoen b Warne	31	(47)	Fall: 13 13 105 119 143 159 190		
*H.H. Streak c Bevan b Ponting	9	(19)	200 200 205		

Bowling: McGrath 6.5–1–26–1; Fleming 6–1–21–2; Warne 10–0–52–2; Bracken 5–0–25–0; Bevan 7–0–25–1; Symonds 8–0–35–2; Ponting 5–0–12–1.

Umpires: D.B. Hair and P.D. Parker.
TV Umpire: S.J.A. Taufel.
Referee: D.T. Lindsay (South Africa).

AUSTRALIA v ZIMBABWE

At Bellerive Oval, Hobart, January 30, 2001. Australia won by six wickets. Toss: Australia. Australia 2 pts. Limited-overs international debut: B.J. Haddin.

In a spirited batting performance, Zimbabwe scored their highest limited-overs total against Australia. Alistair Campbell's brilliant 124 (ten fours and a six) took advantage of some uncharacteristically shoddy Australian fielding, to which the run-out of Guy Whittall by debutant wicket-keeper Brad Haddin, and a superb diving catch by Andrew Symonds were notable exceptions. Stuart Carlisle and Andy Flower provided bright support, and the total looked formidable. If Symonds had been given out to an appeal for a catch to the wicket-keeper off the first ball of the innings, Australia's task might have been difficult, but he survived and hit 12 ferocious fours before he was out to the first ball of the 14th over. Steve Waugh took up where Symonds had left off, belting six fours and two sixes. Mark Waugh proceeded smoothly along, reaching his second century of the tournament thanks to Ian Harvey, who refused numerous runs in the final overs in order to give Waugh the strike to score the runs he needed.

Man of the Match: A.D.R. Campbell. *Attendance:* 11,115.

Zimbabwe

A.D.R. Campbell st Haddin b Warne	124	(142)	D.P. Viljoen b McGrath	1	(2)
G.J. Whittall run out (Haddin)	36	(67)			
S.V. Carlisle c Symonds b Martyn	36	(40)	L-b 6, w 8, n-b 4	18	
†A. Flower c Martyn b Warne	51	(44)			
*H.H. Streak not out	10	(5)	(50 overs, 190 mins) (6 wkts)	279	
G.W. Flower b McGrath	3	(4)	Fall: 94 164 265 266 269 279		

M.L. Nkala, A.J. Mackay, B.C. Strang and B.A. Murphy did not bat.

Bowling: McGrath 10–1–43–2; Fleming 10–0–46–0; Harvey 10–1–54–0; Warne 9–0–51–2; Symonds 7–0–51–0; Martyn 4–0–28–1.

Australia

A. Symonds c Viljoen b Murphy	60	(47)	I.J. Harvey not out	13	(17)
M.E. Waugh not out	102	(112)	B 3, l-b 1, w 3, n-b 2	9	
R.T. Ponting c Mackay b Nkala	6	(7)			
*S.R. Waugh lbw b Murphy	79	(72)	(44 overs, 181 mins) (4 wkts)	282	
†B.J. Haddin c Whittall b Murphy	13	(11)	Fall: 89 114 234 258		

D.R. Martyn, D.S. Lehmann, S.K. Warne, D.W. Fleming and G.D. McGrath did not bat.

Bowling: Streak 10–0–49–0; Strang 6–0–42–0; Nkala 5–0–33–1; Mackay 4–0–33–0; Murphy 10–0–52–3; Viljoen 4–0–28–0; Whittall 5–0–41–0.

Umpires: S. J. Davis and S. J. A. Taufel.
TV Umpire: J. H. Smeaton.
Referee: D. T. Lindsay (South Africa).

WEST INDIES v ZIMBABWE

At WACA Ground, Perth, February 2, 2001. Day/night game. West Indies won by 44 runs. Toss: West Indies. West Indies 2 pts.

There was an element of Sydney in reverse to this match. This time West Indies dug themselves a hole only to watch Zimbabwe dive into it. The West Indies innings included a record-equalling five run-outs, but they stormed back in the field to win easily. A defiant innings from Brian Lara and rapid support from Ricardo Powell added some respectability after a controversial start. In the fifth over Sherwin Campbell was run out without scoring after a mid-pitch collision with Heath Streak. Campbell had a chance to make his ground but stopped in his tracks and watched Trevor Madondo run in from cover and remove the bails. Believing he had been unfairly interfered with, Campbell stood his ground while umpires Darrell Hair and Simon Taufel conferred. They asked Streak if he would like to appeal, and he did. When Zimbabwe batted, Nixon McLean's three early wickets set them back on their heels, and Streak's usual belligerent knock at the end could not retrieve Zimbabwe's hopes of a finals appearance.

Man of the Match: B. C. Lara. *Attendance:* 8,000.

West Indies

D. Ganga run out (Streak/Murphy)	22	(57)	
S. L. Campbell run out (Madondo)	0	(12)	
M. N. Samuels c Campbell b Nkala	10	(34)	
B. C. Lara not out	83	(98)	
R. L. Powell c Campbell b Murphy	37	(36)	
*J. C. Adams run out (Carlisle)	8	(16)	
†R. D. Jacobs run out (A. Flower/Streak)	9	(13)	
L. R. Williams run out (Madondo/Viljoen)	0	(0)	
M. V. Nagamootoo c A. Flower b Viljoen	4	(8)	
N. A. M. McLean c Viljoen b Nkala	0	(3)	
C. E. Cuffy lbw b Viljoen	1	(7)	
L-b 2, w 2	4		
(47.2 overs, 199 mins)	178		

Fall: 4 24 43 105 130 154 160 171 172 178

Bowling: Streak 9–3–20–0; Strang 10–1–30–0; Nkala 8–0–34–2; Murphy 10–0–35–1; Viljoen 6.2–0–31–2; Whittall 4–0–26–0.

Zimbabwe

A. D. R. Campbell c Jacobs b McLean	1	(2)	
G. J. Whittall lbw b Nagamootoo	33	(82)	
S. V. Carlisle c Campbell b McLean	5	(8)	
†A. Flower c Jacobs b McLean	4	(8)	
G. W. Flower c Powell b Cuffy	1	(14)	
T. N. Madondo c Campbell b Williams	10	(15)	
D. P. Viljoen c Jacobs b Samuels	29	(49)	
*H. H. Streak not out	33	(46)	
M. L. Nkala c McLean b Samuels	7	(16)	
B. C. Strang run out (Campbell)	4	(5)	
B. A. Murphy c Williams b Samuels	2	(10)	
L-b 2, w 3	5		
(42.3 overs, 134 mins)	134		

Fall: 2 14 20 25 42 64 104 125 129 134

Bowling: McLean 9–2–21–3; Cuffy 8–4–17–1; Williams 7–0–31–1; Nagamootoo 10–2–31–1; Samuels 7.3–1–25–3; Adams 1–0–7–0.

Umpires: D. B. Hair and S. J. A. Taufel.
TV Umpire: R. J. Woolridge.
Referee: D. T. Lindsay (South Africa).

AUSTRALIA v ZIMBABWE

At WACA Ground, Perth, February 4, 2001. Australia won by one run. Toss: Australia. Australia 2 pts.

Zimbabwe will remember this as the game they nearly stole chasing a mountainous 303 on the bouncy WACA pitch. Brett Lee will remember it as the one where he suffered an injury to his right elbow while fielding that forced him to miss the tour of India. Damien Martyn will remember it for an imperious 144 not out (12 fours) on his home turf, his second limited-overs century for Australia. His score was a record for limited-overs internationals at the WACA, and took his average in international cricket for the season to 352. Ian Harvey will remember it for the 24 runs he took off a Dirk Viljoen over: six, six, six, two, four, out. And Stuart Carlisle will remember it for his fighting 119 (11 fours and a six), his second limited-overs century for Zimbabwe. Zimbabwe needed 26 runs off the last three overs to win but Glenn McGrath returned to the attack to remove Carlisle, who had joined Grant Flower in a Zimbabwean record fourth-wicket stand of 187 off 29 overs. When Flower was run out and Heath Streak was brilliantly caught and bowled by Ian Harvey in the next over, 15 were needed from McGrath's final over. Little-known right-hander Douglas Marillier very nearly wrote his name into the trivia books as he cleverly rocked to the off side to scoop yorkers to the fine-leg fence. But when he was unable to make three runs off the final delivery, Australia had made a clean sweep of the preliminaries.

Man of the Match: D. R. Martyn. *Attendance:* 20,143.

Australia

†A. C. Gilchrist c A. Flower b Streak	.	30	(33)	D. W. Fleming not out	6	(5)
D. R. Martyn not out		144	(149)			
R. T. Ponting run out (Carlisle)		32	(32)	L-b 6, w 1	7	
M. G. Bevan lbw b Murphy		44	(56)			
I. J. Harvey c Carlisle b Viljoen		37	(20)	(50 overs, 206 mins) (5 wkts)	302	
B. Lee b Streak		2	(5)	Fall: 66 110 204 273 282		

*S. R. Waugh, M. E. Waugh, N. W. Bracken and G. D. McGrath did not bat.

Bowling: Streak 10–0–63–2; Mackay 10–0–48–0; Nkala 8–0–45–0; Murphy 9–0–50–1; Viljoen 8–0–63–1; G. W. Flower 5–0–27–0.

Zimbabwe

A. D. R. Campbell c Gilchrist b Lee	. .	27	(34)	D. A. Marillier not out	12	(5)
G. J. Rennie c M. E. Waugh b McGrath	.	0	(4)	D. P. Viljoen not out	1	(1)
S. V. Carlisle c M. E. Waugh b McGrath	119	(144)			
†A. Flower c Gilchrist b Bracken	. . .	24	(30)	L-b 5, n-b 19	24	
G. W. Flower run out						
((sub) Symonds/Harvey)	.	85	(86)	(50 overs, 224 mins) (6 wkts)	301	
*H. H. Streak c and b Harvey	. . . .	9	(6)	Fall: 1 54 91 278 288 288		

M. L. Nkala, A. J. Mackay and B. A. Murphy did not bat.

Bowling: McGrath 10–1–46–2; Fleming 9–1–53–0; Bracken 9–1–46–1; Lee 8–0–72–1; Harvey 9–0–49–1; Bevan 5–0–30–0.

Umpires: S. J. Davis and D. J. Harper.
TV Umpire: D. B. Hair.
Referee: D. T. Lindsay (South Africa).

QUALIFYING TABLE

	Played	Won	Lost	Points	Net run-rate
Australia	8	8	0	16	1.3602
West Indies	8	3	5	6	−0.7248
Zimbabwe	8	1	7	2	−0.5464

Net run-rate was calculated by subtracting runs conceded per over from runs scored per over.

FIRST FINAL

AUSTRALIA v WEST INDIES

At Sydney Cricket Ground, Sydney, February 7, 2001. Day/night game. Australia won by 134 runs. Toss: West Indies.

Australia's crushing victory was soured by another ugly incident involving sledging and Brian Lara. Coming to the crease at two wickets for nought chasing 254, Lara was pricked into action after an exchange of words with Glenn McGrath and Michael Bevan. He went down the pitch at one stage to continue an altercation with Bevan, who was fielding at mid-on. Umpire Simon Taufel tried to calm him, but Lara decided to exact some revenge with his bat. Four of his first five scoring strokes went to the boundary and he hit seven fours in a brief stay before edging a ball from Damien Fleming to Adam Gilchrist. Once Lara was gone, West Indies suffered the fate of many of the crowd-pleasing beach balls confiscated by security guards – the air was squeezed out of them.

Ian Harvey made it two good games in a row, hitting two fours and two sixes to turn a moderate score of six for 179 off 39.4 overs when he came to the crease into a good one. He then took 2/5 off his six overs as Australia delivered another consummate display in the field. The other highlight for the dwindling crowd came with West Indies on nine for 113 when Shane Warne dropped a skied catch off his own bowling that he should have left for Damien Fleming at mid-on. Not only did he miss the ball by some margin, he also fell flat on his back. He was given an identical chance by Sylvester Joseph a few balls later and this time held it, despite a collision with Fleming.

Man of the Match: I.J. Harvey. *Attendance:* 35,797.

Australia

M.E. Waugh c Lara b Cuffy	10	(19)		S.K. Warne c Jacobs b Cuffy	7	(13)
†A.C. Gilchrist run out (Ganga)	44	(55)		D.W. Fleming c Nagamootoo b Samuels	14	(12)
R.T. Ponting c Joseph b Nagamootoo	33	(50)		G.D. McGrath not out	1	(1)
M.G. Bevan c Jacobs b Williams	23	(34)				
*S.R. Waugh c Jacobs b Williams	38	(49)		L-b 5, w 5	10	
D.R. Martyn run out (Williams)	18	(24)				
A. Symonds c Jacobs b McLean	8	(10)		(50 overs, 205 mins) (9 wkts)	253	
I.J. Harvey not out	47	(33)		Fall: 28 72 111 137 168 179 199 219 242		

Bowling: McLean 10–0–47–1; Cuffy 10–1–45–2; Williams 10–0–55–2; Nagamootoo 10–0–55–1; Samuels 10–0–46–1.

West Indies

D. Ganga lbw b McGrath	0	(8)	M. V. Nagamootoo c Warne b Symonds	8	(27)
†R. D. Jacobs c Gilchrist b Fleming	0	(6)	N. A. M. McLean b Martyn b Symonds	0	(3)
M. N. Samuels run out (Bevan)	24	(53)	C. E. Cuffy not out	0	(2)
B. C. Lara c Gilchrist b Fleming	35	(38)			
*J. C. Adams c Gilchrist b Harvey	9	(14)	B 2, l-b 7, w 11, n-b 1	21	
R. L. Powell lbw b Harvey	3	(11)			
S. C. Joseph c and b Warne	18	(47)	(37.2 overs, 148 mins)	119	
L. R. Williams c Ponting b McGrath	1	(16)	Fall: 0 0 58 74 74 77 81 103 103 119		

Bowling: McGrath 10–4–25–2; Fleming 7–2–34–2; Warne 9.2–1–28–1; Harvey 6–2–5–2; Symonds 5–0–18–2.

Umpires: D. J. Harper and S. J. A. Taufel.
TV Umpire: D. B. Hair.
Referee: D. T. Lindsay (South Africa).

SECOND FINAL

AUSTRALIA v WEST INDIES

At Melbourne Cricket Ground, Melbourne, February 9, 2001. Day/night game. Australia won by 39 runs. Toss: West Indies.

On the eve of facing ACB investigator Greg Melick over his alleged involvement with illegal bookmakers, Mark Waugh smashed an Australian record limited-overs score of 173 off 148 balls. He clubbed 16 fours and three sixes on his way to becoming the first Australian to chalk up 8,000 limited-overs runs. Only Sachin Tendulkar, Mohammad Azharuddin, Desmond Haynes and Aravinda de Silva have scored more runs. Waugh's 17th limited-overs century placed him third on the all-time list behind Tendulkar (27) and Saeed Anwar (19). Waugh's innings surpassed Australia's previous best of 154 by Adam Gilchrist at the MCG two years before and anchored Australia's massive total of six for 338, which was another record score on home soil, beating the seven for 337 the previous season in the second final against Pakistan in Sydney.

Marlon Samuels, Wavell Hinds and Ridley Jacobs all contributed spirited knocks as West Indies put up a fight. They helped maintain a scoring rate of above six an over for most of the innings, but wickets fell too often, and West Indies were unable to raise the scoring rate sufficiently towards the end. Brian Lara's miserable tour ended on a dismal note when he was dismissed for a duck by Shane Warne, who bowled dangerously throughout. The disappointing MCG crowd was evidence enough of the ennui that had set in among the public in response to over three months of one-sided international cricket.

Man of the Match: M. E. Waugh.   *Attendance:* 31,915.
Man of the Finals: M. E. Waugh.   *Man of the Preliminaries:* B. C. Lara.

Australia

†A. C. Gilchrist c Hinds b McLean	5	(14)	*S. R. Waugh not out	10	(8)
M. E. Waugh c Lara b Samuels	173	(148)	D. R. Martyn not out	4	(3)
R. T. Ponting c Hinds b Nagamootoo	63	(63)	B 2, l-b 2, w 12	16	
A. Symonds c Nagamootoo b Cuffy	7	(10)			
M. G. Bevan c Williams b Samuels	58	(51)	(50 overs, 204 mins) (6 wkts)	338	
I. J. Harvey c McLean b Samuels	2	(3)	Fall: 12 137 155 291 311 328		

S. K. Warne, D. W. Fleming and G. D. McGrath did not bat.

Bowling: McLean 10–1–58–1; Cuffy 10–0–53–1; Nagamootoo 10 0–54–1; Williams 8–0–72–0; Samuels 10–0–71–3; Adams 2–0–26–0.

West Indies

W. W. Hinds c Ponting b Symonds	... 60	(58)	
R. L. Powell lbw b Warne	 21	(24)	
B. C. Lara c Martyn b Warne	 0	(6)	
M. N. Samuels c Martyn b Warne	 63	(54)	
*J. C. Adams c and b Fleming	 18	(35)	
†R. D. Jacobs c S. R. Waugh b McGrath	59	(61)	
M. V. Nagamootoo b Fleming	 5	(6)	
N. A. M. McLean c S. R. Waugh b Bevan	16	(9)	

D. Ganga b McGrath 18 (19)
L. R. Williams not out 10 (21)
C. E. Cuffy c Martyn b Warne 6 (9)
    B 2, l-b 8, w 8, n-b 5 23

(49.3 overs, 204 mins)   299
Fall: 54 56 128 159 201 218 237
    279 288 299

Bowling: McGrath 10–1–48–2; Fleming 8–0–49–2; Warne 8.3–0–48–4; Harvey 10–0–59–0; Symonds 8–0–55–1; Martyn 2–0–10–0; Bevan 3–0–20–1.

Umpires: S. J. Davis and D. B. Hair.
TV Umpire: D. J. Harper.
Referee: D. T. Lindsay (South Africa).

WORLD SERIES CRICKET RECORDS

Benson & Hedges World Series Cup

Season	Winners	Runners-Up	Third Team	Fourth Team
1979-80	West Indies	England	Australia	–
1980-81	Australia	New Zealand	India	–
1981-82	West Indies	Australia	Pakistan	–
1982-83	Australia	New Zealand	England	–
1983-84	West Indies	Australia	Pakistan	–
1984-85	West Indies	Australia	Sri Lanka	–
1985-86	Australia	India	New Zealand	–
1986-87	England	Australia	West Indies	–
1987-88	Australia	New Zealand	Sri Lanka	–
1988-89	West Indies	Australia	Pakistan	–

Benson & Hedges World Series

1989-90	Australia	Pakistan	Sri Lanka	–
1990-91	Australia	New Zealand	England	–
1991-92	Australia	India	West Indies	–
1992-93	West Indies	Australia	Pakistan	–
1993-94	Australia	South Africa	New Zealand	–
1994-95	Australia	Australia 'A'	England	Zimbabwe
1995-96	Australia	Sri Lanka	West Indies	–

Carlton & United Series

1996-97	Pakistan	West Indies	Australia	–
1997-98	Australia	South Africa	New Zealand	–
1998-99	Australia	England	Sri Lanka	–
1999-00	Australia	Pakistan	India	–

Carlton Series

2000-01	Australia	West Indies	Zimbabwe	–

RESULTS

	M	W	L	NR	T
Australia A	8	3	5	0	0
Australia	237	149	82	4	2
England	55	24	31	0	0
India	40	12	27	0	1
New Zealand	71	27	42	2	0
Pakistan	66	23	41	1	1
Sri Lanka	46	10	36	0	0
South Africa	21	12	9	0	0
West Indies	114	67	44	1	2
Zimbabwe	14	2	12	0	0

HIGHEST INDIVIDUAL SCORES

173	M. E. Waugh	Australia v West Indies at Melbourne	2000-01
158	D. I. Gower	England v New Zealand at Brisbane	1982-83
154	A. C. Gilchrist	Australia v Sri Lanka at Melbourne	1998-99
153*	I. V. A. Richards	West Indies v Australia at Melbourne	1979-80
145	D. M. Jones	Australia v England at Brisbane	1990-91
144*	D. R. Martyn	Australia v Zimbabwe at Perth	2000-01
141	S. C. Ganguly	India v Pakistan at Adelaide	1999-00
138*	G. S. Chappell	Australia v New Zealand at Sydney	1980-81
131	A. C. Gilchrist	Australia v Sri Lanka at Sydney	1998-99
130	M. E. Waugh	Australia v Sri Lanka at Perth	1995-96

Denotes not out.

MOST RUNS

	M	I	NO	R	HS	100s	50s	Avge	S-R
A. R. Border (Aust) . . .	160	148	22	3,899	127*	3	23	30.94	69.67
M. E. Waugh (Aust) . .	109	103	8	3,604	173	8	21	37.94	73.66
D. M. Jones (Aust). . . .	93	90	16	3,456	145	2	28	46.70	70.26
D. C. Boon (Aust)	94	91	9	3,016	122	2	20	36.78	63.31
D. L. Haynes (WI)	83	83	8	2,782	123*	4	21	37.09	59.42
S. R. Waugh (Aust) . . .	134	119	30	2,614	102*	1	13	29.37	70.90
I. V. A. Richards (WI) .	65	60	5	2,563	153*	3	22	46.60	85.26
G. R. Marsh (Aust) . . .	65	64	3	2,197	125*	3	12	36.02	54.35
R. T. Ponting (Aust) . .	58	58	6	2,151	123	3	15	41.37	76.71
M. G. Bevan (Aust) . . .	65	58	23	2,118	105	1	15	60.51	74.03

Denotes not out.

HIGHEST PARTNERSHIPS FOR EACH WICKET

206	for 1st	A. C. Gilchrist and M. E Waugh	Australia v West Indies at Brisbane . .	2000-01
205	for 2nd	D. L. Haynes and I. V. A. Richards	West Indies v Australia at Melbourne	1979-80
224*	for 3rd	D. M. Jones and A. R. Border	Australia v Sri Lanka at Adelaide . . .	1984-85
187	for 4th	S. V. Carlisle and G. W. Flower	Zimbabwe v Australia at Perth	2000-01
159	for 5th	R. T. Ponting and M. G. Bevan	Australia v Sri Lanka at Melbourne . .	1995-96
124	for 6th	C. D. McMillan and C. Z. Harris	New Zealand v South Africa at Adelaide	1997-98
95*	for 7th	S. R. Waugh and I. A. Healy	Australia v England at Melbourne . . .	1990-91
83	for 8th	M. G. Bevan and P. R. Reiffel	Australia v West Indies at Sydney . . .	1995-96
63	for 9th	R. J. Hadlee and G. B. Troup	New Zealand v England at Brisbane .	1982-83
		M. D. Marshall and J. Garner	West Indies v Australia at Sydney . . .	1984-85
45	for 10th	T. J. Laughlin and M. H. N. Walker	Australia v England at Sydney	1979-80

Denotes unbroken partnership.

HIGHEST INNINGS TOTALS

Batting first

6-338	Australia defeated West Indies at Melbourne	2000-01
7-337	Australia defeated Pakistan at Sydney	1999-00
329	Australia defeated India at Adelaide	1999-00
2-323	Australia defeated Sri Lanka at Adelaide	1984-85
3-315	Pakistan defeated Sri Lanka at Adelaide	1989-90
8-310	Australia defeated Sri Lanka at Melbourne	1998-99
6-309	West Indies defeated Sri Lanka at Perth	1984-85
8-302	Australia defeated New Zealand at Melbourne	1982-83
3-302	England lost to Sri Lanka at Adelaide	1998-99
5-302	Australia defeated to Zimbabwe at Perth	2000-01
5-300	Australia defeated at Brisbane	1989-90
6-300	South Africa defeated New Zealand at Brisbane	1997-98

Batting second

9-303	Sri Lanka defeated England at Adelaide	1998-99
6-301	Zimbabwe lost to Australia at Perth	2000-01
299	West Indies lost to Australia at Melbourne	2000-01
9-298	New Zealand lost to South Africa at Brisbane	1997-98
6-297	New Zealand defeated England at Adelaide	1982-83
8-288	Sri Lanka lost to Pakistan at Adelaide	1989-90
3-284	West Indies defeated Australia at Brisbane	1996-97
4-282	Australia defeated Zimbabwe at Hobart	2000-01
6-275	Australia defeated England at Sydney	1998-99
6-273	West Indies defeated Australia at Melbourne	1984-85
6-269	West Indies defeated Australia at Perth	1996-97
267	Sri Lanka lost to Australia at Melbourne	1998-99

LOWEST INNINGS TOTALS

Batting first

63	India lost to Australia at Sydney	1980-81
71	Pakistan lost to West Indies at Brisbane	1992-93
100	India lost to Australia in Sydney	1999-00
102	Sri Lanka lost to West Indies at Brisbane	1995-96
113	India lost to New Zealand at Perth	1985-86

Batting second

69	South Africa lost to Australia	1993-94
70	Australia lost to New Zealand at Adelaide	1985-86
81	Pakistan lost to West Indies at Sydney	1992-93
87	West Indies lost to Australia at Sydney	1992-93
91	Sri Lanka lost to Australia at Adelaide	1984-85
91	West Indies lost to Zimbabwe at Sydney	2000-01

BEST ANALYSES

5/15	G. S. Chappell	Australia v India at Sydney	1980-81
5/15	R. J. Shastri	India v Australia at Perth	1991-92
5/16	C. G. Rackemann	Australia v Pakistan at Adelaide	1983-84
5/17	C. E. L. Ambrose	West Indies v Australia at Melbourne	1988-89
5/21	A. I. C. Dodemaide	Australia v Sri Lanka at Perth	1987-88
5/22	A. M. E. Roberts	West Indies v England at Adelaide	1979-80
5/24	M. E. Waugh	Australia v West Indies at Melbourne	1992-93
5/24	L. Klusener	South Africa v Australia at Melbourne	1997-98
5/25	I. R. Bishop	West Indies v Pakistan at Brisbane	1992-93
5/26	R. J. Hadlee	New Zealand v Australia at Sydney	1980-81
5/26	M. A. Holding	West Indies v Australia at Sydney	1984-85
5/26	C. E. L. Ambrose	West Indies v Australia at Melbourne	1988-89
5/26	A. M. Stuart	Australia v Pakistan at Melbourne	1996-97

MOST WICKETS

	M	O	Mdns	R	W	BB	5W/i	Avge
C. J. McDermott (Australia) ...	82	728	67	2,805	122	4/25	0	22.99
S. K. Warne (Australia)	69	642	36	2,692	120	5/33	1	22.43
G. D. McGrath (Australia)	60	542	64	2,135	111	5/40	1	19.23
S. R. Waugh (Australia)	134	638.5	27	2,716	86	4/33	0	31.58
M. A. Holding (West Indies) ...	49	459.4	44	1,602	74	5/26	1	21.65
P. L. Taylor (Australia)	54	465.1	23	1,878	71	4/38	0	26.45
J. Garner (West Indies)	48	435.5	62	1,381	70	5/31	1	19.73
M. D. Marshall (West Indies) ..	56	497	50	1,748	69	4/18	0	25.33
S. P. O'Donnell (Australia)	52	432	26	1,826	69	4/19	0	26.46
D. K. Lillee (Australia)	40	358.2	55	1,248	68	4/12	0	18.35

MOST CATCHES

A. R. Border (Aust) ...	83 in 160 matches	D. M. Jones (Aust) ...	29 in 93 matches
S. R. Waugh (Aust) ...	52 in 134 matches	P. L. Taylor (Aust) ...	28 in 54 matches
M. E. Waugh (Aust) ..	45 in 109 matches	I. V. A. Richards (WI) ..	28 in 65 matches
S. K. Warne (Aust) ...	37 in 69 matches	M. G. Bevan (Aust) ..	28 in 65 matches
M. A. Taylor (Aust) ..	32 in 53 matches		

MOST DISMISSALS

124 (108ct, 16st) ... I. A. Healy (Aust)
 79 (78ct, 1st) ..... R. W. Marsh (Aust)
 79 (69ct, 10st) .... A. C. Gilchrist (Aust)
 69 (60ct, 9st) ..... P. J. L. Dujon (WI)
 31 (24ct, 7st) ..... Moin Khan (Pak)

30 (27ct, 3st) .... D. J. Richardson (SAf)
29 (26ct, 3st) .... W. B. Phillips (Aust)
25 (21ct, 4st) .... J. R. Murray (WI)
25 (19ct, 6st) .... R. S. Kaluwitharana (SL)

MOST APPEARANCES

	M	Aust	Aust A	Eng	Ind	NZ	Pak	SL	SAf	WI	Zim
A. R. Border (Aust) ..	160	–	–	19	18	35	22	6	13	47	–
S. R. Waugh (Aust) ..	134	–	3	12	17	23	23	14	12	27	3
M. E. Waugh (Aust) ..	109	–	4	13	7	13	16	13	13	27	5
D. C. Boon (Aust)	94	–	4	6	13	21	9	7	10	22	2
D. M. Jones (Aust) ...	93	–	–	10	8	15	14	5	11	30	–
I. A. Healy (Aust)	86	–	3	6	6	10	18	6	10	25	2
D. L. Haynes (WI) ...	83	49	–	8	4	–	18	–	4	–	–
C. J. McDermott (Aust)	82	–	4	1	13	13	8	6	11	25	1
S. K. Warne (Aust) ..	69	–	3	9	1	8	7	11	12	13	5
M. G. Bevan (Aust) ..	69	3	1	7	4	4	10	10	7	14	5

MOST RUNS, 2000-01

	M	I	NO	R	HS	100s	50s	Avge	S-R
M. E. Waugh (Aust) ..	9	7	2	542	173	3	2	108.40	83.00
R. T. Ponting (Aust) ..	9	9	1	393	93	0	4	49.13	89.52
B. C. Lara (WI)	10	10	2	372	116*	1	2	46.50	80.35
A. C. Gilchrist (Aust) .	9	8	0	326	98	0	2	40.75	84.90
D. R. Martyn (Aust) ..	9	6	4	298	144*	1	1	149.00	93.13
A. D. R. Campbell (Zim)	8	8	0	290	124	1	1	36.25	74.74
M. N. Samuels (WI) ..	10	10	0	282	68	0	3	28.20	66.51
S. V. Carlisle (Zim) ..	8	8	0	278	119	1	0	34.75	70.56
M. G. Bevan (Aust) ...	9	7	2	261	74*	0	2	52.20	83.12
R. L. Powell (WI)	10	10	1	252	83*	0	1	28.00	83.44

* *Denotes not out.*

MOST WICKETS, 2000-01

	M	O	Mdns	R	W	BB	Avge
G. D. McGrath (Aust)	9	79.3	14	291	19	5/49	15.32
S. K. Warne (Aust)	9	84.5	5	377	18	4/48	20.94
M. N. Samuels (WI)	10	80.5	2	389	14	3/25	27.79
N. A. M. McLean (WI)	10	90.4	7	401	13	3/21	30.85
C. E. Cuffy (WI)	8	73	8	308	12	4/24	25.67
A. Symonds (Aust)	9	67	3	323	12	4/35	26.92
I. J. Harvey (Aust)	8	67.1	7	277	12	4/28	23.08
G. D. McGrath (Aust)	8	70.3	13	274	11	2/25	24.91
H. H. Streak (Zim)	8	70	10	301	11	4/8	27.36
L. R. Williams (WI)	8	66	2	324	10	3/24	32.40
D. W. Fleming (Aust)	6	50	6	235	9	3/32	26.11

AUSTRALIAN FIRST-CLASS SEASON, 2000-01

FEATURES OF 2000-01

Highest Individual Scores

260	G.S. Blewett	South Australia v Queensland at Brisbane.
233	R.T. Ponting	Tasmania v Queensland at Albion.
231	B.C. Lara	West Indians v Australia A at Hobart.
228*	S.M. Katich	Western Australia v South Australia at Perth.
187*	R.T. Ponting	Tasmania v New South Wales at Hobart.
182	B.C. Lara	West Indies v Australia at Adelaide.
181*	M.A. Higgs	New South Wales v Queensland at Sydney.
176	G.J. Mail	New South Wales v Tasmania at Sydney.
175	J.P. Maher	Queensland v Western Australia at Perth.
173	J.L. Arnberger	Victoria v Tasmania at Hobart.

Denotes not out.

Leading Run-Makers

	M	I	NO	R	HS	100s	50s	Avge
1. S.M. Katich (WAust/Aust A)	12	23	5	1,282	228*	6	3	71.22
2. J. Cox (Tas/Aust A)	11	21	3	1,170	160	5	4	65.00
3. G.S. Blewett (SAust)	9	18	1	1,162	260*	3	6	68.35
4. J.P. Maher (Qld/Aust A)	12	21	3	1,142	175	4	3	63.44
5. B.J. Hodge (Vic/Aust A)	13	23	3	1,129	134†	5	3	56.45
6. J.L. Arnberger (Vic)	12	22	1	1,006	173	2	7	47.90
7. M.L. Love (Qld/Aust A)	10	15	3	910	172*	3	5	75.83
8. S.G. Law (Qld)	11	15	2	814	161	2	4	62.62
9. D.R. Martyn (WAust/Aust A/Aust)	8	15	4	746	122	2	4	67.82
10. R.T. Ponting (Tas/Aust)	7	12	3	726	233	2	3	80.67

Leading Batting Averages

(Qualification: 500 Runs)

	M	I	NO	R	HS	100s	50s	Avge
1. R.T. Ponting (Tas/Aust)	7	12	3	726	233	2	3	80.67
2. M.L. Love (Qld/Aust A)	10	15	3	910	172*	3	5	75.83
3. S.M. Katich (WAust/Aust A)	12	23	5	1282	228*	6	3	71.22
4. G.S. Blewett (SAust)	9	18	1	1162	260*	3	6	68.35
5. D.R. Martyn (WAust/Aust A/Aust)	8	15	4	746	122	2	4	67.82
6. J.P. Maher (Qld/Aust A)	12	21	3	1142	175	4	3	63.44
7. S.G. Law (Qld)	11	15	2	814	161	2	4	62.62
8. M.E. Waugh (NSW/Aust)	7	11	1	590	152	2	3	59.00
9. B.J. Hodge (Vic/Aust A)	13	23	3	1129	134†	5	3	56.45
10. M.G. Bevan (NSW)	8	13	2	557	119	2	2	50.64
11. J.L. Arnberger (Vic)	12	22	1	1006	173	2	7	47.90
12. A. Symonds (Qld)	9	13	1	558	133	1	2	46.50
13. D.S. Lehmann (SAust)	8	16	2	645	146	1	3	46.07
14. B.C. Lara (West Indians)	7	13	0	591	231	2	0	45.46
15. M.L. Hayden (Qld/Aust)	8	13	1	537	118*	1	3	44.75
16. M.T.G. Elliott (Vic)	7	14	1	524	98	0	5	40.31
17. D.J. Marsh (Tas)	9	16	3	514	110	1	3	39.54
18. S.A. Deitz (SAust)	9	18	0	608	114	2	2	33.78
19. M.P. Mott (Vic)	12	22	1	695	154	1	3	33.10
20. M.E. Hussey (WAust)	11	21	1	605	137	1	1	30.25

Notable Partnerships

First Wicket

229*	M.L. Hayden/J.P. Maher, Queensland v Victoria at Albion.
156	M.J. Slater/M.L. Hayden, Australia v West Indies at Adelaide.
147	S.L. Campbell/W.W. Hinds, West Indies v Australia at Sydney.
146	M.J. Slater/C.J. Richards, New South Wales v Tasmania at Hobart.
123	M.T.G. Elliott/J.L. Arnberger, Victoria v Tasmania at Hobart.

Second Wicket

230	S.A. Deitz/G.S. Blewett, South Australia v Queensland at Brisbane.
212	J.P. Maher/M.L. Love, Queensland v Victoria at Melbourne.
203	J.L. Cassell, M.L. Love, Queensland v Tasmania at Hobart.
197	G.J. Mail/M.G. Bevan, New South Wales v Tasmania at Sydney.
195	J. Cox/M.J. Di Venuto, Tasmania v New South Wales at Hobart.

Third Wicket

275	J.P. Maher/S.G. Law, Queensland v Western Australia at Perth.
242	J. Cox/R.T. Ponting, Tasmania v New South Wales at Hobart.
199	D.A. Fitzgerald/D.S. Lehmann, South Australia v New South Wales at Adelaide.
193	S.M. Katich/D.R. Martyn, Western Australia v Tasmania at Hobart.
192	S.M. Katich/D.R. Martyn, Western Australia v New South Wales at North Sydney.

Fourth Wicket

261	M.L. Love/A. Symonds, Queensland v Tasmania at Albion.
183	B.C. Lara/J.C. Adams, West Indies v Australia at Adelaide.
151	B.J. Hodge/J. Moss, Victoria v New South Wales at Sydney.
147	B.J. Hodge/M. Klinger (ret. hurt)/P.Q. Harper, Victoria v West Indians at Melbourne.
145	S.G. Law/A. Symonds, Queensland v South Australia at Brisbane.

Fifth Wicket

264	M.A. Higgs/S. Lee, New South Wales v Queensland at Sydney.
172	B.J. Hodge/I.J. Harvey, Victoria v Queensland at Albion.
167	M.P. Moss/J. Moss, Victoria v Western Australia at Melbourne.
132	S.R. Waugh/R.T. Ponting, Australia v West Indies at Sydney.
124	M.R. Martyn/M.J. Walsh, Western Australia v Tasmania at Hobart.

Sixth Wicket

365	R.D. Jacobs/B.C. Lara, West Indians v Australia A at Hobart.
166	S.M. Katich/A.C. Gilchrist, Western Australia v Queensland at Perth.
147	S.M. Katich/B.P. Julian, Western Australia v South Australia at Perth.
144	D.R. Martyn/A.C. Gilchrist, Western Australia v South Australia at Adelaide.
132	J.M. Vaughan/B.E. Young, South Australia v Western Australia at Adelaide.

Seventh Wicket

132*	B.J. Hodge/P.R. Reiffel, Victoria v New South Wales at Richmond.
122	S.P. Kremerskothen/S.G. Clingeleffer, Tasmania v Western Australia at Hobart.
104	B.A. Johnson/G.A. Manou, South Australia v Tasmania at Adelaide.
95	M.E. Waugh/A.C. Gilchrist, Australia v West Indies at Perth.
89	I.J. Harvey/P.R. Reiffel, Victoria v South Australia at Adelaide.

Eighth Wicket

109	B.P. Julian/J. Angel, Western Australia v New South Wales at North Sydney.
88*	S.M. Katich/M.J. Nicholson, Western Australia v South Australia at Perth.
81	S.R. Waugh/J.N. Gillespie, Australia v West Indies at Melbourne.
61	A.C. Gilchrist/B. Lee, Australia v West Indies at Brisbane.
61	M.J. Walsh/M.J. Nicholson, Western Australia v Queensland at Brisbane.

Ninth Wicket

70	N.T. Adcock/P.C. Rofe, South Australia v Queensland at Adelaide.
60	M.E. Waugh/N.W. Bracken, New South Wales v Tasmania at Hobart.
55	M.J. Phelps/P.A. Jaques, New South Wales v Queensland at Brisbane.
54	D.S. Lehmann/P. Wilson, South Australia v Queensland at Brisbane.
50	B. Lee/S.C.G. MacGill, Australia v West Indies at Brisbane.
50	S. Lee/S.C.G. MacGill, New South Wales v Victoria at Sydney.

Tenth Wicket

63	D.J. Saker/S.B. Tubb, Tasmania v New South Wales at Sydney.
42	C.R. Miller/G.D. McGrath, Australia v West Indies at Sydney.
37	M.D. Pascoe/J.H Dawes, Queensland v Victoria at Melbourne.
27	B.J. Hodge/M.W.H. Inness, Victoria v Queensland at Albion.
27	W.A. Seccombe/J.H. Dawes, Queensland v South Australia at Brisbane.

* Denotes unbroken partnership.

Highest Innings Totals

530	New South Wales v Tasmania at Sydney.
6-499 dec.	New South Wales v Queensland at Sydney.
5-493 dec.	South Australia v Queensland at Brisbane.
492	West Indians v Australia A at Hobart.
8-480 dec.	Western Australia v South Australia at Adelaide.
9-475 dec.	Queensland v South Australia at Adelaide.
7-474 dec.	Western Australia v South Australia at Perth.
4-468 dec.	Queensland v Tasmania at Hobart.
464	New South Wales v Tasmania at Hobart.
452	Australia v West Indies at Sydney.

Highest Fourth-Innings Totals

9-373	Western Australia (Set 387 – drawn) v Tasmania at Hobart.
6-373	Queensland (Set 373 – won by four wickets) v Tasmania at Albion.
342	South Australia (Set 379 – lost by 36 runs) v Western Australia at Perth.
7-287	Victoria (Set 292 – drawn) v Western Australia at Melbourne.
4-286	Tasmania (Set 286 – won by six wickets) v Victoria at Hobart.
286	South Australia (Set 395 – lost by 108 runs) v Victoria at Melbourne.
232	New South Wales (Set 401 – lost by 168 runs) v South Australia at Adelaide.
0-229	Queensland (Set 229 – won by ten wickets) v Victoria at Albion.
6-224	Queensland (Set 224 – won by four wickets) v Victoria at Brisbane.
5-191	Victoria (Set 191 – won by five wickets) v South Australia at Adelaide.

Lowest Innings Totals

78	Western Australia v Queensland at Brisbane.
82	West Indies v Australia at Brisbane.
89	Western Australia v New South Wales at North Sydney.
96	South Australia v Victoria at Melbourne.
109	West Indies v Australia at Melbourne.
112	Tasmania v Queensland at Hobart.
114	West Indians v Victoria at Melbourne.
124	West Indies v Australia at Brisbane.
126	South Australia v Queensland at Brisbane.
130	New South Wales v Western Australia at Perth.

Best Innings Analyses

7/98	J.H. Dawes	Queensland v South Australia at Adelaide.
7/104	S.C.G. MacGill	Australia v West Indies at Sydney.
6/17	G.D. McGrath	Australia v West Indies at Brisbane.
6/19	J.H. Dawes	Queensland v Western Australia at Brisbane.
6/26	M.W.H. Inness	Victoria v West Indians at Melbourne.
6/26	M.W.H. Inness	Victoria v South Australia at Melbourne.
6/40	J.N. Gillespie	Australia v West Indies at Melbourne.
6/98	J.H. Dawes	Queensland v Victoria at Albion.
5/22	N.W. Bracken	New South Wales v Western Australia at North Sydney.
5/26	T.M. Moody	Western Australia v New South Wales at Perth.

Leading Wicket-Takers

		M	O	Mdns	R	W	Avge	5W/i	10W/m	BB
1.	A. J. Bichel (Qld/Aust A/Aust)	10	400.3	99	1,144	49	23.35	3	0	5/60
2.	J. H. Dawes (Qld)	9	358.3	101	1,003	49	20.47	3	1	7/98
3.	S. C. G. MacGill (NSW/Aust)	10	453.4	98	1,390	46	30.22	3	0	7/104
4.	A. C. Dale (Qld)	11	570.3	226	1,076	46	23.39	2	0	5/37
5.	M. W. H. Inness (Vic/Aust A)	13	403.2	126	1,077	43	25.05	2	0	6/26
6.	C. R. Miller (Vic/Aust)	8	377.1	104	998	40	24.95	2	1	5/32
7.	J. Angel (WAust)	9	333.3	109	867	37	23.43	1	0	5/78
8.	B. P. Julian (WAust)	9	266.2	46	934	32	29.19	0	0	4/87
9.	P. R. Reiffel (Vic)	11	325.1	84	824	30	27.47	0	0	4/50
10.	N. W. Bracken (NSW)	6	240.1	65	688	29	23.72	2	0	5/22

Leading Bowling Averages

(Qualification: 20 wickets)

		M	O	Mdns	R	W	Avge	5W/i	10W/m	BB
1.	G. D. McGrath (NSW/Aust)	6	207.5	77	425	23	18.48	1	1	6/17
2.	J. H. Dawes (Qld)	9	358.3	101	1,003	49	20.47	3	1	7/98
3.	B. Lee (NSW/Aust)	4	133	40	411	20	20.55	2	0	5/42
4.	J. N. Gillespie (SAust/Aust)	5	175	51	463	22	21.05	2	0	6/40
5.	T. M. Moody (WAust)	9	189	61	455	20	22.75	1	0	5/26
6.	A. J. Bichel (Qld/Aust A/Aust)	10	400.3	99	1,144	49	23.35	3	0	5/60
7.	A. C. Dale (Qld)	11	570.3	226	1,076	46	23.39	2	0	5/37
8.	J. Angel (WAust)	9	333.3	109	867	37	23.43	1	0	5/78
9.	N. W. Bracken (NSW)	6	240.1	65	688	29	23.72	2	0	5/22
10.	C. R. Miller (Vic/Aust)	8	377.1	104	998	40	24.95	2	1	5/32
11.	M. W. H. Inness (Vic/Aust A)	13	403.2	126	1,077	43	25.05	2	0	6/26
12.	S. Young (Tas)	10	203.3	63	532	21	25.33	0	0	4/33
13.	D. G. Wright (Tas)	6	192.1	43	593	22	26.95	0	0	4/54
14.	P. R. Reiffel (Vic)	11	325.1	84	824	30	27.47	0	0	4/50
15.	B. P. Julian (WAust)	9	266.2	46	934	32	29.19	0	0	4/87
16.	S. C. G. MacGill (NSW/Aust)	10	453.4	98	1,390	46	30.22	3	0	7/104
17.	M. J. Nicholson (WAust)	8	289	86	773	25	30.92	0	0	4/119
18.	M. A. Harrity (SAust)	8	243.3	62	728	23	31.65	0	0	4/55
19.	P. E. McIntyre (SAust)	7	322.2	66	927	28	33.11	1	0	5/102
20.	M. L. Lewis (Vic)	7	246.2	53	772	23	33.57	1	0	5/57

Most Catches in an Innings

4	R. J. Campbell	Western Australia v New South Wales at Perth.
3	M. L. Love	Queensland v Victoria at Albion.
3	A. J. Bichel	Queensland v Victoria at Albion.
3	D. J. Marsh	Tasmania v New South Wales at Hobart.
3	S. A. J. Craig	Victoria v West Indians at Melbourne.
3	M. W. Goodwin	Western Australia v New South Wales at North Sydney.
3	M. E. Hussey	Western Australia v New South Wales at Perth.
3	S. A. Deitz	South Australia v New South Wales at Adelaide.
3	S. M. Katich	Western Australia v Queensland at Brisbane.
3	J. L. Arnberger	Victoria v South Australia at Adelaide.
3	G. S. Blewett	South Australia v Western Australia at Perth.
3	M. J. Di Venuto	Tasmania v Western Australia at Perth.
3	M. A. Higgs	New South Wales v Queensland at Brisbane.

Most Catches in a Match

5	G. S. Blewett	South Australia v Western Australia at Perth.
5	M. J. Di Venutto	Tasmania v Western Australia at Perth.
4	M. E. Hussey	Western Australia v New South Wales at Perth.
4	R. J. Campbell	Western Australia v New South Wales at Perth.

Most Dismissals in an Innings

7	(7ct)	R.D. Jacobs	West Indies v Australia at Melbourne.
6	(6ct)	W.A. Seccombe	Queensland v Western Australia at Perth.
6	(6ct)	W.A. Seccombe	Queensland v Victoria at Albion.
6	(6ct)	M.J. Walsh	Western Australia v South Australia at Perth.
6	(6ct)	W.A. Seccombe	Queensland v New South Wales at Brisbane.
5	(5ct)	B.J. Haddin	New South Wales v Victoria at Richmond.
5	(5ct)	A.C. Gilchrist	Western Australia v West Indians at Perth.
5	(5ct)	A.C. Gilchrist	Australia v West Indies at Brisbane.
5	(5ct)	M.J. Walsh	Western Australia v New South Wales at Perth.
5	(5ct)	W.A. Seccombe	Queensland v Western Australia at Brisbane.

Most Dismissals in a Match

9	(8ct, 1st)	R.D. Jacobs	West Indies v Australia at Melbourne.
9	(8ct, 1st)	W.A. Seccombe	Queensland v New South Wales at Brisbane.
9	(9ct)	M.J. Walsh	Western Australia v South Australia at Perth.
8	(7ct, 1st)	A.C. Gilchrist	Australia v West Indies at Brisbane.
7	(6ct)	W.A. Seccombe	Queensland v Western Australia at Perth.
7	(7ct)	W.A. Seccombe	Queensland v Victoria at Albion.
7	(7ct)	A.C. Gilchrist	Western Australia v West Indians at Perth.
7	(7ct)	R.D. Jacobs	West Indies v Australia at Adelaide.
7	(7ct)	M.J. Walsh	Western Australia v New South Wales at Perth.
7	(7ct)	W.A. Seccombe	Queensland v Victoria at Albion.

FIRST-CLASS AVERAGES, 2000-01

BATTING

* Denotes not out. † Denotes left-handed batsman.

	M	I	NO	R	HS	100s	50s	Avge	Ct/St
† J.C. Adams (West Indians)	8	15	2	213	49	0	0	16.38	7
N.T. Adcock (SAust)	2	4	0	103	48	0	0	25.75	1
M.A. Anderson (Qld)	3	3	1	7	5	0	0	3.50	1
† J. Angel (WAust)	9	11	2	70	37	0	0	7.78	0
J.L. Arnberger (Vic)	12	22	1	1,006	173	2	7	47.90	12
D.S. Berry (Vic)	10	17	1	230	61	0	1	14.38	36/1
† M.G. Bevan (NSW)	8	13	2	557	119	2	2	50.64	4
A.J. Bichel (Qld/Aust A/Aust)	10	13	1	278	61	0	1	23.17	7
M.I. Black (West Indians)	5	9	2	20	11	0	0	2.86	1
G.S. Blewett (SAust)	9	18	1	1,162	260*	3	6	68.35	13
C.J. Borgas (SAust)	2	4	0	28	12	0	0	7.00	0
N.W. Bracken (NSW)	6	7	3	42	30	0	0	10.50	5
S.D. Bradstreet (NSW)	2	4	2	117	60	0	1	58.50	4
C.O. Browne (West Indians)	2	3	1	42	21	0	0	21.00	8
R.J. Campbell (WAust)	5	9	0	167	35	0	0	18.56	10
S.L. Campbell (West Indians)	8	15	0	372	119	1	2	24.80	7
† L.A. Carseldine (Qld)	5	6	0	82	26	0	0	13.67	4
S.R. Cary (WAust)	1	1	1	2	2*	0	0	–	2
J.L. Cassell (Qld)	8	13	1	352	136	1	1	29.33	5
† S. Chanderpaul (West Indians)	3	6	1	177	62*	0	1	35.40	3
A.M. Clark (NSW)	4	4	0	53	24	0	0	13.25	2
S.R. Clark (NSW)	3	5	1	25	13	0	0	6.25	1
M.J. Clarke (NSW)	5	8	1	179	106	1	0	25.57	4
† S.G. Clingeleffer (Tas)	10	14	1	203	50	0	1	15.62	21/4
M.D. Colegrave (Tas)	1	2	0	6	5	0	0	6.00	0
† S.H. Cook (NSW)	1	2	1	6	6*	0	0	6.00	0

	M	I	NO	R	HS	100s	50s	Avge	Ct/St
J. Cox (Tas/Aust A)	11	21	3	1,170	160	5	4	65.00	8
† S. A. J. Craig (Vic)	5	8	0	102	35	0	0	12.75	7
B. N. Creevey (Qld)	1	1	0	0	0	0	0	0.00	0
† G. I. Cullen (WAust)	1	1	0	5	5	0	0	5.00	1
† A. C. Dale (Qld)	11	12	4	139	45*	0	0	17.38	3
C. J. Davies (SAust)	2	4	1	72	52*	0	1	24.00	1
J. M. Davison (Vic)	5	6	0	54	33	0	0	9.00	1
J. H. Dawes (Qld)	9	8	1	55	18	0	0	7.86	2
† S. A. Deitz (SAust)	9	18	0	608	114	2	2	33.78	9
G. J. Denton (Tas)	1	2	2	8	5*	0	0	–	0
† M. J. Di Venuto (Tas)	10	18	1	466	86	0	5	27.41	15
M. Dillon (West Indians)	6	12	0	76	27	0	0	6.33	2
A. G. Downton (Tas)	6	5	0	51	17	0	0	10.20	2
J. A. Dykes (Tas)	4	8	0	125	32	0	0	15.63	3
† M. T. G. Elliott (Vic)	7	14	1	524	98	0	5	40.31	9
D. A. Fitzgerald (SAust)	7	14	0	356	107	1	2	25.43	4
D. W. Fleming (Vic)	3	3	1	28	15	0	0	14.00	0
D. Ganga (West Indians)	7	13	0	145	32	0	0	11.15	2
† A. C. Gilchrist (WAust/Aust)	8	11	2	531	109*	2	3	59.00	29/3
J. N. Gillespie (SAust/Aust)	5	5	0	99	51	0	1	19.80	3
M. W. Goodwin (WAust)	7	13	0	145	59	0	1	11.15	5
B. J. Haddin (NSW/Aust A)	9	15	1	397	93	0	3	28.36	26/3
P. Q. Harper (Vic)	1	1	0	15	15	0	0	15.00	1
M. A. Harrity (SAust)	8	13	8	25	10*	0	0	5.00	1
I. J. Harvey (Vic)	8	14	0	481	100	1	2	34.36	6
† M. L. Hayden (Qld/Aust)	8	13	1	537	118*	1	3	44.75	10
† B. H. Higgins (SAust)	3	6	0	222	65	0	3	37.00	0
† M. A. Higgs (NSW)	7	11	1	413	181*	1	1	41.30	8
† D. F. Hills (Tas)	9	17	0	395	120	1	2	23.24	5
† W. W. Hinds (West Indians)	6	11	0	322	70	0	2	29.27	4
B. J. Hodge (Vic/Aust A)	13	23	3	1,129	134*	5	3	56.45	7
† G. B. Hogg (WAust)	3	4	1	65	35*	0	0	21.67	1
D. A. Horsley (NSW)	1	2	2	11	7*	0	0	–	2
† M. E. Hussey (SAust)	11	21	1	605	137	1	1	30.25	13
† M. W. H. Inness (Vic/Aust A)	13	14	6	20	8	0	0	2.50	3
† R. D. Jacobs (West Indians)	7	13	1	472	131	1	2	39.33	20/1
† P. A. Jaques (NSW)	1	2	0	63	40	0	0	31.50	1
K. C. B. Jeremy (West Indians)	2	2	1	16	9	0	0	16.00	0
† B. A. Johnson (SAust)	5	10	0	260	68	0	2	26.00	2
B. P. Julian (WAust)	9	16	1	367	78	0	2	24.47	4
S. J. Jurgensen (Tas)	2	2	0	13	13	0	0	6.50	0
S. J. Karppinen (WAust)	1	2	0	18	17	0	0	9.00	0
M. S. Kasprowicz (Qld)	1	0	0	0	0	0	0	–	0
† S. M. Katich (WAust/Aust A)	12	23	5	1,282	228*	6	3	71.22	12
M. Klinger (Vic)	9	15	2	358	99*	0	3	27.54	6
† S. P. Kremerskothen (Tas)	9	13	1	435	81	0	2	36.25	6
† J. L. Langer (Aust/Aust)	8	13	0	313	80	0	2	24.08	7
† B. C. Lara (West Indians)	7	13	0	591	231	2	0	45.46	7
S. G. Law (Qld)	11	15	2	814	161	2	4	62.62	10
B. Lee (NSW/Aust)	4	5	2	151	62*	0	1	50.33	1
S. Lee (NSW)	8	11	0	365	114	1	2	33.18	7
† D. S. Lehmann (SAust)	8	16	2	645	146	1	3	46.07	4
M. L. Lewis (Vic)	7	9	5	44	11*	0	0	11.00	1
M. L. Love (Qld/Aust A)	10	15	3	910	172*	3	5	75.83	12
S. C. G. MacGill (NSW/Aust)	10	13	0	89	19	0	0	12.71	6
† J. P. Maher (Qld/Aust A)	12	21	3	1,142	175	4	3	63.44	16
G. J. Mail (NSW)	7	12	0	435	176	1	2	36.25	6
G. A. Manou (SAust)	9	16	2	200	53	0	1	14.29	18/2
D. J. Marsh (Tas)	9	16	3	514	110	1	3	39.54	12
† S. E. Marsh (WAust)	3	5	1	102	46	0	0	25.50	2
D. R. Martyn (WAust/Aust A/Aust) .	8	15	4	746	122	2	4	67.82	10

	M	I	NO	R	HS	100s	50s	Avge	Ct/St
† S. R. Mason (Tas)	1	2	0	9	9	0	0	4.50	0
G. D. McGrath (NSW/Aust)	6	5	0	28	13	0	0	5.60	1
P. E. McIntyre (SAust)	7	12	2	70	29*	0	0	7.00	0
N. A. M. McLean (West Indians)	6	12	0	79	17	0	0	6.58	1
S. W. Meuleman (WAust)	2	4	0	77	46	0	0	19.25	0
C. R. Miller (Vic/Aust)	8	11	3	128	37*	0	0	16.00	3
† M. C. Miller (SAust)	2	3	0	25	15	0	0	8.33	0
T. M. Moody (WAust)	9	14	2	324	57	0	2	27.00	5
J. Moss (Vic)	3	5	0	136	62	0	1	27.20	0
† M. P. Mott (Vic)	12	22	1	695	154	1	3	33.10	15
† M. V. Nagamootoo (West Indians)	2	4	0	128	68	0	1	32.00	0
† B. P. Nash (Qld)	4	6	0	68	44	0	0	11.33	1
D. A. Nash (NSW/Aust A)	9	14	1	255	46	0	0	19.62	2
M. J. Nicholson (WAust)	8	11	2	241	54	0	1	26.78	5
S. Nikitaras (WAust)	1	1	0	0	0	0	0	0.00	0
A. A. Noffke (Qld)	4	4	1	55	43	0	0	18.33	1
† M. J. North (WAust)	6	11	0	277	54	0	2	25.18	4
S. J. O'Leary (Qld)	7	7	3	42	19	0	0	10.50	5
† B. J. Oldroyd (WAust/Aust A)	5	8	5	25	9	0	0	8.33	4
B. C. Oliver (Vic)	1	1	0	0	0	0	0	0.00	1
M. D. Pascoe (Qld)	1	1	1	20	20*	0	0	–	1
† C. J. Peake (Vic)	2	4	1	53	33	0	0	17.67	3
C. T. Perren (Qld)	6	9	1	304	112	1	1	38.00	6
M. J. Phelps (NSW)	1	2	0	70	40	0	0	35.00	6
N. S. Pilon (NSW)	1	1	0	8	8	0	0	8.00	5
T. A. Pinnington (Tas)	1	2	0	9	5	0	0	4.50	0
R. T. Ponting (Tas/Aust)	7	12	3	726	233	2	3	80.67	5
P. R. Reiffel (Vic)	11	17	3	337	70	0	2	24.07	3
C. J. Richards (NSW)	5	9	1	177	69	0	2	22.13	0
P. J. Roach (Vic)	2	4	2	69	51*	0	1	34.50	5
P. C. Rofe (SAust)	3	6	1	48	18	0	0	9.60	0
† G. C. Rummans (NSW)	3	4	1	80	46	0	0	26.67	0
D. J. Saker (Tas)	10	14	3	133	34*	0	0	12.09	1
M. N. Samuels (West Indians)	4	7	1	181	60*	0	1	30.17	2
R. R. Sarwan (West Indians)	5	10	0	88	51	0	1	8.80	2
W. A. Seccombe (Qld)	11	14	2	270	52	0	1	22.50	57/1
M. J. Slater (NSW/Aust)	7	11	1	491	100	1	4	49.10	3
M. J. Smith (SAust)	3	6	0	166	76	0	1	27.67	1
J. Stewart (NSW)	1	2	0	35	23	0	0	17.50	0
C. E. L. Stuart (West Indians)	4	7	3	50	15*	0	0	12.50	1
† B. A. Swain (SAust)	6	11	1	60	21*	0	0	6.00	1
G. G. Swan (WAust)	7	8	5	8	8*	0	0	2.67	4
A. Symonds (Qld)	9	13	1	558	133	1	2	46.50	6
B. S. Targett (Tas)	3	6	2	30	15	0	0	7.50	2
S. B. Tubb (Tas)	1	2	0	42	42	0	0	21.00	0
B. P. Van Deinsen (NSW)	5	9	0	125	29	0	0	13.89	8
J. M. Vaughan (SAust)	5	10	2	350	131*	1	2	43.75	3
G. R. Vimpani (Vic)	1	2	0	26	22	0	0	13.00	1
C. A. Walsh (West Indians)	6	12	4	23	9	0	0	2.88	0
M. J. Walsh (WAust)	8	14	1	195	50	0	1	15.00	33/3
S. K. Warne (Vic)	2	2	0	39	27	0	0	19.50	2
S. R. Watson (Tas)	5	8	2	309	105	1	2	51.50	1
M. E. Waugh (NSW/Aust)	7	11	1	590	152	2	3	59.00	13
S. R. Waugh (NSW/Aust)	6	9	1	394	121*	2	0	49.25	1
C. L. White (Vic)	2	3	2	12	11	0	0	12.00	0
B. A. Williams (WAust)	3	3	1	13	11*	0	0	6.50	2
L. Williams (SAust)	2	4	0	35	16	0	0	8.75	0
P. Wilson (SAust)	5	7	1	54	22	0	0	9.00	1
D. G. Wright (Tas)	6	8	4	47	16*	0	0	11.75	5
B. E. Young (SAust)	1	2	1	85	71*	0	1	85.00	1
† S. Young (Tas)	10	17	4	433	83*	0	3	33.31	5

BOWLING

† *Denotes left-arm bowler.*

	O	M	R	W	BB	5W/i	10W/m	Avge
† J.C. Adams (West Indians)	117.4	24	331	9	2/43	0	0	110.33
N.T. Adcock (SAust)	30	3	119	0	–	0	0	–
† M.A. Anderson (Qld)	111.2	28	271	4	2/39	0	0	67.75
J. Angel (WAust)	333.3	109	867	37	5/78	1	0	23.43
J.L. Arnberger (Vic)	1	0	3	0	–	0	0	–
† M.G. Bevan (NSW)	11	1	49	2	2/23	0	0	24.50
A.J. Bichel (Qld/Aust A/Aust)	400.3	99	1,144	49	5/60	3	0	23.35
M.I. Black (West Indians)	142.2	26	494	12	4/83	0	0	41.17
G.S. Blewett (SAust)	86	19	287	5	1/18	0	0	57.40
† N.W. Bracken (NSW)	240.1	65	688	29	5/22	2	0	23.72
S.D. Bradstreet (NSW)	45.5	8	185	6	2/32	0	0	30.83
† L.A. Carseldine (Qld)	41	12	117	0	–	0	0	–
S.R. Cary (WAust)	27	6	75	0	–	0	0	–
† J.L. Cassell (Qld)	3.3	1	7	0	–	0	0	–
A.M. Clark (NSW)	110.1	26	286	6	2/19	0	0	47.67
S.R. Clark (NSW)	89	25	206	8	2/36	0	0	25.75
M.D. Colegrave (Tas)	33.4	5	131	1	1/76	0	0	131.00
S.H. Cook (NSW)	22	6	60	0	–	0	0	–
J. Cox (Tas/Aust A)	2	1	4	0	–	0	0	–
S.A.J. Craig (Vic)	14	3	49	0	–	0	0	–
B.N. Creevey (Qld)	34	9	101	3	3/42	0	0	33.67
A.C. Dale (Qld)	570.3	226	1,076	46	5/37	2	0	23.39
J.M. Davison (Vic)	194.1	61	488	10	4/90	0	0	48.80
J.H. Dawes (Qld)	358.3	101	1,003	49	7/98	3	1	20.47
S.A. Deitz (SAust)	16	1	56	2	2/17	0	0	28.00
G.J. Denton (Tas)	20	3	90	2	2/90	0	0	45.00
M.J. Di Venuto (Tas)	12	5	30	0	–	0	0	–
M. Dillon (West Indies)	195.4	33	683	20	4/76	0	0	34.15
† A.G. Downton (Tas)	161.5	42	548	16	4/51	0	0	34.25
J.A. Dykes (Tas)	5	1	22	0	–	0	0	–
† M.T.G. Elliott (Vic)	2	1	1	0	–	0	0	–
D.W. Fleming (Vic)	68	21	156	4	2/27	0	0	39.00
D. Ganga (West Indians)	1	0	2	0	–	0	0	–
J.N. Gillespie (SAust/Aust)	175	51	463	22	6/40	2	0	21.05
† M.A. Harrity (SAust)	243.3	62	728	23	4/55	0	0	31.65
I.J. Harvey (Vic)	172.2	54	474	17	4/19	0	0	27.88
M.L. Hayden (Qld/Aust)	4	2	9	0	–	0	0	–
† M.A. Higgs (NSW)	113	16	386	4	2/42	0	0	96.50
D.F. Hills (Tas)	4.1	0	20	2	2/20	0	0	10.00
W.W. Hinds (West Indians)	11	3	42	1	1/18	0	0	42.00
B.J. Hodge (Vic/Aust A)	106.1	27	266	13	4/17	0	0	20.46
† G.B. Hogg (WAust)	79	20	205	4	2/78	0	0	51.25
D.A. Horsley (NSW)	22	3	107	1	1/93	0	0	107.00
M.E. Hussey (WAust)	17	4	63	0	–	0	0	–
† M.W.H. Inness (Vic/Aust A)	403.2	126	1,077	43	6/26	2	0	25.05
R.D. Jacobs (West Indians)	2	2	0	0	–	0	0	–
K.C.B. Jeremy (West Indians)	41	8	127	3	2/42	0	0	42.33
B.A. Johnson (SAust)	28	5	96	1	1/29	0	0	96.00
† B.P. Julian (WAust)	266.2	46	934	32	4/87	0	0	29.19
S.J. Jurgensen (Tas)	70.5	12	250	6	4/113	0	0	41.67
S.J. Karppinen (WAust)	27	8	68	5	3/34	0	0	13.60
M.S. Kasprowicz (Qld)	37	7	110	8	5/29	1	0	13.75
† S.M. Katich (WAust/Aust A)	38.2	3	145	3	3/46	0	0	48.33
S.P. Kremerskothen (Tas)	104	18	402	9	3/64	0	0	44.67
S.G. Law (Qld)	15	0	102	0	–	0	0	–
B. Lee (NSW/Aust)	133	40	411	20	5/42	2	0	20.55
S. Lee (NSW)	151.5	40	463	17	4/43	0	0	27.24
† D.S. Lehmann (SAust)	42.3	9	116	3	2/36	0	0	38.67

	O	M	R	W	BB	5Wi	10W/m	Avge
M.L. Lewis (Vic)	246.2	53	772	23	5/57	1	0	33.57
S.C.G. MacGill (NSW/Aust)	453.4	98	1,390	46	7/104	3	0	30.22
G.J. Mail (NSW)	1	0	4	0	–	0	0	–
† D.J. Marsh (Tas)	216	44	720	18	4/80	0	0	40.00
D.R. Martyn (WAust/Aust A/Aust)	59	11	176	0	–	0	0	–
G.D. McGrath (NSW/Aust)	207.5	77	425	23	6/17	1	1	18.48
P.E. McIntyre (SAust)	322.2	66	927	28	5/102	1	0	33.11
N.A.M. McLean (West Indians)	164	27	566	11	2/69	0	0	51.45
C.R. Miller (Vic/Aust)	377.1	104	998	40	5/32	2	1	24.95
M.C. Miller (SAust)	41	8	131	5	2/30	0	0	26.20
T.M. Moody (WAust)	189	61	455	20	5/26	1	0	22.75
J. Moss (Vic)	55	14	164	4	1/17	0	0	41.00
M.P. Mott (Vic)	56.5	9	215	4	2/42	0	0	53.75
M.V. Nagamootoo (West Indians)	58	6	208	3	3/119	0	0	69.33
D.A. Nash (NSW/Aust A)	243.2	56	730	20	4/57	0	0	36.50
M.J. Nicholson (WAust)	289	86	773	25	4/119	0	0	30.92
† S. Nikitaras (WAust)	31	8	91	2	1/25	0	0	45.50
A.A. Noffke (Qld)	152	29	527	15	5/41	1	0	35.13
M.J. North (WAust)	46	8	152	4	2/64	0	0	38.00
S.J. O'Leary (Qld)	172.2	39	568	9	4/105	0	0	63.11
† B.J. Oldroyd (WAust/Aust A)	142.2	37	410	13	4/90	0	0	31.54
B.C. Oliver (Vic)	25	10	45	3	2/13	0	0	15.00
M.D. Pascoe (Qld)	14	3	46	0	–	0	0	–
C.T. Perren (Qld)	7	2	18	0	–	0	0	–
R.T. Ponting (Tas/Aust)	3	1	14	0	–	0	0	–
P.R. Reiffel (Vic)	325.1	84	824	30	4/50	0	0	27.47
C.J. Richards (NSW)	7	5	4	0	–	0	0	–
P.C. Rofe (SAust)	94	31	261	3	2/69	0	0	87.00
D.J. Saker (Tas)	350	66	1,080	26	5/98	1	0	41.54
M.N. Samuels (West Indians)	102.2	18	319	6	3/100	0	0	53.17
M.J. Smith (SAust)	81	19	262	6	4/81	0	0	43.67
† J. Stewart (NSW)	13	2	42	0	–	0	0	–
C.E.L. Stuart (West Indians)	129.3	19	499	13	3/84	0	0	38.38
† B.A. Swain (SAust)	195.3	44	521	17	4/96	0	0	30.65
G.G. Swan (WAust)	223	52	673	18	3/31	0	0	37.39
A. Symonds (Qld)	139.4	28	424	6	2/79	0	0	70.67
B.S. Targett (Tas)	86	21	265	7	5/62	1	0	37.86
† S.B. Tubb (Tas)	14	2	70	0	–	0	0	–
C.A. Walsh (West Indians)	232.4	61	547	15	4/66	0	0	36.47
S.K. Warne (Vic)	47.5	8	140	9	5/49	1	0	15.56
S.R. Watson (Tas)	74	13	289	11	2/22	0	0	26.27
M.E. Waugh (NSW/Aust)	21	5	42	1	1/10	0	0	42.00
S.R. Waugh (NSW/Aust)	6	3	11	0	–	0	0	–
C.L. White (Vic)	44.3	14	136	4	4/65	0	0	34.00
B.A. Williams (WAust)	82.5	22	220	9	3/31	0	0	24.44
L. Williams (SAust)	0.4	0	4	0	–	0	0	–
P. Wilson (SAust)	179.3	62	406	19	4/23	0	0	21.37
D.G. Wright (Tas)	192.1	43	593	22	4/54	0	0	26.95
† B.E. Young (SAust)	31	8	114	0	–	0	0	–
S. Young (Tas)	203.3	63	532	21	4/33	0	0	25.33

INDIVIDUAL SCORES OF 100 AND OVER

There were 66 three-figure innings in 38 first-class matches in 2000-01, 17 less than in 1999-2000 when 42 matches were played. Of these, four were double-hundreds compared with five in 1999-2000. The list includes 57 hundreds hit in the Pura Cup, the same as in 1999-2000.

Denotes not out.

S. M. Katich (6)
105* WAust v Qld, Perth
152 WAust v Tas, Hobart
117 WAust v NSW, North Sydney
101 WAust v Qld, Brisbane
228* WAust v SAust, Perth
102 WAust v Vic, Melbourne

J. Cox (5)
106 Tas v NSW, Hobart
128* Tas v NSW, Hobart
160 Tas v NSW, Sydney
139* Tas v Vic, Hobart
102 Tas v SAust, Hobart

B. J. Hodge (5)
101* Vic v Qld, Albion
134† Vic v West Indians, Melbourne
104 Vic v SAust, Melbourne
111 Vic v Qld, Melbourne
125 Vic v NSW, Sydney

J.P Maher (4)
175 Qld v WAust, Perth
103* Qld v Vic, Albion
150 Aust A v West Indians, Hobart
113 Qld v NSW, Brisbane

G. S. Blewett (3)
260* SAust v Qld, Brisbane
117 SAust v Vic, Adelaide
138 SAust v WAust, Perth

M. L. Love (3)
161* Qld v Tas, Albion
126 Qld v Vic, Melbourne
172* Qld v Tas, Hobart

J. L. Arnberger (2)
100 Vic v Qld, Melbourne
173 Vic v Tas, Hobart

M. G. Bevan (2)
119 NSW v Tas, Sydney
111 NSW v Qld, Sydney

S. A. Deitz (2)
114 SAust v Vic, Melbourne
106 SAust v Qld, Brisbane

A. C. Gilchrist (2)
109* WAust v Qld, Perth
102 WAust v SAust, Adelaide

B. C. Lara (2)
231 West Indians v Aust A, Hobart
182 West Indies v Aust, Adelaide

S. G. Law (2)
128 Qld v WAust, Perth
161 Qld v SAust, Adelaide

D. R. Martyn (2)
122 WAust v SAust, Adelaide
122 WAust v Tas, Hobart

R. T. Ponting (2)
233 Tas v Qld, Albion
187* Tas v NSW, Hobart

M. E. Waugh (2)
152 NSW v Tas, Hobart
119 Aust v West Indies, Perth

S. R. Waugh (2)
121* Aust v West Indies, Melbourne
103 Aust v West Indies, Sydney

The following each played one three-figure innings:

S. L. Campbell, 119, West Indians v WAust, Perth; J. L. Cassell, 136, Qld v Tas, Hobart; M. J. Clarke, 106, NSW v Vic, Sydney.
D. A. Fitzgerald, 107, SAust v NSW, Adelaide.
I. J. Harvey, 100, Vic v Qld, Albion; M. L. Hayden, 118*, Qld v Vic, Albion; M. A. Higgs, 181*, NSW v Qld, Sydney; D. F. Hills, 120, Tas v Vic, Hobart; M. E. Hussey, 137, WAust v Vic, Melbourne.
R. D. Jacobs, 131, West Indians v Aust A, Hobart.
S. Lee, 114, NSW v Qld, Sydney; D. S. Lehmann, 146, SAust v NSW, Adelaide.
G. J. Mail, 176, NSW v Tas, Sydney; D. J. Marsh, 110, Tas v WAust, Hobart; M. P. Mott, 154, Vic v WAust, Melbourne.
C. T. Perren, 112, Qld v SAust, Adelaide.
M. J. Slater, 100, NSW v Tas, Hobart; A. Symonds, 133, Qld v Tas, Albion.
J. M. Vaughan, 131*, SAust v WAust, Adelaide.
S. R. Watson, 105, Tas v SAust, Hobart.

TEN OR MORE WICKETS IN A MATCH

G. D. McGrath (1)
10/27 Aust v West Indies, Brisbane

C. R. Miller (1)
10/113 Aust v West Indies, Adelaide

J. H. Dawes (1)
10/141 Qld v SAust, Adelaide

FIVE OR MORE WICKETS IN AN INNINGS

A. J. Bichel (3)
5/126   Qld v Tas, Albion
5/60   Aust v West Indies, Melbourne
5/74   Qld v WAust, Brisbane

S. C. G. MacGill (3)
7/104   Aust v West Indies, Sydney
5/125   NSW v Tas, Sydney
5/78   NSW v Qld, Brisbane

J. H. Dawes (3)
6/98   Qld v Vic, Albion
6/19   Qld v WAust, Brisbane
7/98   Qld v SAust, Adelaide

N. W. Bracken (2)
5/22   NSW v WAust, North Sydney
5/68   NSW v Vic, Sydney

A. C. Dale (2)
5/41   Qld v WAust, Perth
5/37   Qld v NSW, Brisbane

J. N. Gillespie (2)
5/89   Aust v West Indies, Adelaide
6/40   Aust v West Indies, Melbourne

M. W. H. Inness (2)
6/26   Vic v West Indians, Melbourne
6/26   Vic v SAust, Melbourne

B. Lee (2)
5/42   NSW v Vic, Richmond
5/61   Aust v West Indies, Perth

C. R. Miller (2)
5/81   Aust v West Indies, Adelaide
5/32   Aust v West Indies, Adelaide

The following each took five wickets or more in an innings on one occasion:

J. Angel, 5/78, WAust v Tas, Perth.
M. S. Kasprowicz, 5/29, Qld v Tas, Hobart.
M. L. Lewis, 5/57, Vic v Qld, Brisbane.
G. D. McGrath, 6/17, Aust v West Indies, Brisbane.
P. E. McIntyre, 5/102, SAust v NSW, Adelaide.
T. M. Moody, 5/26, WAust v NSW, Perth.
A. A. Noffke, 5/41, Qld v Vic, Brisbane.
D. J. Saker, 5/98, Tas v WAust, Hobart.
B. S Targett, 5/62, Tas v SAust, Adelaide.
S. K. Warne, 5/49, Vic v WAust, Perth.

AUSTRALIAN DOMESTIC FIRST-CLASS SEASON, 2000-01

By WARWICK FRANKS

While the same two states again contested the Pura Cup final, the competition was far from a carbon copy of the 1999-2000 season. Certainly, Queensland continued their domination for reasons which Martin Rogers explores earlier in this volume. Suffice it to say here that the men from the north have formed a devastatingly effective unit which, having at last broken through to claim the Sheffield Shield, now appears able to win seemingly at will. As has become customary, Queensland's quick bowlers were incisively effective, Joe Dawes, Adam Dale and Andy Bichel being the three leading wicket-takers in the competition. The batting was similarly productive, and Queenslanders provided four of the 12 highest batting aggregates. Two salutary examples of this richness occurred early in the season. Against Tasmania, when Queensland needed 373 in less than a day, Martin Love and Andrew Symonds joined in a fourth-wicket partnership of 261 from 42 overs in 156 minutes to lead their side to an unlikely victory. Less than a fortnight later, against Victoria, the Queenslanders needed 229 to win in less than two sessions; this time, Matthew Hayden and Jimmy Maher scored the runs speedily and attractively.

Victoria again won the right to contest the final, despite a shaky beginning and conclusion to the season. Their first two matches yielded nothing and they could muster only four points from the final three games, a lack of consistency which contrasted with the relentlessness of the Queenslanders. After two seasons at the bottom of the competition, New South Wales showed a considerable improvement. But for prolonged rain in their penultimate game they may have even made the final, although consistency was still not a hallmark of their performance. Tasmania found form too late but finished confidently with three successive outright wins to share third position with New South Wales. Western Australia fell from grace suddenly and swiftly and had their worst season since 1989-90, while South Australia occupied last position for the third time since winning the competition in 1995-96.

continued over

2000-01 POINTS TABLE

	Played	Won	Lost	Drawn	1st-inns Points	Points	Quotient
Queensland	10	6	1	3	4	40	1.386
Victoria	10	4	3	3	8	32	1.026
Tasmania	10	3	4	3	4	22	0.950
New South Wales	10	3	3	4	4	22	0.911
Western Australia	10	2	4	4	4	16	0.986
South Australia	10	2	5	3	2	14	0.823

Outright win = 6 pts; lead on first innings in a drawn or lost game = 2 pts.

Quotient = runs per wicket scored divided by runs per wicket conceded.

Under Australian Cricket Board playing conditions, a penalty of one run for a no-ball and a wide shall be scored. This penalty shall stand in addition to any other runs which are scored or awarded.

The individual performances gave pause for real consideration. The Australian team has been through a period of success and stability which have naturally fed off one another. The team has been so set that only two specialist batsmen, Matthew Elliott and Darren Lehmann, have made their Test debuts in the last five years. The ageing of the team may now see it on the cusp of change and it will be interesting to see the extent to which performance in the domestic competition is a reliable guide to finding capable replacements. Two of the previous season's consistent performers, Elliott and Michael Hussey, not only failed to advance but were not offered Australian Cricket Board contracts. Greg Blewett headed the aggregates but has disappeared from the national side, while the perennial claims to higher selection of Jamie Cox seem as though they will continue to go unheeded, despite his amassing over 1,000 runs. Martin Love continued to be a model of satisfying consistency and was awarded his first ACB contract ahead of the other consistent run-makers for the season of similar ages in Brad Hodge, Jimmy Maher and Jason Arnberger. Restored to health, Simon Katich scored prolifically and was still the most obviously accomplished and authoritative younger batsman in the country, although, at 26, he is at an age when Australia's most successful Test batsmen were well set in their careers. Of the younger brigade, coaches point to Shane Watson of Tasmania, Michael Klinger of Victoria and Michael Clarke of New South Wales as batsmen of outstanding promise, and it will be a test of this competition as to whether it can temper their mettle for the future.

The bowling, too, was dominated by the quicker men of experience, particularly the Queenslanders mentioned earlier. Nathan Bracken's potential was acknowledged by his selection in the Australian limited-overs side as he pulled ahead of Mathew Inness as that most useful of cricketing possessions, the left-arm quick bowler. Similarly, Ashley Noffke was properly rewarded for his potential and final performance with an Australian Cricket Board contract. Once again, however, there was a lamentable dearth of quality spin bowling. Only Stuart MacGill took more than 30 wickets, although the appearance of Victorian schoolboy leg-spinner Cameron White late in the season was a welcome sign, even if he was consigned to the duties of 12th man in the final.

The renaming of the competition has not been embraced wholeheartedly, with many media organisations still using forms of words which ignore the sponsor's presence. Despite the Australian Cricket Board's official obliteration of the old name, it seems obvious that the appellation of "Sheffield Shield" still has a stubbornly vigorous life. To recognise this fact and to restore it into the title of the competition would seem to make both cricketing and commercial sense.

PURA CUP FINAL, 2000-01

QUEENSLAND v VICTORIA

At Brisbane Cricket Ground, Brisbane, March 23, 24, 25, 26, 27, 2001. Queensland won by four wickets. Toss: Victoria.

This match offered First-class cricket at its most tense and unyielding as each side fought tenaciously to establish its supremacy. Ultimately, the telling factor in Queensland's second successive Final victory over Victoria was being able to dismiss their opponents so cheaply on the first day. Victoria's total of 176 was just not enough, and Queensland were always in the ascendancy thereafter; another 70 runs could have allowed Victoria to exert more crucial pressure in the final innings.

Andy Bichel quickly demonstrated his potency by removing Matthew Elliott and Matthew Mott early, which left Jason Arnberger and Brad Hodge to attempt a rescue operation with a second-wicket stand of 73 in 132 minutes. A decisive period came during mid-afternoon when Ashley Noffke dismissed Hodge, Michael Klinger and Jonathan Moss in the space of 17 scoreless balls, a spell which split the Victorian innings apart at the seams. Despite Arnberger's prolonged and plucky resistance over 283 minutes and 199 balls, too much of the other batting was timid and tentative in the face of a four-pronged pace attack, whose aggression and accuracy had wrapped up the visitors' innings by an hour before stumps. Noffke showed the benefit of being schooled by his experienced colleagues as he exploited a pitch which had plenty of bounce but not much other movement. He conveyed the impression of knowing exactly what to do in the conditions while bowling well within himself.

Forty minutes later, Noffke found himself acting as nightwatchman. Next day, he continued his vigil for an ultimate 254 minutes and 204 balls, during which he showed both defensive competence and application. By tea, with the scoreboard at three for 152, Queensland were looking set for a big lead, but immediately afterwards Hodge removed Noffke and Stuart Law with successive balls, a jolt from which the innings never really recovered. The most eye-catching innings came from Clinton Perren, who batted with aplomb in making an assured 56 in 139 minutes from 103 balls. The bustling Michael Lewis bowled with considerable pugnacity in claiming his best-ever return, while Hodge's off-spin was treated with respect and caution.

The Victorians then set themselves to bat with the most rigid application in trying to clear the arrears with as few losses as possible and then attempting to score enough runs to put pressure on the home side in the final innings. The policy was only partially successful; Mott eschewed anything faintly resembling a stroke for 178 minutes and 141 balls, while Elliott's resistance assumed a monumental quality as it spread over three days, 452 minutes and 340 balls. Surprisingly in the circumstances, he sent 12 of those balls to the boundary. On the other hand, the Queensland bowlers were able to keep chipping away to prevent a match-winning partnership from developing. In the end, it took Darren Berry's experience and skill to produce 61 (133 minutes, 98 balls and nine fours), which left the home batsmen a day and a half to score 224 runs.

A final day of aching tension began with Queensland needing a seemingly comfortable 87 with eight wickets in hand, but Martin Love's calm and composed innings (184 minutes and 144 balls) came to an immediate end with a spectacular catch in the gully. Next ball, Law, on a king pair, was controversially ruled not out by the third umpire after a supremely confident appeal for a diving catch at third slip by Klinger. The Queensland captain was subsequently caught off a no-ball and dropped twice as he rode his considerable luck in guiding his team home to a well-earned victory. A particular delight of this match was the impeccable performances behind the stumps by both Wade Seccombe and Berry, displays which demonstrated amply why many knowledgeable judges rate them as Australia's best two keepers.

Man of the Final: A. A. Noffke. *Attendance:* 15,281.
Close of play: First day, Queensland (1) 1-37 (Maher 22, Noffke 4); Second day, Victoria (2) 0-2 (Arnberger 2, Elliott 0); Third day, Victoria (2) 4-172 (Elliott 88, Moss 5); Fourth day, Queensland (2) 2-137 (Love 50, Perren 25).

Victoria

M. T. G. Elliott c Maher b Bichel	3	– (2) c Cassell b Bichel 98
J. L. Arnberger c Seccombe b Dawes	63	– (1) c Seccombe b Dale 33
M. P. Mott c Seccombe b Bichel	4	– b Dale 19
B. J. Hodge c Seccombe b Noffke	47	– c Perren b Bichel 3
M. Klinger c Seccombe b Noffke	0	– lbw b Dawes 9
J. Moss b Noffke	0	– c Seccombe b Noffke 19
†D. S. Berry c Law b Bichel	2	– c Dawes b Bichel 61
*P. R. Reiffel b Noffke	23	run out (Dawes/Seccombe) 18
J. M. Davison c Perren b Dawes	10	– c Perren b Noffke 10
M. L. Lewis c Dale b Noffke	11	– not out 2
M. W. H. Inness not out	1	– c Seccombe b Bichel 0
L-b 6, n-b 6	12	L-b 1, w 1, n-b 15 17

(75.4 overs, 302 mins)   176   (132.4 overs, 547 mins)   289
Fall: 4 16 89 89 89 112 149   Fall: 49 122 140 149 198 215 260
        153 175 176   287 289 289

Bowling: *First Innings*—Bichel 17–4–42–3; Dale 23–10–34–0; Dawes 17.4–4–53–2; Noffke 18–7–41–5. *Second Innings*—Bichel 30.4–12–44–4; Dawes 28–11–55–1; Noffke 28–7–79–2; Dale 39–14–73–2; Law 7–0–37–0.

Queensland

J. L. Cassell c Elliott b Lewis	9	– lbw b Inness 15
J. P. Maher c Berry b Lewis	25	– c Berry b Inness 37
A. A. Noffke c Elliott b Hodge	43	
M. L. Love c Berry b Lewis	24	– (3) c Mott b Reiffel 52
C. T. Perren c Mott b Lewis	56	– (4) run out (Davison/Berry) 41
*S. G. Law lbw b Hodge	0	– (5) not out 47
B. P. Nash b Reiffel	10	– (6) c Berry b Moss 0
†W. A. Seccombe not out	33	– (7) c Hodge b Inness 12
A. J. Bichel c Hodge b Moss	28	– (8) not out 6
A. C. Dale lbw b Hodge	4	
J. H. Dawes b Lewis	0	
L-b 2, n-b 8	10	B 4, l-b 4, n-b 6 14

(99 overs, 401 mins)   242   (80.3 overs)   (6 wkts) 224
Fall: 22 41 88 152 152 174 174 224 239 242   Fall: 27 76 139 169 169 197

Bowling: *First Innings*—Reiffel 17–4–45–1; Inness 22–9–51–0; Lewis 23–9–57–5; Davison 12–4–29–0; Moss 9–1–24–1; Hodge 12–7–19–3; Mott 4–1–15–0. *Second Innings*—Lewis 18.3–1–82–0; Inness 25–8–48–3; Hodge 5–0–16–0; Reiffel 16–4–34–1; Davison 8–3–19–0; Moss 8–3–17–1.

Umpires: S. J. Davis and S. J. A. Taufel.
TV Umpire: P. D. Parker.

STATISTICS, 2000-01

			For			Against	
	M	Runs	Wickets	Avge	Runs	Wickets	Avge
New South Wales	10	4,085	135	30.26	4,485	135	33.22
Queensland	11	5,339	134	39.84	5,350	184	29.07
South Australia	10	4,792	163	29.40	4,252	119	35.73
Tasmania	10	5,100	151	33.77	5,171	146	35.42
Victoria	11	5,336	173	30.84	5,234	169	30.97
Western Australia	10	4,739	157	30.18	4,899	160	30.62

OVERS BOWLED AND RUNS SCORED, 2000-01

	Overs bowled per hour	Runs scored/ 100 balls
New South Wales.............	15.63	52.50
Queensland..................	15.55	53.07
South Australia..............	15.41	46.06
Tasmania...................	15.80	48.00
Victoria....................	15.79	47.79
Western Australia............	16.78	50.50

LEADING BATTING AVERAGES, 2000-01

(Qualification: 500 runs)

	M	I	NO	R	HS	100s	50s	Avge
M.L. Love (Qld)	9	14	3	834	172*	3	4	75.82
S.M. Katich (WAust).................	10	19	3	1,145	228*	6	2	71.56
G.S. Blewett (SAust)	9	18	1	1,162	260*	3	6	68.35
J. Cox (Tas)	10	19	3	1,070	160	5	3	66.88
S.G. Law (Qld)	11	15	2	814	161	2	4	62.62
D.R. Martyn (WAust)	5	9	0	546	122	2	3	60.67
J.P. Maher (Qld)	11	19	3	946	175	3	3	59.13
B.J. Hodge (Vic)	11	20	2	973	125	4	3	54.06
M.G. Bevan (NSW)	8	13	2	557	119	2	2	50.64
A. Symonds (Qld)	9	13	1	558	133	1	2	46.50

LEADING BOWLING AVERAGES, 2000-01

(Qualification: 15 wickets)

	M	O	Mdns	R	W	BB	5W/i	10W/m	Avge
J.H. Dawes (Qld)	9	358.3	101	1003	49	7/98	3	1	20.47
P. Wilson (SAust)	5	179.3	62	406	19	4/23	0	0	21.37
A.J. Bichel (Qld)	7	318.2	80	872	40	5/74	2	0	21.80
A.C. Dale (Qld)	11	570.3	226	1076	46	5/37	2	1	23.39
J. Angel (WAust)	9	333.3	109	867	37	5/78	1	0	23.43
N.W. Bracken (NSW)	6	240.1	65	688	29	5/22	2	0	23.72
S. Young (Tas)	10	203.3	63	532	21	4/33	0	0	25.33
D.G. Wright (Tas)	6	192.1	43	593	22	4/54	0	0	26.95
S. Lee (NSW)	8	151.5	40	463	17	4/43	0	0	27.24
P.R. Reiffel (Vic)	11	325.1	84	824	30	4/50	0	0	27.47

MOST CATCHES, 2000-01

	M	Ct
J. P. Maher (Qld)	16	22
M. J. Di Venuto (Tas)	15	20
G. S. Blewett (SAust)	13	18
M. E. Hussey (WAust)	12	20
D. J. Marsh (Tas)	12	18
J. L. Arnberger (Vic)	11	22
M. P. Mott (Vic)	11	22
S. M. Katich (WAust)	10	20
S. G. Law (Qld)	10	22
M. L. Love (Qld)	10	18
R. J. Campbell (WAust)	10	10

MOST DISMISSALS, 2000-01

	M	Ct	St	Total
W. A. Seccombe (Qld)	11	57	1	58
D. S. Berry (Vic)	9	31	1	32
M. J. Walsh (WAust)	8	33	3	36
B. J. Haddin (NSW)	8	25	2	27
S. G. Clingeleffer (Tas)	10	21	4	25
G. A. Manou (SAust)	9	18	2	20

AUSTRALIAN DOMESTIC FIRST-CLASS COMPETITION WINNERS

Sheffield Shield

Season	Winner	Season	Winner
1892-93	Victoria	1923-24	Victoria
1893-94	South Australia	1924-25	Victoria
1894-95	Victoria	1925-26	New South Wales
1895-96	New South Wales	1926-27	South Australia
1896-97	New South Wales	1927-28	Victoria
1897-98	Victoria	1928-29	New South Wales
1898-99	Victoria	1929-30	Victoria
1899-00	New South Wales	1930-31	Victoria
1900-01	Victoria	1931-32	New South Wales
1901-02	New South Wales	1932-33	New South Wales
1902-03	New South Wales	1933-34	Victoria
1903-04	New South Wales	1934-35	Victoria
1904-05	New South Wales	1935-36	South Australia
1905-06	New South Wales	1936-37	Victoria
1906-07	New South Wales	1937-38	New South Wales
1907-08	Victoria	1938-39	South Australia
1908-09	New South Wales	1939-40	New South Wales
1909-10	South Australia	1940-41	–
1910-11	New South Wales	1941-42	–
1911-12	New South Wales	1942-43	–
1912-13	South Australia	1943-44	–
1913-14	New South Wales	1944-45	–
1914-15	Victoria	1945-46	–
1915-16	–	1946-47	Victoria
1916-17	–	1947-48	Western Australia
1917-18	–	1949-50	New South Wales
1918-19	–	1950-51	Victoria
1919-20	New South Wales	1951-52	New South Wales
1920-21	New South Wales	1952-53	South Australia
1921-22	Victoria	1953-54	New South Wales
1922-23	New South Wales	1954-55	New South Wales
		1955-56	New South Wales

1956-57	New South Wales	1980-81	Western Australia
1957-58	New South Wales	1981-82	South Australia
1958-59	New South Wales	1982-83	New South Wales
1959-60	New South Wales	1983-84	Western Australia
1960-61	New South Wales	1984-85	New South Wales
1961-62	New South Wales	1985-86	New South Wales
1962-63	Victoria	1986-87	Western Australia
1963-64	South Australia	1987-88	Western Australia
1963-64	South Australia	1988-89	Western Australia
1964-65	New South Wales	1989-90	New South Wales
1965-66	New South Wales	1990-91	Victoria
1966-67	Victoria	1991-92	Western Australia
1967-68	Western Australia	1992-93	New South Wales
1968-69	South Australia	1993-94	New South Wales
1969-70	Victoria	1994-95	Queensland
1970-71	South Australia	1995-96	South Australia
1971-72	Western Australia	1996-97	Queensland
1972-73	Western Australia	1997-98	Western Australia
1973-74	Victoria	1998-99	Western Australia
1974-75	Western Australia		
1975-76	South Australia	**Pura Milk Cup**	
1976-77	Western Australia	1999-00	Queensland
1977-78	Western Australia		
1978-79	Victoria	**Pura Cup**	
1979-80	Victoria	2000-01	Queensland

Note: The Sheffield Shield was not played during World Wars I and II.

FINALS

1982-83	Western Australia lost to New South Wales at Perth by 54 runs.
1983-84	Western Australia defeated Queensland at Perth by four wickets.
1984-85	New South Wales defeated Queensland at Sydney by one wicket.
1985-86	New South Wales drew with Queensland at Sydney.
1986-87	Western Australia drew with Victoria at Perth.
1987-88	Western Australia defeated Queensland at Perth by five wickets.
1988-89	Western Australia drew with South Australia at Perth.
1989-90	New South Wales defeated Queensland at Sydney by 345 runs.
1990-91	Victoria defeated New South Wales at Melbourne by eight wickets.
1991-92	Western Australia defeated New South Wales at Perth by 44 runs.
1992-93	New South Wales defeated Queensland at Sydney by eight wickets.
1993-94	New South Wales defeated Tasmania at Sydney by an innings and 61 runs.
1994-95	Queensland defeated South Australia at Brisbane by an innings and 101 runs.
1995-96	South Australia drew with Western Australia at Adelaide.
1996-97	Western Australia lost to Queensland at Perth by 160 runs.
1997-98	Western Australia defeated Tasmania at Perth by seven wickets.
1998-99	Queensland lost to Western Australia at Brisbane by an innings and 131 runs.
1999-00	Queensland drew with Victoria at Brisbane.
2000-01	Queensland defeated Victoria at Brisbane by four wickets.

Note: Since 1982-83 the winner of the season's competition has been decided by the two top teams at the end of the competition playing a final at the top of the table's choice of venue.

MATCH RESULTS, 1892-93 TO 2000-01

Opponent	Played	Won	Lost	Drawn	Tied
South Australia	669	189	295	184	1
New South Wales	678	292	187	198	1
Victoria	671	249	193	228	1
Queensland	560	154	195	210	1
Western Australia	447	155	127	165	0
Tasmania	217	37	79	101	0
Total	1,621	1,076	1,076	543	2

PLACINGS

	1st	2nd	3rd	4th	5th	6th	Seasons
South Australia	13	21	32	10	19	4	99
New South Wales	42	22	19	9	5	2	99
Victoria	25	33	21	7	6	7	99
Queensland	4	14	15	23	12	1	69
Western Australia	15	7	10	14	8	0	54
Tasmania	0	2	2	6	4	10	24
Total	99	99	99	69	54	24	99

LAST TEN YEARS' PLACINGS

	91-92	92-93	93-94	94-95	95-96	96-97	97-98	98-99	99-00	00-01
South Australia ...	5	5	4	2	1	6	6	4	4	6
New South Wales .	2	1	1	5	5	3	4	6	6	3
Victoria	3	6	5	3	6	5	5	3	2	2
Queensland	4	2	6	1	3	1	3	2	1	1
Western Australia .	1	4	3	4	2	2	1	1	3	5
Tasmania	6	3	2	6	4	4	2	5	5	4

MOST RUNS IN A SEASON

		M	I	NO	R	HS	100s	50s	Avge
G. N. Yallop (Vic)................	1982-83	10	18	0	1,254	246	4	5	69.66
M. G. Bevan (NSW)	1993-94	11	20	5	1,240	203*	5	7	82.67
W. H. Ponsford (Vic)	1927-28	5	8	0	1,217	437	4	1	152.12
D. M. Jones (Vic)	1994-95	10	19	3	1,216	324*	4	3	76.00
G. S. Blewett (SAust)	2000-01	9	18	1	1,162	260*	4	6	68.35
J. Cox (Tas)	1996-97	10	20	1	1,149	143	4	7	60.47
B. A. Richards (SAust)	1970-71	8	13	2	1,145	356	4	3	104.09
S. M. Katich (WAust)	2000-01	10	19	3	1,145	228*	6	2	71.56
J. L. Langer (WAust)	1993-94	10	18	2	1,137	233	1	6	71.06
M. L. Hayden (Qld)..............	1993-94	6	12	3	1,136	173*	7	1	126.22
D. F. Hills (Tas)	1997-98	11	21	1	1,132	265	4	2	56.60
J. D. Siddons (SAust)	1992-93	10	19	2	1,116	197	4	6	65.65
M. T. G. Elliott (Vic)	1995-96	9	17	2	1,116	203	5	3	74.40
D. M. Wellham (NSW)	1982-83	11	20	5	1,109	136*	2	10	73.93
D. S. Lehmann (SAust)	1994-95	11	20	1	1,104	202*	3	6	58.11
D. S. Lehmann (SAust)	1995-96	11	21	1	1,099	161	4	6	54.95
R. B. McCosker (NSW)	1982-83	11	21	3	1,096	124	3	9	60.88
W. H. Ponsford (Vic)	1926-27	5	9	1	1,091	352	5	2	136.37
S. G. Law (Qld)................	1990-91	10	18	4	1,087	142*	3	8	77.64
J. Cox (Tas)...................	2000-01	10	19	3	1,070	160	5	3	66.88
D. S. Lehmann (SAust)	1993-94	10	17	0	1,065	200	4	4	62.65
D. G. Bradman (SAust)...........	1939-40	6	10	2	1,062	267	3	4	132.75
A. D. Ogilvie (Qld)	1977-78	9	18	2	1,060	194	6	2	66.25
T. M. Moody (WAust)	1988-89	11	18	1	1,038	202	4	3	61.06
M. T. G. Elliott (Vic)............	1999-00	10	19	4	1,028	183*	4	4	68.53
K. C. Wessels (Qld)	1981-82	9	15	0	1,015	220	5	2	67.66
D. F. Hills (Tas)................	1993-94	11	21	1	1,015	185*	3	7	50.75
D. W. Hookes (SAust)	1987-88	10	18	1	1,014	132	3	7	59.65
G. M. Wood (WAust)	1987-88	11	16	3	1,014	186*	3	5	78.00
G. S. Chappell (Qld)	1973-74	7	13	2	1,013	180	4	4	92.09
J. Dyson (NSW)	1983-84	10	18	3	1,006	241	3	3	67.07
N. C. O'Neill (NSW)	1957-58	8	14	2	1,005	233	4	3	83.75
M. J. Slater (NSW)	1992-92	9	17	1	1,005	143	3	6	62.81

* Denotes not out.

MOST RUNS IN A CAREER

	M	I	NO	R	HS	100s	50s	Avge
J.D. Siddons (Vic/SAust)....	146	259	21	10,643	245	30	50	44.72
D.S. Lehmann (SAust/Vic) ..	112	203	13	10,164	255	33	43	53.49
D.M. Jones (Vic)	110	194	16	9,622	324*	31	40	54.06
D.W. Hookes (SAust)	120	205	9	9,364	306*	26	44	47.78
R.J. Inverarity (WAust/SAust)	159	275	32	9,341	187	22	46	38.44
J. Cox (Tas)...............	123	226	15	8,941	245	27	38	42.37
D.G. Bradman (NSW/SAust).	62	96	15	8,926	452*	36	20	110.19
T.M. Moody (WAust)	132	228	22	8,853	272	20	46	42.98
G.S. Chappell (SAust/Qld) .	101	173	20	8,762	194	27	44	57.27
S.C. Trimble (Qld)	123	230	13	8,647	252*	22	40	39.85
A.R. Border (NSW/Qld)	108	181	19	8,497	200	19	47	52.45
L.E. Favell (SAust).........	121	220	4	8,269	164	20	43	38.28
D.C. Boon (Tas)	119	203	7	8,029	227	20	43	40.96
I.M. Chappell (SAust)	89	157	13	7,665	205*	22	45	53.22
A.M.J. Hilditch (NSW/SAust)	109	192	11	7,613	230	18	41	42.06
S.G. Law (Qld)	114	188	22	7,532	216	22	38	45.37
M.R.J. Veletta (WAust).....	114	198	20	7,306	262	18	40	41.04
P.J.P. Burge (Qld)	83	138	12	7,084	283	22	31	56.22
G.R. Marsh (WAust)	100	175	12	7,009	355*	21	28	43.00

* Denotes not out.

HIGHEST PARTNERSHIPS FOR EACH WICKET

431	for 1st	M.R.J. Veletta and G.R. Marsh	
		Western Australia v South Australia at Perth	1989-90
378	for 2nd	L.A. Marks and K.D. Walters	
		New South Wales v South Australia at Adelaide	1964-65
390*	for 3rd	J.M. Weiner and J.K. Moss	
		Victoria v Western Australia at St Kilda	1981-82
462*	for 4th	D.W. Hookes and W.B. Phillips	
		South Australia v Tasmania at Adelaide	1986-87
464*	for 5th	M.E. Waugh and S.R. Waugh	
		New South Wales v Western Australia at Perth	1990-91
332	for 6th	N.G. Marks and G. Thomas	
		New South Wales v South Australia at Sydney	1958-59
335	for 7th	C.W. Andrews and E.C. Bensted	
		Queensland v New South Wales at Sydney	1934-35
270	for 8th	V.T. Trumper and E.P. Barbour	
		New South Wales v Victoria at Sydney	1912-13
232	for 9th	C. Hill and E.A. Walkley	
		South Australia v New South Wales at Adelaide	1900-01
307	for 10th	A.F. Kippax and J.E.H. Hooker	
		New South Wales v Victoria at Melbourne	1928-29

* Denotes unbroken partnership.

MOST WICKETS IN A SEASON

		M	Balls	Mdns	R	W	BB	5W/i	10W/m	Avge
C.R. Miller (Tas)	1997-98	11	3,590	159	1,642	67	7/49	5	0	24.51
L.O. Fleetwood-Smith (Vic)	1934-35	6	2,164	25	1,137	60	8/113	8	0	18.95
P.R. Reiffel (Vic)	1999-00	11	2552	118	982	59	5/65	1	0	16.64
C.D. Matthews (WAust)	1987-88	11	2,553	81	1,215	56	8/101	3	0	21.70
J. Garner (SAust)	1982-83	8	2,419	131	976	55	7/78	4	0	17.74
C.J. McDermott (Qld)	1989-90	10	1,392	100	1,375	54	8/44	4	0	25.46
A.J. Bichel (Qld)	1999-00	11	2421	124	989	53	6/45	2	1	18.66
W.J. O'Reilly (NSW)	1939-40	6	1,766	48	705	52	8/23	6	0	13.55
G.R.A. Lock (WAust)	1966-67	8	2,392	104	1,086	51	6/85	3	0	21.29
B.A. Williams (WAust)	1999-00	10	2194	94	1,151	50	6/74	5	0	23.02

MOST WICKETS IN A CAREER

	M	Balls	Mdns	R	W	BB	5W/i	10W/m	Avge
C. V. Grimmett (Vic/SAust)	79	28,465	446	12,976	513	9/180	48	13	25.29
T. M. Alderman (WAust)	97	19,288	778	9,299	384	7/28	17	3	24.21
C. G. Rackemann (Qld)	102	22,400	920	10,079	383	7/43	12	1	26.32
G. F. Lawson (NSW)	103	21,391	873	8,742	367	6/31	12	0	23.82
G. R. J. Matthews (NSW)	116	26,764	1,376	10,518	363	8/52	19	4	28.98
J. R. Thomson (NSW-Qld)	84	16,939	429	8,591	355	7/27	18	3	24.20
A. A. Mallett (SAust)	77	20,906	673	8,173	344	7/57	19	2	23.76
J. Angel (WAust)	84	17,704	818	8,269	343	6/64	11	0	24.11
D. K. Lillee (WAust/Tas)	75	17,814	475	8,086	338	7/36	18	4	23.92
P. R. Reiffel (Vic)	82	18,534	819	7,962	308	6/57	7	2	25.85
C. D. Matthews (WAust/Tas)	79	17,663	614	8,912	307	8/101	18	0	29.03
C. J. McDermott (Qld)	67	14,974	541	7,605	303	8/44	22	2	25.10
G. A. R. Lock (WAust)	63	20,107	544	7,210	302	7/53	16	2	23.87
C. R. Miller (SAust/Vic/Tas)	80	19,492	794	9,303	298	7/49	11	2	31.22
A. N. Connolly (Vic)	71	18,033	365	7,745	297	9/67	12	4	26.00
B. P. Julian (WAust)	87	16,143	612	8,573	292	7/39	15	2	29.36
A. I. C. Dodemaide (Vic)	94	19,892	822	8,884	281	6/67	12	0	31.62
J. W. Martin (NSW/SAust)	77	17,078	242	8,703	273	8/97	12	0	31.87
T. B. A. May (SAust)	80	22,575	931	9,943	270	7/93	15	2	36.83
M. G. Hughes (Vic)	76	16,762	582	8,169	267	7/81	10	2	30.60
M. S. Kasprowicz (Qld)	65	13,992	595	6,686	267	6/47	18	2	25.04
R. Benaud (NSW)	73	17,811	471	7,174	266	7/32	11	3	26.96
G. Dymock (Qld)	75	17,110	449	7,223	266	6/79	8	0	27.15
D. Tazelaar (Qld)	73	15,371	623	7,050	257	6/48	9	1	27.43
P. R. Sleep (SAust)	127	19,467	671	9,893	254	8/133	7	0	38.94
R. J. Bright (Vic)	101	22,789	1,013	8,833	252	6/61	10	0	35.05
M. R. Whitney (NSW)	77	14,983	562	7,314	251	7/75	10	0	29.14

MOST CATCHES IN A CAREER

R. J. Inverarity (WAust/SAust)	189 in 159 matches
J. D. Siddons (Vic/SAust)	189 in 146 matches
M. R. J. Veletta (WAust)	138 in 114 matches
D. W. Hookes (SAust)	123 in 120 matches
M. A. Taylor (NSW)	120 in 85 matches
A. R. Border (NSW/Qld)	117 in 108 matches
I. M. Chappell (SAust)	114 in 89 matches
T. M. Moody (WAust)	114 in 132 matches
D. F. Whatmore (Vic)	109 in 85 matches
G. S. Chappell (SAust/Qld)	103 in 101 matches
S. G. Law (Qld)	103 in 114 matches
G. R. J. Matthews (NSW)	102 in 116 matches

MOST DISMISSALS IN A CAREER

	M	Ct	St	Total
D. S. Berry (SAust/Vic)	114	415	38	453
T. J. Zoehrer (WAust)	107	331	28	359
R. W. Marsh (WAust)	86	311	33	351
P. A. Emery (NSW)	109	298	41	339
J. A. Maclean (Qld)	86	289	24	313
W. A. Seccombe (Qld)	63	303	10	313
T. J. Nielsen (SAust)	92	255	29	284
A. T. W. Grout (Qld)	84	213	63	276
S. J. Rixon (NSW)	94	218	43	261
M. N. Atkinson (Tas)	84	236	25	261
A. C. Gilchrist (NSW/WAust)	57	246	8	254
B. N. Jarman (SAust)	77	193	57	250

MOST APPEARANCES

159	R.J. Inverarity (WAust/SAust)	....	1962-63 – 1984-85
146	J.D. Siddons (Vic/SAust)	....	1984-85 – 1999-00
132	T.M. Moody (WAust)	....	1985-86 – 2000-01
127	P.R. Sleep (SAust)	....	1976-77 – 1992-93
123	S.C. Trimble (Qld)	....	1959-60 – 1975-76
123	J. Cox (Tas)	....	1987-88 – 2000-01
121	L.E. Favell (SAust)	....	1951-52 – 1969-70
120	D.W. Hookes (SAust)	....	1975-76 – 1991-92
119	D.C. Boon (Tas)	....	1978-79 – 1998-99
116	G.R.J. Matthews (NSW)	....	1982-83 – 1997-98
114	M.R.J. Veletta (WAust)	....	1983-84 – 1994-95
114	D.S. Berry (SAust/Vic)	....	1989-90 – 2000-01
114	S.G. Law (Qld)	....	1988-89 – 2000-01
112	D.S. Lehmann (SAust/Vic)	....	1987-88 – 2000-01
110	D.M. Wellham (NSW/Tas/Qld)	....	1980-81 – 1993-94
110	D.M. Jones (Vic)	....	1981-82 – 1997-98
109	G.M. Wood (WAust)	....	1977-78 – 1991-92
109	A.M.J. Hilditch (NSW/SAust)	....	1976-77 – 1991-92
109	P.A. Emery	....	1989-90 – 1998-99
108	A.R. Border (NSW/Qld)	....	1976-77 – 1995-96
107	H.N. Dansie (SAust)	....	1949-50 – 1966-67
107	T.J. Zoehrer (WAust)	....	1980-81 – 1993-94
105	T.V. Hohns (Qld)	....	1972-73 – 1990-91
103	G.F. Lawson (NSW)	....	1977-78 – 1991-92
102	C.G. Rackemann (Qld)	....	1979-80 – 1995-96
101	G.S. Chappell (SAust/Qld)	....	1966-67 – 1983-84
101	R.J. Bright (Vic)	....	1972-73 – 1987-88
100	K.D. Mackay (Qld)	....	1946-47 – 1963-64
100	G.R. Marsh (WAust)	....	1977-78 – 1993-94
100	T.J. Barsby (Qld)	....	1984-85 – 1996-97

PLAYED FOR THREE OR MORE STATES

				Batting				Bowling	
			M	R	Avge	W	Avge	Ct
G.D. Watson	Vic	(1964-65 – 1970-71)	34	1,555	32.40	53	26.57	20
	WAust	(1971-72 – 1974-75)	22	997	31.16	54	24.37	25
	NSW	(1976–77)	4	122	20.33	8	22.50	1
	Total		60	2,674	31.09	115	25.25	46
G.J. Cosier	Vic	(1971-72 & 1980-81)	4	133	22.17	2	43.00	2
	SAust	(1974-75 – 1976-77)	20	1,059	29.42	34	22.18	17
	Qld	(1977-78 – 1979-80)	22	1,295	35.97	16	36.75	22
	Total		46	2,487	31.88	52	27.46	41
T.M. Chappell	SAust	(1972-73 – 1975-76)	14	473	18.92	1	60.00	6
	WAust	(1976-77)	4	160	40.00	–	–	2
	NSW	(1979-80 – 1984-85)	45	2,320	32.68	51	21.06	29
	Total		63	2,953	29.53	52	21.90	37
R.J. McCurdy	Tas	(1980-81)	5	45	4.50	17	34.82	3
	Vic	(1981-82 – 1983-84)	20	239	12.58	67	34.19	7
	SAust	(1984-85)	8	128	12.80	36	29.47	5
	Total		33	412	10.56	120	32.87	15
D.M. Wellham	NSW	(1980-81 – 1986-87)	59	3,812	44.33	0	–	28
	Tas	(1988-89 – 1990-90)	30	1,600	41.03	0	–	12
	Qld	(1991-92 – 1993-94)	21	1,327	39.03	0	–	13
	Total		110	6,739	42.38	0	–	53
C.R. Miller	Vic	(1985-86 & 2000-01)	6	53	6.63	21	33.62	1
	SAust	(1988-89 – 1991-92)	20	274	13.05	67	28.96	6
	Tas	(1992-93 – 1999-00)	54	783	15.35	210	31.70	26
	Total		80	1,110	13.88	298	31.22	25

G. J. Rowell	NSW	(1989-90 – 1990-91)	3	77	25.67	11	26.09	1
	Qld	(1991-92 – 1997-98)	34	400	10.81	116	29.80	18
	Tas	(1998-99)	6	12	4.00	18	25.50	3
Total			43	489	11.37	145	28.99	22

NEW SOUTH WALES

Chief Executive: B. P. Hughes

President: A. K. Davidson AM MBE

Cricket Coach: S. J. Rixon

Captain: S. Lee

Shane Lee

When New South Wales celebrated the centenary of the Sheffield Shield by winning Australia's domestic first-class competition in 1992-93, the then chief executive officer, Robert Radford, struck a commemorative tie for the occasion, immodestly inscribing the white figures "41%" on the royal blue background. New South Wales' 41st triumph in 100 years was followed by another dual success the next summer, again under the coaching mantle of former Test wicket-keeper Steve Rixon, when New South Wales claimed both the Sheffield Shield and the Mercantile Mutual Cup. And then deathly silence. The silverware stopped clinking and the cut glass stopped ringing around New South Wales' trophy cabinet. They won nothing more until this summer, a void of six years, their second-longest barren period after the Shield-less sequence from the mid-1960s through to the early 1980s.

New South Wales' recent captains Mark Taylor and Michael Bevan expressed their concerns for the direction the state was taking in representative cricket without being publicly specific in identifying sources of the trouble. At their prompting and, concerned for the welfare of a state whose prosperity is essential to the national game, the relatively new administration of Bob Horsell and Brian Freedman, two fresh-minded directors appointed to the Australian Cricket Board, initiated a rebuilding plan. New South Wales reappointed Rixon, who had recently coached the New Zealand national team to success, as coach for another term and provided a full-time manager with business acumen in former Test spinner David Sincock.

The strategy brought immediate success in 2000-01. New South Wales won the Mercantile Mutual Cup with a six-wicket defeat of Western Australia at the WACA Ground in Perth, and finished fourth in the Pura Cup despite the abandonment of the game against South Australia at Bankstown Oval without a ball bowled.

Judging by the regrettable evidence of his exclusion from the Australia A team that played the touring West Indians, Michael Bevan is apparently no longer in contention for the Tests. The national team's loss has been New South Wales' gain. Bevan led the state's batting in both competitions, and remains a model for the younger batsmen such as Michael Clarke, Greg Mail, Graeme Rummans and two tyro internationals in Brad Haddin and Mark

Higgs as they continue their development. Higgs, the oldest of the five, is still only 25, so these batsmen could form the nucleus of the state's batting for the next decade, provided they can translate promise into achievement.

The selectors hoped the new leadership role, in Steve Waugh's inevitably frequent and long absences, would bring out the best in Shane Lee, but for a time the international limited-overs all-rounder struggled to come to grips with his new role, in both his personal form and his team responsibilities. By summer's end, however, Lee appeared more comfortable in the position and more assertive in his leadership, batting strongly as New South Wales made their bid for a Pura Cup final position, only to be struck down by a virus before the last game against Queensland at the Gabba when New South Wales needed his experience most. Stuart MacGill led New South Wales ably in Lee's absence, but the loss of their captain compounded by the loss of the toss on a predictably well-grassed pitch proved insurmountable and New South Wales went down by nine wickets.

Once again, New South Wales produced a young pace man of considerable talent in left-arm new-ball bowler Nathan Bracken, who excelled when given his opportunity at international level in the limited-overs arena. Without being a tearaway in the fashion of Brett Lee, Bracken bowled with accuracy, pace and swing. He received his due rewards when named as Australia's Bradman Young Player of the Year and selected in the team for the Ashes tour of England. Brett Lee proved as exciting as he was hostile, and looked a world-class new-ball bowler. He was rarely available from December onwards because of international duties and then, regrettably, his season was cut short by back stress and an elbow injury. Although leg-spinner MacGill played an important part in the Test victories over West Indies, he was still the country's pre-eminent spin bowler in the Pura Cup. The player who created most early attention and then caused later concern was the powerful hitting, fast-bowling all-rounder Don Nash, who electrified the game with some of his strokeplay in the Mercantile Mutual Cup, won Australia A selection as a genuine Ashes tour candidate, then broke down with a torn hamstring muscle and eventually finished out of favour with the state selectors.

Whether Sydney's 20-club system best serves the state's interests remained a vexatious issue. The question has been asked for a decade: Where is the new Ian Craig or "Blinks" Watson or Norman O'Neill or Bob Simpson? Where is New South Wales' next major international batsman after Michael Slater, who made his initial first-class appearance ten years ago? Perhaps it will be Mark Faraday, the New South Wales Under-17s captain, a neat right-handed batsman from Newcastle, and already a member of the New South Wales Colts team. Faraday shows immense promise.

Interstate cricket was once the nursery of Test champions. A similar boast cannot be made so readily today. Regrettably, now that the best players are usually playing elsewhere the old, successful system will never return. The very suggestion of a 15-Test calendar year, on top of the multitude of limited-overs internationals, makes the blood run cold. – PHIL WILKINS.

NEW SOUTH WALES PURA CUP TEAM, 2000-01

Back row: D.J. Sincock (*general manager*), S.J. Rixon (*coach*), S.C.G. MacGill, B.P. Van Deinsen, S. Lee (*captain*), N.W. Bracken, G.J. Mail, A.M. Clark, P. Farhart (*physiotherapist*). *Front row:* M.J. Clarke, S.D. Bradstreet, M.A. Higgs, B.J. Haddin, D.A. Nash, M.G. Bevan. *Absent:* S.R. Clark, S.H. Cook, D.A. Horsley, P.A. Jaques, B.Lee, G.D. McGrath, M.J. Phelps, N.S. Pilon, C.J. Richards, G.C. Rummans, M.J. Slater, J. Stewart, S.M. Thompson, M.E. Waugh, S. R. Waugh.

NEW SOUTH WALES RESULTS, 2000-01

All first-class matches – Played 9: Won 3, Lost 3, Drawn 3, Abandoned 1.
Pura Cup – Played 9: Won 3, Lost 3, Drawn 3, Abandoned 1.
Mercantile Mutual Cup matches – Played 11: Won 7, Lost 4.
Competition placings – Pura Cup, 4th; Mercantile Mutual Cup, 1st.

AUSTRALIAN DOMESTIC FIRST-CLASS RESULTS TABLE

Opponent	M	W	L	D	T
South Australia	193	106	51	36	0
Victoria	199	72	61	65	1
Queensland	142	57	35	50	0
Western Australia	100	40	30	30	0
Tasmania	44	17	10	17	0
Total	678	292	187	198	1

PURA CUP AVERAGES, 2000-01

BATTING

	M	I	NO	R	HS	100s	50s	Avge	Ct/St
M. E. Waugh	2	3	0	251	152	1	1	83.67	2
S. D. Bradstreet	2	4	2	117	60	0	1	58.50	4
M. G. Bevan	8	13	2	557	119	2	2	50.64	4
M. A. Higgs	7	11	1	413	181*	1	0	41.30	8
M. J. Slater	2	3	0	118	100	1	0	39.33	0
G. J. Mail	7	12	0	435	176	1	2	36.25	6
M. J. Phelps	1	2	0	70	40	0	0	35.00	0
S. Lee	8	11	0	365	114	1	2	33.18	7
P. A. Jaques	1	2	0	63	40	0	0	31.50	1
B. J. Haddin	8	14	1	360	93	0	3	27.69	25/2
G. C. Rummans	3	4	1	80	46	0	0	26.67	0
M. J. Clarke	5	8	1	179	106	1	0	25.57	4
C. J. Richards	5	9	1	177	69	0	2	22.13	0
D. A. Nash	8	13	1	225	46	0	0	18.75	2
J. Stewart	1	2	0	35	23	0	0	17.50	0
B. Lee	2	3	0	48	26	0	0	16.00	1
S. R. Waugh	2	3	0	45	25	0	0	15.00	1
B. P. Van Deinsen	5	9	0	125	29	0	0	13.89	8
A. M. Clark	4	4	0	53	24	0	0	13.25	2
S. C. G. MacGill	6	6	2	45	14	0	0	11.25	3
N. W. Bracken	6	7	3	42	30	0	0	10.50	5
N. S. Pilon	1	1	0	8	8	0	0	8.00	5
S. R. Clark	3	5	1	25	13	0	0	6.25	1
S. H. Cook	1	2	1	6	6*	0	0	6.00	0
G. D. McGrath	1	1	0	3	3	0	0	3.00	0
D. A. Horsley	1	2	2	11	7*	0	0	–	2

* *Denotes not out*

BOWLING

	O	M	R	W	BB	5W/i	Avge
N. W. Bracken	240.1	65	688	29	5/22	2	23.72
M. G. Bevan	11	1	49	2	2/23	0	24.50
S. R. Clark.	89	25	206	8	2/36	0	25.75
B. Lee	73.5	19	234	9	5/42	1	26.00
S. Lee	151.5	40	463	17	4/43	0	27.24
S. C. G. MacGill	297.4	59	889	30	5/78	2	29.63
S. D. Bradstreet.	45.5	8	185	6	2/32	0	30.83
G. D. McGrath	24	8	66	2	1/26	0	33.00
D. A. Nash	215.2	53	649	17	4/57	0	38.18
A. M. Clark	110.1	26	286	6	2/19	0	47.67
M. A. Higgs	113	16	386	4	2/42	0	96.50
D. A. Horsley	22	3	107	1	1/93	0	107.00
S. H. Cook.	22	6	60	0	–	0	–
G. J. Mail.	1	0	4	0	–	0	–
C. J. Richards	7	5	4	0	–	0	–
J. Stewart	13	2	42	0	–	0	–
M. E. Waugh.	10	1	27	0	–	0	–
S. R. Waugh	6	3	11	0	–	0	–

At Richmond Cricket Ground, Richmond, October 25 (no play), 26, 27, 28, 2000. NEW SOUTH WALES lost to VICTORIA by 117 runs.

At Bellerive Oval, Hobart, November 7, 8, 9, 10, 2000. NEW SOUTH WALES drew with TASMANIA.

NEW SOUTH WALES v SOUTH AUSTRALIA

At Bankstown Oval, Bankstown, November 15 (no play), 16 (no play), 17 (no play), 18 (no play), 2000. Match abandoned due to rain.

No play was possible on any of the four days due to rain. The Australian Cricket Board ruled that points should not be awarded.

NEW SOUTH WALES v WESTERN AUSTRALIA

At North Sydney Oval, North Sydney, December 1, 2, 3, 4, 2000. New South Wales won by 51 runs. Toss: New South Wales. New South Wales 6 pts. Western Australia 2 pts.

With five players absent on Test duty against West Indies, New South Wales won an extraordinary victory after trailing by 187 runs on the first innings, essentially due to the pace bowling of Nathan Bracken and Don Nash. Batting first, New South Wales were restricted by the early pace of Jo Angel and Brendon Julian, although Brad Haddin hit an enterprising 87 (122 minutes, 121 balls, 14 fours, one six). Simon Katich (196 minutes, 166 balls, 17 fours) and Damien Martyn (190 minutes, 131 balls, 10 fours) added 192 runs in 157 minutes for the third wicket to secure apparent mastery for Western Australia. Greg Mail (279 minutes, 255 balls, eight fours) resisted sternly until the fall of the sixth wicket. Although he and Michael Bevan began the New South Wales revival with a century partnership for the second wicket, Western Australia still required only 141 to win. Bowling on a pitch generally regarded as one of the most benign in the country, Bracken and Nash dismissed Western Australia for 89 in 150 minutes in 35.3 overs, only Brendon Julian's brief flourish showing any defiance.

Man of the Match: N. W. Bracken. *Attendance:* 1,325.

Close of play: First day, Western Australia (1) 1-37 (Campbell 30, Katich 6); Second day, Western Australia (1) 8-401 (Julian 73, Oldroyd 0); Third day, New South Wales (2) 6-246 (Richards 32, Bradstreet 3).

New South Wales

B. P. Van Deinsen b Angel	3	(2) c Katich b Julian	27
G. J. Mail lbw b Swan	3	(1) lbw b Julian	92
M. G. Bevan b Angel	2	run out (Katich)	57
C. J. Richards c Moody b Julian	7	st Walsh b Moody	66
*S. Lee c Goodwin b Julian	26	c Walsh b Julian	17
M. A. Higgs c Hussey b Oldroyd	34	lbw b Angel	1
†B. J. Haddin c Campbell b Oldroyd	87	b Angel	8
S. D. Bradstreet not out	17	lbw b Angel	4
D. A. Nash c Hussey b Julian	0	c Campbell b Oldroyd	32
J. Stewart c Goodwin b Angel	23	c Martyn b Oldroyd	12
N. W. Bracken c Goodwin b Oldroyd	10	not out	0
L-b 6, w 1, n-b 7	14	N-b 11	11

(65 overs, 237 mins)	226	(119.5 overs, 423 mins)	327

Fall: 8 10 14 46 49 163 174 174
207 226

Fall: 57 161 191 221 222 230 252
303 321 327

Bowling: *First Innings*—Angel 18–3–53–3; Swan 16–6–43–1; Moody 5–2–9–0; Julian 12–1–70–3; Oldroyd 14–4–45–3. *Second Innings*—Angel 23–7–64–3; Swan 16–3–51–0; Julian 24–5–73–3; Moody 20–3–55–1; Oldroyd 29.5–11–68–2; Martyn 7–1–16–0.

Western Australia

M. E. Hussey b Bracken	1	(2) lbw b Nash	4
R. J. Campbell c Bradstreet b Bracken	35	(1) b Nash	0
S. M. Katich c Mail b Lee	117	run out (Richards)	5
D. R. Martyn c Higgs b Lee	92	c Bradstreet b Bracken	0
M. W. Goodwin lbw b Nash	0	c Haddin b Bracken	9
*T. M. Moody c Van Deinsen b Bradstreet	23	b Bracken	17
†M. J. Walsh b Bradstreet	14	lbw b Bradstreet	15
B. P. Julian c Haddin b Nash	76	c Bevan b Bracken	32
J. Angel run out (Richards/Haddin)	37	c Haddin b Bracken	4
B. J. Oldroyd c Haddin b Bracken	9	not out	0
G. G. Swan not out	0	b Nash	0
B 3, l-b 4, n-b 2	9	L-b 3	3

(125.1 overs, 471 mins)	413	(35.3 overs, 150 mins)	89

Fall: 13 48 240 241 259 280 291 400 413 413

Fall: 0 6 7 15 23 49 69 77 88 89

Bowling: *First Innings*—Nash 26–5–88–2; Bracken 30.1–6–121–3; Higgs 23–2–65–0; Lee 19–5–58–2; Stewart 13–2–42–0; Bradstreet 14–5–32–2. *Second Innings*—Nash 11.3–2–31–3; Bracken 15–6–22–5; Lee 5–1–13–0; Bradstreet 4–0–20–1.

Umpires: D. M. Brandon and G. J. Lill.
TV Umpire: S. E. Reed.

At WACA Ground, Perth, December 15, 16, 17, 2000. NEW SOUTH WALES lost to WESTERN AUSTRALIA by nine wickets.

At Adelaide Oval, Adelaide, January 4, 5, 6, 7, 2001. NEW SOUTH WALES lost to SOUTH AUSTRALIA by 168 runs.

NEW SOUTH WALES v TASMANIA

At Sydney Cricket Ground, Sydney, February 14, 15, 16, 17, 2001. Drawn. Toss: Tasmania. New South Wales 2 pts.

On a hard, dry pitch, Jamie Cox won a valuable toss and punished New South Wales with his usual relish, batting throughout the first day for his 11th hundred against New South Wales and his fourth at the Sydney Cricket Ground. But only Shaun Young supported Cox, and the last five wickets added just 39 runs after Cox (369 minutes, 336 balls, 27 fours) was dismissed. Greg Mail was a model of resolution in scoring his maiden first-class hundred, (501 minutes, 421 balls, 15 fours), while Bevan (183 minutes, 155 balls, 13 fours, three sixes), batted with his customary elegant relish, their second wicket partnership of 197 offering New South Wales the sort of top-order stability it had lacked for some time. With just over a day left to play, the home side needed quick wickets but Cox (207 minutes, 182 balls, nine fours) again resisted stoutly, Scott Kremerskothen scored a brisk 64, and when David Saker and Shannon Tubb added 63 in 41 minutes for the last wicket a draw was the only possible result.

Man of the Match: J. Cox. Attendance: 1633.

Close of play: First day, Tasmania (1) 4-321 (Cox 156, Young 54); Second day, New South Wales (1) (Mail 87, Clarke 0); Third day, Tasmania (2) 0-33 (Hills 15, Cox 16).

Tasmania

D.F. Hills c Haddin b Lee		25	– c Bracken b MacGill	28
*J. Cox c Haddin b Bracken		160	– c Haddin b Bracken	81
M.J. Di Venuto run out (Clarke/Haddin)		22	– c and b Higgs	0
S.R. Watson c Van Deinsen b MacGill		28	– lbw b Bevan	14
D.J. Marsh c Higgs b Clark		29	– c Van Deinsen b MacGill	13
S. Young b Bracken		67	– c Clark b MacGill	8
S.P. Kremerskothen c Mail b Bracken		20	– b Bracken	64
†S.G. Clingeleffer c Haddin b Bracken		7	– lbw b Bevan	7
S.J. Jurgensen lbw b MacGill		0	– c Clark b MacGill	13
D.J. Saker not out		1	– not out	20
S.B. Tubb c Van Deinsen b MacGill		0	– c Clark b MacGill	42
B 3, l-b 3, w 1, n-b 3		10	B 7, l-b 9	16

(122 overs, 437 mins) 369

Fall: 55 123 199 234 330 353 361 362 368 369

(104 overs, 382 mins) 306

Fall: 53 66 108 133 144 153 203 231 243 306

Bowling: *First Innings*—Nash 14–1–52–0; Bracken 29–8–78–4; Lee 11–4–46–1; MacGill 42–10–117–3; Clark 16–6–41–1; Higgs 10–3–29–0. *Second Innings*—Nash 8–4–25–0; Bracken 25–10–66–2; MacGill 40–11–125–5; Clark 6–2–9–0; Higgs 12–4–26–1; Lee 8–3–16–0; Bevan 5–0–23–2.

New South Wales

B.P. Van Deinsen run out (Young/Marsh)		27		
G.J. Mail b Jurgensen		176		
M.G. Bevan c Clingeleffer b Watson		119	– not out	9
M.J. Clarke lbw b Jurgensen		41		
M.A. Higgs b Watson		12		
*S. Lee c Cox b Young		25		
†B.J. Haddin c Clingeleffer b Kremerskothen		56	– (2) not out	7
D.A. Nash c Cox b Jurgensen		22	– (1) b Jurgensen	2
A.M. Clark c Di Venuto b Jurgensen		24		
S.C.G. MacGill c Watson b Marsh		7		
N.W. Bracken not out		1		
B 7, l-b 8, w 1, n-b 4		20		

(150.5 overs, 551 mins) 530

Fall: 43 240 310 333 380 471 487 512 527 530

(4 overs, 17 mins) (1 wkt) 18

Fall: 2

Bowling: *First Innings*—Saker 23–3–72–0; Jurgensen 33.5–6–113–4; Marsh 30–9–104–1; Young 16–3–40–1; Kremerskothen 18–3–53–1; Tubb 14–2–70–0; Watson 16–3–63–2. *Second Innings*—Jurgensen 2–0–10–1; Watson 2–0–8–0.

Umpires: D. B. Hair and R. L. Parry.
TV Umpire: T. J. Keel.

NEW SOUTH WALES v QUEENSLAND

At Sydney Cricket Ground, Sydney, March 2, 3, 4, 5, 2001. New South Wales won by eight wickets. Toss: New South Wales. New South Wales 6 pts. First-class debut: B. P. Nash.

In hot and humid conditions, Greg Mail batted with such obduracy that he only scored 13 in the first session, and 37 in the second, his 71 ultimately coming in 304 minutes (249 balls, seven fours). Michael Bevan (238 minutes, 197 balls, nine fours, three sixes) proceeded sedately to his 49th first-class hundred, the second wicket partnership of 174 providing New South Wales with an early advantage they never relinquished. Mark Higgs scored an impressive maiden hundred (280 minutes, 235 balls, 21 fours, three sixes), as he and Shane Lee (222 minutes, 171 balls, six fours, three sixes) ransacked Queensland's attack, registering a fifth-wicket partnership of 264, equalling the record for New South Wales against Queensland which had been set by Arthur Morris and Richie Benaud at Brisbane in 1953-54. After Lee's closure in the fifth session, New South Wales' well-balanced attack, led by Nathan Bracken and Stuart MacGill, forced Queensland to follow on 223 runs behind. On a wearing pitch, the local spin trio of MacGill, Higgs and Anthony Clark, the team's new off-spinner, curbed Queensland in capturing 12 wickets between them for the game. Only Stuart Law's defiance (163 minutes, 145 balls, 10 fours) delayed New South Wales' march to victory.

Man of the Match: M. A. Higgs.   Attendance: 2,445.

Close of play: First day, New South Wales (1) 4-287 (Higgs 62, Lee 26); Second day, Queensland (1) 2-113 (Cassell 38, Law 16); Third day, Queensland (2) 4-155 (Law 58, Nash 36).

New South Wales

B. P. Van Deinsen c Law b Dale	1	– run out (Dale/Bichel)	1
G. J. Mail lbw b Bichel	71	– c Seccombe b Bichel	12
M. G. Bevan c O'Leary b Dale	111		
M. J. Clarke b Dale	0	– not out	5
M. A. Higgs not out	181		
*S. Lee c Symonds b Bichel	114		
†B. J. Haddin b Symonds	0		
G. C. Rummans (did not bat)		– (3) not out	6
B 5, l-b 4, w 1, n-b 11	21	L-b 1	1
(141.4 overs, 530 mins) (6 wkts dec)	499	(9.4 overs, 43 mins) (2 wkts)	25
Fall: 1 175 177 235 499 499		Fall: 1 17	

D. A. Nash, S. C. G. MacGill, A. M. Clark and N. W. Bracken did not bat.

Bowling: *First Innings*—Bichel 32–4–134–2; Dale 44–17–81–3; Dawes 25–3–95–0; O'Leary 28–6–122–0; Symonds 9.4–0–27–1; Law 3–0–31–0. *Second Innings*—Bichel 5–0–12–1; Dawes 4.4–2–12–0.

Queensland

J. L. Cassell b Lee	68	– c Higgs b A. M. Clark	31
J. P. Maher c Lee b Bracken	13	– c Haddin b A. M. Clark	21
M. L. Love c Lee b A. M. Clark	46	– c Lee b Higgs	2
*S. G. Law st Haddin b A. M. Clark	27	– c Bracken b MacGill	98
A. Symonds c Clarke b MacGill	54	– lbw b Higgs	0
B. P. Nash b MacGill	0	– c Lee b MacGill	44
†W. A. Seccombe lbw b Bracken	27	– lbw b Lee	21
A. J. Bichel b Bracken	18	– c Nash b MacGill	12
A. C. Dale c Bevan b MacGill	10	– not out	9
S. J. O'Leary not out	5	– lbw b Lee	0
J. H. Dawes b Bracken	4	– lbw b Lee	0
L-b 3, w 1	4	B 5, l-b 1, w 3	9

(105 overs, 372 mins)	276	(71 overs, 258 mins)	247

Fall: 26 93 127 178 183 222 254 261 269 276

Fall: 51 57 57 57 179 216 232 240 247 247

Bowling: *First Innings*—Nash 10–4–25–0; Bracken 21–4–44–4; MacGill 33–3–126–3; A. M. Clark 26–7–52–2; Lee 11–5–14–1; Higgs 3–0–12–0; Bevan 1–1–0–0. *Second Innings*—Bracken 12–4–42–0; Nash 7–0–35–0; A. M. Clark 9–2–19–2; Higgs 12–1–42–2; MacGill 25–4–79–3; Bevan 2–0–14–0; Lee 4–1–10–3.

Umpires: D. M. Brandon and D. B. Hair.
TV Umpire: S. A. Reed.

NEW SOUTH WALES v VICTORIA

At Sydney Cricket Ground, Sydney, March 9, 10, 11, 12, 2001. Drawn. Toss: Victoria. Victoria 2 pts. First-class debuts: N. S. Pilon; J. Moss and C. L. White.

Rain continually interrupted the game and ensured a draw, but it could not prevent a close contest for first-innings points. Revelling in a return to his former state's headquarters and enjoying his hard-earned respect as one of the most consistent openers in Australia, Jason Arnberger (249 minutes, 187 balls, eight fours), was deprived of his century just before stumps on the first day. Brad Hodge (333 minutes, 273 balls, 12 fours) carried on in his stylish, sweet-stroking manner in a 151-run partnership with Michael Klinger before Nathan Bracken brought the innings crumbling to a close with 5/11 from 40 balls. Despite Michael Clarke's cultured maiden century (241 minutes, 211 balls, 16 fours) and Shane Lee's more boisterous innings (172 minutes, 133 balls, eight fours, four sixes), the Victorians' 17-year-old high school student, leg-spinner Cameron White, bowled with composure on his initial first-class appearance to help give his team first-innings points and the satisfaction of eliminating their arch-rivals from the competition final.

Man of the Match: B. J. Hodge. *Attendance:* 1,967.

Close of play: First day, Victoria (1) 3-215 (Hodge 55, Klinger 12); Second day, New South Wales (1) 3-111 (Clarke 13*, S. R. Clark 0); Third day, New South Wales (1) 5-201 (Clarke 46, Lee 13).

Victoria

M. T. G. Elliott c Pilon b A. M. Clark	27	– (2) not out		18
J. L. Arnberger c Lee b S. R. Clark	90	– (1) c Pilon b S. R. Clark		1
M. P. Mott c Pilon b S. R. Clark	18	– not out		2
B. J. Hodge c and b Bracken	125			
M. Klinger lbw b Lee	67			
J. Moss c Mail b MacGill	32			
†D. S. Berry c Pilon b Bracken	17			
*P. R. Reiffel c Pilon b Bracken	0			
C. L. White c A. M. Clark b Bracken	11			
J. M. Davison c MacGill b Bracken	0			
M. W. H. Inness not out	0			
B 5, l-b 8, n-b 9	22			

(141.3 overs, 535 mins)   409   (6 overs, 28 mins)   (1 wkt)   21
Fall: 74 109 186 337 367 391 391 409 409 409   Fall: 19

Bowling: *First Innings*—Bracken 30–11–68–5; S. R. Clark 27–8–53–2; MacGill 26.3–4–88–1; Lee 18–3–53–1; A. M. Clark 26–2–79–1; Higgs 11–0–43–0; Bevan 3–0–12–0. *Second Innings*—Bracken 3–1–11–0; S. R. Clark 3–0–10–1.

New South Wales

G. C. Rummans c Berry b Davison	28	A. M. Clark b White	3
G. J. Mail c Berry b Inness	2	S. C. G. MacGill b Inness	14
M. G. Bevan c Elliott b White	62	N. W. Bracken not out	0
M. J. Clarke c Reiffel b Moss	106		
S. R. Clark c Hodge b Davison	13	B 1, l-b 3, n-b 11	15
M. A. Higgs c Elliott b White	26		
*S. Lee lbw b White	94	(115.3 overs, 440 mins)	371
†N. S. Pilon b Davison	8	Fall: 3 79 111 136 184 290 299 313 363 371	

Bowling: Reiffel 21–3–84–0; Inness 16–2–65–2; Davison 41–12–101–3; Moss 16–3–52–1; White 21.3–6–65–4.

Umpires: D. M. Brandon and S. J. A. Taufel.
TV Umpire: T. M. Donahoo.

At Brisbane Cricket Ground, Brisbane, March 15, 16, 17, 2001. NEW SOUTH WALES lost to QUEENSLAND by nine wickets.

AUSTRALIAN DOMESTIC FIRST-CLASS RECORDS

Highest score for:	452*	D. G. Bradman v Queensland at Sydney	1929-30
Highest score against:	365*	C. Hill (South Australia) at Adelaide	1900-01
Best bowling for:	9/41	W. J. O'Reilly v South Australia at Adelaide	1937-38
Best bowling against:	10/36	T. W. Wall (South Australia) at Sydney	1932-33
Highest total for:	918	v South Australia at Sydney	1900-01
Highest total against:	1,107	by Victoria at Melbourne	1926-27
Lowest total for:	56	v Western Australia at Perth	1998-99
Lowest total against:	27	by South Australia at Sydney	1955-56

MOST RUNS

	M	I	NO	R	HS	100s	50s	Avge
M. G. Bevan	78	137	29	6,526	203*	25	27	59.87
A. F. Kippax	61	95	9	6,096	315*	23	14	70.88
M. A. Taylor	85	147	3	6,090	199	15	34	42.29
M. E. Waugh	72	121	13	5,941	229*	22	23	55.01
J. Dyson	82	150	16	5,648	241	11	29	42.15

	M	I	NO	R	HS	100s	50s	Avge
K. D. Walters.	91	159	16	5,602	253	17	24	39.17
G. R. J. Matthews	116	177	27	5,567	184	8	28	37.11
S. R. Waugh	70	119	13	5,390	216*	17	21	50.85
R. B. McCosker.	70	124	15	5,280	168	17	26	48.44
B. C. Booth	81	128	14	4,943	177	10	25	43.36

HIGHEST PARTNERSHIP FOR EACH WICKET

319	for 1st	R. B. McCosker and J. Dyson v Western Australia at Sydney	1980-81
378	for 2nd	L. A. Marks and K. D. Walters v South Australia at Adelaide	1964-65
363	for 3rd	D. G. Bradman and A. F. Kippax v Queensland at Sydney	1933-34
325	for 4th	N. C. O'Neill and B. C. Booth v Victoria at Sydney	1957-58
464*	for 5th	M. E. Waugh and S. R. Waugh v Western Australia at Perth	1990-91
332	for 6th	N. G. Marks and G. Thomas v South Australia at Sydney	1958-59
255	for 7th	G. Thomas and R. Benaud v Victoria at Melbourne	1961-62
270	for 8th	E. P. Barbour and V. T. Trumper v Victoria at Sydney	1912-13
226	for 9th	C. Kelleway and W. A. S. Oldfield v Victoria at Melbourne	1925-26
307	for 10th	A. F. Kippax and J. E. H. Hooker v Victoria at Melbourne	1928-29

MOST WICKETS

	M	Balls	Mdns	R	W	BB	5W/i	10W/m	Avge
G. F. Lawson	103	21,391	873	8,742	367	6/31	12	0	23.82
G. R. J. Matthews	116	26,764	1,376	10,518	363	8/52	19	4	28.98
R. Benaud	73	17,811	471	7,174	266	7/32	11	3	26.96
J. W. Martin	70	16,034	239	7,949	263	8/97	12	0	30.22
M. R. Whitney	77	14,983	562	7,314	251	7/75	10	0	29.14
A. K. Davidson	62	13,423	270	5,195	246	7/31	10	0	21.12
W. J. O'Reilly	33	10,748	362	3,472	203	9/41	18	7	17.10
R. G. Holland	60	15,435	806	6,250	193	9/83	7	1	32.38
K. J. O'Keeffe	58	11,964	315	5,064	187	6/49	11	1	27.08
L. S. Pascoe	49	9,566	279	4,895	183	8/41	8	2	26.75

MOST DISMISSALS

	M	Ct	St	Total
P. A. Emery	109	298	41	339
S. J. Rixon	94	218	43	261
H. B. Taber	64	179	32	211
W. A. S. Oldfield	51	109	70	179
D. A. Ford	56	107	51	158

MOST CATCHES

M. A. Taylor	120 in 85 matches	R. B. McCosker	91 in 70 matches
G. R. J. Matthews	102 in 116 matches	M. E. Waugh	85 in 72 matches
R. Benaud	92 in 73 matches	J. W. Martin	78 in 70 matches

MOST APPEARANCES

116	G. R. J. Matthews . .	1982-83 – 1997-98	85	M. A. Taylor	1985-86 – 1998-99
109	P. A. Emery	1987-88 – 1998-99	82	J. Dyson	1975-76 – 1988-89
103	G. F. Lawson	1977-78 – 1991-92	81	B. C. Booth	1954-55 – 1968-69
94	S. J. Rixon	1974-75 – 1987-88	78	M. G. Bevan	1990-91 – 2000-01
91	K. D. Walters	1962-63 – 1980-81	77	M. R. Whitney	1980-81 – 1993-94

QUEENSLAND

Chief Executive: G.J. Dixon

President: J.N. McKnoulty

Cricket Coach: B. King

Captain: S.G. Law

Stuart Law

Queensland coach Bennett King handed his players a simple but unique mission when they began the defence of their Pura Cup crown in October. He wanted his players to be found guilty of success, using the three principles that juries use to commit criminals. King reasoned that Queensland needed means (skills), motive (desire) and opportunity (selection) if they wanted to be successful when the Pura Cup final arrived in March. They were eventually found guilty, winning their fourth interstate crown in seven seasons, relying on their experienced playing list combined with the next wave of young players. Old hands Stuart Law, Jimmy Maher, Martin Love, Andy Bichel and Adam Dale provided the foundations, while emerging faces Ashley Noffke and Clinton Perren enhanced Queensland's power base.

On paper, Queensland could not repeat the dominance of the previous season, when they topped the table with 48 points. They managed 40 this time, built on six outright victories and two first-innings results, but King adjudged the season as better than 1999-2000, given the team's personnel and the improvement in the other teams.

The season's highlights included remarkable finishes in the first and last home matches. October's thrilling win over Tasmania, including a memorable partnership from Martin Love and Andrew Symonds, proved the side would again be a force in the new season. But they were forced to wait until the last day of the competition to lever themselves out of a nail-biting and sometimes spiteful final against Victoria.

The win over Tasmania was the work of the batsmen, who needed to hit back after struggling through the previous season. Love, Law and Maher stood out, averaging better than 50, while Matthew Hayden offered his typically professional service when not on Test duty. The batsmen took turns to share the workload, while Perren emerged as a genuine first-class batsman with two innings of substance in the last month.

The bowlers were again outstanding, and set Queensland apart from the other states. Joe Dawes, Bichel and Dale were the competition's leading wicket-takers, while Test pace man Michael Kasprowicz claimed eight wickets in his sole appearance. Dawes' season was the most surprising, as he finally shook off 12th-man duties to justify the confidence Law had long had in him. The policeman proved particularly dangerous against left-handers, topping the wicket-taking list with 49 at 20.47. Bichel returned from Test duty to take 40 wickets at 21.80, again proving a menace for Victoria, while Dale's consistency reaped another 46 wickets at 23.39.

The pace trio were head and shoulders above their rivals in other states, nobody else in the competition taking 40 wickets, but, to underline Queensland's talent, the attention had turned to Noffke by season's end. The 24-year-old, likened to Glenn McGrath for his build and rhythm, was the player of the final as the bowlers routed Victoria in the first innings. That performance helped earn Noffke an Australian Cricket Board contract and left Queensland's selectors with a queue of talented fast bowlers for the 2001-02 season.

Queensland again fielded well and wicket-keeper Wade Seccombe barely missed a beat, fully deserving the recognition of his Ashes tour spot. The team's only blemish came in Sydney, when they allowed the New South Wales batsmen to set up a convincing eight-wicket win. Love was the main casualty of that match, breaking a thumb in the dying overs, and he had to sit in the stands when Queensland extracted revenge against New South Wales two weeks later. The elegant batsman made a surprise return in the final and played a major role in Queensland's win, holding steady in a match in which batsmen struggled.

There are still places available for new talent, most notably a middle-order batting position. Queensland's ability to develop their emerging players into front-line talent will determine whether they can extend their dominance through the decade. – MICHAEL CRUTCHER.

QUEENSLAND RESULTS, 2000-01

All first-class matches – Played 11: Won 7, Lost 1, Drawn 3.
Pura Cup matches – Played 11: Won 7, Lost 1, Drawn 3.
Mercantile Mutual Cup matches – Played 10: Won 4, Lost 5, No result 1.
Competition placings – Pura Cup, 1st; Mercantile Mutual Cup, 4th.

AUSTRALIAN DOMESTIC FIRST-CLASS RESULTS TABLE

Opponent	M	W	L	D	T
New South Wales	142	35	57	50	0
South Australia	137	42	49	45	1
Victoria	136	40	48	48	0
Western Australia	102	23	35	44	0
Tasmania	43	14	6	23	0
Total	560	154	195	210	1

PURA CUP AVERAGES, 2000-01

BATTING

	M	I	NO	R	HS	100s	50s	Avge	Ct/St
M.L. Love.........	9	14	3	834	172*	3	4	75.82	10
M.L. Hayden.......	3	5	1	301	118*	1	1	75.25	2
S.G. Law..........	11	15	2	814	161	2	4	62.62	10
J.P. Maher........	11	19	3	946	175	3	3	59.13	16
A. Symonds........	9	13	1	558	133	1	2	46.50	6
C.T. Perren.......	6	9	1	304	112	1	1	38.00	6
J.L. Cassell......	8	13	1	352	136	1	1	29.33	5
A.J. Bichel	7	10	1	247	61	0	1	27.44	5
W.A. Seccombe	11	14	2	270	52	0	1	22.50	57/1
A.A. Noffke	4	4	1	55	43	0	0	18.33	1
A.C. Dale	11	12	4	139	45*	0	0	17.38	3
L.A. Carseldine......	5	6	0	82	26	0	0	13.67	6
B.P. Nash	4	6	0	68	44	0	0	11.33	1
S.J. O'Leary	7	7	3	42	19	0	0	10.50	5
J.H. Dawes	9	8	1	55	18	0	0	7.86	2
M.A. Anderson......	3	3	1	7	5	0	0	3.50	1
B.N. Creevey	1	1	0	0	0	0	0	0.00	–
M.S. Kasprowicz	1	0	0	0	0	0	0	–	0
M.D. Pascoe	1	1	1	20	20*	0	0	–	1

BOWLING

	O	M	R	W	BB	5W/i	Avge
M.S. Kasprowicz.........	37	7	110	8	5/29	1	13.75
J.H. Dawes..............	358.3	101	1003	49	7/98	3	20.47
A.J. Bichel	318.2	80	872	40	5/74	2	21.80
A.C. Dale	570.3	226	1076	46	5/37	2	23.39
B.N. Creevey	34	9	101	3	3/42	0	33.67
A.A. Noffke	152	29	527	15	5/41	1	35.13
S.J. O'Leary	172.2	39	568	9	4/105	0	63.11
M.A. Anderson	111.2	28	271	4	2/39	0	67.75
A. Symonds	139.4	28	424	6	2/79	0	70.67
L.A. Carseldine	41	12	117	0	–	0	–
J.L. Cassell.............	3.3	1	7	0	–	0	–
M.L. Hayden	2	2	0	0	–	0	–
S.G. Law	15	0	102	0	–	0	–
C.T. Perren.............	7	2	18	0	–	0	–
M.D. Pascoe.............	14	3	46	0	–	0	–

* Denotes not out

At WACA Ground, Perth, October 13, 14, 15, 16, 2000. QUEENSLAND drew with WESTERN AUSTRALIA.

QUEENSLAND v TASMANIA

At Brisbane Cricket Ground, Brisbane, October 26, 27, 28, 29, 2000. Queensland won by four wickets. Toss: Tasmania. Queensland 6 pts. Tasmania 2 pts. First-class debut: S.G. Clingeleffer.

Ricky Ponting gave this extraordinary match a lightning start with a commanding double-century (388 minutes, 326 balls, 37 fours, four sixes) made out of 392 runs scored while he was at the wicket. His easy mastery of the attack took him to the fourth-highest individual innings played for Tasmania. The precision of the bowling of Andy Bichel and Adam Dale is underlined by the fact that their combined 73 overs allowed only one more run than did the 45.2 overs of the other three members of the attack. While Queensland's reply was brisk enough, four of their batsmen reached the 40s

QUEENSLAND PURA CUP TEAM, 2000-01

Back row: A.A. Noffke, M.D. Pascoe, L.A. Carseldine, L.A. Pascoe, T. Oliver *(assistant coach)*, J. Sternes *(technical officer)*, J.L. Cassell, A.L. Dale, A. Anderson, A. Symonds, C.T. Perren, A. Turner, S. Partridge *(physiotherapist)*, B. King *(coach)*. *Front row:* W.A. Seccombe, J. O'Leary, M.L. Love, S.G. Law *(captain)*, A.J. Bichel, J.P. Maher, J.H. Dawes, T. Wilson *(conditioner)*. *Absent:* B.N. Creevey, M.L. Hayden, N.M. Hauritz, J.P. Hopes, M.S. Kasprowicz, B.P. Nash, G.I. Foley, S.A. Prestwidge.

without going on to anything substantial. When Tasmania batted again, Jamie Cox was critical of Queensland skipper Stuart Law for setting offside fields which the Tasmanian captain claimed made reasonable progress almost impossible. He could point to the fact that this time Ponting needed 209 minutes and 187 balls to reach 61. Queensland, having been left with 372 to win from 72 overs, looked shaky when the third wicket fell for 59 in the 20th over. The situation was transformed by a remarkable partnership between Martin Love and Andrew Symonds which produced 261 runs from 42 overs, including one spell during which 100 runs came from 8.3 overs. Love's elegant and undefeated innings occupied 240 minutes and 195 balls, while Symonds was at his exhilarating best for 156 minutes and 122 balls. Each of them hit 19 fours and two sixes as Queensland pushed on to victory in fading light and with only one over remaining.

Man of the Match: M.L. Love. *Attendance:* 1,958.

Close of play: First day, Tasmania (1) 5-356 (Ponting 207, Dykes 23); Second day, Queensland (1) 6-258 (Perren 16, Bichel 26); Third day, Tasmania (2) 5-177 (Marsh 18, Clingeleffer 9).

Tasmania

D.F. Hills c Love b Bichel	25	– c Love b Anderson	2
*J. Cox b Dale	0	– c Seccombe b Bichel	44
M.J. Di Venuto c Hayden b Bichel	5		
R.T. Ponting run out (Symonds)	233	– (3) c Seccombe b Bichel	61
D.J. Marsh c Symonds b Anderson	61	– not out	58
S. Young c Seccombe b Bichel	22	– c Law b Bichel	0
J.A. Dykes c Hayden b Bichel	25	– (4) c Symonds b Anderson	32
†S.G. Clingeleffer c Law b Bichel	1	– (7) c Seccombe b Bichel	24
D.J. Saker c Seccombe b Dale	4	– (8) b Dale	18
D.G. Wright not out	5	– (9) not out	7
A.G. Downton c Noffke b Anderson	9		
L-b 6, w 2, n-b 5	13	L-b 6, w 2, n-b 4	12
(118.2 overs, 437 mins)	403	(107 overs, 396 mins) (7 wkts dec)	258

Fall: 3 11 82 197 296 365 371 386 391 403

Fall: 23 64 140 156 156 210 233

Bowling: *First Innings*—Bichel 36–6–126–5; Dale 37–17–73–2; Noffke 22–1–112–0; Anderson 21.2–4–78–2; Symonds 2–0–8–0. *Second Innings*—Bichel 31–8–105–4; Dale 41–19–70–1; Noffke 14–3–33–0; Anderson 18–4–39–2; Symonds 3–1–5–0.

Queensland

M.L. Hayden c Young b Saker	41	– c Downton b Wright	14
J.P. Maher c Clingeleffer b Wright	47	– b Saker	19
M.L. Love lbw b Saker	35	– not out	161
*S.G. Law c Clingeleffer b Wright	21	– lbw b Saker	0
A. Symonds c and b Marsh	49	– c (sub) Colegrave b Marsh	133
C.T. Perren c Marsh b Downton	23	– (7) lbw b Marsh	2
†W.A. Seccombe b Wright	3	– (8) not out	31
A.J. Bichel c Cox b Marsh	48	– (6) c Dykes b Young	0
A.C. Dale not out	1		
A.A. Noffke lbw b Downton	0		
M.A. Anderson st Clingeleffer b Marsh	0		
L-b 11, w 1, n-b 9	21	B 4, l-b 7, n-b 2	13
(79.5 overs, 306 mins)	289	(71 overs, 269 mins) (6 wkts)	373

Fall: 63 129 140 209 212 220 288 288 288 289

Fall: 20 59 59 320 321 329

Bowling: *First Innings*—Saker 21–4–63–2; Wright 19–4–61–3; Downton 24–8–81–2; Young 3–0–23–0; Marsh 12.5–4–50–3. *Second Innings*—Saker 19–3–88–2; Wright 17–2–72–1; Downton 12–2–81–0; Marsh 17–3–72–2; Ponting 2–0–14–0; Young 4–0–35–1.

Umpires: A.J. McQuillan and P.D. Parker.

QUEENSLAND v VICTORIA

At Allan Border Field, Albion, November 5, 6, 7, 8, 2000. Queensland won by ten wickets. Toss: Victoria. Queensland 6 pts.

Victoria finally had something to smile about in Brisbane when they ended the first day at a respectable four for 229, thanks mainly to three and a quarter hours of patient resistance from Jason Arnberger. Next morning, however, this start was squandered as Andy Bichel and Adam Dale took the last six wickets for 20. Queensland's reply was built on a crisp 81 (154 minutes, 127 balls, ten fours) from Matthew Hayden, who joined Martin Love in an assertive second-wicket partnership of 122. The visitors' second innings was held together by a fifth-wicket partnership of 172 in 179 minutes between the hard-driving Ian Harvey (179 minutes, 177 balls, 12 fours, two sixes) and Brad Hodge (315 minutes, 221 balls, 13 fours). Hodge's mature batting was a sign of things to come during the season. Joe Dawes bowled with pace and accuracy, applying the first trowel of bowling mortar which would cement his place in the team. Chasing 229 runs from 59 overs for victory, Hayden and Jimmy Maher posted the first 50 in an hour and then batted with such freedom and relish that the next 179 runs came in only 109 minutes, and they coasted home with 14.2 overs to spare in under a run a minute. Hayden's domination of the attack (132 balls, 15 fours) was complemented to perfection by Maher (138 balls, 12 fours, one six). Queensland had taken maximum points from their two matches at Albion after resurfacing work had forced them to move from the Gabba.

Man of the Match: M. L. Hayden. *Attendance:* 2,495.

Close of play: First day, Victoria (1) 4-229 (Klinger 37, Harvey 35); Second day, Queensland (2) 4-243 (Symonds 39, Perren 13); Third day, Victoria (2) 4-216 (Hodge 63, Harvey 73).

Victoria

J. L. Arnberger c Love b Dawes	64	–	(2) c Anderson b Dawes	20
S. A. J. Craig c Seccombe b Bichel	23	–	(1) c Bichel b Dawes	35
M. P. Mott c Seccombe b Symonds	31	–	c Seccombe b Dawes	19
B. J. Hodge c Love b Dawes	14	–	not out	101
M. Klinger c Love b Dale	38	–	c Maher b Dawes	2
I. J. Harvey c Seccombe b Bichel	35	–	c Symonds b Dale	100
†D. S. Berry c Seccombe b Bichel	0	–	c Law b Bichel	13
*P. R. Reiffel c Seccombe b Dale	10	–	c Maher b Dawes	7
C. R. Miller c Seccombe b Dale	3	–	c Symonds b Dale	5
M. L. Lewis not out	6	–	c Bichel b Dale	1
M. W. H. Inness b Bichel	0	–	b Dawes	7
L-b 7, n-b 18	25		B 8, l-b 2, n-b 6	16
(94.5 overs, 376 mins)	249		(109.3 overs, 409 mins)	326

Fall: 82 117 137 161 229 229 237 241 248 249

Fall: 45 69 80 83 255 276 286 291 299 326

Bowling: *First Innings*—Bichel 30.5–9–69–4; Dale 31–12–50–3; Dawes 17–1–75–2; Symonds 15–1–47–1; Anderson 1–0–1–0. *Second Innings*—Bichel 26–7–65–1; Dale 34–6–87–3; Dawes 27.3–6–98–6; Anderson 17–8–32–0; Law 5–0–34–0.

Queensland

M. L. Hayden c Klinger b Inness	81	– not out	118
J. P. Maher lbw b Inness	10	– not out	103
M. L. Love c Klinger b Lewis	51		
*S. G. Law c Klinger b Lewis	29		
A. Symonds c Berry b Lewis	49		
C. T. Perren c Berry b Miller	20		
†W. A. Seccombe c Arnberger b Reiffel	35		
A. J. Bichel c Craig b Reiffel	21		
A. C. Dale c Arnberger b Reiffel	25		
J. H. Dawes c Berry b Lewis	2		
M. A. Anderson not out	2		
B 11, l-b 10, n-b 1	22	L-b 5, W 1, n-b 2	8

(99.1 overs, 398 mins)   347   (44.4 overs, 169 mins)   (0 wkts) 229
Fall: 32 154 183 194 253 268 294 342 343 347

Bowling: *First Innings*—Reiffel 13–1–33–3; Inness 22–3–73–2; Harvey 16–6–51–0; Miller 25–5–93–1; Lewis 22.1–5–74–4; Mott 1–0–2–0. *Second Innings*—Reiffel 3–0–20–0; Inness 8–1–32–0; Lewis 6–1–21–0; Miller 11–1–55–0; Harvey 3–0–26–0; Hodge 6.5–0–27–0; Craig 6–0–31–0; Mott 0.5–0–12–0.

Umpires: P. D. Parker and J. F. Torpey.

At Melbourne Cricket Ground, Melbourne, November 29, 30, December 1, 2, 2000. QUEENSLAND drew with VICTORIA.

QUEENSLAND v SOUTH AUSTRALIA

At Brisbane Cricket Ground, Brisbane, December 15, 16, 17, 18, 2000. Drawn. Toss: South Australia. Queensland 2 pts.

Queensland enhanced their reputation as Gabba specialists when they returned to their home ground to dominate the opening two days. Having made four for 329, however, they then lost their way as the last six wickets fell for 49. Half-centuries from Jimmy Maher and Martin Love set the scene for contrasting innings from Stuart Law (277 minutes, 192 balls, 11 fours) and Andrew Symonds (174 minutes, 153 balls, 12 fours). The home side's bowlers then overwhelmed the visitors in only three and a half hours, most of the batsmen showing little relish for getting behind the ball, although Darren Lehmann (117 minutes, 93 balls, nine fours) provided a welcome contrast. Following on before lunch on the third day, South Australia's second innings appeared to have hit the repeat button when they lost David Fitzgerald in the second over. That, however, was Queensland's last slice of joy as Greg Blewett settled in to play an innings of Wagnerian length. He was supported for most of the rest of the day by Shane Deitz (298 minutes, 229 balls, 14 fours) who decided that adhesiveness was the best policy. On the final day, Blewett received consistent support as he resisted for 524 balls which occupied 629 minutes, the fourth-longest innings in Australian domestic cricket (see table, opposite). His innings equalled the 260 of Wayne Phillips at Adelaide in 1981-82 as the highest individual score between these two states.

Man of the Match: G. S. Blewett. *Attendance:* 2,482.

Close of play: First day, Queensland (1) 3-229 (Law 48, Symonds 32); Second day, South Australia (1) 8-110 (Lehmann 56, Wilson 6); Third day, South Australia (2) 3-243 (Blewett 123, Johnson 9).

Queensland

J.L. Cassell b Swain	5	A.C. Dale c Blewett b Wilson	6
J.P. Maher c Blewett b Harrity	62	S.J. O'Leary lbw b Swain	0
M.L. Love c (sub) McIntyre b Blewett	59	J.H. Dawes not out	11
*S.G. Law lbw b Deitz	87		
A. Symonds st Manou b Deitz	85	B 4, l-b 14, w 6, n-b 7	31
L.A. Carseldine c Lehmann b Swain	5		
†W.A. Seccombe c Vaughan b Miller	27	(136 overs, 539 mins)	378
B.N. Creevey lbw b Swain	0	Fall: 17 111 177 322 329 337 337 350 351 378	

Bowling: Wilson 33–20–46–1; Swain 33–6–96–4; Harrity 22–6–69–1; Miller 22–6–62–1; Johnson 10–1–37–0; Blewett 11–5–28–1; Deitz 4–0–17–2; Lehmann 1–0–5–0.

South Australia

S.A. Deitz c Maher b Dale	3	– (2) c Seccombe b Dale 106
D.A. Fitzgerald c Seccombe b Dawes	0	– (1) c Love b Dawes 1
G.S. Blewett lbw b Dale	18	– not out 260
B.A. Johnson c Maher b Dale	10	– (5) lbw b Dale 45
J.M. Vaughan c Seccombe b Dawes	2	– (6) c Love b O'Leary 24
*D.S. Lehmann c Seccombe b Dawes	57	– (7) not out 47
M.C. Miller c Seccombe b Creevey	9	
†G.A. Manou c Carseldine b Creevey	1	
B.A. Swain c O'Leary b Creevey	2	– (4) c Seccombe b Dawes 1
P. Wilson not out	14	
M.A. Harrity b Dale	7	
L-b 1, w 1, n-b 1	3	B 3, l-b 3, W 2, n-b 1 9
(52.2 overs, 210 mins)	126	(176.3 overs, 636 mins)(5 wkts dec) 493
Fall: 0 15 30 35 35 53 55 57 111 126		Fall: 1 231 234 303 382

Bowling: *First Innings*—Dale 24.2–7–42–4; Dawes 17–3–41–3; Creevey 11–4–42–3. *Second Innings*—Dale 37–16–68–2; Dawes 30–10–80–2; Creevey 23–5–59–0; O'Leary 45–9–141–1; Carseldine 11–3–37–0; Symonds 27–6–95–0; Cassell 3.3–1–7–0.

Umpires: A.J. McQuillan and G.C. Zimmer.
TV Umpire: L.D. Musch.

At Bellerive Oval, Hobart, January 3, 4, 5, 2001. QUEENSLAND defeated TASMANIA by an innings and 144 runs.

LONGEST INNINGS – AUSTRALIAN DOMESTIC FIRST-CLASS CRICKET

Minutes

766	M.R.J Veletta (262)	Western Australia v Victoria at Perth	1986-87
708	G. Shipperd (200*)	Tasmania v Western Australia at Perth	1989-90
629	G.S. Blewett (260*)	South Australia v Queensland at Brisbane	2000-01
628	G.R. Marsh (355*)	Western Australia v South Australia at Perth	1989-90
618	D.F. Hills (265)	Tasmania v South Australia at Hobart (Bellerive)	1997-98
605	G. Shipperd (166)	Western Australia v New South Wales at Perth	1982-83
591	M.L. Love (228)	Queensland v New South Wales at Brisbane	1999-00
590	R.B. Simpson (236*)	Western Australia v New South Wales at Perth	1959-60
587	C.L. Badcock (325)	South Australia v Victoria at Adelaide	1935-36
585	W.N. Phillips (205)	Victoria v New South Wales at Sydney	1992-93

QUEENSLAND v WESTERN AUSTRALIA

At Brisbane Cricket Ground, Brisbane, February 18, 19, 20, 2001. Queensland won by eight wickets. Toss: Western Australia. Queensland 6 pts.

Joe Dawes continued his excellent season as Queensland gave Western Australia a frightening return to the Pura Cup after a six-week recess. The visitors were dismissed for 78 shortly after lunch on the first day, with Dawes taking the prized wickets of Simon Katich and Tom Moody. The home side might have been in a similar predicament but for a typically vigilant innings (198 minutes, 143 balls, 14 fours) from Martin Love. Moody, in his final appearance in Brisbane, bowled as cannily as ever. Despite a century of great maturity from Katich (240 minutes, 182 balls, 16 fours), Western Australia were always struggling to catch up and by the end of the second day were only 113 in front with just three wickets in hand. Next morning, Andy Bichel completed another sterling performance. With time not an issue, Jimmy Maher (104 minutes, 87 balls, 11 fours) batted with nonchalance while Andrew Symonds smashed 39 from 23 balls, including three huge sixes into the stands and three fours for good measure.

Man of the Match: J. H. Dawes. *Attendance:* 2,483.

Close of play: First day, Queensland (1) 7-187 (Love 62, Dale 5); Second day, Western Australia (2) 7-253 (Walsh 28, Nicholson 27).

Western Australia

M. E. Hussey c and b Bichel		7	– c Seccombe b Bichel	0
M. J. North lbw b Dale		9	– c Seccombe b Dale	4
S. M. Katich c O'Leary b Dawes		14	– c Symonds b Dawes	101
M. W. Goodwin c Seccombe b Dale		0	– c Seccombe b Bichel	31
*T. M. Moody lbw b Dawes		5	– c Seccombe b Dale	32
G. B. Hogg c Maher b Dawes		0	– c Carseldine b Bichel	7
B. P. Julian c and b Dawes		22	– c Seccombe b Dawes	7
†M. J. Walsh b Bichel		1	– b Dale	35
M. J. Nicholson c Cassell b Dawes		16	– b Bichel	27
J. Angel c Law b Dawes		0	– c Maher b Bichel	0
B. J. Oldroyd not out		0	– not out	4
B 2, n-b 2		4	B 4, l-b 8, w 2, n-b 12	26

(36.3 overs, 155 mins) 78
Fall: 16 21 21 28 33 57 60 62
63 78

(86.5 overs, 346 mins) 274
Fall: 0 12 84 177 190 197 202 263
267 274

Bowling: *First Innings*—Bichel 14–4–38–2; Dale 11–5–19–2; Dawes 11.3–5–19–6. *Second Innings*—Bichel 22.5–4–74–5; Dale 25–6–56–3; Dawes 23–5–73–2; Carseldine 4–1–19–0; Symonds 7–1–28–0; O'Leary 5–2–12–0.

Queensland

J. L. Cassell c Katich b Moody		6	– lbw b Oldroyd	27
J. P. Maher c Goodwin b Nicholson		16	– lbw b Nicholson	59
M. L. Love c Goodwin b Julian		71	– (4) not out	1
*S. G. Law c Katich b Julian		2		
A. Symonds lbw b Moody		26	– (3) not out	39
L. A. Carseldine c Katich b Moody		9		
†W. A. Seccombe c Walsh b Moody		3		
A. J. Bichel lbw b Nicholson		38		
A. C. Dale c Oldroyd b Julian		9		
S. J. O'Leary not out		6		
J. H. Dawes c Julian b Angel		18		
L-b 8, w 2, n-b 4		14	B 6, l-b 1, n-b 2	9

(66 overs, 260 mins) 218
Fall: 21 33 38 80 111 115 164 182 193 218

(29.3 overs, 109 mins) (2 wkts) 135
Fall: 81 133

Bowling: *First Innings*—Angel 15–6–59–1; Nicholson 24–9–54–2; Moody 12–4–38–4; Julian 15–2–59–3. *Second Innings*—Angel 6–3–13–0; Nicholson 10–4–25–1; Julian 4–0–29–0; Moody 4–1–18–0; Oldroyd 5.3–0–43–1.

Umpires: A. J. McQuillan and P. D. Parker.

At Sydney Cricket Ground, Sydney, March 2, 3, 4, 5, 2001. QUEENSLAND lost to NEW SOUTH WALES by eight wickets.

At Adelaide Oval, Adelaide, March 9, 10, 11, 12, 2001. QUEENSLAND defeated SOUTH AUSTRALIA by ten wickets.

QUEENSLAND v NEW SOUTH WALES

At Brisbane Cricket Ground, Brisbane, March 15, 16, 17, 2001. Queensland won by nine wickets. Toss: Queensland. Queensland 6 pts. First-class debuts: D. A. Horsley, P. A. Jaques.

Stuart Law finally won a toss at home and his team had first-innings points by the end of a dramatic first day. New South Wales captain Shane Lee was a last-minute withdrawal because of a virus, forcing the visitors to rush untried batsman Phil Jaques to Brisbane on the morning of the match. He did not arrive until after lunch, by which time the aggression of Adam Dale and Joe Dawes had his side reeling at eight for 70. Jaques (72 minutes, 56 balls, seven fours) then showed commendable defiance as he joined Matthew Phelps in adding 55 runs, the only partnership of substance in the innings. Thanks to a composed innings by Jimmy Maher (298 minutes, 233 balls, nine fours) Queensland built a substantial lead, although stand-in captain Stuart MacGill gave an artistic display of leg-spin bowling. New South Wales made steady progress in their second innings until Dale and Dawes took the second new ball and extinguished the last four wickets for only 24 runs in 8.1 overs. Maher stretched his match aggregate beyond 150 as his side sealed a home final.

Man of the Match: A. C. Dale. *Attendance:* 1,905.

Close of play: First day, Queensland (1) 4-165 (Maher 80, Law 4); Second day, New South Wales (2) 3-93 (Phelps 23).

New South Wales

G. J. Mail lbw b Dale	5	–	(2) c Seccombe b Noffke	23
†B. J. Haddin lbw b Dale	4	–	(7) c Perren b O'Leary	19
M. J. Phelps c Seccombe b Dawes	40	–	st Seccombe b Dale	30
M. J. Clarke c Nash b Dale	2	–	c Maher b Noffke	14
M. A. Higgs c Seccombe b Dale	8	–	c Seccombe b Dale	37
G. C. Rummans c Maher b Dale	0	–	c Seccombe b Dale	46
D. A. Nash c Cassell b Dawes	8	–	(8) c Seccombe b Dawes	35
*S. C. G. MacGill b Dawes	0	–	(9) c Seccombe b Dawes	11
S. R. Clark c Seccombe b Noffke	0	–	(10) c Carseldine b Dale	4
P. A. Jaques c Dale b Dawes	40	–	(1) c (sub) Hopes b Noffke	23
D. A. Horsley not out	4	–	not out	7
B 4, l-b 4, n-b 16, penalties 5	29		B 2, l-b 3, n-b 13	18

(43.5 overs, 190 mins)	140	(89.1 overs, 340 mins)	267
Fall: 15 18 22 46 46 59 67		Fall: 49 58 93 104 165 189 243	
70 125 140		243 253 267	

Bowling: *First Innings*—Dale 17–6–37–5; Dawes 17.5–7–37–4; Noffke 9–0–53–1. *Second Innings*—Dale 26–9–78–4; Dawes 18.1–3–52–2; Noffke 18–3–61–3; O'Leary 11–2–37–1; Perren 5–2–10–0; Carseldine 11–4–24–0.

Queensland

J. L. Cassell c Jaques b Nash	8			
J. P. Maher c Horsley b MacGill	113	– (1) not out		39
C. T. Perren c Higgs b MacGill	28	– not out		13
L. A. Carseldine c Haddin b S. R. Clark	26	– (2) b MacGill		12
B. P. Nash c Higgs b MacGill	12			
*S. G. Law c Higgs b Horsley	63			
†W. A. Seccombe c Horsley b Nash	52			
A. C. Dale c Mail b S. R. Clark	11			
A. A. Noffke c Haddin b MacGill	7			
S. J. O'Leary not out	9			
J. H. Dawes c Clarke b MacGill	5			
L-b 9, n-b 1	10			

(106 overs, 417 mins)   344   (17.1 overs, 67 mins)   (1 wkt)   64
Fall: 30 75 134 159 235 280 305 328 334 344   Fall: 32

Bowling: *First Innings*—Nash 23–7–69–2; S. R. Clark 29–5–74–2; Horsley 18–3–93–1; MacGill 28–7–78–5; Higgs 8–3–21–0. *Second Innings*—S. R. Clark 7–1–14–0; Horsley 4–0–14–0; MacGill 3–0–13–1; Nash 2–0–17–0; Higgs 1.1–0–6–0.

Umpires: P. D. Parker and J. F. Torpey.

FINAL

At Brisbane Cricket Ground, Brisbane, March 23, 24, 25, 26, 27, 2001. QUEENSLAND defeated VICTORIA by four wickets. For details see section on Pura Cup Final, 2000-01, page 369.

AUSTRALIAN DOMESTIC FIRST-CLASS RECORDS

Highest score for:	283*	P. J. P. Burge v New South Wales at Brisbane	1963-64
Highest score against:	452*	D. G. Bradman (New South Wales) at Sydney	1929-30
Best bowling for:	10/61	P. J. Allan v Victoria at Melbourne	1965-66
Best bowling against:	9/67	A. N. Connolly (Victoria) at Brisbane	1964-65
Highest total for:	687	v New South Wales at Brisbane	1930-31
Highest total against:	7-821 dec	by South Australia at Adelaide	1939-40
Lowest total for:	49	v Victoria at Melbourne	1936-37
Lowest total against:	54	by Western Australia at Brisbane	1972-73

MOST RUNS

	M	I	NO	R	HS	100s	50s	Avge
S. C. Trimble	123	230	13	8,647	252*	22	40	39.84
S. G. Law	114	188	22	7,532	216	22	38	45.37
P. J. P. Burge	83	138	12	7,084	283	22	31	56.22
M. L. Hayden	79	144	17	6,903	234	22	29	54.35
A. R. Border	87	143	19	6,779	196	15	37	54.67
K. D. Mackay	100	162	22	6,341	223	14	32	45.29
G. M. Ritchie	94	154	14	6,096	213*	14	34	43.54
T. J. Barsby	100	181	7	6,052	165	13	28	34.78
M. L. Love	72	122	8	5,093	228	13	21	44.68
G. S. Chappell	52	84	11	5,037	194	22	17	69.00

HIGHEST PARTNERSHIP FOR EACH WICKET

388	for 1st	K.C. Wessels and R.B. Kerr v Victoria at St Kilda	1982-83
368*	for 2nd	M.L. Hayden and M.L. Love v Tasmania at Hobart (Bellerive)	1995-96
326	for 3rd	M.L. Love and S.G. Law v Tasmania at Brisbane	1994-95
295	for 4th	P.J.P. Burge and T.R. Veivers v South Australia at Brisbane	1962-63
231	for 5th	K.D. Mackay and R.G. Archer v Victoria at Brisbane	1953-54
		A.R. Border and G.S. Trimble v Victoria at Brisbane	1987-88
211	for 6th	T.R. Veivers and J.D. Bratchford v South Australia at Brisbane	1959-60
335	for 7th	W.C. Andrews and E.C. Bensted v New South Wales at Sydney	1934-35
146	for 8th	T.V. Hohns and G. Dymock v Victoria at Melbourne	1978-79
152*	for 9th	A.T.W. Grout and W.T. Walmsley v New South Wales at Sydney	1956-57
105*	for 10th	W.T. Walmsley and J.E. Freeman v New South Wales at Brisbane	1957-58

MOST WICKETS

	M	Balls	Mdns	R	W	BB	5W/i	10W/m	Avge
C.G. Rackemann	102	22,400	920	10,079	383	7/43	12	1	26.32
J.R. Thomson	77	15,166	404	7,927	328	7/27	17	3	24.17
C.J. McDermott	67	14,974	541	7,605	303	8/44	22	2	25.10
M.S. Kasprowicz	65	13,992	595	6,686	267	6/47	18	2	25.04
G. Dymock	75	17,110	449	7,032	266	6/79	6	0	26.44
D. Tazelaar	73	15,371	623	7,050	257	6/49	9	1	27.43
A.J. Bichel	48	10,756	467	5,108	233	6/45	13	2	21.92
T.V. Hohns	105	16,664	680	7,330	188	6/56	8	1	38.99
P.J. Allan	47	9,840	153	4,603	182	10/61	11	3	25.29
J.N. Maguire	64	12,945	438	5,893	178	6/62	7	1	33.11

MOST DISMISSALS

	M	Ct	St	Total
J.A. Maclean	86	289	24	313
W.A. Seccombe	63	303	10	313
A.T.W. Grout	84	213	63	276
R.B. Phillips	68	214	12	226
D. Tallon	67	145	61	206

MOST CATCHES

S.G. Law	103 in 114 matches	T.J. Barsby	73 in 100 matches
A.R. Border	99 in 87 matches	S.C. Trimble	72 in 123 matches
J.P. Maher	86 in 81 matches	M.L. Hayden	72 in 79 matches
M.L. Love	84 in 72 matches	P.J.P. Burge	70 in 83 matches
G.M. Ritchie	74 in 94 matches	R.B. Kerr	69 in 79 matches

MOST APPEARANCES

123	S.C. Trimble	1959-60 – 1975-76	100	T.J. Barsby	1984-85 – 1996-97
114	S.G. Law	1988-89 – 2000-01	94	G.M. Ritchie	1980-81 – 1991-92
105	T.V. Hohns	1972-73 – 1990-91	87	A.R. Border	1980-81 – 1995-96
102	C.G. Rackemann	1979-80 – 1995-96	86	J.A. Maclean	1968-69 – 1978-79
100	K.D. Mackay	1946-47 – 1963-64	84	A.T.W. Grout	1946-47 – 1965-66

SOUTH AUSTRALIA

Chief Executive: M. Deare

President: I. M. McLaughlan

Cricket Coach: G. S. Chappell

Captain: D. S. Lehmann

Darren Lehmann

It was former Australian captain Greg Chappell's third season at the helm as South Australian state manager of cricket and many wondered if this was the season in which South Australia would again reach the Pura Cup final. But repeatedly fragile first innings, critical batting collapses and a shocking run of injuries prevented them from improving on the fourth place of the previous two seasons. Instead, they descended to the wooden spoon position.

With the other batsmen struggling for consistency, South Australia relied far too heavily on skipper Darren Lehmann and vice-captain Greg Blewett, and the loss of Brad Young to injury after just one match did nothing for team balance. Young's capacity to add variety to the attack was badly missed, while his competent batting down the order could have come in handy. After scoring 71 not out against Western Australia to help his side hold out for a draw in the first match, Young's season ended abruptly. He damaged the anterior cruciate ligament in his left knee while training in Sydney after the match against New South Wales was abandoned because of rain, and was forced to undergo reconstructive surgery.

Blewett scored 1,162 Pura Cup runs for the season at an average of 68.35. He made eight consecutive totals over 50, starting with his heroic unbeaten 260 in the second innings to salvage a draw against Queensland in December. Lehmann scored 645 runs at 46.07 while Shane Deitz was the only other recognised batsman close to the mark with 608 runs at 33.78.

The opening match at Adelaide Oval set a worrying tone, when South Australia managed just 282 in reply to Western Australia's first-innings declaration at eight for 480. But the most glaring example of the South Australians' first-innings woes came when they were bowled out for just 96 in their next match against Victoria, who went on to win by 108 runs. Against Queensland, South Australia conceded a first-innings lead of 252 and were rescued from a crushing defeat only by Blewett's epic performance. When they did secure first-innings points at home against Victoria later in the season, the loss of seven for 22 on the final day cost them the match and dashed their hopes of making the final.

Jeff Vaughan started the year with promise, his unbeaten 131 in the first match being instrumental in the draw against Western Australia. But his season was interrupted in November when he injured his right hand in a limited-overs game against Victoria. After missing a match, Vaughan struggled to regain form and was eventually dropped in the massive clean-out that followed the disastrous five-wicket loss to Victoria in February.

Also struggling for form were fellow middle-order batsman Ben Johnson, who was also dropped during the season, and opener David Fitzgerald, who scored 107 and 51 against New South Wales in January but managed only one other score over 30. A long-term back complaint flared during the match against Victoria in Adelaide and Fitzgerald missed the following two games.

The bowling presented a similarly bleak picture. None of the major members of the attack was available for every match and only the veteran Peter McIntyre, who wheeled away as efficiently as ever, claimed five wickets in an innings. In general, the bowling was respectably accurate rather than ever really threatening the opposition.

With the team out of finals contention and several players injured, the selectors made a raft of changes after the home loss to Victoria in Perth. Opener Luke Williams, 17-year-old batsman Cameron Borgas, pace man Paul Rofe, and Ben Higgins, who made an impressive second-innings 51, debuted as South Australia began rebuilding for season 2001-02. They lost to Western Australia by 36 runs before being thrashed by eventual competition winners Queensland. When Tasmania beat them by an innings and 41 runs in Hobart, South Australia were relegated to the bottom of the table. – VALKERIE MANGNALL.

SOUTH AUSTRALIA RESULTS, 2000-01

All first-class matches – Played 9: Won 2, Lost 5, Drawn 2, Abandoned 1.
Pura Cup matches – Played 9: Won 2, Lost 5, Drawn 2, Abandoned 1.
Mercantile Mutual Cup matches – Played 10: Won 6, Lost 4.
Competition placings – Pura Cup, 6th; Mercantile Mutual Cup, 3rd.

AUSTRALIAN DOMESTIC FIRST-CLASS RESULTS TABLE

Opponent	M	W	L	D	T
New South Wales	193	51	106	36	0
Victoria	194	46	97	51	0
Queensland	137	49	42	45	1
Western Australia	102	28	43	31	0
Tasmania	43	15	7	21	0
Total	669	189	295	184	1

PURA CUP AVERAGES, 2000-01

BATTING

	M	I	NO	R	HS	100s	50s	Avge	Ct/St
B.E. Young	1	2	1	85	71*	0	1	85.00	1
G.S. Blewett	9	18	1	1,162	260*	3	6	68.35	13
J.N. Gillespie	1	1	0	51	51	0	1	51.00	1
D.S. Lehmann	8	16	2	645	146	1	3	46.07	4
J.M. Vaughan	5	10	2	350	131*	1	2	43.75	3
B.H. Higgins	3	6	0	222	65	0	3	37.00	0
S.A. Deitz	9	18	0	608	114	2	2	33.78	9
M.J. Smith	3	6	0	166	76	0	1	27.67	1
B.A. Johnson	5	10	0	260	68	0	2	26.00	2
N.T. Adcock	2	4	0	103	48	0	0	25.75	1
D.A. Fitzgerald	7	14	0	356	107	1	2	25.43	3
C.J. Davies	2	4	1	72	52*	0	1	24.00	1
G.A. Manou	9	16	2	200	53	0	1	14.29	18/2
P.C. Rofe	3	6	1	48	18	0	0	9.60	0
P. Wilson	5	7	1	54	22	0	0	9.00	1
L. Williams	2	4	0	35	16	0	0	8.75	0
M.C. Miller	2	3	0	25	15	0	0	8.33	0
P.E. McIntyre	7	12	2	70	29*	0	0	7.00	1
C.J. Borgas	2	4	0	28	12	0	0	7.00	0
B.A. Swain	6	11	1	60	21*	0	0	6.00	1
M.A. Harrity	8	13	8	25	10*	0	0	5.00	1

* Denotes not out

BOWLING

	O	M	R	W	BB	5W/i	Avge
P. Wilson	179.3	62	406	19	4/23	0	21.37
M.C. Miller	41	8	131	5	2/30	0	26.20
S.A. Deitz.	16	1	56	2	2/17	0	28.00
B.A. Swain	195.3	44	521	17	4/96	0	30.65
M.A. Harrity	243.3	62	728	23	4/55	0	31.65
P.E. McIntyre.	322.2	66	927	28	5/102	1	33.11
D.S. Lehmann	42.3	9	116	3	2/36	0	38.67
M.J. Smith	81	19	262	6	4/81	0	43.67
J.N. Gillespie	34	11	95	2	2/95	0	47.50
G.S. Blewett.	86	19	287	5	1/18	0	57.40
P.C. Rofe	94	31	261	3	2/69	0	87.00
B.A. Johnson	28	5	96	1	1/29	0	96.00
N.T. Adcock.	30	3	119	0	–	0	
L. Williams.	0.4	0	4	0	–	0	
B.E. Young	31	8	114	0	–	0	

SOUTH AUSTRALIA v WESTERN AUSTRALIA

At Adelaide Oval, Adelaide, October 26, 27, 28, 29, 2000. Drawn. Toss: Western Australia. Western Australia 2 pts.

A tenacious unbeaten century by South Australian batsman Jeff Vaughan robbed Western Australia of an outright victory. The home side still trailed by 94 runs at three for 104 in the second innings when play began on the fourth day. Vaughan, however, batted all day to score 131 not out (388 minutes, 330 balls, eight fours) to allow South Australia to hold out for a draw. He was well supported by Brad Young, who contributed 71 (120 minutes, 105 balls, 12 fours) to their unbroken 132-run partnership. The visitors had dominated play throughout the first three days, their first innings being a model of consistency. Damien Martyn batted watchfully for six hours (286 balls, 13 fours, one

SOUTH AUSTRALIA PURA CUP TEAM, 2000-01

Back row: T.J. Nielsen (*assistant coach*), B.A. Swain, M.C. Miller, M.A. Harrity, P.C. Rofe, J.N. Gillespie, P. Wilson, S. Maruan, R.J. Harris, L. Williams, G.S. Chappell (*coach*). *Front row:* P.E. McIntyre, S.A. Deitz, J.M. Vaughan, B.A. Johnson, G.S. Blewett, C.J. Davies, D.A. Fitzgerald, D.J. Harris, G.A. Manou, R. Hunt (*physiotherapist*). *Absent:* N.J.Adcock, C.J. Boras, B.H. Higgins, D.S. Lehmann (*captain*), M.J. Smith, B.E. Young.

six), while Adam Gilchrist was at his flamboyant best, striking the ball with power and precision (110 minutes, 99 balls, 12 fours, two sixes) in a sixth-wicket partnership of 144 runs. Despite three batsmen scoring fifties, South Australia found themselves 198 runs in arrears, but after Western Australia enforced the follow-on, only two wickets fell on the final day.

Man of the Match: A.C. Gilchrist. *Attendance:* 4,701.

Close of play: First day, Western Australia (1) 4-273 (Martyn 56, Moody 47); Second day, South Australia (1) 5-133 (Gillespie 4); Third day, South Australia (2) 3-104 (Lehmann 21, Vaughan 22).

Western Australia

M.E. Hussey c Gillespie b Wilson	48	G.B. Hogg c Young b McIntyre		23
R.J. Campbell c Manou b Gillespie	34	M.J. Nicholson not out		2
J.L. Langer c Deitz b Gillespie	60			
D.R. Martyn c Deitz b Wilson	122	L-b 3, n-b 4		7
S.M. Katich lbw b McIntyre	25			
*T.M. Moody lbw b Wilson	57	(137.2 overs, 515 mins) (8 wkts dec)		480
†A.C. Gilchrist b McIntyre	102	Fall: 43 135 148 190 285 429 473 480		

J. Angel and G.G. Swan did not bat.

Bowling: Gillespie 34–11–95–2; Wilson 30–6–99–3; Blewett 3–0–24–0; McIntyre 35.2–5–130–3; Young 31–8–114–0; Johnson 4–0–15–0.

South Australia

D.A. Fitzgerald c Campbell b Swan	26	– (2) b Nicholson		23
S.A. Deitz lbw b Nicholson	60	– (1) c Gilchrist b Swan		31
G.S. Blewett c and b Hogg	2	– c Katich b Hogg		4
*D.S. Lehmann run out (Campbell/Gilchrist)	38	– c Gilchrist b Hogg		67
J.N. Gillespie lbw b Angel	51			
J.M. Vaughan b Nicholson	0	– (5) not out		131
B.A. Johnson c and b Swan	67	– (6) b Nicholson		19
B.E. Young c Langer b Hogg	14	– (7) not out		71
†G.A. Manou b Swan	0			
P.E. McIntyre not out	16			
P. Wilson b Nicholson	0			
L-b 4, n-b 4	8	L-b 12		12
(104.3 overs, 389 mins)	282	(134 overs, 493 mins) (5 wkts)		358
Fall: 49 72 127 133 133 252 252 253 281 282		Fall: 48 53 63 182 226		

Bowling: *First Innings*—Nicholson 26.3–5–73–3; Angel 19–7–42–1; Swan 21–4–51–3; Hogg 28–7–78–2; Moody 8–3–20–0; Katich 2–0–14–0. *Second Innings*—Nicholson 29–11–50–2; Angel 9–3–19–0; Hogg 35–5–99–2; Swan 16–1–48–1; Moody 24–8–45–0; Martyn 13–1–49–0; Katich 4–0–20–0; Hussey 4–1–16–0.

Umpires: S.J. Davis and J.H. Smeaton.

At Melbourne Cricket Ground, Melbourne, November 23, 24, 25, 26, 2000. SOUTH AUSTRALIA lost to VICTORIA by 108 runs.

SOUTH AUSTRALIA v TASMANIA

At Adelaide Oval, Adelaide, December 1, 2, 3, 4, 2000. South Australia won by 161 runs. Toss: South Australia. South Australia 6 pts.

Four of the home batsmen made fifties, but none went beyond Greg Blewett's 70 (192 minutes, 182 balls, seven fours). The modestly respectable total would have been less substantial but for an important seventh-wicket partnership of 104 between Ben Johnson and Graham Manou. A whole-hearted pace bowling performance from Ben Targett was the outstanding element of the Tasmanian bowling. South Australia's bowlers quickly snuffed out the spirit of the Tasmanian line-up by reducing them to six for 70, a position only faintly redeemed by stern defence from Shaun Young (187 minutes, 133 balls, five fours). The visitors' bowlers then combined to keep the home side in check but they were thwarted by an innings of great character from Jeff Vaughan (227 minutes, 169 balls, seven fours). At their second attempt, the Tasmanian's first five wickets managed only 59, before Dene Hills and Scott Kremerskothen combined for a 51-run stand, Hills having dropped down the order after being struck on the neck while he was fielding during the South Australian second innings. Ultimately, however, the target of 337 on an unfriendly pitch was completely beyond their grasp.

Man of the Match: J. M. Vaughan. *Attendance:* 4,244.

Close of play: First day, South Australia (1) 6-240 (Johnson 37, Manou 17); Second day, South Australia (2) 1-26 (Deitz 3, Blewett 18); Third day, Tasmania (2) 5-95 (Kremerskothen 6, Hills 4).

South Australia

S. A. Deitz c Clingeleffer b Saker	14	– (2) lbw b Wright	3
D. A. Fitzgerald c Clingeleffer b Targett	26	– (1) c Kremerskothen b Wright	5
G. S. Blewett c Cox b Targett	70	– c Saker b Marsh	43
*D. S. Lehmann c Kremerskothen b Targett	5	– c Di Venuto b Saker	1
J. M. Vaughan c Di Venuto b Kremerskothen	63	– not out	85
B. A. Johnson c Wright b Marsh	68	– lbw b Marsh	1
M. C. Miller lbw b Wright	1	– st Clingeleffer b Marsh	15
†G. A. Manou b Targett	53	– b Saker	21
B. A. Swain c Clingeleffer b Targett	7	– run out (Kremerskothen)	1
P. E. McIntyre c Hills b Marsh	1	– b Saker	2
M. A. Harrity not out	0	– b Saker	1
B 3, l-b 2, n-b 3	8	L-b 1	1

(119.5 overs, 443 mins) 316
Fall: 26 50 60 175 189 190 294 306
307 316

(80 overs, 299 mins) 179
Fall: 5 26 27 70 78 116 154 162
173 179

Bowling: *First Innings*—Saker 30–6–74–1; Wright 24–4–68–1; Targett 24–2–62–5; Young 14–5–35–0; Marsh 19.5–3–57–2; Di Venuto 1–0–1–0; Kremerskothen 7–1–14–1. *Second Innings*—Saker 22–6–49–4; Wright 17–5–34–2; Targett 8–1–21–0; Marsh 25–4–53–3; Young 5–0–11–0; Kremerskothen 3–0–10–0.

Tasmania

D. F. Hills lbw b Swain	18	– (7) lbw b Harrity	27
*J. Cox b Manou b Swain	1	– (1) c Lehmann b Swain	10
M. J. Di Venuto run out (Vaughan)	0	– c Johnson b Miller	9
J. A. Dykes lbw b Harrity	9	– (2) lbw b Miller	14
D. J. Marsh b McIntyre	13	– (4) b McIntyre	14
S. Young not out	50	– (5) c Manou b McIntyre	10
S. P. Kremerskothen c Blewett b Miller	7	– (6) lbw b McIntyre	37
†S. G. Clingeleffer b Harrity	15	– lbw b McIntyre	3
D. J. Saker lbw b McIntyre	11	– not out	34
D. G. Wright lbw b Miller	11	– c Manou b Harrity	7
B. S. Targett not out	3	– c Manou b Harrity	4
B 8, l-b 4, n-b 9	21	B 1, l-b 3, n-b 2	6

(57 overs, 237 mins) (9 wkts dec) 159
Fall: 14 19 28 28 54 70 118
137 154

(73.2 overs, 276 mins) 175
Fall: 25 25 35 54 59 110 119 148
161 175

Bowling: *First Innings*—Harrity 17–5–48–2; Swain 9–2–24–2; Miller 9–0–39–2; McIntyre 19–7–26–2; Blewett 3–0–10–0. *Second Innings*—Harrity 18.2–4–51–3; Swain 16–7–27–1; Miller 10–2–30–2; McIntyre 28–11–63–4; Lehmann 1–1–0–0.

Umpires: S. J. Davis and K. D. Perrin.

At Brisbane Cricket Ground, Brisbane, December 15, 16, 17, 18, 2000. SOUTH AUSTRALIA drew with QUEENSLAND.

SOUTH AUSTRALIA v NEW SOUTH WALES

At Adelaide Oval, Adelaide, January 4, 5, 6, 7, 2001. South Australia won by 168 runs. Toss: South Australia. South Australia 6 pts. First-class debut: A. M. Clark.

Contrasting centuries to captain Darren Lehmann and David Fitzgerald steered South Australia into a commanding position. Lehmann blasted 146 (252 minutes, 197 balls, 20 fours) before being caught off the bowling of young pace man Nathan Bracken, who received surprise selection in the national limited-overs squad during the match. Fitzgerald batted much more sedately (322 minutes, 244 balls, 13 fours) before he too fell to Bracken for 107. Peter McIntyre showed the potency of skill and experience as New South Wales were restricted to a first-innings total of 265. They had slumped to five for 67 before a lively innings from Brad Haddin (168 minutes, 141 balls, 13 fours) restored respectability to the total. Half-centuries to Fitzgerald and Greg Blewett allowed Lehmann to set New South Wales a formidable target of 401 in just over a day. Only Shawn Bradstreet (176 minutes, 148 balls, six fours) looked capable of both occupying the crease and scoring runs, while Paul Wilson was accurately effective as the visitors fell well short of the target

Man of the Match: D.S. Lehmann. *Attendance:* 5,099.

Close of play: First day, South Australia (1) 6-352 (Lehmann 131, Manou 4); Second day, New South Wales (1) 8-244 (Bradstreet 34, Nash 14); Third day, New South Wales (2) 1-45 (Mail 17, Bevan 20).

South Australia

S. A. Deitz b Nash	2	– (2) c Van Deinsen b Higgs	21
D.A. Fitzgerald lbw b Bracken	107	– (1) run out (Bevan)	51
G. S. Blewett c and b Nash	80	– c Bradstreet b Lee	69
*D.S. Lehmann c Bradstreet b Bracken	146	– not out	45
J. M. Vaughan c Bevan b Bracken	10	– c Mail b Lee	0
B. A. Johnson b Bradstreet	1	– c Van Deinsen b Bradstreet	12
B. A. Swain c Haddin b Bradstreet	0		
†G. A. Manou c Bracken b Nash	12	– (7) not out	23
P. Wilson b Lee	22		
P.E. McIntyre not out	29		
B 8, l-b 4, w 5, n-b 2	19	B 3, l-b 11, n-b 2	16

(110.2 overs, 427 mins)   (9 wkts dec) 428   (63.5 overs, 271 mins) (5 wkts dec) 237
Fall: 2 127 326 336 341 341 360 380 428   Fall: 44 134 168 168 201

M. A. Harrity did not bat.

Bowling: *First Innings*—Nash 21–6–63–3; Bracken 23–5–66–3; Bradstreet 14–3–68–2; Lee 12.2–1–58–1; Higgs 21–3–93–0; A. M. Clark 18–2–64–0; Mail 1–0–4–0. *Second Innings*—Nash 3.5–2–8–0; Bracken 12–2–38–0; A.M. Clark 9.1–5–22–0; Lee 15–4–59–2; Higgs 10–0–31–1; Bradstreet 13.5–0–65–1.

New South Wales

G. J. Mail c Blewett b Harrity	16	– lbw b Wilson	17
B. P. Van Deinsen c Fitzgerald b McIntyre	23	– lbw b Swain	1
M. G. Bevan st Manou b McIntyre	16	– c Deitz b McIntyre	37
C. J. Richards c Manou b Harrity	0	– c Wilson b McIntyre	0
M. A. Higgs c Blewett b McIntyre	33	– c Deitz b Blewett	31
*S. Lee b Harrity	1	– c Manou b Harrity	13
†B. J. Haddin c Johnson b McIntyre	93	– (8) c Deitz b Wilson	25
S. D. Bradstreet not out	36	– (7) c Blewett b Wilson	60
N. W. Bracken lbw b McIntyre	0	– (10) lbw b Swain	1
D. A. Nash b Wilson	18	– (11) not out	10
A. M. Clark lbw b Wilson	9	– (9) c Swain b Wilson	17
B 3, l-b 10, n-b 7	20	B 9, l-b 6, n-b 5	20

(87 overs, 333 mins)	265	(84.5 overs, 328 mins)	232
Fall: 42 60 62 63 67 149 216 216		Fall: 1 55 64 65 88 121 176 219	
249 265		222 232	

Bowling: *First Innings*—Wilson 21–6–60–2; Swain 12–3–35–0; McIntyre 34–4–102–5; Harrity 15–4–31–3; Blewett 3–1–18–0; Deitz 2–0–6–0. *Second Innings*—Wilson 21.5–9–23–4; Swain 11–1–30–2; McIntyre 30–5–112–2; Harrity 12–4–23–1; Blewett 9–3–22–1; Lehmann 1–0–7–0.

Umpires: P. M. Angley and P. J. Weeks.

SOUTH AUSTRALIA v VICTORIA

At Adelaide Oval, Adelaide, February 19, 20, 21, 22, 2001. Victoria won by five wickets. Toss: South Australia. South Australia 2 pts. Victoria 6 pts.

In a match set to make or break South Australia's season, Victoria shattered the South Australians' faint finals hopes. Having reached four for 261 on the opening day, with a customary century to Greg Blewett (245 minutes, 228 balls, 15 fours), South Australia faded on the second morning. The position was exacerbated when Chris Davies had to retire hurt with the score at seven for 312 when he strained his right knee lunging for the crease to avoid being run out. Off-spinner John Davison returned his best figures for several seasons. At six for 311, the visitors looked to be well set for first-innings points but Mark Harrity then promptly swept through the final four wickets, including that of Ian Harvey who had played a powerfully blustery innings (175 minutes, 123 balls, ten fours). Blewett went within five of a century in each innings as he dominated proceedings (263 minutes, 194 balls, nine fours, one six) but Harvey snared 4/4 from his final ten overs as South Australia collapsed from the relative comfort of four for 164. Victoria made plodding progress towards the target against some probing bowling by Peter McIntyre until Michael Klinger underlined his potential with a refreshingly crisp 66 not out (110 minutes, 92 balls, ten fours).

Man of the Match: I. J. Harvey. *Attendance:* 1,754.

Close of play: First day, South Australia (1) 4-261 (Vaughan 15, Davies 21); Second day, Victoria (1) 5-188 (Roach 0, Harvey 1); Third day, South Australia 3-157 (Blewett 80, Vaughan 13).

South Australia

S. A. Deitz c Roach b Harvey	25	– (2) b Inness	1
D. A. Fitzgerald c Harvey b Davison	50	– (1) c Mott b Lewis	15
G. S. Blewett c Arnberger b Inness	117	– b Harvey	95
*D. S. Lehmann c Arnberger b Davison	21	– lbw b Inness	42
J. M. Vaughan run out (Klinger/Roach)	22	– lbw b Reiffel	13
C. J. Davies retired hurt	52	– (9) b Harvey	9
†G. A. Manou b Lewis	4	– (6) b Harvey	1
B. A. Swain c Harvey b Davison	7	– (7) lbw b Reiffel	0
P. Wilson c Arnberger b Davison	6	– (8) c Roach b Lewis	3
P. E. McIntyre c Mott b Harvey	10	– lbw b Harvey	0
M. A. Harrity not out	10	– not out	0
L-b 10, n-b 6	16	B 2, n-b 5	7

(117.5 overs, 478 mins)	(9 wkts) 340	(73.2 overs, 299 mins) 186
Fall: 56 140 179 236 289 297 312 321 340		Fall: 7 29 128 164 165 167 177
		177 181 186

Bowling: *First Innings*—Reiffel 19-7-43-0; Inness 19-4-53-1; Lewis 25-4-74-1; Harvey 21.5-5-63-2; Mott 4-2-7-0; Davison 29-9-90-4. *Second Innings*—Reiffel 16-2-45-2; Inness 12-5-30-2; Harvey 16.2-10-19-4; Lewis 12-1-37-2; Davison 17-3-53-0.

Victoria

M. T. G. Elliott c Manou b McIntyre	59	– (2) b McIntyre	19
J. L. Arnberger run out ((sub) M.C. Miller/Swain)	11	– (1) c (sub) Miller b McIntyre	9
M. P. Mott b McIntyre	62	– c Lehmann b McIntyre	40
B. J. Hodge c Harrity b Wilson	46	– lbw b Blewett	36
M. Klinger lbw b Wilson	0	– not out	66
†P. J. Roach lbw b Blewett	13	– (7) not out	0
I. J. Harvey c Vaughan b Harrity	87	– (6) c (sub) Miller b McIntyre	19
*P. R. Reiffel c Manou b Harrity	34		
J. M. Davison c Vaughan b Harrity	1		
M. L. Lewis not out	6		
M. W. H. Inness c Manou b Harrity	0		
B 7, l-b 7, w 1, n-b 2	17	L-b 2	2

(112 overs, 454 mins)	336	(67.4 overs, 269 mins) (5 wkts) 191
Fall: 30 91 186 186 222 311 313 336 336		Fall: 28 29 94 134 172

Bowling: *First Innings*—Wilson 26-5-63-2; Swain 17-5-54-0; McIntyre 36-8-107-2; Harrity 18-6-55-4; Lehmann 3-2-8-0; Blewett 10-1-27-1; Deitz 2-0-8-0. *Second Innings*—Wilson 10-2-23-0; Swain 15-3-42-0; McIntyre 24-3-62-4; Harrity 12.4-3-44-0; Blewett 6-0-18-1.

Umpires: D. J. Harper and R. G. Patterson.
TV Umpire: J. S. Booth.

At WACA Ground, Perth, March 2, 3, 4, 5, 2001. SOUTH AUSTRALIA lost to WESTERN AUSTRALIA by 36 runs.

SOUTH AUSTRALIA v QUEENSLAND

At Adelaide Oval, Adelaide, March 9, 10, 11, 12, 2001. Queensland won by ten wickets. Toss: South Australia. Queensland 6 pts.

Queensland wanted to secure a home final, while South Australia were playing for pride alone. The home side, which had lost several players because of injury, struggled against Queensland's disciplined attack, and continued their depressing and repeated batting collapses after the contrasting approaches of Shane Deitz (197 minutes, 157 balls, four fours) and Greg Blewett (203 minutes, 147 balls, nine fours, one six) had produced 132 for the second wicket. Blewett hit his eighth consecutive Pura Cup score over 50. Queensland then occupied the crease for most of two days in setting up a lead of 260. Stuart Law batted with prolonged determination for his 161 (381 minutes, 294 balls, 21 fours, one six), while Clinton Perren was equally patient (250 minutes, 185 balls, 20 fours), their third-wicket partnership realising 185. Mike Smith (210 minutes, 153 balls, seven fours, one six) batted with composure but there was insufficient support and it was left to a ninth-wicket partnership of 70 between Nathan Adcock and Paul Rofe to ensure that Queensland had to bat again. Pace man Joe Dawes gave the batsmen no respite as he returned his best innings analysis to give him ten dismissals for the match.

Man of the Match: J. H. Dawes. *Attendance:* 4,055.

Close of play: First day, South Australia (1) 9-213 (Smith 22, Harrity 0); Second day, Queensland (1) 5-299 (Law 121, Seccombe 3); Third day, South Australia (2) 2-62 (Smith 7, Lehmann 8).

South Australia

L. Williams lbw b Dale	1	– (2) lbw b Dale			12
S. A. Deitz c Seccombe b Bichel	45	– (1) c Seccombe b Symonds			32
G. S. Blewett c Law b Bichel	88	– (5) b Dawes			24
*D. S. Lehmann b Dawes	14	– c Maher b Dawes			45
B. H. Higgins b Symonds	7	– (6) c Bichel b Dawes			10
N. T. Adcock c Seccombe b Dawes	14	– (7) c Perren b Dawes			48
M. J. Smith c Seccombe b Dawes	22	– (3) b Symonds			76
†G. A. Manou c Seccombe b Bichel	13	– c Dale b Dawes			0
P. E. McIntyre run out (Symonds)	1	– c Maher b Dawes			1
P. C. Rofe b Dale	0	– c Seccombe b Dawes			18
M. A. Harrity not out	2	– not out			0
L-b 3, n-b 5	8	B 2, l-b 1, n-b 11			14

(99.1 overs, 388 mins) 215   (105 overs, 404 mins) 280
Fall: 5 137 140 158 175 175 195 202   Fall: 45 46 157 189 205 208 208
213 215   210 280 280

Bowling: *First Innings*—Bichel 26–8–59–3; Dale 27–16–41–2; Dawes 21.1–7–43–3; O'Leary 17–5–56–0; Symonds 8–2–13–1. *Second Innings*—Dawes 35–11–98–7; Dale 29–10–59–1; Symonds 26–4–79–2; O'Leary 13–1–33–0; Perren 2–0–8–0.

Queensland

J. L. Cassell c Deitz b Rofe	4	– not out	13
J. P. Maher c Manou b Harrity	47	– not out	11
C. T. Perren lbw b McIntyre	112		
*S. G. Law c Manou b Rofe	161		
A. Symonds run out (Deitz)	0		
B. P. Nash c Manou b Harrity	2		
†W. A. Seccombe lbw b McIntyre	7		
A. J. Bichel c Deitz b McIntyre	61		
A. C. Dale not out	45		
S. J. O'Leary c Blewett b Lehmann	19		
B 6, l-b 5, n-b 6	17		

(154.3 overs, 590 mins) (9 wkts dec) 475   (8.4 overs, 32 mins) (0 wkts) 24
Fall: 17 76 261 274 294 319 391 429 475

J. H. Dawes did not bat.

Bowling: *First Innings*—Harrity 24–5–82–2; Rofe 31–10–69–2; Smith 19–3–69–0; McIntyre 45–11–139–3; Adcock 18–2–80–0; Lehmann 12.3–4–14–1; Blewett 5–2–11–0. *Second Innings*—Harrity 2–0–6–0; Rofe 4–0–8–0; McIntyre 2–0–6–0; Williams 0.4–0–4–0.

Umpires: J. S. Booth and S. J. Davis.

AUSTRALIAN DOMESTIC FIRST-CLASS RECORDS

Highest score for:	365*	C. Hill v New South Wales at Adelaide	1900-91
Highest score against:	355*	G. R. Marsh (Western Australia) at Perth	1989-90
Best bowling for:	10/35	T. W. Wall v New South Wales at Sydney	1932-33
Best bowling against:	9/40	E. L. McCormick (Victoria) at Adelaide	1936-37
Highest total for:	7-821 dec	v Queensland at Adelaide	1939-40
Highest total against:	918	by New South Wales at Sydney	1900-01
Lowest total for:	27	v New South Wales at Sydney	1955-56
Lowest total against:	41	by Western Australia at Adelaide	1990-91

MOST RUNS

	M	I	NO	R	HS	100s	50s	Avge
D. W. Hookes	120	205	9	9,364	306*	26	44	47.78
L. E. Favell	121	204	8	8,269	164	20	43	38.28
D. S. Lehmann	84	155	9	8,151	255	27	33	55.83
I. M. Chappell	89	157	13	7,665	205*	22	45	53.23
H. N. Dansie	107	196	6	6,692	185	17	32	35.22
G. S. Blewett	73	138	6	6,507	268	16	33	49.30
A. M. J. Hilditch	91	161	11	6,504	230	17	32	43.36
C. Hill	68	126	6	6,270	365*	18	27	52.25
P. R. Sleep	127	211	37	6,106	146*	12	29	35.09
V. Y. Richardson	77	146	7	6,027	203	18	27	43.36
J. D. Siddons	82	150	10	5,940	197	17	26	42.43

HIGHEST PARTNERSHIP FOR EACH WICKET

281	for 1st	L. E. Favell and J. P. Causby v New South Wales at Adelaide	1967-68
308	for 2nd	B. A. Richards and I. M. Chappell v Western Australia at Perth	1970-71
286	for 3rd	G. S. Blewett and D. S. Lehmann v Tasmania at Adelaide	1993-94
462*	for 4th	D. W. Hookes and W. B. Phillips v Tasmania at Adelaide	1986-87
281	for 5th	C. L. Badcock and M. G. Waite v Queensland at Adelaide	1939-40
260	for 6th	D. S. Lehmann and T. J. Nielsen v Queensland at Adelaide	1996-97
198	for 7th	G. A. Bishop and T. B. A. May v Tasmania at Adelaide	1990-91
174	for 8th	D. F. G. O'Connor and A. K. Zesers v Victoria at Adelaide	1984-85
232	for 9th	C. Hill and E. A. Walkley v New South Wales at Adelaide	1900-01
104	for 10th	L. Michael and E. I. Pynor v Victoria at Adelaide	1949-50

MOST WICKETS

	M	Balls	Mdns	R	W	BB	5W/i	10W/m	Avge
C. V. Grimmett	78	28,144	445	12,878	504	9/180	47	13	25.55
A. A. Mallett	77	20.988	673	8,171	344	7/57	19	2	23.75
T. B. A. May	80	22,575	931	9,943	270	7/93	15	2	36.82
P. R. Sleep	127	19,482	671	9,883	252	8/133	7	0	39.22
E. Jones	39	12,145	501	5,516	208	8/157	19	3	26.52
T. J. Jenner	65	13,559	245	6,312	207	7/127	8	1	30.49
P. E. McIntyre	56	16,426	546	8,409	206	6/64	8	2	40.82
G. Giffen	38	11,682	402	5,676	192	9/147	18	7	29.56
G. Noblet	38	11,156	273	3,396	190	7/29	10	2	17.87
G. R. Attenborough	50	11,137	280	5,371	172	7/90	8	2	31.23

MOST DISMISSALS

	M	Ct	St	Total
T. J. Nielsen	92	255	29	284
B. N. Jarman	77	193	57	250
C. W. Walker	57	103	87	190
G. R. A. Langley	46	111	24	135
K. J. Wright	36	102	9	111

MOST CATCHES

D. W. Hookes	128 in 120 matches	V. Y. Richardson	99 in 77 matches
I. M. Chappell	113 in 89 matches	P. R. Sleep	84 in 127 matches
J. D. Siddons	113 in 82 matches	G. A. Bishop	60 in 84 matches

MOST APPEARANCES

127	P. R. Sleep	1976-77 – 1992-93	91	A. M. J Hilditch	1982-83 – 1991-92
121	L. E. Favell	1951-52 – 1969-70	89	I. M. Chappell	1961-62 – 1979-80
120	D. W. Hookes	1975-76 – 1991-92	84	G. A. Bishop	1982-83 – 1992-93
107	H. N. Dansie	1949-50 – 1966-67	84	D. S. Lehmann	1987-88 – 2000-01
92	T. J. Nielsen	1990-91 – 1998-99	82	J. D. Siddons	1991-92 – 1999-00

TASMANIA

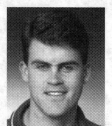

Chief Executive: D. A. Johnston

Chairman: G. Gillies

Cricket Coach: G. Shipperd

Captain: J. Cox

Jamie Cox

Are Tasmania paper Tigers? It is a question which must be asked after the big finish to a season in which they delivered so little. Third place on the Pura Cup table might not suggest that, but in reality the Tasmanians did not begin to snarl until the hunt for a berth in the final was all over. Significantly, Tasmania's wins in the last three games came only after captain Jamie Cox challenged his players to produce "career-defining performances", which until then had been sadly missing. To their credit most players did, even if the awareness that contract-renewal time was nigh may have been as much a motivating factor for some as pride in their own performance.

Cox pulled no punches when he said, "While it was great to finish so well, we can't let it mask the fact that third place flatters the way we performed overall, especially mid-season when we were dreadful. Our top six batters really struggled in that period. We didn't pass 200 in three games and that's the main reason why we lost them." Cox can even designate the punch that ended Tasmania's title bid. "If there was one defining moment in our season it was in Brisbane when Andrew Symonds survived a big leg-before shout first ball which we were convinced was out," he said. "If that had gone our way it would have made Queensland four for 69. Instead, Symonds and Martin Love butchered us to get the 370-odd we'd set them to win."

While the bowlers may have been trampled that day by those two rampaging Queenslanders, it was the batsmen who were to blame for Tasmania languishing so long on the bottom rungs of the ladder. Only Cox, who scored more than twice as many runs as the next best, stood tall. He totalled 1,070 at 66.88 with five centuries to win the national Player of the Year award, but not the nod of the Australian selectors for the tour of England. While he fought like Horatio on the bridge, others fell around him. None was more disappointing than Dene Hills, who with Cox had formed the most successful opening pair in the modern era of domestic first-class cricket. Hills made only 395 runs at 23.24, his tendency to cut up rather than down often bringing about his downfall. Almost as tragic was fellow left-hand dasher Michael Di Venuto, whose 466 at 27.41 underlined his inadequacies against a new ball which he saw far too soon at No. 3. By season's end "Diva", one of several players said to be unhappy under the regime of coach Greg Shipperd, was being courted to move interstate.

Shaun Young presented a much trimmer figure, but too often his batting (433 at 33.31) lacked its beef of old. On the flip side, he took 21 wickets at 25.33, including 7/57 in the last-game rout of South Australia, to become the state's highest-ever first-class wicket-taker. Fellow all-rounder Dan Marsh failed to build on his fine season the summer before, finishing with 514 runs at 39.44 and 18 wickets at 40. To make matters worse, the career of Andrew Dykes (125 at 15.63) nose-dived after promising much the previous season.

Victorian veteran David Saker was recruited to fill the void left by the retirement of pace man Mark Ridgway, and while he was the leading wicket-taker with 26 at a pricey 41.54, his failure to take a wicket between mid-December and mid-March left lingering doubts about his staying power. Of the other quicks, Damien Wright (22 at 26.95) gave Saker the best support. Injury was not kind to the Tasmanian attack, with Gerard Denton playing only one game because of a serious back injury and fellow quicks Wright and Andrew Downton also hampered by injuries.

Happily, there was more to enthuse about among the younger brigade, none better than newcomer Shane Watson. Plucked mid-season from the Australian Cricket Academy, the husky Queenslander showed clear promise for higher honours in the future. Watson scored 309 runs at 51.50 and bowled with genuine pace in taking 11 wickets at 26.27. He responded to the challenge of being moved up the order to No. 4 by making his maiden first-class century against South Australia. Scott Kremerskothen improved steadily to finish with 435 runs at 36.25, but was given limited opportunities at the bowling crease. Former Australian Under-19 keeper Sean Clingeleffer replaced long-time incumbent Mark Atkinson, and his fine glove work and handy batting mark him as one for the national selectors to watch. – DAVID STOCKDALE.

TASMANIA RESULTS, 2000-01

All first-class matches – Played 10: Won 3, Lost 4, Drawn 3.
Pura Cup matches – Played 10: Won 3, Lost 4, Drawn 3.
Mercantile Mutual Cup matches – Played 10: Won 4, Lost 6.
Competition placings – Pura Cup, 3rd; Mercantile Mutual Cup, 5th.

AUSTRALIAN DOMESTIC FIRST-CLASS RESULTS TABLE

Opponent	M	W	L	D	T
Western Australia	44	5	21	18	0
Victoria	43	9	12	22	0
South Australia	43	7	15	21	0
Queensland	43	6	14	23	0
New South Wales	44	10	17	17	0
Total	217	37	79	101	0

PURA CUP AVERAGES, 2000-01

BATTING

	M	I	NO	R	HS	100s	50s	Avge	Ct/St
R. T. Ponting	2	4	1	484	233	2	1	161.33	0
J. Cox.	10	19	3	1,070	160	5	3	66.88	8
S. R. Watson	5	8	2	309	105	1	2	51.50	1
D. J. Marsh.	9	16	3	514	110	1	3	39.54	12
S. P. Kremerskothen . .	9	13	1	435	81	0	2	36.25	6
S. Young	10	17	4	433	83*	0	3	33.31	5
M. J. Di Venuto	10	18	1	466	86	0	5	27.41	15
D. F. Hills.	9	17	0	395	120	1	2	23.24	5
S. B. Tubb	1	2	0	42	42	0	0	21.00	0
J. A. Dykes.	4	8	0	125	32	0	0	15.63	3
S. G. Clingeleffer.	10	14	1	203	50	0	1	15.62	21/4
D. J. Saker	10	14	3	133	34*	0	0	12.09	1
D. G. Wright	6	8	4	47	16*	0	0	11.75	5
A. G. Downton.	6	5	0	51	17	0	0	10.20	2
B. S. Targett.	3	6	2	30	15	0	0	7.50	2
S. J. Jurgensen	2	2	0	13	13	0	0	6.50	0
M. D. Colegrave	1	2	1	6	5	0	0	6.00	0
S. R. Mason	1	2	0	9	9	0	0	4.50	0
T. A. Pinnington	1	2	0	9	5	0	0	4.50	0
G. J. Denton	1	2	2	8	5*	0	0	–	0

* Denotes not out

BOWLING

	O	M	R	W	BB	5W/i	Avge
D. F. Hills	4.1	0	20	2	2/20	0	10.00
S. Young	203.3	63	532	21	4/33	0	25.33
S. R. Watson	74	13	289	11	2/22	0	26.27
D. G. Wright	192.1	43	593	22	4/54	0	26.95
A. G. Downton	161.5	42	548	16	4/51	0	34.25
B. S. Targett	86	21	265	7	5/62	1	37.86
D. J. Marsh	216	44	720	18	4/80	0	40.00
D. J. Saker.	350	66	1,080	26	5/98	1	41.54
S. J. Jurgensen	70.5	12	250	6	4/113	0	41.67
S. P. Kremerskothen	104	18	402	9	3/64	0	44.67
G. J. Denton	20	3	90	2	2/90	0	45.00
M. D. Colegrave	33.4	5	131	1	1/76	0	131.00
J. Cox	2	1	4	0	–	0	–
M. J. Di Venuto	12	5	30	0	–	0	–
J. A. Dykes	5	0	22	0	–	0	–
S. B. Tubb	14	2	70	0	–	0	–
R. T. Ponting	2	0	14	0	–	0	–

At Brisbane Cricket Ground, Brisbane, October 26, 27, 28, 29, 2000. TASMANIA lost to QUEENSLAND by four wickets.

TASMANIA v NEW SOUTH WALES

At Bellerive Oval, Hobart, November 7, 8, 9, 10, 11, 2000. Drawn. Toss: New South Wales. New South Wales 2 pts.

The only winner in this match was the road-like wicket, which drove bowlers to despair as it produced 1,141 runs and five centuries. Sent in, Tasmania were reeling at two for 0 against the blistering pace of Brett Lee before Ricky Ponting (482 minutes, 345

TASMANIA PURA CUP TEAM, 2000-01

Back row: D. Ramshaw (*assistant coach*), S. Clingeleffer, S. Kremerskothen, J.A. Dykes, B. Targett, S. Watson, A. Downton, G. Denton, D. Saker, G. Shipperd (*coach*), L. Coutts (*physiotherapist*). *Middle row:* M. Colegrave, S. Young, M. di Venuto, J. Cox (*captain*), D. Hills, D. Wright, D. Marsh. *Front row:* S. Mason, T. Pinnington, S. Tubb.

balls, 19 fours, one six) joined Jamie Cox (312 minutes, 268 balls, nine fours) to amass 242 for the third wicket. Left-arm pace man Nathan Bracken took 3/0 in seven balls to upend the middle order and restrict Tasmania to 362. New South Wales gained a lead of 102 against an attack depleted by injuries to Andrew Downton and Damien Wright as Michael Slater peeled off an even 100 (205 minutes, 187 balls, 12 fours) and Mark Waugh dispelled doubts about his place in the national side with a fluent 152 (257 minutes, 205 balls, 15 fours). Dan Marsh made the ball dip into a strong wind to collect four wickets, including three catches off his own bowling. A storm at tea on the last day brought a mercifully premature end to proceedings, Cox having taken the opportunity to hit his second century of the match (369 minutes, 308 balls, 11 fours). It was the third time he had achieved the feat against New South Wales, and along the way he passed David Boon as Tasmania's highest run-maker. Michael Di Venuto (217 minutes, 166 balls, 13 fours) contributed to a second-wicket partnership of 195 which dispelled any hopes of a win for the visitors.

Man of the Match: J. Cox. *Attendance:* 1,830.

Close of play: First day, Tasmania (1) 5-279 (Ponting 144, Kremerskothen 11); Second day, New South Wales (1) 4-193 (ME Waugh 7, Bevan 4); Third day, Tasmania (2) 1-119 (Cox 57, Di Venuto 41).

Tasmania

D. F. Hills c Haddin b B. Lee	0	– c S. Lee b MacGill 10
*J. Cox b Bracken	106	– not out 128
M. J. Di Venuto c Haddin b B. Lee	0	– c Haddin b Nash 86
R. T. Ponting not out	187	– b MacGill 3
D. J. Marsh b Bracken	0	– not out 60
S. Young c Haddin b Bracken	5	
S. P. Kremerskothen c Bracken b Nash	15	
†S. G. Clingeleffer c MacGill b S. Lee	21	
D. J. Saker lbw b S. Lee	0	
D. G. Wright c Bevan b MacGill	0	
A. G. Downton b B. Lee	11	
L-b 5, w 1, n-b 11	17	B 3, l-b 10, n-b 15 28

(128.5 overs, 494 mins)	362	(101 overs, 369 mins)	(3 wkts) 315

Fall: 0 0 242 242 250 295 342 342 343 362   Fall: 25 220 224

Bowling: *First Innings*—B. Lee 28.5–8–94–3; Nash 26–11–36–1; MacGill 28–3–74–1; Bracken 26–5–102–3; S. Lee 14–1–47–2; Richards 6–4–4–0. *Second Innings*—B. Lee 17–2–63–0; Nash 12–2–54–1; MacGill 33–10–85–2; Bracken 14–3–30–0; M.E. Waugh 10–1–27–0; S. Lee 8–2–32–0; S.R. Waugh 6–3–11–0; Richards 1–1–0–0.

New South Wales

M. J. Slater c and b Marsh	100	D. A. Nash c (sub) Dykes b Marsh 32
C. J. Richards c and b Marsh	69	N. W. Bracken c Di Venuto b Hills 30
*S. R. Waugh c and b Marsh	7	S. C. G. MacGill not out 0
M. E. Waugh c Cox b Hills	152	
†B. J. Haddin lbw b Saker	1	B 4, l-b 1, n-b 7 12
M. G. Bevan run out ((sub)S. R. Mason)	21	
S. Lee c and b Kremerskothen	14	(118.1 overs, 435 mins) 464
B. Lee c Clingeleffer b Kremerskothen	26	Fall: 146 166 187 188 253 281 343 400 460 464

Bowling: Saker 27–4–97–1; Wright 20.2–4–84–0; Downton 6.4–2–20–0; Young 13–3–38–0; Kremerskothen 25–7–120–2; Marsh 22–2–80–4; Hills 4.1–0–20–2.

Umpires: D. B. Hair and J. H. Smeaton.

TASMANIA v WESTERN AUSTRALIA

At Bellerive Oval, Hobart, November 19, 20, 21, 22, 2000. Drawn. Toss: Western Australia. Tasmania 2 pts. First-class debut: M.D. Colegrave.

Tasmania made Western Australian captain Tom Moody rue his decision to send them in on another Bellerive featherbed. Dan Marsh (242 minutes, 205 balls, 16 fours) led the charge with solid support from Jamie Cox, while Scott Kremerskothen (163 minutes, 143 balls, nine fours, one six) dominated a seventh-wicket partnership of 122. Damien Martyn (247 minutes, 188 balls, 15 fours) continued his run glut at Bellerive with his seventh century there in ten seasons. Mark Walsh beefed up the middle order before Moody declared. With Tasmania's attack crippled by injuries to pace men Gerard Denton and Shaun Young, Cox's second-innings declaration left Western Australia to score 387 off 71 overs. Simon Katich (204 minutes, 168 balls, 19 fours) and Martyn (119 minutes, 99 balls, 14 fours) combined in a rousing third-wicket partnership of 193 to give their side a chance. But then David Saker and Kremerskothen began to create havoc with reverse swing, and Western Australia fell away from two for 223 to nine for 369. Moody drew on his experience to dig in and deny the Tasmanians their first win of the season.

Man of the Match: D.R. Martyn. *Attendance:* 547.

Close of play: First day, Tasmania (1) 4-297 (Marsh 93, Young 43); Second day, Western Australia (1) 4-137 (Martyn 46, Walsh 3); Third day, Tasmania (2) 4-147 (Cox 73, Young 3).

Tasmania

D.F. Hills c Hussey b Julian	15	–	b Julian	3
*J. Cox lbw b Oldroyd	87	–	lbw b Swan	87
M.J. Di Venuto c Katich b Julian	13	–	c Walsh b Oldroyd	51
J.A. Dykes lbw b Moody	13	– (5)	run out (Swan)	2
D.J. Marsh c Walsh b Julian	110	– (4)	b Oldroyd	10
S. Young b Oldroyd	43	–	c Walsh b Moody	48
S.P. Kremerskothen c and b Oldroyd	81	–	st Walsh b Oldroyd	13
†S.G. Clingeleffer c Campbell b Moody	50	– (9)	not out	6
D.J. Saker st Walsh b Oldroyd	9	– (8)	lbw b Moody	1
G.J. Denton not out	5	– (11)	not out	3
M.D. Colegrave not out	1	– (10)	c Swan b Moody	5
L-b 7, w 1, n-b 11	19		L-b 3, n-b 6	9

(150 overs, 541 mins)	(9 wkts dec) 446	
Fall: 33 60 85 172 282 302 424		
438 442		

(60 overs, 222 mins)	(9 wkts dec) 238	
Fall: 3 114 128 136 184 223 223		
225 231		

Bowling: *First Innings*—Nicholson 4–1–13–0; Swan 28–6–109–0; Julian 33–6–94–3; Moody 29–6–82–2; Martyn 15.4–4–31–0; Oldroyd 35–7–90–4; Hussey 5–1–17–0; Katich 1–0–3–0. *Second Innings*—Swan 10–0–54–1; Julian 10–1–53–1; Martyn 5–1–18–0; Oldroyd 24–2–87–3; Moody 11–0–23–3.

Western Australia

M. E. Hussey c Hills b Denton	35	– (2) c Di Venuto b Saker	5
R. J. Campbell lbw b Saker	8	– (1) lbw b Saker	19
S. M. Katich c and b Young	38	– b Kremerskothen	152
D. R. Martyn c Dykes b Saker	122	– c Clingeleffer b Colegrave	90
M. W. Goodwin lbw b Young	3	– (6) c Hills b Saker	12
†M. J. Walsh c Kremerskothen b Denton	50	– (8) c Dykes b Kremerskothen	13
*T. M. Moody not out	20	– not out	22
B. P. Julian lbw b Young	6	– (5) lbw b Saker	39
B. J. Oldroyd not out	5	– (10) b Saker	3
M. J. Nicholson (did not bat)		– (9) b Kremerskothen	9
G. G. Swan (did not bat)		– not out	0
L-b 10, n-b 1	11	B 4, l-b 2, w 1, n-b 2	9

(99.4 overs, 382 mins)	(7 wkts dec) 298	(71 overs, 271 mins)　　(9 wkts) 373

Fall: 13 81 98 124 248
279 286

Fall: 23 30 223 299 317 325 353
364 369

Bowling: *First Innings*—Saker 23–4–66–2; Colegrave 19.4–5–55–0; Denton 20–3–90–2; Young 23–9–37–3; Marsh 8–3–16–0; Kremerskothen 6–1–24–0. *Second Innings*—Saker 21–1–98–5; Colegrave 14–0–76–1; Young 3–0–33–0; Marsh 14–2–74–0; Kremerskothen 14–1–64–3; Dykes 5–0–22–0.

Umpires: K. J. Jones and J. H. Smeaton.
TV Umpire: B. T. Knight.

At Adelaide Oval, Adelaide, December 1, 2, 3, 4, 2000. TASMANIA lost to SOUTH AUSTRALIA by 161 runs.

At Melbourne Cricket Ground, Melbourne, December 14, 15, 16, 17, 2000. TASMANIA lost to VICTORIA by 179 runs.

TASMANIA v QUEENSLAND

At Bellerive Oval, Hobart, January 3, 4, 5, 2001. Queensland won by an innings and 144 runs. Toss: Queensland. Queensland 6 pts. First-class debut: S. R. Watson.

Queensland's win by an innings and plenty with a day to spare reflected the chasm in class and commitment between the competition's top and bottom sides. Sent in to bat, Tasmania scarcely resisted the Queensland pace attack, teenage debutant Shane Watson's 25 not out against his old state underlining how little the more experienced hands contributed. The destroyer was speedster Michael Kasprowicz, in his first game of the season after recovering from shoulder surgery, with the customary support of Joe Dawes. Queensland continued their rampage by amassing a lead of 356 before declaring. The cornerstone was Martin Love's effortless unbeaten 172 (362 minutes, 307 balls, 24 fours), his seventh century against Tasmania, while Jerry Cassell (354 minutes, 278 balls, 15 fours) partnered him in adding 203 for the second wicket. Tasmania fared only a little better the second time around, with Shaun Young's modest 34 the top score. Watson again outshone his more experienced colleagues and completed 189 minutes at the crease in the match without being dismissed. Jamie Cox, in playing his 119th domestic first-class match, joined David Boon as Tasmania's most-capped player.

Man of the Match: M. L. Love. *Attendance:* 957.

Close of play: First day, Queensland (1) 1-121 (Cassell 53, Love 16); Second day, Tasmania (2) 1-18 (Cox 4, Clingeleffer 5).

Tasmania

T. A. Pinnington c Carseldine b Kasprowicz	5	– (2) c O'Leary b Kasprowicz	4
*J. Cox c Law b Dale	2	– (1) c Maher b Kasprowicz	32
M. J. Di Venuto c Seccombe b Kasprowicz	7	– (8) c Symonds b Dawes	9
D. J. Marsh b Dawes	25	– c O'Leary b Dawes	28
S. P. Kremerskothen c Love b Dawes	15	– lbw b O'Leary	18
S. Young c Love b Dawes	10	– lbw b Dawes	34
S. R. Watson not out	25	– not out	22
†S. G. Clingeleffer b Dawes	3	– (3) c Carseldine b Kasprowicz	5
D. J. Saker c Maher b Kasprowicz	0	– b Symonds	13
A. G. Downton c Cassell b Kasprowicz	9	– b O'Leary	17
B. S. Targett c Law b Kasprowicz	0	– b O'Leary	15
L-b 3, w 1, n-b 7	11	L-b 3, n-b 12	15

(47 overs, 197 mins)	112	(82 overs, 303 mins)	212

Fall: 5 14 33 50 67 73 86 88
        108 112

Fall: 8 18 75 83 125 135 149 173
        196 212

Bowling: *First Innings*—Kasprowicz 16–5–29–5; Dale 16–5–26–1; Dawes 13–5–47–4; Symonds 2–0–7–0. *Second Innings*—Kasprowicz 21–2–81–3; Dale 8–5–5–0; Dawes 17–6–39–3; O'Leary 30–11–62–3; Symonds 6–1–22–1.

Queensland

J.L. Cassell c Targett b Downton	136			
J.P. Maher b Watson	48	B 2, l-b 7, n-b 7	16	
M.L. Love not out	172			
*S.G. Law c Clingeleffer b Targett	49	(131.2 overs, 480 mins)	(4 wkts dec)	468
A. Symonds st Clingeleffer b Marsh	47	Fall: 92 296 397 468		

L. A. Carseldine, †W. A. Seccombe, M. S. Kasprowicz, S. J. O'Leary, A.C. Dale and J.H. Dawes did not bat.

Bowling: Saker 21–2–68–0; Downton 20–5–66–1; Targett 24–8–62–1; Young 15–2–63–0; Watson 14–3–45–1; Marsh 29.2–4–119–1; Di Venuto 3–2–4–0; Kremerskothen 5–2–32–0.

Umpires: K. J. Jones and P. V. Mulcahy.

At Sydney Cricket Ground, Sydney, February 14, 15, 16, 17, 2001. TASMANIA drew with NEW SOUTH WALES.

TASMANIA v VICTORIA

At Bellerive Oval, Hobart, March 2, 3, 4, 5, 2001. Tasmania won by six wickets. Toss: Tasmania. Tasmania 6pts. Victoria 2 pts.

Opener Jason Arnberger (380 minutes, 311 balls, 23 fours, two sixes, one of which became stuck in an advertising sign) made Tasmania pay dearly for sending Victoria in by batting with real authority and purpose. On the second day Michael Klinger (213 minutes, 169 balls, 13 fours) became the first batsman in Australian first-class history to be left stranded on 99 by a declaration, after Paul Reiffel decided to push for a quick breakthrough before lunch. Rival skipper Jamie Cox took up the challenge thrown down by Reiffel, declaring 69 runs behind. Opener Dene Hills briefly brightened his dismal season by top-scoring with 120 (389 minutes, 330 balls, 14 fours, one six) and Shane Watson (205 minutes, 151 balls, eight fours) again looked at home in first-class cricket. The Victorians' quest for quick runs to force victory on the last day came unstuck when they were dismissed for 216, with only Reiffel (95 minutes, 78 balls, nine fours) and opener Matthew Elliott (95 minutes, 61 balls, seven fours, two sixes) contributing effectively. Left-arm pace man Andrew Downton again took the bowling honours to give him match figures of 8/146. Amid controversy over two rejected appeals, Cox (315 minutes, 253 balls, 17 fours) ensured that Tasmania reached its victory target of 286 from 83 overs with six wickets and 15 balls to spare. The visitors were hampered by the loss of all-rounder Ian Harvey, who injured his hand while fielding in Tasmania's first innings.

Man of the Match: J. Cox. *Attendance:* 1,330.

Close of play: First day, Victoria (1) 3-290 (Arnberger 161, Klinger 36); Second day, Tasmania (1) 2-202 (Hills 74, Watson 14); Third day, Victoria (2) 8-175 (Reiffel 31, Inness 1).

Victoria

M.T.G. Elliott lbw b Jurgensen	54	– (2) b Downton	55
J.L. Arnberger c Clingeleffer b Downton	173	– (1) c Clingeleffer b Downton	33
M.P. Mott lbw b Downton	20	– (4) c Kremerskothen b Downton	5
B.J. Hodge c Clingeleffer b Downton	3	– (3) run out (Watson)	25
M. Klinger not out	99	– c Young b Marsh	4
I.J. Harvey c Clingeleffer b Downton	12		
†D.S. Berry not out	12	– (6) lbw b Watson	14
*P.R. Reiffel (did not bat)		– (7) c Clingeleffer b Downton	70
J.M. Davison (did not bat)		– (8) lbw b Watson	0
M.L. Lewis (did not bat)		– (9) st Clingeleffer b Marsh	4
M.W.H. Inness (did not bat)		– (10) not out	3
B 1, l-b 10, w 1, n-b 8	20	L-b 2, n-b 1	3

(120 overs, 454 mins)	(5 wkts dec) 393	(58.1 overs, 220 mins)	(9 wkts dec) 216
Fall: 123 164 172		Fall: 63 101 120 120 127 151 151	
314 346		172 216	

Bowling: *First Innings*—Saker 26–6–74–0; Jurgensen 27–5–77–1; Downton 29–4–95–4; Young 15–3–47–0; Watson 12–1–45–0; Marsh 8–2–20–0; Kremerskothen 3–0–24–0. *Second Innings*—Saker 18–4–56–0; Jurgensen 8–1–50–0; Marsh 13–3–33–2; Downton 16.1–5–51–4; Watson 3–0–24–2.

Tasmania

D.F. Hills c Mott b Inness	120	– c Mott b Reiffel	2
*J. Cox c Elliott b Davison	41	– not out	139
M.J. Di Venuto lbw b Hodge	63	– c Klinger b Hodge	60
S.R. Watson c Klinger b Inness	60	– b Lewis	1
D.J. Marsh not out	19	– b Reiffel	35
S. Young not out	4	– not out	29
B 3, l-b 8, n-b 6	17	B 8, l-b 7, W 1, n-b 4	20

(116 overs, 429 mins)	(4 wkts dec) 324	(80.3 overs, 315 mins)	(4 wkts) 286
Fall: 84 179 297 306		Fall: 2 141 142 210	

S.P. Kremerskothen, †S.G. Clingeleffer, D.J. Saker, S.J. Jurgensen, A.G. Downton did not bat.

Bowling: *First Innings*—Reiffel 15–3–47–0; Inness 25–7–77–2; Davison 47–19–89–1; Lewis 17–2–70–0; Mott 4–0–10–0; Hodge 8–3–20–1. *Second Innings*—Reiffel 13.3–1–38–2; Inness 16–4–58–0; Lewis 17–3–60–1; Davison 9–0–38–0; Hodge 11–1–39–1; Mott 12–2–38–0.

Umpires: K.J. Jones and J.H. Smeaton.

At WACA Ground, Perth, March 9, 10, 11, 2001. TASMANIA defeated WESTERN AUSTRALIA by nine wickets.

TASMANIA v SOUTH AUSTRALIA

At Bellerive Oval, Hobart, March 15, 16, 17, 18, 2001. Tasmania won by an innings and 41 runs. Toss: South Australia. Tasmania 6 pts.

Tasmania were on an end-of-season roll, and a woefully undermanned South Australia had no chance of stopping them. An opening stand of 106 by Jamie Cox and Dene Hills laid the foundation for the run deluge which was to follow. The master and his apprentice, Cox (308 minutes, 266 balls, 14 fours) and 19-year-old all-rounder Shane Watson (223 minutes, 172 balls, 14 fours, one six), each hit centuries and combined for a third-wicket partnership of 129. Cox's century was his fifth of the season and Watson's the first of his increasingly promising career. Shaun Young and Scott Kremerskothen finished the job with an unbeaten sixth-wicket partnership of 102. As South Australia stumbled to 185, Young, in dismissing Ben Higgins, became Tasmania's highest first-class wicket-taker, passing Colin Miller's 218 wickets. Forced to follow on, South Australia fared little better. Higgins again flew a lone flag after top-scoring in the first innings, his two innings occupying a total of five hours. Young continued to worry the South Australians, and he had solid support from Damien Wright. On the second day, umpire Barry Jackman was forced from the field by illness, and Tasmanian coach Greg Shipperd stand at square leg for three overs until TCA first-grade umpire Brian Pollard arrived to officiate. John Smeaton became the official replacement for the final two days.

Man of the Match: S. Young. *Attendance:* 921.

Close of play: First day, Tasmania (1) 4-268 (Watson 87, Young 9); Second day, South Australia (1) 4-126 (Higgins 50, Adcock 6); Third day, South Australia (2) 3-71 (Higgins 31, Borgas 5).

Tasmania

D.F. Hills lbw b Smith	50	
*J. Cox b Harrity	102	
M.J. Di Venuto b Smith	0	
S.R. Watson c Adcock b Smith	105	
D.J. Marsh c Manou b Smith	5	
S. Young not out	83	

S.P. Kremerskothen not out	46
B 4, l-b 10, w 1, n-b 7	22
(135 overs, 496 mins) (5 wkts dec)	413
Fall: 106 106 235 254 311	

†S.G. Clingeleffer, D.J. Saker, D.G. Wright, A.G. Downton did not bat.

Bowling: Harrity 26–6–88–1; Rofe 29–11–76–0; Smith 30–10–81–4; McIntyre 26–8–70–0; Blewett 12–4–45–0; Adcock 12–1–39–0.

South Australia

D.A. Fitzgerald lbw b Wright	17	– (2) c Clingeleffer b Wright	10
S.A. Deitz c Marsh b Wright	25	– (1) c Wright b Young	24
*G.S. Blewett c Downton b Watson	27	– b Wright	0
B.H. Higgins c Clingeleffer b Young	52	– c Di Venuto b Young	65
C.J. Borgas lbw b Watson	0	– c Marsh b Wright	7
N.T. Adcock c Marsh b Young	9	– c Marsh b Downton	32
M.J. Smith run out (Cox)	8	– c Hills b Wright	25
†G.A. Manou lbw b Young	38	– c Clingeleffer b Young	2
P.E. McIntyre c Di Venuto b Downton	2	– c Wright b Young	4
P.C. Rofe b Wright	5	– c Di Venuto b Watson	7
M.A. Harrity not out	0	– not out	4
L-b 2	2	B 4, l-b 1, n-b 2	7

(77.1 overs, 305 mins)	185	(56.4 overs, 228 mins)	187
Fall: 35 42 99 105 129 140 140 151		Fall: 12 14 66 76 133 141 146 154	
185 185		175 187	

Bowling: *First Innings*—Saker 12–3–22–0; Wright 11.1–1–42–3; Young 23–12–24–3; Downton 19–5–72–1; Watson 8–2–22–2; Marsh 4–3–1–0. *Second Innings*—Saker 11–2–25–0; Wright 17.4–4–54–4; Watson 5–2–31–1; Downton 11–3–37–1; Young 11–3–33–4; Marsh 1–0–2–0.

Umpires: B.W. Jackman, A.J. McQuillan, B. Pollard and J. Smeaton.

AUSTRALIAN DOMESTIC FIRST-CLASS RECORDS

Highest score for:	265	D. F. Hills v South Australia at Hobart (Bellerive) 1997-98
Highest score against:	306*	D. W. Hookes (South Australia) at Adelaide 1986-97
Best bowling for:	8/95	P. M. Clough v Western Australia at Perth 1983-84
Best bowling against:	8/41	L. S. Pascoe (New South Wales) at Hobart (TCA).....1981-82
Highest total for:	592	v South Australia at Adelaide 1987-88
Highest total against:	673	by South Australia at Adelaide 1987-88
Lowest total for:	76	v New South Wales at Hobart (Bellerive) 1991-92
Lowest total against:	83	by Victoria at Melbourne 1981-82

MOST RUNS

	M	I	NO	R	HS	100s	50s	Avge
J. Cox	123	226	15	8,941	245	27	38	42.37
D. C. Boon.............	119	203	7	8,029	227	20	43	40.96
D. F. Hills	96	179	8	6,701	265	17	36	39.19
M. J. Di Venuto.........	80	141	5	5,525	189	9	40	40.63
S. Young...............	99	168	29	5,306	175*	10	32	38.17
R. T. Tucker...........	90	153	24	4,611	165	7	24	35.74
D. J. Buckingham	75	129	11	4,407	167	9	22	37.35
R. T. Ponting...........	45	83	13	4,382	233	18	13	62.60
R. D. Woolley	68	114	13	4,120	144	7	25	40.79
B. F. Davison...........	41	75	7	3,062	173	9	13	45.03

HIGHEST PARTNERSHIP FOR EACH WICKET

297	for 1st	D. F. Hills and J. Cox v Victoria at Hobart (Bellerive)	1997-98
294	for 2nd	J. Cox and M. J. Di Venuto v New South Wales at Hobart (Bellerive)	1999-00
290	for 3rd	D. F. Hills and R. T. Ponting v South Australia at Adelaide	1993-94
258	for 4th	M. D. Taylor and D. J. Buckingham v South Australia at Adelaide	1987-88
319	for 5th	R. T. Ponting and R. J. Tucker v Western Australia at Hobart (Bellerive) ..	1994-95
213	for 6th	B. F. Davison and R. D. Woolley v South Australia at Adelaide	1980-81
203*	for 7th	B. F. Davison and P. I. Faulkner v Western Australia at Perth	1983-84
148	for 8th	B. F. Davison and P. I. Faulkner v South Australia at Adelaide	1983-84
118*	for 9th	B. F. Davison and P. I. Faulkner v Queensland at Brisbane	1983-84
120	for 10th	S. L. Saunders and P. M. Clough v Western Australia at Perth	1981-82

MOST WICKETS

	M	Balls	Mdns	R	W	BB	5Wi	10Wi/m	Avge
C. R. Miller	54	13,846	556	6,657	210	7/49	8	2	31.70
S. Young	99	16,051	728	7,728	200	5/26	5	1	38.64
M. W. Ridgway	44	9,433	347	5,160	153	6/29	6	0	33.73
C. D. Matthews	35	7,922	272	4,234	119	6/89	7	0	35.57
R. J. Tucker	90	9,139	316	4,561	112	4/56	0	0	40.72
D. R. Gilbert	36	7,345	247	3,513	110	7/127	5	0	31.94
P. M. Clough	28	6,142	226	2,913	102	8/95	5	0	28.56
D. J. Marsh	50	8,273	342	3,991	99	7/57	1	0	40.31
P. T. McPhee	25	5,669	225	2,803	89	6/36	4	1	31.49
R. L. Brown	29	5,146	128	3,197	75	7/80	2	1	42.63

MOST DISMISSALS

	M	Ct	St	Total
M. N. Atkinson	84	237	25	262
R. D. Woolley	43	97	13	110
R. E. Soule	51	103	4	107
J. M. Holyman	9	25	1	26
S. G. Clingeleffer	10	21	4	25

MOST CATCHES

D.C. Boon	93 in 119 matches	
D.F. Hills	67 in 96 matches	
M.J. Di Venuto	64 in 80 matches	
S. Young	61 in 99 matches	
R.J. Tucker	60 in 90 matches	
J. Cox	58 in 123 matches	

MOST APPEARANCES

123	J. Cox	1987-88 – 2000-01
119	D.C. Boon	1978-79 – 1998-99
99	S. Young	1991-92 – 2000-01
96	D.F. Hills	1991-92 – 2000-01
90	R.J. Tucker	1988-89 – 1998-99
84	M.N. Atkinson	1991-92 – 1999-00
80	M.J. Di Venuto	1991-92 – 2000-01
75	D.J. Buckingham	1983-84 – 1993-94
68	R.D. Woolley	1977-78 – 1987-88
54	C.R. Miller	1992-93 – 1999-00

VICTORIA

Paul Reiffel

Chief Executive Officer: K.W. Jacobs

President: R.F. Merriman

Cricket Coach: W.J. Scholes

Captain: P.R. Reiffel

Victoria were described in these pages last year as having "definitively found their level". On bald results alone, it was a standard they maintained but could not better: runners-up (again) to Queensland (again). Such an assessment disguises the heartbreak of their final defeat at the Gabba, where the visitors had a case for thinking they had got the rough end of the pineapple, as the season ended with a last day more dramatic than any in the preceding five months. For all the improvement they had supposedly made, defeat left them with nothing to show for it.

There is no telling how the final act would have been played had either of the umpires, Simon Taufel and Steve Davis, agreed with the Victorians that a first-ball slash from Queensland captain Stuart Law had carried to Michael Klinger at slip. They instead referred it to the third umpire who, working with only three inconclusive camera angles, gave Law the benefit. Law avoided the dubious honour of making a king pair in a final, and Victoria had only themselves to blame for allowing him three further lives and ultimately the luxury of leading his team to victory by four wickets.

Victoria's firm belief going into the final that, this time, things would be different stemmed from a season in which several squad members discovered a maturity to match the elite at this level. In particular, Jason Arnberger with the bat (907 runs at 45.35) and Mathew Inness with the ball (33 wickets at 27.58) continued the calm and steady improvement that makes them the easiest of pupils for coach John Scholes. Inness' taste of life a rung higher while playing for Australia A against the West Indies in Hobart might not be his last.

The rejuvenation of Brad Hodge was a triumph of self-belief, coming as it did after a similarly stellar debut season seven years earlier had been followed by years of inconsistency. His 973 runs at 54.06 featured four centuries, made with the fluency on both sides of the wicket that characterises his game. Perhaps most pleasing was a willingness to dig in when there was hard grafting to be done; Hodge was furious when this steel deserted him at a crucial moment in the final.

Occasionally, the country's premier slow bowlers, Shane Warne and Colin Miller, turned out for their state, but it was the emergence of a 17-year-old schoolboy at season's end that caused most excitement. Cameron White is fair-haired and a leg-spinner, reason enough to set hearts racing in Victoria.

The season was not without controversy. In Hobart in the first week of March, Paul Reiffel declared Victoria's innings closed with Michael Klinger a run short of his maiden first-class century. The public backlash that followed surprised Reiffel, and tested the Victorian ethos that the team comes before the individual. Klinger, who turned 21 in the off-season, is certain to get many more chances.

Darren Berry's decade of service flashed before his eyes when a shoulder injury kept him out of the last match of the regular season, Peter Roach stepping in. Berry's form with the bat had been lamentable, giving rise to talk that the wicket-keeping substitution first aired five seasons before may become permanent. Berry regained his place for the final, and his second-innings 61 and last-day work behind the stumps gave Victoria a winning chance. Despite being arguably the best pure glove-man in the country, his state position remains under siege.

Matthew Elliott missed the first four matches with a knee injury, made 524 runs at 40.31, and failed to score a century for the first time since his debut season of 1992-93. At season's end he lost his Australian Cricket Board contract, turned down all offers of a winter job, put his Gray-Nicolls in the cupboard and was looking forward to watching Australian Rules. Victoria must hope he emerges from hibernation ravenous for runs.

Reiffel himself enjoyed a mixed run – his 30 wickets was a respectable haul, but only half last season's return – and at times seemed as if he was hardly enjoying himself at all, not least in the moments after the final. The absurdity of the situation was not lost on the captain when, after being reported for dissent amid the appeal for Law's dismissal, he was fined a paltry $200. It summed up a season that amounted to nothing. – PETER HANLON.

VICTORIA RESULTS, 2000-01

All first-class matches – Played 11: Won 4, Lost 4, Drawn 3.
Pura Cup matches – Played 10: Won 3, Lost 4, Drawn 3.
Mercantile Mutual Cup matches – Played 10: Won 3, Lost 7.
Competition placings – Pura Cup, 2nd; Mercantile Mutual Cup, 6th.

AUSTRALIAN DOMESTIC FIRST-CLASS RESULTS TABLE

Opponent	M	W	L	D	T
New South Wales	199	61	72	65	1
South Australia	194	97	46	51	0
Queensland	136	48	40	48	0
Western Australia	99	31	26	42	0
Tasmania	43	12	9	22	0
Total	671	249	193	228	1

PURA CUP AVERAGES, 2000-01

BATTING

	M	I	NO	R	HS	100s	50s	Avge	Ct/St
B.J. Hodge	11	20	2	973	125	4	3	54.06	7
J.L. Arnberger......	11	21	1	907	173	2	6	45.35	11
M.T.G. Elliott.......	7	14	1	524	98	0	5	40.31	9
P.J. Roach	2	4	2	69	51*	0	1	34.50	5
I.J. Harvey.........	8	14	0	481	100	1	2	34.36	6
M.P. Mott	11	21	1	677	154	1	3	33.85	11
J. Moss............	3	5	0	136	62	0	1	27.20	0
M. Klinger.........	8	14	2	315	99*	0	3	26.25	6
P.R. Reiffel	11	17	3	337	70	0	2	24.07	3
S.K. Warne	2	2	0	39	27	0	0	19.50	2
C.J. Peake	2	4	1	53	33	0	0	17.67	3
D.S. Berry	9	16	1	230	61	0	1	15.33	31/1
S.A.J. Craig	4	7	0	101	35	0	0	14.43	4
G.R. Vimpani	1	2	0	26	22	0	0	13.00	1
C.L. White	2	3	2	12	11	0	0	12.00	0
D.W. Fleming	2	2	0	22	15	0	0	11.00	0
M.L. Lewis	7	9	5	44	11*	0	0	11.00	1
J.M. Davison.......	5	6	0	54	33	0	0	9.00	1
C.R. Miller	4	6	1	44	26	0	0	8.80	1
M.W.H. Inness	11	14	6	20	8	0	0	2.50	3

* Denotes not out

BOWLING

	O	M	R	W	BB	5W/i	Avge
S.K. Warne............	47.5	8	140	9	5/49	1	15.56
P.R. Reiffel	325.1	84	824	30	4/50	0	27.47
M.W.H. Inness	341	99	910	33	6/26	1	27.58
B.J. Hodge	94.1	21	249	9	3/19	0	27.67
I.J. Harvey	172.2	54	474	17	4/19	0	27.88
M.L. Lewis............	246.2	53	772	23	5/57	1	33.57
C.L. White	44.3	14	136	4	4/65	0	34.00
C.R. Miller	192.2	52	539	15	4/71	0	35.93
J. Moss	55	14	164	4	1/17	0	41.00
D.W. Fleming	38	10	91	2	2/64	0	45.50
J.M. Davison	194.1	61	488	10	4/90	0	48.80
M.P. Mott	56.5	9	215	4	2/42	0	53.75
J.L. Arnberger	1	0	3	0	–	0	–
S.A.J. Craig	14	3	49	0	–	0	–
M.T.G. Elliott	2	1	1	0	–	0	–

VICTORIA v NEW SOUTH WALES

At Richmond Cricket Ground, Richmond, October 25 (no play), 26, 27, 28, 2000. New South Wales won by 117 runs. Toss: Victoria. New South Wales 6 pts.

The Richmond Cricket Ground continued its habit of hosting early-season Victorian matches, and despite rain preventing a ball being bowled until midway through the second day, New South Wales continued their own habit of thrashing Victoria when at full strength. The result was overshadowed by an incident at 6.33 p.m. on day two, when Mark Waugh top-edged a sweep at Colin Miller and Shane Warne misjudged the easiest of skied catches at first slip, breaking the top knuckle on the third finger of his bowling hand. He did not play again for his state until the new year, and missed the entire

A climactic moment for Victoria on the tense final day of the Pura Cup final against Queensland. From left, Matthew Elliott, Jonathan Moss, Brad Hodge (obscured), Michael Klinger, Darren Berry (obscured), captain Paul Reiffel and Matthew Mott erupt in celebration for a brilliant catch at third slip off Stuart Law, from the bowling of Reiffel. The catch was disallowed after the third umpire viewed the inconclusive footage, and the day went sour for the Vics as Law went on to guide his team to victory.

West Indies Test series. Having restricted the visitors to a modest enough total, the Victorians then ran into trouble against the leg-spin of Stuart MacGill before Brad Hodge (231 minutes, 184 balls, seven fours) and Paul Reiffel (167 minutes, 129 balls, five fours) restored some perspective with an unfinished seventh-wicket partnership of 132. Reiffel forfeited the chance of first-innings points in pursuit of a result and Steve Waugh obliged with a target of 261 from 61 overs after the visitors' second innings had rattled along at more than six per over. Brett Lee took 5/17 in eight overs after tea to seal Victoria's fate.

Man of the Match: B. Lee. *Attendance:* 2,599.

Close of play: First day, no play (rain); Second day, New South Wales (1) 6-185 (S. Lee 18, B. Lee 10); Third day, Victoria (1) 6-140 (Hodge 60, Reiffel 34).

New South Wales

C.J. Richards c Miller b Reiffel	30	– (8) not out	5
M.J. Slater c Berry b Reiffel	13	– (1) c (sub) B.C. Oliver b Reiffel	5
*S.R. Waugh c Hodge b Inness	13	– (4) run out (Craig)	25
M.E. Waugh c Warne b Miller	53	– (2) b Mott	46
M.G. Bevan st Berry b Miller	39	– (6) not out	20
S. Lee c Vimpani b Reiffel	53		
†B.J. Haddin c Berry b Miller	2	– (3) b Inness	40
B. Lee c Craig b Miller	14	– (5) b Miller	8
D.A. Nash c Craig b Mott	11	– (7) c (sub) Davison b Miller	46
S.C.G. MacGill not out	13		
G.D. McGrath c Reiffel b Inness	3		
B 2, l-b 3, n-b 1	6	L-b 3, w 4, n-b 8	15

(82 overs, 340 mins)	250	(32 overs, 136 mins) (6 wkts dec)	210
Fall: 19 45 80 147 158 160 190 230 240 250		Fall: 9 70 116 130 138 199	

Bowling: First Innings—Reiffel 21–7–34–3; Inness 22–5–75–2; Miller 22–4–71–4; Warne 12–0–38–0; Craig 2–0–7–0; Mott 3–0–20–1. *Second Innings*—Reiffel 6–0–40–1; Harvey 9–1–53–0; Inness 4–0–20–1; Miller 8–0–60–2; Mott 5–0–34–1.

Victoria

J.L. Arnberger b MacGill	20	– (2) c M.E. Waugh b McGrath	19
G.R. Vimpani c Haddin b B. Lee	4	– (1) c Haddin b B. Lee	22
M.P. Mott c B. Lee b Nash	12	– (5) c S.R. Waugh b MacGill	22
B.J. Hodge not out	85	– (3) c Haddin b B. Lee	32
I.J. Harvey c and b MacGill	0	– (4) st Haddin b MacGill	21
S.A.J. Craig b MacGill	0	– c Haddin b B. Lee	0
†D.S. Berry c S. Lee b McGrath	2	– c Haddin b B. Lee	9
*P.R. Reiffel not out	63	– c M.E. Waugh b B. Lee	13
C.R. Miller (did not bat)		– not out	2
M.W.H. Inness (did not bat)		– lbw b MacGill	0
L-b 6, w 1, n-b 1	8	L-b 7, n-b 2	9

(79 overs, 316 mins)	(6 wkts dec) 194	(39.3 overs, 168 mins) (9 wkts dec)	149
Fall: 4 31 57 59		Fall: 36 48 81 117 121 121 142	
59 62		149 149	

S.K. Warne did not bat.

Bowling: First Innings—McGrath 17–7–40–1; B. Lee 15–5–35–1; Nash 16–4–45–1; S. Lee 6.2–2–14–0; MacGill 24.4–6–54–3. *Second Innings*—McGrath 7–1–26–1; B. Lee 13–4–42–5; MacGill 14.3–1–50–3; Nash 5–0–24–0.

Umpires: D.B. Hair and R.G. Patterson.
TV Umpire: R.L. Parry.

At Allan Border Field, Albion, November 5, 6, 7, 8, 2000. VICTORIA lost to QUEENSLAND by ten wickets.

VICTORIA v SOUTH AUSTRALIA

At Melbourne Cricket Ground, Melbourne, November 23, 24, 25, 26, 2000. Victoria won by 108 runs. Toss: South Australia. Victoria 6 pts.

A match total of 872 runs in four days indicated the dawdling progress of this game. Brad Hodge's first-innings hundred (239 minutes, 189 balls, ten fours, one six) was the major factor in Victoria's achieving a total of minor substance, and helped him to within six of 500 first-class runs for the season from only four matches. Mathew Inness had run through the touring West Indians on the same ground five days earlier, and duplicated those figures of 6/26 on the second day as South Australia crumbled to 96 all out. Victoria's first outright points of the season were virtually ensured, but were still a long time coming as Matthew Mott (243 minutes, 204 balls, 11 fours) led the home side's attempt to stretch out as large a lead as possible. After South Australia were set 395 to win in a day and a half, Greg Blewett and Shane Deitz signalled their intentions by spending 202 minutes assembling an opening partnership of 90. Deitz gave his side something from the game with the slowest first-class century in the MCG's history (438 minutes, 338 balls), outlasting a grateful Dean Jones by half an hour. His ultimate stay at the crease was a sedative 461 minutes and 360 balls with only eight fours.

Man of the Match: M. W. H. Inness. *Attendance:* 2,952.

Close of play: First day, South Australia (1) 0-12 (Fitzgerald 1, Deitz 10); Second day, Victoria (2) 2-138 (Mott 71, Hodge 3); Third day, South Australia (2) 0-82 (Blewett 42, Deitz 35).

Victoria

S. A. J. Craig c Manou b Wilson	30	– (2) c Manou b Swain	5
J. L. Arnberger lbw b Wilson	19	– (1) c (sub) B. H. Higgins b Johnson	56
M. P. Mott c Lehmann b Harrity	12	– lbw b Swain	88
B. J. Hodge c Deitz b Wilson	104	– run out (Wilson)	24
M. Klinger c Blewett b McIntyre	8	– c Davies b Wilson	18
I. J. Harvey lbw b McIntyre	31	– c Fitzgerald b McIntyre	9
†D. S. Berry lbw b Swain	2	– lbw b Swain	7
*P. R. Reiffel lbw b Swain	0	– not out	23
D. W. Fleming c Fitzgerald b Wilson	15	– b Wilson	7
C. R. Miller b Swain	3	– b Wilson	5
M. W. H. Inness not out	0	– c Manou b Harrity	8
B 1, l-b 4, n-b 2	7	B 2, l-b 2, n-b 5	9

(90.1 overs, 363 mins)	231	(102.3 overs, 403 mins)	259

Fall: 41 54 87 127 183 210 210 216 219 231

Fall: 12 121 166 194 206 216 216 231 241 259

Bowling: *First Innings*—Harrity 15–5–44–1; Swain 21–7–33–3; McIntyre 22.1–9–49–4; Blewett 8–1–20–0; McIntyre 20–1–64–2; Lehmann 3–0–15–0; Lehmann 1–0–1–0. *Second Innings*—Wilson 15.3–5–43–3; Swain 22.3–3–66–3; Harrity 17.3–6–32–1; Blewett 2–0–8–0; McIntyre 23–3–46–1; Lehmann 8–2–25–0; Johnson 11–4–29–1; Deitz 3–1–6–0.

South Australia

D. A. Fitzgerald c Berry b Reiffel	16	– (3) c Craig b Fleming	9
S. A. Deitz c Berry b Miller	32	– c Berry b Harvey	114
G. S. Blewett c Berry b Inness	1	– (1) b Harvey	49
*D. S. Lehmann b Inness	0	– c Berry b Inness	43
C. J. Davies lbw b Inness	4	– c Berry b Inness	7
B. A. Johnson run out (Hodge/Berry)	12	– lbw b Reiffel	25
†G. A. Manou not out	14	– b Miller	2
B. A. Swain c Reiffel b Inness	12	– lbw b Fleming	9
P. E. McIntyre b Inness	1	– c Arnberger b Miller	3
P. Wilson c Hodge b Inness	2	– lbw b Miller	7
M. A. Harrity run out (Arnberger/Berry)	0	– not out	1
L-b 2	2	B 2, l-b 5, w 1, n-b 9	17

(38.4 overs, 170 mins)	96	(137.2 overs, 541 mins)	286
Fall: 32 33 33 39 66 66 88		Fall: 90 123 202 216 260 266 266	
90 92 96		274 282 286	

Bowling: *First Innings*—Reiffel 11.4–2–28–1; Fleming 11–2–27–0; Inness 10–3–26–6; Miller 5–1–13–1; Harvey 1–1–0–0. *Second Innings*—Reiffel 18–5–34–1; Fleming 27–8–64–2; Inness 19–7–32–2; Miller 48.2–13–90–3; Harvey 23–7–54–2; Craig 2–1–5–0.

Umpires: R. G. Patterson and A. J. Soulsby.
TV Umpire: R. L. Parry.

VICTORIA v QUEENSLAND

At Melbourne Cricket Ground, Melbourne, November 29, 30, December 1, 2, 2000. Drawn. Toss: Victoria. Victoria 2 pts. First-class debut: S. J. O'Leary.

By lunch on the third day, Victoria seemed to be sniffing a first outright win over Queensland in five years. Jason Arnberger (352 minutes, 286 balls, 12 fours, one six) and Brad Hodge (328 minutes, 260 balls, 15 fours) added 190 circumspect runs for the third wicket. Ian Harvey (156 minutes, 124 balls, ten fours, three sixes) brought a sense of urgency to proceedings which was then backed up by an all-round team performance with the ball that left Paul Reiffel's men 200 runs to the good with five sessions to play. Reiffel's decision to enforce the follow-on appeared a formality, but came under fire as the visitors batted the match to a dour end. Jimmy Maher (389 minutes, 311 balls, ten fours) and Martin Love (469 minutes, 345 balls, ten fours) added 212 for the second wicket in 363 actionless minutes. Victoria effectively played one short, Damien Fleming being selected despite waking on the first morning with a stiff neck. While Fleming convalesced and pace bowler Michael Lewis sat in the dressing room as 12th man, opening batsman Arnberger delivered the last ball of the match – to seven slips and two leg slips – and Adam Dale let it pass by. It summed things up exquisitely.

Man of the Match: I. J. Harvey. *Attendance:* 3,197.

Close of play: First day, Victoria (1) 3-237 (Hodge 103, Klinger 3); Second day, Queensland (1) 5-135 (Carseldine 12, Seccombe 6).

Victoria

J. L. Arnberger c Seccombe b Dale	100	*P. R. Reiffel c Maher b O'Leary	13
S. A. J. Craig lbw b Dale	8	C. R. Miller b O'Leary	26
M. P. Mott c Carseldine b O'Leary	7	M. W. H. Inness not out	1
B. J. Hodge lbw b Dale	111	L-b 5, n-b 11	16
M. Klinger c Cassell b Dawes	3		
I. J. Harvey c Pascoe b O'Leary	93	(141.2 overs, 544 mins) (9 wkts dec)	384
†D. S. Berry c Seccombe b Dawes	6	Fall: 24 44 234 243 267 278 329 373 384	

D. W. Fleming did not bat.

Bowling: Pascoe 14–3–46–0; Dale 46–23–71–3; Dawes 35–12–86–2; O'Leary 23.2–3–105–4; Carseldine 15–4–37–0; Symonds 8–1–34–0.

Queensland

J.L. Cassell lbw b Miller	28	– c Mott b Reiffel	2
J.P. Maher lbw b Inness	3	– c Berry b Reiffel	98
M.L. Love lbw b Miller	30	– lbw b Miller	126
*S.G. Law c Hodge b Harvey	28	– not out	74
A. Symonds c Harvey b Reiffel	18	– c Arnberger b Miller	39
L.A. Carseldine c Berry b Reiffel	12	– lbw b Mott	18
†W.A. Seccombe c Berry b Inness	12	– c and b Mott	3
A.C. Dale c Berry b Reiffel	2	– not out	5
S.J. O'Leary c Berry b Reiffel	3		
M.D. Pascoe not out	20		
J.H. Dawes c Hodge b Harvey	15		
B 4, l-b 2, n-b 7	13	B 5, l-b 3, n-b 7	15

(69.1 overs, 282 mins) 184   (159 overs, 612 mins) (6 wkts) 380
Fall: 10 64 73 109 114 135 144 144 147 184   Fall: 6 218 279 329 362 366

Bowling: *First Innings*—Reiffel 22–10–50–4; Inness 17–3–46–2; Miller 19–8–43–2; Harvey 11.1–3–39–2. *Second Innings*—Reiffel 27–10–44–2; Inness 24–12–49–0; Miller 54–20–114–2; Harvey 27–6–83–0; Mott 14–3–42–2; Hodge 8–2–31–0; Craig 4–2–6–0; Arnberger 1–0–3–0.

Umpires: G.T.D. Morrow and R.L. Parry.

VICTORIA v TASMANIA

At Melbourne Cricket Ground, Melbourne, December 14, 15, 16, 17, 2000. Victoria won by 179 runs. Toss: Tasmania. Victoria 6 pts.

Victoria rounded off three weeks of solid cricket with a comfortable outright win over their southern neighbours, who could have expected a greater contribution from openers Dene Hills and Jamie Cox than a pair each. Matthew Elliott's return from knee surgery was positive and forceful (203 minutes, 154 balls, 11 fours) and he led a second-wicket partnership of 135 with the customarily stubborn Matthew Mott (269 minutes, 240 balls, ten fours). A lower-order flurry helped Victoria to a solid total before Paul Reiffel and Mathew Inness reduced the visitors to three for 1 and then five for 20. Michael Di Venuto (344 minutes, 272 balls, four fours) and Scott Kremerskothen (199 minutes, 141 balls, four fours) added 96 for the sixth wicket in a forlorn attempt to set the innings to rights. Perhaps chastened by his experience against Queensland the previous week, Reiffel opted not to enforce the follow-on. Brad Hodge did not make a century for a change, settling for 81 (126 minutes, 111 balls, 14 fours) amid brisk declaration batting, and Reiffel's three second-innings dismissals took him beyond Alan Connolly's Victorian record of 297 wickets.

Man of the Match: P.R. Reiffel. *Attendance:* 5,891.

Close of play: First day, Victoria (1) 6-250 (Harvey 10, Reiffel 0); Second day, Tasmania (1) 6-134 (Di Venuto 62, Clingeleffer 7); Third day, Tasmania (2) 3-54 (Dykes 16, Young 9).

Victoria

M.T.G. Elliott c Cox b Young	79	– (2) c Di Venuto b Wright	14
J.L. Arnberger lbw b Saker	0	– (1) not out	67
M.P. Mott c Di Venuto b Kremerskothen	78	– lbw b Wright	4
B.J. Hodge lbw b Saker	30	– c Clingeleffer b Young	81
C.J. Peake b Saker	9	– (7) not out	1
I.J. Harvey c Kremerskothen b Saker	15	– (5) c Wright b Kremerskothen	0
†D.S. Berry b Wright	28	– (6) c Targett b Young	20
P.R. Reiffel c and b Young	23		
J.M. Davison c Young b Targett	33		
M.L. Lewis not out	11		
M.W.H. Inness c Cox b Young	0		
L-b 6, n-b 10	16	L-b 2, n-b 3	5

(114.3 overs, 439 mins) 322 (48 overs, 196 mins) (5 wkts dec) 192
Fall: 3 138 192 208 216 250 257 308 322 322 Fall: 22 28 148 152 173

Bowling: *First Innings*—Saker 30–3–102–4; Wright 17–4–52–1; Targett 25–10–87–1; Young 21.3–10–21–3; Kremerskothen 11–2–55–1; Cox 2–1–4–0; Di Venuto 8–3–25–0. *Second Innings*—Saker 12–3–49–0; Wright 11–3–25–2; Targett 5–0–33–0; Young 12–1–55–2; Kremerskothen 8–1–28–1.

Tasmania

D.F. Hills lbw b Inness	0	– c Mott b Reiffel	0
*J. Cox c Elliott b Reiffel	0	– lbw b Inness	0
S.R. Mason c Berry b Inness	0	– (6) c Berry b Reiffel	9
M.J. Di Venuto c Peake b Lewis	66	– (3) c Davison b Lewis	27
J.A. Dykes b Inness	13	– (4) c Berry b Reiffel	17
S. Young lbw b Reiffel	0	– (5) lbw b Davison	18
S.P. Kremerskothen lbw b Harvey	41	– lbw b Harvey	41
†S.G. Clingeleffer c Elliott b Lewis	9	– run out (Hodge/Berry)	38
D.J. Saker c Mott b Davison	1	– c Berry b Harvey	1
D.G. Wright not out	16	– c and b Harvey	0
B.S. Targett c Berry b Lewis	3	– not out	5
B 2, l-b 6, n-b 5	13	B 3, l-b 7, n-b 7	17

(94.5 overs, 382 mins) 162 (67.1 overs, 262 mins) 173
Fall: 1 1 1 19 20 116 136 137 152 162 Fall: 0 12 28 58 70 87 154 167 167 173

Bowling: *First Innings*—Reiffel 19–8–26–2; Inness 18–9–26–3; Harvey 18–6–28–1; Lewis 18.5–5–39–3; Davison 15–5–25–1; Hodge 6–2–10–0. *Second Innings*—Reiffel 13–3–32–3; Inness 10–4–22–1; Lewis 14–5–38–1; Harvey 11–5–17–3; Davison 16.1–6–44–1; Hodge 2–0–6–0; Mott 1–0–4–0.

Umpires: G.T.D. Morrow and R.G. Patterson.

At WACA Ground, Perth, January 4, 5, 6, 2001. VICTORIA defeated WESTERN AUSTRALIA by 77 runs.

At Adelaide Oval, Adelaide, February 19, 20, 21, 22, 2001. VICTORIA defeated SOUTH AUSTRALIA by five wickets.

At Bellerive Oval, Hobart, March 2, 3, 4, 5, 2001. VICTORIA lost to TASMANIA by six wickets.

At Sydney Cricket Ground, Sydney, March 9, 10, 11, 12, 2001. VICTORIA drew with NEW SOUTH WALES.

VICTORIA v WESTERN AUSTRALIA

At Melbourne Cricket Ground, Melbourne, March 15, 16, 17, 18, 2001. Drawn. Toss: Western Australia. Victoria 2 pts. First-class debut: G. I. Cullen.

Western Australia were already out of the running for competition honours, and Victoria's hopes of taking something tangible from this match ended before lunch on the first day with the news that New South Wales were being thrashed and Queensland would host the final. For two days, the lack of interest was palpable as the run-rate failed to reach two per over on a slow pitch with an even slower outfield. Simon Katich (288 minutes, 215 balls, five fours) and Marcus North (252 minutes, 221 balls three fours) set the tone on the first day with a second-wicket partnership of 117 which occupied over four excruciating hours. Brad Hodge (250 minutes, 198 balls, seven fours) was marginally more positive as Victoria gained first-innings points just before lunch on the third day. Suddenly, a bout of urgency broke out as new captain Katich (144 minutes, 146 balls, 11 fours) and Mike Hussey (305 minutes, 216 balls, 16 fours, two sixes) hit centuries for the visitors, the latter his first of a dismal first season as an ACB-contracted player. Chasing 292 in 84 overs, Victoria were four for 94 before Matthew Mott made his highest first-class score (315 minutes, 242 balls, 17 fours) and was well supported by Jonathan Moss (160 minutes, 117 balls, five fours, one six) in a purposeful fifth-wicket partnership of 167. Having made a torpid 23 from 99 balls in the first innings, Mott took that many off two overs from North in the second. Paul Reiffel settled for a draw when six were needed off the last ball.

Man of the Match: S. M. Katich. *Attendance:* 2,994.

Close of play: First day, Western Australia (1) 8-164 (Nicholson 5, Angel 0); Second day, Victoria (1) 5-143 (Hodge 52, Roach 6); Third day, Western Australia (2) 2-231 (Hussey 102, North 17).

Western Australia

M. E. Hussey c Elliott b Inness	2	– (2) c Roach b Lewis	137
S. W. Meuleman c Elliott b Inness	0	– (1) c Arnberger b Inness	4
*S. M. Katich run out (Arnberger)	78	– b Hodge	102
M. J. North c Roach b Lewis	51	– c Klinger b Moss	30
S. E. Marsh c Roach b Hodge	0		
G. I. Cullen c Arnberger b Inness	5		
B. P. Julian run out (Inness/Lewis)	15	– (5) not out	13
†M. J. Walsh b Reiffel	1		
M. J. Nicholson c Inness b Hodge	48		
J. Angel not out	4		
B. A. Williams c Inness b Hodge	1		
B 1, l-b 6, n-b 3	10	B 4, l-b 3, n-b 2	9

(119.2 overs, 460 mins)	215	(80.5 overs, 305 mins) (4 wkts dec)	295
Fall: 2 5 122 125 140 146 147 164 213 215		Fall: 26 179 247 295	

Bowling: *First Innings*—Reiffel 24–11–34–1; Inness 26–9–46–3; Lewis 25–7–48–1; Moss 13–6–22–0; White 18–8–37–0; Hodge 13.2–2–21–3. *Second Innings*—Reiffel 7–2–12–0; Inness 9–2–26–1; Lewis 20.5–4–75–1; Moss 9–1–49–1; Elliott 2–1–1–0; Hodge 20–4–60–1; Mott 8–1–31–0; White 5–0–34–0.

Victoria

M. T. G. Elliott c North b Williams	10	– (2) c Walsh b North	40
J. L. Arnberger c Walsh b Nicholson	17	– (1) lbw b Angel	4
M. P. Mott c Walsh b Williams	23	– c North b Angel	154
B. J. Hodge b Angel	81	– c Nicholson b Julian	3
M. Klinger c Nicholson b Angel	1	– b North	0
J. Moss c Walsh b Julian	23	– c Marsh b Nicholson	62
†P. J. Roach not out	51	– b Angel	5
*P. R. Reiffel c Nicholson b Williams	0	– (9) not out	7
C. L. White not out	0	– (8) not out	1
L-b 10, w 1, n-b 2	13	L-b 8, n-b 3	11

(93 overs, 357 mins)   (7 wkts dec) 219   (84 overs, 339 mins)   (7 wkts) 287
Fall: 15 38 73 80 131 206 211   Fall: 8 85 90 94 261 277 279

M. L. Lewis and M. W. H. Inness did not bat.

Bowling: *First Innings*—Angel 30–10–64–2; Williams 17–6–31–3; Nicholson 23–10–53–1; Julian 14–1–34–1; North 9–1–27–0. *Second Innings*—Angel 21–4–62–3; Williams 14–2–40–0; Nicholson 19–2–79–1; Julian 14–6–34–1; North 16–2–64–2.

Umpires: S. J. Davis and R. L. Parry.
TV Umpire: R. G. Patterson.

FINAL

At Brisbane Cricket Ground, Brisbane, March 23, 24, 25, 26, 27, 2001. VICTORIA lost to QUEENSLAND by four wickets. For details see section on Pura Cup final, 2000-01, page 369.

AUSTRALIAN DOMESTIC FIRST-CLASS RECORDS

Highest score for:	437	W. H. Ponsford v Queensland at Melbourne	1927-28
Highest score against:	357	D. G. Bradman (South Australia) at Melbourne	1935-36
Best bowling for:	9/40	E. L. McCormick v South Australia at Adelaide	1936-37
Best bowling against:	10/44	I. J. Brayshaw (Western Australia) at Perth	1967-68
Highest total for:	1,107	v New South Wales at Melbourne	1926-27
Highest total against:	815	by New South Wales at Sydney	1908-09
Lowest total for:	31	v New South Wales at Melbourne	1906-07
Lowest total against:	49	by Queensland at Melbourne	1936-37

MOST RUNS

	M	I	NO	R	HS	100s	50s	Avge
D. M. Jones	110	194	16	9,622	324*	31	40	54.06
W. M. Lawry	85	139	14	6,615	266	17	41	52.92
M. T. G. Elliott	64	124	10	6,193	203	22	27	54.32
G. N. Yallop	76	137	11	5,881	246	18	31	46.67
A. L. Hassett	58	97	10	5,535	229	18	27	63.62
W. H. Ponsford	43	70	5	5,413	437	21	14	83.28
D. F. Whatmore	85	150	7	5,235	170	10	31	36.61
I. R. Redpath	76	132	11	5,222	261	11	28	43.16
W. W. Armstrong	59	106	7	4,997	250	17	17	50.47
J. D. Siddons	64	109	11	4,703	245	13	24	47.99

HIGHEST PARTNERSHIP FOR EACH WICKET

375	for 1st	W. M. Woodfull and W. H. Ponsford v New South Wales at Melbourne ...	1926-27
314	for 2nd	W. H. Ponsford and H. S. T. L. Hendry v Queensland at Melbourne	1927-28
390*	for 3rd	J. M. Wiener and J. K. Moss v Western Australia at St Kilda	1981-82
301	for 4th	L. P. J. O'Brien and L. S. Darling v Queensland at Brisbane	1932-33
316*	for 5th	L. D. Harper and G. B. Gardener v South Australia at Carlton	1997-98
290	for 6th	M. T. G. Elliott and D. S. Berry v New South Wales at Sydney	1996-97
185	for 7th	P. A. Hibbert and R. J. Bright v New South Wales at Melbourne	1985-86
215	for 8th	R. L. Park and W. W. Armstrong v South Australia at Melbourne	1919-20
143	for 9th	G. R. Hazlitt and A. Kenny v South Australia at Melbourne	1910-11
211	for 10th	M. Ellis and T. J. Hastings v South Australia at Melbourne	1902-03

MOST WICKETS

	M	Balls	Mdns	R	W	BB	5W/i	10W/m	Avge
P. R. Reiffel	82	18,534	819	7,962	308	6/57	7	2	25.85
A. N. Connolly	71	17,973	365	7,745	297	9/67	12	4	26.08
A. I. C. Dodemaide	94	19,892	822	8,884	281	6/67	12	0	31.62
M. G. Hughes	76	16,762	582	8,169	267	7/81	10	2	30.60
R. J. Bright	101	22,899	1,013	8,821	252	6/61	10	0	35.00
L. O. Fleetwood-Smith ...	41	11,576	119	6,034	246	9/135	25	8	24.53
J. D. Higgs	75	14,961	376	7,202	240	8/66	12	2	30.01
M. H. N. Walker	62	15,071	429	6,476	220	6/49	11	0	29.44
H. Ironmonger	44	14,594	432	5,290	215	7/13	16	4	24.60
D. W. Fleming	62	13,902	618	6,284	208	7/90	7	1	30.21

MOST DISMISSALS

	M	Ct	St	Total
D. S. Berry	104	384	35	419
R. D. Robinson	68	213	26	239
R. C. Jordan	70	199	31	230
M. G. D. Dimattina	60	149	19	168
J. L. Ellis	49	111	45	156

MOST CATCHES

D. F. Whatmore	109 in 85 matches	J. D. Siddons	76 in 64 matches
D. M. Jones	96 in 110 matches	W. W. Armstrong ...	68 in 59 matches
M. T. G. Elliott	87 in 64 matches	G. N. Yallop	66 in 76 matches

MOST APPEARANCES

110	D. M. Jones	1981-82 – 1997-98	85	D. F. Whatmore ...	1975-76 – 1988-89
104	D. S. Bright	1990-91 – 2000-01	82	P. R. Reiffel	1987-88 – 2000-01
101	R. J. Bright	1972-73 – 1987-88	76	G. N. Yallop	1972-73 – 1984-85
94	A. I. C. Dodemaide .	1983-84 – 1997-98	76	M. G. Hughes	1981-82 – 1994-95
85	W. M. Lawry	1955-56 – 1971-72	76	I. R. Redpath	1961-62 – 1975-76

WESTERN AUSTRALIA

Simon Katich

Chief Executive Officer: C. M. Smith

President: B. Rakich

Cricket Coach: W. M. Clark

Captain: S. M. Katich

Western Australian cricket is at the crossroads after a turbulent summer. During the season of unrest, some players spoke out angrily against officialdom, coach Wayne Clark announced his retirement in January, captain Tom Moody unexpectedly stood down with two Pura Cup matches remaining, and chief executive Mike Allenby was dumped in February. And then there was the fiasco of a Mercantile Mutual Cup match against Queensland having to be abandoned after five overs because of a dangerous pitch, plus the acute embarrassment of many thousands of fans missing Glenn McGrath's Test hat-trick against West Indies as they waited in surrounding streets, owing to a major ticketing blunder at the WACA Ground. For the first time in five seasons Western Australia did not win one of the two major interstate trophies, after winning the Sheffield Shield in 1997-98 and 1998-99 and the Mercantile Mutual Cup in 1996-97 and 1999-00. A new era is about to begin under a new chief executive, a new coach (Mike Veletta), a new captain to replace the highly successful Moody, and a revamped selection panel, with the long-serving Allan Edwards returning to replace Kim Hughes as chairman.

During the season there were allegations that Murray Goodwin, who was given a state contract ahead of one or two promising young players, had received favoured treatment on his return from Zimbabwe. Ryan Campbell's outburst at being left out of the opening Mercantile Mutual Cup match in favour of Goodwin caused considerable tension. He called the selectors' decision a joke and said their assessment that his knee needed further rest after surgery was nonsense. Damien Martyn had earlier also raised eyebrows when he criticised the standard of pitches at the WACA Ground. He said that for two years variable bounce and the deterioration of pitches in four-day matches had made batting increasingly difficult.

There is no doubt that Western Australia under-achieved in the Pura Cup, with only two outright wins (both at home) from ten matches. Western Australia were dismissed for under 200 six times, and their totals of 78 against Queensland at the Gabba, 139 against Tasmania in Perth and 89 against New South Wales at North Sydney Oval were miserable efforts. The season's outstanding performer was Simon Katich, who became the first Western Australian to score a century against each other state in a first-class season. For good measure he scored two hundreds (105 not out and 101) against Queensland, and his other centuries were 152 (against Tasmania), 117 (against New South Wales), 228 not out (against South Australia) and 102 (against Victoria), to finish the Pura Cup season with 1,145 runs at an average of 71.56. Martyn and Adam Gilchrist each scored two centuries, but international duties forced Martyn to miss five matches and Gilchrist eight. Justin Langer also missed the final eight Pura Cup matches.

Western Australia consistently failed to produce good opening stands. Campbell was dropped for the final five matches after scoring only 167 runs at 18.56. Goodwin, Marcus North and Scott Meuleman all had turns at opening with Mike Hussey, who had his poorest season, scoring 553 Pura Cup runs at 30.72, having failed to reach 50 in the first eight matches. The greatest disappointment was Goodwin, who played in seven Pura Cup matches and managed only 145 runs at 11.15. With Campbell, Hussey and Goodwin failing regularly, the side was constantly battling against odds. Hussey, the most convivial of chaps, tried too hard in his effort to impress the national selectors, and was not his normal relaxed self. Moody, after a season out with back problems, never regained his great prowess with the bat and scored only 288 runs at 26.18 as well as taking 16 wickets at 27.56. Young left-hander North showed glimpses of form, and with work on his technique should develop into a regular player. His ability as an off-spinner will help his cause.

The attack was greatly affected by injuries to fast men Brad Williams and Matthew Nicholson. Williams was fit for only the final three matches, in which he took nine wickets at 24.44. Nicholson required knee surgery in late December and missed three matches before returning and bowling with admirable fire to finish the season with 21 Pura Cup wickets at 33.23. Gavin Swan played in the first six matches, taking 14 wickets at 41.71 before being cast aside. Temperamental left-arm spinner Brad Oldroyd took 13 wickets at 25.76 in four matches, but his future is uncertain. The reliable veteran pair of Jo Angel and Brendon Julian, as so often in the past, formed the backbone of the attack.

Of the 22 players used in Pura Cup matches, four were newcomers to first-class cricket – young batsmen Shaun Marsh, Scott Meuleman and Geoff Cullen and experienced new-ball bowler Stuart Karppinen. Marsh, the elder son of Geoff Marsh, was 17 years and 235 days old when he scored 12 off 27 deliveries against South Australia on debut at the WACA Ground on March 2. The accomplished left-hander followed that with an unbeaten 28 in the

AUSTRALIAN DOMESTIC FIRST-CLASS RESULTS TABLE

Opponent	M	W	L	D	T
New South Wales	100	30	40	30	0
South Australia	102	43	28	31	0
Queensland	102	35	23	44	0
Victoria	99	26	31	42	0
Tasmania	44	21	5	18	0
Total	447	155	127	165	0

second innings and 46 and 16 against Tasmania in the following match. Meuleman, the grandson of former Australian, Victorian and Western Australian batsman Ken, showed tremendous temperament and an excellent technique when he opened in the final two matches. Cullen was rewarded for heavy scoring in club cricket, but was out for five in his only innings against Victoria at the MCG. With the retirements of Moody and Brendon Julian, Western Australia will need plenty from its youngsters if it hopes to return quickly as a force in Australian cricket. – KEN CASELLAS.

WESTERN AUSTRALIA RESULTS, 2000-01

All first-class matches – Played 11: Won 3, Lost 4, Drawn 4.
Pura Cup matches – Played 10: Won 2, Lost 4, Drawn 4.
Mercantile Mutual Cup matches – Played 11: Won 6, Lost 4, No result 1.
Competition placings – Pura Cup, 5th; Mercantile Mutual Cup, 2nd.

PURA CUP AVERAGES, 2000-01

BATTING

	M	I	NO	R	HS	100s	50s	Avge	Ct/St
A.C. Gilchrist	2	3	1	270	109*	2	1	135.00	3/1
S.M. Katich	10	19	3	1,145	228*	6	2	71.56	10
D.R. Martyn	5	9	0	546	122	2	3	60.67	4
M.E. Hussey	10	19	1	553	137	1	1	30.72	12
T.M. Moody	8	13	2	288	57	0	2	26.18	3
S.E. Marsh	3	5	1	102	46	0	0	25.50	2
M.J. North	6	11	0	277	54	0	2	25.18	4
B.P. Julian	8	15	1	335	78	0	2	23.93	4
M.J. Nicholson	7	10	2	187	48	0	0	23.38	5
J.L. Langer	2	3	0	60	60	0	1	20.00	1
S.W. Meuleman	2	4	0	77	46	0	0	19.25	0
R.J. Campbell	5	9	0	167	35	0	0	18.56	10
M.J. Walsh	8	14	1	195	50	0	1	15.00	33/3
M.W. Goodwin	7	13	0	145	59	0	1	11.15	5
G.B. Hogg	2	3	0	30	23	0	0	10.00	1
S.J. Karppinen	1	2	0	18	17	0	0	9.00	0
J. Angel	9	11	2	70	37	0	0	7.78	0
B.J. Oldroyd	4	7	4	21	9	0	0	7.00	2
B.A. Williams	3	3	1	13	11*	0	0	6.50	2
G.I. Cullen	1	1	0	5	5	0	0	5.00	0
G.G. Swan	6	7	5	8	8*	0	0	4.00	4
S.R. Cary	1	1	1	2	2*	0	0	–	2

WESTERN AUSTRALIA PURA CUP TEAM, 2000-01

Back row: C.W. Rogers, R.J. Campbell, R. Baker, S.J. Karppinen, M.J. North, M.E. Hussey, S.E. Marsh, M.J. Walsh. *Middle row:* M.W. Goodwin, B.A. Williams, M. Dighton, B.P. Julian, S.R. Cary, M.J. Nicholson, G.G. Swan, S. Nikitaras, G.B. Hogg. *Front row:* S.M. Katich *(captain)*, M.E. Hussey, T.M. Moody, W.M. Clark *(coach)*, A.C. Gilchrist *(vice-captain)*, D.R. Martyn, J.L. Langer, J. Angel. *Absent:* M.P. Atkinson, K.M. Harvey, D.J. Wates, G.I. Cullen, S.W. Meuleman, B.J. Oldroyd, D.J. Spencer.

BOWLING

	O	M	R	W	BB	5W/i	Avge
S. J. Karppinen	27	8	68	5	3/34	0	13.60
J. Angel	333.3	109	867	37	5/78	1	23.43
B. A. Williams	82.5	22	220	9	3/31	0	24.44
B. J. Oldroyd	109.2	24	335	13	4/90	0	25.77
T. M. Moody	177	54	441	16	5/26	1	27.56
S. M. Katich	22.2	0	83	3	3/46	0	27.67
B. P. Julian	228.2	38	843	28	4/87	0	30.11
M. J. Nicholson	252.1	74	698	21	4/119	0	33.24
M. J. North	46	8	152	4	2/64	0	38.00
G. G. Swan	185	39	584	14	3/34	0	41.71
G. B. Hogg	63	12	177	4	2/78	0	44.25
S. R. Cary	27	6	75	0	–	0	–
M. E. Hussey	15	4	56	0	–	0	–
D. R. Martyn	55	10	162	0	–	0	–

WESTERN AUSTRALIA v QUEENSLAND

At WACA Ground, Perth, October 13, 14, 15, 16, 2000. Drawn. Toss: Western Australia. Queensland 2 pts.

With Queensland cruising at two for 369 in the 120th over shortly before lunch on the second day, Western Australian captain Tom Moody was regretting his decision to send the visitors in on what proved to be a placid pitch. Part-time left-arm wrist-spinner Simon Katich then had opener Jimmy Maher edging a low catch to slip to depart for 175 (453 minutes, 372 balls, 26 fours), and 20 minutes later removed Stuart Law for 128 (332 minutes, 256 balls, 14 fours). Their steady and effective partnership of 275 created a new third-wicket record between these two states. The dismissals precipitated a slump that saw eight wickets crash for 73 runs. Matthew Nicholson took 4/22 off nine overs in a fiery spell after lunch. Adam Dale maintained his marvellous form at the WACA Ground and his 5/41 off 29.1 overs enabled Queensland to dismiss the home side for 195. Law enforced the follow-on and Western Australia were sliding towards defeat at three for 43 before a patient 78 from Damien Martyn and unbeaten centuries from Katich (477 minutes, 392 balls, ten fours) and Adam Gilchrist (232 minutes, 209 balls, 15 fours) steered their side to a well-merited draw. Katich reached his century in 460 minutes off 379 balls, to become the slowest century-maker for his state, beating Geoff Marsh's 100 not out in 408 minutes against Victoria in November 1985.

Man of the Match: J. P. Maher. *Attendance:* 5,645.

Close of play: First day, Queensland (1) 2-283 (Maher 132, Law 86); Second day, Western Australia (1) 5-119 (Hussey 37, Gilchrist 31); Third day, Western Australia (2) 3-148 (Martyn 70, Katich 39).

Queensland

M. L. Hayden lbw b Angel	47	
J. P. Maher c Martyn b Katich	175	
M. L. Love c Campbell b Angel	4	
*S. G. Law st Gilchrist b Katich	128	
A. Symonds c Cary b Nicholson	19	
C. T. Perren b Nicholson	9	
†W. A. Seccombe c Campbell b Nicholson	4	
A. J. Bichel c Gilchrist b Nicholson	15	

A. C. Dale c Katich b Swan	12
A. A. Noffke not out	5
M. A. Anderson c Cary b Katich	5
B 1, l-b 9, n-b 9	19
(149.2 overs, 574 mins)	442
Fall: 87 94 369 382 400 404 405 430 435 442	

Bowling: Angel 33–7–83–2; Cary 27–6–75–0; Nicholson 37–7–119–4; Swan 20–4–58–1; Moody 9–5–19–0; Martyn 8–2–32–0; Katich 15.2–0–46–3.

Western Australia

M. E. Hussey c Seccombe b Noffke	41	– (2) c Perren b Bichel	5
R. J. Campbell lbw b Dale	7	– (1) c Maher b Noffke	25
J. L. Langer c Seccombe b Bichel	0	– c Seccombe b Bichel	0
D. R. Martyn c Love b Noffke	29	– b Bichel	78
S. M. Katich c Seccombe b Noffke	0	– not out	105
*T. M. Moody c Seccombe b Bichel	5	– c Law b Bichel	14
†A. C. Gilchrist c Seccombe b Dale	59	– not out	109
M. J. Nicholson c Seccombe b Dale	35		
J. Angel c Maher b Dale	5		
S. R. Cary not out	2		
G. G. Swan lbw b Dale	0		
L-b 1, n-b 11	12	L-b 5, n-b 8	13

(82.1 overs, 315 mins)   195   (145 overs, 541 mins)   (5 wkts) 349
Fall: 11 12 62 63 74 127 175 184 195 195   Fall: 15 15 43 161 183

Bowling: First Innings—Bichel 19–6–50–2; Dale 29.1–12–41–5; Noffke 13–2–51–3; Symonds 5–0–21–0; Anderson 16–3–31–0. *Second Innings*—Bichel 28–8–54–4; Dale 26–11–65–0; Noffke 30–6–97–1; Anderson 38–9–90–0; Hayden 2–2–0–0; Symonds 21–11–38–0.

Umpires: K. J. Rinaldi and R. J. U. Woolridge.
TV Umpire: B. Bennett.

At Adelaide Oval, Adelaide, October 26, 27, 28, 29, 2000. WESTERN AUSTRALIA drew with SOUTH AUSTRALIA.

At Bellerive Oval, Hobart, November 19, 20, 21, 22, 2000. WESTERN AUSTRALIA drew with TASMANIA.

At North Sydney Oval, North Sydney, December 1, 2, 3, 4, 2000. WESTERN AUSTRALIA lost to NEW SOUTH WALES by 51 runs.

WESTERN AUSTRALIA v NEW SOUTH WALES

At WACA Ground, Perth, December 15, 16, 17, 2000. Western Australia won by nine wickets. Toss: Western Australia. Western Australia 6 pts.

A pitch tinged with green provided great assistance to the new-ball bowlers and the match lasted only two days and 74 minutes, with the rare occurrence of no batsman reaching a half-century. Sent in to bat, the visitors lasted only 52.2 overs, although three catches were dropped. Nine batsmen were caught by wicket-keeper Mark Walsh or in the slips cordon. Jo Angel, Gavin Swan and Brendon Julian capitalised on the conditions, each taking three wickets. Then the New South Wales fast bowlers, Don Nash, Stuart Clark and Shane Lee, dismissed Western Australia for 189, with the young left-hander Marcus North scoring a defiant 47 in three hours. The pitch was still unpredictable when New South Wales batted again. This time it was Tom Moody who took the bowling honours, wrapping up the innings by taking 5/7 off 27 deliveries. Western Australia lost only one second-innings wicket in romping to victory.

Man of the Match: T. M. Moody. *Attendance:* 2,500.

Close of play: First day, Western Australia (1) 4-111 (North 13, Moody 9); Second day, New South Wales 130 all out.

New South Wales

B.P. Van Deinsen c Hussey b Moody	29	– (2) b Swan	13
G.J. Mail c Campbell b Angel	4	– (1) c Walsh b Angel	14
M.G. Bevan c Walsh b Swan	28	– c Walsh b Julian	36
C.J. Richards c Walsh b Julian	0	– c Walsh b Angel	0
*S. Lee c Hussey b Julian	0	– (6) lbw b Moody	8
M.J. Clarke c North b Angel	11	– (7) lbw b Julian	0
†B.J. Haddin c Campbell b Swan	6	– (8) c Walsh b Moody	12
M.A. Higgs c Campbell b Julian	23	– (5) c Hussey b Moody	27
D.A. Nash c Hussey b Swan	9	– c Katich b Moody	0
S.R. Cook c Campbell b Angel	5	– not out	3
S.H. Cook not out	6	– c Walsh b Moody	0
B 3, l-b 3, w 2, n-b 2	10	L-b 8, w 2, n-b 7	17

(52.2 overs, 200 mins) 131
Fall: 14 41 44 50 81 81 88
106 115 131

(51 overs, 198 mins) 130
Fall: 23 51 51 107 111 111 115
115 130 130

Bowling: *First Innings*—Angel 20–9–39–3; Swan 14–5–34–3; Moody 10–3–22–1; Julian 7.2–0–28–3; Oldroyd 1–0–2–0. *Second Innings*—Angel 14–8–25–2; Swan 12–6–14–1; Moody 12–5–26–5; Julian 13–1–57–2.

Western Australia

M.E. Hussey c Haddin b Clark	13	– not out	29
R.J. Campbell c Van Deinsen b Nash	15	– c Haddin b Clark	24
S.M. Katich c Clark b Nash	40	– not out	13
M.W. Goodwin c Haddin b Lee	15		
M.J. North lbw b Lee	47		
*T.M. Moody b Nash	25		
B.P. Julian c Van Deinsen b Nash	6		
†M.J. Walsh c Haddin b Clark	5		
J. Angel c Mail b Lee	9		
B.J. Oldroyd c Higgs b Lee	0		
G.G. Swan not out	8		
B 1, l-b 3, w 1, n-b 1	6	B 4, l-b 1, w 2	7

(81.1 overs, 334 mins) 189
Fall: 24 40 89 91 138 150 159 180 180 189

(15.5 overs, 74 mins) (1 wkt) 73
Fall: 31

Bowling: *First Innings*—Nash 27–4–57–4; Cook 17–4–49–0; Clark 17–8–36–2; Lee 20.1–8–43–4. *Second Innings*—Nash 3–1–20–0; Clark 6–3–19–1; Cook 5–2–11–0; Higgs 1.5–0–18–0.

Umpires: D.B. Hair and R.J.U. Woolridge.

WESTERN AUSTRALIA v VICTORIA

At WACA Ground, Perth, January 4, 5, 6, 2001. Victoria won by 77 runs. Toss: Victoria. Victoria 6 pts. First-class debut: S.J. Karppinen.

Champion leg-spinner Shane Warne's return to first-class cricket after breaking a finger was a significant occasion, and he played a major role in Victoria's victory. Though appearing in his first first-class match for almost three months and bowling on a surface that has traditionally favoured fast bowlers, Warne produced the second-best figures by a leg-spinner in 225 first-class domestic matches at the WACA Ground. His 9/102 has been bettered only by New South Wales' Peter Philpott (11/151 in December 1966). After Gavin Swan had dismissed Victoria's openers, Brendon Julian struck a purple patch when he took 4/17 in 23 deliveries. Half-centuries from Murray Goodwin and Marcus North, plus 40 sundries (including 16 no-balls from Paul Reiffel) were not enough to give the home side first-innings points. Bowlers continued to dominate and 17 wickets fell for 274 runs on the third day as Warne bowled superbly and Simon Katich (138 minutes, 101 balls, 13 fours) batted with combative flair.

Man of the Match: S.K. Warne. *Attendance:* 4,641.
Close of play: First day, Western Australia (1) 1-76 (Goodwin 30, Walsh 0); Second day, Victoria (1) 3-146 (Arnberger 63, Peake 24).

Victoria

M.T.G. Elliott c Martyn b Swan	18	–	(2) c Hussey b Karppinen	30
J.L. Arnberger c Walsh b Swan	45	–	(1) lbw b Angel	63
M.P. Mott c Hussey b Julian	42	–	b Julian	15
B.J. Hodge c Walsh b Julian	22	–	c Walsh b Angel	0
C.J. Peake c Moody b Julian	10	–	c Hussey b Angel	33
I.J. Harvey run out (Julian)	41	–	c Katich b Swan	18
†D.S. Berry c Martyn b Julian	4	–	c Swan b Karppinen	33
S.K. Warne c Moody b Angel	27	–	run out (Katich/North)	12
*P.R. Reiffel c Walsh b Karppinen	19	–	c Swan b Karppinen	14
M.L. Lewis not out	2	–	c Walsh b Angel	1
M.W.H. Inness lbw b Karppinen	0	–	not out	0
B 4, l-b 7, n-b 13	24		B 7, l-b 6, w 2, n-b 5	20
(77 overs, 314 mins)	254		(73.5 overs, 293 mins)	239

Fall: 31 104 134 153 154 158 212 242
254 254

Fall: 59 91 93 146 167 196 210 225
239 239

Bowling: *First Innings*—Angel 20-8-49-1; Swan 18-3-59-2; Karppinen 13-4-34-2; Julian 17-1-87-4; Moody 6-2-6-0; Martyn 3-1-8-0. *Second Innings*—Angel 21.5-4-60-4; Swan 14-1-63-1; Karppinen 14-4-34-3; Julian 14-3-39-1; Moody 6-3-22-0; Martyn 4-0-8-0.

Western Australia

M.E. Hussey lbw b Warne	35	–	c Berry b Lewis	42
M.W. Goodwin run out (Arnberger/Berry)	59	–	c Peake b Reiffel	1
†M.J. Walsh b Warne	10	–	(8) c Mott b Reiffel	5
S.M. Katich c Berry b Warne	6	–	(3) c Peake b Warne	72
D.R. Martyn c Berry b Lewis	5	–	(4) lbw b Warne	8
M.J. North c Harvey b Warne	54	–	(5) c Arnberger b Warne	0
*T.M. Moody c Lewis b Harvey	12	–	(6) c Berry b Lewis	1
B.P. Julian b Harvey	4	–	(7) c Arnberger b Harvey	19
S.J. Karppinen c Warne b Reiffel	1	–	lbw b Warne	17
J. Angel c Harvey b Lewis	9	–	c Inness b Warne	0
G.G. Swan not out	0	–	not out	0
B 4, l-b 10, w 1, n-b 25	40		B 1, l-b 5, n-b 10	16
(63.5 overs, 278 mins)	235		(54 overs, 224 mins)	181

Fall: 74 99 118 129 140 167 187
189 225 235

Fall: 8 78 108 108 129 133 158
175 181 181

Bowling: *First Innings*—Reiffel 14-0-63-1; Inness 8-0-30-0; Lewis 16-5-49-2; Warne 15.5-3-53-4; Harvey 10-2-26-2. *Second Innings*—Reiffel 9-1-38-2; Inness 9-2-25-0; Harvey 5-2-15-1; Warne 20-5-49-5; Lewis 11-1-48-2.

Umpires: K.J. Rinaldi and R.J.U. Woolridge.

At Brisbane Cricket Ground, Brisbane, February 18, 19, 20, 2001. WESTERN AUSTRALIA lost to QUEENSLAND by eight wickets.

WESTERN AUSTRALIA v SOUTH AUSTRALIA

At WACA Ground, Perth, March 2, 3, 4, 5, 2001. Western Australia won by 36 runs. Toss: Western Australia. Western Australia 6 pts. First-class debuts: C.J. Borgas, B.H. Higgins, P.C. Rofe, L. Williams; S.E. Marsh.

Tom Moody's 300th first-class match saw a changing of the guard. Five players made their debuts in first-class ranks and, in a surprise after the match, Moody announced his retirement, as Western Australia, with two Pura Cup matches remaining, had no realistic hope of qualifying for the final. Moody bowed out in style, batting with great panache in the first innings, scoring 55 (86 minutes, 67 balls, nine fours) before chopping a ball from Mike Smith onto his stumps. Simon Katich and Greg Blewett stood above the rest with their splendid batting. Katich, battling a virus and the stifling heat, hit an unbeaten 228 off 331 balls in 458 minutes. Weakened by his illness, he refused dozens of easy singles in a superb innings that included 42 boundaries. Brendon Julian gave one of his periodic imitations of a whirlwind as he dashed to 78 (106 minutes, 87 balls, 13 fours, one six), adding 147 for the sixth wicket with Katich. Blewett was at his imperious best as he pulled and drove aggressively in scoring 138 (283 minutes, 193 balls, 22 fours, one six) and 77. Moody's decision not to enforce the follow-on was vindicated when Western Australia took six wickets in the final session to scramble home. The left-handed Shaun Marsh looked the part, while Ben Higgins, another left-hander, looked the best of the South Australian debutants as he batted for a total of four hours in the match.

Man of the Match: S. M. Katich. *Attendance:* 2,761.

Close of play: First day, Western Australia (1) 6-360 (Katich 152, Walsh 5); Second day, South Australia (1) 5-198 (Blewett 115, Smith 3); Third day, South Australia (2) 1-61 (Deitz 14, Blewett 28).

Western Australia

M. E. Hussey c Smith b Harrity	9	–	c Blewett b Smith		35
M. J. North c Blewett b Harrity	35	–	c Deitz b Blewett		38
S. M. Katich not out	228	–	c Blewett b Lehmann		26
M. W. Goodwin b Harrity	4	–	run out (Blewett)		3
*T. M. Moody b Smith	55				
S. E. Marsh lbw b Rofe	12	–	(5) not out		28
B. P. Julian c Blewett b Swain	78	–	(6) c Manou b Lehmann		7
†M. J. Walsh lbw b Swain	10	–	not out		9
M. J. Nicholson not out	32	–	(7) c Blewett b Harrity		4
B 4, l-b 7	11		B 2, l-b 1, w 6, n-b 1		10

(120 overs, 478 mins)	(7 wkts dec) 474	(59 overs, 227 mins)	(6 wkts dec) 160
Fall: 12 75 87 177 208 355 386		Fall: 70 79 93 127 140 145	

J. Angel and B. A. Williams did not bat.

Bowling: *First Innings*—Harrity 28-3-115-3; Swain 28-4-86-2; Rofe 23-8-98-1; Smith 26-6-94-1; Blewett 7-1-31-0; Deitz 5-0-19-0; Lehmann 3-0-20-0. *Second Innings*—Harrity 16-5-40-1; Swain 11-3-28-0; Rofe 7-2-10-0; Smith 6-0-18-1; Blewett 7-1-25-1; Lehmann 12-0-36-2.

South Australia

L. Williams c Hussey b Angel	6	–	(2) c Walsh b Williams		16
S. A. Deitz c Williams b Angel	4	–	(1) b Angel		66
G. S. Blewett c Marsh b Angel	138	–	c and b Nicholson		77
*D. S. Lehmann c Walsh b Nicholson	23	–	c Williams b North		51
C. J. Borgas c Walsh b Angel	9	–	c Walsh b Julian		12
B. H. Higgins c Walsh b North	29	–	b Julian		59
M. J. Smith c Walsh b Nicholson	7	–	(8) c Katich b Nicholson		28
†G. A. Manou b Julian	7	–	(7) b Williams		9
B. A. Swain not out	21	–	c Walsh b Angel		0
P. C. Rofe c Walsh b Williams	1	–	not out		17
M. A. Harrity c Walsh b Williams	0	–	c Julian b Nicholson		0
B 2, w 3, n-b 6	11		B 2, l-b 3, w 1, n-b 1		7

(86.5 overs, 348 mins)	256	(100.4 overs)	342
Fall: 9 14 49 83 179 203 226 245		Fall: 19 148 182 217 241 257 305	
256 256		306 327 342	

Bowling: *First Innings*—Williams 10.5–4–23–2; Angel 20–9–41–4; Nicholson 21–8–67–2; Julian 14–1–73–1; Moody 10–5–16–0; North 7–0–28–1; Hussey 4–2–6–0. *Second Innings*—Williams 19–4–56–2; Angel 25–6–91–2; Julian 17–4–57–2; Nicholson 20.4–4–80–3; Moody 11–4–40–0; North 8–3–13–1.

Umpires: A.R. Craig and A.J. McQuillan.

WESTERN AUSTRALIA v TASMANIA

At WACA Ground, Perth, March 9, 10, 11, 2001. Tasmania won by nine wickets. Toss: Tasmania. Tasmania 6 pts. First-class debut: S.W. Meuleman.

There was no glorious home-town farewell for retiring captain Tom Moody and coach Wayne Clark as Western Australia's batsmen performed miserably against a vibrant Tasmanian attack. The pace quintet of David Saker, Damien Wright, Andrew Downton, Shaun Young and Shane Watson simply carried too many guns for the home batsmen, who, apart from Mike Hussey in the first innings (305 minutes, 240 balls, 11 fours) and tyros Shaun Marsh and Scott Meuleman, failed to reach 30. Evergreen fast bowler Jo Angel again showed his class and determination in taking 5/78 off 32.4 overs as well as the only wicket to fall in Tasmania's second innings, when Dene Hills became his 400th first-class victim. Watson also impressed with the bat in his innings of 54. Western Australia, trailing by 51 runs on the first innings, folded up without a whimper in the second innings and were dismissed for a paltry 139, their lowest total against Tasmania in Perth.

Man of the Match: S.R. Watson. *Attendance:* 2,521.

Close of play: First day, Western Australia (1) 9-228 (Angel 1); Second day, Tasmania (1) 7-249 (Clingeleffer 8, Saker 10).

Western Australia

M.E. Hussey c Clingeleffer b Wright	90	– (2) c Di Venuto b Saker	15
S.W. Meuleman c Hills b Downton	27	– (1) b Watson	46
*S.M. Katich c Di Venuto b Watson	23	– c Clingeleffer b Downton	0
M.W. Goodwin c Marsh b Young	8	– lbw b Downton	0
M.J. North lbw b Young	0	– c Marsh b Young	9
S.E. Marsh lbw b Wright	46	– c Di Venuto b Young	16
B.P. Julian b Wright	8	– c Marsh b Wright	3
†M.J. Walsh lbw b Saker	0	– c Di Venuto b Saker	27
M.J. Nicholson c Di Venuto b Wright	10	– b Watson	4
J. Angel not out	1	– c Wright b Saker	1
B.A. Williams c Cox b Saker	1	– not out	11
L-b 4, w 1, n-b 10	15	L-b 6, n-b 1	7

(96.1 overs, 365 mins)	229	(54.5 overs, 218 mins)	139

Fall: 43 74 93 93 192 212 215 215   228 229

Fall: 22 33 33 48 74 77 119 125   126 139

Bowling: *First Innings*—Saker 16.1–4–39–2; Wright 26–9–65–4; Downton 15–3–31–1; Young 15–9–17–2; Watson 8–2–26–1; Marsh 12–2–39–0; Kremerskothen 4–0–8–0. *Second Innings*—Saker 17.5–8–38–3; Wright 12–3–36–1; Downton 9–5–14–2; Young 10–3–20–2; Watson 6–0–25–2.

Tasmania

D. F. Hills c Nicholson b Angel	69	– c Walsh b Angel	1
*J. Cox run out (Katich)	20	– not out	30
M. J. Di Venuto c Walsh b Nicholson	0	– not out	48
S. R. Watson c Hussey b Angel	54		
D. J. Marsh c Walsh b Williams	34		
S. Young c Julian b Angel	2		
S. P. Kremerskothen c North b Williams	37		
†S. G. Clingeleffer b Nicholson	14		
D. J. Saker b Angel	20		
D. G. Wright not out	1		
A. G. Downton c Julian b Angel	5		
B 1, l-b 12, w 5, n-b 6	24	L-b 5, n-b 5	10

(105.4 overs, 411 mins)   280   (21 overs, 87 mins)   (1 wkt)   89
Fall: 42 42 147 160 166 221 234 272 274 280   Fall: 1

Bowling: *First Innings*—Williams 17–5–46–2; Angel 32.4–14–78–5; Nicholson 32–11–57–2; Julian 16–5–49–0; North 6–2–20–0; Hussey 2–0–17–0. *Second Innings*—Williams 5–1–24–0; Angel 6–1–25–1; Nicholson 6–2–28–0; Julian 4–1–7–0.

Umpires: D. B. Hair and I. H. Lock.

At Melbourne Cricket Ground, Melbourne, March 15, 16, 17, 18, 2001. WESTERN AUSTRALIA drew with VICTORIA.

AUSTRALIAN DOMESTIC FIRST-CLASS RECORDS

Highest score for:	355*	G. R. Marsh v South Australia at Perth	1989-90
Highest score against:	356	B. A. Richards (South Australia) at Perth	1970-71
Best bowling for:	10/44	I. J. Brayshaw v Victoria at Perth	1967-68
Best bowling against:	8/66	J. D. Higgs (Victoria) at Melbourne	1974-75
Highest total for:	654	v Victoria at Perth	1986-87
Highest total against:	4-601	decby New South Wales at Perth	1990-91
Lowest total for:	41	v South Australia at Adelaide	1989-90
Lowest total against:	52	by Queensland at Perth	1982-83

MOST RUNS

	M	I	NO	R	HS	100s	50s	Avge
T. M. Moody	132	228	22	8,853	272	20	46	42.98
M. R. J. Veletta	114	198	20	7,306	262	18	40	41.04
G. R. Marsh	100	175	12	7,009	355*	21	28	43.00
G. M. Wood	109	174	25	6,904	186*	20	32	46.34
R. J. Inverarity	108	188	18	6,888	187	20	29	40.52
D. R. Martyn	90	159	16	6,416	203*	19	32	44.87
J. L. Langer	67	123	10	6,093	274*	19	21	53.92
B. K. Shepherd	75	127	13	4,934	219	11	26	43.28
M. E. Hussey	65	119	6	4,771	187	11	20	42.22
R. W. Marsh	86	139	9	4,412	168*	6	23	33.94

HIGHEST PARTNERSHIP FOR EACH WICKET

431 for 1st   M.R.J. Veletta and G.R. Marsh v South Australia at Perth 1989-90
254 for 2nd   G.R. Marsh and M.R.J. Veletta v Queensland at Brisbane 1985-86
330 for 3rd   G.M. Wood and G.R. Marsh v New South Wales at Sydney 1983-84
279 for 4th   D.R. Martyn and T.M. Moody v Tasmania at Hobart (Bellerive) 1994-95
301* for 5th   R.B. Simpson and K.D. Meuleman v New South Wales at Perth 1959-60
244 for 6th   J.T. Irvine and R. Edwards v New South Wales at Sydney 1968-69
204 for 7th   G. Shipperd and T.J. Zoehrer v New South Wales at Perth 1982-83
242* for 8th   T.J. Zoehrer and K.H. MacLeay v New South Wales at Perth 1990-91
168* for 9th   K.H. MacLeay and V.J. Marks v New South Wales at Perth 1986-87
91   for 10th I.J. Brayshaw and J.B. Gannon v Queensland at Brisbane 1969-70

MOST WICKETS

	M	Balls	Mdns	R	W	BB	5W/i	10W/m	Avge
T.M. Alderman	97	20,482	778	9,299	384	7/28	17	3	24.22
J. Angel	84	17,704	818	8,269	343	6/64	11	0	24.11
D.K. Lillee	70	16,617	439	7,544	323	7/36	18	4	23.36
G.A.R. Lock	66	20,107	544	7,210	302	7/53	16	2	23.87
B.P. Julian	87	16,143	612	8,573	292	7/39	15	2	29.36
G.D. McKenzie	73	16,566	287	7,322	232	6/100	7	0	31.56
K.H. MacLeay	90	17,761	836	7,033	229	6/93	5	0	30.71
T.M. Moody	132	14,431	673	6,297	220	7/38	5	1	28.62
C.D. Matthews	44	9,741	342	4,678	188	8/101	11	0	24.88
B.A. Reid	49	11,520	496	4,980	181	6/54	7	1	27.51

MOST DISMISSALS

	M	Ct	St	Total
T.J. Zoehrer	107	332	27	359
R.W. Marsh	84	311	33	344
A.C. Gilchrist	48	236	8	244
B.L. Buggins	57	131	18	149
G.C. Becker	39	90	17	107

MOST CATCHES

R.J. Inverarity .... 139 in 108 matches
M.R.J. Veletta .... 138 in 114 matches
T.M. Moody .... 114 in 132 matches
I.J. Brayshaw .... 95 in 91 matches

G.A.R. Lock .... 80 in 66 matches
T.M. Alderman ..... 80 in 90 matches
D.R. Martyn ..... 80 in 97 matches
G.M. Wood .... 77 in 109 matches

MOST APPEARANCES

132 T.M. Moody ...... 1985-86 – 2000-01
114 M.R.J. Veletta ... 1983-84 – 1994-95
109 G.M. Wood ..... 1977-78 – 1991-92
108 R.J. Inverarity .. 1962-63 – 1978-79
107 T.J. Zoehrer ...... 1980-81 – 1993-94

100 G.R. Marsh ..... 1977-78 – 1993-94
97 T.M. Alderman ... 1974-75 – 1992-93
91 I.J. Brayshaw .... 1960-61 – 1977-78
90 K.H. MacLeay ... 1981-82 – 1991-92
90 D.R. Martyn ..... 1990-91 – 2000-01

MERCANTILE MUTUAL CUP, 2000-01

By WARWICK FRANKS

The Mercantile Mutual competition was given a thorough refurbishment, all, naturally, in the cause of faster, brighter and more competitive cricket. The Australian Capital Territory team was declared surplus to needs, the Australian Cricket Board chairman, Denis Rogers, explaining that the board's decision was based on "a philosophical discussion concerning cricket in the ACT". Shorn of its niceties, Canberra cricket authorities were being told that their team was not sufficiently competitive to hold its own and that its immediate future was as a nursery for New South Wales cricketers. The decision did not appear to be a particularly creative way of fostering a wider base and presence for cricket throughout the nation.

The schedule was extended to include both home and away matches so that a more continuous presence during the season might enhance the competition's status beyond a fairly peripheral sideshow in Australian cricket. In an attempt to inject even more urgency into proceedings, a bonus point was offered to teams that could score at a rate 1.25 times that of their opponents, and penalties for slow over rates were introduced. Judged by the appropriate standards for limited-overs cricket, the results were positive. Batsmen played their strokes and plenty of runs were scored, with 28 innings totals of over 240. Fieldsmen were athletic and pitches were prepared that ensured that bowlers did not get above themselves by imagining that they had anything positive to contribute beyond restraining the run rate.

The competition was keenly fought, and on the last weekend of preliminary matches, four of the six teams were still capable of qualifying for a spot in the final. New South Wales eventually seized the moment and won with style, claiming their sixth limited-overs title and their first since the 1993-94 season. It was very much a case of being the better side on the day, as both Western Australia and South Australia had looked to be more consistent and better integrated teams throughout the season. Tasmania improved markedly, but Queensland's inconsistency led to their decline, while Victoria threatened nothing, except the patience of their supporters.

There were a number of landmarks during the season, several of them coming in Western Australia's innings against New South Wales at Perth in January. Murray Goodwin's astonishing 167 from 138 balls set an individual innings record, while his partnership of 257 in 38.1 overs with Mike Hussey, who scored 94, set a third-wicket record and was the second-highest for any wicket in the competition. It was little wonder that Western Australia finished at a record-equalling innings total of five for 325. Don Nash replied in kind in the return match at North Sydney, when he took on the mantle of George Bonnor, his 61 from 28 balls being the second-fastest 50 scored in Australian limited-overs cricket. Darren Lehmann's season brought him another 524 excitingly executed runs at an average of 131.00 and a strike-rate of 111.01, taking him to a career total of 2,249 runs, another record for the competition.

Scott Prestwidge of Queensland made his first appearance in 1991-92 and now lies second on the list of limited-overs wicket-takers with 71 from his 52 matches, but made the last of his three Sheffield Shield appearances in 1996-97. Somewhere in those statistics lies a cautionary tale about the values and assumptions of limited-overs cricket.

2000-01 POINTS TABLE

	Played	Won	Lost	No Result	Bonus Points	Points	Net Run-rate
Western Australia	10	6	3	1	3	29	0.18
New South Wales	10	6	4	0	2	26	0.24
South Australia	10	6	4	0	1	25	−0.08
Queensland	10	4	5	1	2	20	−0.18
Tasmania	10	4	6	0	3	19	0.17
Victoria	10	3	7	0	2	14	−0.29

Net run-rate was calculated by subtracting runs conceded per over from runs scored per over.

FINAL

WESTERN AUSTRALIA v NEW SOUTH WALES

At WACA Ground, Perth, February 25, 2001. New South Wales won by six wickets. Toss: Western Australia.

New South Wales reversed the result of the encounter of the previous month at this ground when Western Australia had thrashed their attack into submission. Initially, Tom Moody mixed exuberance with experience, his partnership with Murray Goodwin adding 103 in 18.5 overs. A pall then fell over the innings as in the next 14.1 overs five wickets fell for the addition of only 52 runs. At this point, Mike Hussey took charge and batted with freedom and power, his 84 coming from only 68 balls and including eight fours and three sixes. He received staunch support from Kade Harvey in an unfinished partnership of 87 in the final 10 overs. The New South Wales innings was a textbook demonstration of Michael Bevan's batting supremacy in this form of the game. He faced only 137 balls, striking 14 fours and a six as he bent the bowlers to his will. The home side paid dearly for Brendon Julian's dropping of a regulation catch at mid-on when Bevan was on 59. Michael Clarke underlined his promise in a second-wicket partnership of 126 in 24 overs as he battled repeated cramping in his right leg, and Mark Higgs and Graeme Rummans gave sensible support to Bevan at a vital period. Perhaps the crucial statistic of the game was that while Western Australia's fourth 50 took 79 balls for the loss of four wickets, in the same period of their innings New South Wales lost no wickets in 52 balls.

Man of the Match: M. G. Bevan. *Man of the Series:* D. S. Lehmann (South Australia) and S. Young (Tasmania). *Attendance:* 9,310.

Western Australia

*T. M. Moody c Higgs b MacGill	 78	(79)	
†R. J. Campbell c Higgs b Bracken	... 10	(11)	
S. M. Katich c Haddin b Bracken	 4	(9)	
M. W. Goodwin c Haddin b Lee	 38	(59)	
B. P. Julian b Lee	 14	(17)	
M. E. Hussey not out	 84	(68)	
M. J. North b Thompson	 14	(25)	

G. B. Hogg c Haddin b Bradstreet ... 1 (4)
K. M. Harvey not out 20 (28)

B 1, l-b 5, w 2, n-b 1 9
———
(50 overs, 220 mins)   (7 wkts) 272
Fall: 23 30 133 139 152 182 185

D. J. Spencer, J. Angel and B. A. Williams did not bat.

Bowling: Bracken 10–2–43–2; Clark 9–0–63–0; Nash 5–0–26–0; Lee 10–1–39–2; MacGill 8–1–46–1; Bradstreet 4–0–24–1; Thompson 4–0–25–1.

New South Wales

M. J. Clarke c Campbell b Spencer ... 57 (84)
†B. J. Haddin c Spencer b Williams 8 (7)
M. G. Bevan not out 135 (137)
*S. Lee c Hussey b Spencer 6 (4)
M. A. Higgs c Moody b Angel 29 (33)

G. C. Rummans not out 30 (27)
L-b 4, w 5, n-b 2 11
———
(48.2 overs, 193 mins)   (4 wkts) 276
Fall: 14 140 146 207

S. M. Thompson, S. D. Bradstreet, D. A. Nash, S. C. G. MacGill, N. W. Bracken and S. R. Clark did not bat.

Bowling: Angel 10–0–40–1; Williams 9–1–44–1; Julian 5–0–23–0; Moody 5–1–29–0; Spencer 7–0–57–2; Harvey 5.2–0–32–0; Hogg 7–0–47–0.

Umpires: D. B. Hair and D. J. Harper.
TV Umpire: R. J. Woolridge.

STATISTICS, 2000-01

			Batting			Bowling	
	M	Runs	Overs	Run-rate	Runs	Overs	Run-rate
Western Australia	10	2,231	432.5	5.15	2,207	444	4.97
New South Wales	10	2,287	452	5.06	2,311	479.5	4.82
South Australia	10	2,275	462.2	4.92	2,372	474	5.00
Queensland	10	1,881	392	4.80	1,830	367	4.99
Tasmania	10	1,696	389.2	4.36	1,696	405.3	4.18
Victoria	10	1,993	476.5	4.18	1,947	435	4.48

Note: Preliminary rounds only. Overs expressed as decimals.

MOST RUNS, 2000-01

	M	I	NO	R	HS	100s	50s	Avge	S-R
M. W. Goodwin (W Aust) .	9	9	2	534	167	1	4	76.29	92.55
D. S. Lehmann (S Aust) ...	7	7	3	524	119*	2	3	131.00	110.08
M. E. Hussey (W Aust) ...	11	9	1	428	94	0	5	53.50	88.80
M. G. Bevan (NSW)	8	8	4	423	135*	1	3	105.75	89.05
J. P. Maher (Qld)	9	9	2	383	87	0	4	54.71	81.84
B. J. Hodge (Vic)	9	9	1	374	87	0	4	46.75	74.80
M. T. G. Elliott (Vic).	7	7	0	328	112	3	0	46.86	90.61
C. J. Davies (S Aust)	10	10	0	322	62	0	3	32.20	65.05
M. L. Love (Qld)	7	6	0	315	124	1	2	52.50	86.54
S. M. Katich (W Aust) ...	8	7	0	300	73	0	4	42.86	81.97

* *Denotes not out.*

MOST WICKETS, 2000-01

	M	O	Mdns	R	W	BB	5W/i	Avge
S.C.G. MacGill (NSW)	11	97	5	500	18	3/41	0	27.78
S.P. Kremerskothen (Tas)	10	38	0	243	14	3/33	0	17.36
G.B. Hogg (W Aust)	11	63.4	2	375	13	3/49	0	28.85
P. Wilson (S Aust)	10	95.7	7	410	13	4/49	0	31.54
S. Young (Tas)	10	72	13	229	13	3/16	0	17.62
J. Angel (W Aust)	11	93	9	386	12	2/23	0	32.17
N.W. Bracken (NSW)	8	66.5	6	275	11	4/36	0	25.00
K.M. Harvey (W Aust)	11	64.2	0	362	11	3/39	0	32.91
J.R. Hopes (Qld)	5	43	3	189	11	5/29	1	17.18
D.J. Spencer (W Aust)	6	40	0	246	11	4/35	0	22.36
J.N. Gillespie (S Aust)	5	46	3	215	10	3/27	0	21.50
M.L. Lewis (Vic)	10	78	8	380	10	2/24	0	38.00

AUSTRALIAN DOMESTIC LIMITED-OVERS WINNERS

Australasian (V & G) Knock-Out Competition

Season	Winner	Runner-up	Season	Winner	Runner-up
1969-70	New Zealanders	Victoria	1970-71	Western Australia	Queensland

Australasian (Coca-Cola) Knock-Out Competition

1971-72	Victoria	South Australia	1972-73	New Zealanders	Queensland

Gillette Cup

1973-74	Western Australia	New Zealanders	1976-77	Western Australia	Victoria
1974-75	Western Australia	Western Australia	1977-78	Western Australia	Tasmania
1975-76	Queensland	Western Australia	1978-79	Tasmania	Western Australia

McDonald's Cup

1979-80	Victoria	New South Wales	1984-85	New South Wales	South Australia
1980-81	Queensland	Western Australia	1985-86	Western Australia	Victoria
1981-82	Queensland	New South Wales	1986-87	South Australia	Tasmania
1982-83	Western Australia	New South Wales	1987-88	New South Wales	South Australia
1983-84	South Australia	Western Australia			

FAI Insurance Cup

1988-89	Queensland	Victoria	1990-91	Western Australia	New South Wales
1989-90	Western Australia	South Australia	1991-92	New South Wales	Western Australia

Mercantile Mutual Cup

1992-93	New South Wales	Victoria	1997-98	Queensland	New South Wales
1993-94	New South Wales	Western Australia	1998-99	Victoria	New South Wales
1994-95	Victoria	South Australia	1999-00	Western Australia	Queensland
1995-96	Queensland	Western Australia	2000-01	New South Wales	Western Australia
1996-97	Western Australia	Queensland			

MATCH RESULTS, 1969-70 TO 2000-01

	M	W	L	NR	T	Won Batting First	Won Batting Second
Australian Capital Territory ..	18	3	15	0	0	16.67%	16.67%
New South Wales	119	69	48	1	1	51.43%	80.00%
New Zealanders	10	7	3	0	0	60.00%	80.00%
Queensland	117	65	48	4	0	52.46%	63.46%
South Australia	113	46	66	0	1	40.38%	41.67%
Tasmania	100	28	71	1	0	27.27%	29.09%
Victoria	117	50	62	4	1	40.30%	51.11%
Western Australia	136	88	43	4	1	68.63%	66.25%
Total	365	356	356	9	2	46.91%	53.09%

RESULTS AT EACH VENUE

	First Game	M	NR	T	Won Batting First	Won Batting Second
Melbourne (MCG)	1969-70	47	1	0	42.55%	57.45%
Perth	1969-70	74	3	1	41.43%	58.57%
Sydney	1969-70	43	1	0	40.48%	59.52%
Adelaide (Adelaide Oval)	1970-71	59	0	1	48.28%	51.72%
Brisbane (Gabba)	1970-71	59	2	0	38.60%	61.40%
Launceston	1970-71	5	0	0	60.00%	40.00%
Hobart (TCA)	1973-74	12	0	0	66.67%	33.33%
Melbourne (Waverley)	1979-80	1	0	0	100.00%	–
Melbourne (St Kilda)	1981-82	1	0	0	–	100.00%
Devonport	1984-85	3	0	0	100.00%	–
Adelaide (Football Park)	1986-87	2	0	0	50.00%	50.00%
Hobart (Bellerive)	1988-89	24	0	0	58.33%	41.67%
North Sydney	1989-90	15	0	0	66.67%	33.33%
Melbourne (Carlton)	1992-93	2	0	0	50.00%	50.00%
Canberra	1997-98	10	0	0	70.00%	30.00%
Bendigo	1997-98	1	0	0	100.00%	–
Melbourne (Richmond)	1999-00	3	0	0	33.33%	66.66%
Brisbane (Albion)	1999-00	2	0	0	50.00%	50.00%
Sydney (Bankstown)	2000-01	1	0	0	–	100.00%

LAST TEN YEARS' PLACINGS

	91-92	92-93	93-94	94-95	95-96	96-97	97-98	98-99	99-00	00-01
Australia Capital Territory	–	–	–	–	–	–	6	6	6	–
New South Wales	1	1	6	3	3	2	2	3	1
Queensland	3	4	4	4	1	2	1	3	2	4
South Australia	5	6	3	2	4	6	4	4	4	3
Tasmania	4	5	6	5	5	5	5	7	6	5
Victoria	6	2	5	1	6	4	7	1	5	6
Western Australia	2	3	2	3	2	1	3	5	1	2

HIGHEST INNINGS SCORES

167	M. W. Goodwin	Western Australia v New South Wales at Perth	2000-01
164	R. B. McCosker	New South Wales v South Australia at Sydney	1981-82
159	S. G. Law	Queensland v Tasmania at Brisbane (Gabba)	1993-94
152*	M. L. Hayden	Queensland v Victoria at Melbourne (MCG)	1998-99
146	J. L. Langer	Western Australia v South Australia at Perth	1999-00
142*	D. S. Lehmann	South Australia v Tasmania at Adelaide	1994-95
140*	P. C. Nobes	South Australia v Western Australia at Perth	1994-95
140	D. R. Martyn	Western Australia v Tasmania at Hobart (Bellerive)	1997-98
139*	D. M. Jones	Victoria v New South Wales at Sydney	1986-87
135	M. G. Bevan	New South Wales v Western Australia at Perth	2000-01

* Denotes not out.

FASTEST HALF-CENTURIES

Balls			
21	D. W. Hookes	South Australia v Western Australia at Perth	1990-91
24	D. A. Nash	New South Wales v Western Australia at North Sydney ..	2000-01
27	I. J. Harvey	Victoria v Tasmania at Hobart (Bellerive)	1998-99
28	D. S. Berry	Victoria v New South Wales at North Sydney	1997-98
30	M. G. Bevan	New South Wales v Victoria at Sydney	1992-93
31	R. W. Marsh	Western Australia v South Australia at Adelaide	1983-84
31	B. J. Hodge	Victoria v Tasmania at Hobart (Bellerive)	1998-99
32	S. G. Law	Queensland v Tasmania at Brisbane (Gabba)	1993-94
32	R. J. Campbell	Western Australia v Victoria at Perth	1996-97
33	W. B. Phillips	South Australia v Tasmania at Hobart (TCA)	1986-87
33	S. M. Small	New South Wales v South Australia at Adelaide	1992-93
33	D. S. Lehmann	South Australia v Tasmania at Hobart (Bellerive)	1996-97

FASTEST CENTURIES

Balls			
74	S. G. Law	Queensland v Tasmania at Brisbane (Gabba)	1998-99
82	R. J. Campbell	Western Australia v Queensland at Perth	1999-00
83	D. S. Lehmann	South Australia v Victoria at Adelaide	2000-01
88	J. P. Maher	Queensland v Western Australia at Perth	1999-00
90	S. Lee	New South Wales v Queensland at Brisbane	1999-00
90	M. L. Hayden	Queensland v South Australia at Adelaide	1999-00
90	M. W. Goodwin	Western Australia v New South Wales at Perth	2000-01
91	D. W. Hookes	South Australia v Western Australia at Adelaide	1984-85
91	S. G. Law	Queensland v Tasmania at Brisbane (Gabba)	1993-94
91	S. G. Law	Queensland v Western Australia at Brisbane (Gabba)	1993-94
91	B. J. Haddin	Australian Capital Territory v Victoria at Canberra	1998-99
91	A. C. Gilchrist	Western Australia v Queensland at Brisbane (Gabba)	1999-00
94	S. G. Law	Queensland v South Australia at Brisbane (Gabba)	1995-96
96	D. M. Jones	Victoria v Tasmania at Carlton	1996-97
98	D. S. Lehmann	South Australia v Tasmania at Adelaide	1994-95

MOST RUNS

	M	I	NO	R	HS	100s	Avge	Stk/Rt
D. S. Lehmann (S Aust/Vic)	59	58	7	2,249	142*	5	44.10	86.57
M. L. Hayden (Qld)	46	46	9	2,162	152*	8	58.43	72.65
D. M. Jones (Vic)	55	52	10	2,122	139*	4	50.52	74.07
J. P. Maher (Qld).........	50	50	8	2,035	128	4	48.45	76.59
T. M. Moody (W Aust)	75	71	12	2,004	102*	2	33.97	72.22
J. L. Langer (W Aust)	55	53	5	1,866	146	1	38.88	65.61
M. G. Bevan (S Aust/NSW)	45	45	17	1,862	135*	1	66.50	74.99
S. G. Law (Qld)..........	64	59	6	1,830	159	5	34.53	91.09
D. C. Boon (W Aust)......	55	52	4	1,725	116	1	35.94	66.22
D. R. Martyn (W Aust)	48	45	7	1,655	140	1	43.55	75.71

* Denotes not out.

HIGHEST PARTNERSHIP FOR EACH WICKET

253	for 1st	R. B. McCosker and J. Dyson,		
		New South Wales v South Australia at Sydney	....	1981-82
260	for 2nd	M. L. Hayden and S. G. Law,		
		Queensland v Tasmania at Brisbane (Gabba)	....	1993-94
257	for 3rd	M. W. Goodwin and M. E. Hussey,		
		Western Australia v New South Wales at Perth	....	2000-01
180	for 4th	G. C. Rummans and S. Lee,		
		New South Wales v Queensland at Brisbane (Gabba)	....	1999-00
156	for 5th	K. J. Roberts and R. Chee Quee,		
		New South Wales v South Australia at Sydney	....	1995-96
173*	for 6th	M. E. Hussey and G. B. Hogg,		
		Western Australia v Victoria at Melbourne (MCG)	....	1999-00
124	for 7th	G. T. Cunningham and C. M. Smart,		
		Australian Capital Territory v Victoria at Richmond	....	1999-00
106*	for 8th	A. C. Gilchrist and B. P. Julian,		
		Western Australia v New South Wales at Sydney	....	1995-96
96*	for 9th	S. M. Thompson and S. D. Bradsteeet,		
		New South Wales v Queensland at North Sydney	....	1998-99
54	for 10th	B. E. McNamara and G. R. Robertson,		
		New South Wales v South Australia at Adelaide	....	1996-97

* Denotes unbroken partnership.

HIGHEST INNINGS TOTALS

Batting First

6-325	South Australia defeated Tasmania at Hobart (TCA)	1986-87
5-325	Western Australia defeated New South Wales at Perth	2000-01
4-320	Queensland defeated Tasmania at Brisbane (Gabba)	1993-94
7-319	New South Wales defeated South Australia at North Sydney	1997-98
4-310	New South Wales defeated South Australia at Sydney	1981-82
5-310	New South Wales defeated Victoria at North Sydney	1991-92
6-310	Western Australia defeated Tasmania at Hobart (Bellerive)	1997-98
7-307	New South Wales defeated Tasmania at North Sydney	1993-94
7-307	South Australia defeated Victoria at Adelaide	1997-98
8-306	Queensland defeated Western Australia at Brisbane	2000-01
7-302	South Australia defeated Western Australia at Perth	1999-00
5-202	New South Wales defeated Western Australia at North Sydney	2000-01
6-301	Western Australia defeated Queensland at Perth	1999-00

Batting Second

7-284	Western Australia defeated Victoria at Perth	1990-91
7-284	Queensland defeated Western Australia at Perth	1997-98
282	South Australia lost to New South Wales at North Sydney	1997-98
5-282	South Australia defeated Victoria at Adelaide	2000-01
6-281	South Australia defeated Western Australia at Perth	1994-95
4-280	Victoria defeated Queensland at Melbourne (MCC)	1998-99
9-278	Queensland lost to New South Wales at Brisbane	2000-01
4-276	New South Wales defeated Western Australia at Perth	2000-01
5-275	South Australia defeated New South Wales at North Sydney	1994-95
6-271	Tasmania defeated Western Australia at Perth	1986-87
9-270	South Australia lost to Queensland at Albion	2000-01

MOST WICKETS

	M	B	Mdns	R	W	BB	5W/i	Avge
T. M. Moody (W Aust)	75	3,205	41	2,131	70	4/30	0	30.44
S. A. Prestwidge (Qld)	45	2,189	18	1,755	67	5/59	1	26.19
P. Wilson (S Aust)	40	2,216	39	1,489	62	4/23	0	24.02
B. P. Julian (W Aust)	54	2,318	19	1,779	59	4/43	0	30.15
J. Angel (W Aust)	53	2,634	42	1,721	59	3/37	0	29.17
B. E. McNamara (NSW)	42	2,005	22	1,281	57	6/25	1	22.47
M. S. Kasprowicz (Qld)	44	2,261	26	1,625	56	4/21	0	29.02
K. M. Harvey (W Aust)	40	1,694	16	1,370	55	4/8	0	24.91
K. H. MacLeay (W Aust)	38	1,896	32	1,165	53	5/30	1	21.98
I. J. Harvey (Vic)	45	1,853	13	1,478	51	5/34	1	28.98

HAT-TRICKS

A. G. Hurst	Victoria v Western Australia at Perth	1978-79
R. M. Baker	Western Australia v Australian Capital Territory at Perth	1999-00

BEST BOWLING ANALYSES

7/34	C. G. Rackemann	Queensland v South Australia at Adelaide	1988-89
6/18	J. R. Thomson	Queensland v South Australia at Brisbane (Gabba)	1978-79
6/25	B. E. McNamara	New South Wales v Tasmania at Sydney	1996-97
5/15	D. L. Boyd	Western Australia v Victoria at Perth	1982-83
5/20	G. D. Watson	Victoria v Western Australia at Melbourne (MCC)	1969-70
5/22	H. J. Howarth	New Zealanders v New South Wales at Sydney	1969-70
5/23	R. J. McCurdy	South Australia v Western Australia at Adelaide	1984-85
5/23	J. P. Marquet	Tasmania v Queensland at Hobart (Bel)	1995-96
5/26	D. J. Hickey	Victoria v Western Australia at Melbourne (MCC)	1985-86
5/27	G. Dymock	Queensland v New South Wales at Sydney	1981-82

MOST CATCHES IN A MATCH

4	J. W. Scholes	Victoria v New Zealanders at Melbourne	1971-72
4	I. M. Chappell	South Australia v New Zealanders at Adelaide	1972-73
4	M. A. Taylor	New South Wales v Queensland at Sydney	1998-99

MOST CATCHES

J. D. Siddons (Vic/S Aust) ... 31 in 62 matches	M. A. Taylor (NSW) ...... 24 in 38 matches
A. R. Border (NSW/Qld) ... 30 in 49 matches	S. G. Law (Qld) .... 24 in 64 matches
D. M. Jones (Vic) .... 28 in 55 matches	M. E. Waugh (NSW) ...... 23 in 41 matches
G. B. Hogg (W Aust) ...... 25 in 44 matches	S. Lee (NSW) .... 23 in 48 matches
T. M. Moody (W Aust) ..... 25 in 75 matches	

MOST DISMISSALS IN A MATCH

6	(all ct)	K. J. Wadsworth......	New Zealanders v New South Wales at Sydney ...	1969-70
5	(all ct)	R. Edwards..........	Western Australia v New Zealanders at Perth	1970-71
5	(all ct)	I. A. Healy	Queensland v Tasmania at Hobart (Bellerive)	1995-96

MOST DISMISSALS

	M	Ct	St	Total
D. S. Berry (S Aust/Vic)	63	77	24	101
P. A. Emery (NSW)	58	70	11	81
W. A. Seccombe (Qld)	38	50	11	61
T. J. Nielsen (S Aust)	45	54	3	57
A. C. Gilchrist (NSW/W Aust)	32	51	5	56
I. A. Healy (Qld)	29	47	7	54
R. W. Marsh (W Aust)	33	51	1	52
M. N. Atkinson (Tas)	35	43	7	50
R.. Campbell (W Aust)	22	43	5	48
T. J. Zoehrer (W Aust)	35	40	4	44

MOST APPEARANCES

75	T. M. Moody (W Aust)	1985-86 – 2000-01
64	S. G. Law (Qld)	1988-89 – 2000-01
63	D. S. Berry (S Aust/Vic)	1989-90 – 2000-01
62	J. D. Siddons (Vic/S Aust)	1985-86 – 1999-00
59	D. S. Lehmann (S Aust/Vic)	1988-89 – 2000-01
58	P. A. Emery (NSW)	1987-88 – 1998-99
57	S. Young (Tas)	1990-91 – 2000-01
55	D. M. Jones (Vic)	1981-82 – 1997-98
55	D. C. Boon (Tas)	1978-79 – 1998-99
55	J. L. Langer (W Aust)	1992-93 – 2000-01

NEW SOUTH WALES

New South Wales' wildly fluctuating form in the Pura Cup was not replicated in the Mercantile Mutual Cup. They began with a resounding eight-wicket win over Victoria at North Sydney and then a seven-wicket win over Queensland at Bankstown, and registered four of their six round-robin wins in their first six games. They were important successes as they indicated the emergence of New South Wales from their long rebuilding phase, confirmed the new management's standing, and provided the young team with early confidence after an extremely difficult era. In these early games, New South Wales had a superbly balanced attack of Glenn McGrath, Brett Lee, Nathan Bracken, Shane Lee and Stuart MacGill, and the impetus from their strike-power had its eventual reward when New South Wales won a splendid final against the titleholders, the Western Warriors, at Perth, where New South Wales had performed ignominiously earlier in the summer.

In the continuing absence of Michael Bevan from the Test squad, the consolation was that he became available with reasonable regularity for New South Wales' limited-overs team, appearing in eight of the 11 games and averaging no less than 105.75 with a century and three half-centuries, typically astonishing figures from the limited-overs champion. Shane Lee, Stuart MacGill and Mark Higgs were the nucleus of the team, playing in all 11 games. However, the season proved a frustrating one for top-order batsman Corey Richards, who was dropped from the side late in the season despite scoring quickly and averaging 51 from his seven appearances. The former internationals Gavin Robertson and Simon Cook also lost their places, and face a struggle to resume their representative careers.

MacGill's 18 wickets made him easily the leading wicket-taker in the competition. His lap of honour at the WACA Ground after New South Wales final triumph was especially enjoyable for him, as he had broken into Test cricket after leaving Western Australia for the better prospects Sydney offered for his type of bowling.

The Australian Capital Territory side were innocent victims of the need to accommodate the expanded Mercantile Mutual Cup competition in an already congested summer. Their readmission to the competition is improbable, despite the fact that the Australian Capital Territory organisation in its three years provided a stepping stone for several promising players, especially the young international Brad Haddin, now wicket-keeper/batsman for New South Wales. Presumably, Canberra players such as Haddin, Higgs and Bevan will again have to move from the region to establish themselves. – PHIL WILKINS.

RESULTS, 2000-01

Mercantile Mutual Cup matches – Played 11: Won 7, Lost 4.
Competition placing – 1st.

DOMESTIC LIMITED-OVERS RESULTS

	M	W	L	NR	T
Australian Capital Territory	3	3	0	0	0
New Zealanders	1	0	1	0	0
Queensland	26	16	10	0	0
South Australia	17	9	8	0	0
Tasmania	19	16	3	0	0
Victoria	25	13	11	1	0
Western Australia	28	12	15	0	1
Total	119	69	48	1	1

MERCANTILE MUTUAL CUP AVERAGES, 2000-01

BATTING

	M	I	NO	R	HS	100s	50s	Avge	Ct/St	S-R
M.G. Bevan	8	8	4	423	135*	1	3	105.75	2	89.05
S.R. Waugh	5	5	2	228	75*	0	1	76.00	1	78.08
C.J. Richards	7	4	1	153	73*	0	2	51.00	2	91.07
M.E. Waugh	5	5	1	160	108*	1	0	40.00	3	68.67
M.A. Higgs	11	8	2	223	46*	0	0	37.17	8	69.04
S. Lee	11	8	0	289	115	1	2	36.13	7	87.05
P.A. Jaques	2	2	0	59	40	0	0	29.50	0	78.67
G.C. Rummans	7	6	2	118	30*	0	0	29.50	1	68.60
G.J. Mail	3	2	1	29	19*	0	0	29.00	2/1	96.67
M.J. Clarke	5	5	1	104	57	0	1	26.00	2	75.36
B.J. Haddin	10	10	0	252	69	0	3	25.20	12/6	108.15
M.J. Slater	9	9	0	205	61	0	2	22.78	1	64.06
B. Lee	5	2	1	18	14*	0	0	18.00	1	66.67
S.D. Bradstreet	7	4	1	53	33	0	0	17.67	0	100.00
S.C.G. MacGill	11	4	2	19	6*	0	0	9.50	4	65.52
S.M. Thompson	3	1	0	7	7	0	0	7.00	2	50.00
S.R. Clark	6	2	0	9	9	0	0	4.50	1	69.23
N.W. Bracken	8	2	0	9	9	0	0	4.50	3	128.57
S.H. Cook	2	0	0	0	0	0	0	–	1	–
G.D. McGrath	4	0	0	0	0	0	0	–	1	–
D.A. Nash	3	1	1	61	61*	0	1	–	0	217.86

* Denotes not out.

BOWLING

	O	M	R	W	BB	5w/i	Avge
M.A. Higgs	47	2	224	9	4/15	0	24.89
M.E. Waugh	4	1	25	1	1/25	0	25.00
N.W. Bracken	66.5	6	275	11	4/36	0	25.00
B. Lee	48	5	207	8	3/41	0	25.88
D.A. Nash	18	1	80	3	2/39	0	26.67
S.C.G. MacGill	97	5	500	18	3/41	0	27.78
S.R. Clark	53	4	244	8	2/30	0	30.50
S.H. Cook	17	1	106	3	2/72	0	35.33
S.D. Bradstreet	43	3	239	6	4/53	0	39.83
G.D. McGrath	40	6	146	3	2/33	0	48.67
S. Lee	80	1	414	8	2/33	0	51.75
S.M. Thompson	11	0	69	1	1/25	0	69.00

NEW SOUTH WALES v VICTORIA

At North Sydney Oval, North Sydney, October 15, 2000. New South Wales won by eight wickets. Toss: New South Wales. New South Wales 5 pts.

Nathan Bracken provided early evidence of the pace and accuracy which were to win him national recognition when he dismantled Victoria's middle order by removing Ian Harvey, Shawn Craig and top-scorer Brad Hodge. Notwithstanding the fine innings by Hodge, the disappointing Victorian batting performance was a continuation of their form of recent seasons, and would have been worse but for Ben Oliver's late intervention. New South Wales' objective became straightforward when Michael Slater and Brad Haddin plundered 107 for the first wicket off 19.1 overs. The enterprising Haddin surpassed Slater for shot-making, hitting three sixes and eight fours in his 52-ball innings of 69. Steve Waugh and Michael Bevan finished off the job with ease, and New South Wales, striking a team total of 19 fours and six sixes, earned a bonus point under the new system when they reached their objective in 35.5 overs.

Man of the Match: B.J. Haddin. *Attendance:* 11,409.

Victoria

G.R. Vimpani c and b S. Lee	17	(29)	*P.R. Reiffel c Bracken b S. Lee	17	(22)
M.P. Mott run out (Higgs)	12	(36)	B.C. Oliver not out	24	(38)
B.J. Hodge c S. Lee b Bracken	87	(92)	D.W. Fleming c Richards b Bracken	4	(9)
I.J. Harvey c MacGill b Bracken	11	(17)			
S.A.J. Craig c Richards b Bracken	8	(29)	L-b 2, w 6, n-b 2	10	
M. Klinger st Haddin b MacGill	1	(15)			
S.K. Warne c and b MacGill	1	(4)	(48.5 overs, 201 mins)	193	
†D.S. Berry run out (Higgs)	1	(4)	Fall: 31 32 52 78 92 94 96 136 183 193		

M.L. Lewis did not bat.

Bowling: McGrath 10–1–48–0; B. Lee 10–1–34–0; S. Lee 9–0–33–2; Bracken 9.5–2–36–4; MacGill 10–0–40–2.

New South Wales

M.J. Slater st Berry b Oliver	61	(80)	L-b 5, w 2, n-b 2	9	
†B.J. Haddin c Reiffel b Oliver	69	(52)			
*S.R. Waugh not out	27	(42)	(35.5 overs, 142 mins)	(2 wkts)	197
M.G. Bevan not out	31	(43)	Fall: 107 138		

C.J. Richards, S. Lee, G.C. Rummans, M.A. Higgs, N.W. Bracken, B. Lee, S.C.G. MacGill, G.D and McGrath did not bat.

Bowling: Fleming 8–1–35–0; Reiffel 6–0–31–0; Lewis 6.5–1–37–0; Warne 6–0–47–0; Oliver 8–0–36–2; Mott 1–0–6–0.

Umpires: D.M. Brandon and S.J.A. Taufel.
TV Umpire: T.M. Donahoo.

NEW SOUTH WALES v QUEENSLAND

At Bankstown Oval, Bankstown, October 22, 2000. New South Wales won by seven wickets. Toss: Queensland. New South Wales 4 pts.

On a wicket regularly considered the best batting strip in Sydney, consistently superior even to that at the Sydney Cricket Ground, Queensland never came to grips with the all-round quality of the New South Wales attack. Despite Martin Love's 82 from 101 balls there was rarely any doubt that the home side would win, and only some bustling work from the tail allowed Queensland to set a decent target. Mark Waugh, opening the innings on the home ground where he launched his career, made a lazy-looking, untroubled 108 not out from 134 balls, sharing a 105-run partnership with Michael

Bevan. New South Wales claimed their win with overs and wickets to spare, Bevan contributing yet another unbeaten innings, this time 51 from 60 balls. Queensland's limited-overs specialists Scott Prestwidge and Andrew Symonds were particularly ineffective against the onslaught.

Man of the Match: M.E. Waugh. *Attendance:* 4,337.

Queensland

M.L. Hayden c Haddin b Bracken	... 14	(18)	S.A. Prestwidge c Slater b B. Lee	... 4	(7)
J.P. Maher c McGrath b MacGill	 48	(61)	A.J. Bichel not out	 15	(16)
M.L. Love c Higgs b S. Lee	 82	(101)	B.N. Creevey not out	 11	(9)
A. Symonds lbw b MacGill	 0	(1)			
*S.G. Law c Haddin b S. Lee	 4	(6)	L-b 7, w 14	 21	
C.T. Perren c Bracken b MacGill	 0	(17)			
L.A. Carseldine c and b B. Lee	 33	(42)	(50 overs, 207 mins)	.......(9 wkts) 247	
†W.A. Seccombe c S.R. Waugh b B. Lee	15	(22)	Fall: 30 88 88 98 116 188 197 215 215		

A.A. Noffke did not bat.

Bowling: McGrath 10–0–43–0; B. Lee 10–0–54–3; Bracken 9–0–39–1; MacGill 10–0–44–3; S. Lee 7–0–42–2; Higgs 4–0–18–0.

New South Wales

M.J. Slater c Perren b Bichel	 29	(45)			
M.E. Waugh not out	108	(134)	L-b 1, w 6, n-b 5	 12	
†B.J. Haddin c Hayden b Bichel	 2	(4)			
*S.R. Waugh c Seccombe b Prestwidge	49	(49)	(47.4 overs, 186 mins)	(3 wkts) 251	
M.G. Bevan not out	 51	(60)	Fall: 50 52 146		

S. Lee, C.J. Richards, M.A. Higgs, B. Lee, G.D. McGrath, N.W. Bracken and S.C.G. MacGill did not bat.

Bowling: Creevey 6–1–32–0; Prestwidge 9–0–57–1; Bichel 9–0–45–2; Noffke 9.4–1–36–0; Symonds 8–0–51–0; Carseldine 6–0–29–0.

Umpires: D.B. Hair and S.J.A. Taufel.
TV Umpire: G.J. Lill.

At Richmond Cricket Ground, Richmond, October 29, 2000. NEW SOUTH WALES lost to VICTORIA by two wickets.

At Bellerive Oval, Hobart, November 11, 2000. NEW SOUTH WALES defeated TASMANIA by seven wickets.

NEW SOUTH WALES v SOUTH AUSTRALIA

At North Sydney Oval, North Sydney, November 19, 2000. South Australia won by six runs. Toss: New South Wales. South Australia 4 pts.

Darren Lehmann showed why he remains one of the most dangerous, effortless and skilful of improvisers in the world limited-overs arena. His unbeaten 115 from 118 balls against the home side's all-international attack was an innings of the highest order, especially as he was batting at No. 5. He shared a partnership of 111 with opener David Fitzgerald for the fourth wicket, and then 87 with Ryan Harris off the last 13.2 overs in an unbroken stand that turned the game into a contest. Although North Sydney enjoys a reputation as one of the quickest-scoring grounds in the competition, New South Wales were unable to dominate the South Australian's pace attack of Paul Wilson, Brett Swain, Jason Gillespie and Paul Rofe. When the sixth wicket fell for 94 in the 28th over the cause looked hopeless, but Corey Richards and Brad Haddin added 116 for the seventh wicket. When they both fell in the 47th over, the target was tantalisingly just out of reach.

Man of the Match: D.S. Lehmann. *Attendance:* 2327.

South Australia

G.S. Blewett c Haddin b B. Lee	.....	2 (16)
D.A. Fitzgerald run out (M.E. Waugh)	50	(83)
S.A. Deitz c S. Lee b Bracken	....	9 (22)
C.J. Davies b McGrath	....	2 (11)
*D.S. Lehmann not out	115	(118)
B.A. Johnson lbw b MacGill	....	0 (2)

†G.A. Manou c Haddin b McGrath	.. 11	(11)
R.J. Harris not out	....	31 (39)
L-b 11, w 12, n-b 2	....	25
(50 overs, 203 mins) (6 wkts)	245	
Fall: 8 25 28 139 140 158		

J.N. Gillespie, B.A. Swain, P.C. Rofe and P. Wilson did not bat.

Bowling: McGrath 10–2–33–2; B. Lee 10–0–49–1; Bracken 10–0–47–1; S. Lee 8–0–51–0; MacGill 9–1–39–1; Higgs 3–0–15–0.

New South Wales

M.J. Slater c Fitzgerald b Wilson	....	1 (18)
M.A. Higgs c Manou b Gillespie	.....	25 (50)
M.E. Waugh lbw b Swain	....	5 (6)
*S.R. Waugh c Lehmann b Rofe	.....	41 (62)
M.G. Bevan run out (Blewett)	....	5 (7)
S. Lee lbw b Rofe	....	9 (18)
C.J. Richards c Deitz b Gillespie	.....	54 (60)
†B.J. Haddin c Fitzgerald b Gillespie	.	63 (58)

B. Lee not out	....	14 (9)
N.W. Bracken b Wilson	....	9 (6)
S.C.G. MacGill not out	....	5 (6)
L-b 4, w 4	....	8
(50 overs, 202 mins) (9 wkts)	239	
Fall: 20 27 58 67 87 94 210 210 223		

G.D. McGrath did not bat.

Bowling: Wilson 10–0–43–2; Swain 10–0–33–1; Gillespie 10–0–42–3; Rofe 10–1–47–2; Harris 5–0–26–0; Blewett 3–0–25–0; Johnson 2–0–19–0.

Umpires: G.J. Lill and S.J.A. Taufel.
TV Umpire: S.E. Reed.

At Brisbane Cricket Ground, Brisbane, December 8, 2000. NEW SOUTH WALES defeated QUEENSLAND by five runs.

At Adelaide Oval, Adelaide, January 14, 2001. NEW SOUTH WALES lost to SOUTH AUSTRALIA by 24 runs.

At WACA Ground, Perth, January 19, 2001. NEW SOUTH WALES lost to WESTERN AUSTRALIA by 72 runs.

NEW SOUTH WALES v WESTERN AUSTRALIA

At North Sydney Oval, North Sydney, February 4, 2001. New South Wales won by 60 runs. Toss: New South Wales. New South Wales 4 pts.

After two successive defeats, New South Wales enjoyed a major victory over formidable opponents, thanks essentially to a whirlwind unbeaten 88-run partnership for the ninth wicket by Don Nash and Michael Clarke. Nash hit six sixes and four fours in an electrifying 61 not out from 28 balls, registering his 50 from just 24 balls as he scored the second fastest fifty in the domestic limited-overs competition. Shane Lee (nine fours, five sixes) had earlier received little support, and what had seemed a likely win for Western Australians when New South Wales were eight for 214 was transformed into New South Wales' most significant, morale-enhancing win of the competition. It put the team in good heart for the run home and eventually the final. Young international Mark Higgs, varying throughout the season from left-arm orthodox to wrist-spin, had the excellent return of 4/15 from 5.1 overs, while pace man Stuart Clark confirmed his value to the team with ten frugal overs for 2/31. Western Australia lost wickets regularly and were always lagging behind the required scoring rate, although their batsmen hit five sixes to bring the day's total to an entertaining 16.

Man of the Match: D.A. Nash. *Attendance:* 4,366.

New South Wales

M. J. Slater c Campbell b Angel	0	(3)
†B. J. Haddin c Hogg b Wates	13	(11)
P. A. Jaques lbw b Moody	19	(34)
*S. Lee c Julian b Hogg	115	(126)
M. A. Higgs c Campbell b Moody	11	(14)
G. C. Rummans b Hogg	29	(56)
S. M. Thompson c and b Julian	7	(14)

M. J. Clarke not out	18	(18)
S. D. Bradstreet st Campbell b Hogg	1	(7)
D. A. Nash not out	61	(28)
L-b 4, w 13, n-b 11	28	

S. C. G. MacGill and S. R. Clark did not bat.

(50 overs, 194 mins)   (8 wkts) 302

Fall: 0 24 58 103 201 208 213 214

Bowling: Angel 10–0–47–1; Wates 5–0–34–1; Spencer 5–0–43–0; Moody 7–0–27–2; Julian 10–0–45–1; Harvey 6–0–53–0; Hogg 7–0–49–3.

Western Australia

†R. J. Campbell c Lee b Nash	1	(10)
J. L. Langer c Haddin b Clark	20	(37)
S. M. Katich lbw b Clark	72	(77)
M. W. Goodwin c Haddin b Nash	44	(64)
*T. M. Moody c Higgs b MacGill	7	(4)
M. E. Hussey c MacGill b Higgs	19	(22)
B. P. Julian st Haddin b MacGill	13	(6)
G. B. Hogg b Higgs	27	(21)

K. M. Harvey b Higgs	13	(23)
D. J. Spencer st Haddin b Higgs	0	(2)
D. J. Wates not out	9	(18)
L-b 4, w 5, n-b 8	17	

J. Angel did not bat.

(46.1 overs, 198 mins)   242

Fall: 4 35 138 148 155 170 212 221 222 242

Bowling: Nash 7–0–39–2; Clark 10–1–31–2; Lee 6–0–27–0; Bradstreet 5–0–32–0; Thompson 4–0–27–0; MacGill 9–0–67–2; Higgs 5.1–0–15–4.

Umpires: T. M. Donahoo and G. J. Lill.

NEW SOUTH WALES v TASMANIA

At Sydney Cricket Ground, Sydney, February 18, 2001. New South Wales won by six wickets. Toss: Tasmania. New South Wales 4 pts.

Tasmania's lacklustre season in the limited-overs sphere was reflected in this performance. Jamie Cox, batting in the unusually low position of No. 5 in an experimental, revamped batting order, made an unbeaten 66, but only all-rounder Shaun Young and the team's talented newcomer Shane Watson offered support before Sean Clingeleffer stayed with his captain to take the score to respectability. Again, the spinners Stuart MacGill and Mark Higgs played important roles for New South Wales in restricting the Tigers to less than 200. The target posed no major difficulties for the home side, despite the loss of two wickets in the first three overs. Michael Bevan was in his element, pacing himself to 75 from 96 balls, Shane Lee hit ten fours in 70 minutes, and Higgs completed a fine match with 46 not out.

Man of the Match: S. C. G. MacGill. *Attendance:* 4,029.

Tasmania

S. P. Kremerskothen c Thompson b Nash	6	(27)
D. J. Marsh c Rummans b Clark	18	(36)
S. R. Watson c Thompson b MacGill	25	(46)
S. Young st Haddin b MacGill	36	(43)
*J. Cox not out	66	(79)
M. J. Di Venuto c Haddin b Clark	6	(8)
G. T. Cunningham b MacGill	2	(4)

B. J. Thomas st Haddin b Higgs	16	(38)
D. J. Saker c and b Higgs	0	(3)
†S. G. Clingeleffer not out	11	(16)
L-b 5, w 5	10	

D. G. Wright and B. Geeves did not bat.

(50 overs, 200 mins)   (8 wkts) 196

Fall: 18 33 87 94 104 109 152 152

Bowling: Nash 6–1–15–1; Bracken 7–0–23–0; Clark 10–1–30–2; Lee 5–0–26–0; MacGill 10–0–41–3; Higgs 9–0–39–2; Thompson 3–0–17–0.

New South Wales

M. J. Clarke b Wright	1	(6)	G. C. Rummans not out	2	(7)	
†B. J. Haddin c Cox b Saker	4	(6)	L-b 6, w 4, n-b 4	14		
M. G. Bevan c Saker b Kremerskothen	75	(96)				
*S. Lee c Cox b Watson	57	(62)	(44 overs, 165 mins)	(4 wkts) 199		
M. A. Higgs not out	46	(91)	Fall: 1 6 99 184			

S. M. Thompson, S. D. Bradstreet, D. A. Nash, S. C. G. MacGill, N. W. Bracken and S. R. Clark did not bat.

Bowling: Saker 5–0–35–1; Wright 10–3–25–1; Geeves 4–0–38–0; Watson 5–0–22–1; Marsh 10–0–34–0; Cox 7–2–29–0; Kremerskothen 3–0–10–1.

Umpires: T. J. Keel and S. J. A. Taufel.
TV Umpire: N. S. Fowler.

FINAL

At WACA Ground, Perth, February 25, 2001. NEW SOUTH WALES defeated WESTERN AUSTRALIA by six wickets. For details see section on Mercantile Mutual Cup, 2000-01, page 451.

RECORDS

Highest score for:	164	R. B. McCosker v South Australia at Sydney	1981-82
Highest score against:	165	M. W. Goodwin (Western Australia) at Perth	2000-01
Best bowling for:	6/25	B. E. McNamara v Tasmania at Sydney	1996-97
Best bowling against:	5/22	H. J. Howarth (New Zealanders) at Sydney	1969-70
Highest total for:	7-319	v South Australia at North Sydney	1997-98
Highest total against:	5-325	by Western Australia at Perth	2000-01
Lowest total for:	92	v Queensland at Brisbane	1972-73
Lowest total against:	80	by Tasmania at Devonport	1984-85

MOST RUNS

	M	I	NO	R	HS	100s	50s	Avge	S-R
M. G. Bevan	43	43	16	1,784	135*	1	15	66.07	75.34
S. R. Waugh	37	36	6	1,415	131	2	9	47.17	81.51
M. E. Waugh	41	40	4	1,269	112	2	8	35.25	78.33
M. A. Taylor	38	38	0	1,218	84	0	12	32.05	59.33
S. Lee	48	43	5	1,177	115	2	6	30.97	88.16
R. Chee Quee	22	22	1	860	131	1	5	40.95	66.62
R. B. McCosker	21	21	2	847	164	2	5	44.58	63.99
M. J. Slater	34	34	0	837	96	0	7	24.62	67.12
C. J. Richards	33	30	3	799	109	1	5	29.59	69.66
J. Dyson	21	21	2	789	101	2	6	41.53	54.90

HIGHEST PARTNERSHIP FOR EACH WICKET

253 for 1st R.B. McCosker and J. Dyson, v South Australia at Sydney 1981-82
199 for 2nd R. Chee Quee and M.G. Bevan, v Western Australia at Sydney 1993-94
240 for 3rd S.R. Waugh and M.E. Waugh, v Victoria at North Sydney 1991-92
180 for 4th G.C. Rummans and S. Lee, v Queensland at Brisbane 1999-00
156 for 5th K.J. Roberts and R. Chee Quee, v South Australia at Sydney 1995-96
105 for 6th M.G. Bevan and G.R.J. Matthews, v Western Australia at Perth 1990-91
116 for 7th C.J. Richards and B.J. Haddin, v South Australia at North Sydney 2000-01
90 for 8th B.E. McNamara and P.A. Emery, v Tasmania at Sydney 1992-93
96* for 9th S.M. Thompson and S.D. Bradstreet, v Victoria at North Sydney 1998-99
54 for 10th B.E. McNamara and G.R. Robertson, v South Australia at Adelaide 1996-97

MOST WICKETS

	M	Balls	Mdns	R	W	BB	5W/i	Avge
B.E. McNamara	42	2,005	22	1,281	57	6/25	1	22.47
S. Lee	48	1,969	12	1,564	50	4/59	0	31.28
G.R.J. Matthews	50	2,302	25	1,500	49	3/29	0	30.61
S.C.G. MacGill	22	1,134	12	916	42	5/40	1	21.81
M.R. Whitney	36	1,926	36	1,188	41	4/30	0	28.98
G.F. Lawson	35	1,811	38	1,053	39	4/31	0	27.00
S.R. Waugh	37	1,092	18	845	34	4/32	0	24.85
W.J. Holdsworth	27	1,295	17	891	30	5/28	1	29.70
T.M. Chappell	23	1,050	11	684	27	4/35	0	25.33
S.R. Clark	22	1,151	14	723	27	4/26	0	26.78

MOST DISMISSALS

	M	Ct	St	Total
P.A. Emery	58	70	11	81
S.J. Rixon	25	25	6	31
B.J. Haddin	16	19	10	29
H.B. Taber	6	8	1	9
G.C. Dyer	10	4	2	6
M. Hendricks	9	3	3	6

MOST CATCHES

M.A. Taylor .... 24 in 38 matches   G.R.J. Matthews .... 15 in 50 matches
M.E. Waugh .... 23 in 41 matches   R. Chee Quee .... 14 in 22 matches
S. Lee .... 23 in 48 matches   S.R. Waugh .... 14 in 37 matches

MOST APPEARANCES

58 P.A. Emery .... 1987-88 – 1998-99   41 M.E. Waugh ..... 1985-86 – 2000-01
50 G.R.J. Matthews .. 1982-83 – 1997-98   38 M.A. Taylor .... 1985-86 – 1998-99
48 S. Lee .... 1992-93 – 2000-01   37 S.R. Waugh ..... 1984-85 – 2000-01
43 M.G. Bevan ...... 1990-91 – 2000-01   36 M.R. Whitney .... 1980-81 – 1993-94
42 B.E. McNamara ... 1989-90 – 1999-00   35 G.F. Lawson ..... 1978-79 – 1991-92

QUEENSLAND

Queensland's limited-overs season was a Jekyll-and-Hyde performance which cost them any chance of a final berth. A six-match winless streak justified the pre-season concerns of coach Bennett King. He was not satisfied with Queensland's attitude towards limited-overs cricket, asking whether they could improve their winning methods. Eventually, with young players ushered in to replace veterans Geoff Foley and Scott Prestwidge, Queensland began a late charge which enabled them to snaffle fourth spot. The fight-back included a comprehensive win over minor premiers Western Australia and a confident away win against South Australia.

The season started on a sound note when Queensland outlasted South Australia in a high-quality match at Allan Border Field. By the time they returned to a resurfaced Gabba, they were on the back foot following a loss to a full-strength New South Wales. The rot spread through the Queensland campaign, culminating in a dismal loss to Tasmania on a cheerless Hobart day as they crashed for 101 before watching Queensland-born Shane Watson steer his side to a seven-wicket victory.

That loss helped spark the change of thinking at selection level. Prestwidge and Foley made way for the likes of James Hopes and Nathan Hauritz as Queensland gambled on new faces. The selectors were rewarded as Hopes took 11 wickets in five matches while the 19-year-old Hauritz bowled his off-spin encouragingly. With other young players showing promise, including Brendan Nash and Ashley Noffke, in the end something was gained from the indifferent season.

Queensland's best performers were the consistent batsmen Jimmy Maher (383 runs at 54.71), Martin Love (315 at 52.50) and Matthew Hayden (247 at 30.88). They helped cover for the likes of captain Stuart Law, who endured an uncharacteristically unproductive season, scoring just 131 runs in 10 matches. Law batted at four different positions in the order as the Queenslanders tinkered with their line-up. The batting ended the season on a strong note when Love and Maher helped orchestrate a win over Western Australia. Their 174-run partnership laid the platform for a 65-run victory and a bonus point.

The bowlers struggled to contain opposition teams early in the season but Adam Dale was typically frugal, conceding 178 runs from his 49 overs. Hopes was also economical, while Michael Kasprowicz made an encouraging return from injury. – MICHAEL CRUTCHER.

RESULTS, 2000-01

Mercantile Mutual Cup matches – Played 10: Won 4, Lost 5, No result 1.
Competition placing – 4th.

DOMESTIC LIMITED-OVERS RESULTS

	M	W	L	NR	T
Australian Capital Territory	3	3	0	0	0
New South Wales	26	10	16	0	0
New Zealanders	1	0	1	0	0
South Australia	20	16	4	0	0
Tasmania	22	14	7	1	0
Victoria	20	11	8	1	0
Western Australia	25	11	12	2	0
Total	117	65	48	4	0

MERCANTILE MUTUAL CUP AVERAGES, 2000-01

BATTING

	M	I	NO	R	HS	100s	50s	Avge	Ct/St	S-R
J.P. Maher	9	9	2	383	87	0	4	54.71	1	81.84
M.L. Love	7	6	0	315	124	1	2	52.50	1	86.54
G.I. Foley...........	2	2	0	67	57	0	1	33.50	0	72.83
M.L. Hayden	8	8	0	247	103	1	0	30.88	2	69.58
B.P. Nash	3	3	1	47	31	0	0	23.50	1	100.00
W.A. Seccombe......	9	9	2	116	45*	0	0	16.57	8/3	100.00
C.T. Perren.........	4	4	0	63	33	0	0	15.75	3	48.09
S.G. Law	10	10	1	131	46	0	0	14.56	4	89.73
A. Symonds	5	4	0	52	32	0	0	13.00	1	115.56
S.A. Prestwidge	5	3	0	27	17	0	0	9.00	0	46.55
J.R. Hopes	5	5	0	33	24	0	0	6.60	1	82.50
A.A. Noffke.........	8	1	0	1	1	0	0	1.00	2	20.00
N.M. Hauritz	5	2	0	1	1	0	0	0.50	1	10.00
G.A.J. Fitness	1	0	0	0	0	0	0	–	0	–
M.S. Kasprowicz.....	6	5	5	27	10*	0	0	–	1	79.41
S.J. O'Leary.........	3	0	0	0	0	0	0	–	0	–
D.A. Turner	1	0	0	0	0	0	0	–	1	–

* Denotes not out.

BOWLING

	O	M	R	W	BB	5w/i	Avge
M.L. Hayden	8	0	32	3	2/16	0	10.67
C.T. Perren..............	4	1	13	1	1/13	0	13.00
J.H. Dawes..............	10	1	29	2	2/29	0	14.50
J.R. Hopes	43	3	189	11	5/29	1	17.18
A.C. Dale	49	3	178	7	2/21	0	25.43
A. Symonds	15.3	0	96	3	2/27	0	32.00
N.M. Hauritz	26.3	0	134	4	2/13	0	33.50
M.S. Kasprowicz.........	47	3	238	7	3/22	0	34.00
A.A. Noffke.............	62	4	291	6	3/32	0	48.50
S.A. Prestwidge	31	0	199	4	2/63	0	49.75
A.J. Bichel.............	59	7	291	4	2/45	0	72.75
B.N. Creevey	16	1	84	1	1/52	0	84.00
L.A. Carseldine	17	0	96	1	1/32	0	96.00
D.A. Turner	3	0	28	0	–	0	–
S.J. O'Leary.............	5	0	35	0	–	0	–

QUEENSLAND v SOUTH AUSTRALIA

At Allan Border Field, Albion, October 8, 2000. Queensland won by three runs. Toss: South Australia. Queensland 4 pts.

Queensland and South Australia provided an entertaining start to the domestic season, treating more than 2,000 fans to a final-over thriller. Queensland made an encouraging start after being sent in, with Jimmy Maher and Martin Love scoring convincing half-centuries in a list of useful contributions. But Queensland's total of seven for 273 was not beyond the visitors' reach in favourable batting conditions. Darren Lehmann and Jeff Vaughan hit brisk fifties and Ben Johnson provided an invaluable 41 not out. South Australia needed seven runs from the final over but young fast bowler Ashley Noffke responded with composure and finished with match-winning figures of 3/32 from 10 overs.

Man of the Match: A. A. Noffke. *Attendance:* 2,413.

Queensland

M. L. Hayden c Manou b Harris	.....	16	(32)	†W. A. Seccombe not out	....	10	(9)
J. P. Maher c Fitzgerald b McIntyre	...	64	(84)	A. C. Dale not out	....	14	(11)
*S. G. Law c Manou b Harris	....	0	(1)			
M. L. Love c Manou b Blewett	.....	63	(69)	B 3, l-b 5, w 11, n-b 1	....	20
A. J. Bichel c Harris b Blewett	....	34	(30)		
C. T. Perren b Rofe	....	30	(44)	(50 overs, 200 mins) (7 wkts) 273
L. A. Carseldine b Wilson	....	22	(21)	Fall: 54 54 115 171 203 241 248

S. A. Prestwidge, D. A. Turner and A. A. Noffke did not bat.

Bowling: Wilson 10–1–46–1; Rofe 10–0–49–1; Harris 7–1–35–2; Harrity 7–0–38–0; McIntyre 10–0–58–1; Blewett 6–0–39–2.

South Australia

G. S. Blewett run out (Turner)	....	36	(57)	P. Wilson c Bichel b Noffke	....	9	(7)
D. A. Fitzgerald lbw b Bichel	....	1	(6)	P. E. McIntyre lbw b Noffke	....	0	(1)
C. J. Davies c Seccombe b Noffke	....	39	(54)	P. C. Rofe not out	....	1	(3)
*D. S. Lehmann run out (Hayden)	....	53	(51)			
J. M. Vaughan lbw b Prestwidge	.....	55	(68)	L-b 4, w 3, n-b 4	....	11
B. A. Johnson not out	....	41	(38)		
†G. A. Manou lbw b Hayden	....	0	(1)	(50 overs, 206 mins) (9 wkts) 270
R. J. Harris c Turner b Hayden	....	24	(18)	Fall: 13 81 81 193 194 195 246 255 264

M. A. Harrity did not bat.

Bowling: Dale 10–0–31–0; Bichel 9–0–63–1; Noffke 10–1–32–3; Prestwidge 10–0–61–1; Carseldine 5–0–35–0; Turner 3–0–28–0; Hayden 3–0–16–2.

Umpires: L. D. Musch and J. F. Torpey.

At Bankstown Oval, Bankstown, October 22, 2000. QUEENSLAND lost to NEW SOUTH WALES by seven wickets.

At WACA Ground, Perth, November 15, 2000. QUEENSLAND and WESTERN AUSTRALIA match abandoned.

QUEENSLAND v NEW SOUTH WALES

At Brisbane Cricket Ground, Brisbane, December 8, 2000. Day/night game. New South Wales won by five runs. Toss: Queensland. New South Wales 4 pts. Competition debut: J. L. Cassell.

With Test players Mark Waugh and Michael Slater in their ranks, New South Wales assumed control of this day/night match from the outset. Mark Higgs' rapid 24 helped prepare the way for Michael Bevan and Slater to add 111 for the third wicket in 23 overs. Corey Richards took real control of the latter part of the innings. Queensland then rode the back of another ruthless innings from Matthew Hayden, who braved the humidity for 103 from 116 balls. Geoff Foley joined him for a 98-run stand in 17.2 overs before Queensland unravelled with a rare dismissal as Hayden was stumped off a wide from Waugh. Queensland were then stopped in their tracks by the bowling of Shawn Bradstreet and, left needing 12 runs from the final over, managed only six.

Man of the Match: M. L. Hayden. *Attendance:* 6,170.

New South Wales

M. A. Higgs c Creevey b Carseldine	..	24	(22)	G. C. Rummans c Law b Prestwidge	. 8 (9)
M. E. Waugh c Carseldine b Dale	....	8	(18)	S. D. Bradstreet not out	.... 19 (9)
M. G. Bevan c Carseldine b Symonds	.	83	(108)	l-b 5, w 2, n-b 6	 13
M. J. Slater c Dale b Creevey	....	50	(73)		
*S. Lee c O'Leary b Prestwidge	.....	5	(7)	(50 overs, 201 mins)	(6 wkts) 283
C. J. Richards not out	....	73	(60)	Fall: 36 37 148 159 229 256	

†G. J. Mail, N. W. Bracken, S. C. G. MacGill and S. R. Clark did not bat.

Bowling: Kasprowicz 6–1–29–0; Carseldine 6–0–32–1; Dale 10–1–49–1; Prestwidge 10–0–63–2; O'Leary 5–0–35–0; Creevey 10–0–52–1; Symonds 3–0–18–1.

Queensland

M. L. Hayden st Mail b Waugh	......103 (116)	S. A. Prestwidge run out	
*S. G. Law c Bracken b Clark	.... 6 (11)	(Waugh/Bradstreet) ..	6 (4)
A. Symonds b MacGill	.... 32 (27)	A. C. Dale not out	.... 9 (10)
J. L. Cassell c Bevan b Bradstreet	.... 13 (27)	M. S. Kasprowicz not out	.... 0 (0)
G. I. Foley c Bevan b Bracken	.... 57 (72)	l-b 4, w 12	 16
†W. A. Seccombe c Waugh b Bradstreet	22 (18)		
L. A. Carseldine b Lee b Bradstreet	... 9 (9)	(50 overs, 210 mins)	(9 wkts) 278
B. N. Creevey b Bradstreet	.... 5 (6)	Fall: 24 92 111 209 237 247 260 260 277	

S. J. O'Leary did not bat.

Bowling: Bracken 10–0–53–1; Clark 5–0–25–1; MacGill 7–0–48–1; Bradstreet 10–0–53–4; Higgs 5–1–24–0; Lee 9–0–46–0; Waugh 4–1–25–1.

Umpires: A. J. McQuillan and G. C. Zimmer.
TV Umpire: L. D. Musch.

At Bellerive Oval, Hobart, January 7, 2001. QUEENSLAND defeated TASMANIA by seven wickets.

QUEENSLAND v VICTORIA

At Brisbane Cricket Ground, Brisbane, January 19, 2001. Day/night game. Victoria won by 63 runs. Toss: Victoria. Victoria 5 pts. Competition debut: N. M. Hauritz and J. R. Hopes.

Queensland's Mercantile Mutual Cup season ground to a halt on a slippery Gabba surface when Victoria achieved a rare win in Brisbane. The visitors were on top from the outset after opener Matthew Elliott, who scored 107 from 107 balls, punished Andy Bichel and Ashley Noffke. The visitors then squeezed handy contributions from their middle order to reach seven for 269. Queensland's reply was always shaky, with none of their batsmen reaching 50. The home team provided Victoria with a bonus point when it slumped to 206 from 43.3 overs, led by Paul Reiffel's haul of 3/28 from seven nagging overs. Queensland, however, had something to smile about in the bowling of their 22-year-old pace bowler James Hopes on his debut.

Man of the Match: M. T. G. Elliott. *Attendance:* 6,046.

Victoria

J. L. Arnberger c Love b Dale	20	(26)		I. S. L. Hewett c Carseldine b Hopes	5	(10)
M. T. G. Elliott st Seccombe b Dale	107	(107)		*P. R. Reiffel not out	22	(20)
B. J. Hodge c Hopes b Kasprowicz	28	(31)				
S. P. Dart st Seccombe b Hopes	38	(60)		L-b 2, w 2, n-b 5	9	
M. Klinger b Hopes	2	(6)				
B. C. Oliver lbw b Hopes	11	(20)		(50 overs, 193 mins) (7 wkts)	269	
†D. S. Berry not out	27	(25)		Fall: 59 92 180 186 210 216 225		

C. R. Miller, D. W. Fleming and M. L. Lewis did not bat.

Bowling: Bichel 4–0–33–0; Noffke 8–0–61–0; Dale 10–0–47–2; Kasprowicz 8–0–45–1; Hauritz 10–0–38–0; Hopes 10–0–43–4.

Queensland

M. L. Hayden run out (Lewis/Berry)	8	(29)		N. M. Hauritz c Berry b Reiffel	0	(6)
J. P. Maher c Oliver b Hewett	30	(31)		A. C. Dale c Oliver b Fleming	10	(18)
*S. G. Law c Hodge b Hewett	46	(38)		M. S. Kasprowicz not out	10	(14)
L. A. Carseldine b Hewett	20	(32)		L-b 3, w 2, n-b 1	6	
A. J. Bichel c Fleming b Miller	36	(48)				
M. L. Love c Reiffel b Miller	28	(28)		(43.3 overs, 181 mins)	206	
J. R. Hopes lbw b Reiffel	1	(5)		Fall: 42 42 109 110 162 163 183		
†W. A. Seccombe c Hewett b Reiffel	11	(13)		186 186 206		

A. A. Noffke did not bat.

Bowling: Fleming 7.3–1–17–1; Lewis 7–0–42–0; Hewett 10–1–47–3; Oliver 3–0–27–0; Miller 9–0–42–2; Reiffel 7–1–28–3.

Umpires: A. J. McQuillan and L. D. Musch.

At Melbourne Cricket Ground, Melbourne, January 26, 2001. QUEENSLAND lost to VICTORIA on run rate.

QUEENSLAND v TASMANIA

At Brisbane Cricket Ground, Brisbane, February 2, 2001. Day/night game. Queensland won on run rate. Toss: Queensland. Queensland 4 pts. Competition debut: B. P. Nash.

This match looked unlikely to proceed after days of heavy rain but Queensland eventually won the battle of wits around four rain delays. The Tasmanian batsmen wobbled through the bad weather, creeping to eight for 134 from their allotted 39 overs on a sodden outfield. Test pace man Michael Kasprowicz pegged down the batting which struggled without a solid partnership. When Queensland crumbled to three for 2, losing Wade Seccombe, Lee Carseldine and Clinton Perren without scoring, the Tasmanians looked on track for victory. Queensland had again reshuffled its batting line-up and it finally paid off when Jimmy Maher and Andy Bichel piled on 55 runs for the eighth wicket at better than a run a ball. They took Queensland to the revised target of 119 runs from 28 overs in a match which stretched close to midnight.

Man of the Match: J. P. Maher. *Attendance:* 1,127.

Tasmania

*J. Cox c Seccombe b Kasprowicz ... 10	(34)		G. T. Cunningham c Bichel b Perren .	3	(7)
M. J. Di Venuto c Seccombe			A. W. Polkinghorne c Maher		
b Kasprowicz ..	0	(1)	b Kasprowicz ..	12	(22)
D. F. Hills c Law b Noffke	14	(43)	†S. G. Clingeleffer not out	0	(2)
S. Young c Seccombe b Hopes	7	(26)	L-b 7, w 6, n-b 15	28	
S. R. Watson not out	28	(66)			
S. P. Kremerskothen run out (Carseldine)	18	(18)	(39 overs, 163 mins) (8 wkts)	134	
D. J. Marsh c Noffke b Hayden	14	(30)	Fall: 3 27 45 45 75 104 107 132		

D. G. Wright and J. P. Marquet did not bat.

Bowling: Bichel 9–0–41–0; Kasprowicz 8–1–22–3; Hopes 6–1–18–1; Noffke 7–2–17–1; Hayden 5–0–16–1; Perren 4–1–13–1.

Queensland

M. L. Hayden run out (Watson)	16	(37)	J. R. Hopes lbw b Polkinghorne	0	(2)
†W. A. Seccombe b Young	0	(4)	A. J. Bichel not out	40	(33)
L. A. Carseldine lbw b Young	0	(4)			
C. T. Perren c Di Venuto b Young	0	(10)	L-b 1, w 1	2	
J. P. Maher not out	52	(57)			
*S. G. Law c Watson b Kremerskothen	11	(8)	(26.2 overs, 119 mins) (7 wkts)	122	
B. P. Nash run out (Young/Clingeleffer)	1	(3)	Fall: 0 0 2 45 64 66 67		

M. S. Kasprowicz, N. M. Hauritz and A. A. Noffke did not bat.

Bowling: Wright 6–2–13–0; Young 6–2–16–3; Marquet 5.2–0–37–0; Polkinghorne 4–0–22–1; Kremerskothen 5–0–33–1.

Umpires: B. N. J. Oxenford and P. D. Parker.

At Adelaide Oval, Adelaide, February 9, 2001. QUEENSLAND defeated SOUTH AUSTRALIA by 101 runs.

QUEENSLAND v WESTERN AUSTRALIA

At Brisbane Cricket Ground, Brisbane, February 16, 2001. Day/night game. Queensland won by 65 runs. Toss: Queensland. Queensland 5 pts.

With no chance of making the final, Queensland's batsmen were intent on collecting a $250,000 jackpot from this match by hitting one of the sponsor's signs posted around the boundary. They failed, but they built a formidable total of eight for 306, thanks largely to Martin Love and Jimmy Maher, who took full advantage of some wayward bowling in a second wicket partnership of 174 in 26.2 overs. Western Australia, who were to host the final the following weekend, were always struggling in reply after slumping to two for 5 in the second over. Murray Goodwin and Mike Hussey hit half-centuries but the Queensland bowlers shared the wickets to finish the season with three consecutive wins.

Man of the Match: M. L. Love.   *Attendance:* 3,241.

Queensland

J. P. Maher c Goodwin b Hogg	87	(96)	†W. A. Seccombe c Moody b Angel .	8	(10)
*S. G. Law c Campbell b Angel	3	(2)	J. R. Hopes run out (North/Campbell)	3	(3)
M. L. Love c Hogg b Harvey	124	(129)			
A. J. Bichel b Harvey	8	(9)	B 8, l-b 8, w 5, n-b 4	25	
L. A. Carseldine b Harvey	23	(33)			
A. Symonds c Angel b Williams	10	(7)	(50 overs, 197 mins) (8 wkts)	306	
B. P. Nash not out	15	(15)	Fall: 4 178 190 254 277 280 295 306		

A. A. Noffke, N. M. Hauritz and J. H. Dawes did not bat.

Bowling: Wates 4–1–20–0; Angel 9–0–52–2; Julian 3–0–32–0; Williams 10–0–52–1; Moody 4–0–33–0; Hogg 10–0–54–1; Harvey 10–0–47–3.

Western Australia

*T. M. Moody c Symonds b Dawes . . .	10	(25)
†R. J. Campbell run out		
(Carseldine/Seccombe) . .	4	(3)
S. M. Katich c Law b Dawes	0	(2)
M. W. Goodwin c Nash b Hopes	59	(71)
M. E. Hussey c Carseldine b Hauritz . . .	57	(74)
M. J. North b Bichel	10	(16)
B. P. Julian c Hauritz b Noffke	0	(1)

G. B. Hogg c Noffke b Symonds	59	(55)
K. M. Harvey c Carseldine b Symonds	23	(31)
D. J. Wates lbw b Hauritz	11	(21)
B. A. Williams not out	0	(0)
L-b 1, w 5, n-b 2	8	
	—	
(49.3 overs, 190 mins)	241	
Fall: 5 5 25 130 137 137 152 212 235 241		

J. Angel did not bat.

Bowling: Bichel 8–2–28–1; Dawes 10–1–29–2; Noffke 10–0–50–1; Hopes 7–0–50–1; Hauritz 10–0–56–2; Symonds 4.3–0–27–2.

Umpires: J. F. Torpey and G. C. Zimmer.

RECORDS

Highest score for:	159	S. G. Law v Tasmania at Brisbane	 1993-94
Highest score against:	131	S. R. Waugh (New South Wales) at Brisbane	 1992-93
Best bowling for:	7/34	C. G. Rackemann v South Australia at Adelaide	 1988-89
Best bowling against:	5/23	J. P. Marquet (Tasmania) at Hobart (Bellerive)	 1995-96
Highest total for:	4-320	v Tasmania at Brisbane	 1993-94
Highest total against:	6-301	by Western Australia at Perth	 1999-00
Lowest total for:	62	v Western Australia at Perth	 1976-77
Lowest total against:	77	by Western Australia at Perth	 1976-77

MOST RUNS

	M	I	NO	R	HS	100s	50s	Avge	S-R
M. L. Hayden	46	46	9	2,162	152*	8	11	58.43	72.65
J. P. Maher	50	50	8	2,035	128	4	12	48.45	76.59
S. G. Law	64	59	5	1,830	159	5	5	34.53	91.09
M. L. Love	47	44	6	1,321	124	1	7	34.76	74.97
T. J. Barsby	42	41	2	1,145	101	1	10	29.36	61.10
A. R. Border	43	40	8	1,049	97	0	9	32.78	72.60
G. M. Ritchie	27	24	4	825	114	1	5	41.25	74.93
G. S. Chappell	20	20	0	682	92	0	7	34.10	78.66
G. I. Foley	41	34	7	677	66	0	3	25.07	65.79
A. Symonds	38	35	4	673	85	0	1	21.71	90.70

HIGHEST PARTNERSHIP FOR EACH WICKET

250	for 1st	M. L. Hayden and J. P. Maher, v Australian Capital Territory at Canberra . .	1999-00
260	for 2nd	M. L. Hayden and S. G. Law, v Tasmania at Brisbane	1993-94
187	for 3rd	J. M. Thomas and S. G. Law, v Western Australia at Brisbane	1993-94
158	for 4th	S. G. Law and G. I. Foley, v New South Wales at Brisbane	1996-97
98	for 5th	G. M. Ritchie and G. S. Trimble, v South Australia at Brisbane	1984-85
86	for 6th	P. L. Taylor and I. A. Healy, v Tasmania at Brisbane	1990-91
91	for 7th	J. N. Langley and J. A. Maclean, v South Australia at Brisbane	1975-76
55*	for 8th	S. A. Prestwidge and A. J. Bichel, v New South Wales at Sydney	1997-98
62	for 9th	S. A. Prestwidge and M. S. Kasprowicz, v New South Wales at Brisbane . .	1997-98
33	for 10th	M. L. Love and C. G. Rackemann, v New South Wales at Brisbane	1993-94

MOST WICKETS

	M	Balls	Mdns	R	W	BB	5W/i	Avge
S. A. Prestwidge	40	2,003	18	1,556	63	5/59	1	24.70
M. S. Kasprowicz	38	1,979	23	1,387	49	4/21	0	28.31
C. G. Rackemann	36	1,975	38	1,249	48	7/34	1	26.02
G. Dymock	23	1,300	20	749	39	5/27	1	19.21
A. J. Bichel	31	1,621	19	1,158	36	4/45	0	32.17
J. R. Thomson	25	1,273	19	821	35	6/19	1	23.46
C. J. McDermott	25	1,250	27	783	30	4/14	0	26.10
A. C. Dale	21	1,157	17	664	29	4/26	0	22.90
G. S. Chappell	20	761	9	492	27	4/35	0	18.22
B. N. Creevey	22	1,027	12	809	27	3/26	0	29.96

MOST DISMISSALS

	M	Ct	St	Total
W. A. Seccombe	38	50	11	61
I. A. Healy	29	47	7	54
J. A. Maclean	19	32	1	33
R. B. Phillips	18	22	0	22
P. W. Anderson	6	4	0	4

MOST CATCHES

A. R. Border	26 in 43 matches	J. P. Maher	18 in 50 matches
S. G. Law	24 in 64 matches	A. Symonds	17 in 38 matches
M. L. Love	18 in 47 matches	M. L. Hayden	14 in 38 matches

MOST APPEARANCES

64	S. G. Law	1988-89 – 2000-01	45	S. A. Prestwidge	1992-93 – 2000-01
50	J. P. Maher	1993-94 – 2000-01	44	M. S. Kasprowicz	1989-90 – 2000-01
47	M. L. Love	1993-94 – 2000-01	41	G. I. Foley	1989-90 – 2000-01
46	M. L. Hayden	1992-93 – 2000-01	39	A. J. Bichel	1992-93 – 2000-01

SOUTH AUSTRALIA

Two crucial losses late in the season proved costly for a South Australian side that had started the summer with so much promise. Five of South Australia's first six matches came down to just a handful of runs at the end, with the South Australians clinching three of those and recording a convincing six-wicket away win over Victoria.

The South Australians' confidence peaked when they beat a full-strength New South Wales outfit in Sydney. Captain Darren Lehmann was largely responsible for the win as he smacked an unbeaten 115 from 118 deliveries. Opener David Fitzgerald provided welcome support with a neat 50 from 83 balls. But it was a 33-run away loss to Tasmania on January 21, in the absence of Lehmann, their regular match-winner, that put the pressure on South Australia. They were bowled out for just 161 in reply to Tasmania's modest total of nine for 194. As a result, South Australia went into their home game against Queensland nearly three weeks later needing to win to give themselves some breathing space in the lead-up to the final. But, with Lehmann again away on international duties, none of the South Australian batsmen stepped up to take his place. Graham Manou, who scored 42, was the only batsman to pass 30 as new Queensland all-rounder James Hopes took five wickets to lead Queensland to a 101-run victory, despite being out of finals contention.

The devastating defeat left South Australia in a precarious position going into the last minor-round match against a Victorian side which could not make the top two. If they were to reach the final, South Australia had to beat Victoria with a bonus point to avoid relying on Tasmania defeating New South Wales the following day. Again Lehmann led the way with an unbeaten 119 from 88 balls with Chris Davies contributing a valuable 56 as the South Australians won by five wickets. But it was not enough to claim the vital extra point. Eventual premiers New South Wales beat the Tigers by six wickets in Sydney to advance to the final against Western Australia, while South Australia had to settle for a bitter third place, missing out by just one point.

Lehmann was by far the best of the South Australian batsmen, scoring 524 runs at an average of 131, Davies following with the best aggregate of 322 runs, at an average of 32.20. – VALKERIE MANGNALL.

RESULTS, 2000-01

Mercantile Mutual Cup matches – Played 10: Won 6, Lost 4.
Competition placing – 3rd.

DOMESTIC LIMITED-OVERS RESULTS

	M	W	L	NR	T
Australian Capital Territory	3	3	0	0	0
New South Wales	17	8	9	0	0
New Zealanders	2	0	2	0	0
Queensland	20	4	16	0	0
Tasmania	18	12	6	0	0
Victoria	24	8	15	0	1
Western Australia	29	11	18	0	0
Total	113	46	66	0	1

MERCANTILE MUTUAL CUP AVERAGES, 2000-01

BATTING

	M	I	NO	R	HS	100s	50s	Avge	Ct	S-R
D.S. Lehmann	7	7	3	524	119*	2	3	131.00	5	110.08
R.J. Harris	7	4	3	58	31*	0	0	58.00	3	98.31
M.C. Miller	5	5	2	102	82*	0	1	34.00	2	103.03
C.J. Davies	10	10	0	322	62	0	3	32.20	2	65.05
D.A. Fitzgerald	9	9	0	266	103	1	1	29.56	6	66.83
S.A. Deitz	5	5	0	134	44	0	0	26.80	2	64.11
G.A. Manou	10	7	3	106	42*	0	0	26.50	15	84.80
B.E. Young	3	3	2	26	14*	0	0	26.00	2	104.00
B.A. Johnson	9	9	2	167	41*	0	0	23.86	3	72.29
G.S. Blewett	10	10	0	238	45	0	0	23.80	4	62.63
J.M. Vaughan	8	7	0	135	57	0	2	19.29	3	74.59
P. Wilson	10	3	1	35	14*	0	0	17.50	0	94.59
N.T. Adcock	1	1	0	2	2	0	0	2.00	1	25.00
P.E. McIntyre	3	3	0	1	1	0	0	0.33	0	10.00
B.A. Swain	8	1	0	0	0	0	0	0.00	1	0.00
B.H. Higgins	1	1	0	0	0	0	0	0.00	0	0.00
J.N. Gillespie	5	1	0	0	0	0	0	0.00	0	0.00
P.C. Rofe	4	1	1	1	1*	0	0	–	0	33.33
M.A. Harrity	5	0	0	0	0	0	0	–	2	–

* Denotes not out.

BOWLING

	O	M	R	W	BB	5w/i	Avge
D.S. Lehmann	7	0	44	3	3/25	0	14.67
J.N. Gillespie	46	3	215	10	3/27	0	21.50
B.E. Young	10	0	52	2	1/10	0	26.00
G.S. Blewett	38	0	268	9	4/33	0	29.78
P. Wilson	95	7	410	13	4/49	0	31.54
B.A. Johnson	13	0	100	3	1/20	0	33.33
M.A. Harrity	45	2	220	6	2/46	0	36.67
M.C. Miller	37	4	184	5	3/27	0	36.80
P.E. McIntyre	26	0	122	3	2/28	0	40.67
R.J. Harris	36	1	216	5	2/29	0	43.20
B.A. Swain	75	5	281	6	2/33	0	46.83
P.C. Rofe	39	2	183	3	2/47	0	61.00
N.T. Adcock	5	0	38	0	–	0	–

At Allan Border Field, Albion, October 8, 2000. SOUTH AUSTRALIA lost to QUEENSLAND by three runs.

SOUTH AUSTRALIA v TASMANIA

At Adelaide Oval, Adelaide, October 14, 2000. South Australia won by four runs. Toss: Tasmania. South Australia 4 pts. Competition debuts: S. G. Clingeleffer, B. Geeves.

A quickfire 124 off 130 balls by Michael Di Venuto was not quite enough to push Tasmania past South Australia in a match which started 85 minutes late because of rain. With each innings reduced to 43 overs, the South Australian top order pulled together to post a total of 248. David Fitzgerald and Chris Davies got their side away to a solid start which was then enhanced by Darren Lehmann and Jeff Vaughan who added 106 for the fourth wicket in 13.1 overs. Di Venuto and Ricky Ponting kept the visitors in touch with a second wicket partnership of 137 in 24.1 overs. Tasmania needed to score 12 off the last over but managed only seven.

Man of the Match: M. J. Di Venuto. *Attendance:* 1,507.

South Australia

D. A. Fitzgerald c Di Venuto b Young	46	(78)
G. S. Blewett b Saker	8	(18)
C. J. Davies c Clingeleffer b Geeves	54	(74)
*D. S. Lehmann c Wright		
b Kremerskothen	44	(33)
J. M. Vaughan c Cox b Kremerskothen	57	(57)
B. A. Johnson c Cox b Kremerskothen	2	(3)

B. E. Young not out	3	(2)
†G. A. Manou not out	2	(1)
L-b 9, w 13, n-b 10	32	
	—	
(43 overs, 183 mins)	(6 wkts)	248
Fall: 28 125 128 234 241 246		

R. J. Harris, J. N. Gillespie, B. A. Swain and P. Wilson did not bat.

Bowling: Saker 9–1–38–1; Wright 9–0–32–0; Denton 3–0–40–0; Geeves 9–1–31–1; Young 7–0–44–1; Kremerskothen 6–0–54–3.

Tasmania

*J. Cox c Young b Swain	21	(27)
M. J. Di Venuto run out (Harris/Manou)	124	(130)
R. T. Ponting c Manou b Wilson	68	(75)
S. Young c and b Young	3	(4)
D. J. Marsh not out	13	(19)
D. F. Hills b Gillespie	1	(2)

D. G. Wright not out	2	(1)
L-b 2, w 10	12	
	—	
(43 overs, 179 mins)	(5 wkts)	244
Fall: 57 194 201 240 242		

B. Geeves, S. P. Kremerskothen, G. J. Denton, D. J. Saker and †S. G. Clingeleffer did not bat.

Bowling: Gillespie 9–0–53–1; Swain 9–0–42–1; Wilson 9–0–31–1; Harris 5–0–35–0; Young 7–0–42–1; Blewett 4–0–39–0.

Umpires: J. S. Booth and S. J. Davis.

At WACA Ground, Perth, October 20, 2000. SOUTH AUSTRALIA lost to WESTERN AUSTRALIA by three runs.

At Richmond Cricket Ground, Richmond, November 12, 2000. SOUTH AUSTRALIA defeated VICTORIA by six wickets.

At North Sydney Oval, North Sydney, November 19, 2000. SOUTH AUSTRALIA defeated NEW SOUTH WALES by six runs.

SOUTH AUSTRALIA v WESTERN AUSTRALIA

At Adelaide Oval, Adelaide, December 9, 2000. South Australia won by two runs. Toss: Western Australia. South Australia 4 pts.

Darren Lehmann became the highest run-scorer in Australian domestic limited-overs cricket, passing Dean Jones' total of 2,122 when he smashed 63 (four fours, four sixes) from 44 balls. David Fitzgerald made a valuable 103 and batted for all but two balls of the innings. Justin Langer and Murray Goodwin added 126 in 29 overs which prepared the way for the usual Adam Gilchrist onslaught, he and Langer adding another 74 runs in 9.5 overs. Just as the visitors were closing in on the target and the pressure was building, Greg Blewett took four wickets to help his side snare a thrilling win.

Man of the Match: D. A. Fitzgerald. *Attendance:* 2,655.

South Australia

D. A. Fitzgerald run out				M. C. Miller c Goodwin b Julian	5	(8)
	(Karppinen/Harvey)	103	(127)	†G. A. Manou not out	4	(3)
G. S. Blewett c Gilchrist b Julian		20	(49)	R. J. Harris not out	2	(1)
C. J. Davies b Harvey		27	(42)	L-b 8, w 1, n-b 2	11	
*D. S. Lehmann c Hogg b Angel		63	(44)			
B. A. Johnson lbw b Julian		25	(25)	(50 overs, 202 mins) (7 wkts)	260	
J. M. Vaughan lbw b Julian		0	(1)	Fall: 59 117 203 240 240 248 257		

B. A. Swain, P. Wilson and P. C. Rofe did not bat.

Bowling: Angel 10-0-46-1; Karppinen 9-1-55-0; Moody 6-1-14-0; Julian 10-2-41-4; Harvey 7-0-38-1; Nikitaras 5-0-25-0; Hogg 3-0-33-0.

Western Australia

R. J. Campbell c Miller b Wilson		5	(13)	G. B. Hogg not out	2	(2)
J. L. Langer run out (Wilson/Miller)		88	(134)	K. M. Harvey not out	1	(1)
M. W. Goodwin c Swain b Harris		70	(89)			
†A. C. Gilchrist c Harris b Blewett		46	(33)	L-b 9, w 2, n-b 1	12	
*T. M. Moody b Blewett		21	(20)			
B. P. Julian b Blewett		11	(6)	(50 overs, 218 mins) (7 wkts)	258	
M. E. Hussey c Davies b Blewett		2	(3)	Fall: 6 132 206 240 252 253 256		

S. J. Karppinen, S. Nikitaras and J. Angel did not bat.

Bowling: Wilson 10-0-45-1; Swain 10-1-29-0; Rofe 10-0-46-0; Miller 8-0-48-0; Harris 5-0-29-1; Lehmann 2-0-19-0; Blewett 5-0-33-4.

Umpires: P. M. Angley and P. J. Weeks.
TV Umpire: S. J. Davis.

SOUTH AUSTRALIA v NEW SOUTH WALES

At Adelaide Oval, Adelaide, January 14, 2001. Day/night game. South Australia won by 24 runs. Toss: South Australia. South Australia 4 pts. Competition debut: M. J. Clarke.

All-rounder Michael Miller allowed South Australia to leapfrog New South Wales into top spot on the table with a comfortable win. With the innings at the crossroads, the former Queenslander blasted an unbeaten 82 off just 58 deliveries, including eight fours and two sixes, as he and Graham Manou took 98 from 11.4 overs. The top order of the New South Wales batting performed consistently but, after a forthright 66 off 56 balls by Shane Lee, the innings folded.

Man of the Match: M. C. Miller. *Attendance:* 2,062.

South Australia

*G. S. Blewett c Clark b MacGill	....	45	(49)	†G. A. Manou run out (Slater)	......	28	(29)
D. A. Fitzgerald c MacGill b Clark	...	18	(16)	R. J. Harris not out	....	1	(1)
C. J. Davies c Lee b MacGill	....	35	(39)			
B. A. Johnson c and b Higgs	....	39	(57)	B 3, l-b 2, w 1, n-b 2	......	8
J. M. Vaughan c and b Cook	....	4	(7)		
S. A. Deitz c Mail b Clark	....	33	(46)	(50 overs, 209 mins)	(7 wkts) 293
M. C. Miller not out	....	82	(58)	Fall: 34 82 128 135 151 189 287

B. A. Swain, P. Wilson and M. A. Harrity did not bat.

Bowling: Clark 10–1–48–2; Cook 7–0–34–1; Bradstreet 7–0–58–0; MacGill 10–1–60–2; Lee 10–0–62–0; Higgs 6–0–26–1.

New South Wales

C. J. Richards c Blewett b Wilson	....	16	(25)	†G. J. Mail not out	....	19	(19)
B. J. Haddin c Harrity b Swain	......	26	(17)	S. C. G. MacGill run out		
M. A. Higgs b Harrity	....	42	(54)	(Fitzgerald/Manou)	..	3	(2)
M. J. Slater c Miller b Harrity	....	27	(45)	S. R. Clark run out		
*S. Lee c Vaughan b Johnson	......	66	(56)	(Swain/Blewett/Manou)	..	9	(10)
G. C. Rummans run out	....			L-b 3, w 4, n-b 2	....	9
(Harrity/Fitzgerald)	..	28	(35)		
M. J. Clarke c Harrity b Blewett	.....	24	(25)	(48 overs, 202 mins)	269
S. D. Bradstreet c Harris b Blewett	...	0	(2)	Fall: 28 63 114 121 192 228 234 242 247 269

S. H. Cook did not bat.

Bowling: Wilson 9–0–42–1; Swain 10–0–60–1; Miller 4–0–20–0; Harrity 10–0–46–2; Harris 4–0–32–0; Johnson 5–0–40–1; Blewett 6–0–26–2.

Umpires: S. D. Fry and K. D. Perrin.

At Devonport Oval, Devonport, January 21, 2001. SOUTH AUSTRALIA lost to TASMANIA won by 33 runs.

SOUTH AUSTRALIA v QUEENSLAND

At Adelaide Oval, Adelaide, February 9, 2001. Queensland won by 101 runs. Toss: Queensland. Queensland 5 pts.

South Australia needed to defeat Queensland to ease some of the pressure going into the final minor-round match against Victoria. But Queensland newcomer James Hopes had other ideas. With his team out of finals contention, Hopes was both accurate and penetrating in destroying the home side's batting as they were bowled out for 143 with nearly 10 overs remaining. Earlier Queensland had batted consistently until a late flurry of runs from Wade Seccombe had ensured Queensland a sizeable total to defend.

Man of the Match: J. R. Hopes. *Attendance:* 3,822.

Queensland

M. L. Hayden c Johnson b Miller	.....	48	(57)	†W. A. Seccombe not out	....	45	(32)
J. P. Maher c Manou b Miller	....	17	(32)	J. R. Hopes c Vaughan b Gillespie	.	5	(7)
*S. G. Law c Johnson b Harrity	......	4	(16)	M. S. Kasprowicz not out	....	3	(3)
A. J. Bichel c Manou b Miller	....	13	(14)	L-b 4, w 4, n-b 3	....	11
L. A. Carseldine c Manou b Gillespie	.	34	(52)		
C. T. Perren run out (Vaughan)	......	33	(60)	(50 overs, 212 mins)	(8 wkts) 244
B. P. Nash c Manou b Blewett	....	31	(29)	Fall: 55 74 74 96 140 187 200 219

N. M. Hauritz and A. A. Noffke did not bat.

Bowling: Wilson 10–1–54–0; Gillespie 10–0–49–2; Miller 10–3–27–3; Harrity 10–2–41–1; McIntyre 6–0–36–0; Blewett 4–0–33–1.

South Australia

*G. S. Blewett run out (Hopes)	29	(58)	J. N. Gillespie b Hopes	0	(5)
D. A. Fitzgerald c Perren b Kasprowicz	5	(12)	P. Wilson b Hauritz	12	(19)
C. J. Davies c Perren b Hopes	18	(40)	P. E. McIntyre c Kasprowicz b Hauritz	0	(4)
B. A. Johnson c Hayden b Hopes	14	(32)			
J. M. Vaughan b Hopes	8	(19)	L-b 1, n-b 6	7	
S. A. Deitz run out (Hauritz/Bichel)	4	(11)			
M. C. Miller b Hopes	4	(8)	(40.3 overs, 171 mins)	143	
†G. A. Manou not out	42	(41)	Fall: 10 41 58 78 81 88 89 89 132 143		

M. A. Harrity did not bat.

Bowling: Bichel 10–4–16–0; Kasprowicz 10–1–59–1; Noffke 8–0–25–0; Hopes 10–1–29–5; Hauritz 2.3–0–13–2.

Umpires: J. S. Booth and K. D. Perrin.
TV Umpire: M. A. Bartlett.

SOUTH AUSTRALIA v VICTORIA

At Adelaide Oval, Adelaide, February 17, 2001. South Australia won by five wickets. Toss: Victoria. South Australia 4 pts. Competition debut: B. H. Higgins

South Australia had to beat Victoria and earn a bonus point, otherwise they would have to rely on Tasmania beating New South Wales the following day if they were to secure a finals berth. The South Australian selectors made a number of changes to the side that lost to Queensland, but it was Darren Lehmann, returning from international limited-overs duties, who led his side to victory with an unbeaten 119 from 88 balls. He was well supported by Chris Davies in a third wicket partnership of 153 in 25.1 overs. Earlier, Matthew Elliott had scored a competent century, although the Victorians were held in check by Paul Wilson's accuracy and three late wickets from Lehmann. Despite all the good work, the vital bonus point eluded the home side.

Man of the Match: D. S. Lehmann. *Attendance:* 2,092.

Victoria

M. T. G. Elliott c Lehmann b Wilson	102	(106)	I. S. L. Hewett b Lehmann	1	(2)
J. L. Arnberger c Adcock b Wilson	9	(19)	*P. R. Reiffel not out	12	(15)
B. J. Hodge b Wilson	4	(3)	J. M. Davison not out	11	(8)
S. P. Dart c Blewett b Harrity	27	(52)			
I. J. Harvey c Manou b Wilson	56	(42)	L-b 1, w 4, n-b 1	6	
M. Klinger c Deitz b Lehmann	30	(35)			
J. Moss c and b Lehmann	16	(13)	(50 overs, 206 mins)	(9 wkts) 277	
†P. J. Roach c Manou b Harrity	3	(6)	Fall: 32 36 96 199 204 230 237 242 259		

M. L. Lewis did not bat.

Bowling: Wilson 10–0–49–4; Swain 10–1–26–0; Harrity 8–0–54–2; Miller 5–0–27–0; Adcock 5–0–38–0; Harris 3–0–30–0; Blewett 4–0–27–0; Lehmann 5–0–25–3.

South Australia

S. A. Deitz c and b Harvey	44	(53)
G. S. Blewett c Reiffel b Harvey	39	(43)
C. J. Davies c Reiffel b Hewett	56	(83)
*D. S. Lehmann not out	119	(88)
N. T. Adcock lbw b Harvey	2	(8)
B. H. Higgins b Lewis	0	(7)

M. C. Miller not out	5	(5)
B 3, l-b 3, w 7, n-b 4	17	
(47.1 overs, 206 mins) (5 wkts)	282	
Fall: 84 90 243 260 261		

R. J. Harris, †G. A. Manou, B. A. Swain, P. Wilson and M. A. Harrity did not bat.

Bowling: Reiffel 4–0–19–0; Lewis 8.1–1–52–1; Moss 7–0–55–0; Harvey 8–0–45–3; Hewett 10–0–39–1; Davison 6–1–44–0; Hodge 4–0–22–0.

Umpires: S. D. Fry and D. J. Harper.
TV Umpire: M. A. Bartlett.

RECORDS

Highest score for:	142	D. S. Lehmann v Tasmania at Adelaide	1994-95
Highest score against:	164	R. B. McCosker (New South Wales) at Sydney	1981-82
Best bowling for:	5/23	R. J. McCurdy v Western Australia at Adelaide	1984-85
Best bowling against:	7/34	C. G. Rackemann (Queensland) at Adelaide	1988-89
Highest total for:	6-325	v Tasmania at Hobart (TCA)	1986-87
Highest total against:	7-310	by New South Wales at North Sydney	1997-98
Lowest total for:	87	v Western Australia at Perth	1989-90
Lowest total against:	119	by Queensland at Adelaide	1993-94

MOST RUNS

	M	I	NO	R	HS	100s	50s	Avge	S-R
D. S. Lehmann	48	48	6	2,057	142*	5	13	48.98	88.59
G. S. Blewett	50	48	5	1,597	101*	1	10	32.47	63.52
J. D. Siddons	42	40	4	1,169	102	1	8	32.47	78.77
D. W. Hookes	38	38	1	1,149	101	1	6	31.05	80.07
P. R. Sleep	30	28	4	846	90	0	4	35.25	65.58
D. A. Fitzgerald	26	26	1	806	114	2	5	32.24	73.34
P. C. Nobes	27	27	4	745	140*	1	4	32.39	58.43
C. J. Davies	25	24	0	728	125	1	5	30.33	67.97
G. A. Bishop	26	25	1	708	119*	2	2	29.50	66.48
A. M. J. Hilditch	24	23	1	691	109	2	2	31.41	59.88

HIGHEST PARTNERSHIP FOR EACH WICKET

217*	for 1st	D. S. Lehmann and P. C. Nobes, v Tasmania at Adelaide	1994-95
145	for 2nd	B. A. Richards and I. M. Chappell, v Queensland at Adelaide	1970-71
153	for 3rd	C. J. Davies and D. S. Lehmann, v Victoria at Adelaide	2000-01
125	for 4th	G. S. Chappell and K. G. Cunningham, v Western Australia at Perth	1972-73
133*	for 5th	A. M. J. Hilditch and M. D. Haysman, v Queensland at Brisbane	1984-85
88	for 6th	P. R. Sleep and J. K. Pyke, v New South Wales at Sydney	1987-88
106*	for 7th	J. K. Pyke and C. M. Killen, v Victoria at Adelaide	1987-88
64*	for 8th	D. S. Lehmann and B. A. Swain, v Australian Capital Territory at Canberra	1999-00
61*	for 9th	M. Hendrick and A. A. Mallett, v Western Australia at Perth	1974-75
32	for 10th	T. B. A. May and C. J. Owen, v Tasmania at Adelaide	1991-92

MOST WICKETS

	M	Balls	Mdns	R	W	BB	5W/i	Avge
P. Wilson	40	2,216	39	1,489	62	4/23	0	24.02
G.S. Blewett	50	1,770	10	1,482	42	4/33	0	35.29
M.A. Harrity	23	1,233	13	920	35	5/42	1	26.29
J.C. Scuderi	37	1,759	13	1,357	32	3/36	0	42.41
S.P. George	20	1,049	7	881	29	4/33	0	30.28
B.N. Wigney	26	1,318	23	876	29	3/24	0	30.21
T.B.A. May	24	1,318	18	818	27	4/9	0	30.30
J.N. Gillespie	15	870	14	611	27	4/46	0	22.63
A.A. Mallett	15	881	9	589	23	3/43	0	25.61
B.E. Young	27	1,129	6	960	23	4/24	0	41.74

MOST DISMISSALS

	M	Ct	St	Total
T.J. Nielsen	45	54	3	57
W.B. Phillips	24	23	0	23
G.A. Manou	15	21	0	21
K.J. Wright	10	7	2	9
D.S. Berry	4	5	2	7
D.B. Yagmich	2	5	1	6

MOST CATCHES

D.W. Hookes	22 in 38 matches		B.E. Young	15 in 27 matches
J.D. Siddons	20 in 42 matches		D.S. Lehmann	15 in 48 matches
G.S. Blewett	19 in 50 matches		B.A. Johnston	14 in 23 matches

MOST APPEARANCES

50	G.S. Blewett	1992-93 – 2000-01	37	J.C. Scuderi	1988-89 – 1998-99
48	D.S. Lehmann	1988-89 – 2000-01	37	B.A. Johnson	1994-95 – 2000-01
42	J.D. Siddons	1991-92 – 1999-00	30	P.R. Sleep	1978-79 – 1992-93
40	P. Wilson	1993-94 – 2000-01	27	P.C. Nobes	1988-89 – 1995-96
38	D.W. Hookes	1975-76 – 1991-92	27	B.E. Young	1996-97 – 2000-01

TASMANIA

Tasmania are not yet out of the Mercantile Mutual Cup wilderness of the past decade, but there are signs that they may be finding their way. The Tigers came fifth with a 4-6 win-loss record, but they could have finished 6-4 had they not squandered their chances in the away game against South Australia and the home game against Western Australia. They failed by five runs against South Australia because their prodigal bowlers gave away extra runs and overs with 13 wides and 10 no-balls. Against Western Australia, the Tigers finished three runs short after their later batsmen tried to belt the ball to the well-protected boundaries rather than work it into the gaps.

Generally the batting showed more authority than in recent seasons, with one century and 10 fifties. That was especially evident when Ricky Ponting (153 runs at 51.00, with a strike rate of 82.70) was available for the early games. Captain Jamie Cox, Michael Di Venuto and Shaun Young all topped 200 runs. Cox, who moved himself up and down the order, looks a more assured one-day player for his profitable time in English county cricket.

Of the bowlers, Scott Kremerskothen was the leading wicket-taker with 14 (second in the competition), but they came at a cost of 6.39 runs an over. Tight as well as effective were Young (13 at 3.18), who was the joint winner of the national Mercantile Mutual Player of the Year award, and Damien Wright (nine at 3.36). Brett Geeves, an 18-year-old fast bowler, also showed considerable promise. Tasmania used 21 players in an effort to find the right mix for success. – DAVID STOCKDALE.

RESULTS, 2000-01

Mercantile Mutual Cup matches – Played 10: Won 4, Lost 6.
Competition placing – 5th.

DOMESTIC LIMITED-OVERS RESULTS

	M	W	L	NR	T
Australian Capital Territory	3	2	1	0	0
New South Wales	19	3	16	0	0
New Zealanders	1	0	1	0	0
Queensland	22	7	14	1	0
South Australia	18	6	12	0	0
Victoria	16	6	10	0	0
Western Australia	21	4	17	0	0
Total	100	28	71	1	0

MERCANTILE MUTUAL CUP AVERAGES, 2000-01

BATTING

	M	I	NO	R	HS	100s	50s	Avge	Ct/St	S-R
R. T. Ponting	4	4	1	153	68	0	2	51.00	4	82.70
J. Cox	9	9	1	277	66*	0	3	34.63	6	67.23
D. J. Marsh	9	8	2	177	57*	0	1	29.50	5	68.60
M. J. Di Venuto	9	9	1	223	124	1	1	27.88	3	77.43
S. R. Watson	6	6	2	103	28*	0	0	25.75	3	50.00
S. Young	10	9	1	203	76	0	2	25.38	6	65.27
S. P. Kremerskothen	10	7	1	134	47	0	0	22.33	3	73.22
J. A. Dykes	3	2	1	20	15	0	0	20.00	0	68.97
D. F. Hills	8	7	0	137	42	0	0	19.57	3	54.37
G. T. Cunningham	5	4	0	77	68	0	1	19.25	1	122.22
S. G. Clingeleffer	10	6	4	35	22*	0	0	17.50	11/1	70.00
B. J. Thomas	2	2	0	32	16	0	0	16.00	0	45.71
T. A. Pinnington	3	3	0	42	38	0	0	14.00	0	54.55
A. W. Polkinghorne	2	2	0	22	12	0	0	11.00	0	64.71
D. J. Saker	7	3	0	28	26	0	0	9.33	1	90.32
K. M. Munday	1	1	0	1	1	0	0	1.00	0	33.33
D. G. Wright	8	4	4	26	15*	0	0	–	1	68.42
G. J. Denton	1	0	0	0	0	0	0	–	0	–
B. Geeves	6	0	0	0	0	0	0	–	1	–
J. P. Marquet	6	0	0	0	0	0	0	–	0	–
S. R. Mason	1	0	0	0	0	0	0	–	0	–

* Denotes not out.

BOWLING

	O	M	R	W	BB	5w/i	Avge
B. J. Thomas	5	0	15	1	1/15	0	15.00
S. P. Kremerskothen	38	0	243	14	3/33	0	17.36
S. Young	72	13	229	13	3/16	0	17.62
A. W. Polkinghorne	4	0	22	1	1/22	0	22.00
D. G. Wright	66.4	9	224	9	3/16	0	24.89
J. P. Marquet	48.3	1	226	9	3/29	0	25.11
D. J. Marsh	39.3	1	162	6	2/30	0	27.00
D. J. Saker	61	4	258	8	2/26	0	32.25
B. Geeves	42	4	180	4	1/23	0	45.00
S. R. Watson	15	0	73	1	1/22	0	73.00
J. Cox	7	2	29	0	–	0	–
G. J. Denton	3	0	40	0	–	0	–
J. A. Dykes	10	0	55	0	–	0	–
D. F. Hills	1	0	21	0	–	0	–

At Adelaide Oval, Adelaide, October 14, 2000. SOUTH AUSTRALIA defeated TASMANIA by four runs.

TASMANIA v NEW SOUTH WALES

At Bellerive Oval, Hobart, November 11, 2000. New South Wales won by seven wickets. Toss: New South Wales. New South Wales 5 pts.

With the game restricted to 38 overs because of a rain-affected wicket, the New South Wales bowlers vindicated Steve Waugh's decision to put Tasmania in by restricting the home side to eight for 162. Pace man Nathan Bracken did the early damage as Tasmania crashed to four for 21, before Dan Marsh and Dene Hills combined in a careful fifth-wicket stand of 73. After the loss of two quick wickets, a cavalier stand of 86 in eight overs between Steve Waugh and Mark Bevan saw the visitors rattle off the target in just 24.3 overs and pick up the bonus point.

Man of the Match: S. R. Waugh. *Attendance:* 1,303.

Tasmania

*J. Cox run out (B. Lee)	0	(2)
M.J. Di Venuto c Haddin b Bracken ..	10	(13)
R.T. Ponting c M.E. Waugh		
b Bracken ..	1	(15)
S. Young c Higgs b Bradstreet	1	(16)
D.F. Hills st Haddin b MacGill	40	(77)
D.J. Marsh not out	57	(63)
J.A. Dykes c Haddin b S. Lee	15	(19)

B. Geeves and J.P. Marquet did not bat.

S.P. Kremerskothen c M.E. Waugh		
b S. Lee ..	23	(19)
D.J. Saker b B. Lee	2	(4)
†S.G. Clingeleffer not out	1	(1)
B 1, l-b 3, w 7, n-b 1	12	
(38 overs, 166 mins) (8 wkts)	162	
Fall: 0 11 12 21 94 124 156 159		

Bowling: B. Lee 8–1–29–1; Bracken 7–2–21–2; Bradstreet 7–2–22–1; S. Lee 7–0–40–2; MacGill 7–0–27–1; Higgs 2–0–19–0.

New South Wales

M.J. Slater b Marquet	18	(14)
†B.J. Haddin c Young b Saker	2	(5)
M.E. Waugh run out (Ponting)	22	(32)
*S.R. Waugh not out	75	(73)
M.G. Bevan not out	43	(23)

S. Lee, C.J. Richards, M.A. Higgs, S.D. Bradstreet, B. Lee, N.W. Bracken and S.C.G. MacGill did not bat.

B 1, l-b 1, w 3	5
(24.3 overs, 102 mins) (3 wkts)	165
Fall: 13 22 79	

Bowling: Saker 8–1–34–1; Marquet 7–0–54–1; Geeves 6–0–36–0; Kremerskothen 2–0–21–0; Marsh 1.3–0–18–0.

Umpires: K.J. Jones and P.V. Mulcahy.
TV Umpire: B.W. Jackman.

TASMANIA v WESTERN AUSTRALIA

At Bellerive Oval, Hobart, November 18, 2000. Western Australia won by two runs. Toss: Western Australia. Western Australia 4 pts.

If ever a game was the one that got away for Tasmania this was it. On a good wicket, the home side had the Western Australians in early bother until Simon Katich and Tom Moody joined forces in a belligerent fifth-wicket stand of 125 in 19.4 overs. Jamie Cox made a costly error of judgment when he brought on part-time spinner Dene Hills and the duo obligingly bludgeoned 21 off his only over. Cox and Shaun Young put Tasmania within sight of victory, only for the later batsmen to lose their way when only 26 runs were required off the last six overs.

Man of the Match: S. Young. *Attendance:* 628.

Western Australia

†A.C. Gilchrist b Marquet	5	(9)
R.J. Campbell b Saker	13	(19)
D.R. Martyn c Ponting b Geeves	34	(67)
J.L. Langer c Ponting b Young	17	(30)
S.M. Katich run out		
(Hills/Marsh/Clingeleffer) ..	73	(87)
*T.M. Moody c Cox b Kremerskothen	68	(59)
M.E. Hussey c Ponting b Marsh	5	(9)

S. Nikitaras and J. Angel did not bat.

G.B. Hogg not out	10	(12)
K.M. Harvey b Kremerskothen	5	(4)
S.J. Karppinen not out	5	(5)
B 1, l-b 4, w 5, n-b 1	11	
(50 overs, 194 mins) (8 wkts)	246	
Fall: 13 26 64 91 216 223 227 236		

Bowling: Saker 10–0–51–1; Marquet 10–0–45–1; Young 10–0–36–1; Geeves 7–1–23–1; Dykes 5–0–31–0; Marsh 4–0–21–1; Kremerskothen 3–0–13–2; Hills 1–0–21–0.

Tasmania

*J. Cox lbw b Karppinen	61	(78)	J. A. Dykes not out		5	(10)
M. J. Di Venuto c and b Angel	13	(18)	S. P. Kremerskothen not out		6	(8)
R. T. Ponting c Gilchrist b Karppinen	20	(26)	B 1, l-b 2, w 4, n-b 1		8	
S. Young c Katich b Martyn	76	(86)				
D. J. Marsh b Harvey	35	(51)	(50 overs, 199 mins)	(6 wkts)	244	
D. F. Hills c Hogg b Martyn	20	(24)	Fall: 35 79 111 181 224 234			

†S. G. Clingeleffer, D. J. Saker, B. Geeves and J. P. Marquet did not bat.

Bowling: Nikitaras 8–0–43–0; Angel 10–2–25–1; Harvey 10–0–67–1; Karppinen 10–0–44–2; Moody 4–0–20–0; Hogg 5–0–30–0; Martyn 3–0–12–2.

Umpires: B. W. Jackman and P. V. Mulcahy.
TV Umpire: K. J. Jones.

At Melbourne Cricket Ground, Melbourne, December 10, 2000. TASMANIA defeated VICTORIA by nine wickets.

TASMANIA v QUEENSLAND

At Bellerive Oval, Hobart, January 7, 2001. Tasmania won by seven wickets. Toss: Tasmania. Tasmania 5 pts.

From the moment they won the toss and put Queensland in on a wicket with some early life, Tasmania did not put a foot wrong. They skittled the visitors for 101 in 32.4 overs, Damien Wright making the early inroads, and Shaun Young and David Saker pressing home the advantage. No batsman made 20 and Scott Prestwidge lasted 47 balls to play the longest innings in the sad procession. Tasmania took only 21.2 overs to pick off the required runs, Young's crunching 51 not out off 52 balls with seven fours and two sixes ensuring him the Man of the Match award and the Tigers the bonus point.

Man of the Match: S. Young. *Attendance:* 1,107.

Queensland

J. P. Maher c Clingeleffer b Wright	15	(27)	S. A. Prestwidge c Hills b Kremerskothen	17	(47)
*S. G. Law c Clingeleffer b Wright	12	(25)	A. C. Dale c Kremerskothen b Geeves	5	(16)
A. Symonds c Kremerskothen b Saker	10	(10)	M. S. Kasprowicz not out	6	(13)
M. L. Love b Young	16	(21)	A. A. Noffke c Clingeleffer b Wright	1	(5)
G. I. Foley c Clingeleffer b Young	10	(20)	L-b 3, w 2	5	
L. A. Carseldine lbw b Saker	0	(6)			
†W. A. Seccombe run out			(32.4 overs, 138 mins)	101	
(Kremerskothen)	4	(6)	Fall: 20 34 38 60 65 65 72 90 99 101		

S. J. O'Leary did not bat.

Bowling: Wright 7.4–1–16–3; Saker 9–0–39–2; Young 9–4–15–2; Geeves 6–1–25–1; Kremerskothen 1–0–3–1.

Tasmania

T. A. Pinnington c Seccombe					
b Kasprowicz	0	(1)			
D. F. Hills c Seccombe b Dale	3	(9)	L-b 1, w 3, n-b 1	5	
*J. Cox lbw b Dale	27	(39)			
S. Young not out	51	(52)	(21.2 overs, 88 mins)	(3 wkts)	102
S. R. Watson not out	16	(28)	Fall: 0 8 55		

G. T. Cunningham, S. P. Kremerskothen, D. J. Marsh, †S. G. Clingeleffer, D. G. Wright, D. J. Saker and B. Geeves did not bat.

Bowling: Kasprowicz 6–0–28–1; Dale 9–2–21–2; Noffke 4.2–0–34–0; Prestwidge 2–0–18–0.

Umpires: K. J. McGuinness and J. H. Smeaton.
TV Umpire: P. V. Mulcahy.

TASMANIA v SOUTH AUSTRALIA

At Devonport Oval, Devonport, January 21, 2001. Tasmania won by 33 runs. Toss: South Australia. Tasmania 4 pts.

Tasmania triumphed on a wicket of variable bounce on which no batsman was able to reach 50. A number of useful contributions headed by Dan Marsh and Jamie Cox made up the home team's nine for 194. Despite losing David Saker with a calf injury in the pre-match warm-up, the Tasmanians clawed their way back into the game. They bundled South Australia out for 161, Josh Marquet taking three wickets cheaply, including those of the threatening Greg Blewett and top-scorer Shane Deitz.

Man of the Match: D.J. Marsh. *Attendance:* 2,303.

Tasmania

T.A. Pinnington b Swain	4	(12)
M.J. Di Venuto c Johnson b Wilson	15	(21)
*J. Cox c Fitzgerald b Miller	30	(50)
S. Young c Manou b Harrity	22	(72)
D.J. Marsh b McIntyre	33	(49)
D.F. Hills lbw b McIntyre	17	(35)
S.R. Watson run out (Harrity)	6	(14)
S.P. Kremerskothen c Blewett b Miller	20	(25)

J.P. Marquet did not bat.

†S.G. Clingeleffer not out	22	(21)
K.M. Munday run out (Wilson)	1	(3)
D.G. Wright not out	4	(4)
L-b 1, w 13, n-b 6	20	

(50 overs, 208 mins)　　　(9 wkts) 194

Fall: 22 22 81 85 118 141 145 171 174

Bowling: Wilson 10–2–29–1; Swain 10–1–33–1; Miller 10–1–62–2; Harrity 10–0–41–1; McIntyre 10–0–28–2.

South Australia

D.A. Fitzgerald c Hills b Wright	0	(6)
*G.S. Blewett c Kremerskothen b Marquet	32	(40)
C.J. Davies c Clingeleffer b Marquet	12	(28)
B.A. Johnson c Clingeleffer b Young	24	(49)
J.M. Vaughan c Clingeleffer b Young	2	(14)
S.A. Deitz b Marquet	44	(77)
M.C. Miller c and b Marsh	6	(20)

M.A. Harrity did not bat.

†G.A. Manou c Hills b Kremerskothen	19	(39)
B.A. Swain b Marsh	0	(1)
P. Wilson not out	14	(11)
P.E. McIntyre b Kremerskothen	1	(5)
L-b 2, w 3, n-b 2	7	

(48 overs, 190 mins)　　　161

Fall: 0 40 47 52 82 91 141 141 158 161

Bowling: Wright 10–1–37–1; Marquet 9–0–29–3; Watson 5–0–18–0; Young 10–2–27–2; Marsh 10–1–30–2; Kremerskothen 4–0–18–2.

Umpires: K.J. Jones and J.H. Smeaton.

At WACA Ground, Perth, January 26, 2001. TASMANIA lost to WESTERN AUSTRALIA by 64 runs.

At Brisbane Cricket Ground, Brisbane, February 2, 2001. TASMANIA lost to QUEENSLAND on run rate.

TASMANIA v VICTORIA

At Launceston Oval, Launceston, February 10, 2001. Tasmania won by 41 runs. Toss: Victoria. Tasmania 5 pts.

The match doubled as a celebration of the 150th anniversary of the first first-class match in Australia, which the two colonies played in Launceston in February 1851. Sadly, the intervening years had not improved the wicket. Tasmania were reeling at four for 14 before Jamie Cox and Scott Kremerskothen turned the game around with a feisty fifth-wicket partnership of 109 which helped raise the score to 183. Victoria had no such saviours, and Darren Berry's 27 was the top score as they were bowled out for 142 with nearly six overs to spare. The consistent Tasmanian attack shared the wickets and picked up what had seemed an unlikely bonus point.

Man of the Match: J. Cox.　*Attendance:* 2,402.

Tasmania

M.J. Di Venuto c Berry b Lewis	0	(2)	A.W. Polkinghorne b Reiffel	10	(12)
D.J. Marsh b Miller	7	(6)	†S.G. Clingeleffer c Berry b Reiffel	1	(7)
S.R. Watson b Lewis	3	(7)	D.G. Wright not out	15	(25)
S. Young c Berry b Miller	0	(2)			
S.P. Kremerskothen run out (Lewis)	47	(70)	L-b 7, w 8, n-b 7	22	
*J. Cox c Berry b Miller	58	(90)		—	
G.T. Cunningham c Elliott b Miller	4	(6)	(42.2 overs, 175 mins)	183	
B.J. Thomas c Reiffel b Hewett	16	(32)	Fall: 0 11 11 14 123 132 138 157 160 183		

J.P. Marquet did not bat.

Bowling: Lewis 9–0–34–2; Miller 10–1–36–4; Reiffel 10–1–34–2; Hewett 4.2–0–26–1; Moss 5–0–19–0; Oliver 3–0–21–0; Hodge 1–0–6–0.

Victoria

J.L. Arnberger c Di Venuto b Wright	6	(38)	I.S.L. Hewett c Watson b Marsh	7	(9)
M.T.G. Elliott c Cunningham b Young	2	(5)	*P.R. Reiffel not out	6	(21)
B.J. Hodge c Marsh b Young	12	(19)	C.R. Miller c Watson b Marquet	12	(16)
S.P. Dart c Marsh b Marquet	8	(26)			
M. Klinger c Young b Marsh	20	(34)	L-b 2, w 2, n-b 3	7	
J. Moss c Cox b Thomas	19	(34)		—	
†D.S. Berry c Marsh b Wright	27	(40)	(44.1 overs, 165 mins)	142	
B.C. Oliver run out (Cox/Clingeleffer)	16	(26)	Fall: 3 19 26 35 65 86 113 115 126 142		

M.L. Lewis did not bat.

Bowling: Wright 10–1–29–2; Young 10–2–30–2; Marquet 7.1–1–15–2; Marsh 10–0–38–2; Thomas 5–0–15–1; Kremerskothen 2–0–13–0.

Umpires: P.V. Mulcahy and J.H. Smeaton.

At Sydney Cricket Ground, Sydney, February 18, 2001. TASMANIA lost to NEW SOUTH WALES by six wickets.

RECORDS

Highest score for:	129*	M.J. Di Venuto v South Australia at Hobart (Bellerive) 1996-97
Highest score against:	159	S.G. Law (Queensland) at Brisbane 1993-94
Best bowling for:	5/23	J.P. Marquet v Queensland at Hobart (Bellerive) 1995-96
Best bowling against:	6/25	B.E. McNamara (New South Wales) at Sydney 1996-97
Highest total for:	6-271	v Western Australia at Perth 1986-87
Highest total against:	6-325	by South Australia at Hobart (TCA) 1986-87
Lowest total for:	80	v New South Wales at Devonport 1984-85
Lowest total against:	133	by Western Australia at Hobart (TCA) 1978-79

MOST RUNS

	M	I	NO	R	HS	100s	50s	Avge	S-R
D.C. Boon	55	52	4	1,725	116	1	16	35.94	66.22
J. Cox	53	52	2	1,412	99	0	12	28.24	64.65
S. Young	57	50	5	1,320	96	0	9	29.33	67.62
M.J. Di Venuto	49	48	7	1,261	129*	2	5	30.76	80.17
D.F. Hills	40	37	3	1,108	81	0	8	32.59	56.79
R.J. Tucker	39	38	2	869	75	0	6	24.14	76.56

	M	I	NO	R	HS	100s	50s	Avge	S-R
R.T. Ponting	27	27	4	727	87*	0	5	31.61	73.14
D.J. Marsh	31	28	7	657	78*	0	3	31.29	70.72
D.J. Buckingham	22	22	4	506	61	0	2	28.11	74.41
R.D. Woolley	22	20	2	454	80*	0	2	25.22	77.53

HIGHEST PARTNERSHIP FOR EACH WICKET

210 for 1st	J. Cox and D.C. Boon, v New South Wales at Hobart (Bellerive)	1998-99
137 for 2nd	M.J. Di Venuto and R.T. Ponting, v South Australia at Adelaide	2000-01
152 for 3rd	G.W. Goodman and J.H. Hampshire, v Queensland at Brisbane	1978-79
118 for 4th	S. Young and R.J. Tucker, v New South Wales at Hobart (Bellerive)	1994-95
127 for 5th	S. Young and D.F. Hills, v Western Australia at Perth	1998-99
91* for 6th	R.D. Woolley and R.E. Soule, v South Australia at Adelaide	1986-87
96* for 7th	T.W. Docking and J. Simmons, v Western Australia at Hobart (TCA)	1978-79
39 for 8th	R.E. Soule and R.L. Brown, v South Australia at Hobart (TCA)	1986-87
67 for 9th	G.T. Cunningham and D.J. Saker, v Western Australia at Perth	2000-01
28 for 10th	M.G. Farrell and M.W. Ridgway, v Western Australia at Hobart (Bellerive)	1996-97

MOST WICKETS

	M	Balls	Mdns	R	W	BB	5W/i	Avge
S. Young	57	2,324	38	1,595	40	3/16	0	39.88
R.J. Tucker	39	1,461	4	1,263	34	4/31	0	37.15
C.R. Miller	33	1,843	31	1,267	34	4/48	0	37.26
M.W. Ridgway	21	1,170	22	868	28	4/37	0	31.00
M.G. Farrell	28	1,224	3	885	27	4/51	0	32.78
D.G. Wright	17	898	16	530	24	3/16	0	22.08
P.J. Marquet	14	759	7	564	21	5/23	1	26.86
D.J. Marsh	31	841	2	683	15	3/47	0	45.53
S.P. Kremerskothen	18	396	1	405	15	3/33	0	27.00
J. Simmons	11	613	8	280	14	4/17	0	20.00

MOST DISMISSALS

	M	Ct	St	Total
M.N. Atkinson	35	43	7	50
R.D. Woolley	22	16	1	17
S.G. Clingeleffer	10	11	1	12
R.E. Soule	11	9	0	9
L.G. Allen	3	5	0	5
T.A. Pinnington	4	2	1	3

MOST CATCHES

S. Young . . . . 21 in 57 matches	D.C. Boon . . . . 16 in 55 matches
M.J. Di Venuto . . . . . . 19 in 49 matches	R.J. Tucker . . . . 13 in 39 matches
D.J. Marsh . . . . 17 in 31 matches	J. Cox . . . . 13 in 53 matches

MOST APPEARANCES

57 S. Young . . . . 1990-91 – 2000-01	39 R.J. Tucker . . . . . . 1987-88 – 1998-99
55 D.C. Boon . . . . 1978-79 – 1998-99	35 M.N. Atkinson . . . 1992-93 – 2000-01
53 J. Cox . . . . 1988-89 – 2000-01	33 C.R. Miller . . . . . . 1992-93 – 1999-00
49 M.J. Di Venuto . . . 1992-93 – 2000-01	31 D.J. Marsh . . . . 1996-97 – 2000-01
40 D.F. Hills . . . . 1992-93 – 2000-01	28 M.G. Farrell . . . . . 1990-91 – 1996-97

VICTORIA

The heady days of victory in this competition just two seasons ago were but a distant memory after another lamentable campaign left the Victorians rock bottom with three wins. The introduction of a bonus points system, providing incentive for reaching targets or dismissing opponents in quick time, was as disastrous for the Victorians as it was profitable for anyone who met them; three times in their first four matches they coughed up an extra point to the opposition.

Of the 23 players used, only a handful contributed usefully. Matthew Elliott was either red hot or definitely not, hitting three centuries but somehow finishing with only 328 runs from his seven trips to the crease. Brad Hodge batted as he did in both forms of the game; although he failed to score a century, his 374 runs were a team high and he matched Elliott's average of a shade over 46. Apart from the odd cameo from Michael Klinger and Ian Harvey, that was about it.

There were a couple of flickers of sunshine, most notably the form of 21-year-old all-rounder Ben Oliver. Hailing from famous country Victorian sporting stock, Oliver gave every indication that he was ready to carve out a name for himself. Playing nine of the 10 matches, he hit 147 runs in the lower middle order at just under 25, batting with great maturity as all around him went to water. Oliver also bowled tightly and cleverly against daunting opposition, and was solid and at times spectacular in the field.

Another plus came like a bolt from the blue – or in this case, the Blues – in the form of Jonathan Moss. The all-rounder was still playing Sydney grade cricket at Christmas time, convinced his state aspirations had passed him by. A month later, on Australia Day, he took five wickets on debut for Victoria to secure that rarity of results, victory over Queensland.

In fact it was Victoria's second defeat of Queensland in a week, a high water mark in a dreary campaign. Coach John Scholes stressed at the start of the season how prominently success in the limited-overs arena featured in his plans. After a showing that could hardly have been worse, Victoria made a concerted early-winter push to secure the services of West Australian

RESULTS, 2000-01

Mercantile Mutual Cup matches – Played 10: Won 3, Lost 7.
Competition placing – 6th.

DOMESTIC LIMITED-OVERS RESULTS

	M	W	L	NR	T
Australian Capital Territory	3	1	2	0	0
New South Wales	25	11	13	1	0
New Zealanders	2	1	1	0	0
Queensland	20	8	11	1	0
South Australia	24	15	8	0	1
Tasmania	16	10	6	0	0
Western Australia	27	4	21	2	0
Total	117	50	62	4	1

batsman and sometime wicket-keeper Ryan Campbell. It failed, but it demonstrated a recognition that something needs to change. – PETER HANLON.

MERCANTILE MUTUAL CUP AVERAGES, 2000-01

BATTING

	M	I	NO	R	HS	100s	50s	Avge	Ct/St	S-R
M.T.G. Elliott	7	7	0	328	112	3	0	46.86	2	90.61
B.J. Hodge	9	9	1	374	87	0	4	46.75	4	74.80
B.C. Oliver	9	8	2	147	39*	0	0	24.50	4	59.04
D.S. Berry	9	8	2	143	36	0	0	23.83	13/5	63.56
I.J. Harvey	6	6	0	123	56	0	1	20.50	4	81.46
M. Klinger	10	10	1	182	41*	0	0	20.22	1	59.67
J.L. Arnberger	6	6	0	117	75	0	1	19.50	0	60.31
S.P. Dart	5	5	0	92	38	0	0	18.40	1	53.80
P.R. Reiffel	9	9	5	70	22*	0	0	17.50	6	66.04
J. Moss	3	2	0	35	19	0	0	17.50	1	74.47
G.R. Vimpani	1	1	0	17	17	0	0	17.00	0	58.62
P.Q. Harper	3	3	0	51	27	0	0	17.00	0	51.52
S.A.J. Craig	3	3	0	41	28	0	0	13.67	0	37.96
M.P. Mott	4	4	0	44	16	0	0	11.00	1	36.97
C.R. Miller	7	3	1	20	12	0	0	10.00	1	68.97
D.W. Fleming	4	3	1	19	15*	0	0	9.50	1	90.48
C.J. Peake	3	3	0	19	14	0	0	6.33	2	41.30
I.S.L. Hewett	5	4	0	22	9	0	0	5.50	1	52.38
P.J. Roach	1	1	0	3	3	0	0	3.00	0	50.00
S.K. Warne	2	2	0	1	1	0	0	0.50	0	20.00
J.M. Davison	3	3	3	19	11*	0	0	–	0	95.00
M.W.H. Inness	1	0	0	0	0	0	0	–	0	–
M.L. Lewis	10	0	0	0	0	0	0	–	3	–

BOWLING

	O	M	R	W	BB	5w/i	Avge
M.P. Mott	2	0	8	2	2/2	0	4.00
I.S.L. Hewett	36.1	1	177	9	3/38	0	19.67
J. Moss	22	0	121	5	5/47	1	24.20
C.R. Miller	58	2	228	9	4/36	0	25.33
B.J. Hodge	8	0	53	2	2/25	0	26.50
I.J. Harvey	32.1	2	164	6	3/45	0	27.33
D.W. Fleming	34.3	5	116	4	3/30	0	29.00
S.K. Warne	16	2	95	3	3/48	0	31.67
P.R. Reiffel	57	4	257	7	3/28	0	36.71
M.L. Lewis	78	8	380	10	2/24	0	38.00
B.C. Oliver	51.3	1	235	5	2/36	0	47.00
S.P. Dart	1	0	2	0	–	0	–
J.M. Davison	8	1	49	0	–	0	–
M.W.H. Inness	4	0	21	0	–	0	–

At North Sydney Oval, North Sydney, October 15, 2000. VICTORIA lost to NEW SOUTH WALES by eight wickets.

VICTORIA v NEW SOUTH WALES

At Richmond Cricket Ground, Richmond, October 29, 2000. Victoria won by two wickets. Toss: Victoria. Victoria 4 pts.

On a good pitch and close to full strength, both teams made this anything but a Sunday stroll. The six Test batsmen in the New South Wales side could only muster 62 runs between them against a chokingly steady attack. Needing only to overtake a modest target of 129 in 40.1 overs to achieve a bonus point, Victoria failed by 10 balls but were happy just to get there at all, winning with two wickets in hand. With their side teetering at five for 60, 20-year-olds Ben Oliver and Michael Klinger put on 39 to right the ship, and Darren Berry saw off Brett Lee's final burst.

Man of the Match: B.C. Oliver. *Attendance:* 3,306.

New South Wales

M.E. Waugh st Berry b Harvey	17 (43)	B. Lee c Mott b Miller	4 (18)
M.J. Slater c Berry b Lewis	0 (2)	S.C.G. MacGill c Lewis b Mott	5 (10)
†B.J. Haddin c Klinger b Lewis	7 (19)	N.W. Bracken st Berry b Mott	0 (1)
*S.R. Waugh c Harvey b Oliver	36 (66)		
M.G. Bevan c and b Harvey	0 (1)	B 1, l-b 2, w 5, n-b 3	11
S. Lee c Hodge b Miller	17 (33)		
C.J. Richards lbw b Miller	10 (23)	(42 overs, 181 mins)	129
M.A. Higgs not out	22 (39)	Fall: 3 11 60 60 80 93 100 120 126 129	

G.D. McGrath did not bat.

Bowling: Reiffel 8–0–30–0; Lewis 7–2–24–2; Harvey 6–2–14–2; Oliver 9–1–32–1; Miller 9–0–19–3; Davison 2–0–5–0; Mott 1–0–2–2.

Victoria

J.L. Arnberger run out (Haddin/B. Lee)	3 (14)	†D.S. Berry not out	14 (36)
M.P. Mott b MacGill	10 (20)	*P.R. Reiffel b B. Lee	1 (12)
B.J. Hodge run out (Haddin)	13 (26)	J.M. Davison not out	0 (5)
I.J. Harvey b B. Lee	21 (30)	L-b 4, w 8, n-b 3	15
S.A.J. Craig b MacGill	5 (14)		
M. Klinger lbw b McGrath	19 (51)	(41.5 overs, 181 mins) (8 wkts)	130
B.C. Oliver b B. Lee	29 (46)	Fall: 7 21 38 52 60 99 117 120	

C.R. Miller and M.L. Lewis did not bat.

Bowling: McGrath 10–3–22–1; B. Lee 10–3–41–3; MacGill 10–2–26–2; Bracken 4–0–13–0; Higgs 7.5–1–24–0.

Umpires: G.T.D. Morrow and R.L. Parry.
TV Umpire: R.G. Patterson.

VICTORIA v SOUTH AUSTRALIA

At Richmond Cricket Ground, Richmond, November 12, 2000. South Australia won by six wickets. Toss: South Australia. South Australia 5 pts.

The drizzle that reduced this to a 37-over contest did not last long enough for Victoria, who scraped together just 141 against a slippery Jason Gillespie on a damp pitch and damper outfield. Only Michael Klinger's robust 41 from 38 balls prevented serious embarrassment. After Paul Reiffel provided a flicker of early hope with the ball, Chris Davies saw South Australia home with a measured 62 off 79 balls as the ground – and the hosts – dried up.

Man of the Match: C.J. Davies. *Attendance:* 2,044.

Victoria

J.L. Arnberger c Manou b Wilson	4	(9)	
S.A.J. Craig c Manou b Harris	28	(65)	
B.J. Hodge lbw b Harris	34	(59)	
I.J. Harvey b Young	6	(15)	
M.P. Mott c Lehmann b Gillespie	6	(13)	
M. Klinger not out	41	(38)	
B.C. Oliver c Lehmann b Johnson ...	7	(12)	

†D.S. Berry b Gillespie	1	(2)
*P.R. Reiffel c Manou b Gillespie ..	1	(2)
J.M. Davison not out	8	(7)
B 1, l-b 3, w 1	5	

C.R. Miller and M.L. Lewis did not bat.

(37 overs, 149 mins)   (8 wkts) 141

Fall: 9 66 75 82 85 112 113 117

Bowling: Wilson 8–3–26–1; Swain 7–0–25–0; Harris 7–0–29–2; Gillespie 8–1–27–3; Johnson 4–0–20–1; Young 3–0–10–1.

South Australia

D.A. Fitzgerald c Berry b Reiffel	11	(22)	
G.S. Blewett c Berry b Reiffel	1	(15)	
C.J. Davies c Berry b Lewis	62	(79)	
*D.S. Lehmann c Lewis b Oliver ...	39	(46)	
B.E. Young not out	14	(10)	

B.A. Johnson not out	0	(1)
l-b 3, w 9, n-b 4	16	

(28.1 overs, 124 mins)   (4 wkts) 143

Fall: 13 17 107 136

J.M. Vaughan, †G.A. Manou, R.J. Harris, B.A. Swain, J.N. Gillespie and P. Wilson did not bat.

Bowling: Reiffel 6–1–24–2; Lewis 6–1–33–1; Harvey 2.1–0–19–0; Oliver 8–0–37–1; Miller 6–0–27–0.

Umpires: R.L. Parry and A.J. Soulsby.
TV Umpire: R.G. Patterson.

VICTORIA v TASMANIA

At Melbourne Cricket Ground, Melbourne, December 10, 2000. Tasmania won by nine wickets. Toss: Tasmania. Tasmania 5 pts. Competition debut: S.P. Dart and P.Q. Harper.

Ricky Ponting's debut as Tasmanian captain was a happy (albeit short) affair, as his side reduced Victoria to a fourth successive score of less than 200 in the competition. The hosts presented their opposition with a bonus point for the third time in four matches as Ponting (six fours and three sixes) and Michael Di Venuto knocked off the runs in 37 overs. In his first state outing of the season, Matthew Elliott made a three-ball duck and grassed a simple slips catch. It was left to Ben Oliver and Darren Berry to add a whiff of respectability to the total by adding 67 for the eighth wicket.

Man of the Match: R.T. Ponting. *Attendance:* 2,796.

Victoria

M.T.G. Elliott c Young b Saker	0	(3)	
P.Q. Harper c Geeves b Wright	22	(41)	
I.J. Harvey c Young b Wright	6	(20)	
C.J. Peake run out (Clingeleffer)	1	(2)	
M.P. Mott c Ponting b Saker	16	(50)	
M. Klinger lbw b Young	11	(36)	
S.P. Dart lbw b Geeves	4	(18)	

B.C. Oliver not out	39	(56)
†D.S. Berry c Young b Kremerskothen	36	(73)
*P.R. Reiffel not out	6	(6)
B 1, l-b 4, w 13, n-b 5	23	

C.R. Miller and M.L. Lewis did not bat.

(50 overs, 202 mins)   (8 wkts) 164

Fall: 2 25 26 38 61 70 77 144

Bowling: Saker 10–1–26–2; Wright 7–1–17–2; Young 10–3–20–1; Geeves 10–1–27–1; Kremerskothen 8–0–45–1; Dykes 5–0–24–0.

Tasmania

T. A. Pinnington c Harvey b Lewis	... 38	(64)
M. J. Di Venuto not out	 54	(90)
*R. T. Ponting not out	 64	(69)
L-b 2, w 6, n-b 1	 9	

(37 overs, 151 mins)   (1 wkt) 165
Fall: 62

†S. G. Clingeleffer, S. Young, S. R. Mason, J. A. Dykes, S. P. Kremerskothen, D. F. Hills, D. G. Wright, D. J. Saker and B. Geeves did not bat.

Bowling: Reiffel 6–0–40–0; Lewis 9–0–43–1; Harvey 6–0–19–0; Oliver 5–0–14–0; Miller 10–0–45–0; Dart 1–0–2–0.

Umpires: R. L. Parry and R. G. Patterson.
TV Umpire: G. T. D. Morrow.

At WACA Ground, Perth, January 2, 2001. VICTORIA lost to WESTERN AUSTRALIA by seven runs.

VICTORIA v WESTERN AUSTRALIA

At Melbourne Cricket Ground, Melbourne, January 16, 2001. Western Australia won by seven wickets. Toss: Western Australia. Western Australia 5 pts.

Victoria's tiny hopes of reaching the limited-overs final collapsed in a hurry as the hosts conceded a bonus point for the fourth time in six matches. Only Brad Hodge stood firm against consistent bowling on a moist pitch. Victoria's bowlers, on the other hand, looked innocuous as Western Australia's openers, Ryan Campbell and Justin Langer, took due care as they knocked off 113 of the 184 needed before Brendon Julian iced the Western Australians victory cake with 30 off 22 balls.

Man of the Match: B. J. Hodge. *Attendance:* 2,278.

Victoria

M. T. G. Elliott lbw b Wates	 4	(20)	*P. R. Reiffel b Harvey	 0	(1)
P. Q. Harper c Spencer b Angel	 2	(13)	C. R. Miller run out (Hussey/Campbell)	3	(6)
B. J. Hodge st Campbell b Hogg	 84	(109)	D. W. Fleming not out	 15	(11)
C. J. Peake c Campbell b Julian	 4	(20)			
M. Klinger c and b Harvey	 23	(41)	L-b 3, w 11, n-b 1	 15	
B. C. Oliver c Hussey b Hogg	 13	(31)			
I. S. L. Hewett c Wates b Harvey	 9	(21)	(49.1 overs, 193 mins)	 183	
†D. S. Berry c Moody b Spencer	 11	(23)	Fall: 7 8 56 118 141 146 154 155 162 183		

M. L. Lewis did not bat.

Bowling: Angel 10–3–34–1; Wates 6–2–18–1; Julian 5–0–21–1; Moody 5–0–20–0; Spencer 5.1–0–23–1; Harvey 10–0–39–3; Hogg 8–0–25–2.

Western Australia

†R. J. Campbell c Berry b Hewett	 57	(89)	B 4, l-b 2, w 7	 13	
J. L. Langer c Peake b Hewett	 57	(94)			
B. P. Julian c Peake b Hewett	 30	(22)			
K. M. Harvey not out	 6	(8)	(38.5 overs, 160 mins) (3 wkts) 186		
M. W. Goodwin not out	 23	(20)	Fall: 113 138 156		

*T. M. Moody, M. J. North, M. E. Hussey, G. B. Hogg, D. J. Spencer, D. J. Wates and J. Angel did not bat.

Bowling: Fleming 9–1–34–0; Lewis 10–1–47–0; Reiffel 7–1–26–0; Oliver 2–0–9–0; Miller 4–0–26–0; Hewett 6.5–0–38–3.

Umpires: R. G. Patterson and A. J. Soulsby.

At Brisbane Cricket Ground, Brisbane, January 19, 2001. VICTORIA defeated QUEENSLAND by 63 runs.

VICTORIA v QUEENSLAND

At Melbourne Cricket Ground, Melbourne, January 26, 2001. Victoria won on run rate. Toss: Queensland. Victoria 5 pts. Competition debut: J. Moss.

Matthew Elliott scored a second limited-overs century against Queensland in a week, helping Victoria to achieve back-to-back wins over a much-vaunted opponent. Jason Arnberger joined him in an opening stand that produced 161 in only 29.1 overs, while Brad Hodge also scored freely. Only Adam Dale was able to contain the onslaught. Queensland started well enough, with Jimmy Maher, in particular, looking in fine fettle. Once they began to lose wickets to fine pace bowling from ex-Sydneysider Jonathan Moss in his debut match, they lost their way. They sank to the bottom of the table after the Duckworth/Lewis calculations consigned them to a 59-run loss.

Man of the Match: M. W. Goodwin. *Attendance:* 2,358.

Victoria

M.T.G. Elliott c Seccombe b Kasprowicz	112	(118)	C.R. Miller not out	5	(7)
J.L. Arnberger c Law b Dale	75	(88)	B 1, l-b 8, w 1, n-b 4	14
B.J. Hodge not out	50	(57)		
S.P. Dart st Seccombe b Noffke	15	(15)	(48 overs, 195 mins) (4 wkts)	271
M. Klinger b Dale	0	(7)	Fall: 161 215 248 252

B.C. Oliver, *†D.S. Berry, I.S.L. Hewett, M.L. Lewis, J. Moss and M.W.H. Inness did not bat.

Bowling: Bichel 10–1–65–0; Dale 10–0–30–2; Kasprowicz 9–0–55–1; Hopes 10–1–49–0; Hauritz 4–0–27–0; Noffke 5–0–36–1.

Queensland

M.L. Hayden c Hodge b Hewett	36	(53)	N.M. Hauritz c Berry b Moss	1	(4)
J.P. Maher c Dart b Moss	64	(67)	A.C. Dale c Lewis b Oliver	6	(7)
*S.G. Law c Miller b Lewis	37	(34)	M.S. Kasprowicz not out	8	(4)
A.J. Bichel lbw b Moss	19	(23)	L-b 1, w 4	5
M.L. Love c and b Moss	2	(16)		
L.A. Carseldine c Berry b Hodge	23	(28)	(43.3 overs, 187 mins)	226
J.R. Hopes c Oliver b Hodge	24	(23)	Fall: 80 128 161 162 176 210 211
†W.A. Seccombe c Oliver b Moss	1	(2)	211 213 226

A.A. Noffke did not bat.

Bowling: Inness 4–0–21–0; Miller 10–1–33–0; Lewis 5–0–38–1; Oliver 6.3–0–34–1; Hewett 5–0–27–1; Moss 10–0–47–5; Hodge 3–0–25–2.

Umpires: R.L. Parry and R.G. Patterson.

At Launceston Oval, Launceston, February 10, 2001. VICTORIA lost to TASMANIA by 41 runs.

At Adelaide Oval, Adelaide, February 17, 2001. VICTORIA lost to SOUTH AUSTRALIA by five wickets.

RECORDS

Highest score for:	139*	D. M. Jones v New South Wales at Sydney	1986-87
Highest score against:	150*	M. L. Hayden (Queensland) at Melbourne	1998-99
Best bowling for:	5/20	G. D. Watson v Western Australia at Melbourne	1969-70
Best bowling against:	5/15	D. L. Boyd (Western Australia) at Perth	1982-83
Highest total for:	5-282	v Western Australia at Perth	1990-91
Highest total against:	5-310	by New South Wales at North Sydney	1991-92
Lowest total for:	78	v Queensland at Brisbane	1989-90
Lowest total against:	59	by Western Australia at Melbourne	1969-70

MOST RUNS

	M	I	NO	R	HS	100s	50s	Avge	S-R
D. M. Jones	55	52	10	2,122	139*	4	12	50.52	74.07
B. J. Hodge	47	45	5	1,512	118*	2	11	37.80	72.28
M. T. G. Elliott	42	40	3	1,156	112	4	4	31.24	65.98
J. M. Wiener	20	20	2	1,003	108*	1	10	55.72	66.52
I. J. Harvey	45	40	3	722	71	0	4	19.51	79.43
G. M. Watts	19	19	0	590	85	0	6	31.05	51.39
G. N. Yallop	24	24	2	586	91	0	3	26.64	68.50
D. S. Berry	59	44	13	530	64*	0	1	17.10	66.08
G. R. Vimpani	19	19	0	467	92	0	2	24.58	63.54
A. I. C. Dodemaide	38	30	8	454	40	0	0	20.64	58.13
W. J. Scholes	17	16	2	443	95	0	4	31.64	68.49

HIGHEST PARTNERSHIP FOR EACH WICKET

194	for 1st	M. T. G. Elliott and G. R. Vimpani, v New South Wales at North Sydney	1999-00
114	for 2nd	J. M. Wiener and G. N. Yallop, v Western Australia at Perth	1983-84
135	for 3rd	D. M. Jones and M. T. G. Elliott, v Tasmania at Hobart (Bellerive)	1995-96
127	for 4th	G. N. Yallop and J. K. Moss, v Western Australia at Perth	1978-79
124*	for 5th	B. J. Hodge and S. A. J. Craig, v Australian Capital Territory at Canberra	1998-99
92	for 6th	B. J. Hodge and P. R. Reiffel, v New South Wales at North Sydney	1997-98
98*	for 7th	T. J. Laughlin and R. J. Bright, v New South Wales at Sydney	1976-77
73*	for 8th	A. M. Smith and A. I. C. Dodemaide, v Queensland at Melbourne	1996-97
73	for 9th	R. C. Jordon and R. K. Rowan, v South Australia at Adelaide	1970-71
30	for 10th	D. W. Fleming and D. J. Saker, v Western Australia at Melbourne	1995-96

MOST WICKETS

	M	Balls	Mdns	R	W	BB	5W/i	Avge
I. J. Harvey	45	1,853	13	1,478	51	5/34	1	28.98
D. W. Fleming	39	2,064	39	1,333	42	3/25	0	31.74
P. R. Reiffel	40	1,844	35	1,201	37	4/14	0	32.46
A. I. C. Dodemaide	38	2,019	34	1,268	35	3/11	0	36.23
M. G. Hughes	30	1,523	26	1,147	33	4/34	0	34.76
D. J. Saker	27	1,344	32	869	27	4/35	0	32.19
S. K. Warne	16	815	11	595	25	5/35	0	23.80
M. H. N. Walker	18	1,098	18	583	24	4/37	0	24.29
P. W. Jackson	14	754	13	502	22	4/26	0	22.82
S. F. Graf	15	815	14	537	22	4/15	0	24.41

MOST DISMISSALS

	M	Ct	St	Total
D.S. Berry	59	72	22	94
M.G.D. Dimattina	18	16	2	18
R.D. Robinson	17	11	4	15
P.G. Sacristani	4	8	0	8
N.M. Carlyon	3	6	1	7

MOST CATCHES

D.M. Jones	28 in 55 matches	I.J. Harvey	12 in 45 matches
M.T.G. Elliott	20 in 42 matches	P.R. Reiffel	12 in 40 matches
B.J. Hodge	19 in 47 matches	J.D. Siddons	11 in 20 matches

MOST APPEARANCES

59	D.S. Berry	1990-91 – 2000-01	40	P.R. Reiffel	1987-88 – 2000-01
55	D.M. Jones	1981-82 – 1997-98	39	D.W. Fleming	1988-89 – 2000-01
46	B.J. Hodge	1993-94 – 2000-01	38	A.I.C. Dodemaide	1983-84 – 1997-98
45	I.J. Harvey	1993-94 – 2000-01	30	M.G. Hughes	1981-82 – 1994-95
42	M.T.G. Elliott	1992-93 – 2000-01	27	D.J. Saker	1994-95 – 1999-00

WESTERN AUSTRALIA

Murray Goodwin's dazzling, record-breaking innings of 167 against New South Wales at the WACA Ground was the highlight of a topsy-turvy season in which the side won four in a row before ending with three successive defeats. Western Australia's weak bowling was aptly illustrated when New South Wales scored eight for 302 at North Sydney Oval and Queensland amassed eight for 306 at the Gabba, and the batting was unable to approach such huge targets. Then came the final, which Western Australia also lost to a superb batting display by Michael Bevan. Before this season, Western Australia had only once conceded in excess of 300 – when South Australia rattled up seven for 302 against an inexperienced attack at the WACA Ground in 1999-00.

Western Australia's fielding standard was generally high, but the bowlers must learn to be more frugal. Veteran Jo Angel stood out as the most consistent bowler, taking 12 wickets at an average of 32.17 and conceding 4.15 runs an over. Left-arm wrist-spinner Brad Hogg again proved a success in this form of cricket, taking 13 wickets at 28.85, although he conceded 5.91 an over. Medium-pacer Kade Harvey's 11 wickets cost 5.63 an over, Duncan Spencer's 11 wickets cost 6.15 an over; Brendon Julian's nine wickets cost 5.25 an over, while Tom Moody was a fading force, with his five wickets coming at a costly average of 50.60 and conceding 4.43 an over. Swing bowler Darren Wates showed promise in five matches in the latter half of the season, his five wickets at 27.60 costing only 3.94 runs an over.

Without international representatives Adam Gilchrist and Damien Martyn for most of the 11 matches, Western Australia performed below par with the bat. Goodwin's spectacular 167 was the side's only century. When Western Australia took the title the previous summer, its batsmen had scored five centuries in eight matches. Ryan Campbell, an explosive opener a few seasons earlier, again performed poorly, managing only 135 runs at an average of 15.00. Goodwin, enjoying the freedom of restricted field placings, was the most successful batsman in the competition, amassing 534 runs at 76.29. Simon Katich hit four half-centuries from seven innings, Justin Langer had his moments, and Moody scored some useful runs. However, Mike Hussey, for so long considered unsuited to the helter-skelter of limited-overs cricket, was a shining light with his diligent application, composure, sparkling running between wickets and improvised strokeplay.

Without Moody, for so long a guiding light in limited-overs cricket, Western Australia must redefine its strategies under new coach Mike Veletta in this hectic form of the game. The priority will be to mould a potent attack, one that can take early wickets and control the flow of runs. Much may depend on Matthew Nicholson (who has yet to bowl in the limited-overs domestic competition) getting his act together and developing into a lethal performer in this type of cricket. – KEN CASELLAS.

RESULTS, 2000-01

Mercantile Mutual Cup matches – Played 11: Won 6, Lost 4, No result 1.
Competition placing – 2nd.

DOMESTIC LIMITED-OVERS RESULTS

	M	W	L	NR	T
Australian Capital Territory	3	3	0	0	0
New South Wales	28	15	12	0	1
New Zealanders	3	2	1	0	0
Queensland	25	12	11	2	0
South Australia	29	18	11	0	0
Tasmania	21	17	4	0	0
Victoria	27	21	4	2	0
Total	136	88	43	4	1

MERCANTILE MUTUAL CUP AVERAGES, 2000-01

BATTING

	M	I	NO	R	HS	100s	50s	Avge	Ct/St	S-R
M. W. Goodwin	9	9	2	534	167	1	4	76.29	2	92.55
M. E. Hussey	11	9	1	428	94	0	5	53.50	3	88.80
G. B. Hogg	11	8	5	131	59	0	1	43.67	7	97.76
S. M. Katich	8	7	0	300	73	0	4	42.86	3	81.97
T. M. Moody	11	8	1	240	78	0	2	34.29	5	102.13
J. L. Langer..........	8	7	0	228	88	0	2	32.57	2	56.72
D. R. Martyn........	4	3	0	73	39	0	0	24.33	1	51.41
A. C. Gilchrist.......	4	3	0	69	46	0	0	23.00	2/1	97.18
D. J. Wates	5	2	1	20	11	0	0	20.00	1	51.28
K. M. Harvey	11	8	4	74	23	0	0	18.50	1	70.48
R. J. Campbell	10	9	0	135	57	0	1	15.00	18/3	69.95
M. J. North	4	3	1	27	14	0	0	13.50	1	62.79
B. P. Julian	8	8	0	100	30	0	0	12.50	2	112.36
D. J. Spencer........	6	2	0	4	4	0	0	2.00	3	66.67
S. J. Karppinen	4	2	2	5	5*	0	0	–	0	100.00
B. A. Williams	3	1	1	0	0*	0	0	–	0	–
J. Angel.............	11	0	0	0	0	0	0	–	2	–
M. P. Atkinson.......	1	0	0	0	0	0	0	–	1	–
S. Nikitaras........	3	0	0	0	0	0	0	–	0	–

BOWLING

	O	M	R	W	BB	5w/i	Avge
D. R. Martyn...........	3	0	12	2	2/12	0	6.00
D. J. Spencer...........	40	0	246	11	4/35	0	22.36
D. J. Wates	35	6	138	5	2/21	0	27.60
G. B. Hogg	63.4	2	375	13	3/49	0	28.85
B. P. Julian	51	2	268	9	4/41	0	29.78
J. Angel...............	93	9	386	12	2/23	0	32.17
K. M. Harvey	64.2	0	362	11	3/39	0	32.91
B. A. Williams	27	1	139	3	1/43	0	46.33
T. M. Moody	57	3	253	5	2/27	0	50.60
M. P. Atkinson	8	0	53	1	1/53	0	53.00
S. J. Karppinen	24	1	126	2	2/44	0	63.00
S. Nikitaras.............	15	1	71	0	–	0	–

WESTERN AUSTRALIA v SOUTH AUSTRALIA

At WACA Ground, Perth, October 20, 2000. Western Australia won by three runs. Toss: Western Australia. Western Australia 4 pts.

The match was reduced to 44 overs a side after rain delayed the start by 75 minutes. South Australia paid dearly for fielding errors. Simon Katich was dropped on four at short mid-wicket by a diving Darren Lehmann, and Murray Goodwin, on 20, was dropped by Chris Davies at deep mid-wicket. They put on 103 for the fourth wicket at a run a ball. Brilliant catches by Damien Martyn and Brad Hogg removed South Australia's dangerous openers. Lehmann then assumed control and with five wickets in hand the visitors needed ten to win off the final over, from Brad Williams. Brad Young needed to hit a four off the final delivery, but he lofted a drive and was caught by Tom Moody at long-off.

Man of the Match: S. M. Katich. *Attendance:* 3,630.

Western Australia

†A.C. Gilchrist c Fitzgerald b Swain	. 18	(29)	G.B. Hogg not out	5	(3)
J.L. Langer c Blewett b Swain	0	(2)			
D.R. Martyn c Fitzgerald b Gillespie	. 39	(72)	L-b 3, w 2	5	
S.M. Katich c Davies b Johnson	69	(74)		—	
M.W. Goodwin not out	62	(65)	(44 overs, 190 mins)	(5 wkts) 233	
M.E. Hussey c Vaughan b Wilson	35	(20)	Fall: 4 37 68 171 227		

*T.M. Moody, K.M. Harvey, M.P. Atkinson, B.A. Williams and J. Angel did not bat.

Bowling: Wilson 9–0–45–1; Swain 9–2–33–2; Gillespie 9–2–44–1; Rofe 9–1–41–0; Blewett 6–0–46–0; Johnson 2–0–21–1.

South Australia

G.S. Blewett c Martyn b Atkinson	... 26	(35)	B.E. Young c Moody b Williams	9	(13)
D.A. Fitzgerald c Hogg b Harvey	 32	(48)			
C.J. Davies st Gilchrist b Hogg	17	(45)	L-b 10, w 11, n-b 3	24	
*D.S. Lehmann not out	91	(96)		—	
J.M. Vaughan c Atkinson b Moody	.. 9	(15)	(44 overs, 189 mins)	(6 wkts) 230	
B.A. Johnson lbw b Harvey	22	(24)	Fall: 47 75 121 140 199 230		

†G.A. Manou, P.C. Rofe, B.A. Swain, J.N. Gillespie and P. Wilson did not bat.

Bowling: Angel 7–0–26–0; Williams 8–0–43–1; Atkinson 8–0–53–1; Harvey 7–0–33–2; Hogg 7–1–31–1; Moody 7–0–34–1.

Umpires: B. Bennett and K.J. Rinaldi.

WESTERN AUSTRALIA v QUEENSLAND

At WACA Ground, Perth, November 15, 2000. No result. Toss: Queensland. Western Australia 2 pts. Queensland 2 pts.

For the first time in 343 limited-overs domestic matches in Australia, the contest was abandoned because of a dangerous pitch. Curator Richard Winter had prepared the pitch that was used in the four-day match between Western Australia and the West Indies which finished three days earlier, but after three days of high temperatures the pitch was badly cracked. Play lasted only 23 minutes and five overs. The fifth delivery of the second over (from Steve Nikitaras) skidded along the ground to Jimmy Maher, and the next delivery leapt viciously and struck Maher on the chest. Western Australia's captain Tom Moody spoke to the umpires, and after discussions with the match referee, Ric Evans, the match was called off.

Attendance: 1,285.

Queensland

M. L. Hayden c Katich b Angel	6	(13)
J. P. Maher not out	6	(13)
*S. G. Law not out	8	(5)

(5 overs, 23 mins)   (1 wkt) 20
Fall: 12

A. Symonds, M. L. Love, L. A. Carseldine, S. A. Prestwidge, B. N. Creevey, †G. A. J. Fitness, A. J. Bichel, A. C. Dale and S. J. O'Leary did not bat.

Bowling: Angel 3–0–17–1; Nikitaras 2–1–3–0.

Western Australia

M. E. Hussey, R. J. Campbell, J. L. Langer, †A. C. Gilchrist, D. R. Martyn, S. M. Katich, *T. M. Moody, K. M. Harvey, G. B. Hogg, S. J. Karppinen, S. Nikitaras, J. Angel.

Umpires: K. J. Rinaldi and R. J. U. Woolridge.

At Bellerive Oval, Hobart, November 18, 2000. WESTERN AUSTRALIA defeated TASMANIA by two runs.

At Adelaide Oval, Adelaide, December 9, 2000. WESTERN AUSTRALIA lost to SOUTH AUSTRALIA by two runs.

WESTERN AUSTRALIA v VICTORIA

At WACA Ground, Perth, January 2, 2001. Western Australia won by seven runs. Toss: Western Australia. Western Australia 4 pts.

This was a match of successful comebacks by bowlers. Duncan Spencer was making his first interstate appearance since February 1994 and Victoria's champion leg-spinner Shane Warne was resuming after fracturing a finger in October. Victoria began magnificently, having the home side reeling at three for 5 in the third over and still struggling at three for 14 after 11 overs. Michael Lewis had 2/4 off his first five overs. Simon Katich and Mike Hussey rebuilt the innings before Warne dismissed Katich, Tom Moody and Brendon Julian. Victoria were penalised one over and fell just short of the target. Spencer bowled fast and straight and was rewarded with four wickets.

Man of the Match: M. E. Hussey. *Attendance:* 8,837.

Western Australia

†R. J. Campbell c Elliott b Fleming	4	(9)	K. M. Harvey b Fleming	4	(8)
M. W. Goodwin c Berry b Lewis	0	(3)	D. J. Spencer c Hodge b Harvey	4	(4)
D. R. Martyn b Lewis	0	(3)	S. J. Karppinen not out	0	(0)
S. M. Katich c Reiffel b Warne	50	(75)			
M. E. Hussey b Fleming	79	(118)			
*T. M. Moody st Berry b Warne	32	(30)	L-b 5, w 13, n-b 7	25	
B. P. Julian st Berry b Warne	9	(21)			
G. B. Hogg not out	23	(32)	(50 overs, 220 mins) (9 wkts)	230	

Fall: 4 4 5 82 127 159 207 222 229

J. Angel did not bat.

Bowling: Fleming 10–2–30–3; Lewis 10–2–30–2; Oliver 7–0–25–0; Harvey 10–0–67–1; Warne 10–2–48–3; Reiffel 3–0–25–0.

Victoria

P. Q. Harper c Hussey b Spencer	27	(45)
M. T. G. Elliott c Campbell b Angel	1	(3)
B. J. Hodge c and b Hogg	62	(104)
C. J. Peake lbw b Spencer	14	(24)
I. J. Harvey c Katich b Julian	23	(27)
M. Klinger c Moody b Hogg	35	(42)
B. C. Oliver b Harvey	8	(20)
†D. S. Berry run out (Campbell)	26	(22)

S. K. Warne lbw b Spencer	0	(1)
*P. R. Reiffel not out	5	(7)
D. W. Fleming c Campbell b Spencer	0	(1)
B 1, l-b 8, w 10, n-b 3	22	
	—	
(48.5 overs, 208 mins)	223	
Fall: 3 47 81 127 164 185 208		
209 223 223		

M. L. Lewis did not bat.

Bowling: Angel 10–2–25–1; Karppinen 5–0–27–0; Moody 7–0–34–0; Spencer 9.5–0–43–4; Julian 5–0–29–1; Harvey 6–0–31–1; Hogg 6–1–25–2.

Umpires: B. Bennett and K. J. Rinaldi.

At Melbourne Cricket Ground, Melbourne, January 16, 2001. WESTERN AUSTRALIA defeated VICTORIA by seven wickets.

WESTERN AUSTRALIA v NEW SOUTH WALES

At WACA Ground, Perth, January 19, 2001. Western Australia won by 72 runs. Toss: Western Australia. Western Australia 5 pts.

Murray Goodwin, back in the Western Australian side after a stint with Zimbabwe, went on the rampage. His dazzling 167 off 137 balls was highest individual score in the 32-year history of the domestic limited-overs competition, beating Rick McCosker's 164 in 1981-82. The home side's total of five for 325 equalled the highest in the competition, South Australia's six for 325 in 1986-87. For good measure, Ryan Campbell took five catches and made one stumping to set a new mark for wicket-keepers. The partnership of 257 off 38.1 overs between Goodwin and Mike Hussey was the highest for the third wicket in the competition and the second-highest for any wicket. The run-out of opener Brad Haddin for 58 effectively ended New South Wales' prospects.

Man of the Match: M. W. Goodwin. *Attendance:* 7,661.

Western Australia

†R. J. Campbell c Clarke b Cook	13	(13)
J. L. Langer c Mail b Cook	20	(34)
M. W. Goodwin c Lee b Clark	167	(138)
M. E. Hussey c and b Higgs	94	(104)
B. P. Julian c Clarke b Higgs	1	(2)
*T. M. Moody not out	14	(7)

M. J. North not out	3	(2)
L-b 2, w 11	13	
	—	
(50 overs, 218 mins) (5 wkts)	325	
Fall: 22 44 301 303 310		

D. J. Spencer, G. B. Hogg, D. J. Wates, K. M. Harvey and J. Angel did not bat.

Bowling: Clark 9–1–47–1; Cook 10–1–72–2; Bradstreet 10–1–50–0; Lee 9–0–48–0; MacGill 7–0–62–0; Higgs 5–0–44–2.

New South Wales

B. J. Haddin run out (North)	58	(54)
M. A. Higgs c Campbell b Angel	24	(20)
M. J. Slater c Campbell b Wates	19	(40)
*S. Lee c North b Spencer	14	(26)
G. C. Rummans c Campbell b Moody	21	(38)
M. J. Clarke c Campbell b Spencer	4	(5)
P. A. Jaques st Campbell b Hogg	40	(41)
S. D. Bradstreet c and b Hogg	33	(35)

†G. J. Mail c Langer b Spencer	10	(11)
S. C. G. MacGill not out	6	(11)
S. R. Clark c Campbell b Spencer	0	(3)
L-b 14, w 8, n-b 2	24	
	—	
(47 overs, 187 mins)	253	
Fall: 49 100 111 149 161 165 237		
238 253 253		

S. H. Cook did not bat.

Bowling: Wates 10–1–45–1; Angel 7–0–51–1; Julian 6–0–27–0; Moody 7–1–22–1; Spencer 8–0–35–4; Hogg 6–0–37–2; Harvey 3–0–22–0.

Umpires: A.R. Craig and R.J.U. Woolridge.

WESTERN AUSTRALIA v TASMANIA

At WACA Ground, Perth, January 26, 2001. Western Australia won by 64 runs. Toss: Tasmania. Western Australia 5 pts.

Surprisingly, Jamie Cox sent the home side in on an easy-paced pitch, and Western Australia were no wicket for 44 after six overs. Most of the batsmen made worthwhile contributions, with Murray Goodwin and Mike Hussey again showing the way in a fourth-wicket partnership of 107. Scott Kremerskothen cashed in on some late big hitting to take three wickets, but the persistent David Saker was Tasmania's best bowler. The contest was virtually over when Darren Wates and Jo Angel reduced Tasmania to four for 13, and Ryan Campbell snapped up six catches behind the stumps as Western Australia cruised to victory.

Man of the Match: M.W. Goodwin. *Attendance:* 4,788.

Western Australia

†R.J. Campbell c Clingeleffer b Young	28	(26)	B.P. Julian b Kremerskothen	22	(14)
J.L. Langer c Clingeleffer b Marquet	26	(71)	G.B. Hogg not out	4	(5)
S.M. Katich c Clingeleffer b Marquet	32	(42)	K.M. Harvey not out	2	(2)
M.W. Goodwin st Clingeleffer b Marsh	71	(68)	B 4, l-b 2, w 13, n-b 3	22	
M.E. Hussey c Marsh b Kremerskothen	53	(64)			
*T.M. Moody c Young			(50 overs, 208 mins) (7 wkts)	270	
b Kremerskothen	10	(11)	Fall: 50 90 108 215 235 253 267		

D.J. Wates, D.J. Spencer and J. Angel did not bat.

Bowling: Saker 10–1–35–0; Wright 7–0–55–0; Young 10–0–41–1; Marquet 10–0–46–2; Watson 5–0–33–0; Marsh 4–0–21–1; Kremerskothen 4–0–33–3.

Tasmania

*J. Cox c Campbell b Wates	4	(13)	†S.G. Clingeleffer c Campbell b Julian	0	(3)
M.J. Di Venuto c Campbell b Wates	1	(5)	D.J. Saker c Spencer b Hogg	26	(24)
S. Young c Campbell b Angel	7	(10)	D.G. Wright not out	5	(8)
D.J. Marsh c Campbell b Angel	0	(4)			
S.R. Watson b Julian	25	(45)	L-b 3, w 6, n-b 5	14	
D.F. Hills c Langer b Moody	42	(62)			
G.T. Cunningham c Campbell b Hogg	68	(46)	(38.4 overs, 159 mins)	206	
S.P. Kremerskothen run out (Hussey)	14	(16)	Fall: 6 13 13 13 83 99 122 122 189 206		

J.P. Marquet did not bat.

Bowling: Wates 10–2–21–2; Angel 7–2–23–2; Spencer 5–0–45–0; Julian 7–0–50–2; Moody 5–0–20–1; Hogg 4.4–0–44–2.

Umpires: I.H. Lock and R.J.U. Woolridge.

At North Sydney Oval, North Sydney, February 4, 2001. WESTERN AUSTRALIA lost to NEW SOUTH WALES by 60 runs.

At Brisbane Cricket Ground, Brisbane, February 16, 2001. WESTERN AUSTRALIA lost to QUEENSLAND by 65 runs.

FINAL

At WACA Ground, Perth, February 25, 2001. WESTERN AUSTRALIA lost to NEW SOUTH WALES by six wickets. For details see section on Mercantile Mutual Cup, 2000-01, page 451.

RECORDS

Highest score for:	167	M. W. Goodwin v New South Wales at Perth	2000-01
Highest score against:	140*	P. C. Nobes (South Australia) at Perth	1994-95
Best bowling for:	5/15	D. L. Boyd v Victoria at Perth	1982-83
Best bowling against:	5/23	R. J. McCurdy (South Australia) at Adelaide	1984-85
Highest total for:	5-325	v New South Wales at Perth	2000-01
Highest total against:	8-306	by Queensland at Brisbane	2000-01
Lowest total for:	59	v Victoria at Melbourne	1969-70
Lowest total against:	62	by Queensland at Perth	1976-77

MOST RUNS

	M	I	NO	R	HS	100s	50s	Avge	S-R
T. M. Moody	75	71	12	2,004	102*	2	14	33.97	72.22
J. L. Langer	55	53	5	1,866	146	1	16	38.88	65.61
D. R. Martyn	48	45	7	1,655	140	2	12	43.55	75.71
G. R. Marsh	38	37	7	1,596	110	3	12	53.20	62.30
M. E. Hussey	35	32	3	1,098	100*	1	9	37.86	76.04
M. R. J. Veletta	42	39	8	1,077	105*	1	8	34.74	62.18
S. M. Katich	28	27	3	885	116	1	7	36.88	75.32
A. C. Gilchrist	30	27	3	855	115	1	6	35.63	85.67
R. J. Campbell	42	41	0	852	108	1	5	20.78	82.56
G. M. Wood	42	38	3	851	108*	1	4	24.31	57.46

HIGHEST PARTNERSHIP FOR EACH WICKET

171	for 1st	G. R. Marsh and M. W. McPhee, v Queensland at Perth	1990-91
188*	for 2nd	J. L. Langer and D. R. Martyn, v Victoria at Melbourne	1997-98
257	for 3rd	M. W. Goodwin and M. E. Hussey, v New South Wales at Perth	2000-01
110	for 4th	G. R. Marsh and M. R. J. Veletta, v New South Wales at Perth	1990-91
129	for 5th	J. L. Langer and W. S. Andrews, v Queensland at Brisbane	1992-93
173	for 6th	M. E. Hussey and G. B. Hogg, v Victoria at Melbourne	1999-00
111*	for 7th	R. W. Marsh and B. Yardley, v New South Wales at Sydney	1973-74
106*	for 8th	A. C. Gilchrist and B. P. Julian, v New South Wales at Sydney	1995-96
57	for 9th	D. R. Martyn and B. P. Julian, v Queensland at Brisbane	1997-98
36	for 10th	K. H. MacLeay and P. M. Clough, v New South Wales at Perth	1984-85

MOST WICKETS

	M	Balls	Mdns	R	W	BB	5W/i	Avge
T. M. Moody	75	3,205	41	2,131	70	4/30	0	30.40
B. P. Julian	54	2,318	19	1,779	59	4/41	0	30.15
J. Angel	53	2,634	42	1,721	59	3/37	0	29.17
K. M. Harvey	40	1,694	16	1,370	55	4/8	0	24.91
K. H. MacLeay	38	1,896	32	1,165	53	5/30	1	21.98
D. K. Lillee	26	1,505	32	766	48	4/21	0	15.96
T. M. Alderman	35	1,938	34	1,169	40	4/14	0	29.23
J. Stewart	32	1,564	9	1,243	36	4/34	0	31.03
M. P. Atkinson	27	1,325	11	984	34	4/38	0	28.94
B. A. Reid	23	1214	19	724	28	4/40	0	25.86

MOST DISMISSALS

	M	Ct	St	Total
A.C. Gilchrist	30	51	5	56
R.W. Marsh	33	51	1	52
R.J. Campbell	22	43	5	48
T.J. Zoehrer	35	40	4	44
K.J. Wright	10	8	1	9

MOST CATCHES

G.B. Hogg .... 25 in 44 matches	G.R. Marsh .... 19 in 38 matches
T.M. Moody .... 25 in 77 matches	M.R.J. Veletta ...... 19 in 42 matches
J.L. Langer .... 20 in 55 matches	M.E. Hussey .... 18 in 35 matches

MOST APPEARANCES

75	T.M. Moody ...... 1985-86 – 2000-01	44	G.B. Hogg .... 1993-94 – 2000-01
55	J.L. Langer .... 1991-92 – 2000-01	42	M.R.J. Veletta .... 1983-84 – 1994-95
54	B.J. Julian .... 1991-92 – 2000-01	42	G.M. Wood ...... 1977-78 – 1991-92
53	J. Angel .... 1992-93 – 1998-99	42	R.J. Campbell .... 1992-93 – 2000-01
48	D.R. Martyn ...... 1991-92 – 2000-01	40	K.M. Harvey ..... 1994-95 – 2000-01

MINOR CRICKET IN AUSTRALIA, 2000-01

By KEN PIESSE

Australia's Young Cricketer of the Year, Ashes squad member Nathan Bracken, rocketed from obscurity to the front line in 2000-01. The finely built fast bowler from the Blue Mountains township of Springwood began with dozens of hopefuls in the ACB Cup for Second Eleven and Colts prospects, returning the extremely modest match figures of 1/109 and making a fourth-ball duck for the New South Wales Second XI against Western Australian Second XI in Perth in October. So rapid was his improvement afterwards, however, that he was selected for Australia's one-day team, having played just ten first-class games in three fragmented seasons with New South Wales.

Western Australia won the overall competition, with Queensland second, Victoria third, New South Wales fourth, Tasmania fifth, Australian Capital Territory sixth, Australian Cricket Academy seventh and South Australia eighth. The second season of the restructured, extended competition again allowed state selectors to look at emerging players in four-day preludes to the real thing. A number of Pura Cup players also used the competition for extra match practice. At various times of the summer, back-to-back champions Queensland played five of their title-winning team in their Second Eleven: fast bowlers Joe Dawes and Ashley Noffke and batsmen Brendan Nash, Clinton Perren and Jerry Cassell.

In March, South Australia named three first-class newcomers, Luke Williams, Cameron Borgas and Ben Higgins, direct from the ACB Cup. Williams, a 21-year-old right-hander, shared one of the highest partnerships of the minor summer, 302 for the second wicket at four an over, while representing the Academy against South Australian Second XI at Adelaide Oval. On the fourth day of the game, Williams (201 not out) and Wollongong's Phil Jaques (135) carried the Academy score from one for 37 to 308 before Jaques was caught. Williams batted for 427 minutes and hit 22 fours. Just one week earlier, Jaques, 21, had also shared a double-century stand with the West Indian Ramnaresh Sarwan in a one-day game for the Academy against Tasmania. He made his first-class debut, as an eleventh-hour inclusion, in New South Wales' final Pura Cup game of the season in Brisbane, after being part of the state squad that played two games against Wellington in New Zealand in November.

Seventeen-year-old Borgas played more cricket in one season than most do in two, playing for his state at Under-17s, Under-19s, Second Eleven and first-class levels all in the space of three months. South Australia's coach Greg Chappell says that although the talented youngster has much to learn with both his batting and fielding, "At least he has had a taste of it now and knows what he must do to improve." Higgins, an experienced left-handed batsman, captained the South Australian Second XI in several Cup matches and after a fine double of 46 and 177 against the Tasmanian Second XI in Adelaide was also rewarded with senior team selection. Left-arm pace man

Mark Harrity claimed ten wickets for 163 in the same match. A former Australian youth representative, Harrity also took 6/31 and 2/18 against a Queensland Academy of Sport team in Adelaide.

Two more 17-year-olds, Victoria's Cameron White and Western Australia's Shaun Marsh, also used the Cup as a stepping stone into first-class ranks. White took 5/55 from 15 overs against an Australian Capital Territory team that included Rod Tucker at Richmond and soon afterwards was named for Victoria against New South Wales and took four wickets on debut. Marsh scored 112 from 167 balls for the Western Australian Second XI against the Tasmanian Second XI in Perth to earn his promotion. Tasmania's promising 18-year-old all-rounder Shane Watson had begun the season in Brisbane with the Redlands Tigers and represented the Queensland Colts in several matches, including the annual Syd Gregory Cup contest with the New South Wales Colts. Originally from Ipswich Grammar, the same school as Craig McDermott, he was also a front-line player for the Academy.

AUSTRALIAN CRICKET BOARD CUP, 2000-01

2000-01 POINTS TABLE

	Played	WO	WI	D	LI	LO	T	Points	Quotient
Western Australia Second XI . .	5	4	0	0	0	1	0	36.4	1.283
Queensland Academy of Sport .	5	3	0	1	1	0	0	25.2	1.611
Victoria Second XI	4	2	1	0	0	1	0	24.5	1.208
New South Wales Second XI . .	4	2	0	2	0	0	0	21.0	1.361
Tasmania Second XI	5	2	0	0	0	3	0	16.8	0.932
AIS Cricket Academy	7	1	1	1	0	4	0	12.0	0.819
Australian Capital Territory. . .	4	1	0	0	0	3	0	10.5	0.663
South Australia Second XI	4	0	0	0	1	3	0	3.5	0.703

Quotient = runs per wicket scored divided by runs per wicket conceded.

Western Australia obtained 1st innings points but lost outright to New South Wales in Perth.

Points are determined by multiplying game points by 7 then dividing by the number of games to be played by each team. Allotted games for each team: 7 – ACA, 5 – Qld, Tas, WA, 4 – ACT, NSW, SA, Vic.

AUSTRALIAN CRICKET BOARD CUP AVERAGES, 2000-01

BATTING

(Qualification: 200 runs)

	M	I	NO	R	HS	100s	50s	Avge
L. W. Kahler (Qld)	2	4	1	252	137*	2	0	84.00
A. J. Sainsbury (NSW)	3	5	2	218	196*	1	0	72.67
S. P. Dart (Vict)	3	5	1	264	90*	0	4	66.00
L. Williams (ACA/SAust)	7	11	2	585	201*	3	2	65.00
B. P. Nash (Qld)	4	7	3	250	98	0	2	62.50
S. E. Marsh (WAust)	4	6	1	309	112	1	2	61.80
M. J. North (WAust)	3	6	1	279	101	1	1	55.80
B. H. Higgins (SAust)	4	7	0	352	177	1	1	50.29
C. J. L. Rogers (WAust)	5	9	1	382	84	0	4	47.75
C. Brown (ACT)	4	8	0	377	128	1	3	47.13

BOWLING

(Qualification: 10 wickets)

	M	O	Mdns	R	W	BB	5Wi	10Wm	Avge
M. A. Harrity (SAust)....	2	77	18	212	18	6/31	2	1	11.78
J. Moss (Vic)	2	72.1	26	172	13	6/35	1	0	13.23
S. J. O'Leary (Qld)	2	82	24	183	12	5/68	1	0	15.25
B. S. Targett (Tas)	3	78	23	223	13	5/3	1	0	17.15
P. C. Rofe (SAust/ACA) .	6	194.5	39	522	30	6/63	1	1	17.40
M. J. Petrie (Qld/ACA) ..	4	114	33	285	16	3/33	0	0	17.81
S. R. Cary (WAust)......	2	75.1	19	214	12	5/53	1	0	17.83
E. Kellar (ACT)	4	157.2	46	387	21	6/41	2	1	18.43
S. Nikitaras (WAust)	2	70.5	17	190	10	5/23	1	0	19.00
J. J. Taylor (Vic)	2	55.3	8	203	10	4/32	0	0	20.30

Note: All games played in this competition were not first-class.

TASMANIA SECOND XI v VICTORIA SECOND XI

At New Town Oval, October 30, 31, November 1, 2, 2000. Tasmania Second XI won by 168 runs. Toss: Victoria Second XI.

Tasmania Second XI

J. P. Miller c Roach b Lewis	8	– b Taylor	8
C. W. G. Bassano c Roach b Lewis	5	– b Street	0
*†M. N. Atkinson lbw b Oliver	19	– c Roach b Lewis	2
S. P. Kremerskothen c Harper b Street	4	– b Taylor	12
G. T. Cunningham b Street	0	– lbw b Street	19
B. J. Thomas c Roach b Taylor	14	– c and b Taylor	68
J. G. J. Selby not out	40	– lbw b Oliver	15
S. B. Tubb b Taylor	1	– c McDonald b Lewis	34
B. S. Targett c Harper b Street	12	– b Lewis	9
G. J. Denton b Oliver	15	– b Taylor	2
B. Geeves b Lewis	1		
X. J. Doherty (did not bat)		– not out	1
B 1, l-b 4, w 3, n-b 12	20	B 4, l-b 6, n-b 2	12

(46.1 overs, 229 mins)	139	(53 overs, 210 mins)	182

Fall: 15 16 21 21 48 62 70 103 130 139   Fall: 0 5 24 25 66 91 163 179 179 182

Bowling: *First Innings*—Lewis 9.1–3–22–3; Street 13–2–35–3; Taylor 9–3–30–2; Oliver 10–3–21–2; McDonald 3–0–20–0; Davison 2–0–6–0. *Second Innings*—Lewis 11–1–42–3; Street 11–4–14–2; Taylor 11–1–32–4; Oliver 5–1–21–1; Smart 6–1–24–0; Davison 4–0–14–0; McDonald 5–1–25–0.

Victoria Second XI

P. Q. Harper run out (Kremerskothen)	34	–	(2) b Kremerskothen	12
T. P. Gloury c Tubb b Thomas	6	–	(1) b Targett	0
A. J. Kent b Thomas	0	–	c Cunningham b Targett	0
C. J. Peake lbw b Kremerskothen	0	–	c Atkinson b Targett	3
B. C. Oliver c Atkinson b Kremerskothen	4	–	lbw b Targett	2
C. M. Smart lbw b Kremerskothen	6	–	lbw b Targett	0
A. B. McDonald lbw b Targett	13	–	lbw b Kremerskothen	1
*†P. J. Roach c Doherty b Denton	15	–	b Geeves	3
M. L. Lewis b Targett	0			
J. J. Taylor c Kremerskothen b Geeves	9	–	b Denton	14
J. M. Davison not out	0	–	(9) lbw b Geeves	1
C. B. D. Street (did not bat)		–	not out	0
B 2, l-b 11, w 7, n-b 4	24		L-b 6	6

(51 overs, 202 mins)	111	(20.3 overs, 86 mins)	42
Fall: 36 42 44 50 60 77 92 92 111 111		Fall: 0 0 12 22 22 22 24 25 42 42	

Bowling: First Innings—Denton 12–2–23–1; Geeves 9–2–24–1; Thomas 7–1–11–2; Targett 12–4–19–2; Kremerskothen 10–3–18–3; Doherty 1–0–3–0. *Second Innings*—Targett 7–4–3–5; Thomas 4–1–16–0; Kremerskothen 4–2–4–2; Geeves 3.3–0–11–2; Denton 2–1–2–1.

Umpires: B. W. Jackman and K. J. Jones.

SOUTH AUSTRALIA SECOND XI v QUEENSLAND ACADEMY OF SPORT

At Adelaide Oval, November 6, 7, 8, 9, 2000. Queensland Academy of Sport won by seven wickets. Toss: South Australia Second XI.

South Australia Second XI

†D. A. Reeves c Petrie b Creevey	33	–	(9) lbw b Pascoe	25
L. Williams c Turner b Petrie	5	–	c Foley b Petrie	8
*C. J. Davies lbw b Creevey	9	–	st Fitness b O'Leary	11
B. H. Higgins b Petrie	8	–	(5) c Betts b Turner	6
M. J. Smith c Cassell b O'Leary	58	–	(6) c Fitness b Turner	20
M. C. Miller c Fitness b Pascoe	3	–	(7) st Fitness b O'Leary	21
B. P. Cameron c Nash b Petrie	9	–	(8) c Nash b O'Leary	1
A. M. Smith c Foley b Pascoe	5	–	(1) c Betts b Turner	45
R. J. Harris c Betts b O'Leary	10	–	(4) lbw b Turner	9
R. W. Bulger lbw b O'Leary	6	–	(11) not out	0
P. C. Rofe not out	2	–	(10) run out (Nash/Fitness)	0
L-b 8, n-b 2	10		L-b 3	3

(71.3 overs, 264 mins)	158	(83.3 overs, 286 mins)	149
Fall: 34 49 57 63 79 91 106		Fall: 13 46 67 81 88 103 104	
129 135 158		149 149 149	

M. A. Harrity did not bat.

Bowling: First Innings—Creevey 18–10–34–2; Pascoe 18–7–40–2; Petrie 16–6–33–3; O'Leary 9.3–4–16–3; Hopes 5–1–11–0; Turner 5–1–16–0. *Second Innings*—Creevey 4–0–5–0; Pascoe 10–6–13–1; Petrie 10–4–19–1; O'Leary 35.3–11–61–3; Turner 24–8–48–4.

Queensland Academy of Sport

D. M. Betts lbw b Harrity	0	– c Reeves b Rofe	8
J. L. Cassell c Reeves b Harrity	46	– lbw b Harrity	7
M. R. Hayward c Harris b Harrity	2		
*G. I. Foley b Harrity	58	– (3) c Reeves b Harrity	0
B. P. Nash c A. M. Smith b Harris	98	– (4) not out	8
J. R. Hopes c Reeves b Harrity	0	– (5) not out	1
†G. A. J. Fitness c Reeves b Harrity	2		
D. A. Turner b Miller	12		
B. N. Creevey c M. J. Smith b Rofe	34		
M. D. Pascoe lbw b A. M. Smith	0		
S. J. O'Leary not out	10		
B 2, l-b 12, w 1, n-b 5	20	B 2	2

(87.5 overs, 352 mins)	**282**	(5.4 overs, 27 mins) (3 wkts) **26**
Fall: 1 17 81 170 170 176 225 242 245 282		Fall: 17 17 25

M. J. Petrie did not bat.

Bowling: *First Innings*—Harrity 21–9–31–6; Rofe 12.5–4–38–1; Harris 17–3–66–1; Miller 13–3–48–1; Bulger 15–3–58–0; M. J. Smith 2–0–9–0; A. M. Smith 7–1–18–1. *Second Innings*—Harrity 3–0–18–2; Rofe 2.4–1–6–1.

Umpires: K. D. Perrin and P. J. Weeks.

NEW SOUTH WALES SECOND XI v AIS CRICKET ACADEMY

At Bradman Oval, Bowral, November 13, 2000. Drawn. Toss: New South Wales Second XI.

New South Wales Second XI

B. P. Van Deinsen not out	121	N-b 4	4
†G. J. Mail c Stanton b Rofe	57		
A. J. Sainsbury c Hartley b Rofe	9		
M. A. Higgs run out	21	(56.2 overs, 224 mins) (3 wkts) **214**
M. J. Phelps not out	2	Fall: 131 163 209

R. J. Brewster, M. G. Betsey, G. C. Rummans, *S. D. Bradstreet, J. M. Heath, A. M. Clark and S. H. Cook did not bat.

Bowling: Rofe 19–5–71–2; Griffith 6–1–32–0; O'Brien 9–1–36–0; Watson 9.2–5–19–0; McDonald 3–0–23–0; Hauritz 10–2–33–0.

AIS Cricket Academy

M. J. Clarke, †C. D. Hartley, N. M. Hauritz, P. A. Jaques, A. B. McDonald, A. W. O'Brien, S. D. Stanton, *S. R. Watson, L. Williams, P. C. Rofe, A. R. Griffith, A. J. Kent.

Umpires: J. Evans and P. Hughes.

SOUTH AUSTRALIA SECOND XI v TASMANIA SECOND XI

At Adelaide Oval, November 13, 14, 15, 16, 2000. Tasmania Second XI won by four wickets. Toss: Tasmania Second XI.

South Australia Second XI

A. M. Smith b Denton	7	– c and b Denton	4
T. K. Koch c Tubb b Thomas	7	– c and b Colegrave	43
*B. H. Higgins lbw b Colegrave	46	– lbw b Denton	177
M. C. Miller lbw b Colegrave	12	– c Colegrave b Denton	15
M. J. Smith c Atkinson b Targett	15	– lbw b Selby	46
B. P. Cameron lbw b Targett	15	– lbw b Selby	1
†D. A. Reeves c Targett b Thomas	23	– st Atkinson b Selby	0
R. J. Harris c Dykes b Thomas	26		
D. A. Ross lbw b Doherty	5	– (8) st Atkinson b Selby	0
M. A. Harrity lbw b Tubb	6	– c Dykes b Colegrave	27
S. M. Maraun not out	20	– (9) b Denton	7
R. W. Bulger (did not bat)		– not out	10
B 8, l-b 15, w 3, n-b 5	31	B 1, l-b 9, n-b 5	15

(88.2 overs, 326 mins)	213	(101.3 overs, 395 mins)	345

Fall: 15 32 63 107 121 132 177 187 187 213

Fall: 5 116 147 231 237 237 237 248 319 345

Bowling: *First Innings*—Denton 19–5–49–1; Colegrave 22–8–42–2; Targett 13–4–26–2; Tubb 5.2–1–8–1; Thomas 15–3–35–3; Doherty 14–5–30–1. *Second Innings*—Denton 18–2–70–4; Colegrave 22.3–6–58–2; Dykes 3–0–7–0; Targett 14–3–55–0; Thomas 2–0–11–0; Tubb 17–2–76–0; Doherty 15–6–38–0; Selby 10–5–20–4.

Tasmania Second XI

S. R. Mason c Reeves b Miller	90	– c Koch b Harrity	2
A. J. Daly lbw b Harrity	0	– c Koch b Harrity	91
J. A. Dykes lbw b Harris	33	– c Reeves b Harrity	7
J. P. Miller retired hurt	14		
J. G. J. Selby c Reeves b Bulger	30	– c Reeves b Harrity	15
B. J. Thomas c Cameron b Harrity	56	– (4) c Reeves b Harrity	78
*†M. N. Atkinson c Maraun b M. J. Smith	43	– not out	23
S. B. Tubb c Reeves b Harrity	0	– (6) c A. M. Smith b Harrity	4
B. S. Targett lbw b Harrity	8	– (8) not out	7
M. D. Colegrave c Cameron b Miller	7		
G. J. Denton not out	12		
B 9, l-b 7, n-b 12	28	B 1, l-b 7, w 1, n-b 3	12

(119.1 overs, 451 mins)	(9 wkts dec) 321	(68.2 overs, 290 mins)	(6 wkts) 239

Fall: 9 63 178 194 270 274 292 300 321

Fall: 5 13 189 190 196 211

X. J. Doherty did not bat.

Bowling: *First Innings*—Harrity 32–6–100–4; Miller 16.1–6–24–2; Maraun 11–3–24–0; Harris 8–2–24–1; M. J. Smith 10–1–32–1; Bulger 27–9–67–1; Ross 13–4–33–0; Smith 2–1–1–0. *Second Innings*—Harrity 21–3–63–6; Miller 9–2–27–0; Maraun 3–1–8–0; Bulger 11.2–0–53–0; M. J. Smith 10–0–45–0; Smith 14–2–35–0.

Umpires: J. S. Booth and L. G. Donsithorpe.

WESTERN AUSTRALIA SECOND XI v TASMANIA SECOND XI

At WACA Ground, Perth, November 20, 21, 22, 23, 2000. Western Australia Second XI won by 28 runs. Toss: Western Australia.

Western Australia Second XI

C.J.L. Rogers c Atkinson b Jurgensen	15	– (2) lbw b Griffith	12
S.W. Meuleman lbw b Jurgensen	1	– (1) c Atkinson b Jurgensen	2
*M.J. North c Atkinson b Geeves	80	– c Pinnington b Selby	101
S.E. Marsh c Atkinson b Griffith	112	– c Pinnington b Selby	27
D.C. Bandy b Doherty	38	– c Pinnington b Jurgensen	15
G.I. Cullen b Tubb	0	– c Atkinson b Polkinghorne	14
K.M. Harvey c Mason b Jurgensen	68	– c Pinnington b Jurgensen	34
†L. Ronchi c Pinnington b Doherty	25	– c Atkinson b Selby	0
S.J. Karppinen run out (Mason)	59	– c Atkinson b Jurgensen	13
A. Gray not out	6	– lbw b Selby	0
M.J. Thistle c Atkinson b Griffith	2		
S.R. Cary (did not bat)		– not out	9
B 1, l-b 4, w 6, n-b 3	14	L-b 1, w 3, n-b 1	5
(115.4 overs, 452 mins)	**420**	**(67.2 overs, 279 mins)**	**232**

Fall: 4 24 176 254 258 262 317 395 413 420

Fall: 11 17 82 111 138 205 209 215 215 232

Bowling: *First Innings*—Griffith 19.4–7–47–2; Jurgensen 30–8–111–3; Geeves 17–0–76–1; Polkinghorne 8–1–32–0; Doherty 27–9–86–2; Tubb 14–3–63–1. *Second Innings*—Jurgensen 24.2–9–57–4; Griffith 10–1–44–1; Polkinghorne 10–0–56–1; Selby 20–3–58–4; Doherty 3–1–16–0.

Tasmania Second XI

S.R. Mason b Cary	77	– c Ronchi b Thistle	6
T.A. Pinnington c Ronchi b Thistle	27	– c North b Cary	87
A.J. Daly c Ronchi b Thistle	0	– lbw b Harvey	51
C.W.G. Bassano c Ronchi b Karppinen	100	– lbw b Harvey	27
J.G.J. Selby b Harvey	27	– c Ronchi b Karppinen	22
S.B. Tubb c Harvey b Thistle	21	– (7) c Ronchi b Cary	43
*†M.N. Atkinson b Harvey	9	– (8) not out	34
A.W. Polkinghorne lbw b Thistle	32	– (6) c Rogers b Karppinen	11
S.J. Jurgensen c Gray b Thistle	2	– run out (Ronchi)	0
A.R. Griffith c Ronchi b Cary	4	– lbw b Cary	0
X.J. Doherty not out	0	– c Ronchi b Karppinen	14
B 1, l-b 4, n-b 7	17	B 2, l-b 6, n-b 5	13
(104.4 overs, 395 mins)	**316**	**(87.5 overs, 342 mins)**	**308**

Fall: 45 49 162 217 246 275 289 309 316 316

Fall: 20 139 159 196 213 213 274 274 274 308

B. Geeves did not bat.

Bowling: *First Innings*—Cary 24–4–77–2; Karppinen 23–3–79–1; Thistle 20.4–5–61–5; Harvey 26–5–62–2; Gray 11–2–27–0. *Second Innings*—Karppinen 24.5–7–82–3; Thistle 15–5–52–1; Cary 21–6–60–3; Harvey 16–5–73–2; Gray 11–0–33–0.

Umpires: A.R. Craig and I.H. Lock.

AUSTRALIAN CAPITAL TERRITORY v NEW SOUTH WALES SECOND XI

At Boomanulla Oval, Canberra, November 27, 28, 29, 30, 2000. New South Wales Second XI won by five wickets. Toss: Australian Capital Territory.

Australian Capital Territory

A.D. McQuire c Clark b Thornely	36	– b Clark	39
C. Brown c Thornely b Betsey	128	– c Sainsbury b Heath	4
D.M. Jeffrey lbw b Thornely	56	– c Betsey b Lambert	9
S.P. Heaney c Williams b Cook	34	– c Pilon b Lambert	22
*R.J. Tucker c Thornely b Heath	44	– b Lambert	31
J.J. Swift c Pilon b Horsley	0	– c Betsey b Cook	1
J. Robson b Heath	21	– c Betsey b Thornely	10
†S.A. Holcombe not out	4	– b Clark	16
M.H. Ramage (did not bat)		– c Sainsbury b Horsley	1
A.C.L. James (did not bat)		– not out	6
E. Kellar (did not bat)		– c Horsley b Lambert	0
B 5, l-b 1, n-b 10	16	B 4, l-b 4, n-b 6	14

(114.1 overs, 380 mins)   (7 wkts dec) 339   (66.1 overs, 285 mins) 153

Fall: 80 203 250 293 298   Fall: 18 52 70 81 103 126 138 139
330 339   152 153

G.L. Miller did not bat.

Bowling: *First Innings*—Cook 22–8–45–1; Heath 15.1–0–61–2; Horsley 15–4–53–1; Thornely 23–8–59–2; Clark 20–3–59–0; Rummans 11–3–37–0; Betsey 7–3–17–1; Sainsbury 1–0–2–0. *Second Innings*—Cook 15.4–4–47–1; Heath 10–5–21–1; Horsley 16–5–19–1; Clark 9–3–29–2; Lambert 11.1–3–27–4; Thornely 5–3–2–1.

New South Wales Second XI

V.M. Williams c McQuire b Ramage	70	– st Holcombe b James	1
R.J. Brewster lbw b James	21	– b Kellar	13
G.M. Lambert lbw b Kellar	26	– (6) not out	23
A.J. Sainsbury not out	196	– (7) not out	1
*G.C. Rummans c Holcombe b Ramage	6	– (3) lbw b James	1
M.G. Betsey st Holcombe b Robson	69		
D.J. Thornely not out	7	– (4) c Holcombe b Kellar	2
†N.S. Pilon (did not bat)		– (5) c Robson b Ramage	39
L-b 13, n-b 4	17	L-b 1, n-b 3	4

(104 overs, 386 mins)   (5 wkts dec) 412   (22.5 overs, 90 mins)   (5 wkts) 84

Fall: 37 81 146 164 385   Fall: 3 9 12 43 79

A.M. Clark, J.M. Heath, S.H. Cook and D.A. Horsley did not bat.

Bowling: *First Innings*—James 20–3–84–1; Miller 16–2–72–0; Kellar 20–7–40–1; Ramage 20–6–72–2; Robson 17–2–68–1; Swift 8–1–51–0; Tucker 3–1–12–0. *Second Innings*—James 6–1–35–2; Kellar 11–3–29–2; Miller 2–0–13–0; Ramage 3.5–2–6–1.

Umpires: J.C. Hannaford and W.F. Ruce.

WESTERN AUSTRALIA SECOND XI v AIS CRICKET ACADEMY

At Richardson Park, Perth, November 27, 28, 29, 30, 2000. Western Australia Second XI won by eight wickets. Toss: Western Australia Second XI.

AIS Cricket Academy

L. Williams c Ronchi b Nikitaras	9	– (2) c Rogers b Wates	58
D. J. Harris c Wates b Nikitaras	0	– (1) c Cullen b Wates	19
P. A. Jaques c Meuleman b Nikitaras	0	– st Ronchi b Gray	110
S. R. Watson c Ronchi b Nikitaras	0	– c Wates b Nikitaras	86
A. J. Kent c Wates b Nikitaras	0	– c Ronchi b Wates	26
A. B. McDonald c Ronchi b Wates	2	– c Cullen b Harvey	31
†S. D. Stanton c Ronchi b Karppinen	40	– c Ronchi b Harvey	5
*A. C. Voges c Rogers b Karppinen	17	– not out	27
N. M. Hauritz c Ronchi b Karppinen	6	– c Ronchi b Karppinen	5
D. R. MacKenzie b Harvey	8	– c Ronchi b Nikitaras	12
A. R. Griffith not out	0	– lbw b Nikitaras	0
L-b 1, n-b 1	2	B 4, l-b 11, n-b 7	22

(33 overs, 124 mins)	84	(135 overs, 516 mins) 401
Fall: 7 7 7 7 10 12		Fall: 64 122 270 302 328 356 357
44 73 82 84		374 401 401

P. C. Rofe did not bat.

Bowling: *First Innings*—Nikitaras 10–3–23–5; Wates 11–4–19–1; Karppinen 7–0–20–3; Harvey 5–0–21–1. *Second Innings*—Nikitaras 26–6–75–3; Karppinen 33–6–122–1; Wates 26–9–71–3; Harvey 26–4–69–2; Gray 24–3–49–1.

Western Australia Second XI

C. J. L. Rogers b McDonald	27	– (2) not out	78
S. W. Meuleman c Stanton b Rofe	21	– (1) c Stanton b Rofe	4
*M. J. North lbw b MacKenzie	18	– (4) not out	39
S. E. Marsh c Watson b MacKenzie	0		
D. C. Bandy c Stanton b McDonald	16		
G. I. Cullen c Voges b Watson	51		
K. M. Harvey c Griffith b Hauritz	70		
D. J. Wates c Voges b Hauritz	37		
S. J. Karppinen b Watson	35		
†L. Ronchi not out	30		
A. Gray c Stanton b Watson	5	– (3) lbw b Griffith	28
L-b 10, n-b 5	15	B 5, l-b 3, n-b 3	11

(94.4 overs, 367 mins)	325	(51.2 overs, 191 mins) (2 wkts) 160
Fall: 39 69 69 69 110 167 248 255 301 325		Fall: 9 102

S. Nikitaras did not bat.

Bowling: *First Innings*—Rofe 22–6–55–1; MacKenzie 17–6–56–2; Griffith 15–1–62–0; McDonald 11–2–45–2; Watson 9.4–5–26–3; Hauritz 17–2–55–2; Voges 3–0–16–0. *Second Innings*—Rofe 11–1–24–1; MacKenzie 7–2–15–0; McDonald 7–2–26–0; Watson 5–0–21–0; Hauritz 11.2–3–31–0; Voges 4–0–10–0; Griffith 6–0–25–1.

Umpires: A. R. Craig and A. Dix.

VICTORIA SECOND XI v AIS CRICKET ACADEMY

At Albert Ground, Melbourne, December 11, 12, 13, 14, 2000. Victoria Second XI won by 99 runs. Toss: Victoria Second XI.

Victoria Second XI

S. A. J. Craig c Stanton b Goldsmith	1	– (2) lbw b Rofe	9
P. Q. Harper c Kent b Rofe	24	– (1) b Rofe	94
D. M. Dempsey c Williams b Rofe	0	– c Stanton b Rofe	8
S. P. Dart lbw b Rofe	52	– c McInnes b Rofe	69
T. P. Gloury b Watson	9	– c Stanton b Rofe	2
R. A. Bartlett c Stanton b Rofe	102	– c Goldsmith b Rofe	18
*†P. J. Roach b Watson	39	– lbw b Watson	28
J. Moss lbw b Watson	12	– c and b McInnes	16
J. J. Taylor c Rofe b Voges	40	– lbw b Watson	6
J. M. Davison c Griffith b Voges	0		
B. J. Jenkinson not out	6	– (10) b Watson	20
B. E. McGain (did not bat)		– not out	0
L-b 13, n-b 4	17	B 2, l-b 5, w 1, n-b 1	9
(81.5 overs, 342 mins)	302	(74.2 overs, 305 mins)	279

Fall: 5 15 30 43 165 224 247
288 289 302

Fall: 23 55 182 185 188 217 250
259 276 279

M. L. Quinn did not bat.

Bowling: *First Innings*—Rofe 22–4–48–4; Goldsmith 14–1–48–1; Watson 14–2–48–3; Griffith 19–5–73–0; McDonald 7–1–35–0; McInnes 4–0–35–0; Voges 1.5–0–2–2. *Second Innings*—Rofe 23–4–63–6; Goldsmith 13–1–44–0; Griffith 3–0–17–0; Watson 17.2–1–68–3; McInnes 15–2–56–1; Voges 3–0–24–0.

AIS Cricket Academy

D. J. Harris b Moss	20	– (2) b Taylor	3
L. Williams run out (Dart/Roach)	5	– (1) c Harper b Jenkinson	12
P. A. Jaques c Dempsey b Taylor	9	– c McGain b Taylor	31
S. R. Watson run out (Bartlett/Moss)	74	– lbw b Jenkinson	9
*A. J. Kent c Bartlett b Jenkinson	5	– c Roach b McGain	76
A. B. McDonald c Taylor b Moss	26	– lbw b Jenkinson	3
†S. D. Stanton lbw b Taylor	72	– lbw b McGain	20
A. C. Voges lbw b Moss	50	– c Craig b Jenkinson	12
M. A. W. Goldsmith c and b Bartlett	16	– lbw b McGain	6
A. R. Griffith c and b Moss	18	– c Moss b Jenkinson	2
M. W. McInnes not out	2	– not out	0
B 1, l-b 7, n-b 2	10	L-b 1	1
(110.3 overs, 425 mins)	307	(53.2 overs, 216 mins)	175

Fall: 12 28 48 57 138 146 232 261
301 307

Fall: 14 28 42 60 71 124 155 166
175 175

P. C. Rofe did not bat.

Bowling: *First Innings*—Jenkinson 23–7–46–1; Taylor 24.3–4–81–2; Moss 29–8–70–4; Davison 15–3–31–0; Bartlett 6–1–29–1; McGain 6–1–15–0; Dart 6–1–27–0; Craig 1–1–0–0. *Second Innings*—Jenkinson 17–5–49–5; Taylor 11–0–60–2; Moss 9–4–27–0; Quinn 9–2–18–0; McGain 7.2–2–20–3.

Umpires: A. Barrow and J. Ward.

TASMANIA SECOND XI v AIS CRICKET ACADEMY

At TCA Ground, Hobart, December 18, 19, 20, 21, 2000. AIS Cricket Academy won by seven wickets. Toss: Tasmania Second XI.

Tasmania Second XI

A. J. Daly c Jaques b Rofe	17	– lbw b Rofe	9
M. R. Nutting run out (Williams)	6	– lbw b Rofe	16
G. T. Cunningham c Stanton b O'Brien	33	– c Voges b Watson	24
C. W. G. Bassano lbw b Rofe	4	– c Hartley b Watson	16
A. W. Polkinghorne c Hartley b Watson	75	– lbw b O'Brien	0
*†M. N. Atkinson c Stanton b Rofe	8	– (7) b Griffith	75
J. G. J. Selby b Griffith	13	– (6) c Kent b Watson	15
S. J. Jurgensen lbw b Rofe	23	– b Watson	21
S. B. Tubb lbw b Watson	21	– (10) not out	18
M. D. Colegrave lbw b Watson	5	– (11) lbw b Watson	8
L. B. O'Shea not out	2		
A. G. Downton (did not bat)	–	(9) run out (Williams)	2
L-b 11, w 2, n-b 3	16	B 6, l-b 15, n-b 3	24
	—		—
(51.3 overs, 212 mins)	223	(103.5 overs, 379 mins)	228

Fall: 15 57 65 68 84 143 181 197 208 223

Fall: 26 26 66 69 73 94 156 175 212 228

Bowling: *First Innings*—Rofe 16–2–56–4; Watson 17.3–1–81–3; O'Brien 6–0–27–1; Griffith 10–3–31–1; Voges 2–0–17–0. *Second Innings*—Rofe 28–6–67–3; Watson 21.5–8–44–4; Griffith 11–4–20–1; O'Brien 31–9–62–1; Hauritz 12–9–14–0.

AIS Cricket Academy

S. D. Stanton run out (Tubb)	0	– c Polkinghorne b Jurgensen	2
L. Williams lbw b Colegrave	124	– not out	56
D. J. Harris c Cunningham b Colegrave	14	– lbw b Tubb	6
P. A. Jaques c Tubb b Jurgensen	6	– c Polkinghorne b Tubb	8
A. J. Kent c Cunningham b Jurgensen	0	– not out	15
*S. R. Watson lbw b Selby	44		
A. W. O'Brien c Atkinson b Jurgensen	19		
A. C. Voges c Selby b Jurgensen	59		
†C. D. Hartley c Downton b Polkinghorne	28		
A. R. Griffith c Tubb b Downton	33		
P. C. Rofe not out	0		
B 5, l-b 4, w 2, n-b 20	31	B 2, l-b 4, n-b 1	7
	—		—
(123.4 overs, 459 mins)	358	(35.1 overs, 128 mins) (3 wkts)	94

Fall: 0 43 57 57 147 202 244 312 339 358

Fall: 11 32 46

N. M. Hauritz did not bat.

Bowling: *First Innings*—Colegrave 35–11–103–2; Jurgensen 30–5–81–4; Selby 14–6–24–1; O'Shea 12–3–27–0; Tubb 15–4–43–0; Polkinghorne 8–0–37–1; Downton 9.4–0–34–1. *Second Innings*—Downton 7–4–10–0; Colegrave 5–1–10–0; Jurgensen 5–0–13–1; O'Shea 7–3–5–0; Polkinghorne 3–1–8–0; Tubb 7.1–1–38–2; Selby 1–0–4–0.

Umpires: B. W. Jackman and P. V. Mulcahy.

WESTERN AUSTRALIA SECOND XI v SOUTH AUSTRALIA SECOND XI

At Cresswell Park, Perth, January 8, 9, 10, 11, 2001. Western Australia Second XI won by 74. Toss: Western Australia Second XI.

Western Australia Second XI

C. J. L. Rogers c Reeves b Rofe	59	– (2) c and b Maraun	84
S. W. Meuleman c Reeves b M. J. Smith	41	– (1) c Davies b Thomas	94
D. C. Bandy lbw b Rofe	6	– c Koch b M. J. Smith	28
*M. G. Dighton c Higgins b Harden	33	– c Higgins b Rofe	1
G. I. Cullen c and b Maraun	26	– c Reeves b Rofe	10
D. J. Wates b M. J. Smith	43	– lbw b Rofe	0
P. C. Worthington c Rofe b Maraun	3	– c Koch b Crook	8
D. J. Spencer c Thomas b Rofe	8	– c Harden b Crook	53
G. A. Wates b M. J. Smith	4	– lbw b Harris	1
B. Casson lbw b M. J. Smith	1	– c Reeves b Rofe	19
†L. Ronchi not out	0	– not out	11
L-b 6, n-b 6	12	B 4, l-b 9, n-b 12	25

(79.2 overs, 304 mins)   236   (100.2 overs, 380 mins)   334
Fall: 89 107 119 162 173 189 201   Fall: 155 211 214 226 230 230 265
    234 235 236   266 316 334

B. J. Oldroyd did not bat.

Bowling: *First Innings*—Harden 15–4–39–1; Rofe 19–1–50–3; Crook 19–4–69–0; Maraun 8–0–39–2; M. J. Smith 13.2–5–29–4; A. M. Smith 5–1–4–0. *Second Innings*—Rofe 19.2–5–44–4; Harden 9–1–29–0; A. M. Smith 7–2–12–0; M. J. Smith 15–4–53–1; Harris 12–2–40–1; Crook 16–2–64–2; Thomas 9–1–34–1; Maraun 13–1–45–1.

South Australia Second XI

T. K. Koch c Cullen b D. J. Wates	10	– c Bandy b Worthington	21
W. D. Thomas c Cullen b Oldroyd	17	– c Bandy b D. J. Wates	2
C. J. Davies c Bandy b Worthington	74	– c D. J. Wates b Oldroyd	52
*B. H. Higgins c Dighton b Oldroyd	0	– c Ronchi b Casson	45
A. M. Smith c Ronchi b Worthington	55	– b Casson	11
M. J. Smith lbw b Bandy	8	– c Ronchi b Oldroyd	43
†D. A. Reeves lbw b D. J. Wates	28	– st Ronchi b Casson	11
R. J. Harris lbw b D. J. Wates	57	– c Ronchi b Oldroyd	8
A. R. Crook c Dighton b D. J. Wates	0	– lbw b Casson	1
S. M. Maraun c Bandy b Worthington	10	– (11) c Worthington b Oldroyd	19
P. C. Rofe not out	0	– (10) not out	3
L-b 7, w 1, n-b 7	15	B 1, l-b 3, w 1, n-b 1	6

(107.1 overs, 378 mins)   274   (90.3 overs, 312 mins)   222
Fall: 21 54 54 163 174 178 216   Fall: 4 39 104 121 141 171 193
    216 274 274   200 200 222

M. J. Harden did not bat.

Bowling: *First Innings*—Spencer 19–4–52–0; D. J. Wates 30–13–64–4; Oldroyd 19–5–57–2; Worthington 24.1–2–79–3; Bandy 7–4–6–1; Casson 8–2–9–0. *Second Innings*—Spencer 12–3–24–0; D. J. Wates 10–3–14–1; Worthington 12–5–28–1; Oldroyd 27.3–6–68–4; Casson 28–7–76–4; Bandy 1–0–8–0.

Umpires: A. R. Dix and I. H. Lock.

QUEENSLAND ACADEMY OF SPORT v VICTORIA SECOND XI

At Allan Border Field, Albion, January 29, 30, 31, February 1 (no play), 2001. Drawn.
Toss: Queensland Academy of Sport.

Queensland Academy of Sport

D. M. Betts b Hewett	1	– b Lewis	19
B. P. Nash c P. Q. Harper b Moss	13	– c Hewett b Moss	29
L. A. Carseldine lbw b Moss	17	– c L. D. Harper b Moss	33
*C. T. Perren run out (Lewis)	13	– not out	80
L. W. Kahler c Roach b Moss	4	– lbw b Moss	5
J. R. Hopes c Dart b Moss	69	– (7) not out	4
†C. D. Hartley c L. D. Harper b Hewett	0		
N. M. Hauritz c L. D. Harper b Hewett	0	– (6) lbw Hewett	23
A. A. Noffke c White b Moss	13		
J. H. Dawes c Davison b Moss	21		
M. A. Anderson not out	4		
L-b 2, n-b 5	7	B 5, l-b 3, n-b 8	16

(60.1 overs, 219 mins)	162	(78 overs, 295 mins) (5 wkts)	209

Fall: 1 25 44 48 58 68 69 133 138 162

Fall: 50 62 139 145 196

M. J. Petrie did not bat.

Bowling: *First Innings*—Lewis 14–4–38–0; Hewett 13–5–38–3; Moss 15.1–4–35–6; Davison 8–1–22–0; White 10–3–27–0. *Second Innings*—Lewis 17–4–49–1; Hewett 19–3–50–1; Moss 19–10–40–3; Davison 13–3–40–0; White 5–0–11–0; Dart 3–0–9–0; Mott 2–1–2–0.

Victorian Second XI

P. Q. Harper c Perren b Anderson	50	I. S. L. Hewett c Nash b Perren	28
M. P. Mott c Nash b Petrie	78	J. M. Davison c Nash b Petrie	11
*L. D. Harper c Carseldine b Hauritz	0	C. L. White c (sub) Stevens b Noffke	8
S. P. Dart c Anderson b Hauritz	0		
M. Klinger c Dawes b Noffke	58	B 8, l-b 1, w 4, n-b 28	41
C. J. Peake c Perren b Petrie	0		
†P. J. Roach not out	47	(112.1 overs, 422 mins)	321
J. Moss hit wicket b Noffke	0	Fall: 110 115 115 198 198 222 222 283 304 321	

M. L. Lewis did not bat.

Bowling: Dawes 12–2–49–0; Noffke 22.1–4–59–3; Petrie 24–8–69–3; Hopes 6–1–26–0; Hauritz 24–7–54–2; Anderson 21–9–47–1; Perren 3–1–8–1.

Umpires: G. Cubit and N. MacNamara.

WESTERN AUSTRALIA SECOND XI v AUSTRALIAN CAPITAL TERRITORY

At WACA Ground, Perth, February 6, 7, 8, 2001. Western Australia Second XI won by an innings and 1 run. Toss: Western Australia Second XI.

Australian Capital Territory

J. K. Smith c Campbell b Cary	56	– b Nicholson	0
C. Brown c Campbell b Cary	10	– c Dighton b Ellis	63
A. D. McQuire lbw b Williams	40	– c Nicholson b Cary	0
S. P. Heaney c Campbell b Williams	41	– c Marsh b Cary	3
*R. J. Tucker c Marsh b Nicholson	15	– c Ellis b Oldroyd	70
M. J. Dawn c Campbell b Cary	4	– c Campbell b Thistle	4
J. D. Robson c Campbell b Nicholson	1	– c Cullen b Nicholson	19
†S. A. Holcombe run out (Glew)	9	– c Thistle b Oldroyd	7
G. L. Miller c Rogers b Cary	25	– c Thistle b Oldroyd	13
A. C. L. James not out	18	– b Williams	0
E. Kellar c Dighton b Cary	1	– not out	0
L-b 8, n-b 2	10	B 1, l-b 3, w 1	5

(85.1 overs, 323 mins) 230
Fall: 38 100 110 134 141 148 183 187
218 230

(51.5 overs, 210 mins) 184
Fall: 0 6 22 93 98 146 169 177
182 184

D. Reynolds did not bat.

Bowling: *First Innings*—Williams 17–3–61–2; Ellis 13–7–25–0; Nicholson 13–5–23–2; Cary 21.1–6–53–5; Thistle 9–1–25–0; Oldroyd 12–4–35–0. *Second Innings*—Nicholson 15–4–40–2; Cary 9–3–24–2; Williams 6–3–14–1; Thistle 8–0–38–1; Ellis 6–0–31–1; Oldroyd 7.5–2–33–3.

Western Australia Second XI

C. J. L. Rogers c Holcombe b Kellar	29
M. G. Dighton c Miller b Smith	115
G. I. Cullen c Smith b Reynolds	63
S. E. Marsh c McQuire b Kellar	55
*†R. J. Campbell c Smith b Robson	107
S. A. Glew lbw b Kellar	0
M. J. Nicholson b Kellar	0
B. J. Oldroyd c Tucker b Kellar	2
M. J. Thistle c Tucker b Robson	0
S. R. Cary not out	23
B. A. Williams run out (Smith)	4
L-b 9, w 1, n-b 7	17

(102.2 overs, 403 mins) 415
Fall: 64 149 264 276 276 277 309 310 403 415

D. Ellis did not bat.

Bowling: James 15–3–78–0; Miller 20–2–111–0; Robson 17.2–1–74–2; Kellar 28–9–60–5; Reynolds 15–4–41–1; Tucker 3–0–25–0; Smith 4–1–17–1.

Umpires: B. Bennett and A. R. Craig.

VICTORIA SECOND XI v AUSTRALIAN CAPITAL TERRITORY

At Richmond Cricket Ground, Richmond, February 12, 13, 14, 15, 2001. Victoria Second XI won by 143 runs. Toss: Australian Capital Territory.

Victoria Second XI

*S. A. J. Craig c Holcombe b Kellar	1	– (2) c Heaney b James	8
P. Q. Harper c Holcombe b Reynolds	17	– (1) c McQuire b Kellar	6
S. P. Dart c Smith b James	53	– not out	90
M. Klinger lbw b Robson	92	– run out (Dawn/Holcombe)	27
C. J. Peake c Reynolds b Ramage	96	– not out	59
†P. J. Roach lbw b James	14		
B. C. Oliver not out	50		
C. L. White c McQuire b James	0		
T. H. Welsford b Kellar	19		
A. J. Dickinson lbw b Ramage	17		
B. E. McGain c James b Ramage	13		
B 6, l-b 7, w 1, n-b 8	22	L-b 2, n-b 3	5

(117 overs, 446 mins)   394   (62 overs, 226 mins)   (3 wkts dec) 195
Fall: 9 36 108 240 289 291 291 336 371 394   Fall: 9 21 71

W. N. Carr and †M. A. A. Butera did not bat.

Bowling: *First Innings*—James 27–2–89–3; Kellar 32–9–76–2; Reynolds 18–0–71–1; Tucker 7–4–20–0; Ramage 22–3–86–3; Robson 9–1–29–1; Smith 2–0–10–0. *Second Innings*—James 15–2–44–1; Kellar 17–4–42–1; Robson 5–0–12–0; Reynolds 12–1–42–0; Ramage 10–0–33–0; Smith 3–0–20–0.

Australian Capital Territory

J. K. Smith c Roach b McGain	29	– b White	41
C. Brown lbw b Welsford	96	– c Peake b Carr	2
A. D. McQuire lbw b McGain	0	– lbw b Carr	26
S. P. Heaney st Roach b McGain	7	– (5) c Craig b White	7
M. J. Dawn c and b McGain	3	– (7) c and b White	5
*R. J. Tucker c Oliver b McGain	89	– (4) c Welsford b White	0
J. D. Robson lbw b Dart	27	– (6) lbw b Carr	51
†S. A. Holcombe lbw b Carr	8	– lbw b White	2
A. C. L. James not out	15	– b Carr	12
M. H. Ramage c Harper b Dickinson	3	– not out	0
D. J. Reynolds b Dickinson	0	– b Carr	2
B 1, l-b 10, n-b 5	16	B 1, l-b 3, n-b 1	5

(106 overs, 388 mins)   293   (52.4 overs, 194 mins)   153
Fall: 70 74 90 102 221 264 267 286   Fall: 3 69 71 71 101 113 130 144
      289 293   151 153

E. Kellar did not bat.

Bowling: *First Innings*—Carr 31–12–64–1; Dickinson 14–2–44–2; Oliver 10–3–40–0; Welsford 14–2–45–1; McGain 25–10–46–5; White 5–2–10–0; Peake 3–1–15–0; Dart 4–0–18–1. *Second Innings*—Carr 12.4–0–35–5; Dickinson 4–1–5–0; Welsford 9–2–21–0; Oliver 5–2–7–0; White 15–4–55–5; McGain 7–0–26–0.

Umpires: A. J. Barrow and J. D. Ward.

QUEENSLAND ACADEMY OF SPORT v TASMANIA SECOND XI

At Allan Border Field, Albion, February 19, 20, 21, 22, 2001. Queensland Academy of Sport won by 124 runs. Toss: Queensland.

Queensland Academy of Sport

L. W. Kahler c Polkinghorne b Wright	106	– not out	137
B. P. Nash b Targett	4	– (8) not out	51
A. M. Rowe c Selby b Polkinghorne	29	– b Polkinghorne	0
*C. T. Perren c Cunningham b Polkinghorne	20	– c Cunningham b Wright	11
J. R. Hopes c Cunningham b Targett	19	– c Pinnington b Wright	0
C. A. Phillipson c Doherty b Wright	12	– c Pinnington b Thomas	8
N. M. Hauritz c Pinnington b Geeves	23	– c Wright b Targett	26
†G. A. J. Fitness not out	85	– (2) c Mason b Wright	10
M. D. Pascoe c Pinnington b Targett	20		
D. R. MacKenzie not out	3		
L-b 9, n-b 10	19	B 7, l-b 3, w 1, n-b 4	15

(116 overs, 441 mins) (8 wkts dec) 340 (72 overs, 278 mins) (6 wkts dec) 258
Fall: 23 96 169 169 190 211 300 323 Fall: 25 27 47 49 82 152

M. A. Anderson and M. J. Petrie did not bat.

Bowling: *First Innings*—Wright 32–6–80–2; Targett 22–5–86–3; Thomas 8–2–14–0; Geeves 20–8–46–1; Polkinghorne 20–2–80–2; Doherty 14–5–25–0. *Second Innings*—Wright 19–3–71–3; Polkinghorne 13–0–52–1; Geeves 11–1–44–0; Thomas 6–2–21–1; Targett 10–3–34–1; Doherty 13–4–26–0.

Tasmania Second XI

S. R. Mason c Anderson b Pascoe	13	– c Fitness b Petrie	5
M. R. Nutting c Fitness b Pascoe	7	– lbw b Pascoe	0
G. T. Cunningham c Hopes b Pascoe	69	– c Hauritz b Petrie	13
*B. J. Thomas c Perren b Petrie	39	– c Perren b MacKenzie	3
C. W. G. Bassano b Hopes	50	– c Fitness b Hopes	2
†T. A. J. Pinnington c Kahler b Hauritz	29	– run out (Hauritz)	22
A. W. Polkinghorne c Fitness b Pascoe	20	– c Hauritz b Hopes	122
D. G. Wright c Fitness b Hopes	9	– lbw b Hauritz	7
B. S. Targett not out	34	– (10) c Fitness b Hopes	0
X. J. Doherty (did not bat)		– (11) not out	0
J. G. J. Selby (did not bat)		– (9) c Fitness b Hopes	2
L-b 5, w 1, n-b 11	17	B 6, l-b 4, n-b 1	11

(102 overs, 356 mins) (8 wkts dec) 287 (61.5 overs, 232 mins) 187
Fall: 20 29 129 144 191 225 Fall: 1 17 22 26 26 122 181 183
241 287 187 187

B. Geeves did not bat.

Bowling: *First Innings*—Pascoe 26–7–58–4; Petrie 19–5–39–1; MacKenzie 10–0–65–0; Hopes 10–1–28–2; Anderson 15–8–44–0; Hauritz 22–7–48–1. *Second Innings*—Pascoe 14–5–49–1; Petrie 6–4–6–2; Hopes 14.5–5–31–4; MacKenzie 6–3–25–1; Hauritz 13–5–33–1; Anderson 8–3–33–0.

Umpires: K. N. Horton and J. M. Rowe.

AUSTRALIAN CAPITAL TERRITORY v AIS CRICKET ACADEMY

At Manuka Oval, Canberra, March 12, 13, 14, 15, 2001. Australian Capital Territory won by three wickets. Toss: Australian Capital Territory.

AIS Cricket Academy

S. R. Mason lbw b Robson	93	– (2) c Reynolds b Kellar	11
D. M. Betts lbw b Kellar	0	– (1) c Heaney b Reynolds	31
R. J. Brewster lbw b Pascoe	37	– c McQuire b Heading	0
A. J. Kent c Smith b Robson	51	– c Dawson b Kellar	0
D. C. Bandy c Dawson b Heading	46	– b Kellar	0
*A. C. Voges c Dawson b Reynolds	3	– c Dawson b Kellar	44
B. P. Cameron c Dawson b Kellar	44	– lbw b Kellar	17
†L. Ronchi b Kellar	0	– c Heaney b Smith	46
A. R. Griffith c Dawson b Reynolds	25	– c Dawson b Robson	4
M. A. W. Goldsmith b Kellar	2		
S. P. Coombes not out	2	– (10) c Dawson b Kellar	0
M. J. Petrie (did not bat)		– not out	0
L-b 2, n-b 14	16	B 3, l-b 4, n-b 6	13

(115.1 overs, 416 mins)	319	(58.2 overs, 205 mins)	166

Fall: 5 87 189 200 203 281 286 294
305 319

Fall: 28 33 38 38 54 89 155 166
166 166

Bowling: *First Innings*—Kellar 30–6–99–4; Reynolds 22.1–7–49–2; Heading 21–3–82–1; Pascoe 18–8–40–1; Tucker 7–0–15–0; Robson 16–7–32–2; Smith 1–1–0–0. *Second Innings*—Kellar 19.2–8–41–6; Heading 7–2–17–1; Robson 15–6–37–1; Reynolds 5–1–20–1; Pascoe 9–2–32–0; Smith 3–0–12–1.

Australian Capital Territory

J. K. Smith c Kent b Petrie	2	– c Cameron b Bandy	31
C. Brown c Griffith b Bandy	17	– (3) c Cameron b Goldsmith	57
A. D. McQuire c Bandy b Goldsmith	6	– (2) lbw b Petrie	15
S. P. Heaney lbw b Goldsmith	0	– c Ronchi b Petrie	24
*R. J. Tucker b Petrie	0	– c Betts b Petrie	52
S. L. Maxwell c Ronchi b Bandy	16	– c Brewster b Goldsmith	2
†D. G. Dawson c Bandy b Petrie	22	– not out	54
J. D. Robson lbw b Bandy	0	– b Goldsmith	5
A. J. Heading lbw b Bandy	94	– not out	35
E. Kellar c Petrie b Coombes	40		
D. C. Pascoe not out	1		
L-b 4, n-b 3	7	L-b 2, n-b 4	6

(76.4 overs, 274 mins)	205	(80.5 overs, 315 mins) (7 wkts)	281

Fall: 6 16 16 17 37 47 47 70 203 205

Fall: 23 53 120 139 141 199 205

D. J. Reynolds did not bat.

Bowling: *First Innings*—Petrie 15–2–46–3; Goldsmith 15–4–35–2; Griffith 14–5–32–0; Bandy 15–3–40–4; Coombes 11.4–5–26–1; Voges 6–1–22–0. *Second Innings*—Goldsmith 21–3–81–3; Petrie 24–4–73–3; Bandy 9–1–28–1; Griffith 12–2–38–0; Cameron 6–0–31–0; Coombes 6–0–21–0; Voges 2.5–0–7–0.

Umpires: D. Harris and A. Shelley.

KWAZULU-NATAL VISIT

WESTERN AUSTRALIA v KWAZULU-NATAL

At Kingsway Sports Ground, Perth, September 13, 2000. Western Australia won by 79 runs. Toss: Western Australia.

Western Australia

†A.C. Gilchrist retired	....	101(105)	C.J.L. Rogers not out	....	0	(1)
M.E. Hussey retired	....	55 (95)	B 2, l-b 2, w 5, n-b 3	....	12	
M.G. Dighton c Stewart b Kent	......	0 (1)				
*T.M. Moody c Baptiste b Kent	.....	55 (51)	(50 overs, 207 mins)	(4 wkts)	245	
S.E. Marsh not out	....	22 (48)	Fall: 163 163 163 244			

D.J. Hussey, K.M. Hussey, J. Angel, M.J. Nicholson, S.R. Cary and S. Nikitaras did not bat.

Bowling: Veenstra 10–0–31–0; Gilder 10–1–57–0; Kent 10–2–31–2; Baptiste 9–0–28–0; Pietersen 6–0–44–0; Wingfield 3–0–20–0; Bodi 2–0–30–0.

KwaZulu-Natal

R. Gobind c Gilchrist b Cary	....	4 (12)	K.P. Pietersen c Dighton b Nikitaras	30 (30)		
D.L. Brown lbw b Nikitaras	....	8 (51)	R.E. Veenstra not out	....	14 (34)	
A.M. Amla c D.J. Hussey b Harvey	..	31 (63)	G.M. Gilder b Harvey	....	2 (5)	
J.C. Kent c M.E. Hussey b Nikitaras	..	22 (20)				
A.C. Hudson lbw b Angel	....	7 (14)	L-b 5, w 6, n-b 6	....	17	
†E.L.R. Stewart b Harvey	....	5 (19)				
*E.A.E. Baptiste c Marsh b Cary	....	14 (24)	(46.5 overs, 193 mins)		166	
G.H. Bodi c Gilchrist b Cary	....	12 (27)	Fall: 9 44 72 78 84 94 112 118 164 166			

W.R. Wingfield did not bat.

Bowling: Cary 10–1–34–3; Angel 9–0–21–1; Nikitaras 9–0–26–3; Nicholson 10–0–49–0; Harvey 8.5–1–31–3.

WESTERN AUSTRALIA v KWAZULU-NATAL

At Kingsway Sports Ground, Perth, September 14, 2000. KwaZulu-Natal. Toss: Western Australia.

Western Australia

M.W. Goodwin c Pietersen b Kent	...	15 (53)	†M.J. Walsh not out	....	13 (23)	
M.G. Dighton b Veenstra	....	0 (3)	M.J. Nicholson not out	....	7 (17)	
D.R. Martyn b Veenstra	....	3 (10)				
G.B. Hogg run out (Hudson)	....	20 (56)	B 4, l-b 11, w 7	....	22	
*B.P. Julian c Hudson b Kent	....	0 (6)				
D.J. Hussey b Kent	....	1 (9)	(40 overs, 171 mins)	(7 wkts)	112	
M.E. Hussey c Stewart b Kent	......	31 (37)	Fall: 1 11 37 38 42 89 90			

S.J. Karppinen, S.R. Cary and B.A. Williams did not bat.

Bowling: Veenstra 8–2–14–2; Gilder 8–1–23–0; Adam 8–4–8–0; Kent 8–2–20–4; Pietersen 8–1–32–0.

KwaZulu-Natal

†D.L. Brown run out (Hogg)	....	54 (62)	B 1, w 4	....	5
A. Mall c M.E. Hussey b Hogg	......	25 (45)			
A.M. Amla not out	....	24 (27)	(25.2 overs, 100 mins)	(2 wkts)	113
A.C. Hudson not out	....	5 (17)	Fall: 79 87		

*E.L.R. Stewart, J.C. Kent, K.P. Pietersen, R.E. Veenstra, G.M. Gilder, S.M. Adam, G.H. Bodi and R. Gobind did not bat.

Bowling: Cary 5–0–23–0; Karppinen 6–0–35–0; Nicholson 6–1–20–0; Hogg 5.2–0–26–1; M.E. Hussey 3–1–8–0.

Umpires: B. Bennett and K.J. Rinaldi.

WESTERN AUSTRALIA v KWAZULU-NATAL

At Lilac Hill, Perth, September 16, 2000. Match abandoned.

Western Australia

*T.M. Moody, J. Angel, D. Bandy, M.W. Goodwin, S. Howman, D.J. Hussey, S.J. Karppinen, S.E. Marsh, S. Nikitaras, C.J.L. Rogers, G.G. Swan, †M.J. Walsh, M.J. Wates.

KwaZulu-Natal

*E.A.E. Baptiste, S.M. Adam, A.M. Amla, G.H. Bodi, D.L. Brown, G.M. Gilder, R. Gobind, A.C. Hudson, J.C. Kent, A. Mall, K.P. Pietersen, †E.L.R. Stewart, R.E. Veenstra, W.R. Wingfield.

WESTERN AUSTRALIA v KWAZULU-NATAL

At Lilac Hill, Perth, September 17, 2000. Tied. Toss: Western Australia.

KwaZulu-Natal

K.P. Pietersen c Goodwin b Swan	0	(13)	†D.L. Brown not out 56	(70)
A. Mall c Hussey b Karppinen	1	(29)	R. Gobind not out 1	(2)
A.M. Amla lbw b Swan	0	(1)	L-b 6, w 17, n-b 3 26	
A.C. Hudson b Swan	7	(27)		
*E.L.R. Stewart run out (Rogers)	20	(39)	(45 overs, 179 mins) (6 wkts) 181	
J.C. Kent c Hussey b Karppinen	70	(98)	Fall: 5 5 14 19 67 169	

Bowling: Angel 8–4–26–0; Swan 9–4–8–3; Karppinen 8–045–2; Wates 9–0–48–2; Howman 6–0–23–0; Hussey 5–0–25–0.

Western Australia

C.J.L. Rogers st Brown b Pietersen ..	28	(54)	D.J. Wates not out 12	(8)
D. Bandy c Mall b Kent	21	(39)	L-b 2, w 6 n-b 1 9	
M.W. Goodwin c Stewart b Veenstra .	62	(91)		
*T.M. Moody c Gilder b Pietersen ...	22	(42)	(45 overs, 181 mins) (4 wkts) 181	
D.J. Hussey not out	27	(35)	Fall: 37 68 111 164	

†M.J. Walsh, S.E. Marsh, S.J. Karppinen, S. Howman, J. Angel and G.G. Swan did not bat.

Bowling: Veenstra 9–0–41–1; Gilder 9–1–24–0; Adam 9–1–45–0, Kent 9–0–29–1; Pietersen 9–0–39–2.

Umpires: A. Dix and R.J.U. Woodridge.

WESTERN AUSTRALIA v KWAZULU-NATAL

At Lilac Hill, Perth, September 19, 20, 21, 2000. Drawn. Toss: Western Australia.
Close of play: First day, KwaZulu-Natal (1) 1-24 (Mall 6, Amla 13). Second day, Western Australia (2) 3-91 (Bandy 28, Campbell 16).

Western Australia

*M.E. Hussey lbw b Adam	9	– (2) c Bodi b Pietersen 22
J. Meuleman c Stewart b Gilder	3	– (1) c Stewart b Gilder 7
M.G. Dighton c Hudson b Kent	10	
M.J. North lbw b Kent	52	– (6) c Stewart b Kent 0
R.J. Campbell st Stewart b Pietersen	44	– c Stewart b Kent 28
S.A. Glew lbw b Adam	10	– (4) c Stewart b Pietersen 12
D.J. Hussey b Adam	70	
A.C. Voges not out	59	– (9) not out 36
M.J. Nicholson not out	9	– (8) c Brown b Pietersen 2
D. Bandy (did not bat)	–	(3) b Gilder 55
†L. Ronchi (did not bat)	–	(7) lbw b Pietersen 4
S.J. Karppinen (did not bat)	–	(10) st Stewart b Pietersen 0
J. Angel (did not bat)	–	(11) not out 27
B 4, l-b 12, n-b 6	22	B 1, l-b 2, w 4, n-b 2 9

(88 overs, 361 mins)	(7 wkts dec) 288	(74 overs, 279 mins) (9 wkts dec) 202

Fall: 13 21 25 100 123
154 266

Fall: 17 48 69 112 112 130 135
144 144

P. Davis did not bat.

Bowling: *First Innings*—Gilder 16–4–50–1; Adam 16–5–52–3; Kent 14–4–50–2; Baptiste 12–2–32–0; Pietersen 17–4–40–1; Bodi 10–0–47–0; Gobind 1–0–1–0. *Second Innings*—Gilder 15–4–35–2; Adam 12–2–33–0; Kent 11–4–35–2; Pietersen 24–4–61–5; Bodi 12–0–35–0.

KwaZulu-Natal

R. Gobind c Dighton b Angel	0	– c Karppinen b Angel 2
A. Mall c Ronchi b Davis	25	– b Angel 0
A.M. Amla b Karppinen	49	– c M.E. Hussey b Nicholson 25
A.C. Hudson lbw b Angel	63	– c Glew b Nicholson 37
†E.L.R. Stewart c M.E. Hussey b Karppinen	6	– lbw b Karppinen 12
J.C. Kent c Ronchi b Karppinen	15	– c Ronchi b Nicholson 2
D.L. Brown not out	51	– not out 15
K.P. Pietersen c Ronchi b Nicholson	15	– c and b North 34
G.H. Bodi not out	2	
*E.A.E. Baptiste (did not bat)	–	(9) not out 27
L-b 5, w 1, n-b 7	13	N-b 4 4

(79.3 overs, 299 mins)	(7 wkts dec) 239	(62 overs, 242 mins) (7 wkts) 158

Fall: 0 71 87 111 140 184 227

Fall: 1 6 36 76 78 82 124

G.M. Gilder and S.M. Adam did not bat.

Bowling: *First Innings*—Angel 21–7–35–2; Nicholson 18.3–5–49–1; Davis 12–2–33–1; Karppinen 15–5–42–3; Voges 7–1–44–0; North 6–1–31–0. *Second Innings*—Angel 11–5–19–2; Nicholson 16–10–34–3; Karppinen 17–7–30–1; Davis 6–2–10–0; North 7–2–32–1; Voges 5–0–33–0.

Umpires: A. Craig and K.J. Rinaldi.

WESTERN AUSTRALIA v KWAZULU-NATAL

At Male Oval, Broome, September 24, 2000. KwaZulu-Natal won by six wickets. Toss: KwaZulu-Natal.

Western Australia

*T. M. Moody c Hudson b Veenstra	..	5	(12)	M. W. Goodwin c Gobind b Gilder ..	18 (28)
B. P. Julian c Brown b Baptiste	......	40	(90)	G. B. Hogg not out	7 (8)
D. R. Martyn c Stewart b Veenstra	...	5	(9)		
M. E. Hussey run out (Mall)	....	46	(80)	B 1, l-b 4, w 15, n-b 8	28
K. M. Harvey lbw b Pietersen	....	3	(16)		
M. G. Dighton not out	....	55	(63)	(50 overs, 216 mins) (7 wkts)	208
M. J. North st Brown b Pietersen	.....	1	(3)	Fall: 13 30 88 95 154 159 194	

D. J. Wates, †M. J. Walsh and J. Angel did not bat.

Bowling: Veenstra 10–1–35–2; Kent 3–0–15–0; Gilder 10–1–35–1; Adam 10–1–38–0; Baptiste 7–0–28–1; Pietersen 10–0–52–2.

KwaZulu-Natal

D. L. Brown c Harvey b Angel	......	0	(5)	J. C. Kent not out	20 (18)
R. Gobind c Goodwin b Martyn	.....	17	(44)	L-b 1, w 4	5
A. Mall lbw b Angel	....	15	(25)		
A. C. Hudson not out	....	102	(122)	(47.2 overs, 193 mins) (4 wkts)	210
†E. L. R. Stewart c Dighton b Hogg	...	51	(71)	Fall: 0 18 63 178	

G. H. Bodi, G. M. Gilder, S. M. Adam, *E. A. E. Baptiste, R. E. Veenstra and K. P. Pietersen did not bat.

Bowling: Angel 10–2–29–2; Wates 8–1–33–0; Martyn 7–1–31–1; Harvey 9–0–46–0; North 6–0–31–0; Hogg 7.2–0–38–1.

Umpires: B. Bennett and R. J. U. Woolridge.

PRE-SEASON MATCHES

QUEENSLAND v AUSTRALIANS

At Allan Border Field, Albion, August 11, 2000. Australians won by 75 runs. Toss: Queensland.

Australian XI

†A. C. Gilchrist c Seccombe b Pascoe	.	1	(8)	S. Lee run out	31 (31)
M. E. Waugh c Cassell b Creevey	....	77	(103)	I. J. Harvey not out	9 (4)
R. T. Ponting c Creevey b Bichel	.....	9	(22)		
M. G. Bevan c Seccombe b Prestwidge		17	(42)	L-b 3, w 12, n-b 12	27
*S. R. Waugh c Creevey b Prestwidge		9	(28)		
D. R. Martyn not out	....	53	(69)	(50 overs, 209 mins) (7 wkts)	238
A. Symonds run out (Hopes)	....	5	(6)	Fall: 8 27 99 135 146 158 213	

B. Lee and J. N. Gillespie did not bat.

Bowling: Bichel 5–1–16–1; Pascoe 6–0–41–1; May 6–1–20–0; Prestwidge 9–0–36–2; Creevey 10–0–35–1; Anderson 10–1–66–0; Hopes 4–0–21–0.

Queensland

*J.P. Maher c Gilchrist b S. Lee	47	(75)	
J.L. Cassell c Symonds b B. Lee	4	(16)	
B.K.D. May c Gillespie b S. Lee	8	(30)	
L.A. Carseldine c Gilchrist b B. Lee	26	(41)	
†W.A. Seccombe b B. Lee	19	(33)	
S.A. Prestwidge b Symonds	0	(6)	
A.J. Bichel c Gillespie b Symonds	3	(10)	
B.N. Creevey c Gillespie b S. Lee	13	(23)	

J.R. Hopes c S.R. Waugh b Bevan	7	(13)
M.D. Pascoe not out	12	(11)
S.A. Muller b Bevan	4	(10)
L-b 8, w 10, n-b 2	20	
(44.4 overs, 188 mins)	163	
Fall: 18 66 69 109 110 120 125		
141 149 163		

M.A. Anderson did not bat.

Bowling: Gillespie 8–1–22–0; B. Lee 8–0–30–3; S. Lee 8–0–42–3; Harvey 7–1–22–0; Symonds 8–1–24–2; Martyn 1–0–1–0; Bevan 4.4–0–14–2.

Umpires: A.J. McQuillan and P.D. Parker.

QUEENSLAND v AUSTRALIANS

At Allan Border Field, Albion, August 13, 2000. Australians won by one wicket. Toss: Queensland.

Queensland

J.L. Cassell lbw b Harvey	10	(40)
L.A. Carseldine c Gilchrist b S. Lee	40	(67)
†W.A. Seccombe c Gilchrist b S. Lee	35	(58)
*J.P. Maher b Warne	12	(30)
B.N. Creevey c B. Lee b Warne	3	(10)
A.J. Bichel c Symonds b Warne	0	(5)
S.A. Prestwidge lbw b B. Lee	11	(10)
D.A. Turner run out (Harvey)	28	(40)

J.R. Hopes c Harvey b Gillespie	11	(13)
L.M. Stevens run out (Harvey)	19	(27)
M.D. Pascoe not out	1	(2)
W 1, n-b 2	3	
(50 overs, 210 mins)	173	
Fall: 25 84 87 94 101 106 120 134		
171 173		

S.A. Muller did not bat.

Bowling: McGrath 8–1–18–0; B. Lee 8–0–34–1; Harvey 9–2–33–1; Gillespie 9–2–28–1; S. Lee 8–0–36–2; Warne 8–1–24–3.

Australians

M.E. Waugh b Bichel	14	(30)
†A.C. Gilchrist c Prestwidge b Bichel	29	(34)
†R.T. Ponting b Carseldine	21	(13)
*S.R. Waugh c Cassell b Creevey	29	(45)
D.R. Martyn run out (Prestwidge/Turner)	27	(42)
A. Symonds c Pascoe b Turner	18	(19)
S. Lee c Creevey b Bichel	16	(21)
I.J. Harvey c Turner b Prestwidge	11	(9)

S.K. Warne c Maher b Prestwidge	0	(3)
B. Lee not out	2	(3)
J.N. Gillespie not out	2	(4)
L-b 2, w 3	5	
(37.1 overs, 163 mins)	174	
Fall: 41 44 67 111 136 142 165 169 169		

G.D. McGrath did not bat.

Bowling: Bichel 10–0–54–3; Carseldine 10–3–32–1; Muller 2–0–21–0; Creevey 7–1–31–1; Prestwidge 5.1–1–20–2; Turner 3–0–14–1.

Umpires: A.J. McQuillan and P.D. Parker.

QUEENSLAND v NEW ZEALANDERS

At Allan Border Field, Albion, August 14, 2000. New Zealanders won by 127 runs. Toss: New Zealanders.

New Zealanders

C. J. Nevin c Seccombe b Creevey ...	7	(9)
D. L. Vettori c Hopes b Muller	4	(5)
*S. P. Fleming c Maher b Muller	15	(22)
†R. G. Twose c Seccombe b Pascoe ..	32	(49)
C. L. Cairns c Muller b O'Leary	100	(89)
C. D. McMillan c Prestwidge b S. J. Hopes ..	103	(109)

C. Z. Harris not out	38	(23)
B 2, l-b 7, w 7, n-b 6	22	
(50 overs, 211 mins)　　(6 wkts)	321	

Fall: 9 13 49 106 223 321

S. B. Styris, G. I. Allott, P. J. Wiseman, D. R. Tuffey and S. B. O'Connor did not bat.

Bowling: Muller 7–0–56–2; Creevey 6–0–22–1; Pascoe 7–1–29–1; Carseldine 10–0–44–0; Bichel 4–0–21–0; O'Leary 10–0–76–1; Prestwidge 4–0–43–0; Hopes 2–0–21–1.

Queensland

J. L. Cassell c Tuffey b Harris	58	(109)
*J. P. Maher lbw b Allott	14	(18)
L. A. Carseldine lbw b Allott	1	(8)
B. K. D. May lbw b O'Connor	13	(23)
S. A. Prestwidge c and b Harris	31	(35)
B. N. Creevey st (sub) Fitness b Vettori	25	(32)
†W. A. Seccombe c Wiseman b Harris .	0	(2)
J. R. Hopes c and b O'Connor	24	(36)

M. D. Pascoe c Styris b O'Connor ...	15	(20)
S. J. O'Leary not out	5	(11)
S. A. Muller not out	1	(6)
L-b 4, w 3	7	
(50 overs, 211 mins)　　(9 wkts)	194	

Fall: 23 29 49 115 129 129 168 182 191

A. J. Bichel did not bat.

Bowling: Allott 7–1–26–2; Cairns 3–0–13–0; Tuffey 5–1–22–0; O'Connor 7–1–24–3; Styris 4–1–10–0; Vettori 10–0–47–1; Harris 8–1–23–3; Wiseman 6–0–25–0.

Umpires: L. D. Musch and J. F. Torpey.

QUEENSLAND v NEW ZEALANDERS

At Allan Border Field, Albion, August 15, 2000. Queensland won by 23 runs. Toss: Queensland.

Queensland

J. L. Cassell c Tuffey b Cairns	7	(10)
*J. P. Maher c O'Connor b Allott	6	(26)
J. R. Hopes run out	37	(75)
B. K. D. May lbw b Allott	0	(3)
D. A. Turner lbw b O'Connor	5	(4)
S. A. Prestwidge c Tuffey b Vettori ...	29	(44)
L. A. Carseldine b Harris	42	(70)
†W. A. Seccombe c Styris b Wiseman .	3	(13)

B. N. Creevey not out	36	(39)
M. D. Pascoe b Styris	6	(13)
S. A. Muller not out	3	(4)
B 4, l-b 6, w 6, n-b 1	17	
(50 overs, 194 mins)　　(9 wkts)	191	

Fall: 13 17 18 27 66 109 117 140 174

M. A. Anderson did not bat.

Bowling: Allott 4–0–14–2; Cairns 4–1–11–1; O'Connor 5–0–21–1; Tuffey 7–0–40–0; Vettori 9–2–20–1; Wiseman 10–0–35–1; Harris 9–0–25–1; Styris 2–0–15–1.

New Zealanders

D.L. Vettori c May b Muller	0	(2)	
S.B. Styris c May b Muller	4	(7)	
C.L. Cairns c Seccombe b Carseldine	13	(14)	
*S.P. Fleming b Carseldine	14	(27)	
†A.C. Parore c Seccombe b Pascoe	16	(24)	
C.D. McMillan c and b Turner	39	(69)	
C.Z. Harris c Anderson b Pascoe	6	(14)	
D.R. Tuffey b Pascoe	0	(2)	

R.G. Twose did not bat.

P.J. Wiseman c Maher b Creevey	38	(62)	
S.B. O'Connor not out	25	(47)	
G.I. Allott st Seccombe b Turner	1	(5)	
B 1, w 3, n-b 8	12		
(44.1 overs, 183 mins)	168		

Fall: 1 16 24 45 54 73 74 124 163 168

Bowling: Muller 8–0–51–2; Carseldine 7–2–13–2; Creevey 10–1–32–1; Pascoe 5–0–18–3; Turner 8.1–1–27–2; Anderson 5–0–25–0; Hopes 1–0–1–0.

Umpires: J.F. Torpey and J. Rowe.

WESTERN AUSTRALIA v VICTORIA

At Lilac Hill Park, Perth, September 20, 2000. Western Australia won by eight wickets. Toss: Western Australia.

Victoria

G.R. Vimpani c Walsh b Johnston	24	(62)	
M.P. Mott c G. Wates b Johnston	9	(30)	
B.J. Hodge c Walsh b Atkinson	34	(84)	
L.D. Harper lbw b D.J. Wates	25	(51)	
M. Klinger c Rogers b D.J. Wates	1	(10)	
S.A.J. Craig not out	33	(41)	
C.J. Peake b Atkinson	8	(16)	

D.W. Fleming, M.W.H. Inness and M.L. Lewis did not bat.

†P.J. Roach lbw b G. Wates	1	(4)	
*P.R. Reiffel not out	20	(14)	
L-b 3, w 13, n-b 2	18		
(50 overs)	(7 wkts) 173		

Fall: 21 48 96 100 128 146 147

Bowling: Atkinson 10–1–19–2; Harvey 10–1–34–0; G Wates 8–1–21–1; Johnston 10–0–34–2; DJ Wates 7–0–30–2; Hogg 5–0–32–0.

Western Australia

C.J.L. Rogers c Roach b Reiffel	29	(56)	
M.G. Dighton b Peake	73	(134)	
*D.R. Martyn not out	53	(60)	
M.W. Goodwin not out	8	(23)	

L-b 2, w 8, n-b 1	11		
(44 overs)	(2 wkts) 174		

Fall: 49 150

G.B. Hogg, †M.J. Walsh, M.P. Atkinson, K.M. Harvey, D.J. Wates, M. Johnston, G. Wates and B.P. Julian did not bat.

Bowling: Fleming 10–4–45–0; Inness 6–2–16–0; Reiffel 7–1–14–1; Lewis 6–1–25–0; Mott 3–0–22–0; Hodge 7–0–37–0; Peake 5–0–13–1.

Umpires: B. Callender and R. Pease.

WESTERN AUSTRALIA v VICTORIA

At Lilac Hill Park, Perth, September 21, 2000. Victoria won by three wickets. Toss: Western Australia.

Western Australia

†A.C. Gilchrist c Hodge b Inness	....	6	(24)	M.P. Atkinson c Hodge b Dart	.....	23 (33)
M.W. Goodwin lbw b Inness	....	0	(1)	G.G. Swan b Oliver	....	9 (22)
*D.R. Martyn b Oliver	....	37	(64)	S. Howman not out	....	6 (13)
T.M. Moody c Dart b Lewis	....	13	(31)			
B.P. Julian c and b Harwood	....	24	(26)	L-b 1, w 8, n-b 3	....	12
G.B. Hogg not out	....	34	(80)			
K.M. Harvey lbw b Oliver	....	2	(10)	(50 overs, 208 mins)	(9 wkts)	166
D.J. Wates lbw b Oliver	....	0	(2)	Fall: 1 14 50 78 88 91 91 133 151		

Bowling: Inness 10–2–25–2; Harwood 10–0–45–1; Lewis 10–0–36–1; Oliver 10–2–21–4; Peake 5–0–25–0; Dart 5–0–13–1.

Victoria

G.R. Vimpani b Wates	....	27	(40)	B.C. Oliver lbw b Martyn	....	3 (12)
J.L. Arnberger c Gilchrist b Swan	....	0	(6)	†P.J. Roach not out	....	1 (3)
B.J. Hodge c Gilchrist b Howman	...	53	(79)			
M. Klinger c Martyn b Hogg	....	19	(53)	B 1, l-b 10, w 11, n-b 1	....	23
C.J. Peake c Howman b Hogg	....	23	(37)			
*L.D. Harper run out (Howman)	.....	11	(23)	(45.1 overs, 188 mins)	(7 wkts)	167
S.R. Dart not out	....	7	(26)	Fall: 9 48 110 119 147 154 159		

M.W.H. Inness, S.M. Harwood and M.L. Lewis did not bat.

Bowling: Swan 6–1–29–1; Wates 6–3–13–1; Atkinson 6–1–15–0; Thistle 6.1–1–36–0; Hogg 10–1–33–2; Howman 5–0–20–1; Martyn 6–2–10–1.

Umpires: A. Dix and I. Lock.

WESTERN AUSTRALIA v VICTORIA

At Male Oval, Broome, September 23, 2000. Western Australia won by eight wickets. Toss: Western Australia.

Victoria

J.L. Arnberger b Wates	....	27	(50)	S.M. Harwood run out (North)	.....	4 (11)
G.R. Vimpani c Walsh b Harvey	.....	9	(28)	D.W. Fleming c Hussey b Hogg	....	2 (9)
S.P. Dart c North b Martyn	....	28	(65)	M.L. Lewis c sub (Dighton) b Harvey		6 (15)
L.D. Harper b Wates	....	0	(1)	L-b 1, w 7	....	8
M.P. Mott not out	....	51	(89)			
S.A.J. Craig b Martyn	....	8	(12)	(48.2 overs, 191 mins)		145
†P.J. Roach lbw b Martyn	....	0	(2)	Fall: 22 52 52 93 105 105 116 123		
B.C. Oliver b Hogg	....	2	(8)	126 145		

*P.R. Reiffel did not bat.

Bowling: Williams 8–1–19–0; Angel 9–1–28–0; Harvey 8.2–1–23–2; Wates 8–0–22–2; Hogg 10–1–42–2; Martyn 5–2–10–3.

Western Australia

R.J. Campbell st Roach b Oliver	.....	60	(84)	L-b 3, w 3, n-b 4	....	10
M.W. Goodwin c and b Craig	....	43	(74)			
D.R. Martyn not out	....	26	(60)	(38.1 overs, 146 mins)	(2 wkts)	148
M.E. Hussey not out	....	9	(15)	Fall: 90 134		

*T.M. Moody, M.J. North, G.B. Hogg, †M.J. Walsh, D.J. Wates, K.M. Harvey, B.A. Williams and J. Angel did not bat.

Bowling: Fleming 6–0–24–0; Harwood 8–0–47–0; Lewis 6–0–23–0; Oliver 7–1–21–1; Reiffel 5–1–12–0; Craig 4–0–9–1; Mott 2.1–0–9–0.

Umpires: B. Bennett and R.J.U. Woolridge.

WESTERN AUSTRALIA v VICTORIA

At Creswell Park, Perth, September 26, 27, 2000. Drawn. Toss: Victoria.
Close of play: First day, Victoria (1) 6-318 (Oliver 51, Roach 29).

Victoria

J. L. Arnberger c Walsh b Cary	7	B. C. Oliver not out	51
S. A. J. Craig c Hussey b Karppinen	39	†P. J. Roach not out	29
M. P. Mott c North b Karppinen	78	B 1, l-b 4, w 3, n-b 16	24
B. J. Hodge c Campbell b Swan	14		
M. Klinger c North b Mason	46	(96 overs, 379 mins) (6 wkts dec)	318
C. J. Peake c North b Nicholson	30	Fall: 19 70 108 170 217 250	

S. P Dart, *P. R. Reiffel, M. W. H. Inness and M. L. Lewis did not bat.

Bowling: Nicholson 15–3–39–1; Cary 18–5–49–1; Swan 13–2–64–1; Karppinen 18–2–53–2; Hogg 14–3–67–0; Mason 10–5–16–1; North 8–0–25–0.

Western Australia

R. J. Campbell c Hodge b Inness	0	M. J. Nicholson c Oliver b Dart	0
*M. E. Hussey c Klinger b Lewis	27	S. R. Cary not out	7
M. W. Goodwin c Craig b Inness	66	S. J. Karppinen lbw b Inness	0
M. J. North c Klinger b Peake	34		
S. W. Meuleman run out (Oliver/Roach)	26	B 4, l-b 5, w 2, n-b 15	26
C. G. Mason lbw b Hodge	9		
G. B. Hogg c Craig b Lewis	48	(85.5 overs, 329 mins)	261
†M. J. Walsh b Dart	18	Fall: 7 81 125 164 182 186 246 247 260 261	

G. G. Swan did not bat.

Bowling: Lewis 14–1–52–2; Inness 12.5–5–21–3; Oliver 16–2–65–0; Mott 3–1–7–0; Hodge 18–6–45–1; Craig 11–2–28–0; Peake 8–0–27–1; Dart 3–0–7–2.

Umpires: C. R. Allen and R. J. U. Woolridge.

NEW SOUTH WALES v AUSTRALIAN CAPITAL TERRITORY

At Caringbah Oval, Sydney, October 1, 2000. Tied. Toss: New South Wales.

New South Wales

†G. J. Mail c and b Day	58	D. A. Nash b James	3
*M. J. Slater c Heaney b James	21	J. Stewart c Swift b Day	7
B. P. van Deinsen c Brown b Stuart	48	N. W. Bracken not out	1
C. J. Richards run out	18	B 3, l-b 5, w 4, n-b 3	15
G. C. Rummans not out	32		
M. J. Clarke c Holcombe b Stuart	2	(50 overs, 187 mins) (8 wkts)	206
S. D. Bradstreet b James	1	Fall: 54 102 148 154 162 176 180 198	

S. R. Clark and S. C. G. MacGill did not bat.

Bowling: Stuart 8–0–34–2; Kellar 10–2–30–0; James 7–0–36–3; Ramage 10–0–31–0; Day 10–1–43–2; Jeffrey 5–0–24–0.

Australian Capital Territory

A. D. McQuire st Mail b MacGill	65
C. Brown c Mail b Bradstreet	57
D. M. Jeffrey lbw b Stewart	20
S. P. Heaney run out	37
J. J. Swift lbw b Stewart	0
*R. J. Tucker run out	1
M. D. Day b Clark	1
A. M. Stuart not out	6
B 4, l-b 7, w 7, n-b 1	19
(50 overs, 191 mins) (7 wkts)	206

Fall: 112 144 179 179 190 191 206

†S. A. Holcombe, E. Kellar, A. C. L. James and M. H. Ramage did not bat.

Bowling: Nash 6–1–15–0; Bracken 10–1–33–0; Bradstreet 7–0–24–1; Clark 7–1–40–1; MacGill 10–0–48–1; Stewart 10–0–35–2.

Umpires: T. J. Keel and S. J. A. Taufel.

SYDNEY GREGORY CUP

NEW SOUTH WALES COLTS v QUEENSLAND COLTS

At Hurstville Oval, Sydney, November 6, 7, 8, 9, 2000. Drawn. Toss: Queensland Colts. *Close of play:* First day: Queensland Colts (1) 4-250 (Rowe 112, Hartley 7); Second day, New South Wales Colts (1) 8-236 (Hoare 39, Barry 3); Third day, New South Wales Colts (2) 0-6 (Stanton 6, Brewster 0).

Queensland Colts

C. P. Simpson lbw b Luiters	35	– (2) c Scott b Byrom	12
N. J. Kruger c Stanton b O'Brien	16	– (1) lbw b O'Brien	25
*S. R. Watson c and b Eriksson	63	– run out	13
A. M. Rowe c Stanton b Scott	115	– c Stanton b Byrom	41
R. A. Broad c O'Brien b Byrom	6		
†C. D. Hartley not out	20	– (5) c Hoare b Eriksson	30
N. M. Hauritz c Stanton b O'Brien	3	– (6) not out	74
D. R. MacKenzie b Scott	15	– (7) c Hoare b Baker	12
T. J. M. Orr (did not bat)		– (8) b Eriksson	21
S. J. Magoffin not out	0	– (9) not out	23
L-b 7, w 1, n-b 6	14	L-b 1, n-b 5	6
(106 overs, 420 mins)	287	(83 overs, 329 mins) (7 wkts dec)	257

Fall: 58 68 185 221 255 262 279

Fall: 21 50 50 114 123 135 186

N. J. Rimmington and J. G. Dellit did not bat.

Bowling: *First Innings*—Byrom 18–7–32–1; Scott 18–6–35–2; Baker 13–4–21–0; Barry 10–1–29–0; O'Brien 24–7–84–2; Luiters 7–1–39–1; Eriksson 16–6–40–1. *Second Innings*—Byrom 16–2–52–2; Scott 16–1–74–0; Barry 5–2–10–0; Baker 10–3–25–1; O'Brien 26–11–40–1; Eriksson 9–2–40–2; Luiters 1–0–15–0.

New South Wales Colts

†S.D. Stanton c Orr b Magoffin	0	– c Simpson b Hauritz	39
*R.J. Brewster b Hauritz	52	– b MacKenzie	8
A.W. O'Brien b Hauritz	75	– c Hartley b Magoffin	70
S.G. Karam run out	4	– b Magoffin	1
K.J.J. Luiters lbw b Orr	0	– c Broad b Hauritz	42
S.J. Phillips c Dellit b Orr	16	– lbw b Rimmington	20
T. Hoare not out	39	– not out	23
B.A. Eriksson lbw b Watson	11	– not out	6
M.J. Baker c Watson b Hauritz	17		
C.P. Barry c Hartley b Magoffin	3		
P.J. Byrom c Hartley b Magoffin	0		
B 5, l-b 3, w 1, n-b 11	20	B 7, l-b 17, w 3, n-b 9	36
(86.2 overs, 311 mins)	237	(107 overs, 387 mins)	245
Fall: 0 137 138 139 159 161 196 231 237 237		Fall: 16 133 137 137 184 222	

A.R. Scott did not bat.

Bowling: *First Innings*—Magoffin 4.2–1–10–3; Rimmington 6–0–40–0; MacKenzie 8–1–30–0; Hauritz 32–14–46–3; Dellit 7–1–24–0; Watson 11–2–35–1; Orr 16–2–38–2; Rowe 2–0–6–0. *Second Innings*—MacKenzie 22–5–47–1; Magoffin 23–8–43–2; Rimmington 13–2–30–1; Hauritz 35–17–58–2; Simpson 5–1–13–0Watson 8–1–27–0; Rowe 1–0–3–0.

Umpires: N. Fowler and R. Furtner.

NEW SOUTH WALES IN NEW ZEALAND, 2000-01

WELLINGTON v NEW SOUTH WALES

At Basin Reserve, Wellington, November 21, 22, 2000. Drawn. Toss: Wellington.
Close of play: First day, New South Wales 388.

New South Wales

B.P. van Deinsen c Patel b Bulfin	1	S.D. Bradstreet b Walker	25
†G.J. Mail run out (Patel)	26	D.A. Nash c Bell b Walker	56
C.J. Richards c Jefferson b Walker	23	N.W. Bracken not out	0
P.A. Jaques c Donaldson b Patel	106		
*S. Lee c Franklin b Gillespie	24	B 8, l-b 5, w 1, n-b 13	27
J. Stewart c Walker b Patel	27		
M.A. Higgs run out (Bell)	14	(99.5 overs)	388
M.J. Phelps st Howell b Jefferson	59	Fall: 7 57 75 131 208 234 249 312 370 388	

M.J. Clarke did not bat.

Bowling: Bulfin 14–2–51–1; Gillespie 20–2–81–1; Franklin 19–2–81–0; Walker 21.5–2–95–3; Patel 16–5–41–2; Jefferson 9–3–26–1.

Wellington

*M.D. Bell st Mail b Higgs	46	M.D.J. Walker not out	53
M. Blackmore b Nash	0	M.R. Jefferson not out	38
R.A. Jones c Mail b Bracken	40	B 3, l-b 3, w 2	8
G.T. Donaldson c van Deinsen b Stewart	6		
J.E.C. Franklin c and b Higgs	63	(100 overs) (6 wkts)	338
†C.J. Nevin c Lee b Higgs	84	Fall: 0 74 83 100 241 249	

M.R. Gillespie, C.E. Bulfin, J.S. Patel and G.A. Howell did not bat.

Bowling: Nash 18–3–80–1; Bracken 18–6–59–1; Lee 13–6–38–0; Stewart 22–8–57–1; Higgs 19–7–67–3; Bradstreet 9–2–23–0; Richards 1–0–8–0.

Umpires: D. Ellwood and E.A. Watkin.

WELLINGTON v NEW SOUTH WALES

At Westpac Trust Stadium, Wellington, November 23, 2000. Day/night game. New South Wales won by seven wickets. Toss: Wellington.

Wellington

†C. J. Nevin c and b Bradstreet	55	(46)	S. B. Golder b Lee	8	(18)
*M. D. Bell lbw b Bracken	1	(5)	P. A. Hitchcock not out	0	(7)
S. R. Mather c Lee b Bradstreet	12	(21)	C. E. Bulfin b Bracken	0	(5)
R. G. Twose c and b Lee	29	(44)			
G. T. Donaldson b Nash	4	(7)	B 2, l-b 3, w 3	8	
R. G. Petrie c and b Nash	3	(18)			
M. D. J. Walker c Haddin b Lee	4	(20)	(35 overs)	131	
M. R. Jefferson run out (Higgs)	7	(19)	Fall: 9 55 85 90 100 110 115 125 130 131		

J. S. Patel did not bat.

Bowling: Nash 10–1–38–2; Bracken 5–1–24–2; Higgs 4–0–25–0; Bradstreet 7–3–18–2; Lee 6–0–15–3; van Deinsen 3–0–6–0.

New South Wales

B. P. van Deinsen b Patel	28	(31)	B 3, l-b 1, w 4, n-b 2	10	
M. A. Higgs c and b Jefferson	59	(59)			
C. J. Richards c Bell b Patel	19	(27)			
*S. Lee not out	14	(25)	(24.5 overs)	132	
†B. J. Haddin not out	2	(9)	Fall: 62 91 125		

P. A. Jaques, M. J. Clarke, G. J. Mail, N. W. Bracken, S. D. Bradstreet, D. A. Nash and M. J. Phelps did not bat.

Bowling: Bulfin 4–0–32–0; Patel 9–0–50–2; Hitchcock 5–0–21–0; Jefferson 3.5–0–15–1; Walker 3–1–10–0.

Umpires: D. Kinsey and E. A. Watkin.

PRACTICE ONE-DAY MATCH

VICTORIA v AUSTRALIANS

At Junction Oval, Melbourne, January 9, 2001. Australians won by two runs.

Australians

*†A. C. Gilchrist run out	3	S. K. Warne c Klinger b Oliver	3
M. E. Waugh st Berry b Oliver	46	D. R. Martyn not out	21
R. T. Ponting retired	60	N. W. Bracken run out	10
M. G. Bevan c Lewis b Hewett	13		
D. R. Martyn c Berry b Hewett	0	B 1, w 5, nb 6	12
D. S. Lehmann retired	47		
A. Symonds c Bartlett b Lewis	41	(50 overs, 211 mins)	271
I. J. Harvey c Harper b Inness	15	Fall: 4 92 125 125 129 205 233 238 239 271

G. D. McGrath did not bat.

Bowling: Inness 10–1–51–1; Lewis 9–0–55–1; Oliver 10–0–51–2; Bartlett 1–0–10–0; Hewett 10–2–45–2; Davison 10–0–58–0.

Victoria

M. T. G. Elliott c Gilchrist b Lehmann 84	*†D. S. Berry c Symonds b Warne 16
J. L. Arnberger b McGrath 37	J. M. Davison b Harvey 0
P. Q. Harper c Gilchrist b Symonds 6	C. J. Peake not out 0
M. P. Mott c Warne b Harvey 54	
M. Klinger c Martyn b Bracken 8	L-b 3, w 1, n-b 4 8
R. A. Bartlett run out 2	
I. S. L. Hewett st Gilchrist b Warne 42	(49.1 overs, 199 mins) 269
B. C. Oliver st Gilchrist b Warne 12	Fall: 49 68 175 190 193 197 237 269 269 269

M. L. Lewis and M. W. H. Inness did not bat.

Bowling: McGrath 7–1–36–1; Bracken 10–0–46–1; Symonds 10–0–46–1; Harvey 9.1–0–61–2; Warne 10–1–61–3; Lehmann 3–0–16–1.

SUPPLEMENTARY FIXTURE

ROCKINGHAM-MANDURAH v NEW SOUTH WALES

At Settlers Hill, Baldivis. January 17, 2001. New South Wales won by 184 runs. Toss: New South Wales.

New South Wales

M. A. Higgs c Rennie b Symington 39	S. D. Bradstreet not out 5
M. J. Slater c & b Symington 28	†G. J. Mail not out 4
*S. Lee c Cook b Heal 30	
G. C. Rummans retired 101	Extras 23
M. J. Clarke retired 47	
P. A. Jaques c Symington b Meuleman 18	(50 overs) 300
B. J. Haddin b Cook 5	Fall: 69 94 154 287 294

S. C. G. MacGill, S. H. Cook and S. R. Clark did not bat.

Bowling: Cook 9–0–45–1; Hatch 10–1–45–0; Hopkinson 9–0–56–0; Symington 10–0–59–2; Heal 7–0–40–1; Simmons 3–0–37–0; Meuleman 2–0–10–1.

Rockingham-Mandurah

*J. Meuleman c Mail b Lee 18	S. J. Cook lbw b MacGill 19
C. Simmons c Lee b Clark 4	M. Rennie b MacGill 0
O. A. Shah c Jaques b Lee 8	A. Heal not out 10
B. L. Hutton c Mail b Bradstreet 2	
K. Trevenen c Slater b Lee 0	Extras 19
J. Smith c and b Higgs 17	
C. Hopkinson c Mail b Lee 6	(31.4 overs) 116
M. Symington c Clarke b Higgs 13	Fall: 19 37 44 44 44 59 83 86 86 116

N. G. Hatch did not bat.

Bowling: Cook 5–0–15–0; Clark 5–0–19–1; Lee 4–1–15–4; Bradstreet 4–1–11–1; Higgs 5–1–13–2; MacGill 6.4–1–22–2; Clarke 2–0–15–0.

Umpires: R. Evans and B. Rennie.

CHAMPIONS CUP

CENTRAL DISTRICTS v KWAZULU-NATAL

At WACA Ground, Perth, March 29, 2001. Day/night game. KwaZulu-Natal won by seven wickets. Toss: KwaZulu-Natal.

Central Districts

D. P. Kelly c Watson b Gilder	6	(8)	†B. B. J. Griggs run out (Benkenstein)	20	(21)
*C. M. Spearman c Benkenstein b Kent	15	(13)	A. M. Schwass run out (Benkenstein)	3	(3)
B. F. Smith c Watson b Wingfield	75	(123)	E. P. Thompson not out	6	(7)
G. P. Sulzberger c Bruyns			B. E. Hefford not out	1	(1)
b E. A. E. Baptiste	5	(19)	L-b 2, w 4, n-b 3	9	
M. W. Douglas c Stewart b Wingfield	2	(8)			
J. D. P. Oram c Watson b Bodi	30	(38)	(50 overs, 208 mins) (9 wkts)	222	
J. M. H. How c Bruyns b Gilder	50	(62)	Fall: 7 28 45 65 124 157 211 215 216		

Bowling: Kent 10–2–43–1; Gilder 10–3–51–2; Wingfield 8–1–30–2; Baptiste 6–0–18–1; Tweedie 9–0–44–0; Bodi 7–0–34–1.

KwaZulu-Natal

D. J. Watson not out	76	(117)			
A. Mall c Spearman b Thompson	12	(10)	L-b 4, w 7	11	
W. R. Wingfield c Douglas b Oram	61	(83)			
M. L. Bruyns c Griggs b Sulzberger	29	(30)	(43 overs, 172 mins) (3 wkts)	225	
*D. M. Benkenstein not out	36	(17)	Fall: 16 136 177		

J. C. Kent, †E. L. R. Stewart, G. H. Bodi, E. A. H. Baptiste, A. N. W. Tweedie and G. M. Gilder did not bat.

Bowling: Thompson 9–0–46–1; Hefford 8–2–35–0; Oram 8–1–21–1; Schwass 8–1–38–0; Sulzberger 10–0–67–1.

Umpires: R. L. Parry and R. J. U. Woolridge.
TV Umpire: P. D. Parker.

WESTERN AUSTRALIA v MUMBAI

At WACA Ground, Perth, March 30, 2001. Day/night game. Western Australia won by seven wickets. Toss: Mumbai.

Mumbai

R. F. Morris c Harvey b Nicholson	32	(73)	R. R. Powar c Hussey b Harvey	5	(10)
W. Jaffer c Katich b Williams	82	(108)	A. P. Dani run out (Campbell)	1	(2)
J. V. Paranjpe c Campbell b Harvey	0	(4)	N. M. Kulkarni not out	2	(2)
V. R. Mane run out (Harvey/Campbell)	22	(40)	B 2, l-b 1, w 15, n-b 6	24	
V. G. Kambli c Angel b Williams	5	(13)			
S. V. Bahutule not out	32	(32)	(50 overs, 213 mins) (8 wkts)	231	
*†S. S. Dighe b Harvey	26	(22)	Fall: 98 98 154 159 162 211 221 223		

S. R. Saxena did not bat.

Bowling: Wates 8–1–38–0; Angel 10–1–32–0; Williams 10–0–61–2; Nicholson 8–0–35–1; Harvey 9–1–40–3; Hogg 5–0–22–0.

Western Australia

†R. J. Campbell c and b Saxena	10	(8)
*J. L. Langer not out	119	(149)
S. M. Katich st Dighe b Bahutule	30	(57)
M. W. Goodwin c Dighe b Kulkarni	30	(40)
M. E. Hussey not out	32	(33)

W 6, n-b 7 13
—
(46.5 overs, 180 mins)   (3 wkts) 234
Fall: 13 85 139

K. M. Harvey, G. B. Hogg, M. J. Nicholson, D. J. Wates, B. A. Williams and J. Angel did not bat.

Bowling: Saxena 7.5–0–37–1; Dani 9–2–42–0; Powar 10–0–35–0; Morris 5–0–35–0; Bahutule 7–0–43–1; Kulkarni 8–0–42–1.

Umpires: I. H. Lock and P. D. Parker.
TV Umpire: R. J. Woolridge.

WESTERN AUSTRALIA v KWAZULU-NATAL

At WACA Ground, Perth, March 31, 2001. Day/night game. Western Australia won by 81 runs. Toss: KwaZulu-Natal.

Western Australia

†R. J. Campbell c Kent b Wingfield	42	(47)	M. J. Nicholson not out	8	(11)
*J. L. Langer c Mall b Gilder	0	(2)	B 1, l-b 8, w 9, n-b 3	21	
S. M. Katich run out (Bodi/Bender)	68	(108)			
M. W. Goodwin c Gilder b Wingfield	69	(90)	(50 overs, 200 mins) (4 wkts)	270	
M. E. Hussey not out	62	(44)	Fall: 4 60 180 216		

G. B. Hogg, K. M. Harvey, M. J. North, D. J. Wates and J. Angel did not bat.

Bowling: Kent 9–0–61–0; Gilder 9–0–43–1; Wingfield 9–1–42–2; Tweedie 6–1–25–0; Bodi 9–0–49–0; Bender 8–0–41–0.

KwaZulu-Natal

D. J. Watson c Langer b Nicholson	12	(37)	K. S. Bender b Hogg	19	(44)
A. Mall c Hussey b Wates	44	(45)	A. N. W. Tweedie not out	70	(68)
W. R. Wingfield c Campbell b Wates	11	(28)	G. M. Gilder c North b Hogg	1	(5)
M. L. Bruyns lbw b Harvey	2	(14)			
*D. M. Benkenstein c Langer b Angel	1	(18)	L-b 5, w 17, n-b 1	23	
G. H. Bodi c Campbell b Wates	0	(4)			
J. C. Kent c Hogg b Hussey	3	(6)	(47 overs, 181 mins)	189	
†E. L. R. Stewart c Campbell b Hussey	3	(15)	Fall: 57 65 79 83 83 87 89 93 164 189		

Bowling: Angel 10–3–38–1; Wates 8.3–1–27–3; Nicholson 8–2–34–1; Harvey 6–1–16–1; Hussey 6.3–2–19–2; Hogg 6–0–35–2; Katich 2–0–15–0.

Umpires: P. D. Parker and R. L. Parry.
TV Umpire: I. H. Lock.

KWAZULU-NATAL v MUMBAI

At WACA Ground, Perth, April 1, 2001. Day/night game. KwaZulu-Natal won by six wickets. Toss: Mumbai.

Mumbai

R.F. Morris c Stewart b Kent	30	(39)	R.R. Powar c Benkenstein b Tweedie	.	19	(19)
W. Jaffer c Stewart b Tweedie	5	(5)	N.M. Kulkarni not out		2	(10)
V.G. Kambli c Amla b Gilder	16	(16)	S.R. Saxena b Kent		0	(2)
J.V. Paranjpe c Amla b Baptiste	34	(55)				
S.V. Bahutule run out (Kent)	15	(36)	B 4, l-b 2, w 6, n-b 3		15	
A.P. Dani c Watson b Benkenstein	16	(37)				
*†S.S. Dighe c Kent b Benkenstein	3	(22)	(47.3 overs, 200 mins)		186	
P.L. Mhambrey b Kent	31	(45)	Fall: 7 34 66 110 110 120 136 164 186 186			

Bowling: Gilder 8–0–26–1; Tweedie 9–1–53–2; Kent 8.3–1–25–3; Baptiste 8–1–20–1; Wingfield 9–1–29–0; Benkenstein 5–0–27–2.

KwaZulu-Natal

D.J. Watson run out (Jaffer)	30	(43)	W.R. Wingfield not out		51	(83)
A. Mall run out (Dani)	23	(25)	L-b 4, w 5, n-b 2		11	
J.C. Kent c Dighe b Mhambrey	6	(16)				
M.L. Bruyns not out	54	(75)	(45 overs, 181 mins)	(4 wkts)	190	
A.M. Amla c Dighe b Saxena	15	(31)	Fall: 45 67 67 90			

*D.M. Benkenstein, †E.L.R. Stewart, E.A.E. Baptiste, A.N.W. Tweedie and G.M. Gilder did not bat.

Bowling: Mhambrey 10–1–24–1; Saxena 10–0–57–1; Bahutule 10–1–41–0; Kulkarni 7–1–24–0; Dani 7–0–33–0; Morris 1–0–7–0.

Umpires: I.H. Lock and R.J.U. Woolridge.
TV Umpire: R.L. Parry.

CENTRAL DISTRICTS v MUMBAI

At WACA Ground, Perth, April 2, 2001. Day/night game. Central Districts won by 106 runs. Toss: Mumbai.

Central Districts

D.P. Kelly c Dighe b Saxena	6	(11)	A.M. Schwass run out (Paranjpe)		22	(16)
J.M.H. How run out (Kulkarni)	40	(73)	E.P. Thompson not out		6	(8)
C.M. Spearman c Kannan b Saxena	12	(16)	B.E. Hefford not out		2	(1)
B.F. Smith lbw b Saxena	2	(9)				
*J.D.P. Oram c Mhambrey b Kulkarni	74	(65)	L-b 4, w 4, n-b 2		10	
†M.W. Douglas c and b Kulkarni	8	(18)				
G.P. Sulzberger c Dighe b Kulkarni	57	(60)	(50 overs, 212 mins)	(9 wkts)	268	
G.R. Todd b Mhambrey	29	(27)	Fall: 11 35 41 74 88 196 218 255 266			

Bowling: Mhambrey 9–0–56–1; Saxena 10–0–39–3; Kannan 10–0–54–0; Kulkarni 10–0–38–3; Bahutule 6–0–37–0; Morris 5–0–40–0.

Mumbai

R.F. Morris c Kelly b Hefford	4	(11)	S. Kannan b E.P. Schwass		1	(4)
W. Jaffer run out (Smith)	0	(6)	N.M. Kulkarni lbw b Oram		6	(12)
V.G. Kambli c Spearman b Thompson	4	(9)	S.R. Saxena not out		10	(9)
V.R. Mane c Kelly b Schwass	53	(71)				
J.V. Paranjpe run out (Todd/Douglas)	14	(47)	L-b 4, w 19, n-b 5		28	
S.V. Bahutule c Todd b Sulzberger	38	(46)				
†S.S. Dighe c Sulzberger b Schwass	2	(9)	(38.3 overs, 174 mins)		162	
P.L. Mhambrey c and b Sulzberger	2	(8)	Fall: 4 7 11 65 138 141 142 146 148 162			

Bowling: Thompson 8–0–38–1; Hefford 7–1–14–1; Oram 6.3–0–18–1; Schwass 7–1–41–3; Todd 3–0–19–0; Sulzberger 7–0–28–2.

Umpires: P.D. Parker and R.J.U. Woolridge.
TV Umpire: I.H. Lock.

WESTERN AUSTRALIA v CENTRAL DISTRICTS

At WACA Ground, Perth, April 3, 2001. Day/night game. Western Australia won by 108 runs. Toss: Western Australia.

Western Australia

†R.J. Campbell c How b Hefford	4	(9)
G.B. Hogg c Spearman b Schwass	29	(53)
M.J. North b Sulzberger	56	(80)
P.C. Worthington c (sub) West b Sulzberger	54	(63)
*J.L. Langer c (sub) West b Thompson	60	(64)
M.W. Goodwin c Sulzberger b Oram	10	(10)
M.E. Hussey b Schwass	7	(9)

M.J. Nicholson run out (Oram/Schwass)	3	(4)
S.J. Karppinen not out	3	(7)
S.M. Katich not out	5	(3)
L-b 10, w 15, n-b 1	26	
(50 overs, 218 mins) (8 wkts)	257	
Fall: 6 89 112 207 230 243 247 251		

B.A. Williams did not bat.

Bowling: Thompson 9–0–49–1; Hefford 10–0–49–1; Oram 10–1–39–1; Schwass 10–0–55–2; Sulzberger 9–1–38–2; Todd 2–0–17–0.

Central Districts

J.M.H. How c Worthington b Karppinen	39	(72)
D.P. Kelly b Williams	5	(9)
C.M. Spearman b Williams	13	(13)
B.F. Smith c Hogg b Karppinen	0	(3)
*J.D.P. Oram b Nicholson	25	(27)
†M.W. Douglas run out (Hussey/North)	13	(21)
G.P. Sulzberger c Katich b North	20	(21)
G.R. Todd lbw b North	1	(5)

A.M. Schwass c Campbell b Hogg	7	(10)
E.P. Thompson not out	9	(6)
B.E. Hefford c Goodwin b Hogg	2	(9)
L-b 3, w 10, n-b 2	15	
(32.2 overs, 137 mins)	149	
Fall: 16 35 47 79 95 117 124 131 145 149		

Bowling: Karppinen 10–0–40–2; Williams 5–0–22–2; Nicholson 6–2–28–1; Hogg 6.2–0–33–2; North 4–0–20–2; Worthington 1–0–3–0.

Umpires: I.H. Lock and D.L. Parry.
TV Umpire: P.D. Parker.

FINAL

WESTERN AUSTRALIA v KWAZULU-NATAL

At WACA Ground, Perth, April 4, 2001. Day/night game. Western Australia won by six wickets. Toss: KwaZulu-Natal.

KwaZulu-Natal

D.J. Watson c Campbell b Angel	13	(34)
A. Mall c Campbell b Nicholson	21	(33)
W.R. Wingfield run out (Langer/Campbell)	28	(53)
G.H. Bodi c Angel b Nicholson	4	(10)
M.L. Bruyns c and b Hogg	33	(41)
*D.M. Benkenstein c Campbell b Angel	7	(10)
J.C. Kent not out	81	(82)

†E.L.R. Stewart b Harvey	46	(42)
K.S. Bender b I.J. Harvey	0	(1)
A.N.W. Tweedie not out	0	(0)
B 1, l-b 2, w 4, n-b 3	10	
(50 overs, 204 mins) (8 wkts)	243	
Fall: 34 34 41 96 106 133 228 228		

E.A.E. Baptiste did not bat.

Bowling: Angel 10–2–39–2; Williams 10–1–63–0; Nicholson 10–0–50–2; Harvey 10–0–44–2; North 2–0–12–0; Hogg 8–0–32–1.

Western Australia

†R. J. Campbell c and b Wingfield	... 29 (27)	M. E. Hussey not out	.... 16 (15)
M. J. North c Benkenstein b Baptiste	.. 55 (89)	L-b 3, w 18, n-b 1	 22
*J. L. Langer c Bender b Baptiste	.... 34 (53)		
S. M. Katich not out	.... 67 (65)	(49.1 overs, 216 mins) (4 wkts) 244	
M. W. Goodwin c Kent b Tweedie	... 21 (48)	Fall: 60 122 142 189	

G. B. Hogg, K. M. Harvey, M. J. Nicholson, B. A. Williams and J. Angel did not bat.

Bowling: Wingfield 8.1–0–46–1; Tweedie 6–0–37–1; Bender 10–0–38–0; Kent 10–0–53–0; Baptiste 10–0–40–2; Bodi 5–0–27–0.

Umpires: P. D. Parker and R. L. Parry.
TV Umpire: R. J. U. Woolridge.

OTHER MINOR CRICKET

ATSIC CHAIRMAN'S XI V PRIME MINISTER'S XI

At Manuka Oval, Canberra, April 19, 2001. ATSIC Chairman's XI won by seven wickets. Toss: ATSIC Chairman's XI.

This match was part of the national reconciliation process and an important opportunity for cricket to begin an examination of both its relationship with and place in indigenous communities. The teams competed for the handsome trophy commemorating the cricketing skills and life of the dominating presence on the 1868 Aboriginal tour of England, Johnny Mullagh. The Prime Minister's XI drew on the services of Belinda Clark, captain of the Australian women's team, Joe Hockey, Federal Minister for Financial Services and Ashley Mallett, who is currently writing a book on the 1868 tour. Geoff Clark, chairman of ATSIC, made an appearance for his side, as did runner Nova Peris, Senator Aden Ridgway, actor Aaron Pederson, hurdler Kyle Vander-Kuyp and rugby league player turned boxer Anthony Mundine. The Prime Minister's XI innings was held together by Tim Dann, an indigenous player from Perth, who batted with composure for 103 balls. Glen Martin, a first grader with Northern Districts in Brisbane, was lively and penetrating, while Ryan Bulger, a Glenelg A grader, bowled his leg-breaks with skill. The Chairman's XI won with wickets to spare, thanks to a rousing innings from Clinton Dann of the Perth club, who was ably supported by Sydney players Matthew Bradley and Damien Duroux.

Player of the Match: C Dann.
Attendance: 3,000 (approx).

Prime Minister's XI

M. A. Higgs c Redpath b Martin	..... 16 (17)	P. Thomas c Vander-Kuyp b Bulger	. 14 (19)
M. Klinger c Dann b Trindall	.... 0 (4)	M. G. Johnson not out	.... 22 (19)
T. Dann lbw b Bulger	.... 74 (103)	N. W. Bracken not out	.... 6 (6)
*S. R. Waugh c Bulger b Hoffman	... 11 (20)		
†S. G. Clingeleffer c Trindall b Dann	. 17 (31)	L-b 7, w 14, n-b 1	 22
B. J. Clark b Martin	.... 10 (15)		
J. Hockey lbw b Martin	.... 0 (1)	(40 overs, 166 mins) (9 wkts) 194	
K. Thomas st Sarra b Bulger	.... 2 (6)	Fall: 6 25 59 104 141 141 144 157 170	

A. A. Mallett and A. C. L. James did not bat.

Bowling: Martin 8–0–45–3; Trindall 7–2–22–1; Redpath 6–0–47–0; Hoffman 6–2–18–1; Dann 5–0–23–1; Bulger 8–1–32–3.

ATSIC Chairman's XI

I. Redpath c Higgs b Johnson	1	(17)
C. Dann not out	87	(125)
M. S. Bradley c and b James	40	(46)
†J. Sarra c Higgs b K Thomas	2	(18)
D. Duroux not out	41	(40)

L-b 1, w 14, n-b 9 24

—

(39.3 overs, 161 mins)   (3 wkts) 195

Fall: 13 77 99

G. Clark, A. Hoffman, R. W. Bulger, C. A. Trindall, G Martin, *J. N. Gillespie, A. Mundine, A. Ridgway, N. Peris, A. Pedersen and K. Vander-Kuyp did not bat.

Bowling: Bracken 5–1–15–0; Johnson 7–2–37–1; James 5–1–37–1; K Thomas 7–2–20–1; Mallett 5–0–27–0; Higgs 7.3–0–40–0; P Thomas 3–0–18–0.

Umpires: P. D. Chapman and D. B. Harris.
TV Umpire: G. R. Clifton.

AUSTRALIAN CRICKET ACADEMY, 2000-01

By KEN PIESSE

Australian cricket's renowned finishing school took on an international air in 2000 when five young West Indians were among a growing band of overseas cricketers to spend time in Adelaide. Guyana's Ramnaresh Sarwan, Trinidad and Tobago's Daren Ganga and Jamaicans Chris Gayle, Jermaine Lawson and Ricardo Powell all had stints, alongside the 13 full-time Australian scholars. Academy head coach Rod Marsh and his assistant Wayne Phillips are actively encouraging the best youngsters from overseas to come to Australia – at a fee – especially in the months from January to April in between Academy intakes when the heritage-listed guest house at Henley Beach is less than full. In addition to the West Indian brigade, three lads from India are sent annually via the Border–Gavaskar scholarships, and the Zimbabwean Douglas Marillier spent a fortnight there, as did cricketers from England, Bangladesh, South Africa and even Tonga.

Marsh was delighted that the West Indies Cricket Board preferred to send some of their most promising players to the Academy for four to six-week periods rather than involving them in the ICC mini-World Cup in Kenya. Three of the West Indian guests were to play in the internationals in the following months, Sarwan and Ganga in the Tests and Ganga and Powell in the Carlton Series. Marsh was particularly impressed with Sarwan, who played one of the most memorable innings of the Academy summer when he stroked 112 from 110 balls in a practice match against a full-strength Tasmania in Adelaide in early October. He and New South Wales' Phil Jacques, who scored 88, took the score from three for 12 to four for 222, their stand hurtling along at six an over. Chasing 296, the Academy finished at eight for 282 after an exhilarating run chase. Four of the five West Indians played in the game. Lawson, a teenage fast bowler, also played for the Academy against the Queensland Academy of Sport in Brisbane.

In addition to the annual involvement of notables such as Ian Chappell, Dennis Lillee and Terry Jenner, the 2000 intake had the benefit of a visit from Mark Taylor. For four days the former Australian captain shared meals with the boys, chatted and coached. He gave one formal talk on captaincy, which according to one of the scholars, Melbourne teenager Andrew Kent, was one of the highlights of his eight-month stint. "He spoke for two hours and the time just flew by," said Kent. "We hung on his every word."

Kent, one of the most promising youngsters in the batch, says the opportunity to go to the Academy is a once-in-a-lifetime experience which reinforces a player's strengths and shores up his weaknesses. "For me it was learning to adapt better to the short ball rather than looking to play all the time off the front foot. Striking a balance is important." The Academy staff included for the first time the former Tasmanian pace bowler Troy Cooley, while South Australia's David Fitzgerald was a specialist coach. In 2001 his role was taken by the Victorian fast bowler Mathew Inness.

The 2000 Academy scholars were: Michael Clarke, Phil Jacques, Aaron O'Brien and Shane Stanton (NSW), Chris Hartley, Nathan Hauritz, Shane Watson and Mitchell Johnson (Qld), Paul Rofe and Luke Williams (SAust), Andrew Kent and Andrew McDonald (Vic) and Adam Voges (WAust). In addition to playing virtually non-stop from October to December in the ACB Cup, as well as in other representative games around Australia, many of the boys went overseas, to India and Bangladesh. Rofe and Watson spent time at the MRF Pace Foundation in Chennai, while Kent, McDonald, Voges and Stanton had two weeks at the Indian Cricket Academy.

In January 2001, an Academy team bolstered by several invitational players, including Western Australian Shane Marsh and Victoria's Tim Welsford, toured Bangladesh for three three-day games and four limited-overs games. The wickets were hard and flat and spun considerably. Among the opposition were many of Bangladesh's recently capped Test cricketers. Marsh, with two centuries, was outstanding, and on his return soon made his first-class debut with Western Australia.

During the ACB Cup several players shared the captaincy responsibilities as part of their cricketing education. Sent in against the ultimate champions, Western Australia, at Richardson Park, the Academy lost six for 12 before being bowled out for 84, Stanton top-scoring with 40. In the second innings they made 401 with Jacques (who made 110), Watson and Williams in the runs. Williams was the leading run-maker in the ACB Cup games with 585 runs at an average of 65 in seven matches. Jacques made 323 in six. Watson was also impressive, making 271 runs (at 38.71) and taking 17 wickets (at 25.64) in six games. Rofe, a tall pace bowler, took 30 wickets in six games at the rate of a wicket every 35 balls.

AUSTRALIAN CRICKET ACADEMY v TASMANIA

At Adelaide Oval No. 2, October 9, 2000. Tasmania won by 13 runs. Toss: Tasmania.

Tasmania

*J. Cox c Sarwan b Voges	76 (93)	S. P. Kremerskothen not out	8 (6)
M. J. Di Venuto c and b Geeves	45 (54)	L-b 3, w 5, nb 5	13
S. Young c Hauritz b Thomas	62 (67)		
D. F. Hills not out	63 (59)	(50 overs, 209 mins)　(4 wkts)	295
G. T. Cunningham c Hauritz b Geeves	28 (26)	Fall: 87 169 215 264	

D. J. Saker, D. G. Wright, A. G. Downton, B. S. Targett, G. J. Denton and †S. G. Clingeleffer did not bat.

Bowling: Lawson 6–0–46–0; Watson 7–0–50–0; Geeves 10–1–50–2; Thomas 6–0–40–1; Hauritz 10–0–37–0; Gayle 2–0–11–0; Voges 4–0–22–1; Jaques 5–0–36–0.

Australian Cricket Academy

†S. D. Stanton c Clingeleffer b Wright	8 (13)	*A. C. Voges c Hills b Downton	25 (17)
D. Ganga b Wright	1 (22)	N. M. Hauritz not out	12 (11)
C. H. Gayle c Clingeleffer b Wright ..	0 (3)	O. C. Thomas not out	2 (3)
P. A. Jaques run out (Di Venuto)	88 (110)	B 4, l-b 2, n-b 11	17
R. R. Sarwan c Wright b Kremerskothen	112 (110)		
A. J. Kent c Wright b Kremerskothen .	7 (10)	(50 overs, 208 mins) (8 wkts)	282
S. R. Watson run out (Cox)	10 (12)	Fall: 9 9 12 222 223 233 249 274	

B. Geeves and J. Lawson did not bat.

Bowling: Saker 10–2–41–0; Wright 7–2–22–3; Downton 8–1–40–1; Denton 8–0–57–0; Cox 4–0–26–0; Targett 2–0–16–0; Young 6–0–42–0; Kremerskothen 5–0–32–2.

Umpires: S. D. Fry and R. Thomas.

AUSTRALIAN CRICKET ACADEMY IN BANGLADESH, 2000-01

BANGLADESH CRICKET BOARD UNDER-21s v AUSTRALIAN CRICKET ACADEMY

At Bangladesh Krira Shixa Protisthan Ground, Dhaka, January 7, 8, 9, 2001. Drawn. Toss: Australian Cricket Academy.

Close of Play: Day 1: Bangladesh Cricket Board Under-21s (1) 0-23 (Mohammed Ashraful 4, Sajjadul Hassan Shetu 16). Day 2: Australian Cricket Academy (2) 2-96 (O'Brien 43, Voges 16).

Australian Cricket Academy

D. J. Harris b Tapash Kumar Baisno	25	– (2) c Mohammed Salim b Ranjan Das	4
L. Williams c Mohammed Salim b Ranjan Das	5	– (1) b Manjural Islam	33
S. D. Stanton c Manjural Islam b Mohammed Shariff	88		
S. E. Marsh not out	106		
A. J. Kent c Ranjan Das b Shabir Ahmed	19		
A. B. McDonald not out	9		
A. W. O'Brien (did not bat)		– (3) b Mohammed Shariff	48
A. C. Voges (did not bat)		– (4) lbw b Mohammed Shariff	74
T. H. Welsford (did not bat)		– (5) c Sajjadul Hassan Shetu b Shabir Ahmed ..	4
†C. D. Hartley (did not bat)		– (6) not out	51
*N. M. Hauritz (did not bat)		– (7) not out	11
B 15, l-b 5, n-b 1	21	L-b 1, w 1	2

(83.5 overs, 395 mins)	(4 wkts) 273	(52 overs, 243 mins) (5 wkts dec) 227
Fall: 25 47 214 248		Fall: 23 78 109 138 205

Bowling: *First Innings*—Ranjan Das 16–6–31–1; Mohammed Shariff 14–1–43–1; Tapash Kumar Baisno 13–0–54–1; Shabir Ahmed 17–3–41–1; Mohammed Ashraful 7.5–2–37–0; Manjural Islam 16–2–47–0. *Second Innings*—Ranjan Das 10–1–37–1; Mohammed Shariff 11–0–53–2; Tapash Kumar Baisno 6–0–33–0; Shabir Ahmed 15–5–46–1; Manjural Islam 7–0–41–1; Mohammed Ashraful 3–1–16–0.

Bangladesh Cricket Board Under-21s

Mohammed Ashraful c Hartley b Welsford	19	– (2) c Hartley b Hauritz	27
Sajjadul Hassan Shetu c Hartley b McDonald	17	– (1) c Welsford b O'Brien	31
Rajin Salah c Hartley b McDonald	10	– c Hartley b O'Brien	81
†Mohammed Salim c Stanton b McDonald	13	– c Harris b McDonald	14
Mazharol Hoq Mridul c and b Voges	34	– c Hauritz b O'Brien	26
Tusher Imran b Voges	48	– not out	25
Manjural Islam not out	13	– Manjural Islam not out	0
*Shabir Ahmed lbw b Voges	0		
Mohammed Shariff b McDonald	30		
Tapash Kumar Baisno c Stanton b McDonald	2		
Ranjan Das b McDonald	0		
B 1, l-b 6, n-b 2	9	B 4, l-b 7, w 1, n-b 2	14

(68.5 overs, 257 mins)   195
Fall: 33 39 58 63 137 157 157 193 195 195

(71 overs, 240 mins)   (5 wkts) 218
Fall: 53 64 112 163 218

Bowling: *First Innings*—Welsford 19–2–55–1; Hauritz 8–3–24–0; McDonald 13.5–3–28–6; Marsh 3–0–13–0; O'Brien 11–4–19–0; Voges 14–2–49–3. *Second Innings*—Welsford 11–3–25–0; McDonald 9–1–31–1; Hauritz 22–8–58–1; O'Brien 14–5–24–3; Stanton 2–1–6–0; Kent 2–0–12–0; Voges 9–1–31–0; Marsh 2–0–20–0.

Umpires: Samiur Rahman and Mahbubur Rahman.

BANGLADESH CRICKET BOARD PRESIDENT'S XI v AUSTRALIAN CRICKET ACADEMY

At Rajshahi District Stadium, Rajshahi, January 12, 13, 14, 2001. Drawn. Toss: Bangladesh Cricket Board President's XI.

Close of Play: Day 1: Australian Cricket Academy 0-11 (Harris 4, Williams 3). Day 2: Bangladesh Cricket Board President's XI 2-7 (Mossadek Hossain 0, Rajin Salah 0).

Bangladesh Cricket Board President's XI

Shahriar Hossain st Hartley b O'Brien	36	– c O'Brien b Chaitra	3
Rafiqul Islam c Williams b O'Brien	11	– c Hartley b Chaitra	3
Nasirul Alam Nahid c and b O'Brien	2	– (5) c Hartley b McDonald	0
Rajin Salah c Hartley b McDonald	0	– c Stanton b McDonald	4
Mushfiqur Rahman not out	100	– (6) b McDonald	36
*†Khaled Mashud c Chaitra b O'Brien	8	– (8) b McDonald	75
Anisur Rehman c and b McDonald	83	– b O'Brien	26
Fahim Muntasir c Hartley b Voges	34	– c Sumit Panda b McDonald	14
Ahsanullah Hasan not out	8	– run out (Hartley)	1
Mossadek Hossain (did not bat)		– (3) lbw b Chaitra	53
Habibul Hossain (did not bat)		– not out	9
L-b 3, w 1, n-b 1	5	B 1, w 5 n-b 4	10

(88 overs, 300 mins)   (7 wkts dec) 287
Fall: 40 49 50 56 90 224 274

(89 overs)   234
Fall: 6 7 18 18 95 118 140 189 202 234

Aminul Islam jnr did not bat.

Bowling: *First Innings*—Sumit Panda 15–2–44–0; Chaitra 8–3–10–0; O'Brien 26–12–68–4; McDonald 9–3–41–2; Hauritz 15–4–50–0; Voges 15–0–71–1. *Second Innings*—Sumit Panda 13–8–11–0; Chaitra 18–7–46–3; McDonald 17–7–44–5; O'Brien 15–1–46–1; Voges 6–1–19–0; Hauritz 17–4–53–0; Stanton 3–0–14–0.

Australian Cricket Academy

D. J. Harris c Khaled Mashud b Fahim Muntasir	...	49	
L. Williams c Aminul Islam jnr b Fahim Muntasir	..	27	
S. D. Stanton c Mushfiqur Rahman b Ahsanullah Hasan	..	46	– not out 18
S. E. Marsh c Khaled Mashud b Mushfiqur Rahman		95	
A. J. Kent c Shahriar Hossain b Mushfiqur Rahman		53	
A. B. McDonald c Shahriar Hossain b Aminul Islam jnr		21	
A. W. O'Brien not out	....	7	
A. C. Voges c Shahriar Hossain b Aminul Islam jnr	.	2	– (1) b Mushfiqur Rahman 46
†C. D. Hartley (did not bat)	....		– c and b Aminul Islam jnr 7
*N. M. Haurtiz (did not bat)	....		– not out 1
B 3, l-b 4, w 3, n-b 3	....	13	B 1, w 1, n-b 1 3

(90.1 overs, 306 mins)	(7 wkts dec) 313	(13 overs) (2 wkts) 75
Fall: 64 109 166 251 300 304 313		Fall: 30 74

Sumit Panda and G. Chaitra did not bat.

Bowling: *First Innings*—Habibul Hossain 15–1–59–0; Aminul Islam jnr 22.1–4–76–2; Fahim Muntasir 24–8–61–2; Mossadek Hossain 12–1–40–0; Mushfiqur Rahman 8–1–35–2; Ahsanullah Hasan 9–1–35–1. *Second Innings*—Habibul Hossain 4–0–33–0; Aminul Islam jnr 4–0–23–1; Mushfiqur Rahman 3–0–13–1; Fahim Muntasir 2–0–5–0.

Umpires: S. B. Chowdhury and S. R. Chinu.

BANGLADESH CRICKET BOARD PRESIDENT'S XI v AUSTRALIAN CRICKET ACADEMY

At Rajshahi District Stadium, Rajshahi, January 15, 2000. Australian Cricket Academy won by four wickets. Toss: Bangladesh Cricket Board President's XI.

Bangladesh Cricket Board President's XI

Rashedul Hoque Suman c Marsh b McDonald	..	9	(29)	Fahim Muntasir not out 27	(26)
Reshadur Rahman Ranim b Sumit Panda	21	(28)		Mossadek Hossain c Stanton b Voges 7	(12)
Rajin Salah b Hauritz	....	16	(49)	Saiful Islam lbw b Welsford 0	(1)
Nasirul Alam Nahid c Marsh b O'Brien	24	(29)		B 4, l-b 6, n-b 22 32	
Mushfiqur Rahman c Stanton b O'Brien	0	(1)			
Anisur Rehman run out (Stanton)	....	31	(50)	(46.5 overs) 194	
*†Khaled Mashud b McDonald	......	23	(40)	Fall: 40 41 78 80 105 146 153 164	
Alok Kapali run out (Stanton)	....	4	(7)	189 194	

Tapash Kumar Baisno did not bat.

Bowling: Welsford 5.5–0–39–1; Sumit Panda 8–0–29–1; McDonald 8–1–32–2; O'Brien 10–1–39–2; Hauritz 10–0–28–1; Voges 5–0–23–1.

Australian Cricket Academy

†S. D. Stanton b Tapash Kumar Baisno	17	(31)	*N. M. Hauritz c M. Rahman b M. Hossain	..	2	(8)
L. Williams run out (Khaled Mashud)	.	73	(112)	A. C. Voges not out 11	(8)
D. J. Harris b Saiful Islam	....	5	(17)	L-b 5, w 13, n-b 2 20	
C. D. Hartley c Khaled Mashud b Mossadek Hossain	..	46	(79)	(48 overs, 192 mins) (6 wkts) 195	
A. J. Kent c and b Mossadek Hossain	.	4	(5)	Fall: 25 35 141 146 173 184	
S. E. Marsh not out	....	17	(30)		

T. H. Welsford, A. W. O'Brien, A. B. McDonald and Sumit Panda did not bat.

Bowling: Tapash Kumar Baisno 9–1–22–1; Saiful Islam 10–1–32–1; Mushfiqur Rahman 9–0–30–0; Alok Kapali 3–0–20–0; Fahim Muntasir 7–0–30–0; Rashedul Hoque Suman 4–0–23–0; Mossadek Hossain 6–0–33–3.

Umpires: Shawkatur Rahman Chinu and Khondokar Ziaul Islam Masud.

BANGLADESH CRICKET BOARD v AUSTRALIAN CRICKET ACADEMY

At Bangabandhu National Stadium, Dhaka, January 17, 18, 19, 20 2001. Australian Cricket Academy won by 155 runs. Toss: Bangladesh Cricket Board.
Close of Play: Day 1: Australian Cricket Academy 6-297 (Kent 61, Voges 11). Day 2: Bangladesh Cricket Board 6-226 (Mazharol Hoq Mridul 97, Khaled Mashud 0). Day 3: Australian Cricket Academy 3-235 (Marsh 55, O'Brien 17).

Australian Cricket Academy

*L. Williams c Khaled Mashud b Mushfiqur Rahman	23	– lbw b Mossadek Hossain 80
D.J. Harris c Khaled Mashud b Aminul Islam jnr ..	14	– b Mohammad Rafique 29
S.D. Stanton lbw b Hasibul Hussain	45	– c Mohammad Rafique b Anisur Rehman .. 43
S.E. Marsh c Khaled Mashud b Mushfiqur Rahman	92	– c and b Mohammad Rafique 89
A.W. O'Brien lbw b Mushfiqur Rahman	11	– b Fahim Muntasir 70
A.J. Kent c Rajin Salah b Aminul Islam jnr	61	– b Mohammad Rafique 1
A.B. McDonald c Khaled Mashud b Mushfiqur Rahman ..	21	– not out 0
A.C. Voges c Khaled Mashud b Hasibul Hussain ..	15	
†C.D. Hartley c Mushfiqur Rahman b Aminul Islam jnr	0	
T.H. Welsford c Mushfiqur Rahman b Aminul Islam jnr	0	
Sumit Panda not out	0	
B 4, l-b 6, w 1, n-b 8	19	L-b 16, n-b 4 20
(97.1 overs, 314 mins)	301	(86.1 overs, 334 mins) (6 wkts dec) 332
Fall: 38 40 176 190 201 276 297 297 301 301		Fall: 97 132 195 326 332 332

G. Chaitra did not bat.

Bowling: *First Innings*—Aminul Islam jnr 23–6–42–4; Hasibul Hussain 20.1–4–74–2; Mushfiqur Rahman 26–6–73–4; Mohammad Rafique 17–4–60–0; Fahim Muntasir 8–30–0; Mossadek Hossain 3–1–12–0. *Second Innings*—Aminul Islam jnr 5–0–25–0; Hasibul Hussain 14–0–42–0; Mushfiqur Rahman 17–2–66–0; Fahim Muntasir 11.1–1–51–1; Mohammad Rafique 21–3–60–3; Mossadek Hossain 7–2–23–1; Anisur Rehman 11–1–49–1.

Bangladesh Cricket Board

Rashedul Hoque Suman b Welsford	8	– b Welsford 0
†Hannan Sarker b McDonald	4	– b Welsford 5
Rajin Salah b Welsford	0	– lbw McDonald 0
Mazharol Hoq Mridul c Hartley b McDonald ...	144	– c Hartley b McDonald 10
Mushfiqur Rahman c Hartley b O'Brien	9	– lbw Williams 16
Mossadek Hossain b Welsford	12	– (8) c Williams b O'Brien 17
Anisur Rehman c and b Voges	73	– (6) run out (Hartley) 1
*Khaled Mashud c Hartley b Chaitra	49	– (7) c Welsford b O'Brien 18
Fahim Muntasir c Welsford b Chaitra	0	– (10) c Voges b McDonald 11
Mohammad Rafique not out	4	– (9) c Chaitra b Voges 52
Hasibul Hussain b Mcdonald	1	– not out 2
B 4, l-b 5, w 5, n-b 20	34	B 2, l-b 5, w 1 8
(107.1 overs, 425 mins)	338	(65.5 overs, 246 mins) 140
Fall: 13 13 13 58 85 214 322 329 337 338		Fall: 0 1 9 29 33 54 64 97 131 140

Aminul Islam jnr did not bat.

Bowling: *First Innings*—Welsford 22–2–61–3; McDonald 21.1–7–55–3; Chaitra 15–2–47–2; O'Brien 24–6–77–1; Sumit Panda 15–5–40–0; Voges 10–1–49–1. *Second Innings*—Welsford 10–6–18–2; McDonald 15.5–7–23–3; Chaitra 6–4–6–0; Sumit Panda 3–1–11–0; O'Brien 15–4–31–2; Williams 5–2–9–1; Vogues 11–4–35–1.

Umpires: Sayeed Mahbubullah and Akhteruddin.

BANGLADESH CRICKET BOARD v AUSTRALIAN CRICKET ACADEMY

At Bangabandhu National Stadium, Dhaka, January 23, 2001. Day/night match. Australian Cricket Academy won by 154 runs. Toss: Bangladesh Cricket Board

Australian Cricket Academy

*L. Williams c Anwar Hossain b Enamul Hoque .. 48 (53)	A. B. McDonald c Aminul Islam b Shafiuddin Ahmed .. 22 (32)
D. J. Harris c Anisur Rehman b Aminul Islam .. 40 (67)	T. H. Welsford c Aminul Islam b Manjural Islam .. 31 (20)
A. C. Voges b Enamul Hoque 76 (69)	†C. D. Hartley not out 1 (1)
S. E. Marsh b Aminul Islam 2 (4)	
A. J. Kent c Anwar Hossain b Enamul Hoque .. 18 (32)	B 1, l-b 9, w 6 16
A. W. O'Brien c Tusher Imran b Ehsan-ul-Haque .. 20 (23)	(50 overs, 208 mins) (9 wkts) 274
S. D. Stanton c Anwar Hossain b Enamul Hoque ... 0 (1)	Fall: 69 138 145 188 197 197 238 265 274

Sumit Panda and G Chaitra did not bat.

Bowling: Manjural Islam 10–1–47–1; Shafiuddin Ahmed 10–0–47–1; Enamul Hoque 10–1–45–4; Shabbir Khan 5–0–45–0; Mohammed Ashraful 3–0–21–0; Aminul Islam 10–0–45–2; Ehsan–ul–Haque 2–0–15–1.

Bangladesh Cricket Board

Mohammed Ashraful c Voges b Welsford 8 (13)	Enamul Hoque c Harris b O'Brien .. 8 (26)
†Nafis Iqbal Khan lbw b Welsford ... 0 (1)	Anwar Hossain c Marsh b Voges ... 5 (29)
Ehsan-ul-Haque b Chaitra 0 (4)	Shafiuddin Ahmed not out 0 (1)
*Aminul Islam c Hartley b Welsford . 0 (1)	
Mazharul Islam c Hartley b Welsford . 30 (43)	L-b 1, w 22, n-b 5 28
Anisur Rehman c Hartley b McDonald 18 (26)	
Tusher Imran c Hartley b McDonald .. 21 (38)	(33.1 overs, 137 mins) 120
Shabbir Khan c Harris b O'Brien 2 (22)	Fall: 5 9 11 17 58 79 102 102 120 120

Manjural Islam did not bat.

Bowling: Welsford 8–0–42–4; Sumit Panda 4–1–6–0; Chaitra 6–0–23–1; McDonald 6–1–26–2; O'Brien 9–3–22–2; Voges 0.1–0–0–1.

Umpires: D. J. Harper and Mohammad Asgar.

BANGLADESH CRICKET BOARD v AUSTRALIAN CRICKET ACADEMY

At Bangabandhu National Stadium, Dhaka, January 24, 2001. Day/night match. Australian Cricket Academy won by five wickets. Toss: Bangladesh Cricket Board.

Bangladesh Cricket Board

Nafis Iqbal Khan c Stanton b Sumit Panda	28	(67)		Sarfuddula Saikat lbw b McDonald ..	3	(10)
Mehrab Hossain c Hartley b Chaitra ..	0	(1)		†Mukhtar Siddique not out	23	(27)
Sajjad Ahmed c McDonald b Williams	68	(90)		Ranjan Das not out	2	(2)
Hasannuzzaman run out (Kent)	0	(3)				
*Naimur Rahman c Stanton b O'Brien	51	(41)		L-b 3, w 13, n-b 2	18	
Asadullah Khan run out (McDonald) .	7	(16)			—	
Mushfiqur Rahman c Harris b McDonald	30	(32)		(50 overs, 211 mins) (9 wkts)	236	
Fahim Muntasir c and b O'Brien	6	(13)		Fall: 0 77 82 123 146 168 181 197 231		

Ashfaq Ali Rahat did not bat.

Bowling: Welsford 10–1–50–0; Chaitra 6–0–16–1; McDonald 10–1–46–2; Sumit Panda 10–0–31–1; O'Brien 7–0–54–2; Williams 7–0–36–1.

Australian Cricket Academy

S.D. Stanton c Ashfaq Ali Rahat				A.W. O'Brien c Mukhtar Siddique		
b Mushfiqur Rahman ..	14	(29)		b Ashfaq Ali Rahat .	9	(15)
*L. Williams run out (Nafis Iqbal Khan)	13	(11)		A.C. Voges not out	10	(16)
D.J. Harris run out (Mukhtar Siddique)	65	(84)		L-b 4, w 18, n-b 1	23	
S.E. Marsh not out 105		(118)			—	
A.J. Kent c Asadullah Khan				(45.2 overs, 201 mins) (5 wkts)	240	
b Ashfaq Ali Rahat ...	1	(2)		Fall: 19 39 169 176 208		

†C.D. Hartley, A.B. Mcdonald, Sumit Panda, T.H. Welsford and G. Chaitra did not bat.

Bowling: Ranjan Das 8–0–28–0; Ashfaq Ali Rahat 10–0–52–2; Mushfiqur Rahman 10–0–45–1; Fahim Muntasir 7–0–35–0; Sarfuddula Saikat 5–0–34–0; Naimur Rahman 5–0–34–0; Hasannuzzaman 0.2–0–8–0.

Umpires: D.J. Harper and Sailab Hossain Tutul.

BANGLADESH CRICKET BOARD v AUSTRALIAN CRICKET ACADEMY

At Bangabandhu National Stadium, Dhaka, January 25, 2001. Day/night match. Australian Cricket Academy won by six wickets. Toss: Bangladesh Cricket Board.

Bangladesh Cricket Board

Mohammad Ashraful not out 110		(139)		Mohammad Rafique not out	38	(26)
Javed Omar c Hartley b Chaitra	3	(14)				
Habibul Bashar c O'Brien b Welsford .	4	(17)		B 1, l-b 4, w 7	12	
Anisur Rehman c O'Brien b McDonald .	25	(39)			—	
*Akram Khan c Harris b Voges	38	(39)		(50 overs, 209 mins) (5 wkts)	255	
Sanuar Hossain c Kent b McDonald ..	25	(26)		Fall: 21 36 81 150 202		

†Golam Mortuja, Mushfiqur Rahman, Saiful Islam, Mohammed Shariff and Nasirul Alam Nahid did not bat.

Bowling: Welsford 8–3–20–1; Chaitra 10–0–46–1; O'Brien 10–0–46–0; McDonald 10–0–59–2; Voges 5–0–34–1; Sumit Panda 7–0–45–0.

Australian Cricket Academy

A.J. Kent b Mohammad Rafique	96	(91)	T.H. Welsford not out	16 (16)
†C.D. Hartley c Golam Mortuja				
b Mohammad Rafique	31	(71)	B 4, l-b 21, w 10, n-b 1	36
S.D. Stanton b Mohammed Shariff	26	(56)		
A.W. O'Brien c and b Habibul Bashar	12	(16)	(49.3 overs, 222 mins)	(4 wkts) 256
A.B. McDonald not out	39	(48)	Fall: 59 92 125 232	

D.J. Harris, A.C. Voges, S.E. Marsh, Sumit Panda, G. Chaitra and *L. Williams did not bat.

Bowling: Mohammed Shariff 10–0–44–1; Mushfiqur Rahman 9–2–32–0; Saiful Islam 9–0–36–0; Mohammad Rafique 9.3–0–56–2; Habibul Bashar 9–0–39–1; Sanuar Hossain 2–0–10–0; Mohammed Ashraful 1–0–14–0.

Umpires: D.J. Harper and Mahbubar Rahman.

NEW ZEALAND CRICKET ACADEMY IN AUSTRALIA, 2000-01

AUSTRALIAN CRICKET ACADEMY v NEW ZEALAND CRICKET ACADEMY

At Park 25, Adelaide, April 21, 2001. One day match. New Zealand Cricket Academy won by seven wickets.

Australian Cricket Academy

S.W. Meuleman b McSkimming	132	(126)	M.G. Johnson c N.L. McCullum	
D.M. Betts c B.B. McCullum			b McSkimming	8 (11)
b Cornelius	3	(17)	†D. Smith c Horsley b Whiteman	3 (7)
S.E. Marsh c B.B. McCullum			X.J. Doherty not out	1 (1)
b Whiteman	30	(47)	B. Geeves run out	0 (2)
R.J. Brewster c Young b Woodcock	22	(32)	L-b 2, w 7, n-b 6	15
*T.H. Welsford c B.B. McCullum				
b Cornelius	26	(29)	(49.4 overs)	253
M.J. Cosgrove lbw b N.L. McCullum	1	(6)	Fall: 11 82 135 204 213 231 245	
B. Casson b Whiteman	12	(24)	250 251 253	

M.J. Thistle did not bat.

Bowling: Cornelius 10–1–41–2; McSkimming 8–0–25–2; Todd 8–1–44–0; Whiteman 9.4–0–53–3; N.L. McCullum 8–0–46–1; Woodcock 6–0–42–1.

New Zealand Cricket Academy

J.M.H. How b Geeves	110	(149)	B 3, l-b 8, w 5, n-b 3	19
G.R. Todd c Doherty b Casson	32	(61)		
N.K.W. Horsley c Welsford b Casson	17	(34)		
S.L. Stewart not out	65	(49)	(49.5 overs)	(3 wkts) 254
J.P. McNamee not out	11	(9)	Fall: 85 132 223	

†B.B. McCullum, R.A. Young, W.C. McSkimming, S. Whiteman, N.L. McCullum, L. Woodcock and W.A.N. Cornelius did not bat.

Bowling: Johnson 7–1–51–0; Thistle 7.5–4–33–0; Geeves 8–0–41–1; Welsford 4–0–25–0; Casson 10–1–33–2; Doherty 10–1–32–0; Marsh 3–0–28–0.

AUSTRALIAN CRICKET ACADEMY v NEW ZEALAND CRICKET ACADEMY

At Adelaide Oval No. 2, April 23, 24, 2001. Drawn.
Close of Play: First day: Australian Cricket Academy 320.

Australian Cricket Academy

D. M. Betts c McSkimming b Cornelius	 8	J.J. Taylor c and b N.L. McCullum	 1
M.J. Cosgrove c Cornelius b Robin	 78	X.J. Doherty c B.B. McCullum b N.L.	
S.E. Marsh c McNamee b Cornelius	 14	McCullum	.. 0
R.J. Brewster c Horsley b Cornelius	 0	B. Geeves not out	 11
*T.H. Welsford c McNamee b Cornelius	... 51	L-b 6, w 1, n-b 4	 11
D. Smith c Robin b Geeves	 78		
B. Casson c Young b Cornelius	 9	(78.5 overs, 333 mins)	320
†L. Ronchi c N.L. McCullum b Arnel	 59	Fall: 18 36 39 107 224 244 276 278 278 320	

S. J. Magoffin did not bat.

Bowling: Cornelius 24–4–67–6; McSkimming 13–1–52–0; Arnel 5.5–1–31–1; Robin 13–2–65–1; N.L. McCullum 17–4–55–2; Woodcock 6–0–44–0.

New Zealand Cricket Academy

J.M.H. How c Ronchi b Geeves	 5	W.C. McSkimming b Welsford	 0
†R.A. Young lbw b Geeves	 0	N.L. McCullum not out	 14
N.K.W Horsley c Taylor b Geeves	 20	B.J. Arnel not out	 0
S.L. Stewart lbw b Magoffin	 11	B 1, l-b 7, w 2, n-b 12	 22
J.P. McNamee lbw b Welsford	123		
*B.B. McCullum c Welsford b Casson	 56	(101 overs, 394 mins) (8 wkts dec)	322
L. Woodcock lbw b Casson	 71	Fall: 1 20 46 47 146 300 302 310	

T. P. Robin and W. A. N. Cornelius did not bat.

Bowling: Magoffin 10–2–35–1; Geeves 21–7–41–3; Taylor 15–2–43–0; Cosgrove 4–1–13–0; Doherty 20–4–65–0; Casson 23–2–99–2; Welsford 8–3–18–2.

Umpires: R. A. Falk and A. Willoughby.

AUSTRALIAN CRICKET ACADEMY v NEW ZEALAND CRICKET ACADEMY

At Adelaide Oval No. 2, April 25, 26, 2001. Drawn. Toss: New Zealand Cricket Academy.
Close of Play: First day: Australian Cricket Academy 1-38 (Meuleman 23, Marsh 6).

New Zealand Cricket Academy

J.M.H. How c Smith b Johnson	 4	J.P. McNamee c Marsh b Casson	 4
†R.A. Young c Marsh b Doherty	 46	L. Woodcock c sub (Geeves) b Doherty	... 1
N.K.W. Horsley run out	123	B.J. Arnel not out	 0
S.L. Stewart c Marsh b Doherty	 95		
G.R. Todd c Betts b Welsford	 9	B 13, l-b 10, w 2, n-b 3	 28
B.B. McCullum c Brewster b Doherty	 26		
*N.L. McCullum st Smith b Casson	 41	(78.5 overs, 320 mins)	399
S. Whiteman st Smith b Casson	 22	Fall: 11 121 271 300 306 346 393 394 395 399	

T. P. Robin did not bat.

Bowling: Johnson 5–1–11–1; Scott 14–3–51–0; Hilfenhaus 9–1–50–0; Welsford 12–2–64–1; Casson 17.5–2–69–3; Doherty 19–2–107–4; Meuleman 2–0–24–0.

Australian Cricket Academy

D. M. Betts c Young b Arnel	0	B. Casson b Whiteman	55
S. W. Meuleman lbw b Arnel	33	†D. Smith not out	0
S. E. Marsh c How b N. L. McCullum	77	B 14, l-b 6, w 4, n-b 5	29
R. J. Brewster c How b N. L. McCullum	72		
*T. H. Welsford c Todd b N. L. McCullum	10	(94.1 overs, 389 mins) (6 wkts)	400
L. Ronchi not out	124	Fall: 12 54 180 206 214 383	

M. G. Johnson, A. R. Scott, B. Hilfenhaus and X. J. Doherty did not bat.

Bowling: Robin 21–6–75–0; Arnel 25–8–84–2; N. L. McCullum 24–5–86–3; Whiteman 12.1–0–66–1; Todd 4–0–41–0; Woodcock 7–1–24–0; How 1–0–4–0.

Umpires: L. G. Donisthorpe and P. J. Weeks.

AUSTRALIAN CRICKET ACADEMY v NEW ZEALAND CRICKET ACADEMY

At Park 25, Adelaide, April 28, 2001. Australian Cricket Academy won by four wickets.
Toss: New Zealand Cricket Academy.

New Zealand Cricket Academy

†B. B. McCullum b Thistle	33	(39)	S. Whiteman st Ronchi b Casson	9	(23)
N. K. W. Horsley c Ronchi b Welsford	9	(17)	T. P. Robin not out	4	(21)
J. M. H. How lbw b Cosgrove	7	(26)	W. A. N. Cornelius c Ronchi b Casson	4	(4)
S. L. Stewart c Ronchi b Welsford	15	(25)			
J. P. McNamee c Ferguson b Casson	8	(12)	B 4, l-b 6, w 6	16	
G. R. Todd run out	0	(5)			
W. C. McSkimming c Ferguson b Doherty	8	(25)	(34.3 overs, 137 mins)	113	
*N. L. McCullum c Welsford b Casson	0	(10)	Fall: 41 49 76 76 83 88 92 94 103 113		

B. J. Arnel did not bat.

Bowling: Geeves 3–0–20–0; Thistle 6–1–21–1; Welsford 6–2–24–2; Cosgrove 6–1–16–1; Casson 8.3–4–15–4; Doherty 5–3–7–1.

Australian Cricket Academy

D. M. Betts run out	14	(55)	†L. Ronchi b Whiteman	9	(16)
M. J. Cosgrove c BB McCullum b McSkimming	10	(14)	D. Smith not out	16	(16)
S. E. Marsh lbw b McSkimming	6	(10)	L-b 2, w 5, n-b 4	11	
C. J. Ferguson run out (Whiteman)	0	(7)			
C. J. Borgas c Todd b McSkimming	1	(8)	(29.4 overs, 129 mins) (6 wkts)	114	
*T. H. Welsford not out	47	(56)	Fall: 14 20 20 22 52 80		

B. Casson, X. J. Doherty, M. J. Thistle and B. Geeves did not bat.

Bowling: Cornelius 10–2–30–0; McSkimming 9.4–2–39–3; Robin 5–0–17–0; Arnel 2–0–7–0; Whiteman 3–0–19–1.

Umpires: C. Thiele and P. J. Weeks.

AUSTRALIAN CRICKET ACADEMY v NEW ZEALAND CRICKET ACADEMY

At Park 25, Adelaide, April 29, 2001. New Zealand Cricket Academy won by two wickets. Toss: New Zealand Cricket Academy.

Australian Cricket Academy

D. M. Betts c Young b Whiteman	 21	(37)	B. Casson run out (McNamee)	 7	(10)
C. J. Ferguson c Young b McSkimming	9	(35)	X. J. Doherty c How b Whiteman	... 6	(12)
†D. Smith c McSkimming b Arnel	... 6	(17)	M. J. Thistle not out	 1	(2)
S. E. Marsh c McSkimming b Todd	... 23	(39)			
C. J. Borgas c Stewart b Cornelius	 29	(49)	B 3, l-b 8, w 11, n-b 2	 24	
*T. H. Welsford c How b McSkimming	56	(48)			
L. Ronchi c Cornelius b Todd	 24	(36)	(49.1 overs, 233 mins)		206
M. J. Cosgrove c How b Cornelius	... 0	(1)	Fall: 30 42 43 90 109 164 164 175 204 206		

B. Geeves did not bat.

Bowling: Cornelius 10–1–35–2; McSkimming 9.1–3–22–2; Arnel 10–0–35–1; Whiteman 10–2–29–2; Woodcock 3–0–19–0; Todd 7–0–56–2.

New Zealand Cricket Academy

S. L. Stewart b Casson	 62	(105)	W. C. McSkimming c Smith b Welsford	4	(8)
J. P. McNamee b Thistle	 12	(18)	L. Woodcock not out	 14	(25)
J. M. H. How c Betts b Geeves	 8	(10)	S. Whiteman not out	 17	(26)
N. K. W. Horsley c Borgas b Cosgrove	20	(26)	B 5, l-b 5, w 7, n-b 3	 20	
*B. B. McCullum lbw b Cosgrove	 10	(9)			
G. R. Todd c Thistle b Doherty	 28	(55)	(48.5 overs, 200 mins)	(8 wkts) 207	
†R. A. Young b Doherty	 12	(12)	Fall: 19 30 72 83 148 154 172 172		

B. J. Arnel and W. A. N. Cornelius did not bat.

Bowling: Geeves 7–1–28–1; Thistle 9–3–31–1; Welsford 7.5–1–34–1; Cosgrove 6–1–22–2; Casson 10–1–37–1; Doherty 9–0–45–2.

Umpires: M. A. Bartlett and A. Willoughby.

AUSTRALIAN UNDER-19s, 2000-01

By KEN PIESSE

Nathan Hauritz enjoyed a multiple celebration in 2000-01, leading Queensland to their fourth Australian Under-19s championship, co-captaining Australia to a near clean sweep in the youth series against Sri Lanka, captaining the Australian Cricket Academy team to Bangladesh, and making his representative debut in the Mercantile Mutual Cup. Fellow Queenslanders Chris Hartley and left-arm pace bowler Mitchell Johnson joined Hauritz for the seven-match programme against the touring Sri Lankans in March and April. The young Australians took the series 3-0, winning by ten wickets at St Peter's College in Adelaide and Lilac Hill in Perth and by six wickets at Fletcher Park, also in Perth. The international limited-overs series was tied 1-1. Australia won an additional limited-overs game at the end of the tour when the third youth Test finished early.

Hauritz, an all-rounder from Hervey Bay, and Tasmanian pace bowler Brett Geeves both made their state limited-overs debuts while Victoria's Cameron White and Western Australia's Shaun Marsh, son of Geoff Marsh, played in their maiden first-class matches. Seventeen-year-old White, the youngest first-class representative in 15 years, played two of the three youth Tests, having been unavailable for the first, his selection in Victoria's Pura Cup final team taking priority. A tall leg-spinner from Bairnsdale, who had been inspired to experiment with leg-spin by Shane Warne's wicket-taking feats, White took 3/55 in the Second Youth Test and top-scored with 53 in the third. Marsh, also 17, was one of the most prominent in the youth series, scoring a polished 123 with 18 fours in the second Test at Lilac Hill. In the final match of the tour, a one-day game at Fletcher Park, his top score of 73 included four fours and four sixes. Marsh had represented Australia in the 1999-2000 youth World Cup in Sri Lanka.

Western Australian all-rounder Beau Casson took eight wickets in the three youth Tests with his left-arm wrist-spin, including 5/52 from 21 overs in the first international at St Peter's College. This match had earlier been dominated by Hauritz and Hartley, a left-handed batsman and wicket-keeper from Brisbane Boys' College, who added 106 for the seventh wicket in a match-winning stand.

Others to represent Australia in the youth Tests were Travis Birt and Peter Dickson (Victoria), Cameron Borgas and Mark Cosgrove (South Australia), Andrew James (Australian Capital Territory) and Aaron O'Brien (New South Wales). Borgas, from Immanuel College in Adelaide, also played first-class cricket with South Australia, having earlier in the summer represented the state Under-17s and Under-19s teams. His brother, Jason, 19, a left-hander from Sturt, also played for South Australia in the Under-19s titles.

Co-captain of the Australian team against the Sri Lankans was Victoria's Tim Welsford, an accurate pace bowler and enterprising batsman from Northcote, who was the leading carnival wicket-taker with 14 wickets in five matches, just ahead of Tasmania's Xavier Doherty and South Australia's

Matthew Burr, each with 12. Welsford helped the Victorians maintain their three-year unbeaten record through to the low-scoring final at Bellerive Oval which the Queenslanders won after a Victorian collapse on the second day. Having reached three for 83, chasing 232, mid-way through the fourth session of the match, the young Victorians collapsed to 116 all out, Nathan Rimmington, from Sandgate–Redcliffe, taking 4/36.

It was a meritorious win for the young Queenslanders, whose three previous titles had all been shared victories. They had been humbled on the opening day of the tournament by Victoria, who bowled them out for just 74 at the University Oval in Hobart. Throughout the two weeks Queensland were without two injured front-line players, Johnson and Wynnum batsman Ryan Broad, son of former Queensland batsman Wayne Broad.

Victoria were the only team to win all three qualifying matches. They defeated South Australia in the semi-final and entered the two-day final against Queensland as favourites. Throughout the carnival the Victorians were best served by Welsford, Stuart Brohaska, a wicket-keeper/batsman, Birt, Dickson and Mark Simpson, an all-rounder who also played his maiden matches of premier league cricket with Richmond. White, on the verge of his first representative games at senior level, impressed against New South Wales in particular with 5/80. He also batted aggressively late in the order, averaging over 40 with two half-centuries.

Third-placed Western Australia lacked the batting depth of the top two states. Against Northern Territory, however, at Hutchins, Marsh and Jim Allenby, from Claremont–Nedlands, shared the highest stand of the carnival, 224 for the second wicket, Marsh making 111 and Allenby 180, the highest score of the tournament, with 23 fours and four sixes. Casson topped the batting aggregates with 261 runs at an average of 52. He also took 11 wickets at 20.

New South Wales, who finished fourth, had six prominent players in Jarrod Burke, Denis Lonergan, Ed Cowan and Daniel Smith, all batsmen, Brett Eriksson, an all-rounder, and O'Brien, who bowls left-arm orthodox spin. In addition to the Borgas brothers, fifth-placed South Australia also included two very promising batsmen, Cosgrove and Callum Ferguson, the Australian Under-17s captain. Tasmania's best players were Geeves, George Bailey and Doherty, who in April was the youngest of nine Australians to gain valuable experience on an eight-day coaching camp in Chennai.

Thanks to Adam Heading, Australian Capital Territory made the highest score of the carnival, eight for 425, in a consolation final against Northern Territory at Kingston Beach. Heading scored the fastest century of the championships, making 106 not out from just 86 balls with 11 fours and two sixes. Australian Capital Territory also had promising batsmen in Peter Colbourne and Stewart Heaney. Northern Territory's leading players were Shane Chatto, whose 254 runs placed him second in the competition aggregates, and their left-handed opener, Philip Sutherland. Chatto is in his third year at the Northern Territory Institute of Sport. Sutherland and Blayne Cornford, the side's leg-spinner, also played at grade level in Adelaide, the Northern Territory season being played from March to September.

ROUND ONE

Group A

At TCA Ground, Hobart, December 4, 5, 2000. Tasmania won by 86 runs. Tasmania 303 (G. J. Bailey 91, N. King 56, N. G. Webb 54, J. Leatherbarrow 50; J. Shaw 3/47, M. J. Sutherland 2/34, J. N. Burke 2/36); New South Wales 217 (D. G. Lonergan 53, J. N. Burke 39, A. W. O'Brien 34; B. Geeves 3/39, B. Hilfenhaus 3/52, X. J. Doherty 2/40).

At University Oval, Hobart, December 4, 5, 2000. Victoria won on first innings. Queensland 74 (T. H. Welsford 3/6, B. T. Anderton 3/25, C. L. White 2/4) and two for 116 (A. P. Maynard 55*); Victoria 287 (M. G. Simpson 56, C. L. White 54, V. J. Ion 36; C. Summers 3/24, L. R. Davis 3/72).

Group B

At New Town Oval, Hobart, December 4, 5, 2000. Drawn. Australian Capital Territory 248 (S. P. Heaney 71, D. G. Dawson 42, P. Colebourne 38; T. Crook 3/39, A. Heal 3/57, K. Wulff 2/15) drew with Western Australia nine for 245 (M. Smart 51, B. Casson 39, B. Jones 38; A. C. L. James 4/61, B. Wilson 2/18, D. C. Pascoe 2/38).

At Lindisfarne Oval, Hobart, December 4, 5, 2000. South Australia won on first innings. Northern Territory 146 (M. Patrick 38, S. McNally 36, S. Redfern 35; B. J. Pahl 3/42, M. R. Burr 2/22, S. W. Tait 2/23) and five for 151 (P. Sutherland 41, S. Chatto 40, B. M. Cornford 34; D. Kendrick 2/31, M. R. Burr 2/40); South Australia five for 306 declared (J. Whetstone 114*, M. J. Cosgrove 104; M. Patrick 2/49).

ROUND TWO

Group A

At Kingston Beach Oval, Hobart, December 6, 7, 2000. Victoria won by 66 runs. Victoria nine for 335 declared (P. J. Dickson 94, T. R Birt 71, M. G. Simpson 48; J. N. Burke 3/79, M. J. Sutherland 2/44, A. W. O'Brien 2/54); New South Wales 269 (J. N. Burke 65, D. G. Lonergan 44, D. Smith 38; C. L. White 5/80, B. T. Anderton 3/44).

At Lindisfarne Oval, Hobart, December 6, 7, 2000. Queensland won by 34 runs. Queensland 222 (A. P. Maynard 38, N. J. Kruger 32; X. J. Doherty 5/35, K. M. Munday 2/18, B. Hilfenhaus 2/30) and three for 78 (C. A. Phillipson 44*); Tasmania 188 (M. Singh 33, G. J. Bailey 32; C. A. Phillipson 3/26, N. M. Hauritz 2/55).

Group B

At Queenborough Oval, Hobart, December 6, 7, 2000. Australian Capital Territory won by 18 runs. Australian Capital Territory 292 (P. Colebourne 83, S. A. Holcombe 48, S. Dejong 45, S. P. Heaney 45; S. K. Skewes 3/30, S. Redfern 2/40, M. Keith 2/48); Northern Territory 274 (P. Sutherland 76, S. Chatto 67, M, Keith 47; D. J. Reynolds 5/56, D. C. Pascoe 2/37).

At King George V Oval, Hobart, December 6, 7, 2000. Drawn. Western Australia nine for 282 declared (B. Casson 82, M. Swart 49, B. Jones 45; S. P. Crook 3/40, M. R. Burr 2/60); South Australia nine for 209 (C. J. Ferguson 72, J. Whetstone 32; A. Andrich 2/34, B. Casson 2/34, R. Slowey 2/39).

ROUND THREE

Group A

At King George V Oval, Hobart. December 9, 10, 2000. Queensland won by 153 runs. New South Wales 172 (J.N. Burke 31, D.G. Lonergan 31; C.J. McCabe 4/21, N.J. Rimmington 2/28, C.A. Phillipson 1/11); Queensland 325 (C.D. Hartley 102*, A.P. Maynard 47, N.J. Kruger 42; B.A. Iriksson 4/55, M.J. Sutherland 4/67).

At TCA Ground, Hobart, December 9, 10, 2000. Victoria won on first innings. Victoria 272 (L. Mash 61, C.L. White 57, P.J. Dickson 45; X.J. Doherty 4/60, B. Hilfenhaus 3/29, B. Coombs 2/20) and none for 60 (P.J. Dickson 28*, T.H. Welsford 26); Tasmania 155 (N.G. Webb 60; T.H. Welsford 4/25, B. Waterman 2/36).

Group B

At New Town Oval, Hobart, December 9, 10, 2000. South Australia won by 173 runs. Australian Capital Territory 142 (S.A. Holcombe 39, S.P. Heaney 27, C.J. Males 24; D. Kendrick 3/29, M.J. Cosgrove 2/7, S.P. Crook 2/40); South Australia three for 315 (J.D. Borgas 109*, M.J. Cosgrove 81, C.J. Borgas 63).

At Hutchins School Oval, Hobart, December 9, 10, 2000. Western Australia won by 116 runs. Western Australia seven for 401 declared (J. Allenby 180, S.E. Marsh 111, B. Casson 45; J. Leeder 3/44, S. Redfern 2/84); Northern Territory 285 (S. McNally 89, S. Chatto 75, J. Leeder 29; B. Casson 4/83, A. Andrich 2/26).

QUALIFYING FINALS

At Queenborough Oval, Hobart, December 12, 13, 2000. New South Wales won on first innings. Northern Territory 157 (S. Chatto 62, A. Marshall 41; K. Daley 4/48, A.W. O'Brien 3/34, D. Christian 2/19) and three for 36; New South Wales eight for 378 declared (A.W. O'Brien 86, T.D. Cruikshank 82, B.A. Eriksson 54*; L. Mauger 2/41, K. Wyles 2/53, M. Keith 2/81).

At Lindisfarne Oval, Hobart, December 12, 13, 2000. Queensland won by three runs. Tasmania 196 (G.J. Bailey 66, N. King 32, N.G. Webb 22; N.M. Hauritz 3/34, C.A. Phillipson 2/17, N.J. Rimmington 2/24); Queensland six for 199 (C.A. Phillipson 77*, N.M. Hauritz 53; B. Geeves 3/66).

At King George V Oval, Hobart, December 12, 13, 2000. Western Australia won by 78 runs. Western Australia 275 (B. Casson 95, C. Robertson 56, S. Mason 34; A.C.L. James 3/53, D.C. Pascoe 2/17); Australian Capital Territory 197 (S.A. Holcombe 35, A.C.L. James 35, A. Rhynhart 33; B. Casson 4/56, K. Wulff 3/32, B. Jones 2/21).

At TCA Ground, Hobart, December 12, 13, 2000. Victoria won by 68 runs. Victoria 295 (T.R. Birt 79, L. Mash 65, J. Seeary 30; M.J. Cosgrove 3/42, S.P. Crook 3/57, M.R. Burr 3/85); South Australia 227 (C.J. Borgas 69, J. Whetstone 44; T.H. Welsford 6/73, C.L. White 2/65).

CONSOLATION FINALS

7TH AND 8TH PLACES

AUSTRALIAN CAPITAL TERRITORY v NORTHERN TERRITORY

At Kingston Beach Oval, Hobart, December 14, 15, 2000. Australian Capital Territory won on first innings. Toss: Australian Capital Territory.

Close of play: First day, Australian Capital Territory 7-327 (Heading 29, James 22).

Australian Capital Territory

S. Dejong b Wyles	5 (10)	A.J. Heading not out	106 (86)
P. Colebourne c Brown b Leeder	79 (137)	A.C.L. James b Leeder	44 (55)
*†S.A. Holcombe lbw b Redfern	22 (63)		
S.P. Heaney c Cornford b Skewes	6 (21)	B 2, l-b 6, n-b 2	10
D.G. Dawson c Brown b Skewes	50 (87)		
C.J. Males b Keith	44 (117)	(111 overs, 397 mins) (8 wkts dec)	425
A. Rhynhart c Brown b Leeder	59 (91)	Fall: 18 79 96 128 171 265 281 425	

D.J. Reynolds, D.C. Pascoe and D. De Cruz did not bat.

Bowling: Wyles 22–5–79–1; Skewes 20–4–81–2; Leeder 23–2–76–3; Keith 17–0–69–1; Redfern 16–2–62–1; Mauger 13–4–50–0.

Northern Territory

P. Sutherland c Rhynhart b James	64 (122)	B.M. Cornford c De Cruz b Pascoe	11 (34)
S. McNally b Males	56 (144)	L. Mauger not out	39 (67)
S. Chatto c Colebourne b Rhynhart	6 (37)	B 11, l-b 3, w 2, n-b 7	23
*J. Leeder lbw b Dawson	6 (27)		
A. Marshall not out	43 (121)	(93 overs, 320 mins) (6 wkts)	248
†M.M. Brown lbw b Reynolds	0 (13)	Fall: 113 140 142 152 159 180	

K. Wyles, K.J. Skewes, M. Keith and S. Redfern did not bat.

Bowling: James 12–1–48–1; Reynolds 12–3–24–1; Pascoe 20–5–47–1; De Cruz 14–2–38–0; Dejong 5–0–13–0; Males 14–3–34–1; Rhynhart 6–2–5–1; Dawson 8–5–13–1; Colebourne 1–0–1–0; Heaney 1–0–11–0.

Umpires: J. Martin and A.S. Ward.

5TH AND 6TH PLACES

NEW SOUTH WALES v SOUTH AUSTRALIA

At New Town Oval, Hobart, December 14, 15, 2000. New South Wales won on first innings. Toss: South Australia.

Close of play: First day, New South Wales 1-33 (Cowan 14).

South Australia

M.J. Cosgrove st Smith b Shaw	43	(64)	S.P. Crook lbw b Burke	0	(5)
T.C. Plant b Christian	7	(30)	D. Kendrick not out	21	(34)
*J.D. Borgas b O'Brien	28	(111)	B.J. Pahl c Cowan b O'Brien	0	(5)
C.J. Borgas run out (Burke)	42	(128)	N-b 5	5	
C.J. Ferguson b Eriksson	13	(87)			
J. Whetstone c Lonergan b Burke	0	(1)	(96.5 overs, 315 mins)	201	
†J.W. Plant st Smith b Burke	22	(67)	Fall: 26 57 110 138 138 138 172		
M.R. Burr c Lonergan b O'Brien	20	(54)	177 186 201		

J. Worthley did not bat.

Bowling: Daley 9–2–41–0; Christian 8–2–24–1; Shaw 8–3–18–1; Burke 26–11–54–3; O'Brien 19.5–10–28–3; Sutherland 16–8–22–0; Eriksson 10–4–14–1.

New South Wales

T.D. Cruikshank b Worthley	17	(27)	S.G. Karam not out	2	(2)
E.J.M. Cowan c Ferguson b Burr	75	(132)			
*A.W. O'Brien c Crook b Burr	42	(61)	B 1, l-b 3, w 1	5	
D.G. Lonergan not out	35	(77)			
†D. Smith b Crook	14	(30)	(59 overs, 205 mins) (5 wkts)	203	
J.N. Burke c Worthley b Burr	13	(25)	Fall: 33 113 148 168 201		

B.A. Eriksson, D. Christian, M.J. Sutherland, J. Shaw and K. Daley did not bat.

Bowling: Crook 12–0–59–1; Pahl 6–2–14–0; Worthley 9–2–24–1; Burr 22–5–57–3; Cosgrove 4–0–21–0; Kendrick 6–0–24–0.

Umpires: B.N.J. Oxenford and A. Shelley.

3RD AND 4TH PLACES

TASMANIA v WESTERN AUSTRALIA

At University Oval, Hobart, December 14, 15, 2000. Western Australia won on first innings. Toss: Tasmania.
Close of play: First day, Western Australia 2-22 (Marsh 10, Casson 0).

Tasmania

N. King b Andrich	3	(6)	B. Geeves b Allenby	0	(8)
T. Little lbw b Allenby	18	(68)	B. Coombs c Swart b Slowey	17	(43)
†T.D. Paine c Mason b Casson	34	(88)	D. Tueon not out	10	(12)
K.M. Munday lbw b Wulff	0	(6)			
*N.G. Webb lbw b Allenby	37	(90)	L-b 3, w 1, n-b 1	5	
G.J. Bailey c Mason b Crook	3	(21)			
X.J. Doherty run out	25	(124)	(78 overs, 278 mins)	152	
J. Leatherbarrow c Mason b Allenby	0	(2)	Fall: 3 50 51 59 70 105 105 109 137 152		

B. Hilfenhaus did not bat.

Bowling: Crook 12–2–27–1; Andrich 12–6–17–1; Slowey 8–1–32–1; Wulff 17–4–28–1; Allenby 13–5–18–4; Casson 16–3–27–1.

Western Australia

M. Swart c Tucon b Coombs 10 (46)
J. Allenby b Geeves 0 (2)
S.E. Marsh c Paine b Geeves 21 (95)
B. Casson lbw b Geeves 0 (23)
*B. Jones not out 62 (180)

C. Simmonds not out 50 (164)
  B 2, l-b 6, w 2 10

(85 overs, 273 mins)   (4 wkts) 153
Fall: 3 20 22 39

T. Crook, A. Andrich, R. Slowey, K. Wulff, †S. Mason, and A. Heal did not bat.

Bowling: Geeves 24–14–33–3; Hilfenhaus 15–5–25–0; Coombs 17–2–29–1; Doherty 8–3–14–0; Tucon 9–2–25–0; Webb 11–4–18–0; Leatherbarrow 1–0–1–0.

Umpires: S.D. Fry and K.J. McGinness.

CHAMPIONSHIP FINAL

QUEENSLAND v VICTORIA

At Bellerive Oval, Hobart. December 14, 15, 2000. Queensland won on first innings.
Toss: Victoria.
Close of Play: First day, Victoria 2-19 (Brohaska 1, Geisler 0).

Queensland

N.J. Kruger lbw b Waterman 61 (148)
C.P. Simpson lbw b Waterman 16 (72)
A.P. Maynard c Brohaska b Simpson . 12 (38)
M.J. Chapman lbw b Simpson 1 (8)
†C.D. Hartley c Brohaska b Seeary .. 16 (54)
*N.M. Hauritz c Mash b Anderton ... 18 (88)
C.A. Phillipson c Ion b White 11 (25)

J.G. Dellit not out 46 (74)
C.J. McCabe c and b Simpson 22 (39)
N.J. Rimmington not out 3 (4)
  B 11, l-b 9, w 2, n-b 4 26

(91 overs, 333 mins)   (8 wkts dec) 232
Fall: 42 81 84 113 132 143 165 215

S. Brant and L.R. Davis did not bat.

Bowling: Welsford 13–5–20–0; Anderton 17–3–49–1; Seeary 15–6–28–1; Waterman 15–5–25–2; Geisler 4–0–14–0; Simpson 9–1–31–3; White 18–7–45–1.

Victoria

T.R. Birt run out (McCabe) 15 (21)
P.J. Dickson lbw b Rimmington 1 (16)
†S. Brohaska run out (Davis) 30 (80)
N. Geisler c Hartley b Rimmington .. 8 (17)
*T.H. Welsford c Chapman b McCabe 23 (45)
L. Mash c Hartley b Brant 2 (10)
V.J. Ion c Hartley b McCabe 4 (12)
M.G. Simpson c Hartley b Rimmington 2 (15)

C.L. White not out 20 (29)
J. Seeary b Rimmington 0 (7)
B. Waterman b Hauritz 3 (5)

  L-b 3, w 1, n-b 4 8

(42.1 overs, 159 mins)   116
Fall: 16 16 39 83 83 85 90 100 107 116

B.T. Anderton did not bat.

Bowling: Rimmington 12–2–36–4; Simpson 6–1–18–0; Dellit 6–2–12–0; Brant 8–4–11–1; McCabe 7–2–18–2; Phillipson 1–0–6–0; Hauritz 2.1–0–12–1.

Umpires: B. Bennett and N.S. Fowler.

UNDER-19s CRICKET CHAMPIONSHIPS RECORDS

Kookaburra Shield

Series	*Venue*	*Winner*	*Player of the Year*
1969-70	Melbourne	Victoria	no award
1970-71	Sydney	Victoria	no award
1971-72	Adelaide	Victoria	R. Wallace (Qld)
1972-73	Canberra	New Zealand	G.C. Hughes (NSW)
1973-74	Melbourne	South Australia	D.W. Hookes (SAust)
1974-75	Brisbane	Victoria	D. Brown (Qld)
1975-76	Perth	New South Wales	D.M. Wellham (NSW)
1976-77	Hobart	New Zealand	J.J. Crowe (NZ)
1977-78	Christchurch	New South Wales	P.S. Clifford (NSW)
1978-79	Sydney	Western Australia	R.J. Thomas (NZ)
1979-80	Adelaide	Western Australia/Victoria	M.D. Crowe (NZ)
1980-81	Brisbane	Victoria	D. Knox (NSW)
1981-82	Canberra	Victoria	M.R.J. Veletta (WAust)

Barclays Championship

1982-83	Perth	Victoria	I.A. Healy (Qld)
1983-84	Melbourne	South Australia	S.R. Waugh (NSW)
1984-85	Hobart	Victoria	J.K. Pyke (ACT)
1985-86	Sydney	Queensland/New South Wales	J.C. Scuderi (Qld)
1986-87	Adelaide	New South Wales	G.R. Parker (Vic)
1987-88	Brisbane	Western Australia	R.C. Kelly (WAust)
1988-89	Canberra	New South Wales	M.G. Bevan (ACT)
1989-90	Melbourne	New South Wales	J.E.R. Gallian (NSW)
1990-91	Sydney	South Australia	A.C. Gilchrist (NSW)
1991-92	Perth	Western Australia	A.D. McQuire (NSW)
1992-93	Brisbane	Victoria	J. Bray (NSW)
1993-94	Melbourne	Western Australia	J.L. Cassell (Qld)

ACI Pink Batts Cup

1994-95	Sydney	Queensland/New South Wales	B.A. Clemow (NSW)
1995-96	Adelaide	Victoria	P.A. Sutherland (NSW)

Australian Under-19s Youth Championship

1996-97	Canberra	New South Wales	D.J. McLauchlan (NSW)

Torpedoes Cup

1997-98	Melbourne	South Australia	G.A. Manou (SAust)
1998-99	Adelaide	New South Wales	M. Klinger (Vic)
1999-00	Perth	Victoria/Queensland	L. Buchanan (Vic)

Australian Under-19s Youth Championship

2000-01	Hobart	Queensland	B. Casson (WAust)

LAST TEN YEARS' PLACINGS

	91-92	92-93	93-94	94-95	95-96	96-97	97-98	98-99	99-00	00-01
Australian Capital Territory .	7	5	7	8	7	6	7	6	7	7
New South Wales .	2	2	3	1	2	1	2	1	3	4
Northern Territory	8	7	8	7	8	8	8	8	8	8
Queensland	3	3	5	1	3	5	3	2	1	1
South Australia ...	5	6	4	6	5	3	1	4	5	5
Tasmania	6	8	6	5	6	7	6	7	4	6
Victoria	4	1	2	3	1	2	5	3	1	2
Western Australia .	1	4	1	4	4	4	4	5	6	3

HIGHEST INDIVIDUAL SCORES

244	G. H. Armstrong, Australian Capital Territory v Queensland at Brisbane	1987-88
242	R. J. Davison, New South Wales v Northern Territory at Brisbane	1987-88
222*	M. P. Mott, Queensland v Northern Territory at Perth	1991-92
215*	G. S. Milliken, New South Wales v Tasmania at Perth	1982-83
214	D. A. Tuckwell, Queensland v Northern Territory at Sydney	1985-86
206*	M. L. Love, Queensland v South Australia at Brisbane	1992-93
205*	B. Zacny, ACT v Northern Territory at Melbourne	1997-98
202*	G. S. Blewett, South Australia v Northern Territory at Melbourne	1989-90
201	R. Bowden, Northern Territory v Australian Capital Territory at Sydney	1990-91

MOST RUNS

	I	NO	R	HS	Avge
M. L. Love (Qld)	12	4	831	206*	103.87
D. R. Reynolds (Qld)	12	1	724	122	65.82
J. J. Crowe (NZ)	17	6	705	97	64.09
J. K. Pyke (ACT)	23	6	695	135*	40.88
W. G. Ayres (Vic)	25	2	671	108	29.17
B. J. Opperman (SA)	14	1	668	156	51.38

HIGHEST PARTNERSHIP FOR EACH WICKET

318 for 1st	V. W. Williams and D. S. Wotherspoon, NSW v South Australia at Canberra .	1996-97
224 for 2nd	J. Allenby and S. E. Marsh, Western Australia v Northern Territory at Hobart .	2000-01
339 for 3rd	M. Armstrong and S. P. Heaney, ACT v Northern Territory at Perth	1999-00
240 for 4th	A. I. C. Dodemaide and A. Grant, Victoria v South Australia at Perth	1982-83
231 for 5th {	D. M. Wellham and M. Cox, NSW v Australian Capital Territory at Perth ..	1975-76
	M. L. Love and A. Walduck, Queensland v Tasmania at Perth	1991-92
185 for 6th	K. K. Beazleigh and P. Holland, New South Wales v Victoria at Melbourne .	1991-92
251 for 7th	C. Mason and K. M. Harvey, Western Australia v Queensland at Melbourne .	1993-94
144 for 8th	A. J. Heading and A. C. L. James, ACT v Northern Territory at Hobart	2000-01
117 for 9th	B. A. Birrell and A. McDonald, South Australia v Tasmania at Sydney	1994-95
98* for 10th	S. Bannerman and J. Cooper, ACT v South Australia at Melbourne	1989-90

MOST WICKETS

	O	M	R	W	Avge
M. C. Dolman (SAust)	256.1	41	784	52	15.07
R. J. Thomas (NZ)	156.2	22	432	39	11.07
R. P. Done (ACT)	232.3	37	546	38	14.37
K. Sheppard (WAust)	186.3	33	460	37	12.43
R. Wallace (Qld)	206.5	38	464	36	12.88

BEST BOWLING IN AN INNINGS

9/11	D. J. McLauchlan, New South Wales v South Australia at Canberra	1996-97
9/70	M. C. Dolman, South Australia v Western Australia at Sydney	1978-79
8/13	C. Simpson, Queensland v Northern Territory at Melbourne	1997-98
8/25	M. Reidy-Crofts, Western Australia v ACT at Adelaide	1979-80
8/31	S. Hill, Western Australia v New Zealand at Sydney	1978-79
8/41	M. L. Clews, ACT v South Australia at Melbourne	1969-70
8/46	I. Woolf, Victoria v South Australia at Adelaide	1971-72
8/49	R. J. Thomas, New Zealand v ACT at Sydney	1978-79
8/58	P. Walker, ACT v Tasmania at Adelaide	1971-72
8/78	M. White, ACT v South Australia at Sydney	1978-79
8/84	S. P. Davis, Victoria v Tasmania at Christchurch	1977-78

BEST BOWLING IN A MATCH

14/15	D. J. McLauchlan, New South Wales v South Australia at Canberra	1996-97
13/18	C. Simpson, Queensland v Northern Territory at Melbourne	1997-98
10/43	D. W. Fleming, Victoria v Northern Territory at Canberra	1988-89
10/59	A. J. De Winter, Tasmania v Western Australia at Sydney	1985-86

HAT-TRICKS

D. A. Johnston, South Australia v Tasmania at Canberra	1972-73
R. Bucholz, Queensland v Victoria at Adelaide	1979-80
H. V. Hammelman, Queensland v South Australia at Perth	1982-83
A. J. De Winter, Tasmania v Western Australia at Sydney	1985-86
M. G. Bevan, ACT v New South Wales at Adelaide	1986-87
I. Connell, Tasmania v ACT at Brisbane	1992-93
J. Southam, Northern Territory v South Australia at Adelaide	1995-96
S. G. Busbridge, South Australia v ACT at Canberra	1996-97
P. D. Waite, Western Australia v Queensland at Canberra	1996-97
D. R. Mackenzie, Queensland v South Australia at Adelaide	1998-99

UNDER-19s CRICKET CHAMPIONSHIP, 2000-01

POINTS TABLE

Group A	P	WO	W1	D	L1	LO	T	Points	Quotient
Victoria	3	0	3	0	0	0	0	18	1.714
Queensland	3	0	2	0	1	0	0	12	1.111
Tasmania	3	0	1	0	2	0	0	6	0.837
New South Wales	3	0	0	0	3	0	0	0	0.638
Group B									
South Australia	3	0	2	1	0	0	0	12	2.302
Western Australia	3	0	1	2	0	0	0	6	1.452
Australian Capital Territory	3	0	1	1	1	0	0	6	0.600
Northern Territory	3	0	0	0	3	0	0	0	0.539

Quotient = runs per wicket scored divided by runs per wicket conceded.

FINAL PLACINGS

1st	Queensland
2nd	Victoria
3rd	Western Australia
4th	New South Wales
5th	South Australia
6th	Tasmania
7th	Australian Capital Territory
8th	Northern Territory

HIGHEST INDIVIDUAL SCORE

180	J. Allenby	Western Australia v Northern Territory at Hutchins School Oval
114*	J. Whetstone	South Australia v Northern Territory at Lindisfarne Oval
111	S.E. Marsh	Western Australia v Northern Territory at Hutchins School Oval
109	J.D. Borgas	South Australia v Australian Capital Territory at New Town Oval
106	A.J. Heading	Australian Capital Territory v Northern Territory at Kingston Beach Oval
104	M.J. Cosgrove	South Australia v Northern Territory at Lindisfarne Oval
102*	C.D. Hartley	Queensland v New South Wales at King George V Oval

MOST RUNS

	M	I	NO	R	HS	100s	50s	Avge
B. Casson (WAust) . . .	5	5	0	261	95	0	2	52.20
S. Chatto (NT)	5	6	0	254	75	0	3	42.33
M.J. Cosgrove (SAust)	5	5	0	242	104	1	1	48.40
J. Allenby (WAust) . . .	5	5	0	230	180	1	0	46.00
A.W. O'Brien (NSW) .	5	5	0	213	86	0	1	42.60
P.J. Dickson (Vic)	5	6	1	211	94	0	1	42.20
G.J. Bailey (Tas)	5	5	0	208	91	0	2	41.60
P. Colebourne (ACT) .	5	5	0	206	83	0	2	41.20
S. McNally (NT)	5	6	0	204	89	0	2	34.00
P. Sutherland (NT) . . .	5	6	0	202	76	0	2	33.66

MOST WICKETS

	M	O	Mdns	R	W	BB	5W/i	10W/m	Avge
T.H. Welsford (Vic)	5	78	18	180	14	6/73	1	0	12.85
X.J. Doherty (Tas)	5	106.4	43	184	12	5/35	1	0	15.33
M.R. Burr (SAust)	4	95.2	27	264	12	3/57	0	0	22.00
B. Casson (WAust)	5	104.3	31	222	11	4/56	0	0	20.18
B.T.Anderson (Vic)	5	72	17	179	10	3/25	0	0	17.90
B. Hilfenhaus (Tas)	5	95.5	30	211	10	3/29	0	0	21.10
B. Geeves (Tas)	4	95.1	29	234	10	3/33	0	0	23.40
S.P. Crook (SAust)	5	77.5	14	236	10	3/40	0	0	23.60
C.L. White (Vic)	5	114.1	33	239	10	5/80	1	0	23.90

HIGHEST TOTALS

8d-425	Australian Capital Territory v Northern Territory at Kingston Beach Oval
7d-401	Western Australia v Northern Territory at Hutchins School Oval
8d-378	New South Wales v Northern Territory at Queenborough Oval
335	Victoria v New South Wales at Kingston Beach Oval
9d-325	Queensland v New South Wales at King George V Oval
3-315	South Australia v Australian Capital Territory at New Town Oval
5d-306	South Australia v Northern Territory at Lindisfarne Oval
303	Tasmania v New South Wales at TCA Ground

LOWEST TOTAL

74 Queensland v Victoria at University Oval

SRI LANKAN UNDER-19s IN AUSTRALIA, 2000-01

SRI LANKAN UNDER-19s TOURING SQUAD

S. H. T. Kandamby (*captain*), M. Pushpakumara (*vice-captain*), K. S. Lokuarachchi, G. M. C. Nilantha, D. Niroshan, D. N. Pathirana, M. S. P. Peiris, R. T. Peiris, K. G. M. H. Perera, M. D. K. Perera, N. A. N. N. Perera, D. A. Ranatunga, K. G. N. Randika, M. I. Ratnayake, G. C. Wijesinghe, O. L. A. Wijesiriwardene. *Coach:* O. Mottau.

SOUTH AUSTRALIA INVITATION UNDER-19s
v SRI LANKA UNDER-19s

At Adelaide Oval No. 2, March 13, 14, 2001. Drawn. Toss: South Australia Invitation Under-19s.

Close of Play: First day, Sri Lanka Under-19s 1-25 (M. S. P. Peiris 18, Ranatunga 6).

South Australia Invitation Under-19s

J. D. Borgas c N. A. N. N. Perera b Wijesiriwardene .	32	– not out	50
T. C. Plant c Lokuarachchi b Wijesiriwardene	12	– not out	13
C. J. Ferguson c Nilantha b Wijesiriwardene	3		
S. Williams c Niroshan b Nilantha	9		
*A. R. Crook c R. T. Peiris b Lokuarachchi	79		
B. T. Symes c Kandamby b Nilantha	31		
†J. W. Plant not out	49		
M. R. Burr lbw b Nilantha	0		
O. C. Thomas c Wijesiriwardene b Nilantha	4		
S. P. Crook c Ranatunga b Pushpakumara	29		
R. W. Bulger lbw b Ratnayake	12		
B 1, l-b 9, n-b 4	14		
(86.3 overs, 318 mins)	274	(16 overs, 61 mins)	63

Fall: 13 28 46 87 141 201 201 213 253 274

B. J. Pahl did not bat.

Bowling: *First Innings*—Wijesiriwardene 10–3–50–3; Ratnayake 14.3–3–40–1; Nilantha 9–3–18–4; Pushpakumara 17–4–55–1; Niroshan 2–0–10–0; Lokuarachchi 19–10–36–1; Randika 10–2–33–0; Kandamby 5–1–22–0. *Second Innings*—Niroshan 5–0–17–0; Ratnayake 5–0–31–0; Pathirana 3–1–13–0; MSP Peiris 3–1–2–0.

Sri Lanka Under-19s

M. S. P. Peiris lbw b Thomas	33	†R. T. Peiris b Thomas	11
N. A. N. N. Perera c J. W. Plant b S. P. Crook	1	M. D. K. Perera c Borgas b Thomas	3
D. A. Ranatunga c J. W. Plant b Pahl	12	O. L. A. Wijesiriwardene not out	1
*S. H. T. Kandamby b S. P. Crook	56		
D. N. Pathirana c J. W. Plant b S. P. Crook	10	L-b 8, n-b 8	16
M. Pushpakumara lbw b Burr	56		
K. S. Lokuarachchi c J. W. Plant b Williams	23	(89 overs, 324 mins)	254
K. G. N. Randika c Pahl b Thomas	32	Fall: 15 51 53 65 157 189 211 234 252 254	

D. Niroshan, M. I. Ratnayake and G. M. C. Nilantha did not bat.

Bowling: S. P. Crook 16–5–51–3; Pahl 14–2–31–1; Burr 15–6–36–1; Thomas 17–4–28–4; A. R. Crook 12–2–41–0; Bulger 10–1–45–0; Williams 5–2–14–1.

Umpires: R. A. Falk and P. J. Weeks.

AUSTRALIA v SRI LANKA

First Limited-Overs International

At University Oval, Adelaide, March 16, 2001. No result. Toss: Sri Lanka.

Australia

T. R. Birt not out	5	(34)
M. J. Cosgrove not out	18	(23)
L-b 1, n-b 2	3	

(9.1 overs, 44 mins) (0 wkts) 26

P. J. Dickson, A. W. O'Brien, D. G. Lonergan, M. G. Simpson, *T. H. Welsford, N. M. Hauritz, B. Geeves, †C. D. Hartley, J. N. Burke and M. G. Johnson did not bat.

Bowling: Wijesiriwardene 5–1–15–0; Niroshan 4.1–0–10–0.

Sri Lanka

*S. H. T. Kandamby, M. Pushpakumara, K. S. Lokuarachchi, †R. T. Peiris, K. G. N. Randika, N. A. N. N. Perera, O. L. A. Wijesiriwardene, M. S. P. Peiris, M. D. K. Perera, D. Niroshan, D. N. Pathirane, G. M. C. Nilantha.

Umpires: R. A. Falk and C. Hollard.

AUSTRALIA v SRI LANKA

Second Limited-Overs International

At University Oval, Adelaide, March 18, 2001. Sri Lanka won by two wickets. Toss: Sri Lanka.

Australia

T. R. Birt c R. T. Peiris b Niroshan	13	(33)
M. J. Cosgrove c Nilantha b Niroshan	4	(7)
P. J. Dickson c sub (Wijesinghe) b Nilantha	4	(30)
A. W. O'Brien b Pushpakumara	30	(88)
D. G. Lonergan run out (Kandamby)	19	(69)
N. M. Hauritz not out	41	(46)
†C. D. Hartley c sub (Wijesinghe) b Wijesiriwardene	18	(23)
*T. H. Welsford run out (N. A. N. N Perera)	12	(7)
M. G. Simpson not out	0	(1)
B 3, l-b 4, w 11, n-b 4	22	

(50 overs, 203 mins) (7 wkts) 163

Fall: 11 26 35 84 90 128 162

J. N. Burke, M. G. Johnson and B. Geeves did not bat.

Bowling: Wijesiriwardene 10–1–33–1; Niroshan 7–0–18–2; Nilantha 10–3–20–1; Pushpakumara 10–2–28–1; Lokuarchchi 10–0–29–0; Pathirane 3–0–28–0.

Sri Lanka

M. S. P. Peiris c and b Geeves	22	(32)	K. S. Lokuarachchi c Simpson b Hauritz	10	(15)
N. A. N. N. Perera b Welsford	3	(5)	†R. T. Peiris b O'Brien	7	(7)
K. G. N. Randika c Burke b Welsford	12	(61)	O. L. A. Wijesiriwardene not out	5	(11)
M. D. K. Perera c Hartley b Cosgrove	7	(23)	L-b 3, w 7, n-b 3	13	
*S. H. T. Kandamby not out	57	(90)		—	
M. Pushpakumara lbw b Cosgrove	5	(9)	(47.4 overs, 197 mins) (8 wkts)	164	
D. N. Pathirane run out (Hauritz/O'Brien)	23	(36)	Fall: 8 30 48 49 57 93 126 141		

D. Niroshan and G. M. C. Nilantha did not bat.

Bowling: Johnson 6–1–17–0; Welsford 10–1–18–2; Geeves 8.4–0–33–1; Cosgrove 5–1–22–2; Simpson 4–0–15–0; O'Brien 7–0–32–1; Hauritz 7–0–24–1.

Umpires: S. Knobben and B. Stewart.

AUSTRALIA v SRI LANKA

Third Limited-Overs International

At Adelaide Oval, March 19, 2001. Australia won by 60 runs. Toss: Australia.

Australia

T. R. Birt lbw b Randika	32	(65)	*N. M. Hauritz c Pathirane		
M. J. Cosgrove run out	28	(43)	b Pushpakumara	6	(15)
J. N. Burke st R. T. Peiris b Lokuarchchi	9	(14)	T. H. Welsford lbw b Pushpakumara	2	(8)
M. G. Simpson run out	23	(20)	P. J. Dickson not out	0	(6)
B. Casson c Wijesiriwardene					
b Pushpakumara	22	(33)	B 1, l-b 2, n-b 1	4	
A. W. O'Brien st R. T. Peiris				—	
b Pushpakumara	28	(29)	(44.1 overs, 190 mins)	177	
D. G. Lonergan b Niroshan	15	(17)	Fall: 61 68 82 102 128 153 165 175		
†C. D. Hartley lbw b Lokuarchchi	8	(16)	177 177		

A. C. L. James did not bat.

Bowling: Wijesiriwardene 6–0–20–0; Niroshan 8–2–31–1; Nilantha 5–0–27–0; Pushpakumara 8.1–1–26–4; Randika 10–0–49–1; Lokuarchchi 7–1–21–2.

Sri Lanka

M. S. P. Peiris c Casson b Welsford	4	(9)	K. G. N. Randika b Casson	21	(74)
†R. T. Peiris c Lonergan b James	9	(17)	O. L. A. Wijesiriwardene b Casson	3	(13)
K. G. M. H. Perera lbw b Welsford	0	(1)	D. Niroshan not out	8	(17)
*S. H. T. Kandamby b James	10	(14)			
D. N. Pathirane c Hartley b James	4	(11)	B 1, l-b 3, w 10, n-b 4	18	
M. Pushpakumara c Hartley b Simpson	10	(19)		—	
K. S. Lokuarachchi c Hartley b Welsford	2	(9)	(35 overs, 152 mins)	117	
M. D. K. Perera c Dickson b Burke	28	(31)	Fall: 12 12 25 28 33 37 67 86 90 117		

G. M. C. Nilantha did not bat.

Bowling: James 8–0–41–3; Welsford 7–1–24–3; Simpson 6–1–26–1; Burke 8–1–9–1; Casson 6–0–13–2.

Umpires: R. A. Falk and C. Hollard.

AUSTRALIA v SRI LANKA

Fourth Limited-Overs International

At Adelaide Oval, March 20, 2001. No result. Toss: Australia.

Australia

T.R. Birt c Pushpakumara b M.D.K. Perera	60	(91)
D.G. Lonergan b Wijesiriwardene	0	(7)
S.E. Marsh lbw b M.D.K. Perera	40	(58)
M.G. Simpson c Niroshan b M.D.K. Perera	6	(14)
A.W. O'Brien run out (Wijesinghe)	1	(2)
B. Casson run out	16	(42)
*T.H. Welsford run out	0	(0)
N.M. Hauritz c Wijesiriwardene b Pushpakumara	14	(35)

†C.D. Hartley c and b Pushpakumara	10	(20)
J.N. Burke b Lokuarchchi	4	(17)
M.G. Johnson not out	5	(12)
L-b 9, w 4, n-b 1	14	
(49.3 overs, 188 mins)	170	

A.C.L. James did not bat.

Fall: 4 107 115 117 124 124 149 150 157 170

Bowling: Wijesiriwardene 7–0–25–1; Niroshan 6–1–22–0; Nilantha 3–1–14–0; Pushpakumara 9.3–0–29–2; Lokuarchchi 10–2–28–1; M.D.K. Perera 9–1–31–3; Randika 5–0–12–0.

Sri Lanka

M.S.P. Peiris, N.A.N.N. Perera, M.D.K. Perera, *S.H.T. Kandamby, C.G. Wijesinghe, M. Pushpakumara, K.G.N. Randika, †R.T. Peiris, K.S. Lokuarachchi, G.M.C. Nilantha, D. Niroshan, O.L.A. Wijesiriwardene.

Umpires: K.D. Perrin and R. Thomas.

AUSTRALIA v SRI LANKA

First Youth Test

At St Peter's College, Adelaide, March 22, 23, 24, 25, 2001. Australia won by ten wickets. Toss: Sri Lanka.
Close of Play: First day, Australia (1) 7-294 (Hartley 48, Welsford 9); Second day, Sri Lanka (1) 8-110 (Randika 12, R.T. Periris 3*); Third day, Sri Lanka Under-19s (2) 7-127 (Randika 2*, Lokuarachchi 2*).

Australia

T.R. Birt c R.T. Peiris b Wijesiriwardene	35			
M.J. Cosgrove c R.T. Peiris b Wijesiriwardene	5			
P.J. Dickson c R.T. Peiris b Niroshan	13			
S.E. Marsh c sub (D.N. Pathirane) b Wijesiriwardene	69			
C.J. Borgas c and b Lokuarchchi	7	– (1) not out	1	
A.W. O'Brien b Niroshan	1			
*N.M. Hauritz c Ranatunga b Kandamby	85			
†C.D. Hartley st R.T. Peiris b Pushpakumara	80			
T.H. Welsford c M.D.K. Perera b Wijesiriwardene	10			
B. Casson c K.G.M.H. Perera b Niroshan	26			
M.G. Johnson not out	0	– (2) not out	13	
B 2, l-b 3, w 1, n-b 21	27	N-b 1	1	
(112.2 overs, 455 mins)	358	(1.3 overs)	(0 wkts)	15

Fall: 7 36 91 112 125 165 271 301 356 358

A.C.L. James did not bat.

Bowling: *First Innings*—Wijesiriwardene 30–5–104–4; Niroshan 18.2–2–48–3; Wijesinghe 3–1–5–0; Pushpakumara 27–2–94–1; Randika 10–3–34–0; Lokuarchchi 15–6–40–1; Kandamby 9–1–28–1. *Second Innings*—Wijesiriwardene 1–0–7–0; Niroshan 0.3–0–8–0

Sri Lanka

M. S. P. Peiris c Hartley b Johnson	1	– c Hartley b Casson	47
M. D. K. Perera c Hartley b James	16	– c James b O'Brien	4
K. G. M. H. Perera c Marsh b Welsford	1	– b Johnson	5
D. A. Ranatunga c Hartley b Welsford	29	– (5) c Marsh b O'Brien	2
*S. H. T. Kandamby run out (Cosgrove)	0	– (4) c Marsh b Hauritz	0
C. G. Wijesinghe c Hauritz b Casson	32	– lbw b Casson	42
M. Pushpakumara run out	0	– c Hauritz b Casson	16
K. G. N. Randika not out	40	– not out	27
K. S. Lokuarachchi c Hauritz b James	9	– c Hartley b Johnson	45
†R. T. Peiris c James b Welsford	21	– b Casson	10
O. L. A. Wijesiriwardene c Hartley b Welsford	1	– lbw b Casson	6
B 1, l-b 4, n-b 4	9	B 2, l-b 2, w 2, n-b 2	8

(95.5 overs, 343 mins)	159	(123 overs)	212
Fall: 10 20 20 25 79 80 88		Fall: 13 20 27 37 97 118 125	
99 142 159		182 201 213	

D. Niroshan did not bat.

Bowling: *First Innings*—Johnson 9–4–10–1; James 21–5–45–2; Welsford 17.5–8–25–4; O'Brien 15–10–11–0; Cosgrove 4–1–9–0; Hauritz 10–3–19–0; Casson 13–5–27–1; Dickson 6–1–8–0. *Second Innings*—Johnson 13–7–18–2; Cosgrove 4–1–7–0; James 17–6–35–0; Hauritz 32–10–43–1; O'Brien 18–9–26–2; Welsford 14–5–25–0; Dickson 4–2–3–0; Casson 21–7–52–5.

Umpires: M. Bartlett and P. J. Weeks.

AUSTRALIA v SRI LANKA

Second Youth Test

At Lilac Hill, Perth, March 29, 30, 31, April 1, 2001. Australia won by ten wickets. Toss: Sri Lanka.

Close of Play: First day, Australia (1) 1-5 (Cosgrove 0, Marsh 5). Second day, Australia (1) 7-300 (Hartley 12, Welsford 28). Third day, Sri Lanka (2) 8-169 (R. T. Peiris 23, Wijesiriwardene 8).

Sri Lanka

M. S. P. Peiris c Hartley b O'Brien	73	– c Geeves b O'Brien	59
N. A. N. N. Perera c Hartley b Welsford	0	– lbw b Welsford	0
*S. H. T. Kandamby c White b Geeves	28	– c Birt b White	37
D. A. Ranatunga lbw b James	1	– (5) c White b Hauritz	5
C. G. Wijesinghe c Hartley b White	18	– (4) lbw b White	2
M. Pushpakumara c Geeves b Casson	19	– (7) c Borgas b Hauritz	1
K. G. N. Randika c Marsh b O'Brien	19	– (6) c Hartley b Geeves	2
K. S. Lokuarachchi lbw b White	4	– c Hartley b Geeves	22
†R. T. Peiris not out	60	– c and b White	45
O. L. A. Wijesiriwardene lbw b White	1	– st Hartley b Hauritz	8
D. Niroshan c White b Geeves	0	– not out	0
L-b 8, n-b 2	10	B 9, l-b 1, n-b 1	11

(89.1 overs, 332 mins)	233	(79.1 overs, 284 mins)	192
Fall: 3 49 50 83 121 167 168		Fall: 2 62 64 77 102 107 134	
172 174 233		134 192 192.	

G. M. C. Nilantha did not bat.

Bowling: *First Innings*—James 11–2–37–1; Welsford 13–6–27–1; Geeves 14.1–4–30–2; Hauritz 12–3–26–0; White 16–5–41–3; Casson 12–3–37–1; O'Brien 11–6–27–2. *Second Innings*—Geeves 16–5–26–2; Welsford 8–2–13–1; James 8–1–33–0; Hauritz 24.1–10–32–3; White 18–6–55–3; O'Brien 5–1–23–1.

Australia

T. R. Birt b Wijesiriwardene	0	– not out	17
M. J. Cosgrove c Perera b Lokuarachchi	37	– not out	7
S. E. Marsh c R. T. Peiris b Pushpakumara	123		
N. M. Hauritz lbw b Lokuarachchi	1		
A. W. O'Brien c and b Pushpakumara	51		
C. J. Borgas c Lokuarachchi b Wijesiriwardene	11		
†C. D. Hartley not out	72		
C. L. White c sub (M. D. K. Perera) b Pushpakumara	26		
*T. H. Welsford lbw b Wijesiriwardene	34		
B. Casson c Randika b Pushpakumara	29		
B. Geeves run out	3		
B 6, l-b 3, n-b 5	14	N-b 1	1
(103 overs, 389 mins)	401	(8.3 overs, 33 mins) (0 wkts)	25

Fall: 0 63 77 190 233 233 260 318 383 401

A. C. L. James did not bat.

Bowling: *First Innings*—Wijesiriwardene 22–5–72–2; Niroshan 14–5–51–0; Lokuarachchi 24–8–57–2; Pushpakumara 27–9–52–3; Nilantha 5–1–13–0; Randika 6–1–18–0; Kandamby 4–0–28–0; M. S. P. Peiris 1–0–2–0. *Second Innings*—Wijesiriwardene 4–1–15–0; Pushpakumara 4–1–9–0; Perera 0.3–0–1–0.

Umpires: B. Bennett and A.R. Craig.

AUSTRALIA v SRI LANKA

Third Youth Test

At Fletcher Park, Perth, April 4, 5, 6, 2001. Australia won by six wickets. Toss: Sri Lanka.

Close of play: First day, Australia (1) 2-17 (Birt 7, Marsh 3). Second day, Sri Lanka (2) 2-9 (Kandamby 3, Randika 0).

Sri Lanka

M. S. P. Peiris b White	29	– c Hauritz b Johnson	4
M. D. K. Perera b Johnson	2	– c White b Geeves	0
*S. H. T. Kandamby c Hartley b Geeves	21	– c Hartley b Welsford	16
M. Pushpakumara b Geeves	3	– (7) c and b O'Brien	13
K. G. M. H. Perera c Hartley b Welsford	20	– c Birt b Geeves	9
D. N. Pathirana c Marsh b Hauritz	64	– c Birt b Geeves	10
†R. T. Peiris c Marsh b Casson	1	– (8) c Hartley b O'Brien	36
K. G. N. Randika c Welsford b Hauritz	21	– (4) c Cosgrove b Geeves	0
K. S. Lokuarachchi c Hartley b O'Brien	1	– b O'Brien	20
O. L. A. Wijesiriwardene st Hartley b O'Brien	0	– c Hartley b Johnson	6
D. Niroshan not out	0	– not out	3
L-b 2, n-b 5	7	B 3, l-b 3, w 1, n-b 5	12
(76.4 overs, 312 mins)	169	(57 overs)	129

Fall: 6 45 55 70 100 103 150 151 157 169   Fall: 2 6 10 27 42 56 71 116 123 129

M. I. Ratnayake did not bat.

Bowling: *First Innings*—Johnson 7–1–23–1; Welsford 16–7–31–1; Geeves 15–6–32–2; Cosgrove 8–4–14–0; White 7–0–22–1; Hauritz 5.4–2–20–2; Casson 14–7–23–1; Marsh 1–1–0–0; O'Brien 3–2–2–2. *Second Innings*—Johnson 10–5–13–2; Geeves 19–4–53–4; Cosgrove 6–3–5–0; Welsford 6–2–6–1; O'Brien 11–8–14–3; White 5–0–32–0.

Australia

M. J. Cosgrove c M. S. P. Peiris b Ratnayake	1	– (4)	not out	32
T. R. Birt c and b Pushpakumara	31	– (5)	lbw Pushpakumara	3
P. J. Dickson c R. T. Peiris b Ratnayake	5	– (1)	c Kandamby b Niroshan	24
S. E. Marsh c R. T. Peiris b Niroshan	5	– (6)	not out	5
A. W. O'Brien c R. T. Peiris b Ratnayake	12			
*N. M. Hauritz c Pathirana b Niroshan	0			
†C. D. Hartley c R. T. Peiris b Niroshan	6			
C. L. White st R. T. Peiris b Lokuarachchi	53			
T. H. Welsford c Niroshan b Lokuarachchi	50			
B. Casson not out	11	– (3)	c Pathirana b Pushpakumara	22
M. G. Johnson lbw b M. D. K. Perera	17	– (2)	c R. T. Peiris b M. D. K. Perera	9
L-b 3, n-b 8	11		L-b 3	3

(103.2 overs, 388 mins)   202   (26.1 overs, 100 mins)   (4 wkts)   98
Fall: 2 12 19 41 46 54 80 169 176 202   Fall:14 42 73 93

B. Geeves did not bat.

Bowling: *First Innings*—Wijesiriwardene 13–3–30–0; Niroshan 17–7–30–3; Ratnayake 17–4–37–3; M. D. K. Perera 2.2–1–1–1; Pushpakumara 31–13–52–1; Lokuarachchi 17–5–30–2; Randika 2–0–5–0; Kandamby 4–0–14–0. *Second Innings*—Wijesiriwardene 4–2–10–0; Niroshan 5–1–21–1; M. D. K. Perera 3–0–7–1; Pushpakumara 9–4–13–2; Ratnayake 1–0–12–0; Lokuarachchi 3–0–21–0; Kandamby 1.1–0–11–0.

Umpires: J. Brookes and A.R. Craig.

AUSTRALIAN UNDER-17s, 2000-01

By KEN PIESSE

South Australia won the R. J. Parish Trophy for the first time since 1988-89 when they drew the final against New South Wales at Northgate in Brisbane. South Australia's captain Cameron Borgas top-scored with 149 in the final, joining Tom Plant (122) in adding 187 for the third wicket as South Australia, the top-ranked team, batted well into the second day, scoring almost 500. Having narrowly defeated New South Wales by just 12 runs in the high-scoring opening game of the carnival, the strong batting of the young South Australians had only to ensure a draw in the final to win the title.

"Our side was strong in batting and in camaraderie. There was a lot of enthusiasm and respect for each other," said South Australian coach Dean Sayers. "The boys had the very best of facilities, with the wickets at Northgate being good enough to host a Pura Cup match." A bonus for the best-performed players was their selection in a development squad which played England Under-17s in Adelaide in what is likely to be the first of a regular representative program, as cricket continues to look to the future in providing a pathway to representative ranks.

Callum Ferguson, South Australia's opening batsman, captained Australia in the two representative matches against England, a one-day match, which the Australians won by three wickets, and a three-day match, which the Australians won by 90 runs. Two of the outstanding batsmen of the carnival, Victoria's Simon Hill (107 in the one-day match) and Matthew Berriman (32 and 82 in the three-day match) were again prominent against England. So were Western Australian medium-pacer Ian Hyland, who took 4/28 from nine overs in the one-day match, and Queensland's Luke Davis, a wrist-spinner, who took 1/23 and 5/25 in the three-day match. Earlier, the English team won two one-day games against South Australia Under-17s. Capping his summer, Ferguson, who is eligible for Under-17s selection again next summer, also played for Prospect in their Adelaide A-grade premiership side.

The Australian squad was: Callum Ferguson (captain), Cameron Borgas, Mark Cosgrove and Matthew Burr (South Australia), Aaron Bird, Mark Faraday, Greg Hunt and Cameron Nupier (New South Wales), Matthew Berriman, Simon Hill and Shane Jones (Victoria), Ken Skewes (Northern Territory), Tim Paine (Tasmania), Luke Davis and Grant Sullivan (Queensland) and Ian Hyland (Western Australia). The squad was selected by Australian Academy assistant coach Troy Cooley and the ACB's coaching consultant Brian Taber in consultation with state and territory team coaches.

South Australia won two of their three qualifying games but lost to Queensland by 83 runs, before winning their semi-final against Western Australia and drawing the final with New South Wales. Cosgrove, who also played in the Under-19s carnival, dominated the semi-final, making 55 and taking 4/31 including a hat-trick to finish the match. Burr, a rangy off-spinner from Sturt, was the cornerstone of the attack.

New South Wales were best served by their captain, Faraday, and Hunt, whose prolific tournament included 107 against Queensland and 98 against Victoria in the semi-final. Titleholders Victoria, who finished third this time, were also strongest in batting. Hill, from Camberwell, batted four and a half hours for 154 against New South Wales, and Berriman scored 86 against Queensland and 125 against New South Wales, before making his premier league debut in the final round of the Melbourne club season for Prahran.

Queensland won only one of their first three games before defeating Australian Capital Territory in a consolation final to finish fourth, after Peter Reimers, who made 107, and Murray Bragg added 125 for the seventh wicket. Tasmania's best players were Paine, who combined captaincy and wicket-keeping, Brent Mullet, James Westcombe and Clinton Viney. Western Australia, who finished sixth, had key batting contributions from Liam Davis, who made a century in the second innings against Tasmania, Dean Brownlie and Chad Jones, the wicket-keeper. Ryan Pack and Hyland were the leading wicket-takers. Australian Capital Territory and Northern Territory again struggled to be competitive, but Skewes, from Northern Territory, is an exceptional prospect and is eligible for Under-17s selection again in 2001-02.

ROUND ONE

Group A

At Northgate No. 3 Ground, Brisbane, January 1, 2, 2001. South Australia won by 12 runs. South Australia seven for 320 declared (C. Ferguson 113, M. Cosgrove 51, N. Kurzel 44; A. Bird 3/50, M. Bright 2/62, L. Reynolds 1/30) and none for 10; New South Wales 308 (M. Hughston 99, M. Faraday 97, L. Reynolds 34; M. Cosgrove 3/31, D. Franco 2/31).

At Northgate No. 4 Ground, Brisbane, January 1, 2, 2001. Victoria won by 79 runs. Queensland 211 (C. Mercant 88, P. Reimers 35, M. Bragg 30; A Digiacomo 4/29, S. Jones 2/45) and none for 34 (C. Mengel 23); Victoria 290 (M. Berriman 86, M. Gale 50, B. McDonald 42; G. Sullivan 2/38, D. Watts 2/44).

Group B

At Northgate No. 1 Ground, Brisbane, January 1, 2, 2001. Western Australia won on first inmnings. Australian Capital Territory 161 (C. Johnston 46, M. Shaw 41, O. Webb 16; R. Pack 4/48, G. Atkinson 2/25, R. Head 1/15) and two for 63 (W. Baker 31, A. Pickard 16*); Western Australia 201 (C. Jones 69, T. Doropoulos 41, P. Scott 24; D. Pascoe 5/70).

At Northgate No. 2 Ground, Brisbane, January 1, 2, 2001. Tasm,ania won by 45 runs. Northern Territory 245 (K. Skewes 104, T. Clements 38, D. Richards 20; C. Viney 2/20, S. Butterworth 2/21); Tasmania six for 290 (T. Paine 100, J. Westcombe 79*, N. Aird 39; S. McCrystal 3/40).

ROUND TWO

Group A

At Northgate No. 1 Ground, Brisbane, January 3, 4, 2001. New South Wales won on first innings. New South Wales 339 (G. Hunt 107, B. Burgess 57, M. Faraday 50; L. Davis 6/87, P. Reimers 2/43) and two for 33; Queensland 191 (C. Merchant 45, J. Nielsen 30, A. Hicks 24; V. Sithloo 4/64, B. Drew 2/28, M. Bright 2/37).

At Northgate No. 2 Ground, Brisbane, January 3, 4, 2001. South Australia won by 100 runs. Victoria 221 (B. McDonald 66, A. Crosthwaite 43, A. Connaughton 33; M. Cosgrove 3/39, M. Burr 3/57, D. Franco 2/31); South Australia five for 331 (C. Ferguson 103, T. Plant 87, C. Borgas 70*; M. Digiacomo 2/65).

Group B

At Northgate No. 3 Ground, Brisbane, January 3, 4, 2001. Tasmania won by 181 runs. Australian Capital Territory 157 (W. Baker 35, O. Web 34, A. Pickard 29; S. Stevenson 3/41, P. Doherty 2/31, S Leatherbarrow 1/2); Tasmania 338 (J. Westcombe 98, S. Butterworth 49, C. Viney 46; A. Pickard 2/8, M. Shaw 2/51, S. Morrison 2/33).

At Northgate No. 4 Ground, Brisbane, January 3, 4, 2001. Western Australia won on first innings. Western Australia 202 (C. Jones 42, L. Davis 32, B. Mills 27; S. McCrystal 4/37, N. Ingall 2/22, P. Cook 2/36) and three for 118 (L. Davis 46, D. Brownlie 44*); Northern Territory 174 (D. Richards 38, R. McDonald 32, K. Skewes 26; G. Atkinson 3/30, R. Scali 2/23).

ROUND THREE

Group A

At Northgate No. 3 Ground, Brisbane, January 6, 7, 2001. Queensland won on first innings. Queensland seven for 251 declared (C. Mengel 75, C. Howe 48, M. Bragg 37*; M. Cosgrove 2/40, D. Franco 2/47) and five for 92 (J. Nielsen 40*, C. Howe 20, C. Mengel 14; J. Hume 2/27, M. Cosgrove 1/14); South Australia 168 (C. Borgas 26, N. Kurzel 25, J. Tamblyn 23; L. Davis 3/40, G. Sullivan 3/45, M. Jennings 2/25).

At Northgate No. 4 Ground, Brisbane, January 6, 7, 2001. Victoria won on first innings. New South Wales 279 (M. Bright 67, M. Hughston 60, M. O'Connor 53; S. Jones 3/67, M. Berriman 2/14, L. Blake 2/25) and one for 38 (B. Burgess 21, M. Hughston 14*); Victoria nine for 287 declared (M. Berriman 125, S. Jones 70, J. Bartel 18, A. Crosthwaite 18*; C. Nupier 4/35, A. Bird 2/55).

Group B

At Northgate No. 1 Ground, Brisbane, January 6, 7, 2001. Northern Territory won on first innings. Northern Territory seven for 255 (K. Skewes 97, M. Brown 71, D. Richards 33; D. Pascoe 3/81, S. Morrison 2/30, J. Herdegan 1/30) and two for 25; Australian Capital Territory 116 (A. Mansfield 37*, M. Shaw 23; M. Donfield 4/16, S. McCrystal 2/17, P. Cook 2/24).

At Northgate No. 2 Ground, Brisbane, January 6, 7, 2001. Western Australia won on first innings. Western Australia seven for 291 declared (D. Brownlie 91, T. Doropoulos 61, C. Jones 37; B. Holland 2/40, N. Aird 122) and four for 197 (L. Davis 104, R. Head 53*, B. Mills 22; S. Butterworth 3/56, C. Viney 128); Tasmania 114 (S. Stevenson 29*, M. Knight 23, S. Butterworth 18; B. Mills 3/10, R. Pack 3/36, L. Hyland 2/16).

QUALIFYING FINALS

At Albury Oval, Brisbane, January 8, 9, 2001. New South Wales won by 23 runs. New South Wales eight for 369 declared (G. Hunt 98, M. Faraday 72, M. O'Connor 59; J. Bartel 3/35, S. Jones 2/93); Victoria 346 (S. Hill 154, S. Jones 55, B. McDonald 35; A. Bird 3/40, C. Nupier 3/52, M. Ross 2/67).

At Norm McMahon Oval, Brisbane, January 8, 9, 2001. Queensland won by 120 runs. Australian Capital Territory 190 (D. King 90, D. Pascoe 25*, A. Pickard 21; P. Reimers 3/16, D. Watts 1/4, B. Teece 1/15); Queensland six for 310 (P. Reimers 107*, M. Bragg 50*, J. Nielsen 41; D. Pascoe 4/93, M. Shaw 2/79).

At Peter Easton Oval, Brisbane, January 8, 9, 2001. South Australia won by 64 runs. South Australia 220 (C. Borgas 61, M. Cosgrove 55, M. Burr 36; I. Hyland 5/23, B. Mills 2/10, R. Pack 2/43); Western Australia 154 (R. Morgan 58, L. Davis 32, P. Scott 22; M. Cosgrove 4/31, M. Burr 3/53, D. Franco 2/30).

At Trevor Barsby Oval, Brisbane, January 8, 9, 2001. Tasmania won on first innings. Northern Territory 117 (M. Brown 29, N. Ingall 20; B. Mullett 3/11, S. Butterworth 2/13, B. Holland 1/8) and seven for 139 (R. McDonald 25, M. Brown 24, S. McCrystal 24*; S. Leatherbarrow 2/20, B. Mullett 2/26, C. Viney 1/7); Tasmania 242 (C. Viney 73*, T. Paine 37, M. Knight 24; K. Skews 3/39, K. Smith 2/22, S. McCrystal 2/34).

CONSOLATION FINALS

AUSTRALIAN CAPITAL TERRITORY v NORTHERN TERRITORY

At Brisbane Grammar School Oval No. 3. Brisbane, January 10, 11, 2001. Australian Capital Territory won on first innings. Toss: Northern Territory. Northern Territory 151 (N. Brown 71, D. Richards 20; R. Bissell 2/14, S. Morrison 2/22, D. Harris 2/32); Australian Capital Territory six for 255 (C. Johnston 77, W. Baker 61, A. Mansfield 27, D. Harris 26).

QUEENSLAND v WESTERN AUSTRALIA

At Northgate No. 2 Ground, Brisbane, January 10, 11, 2001. Queensland won on first innings. Toss: Queensland. Queensland 258 (J. Nielsen 58, P. Reimers 47, T. Hardingham 47*, M. Bragg 34; T. Houston 3/31, G. Atkinson 3/49) and one for 42; Western Australia 198 (R. Morgan 92, R. Head 32, T. Doropoulos 20, L. Davis 19; C. Howe 2/52).

TASMANIA v VICTORIA

At Northgate No. 4 Ground, Brisbane, January 10, 11, 2001. Match tied. Toss: Victoria. Victoria seven for 348 declared (A. Connaughton 82, J. Bartel 45, S. Jones 39, A. Crosthwaite 39, A. Diagiacomo 31; B. Godfrey 4/48, S. Leatherbarrow 2/45); Tasmania nine for 348 (T. Paine 122, C. Viney 49*, S. Stevenson 33, B. Mullett 32, S. Butterworth 28; L. Blake 3/42, A. Connaughton 2/44).

CHAMPIONSHIP FINAL

NEW SOUTH WALES v SOUTH AUSTRALIA

At Northgate No. 1 Ground, Brisbane, January 10, 11, 2001. Drawn. Toss: South Australia.

South Australia

M. Cosgrove c Hunt b Nupier	1	(3)	R. Crane c and b Bright	4	(19)
T. Plant c Burgess b Drew	122	(293)	D. Franco c and b Sithloo	0	(2)
C. Ferguson c Nupier b Bird	82	(130)	J. Corbett not out	6	(12)
*C. Borgas c Hunt b Nupier	149	(317)	B 3, l-b 3, w 4, n-b 6	16	
N. Kurzel c Drew b Sithloo	62	(126)			
M. Burr c O'Connor b Sithloo	32	(39)	(159.2 overs, 504 mins)	484	
†J. McLean lbw b Bright	9	(16)	Fall: 1 125 312 404 453 466 474		
C. Bailey c Allsop b Sithloo	1	(9)	474 474 484		

J. Hume did not bat.

Bowling: Bird 22–3–57–1; Nupier 18–3–75–2; Ross 18–3–66–0; Bright 37.2–8–76–2; Drew 22–3–69–1; Sithloo 33–10–90–4; Hunt 2–0–9–0; O'Connor 7–2–16–0.

New South Wales

B. Burgess c McLean b Cosgrove	16	(42)	A. Bird not out	48	(64)
M. Hughston not out	74	(166)	†J. Allsopp not out	0	(0)
G. Hunt c McLean b Cosgrove	4	(6)	L-b 3, n-b 3	6	
*M. Faraday st McLean b Bailey	47	(38)			
M. Bright c Corbett b Bailey	7	(18)	(56 overs, 185 mins) (5 wkts)	204	
M. O'Connor c Corbett b Bailey	2	(5)	Fall: 40 44 111 123 129		

C. Nupier, M. Ross, B. Drew and V. Sithloo did not bat.

Bowling: Franco 6–0–27–0; Corbett 6–4–8–0; Cosgrove 12–1–37–2; Burr 8–0–34–0; Crane 3–1–14–0; Bailey 14–2–47–3; Hume 6–1–24–0; Kurzel 1–0–10–0.

Umpires: S. Knobben and A. Craig.

UNDER-17s CRICKET CHAMPIONSHIPS RECORDS

Under-17s Championships

Series	Venue	Winner	Player of the Year
1986-87	Melbourne	New South Wales	M. Galbraith (Vic)
1987-88	Launceston	New South Wales	J.C. Young (NSW)
1988-89	Sydney	South Australia	M.J.P. Minagall (SA)
1989-90	Adelaide	Victoria	T.F. Corbett (Vic)
1990-91	Brisbane	New South Wales	J.P. Maher (Qld)
1991-92	Canberra	New South Wales	B.J. Hodge (Vic)
1992-93	Hobart	New South Wales	B.A. Clemow (NSW)
1993-94	Adelaide	New South Wales	M.D. Pascoe (Qld)
1994-95	Perth	New South Wales	D.J. Thornely (NSW)
1995-96	Melbourne/Geelong	Queensland	M.J. North (WAust)
1996-97	Brisbane	New South Wales	L. Williams (SAust)
1997-98	Hobart	Victoria	A. Kent (Vic)
1998-99	Sydney	New South Wales	E. Cowan (NSW)
1999-00	Brisbane	Victoria	P. Boraston (Vic)
2000-01	Brisbane	South Australia	C.J. Borgas (SAust)

TEN YEARS' PLACINGS

	91-92	92-93	93-94	94-95	95-96	96-97	97-98	98-99	99-00	00-01
Australia										
Capital Territory .	7	7	4	6	7	7	7	5	7	7
New South Wales .	1	1	1	1	6	1	6	1	2	2
Northern Territory	8	8	8	8	8	8	4	7	8	8
Queensland	4	4	3	1	1	2	8	2	4	4
South Australia ...	6	2	6	4	2	4	5	8	3	1
Tasmania	5	5	7	5	5	6	3	6	6	5
Victoria	3	6	2	3	3	5	1	4	1	3
Western Australia .	2	3	5	7	4	3	2	3	5	6

UNDER-17s CRICKET CHAMPIONSHIP, 2000-01

POINTS TABLE

Group A	P	WO	W1	D	L1	LO	T	Points	Quotient
South Australia	3	0	2	0	1	0	0	12	1.38
Victoria	3	0	2	0	1	0	0	12	0.79
New South Wales	3	0	1	0	2	0	0	6	0.97
Queensland	3	0	1	0	2	0	0	6	0.94
Group B									
Western Australia	3	0	3	0	0	0	0	18	1.85
Tasmania	3	0	2	0	1	0	0	12	0.83
Northern Territory	3	0	1	0	2	0	0	6	0.76
Australian Capital Territory	3	0	0	0	3	0	0	0	0.66

Quotient = runs per wicket scored divided by runs per wicket conceded.

FINAL PLACINGS

1st	South Australia
2nd	New South Wales
3rd	Victoria
4th	Queensland
5th	Tasmania
6th	Western Australia
7th	Australian Capital Territory
8th	Northern Territory

HIGHEST INDIVIDUAL SCORE

154	S. Hill	Victoria v New South Wales at Albury Oval
149	C. Borgas	South Australia v New South Wales at Northgate No. 1 Ground
125	M. Berriman	Victoria v New South Wales at Northgate No. 4 Ground
122	T. Paine	Tasmania v Victoria at Northgate No. 4 Ground
122	T. Plant	South Australia v New South Wales at Northgate No. 1 Ground
113	C. Ferguson	South Australia v New South Wales at Northgate No. 3 Ground
107	G. Hunt	New South Wales v Queensland at Northgate No. 1. Ground
107*	P. Reimers	Queensland v Australian Capital Territory at Norm McMahon Oval
104	L. Davis	Western Australia v Tasmania at Northgate No. 2 Ground
104	K. Skewes	Northern Territory v Tasmania at Northgate No. 2 Ground
103	C. Ferguson	South Australia v Victoria at Northgate No. 2 Ground
100	T. Paine	Tasmania v Northern Territory at Northgate No. 2 Ground

MOST RUNS

	M	I	NO	R	HS	100s	50s	Avge
C. Borgas (SAust)	5	5	1	342	149	1	2	85.50
M. Berriman (Vic)	5	5	0	328	125	1	1	65.60
C. Ferguson (SAust)	5	5	0	323	113	2	1	64.60
M. Faraday (NSW)	5	5	0	306	97	0	3	61.20
M. Hughston (NSW)	5	6	2	280	99	0	3	70.00
T. Paine (Tas)	5	5	0	270	122	2	0	54.00
L. Davis (WAust)	5	7	0	263	104	1	0	37.57
G. Hunt (NSW)	5	5	0	249	107	1	1	49.80
S. Hill (Vic)	5	5	0	248	154	1	0	49.60
K. Skewes (NT)	5	6	0	243	104	1	1	40.50

MOST WICKETS

	M	O	Mdns	R	W	BB	5W/i	10W/m	Avge
D. Pascoe (ACT)	5	146.4	50	304	15	5/70	1	0	20.27
M. Cosgrove (SAust)	5	78.3	22	187	14	4/31	0	0	13.36
S. McCrystal (NT)	5	74.4	13	177	12	4/37	0	0	14.75
R. Pack (WAust)	5	94.2	29	223	11	4/48	0	0	22.27
A. Bird (NSW)	5	96	20	241	10	3/40	0	0	24.10
L. Davis (Qld)	5	109.5	35	235	10	6/87	1	0	23.50
G. Sullivan (Qld)	5	78.3	21	181	10	3/45	0	0	18.10

BEST BOWLING

6/87	L. Davis	Queensland v New South Wales at Northgate No. 1 Ground
5/23	I. Hyland	Western Australia v South Australia at Peter Easton Oval
5/70	D. Pascoe	Australian Capital Territory v Western Australia at Northgate No. 1 Ground

HIGHEST TOTALS

484	South Australia v New South Wales at Northgate No. 1 Ground
8d-369	New South Wales v Victoria at Albury Oval
7d-348	Victoria v Tasmania at Northgate No. 4 Ground
9-348	Tasmania v Victoria at Northgate No. 4 Ground
346	Victoria v New South Wales at Albury Oval
339	New South Wales v Queensland at Northgate No. 1 Ground
338	Tasmania v Australian Capital Territory at Northgate No. 3 Ground
5d-331	South Australia v Victoria at Northgate No. 2 Ground
7d-320	South Australia v New South Wales at Northgate No. 3 Ground
6d-310	Queensland v Australian Capital Territory at Norm McMahon Oval
308	New South Wales v South Australia at Northgate No. 3 Ground

LOWEST TOTAL

114	Tasmania v Western Australia at Northgate No. 2 Ground
116	Australian Capital Territory v Northern Territory at Northgate No. 1 Ground
117	Northern Territory v Tasmania at Trevor Barsby Oval

ENGLAND UNDER-17s IN AUSTRALIA, 2000-01

ENGLAND TOURING SQUAD

J. J. Sayers (Yorkshire) *(captain)*, G. M. Andrew (Somerset), D. J. Barrick (Yorkshire), D. L. Broadbent (Yorkshire), T. T. Bresnan (Yorkshire), A. J. Coleman (Middlesex), A. W. Gale (Yorkshire), C. R. Gilbert (Yorkshire), A. J. Hodd (Sussex), T. Paine (Yorkshire), S. Patel (Nottinghamshire), T. Rees (Lancashire), G. M. Scott (Durham), B. M. Shafayat (Nottinghamshire), D. A. Stiff (Yorkshire). *Coach/Manager:* K. Tomlins.

SOUTH AUSTRALIA v ENGLAND

At Adelaide Oval No. 2, April 3, 2001. England won by eight wickets. Toss: South Australia.

South Australia

C. B. Bailey b Bresnan 8	†J. L. McLean c Patel b Gilbert 24
B. Gunning c Patel b Stiff 0	R. A. Crane not out 7
*C. J. Ferguson st Andrews b Barrick 69	
B. T. Symes c Hodd b Bresnan 12	B 4, l-b 11, w 9, n-b 5 29
J. P. Tamblyn c Rees b Patel 14	
M. R. Burr c Gale b Barrick 0	(50 overs, 191 mins) (7 wkts) 199
H. Thorpe not out 36	Fall: 1 34 62 111 111 113 171

D. J. Franco, J. A. Hume and J. R. Corbett did not bat.

Bowling: Stiff 10–2–36–1; Andrews 7–2–19–0; Gilbert 7–1–30–1; Bresnan 9–2–38–2; Barrick 10–1–29–2; Patel 7–0–32–1.

England

B. M. Shafayat not out 86	L-b 1, w 8, n-b 3 12
*J. J. Sayers c McLean b Corbett 1	
A. W. Gale run out 58	(48.3 overs, 171 mins) (2 wkts) 202
S. Patel not out 45	Fall: 2 118

T. Rees, G. M. Andrews, †A. J. Hodd, T. T. Bresnan, D. J. Barrick, D. A. Stiff, C. R. Gilbert and G. M. Scott did not bat.

Bowling: Franco 5–0–19–0; Corbett 8–1–33–1; Crane 7–0–31–0; Hume 3–0–14–0; Burr 10–0–40–0; Bailey 10–2–41–0; Ferguson 3–0–12–0; Gunning 2.3–0–11–0.

Umpires: R. A. Falk and D. Little.

SOUTH AUSTRALIA v ENGLAND

At Adelaide Oval No. 2, Adelaide, April 5, 2001. England won by two wickets. Toss: South Australia.

South Australia

C.B. Bailey c Hodd b Coleman	22	R.A. Crane b Gilbert 30
M.R. Burr c Sayers b Gilbert	7	J.A. Hume b Andrew 0
*C.J. Ferguson b Coleman	5	J.R. Corbett not out 0
B.G. Gunning c Sayers b Barrick	7	
B.T. Symes c Hodd b Broadbent	35	B 4, l-b 7, w 13, n-b 2 26
H.J. Thorpe c Scott b Broadbent	9	
J.P. Tamblyn c and b Barrick	0	(47.1 overs, 175 mins) 161
†J.L. McLean run out	20	Fall: 12 21 44 59 92 93 99 161 161 161

D.J. Franco did not bat.

Bowling: Andrew 10–0–32–1; Gilbert 6.1–1–25–2; Coleman 4–0–22–2; Barrick 10–1–20–2; Broadbent 10–1–19–2; Scott 7–2–19–0; Patel 5–0–13–0.

England

*J.J. Sayers lbw b Gunning	20	S. Patel b Franco 2
T. Rees c McLean b Franco	4	D.J. Barrick c Gunning b Franco 0
G.M. Andrew c Ferguson b Franco	1	D.L. Broadbent not out 2
G.M. Scott c Crane b Tamblyn	34	L-b 6, w 19, n-b 4 29
†A.J. Hodd b Burr	11	
A.J. Coleman c Symes b Tamblyn	31	(49.4 overs, 196 mins) (8 wkts) 163
B.M. Shafayat not out	29	Fall: 19 21 53 81 101 142 147 153

C.R. Gilbert and D.A. Stiff did not bat.

Bowling: Franco 8–2–9–4; Corbett 4–0–25–0; Crane 6–1–14–0; Burr 10–3–27–1; Gunning 4–0–15–1; Tamblyn 5–0–28–2; Ferguson 5–2–14–0; Bailey 7.4–0–25–0.

Umpires: M. Bartlett and R.A. Falk.

AUSTRALIA v ENGLAND

At St Peter's College, Adelaide, April 9, 10, 11, 2001. Australia won by 90 runs. Toss: Australia

Close of Play: First day, England 1-38 (Sayers 5, Patel 2); Second day, Australia 2-120 (Berriman 63, Farraday 17).

Australia

*C.J. Ferguson c Shafayat b Andrew	34	– b Stiff	9
G.I. Hunt lbw b Andrew	28	– lbw b Barrick	28
M. Berriman c Patel b Stiff	32	– b Patel	82
M.W.B. Faraday c Bresnan b Broadbent	8	– run out	43
S.F Hill c Gale b Scott	45	– b Patel	9
K.J Skewes c Gale b Bresnan	51	– not out	0
†T.D Paine not out	37		
M.R Burr c Hodd b Stiff	15		
L.R Davis not out	10		
L-b 11, w 1, n-b 5	17	B 2, l-b 4, w 1, n-b 1	8
(89 overs, 305 mins) (7 wkts dec) 277		(41.3 overs, 147 mins) (5 wkts dec) 179	
Fall: 67 70 85 121 180 229 246		Fall: 20 72 165 179 179	

I.P. Hyland, A.C. Bird and G.J. Sullivan did not bat.

Bowling: *First Innings*—Stiff 17–9–20–2; Gilbert 13–3–61–0; Bresnan 9–1–40–1; Barrick 8–1–31–0; Andrew 5–1–17–2; Broadbent 6–0–19–1; Patel 16–8–30–0; Scott 15–4–48–1. *Second Innings*—Stiff 9–0–39–1; Gilbert 8–0–34–0; Andrew 2–0–14–0; Broadbent 5–0–14–0; Barrick 9–0–31–1; Scott 3–0–20–0; Patel 4.3–2–16–2; Bresnan 1–0–5–0.

England

A. W. Gale c Berriman b Sullivan	18	– st Paine b Burr	36
*J. J. Sayers c Paine b Burr	31	– c Paine b Sullivan	6
S. Patel lbw b A. C. Bird	17	– (4) c Hill b Burr	17
B. M. Shafayat c Hill b Sullivan	32	– (3) lbw b Davis	30
G. M. Scott c Paine b Sullivan	6	– lbw b Burr	0
†A. J. Hodd c Paine b Sullivan	0	– lbw b Burr	19
D. J. Barrick b Burr	33	– lbw b Davis	18
T. T. Bresnan c Paine b Hyland	4	– lbw b Davis	20
C. R. Gilbert c Burr b Davis	1	– c Burr b Davis	14
D. A. Stiff b A. C. Bird	26	– b A. C. Bird	0
D. L. Broadbent not out	0	– not out	0
L-b 6, w 2, n-b 15	23	B 2, l-b 8, n-b 5	15

(77.4 overs, 303 mins) **191** (74.4 overs, 264 mins) **175**

Fall: 25 73 98 123 123 130 147 Fall: 31 62 96 96 100 125 150
154 191 191 163 175 175

G. M. Andrew did not bat.

Bowling: *First Innings*—Sullivan 17–3–57–4; Hyland 14–4–32–1; AC Bird 17–3–31–2; Burr 16.4–4–41–2; Davis 12.2–2–23–1; Skewes 1–0–1–0. *Second Innings*—Sullivan 11–2–28–1; AC Bird 11–2–23–1; Burr 31–10–81–3; Hyland 4–1–8–0; Davis 17.4–7–25–5.

Umpires: P. J. Weeks and G. G. Smith.

AUSTRALIAN CAPITAL TERRITORY FIRST-GRADE CRICKET, 2000-01

By ADAM MOREHOUSE

The Australian Capital Territory Cricket Association season was marked by positive play throughout. Four clubs dominated the season, but the third and fourth teams made it to the final, which Weston Creek won for the first time in their 20-year history. They had the strongest batting line-up in Cade Brown (750 runs), Anthony McQuire (849 runs), Jack Smith (564 runs) and Sean Maxwell (642 runs). Their bowling was also strong, led by the Australian Under-19s representative Andrew James with 24 wickets at 17.70.

Queanbeyan exceeded their expectations by reaching the final, principally through the all-round excellence of their captain, Jason Swift, who scored 798 runs and took 25 wickets with his spin bowling. Their bowling was led by the pace of Grant Miller, who took 22 wickets, but the lack of a regular wicket-keeper hampered the side.

The losing semi-finalists, Tuggeranong Valley and Eastlake, led the other teams during the season. Tuggeranong's batting was not as reliable as in previous seasons but their bowling was as strong as ever, with Evan Kellar their leading wicket-taker with 35 wickets. Tim Ferguson took 34 wickets and Chris Males chimed in with 29. Rod Tucker led Eastlake in both batting and bowling with 751 runs and 29 wickets, while spinner Matt Ramage took 38 wickets.

Ginninderra had their best season for eight years, finishing just outside the top four. David Dawson starred with the bat, scoring 646 runs, while Luke Bulkeley showed his promise by taking 39 wickets. North Canberra struggled again but Bruce Mikkelsen headed the competition's wicket-takers with 42 wickets, ably supported by captain Heath Axelby with 32.

Western District and Australian National University finished seventh and eighth again respectively. Australian National University missed the experience of Hall O'Meagher, while Western District had lost a number of experienced players, and their season was one of rebuilding. Daniel Pascoe of Australian National University was rewarded for good performances with selection for the Australian Capital Territory side, while Ben Keens continued his good form with 39 wickets.

Albury & Border finished as runners-up again in the Konica Cup competition, this time to Tuggeranong Valley. Wagga Wagga narrowly missed the semi-finals, and Goulburn's season showed signs of improvement despite their position on the table.

AUSTRALIAN CAPITAL TERRITORY
FIRST-GRADE TABLE, 2000-01

	M	WO	W1	D	LI	LO	T	Points
Tuggeranong Valley	11	1	7	1	2	0	0	52
Eastlake	11	1	6	1	3	0	0	46
Weston Creek	11	0	7	1	3	0	0	42
Queanbeyan	11	0	6	2	2	1	0	36
Ginninderra West Belconnen	11	0	5	0	6	0	0	30
North Canberra–Gungahlin	11	0	4	0	6	1	0	24
Western District	11	0	3	0	8	0	0	18
Australian National University	11	0	1	1	9	0	0	6

AUSTRALIAN CAPITAL TERRITORY
FIRST-GRADE AVERAGES, 2000-01

BATTING

(Qualification: 400 runs)

	M	I	NO	R	HS	100s	50s	Avge
A. D. McQuire (Weston Creek)	16	15	3	849	150	3	5	70.75
C. Brown (Weston Creek)	17	15	3	750	164*	3	3	62.50
J. J. Swift (Queanbeyan)	16	17	3	798	152*	3	3	57.00
M. J. Dawn (Eastlake)	14	14	3	594	159	2	4	54.00
D. G. Dawson (Ginninderra W. Belconnen)	14	14	2	646	160	2	3	53.83
D. S. Hazell (Weston Creek)	20	18	7	558	150*	1	5	50.72
R. J. Tucker (Eastlake)	17	18	3	751	149*	1	6	50.06
J. K. Smith (Weston Creek)	16	15	2	564	103	1	5	43.38
S. L. Maxwell (Weston Creek)	20	19	4	642	120	1	4	42.79
S. P. Heaney (Tuggeranong Valley)	14	13	2	453	128*	1	3	41.18

* Denotes not out.

BOWLING

(Qualification: 25 wickets)

	M	O	Mdns	R	W	BB	5Wi	10W/m	Avge
R. J. Tucker (Eastlake)	17	149.5	35	285	29	4/10	0	0	9.82
T. J. Ferguson (T. Valley)	17	207.3	45	484	34	7/25	1	0	14.23
B. M. Keens (W. District)	15	254.1	60	576	39	6/54	3	0	14.76
J. D. Robson (T. Valley)	16	191	62	405	26	5/33	1	0	15.57
J. J. Swift (Queanbeyan)	16	175.3	42	401	25	5/80	1	0	16.04
E. Kellar (T. Valley)	16	263.2	70	567	35	5/34	1	0	16.20
J. Henri (Eastlake)	14	181	26	519	31	6/15	2	0	16.74
M. A. Hatton (W. District)	16	273.1	80	579	33	5/33	1	0	17.54
L. J. Bulkeley (Ginninderra)	16	214.1	43	705	39	5/20	2	0	18.07
B. A. Mikkelsen (Norths)	15	290.2	62	840	42	5/15	3	0	20.00

AUSTRALIAN CAPITAL TERRITORY
FIRST-GRADE SEMI-FINALS, 2000-01

TUGGERANONG VALLEY v QUEANBEYAN

At Manuka Oval, March 24, 25, 26, 2001. Queanbeyan won on first innings. Tuggeranong Valley 352 (S. A. Holcombe 187); Queanbeyan seven for 353 (J. J. Swift 152*, C. J. Hamill 54; T. J. Ferguson 3/60).

EASTLAKE v WESTON CREEK

At Boomanulla Oval, March 24, 25, 26, 2001. Weston Creek won on first innings. Weston Creek nine for 488 declared (C. Brown 112, A. D. McQuire 95, J. K. Smith 82, D. S. Hazell 66; J. Henri 3/100, R. Mongan 3/121, M. H. Ramage 3/141); Eastlake 273 (M. J. Dawn 159; E. A. Mackenzie 5/74).

AUSTRALIAN CAPITAL TERRITORY FINAL, 2000-01

WESTON CREEK v QUEANBEYAN

At Manuka Oval on March 31, April 1, 2, 2001. Weston Creek won on first innings. Toss: Queanbeyan.

For the first time since the 1976-77 season, teams that had finished third and fourth battled it out for the Douglas Cup. Queanbeyan won the toss and batted under a blue sky and on a hard Manuka wicket. Weston Creek took two early wickets, which brought Queanbeyan captain Jason Swift to the crease. He dominated the innings with his 106, which included 18 boundaries, but the batting collapsed after his dismissal. Anthony McQuire overcame a bout of conjunctivitis to lead Weston Creek to victory with his 110, receiving sound support from Sean Maxwell and Dave Hazell. With Weston Creek in a commanding position at stumps on the second of three scheduled days, Jason Swift conceded the match.

Close of Play: First day, Queanbeyan 9/278 (Collier 5, Miller 13); Second day, Weston Creek 5/298 (Hazell 50, Mowbray 30).

Queanbeyan

M. J. Frost b Mowbray 8	M. Stachow c Brown b Freemantle 5
P. W. Coleborne c McQuire b Freemantle . . 23	R. Collier not out 5
D. Mansfield c Maxwell b Reynolds 32	G. L. Miller b Mowbray 14
*J. J. Swift c Mowbray b Mackenzie 106	
A. J. Heading c Maxwell b Hunter 16	B 2, l-b 5, n-b 2 9
C. J. Hamill c Hazell b Mowbray 14	
J. Anderson c Maxwell b Hazell 38	(93.1 overs, 360 mins) 279
M. Heading c Maxwell b Mowbray 9	Fall: 13 53 86 141 174 246 246 260 260 279

Bowling: Reynolds 16–5–40–1; Mowbray 20.1–3–50–4; Hunter 17–6–52–1; Freemantle 13–2–46–2; Mackenzie 19–8–50–1; Smith 4–0–19–0; Hazell 4–0–15–1.

Weston Creek

J. K. Smith b Miller 8	D. D. Mowbray not out 30
A. D. McQuire c Anderson b Swift 110	
*C. Brown c Swift b Collier 21	B 4, l-b 3, w 1, n-b 3 11
†S. L. Maxwell c Swift b Anderson 67	
D. S. Hazell not out 50	(90 overs, 350 mins) (5 wkts) 298
M. F. Densten b Mowbray 1	Fall: 20 92 175 236 242

L. F. Freemantle, E. A. Mackenzie, C. Hunter and D. J. Reynolds did not bat.

Bowling: Miller 18–2–69–1; A. J. Heading 14–2–52–0; Swift 19–7–57–1; Collier 8–1–36–1; Anderson 19–5–44–2; Stachow 8–2–23–0; Frost 4–1–10–0.

Umpires: J. C. Hannaford and W. F. Ruse.

SYDNEY FIRST-GRADE CRICKET

By ADRIAN WARREN

St George won their 13th Sydney first-grade premiership and their first for four years, in a season dominated by disaffection over the competition format. In late November, the New South Wales Cricket Association board decided to reduce the competition in future seasons from 20 to 16 clubs, claiming it would lead to a "more competitive environment" and "correspondingly increase the average quality of players" and "create the opportunity for a more representative type of cricket to be played".

The board met all 20 clubs over the first weekend of March and subsequently asked ten of them, in four separate groups, to discuss the possibility of merging. In April, the board effectively earmarked Randwick, Hawkesbury, Petersham and Mosman as the teams to be cut, telling them they might be "adversely affected" after making a "preliminary identification" of the 16 clubs it intended inviting to participate in the 2001-02 competition. Before making its final decision, the board met the four endangered clubs in late April. On May 7 it resolved to retain the 20-team format for the next two seasons while pledging to continue its review of the competition over that period.

"The Board remains adamant that standards of play have fallen in grade cricket over the last decade. This view is supported by players and administrators across the game in polls commissioned by Cricket NSW over the last 10 years," said the board's chairman, Bob Horsell. "Despite the significant improvements to wickets, grade cricket infrastructure, and our national representation, we are not satisfied that the grade competition is performing at the optimal level. For example, NSW has not produced a specialist Test batsman since Michael Bevan debuted in 1994-95 and too few of our top-scoring grade batsmen have gone on to significant and sustainable first-class careers in the last 10 years. This is not good enough."

The board said it would continue to promote and support club mergers which were in the best interests of the competition, and would consider the possible admission in 2003-04 of a club centred on the Blacktown/Rouse Hill area. "The Board has the right to set the size of the Sydney grade cricket competition. The exercise we have just completed, while distressing in some instances, must serve as a wake-up call that no club has intrinsic rights to be a member of the grade competition," Horsell said.

On the field, St George went one better than the previous season, when they had been beaten in the final by Bankstown–Canterbury. They were entrenched in the top four for virtually the whole season, and won the minor premiership, leapfrogging Manly at the end of the season when Manly's final match was washed out.

St George's opening batsman Brett van Deinsen headed the competition run aggregates for the second successive season, though for much of the summer it looked as if Rodney Davison would finish on top, despite moving to Queensland at the turn of the year. Davison accumulated 789 runs from just

10 innings, failing to reach 50 only three times. His phenomenal average of 157.80 was the fifth-best in Sydney first-grade history for players scoring over 500 runs. It placed him behind a quartet of cricketing greats in Monty Noble (273.00, 1898-99), Victor Trumper (204.20, 1897-98), Donald Bradman (170.66, 1932-33) and Geoff Boycott (165.71, 1976-77). Van Deinsen, who batted twice as often as Davison, overtook him during his score of 172 in the final.

St George also boasted the leading wicket-taker, Scott Thompson, whose haul of 54 was one ahead of Sydney University spinner Jamie Stewart. Thompson underlined his versatility and value by scoring 762 runs, the sixth-highest tally in the competition. Opening batsman Nathan Catalano (737 runs) and bowlers James Turner and Peter Wooden (40 and 39 wickets respectively) were other major contributors to the St George cause.

Eventual runners-up Eastern Suburbs moved up from eighth the previous season and scraped into the finals in fifth spot despite losing their last match outright. Their stalwart batsman Mark Patterson scored a century in both the qualifying final and semi-final, and in the process surpassed the club run-scoring record established by the great Alan Kippax. Former Australian limited-overs fast bowler Anthony Stuart was another inspirational figure for Easts, capturing 49 wickets.

Bankstown–Canterbury had an indifferent summer after their success in 1999-2000 and failed to make the finals for the first time in several seasons. Their plight paled in comparison to that of the hapless Gordon, who failed to score a single point on the way to collecting their third consecutive wooden spoon.

Manly took the limited-overs title with a 98-run victory over Northern District, while the O'Reilly Medal for the first-grade Player of the Year was won by Parramatta all-rounder Bob Aitken (675 runs at 48.21 and 42 wickets at 17.78).

SYDNEY FIRST-GRADE TABLE, 2000-01

	M	WO	W1	D	L1	LO	Points	Quotient
St George	16	3	8	1	4	0	74	1.5908
Manly–Warringah	16	3	7	2	4	0	72	1.4244
Balmain	16	1	9	1	4	1	64	1.3025
Western Suburbs	16	1	9	3	3	0	64	1.2903
Eastern Suburbs	16	2	6	3	3	2	60	0.9129
Sydney University	16	2	6	4	3	1	59	1.1758
Northern District	16	1	8	4	3	0	58	1.0709
North Sydney	16	2	6	1	3	4	56	0.9033
Penrith	16	1	6	2	7	0	46	1.0855
Fairfield–Liverpool	16	1	6	1	8	0	46	0.8999
Mosman	16	0	7	3	6	0	45	1.1738
Bankstown	16	0	7	3	5	1	42	1.1391
Campbelltown–Camden	16	0	6	4	5	1	39	0.8214
Sutherland	16	0	6	3	7	0	36	0.8376
Hawkesbury	16	0	6	0	9	1	36	0.7454
Parramatta	16	0	5	2	7	2	34	1.0383
Randwick	16	0	5	3	7	1	30	1.0280
University of NSW	16	0	4	3	9	0	27	0.8864
Petersham–Marrickville	16	0	2	2	9	2	18	0.7015
Gordon	16	0	0	1	13	2	0	0.6118

SYDNEY FIRST-GRADE AVERAGES, 2000-01

BATTING

(Qualification: 500 runs)

	M	I	NO	Runs	HS	100s	50s	Ave
R. J. Davison (Sydney University)	10	10	5	789	168*	3	4	157.80
C. J. Adams (University of NSW)	9	11	3	577	109*	3	2	72.12
P. Maraziotis (Bankstown)	16	17	6	706	138*	3	2	64.18
C. J. Richards (Bankstown)	12	13	3	605	130*	2	4	60.50
M. T. Haywood (Mosman)	16	16	4	686	136*	2	3	57.16
S. D. Bradstreet (Manly–Warringah)	13	12	4	450	90	0	4	56.25
M. J. Clarke (Western Suburbs)	15	15	1	770	119	3	4	55.00
S. D. Stanton (Sydney University)	13	14	4	506	64	0	5	50.59
B. P. Van Deinsen (St George)	18	20	1	919	172	3	3	48.36
R. C. Aitken (Parramatta)	16	19	5	675	82	0	6	48.21

Denotes not out.

BOWLING

(Qualification: 30 wickets)

	M	O	Mdns	R	W	BB	5Wi	10W/m	Avge
P. M. Wooden (St George)	18	167.3	43	458	39	5/24	1	0	11.74
S. D. Bradstreet (Manly–Warringah)	13	150.5	34	430	36	9/55	1	1	11.94
D. A. Horsley (Western Suburbs)	12	257.4	67	638	49	6/16	5	0	13.02
S. M. Thompson (St George)	19	267.3	51	817	54	7/64	5	0	15.12
J. A. Turner (St George)	19	250.4	75	623	40	5/17	2	0	15.57
B. J. Newman (Penrith)	16	154.2	32	519	33	5/43	2	0	15.72
D. Jackson (Parramatta)	14	175.4	41	521	32	4/42	0	0	16.28
M. J. Baker (North Sydney)	11	200.4	40	616	36	6/22	3	1	17.11
R. C. Aitken (Parramatta)	16	282	64	747	42	4/6	0	0	17.78
M. A. W. Goldsmith (Penrith)	16	276.2	58	772	42	7/36	1	1	18.38

SYDNEY FIRST-GRADE QUALIFYING FINALS, 2000-01

ST GEORGE v SYDNEY UNIVERSITY

At Bankstown Oval, Bankstown, March 17, 18, 2001. St George won by seven wickets. Sydney University 161 (I. Moran 68, P.J. Byrom 50*; S.M. Thompson 6/42) and seven for 182 declared (S.D. Stanton 51*; P.J. Stanbridge 28, W.J. Knight 24, I. Moran 23, E.J.M. Cowan 22; J.A. Turner 5/67); St George 183 (N.J. Catalano 41, N.S. Pilon 41, J. Shaw 31; P.J. Byrom 6/44, A.R. Scott 3/65) and three for 161 (P.J. Ryan 59, N.J. Catalano 47*, B.P. Van Deinsen 33).

MANLY–WARRINGAH v EASTERN SUBURBS

At Manly Oval, Manly, March 17, 18, 2001. Eastern Suburbs won on first innings. Eastern Suburbs 267 (M.W. Patterson 142, D.J. Hunter 31, B.M. Day 24, A. Jeffrey 22†; S.L. Waddington 3/35, J.M. Heath 2/46, M.W. McInnes 2/66); Manly–Warringah 248 (S.D. Bradstreet 90, S. Spoljaric 57, T.D. Cruickshank 54; A.M. Stuart 3/65, E.P.M. Holland 2/20, J. Dery 2/58, A.E. Tucker 2/63).

BALMAIN v WESTERN SUBURBS

At Drummoyne Oval, Drummoyne, March 17, 18, 2001. Balmain won on first innings. Western Suburbs three for 298 declared (P.A. Burkhart 116, M.R. Clarke 89, S.J. Phillips 43*, N.W. Austin 39*); Balmain six for 300 (G.J. Mail 101, M. Schenke 67, G. Everest 52*; M.J. Clarke 2/25, J.N. Sullivan 2/37, D.A. Horsley 2/57).

SYDNEY FIRST-GRADE SEMI-FINALS, 2000-01

BALMAIN v EASTERN SUBURBS

At Drummoyne Oval, Drummoyne. March 24, 25, 2001. Eastern Suburbs won on first innings. Eastern Suburbs eight for 310 declared (M.W. Patterson 122, D.J. Hunter 73, A.E. Tucker 34, J.R. McCallum 32; R.R.T. Burton 5/71, S.H. Cook 3/56); Balmain 125 (K.K. Wong 36, M. Schenke 28, B.P. Schutz 24; A.E. Tucker 3/23, J. Dery 3/26, M. Macleannan 2/12).

ST GEORGE v MANLY–WARRINGAH

At Hurstville Oval, Hurstville, March 24, 25, 2001. St George won on first innings. St George 232 (P.J. Ryan 60, B.P. Van Deinsen 40, J. Shaw 30; J.M. Heath 3/83, W.F. Newell 2/17, S.D. Bradstreet 2/30); Manly–Warringah 193 (T.D. Cruickshank 97, S.C.G. MacGill 3/44, B.P. Van Deinsen 3/45, P.M. Wooden 2/6, S.M. Thompson 2/46).

SYDNEY FIRST-GRADE FINAL, 2000-01

ST GEORGE v EASTERN SUBURBS

At Bankstown Oval, Bankstown, March 30, 31, April 1, 2001. St George won on first innings. Toss: Eastern Suburbs.

A monumental innings of 172 from opening batsman Brett Van Deinsen steered St George to a first-innings win and showed the state selectors that he still had plenty to offer. Dropped by New South Wales shortly before the end of the season after a modest return of 125 runs at 13.88 from five Pura Cup appearances, van Deinsen responded with a marathon innings which lasted just a few minutes short of eight hours. He displayed great concentration against an attack which included two Australian representatives in Anthony Stuart and Greg Matthews. Renowned more for the sort of explosive strokeplay he displayed during his thrilling cameo in the previous season's final, van Deinsen held his side together after it had faltered in pursuit of a modest target of 188.

Easts won the toss and Stuart opted to bat, but they lost two for one as Scott Thompson picked up a wicket in each of his first two overs. Opening batsman Lee Kirk, who was 12th man in Easts' last premiership-winning team in 1991-92, defied the bowlers for almost five hours but lacked adequate support, apart from Matthews, during a 64-run stand for the fifth wicket. Mark Patterson, who had scored a century in each of Easts' earlier finals games, tore a hamstring and had to retire before later resuming his innings. Test leg-spinner Stuart MacGill chipped away at Easts' middle order.

In reply St George looked comfortable at two for 80 after a third-wicket stand of 64 between Van Deinsen and his captain Paul Ryan. Then Matthews took two wickets to leave St George four for 99 and the match in the balance. Though Matthews gave van Deinsen some anxious moments the youngster and wicket-keeper Nathan Pilon added a fifth-wicket partnership of 81, and a seventh-wicket stand of 58 between van Deinsen and Peter Wooden effectively ended Easts' hopes. Van Deinsen remained at the crease until he was ninth out in the 116th over on the last day.

Trailing by 118 on the first innings and without time to push for an outright win, Easts batted for 19 overs in their second innings before the captains agreed to end the game.

Man of the Match (Benaud Medal): – B. P Van Deinsen.

Close of play: First day, St George 0-10 (Van Deinsen 6, Catalano 4); Second day, St George 7-265 (Van Deinsen 153, MacGill 2).

Eastern Suburbs

L. R. Kirk run out (Rummans)	62	– c Pilon b Turner	3
J. Dery c Catalano b Thompson	0		
J.R. McCallum b Thompson	0	– not out	11
B.M. Day c and b Van Deinsen	23		
M.W. Patterson c Catalano b MacGill	30		
†D.J. Hunter lbw b Thompson	0	– (2) not out	42
G.R.J. Matthews c Rummans b MacGill	27		
*A.M. Stuart st Pilon b MacGill	0		
A.E. Tucker c MacGill b Wooden	16		
S. Musgrave c Ryan b MacGill	7		
E.P.M. Holland not out	7		
L-b 9, n-b 6	15	W 1, n-b 4	5

(92.4 overs, 347 mins)	187	(19 overs, 116 mins)	(1 wk)	61

Fall: 1 1 46 74 138 138 139 163 171 187

Fall: 9

Bowling: *First Innings*—Thompson 18–8–36–3; Turner 12–5–20–0; Shaw 9–5–7–0; MacGill 34–7–84–4; Van Deinsen 4–2–6–1; Wooden 15.4–5–25–1. *Second Innings*—Thompson 7–2–17–0; Turner 6–5–2–1; MacGill 13–3–18–0; Wooden 12–4–24–0.

St George

B. P. Van Deinsen c (sub) M. Maclennan b Tucker	172	S. C. G. MacGill c Hunter b Stuart	9
N. J. Catalano c Kirk b Stuart	10	J. A. Turner not out	12
G. C. Rummans c Hunter b Dery	0	J. Shaw c Stuart b Tucker	1
*P. J. Ryan c Hunter b Matthews	32		
S. M. Thompson b Matthews	11	B 2, l-b 1, w 1, n-b 2	6
†N. S. Pilon lbw b Stuart	32		
C. M. Porter b Dery	4	(117.2 overs, 481 mins)	305
P. M. Wooden lbw b Stuart	16	Fall: 17 17 81 99 180 199 257 273 301 305	

Bowling: Stuart 33–8–89–4; Dery 27–9–71–2; Tucker 18.2–4–43–2; Holland 10–1–28–0; Matthews 24–5–52–2; Musgrave 5–1–19–0.

Umpires: D. M. Brandon and S. J. A. Taufel.

BRISBANE FIRST-GRADE CRICKET

By STEPHEN GRAY

After three premierships in a row, the reign of the mighty Sandgate–Redcliffe came to an end as Redlands, University and South Brisbane all narrowed the gap. Sandgate claimed the minor premiership by 15 points from the Redlands Tigers (formerly Easts–Redlands), but it was South Brisbane who successfully bridged the gap. Souths had squeaked into the top four by little more than a point after a late string of victories, and they continued their improvement through the finals to win their first premiership in a decade.

The Queensland selectors signalled that performances in grade cricket were no longer paramount in their selection criteria, with the leading run-scorer and wicket-taker absent from the 2001-02 Queensland squad and the Peter Burge Medal winner for the best grade cricketer, Souths all-rounder Dale Turner, also overlooked. The current depth of Queensland cricket is set to ensure that many fine grade cricketers may look elsewhere for first-class opportunity in the immediate future.

The case of Toombul's Matthew Pascoe certainly suggests that outcome. His 46 wickets at 21.26 put him at the top of the wicket-taking list, yet he missed a state contract despite being a squad member, and playing a first-class match, last season. Turner, a member of Queensland's Mercantile Mutual Cup side for the past two seasons, who finished second behind Pascoe with 41 wickets at 18.58 as well as scoring 752 runs at 83.55, returned to New South Wales to seek his fortune, but not before helping Souths to the premiership. In round ten against Beenleigh–Logan he hit 210 not out, including 156 in a session, scoring his first career double-century off 199 balls.

It is much the same story for the batsmen. Sunshine Coast right-hander Jeff Thomas, an irregular Queensland player in the early 1990s, scored 790 runs at 60.76 with four centuries to be the leading scorer, while Souths left-hander Lance Kahler, another fringe state batsman, amassed 785 runs at 49.06. Thomas at least has something more to occupy him, taking on the job as Canadian national coach for the ICC Trophy tournament in Canada.

Queensland opener Jimmy Maher also notched up a double-century, with his 222 not out for Redlands against University the highest individual score in first-grade. The outstanding bowling performance came from Norths all-rounder James Hopes, who prefaced his call-up to the Queensland limited-overs team with a haul of 8/21 against Sunshine Coast.

Valley defeated Western Suburbs to secure the K & R Plumbing limited-overs competition, thanks to a comprehensive batting display by Matthew Hayden, Brendan Shinnick and teenage Englishman Richard Clinton in the final at Allan Border Field. Shinnick, whose big-hitting feats are renowned in Brisbane, clouted 69 off 42 balls with six sixes and three fours while Hayden, in his final innings before the tour of India, gave a taste of things to come with 83 not out off 91 balls. Valley scored one for 200 in reply to Wests' total of 199.

Brett Henschell, the Valley and Queensland all-rounder, whose grade cricket journey started in 1979-80 as a 17-year-old with weekly trips from his Darling Downs home of Dalby, announced his retirement from first-grade after 22 years. Henschell, who played 66 first-class matches, set a swag of individual records for Valley, including a career total of 7,759 runs.

The women's premiership was restructured, with a Premier League featuring four zone-based teams replacing the previous first-grade competition. Northern Zone won the inaugural title, based on the overall points total, after the final against Western Zone was washed out.

BRISBANE FIRST-GRADE TABLE, 2000-01

	M	WO	W1	D	L1	LO	Points
Sandgate–Redcliffe	11	0	8	0	3	0	157.98
Redlands	11	0	7	1	3	0	142.83
University	11	1	5	1	4	0	138.03
South Brisbane	11	0	6	1	4	0	133.06
Valley	11	0	6	1	4	0	131.57
Northern Suburbs	11	0	5	2	4	0	121.82
Sunshine Coast	11	0	5	2	3	1	121.70
Gold Coast	11	0	4	2	5	0	98.81
Western Suburbs	11	1	2	2	6	0	95.29
Wynnum–Manly	11	0	3	3	5	0	91.82
Toombul	11	0	2	1	8	0	79.84
Beenleigh–Logan	11	0	2	2	6	1	74.36

BRISBANE FIRST-GRADE AVERAGES, 2000-01

BATTING

(Qualification: 300 runs)

	M	I	NO	R	HS	100s	50s	Avge
J.P. Maher (Redlands)	5	5	1	371	222*	2	0	92.75
D.A. Turner (South Brisbane)	13	15	6	752	210*	3	3	83.55
C.T. Perren (Northern Suburbs)	7	8	3	356	143*	1	2	71.20
R.D. Poole (Wynnum-Manly)	6	7	2	347	171*	1	2	69.40
A.B. Henschell (Valleys)	10	12	4	521	117	1	4	65.12
J.M. Thomas (Sunshine Coast)	11	15	2	790	185*	4	1	60.76
D.M. Payne (Redlands)	12	14	3	657	176	2	3	59.72
B.P. Nash (Northern Suburbs)	9	10	0	580	167	2	3	58.00
M.L. Love (University)	7	7	1	339	136	1	2	56.50
K.J. Healy (Wynnum-Manly)	9	10	2	432	134	1	1	54.00

* Denotes not out.

BOWLING

(Qualification: 20 wickets)

	M	O	Mdns	R	W	BB	5W/i	10W/m	Avge
J.H. Dawes (Valleys)	8	145.4	41	389	25	5/27	1	0	15.56
C.R. Swan (Gold Coast)	11	218.5	51	630	36	6/56	1	0	17.50
J.R. Hopes (Northern Suburbs)	10	205.3	59	526	29	8/21	2	1	18.13
M.A. Anderson (Sandgate–Redcliffe)	10	200.1	67	534	29	7/67	1	0	18.41
M.A. Shackel (University)	8	197.1	67	498	27	6/34	1	0	18.44
D.A. Turner (South Brisbane)	13	330.2	102	762	41	6/58	4	0	18.58
D.R. Turner (Valleys)	11	216.1	48	659	34	5/32	3	0	19.38

	M	O	Mdns	R	W	BB	5Wi	10W/m	Avge
M.S. Dann (Wynnum–Manly)	11	173.5	29	569	28	5/44	1	0	20.32
M.D. Pascoe (Toombul)	11	272	52	978	46	7/57	3	0	21.26
J.J. Bird (South Brisbane)	13	251.3	63	768	35	5/70	1	0	21.94

BRISBANE FIRST-GRADE SEMI-FINALS, 2000-01

SANDGATE–REDCLIFFE v SOUTH BRISBANE

At Albury Oval, Deagon. March 17, 18, 2001. South Brisbane won on first innings. Sandgate–Redcliffe 204 (G.A.J. Fitness 115*; B.W. Ambrose 4/59, J.J. Anning 3/48, J.J. Bird 2/41); South Brisbane seven for 273 (D.A. Turner 140*, M. Sippel 50, A.S. Holznagel 37; B.N. Creevey 3/90, B.R. Mortimer 2/63).

REDLANDS v UNIVERSITY

At Peter Burge Oval, Wellington Point. March 17, 18, 2001. University won on first innings. Redlands 112 (D.M. Payne 72; B.P. Boardman 6/19, M.A. Shackel 3/36); University eight for 267 (B.P. Boardman 79, C.A. Torrisi 35, D. Schweitzer 30*; M.J. Petrie 3/40, D.R. Mackenzie 2/33).

BRISBANE FIRST-GRADE FINAL, 2000-01

SOUTH BRISBANE v UNIVERSITY

At Allan Border Field, Albion, March 24, 25, 31, April 1, 2001. South Brisbane won by 128 runs. Toss: South Brisbane.

Both teams started the match without their Queensland representative players, as the Pura Cup final coincided with the first weekend of play. Along with the returning state players, Michael Kasprowicz arrived home after the Australian tour of India to find himself playing on the second weekend. By then, however, the result was all but settled, thanks to an inspired spell by Souths' young pace bowler Jarrod Bird late on the opening day.

After Souths had made 208, thanks largely to a fighting 78 from Michael Sippel, a cousin of team-mate Andy Bichel, Bird swept through the University top order to leave them reeling at four for 27 at stumps. Bird finished with 5/70 as University's first innings fell just short, despite a game recovery from Chris Torrisi, young wicket-keeper David Schweitzer and Brett Boardman. Souths captain Brad Ruddell, an AIS Cricket Academy graduate in 1990, did not need the five-day break to plan his team's approach for the second weekend: bat, and keep batting.

With such clear instructions, Ashley Holznagel, Matthew Lunn and Andrew Harris combined to push the total past 300. After a quick flourish from Bichel, University faced a fourth-innings chase of 381 if they were to defy the odds on the fourth day. Despite the presence of Martin Love, University's challenge petered out at 252. Bichel took 4/87 while Bird collected three more wickets to finish with eight for the match.

Close of play: First day, University (1) 4-27 (G.I. Foley 17, C.A. Torrisi 0); Second day, South Brisbane (2) 3-107 (M.N. Lunn 18, D.A. Turner 10); Third day, University (2) 2-18 (M.L. Love 3, G.I. Foley 0).

South Brisbane

T. Sawyer lbw b Dever	5	– c Schweitzer b Boardman	2
A. S. Holznagel c Schweitzer b Boardman	1	– c Ellison b Foley	70
L. W. Kahler c Philipson b Dever	21	– lbw b Boardman	0
M. N. Lunn lbw b Shackel	18	– c Foley b Boardman	70
D. A. Turner c Farrell b Dever	2	– c Foley b Kasprowicz	25
A. C. Harris lbw b Shackel	8	– c Stevens b Kasprowicz	71
M. Sippel c Foley b Shackel	78	– (8) c Philipson b Shackel	31
*†B. J. Ruddell c Foley b Philipson	46	– (9) c Thornton b Boardman	9
J. J. Anning c Torrisi b Dever	13		
B. W. Ambrose c Foley b Philipson	0	– c Boardman b Foley	14
J. J. Bird not out	1	– not out	0
A. J. Bichel (did not bat)		– c Seccombe b Kasprowicz	39
L-b 6, w 1, n-b 8	15	B 10, l-b 11, w 1, n-b 9	31

(75.4 overs, 304 mins)	208	(116.2 overs, 456 mins)	362

Fall: 2 23 35 43 61 67 191
204 204 208

Fall: 39 57 85 133 244 297 307
321 361 362

Bowling: *First Innings*—Boardman 20–7–45–1; Shackel 22–8–47–3; Dever 11.4-4–38–4; Stevens 8–1–17–0; Foley 10–2–37–0; Philipson 4–0–18–2. *Second Innings*—Shackel 23.2–12–44–1; Boardman 33–5–129–4; Foley 20–6–62–2; Dever 7–1–17–0; Kasprowicz 30–7–81–3; Stevens 3–1–8–0.

University

M. Ellison b Bird	0		
S. J. Farrell c Ruddell b Bird	1	– (1) c Kahler b Bird	9
*M. G. Thornton c Ruddell b Bird	8	– (2) c Holznagel b Bird	0
G. I. Foley lbw b Ambrose	17	– c Lunn b Bichel	27
C. A. Philipson lbw b Bird	1	– (6) c Lunn b Bichel	32
C. A. Torrisi c Turner b Anning	43	– (7) hit wicket b Bichel	10
L. M. Stevens st Ruddell b Turner	32	– (8) not out	37
†D. Schweitzer not out	43		
B. P. Boardman c Turner b Anning	37	– (10) c Lunn b Bird	23
M. A. Shackel c Ruddell b Bird	0	– (11) b Ambrose	40
N. Dever c Kahler b Anning	2		
M. L. Love (did not bat)		– (3) b Bichel	12
W. A. Seccombe (did not bat)		– (5) c Ambrose b Turner	28
M. S. Kasprowicz (did not bat)		– (9) b Turner	22
B 1, l-b 1, n-b 4	6	B 7, w 2, n-b 3	12

(74.1 overs, 281 mins)	190	(75.2 overs, 297 mins)	252

Fall: 1 2 25 27 37 107 109
185 185 190

Fall: 8 15 35 66 106 124 129
160 193 252

Bowling: *First Innings*—Ambrose 24–5–73–1; Bird 21–7–70–5; Turner 21–12–24–1; Anning 8.1–2–21–3. *Second Innings*—Bichel 25–6–87–4; Bird 18–3–50–3; Sippel 5–0–19–0; Ambrose 6.2–1–18–1; Turner 21–3–71–2.

Umpires: A. J. McQuillan and J. F. Torpey.

ADELAIDE A-GRADE CRICKET

By LAURIE COLLIVER

In a season when the ball dominated the bat, Prospect's strong attack helped the club to end a drought of 30 seasons and capture the 2000-01 premiership. Martin Faull, who had also led Tea Tree Gully to their first flag in 1995-96, had two of the competition's best bowlers in his side, Joel Southam (33 wickets at 13.24) and Michael Harden (52 at 16.78), with sound support from Michael Carter (25 at 24.92). Faull led by example with the bat (474 runs at 33.85) and had support from left-hander Sam Ellicott (416 at 32.00). The Pirates also unearthed a young batsman in Callum Ferguson, who at barely 17 years of age played some innings of immense promise.

Adelaide had appeared to be the team to beat in the finals, but their batting, which had been strong, let them down. Chris Davies' efforts were a highlight, and Luke Williams (389 at 43.22) played some important hands, which resulted in his promotion to interstate ranks. But it was in bowling that Adelaide were strong. Ben Johnson responded well to his omission from the state team, and Ben Southam (23 wickets at 19.43) and Shane Maraun (33 at 21.33) also bowled purposefully.

Sturt lost their third consecutive semi-final but unearthed a future player of quality in right-handed teenage batsman Cameron Borgas. Skipper James Orchard (467 at 33.35) batted well when required, but the Blues are another club which is stronger in bowling than batting. Matthew King continued his improvement and Tea Tree Gully premiership player Matthew Stokes turned up to play a pivotal role.

Last season's premiers, Kensington, finished the season tamely. Again John Lee made a more than worthwhile contribution and as skipper Dean Waugh (529 runs at 35.26) played well after considering a move to Port Adelaide. All-rounder Barry Steele (324 runs and 33 wickets) continues to be ignored by the state selectors, even for a game at second eleven level.

One of the big improvers were fifth-placed Tea Tree Gully, under the new leadership of Garry Chillingworth, who took 20 wickets in addition to his valuable runs in the middle order. The Gullies also managed to revive the career of Garry Wright, and with Peter McIntyre available after missing a lot of the previous season with a shoulder injury they finished the season strongly. The likes of Wes Thomas and Ben Cameron need to convert starts into big scores if Tea Tree Gully are to press for the top four next season.

University could rejoice in their all-rounder Michael Smith winning his first Bradman Medal. Some of the University faithful felt he should have won it the previous season but this year his efforts were fully rewarded, not only with the medal but also with state selection in the last three matches. The Blacks' batting was like many other clubs, thin, with Adam Kimber (360 at 30.00) the only player to find consistency. Glenelg spent most of the season in the four but fell away badly in the last three matches. Ben Hook (529 at 37.79), who moved from Adelaide, carried the batting, while pace bowler

Neil Rowe deservedly won a place in the grade Team of the Year for his efforts.

Anthony Heidrich and veteran Peter Cameron (455 at 37.92) were the main players for Northern Districts. Mark Cosgrove averaged over 40, but he made his two centuries in the second innings, when the pressure had fallen away. Nevertheless the Under-19s Australian representative is a player of promise. Steven Crook (30 wickets at 18.33) also has the ability to play at the next level. East Torrens at one stage led the table but collapsed after the Christmas break. Cos Lanzoni (315 at 39.38) was the club's most consistent batsman, while it was heartening for the club that Paul Rofe progressed to state ranks. East Torrens need to blood some more youth through the grades if they are to improve.

West Torrens slumped from runners-up to tenth. While Andrew Haslett and Ben Smith batted well, they found little support, and in the bowling only Smith (20 at 22.70) reached 20 wickets. Ageing captain-coach Brad Wigney missed most of the second half of the season through injury. Woodville also fell several spots. They perhaps unwisely rejected an approach from a neighbouring club for merger talks. Daniel Harris (469 at 36.08) carried the batting, while Mick Miller was a welcome recruit from Queensland.

Southern Districts and Port Adelaide occupied the bottom positions on the ladder. Shane Deitz was not available enough for the Southerners' liking, but they were heartened by the continued development of off-spinner Dwayne Ross (38 wickets at 18.42) who was rewarded with Team of the Year status. Port Adelaide sadly continue to be the worst-performed club of the competition, although Jamie Marsh (23 wickets at 29.65) worked hard after transferring from Sturt.

ADELAIDE A-GRADE TABLE, 2000-01

	M	WO	W	D	T	L	LO	Match Points	Bonus Points	O/rate Points	Total Points
Prospect	12	0	9	0	0	3	0	135	70.52	–	205.52
Sturt	12	1	7	0	0	4	0	125	69.40	–	194.40
Adelaide	12	1	7	0	0	4	0	125	69.50	0.25	194.25
Kensington	12	0	8	0	0	4	0	120	71.34	1.00	190.34
Tea Tree Gully	12	1	6	0	0	5	0	110	68.05	–	178.05
University	12	2	4	0	1	5	0	107.5	69.43	–	176.93
Glenelg	12	0	7	1	0	3	1	105	67.55	–	172.55
North Districts	12	3	2	1	0	6	0	90	77.73	0.50	167.23
East Torrens	12	1	5	1	1	4	0	95	61.36	–	156.36
West Torrens	12	0	4	0	0	7	1	60	65.62	0.25	125.37
Woodville	12	0	4	0	0	7	1	60	64.49	1.00	123.49
Southern Districts	12	0	2	1	0	7	2	30	61.35	1.00	90.35
Port Adelaide	12	0	1	0	0	7	4	15	60.94	1.00	74.94

ADELAIDE A-GRADE AVERAGES, 2000-01

BATTING

(Qualification: 400 runs)

	M	I	NO	R	HS	100s	50s	Avge
C. J. Davies (Adelaide)	8	8	3	432	139*	1	3	86.40
J. D. Lee (Kensington)	10	13	2	673	164	2	1	61.18
B. B. Smith (West Torrens)	12	13	3	528	151	1	2	52.80
C. J. Borgas (Sturt)	9	11	2	405	90	0	3	45.00
M. J. Cosgrove (Salisbury)	10	16	2	586	125*	2	2	41.86
M. Chilton (East Torrens)	11	13	3	410	174*	1	2	41.00
G. J. Wright (Tea Tree Gully)	10	13	1	483	152	1	2	40.25
A. S. Haslett (West Torrens)	10	14	1	521	179	1	3	40.08
M J. Smith (University)	11	12	0	471	110	1	2	39.25
G. A. Chillingworth (Tea Tree Gully) .	12	13	2	428	79	0	2	38.91

* Denotes not out.

BOWLING

(Qualification: 25 wickets)

	M	O	Mdns	R	W	BB	5W/i	10W/m	Avge
M. J. Smith (University)	11	239	75	541	48	5/12	5	1	11.27
M. D. King (Sturt)	12	223.4	70	489	39	6/20	3	0	12.53
M. K. Stokes (Sturt)	7	149.2	34	384	30	4/33	0	0	12.80
J. T. Southam (Prospect)	11	148.3	33	437	33	5/52	2	0	13.24
B. A. Johnson (Adelaide)	7	174.1	47	431	32	6/42	3	0	13.46
A. P. Heidrich (Northern Districts) . .	12	152.2	38	400	29	4/40	0	0	13.79
N. A. Roberts (Unviersity)	8	151.1	27	430	29	4/36	0	0	14.83
P. E. McIntyre (Tea Tree Gully)	8	215	76	459	30	5/44	1	0	15.30
N. M. Rowe (Glenelg)	12	225.5	63	538	35	4/29	0	0	15.37
P. C. Rofe (East Torrens)	7	164.3	33	399	24	7/57	2	0	16.63

ADELAIDE A-GRADE SEMI-FINALS, 2000-01

ADELAIDE v STURT

At Adelaide Oval No. 2, Adelaide, March 17, 18, 2001. Adelaide won on first innings. Adelaide 171 (M. D. King 5/41); Sturt 138 (J. R. Orchard 58; B. A. Johnson 4/52).

PROSPECT v KENSINGTON

At Adelaide Oval, March 17, 18, 2001. Prospect won on first innings.. Prospect 212 (P. Richardson 45, M. A. Carter 42; B. H. Steele 6/53); Kensington 166 (J. T. Southam 4/48).

ADELAIDE A-GRADE FINAL, 2000-01

PROSPECT v ADELAIDE

At Adelaide Oval, March 17, 18, 2001. Prospect won on first innings. Toss: Prospect.

Prospect capped off a splendid season with a hard-fought victory to capture their first senior pennant since 1970-71. The final produced the lowest aggregate for many years but that did not detract from a riveting contest. As in the semi-final, Prospect's opening batsman Stuart Ellicott left early, but left-hander Paul Duffett and Jeff Vaughan steadied, adding 43 in an hour and a quarter before Erin Bernhardt struck a double blow for the Buffaloes, enticing Duffett and captain-coach Martin Faull to edge to second slip, and Prospect were in trouble at three for 47. As Ben Johnson began his demolition of the middle and lower order, Vaughan continued the struggle for runs, seeing his side past 100 before he was seventh out after 201 minutes of resistance. Then semi-final heroes Peter Richardson and Michael Carter went in consecutive balls to reduce Prospect to nine for 109. This brought strike bowler Mike Harden to the crease, and he and Joel Southam resisted for over an hour to take the team to a more respectable 170. Southam finished unbeaten on 51, hitting seven fours in 100 minutes of spirited batting that helped swing the momentum back Prospect's way.

The Adelaide openers wasted no time, adding four an over before Luke Williams edged to the keeper and David Agars was trapped in front in the space of six balls. A vehement leg-before shout was rejected in the last over of the day, and at stumps Adelaide needed 138 with eight wickets in hand for their second flag in three seasons. Tarkin Brown went early on the second day, and three overs later Johnson fell for just a single as Adelaide slumped to four for 37. Knott found an able partner in Adam Smith and these two added 42, before Smith was bowled on the stroke of lunch, leaving 91 to get. When Knott's vigilance ended after nearly two and a half hours the end was nigh. Bernhardt, who had made valuable runs in the semi-final, clouted a four and a six before giving Harden his fifth wicket and then Sam Williams, who had resisted doggedly for 90 minutes without getting to double figures, gave Duffett a catch and Prospect had broken their 30-year drought.

David Hookes Medallist: J.T. Southam.

Close of play: First day, Adelaide 2-33 (Knott 0, Brown 3).

Prospect

Stuart Ellicott c Southam b Johnson		1
P.G. Duffett c Southam b Bernhardt		30
J.M. Vaughan c W. Smith b Southam		32
*M.P. Faull c Southam b Bernhardt		0
Sam Ellicott lbw b Maraun		5
C.J. Ferguson c W. Smith b Johnson		7
C. Hanna lbw b Johnson		6
†P.J. Richardson c and b Johnson		15
J.T. Southam not out		51
M. Carter lbw b Johnson		0
M. J Harden run out		
(S. Williams/A.M. Smith)		11
B 1, l-b 9, n-b 2		12
		—
(79.2 overs, 317 mins)		170
Fall: 3 47 47 66 76 89 101 109 109 170		

Bowling: Maraun 21–7–49–1; Johnson 26–12–51–5; Bernhardt 16–9–22–2; Southam 9–3–21–1; A.M. Smith 5.2–2–10–0; S. Williams 2–1–7–0.

Adelaide

L. Williams c Richardson b Southam		10
D. Agars lbw b Harden		14
P. Knott lbw b Stuart Ellicott		29
T. Brown c Richardson b Southam		4
*B.A. Johnson lbw b Harden		1
A.M. Smith b Carter		25
S. Williams c Duffett b Southam		9
B.S. Southam c Vaughan b Harden		1
†W. Smith c Sam Ellicott b Harden		2
E.C. Bernhardt c Richardson b Harden		10
S.M. Maraun not out		1
L-b 3, n-b 11		14
		—
(53 overs, 219 mins)		120
Fall: 24 29 35 37 79 98 101 106 118 120		

Bowling: Harden 18–3–52–5; Southam 13–3–32–3; Carter 8–3–13–1; Vaughan 7–4–9–0; Stuart Ellicott 7–4–11–1.

Umpires: S.J. Davis and K.D. Perrin

TASMANIAN CRICKET ASSOCIATION FIRST-GRADE CRICKET, 2000-01

By COLIN CHUNG

The Tasmanian Cricket Association season was marred by two major controversies, one of which occurred during the semi-finals. The semi-final between top side Lindisfarne and fourth-placed New Town was scheduled for Lindisfarne's home ground at Anzac Park. Although the square was covered on the Thursday night, only the small pitch cover was used on the Friday night despite a forecast of heavy rain. The rain came down in bucketloads overnight and, with overcast conditions all weekend, the pitch was unfit for play and the game had to be abandoned.

Lindisfarne advanced to the final because they had finished ahead of New Town. New Town fired in a letter of protest, claiming the Lindisfarne club had not made a proper effort to prepare its ground. The TCA pennant committee upheld the protest and Lindisfarne forfeited their grand final place, but on appeal to the TCA permit committee they won it back. The ruling proved crucial as it allowed Lindisfarne to beat South Hobart–Sandy Bay in the final, and win their inaugural first-grade premiership since entering the TCA competition nine years ago.

The other controversy happened in round six when University were penalised a massive nine points for not completing their minimum number of overs against Kingborough. The penalty ultimately cost University third spot and the club had to settle for fifth.

The season itself started slowly with rain virtually washing out the first two rounds. North Hobart then set the early pace and emerged as almost unbackable favourites for the premiership with six consecutive wins. However, after a loss of form in the second half of the season they finished second, and bowed out in the semi-final to the surprise packet of the competition, South Hobart–Sandy Bay.

Having lost a number of experienced players, South Hobart–Sandy Bay looked to be in for a lean season before the unexpected arrival of former South Australian Adam Polkinghorne. Rarely has a newcomer had such an incisive impact on the TCA competition. His aggressive batting (363 runs at 40.33) and bowling (41 wickets at 15.61) not only won games for the club but earned him the TCA Medal.

Of the other clubs, Lindisfarne were always going to be hard to beat, New Town, with seven state squad members, could consider themselves a little unlucky, while regular finalists Kingborough and University missed out, the latter gaining some consolation by winning their third consecutive state limited-overs title. Glenorchy finished the season well to be seventh but Clarence, a regular semi-finalist in recent years, finished last.

In a lean season for batsmen, with only three passing 400 runs, the batting aggregate was won by newcomer Mark Nutting, who scored 476 runs at 36.62 opening for Lindisfarne, while Polkinghorne was the top wicket-taker, just ahead of Lindisfarne's Shane Jurgensen with 39 wickets at 14.

TASMANIAN CRICKET ASSOCIATION
FIRST-GRADE LADDER, 2000-01

	M	WO	WI	D	L1	LO	Points
Lindisfarne	10	1	6	2	1	0	107.71
North Hobart	10	0	7	0	2	1	101.03
South Hobart–Sandy Bay	10	0	5	0	4	1	81.52
New Town	10	1	2	2	5	0	80.35
University	10	1	3	2	4	0	76.04
Kingborough	10	0	3	2	4	1	71.29
Glenorchy	10	0	2	4	4	0	67.60
Clarence	10	0	2	2	6	0	65.58

TASMANIAN CRICKET ASSOCIATION
FIRST-GRADE AVERAGES, 2000-01

BATTING

(Qualification: 300 runs)

	I	NO	R	HS	100s	50s	Avge
A.G. Downton (New Town)	8	2	326	103	1	2	54.33
M.N. Atkinson (Lindisfarne)	12	4	366	107	1	3	45.75
T.A. Pinnington (North Hobart)	11	2	400	132	1	3	44.44
A.S. Wyver (Glenorchy)	10	1	386	76	0	3	42.89
M.R. Harry (North Hobart)	11	3	332	69	0	3	41.50
A.W. Polkinghorne (Sth Hobart–S. Bay)	9	0	363	109	1	3	40.33
G. Cunningham (New Town)	11	0	407	79	0	4	37.00
M.R. Nutting (Lindisfarne)	16	3	476	102	1	3	36.62
P. Di Venuto (Kingborough)	13	1	437	84	0	3	36.42
B.L. Harris (Clarence)	14	2	384	80*	0	2	32.00

* Denotes not out.

BOWLING

(Qualification: 20 wickets)

	O	Mdns	R	W	BB	5W/i	10W/m	Avge
J.P. Marquet (University)	123.1	35	263	23	6/28	2	0	11.43
A.G. Downton (New Town)	151	54	297	23	5/43	1	0	12.91
S.J. Jurgensen (Lindisfarne)	240.1	75	546	39	8/40	3	1	14.00
R.A. Allanby (Lindisfarne)	157.2	46	399	27	5/44	2	0	14.78
L. O'Shea (North Hobart)	145.1	49	299	20	5/28	1	0	14.95
A.W. Polkinghorne (Sth Hobart–S. Bay)	254.4	72	640	41	7/55	5	1	15.61
S.N.B. Bakes (University)	116.4	25	376	24	7/60	2	0	15.67
M.R. Harry (North Hobart)	158.2	44	465	29	6/37	3	0	16.03
R.J. Pears (Lindisfarne)	188.2	58	414	25	5/21	2	0	16.56
A.R. Griffith (North Hobart)	215.5	67	490	29	5/23	2	1	16.90

TASMANIAN CRICKET ASSOCIATION
FIRST-GRADE SEMI-FINALS, 2000-01

LINDISFARNE v NEW TOWN

At Anzac Park, Lindisfarne, March 17, 18, 2001. Abandoned without a ball bowled.
Lindisfarne advanced to the final because of their superior ladder position.

NORTH HOBART v SOUTH HOBART–SANDY BAY

At TCA Ground, Hobart, March 17, 18, 2001. South Hobart–Sandy Bay won on first innings. South Hobart–Sandy Bay five for 168 (A. W. Polkinghorne 108*; A. R. Griffith 3/16); North Hobart 134 (P. W. Collins 41; A. W. Polkinghorne 5/59).

TASMANIAN CRICKET ASSOCIATION FIRST-GRADE FINAL, 2000-01

LINDISFARNE v SOUTH HOBART–SANDY BAY

At Bellerive Oval, Hobart, March 24, 25, 2001. Lindisfarne won on first innings. Toss: Lindisfarne.

Against a side brimming with current and former state players, South Hobart–Sandy Bay started as underdogs. Their chances were not helped when Lindisfarne won the toss and chose to bowl first on a wicket offering some early movement. Openers Colin Lamont and Brad Kelly survived the early pace onslaught from Shane Jurgensen and Richard Pears, but the turning point of the match came with the introduction of state all-rounder Shane Watson into the attack. He took four wickets in his first spell including the dangerous Adam Polkinghorne for 36 (eight fours) to put Lindisfarne in the box seat at lunch with South Hobart–Sandy Bay five for 102. While the lower order offered some resistance during the middle session, wickets continued to fall and South Hobart–Sandy Bay were dismissed for 198 overs just after tea.

Lindisfarne recovered from the early loss of Mark Nutting for seven to wipe 75 runs off the run chase by stumps, state captain Jamie Cox leading the way with 52 not out. Less than one session was required the next day for Lindisfarne to wrap up their first TCA premiership, thanks to a dominant batting display by Cox and Watson. Cox finished on 107 not out (157 balls, 16 fours and one six) while Watson smashed 67 not out (75 balls and nine fours) to earn Man of the Match honours.

Man of the Match: S. R. Watson.

Close of play: First day, Lindisfarne 1-75 (Cox 52).

SOUTH HOBART–SANDY BAY

B. Kelly c Atkinson b Pears	13	*B. S. Targett not out	24
C. Lamont b Watson	24	J. Pearson c Cox b Pears	10
P. Stewart lbw b Watson	5	M. Parbs lbw b Jurgensen	0
B. Lamont c Allen b Watson	21	J. Taylor lbw b Jurgensen	3
A. W. Polkinghorne c Cox b Watson	36	Extras	10
D. Stevens lbw b Cox	26		
A. Hingston c Atkinson b Watson	26	(70 overs)	198

Fall: 23 32 55 86 102 140 167 183 196 198

J. Sales did not bat.

Bowling: Jurgensen 22–8–62–2, Pears 12–6–21–2; Watson 13–4–48–5; Allanby 5–0–28–0; Allen 7–1–19–0; Cox 11–3–15–1.

Lindisfarne

M. R. Nutting c Targett b Polkinghorne	 7		Extras	 6
J. Cox not out	107			
A. Towns lbw b Targett	 13		(51.1 overs)	(2 wkts) 199
S. R. Watson not out	 67		Fall: 17 81	

S. J. Reid, *R. G. Allanby, M. Allen, R. Pears, †M. N. Atkinson, A. J. De Winter, S. J. Jurgensen did not bat.

Bowling: Polkinghorne 16–0–67–1; Targett 14–1–60–1; Parbs 13–3–33–0; Stewart 3–1–8–0; Taylor 1–0–5–0; B. Lamont 3–0–18–0; Hingston 1–0–3–0; Sales 0.1–0–4–0.

VICTORIAN PREMIER CRICKET, 2000-01

By KEN WILLIAMS

St Kilda won their 14th VCA premiership when they defeated Essendon by four wickets in a low-scoring and hard-fought final. Despite a particularly warm and dry summer, bowlers were generally on top throughout the season and only three of the 153 matches played before the finals ended in draws. The season proved one of the most evenly contested for several years, several clubs emerging as strong flag contenders.

In the event, St Kilda's win was well deserved. They ended the home-and-away programme in second place and qualified for the final after winning a tightly contested semi-final against Hawthorn–Waverley. One of the highlights of their season was a remarkable ten-wicket win over South Melbourne in the final round, in which they became only the second team since the start of the competition to win outright without losing a wicket. A well-balanced combination, their leading run-scorers were Shaun Craig (818 at 62.92), skipper Tim O'Sullivan (512 at 28.44), Michael Klinger (494 at 61.75) and Nick Jewell (490 at 32.66). Craig and Klinger each scored two centuries. Opening bowler Adrian Jones (36 wickets) was the leading wicket-taker, and was well supported by spinner John Davison (33 at 18.12), Jamie Murch and Simon Burriss (25 wickets each) and Jewell (22). Shane Warne failed to take a wicket in his three matches.

Well led by the veteran David Tate, Essendon went close to winning the premiership. Their spirit was exemplified in the semi-final against Geelong when their last pair put on 24 runs to give them victory with two balls to spare. Their leading run-scorer was the hard-hitting Justin Baker (711 runs at 35.55), who had played only a handful of senior games before the season. Craig Berger (682 runs at 42.62) headed the batting averages and also captured 21 wickets. Stuart Clark, formerly of Camberwell Magpies, captured 41 wickets, and was well supported by Jody Hutchinson (30 wickets) and newcomer Clinton Chugg (28). Mathew Inness, available for half the matches, captured 27 wickets at a low cost. Wicket-keeper Brent Hutchinson (328 runs and 43 dismissals) also did well.

Geelong, who had considerable all-round depth, finished the home-and-away programme in top place after losing only four matches. Clinton Peake (714 runs at 54.92) was their top batsman, and they were well served by new all-rounder Ian Redpath (no relation to the former Test player) who scored 484 runs and took 30 wickets. Liam Buchanan (439 runs) continued to impress as one of the state's best young prospects.

Hawthorn–Waverley, the only team to reach the finals in each of the past four seasons, were well in contention until their semi-final loss to St Kilda. In contrast to recent seasons, batting was their strong point. They were again well led by Peter Roach, who in addition to keeping wickets was their leading run-scorer with 662 runs at 41.37. Simon Dart was their other outstanding player, scoring 624 runs at 41.60 and heading the competition's bowling averages with 24 wickets at 12.21. Other batsmen to do well were Chris

Bambury (404 runs at 57.71), who returned mid-way through the season to head the batting averages and Corey Booth (527 runs). For the second year in a row Hawthorn–Waverley won the Club Championship, awarded to the club with the best record over all four grades.

Defending premiers Richmond struggled to make the finals despite an outstanding contribution from the Durham all-rounder Paul Collingwood, playing in Australia on a Crusaders scholarship, who scored 600 runs at 40.00 and captured 33 wickets at 12.66. In the final home-and-away match against Carlton his 83 and 5/27 and 6/48 enabled Richmond to win outright and move into the top six. Other Richmond players to do well were bowlers Matthew Albers and Allan Wise (32 wickets each), while state opener Jason Arnberger maintained his excellent record with 386 runs at 77.20 from limited appearances.

Sixth-placed North Melbourne, who appeared in the finals for the first time in 40 years, were the season's biggest improvers, after finishing last in 1998-99 and second-last in 1999-2000. Opening bowler Adam McGinty (47 wickets at 18.36) was the leading wicket-taker in the competition, and was well supported by former Northcote pace man Shannon Waters (39). Their leading run-scorers were Gene Maurice (639 runs), Brent Skinner (557) and experienced skipper Earl Eddings (472).

Fitzroy–Doncaster, in the top six for most of the season, slipped to seventh place after a dramatic outright loss to North Melbourne in the final round. Skipper Brendan Joyce (796 runs), David Plumpton (591) and Robbie Bartlett (545) all scored heavily. Dandenong, strengthened by the acquisition of the experienced Ian Wrigglesworth from Carlton, improved from 15th to eighth. Seventeen-year-old all-rounder Cameron White showed great promise, scoring two centuries and capturing 28 wickets with his leg-breaks, including a remarkable 6/6, including a hat-trick, against South Melbourne. Other leading players were opening bowler William Carr (46 wickets) and batsman Tim Hooper (730 runs).

Despite a successful recruiting campaign, Carlton could finish no higher than ninth. Their attack was arguably the best in the competition, with Andrew Dickinson (46 wickets), John Taylor (35), Ashley Gilbert (36) and Craig Sheedy (37) all averaging under 18 runs per wicket, but the batting, apart from Paul Hetherington (579 runs) was brittle. Tenth-placed University were well served by Peter Harper (743 runs at 46.43), whose 195 against South Melbourne was the highest individual score of the season. Melbourne, runners-up in 1999-2000, slipped to 11th place, missing the finals for only the second time in 15 years. Their captain, Warren Ayres, became only the fifth player to reach 10,000 runs in the competition, joining Peter McAlister, Jack Ryder, John Scholes and Gary Watts. A bright spot for 12th-placed Northcote was the form of Travis Gloury, who scored four centuries and was the season's leading run-scorer with 827 runs at 55.13.

Two long-serving players, Gary Watts and Wayne Phillips, announced their retirements at the end of the season. Watts, who at the start of the season became the highest run-maker in the history of the competition, began his career with Fitzroy-Doncaster (then Fitzroy) in 1975-76, scoring 12,933 runs at 42.26 including 25 centuries. Phillips, who commenced at South Melbourne in 1980-81, scored 8,438 runs and took 125 wickets. Each has won the Ryder Medal, Phillips in 1987-88 and Watts in 1993-94.

For the first time since its inception in 1973 there were joint Ryder Medallists, when Collingwood and Ringwood's Darren Dempsey finished level on 34 votes. Dempsey, who scored 630 runs at 42.00, has since announced his intention of moving to Adelaide in an attempt to break into first-class cricket. Craig Berger was third with 32 votes. The following players made up the Premier Cricket team of the season: Craig Berger, William Carr, Paul Collingwood, Shawn Craig, Darren Dempsey, Travis Gloury, Peter Harper, Brendan Joyce, Adam McGinty, Clinton Peake, Peter Roach (captain) and Cameron White.

VICTORIAN PREMIER CRICKET
FIRST ELEVEN TABLE, 2000-01

	M	WO	W1	W2	D	LO	L2	L1	T	Points	Quotient
Geelong	17	0	7	6	0	0	4	0	0	78	1.400
St Kilda	17	1	3	7	0	0	2	3	1	73	1.447
Hawthorn–Waverley	17	0	5	7	1	0	2	2	0	72	1.497
Essendon	17	0	5	6	1	0	3	2	0	66	1.208
Richmond	17	1	5	4	0	0	5	2	0	64	0.288
North Melbourne . . .	17	1	4	4	0	0	5	3	0	58	0.985
Fitzroy–Doncaster . .	17	0	5	4	1	2	3	1	1	57	1.043
Dandenong	17	0	2	7	0	0	3	5	0	54	1.172
Carlton	17	2	2	3	0	1	4	5	0	50	−0.425
Melbourne University	17	0	2	6	0	0	4	5	0	48	1.005
Melbourne	17	0	5	3	1	0	6	2	0	48	0.862
Northcote	17	0	2	5	0	0	5	5	0	42	0.966
Ringwood	17	0	1	6	0	0	4	6	0	42	0.851
Camberwell Magpies	17	0	5	2	1	0	7	2	0	42	−0.277
Prahan	17	1	2	4	0	0	5	5	0	42	−0.472
Footscray–Vic. Uni. .	17	0	3	2	0	2	6	4	0	34	0.718
South Melbourne . . .	17	0	3	2	0	1	7	4	0	30	0.566
Frankston Peninsula .	17	0	1	3	1	0	6	6	0	24	0.665

VICTORIAN PREMIER CRICKET
FIRST ELEVEN AVERAGES, 2000-01

BATTING

(Qualification: 300 runs)

	M	I	NO	R	HS	100s	50s	Avge
M.T.G. Elliott (Camberwell–Magpies)	4	4	0	421	133	3	1	105.25
J.L. Arnberger (Richmond)	6	6	1	386	152	1	3	77.20
M.P. Mott (Frankston Peninsular)	8	8	1	520	169	2	2	74.29
S.A.J. Craig (St Kilda)	16	18	5	818	168*	2	5	62.92
M. Klinger (St Kilda)	12	11	3	494	131	2	1	61.75
C.J. Bambury (Hawthorn–Waverley) .	7	8	1	404	102*	1	3	57.71
T.P. Gloury (Northcote)	17	18	3	827	167*	4	2	55.13
C.J. Peake (Geelong)	16	15	2	714	171*	1	3	54.92
B.A. Joyce (Fitzroy–Doncaster)	17	19	3	796	144*	3	2	49.75
P.Q. Harper (Melbourne University) . .	16	17	1	743	195	2	1	46.44

* Denotes not out.

BOWLING

(Qualification: 20 wickets)

	M	O	Mdns	R	W	BB	5Wi	10Wm	Avge
S.P.Dart (Hawthorn–Waverley)	18	110.4	14	293	24	4/16	0	0	12.21
M.W. Inness (Essendon)	10	153.2	48	341	27	5/38	1	0	12.63
P.D. Collingwood (Richmond)	15	138.5	27	418	33	6/48	2	1	12.67
M. Lawrence (Dandenong)	16	155.4	37	339	23	4/37	0	0	14.74
A. Dickinson (Carlton)	16	206.5	48	679	46	5/20	2	0	14.76
M.L. Lewis (Nortcote)	9	142	25	422	27	6/59	2	0	15.63
J. Taylor (Carlton)	14	201.4	45	555	35	6/47	1	1	15.86
A. Gilbert (Carlton)	15	246	89	575	36	5/12	2	0	15.97
I.M. Redpath (Geelong)	18	165	40	489	30	5/59	1	0	16.30
W. Carr (Dandenong)	17	275.2	63	750	46	5/39	2	0	16.30

VICTORIAN PREMIER CRICKET
FIRST ELEVEN SEMI-FINALS, 2000-01

GEELONG v ESSENDON

At Geelong Cricket Ground, Geelong, March 24, 25, 2001. Essendon won on first innings. Geelong 205 (I.M. Redpath 93, C.J. Peake 48, G.P. Lindsay 22; C.M. Chugg 4/47, J.C. Hutchison 4/65, D.A. Tait 2/4); Essendon nine for 206 (R.G Marcy 57, B.R. Hutchison 51*, V.J. Ion 46; B.C. Oliver 3/42, I.M. Redpath 1/19, L. Buchanan 1/21, J.P. Miller 1/27, J.R. Bakker 1/48).

ST KILDA v HAWTHORN–WAVERLEY

At Junction Oval, St Kilda, March 24, 25, 2001. St Kilda won on first innings. St Kilda five for 172 declared (T.D.B. O'Sullivan 104*, S.A.J. Craig 25, S.P. Richardson 10; B.J. Jenkinson 1/12, S.R. Dart 1/22, C.J. Bambury 1/29, D. Bryant 1/45); Hawthorn–Waverley 129 (S.R. Dart 35, G. Kellar 32, P.J. Roach 29; J.C.T. Murch 4/24, A.P. Jones 3/34, S.C. Burriss 2/22).

VICTORIAN PREMIER CRICKET
FIRST ELEVEN FINAL, 2000-01

ESSENDON v ST KILDA

At Albert Ground, Melbourne, March 30, 31, April 1, 2001. St Kilda won by four wickets. Toss: Essendon.

The first meeting between these teams in a final was an engrossing and low-scoring contest with only one individual score over 50. St Kilda had not appeared in a final since they defeated Collingwood in 1991-92, while Essendon, striving to win their first premiership since 1969-70, had last appeared in a final in 1983-84. The opposing captains, St Kilda's Tim O'Sullivan (when playing for Northcote) and Essendon's David Tate, were the only participants to have previously appeared in a final. St Kilda's hard-earned win gave them their 14th VCA premiership, while Essendon, who went into the match as underdogs, proved worthy finalists.

Batting first after winning the toss, Essendon got off to a flying start as Justin Baker and Ricky Marcy put on 47 in 34 minutes for the first wicket. However, the dismissal of Baker triggered a collapse and they slumped to eight for 83, before a determined 30 in 73 minutes from tail-ender Stuart Clark enabled them to reach a modest 138. This total appeared to pose few problems for St Kilda's strong batting line-up and, passing 100 for the loss of three wickets, with Michael Klinger and Nick Jewell well set, they seemed likely to establish a big first-innings lead. However, Essendon, showing the spirit which had characterised their progression to the final, staged a remarkable fight-back, as fast bowlers Mathew Inness and Clark ran through the middle order and Craig Berger brilliantly ran out Jewell. By stumps St Kilda were precariously placed at nine for 133, still six runs short of a first-innings lead. In an engrossing opening day's play, in good batting conditions, nineteen wickets had fallen for 271 runs. Next morning St Kilda secured a slender first-innings lead, thanks to a determined innings from No. 11 batsman Simon Burriss, who withstood some fiery bowling from Inness.

Essendon soon cleared the arrears as Baker and Marcy again opened with a flourish, putting on 48 in quick time for the first wicket. However, after Baker's dismissal the innings steadily fell away, as Essendon's batsmen fell to a succession of ambitious shots. All their recognised batsmen made a start, but none exceeded 30. St Kilda bowled and fielded well, with John Davison extracting considerable turn with his off-spin to finish with four wickets. Essendon's innings was ended by two brilliant run-outs effected by Klinger and Davison. Set a modest target of 156, St Kilda were made to fight and by the close of the second day they still needed 90 runs with six wickets in hand. Next morning, after the dismissal of opener Richard Sherman, who made a patient 31 in two and three-quarter hours, with St Kilda still needing 72 to win, Essendon still held a good chance of victory. However, Jewell, nine not out at the start of play, stood firm and took part in two key partnerships that steered St Kilda to victory. First he added 38 runs for the sixth wicket with Shaun Richardson and then an unbroken 35 for the seventh with Davison, who hit three fours and a six in a breezy unbeaten 21. Jewell, a 23-year-old all-rounder, was St Kilda's hero. His 36 in the first innings and unbeaten 53 in two and a half hours in the second were the two highest scores in the match, and he also captured three handy wickets.

The low scoring was attributable to the pressure of playing in a final and good quality bowling, rather than to any shortcomings in the wicket which, though providing some bounce and movement, played well throughout.

Man of the Match: N. Jewell.

Close of play: First day, St Kilda 9/133; Second day, St Kilda 4/66.

Essendon

J.T. Baker c Richardson b Jones	27	– (2) c Rowan b Davison	30
R.G. Marcy c Rowan b Jones	19	– (1) lbw b Jewell	16
N.C. Petricola run out (Rowan)	4	– lbw b Davison	12
C.A.C. Berger lbw b Jewell	4	– c Rowan b Murch	23
J.C. Hutchinson c Klinger b Jones	2	– (8) c O'Sullivan b Davison	6
*D.A. Tate c Rowan b Jewell	2	– (5) c Richardson b Jones	20
V.J. Ion c Sherman b Davison	5	– b Jones	25
†B.R. Hutchinson c Rowan b Burriss	17	– (6) c O'Sullivan b Davison	20
C.M. Chugg c Craig b Murch	7	run out (Klinger)	12
S.W. Clark b Davison	30	– not out	0
M.W.H. Inness not out	9	run out (Davison)	0
B 4, l-b 6, n-b 2	12	B 4, n-b 4	8

(51.3 overs, 206 mins)	138	(56.4 overs, 223 mins)	172

Fall: 47 56 57 59 65 68 72
83 110 138

Fall: 48 50 64 100 122 147 159
165 172 172

Bowling: *First Innings*—Burriss 10–2–41–1; Jones 15–3–44–3; Jewell 9–6–10–2; Davison 10.3–4–19–2; Murch 7–3–14–1. *Second Innings*—Burriss 4–0–27–0; Jones 12.4–1–36–2; Jewell 12–4–26–1; Davison 18–3–55–4; Craig 4–2–5–0; Murch 6–2–19–1.

St Kilda

R. Sherman b Chugg	22	– (2) c Berger b Inness	31
*T. D. B. O'Sullivan lbw b Inness	7	– (1) lbw b Clark	2
S. A. J. Craig b Chugg	18	– lbw b Inness	9
M. Klinger b Clark	33	– c B. R. Hutchinson b Berger	22
N. Jewell run out	36	– (6) not out	53
S. P. Richardson lbw b Inness	1	– c Ion b Inness	12
J. M. Davison c Petricola b Clark	2	– not out	21
A. P. Jones c Petricola b Clark	4		
J. C. T. Murch b Inness	6	– (5) lbw b Inness	0
†D. N. Rowan b Inness	0		
S. C. Burriss not out	23		
B 1, l-b 1, n-b 1	3	B 1, l-b 5, n-b 1	7

(51 overs, 232 mins)　　　　　　　　　155　　(60.2 overs, 271 mins)　　(6 wkts) 157
Fall: 7 44 53 113 118 120 128 128 155　　　Fall: 3 16 52 57 84 122

Bowling: *First Innings*—Inness 21–7–63–4; Clark 18–6–45–3; Chugg 6–0–28–2; J.C. Hutchinson 5–1–14–0; Tate 1–0–3–0. *Second Innings*—Inness 19.2–5–56–4; Clark 15–3–39–1; Chugg 11–4–23–0; J.C. Hutchinson 6–2–22–0; Berger 3–2–1–1; Petricola 3–1–6–0; Tate 3–2–4–0.

Umpires: G. T. D. Morrow and R. G. Patterson.

PERTH FIRST-GRADE CRICKET, 2000-01

By KEN CASELLAS

Nobody approaches his cricket in Western Australia with greater gusto and dedication than Brad Hogg, so it was fitting that the energetic left-hander became the highest individual scorer in the 115-year history of the Perth first-grade competition. Playing for Willetton in an elimination final of the Sunsmart League at Burrendah Reserve, Hogg gave a flawless display as he pummelled the Bayswater–Morley attack for 285. Before his dismissal in the final over before lunch on the second day, he had not given a chance, hitting 35 fours and two sixes in 472 minutes. It was Hogg's 16th first-grade century, but sport is a great leveller, and a week later in a semi-final against Wanneroo he was out for a first-ball duck. Hogg finished the season with 875 first-grade runs at an average of 72.91, and also scored 295 runs at 59.00 for Willetton in the limited-overs BankWest Cup competition.

Hogg's double-century enabled him to take the honour as the season's leading run-scorer from Claremont–Cottesloe left-hander Geoff Cullen, who was most impressive in amassing 852 runs at 56.80. Next in the aggregate came Fremantle opener Ryan Shuttleworth (719 runs at 47.93), Scarborough's Kade Harvey (681 at 56.75 – he also took 29 wickets at 17.79), and Mount Lawley veteran Mike Veletta (664 at 51.07). Swing bowler Sean Cary (Willetton) was the leading wicket-taker with 52 at 17.77, followed by Subiaco–Floreat's Gavin Swan (49 at 12.14) and University's Matthew Healey (49 at 19.81).

The most promising of the young batsmen in the competition included Cullen, Marcus North, Shaun Marsh, Scott Meuleman and Kosta Kapinkoff. The best young wicket-keeping prospect is Perth's Luke Ronchi, who should soon develop into the state's second keeper behind Adam Gilchrist. Scarborough's young left-arm wrist-spinner Beau Casson also has the ability to graduate to first-class ranks. Once again there was a disturbing lack of emerging young fast bowlers. However, Bayswater–Morley right-armer Michael Thistle shows good promise. He took 40 wickets at 20.47 in the first-grade competition. He is not an express bowler, but swings the ball deftly. Another to catch the eye was tall Subiaco–Floreat left-arm pace bowler Michael Clark, a son of former Test opening bowler Wayne Clark. His 35 wickets at 15.20 should earn him a chance with the state squad in the coming season. Midland–Guildford's hard-working young all-rounder Peter Worthington is another destined to make his mark in higher company after a fine double of 570 runs and 41 wickets.

PERTH FIRST-GRADE TABLE, 2000-01

	M	WO	W1	D	L1	LO	T	Points
Subiaco–Floreat	13	2	9	0	3	0	0	184.71
Willetton	13	0	10	0	3	0	0	164.79
Mount Lawley	13	0	10	0	3	0	0	163.92
Scarborough	13	2	5	1	5	0	0	151.56
Bayswater–Morley	13	1	6	1	5	0	0	142.26
Wanneroo	13	1	6	0	5	1	0	140.80
Midland-Guildford	13	1	6	0	6	0	0	138.62
South Perth	13	0	7	1	4	0	1	134.83
Fremantle	13	0	6	1	6	0	0	122.96
Joondalup	13	0	6	0	7	0	0	118.70
University	13	1	5	1	6	1	0	117.94
Claremont–Nedlands	13	0	5	1	5	1	1	113.56
Melville	13	0	4	2	7	0	0	100.40
Gosnells	13	0	4	0	7	2	0	98.52
Rockingham–Mandurah	13	0	2	0	9	2	0	71.08
Perth	13	0	1	0	11	1	0	65.65

PERTH FIRST-GRADE AVERAGES, 2000-01

BATTING

(Qualification: 400 runs)

	I	NO	R	HS	100s	50s	Avge
G. B. Hogg (Willetton)	15	3	875	285	3	2	72.92
N. North (Bayswater–Morley)	11	1	623	192	3	2	62.30
G. I Cullen (Claremont–Nedlands)	16	1	852	162	1	7	56.80
K. M. Harvey (Scarborough)	15	3	681	145*	2	3	56.75
S. E. Marsh (Willetton)	9	1	440	110	2	2	55.00
P. Worthington (Midland-Guildford)	14	3	570	108	2	3	51.82
M. R. J. Veletta (Mount Lawley)	14	1	664	123	3	3	51.07
R. Shuttleworth (Fremantle)	19	4	719	117	3	2	47.93
M. P. Lavender (Midland-Guildford)	13	1	564	144	2	2	47.00
J. Batty (Mount Lawley)	15	5	438	108	1	1	43.80

BOWLING

(Qualification: 25 wickets)

	O	Mds	R	W	BB	5W/i	10W/m	Avge
C. McDonald (Mount Lawley)	236	95	383	34	4/27	0	0	11.26
G. G. Swann (Subiaco–Floreat)	267	67	595	49	7/52	2	0	12.14
D. J. Spencer (Melville)	115.1	35	334	27	5/32	1	0	12.37
G. Holt (Willetton)	325	129	601	44	7/50	4	0	13.66
M. Clark (Subiaco–Floreat)	209	57	532	35	5/51	3	0	15.20
J. Parry (Willetton)	199.2	44	583	37	5/43	1	0	15.75
P. Henryon (Subiaco–Floreat)	142	38	430	27	5/44	1	0	15.93
D. J. Wates (Subiaco–Floreat)	230.4	57	552	33	5/43	2	0	16.73
S. Howman (Subiaco–Floreat)	229	63	518	30	7/58	1	0	17.27
M. Mason (Willetton)	324	111	622	36	6/21	1	0	17.27

PERTH FIRST-GRADE SEMI-FINALS, 2000-01

SUBIACO–FLOREAT v SCARBOROUGH

At Richardson Park, South Perth, March 24, 25, 2001. Subiaco–Floreat won on first innings. Subiaco–Floreat 206 (M.W. Goodwin 120; R. Daly 4/36, K.M. Harvey 3/57) and 2 for 50 defeated Scarborough 87 (R.J. Campbell 57; G.G. Swan 7/52).

WILLETTON v WANNEROO

At Tompkins Reserve, Tompkins, March 24, 25, 2001. Wanneroo won on first innings. Willetton 215 (C. Whisson 43, A. Scragg 43, B. Saunders 28; W. Robinson 4/68, J. Parry 3/27) lost to Wanneroo six for 216 (M.E. Hussey 94, V. Lawes 43; S.R. Cary 3/68).

PERTH FIRST-GRADE FINAL, 2000-01

SUBIACO–FLOREAT v WANNEROO

At Richardson Park, South Perth, March 31, 2001. Subiaco–Floreat won on first innings. Toss: Wanneroo.

The showpiece of the Perth club competition was a fizzer, as Subiaco–Floreat simply outplayed Wanneroo. After winning the toss and batting, Wanneroo were routed for 84 off 47.3 overs. At 5.02 p.m. on the first of two scheduled days, with Subiaco–Floreat in total command at two for 141 off 35 overs, Wanneroo conceded the match. The hero of the victory was Subiaco–Floreat's captain Gavin Swan, who generated considerable pace and moved the ball menacingly off the pitch to take 5/24 off 18 overs. A week earlier, he had played a major part in Subiaco–Floreat's semi-final victory over the powerful Scarborough side by taking 7/52. Swan was ably assisted by left-armer Michael Clark, who took two early wickets, and young swing bowler Sam Howman. Not one of the Wanneroo batsmen was able to counter the Subiaco–Floreat attack.

Left-handed openers David Bolton and Brett Jones gave Subiaco–Floreat a flying start before Jones drove uppishly at Matt Mason and was caught at mid-off for 29 off 33 deliveries. When Bolton glided the second ball of the 22nd over to third man for two, Subiaco–Floreat had overhauled Wanneroo's miserable total. Subiaco–Floreat's premiership was a triumph for Noel Knight in his first year as coach. The 49-year-old had also coached first-grade premiership sides Scarborough in 1995 and Bayswater–Morley in 1999. He is a well-organised coach, a strong disciplinarian who plays no favourites and demands dedication and hard work from his players.

Wanneroo

D. Page c Howman b Clark	....	7
J. Charles c Simpson b Swan	....	0
A. Slattery run out	....	12
*D. Hussey c Bolton b Clark	....	2
W. Robinson c Simpson b Swan	....	11
V. Lawes c Campbell b Swan	....	13
B. Kelly b Howman	....	0
C. Thorp c Glew b Swan	....	10
†A. Lucas c Glew b Swan	....	10
J. Parry c Simpson b Howman	....	2
M. Mason not out	....	5
L-b 8, w 4	....	12
(47.3 overs)		84

Fall: 4 8 11 26 39 42 62 69 74 84

Bowling: Swan 18–4–24–5; Howman 7.3–3–9–2, Clark 16–5–27–2; Campbell 6–0–16–0.

Subiaco–Floreat

D. Bolton not out	55	L-b 2, n-b 11	13
B. Jones c Parry b Mason	29		
S. Moody b Robinson	10	(35 overs)	(2 wkts) 141
S. A Glew not out	34	Fall: 41 64	

K. Kapinkoff, B. Hart, †M. Simpson, S. Howman, *G. G Swan, M. Clark and B. Campbell did not bat.

Bowling: Mason 11–2–32–1; Thorp 9–0–36–0, Robinson 9–2–32–1, Parry 6–0–39–0.

Umpires: J. Brookes and C. Allen

NATIONAL COUNTRY CRICKET CHAMPIONSHIPS, 2000-01

By WARWICK TORRENS

New South Wales regained the top position in the National Country Cricket Championships, which were played at Albany and Mount Barker in Western Australia. They began with a strong performance against last year's winners, Queensland, exceeding 400 in an innings for the first time. In doing so, they became the last of the six competing teams to achieve the 400 mark.

From winning that first game New South Wales never lost their grip on the title and in the end won by a comfortable margin, though at all times they were mindful of the position of their nearest rivals, Australian Capital Territory. Yet in the third-round game they had dismissed the players of the national capital for 103, equal to the lowest total recorded by the Territorians at Townsville in 1990-91. After a good start New South Wales struggled for runs and were dismissed for just 200.

Queensland generally struggled, and finished with only one victory, against South Australia, who failed to win a game. Yet Queensland had one of the most prolific batsmen, Brian May, who recorded three centuries to equal the effort of Mark Curry in 1991-92. May fell just eight runs short of the aggregate of Anthony McQuire of Australian Capital Territory, who hit 382 runs.

After losing their first two games, Western Australia improved to win their remaining three matches and secure fourth place. Included in their victories was a win over Victoria who at one time seemed the most likely team to challenge New South Wales. But in the fourth-round fixture, reduced to a one-day game because of rain, Victoria lost decisively to the eventual champions. It was in this fourth round that South Australia were required to bat second on a wicket that became more favourable to the bowlers as the game progressed and they fell for 59, their lowest ever total in the championships.

During the season three new partnership records were created, all coming at a time of need. Two came in the opening round when on the second day Brad Campbell and Brad Glenn added 212 for Victoria's sixth wicket to right a poor response of five for 79 to South Australia's 233. On the opening day South Australia were eight for 95 when wicket-keeper Dan Stratford joined the elegant Shane Sweet to share in a ninth-wicket partnership of 138. Then in the final round New South Wales were in danger of defeat by South Australia when Steve Lockhart joined wicket-keeper Randall Starr at six for 107 and they added an unbroken 142 to carry their team to victory.

Though there were some good bowling efforts in the series, one performance stands out: that of Doug Ellis of Western Australia. After failing to capture a wicket in the first round and being relegated to 12th man for the second, Ellis captured 8/84 in the third-round match against Victoria, bowling his way into the Australian Country twelve. He went on to be the leading wicket-taker of the series with 15, one more than Craig Tonkin of Western Australia and Brad Campbell.

Player of the Series: B.K.D. May (Qld)
Don Bradman Batting Trophy: A.D. McQuire (ACT)
Bill O'Reilly Bowling Trophy: D. Ellis (WA)
Fieldsman of the Series: B.D. Ward (WA) and R. Starr (NSW)

ROUND ONE

At North Road Sporting Complex West Ground, Albany, January 3, 4, 2001. Australian Capital Territory won on first innings. Australian Capital Territory nine for 300 (J.D. Robson 59, A.D. McQuire 58, A.J. Heading 53, C. Brown 49; P. Tomasi 4/85, C. Tonkin 3/31) and one for 52; Western Australia 242 (L.G. Burns 52, D. Gaby 49, K.N. Elliot 43; J.D. Robson 3/40, T.J. Ferguson 3/39).

At North Road Sporting Complex East Ground, Albany, January 3, 4, 2001. New South Wales won by 169 runs. Queensland 263 (B.K.D. May 120, D.A. Todd 55; M.A. Cameron 3/47); New South Wales six for 432 (J. Henderson 156, R. Starr 79*, C.J. Haworth 76, G.P. Smith 40).

At North Road Sporting Complex North Ground, Albany, January 3, 4, 2001. Victoria won by 130 runs. South Australia 233 (S.A. Sweet 119, D.M. Stratford 47*; S.J. Phillips 3/35, B.L. Campbell 3/89); Victoria eight for 363 (B.J. Glenn 119, B.L. Campbell 115; P.A. Attard 4/76).

ROUND TWO

At North Road Sporting Complex East Ground, Albany, January 5, 6, 2001. South Australia won on first innings. Australian Capital Territory seven for 344 (J.K. Smith 83, J.D. Robson 82, D.G. Dawson 47, S.P. Heaney 40; S.W. Tait 2/46, S.J. Merkel 2/49) and none for 81 (C. Brown 59*); South Australia 190 (M.J. Whitelum 53, S.A. Sweet 39; G.L. Miller 4/46).

At North Road Sporting Complex North Ground, Albany, January 5, 6, 2001. Victoria won on first innings. Victoria nine for 270 declared (P.A. Barber 79, B.M. Stewart 47, T.D. Wrigglesworth 34*; C.W. Jesberg 2/21, K.E. Johnson 2/21, C.E. Window 2/29) and three for 87 (K.J. Burdett 46, C.D. Pinniger 29); Queensland 231 (D.A. Todd 48, M.D. Brennan 42*, S.A. Baker 35; S.J. Phillips 3/49, P.A. Barber 2/34).

At Sounness Park, Mount Barker, January 5, 6, 2001. New South Wales won by 199 runs. Western Australia 199 (C. Tonkin 65; M.A. Cameron 5/36, S.J. Lockhart 2/42); New South Wales 398 (G.P. Smith 91, C.J. Haworth 80, S.J. Mace 55, R. Starr 52; C. Tonkin 4/78, N. Herbert 2/87).

ROUND THREE

At North Road Sporting Complex North Ground, Albany, January 8, 9, 2001. New South Wales won on first innings. Australian Capital Territory 103 (D.M. Jeffrey 38; M.A. Cameron 3/25, P.D. Stepto 3/35, A.J. Starr 2/10, G.P. Smith 2/18) and three for 257 (A.D. McQuire 143*, J.K. Smith 67; G.P. Smith 2/23); New South Wales 200 (G.A. Grimmond 64, S.G. Moore 42, J. Henderson 33; G.L. Miller 3/47, J.D. Robson 2/36).

At Sounness Park, Mount Barker, January 5, 6, 2001. Queensland won by 27 runs. South Australia 333 (S.J. Merkel 65, J.R. Mosey 56, M.J. Whitelum 39, M.B. Johnson 39, B.B. Seebaran 36*; M.D. Brennan 5/107, S.B. Connor 2/73); Queensland 360 (B.K.D. May 125, M.D. Brennan 47, D.A. Todd 42, S.A. Baker 39, S.B. Connor 31; B.B. Seebaran 4/78, P.A. Attard 3/81, S.W. Tait 2/88).

At North Road Sporting Complex West Ground, Albany, January 5, 6, 2001. Western Australia won on first innings. Western Australia nine for 311 declared (L. Sorfleet 90, L. G. Burns 50, B. P. King 41, G. J. Dehring 39; G Pearse 3/75, P. A. Barber 2/45, B. L. Campbell 2/72) and two for 12; Victoria 282 (C. M. Brittain 77, J. Murphy 55, B. J. Glenn 42, B. L. Campbell 30; D. Ellis 8/84, P. Tomasi 2/50).

ROUND FOUR

At North Road Sporting Complex West Ground, Albany, January 12, 2001. Australian Capital Territory won by 51 runs. Australian Capital Territory 233 (A. D. McQuire 79, C. Brown 49, J. K. Smith 29; C. W. Jesberg 4/44, L. A. Wilson 3/43); Queensland 182 (R. J. Colville 47, D. A. Todd 28, M. D. Brennan 24, B. K. D. May 23; E. Kellar 3/28, D. M. Jeffrey 3/35, M. H. Ramage 3/49).

At North Road Sporting Complex East Ground, Albany, January 12, 2001. New South Wales won by 96 runs. New South Wales 259 (G. A. Grimmond 86, S. G. Moore 46, A. J. Starr 28*; C. J. Keady 3/31, G. Pearse 2/33); Victoria 163 (B. M. Stewart 36, C. M. Brittain 28, C. J. Keady 21, G. Pearse 20; S. J. Lockhart 4/44, P. D. Stepto 2/33).

At North Road Sporting Complex North Ground, Albany, January 12, 2001. Western Australia won by 122 runs. Western Australia nine for 181 (G. J. Dehring 63, B. Ward 22, P. Tomasi 22; S. W. Tait 4/21, L. J. Knight 2/38); South Australia 59 (B. B. Seebaran 18*; C. Tonkin 4/27, J. Partington 3/10, D. Ellis 3/11.

ROUND FIVE

At North Road Sporting Complex North Ground, Albany, January 13, 2001. Victoria won by one run. Australian Capital Territory nine for 230 (A. D. McQuire 76, D. G. Dawson 53*; B. L. Campbell 3/36, G. Pearse 2/58); Victoria six for 231 (B. L. Campbell 73*, J. Murphy 60, G. Pearse 28*; P. A. Barber 21; E. Kellar 2/43, A. J. Heading 2/57).

At North Road Sporting Complex West Ground, Albany, January 13, 2001. New South Wales South won by one run. Australian six for 248 (M. J. Whitelum 104, S. J. Merkel 65, M. B. Johnson 31); New South Wales six for 249 (R. Starr 143*, S. J. Lockhart 61*, S. G. Moore 25; L. J. Knight 3/53).

At North Road Sporting Complex East Ground, Albany, January 13, 2001. Western Australia won by eight runs. Western Australia nine for 232 (G. J. Dehring 58, R. D. Elliot 51, L. G. Burns 49; M. D. Brennan 3/53, C. W. Jesberg 2/34, K. E. Johnson 2/55); Queensland 224 (B. K. D. May 103, M. D. Brennan 32, C. E. Window 26; D. Ellis 4/46, C. Tonkin 3/45).

POINTS TABLE, 2000-01

	Played	Won	Lost	Drawn	Points
New South Wales	5	5	0	0	50.50
Australian Capital Territory	5	3	2	0	38.37
Victoria	5	3	2	0	37.62
Western Australia	5	3	2	0	35.71
Queensland	5	1	4	0	22.94
South Australia	5	0	5	0	15.06

CHAMPIONSHIP WINNERS

Season	Venue	Winner
1984-85	Beenleigh (Queensland)	New South Wales
1985-86	Riverlands (SAust)	New South Wales
1986-87	Dubbo (NSW)	Australian Capital Territory
1987-88	Canberra (ACT)	Queensland
1988-89	Bunbury (WAust)	New South Wales
1989-90	Bendigo (Victoria)	New South Wales
1990-91	Townsville (Queensland)	Victoria
1991-92	Riverlands (SA)	New South Wales
1992-93	Newcastle (NSW)	New South Wales
1993-94	Canberra (ACT)	Australian Capital Territory
1994-95	Albany (WAust)	Queensland
1995-96	Sale (Victoria)	New South Wales
1996-97	Toowoomba (Queensland)	Queensland
1997-98	Mt Gambier (SAust)	Western Australia
1998-99	Barooga (NSW-Victoria)	New South Wales
1999-00	Canberra (ACT)	Queensland
2000-01	Albany–Mt Barker (WAust)	New South Wales

AUSTRALIAN COUNTRY v WESTERN AUSTRALIA

At North Road Sporting Complex North Ground, Albany, January 10, 2001. Western Australia won by 61 runs. Toss: Australian Country.

Sent in to bat, Western Australia began with a flurry of runs from Ryan Campbell, after which Murray Goodwin and Mike Hussey added 150. The middle order collapsed, and the score was seven for 212 before the former Australian Capital Territory player Stuart Karppinen dominated an eighth-wicket partnership of 40. Local player Doug Ellis bowled well to keep the batsmen in check and the veteran slow left-armer John Robson, another former Australian Capital Territory representative, also bowled impressively, capturing two top-order wickets. When the Country team batted most of the earlier batsmen made a start but only Craig Haworth, a former New South Wales Colts representative and now playing at Coffs Harbour, passed 50. In the end the target was just too much for the Country team in the face of some accurate bowling, especially by Karppinen.

Western Australia

R. J. Campbell c and b Ellis	27	(25)	†M. J. Walsh run out (Ellis)	3	(5)
M. W. Goodwin c May b Robson	74	(81)	S. J. Karppinen not out	39	(40)
M. E. Hussey c Glenn b Smith	76	(88)	S. Nikitaras not out	1	(1)
M. J. North b Robson	11	(25)	B 1, l-b 4, w 8	13	
G. B. Hogg run out	2	(2)			
D. Hussey c Campbell b Cameron	17	(32)	(50 overs, 192 mins) (8 wkts)	263	
K. M. Harvey c Glenn b Smith	0	(6)	Fall: 34 184 193 199 202 207 212 252		

S. R. Cary and G. G. Swan did not bat.

Bowling: Cameron 10–0–54–1; Ellis 10–1–42–1; Campbell 10–0–64–0; Robson 10–0–48–2; Smith 10–3–50–2.

Australian Country

L. G. Burns c Walsh b Karppinen	3	(14)
A. D. McQuire c Walsh b Cary	22	(41)
B. K. D. May b Harvey	34	(80)
D. A. Todd c Swan b Hogg	23	(40)
*C. J. Haworth st Campbell b Hogg	52	(58)
S. A. Sweet c Campbell b Nikitaras	2	(7)
G. P. Smith lbw b Nikitaras	0	(2)
B. L. Campbell b Karppinen	17	(25)
J. D. Robson c Swan b Karppinen	20	(30)
*B. J. Glenn run out (Hogg)	3	(7)
M. A. Cameron not out	8	(7)
L-b 3, w 10, n-b 5	18	
(50 overs, 214 mins)	202	

D. Ellis did not bat.

Fall: 14 54 92 135 148 148 156 180 185 202

Bowling: Swan 10–1–55–0; Karppinen 9–1–22–3; Nikitaras 9–0–34–2; Cary 7–2–25–1; Harvey 7–0–30–1; Hogg 7–0–27–2; Walsh 1–0–6–0.

Umpires: J. Brooks and K. Hulcup.

AUSTRALIAN COUNTRY v ZIMBABWEANS

At Bradman Oval, Bowral, January 19, 2001. Australian Country won by 51 runs. For details see section on Zimbabweans in Australia, 2000-01, page 333.

SCHOOLS' CRICKET, 2000-01

By Dr GREG McKIE

Last year's *Wisden Australia* mentioned that Australian schools' cricket was going through a readjustment period. Unfortunately, the problems identified then have not gone away. Accordingly, the past season was not a vintage one.

The governing body for schools' cricket, the Australian Schools' Cricket Council, is still not in a position to run their competition for the Australian champion school cricket team. This competition ran successfully between 1988 and 1996 with Gillette sponsorship. The ASCC and the Australian Cricket Board then jointly funded the competition in 1997 and 1998. Since then, the ASCC has been unable to attract a corporate sponsor. Last year it found that the Sydney Olympics greatly restricted the amount of potential sponsorship. The ASCC also faces the problem of individual state sponsorship. A potential national sponsor has come forward, but it is only interested if it can sponsor all aspects of the school game in every state and territory. This means that the ASCC will have to wait until existing state sponsorship agreements have run their course. A national sponsor may not be prepared to wait so long.

It is now three years since the national schools competition was held, and if it is not held again soon the ASCC may not survive. The ASCC has been holding together the national schools' cricket structure for almost 30 years. Without a role in running a national competition, the ASCC probably has no future, despite the continued support it has been receiving from Kookaburra Sport. Without the ASCC, international schools touring teams would have no point of contact to arrange fixtures in Australia. Australian state and territory school cricket bodies would also have no central focus or a forum for discussing matters of common interest.

The ACB has been sympathetic to the ASCC's needs, but after sponsoring the national competition for two years, it now feels that its money can be put to better use providing development programs in schools throughout Australia. Also, as most states are now running the school game themselves, the annual ASCC conferences have only limited use, as similar issues would have already been discussed at ACB development managers' meetings.

Without the spur of an interstate schools' competition, some states have experienced a drop-off in interest for their own competitions. It seems that some schools are simply not entering the elimination series at state level in the absence of the incentive of competition at national level.

State competitions are still being held, however. The largest two are in New South Wales and Victoria, where more than 500 schools in each state contest the elimination series. The New South Wales winner for 2001 was Barker College and the Victorian winner for 2000 was Wesley College, with St Kevin's College already into the final for the 2001 competition. In Western Australia the Coca-Cola Shield final was won by Kent Street Senior High School over Wesley College. In the Northern Territory, St Phillip's College won the southern section and Kormilda College the northern; in the best-of-three final Kormilda won the deciding match by five wickets.

Many problems are starting to manifest themselves at school cricket level. State association under-age fixtures have increased dramatically in scope, and these competitions are pushing school games into the background. The creation of cricket "pathways" by most state associations has given a clear message to school players that if they want to progress in the game, they must do it through playing in certain approved competitions. School games have never been part of these "pathways" (and have never wanted to be), so that if a clash occurs, the schoolboy player feels pressured to choose the game which can lead him on to higher rewards.

The existence of this choice last year meant that certain school cricket associations did not compete in the annual inter-association fixtures because their better players were playing in state association under-age fixtures instead. The school associations did not want to be obliged to award selection to boys who were effectively their second or even third eleven. In the competitions that took place, the resultant cricket was not a good showcase for the health of the game in the schools.

Several state school cricket bodies are also experiencing a drop-off in the numbers of teachers who are prepared to become involved in cricket administration. With the increase in the age of the people who are involved, the situation is starting to become critical. Effectively the same personnel has been running the school game in each state for up to 25 years. The Victorian Schools' Cricket Association recently approached the Victorian Cricket Association to take over the game in schools, arguing that the majority of VSCA members were now ex-teachers because of age retirement. Without an increase in teacher numbers onto their committee, there was no guarantee that programs could be maintained. The VCA has a Schools' Officer, who would be ideally placed to administer schools' cricket. A VCA takeover would also ensure that fixture clashes became a thing of the past. This may well be the way of the future for schools' cricket. State associations have the resources and the knowhow to run large-scale competitions, and the financial backing to make such competitions viable.

As a reflection of some of these problems, the longest-running interstate schools cricket fixture, South Australia versus Victoria Under-19s schools, was cancelled last year. The clash of fixtures which occurred during both states' schools' series meant that any team they picked would not be representative of schools' cricket in the state. This three-day match may still be played later this year if fixture clashes can be avoided. The annual Queensland versus New South Wales Under-19s schools fixture did take place, however.

All is not lost, because some aspects of the game in schools are still extremely positive. Girls' school cricket goes from strength to strength, with a healthy increase in numbers each year. The skill level of the girls has also dramatically increased. Most of the teams now field very competently and bowl with reasonable accuracy. At the lower age levels, batting skills still need refining, but the enthusiasm and interest are first-rate. Some state associations are encouraging senior women's teams to "sponsor" a junior team. This has terrific advantages for a school. The team (usually at the Under-17s age level) plays its matches on a Friday night so there is no clash with other school activities. The local club provides a ground, umpires, coaching and all necessary equipment. The girls enjoy the games and the club naturally hopes that some of the girls will join the senior club in coming years.

Fun competitions such as "Super Eights" are increasingly popular. These games are an ideal way to get more students involved in cricket. Every player is involved throughout a Super Eights game. A game takes only about 40 minutes, and as everyone must bowl, and field in every position, no one misses out. As a separate bowling or batting team can be used, these games can involve more students than in regular cricket. The captain of a Super Eights team has to make crucial decisions continually, and all aspects of the game are covered in a fun, non-confronting way. These games are not just "hit and giggle". Schools put a lot of time into training their teams. Some non-government schools have even hired state players as professional coaches. The existence of such competitions has encouraged some schools to raise a cricket team for the first time.

An innovation introduced successfully during the season was the Australian Schools 15-Years Championship for boys. School Sport Australia staged the inaugural championship on the Gold Coast in April. Players were selected from both government and non-government schools, and all states and territories competed in what may become an annual event. (See the separate report below.)

SCHOOLS 15-YEARS CHAMPIONSHIPS, 2001

By WARWICK TORRENS

The inaugural 15-Years Championships were conducted in Buderim, Queensland. All six states and both territories entered teams. With only a small base from which to choose, Northern Territory included four Queensland players in their squad of 13. Of the 103 players on view many showed great promise.

South Australia claimed the title after an eventful week. Players were required to have not reached 16 years of age as at September 1, 2001. On the second day it was discovered that every member of the New South Wales team was too old, owing to a misinterpretation of the age conditions. The organising committee met and decided that New South Wales should be allowed to continue playing but that their team and players would not be eligible for any trophies.

The other major problem of the week was the weather. On the second afternoon heavy rain ended the three games at Elizabeth Daniels Park soon after 30 of the scheduled 50 overs had been completed in all three second innings. Conditions of play stated that in such an event the match would be decided on comparative scores at the same stage of the innings. The match at Ballinger Park was played to a finish without interruption.

Within a quarter of an hour of play commencing on the third day, torrential rain drenched both grounds and continued to fall for some time. The committee sensibly concluded that the matches should be abandoned and rescheduled for the following day, which had been programmed as an educational excursion day. The excursion was quickly brought forward a day. The rest of the matches were affected only by some lingering dampness in the outfields.

The final day produced some exciting cricket. The Victorian attack managed to keep the South Australian batting to a competitive total of 159, taking the final wicket with an over to spare. Supported by good fielding, the South Australian bowlers kept up the pressure. Despite some valiant efforts from the Victorian lower order, South Australia finally claimed a comfortable victory with more than seven overs to spare, keeping their undefeated record intact and claiming the title.

At Ballinger Park, Australian Capital Territory, with half-centuries from Hay and Johnson, built a useful total and then proceeded to dispose of the Tasmanians, whose only real resistance came from Licht and Biffin. Queensland went down to New South Wales, though they did have the honour of recording the highest team total of the week against New South Wales, who not surprisingly won all their matches.

Next year the championships will be played in the Victorian city of Bendigo.

ROUND ONE

At John Blanck Oval, Buderim, April 2, 2001. Victoria won on first innings. Victoria nine for 242 (M. Harrison 120, S. A. Sanders 35; C. Watt 2/39, J. Wyatt 3/42); Northern Territory Combined 53 (L. J. Crawford 2/12, T. M. O'Brien 5/16).

At Ron McMullin Oval, Buderim, April 2, 2001. South Australia won on first innings. South Australia 161 (S. W. Hurn 65, T. F. Kurzel 36; S. Graham 2/20, B. L. Burgess 3/18, N. G. Hitartzidis 3/38); Tasmania nine for 105 (G. D. Putland 4/12, J. E. Nash 2/14, R. Biar 2/20).

At Kev Hackney Oval, Buderim, April 2, 2001. New South Wales won on first innings. New South Wales four for 251 (E. R. J. McCarthy 32, S. J. Hinton 78, M. Littlewood 84*, B. Crawley 40; D. Poidevin 2/47); Australian Capital Territory eight for 120 (G. M. Fitzgibbon 37).

At Ballinger Park, Buderim, April 2, 2001. Western Australia won on first innings. Western Australia eight for 119 (D. N. Porter 32; B. J. Daniels 2/18); Queensland 101 (B. J. Wright 4/11, D. N. Porter 2/20).

ROUND TWO

At John Blanck Oval, Buderim, April 3, 2001. South Australia won on first innings on run rate. Western Australia 106 (B. D. Hansberry 31; G. D. Putland 2/20, J. E. Nash 2/16, S. C. Wiese 3/12); South Australia five for 94 (J. H. T. Hartford 43).

At Ron McMullin Oval, Buderim, April 3, 2001. Victoria won on first innings. Australian Capital Territory nine for 139 (D. Poidevin 57, P. Gordon 33; N. W. Owen 2/11, T. M. O'Brien 2/39); Victoria four for 117 (C. I. Armstrong 40; W. Hay 2/3) on run rate.

At Kev Hackney Oval, Buderim, April 3, 2001. Tasmania won on first innings. Queensland six for 191 (B. J. Couper 30; Z. E. Turner 32, B. S. Barnes 42, A. C. Eden 34*; J. M. Sherman 2/35); Tasmania two for 97 (J. W. Licht 34, H. Fenton 32*) on run rate.

At Ballinger Park, Buderim, April 3, 2001. New South Wales won on first innings. New South Wales five for 245 (D. M. Badger 32, S. O'Keefe 114*; A. Knezevic 2/25); Northern Territory Combined 95 (S. Cook 2/15, D. M. Badger 3/0).

ROUND THREE

At John Blanck Oval, Buderim, April 5, 2001. Australian Capital Territory won on first innings. Australian Capital Territory seven for 175 (D. Poidevin 56, W. Hay 42; N. J. Drummond 2/35, K. S. Anand 3/34); Northern Territory Combined seven for 141 (M. I. Brandon 51; W. Hay 2/10, L. J. Kiel 2/20).

At Ron McMullin Oval, Buderim, April 5, 2001. South Australia won on first innings. Queensland nine for 140 (G. I. Skennar 32, B. J. Couper 39; S. C. Wiese 2/24, C. H. Harper 2/14); South Australia eight for 142 (J. P. Pratt 34, S. W. Hurn 54*; T. J. Roy 2/33, G. W. Dobbie 3/25).

At Kev Hackney Oval, Buderim, April 5, 2001. New South Wales won on first innings. New South Wales 141 (S. O'Keefe 45; N. W. Owen 2/5, R. J. Livera 2/33, T. M. O'Brien 2/26, N. L. Allen 2/19); Victoria 113 (M. Harrison 33; T. J. Harrington 2/21, V. Sithloo 2/17, S. O'Keefe 3/18, S. Cook 2/26).

At Ballinger Park, Buderim, April 5, 2001. Tasmania won on first innings. Western Australia five for 114 (B. J. Wright 33, D. N. Porter 31*); Tasmania eight for 115 (M. J. Johnston 2/24, T. J. Kingdon 2/15, B. J. Wright 2/20).

SEMI-FINAL ROUND

At John Blanck Oval, Buderim, April 6, 2001. New South Wales won on first innings. New South Wales seven for 222 (M. Littlewood 51, S. J. Hinton 74, M. Friedrich 50*; R. T. Roles 2/46); Western Australia eight for 124 (T. J. Harrington 3/15, S. Cook 2/32).

At Ron McMullin Oval, Buderim, April 6, 2001. Victoria won on first innings. Tasmania eight for 143 (A. Biffin 38*; J. L. Wood 2/33, N. L. Allen 3/17, B. MacRae 2/10); Victoria six for 144 (B. MacRae 39, R. J. Livera 53; G. S. Kerr 3/14).

At Kev Hackney Oval, Buderim, April 6, 2001. South Australia won on first innings. Australian Capital Territory 140 (T. M. Dennett 37, J. W. Rogers 40; J. E. Nash 2/21, P. L. Maddocks 2/24); South Australia two for 141 (A. Murphy 67, J. H. T. Hartford 44*).

At Ballinger Park, Buderim, April 6, 2001. Queensland won on first innings. Northern Territory Combined 107 (T. N. Devereux 40; A. I. Greig 2/9, G. W. Dobbie 3/21, R. A. Stenhouse 4/10); Queensland eight for 108 (A. Knezevic 2/12, J. Wyatt 2/19).

FINALS ROUND

Playoff for 1st and 2nd

At John Blanck Oval, Buderim, April 7, 2001. South Australia won on first innings. South Australia 159 (J. H. T. Harford 39; L. J. Crawford 2/22, N. W. Owen 2/10, R. J. Livera 2/7); Victoria 98 (G. D. Putland 2/21).

Playoff for 3rd and 4th

At Ballinger Park, Buderim, April 7, 2001. Australian Capital Territory won on first innings. Australian Capital Territory seven for 174 (W. Hay 59, D. A. Johnson 51; S. Graham 2/32, Z. P. Littlejon 2/45); Tasmania 136 (J. W. Licht 36, A. Biffin 35; W. Hay 2/9, L. J. Kiel 5/33).

At Ron McMullin Oval, Buderim, April 7, 2001. New South Wales won on first innings. Queensland 152 (A. C. Eden 56; T. J. Harrington 2/24, S. Cook 2/32, S. O'Keefe 2/17); New South Wales five for 156 (S. J. Hinton 74, M. Friedrich 32*).

At Kev Hackney Oval, Buderim, April 7, 2001. Western Australia won on first innings. Western Australia five for 241 (J. Addison 32, R. D. Blight 58, C. R. Verco 59*, B. J. Wright 43); Northern Territory Combined eight for 120 (R. D. Bhasin 34; C. R. Verco 4/18, S. G. Lamont 2/24).

WOMEN'S CRICKET, 2000-01

By ERICA SAINSBURY

Australia relinquished their world crown to New Zealand in the Women's Cricket World Cup in Christchurch, New Zealand, in December 2000. The Australians lost only one match during the tournament – the final, by a margin of only four runs. The month-long festival highlighted the massive differences in standards even among the top nations, and underlined the challenges facing a revitalised International Women's Cricket Council, headed by the Australian administrator Christine Brierley. Australia now enters a rebuilding phase in order to prepare for the next World Cup (scheduled for South Africa in 2005), starting with the 2001 Tour of England under new coach Steve Jenkin. Australia's Lisa Keightley won the Player of the Tournament award, from Karen Rolton of Australia and Anna O'Leary of New Zealand, who were equal second. Rolton was the tournament's highest and fastest scorer – 393 runs at an average of 131.00, and a strike-rate of 106.21 per 100 balls faced – and Australia's Charmaine Mason took the most wickets – 17 at an average of 10.76.

WOMEN'S WORLD CUP, 2000-01

AUSTRALIAN TOUR PARTY

B. J. Clark (New South Wales) (*captain*), K. L. Rolton (South Australia) (*vice-captain*), C. Bambury (Western Australia), J. Broadbent (South Australia), L. Broadfoot (Victoria), A. J. Fahey (Western Australia), C. L. Fitzpatrick (Victoria), Z. J. Goss (Western Australia), J. Hayes (New South Wales), L. M. Keightley (New South Wales), O. J. Magno (South Australia), C. L. Mason (Victoria), T. A. McGregor (New South Wales), J. C. Price (Queensland).

Coach: J. C. Harmer. *Manager:* J. Stainer. *Physiotherapist:* L. Ross. *Assistant coach:* S. Jenkin. *Scorer/statistician:* E. J. Sainsbury. *Physical fitness coordinator:* S. Bailey.

MATCHES NOT INVOLVING AUSTRALIA

England v Netherlands at Bert Sutcliffe Oval, Lincoln, November 30, 2000. England three for 256 defeated Netherlands nine for 116 by 140 runs.

India v South Africa at Hagley Oval, Christchurch, November 30, 2000. India two for 129 defeated South Africa eight for 128 by eight wickets.

New Zealand v Ireland at Bert Sutcliffe Oval, Lincoln, December 1, 2000. Ireland 99 lost to New Zealand two for 102 by eight wickets.

England v South Africa at Bert Sutcliffe Oval, Lincoln, December 2, 2000. England 143 lost to South Africa five for 144 by five wickets.

India v Netherlands at Lincoln Green, Lincoln, December 2, 2000. India four for 275 defeated Netherlands six for 121 by 154 runs.

New Zealand v Sri Lanka at Lincoln Green, Lincoln, December 3, 2000. New Zealand four for 210 defeated Sri Lanka 88 by 122 runs.

England v India at Lincoln Green, December 4, 2000. England 147 lost to India seven for 155 by eight runs.

Netherlands v South Africa at Hagley No. 2 Oval, Christchurch, December 4, 2000. Netherlands 92 lost to South Africa six for 93 by four wickets.

Ireland v Sri Lanka at Lincoln Green, Lincoln, December 5, 2000. Sri Lanka 129 defeated Ireland 110 by ten runs

New Zealand v Netherlands at Hagley No. 2 Oval, Christchurch, December 6, 2000. Netherlands 80 lost to New Zealand two for 81 by eight wickets.

England v Ireland at Bert Sutcliffe Oval, Lincoln, December 7, 2000. Ireland 103 lost to England two for 105 by eight wickets.

South Africa v Sri Lanka at Lincoln Green, Lincoln, December 8, 2000. Sri Lanka nine for 134 lost to South Africa four for 135 by six wickets.

New Zealand v India at Bert Sutcliffe Oval, Lincoln, December 9, 2000. New Zealand five for 224 defeated India seven for 150 by 74 runs.

Netherlands v Sri Lanka at Hagley No. 2 Oval, Christchurch, December 10, 2000. Sri Lanka 139 defeated Netherlands 113 by 26 runs.

India v Ireland at Hagley No. 2 Oval, Christchurch, December 11, 2000. India nine for 199 defeated Ireland 169 by 30 runs.

New Zealand v South Africa at Lincoln Green, Lincoln, December 11, 2000. New Zealand five for 265 defeated South Africa 107 by 158 runs.

England v Sri Lanka at Bert Sutcliffe Oval, Lincoln, December 12, 2000. England four for 242 defeated Sri Lanka nine for 137 by 105 runs.

New Zealand v England at Bert Sutcliffe Oval, Lincoln, December 14, 2000. New Zealand eight for 238 defeated England 145 by 93 runs.

Ireland v Netherlands at Hagley Oval, Christchurch, December 14, 2000. Ireland six for 232 defeated Netherlands eight for 191 by 41 runs.

India v Sri Lanka Sri Lanka at Lincoln Green, Lincoln, December 15, 2000. India four for 230 defeated Sri Lanka 89 by 141 runs.

Ireland v South Africa at Hagley Oval, Christchurch, December 16, 2000. Ireland nine for 176 lost to South Africa one for 177 by nine wickets.

AVERAGES

AUSTRALIA – BATTING

	M	I	NO	R	HS	100s	50s	Avge	Ct/St	S-R
K.L. Rolton	9	7	4	393	154*	2	2	131.00	2	106.21
L.M. Keightley	8	8	3	375	91*	0	4	75.00	3	66.13
B.J. Clark	9	9	3	351	91	0	2	58.50	5	71.63
T.A. McGregor	7	2	1	40	21*	0	0	40.00	2	66.66
O.J. Magno........	8	5	2	98	38	0	0	32.66	3	70.50
Z.J. Goss.	7	2	0	50	49	0	0	25.00	1	55.55
J.C. Price	9	3	1	48	23*	0	0	24.00	8/2	80.00
C.L. Fitzpatrick	9	2	1	24	18*	0	0	24.00	2	82.75
C. Bambury	7	4	0	63	38	0	0	15.75	6	46.32
J. Broadbent	5	3	0	41	25	0	0	13.66	1	31.53
C.L. Mason	8	1	0	11	11	0	0	11.00	3	84.61
A.J. Fahey	7	1	1	3	3*	0	0	–	1	75.00
J. Hayes.	4	–	–	–	–	–	–	–	–	–
L.C. Broadbent	2	–	–	–	–	–	–	–	–	–

Denotes not out.

BOWLING

	O	M	R	W	BB	5W/i	Avge
J. Broadbent	4	2	3	1	1/3	0	3.00
Z.J. Goss.	20.3	6	66	7	4/10	0	9.42
C.L. Mason	69.3	18	183	17	3/20	0	10.76
A.J. Fahey	45	6	153	13	3/11	0	11.76
J. Hayes.	31	14	69	5	2/16	0	13.80
T.A. McGregor	63	16	156	10	4/18	0	15.60
L.C. Broadbent	5	0	16	1	1/16	0	16.00
C.L. Fitzpatrick	84.4	15	287	11	3/22	0	26.09
K.L. Rolton	47	8	124	4	2/41	0	31.00
O.G. Magno	55	5	177	3	1/12	0	59.00

NEW ZEALAND v AUSTRALIA WOMEN

At Bert Sutcliffe Oval, Lincoln. November 29, 2000. Australia won by six wickets. Toss: Australia.

That this match took place at all was a minor miracle of ground maintenance, as dedicated staff worked literally throughout the night to remove an estimated 10,000 litres of water from the playing surface, to allow a start with only one hour's delay. After Australia won the toss, World Cup debutante Therese McGregor ran through the New Zealand top order to collect the first four wickets and the Player of the Match award, and Cathryn Fitzpatrick caused New Zealand captain Emily Drumm to retire hurt with a painful blow to the arm. Drumm returned to the crease with her team teetering at five for 48 in the 24th over, but her spirited innings could only push the total to 166, which never looked likely to be adequate. Karen Rolton played the innings of the day, building on the solid foundation provided by Lisa Keightley and Joanne Broadbent to see the Australians safely home with 15 balls to spare. She finished with 51 not out from only 55 balls, including a straight-driven six from spinner Catherine Campbell.

Player of the Match: T.A. McGregor.

New Zealand

A.M. O'Leary c Keightley b McGregor	7 (21)	C.M. Nicholson not out	19 (23)
†R.J. Rolls c Price b McGregor	0 (2)	K.M. Keenan c Bambury b Mason . .	7 (18)
*E.C. Drumm c Magno b Rolton	74 (111)	C.A. Campbell not out	1 (1)
D.A. Hockley c Mason b McGregor . .	11 (30)		
H.M. Tiffen lbw b McGregor	2 (9)	L-b 5, w 3, n-b 1	9
K.A. Ramel c Mason b Fahey	32 (60)		
H.M. Watson c Price b Mason	1 (20)	(50 overs, 178 mins) 166	
R.J. Pullar c Bambury b Rolton	3 (6)	Fall: 2 13 35 39 48 119 138 138 165	

Bowling: Fitzpatrick 10–1–26–0; McGregor 10–2–18–4; Mason 10–2–29–2; Magno 5–0–17–0; Rolton 9–0–41–2; Fahey 6–0–30–1.

Australia

L.M. Keightley c Nicholson b Campbell	44 (83)	O.J. Magno not out	0 (2)
*B.J. Clark b Keenan	1 (10)	B 1, l-b 1, w 6	8
J. Broadbent c and b Ramel	25 (77)		
K.L. Rolton not out	51 (54)	(47.3 overs, 179 mins) . . . . .(4 wkts)167	
C. Bambury run out (Pullar/Nicholson)	38 (59)	Fall: 8 67 84 155	

†J.C. Price, C.L. Fitzpatrick, C.L. Mason, A.J. Fahey and T.A. McGregor did not bat.

Bowling: Keenan 10–1–26–1; Nicholson 9.3–2–30–0; Pullar 9–1–30–0; Tiffen 6–0–21–0; Ramel 6–0–27–1; Campbell 6–0–22–1; Hockley 1–0–9–0.

Umpires: B.F. Bowden and B.G. Jerling.

AUSTRALIA v SRI LANKA

At Hagley Oval, Christchurch. December 1, 2000. Australia won by 200 runs. Toss: Australia.

Australia completely dominated this first-ever clash between the two nations. Although the Sri Lankans showed considerable tenacity in the early stages of both innings, they lacked depth in both batting and bowling, and the Australians punished them mercilessly in all facets of the game. Karen Rolton continued her form from the first match with a blistering unbeaten 154 from a mere 118 balls, and she was ably supported in century stands by both Lisa Keightley and Olivia Magno. Julie Hayes celebrated her international debut with two wickets in one over, and Avril Fahey returned the outstanding figures of 3/11 as the Sri Lankans managed only 82.

Player of the Match: K. L. Rolton.

Australia

*B. J. Clark c Ekanayake b Silva	18 (39)	L-b 4, w 12	16
L. M. Keightley b Abeysinghe	56 (94)		
K. L. Rolton not out	154 (118)	(50 overs, 178 mins) (3 wkts)	282
O. J. Magno run out (Ekanayake)	38 (49)	Fall: 36 153 282	

Z. J. Goss, C. L. Fitzpatrick, J. Hayes, A. J. Fahey, J. Broadbent, C. L. Mason and †J. C. Price did not bat.

Bowling: Silva 10–1–37–1; Senevirathne 10–2–49–0; Indralatha 2–0–24–0; Sugathadasa 4–0–22–0; Mala 10–1–49–0; Perera 4–0–28–0; Abeysinghe 5–0–36–1; Fernando 5–0–33–0.

Sri Lanka

K. H. Liyanarachchi c Keightley b Fitzpatrick	0 (7)	A. A. D. Indralatha b Fahey	12 (33)
L. D. V. W. de Silva b Hayes	17 (30)	K. R. Perera b Magno	2 (30)
H. D. W. Fernando c and b Fahey	15 (44)	†T. P. Ekanayake not out	6 (17)
*S. A. R. C. Silva c Broadbent b Hayes	0 (3)	A. D. J. Mala run out (Goss/Price)	6 (9)
G. C. P. Sugathadasa b Mason	0 (15)	B 1, l-b 5, w 4	10
C. R. Senevirathne c Keightley b Fahey	6 (21)	(39 overs, 121 mins)	82
A. D. H. Abeysinghe b Goss	8 (25)	Fall: 0 29 36 37 53 53 67 75 82	

Bowling: Fitzpatrick 7–2–17–1; Hayes 7–3–16–2; Mason 5–2–10–1; Fahey 7–1–11–3; Goss 6–3–10–1; Magno 7–2–12–1.

Umpires: B. F. Bowden and K. Cross.

AUSTRALIA v IRELAND

At Hagley Park No. 2, Christchurch. December 3, 2000. Australia won by ten wickets. Toss Ireland.

By the end of this match all members of the touring party had played at least once, and all had made a valid claim for inclusion in the top eleven. Zoe Goss snared four wickets to be named Player of the Match, Louise Broadfoot made her debut and claimed her first wicket, and Joanne Broadbent also made a rare, and successful, return to the bowling crease. At four for 20 the Irish seemed in danger of posting their lowest total against Australia, but their next two pairs added 60 before Goss triggered a collapse. Belinda Clark and Lisa Keightley were untroubled in quickly posting the required 91 runs. Australia have never lost a wicket batting second against Ireland.

Player of the Match: Z. J. Goss.

Ireland

K. N. Young c Rolton b McGregor	...	2	(26)	S. A. Young lbw b Goss	0	(5)
†A. Linehan c Fitzpatrick b Goss	....	5	(26)	L. D. Molins b Goss	0	(6)
C. M. Beggs b Rolton		18	(77)	I. M. Joyce not out	4	(3)
*M. E. Grealey b Goss		5	(6)			
C. M. O'Leary st Price b Hayes	.....	0	(15)	B 1, l-b 2, w 16	19	
C. O'Neill run out (Broadfoot/Goss)	..	28	(107)			
C. M. A. Shillington c Clark b Broadfoot		9	(25)	(49.3 overs, 161 mins)	90	
B. M. McDonald lbw b Broadbent	....	0	(2)	Fall: 9 10 17 20 60 80 80 81 83 90		

Bowling: Fitzpatrick 9–2–31–0; McGregor 10–4–14–1; Goss 9.3–3–10–4; Hayes 7–3–5–1; Rolton 5–3–8–1; Broadfoot 5–0–16–1; Broadbent 4–2–3–1.

Australia

L. M. Keightley not out		49	(71)
*B. J. Clark not out		40	(52)
L-b 1, w 1		2	
(20.3 overs, 63 mins)	(0 wkts)	91	

K. L. Rolton, J. Broadbent, L. C. Broadfoot, †J. C. Price, C. L. Fitzpatrick, Z. J. Goss, J. Hayes, C. Bambury and T. A. McGregor did not bat.

Bowling: McDonald 5.3–0–24–0; O'Neill 7–0–25–0; S. A. Young 3–0–15–0; Joyce 3–0–18–0; K. N. Young 2–0–8–0.

Umpires: B. F. Bowden and D. M. Quested

AUSTRALIA v INDIA

At Bert Sutcliffe Oval, Lincoln. December 6, 2000. Australia won by 51 runs. Toss: Australia.

In the first encounter between the two teams since the tensely fought semi-final in the 1997 World Cup, Australia ran out comfortable winners by 51 runs, although not before some nervous moments. In front of an appreciative crowd, many taking a break from an international soil science conference at the Lincoln University campus, Karen Rolton continued on her merry way with another half-century, taking her aggregate to 266 runs from three innings and only one dismissal. Lisa Keightley again provided a solid foundation for the innings, and an enterprising partnership between Olivia Magno and Julia Price added 42 vital runs in 19 minutes at the end. In reply India began confidently, putting on 59 runs before losing Anju Jain to a direct hit from Magno. At three for 154 India were threatening, but the experienced Australian attack regained control, backed up by some excellent fielding. Cathryn Fitzpatrick and Charmaine Mason smothered the Indian strokeplay, and the last five wickets fell for 11 runs, leaving India well short.

Player of the Match: L. M. Keightley.

Australia

*B. J. Clark c and b Shastri		27	(53)	†J. C. Price not out	23	(14)
L. M. Keightley b Rau		74	(116)			
K. L. Rolton run out (Shastri/Jain)	....	61	(72)	L-b 3, w 4	7	
C. Bambury c Harikrishna b Rau	.....	1	(8)			
J. Broadbent c Jain b David		6	(13)	(50 overs, 183 mins)	(5 wkts) 223	
O. J. Magno not out		24	(24)	Fall: 55 165 169 170 181		

C. L. Fitzpatrick, C. L. Mason, A. J. Fahey and T. A. McGregor did not bat.

Bowling: Harikrishna 7–1–31–0; Margrate 7–2–23–0; David 10–0–58–1; Shastri 9–0–44–1; Kulkarni 9–0–29–0; Rau 8–0–35–2.

India

*†A. Jain run out (Magno)	36	(65)
A. Chopra c Bambury b McGregor	47	(105)
P. Rau c Bambury b McGregor	25	(44)
C. Kaul b McGregor	24	(23)
H. Kala run out (Clark)	9	(17)
R. Shastri c Price b Fitzpatrick	0	(7)
S. Harikrishna not out	7	(16)

R. Margrate b Mason	0	(2)
K. Arundhati c Clark b Mason	0	(4)
D. M. Kulkarni c not out	2	(17)
B 1, l-b 11, w 10	22	
(50 overs, 182 mins) (8 wkts)	172	
Fall: 59 114 140 154 157 163 165 165		

N. David did not bat.

Bowling: Fitzpatrick 10–2–26–1; McGregor 10–0–38–3; Rolton 6–0–25–0; Mason 10–3–22–2; Magno 7–1–24–0; Fahey 7–1–25–0.

Umpires: K. Cross and S. J. A. Taufel.

AUSTRALIA v ENGLAND

At Lincoln Green, December 10, 2000. Australia won by 54 runs. Toss: Australia.

England showed some glimmers of their potential but were outclassed by an Australian side which demonstrated its all-round depth after a shaky start. Veteran England medium-pacer Clare Taylor set Australia back by dismissing the top three – Clark, Keightley and Rolton – but when her overs were finished, the Australians set about regaining control. Zoe Goss played sensibly and was unlucky to miss out on a half-century, but the real difference between the sides was highlighted by the critical contribution of the middle and lower order. Olivia Magno, Julia Price, Therese McGregor and Cathryn Fitzpatrick accelerated the scoring rate making 30 runs in the last three overs, to push the total beyond the English reach. Fitzpatrick removed both England openers in her opening overs, and combined with Charmaine Mason to mop up the tail. In between, Avril Fahey continued her fine form to destroy the middle order. The one note souring this victory was a hamstring injury to Australia's Joanne Broadbent which ruled her out of the remainder of the tournament.

Player of the Match: C. L. Fitzpatrick.

Australia

L. M. Keightley b C. E. Taylor	10	(32)
*B. J. Clark c Holden b C. E. Taylor	2	(10)
K. L. Rolton c Pearson b C. E. Taylor	17	(38)
Z. J. Goss lbw b Reynard	49	(79)
J. Broadbent b Connor	10	(40)
O. J. Magno c Daniels b Reynard	32	(51)
†J. C. Price lbw b Connor	15	(18)

T. A. McGregor not out	21	(23)
C. L. Fitzpatrick not out	18	(10)
L-b 2, w 13, n-b 1	16	
(50 overs, 169 mins) (7 wkts)	190	
Fall: 4 26 35 66 133 134 158		

C. L. Mason and A. J. Fahey did not bat.

Bowling: C. E. Taylor 10–3–30–3; Pearson 10–0–40–0; Collyer 10–0–20–0; Connor 10–0–48–2; Holden 5–0–26–0; Reynard 5–0–24–2.

England

C. M. Edwards b Fitzpatrick	0	(2)		
K. M. Leng b Fitzpatrick	12	(22)		
B. Daniels b Mason	28	(66)		
S. C. Taylor c McGregor b Fahey	45	(85)		
†J. Cassar c Price b Rolton	0	(11)		
*C. J. Connor c Clark b Fahey	22	(35)		
M. Reynard lbw b Mason	15	(30)		
S. V. Collyer c Magno b Fahey	2	(7)		

C.E. Taylor c sub (J. Hayes) b Fitzpatrick ... 3 (13)
D..Holden b Mason 2 (11)
L. C. Pearson not out 0 (3)

B 3, w 4 7

(47.3 overs, 156 mins)   136
Fall: 0 13 65 77 93 117 125 130 136 136

Bowling: Fitzpatrick 9–3–22–3; McGregor 7–1–14–0; Mason 8.3–3–20–3; Magno 8–0–25–0; Rolton 4–0–11–1; Fahey 6–0–23–3; Goss 5–0–18–0.

Umpires: R. S. Dunne and P. R. Williams.

AUSTRALIA v SOUTH AFRICA

At Bert Sutcliffe Oval, Lincoln. December 13, 2000. Australia won by nine wickets. Toss: South Africa.

South Africa hit their highest score against Australia, thanks largely to an enterprising 74-run partnership between Cindy Eksteen and Anina Burger. Cathryn Fitzpatrick and Charmaine Mason were again Australia's most potent weapons, confirming their standing as the most effective final-overs bowling partnership in the world. Karen Rolton then blasted her second century of the tournament in a display of power and precision hitting to take Australia to victory in half the allotted overs. Rolton and Belinda Clark, for once taking the back seat, took less than 90 minutes to overhaul the target. Along the way, Rolton broke the record for the fastest limited-overs century by a woman, ironically taking the record from Clark's 64-ball century at the last World Cup. Rolton took seven balls from the record, and her second fifty came in only 21 balls, including at one stage nine boundaries from 13 deliveries. Regardless of where the ball was bowled, Rolton had a shot for it. With this victory, Australia was guaranteed first place on the points table.

Player of the Match: K. L. Rolton.

South Africa

L. Olivier c Mason b Hayes	34	(74)		
H. Strydom c Price b Mason	7	(32)		
†M. Terblanche c Rolton b Goss	22	(50)		
A. A. Burger b Fitzpatrick	44	(70)		
C. E. Eksteen b Mason	46	(62)		
S. Viljoen b Fitzpatrick	3	(6)		
D. J. Reid b Mason	0	(5)		

Y. van der Merwe not out 0 (1)
A. Kuylaars run out (Hayes/Mason) . 0 (1)

L-b 6, w 5, n-b 2 13

(50 overs, 165 mins)   (8 wkts) 169
Fall: 18 53 71 145 165 168 169 169

*K. Price and S. D. van Zyl did not bat.

Bowling: Fitzpatrick 10–2–37–2; McGregor 6–0–15–0; Mason 10–1–29–3; Magno 10–1–33–0; Hayes 9–3–32–1; Goss 3–0–8–1; Rolton 2–0–9–0.

Australia

*B. J. Clark not out	49	(71)	
C. Bambury b van der Merwe	10	(12)	
K. L. Rolton not out	107	(67)	
W 5	5		

(25 overs, 93 mins)   (1 wkt) 171
Fall: 20

Z. J. Goss, O. J. Magno, †J. C. Price, C. L. Fitzpatrick, L. C. Broadfoot, C. L. Mason, J. Hayes and T. A. McGregor did not bat.

Bowling: van der Merwe 8–0–40–1; van Zyl 5–0–39–0; Eksteen 8–0–65–0; Price 4–0–27–0.

Umpires: B. G. Jerling and D. M. Quested.

AUSTRALIA v NETHERLANDS

At Lincoln Green, December 16, 2000. Australia won by ten wickets. Toss: Netherlands.

Australia recorded an emphatic victory over Netherlands at breakneck pace to finish undefeated. The Australians were asked to bowl first, and soon had the Dutch in deep trouble at two for eight from 13 overs, with Julie Hayes and Charmaine Mason giving nothing away. A solid partnership between Pauline te Beest and Rowan Milburn pushed the total above 50, but Avril Fahey ripped through the middle order to return her third three-wicket haul of the tournament, and restrict the Dutch to seven for 107. Such was the pace with which the Australian bowlers sped through their overs – they had bowled 22 in the first hour and 42 by the end of the second hour – that the Australian openers were required to begin their innings before the lunch break, and they did so in fine form. After seven overs, they had scored 43 of the required runs, with Belinda Clark on 17 and Lisa Keightley on 19. After lunch the momentum slowed, but the openers still reached the target in the 24th over.

Player of the Match: L. M. Keightley.

Netherlands

M. A. Koster b Mason	2	(32)		L. Hoitink c Bambury b Fahey	0	(10)
H. Rambaldo c Price b Hayes	4	(15)		M. De Boer st Price b Fahey	12	(14)
*P. te Beest c sub (L. C. Broadfoot)				C. de Fouw not out	2	(21)
b Magno	42	(69)		L-b 3, w 11	14	
†R. C. Milburn c Clark b Fahey	16	(68)				
C. Salomons run out (Keightley/Magno)	3	(8)		(50 overs, 143 mins)	(7 wkts) 107	
T. van der Gun not out	12	(63)		Fall: 4 8 61 66 75 75 97		

S. Kottman and E. Reynolds did not bat.

Bowling: Mason 7–5–4–1; Hayes 8–5–16–1; Fitzpatrick 10–1–28–0; Magno 7–0–23–1; Fahey 8–3–19–3; Rolton 7–4–8–0; Goss 3–0–6–0.

Australia

L. M. Keightley not out	51	(70)
*B. J. Clark not out	48	(74)
W 10	10	

(24 overs, 65 mins)   (0 wkts) 109

K. L. Rolton, C. Bambury, O. J. Magno, Z. J. Goss, †J. C. Price, C. L. Fitzpatrick, C. L. Mason, A. J. Fahey and J. Hayes did not bat.

Bowling: Reynolds 7–0–39–0; Kottman 7–0–24–0; De Boer 5–1–10–0; Salomons 4–0–22–0; de Fouw 1–0–14–0.

Umpires: K. Cross and P. R. Williams.

QUALIFYING TABLE

	Played	Won	Lost	Points	Net run-rate
Australia	7	7	0	14	1.984
New Zealand	7	6	1	12	2.002
India	7	5	2	10	0.711
South Africa	7	4	3	8	−0.403
England	7	3	4	6	0.440
Sri Lanka	7	2	5	4	−1.572
Ireland	7	1	6	2	−0.975
Netherlands	7	0	7	0	−2.098

Net run-rate was calculated by subtracting runs conceded per over from runs scored per over.

FIRST SEMI-FINAL

AUSTRALIA v SOUTH AFRICA

At Bert Sutcliffe Oval, Lincoln. December 18, 2000. Australia won by nine wickets. Toss: Australia.

Australia repeated their nine-wicket victory of the round robin, after South Africa had once again registered their highest score against Australia. The South Africans played their shots from the beginning and scored the highest total against Australia so far in the tournament. Charmaine Mason made the initial breakthrough, with Hanri Strydom caught behind by Julia Price in the 15th over. This took both participants to new Australian records – Mason passing Lyn Fullston as the highest wicket-taker, and Price, with her 50th dismissal, overtaking Christina Matthews as the most prolific wicket-keeper. Opening batter Linda Olivier top-scored with 41, but the highlight was a stylish 28 from 33 balls by 17-year-old Sunette Viljoen. Belinda Clark and Lisa Keightley then demonstrated why they are the best opening pair in world cricket. They played every ball on its merits, but when they unleashed their strokes, their power, timing and grace were exceptional. For Clark, the innings represented something of a return to form, while Keightley continued in the same relentless fashion she had shown all through the carnival, and collected her third Player of the Match award. Only Cindy Eksteen showed some ability to restrain the scoring rate. In the other semi-final two days later New Zealand comprehensively defeated a disappointing Indian team to set up the long-expected final clash.

Player of the Match: L. M. Keightley.

South Africa

L. Olivier c Fitzpatrick b Fahey	41	(101)
H. Strydom c Price b Mason	22	(39)
†M. Terblanche lbw b Magno	10	(17)
A. A. Burger b Mason	14	(19)
C.E. Eksteen c Goss b Fahey	16	(29)
S. Viljoen c Magno b Fitzpatrick	28	(33)
A. Hodgkinson run out (Magno/Price)	22	(49)
Y. van der Merwe b Mason	2	(6)
D.J. Reid not out	5	(7)
A. Kuylaars not out	3	(2)
B 1, l-b 4, w 10, n-b 2	17	
(50 overs, 174 mins) (8 wkts)	180	

Fall: 38 54 80 107 107 164 168 176

*K. Price did not bat.

Bowling: Fitzpatrick 10–0–48–1; McGregor 10–4–31–0; Mason 10–0–39–3; Magno 5–1–21–1; Rolton 8–1–10–0; Fahey 7–1–26–2.

Australia

*B.J. Clark st Terblanche b Eksteen	75	(79)
L.M. Keightley not out	91	(97)
K.L. Rolton not out	2	(14)
L-b 1, w 10, n-b 2	13	
(31.2 overs, 111 mins) (1 wkt)	181	

Fall: 170

T. A. McGregor, †J.C. Price, A.J. Fahey, C.L. Fitzpatrick, Z.J. Goss, C.L. Mason, C. Bambury and O.J. Magno did not bat.

Bowling: van der Merwe 7–1–34–0; Strydom 6.2–0–38–0; Price 4–0–30–0; Eksteen 9–0–39–1; Viljoen 5–0–39–0.

Umpires: B.F. Bowden and R.S. Dunne.
TV Umpire: P.R. Williams.

SECOND SEMI-FINAL

NEW ZEALAND v INDIA

At Bert Sutcliffe Oval, Lincoln. December 20, 2000. New Zealand won by nine wickets. Toss: India. India 117 (P. Rau 67, A. Jain 16; K. A. Ramel 2/12, C. M. Nicholson 2/15, R. J. Pullar 2/29); New Zealand one for 121 (A.M. O'Leary 50*, E. C. Drumm 47*, R.J. Rolls 23).

FINAL

NEW ZEALAND v AUSTRALIA

At Bert Sutcliffe Oval, Lincoln. December 23, 2000. New Zealand won by four runs. Toss: New Zealand.

In a day of fluctuating weather, fortunes and power supply, New Zealand did just enough to sneak over the line for a four-run victory. New Zealand captain Emily Drumm won the toss and chose to bat first. After a 31-minute rain interruption – the only time lost to the weather since the first match of the tournament – Therese McGregor got the Australians off to a flying start, dismissing Anna O'Leary and Drumm and catching a big hit from Rebecca Rolls on the mid-wicket boundary. Avril Fahey claimed the prize scalp of Debbie Hockley, Zoe Goss chimed in with the wicket of Haidee Tiffen, and Charmaine Mason and Cathryn Fitzpatrick cleaned up the tail. Karen Rolton finished the innings off with a direct hit which found Catherine Campbell short of her ground, and the Australians needed 185 to take home their fifth World Cup title.

Under clearing skies, disaster struck in the first over with Lisa Keightley edging Katrina Keenan to wicket-keeper Rolls for a duck. The innings fell into further disarray when Karen Rolton, the tournament's top run-scorer, was fractionally short of her crease on a quick single, leaving Australia two for 2 in the third over. Belinda Clark gradually took control, and she and Cherie Bambury took Australia to 85 before Bambury chipped a leading edge to Hockley from the bowling of Rachel Pullar. Zoe Goss provided Catherine Campbell with the opportunity to draw level with Charmaine Mason as the world's leading wicket-taker as she was beaten by a sharply turning delivery, and Olivia Magno was bowled by a beauty from Keenan. Therese McGregor played sensibly in support of Clark, who was steadily taking her side closer to victory, and the two put on 35 valuable runs before Clark finally played the wrong line to a straight one from Clare Nicholson and was bowled behind her legs. Sensing that Clark's was the critical wicket, the New Zealanders piled on the pressure, but McGregor, Fitzpatrick, Mason and Fahey continued to work the ball for singles and the occasional boundary. Fitzpatrick was given out in what is possibly the first time a third umpire has had to adjudicate on a "bowled" decision. Brian Jerling ruled that Kathryn Ramel's delivery had indeed brushed Fitzpatrick's stumps. With nine wickets down, Australia needed five runs off the last over, but Mason edged the first ball to the wicket-keeper, and New Zealand were the world champions.

Player of the Match: B.J. Clark. *Player of the Tournament:* L.M. Keightley.

New Zealand

A. M. O'Leary b McGregor	1	(8)	R. J. Pullar not out	9	(5)
†R. J. Rolls c McGregor b Mason	34	(47)	K. M. Keenan b Fitzpatrick	0	(2)
*E. C. Drumm c Price b McGregor	21	(29)	C. A. Campbell run out (Rolton)	0	(1)
D. A. Hockley lbw b Fahey	24	(69)	L-b 9, w 8, n-b 1	18	
H. M. Tiffen c Bambury b Goss	14	(33)			
K. A. Ramel c Clark b Fitzpatrick	41	(63)	(48.4 overs, 174 mins)	184	
H. M. Watson b Fitzpatrick	11	(15)	Fall: 17 60 60 92 121 136 172 175		
C. M. Nicholson b Mason	11	(21)	184 184		

Bowling: Fitzpatrick 9.4–2–52–3; McGregor 10–5–26–2; Mason 9–2–30–2; Magno 6–0–22–0; Goss 4–0–14–1; Rolton 6–0–12–0; Fahey 4–0–19–1.

Australia

L. M. Keightley c Rolls b Keenan	0	(4)	C. L. Fitzpatrick b Ramel	6	(19)
*B. J. Clark b Nicholson	91	(102)	C. L. Mason c Rolls b Nicholson	11	(13)
K. L. Rolton run out (Watson)	1	(7)	A. J. Fahey not out	3	(4)
C. Bambury c Hockley b Pullar	14	(57)			
Z. J. Goss b Campbell	1	(11)	B 1, l-b 6, w 12, n-b 1	20	
O. J. Magno b Keenan	4	(13)			
†J. C. Price b Pullar	10	(28)	(49.1 overs, 200 mins)	180	
T. A. McGregor run out (Watson)	19	(37)	Fall: 0 2 85 88 95 115 150 159 175 180		

Bowling: Keenan 10–3–19–2; Pullar 10–0–35–2; Tiffen 5–1–27–0; Ramel 5–0–26–1; Campbell 10–2–28–1; Nicholson 9.1–1–38–2.

Umpires: P. D. Parker and D. M. Quested.
TV Umpire: B. G. Jerling.

AUSTRALIAN WOMEN'S NATIONAL CRICKET LEAGUE, 2000-01

The New South Wales Institute of Sport retained their national title, but the 2000-01 season saw some changes in relative strength among the other competing states. Queensland, the only team to beat New South Wales during the season, rose from fourth to take part in their first finals series at national level. Last season's finalists Western Australia slumped to finish fourth, Victoria slid from third to last, while South Australia rose from last to third. New South Wales have now taken on, and defeated, each of the other four states in the past four finals. Based on the season's results, it is difficult to foresee anything other than continued dominance by New South Wales in 2001-02.

South Australia's Karen Rolton topped the batting statistics with 492 runs at 70.28 to take out the Player of the Series award. Zoe Goss of Western Australia (342 runs at 57.00) and Belinda Clark of New South Wales (451 at 56.37) had the only other batting averages over 40. New South Wales left-arm seamer Emma Liddell set a wicket-taking record with 17 wickets at 13.05, and her team-mate, pace bowler Bronwyn Calver, was not far behind with 15 wickets at 17.66. Australian wicket-keeper Julia Price demonstrated her all-round ability in scoring Queensland's maiden century in the league, while Clark pushed her league run total over 2,000, and evergreens Calver and Cathryn Fitzpatrick of Victoria took their wicket tallies past 50.

At Adelaide Oval No. 2, Adelaide, October 14, 2000. New South Wales won by seven wickets. Toss: New South Wales. South Australia five for 172 (K. L. Rolton 75, J. Broadbent 60); New South Wales three for 176 (L. M. Keightley 85*, B. J. Clark 51).

At Adelaide Oval No. 2, Adelaide, October 15, 2000. New South Wales won by 22 runs. Toss: New South Wales. New South Wales nine for 179 (M. A. J. Goszko 65, E. Liddell 35*; K. L. Rolton 2/32, N. Simon 2/39); South Australia eight for 157 (K. L. Rolton 84, J. Broadbent 41; B. L. Calver 3/18, J. Hayes 2/38).

At Lilac Hill Oval, Perth, October 21, 2000. Western Australia won by seven wickets. Toss: Western Australia. Victoria eight for 130 (L. Broadfoot 44; A.J. Fahey 2/19, Z.J. Goss 2/21, J. Burnett 2/21); Western Australia three for 132 (E.P. Campbell 66).

At Melvista Oval, Perth, October 22, 2000. Victoria won by 19 runs. Toss: Victoria. Victoria five for 212 (L. Broadfoot 91, M. Jones 50; C. Bambury 2/31); Western Australia eight for 193 (Z.J. Goss 66; C.L. Mason 4/30, C.R. Smith 2/30).

At Brisbane Grammar School, Brisbane, October 28, 2000. New South Wales won by 19 runs. Toss: New South Wales. New South Wales nine for 167 (B.J. Clark 59, A.J. Owens 31*; K. Klibbe 4/35, C. Kross 2/25, A.J. Farrell 2/31); Queensland 148 (T. Brown 48; J. Hayes 3/11, B.L. Calver 2/18, T.A. McGregor 2/22).

At Woodville Oval, Adelaide, October 28, 2000. Western Australia won by 1 run. Toss: Western Australia. Western Australia eight for 143 (Z.J. Goss 68; N. Simon 2/23, K.L. Rolton 2/24); South Australia nine for 142 (K.L. Rolton 52; Z.J. Goss 3/18).

At Brisbane Grammar School, Brisbane, October 29, 2000. Queensland won by 2 runs. Toss: New South Wales. Queensland eight for 176 (M. Bulow 47, S. Cooper 45; D. Nelson 3/27, T.A. McGregor 2/23); New South Wales 174 (B.J. Clark 40, L.C. Sthalekar 31; C. Kross 2/17, L. Shields 2/26, B. Buckley 2/29).

At Woodville Oval, Adelaide, October 29, 2000. South Australia won by 5 runs. Toss: South Australia. South Australia four for 155 (K.L. Rolton 45, J. Broadbent 34); Western Australia 150 (Z.J. Goss 55; J. Broadbent 3/20).

At Harry Trott Oval, Melbourne, November 4, 2000. Victoria won by 43 runs. Toss: Victoria. Victoria six for 152 (S. Theodore 45; B. Buckley 2/11); Queensland 109 (M. Bulow 54; L. Broadfoot 3/24, M. Foster 2/24).

At Harry Trott Oval, Melbourne, November 5, 2000. Queensland won by three wickets. Toss: Victoria. Victoria eight for 166 (J. Franklin 49; B. Buckley 2/24, S. Cooper 2/38); Queensland seven for 167 (M. Bulow 62, J.C. Price 49).

At Hurstville Oval, Sydney, November 11, 2000. New South Wales won by 102 runs. Toss: New South Wales. New South Wales seven for 208 (B.J. Clark 122*; J. Burnett 2/42); Western Australia 106 (E. Liddell 3/19, L.C. Sthalekar 3/23).

At Hurstville Oval, Sydney, November 12, 2000. New South Wales won by four wickets. Toss: Western Australia. Western Australia 104 (A. Gray 42; D. Nelson 3/9, J. Hayes 2/12, T.A. McGregor 2/14, E. Liddell 2/26); New South Wales six for 105 (M.A.J. Goszko 38; Z.J. Goss 2/18, J. Burnett 2/19).

At Allan Border Field, Brisbane, January 13, 2001. Queensland won by one wicket. Toss: South Australia. South Australia 155 (K.L. Rolton 45; C. Kross 3/21, K. Klibbe 2/33, T. Brown 2/33); Queensland nine for 156 (J.C. Price 73; J. Broadbent 3/28).

At Lavington Oval, Albury, January 13, 2001. New South Wales won by six wickets. Toss: Victoria. Victoria six for 160 (M. Jones 47, J.A. Franklin 42, S. Theodore 34*; B.L. Calver 2/34); New South Wales four for 161 (L.M. Keightley 74*, M.A.J. Goszko 53; M. Foster 2/37).

At Allan Border Field, Brisbane, January 14, 2001. South Australia won by six wickets. Toss: Queensland. Queensland 139 (S. Cooper 51, M. Bulow 34; O.J. Magno 5/25, K.L. Rolton 2/24, N. Simon 2/24); South Australia four for 140 (S. Nitschke 43, J. Broadbent 34*).

At Lavington Oval, Albury, January 14, 2001. New South Wales won by 69 runs. Toss: Victoria. New South Wales eight for 142 (B.J. Clark 53; C.L. Fitzpatrick 3/28, M. Foster 2/15); Victoria 73 (L.C. Sthalekar 4/7, B.L. Calver 2/11, T.A. McGregor 2/12, E. Liddell 2/12).

At the WACA Ground, Perth, January 20, 2001. Queensland won by 29 runs. Toss: Queensland. Queensland five for 258 (J.C. Price 112*, S. Cooper 60, M. Bulow 37; Z.J. Goss 2/41, D. Brown 2/52); Western Australia 229 (Z.J. Goss 66, A. Gray 38, A.J. Fahey 36*, E. Campbell 30; T. Brown 3/39, A.J. Farrell 2/37, B. Buckley 2/50).

At Punt Road Oval, Melbourne, January 20, 2001. Victoria won by 2 runs. Toss: Victoria. Victoria 138 (C.L. Fitzpatrick 39; J. Broadbent 2/27, N. Simon 2/29); South Australia 136 (K.L. Rolton 62, J. Broadbent 34; L. Broadfoot 4/14).

At WACA Ground, Perth, January 21, 2001. Western Australia won by nine wickets. Toss: Queensland. Queensland 89 (Z.J. Goss 3/14, A.J. Fahey 3/18, D. Brown 2/15); Western Australia one for 90 (H. Taylor 33, A. Gray 31*).

At Punt Road Oval, Melbourne, January 21, 2001. South Australia won by six wickets. Toss: Victoria. Victoria nine for 156 (L. Ebsary 3/21, K.L. Rolton 2/31); South Australia four for 157 (K.L. Rolton 100*; M. Foster 2/15).

POINTS TABLE, 2000-01

	Played	Won	Lost	Points	Net run-rate
New South Wales	8	7	1	42	0.623
Queensland	8	4	4	24	−0.382
South Australia	8	3	5	18	0.017
Western Australia	8	3	5	18	−0.106
Victoria	8	3	5	18	−0.154

Net run-rate was calculated by subtracting runs conceded per over from runs scored per over.

FIRST FINAL

NEW SOUTH WALES v QUEENSLAND

At Bankstown Memorial Oval, Bankstown, January 26, 2001. New South Wales won by 33 runs. Toss: New South Wales.

New South Wales made a solid if unspectacular start to their title defence, with Australian openers Belinda Clark and Lisa Keightley subdued by a tight spell from Cindy Kross, whose ten overs cost only 16 runs. The fireworks began after the two departed with the score on 65, bringing together Michelle Goszko and Lisa Sthalekar for the critical partnership of the game. Goszko was in sparkling form, placing her powerful shots to all parts of the ground, and clearing the boundary for a memorable six. The pair put on 116 runs in just 72 minutes. Shannon Cunneen, in her first-class debut, continued the run spree together with the experienced Julie Hayes and Bronwyn Calver to push the New South Wales total to a formidable 234. Queensland started the chase confidently, if slowly, to amass 70 runs without loss, but the introduction of Emma Liddell and Lisa Sthalekar turned the tide inexorably in New South Wales's favour. Sthalekar bowled superbly to concede a mere 20 runs from 10 overs, while Liddell's four wickets cut a swathe through the top order. The shining star for Queensland was left-hander Sally Cooper, who showed skill and persistence to finish unbeaten on 78 from only 63 balls, but she received too little support.

New South Wales

*B. J. Clark c Brown b Farrell	34	(67)		B. L. Calver not out	11	(7)
L. M. Keightley c Brandon b Klibbe	11	(27)				
M. A. J. Goszko c Thompson b Brown	80	(101)		L-b 5, w 16, n-b 1	22	
L. C. Sthalekar c Buckley b Brown	43	(64)				
S. Cunneen not out	21	(23)		(50 overs, 169 mins)	(5 wkts) 234	
J. Hayes c Pickering b Klibbe	12	(12)		Fall: 30 65 181 187 211		

A. Owens, E. Liddell, T. A. McGregor, †L. Coleman and D. Nelson did not bat.

Bowling: Brown 10–0–57–2; Kross 10–4–16–0; Klibbe 10–0–58–2; Farrell 8–0–41–1; Buckley 9–0–39–0; Shields 3–0–18–0.

Queensland

V. Pickering lbw b Liddell	35	(90)		L. Shields run out (Sthalekar/McGregor)	1	(4)
M. Bulow c Owens b Liddell	37	(80)		H. Thompson b Calver	0	(2)
*†J. C. Price c Calver b Liddell	15	(37)		B. Buckley run out (Clark)	1	(1)
S. Cooper not out	78	(80)		L-b 5, w 8	13	
M. Brandon b Liddell	1	(3)				
K. Klibbe run out (Nelson)	10	(6)		(48.3 overs, 168 mins)	201	
T. E. Brown c Clark b Calver	10	(7)		Fall: 70 80 124 126 149 189 194 197		
C. Kross c and b Calver	0	(1)		199 201		

A. Farrell did not bat.

Bowling: Calver 9.3–0–48–3; McGregor 8–0–45–0; Hayes 9–1–38–0; Sthalekar 10–1–20–0; Liddell 10–2–33–4; Nelson 2–0–12–0.

Umpires: R. Furtner and B. Hendricks.
TV Umpire: C. Laden.

SECOND FINAL

NEW SOUTH WALES v QUEENSLAND

At Bankstown Memorial Oval, January 27, 2001. New South Wales won by seven wickets. Toss: Queensland.

Needing a victory, Queensland took the initiative and chose to bat first, but they were unable to continue their form of the previous day and were dismissed for only 137. Melissa Bulow and Vanessa Pickering again provided a half-century opening partnership, but Queensland never recovered from the key loss of Sally Cooper. Kelly Klibbe played some useful shots, and Angela Farrell struck a massive six, but she was clean bowled from the following delivery to mark the end of the innings. In reply, New South Wales were untroubled, despite a brief flurry of wickets with the score at 70, and marched to their fifth consecutive title thanks to a typically dominant innings from Belinda Clark. The Australian captain was back to her best form, with a combination of deft placement and elegance, and she was well supported by Shannon Cunneen. Together the pair accumulated the necessary 68 runs for victory, with 16 overs to spare. Queensland were not disgraced, but they were outplayed by a team superior in all aspects of the game. The result was a fitting tribute to retiring New South Wales coach Steve Jenkin, who accepted the position of head coach of the Australian team from April.

Player of the Finals: E. Liddell. *Player of the Series:* K. L. Rolton (South Australia).

Queensland

M. Bulow lbw b Hayes	30	(63)	
V. Pickering c Hayes b Nelson	20	(32)	
S. Cooper c Sthalekar b Hayes	14	(25)	
*†J.C. Price c Hayes b Liddell	13	(41)	
L. Shields run out (McGregor/Coleman)	6	(33)	
T.E. Brown c Cunneen b Liddell	2	(11)	
M. Brandon c Calver b Liddell	12	(27)	
C. Kross c Cunneen b Sthalekar	0	(3)	

K. Klibbe c Keightley b Calver	19	(22)	
B. Buckley not out	4	(33)	
A. Farrell b McGregor	9	(8)	
B 1, l-b 1, w 6	8		
(49.3 overs, 164 mins)	137		

L. Randall did not bat.

Fall: 52 54 69 88 88 93 96 112 124 137

Bowling: Calver 10–0–28–1; McGregor 6.3–2–25–1; Nelson 5–1–13–1; Hayes 10–2–26–2; Sthalekar 10–2–18–1; Liddell 8–1–25–3.

New South Wales

L.M. Keightley c Pickering b Kross	4	(15)	
*B.J. Clark not out	76	(87)	
M.A.J. Goszko b Buckley	22	(43)	
L.C. Sthalekar c and b Buckley	0	(2)	
S. Cunneen not out	16	(57)	

L-b 1, w 19	20		
(34 overs, 119 mins)	(3 wkts)	138	

Fall: 17 70 70

A. Owens, B.L. Calver, T.A. McGregor, J. Hayes, E. Liddell, †L. Coleman and D. Nelson did not bat.

Bowling: Brown 4–0–23–0; Kross 10–3–24–1; Klibbe 7–0–38–0; Buckley 9–0–35–2; Farrell 3–0–15–0; Randall 1–0–2–0.

Umpires: R. Furtner and C. Laden.
TV Umpire: B. Hendricks.

PART FIVE: AUSTRALIANS OVERSEAS IN 2000-01

THE AUSTRALIANS IN INDIA, 2000-01

By MIKE COWARD

Failure to win in India and conquer what many regarded as the Australian team's "last frontier" should not diminish the greatness of Steve Waugh's side, which won 16 consecutive Tests before perhaps the most remarkable turnaround in the history of Test cricket at Kolkata (formerly known as Calcutta). Clearly such a subduing defeat, after being within a solitary wicket of a series win in perhaps just six playing days, will temper the argument that the team should be bracketed with Sir Donald Bradman's 1948 "Invincibles". By the tenor of his public statements in advance of the tour Steve Waugh realised that only the first Australian victory in India since 1969-70 would gain his team immortality. Victory would have been Australia's but for one of the greatest innings ever played – the consummate, chanceless 281 by the tall, amiable V. V. S. Laxman which so dramatically changed the direction of the Second Test and the series.

And, while much criticism can be levelled at the Australian batsmen, who again failed to come to terms with subcontinental conditions – 13 ducks for the series is a damning statistic – the mental strength, physical courage, self-belief and strength of character and resourcefulness of Waugh's men were beyond question. And these qualities were never more evident than in the final Test at Chennai, when time and again they somehow hauled themselves from the mat and in the end were just two wickets shy of an improbable win that would have seen them retain the Border–Gavaskar Trophy.

Laxman not only provided India with the impetus to win the series, but with the help of coach John Wright and aggressive captain Saurav Ganguly he changed the mindset of the Indian dressing room and lifted morale to new and spectacular heights. The metamorphosis was magical. Within a week there was no sign of the dispirited, erratic band brushed aside in Mumbai in three days and compelled to follow on 274 runs behind at Kolkata. In every respect the team was unrecognisable from the party humiliated in Australia just 14 months earlier and then badly beaten at home by South Africa.

Waugh, arguably the most influential thinker in the game now, was gracious in defeat, and with characteristically impeccable timing again promoted the joys of Test cricket. "For everyone watching these matches, they were great games," he said. "Either side could have probably won all three. If you like Test cricket, these are three of the best Tests you could ever want to see." This was unquestionably so. The cricket was often exceptional and the series was played to a backcloth of high drama and the customary quota of controversy before vast crowds. While the exact number of

THE AUSTRALIAN TOURING PARTY IN INDIA, 2000-01

Back row: J. Campbell *(fitness adviser)*, E.L. Alcott *(physiotherapist)*, D.R. Martyn, D.W. Fleming, M.S. Kasprowicz, J.N. Gillespie, C.R. Miller, M.L. Hayden, M.J. Walsh *(assistant manager/cricket analyst)*. *Front row:* J. Langer, R.T. Ponting, S.K. Warne, J.M. Buchanan *(coach)*, S.R. Waugh *(captain)*, A.C. Gilchrist *(vice-captain)*, S.R. Bernard *(manager)*, M.E. Waugh, G.D. McGrath, M.J. Slater. *Absent:* B.J. Haddin, N.W. Bracken, P.J. Farhart, I.J. Harvey, S. Lee, D.S. Lehmann, A. Symonds.

spectators at the three Tests will never be known – by necessity India is a land of approximations – a sensibly conservative aggregate is 550,000. The series also generated record television ratings and, presumably, advertising revenue.

The series arrested the attention of the international cricket community and substantially bolstered the image of the Border–Gavaskar Trophy at a time when renowned prizes such as the Ashes and the Frank Worrell Trophy had lost some of their lustre. More importantly, it may have reignited interest in Test cricket in a country notorious for its unhealthy preoccupation with the limited-overs game. Nothing, not even the World Cup, can generate the excitement and nerve-racking tension the cricket generated at Kolkata and Chennai. The euphoria which accompanied the triumph should prompt the often avaricious and self-serving administrators in India to rethink their responsibility to the game's traditional form and traditional values. For too long, all major reference points in Indian cricket have related to the compressed game.

Certainly as captain, and successor to the universally admired Sachin Tendulkar, Ganguly needs to pay greater heed to the history and conventions of the game. To his credit, he managed to ignore barbs about poor form and alleged indiscretions in his private life to eradicate the mental softness which has often retarded the progress of Indian teams. But while he showed a healthy willingness to fire a salvo or two across Waugh's bow, in the psychological battle which is so much a part of the contemporary game, his disregard or ignorance of the game's etiquette was unsettling. That he deliberately kept Waugh waiting for some minutes before the coin-tossing ceremony at Kolkata and Chennai brought no credit upon Ganguly, who was loudly jeered by crowds at the presentation ceremonies in Mumbai and Chennai. Little love was lost between Waugh, a proud, uncompromising, single-minded warrior from Sydney's working-class western suburbs, and Ganguly, a silky autocrat born to wealth and privilege in Kolkata. The tension was palpable each time they were required to be together.

Rarely can a series have been so dominated by the exploits of a handful of individuals. More remarkable is the fact that the outstanding performers, Laxman, Harbhajan Singh and Matthew Hayden, were generally regarded as peripheral players at the start of the series. Hayden accumulated a staggering 549 runs at 109.80, Laxman came of age as a Test cricketer in the most imposing manner, while Harbhajan revived memories of the legendary exploits of India's greatest spin bowlers. At the age of 20 and still very much learning his sophisticated off-spinning craft, Harbhajan took 32 wickets at 17.03, the second-best analysis for India in Test series and the fourth-best analysis in a three-Test series in the history of the game. And to think that at the start of the series the Indian cricket community was understandably despairing at the absence through injury of the gifted Anil Kumble.

AUSTRALIAN TOURING PARTY

S.R. Waugh (New South Wales) (*captain*), A.C. Gilchrist (Western Australia) (*vice-captain*), D.W. Fleming (Victoria), M.L. Hayden (Queensland), J.N. Gillespie (South Australia), M.S. Kasprowicz, (Queensland), J.L. Langer (Western Australia), D.R. Martyn (Western Australia), G.D. McGrath (New South Wales), C.R. Miller (Victoria), R.T. Ponting (Tasmania), M.J. Slater (New South Wales), S.K. Warne (Victoria) and M.E. Waugh (New South Wales).

B.J. Haddin (New South Wales) was called to join the touring party on standby for Gilchrist.

The Australian touring party for the international limited-overs series was as follows: S.R. Waugh (New South Wales) (*captain*), A.C. Gilchrist (Western Australia) (*vice-captain*), M.G. Bevan (New South Wales), N.W. Bracken (New South Wales), D.W. Fleming (Victoria), I.J. Harvey (Victoria), M.L. Hayden (Queensland), S. Lee (New South Wales), D.S. Lehmann (South Australia), G.D. McGrath (New South Wales), D.R. Martyn (Western Australia), R.T. Ponting (Tasmania), A. Symonds (Queensland), S.K. Warne (Victoria) and M.E. Waugh (New South Wales).

Manager: S.R. Bernard. *Coach:* J.M. Buchannan. *Physiotherapist:* P.J. Farhart. *Fitness Adviser:* J. Campbell. *Cricket Analyst:* M.J. Walsh.

AUSTRALIAN TOUR RESULTS

Test matches – Played 3: Won 1, Lost 2.
First-class matches – Played 6: Won 1, Lost 2, Drawn 3.
Wins – India.
Losses – India A, Mumbai, India Board President's XI, India (2).
Limited-overs internationals – Played 5: Won 3, Lost 2.
Other matches: Lost – Indian XI.

TEST MATCH AVERAGES

INDIA – BATTING

	M	I	NO	R	HS	100s	50s	Avge	Ct/St
V.V.S. Laxman	3	6	0	503	281	1	3	83.83	3
R.S. Dravid	3	6	0	338	180	1	1	56.33	6
S.R. Tendulkar	3	6	0	304	126	1	2	50.67	1
S.S. Das	3	6	0	173	84	0	1	28.83	5
S. Ramesh	3	6	0	162	61	0	1	27.00	3
S.S. Dighe	1	2	1	26	22*	0	0	26.00	0/1
S.V. Bahutule	1	2	1	21	21*	0	0	21.00	1
N.R. Mongia	2	4	1	60	28	0	0	20.00	5/1
S.C. Ganguly	3	6	0	106	48	0	0	17.67	4
Harbhajan Singh	3	6	3	34	17*	0	0	11.33	2
Zaheer Khan	2	4	1	30	23*	0	0	10.00	1
J. Srinath	1	2	0	12	12	0	0	6.00	1
N.M. Kulkarni	1	1	0	4	4	0	0	4.00	0
S.L. Venkatapathy Raju	1	1	0	4	4	0	0	4.00	0
R.L. Sanghvi	1	2	0	2	2	0	0	1.00	0
A.B. Agarkar	1	2	0	0	0	0	0	0.00	0
B.K. Venkatesh Prasad	1	1	1	7	7*	0	0	–	0

* *Denotes not out.*

BOWLING

	O	M	R	W	BB	5W/i	10W/m	Avge
Harbhajan Singh........	178.3	44	545	32	8/84	4	1	17.03
A. B. Agarkar	13	1	58	2	2/50	0	0	29.00
J. Srinath...............	18	3	77	2	2/60	0	0	38.50
R. L. Sanghvi	12.2	3	78	2	2/67	0	0	39.00
S. R. Tendulkar........	48	5	151	3	3/31	0	0	50.33
S. V. Bahutule..........	30	3	102	2	1/32	0	0	51.00
Zaheer Khan...........	55.4	15	189	3	2/89	0	0	63.00
S. C. Ganguly..........	17.2	4	65	1	1/44	0	0	65.00
S. L. V. Raju	35	5	116	1	1/58	0	0	116.00
N. M. Kulkarni	53	16	137	1	1/70	0	0	137.00
B. K. V. Prasad	33	6	102	0	–	0	0	–

AUSTRALIA – BATTING

	M	I	NO	R	HS	100s	50s	Avge	Ct
M. L. Hayden........	3	6	1	549	203	2	2	109.80	3
S. R. Waugh........	3	5	0	243	110	1	0	48.60	4
G. D. McGrath.......	3	5	4	47	21*	0	0	47.00	1
M. J. Slater..........	3	6	1	166	48	0	0	33.20	0
J. L. Langer	3	5	0	161	58	0	1	32.20	0
M. E. Waugh	3	5	0	149	70	0	2	29.80	8
A. C. Gilchrist	3	5	0	124	122	1	0	24.80	13
M. S. Kasprowicz	1	2	1	20	13*	0	0	20.00	0
J. N. Gillespie	3	5	0	54	46	0	0	10.80	0
S. K. Warne	3	5	0	50	39	0	0	10.00	2
D. W. Fleming.......	1	1	0	6	6	0	0	6.00	0
R. T. Ponting........	3	5	0	17	11	0	0	3.40	7
C. R. Miller	1	2	0	2	2	0	0	1.00	1

* Denotes not out.

BOWLING

	O	M	R	W	BB	5W/i	10W/m	Avge
G. D. McGrath	136.2	60	261	17	4/18	0	0	15.35
J. N. Gillespie	126.3	31	394	13	3/45	0	0	30.31
C. R. Miller.............	55	7	201	6	3/41	0	0	33.50
M. E. Waugh	36	6	106	3	3/40	0	0	35.33
S. K. Warne............	152.1	31	505	10	4/47	0	0	50.50
M. S. Kasprowicz	48	8	178	2	2/39	0	0	89.00
D. W. Fleming	30	4	99	1	1/55	0	0	99.00
M. J. Slater	2	1	4	0	–	0	0	–
M. L. Hayden	7	0	31	0	–	0	0	–
R. T. Ponting..........	14	2	43	0	–	0	0	–
J. L. Langer............	1	0	3	0	–	0	0	–

AUSTRALIAN FIRST-CLASS TOUR AVERAGES

BATTING

	M	I	NO	R	HS	100s	50s	Avge	Ct/St
M. S. Kasprowicz	3	6	3	194	92	0	1	64.67	0
M. L. Hayden........	6	12	1	709	203	2	2	64.45	4
S. R. Waugh.........	6	10	2	509	110	3	0	63.63	6
M. E. Waugh	5	7	0	375	164	1	3	53.57	9
R. T. Ponting	6	11	1	348	102*	2	2	34.80	12
G. D. McGrath.......	4	6	4	66	21*	0	0	33.00	1
J. L. Langer	6	11	0	346	115	1	1	31.45	1
D. R. Martyn	2	4	0	115	54	0	1	28.75	1
M. J. Slater..........	6	12	1	270	48	0	0	24.55	2
A. C. Gilchrist	5	9	0	176	122	1	0	19.56	18/2
J. N. Gillespie	4	7	0	116	57	0	1	16.57	0
B. J. Haddin	1	2	0	32	24	0	0	16.00	1
D. W. Fleming	4	6	2	64	29*	0	0	16.00	4
S. K. Warne	4	7	0	59	39	0	0	8.43	2
C. R. Miller	4	6	1	8	5	0	0	1.60	1

* Denotes not out.

BOWLING

	O	M	R	W	BB	5W/i	10W/m	Avge
G. D. McGrath	168.2	70	338	21	4/18	0	0	16.10
M. E. Waugh...........	46	8	133	5	3/40	0	0	26.60
J. N. Gillespie	145.3	39	449	15	3/45	0	0	29.93
C. R. Miller............	156.4	34	503	15	6/90	1	0	33.53
S. K. Warne	192.4	40	642	18	7/56	1	0	35.67
R. T. Ponting..........	23	2	76	2	2/10	0	0	38.00
M. S. Kasprowicz......	88.4	13	349	6	3/68	0	0	58.17
M. L. Hayden	15	0	70	1	1/37	0	0	70.00
D. W. Fleming	91	19	299	3	1/27	0	0	99.67
M. J. Slater	2	1	4	0	–	0	0	–
D. R. Martyn	4	1	11	0	–	0	0	–
J. L. Langer	1	0	3	0	–	0	0	–

INTERNATIONAL LIMITED-OVERS AVERAGES

INDIA – BATTING

	M	I	NO	R	HS	100s	50s	Avge	Ct/St	S-R
V. V. S. Laxman	5	5	0	291	101	1	2	58.20	0	85.59
V. K. Shewag	1	1	0	58	58	0	1	58.00	0	107.41
S. R. Tendulkar.....	5	5	0	280	139	1	1	56.00	2	120.17
H. K. Badani........	5	5	0	166	100	1	0	33.20	2	87.37
R. S. Dravid	5	5	0	146	80	0	1	29.20	1	74.49
Harbhajan Singh....	5	4	2	56	46	0	0	28.00	1	127.27
Zaheer Khan........	5	5	3	52	29	0	0	26.00	1	110.64
Yuvraj Singh	1	1	0	19	19	0	0	19.00	1	90.48
S. B. Joshi	1	1	0	19	19	0	0	19.00	0	82.61
V. Dahiya	5	5	1	75	51	0	1	18.75	6/1	93.75
S. C. Ganguly	5	5	0	93	74	0	1	18.60	4	49.73
R. R. Singh	1	1	0	16	16	0	0	16.00	0	50.00
J. Srinath..........	5	3	2	12	7*	0	0	12.00	1	109.09
D. Mongia..........	2	2	0	6	4	0	0	3.00	0	54.55
A. B. Agarkar	4	3	0	23	13	0	0	7.67	2	63.89
R. P. Singh	0	0	0	0	0	0	0	–	0	–

* Denotes not out.

BOWLING

	O	M	R	W	BB	Avge
V. K. Shewag	9	0	59	3	3/59	19.67
J. Srinath	43.2	2	239	9	3/49	26.56
S. R. Tendulkar	21	0	106	3	3/35	35.33
S. C. Ganguly	14	0	78	2	1/15	39.00
A. B. Agarkar	31	0	200	5	3/38	40.00
Zaheer Khan	39	0	225	4	2/34	56.25
Harbhajan Singh	47	0	237	4	3/37	59.25
R. R. Singh	6	0	37	0	–	–
Yuvraj Singh	3	0	16	0	–	–
S. B. Joshi	9.1	0	54	0	–	–

AUSTRALIA – BATTING

	M	I	NO	R	HS	100s	50s	Avge	Ct/St	S-R
M. E. Waugh	2	2	1	138	133*	1	0	138.00	3	95.17
M. G. Bevan	5	5	3	218	87*	0	1	109.00	1	79.85
M. L. Hayden	4	4	0	303	111	1	2	75.75	1	92.94
A. C. Gilchrist	5	4	0	172	76	0	2	43.00	4/1	105.52
R. T. Ponting	4	4	0	137	101	1	0	34.25	2	86.16
S. R. Waugh	5	4	0	93	35	0	0	23.25	3	84.55
I. J. Harvey	3	3	1	43	25*	0	0	21.50	1	78.18
S. K. Warne	4	2	0	31	18	0	0	15.50	3	62.00
D. R. Martyn	4	2	0	20	19	0	0	10.00	2	86.96
D. W. Fleming	4	2	1	9	9	0	0	9.00	1	112.50
A. Symonds	3	2	0	12	7	0	0	6.00	0	80.00
D. S. Lehmann	3	3	0	3	1	0	0	1.00	2	25.00
G. D. McGrath	5	2	1	0	0*	0	0	0.00	2	0.00
S. Lee	1	1	1	25	25*	0	0	–	1	227.27
N. W. Bracken	3	0	0	0	0	0	0	–	1	–

* Denotes not out.

BOWLING

	O	M	R	W	BB	Avge
S. R. Waugh	6	0	29	3	3/29	9.67
N. W. Bracken	27	3	112	5	2/21	22.40
G. D. McGrath	45.5	1	260	10	3/52	26.00
D. W. Fleming	38	3	188	6	2/34	31.33
I. J. Harvey	30	1	165	5	2/49	33.00
S. K. Warne	38	0	222	4	3/38	55.50
D. R. Martyn	15	0	100	1	1/25	100.00
A. Symonds	22	0	118	1	1/40	118.00
M. G. Bevan	5	0	52	0	–	–
S. Lee	3	0	11	0	–	–
D. S. Lehmann	6	0	37	0	–	–
M. E. Waugh	9	0	64	0	–	–

INDIA A v AUSTRALIANS

At Vidarbha CA Ground, Nagpur, February 17, 18, 19, 2001. Drawn. Toss: Australians.

Fortunately for the Australians, the four batsmen who managed to reach double figures made substantial contributions after left-arm seamer Ashish Nehra had made early inroads. While Matthew Hayden batted with circumspection and Ricky Ponting was at his exuberant best, a scorecard of seven for 133 boded ill for a total of substance. Michael Kasprowicz (12 fours and a six) and Jason Gillespie then settled in to a partnership of 155 in 160 minutes in which their batting developed from watchfulness into real authority. Slow left-armer Rahul Sanghvi then promptly wrapped up the innings, although, significantly, off-spinner Harbhajan Singh showed an ability to test the Australian batsmen. The local innings was dominated by a stroke-filled second-wicket partnership of 195 between Sadagopan Ramesh and V. V. S. Laxman, both of whom dominated the Australian attack, for whom Colin Miller bowled with skilful persistence. The Australians used the last day for batting practice, which was fully utilised by Justin Langer for 237 minutes.

Close of play: First day, India A (1) 1-71 (Ramesh 43, Laxman 6); Second day, Australians (2) 1-39 (Hayden 20, Langer 0).

Australians

M. J. Slater b A.D. Nehra	5	– (2) c Balaji b Harbhajan Singh	11
M.L. Hayden c Mohanty b Sanghvi	49	– (1) c Badani b Harbhajan Singh	37
J.L. Langer lbw b A.D. Nehra	8	– c Laxman b Harbhajan Singh	115
*S.R. Waugh c N.R. Mongia b A.D. Nehra	0	– c Das b Balaji	17
R.T. Ponting c Mohanty b Harbhajan Singh	56	– lbw b Laxman	68
D.R. Martyn c Das b Harbhajan Singh	6	– (7) b Badani	53
†A.C. Gilchrist c Harbhajan Singh b Sanghvi	5	– (6) run out (Badani/Laxman)	21
J.N. Gillespie c and b Sanghvi	57	– c Badani b Balaji Rao	5
M. S. Kasprowicz c Monghia b Sanghvi	92	– not out	15
D.W. Fleming c (sub) Kaif b Sanghvi	0	– c Laxman b Balaji Rao	2
C.R. Miller not out	0		
L-b 4, n-b 9	13	B 2, l-b 14, n-b 5	21
(69.1 overs, 300 mins)	291	(95.1 overs, 399 mins) (9 wkts)	365

Fall: 6 24 25 116 128 128 133
288 288 291

Fall: 31 62 111 260 287 300
324 354 365

Bowling: *First Innings*—Mohanty 12–2–62–0; Nehra 13–2–78–3; Harbhajan Singh 20–3–63–2; Sanghvi 18.1–8–40–5; Balaji Rao 6–0–44–0. *Second Innings*—Mohanty 16–5–51–0; Nehra 15–4–52–0; Harbhajan Singh 20–3–81–3; Sanghvi 5–1–16–0; Balaji Rao 18.1–1–100–3; Laxman 9–2–22–1; D. Mongia 8–2–21–0; Badani 4–2–6–1.

India A

S.S. Das run out (Waugh/Gilchrist)	12	R.L. Sanghvi lbw b Miller	1
S. Ramesh c Gilchrist b Gillespie	101	D.S. Mohanty c Slater b Miller	28
*V. V. S. Laxman c S.R. Waugh b Gillespie	94	A. Nehra c Slater b Kasprowicz	4
D. Mongia c Gilchrist b Miller	0		
H.K. Badani c S.R. Waugh b Miller	0	B 13, l-b 10, w 1, n-b 15	39
†N.R. Mongia not out	71		
W.D. Balaji Rao c Fleming b Miller	6	(97.4 overs, 394 mins)	368
Harbhajan Singh st Gilchrist b Miller	12	Fall: 36 231 232 232 232 264 281 287 362 368

Bowling: Gillespie 19–8–55–2; Fleming 21–4–74–0; Miller 32–10–90–6; Kasprowicz 22.4–2–103–1; Ponting 3–0–23–0.

Umpires: S. V. Ramani and Dr. B. K. Sadashiv.

MUMBAI v AUSTRALIANS

At Brabourne Stadium, Mumbai, February 22, 23, 24, 2001. Drawn. Toss: Mumbai.

The Ranji Trophy champions had stumbled to five for 82 shortly after lunch on the opening day before Sameer Dighe found an ally in Sairaj Bahutule in adding 117 for the sixth wicket in 128 minutes. Ramesh Powar enlivened the latter part of the day, his fifty coming from 49 balls. The Australian innings was a lacklustre affair apart from the customary authority of Steve Waugh, whose century included ten fours and three sixes. Shane Warne showed all of his wares as he took seven wickets on the third morning, but it again required Steve Waugh's steadfastness to steer the side into the calm waters of a draw. Mark Waugh injured a finger while fielding on the first day and took no further part in the match.

Close of play: First day, Mumbai (1) 9-328 (Powar 65, Kulkarni 14); Second day, Mumbai (2) 0-83 (Mane 45, Jaffer 36).

Mumbai

V.R. Mane b Hayden	19	– c Gilchrist b McGrath		57
W. Jaffer c M.E. Waugh b McGrath	16	– c Ponting b Warne		52
J.V. Paranjpe c Fleming b Warne	27	– c Langer b Warne		35
A.A. Muzumdar lbw b Miller	1	– (7) c (sub) D.R. Martyn b Warne		17
V.G. Kambli c Ponting b McGrath	0	– (4) c Hayden b Warne		2
*†S.S. Dighe c Gilchrist b Fleming	84	– (8) c (sub) D.R. Martyn b Warne		5
S.V. Bahutule lbw b Ponting	51	– (9) not out		7
R.F. Morris c Gilchrist b Ponting	2	– (5) st Gilchrist b Warne		0
R.R. Powar not out	65	– (6) c Fleming b Warne		13
P.L. Mhambrey c Fleming b McGrath	19			
N.M. Kulkarni not out	14			
B 5, l-b 16, n-b 9	30	L-b 2, n-b 1		3

(94 overs, 362 mins)   (9 wkts dec) 328
Fall: 27 52 57 57 82 199 202 265 296

(67.3 overs, 251 mins) (8 wkts dec) 191
Fall: 103 121 123 123 154 166 177 191

Bowling: *First Innings*—McGrath 19–6–46–3; Fleming 19–4–56–1; Miller 21–6–64–1; Hayden 7–0–37–1; Warne 19–4–81–1; M.E. Waugh 3–0–13–0; Ponting 6–0–10–2. *Second Innings*—McGrath 13–4–31–1; Fleming 11–4–43–0; Warne 21.3–5–56–7; Miller 21–3–57–0; Hayden 1–0–2–0.

Australians

M.J. Slater c Muzumdar b Mhambrey	11	– (2) st Dighe b Bahutule		32
M.L. Hayden lbw b Kulkarni	11	– (1) c Dighe b Mhambrey		6
J.L. Langer c and b Kulkarni	25	– c Mane b Bahutule		18
R.T. Ponting c Dighe b Mhambrey	1	– st Dighe b Bahutule		2
*S.R. Waugh not out	106	– (6) not out		34
†A.C. Gilchrist c Dighe b Mhambrey	22	– (5) b Bahutule		4
S.K. Warne c Dighe b Bahutule	1	– run out (Morris)		8
D.W. Fleming lbw b Kulkarni	5	– not out		22
C.R. Miller b Kulkarni	0			
G.D. McGrath lbw b Mhambrey	19			
L-b 1, n-b 1	2	B 4, l-b 4, n-b 7		15

(64.3 overs, 245 mins)   203
Fall: 13 25 28 70 103 118 129 133 203

(55 overs, 200 mins)   (6 wkts) 141
Fall: 6 47 57 61 64 80

M.E. Waugh did not bat.

Bowling: *First Innings*—Mhambrey 15.3–2–59–4; Morris 4–1–8–0; Kulkarni 25–11–39–4; Powar 7–1–42–0; Bahutule 13–0–54–1. *Second Innings*—Mhambrey 9–3–21–1; Morris 7–1–34–0; Kulkarni 18–7–27–0; Bahutule 15–4–38–4; Powar 5–3–6–0; Kambli 1–0–7–0.

Umpires: Dr. M.S. Mahal and A.M. Saheba.

INDIA v AUSTRALIA

First Test Match

At Wankhede Stadium, Mumbai, February 27, 28, March 1, 2001. Australia won by ten wickets. Toss: Australia. Test debut: R.L. Sanghvi.

The euphoria at Australia's record 16th consecutive Test match victory was tempered by the outpourings of grief at the death of Sir Donald Bradman on February 25. Players of both teams wore black armbands throughout the match and observed a two-minute silence before play on the first day. When the President of the Mumbai Cricket Association, Shri Sharad Pawar, made reference to Sir Donald's record during a tribute speech there was a spontaneous roar from the bleachers – the people's tribute to the Don. Sachin Tendulkar and Shane Warne, who had called on Sir Donald at his Adelaide home in 1998, and Steve Waugh, who visited the following year, paid special tributes that were widely reported.

Waugh, declaring that he and his men could best honour the life and record of Sir Donald by winning the Test, surprised observers by electing to bowl. The absence of Brett Lee did not cause him to modify his view that regardless of the conditions fast bowlers were most likely to pave the way to a series victory. To Waugh's indignation, his counterpart Saurav Ganguly had appealed for the preparation of slow turning pitches. However, curator Nadeem Memon paid Ganguly no heed, fervently believing that the pitch should provide an opportunity for everyone to showcase their wares. As it happened, the conditions were challenging for the batsmen, as the ball jumped, spat, turned, bounced and skidded on the dusty, tawny surface from the second session. Spinners took 14 of the 30 wickets to fall, but the pitch was certainly not a slow turner.

Only Sachin Tendulkar, Adam Gilchrist and Matthew Hayden showed the temperament and technique required to conquer the conditions. India reached four for 130, but as is so often the case the innings disintegrated when Tendulkar was dismissed, this time by his celebrated adversary Glenn McGrath for a luscious 76, with 13 fours. As Tendulkar returned to the pavilion and the acclamation of his devotees, Dicky Rutnagur, a respected old hand in the press boxes of the world, observed reverentially: "The Don would have enjoyed that."

The batsmanship of the Australian left-handers was something to behold. They made light of the treacherous going for a record sixth-wicket partnership of 197 and hauled Australia from the mire of five for 99 in pursuit of India's seemingly modest total of 176. Even Tendulkar must have found himself gasping in admiration at the batting of Gilchrist. While patience and persistence were the hallmarks of Hayden's hand, Gilchrist unleashed a spectacular attack on the Indian bowling, especially the spinners, Harbhajan Singh and Rahul Sanghvi. He faced 15 balls before scoring, but took only 84 balls to reach his second century in Tests, the ninth-fastest, calculated on balls faced, in the history of Test cricket. He was finally and inadvertently stumped by Nayan Mongia, when the ball bounced off the wicket-keeper's gloves, for 122 from 112 deliveries with 15 fours and four sixes. However, it is problematic whether Gilchrist could have played such a hand without the reassuring influence of Hayden, whose concentration and shot selection were exemplary. As it turned out, his innings of 119, from 172 deliveries in 283 minutes, with 17 fours and a six, breathed new life into his international career.

The confidence the Australians brought into the match was evident not only in the batting of Gilchrist and Hayden but also in the catching. Hayden, assuming great responsibility in the slips cordon while Mark Waugh nursed three stitches in the webbing of his left hand, and Ricky Ponting were especially conspicuous. Ponting took a freakish catch in the second innings to dismiss Tendulkar from a lusty pull which ricocheted off the shoulder of Justin Langer at short leg. India lost eight for 65 from the moment Tendulkar departed. As the victorious Australians took their bows, the crowd booed Ganguly, the home captain.

During the Indian second innings Michael Slater remonstrated aggressively after umpire Srinivas Venkataraghavan disallowed his emphatic appeal for a catch against Rahul Dravid. To the surprise of many officials and observers from both countries the match referee, Cammie Smith, regarded the incident as insignificant.

Man of the Match: A.C. Gilchrist.

Close of play: First day, Australia (1) 1-49 (Hayden 28, Langer 10); Second day, India (2) 2-58 (Dravid 6, Tendulkar 0).

India

S. S. Das c Hayden b Gillespie	14	– c S.R. Waugh b Gillespie	7
S. Ramesh c Gilchrist b McGrath	2	– c Ponting b McGrath	44
R. S. Dravid c Gilchrist b Fleming	9	– b Warne	39
S. R. Tendulkar c Gilchrist b McGrath	76	– (5) c Ponting b M.E. Waugh	65
*S.C. Ganguly c Hayden b Warne	8	– (6) run out (Slater/Warne)	1
V. V. S. Laxman c Ponting b McGrath	20	– (7) c Gilchrist b M.E. Waugh	12
†N. R. Mongia not out	26	– (4) c Gilchrist b Gillespie	28
A. B. Agarkar c and b Warne	0	– b M.E. Waugh	0
J. Srinath c M.E. Waugh b Warne	12	– (11) b McGrath	0
Harbhajan Singh c S.R. Waugh b Warne	0	– (9) not out	17
R.L. Sanghvi c Gilchrist b Gillespie	2	– (10) b Gillespie	0
B 2, l-b 3, w 1, n-b 1	7	B 5, n-b 1	6

(71.3 overs, 300 mins)	176	(94.1 overs, 393 mins)	219

Fall: 7 25 31 55 130 139 140 165 166 176

Fall: 33 57 154 156 174 174 193 210 216 219

Bowling: *First Innings*—McGrath 19–13–19–3; Fleming 15–3–55–1; Gillespie 15.3–4–50–2; Warne 22–7–47–4. *Second Innings*—McGrath 17.1–9–25–2; Fleming 15–1–44–0; Warne 28–11–60–1; Gillespie 19–8–45–3; M.E. Waugh 15–5–40–3.

Australia

M. J. Slater b Agarkar	10	– (2) not out	19
M.L. Hayden c Mongia b Srinath	119	– (1) not out	28
J.L. Langer c Dravid b Harbhajan Singh	19		
M. E. Waugh c Ganguly b Harbhajan Singh	0		
*S. R. Waugh c Dravid b Sanghvi	15		
R. T. Ponting c Das b Harbhajan Singh	0		
†A.C. Gilchrist st Mongia b Harbhajan Singh	122		
S. K. Warne c Tendulkar b Sanghvi	39		
J. N. Gillespie c Mongia b Srinath	0		
D. W. Fleming c Srinath b Agarkar	6		
G.D. McGrath not out	0		
B 13, l-b 3, n-b 3	19		

(73.2 overs, 333 mins)	349	(7 overs, 25 mins)	(0 wkts) 47

Fall: 21 71 71 98 99 296 326 327 349 349

Bowling: *First Innings*—Srinath 16–3–60–2; Agarkar 12–1–50–2; Harbhajan Singh 28–3–121–4; Sanghvi 10.2–2–67–2; Tendulkar 7–1–35–0. *Second Innings*—Srinath 2–0–17–0; Agarkar 1–0–8–0; Harbhajan Singh 2–0–11–0; Sanghvi 2–1–11–0.

Umpires: D. S. Shepherd (England) and S. Venkataraghavan.
TV Umpire: Narendra Menon.
Referee: C. W. Smith (West Indies).

INDIAN BOARD PRESIDENT'S XI v AUSTRALIANS

At Feroze Shah Kotla Ground, Delhi, March 6, 7, 8, 2001. Drawn. Toss: Australians.

The Australians raced to eight for 413 on the first day, with century-makers Steve Waugh and Ricky Ponting combining in a fifth-wicket partnership of 171 which was filled with handsome and daring strokeplay. The batting of the President's XI lacked both form and substance apart from two hours of controlled aggression from Dinesh Mongia during which he hit nine fours and three sixes. Apart from his squandering of 13 no-balls, Michael Kasprowicz gave a reminder of his bowling usefulness in Indian conditions. Although the Australians began the final day in a strong position to force a victory, instead they just used the time for batting practice. Ponting completed his second dazzling century for the match, while Mark Waugh hit 17 fours and seven sixes. In what passed for tactical acumen, Ganguly used off-spinner Sarandeep Singh for only three overs in the second innings, thus signalling the bowler's likely appearance in the next Test.

Close of play: First day, Australians (1) 8-413 (Kasprowicz 27, Fleming 4); Second day, Australians (2) 1-53 (Slater 24, Langer 0).

Australians

M. J. Slater c Martin b Patel	19	– c Mongia b Hirwani	26
M. L. Hayden c Martin b Sarandeep Singh	31	– c Dahiya b Hirwani	26
J. L. Langer lbw b Patel	4	– c Mongia b Hirwani	15
M. E. Waugh lbw b Hirwani	62	– c Dahiya b B. P. Patel	164
*S. R. Waugh c Surendra Singh b Sarandeep Singh	109		
R. T. Ponting c and b Sarandeep Singh	102	– not out	102
D. R. Martyn c Ganguly b Hirwani	2	– (5) c (sub) Gambhir b Hirwani	54
†B. J. Haddin st Dahiya b Sarandeep Singh	24	– (7) b B. P. Patel	8
M. S. Kasprowicz c Sarandeep Singh b Hirwani	35	– not out	32
D. W. Fleming not out	29		
C. R. Miller c Ganguly b Sarandeep Singh	5	– (8) c (sub) Powar b Hirwani	1
B 3, l-b 9, n-b 17	29	B 1, l-b 6, w 5, n-b 21	33

(100 overs, 395 mins)	451

Fall: 25 35 97 164 335 355 357 403 433 451

(93 overs, 393 mins)	(7 wkts)	461

Fall: 50 60 90 232 345 384 393

Bowling: *First Innings*—Surendra Singh 16–7–48–0; Patel 14–0–84–2; Hirwani 23–5–120–3; Sarandeep Singh 26–3–114–5; Sriram 17–4–63–0; Ganguly 4–0–10–0. *Second Innings*—Patel 22–3–113–2; Surendra Singh 15–1–68–0; Hirwani 38–3–168–5; Sarandeep Singh 3–0–10–0; Sriram 10–0–61–0; Mongia 5–0–34–0.

Indian Board President's XI

†V. Dahiya lbw b Fleming	0	Sarandeep Singh run out (Ponting)	0
S. Sriram c Haddin b Kasprowicz	27	Surendra Singh run out (M. E. Waugh/Haddin)	7
M. Kaif c Martyn b Miller	33	N. D. Hirwani not out	0
*S. C. Ganguly b M. E. Waugh	40		
D. Mongia c Ponting b Kasprowicz	66	B 8, l-b 2, n-b 13	23
J. J. Martin c Ponting b M. E. Waugh	10		
H. H. Kanitkar c Ponting b Kasprowicz	2	(66.4 overs, 253 mins)	221
R. B. Patel b Miller	13	Fall: 0 55 71 163 187 189 204 205 221 221	

Bowling: Fleming 10–3–27–1; Kasprowicz 18–3–68–3; Miller 27.4–8–91–2; Martyn 4–1–11–0; M. E. Waugh 7–2–14–2.

Umpires: S. Banerjee and S. Rao.

INDIA v AUSTRALIA

Second Test Match

At Eden Gardens, Kolkata, March 11, 12, 13, 14, 15, 2001. India won by 171 runs. Toss: Australia.

A peripheral player best known by his initials rather than by one of his given names single-handedly engineered one of the most remarkable victories in Test cricket. V. V. S. (Vangipurappu Venkat Sai) Laxman hit India's highest individual Test score as he converted a massive first innings deficit of 274 into a head-spinning advantage of 383. Such was his achievement that other heroic deeds that would normally have demanded attention paled by comparison. The young off-spinner Harbhajan Singh became the first Indian to take a Test hat-trick (dismissing Ricky Ponting, Adam Gilchrist and Shane Warne) on his way to a stunning match haul of 13 wickets, Rahul Dravid silenced his strident critics with a timely innings of immense character, and the redoubtable Steve Waugh crafted a thrilling century before a crowd that embraced him as one of their own. But this Test must inevitably become known as "Laxman's match".

The euphoria throughout the Indian cricket community that followed this remarkable win was unthinkable after the first two days. The country's cricket stocks were at their lowest, and the players' morale was around their ankles. The restructuring of the attack, with the inclusion of the red-blooded young fast bowler Zaheer Khan and the reinstatement of seasoned campaigners Venkatesh Prasad and Venkatapathy Raju, failed to raise their spirits after the heavy defeat at Mumbai. Dropped catches and fielding lapses enabled the Australians to recover after the loss of six wickets for 76 had squandered the splendid start provided by Matthew Hayden, Michael Slater and Justin Langer. Once again it was Steve Waugh who led the fight-back, with his 25th Test century, and one he marked with an unusually overt display of emotion – a run in an arc beyond the wicket and a series of joyful punches at the dusty sky. Jason Gillespie supported him in a ninth-wicket partnership of 133 in 190 minutes before Glenn McGrath enabled Waugh to reach his century as the pair added a breezy 43 in only 37 minutes for the last wicket.

It seemed the final humiliation for India. They batted as though they were collectively beyond therapy, with only Laxman, who hit 12 fours, offering any resistance to an Australian attack superbly directed by McGrath, who again claimed the precious wicket of Sachin Tendulkar in his figures of 4/18.

The criticism later directed at Waugh for enforcing the follow-on was unwarranted. The decision was in keeping with his attacking philosophy, which had brought the team success in the previous 16 Tests and changed the mood of Test cricket the world over. Furthermore, India's first innings had occupied just 58.1 overs. There was no questioning of Waugh's judgment when Gillespie accounted for Tendulkar for 10 with a pearl of a delivery and India were three for 115 and still a colossal 159 runs in arrears. Indeed, such was the frustration of spectators that a water pouch was thrown at Tendulkar as he departed. To the unease of officials and the constabulary a sense of frustration and despair was palpable as Saurav Ganguly joined Laxman in the middle.

It says much for Laxman's temperament that he was unaffected by the chaos which surrounded him. Before Laxman had removed his pads in the first innings Ganguly told him he would be granted his long-held wish to bat at No. 3 in the second innings. The promotion inspired him to take his heady form in domestic cricket into the international arena, and he played with the freedom and flair that he had only occasionally shown in his previous 20 Tests, as he used his reach to pulverise the bowling of Shane Warne. First he elicited support from the struggling Ganguly, adding 117 in 128 minutes for the fourth wicket, before he was joined by Dravid, whom he had displaced in the No. 3 spot. Dravid set about regaining form and confidence and rebuilding his reputation as a world-class player. So effective was his rehabilitation that he stayed with Laxman throughout the fourth day, a day many thought would not have been required, adding a colossal 335 runs off the regulation 90 overs. (On the same day, March 14, two years earlier, the Australians had failed to take a wicket when Brian Lara and Jimmy Adams batted through the day, adding 340 runs for West Indies at Kingston.)

Ganguly's greatest challenge in the end was the timing of his declaration. He left it late, batting on even after Laxman failed to reach the triple century so fervently anticipated by the vast crowd. (The aggregate attendance figure was in the region of 330,000.) But the Australians, unused to being so aggressively challenged, capitulated before the guileful Harbhajan and Tendulkar, losing their last nine wickets for 106 after Hayden and Slater had again provided a sound foundation. Rather than dwelling on marginal umpiring decisions, which are inevitable when slow bowlers are on top, the Australians needed to examine just why their technique and temperament were inadequate against Harbhajan. For one thing, they would have been much better served by the use of perpendicular bats.

In the end India won easily, inflicting Australia's first defeat since Kandy in September 1999. It was only the third time a team had followed on and won a Test match. Each time the losing side has been Australia.

Man of the Match: V. V. S. Laxman.

Close of play: First day, Australia (1) 8-291 (S. R. Waugh 29, Gillespie 6); Second day, India (1) 8-128 (Laxman 26, Raju 3); Third day, India (2) 4-254 (Laxman 109, Dravid 7); Fourth day, India (2) 4-589 (Laxman 275, Dravid 165).

Australia

M. J. Slater c Mongia b Zaheer Khan	42	–	(2) c Ganguly b Harbhajan Singh	43
M. L. Hayden c (sub) Badani b Harbhajan Singh	97	–	(1) lbw b Tendulkar	67
J. L. Langer c Mongia b Zaheer Khan	58	–	c Ramesh b Harbhajan Singh	28
M. E. Waugh c Mongia b Harbhajan Singh	22	–	lbw b Venkatapathy Raju	0
*S. R. Waugh lbw b Harbhajan Singh	110	–	c (sub) Badani b Harbhajan Singh	24
R. T. Ponting lbw b Harbhajan Singh	6	–	c Das b Harbhajan Singh	0
†A. C. Gilchrist lbw b Harbhajan Singh	0	–	lbw b Tendulkar	0
S. K. Warne c Ramesh b Harbhajan Singh	0	–	(9) lbw b Tendulkar	0
M. S. Kasprowicz lbw b Ganguly	7	–	(10) not out	13
J. N. Gillespie c Ramesh b Harbhajan Singh	46	–	(8) c Das b Harbhajan Singh	6
G. D. McGrath not out	21	–	lbw b Harbhajan Singh	12
B 19, l-b 10, n-b 7	36		B 6, n-b 8, penalty 5	19

(131.5 overs, 575 mins)   445
Fall: 103 193 214 236 252 252 252
     269 402 445

(68.3 overs, 272 mins)   212
Fall: 74 106 116 166 166 167 173
     174 191 212

Bowling: *First Innings*—Zaheer Khan 28.4–6–89–2; Venkatesh Prasad 30–5–95–0; Ganguly 13.2–3–44–1; Venkatapathy Raju 20–2–58–0; Harbhajan Singh 37.5–7–123–7; Tendulkar 2–0–7–0. *Second Innings*—Zaheer Khan 8–4–30–0; Venkatesh Prasad 3–1–7–0; Harbhajan Singh 30.3–8–73–6; Venkatapathy Raju 15–3–58–1; Tendulkar 11–3–31–3; Ganguly 1–0–2–0.

India

S. S. Das c Gilchrist b McGrath	20	–	hit wicket b Gillespie	39
S. Ramesh c Ponting b Gillespie	0	–	c M. E. Waugh b Warne	30
R. S. Dravid b Warne	25	–	(6) run out (S. R. Waugh/Kasprowicz)	180
S. R. Tendulkar lbw b McGrath	10	–	c Gilchrist b Gillespie	10
*S. C. Ganguly c S. R. Waugh b Kasprowicz	23	–	c Gilchrist b McGrath	48
V. V. S. Laxman c Hayden b Warne	59	–	(3) c Ponting b McGrath	281
†N. R. Mongia c Gilchrist b Kasprowicz	2	–	b McGrath	4
Harbhajan Singh c Ponting b Gillespie	4	–	(9) not out	8
Zaheer Khan b McGrath	3	–	(8) not out	23
S. L. Venkatapathy Raju lbw b McGrath	4			
B. K. Venkatesh Prasad not out	7			
L-b 2, n-b 12	14		B 4, l-b 14, W 2, n-b 14	34

(58.1 overs, 258 mins)   171
Fall: 0 34 48 88 88 92 97 113 129 171

(178 overs, 737 mins) (7 wkts dec)   657
Fall: 52 97 115 232 606 624 629

Bowling: *First Innings*—McGrath 14–8–18–4; Gillespie 11–0–47–2; Kasprowicz 13–2–39–2; Warne 20.1–3–65–2. *Second Innings*—McGrath 39–12–103–3; Gillespie 31–6–115–2; Warne 34–3–152–1; M. E. Waugh 18–1–58–0; Kasprowicz 35–6–139–0; Ponting 12–1–41–0; Hayden 6–0–24–0; Slater 2–1–4–0; Langer 1–0–3–0.

Umpires: P. Willey (England) and S. K. Bansal.
TV Umpire: S. N. Bandekar.
Referee: C. W. Smith (West Indies).

INDIA v AUSTRALIA

Third Test Match

At M. A. Chidambaram Stadium (Chepauk), Chennai, March 18, 19, 20, 21, 22, 2001.
India won by two wickets. Toss: Australia. Test debuts: S. V. Bahutule, S. S. Dighe.

Memories of the 1986-87 tied Test at this ground were vividly evoked in a tense,
hard-fought conclusion to the series. India managed to maintain its imposing home
record against Australia and inflict the first series defeat on Steve Waugh's team since
Sri Lanka's victory in 1999-00.

In the end, the Australians did not have enough runs with which to manoeuvre,
despite more remarkable batting by Matthew Hayden on the first two days. He carried
all before him, this time compiling a consummate double-century to take his aggregate
of runs for the series beyond 500. Hayden, who again swept spectacularly, provided his
team-mates with the opportunity to bat India out of the game, but they lacked the nous
or the ability to do it. Australian batsmen have a history of insecurity against the best off-
spin bowling, but on this occasion the middle and lower order were guilty of impulsive,
thoughtless batting after a first day that had realised a handsome stumps score of three
for 326. Hayden was the ninth batsman dismissed after almost eight hours at the crease
in the enervating conditions for which the cement cauldron at Chennai is renowned. He
faced 320 balls and struck 15 fours and six sixes in a thrilling assault on the Indian
spinners. After taking 1/100 off 26 unusually nervous overs Harbhajan Singh again
tormented the Australian batsmen with his turn, bounce and subtle variations in line,
finishing the innings 7/133 on his way to becoming only the 12th bowler and the
second Indian to take 15 wickets in a Test.

Hayden's only substantial support came from the Waugh brothers. Not for the first
time Mark Waugh again regained touch when he most needed it, surviving a stumping
chance on nine to score 70 and follow it with the only half-century of the second innings.
Steve Waugh, customarily the most vigilant and calculating of batsmen, had a rare lapse
in concentration and became just the sixth player in 1,539 Tests to be out handled the
ball. He had survived a leg before wicket appeal from Harbhajan, but as the ball bounced
back towards him, he reflexively fended it away from the stumps with the palm of his
right hand. His dramatic dismissal prompted another batting collapse, seven wickets
falling for 51, the last six of them to Harbhajan.

At last there was an equitable distribution of the Indian batting workload. Shiv Sunder
Das and his opening partner Sadagopan Ramesh provided delightful cameos in their
partnership of 123, while V. V. S. Laxman and Rahul Dravid managed to clamber down
from the clouds of Kolkata and score telling half-centuries. After failing to impose
himself on the first two Tests, Sachin Tendulkar scored his 25th Test century a month
in advance of his 28th birthday. He willed himself to score heavily and occupied the
crease for 336 minutes, striking 15 fours and two sixes. There was an inevitability about
his hundred, although Michael Slater at mid-wicket should have held the straightforward
catch Tendulkar offered at 82 off the bowling of Colin Miller.

The marauding Harbajan never allowed Australia to take control of their second
innings, taking 8/84 and finishing the series with 32 wickets (the next-best Indian bowler
took three) and a richly deserved Man of the Series triumph. Then, in pursuit of a
seemingly modest 155 on a pitch that, despite its appearance, remained hard and true,
India were three for 101 when they collectively lost their nerve to plunge to seven for
135 and then eight for 151. As ever, the Australian bowlers, most notably the
indefatigable Glenn McGrath and Jason Gillespie, endeavoured to atone for the
deficiencies of their batting colleagues, and with the help of Miller went perilously close
to defying extraordinary odds. But at the end, fittingly, Harbhajan struck the winning
runs, and the Indian team, ridiculed just 10 days earlier, held aloft the glittering prize –
the Border–Gavaskar Trophy.

Man of the Match: M.L. Hayden and Harbhajan Singh.
Man of the Series: Harbhajan Singh.
Close of play: First day, Australia (1) 3-326 (Hayden 147, S.R. Waugh 43); Second day, India (1) 1-211 (Das 84, Laxman 59); Third day, India (2) 4-480 (Bahutule 4, Kulkarni 0); Fourth day, Australia (2) 7-241 (S.R. Waugh 43).

Australia

M.J. Slater c Laxman b Zaheer Khan	4	– (2) c Laxman b Harbhajan Singh .. 48
M.L. Hayden c Ganguly b Harbhajan Singh	203	– (1) c Zaheer b Kulkarni 35
J.L. Langer c Dravid b Harbhajan Singh	35	– (4) c Laxman b Bahutule 21
M.E. Waugh c (sub) Badani b Bahutule	70	– (5) c Dravid b Harbhajan Singh 57
*S.R. Waugh handled ball	47	– (6) c Das b Harbhajan Singh 47
R.T. Ponting st Dighe b Harbhajan Singh	0	– (7) c Dravid b Harbhajan Singh ... 11
†A.C. Gilchrist lbw b Harbhajan Singh	1	– (3) lbw b Harbhajan Singh 1
S.K. Warne c Das b Harbhajan Singh	0	– lbw b Harbhajan Singh 11
J.N. Gillespie c Ganguly b Harbhajan Singh	0	– c Dravid b Harbhajan Singh 2
C.R. Miller c Bahutule b Harbhajan Singh	0	– lbw b Harbhajan Singh 2
G.D. McGrath not out	3	– not out 11
B 8, l-b 10, n-b 10	28	B 8, l-b 6, n-b 4 18

(115.2 overs, 474 mins)   391
Fall: 4 67 217 340 340 344 374
   376 385 391

(97.5 overs, 373 mins)   264
Fall: 82 84 93 141 193 211 241
   246 251 264

Bowling: *First Innings*—Zaheer Khan 15-5-57-1; Ganguly 2-1-11-0; Harbhajan Singh 38.2-6-133-7; Kulkarni 23-5-67-0; Bahutule 21-3-70-1; Tendulkar 16-1-35-0. *Second Innings*—Zaheer Khan 4-0-13-0; Ganguly 1-0-8-0; Harbhajan Singh 41.5-20-84-8; Kulkarni 30-11-70-1; Tendulkar 12-0-43-0; Bahutule 9-0-32-1.

India

S.S. Das lbw b McGrath	84	– c and b McGrath 9
S. Ramesh c Ponting b Warne	61	– run out (Ponting/Gilchrist) 25
V.V.S. Laxman c M.E. Waugh b McGrath	65	– c M.E. Waugh b Miller 66
S.R. Tendulkar c Gilchrist b Gillespie	126	– c M.E. Waugh b Gillespie 17
*S.C. Ganguly c Gilchrist b McGrath	22	– c M.E. Waugh b Gillespie 4
R.S. Dravid c Gilchrist b Gillespie	81	– c S.R. Waugh b Miller 4
†S.S. Dighe lbw b Warne	4	– not out 22
S.V. Bahutule not out	21	– c Warne b Miller 0
Zaheer Khan c and b Miller	4	– c M.E. Waugh b McGrath 0
Harbhajan Singh c M.E. Waugh b Miller	2	– not out 3
N.M. Kulkarni lbw b Miller	4	
B 19, l-b 2, w 1, n-b 5	27	L-b 3, n-b 2 5

(165 overs, 697 mins)   501
Fall: 123 211 237 284 453 468 470 475 477 501

(41.1 overs, 217 mins)   (8 wkts) 155
Fall: 18 76 101 117 122 135 135 151

Bowling: *First Innings*—McGrath 36-15-75-3; Gillespie 35-11-88-2; Miller 46-6-160-3; Warne 42-7-140-2; Ponting 2-1-2-0; M.E. Waugh 3-0-8-0; Hayden 1-0-7-0. *Second Innings*—McGrath 11.1-3-21-2; Gillespie 15-2-49-2; Miller 9-1-41-3; Warne 6-0-41-0.

Umpires: R.E. Koertzen (South Africa) and A.V. Jayaprakash.
TV Umpire: C.R. Vijayaraghavan.
Referee: C.W. Smith (West Indies).

†INDIA XI v AUSTRALIA EXHIBITION MATCH

At MA Chidambaram Stadium (Chepauk), Chennai, March 23, 2001. India XI won by 154 runs. Toss: India XI.

This match was played to assist in raising funds for victims of the disastrous earthquake in Gujarat. Quick runs were the order of the day, and Sachin Tendulkar set the tone in an innings which occupied only 49 balls, during which he struck 18 fours and two sixes. He had plenty of support against some amiable bowling, but only Michael Bevan and Justin Langer lasted long for the visitors.

India XI

S. Ramesh st Phillips b Matthews	35	(35)	
S.R. Tendulkar c Bracken b Kasprowicz	93	(49)	
H.K. Badani c Kasprowicz b Bevan	55	(41)	
D. Mongia c Lehmann b Miller	29	(32)	
V.K. Shewag c Harvey b Lehmann	19	(12)	
R.R. Singh c Martyn b Harvey	33	(26)	
†V. Dahiya b Campbell	50	(32)	

S.B. Joshi c Lehmann b Campbell	5	(7)	
*R.S. Dravid not out	0	(1)	
A.B. Agarkar not out	1	(1)	
B 4, l-b 3, w 6, n-b 5	18		
(40 overs)	(8 wkts)	338	

Fall: 127 133 203 231 239 315 335 337

J. Srinath, Zaheer Khan and Harbhajan Singh did not bat.

Bowling: Fleming 4–0–48–0; Bracken 6–0–50–0; Harvey 4–0–34–1; Kasprowicz 4–0–29–1; Matthews 4–0–26–1; Martyn 5–0–37–0; Miller 4–0–30–1; Bevan 4–0–37–1; Lehmann 2–0–15–1; Langer 2–0–22–0; Campbell 1–0–3–2.

Australian XI

D.R. Martyn b Agarkar	1	(4)	
*D.S. Lehmann b Srinath	24	(9)	
M.G. Bevan c and b Shewag	58	(35)	
I.J. Harvey c Badani b Srinath	7	(10)	
J.L. Langer c Joshi b Mongia	53	(39)	
D.W. Fleming c Badani b Shewag	0	(1)	
M.S. Kasprowicz c Badani b Shewag	5	(12)	
N.W. Bracken b Joshi	8	(19)	

G.R.J. Matthews c Singh b Ramesh	16	(20)	
C.R. Miller c and b Badani	1	(6)	
†R.B. Phillips not out	6	(8)	
B 1, l-b 4	5		
(27.1 overs)	184		

Fall: 11 33 75 99 99 121 148 164 170 184

D. Fordan and J. Campbell did not bat.

Bowling: Srinath 5–0–46–2; Agarkar 5–0–37–1; Singh 3–0–17–0; Harbhajan Singh 3–0–17–0; Shewag 3–0–19–3; Joshi 4–0–23–1; Mongia 3–0–21–1; Ramesh 2.1–0–4–1; Badani 2–0–12–1.

Umpires: K.G. Lakshiminarayanan and K.R. Shanker.

†INDIA v AUSTRALIA

First Limited-Overs International

At M Chinnaswamy Stadium, Bangalore, March 25, 2001. India won by 60 runs. Toss: India.

After their defeat in the Tests, Australia seemed dispirited and incapable of preventing a rampant victory by India in the first of this five-match series. By contrast, the Indians took the field eagerly, spurred on by the usual full house of supporters. After Saurav Ganguly's dismissal, India batted at a cracking pace, Sachin Tendulkar hitting 19 off one over from Glenn McGrath and V. V. S. Laxman belting seven fours and a six. Rahul Dravid and newcomer Virender Shewag, who played in a borrowed shirt with the name on the back covered with tape, added 100 runs in 16 overs before Vijay Dahiya joined Dravid to add 61 off 40 balls. Shewag then put the lacklustre performance of the Australian bowlers in perspective as he took three wickets with his off-spin, including the wicket of Matthew Hayden, who had been the linchpin of the innings until perhaps unluckily adjudged leg-before on 99. Although they maintained the required run-rate for most of their innings, Australia lost wickets too regularly to pose a threat for long, and spectators became so bored as the innings ambled along to the inevitable conclusion that they lit a series of fires in the stands.

Man of the Match: V. K. Shewag.

India

*S. C. Ganguly c M. E. Waugh b Fleming	6	(27)	Harbhajan Singh c Ponting b Harvey	0	(1)
S. R. Tendulkar run out (Bevan)	35	(26)	Zaheer Khan not out	1	(1)
V. V. S. Laxman c Martyn b Harvey	45	(34)	J. Srinath c Martyn b McGrath	2	(5)
R. S. Dravid c Harvey b Martyn	80	(85)			
H. K. Badani c M. E. Waugh b Warne	11	(18)	W 7, n-b 6	13	
V. K. Shewag b Fleming	58	(54)			
†V. Dahiya run out (Bevan)	51	(39)	(49.5 overs, 222 mins)	315	
A. B. Agarkar c and b McGrath	13	(15)			

Fall: 16 52 102 122 222 284 306 311 312 315

Bowling: McGrath 9.5–0–60–2; Fleming 10–0–62–2; Harvey 10–0–68–2; Warne 10–0–58–1; M. E. Waugh 6–0–42–0; Martyn 4–0–25–1.

Australia

M. L. Hayden lbw b Shewag	99	(89)	S. K. Warne b Srinath	13	(18)
M. E. Waugh b Srinath	5	(7)	D. W. Fleming not out	0	(0)
R. T. Ponting c Dravid b Zaheer Khan	9	(14)	G. D. McGrath lbw b Srinath	0	(2)
M. G. Bevan c (sub) Singh b Ganguly	49	(56)	L-b 3, w 8, n-b 6	17	
*S. R. Waugh lbw b Shewag	18	(24)			
D. R. Martyn c Dahiya b Shewag	1	(6)	(43.3 overs, 209 mins)	255	
†A. C. Gilchrist b Zaheer Khan	27	(28)			
I. J. Harvey c Ganguly b Agarkar	17	(22)			

Fall: 16 44 153 174 179 212 230 252 254 255

Bowling: Srinath 7.3–0–49–3; Zaheer Khan 8–0–34–2; Agarkar 8–0–54–1; Harbhajan Singh 8–0–41–0; Shewag 9–0–59–3; Ganguly 3–0–15–1.

Umpires: D. D. Sharma and S. K. Sharma.
TV Umpire: T. G. Laxmi Narayan.
Referee: C. W. Smith (West Indies).

INDIA v AUSTRALIA

Second Limited-Overs International

At Pandit Jawaharlal Nehr Stadium, Pune, March 28, 2001. Australia won by eight wickets. Toss: India. International limited-overs debut: D. Mongia.

The Australians snapped out of their lethargy, led by that most languid of cricketers, Mark Waugh. After Sachin Tendulkar's customary lightning start India were restricted to a surmountable 248, their innings notable for a polished and speedy century by left-hander Hemang Badani (ten fours and two sixes), who had been overlooked for the Test series. The match was virtually Australia's by the time the first Australian wicket fell at 143 in the 26th over with the dismissal of Matthew Hayden. Then came an incident in which Darren Lehmann was unlucky to be adjudged run out. He was stranded mid-pitch in a mix-up with Mark Waugh, and television replays indicated that the batsmen may have crossed, which should have cost Waugh his wicket. The volatile Indian captain Saurav Ganguly berated the umpires, who meekly accepted his request for an adjudication by the third umpire. With the television pictures inconclusive, Waugh, who had also been vocal, was able to stay at the crease to compile 133 not out (15 fours and a six) and carry Australia to an easy victory.

Man of the Match: M. E. Waugh.

India

*S.C. Ganguly b McGrath	4	(15)	Zaheer Khan b McGrath	15	(10)
S.R. Tendulkar c Lehmann b Fleming	32	(29)	Harbhajan Singh not out	1	(1)
V.V.S. Laxman run out (S.R. Waugh)	51	(86)	J. Srinath not out	3	(2)
R.S. Dravid run out (Bevan/Martyn)	13	(23)			
H.K. Badani c Lehmann b Bracken	100	(98)	L-b 2, w 4	6	
D. Mongia run out (M Waugh/					
S Waugh/Fleming	2	(6)	(50 overs, 212 mins) (9 wkts)	248	
†V. Dahiya c Bracken b Fleming	2	(7)	Fall: 29 37 60 153 157 162 221		
S.B. Joshi c M.E. Waugh b Bracken	19	(23)	239 244		

Bowling: McGrath 10–1–49–2; Fleming 10–1–39–2; Bracken 10–1–54–2; Martyn 7–0–41–0; Symonds 10–0–41–0; M.E. Waugh 3–0–22–0.

Australia

M.E. Waugh not out	133	(138)			
M.L. Hayden c Ganguly b Zaheer Khan	57	(81)	B 4, l-b 10, w 7, n-b 4	25	
D.S. Lehmann run out ((sub)Yuvraj					
Singh/Dahiya)	1	(4)	(45.1 overs, 205 mins) (2 wkts)	249	
M.G. Bevan not out	33	(52)	Fall: 143 163		

A. Symonds, *S.R. Waugh, D.R. Martyn, †A.C. Gilchrist, D.W. Fleming, N.W. Bracken and G.D. McGrath did not bat.

Bowling: Srinath 7–0–33–0; Zaheer Khan 6–0–26–1; Harbhajan Singh 10–0–46–0; Joshi 9.1–0–54–0; Ganguly 3–0–17–0; Tendulkar 10–0–59–0.

Umpires: S.C. Gupta and I. Sivaram.
TV Umpire: C.R. Mohite.
Referee: C.W. Smith (West Indies).

†INDIA v AUSTRALIA

Third Limited-Overs International

At Nehru Stadium, Indore, March 31, 2001. India won by 118 runs. Toss: Australia.

After two brilliant but brief innings in the previous two matches, the Indian master Sachin Tendulkar claimed this match as his own as he blasted 139 from a hard-working Australian attack, becoming on the way the first batsman to score 10,000 runs in international limited-overs cricket. On the tiny ground he hit 19 fours, and his second fifty came in just 28 balls as he turned good balls into boundaries at will. India's second Test batting hero V. V. S. Laxman played an uncharacteristic supporting role in a partnership of 199 off 29.2 overs. The three Australians making up the team's "fifth bowler" conceded 94 runs in their ten overs. Facing a run chase of six an over Australia could do nothing but risk wickets in all-out attack, but the Indian bowlers stuck to their guns, and after Adam Gilchrist fell at two for 102 in the 20th over, the innings petered out to a miserable 181. In another sour incident between the captains, Saurav Ganguly claimed to have won the toss, and elected to bat. Steve Waugh called in the referee and was awarded the toss, but averted further rancour by going out to field.

Man of the Match: S. R. Tendulkar.

India

R. S. Dravid c Gilchrist b Fleming	 15	(34)	†V. Dahiya b McGrath	 0	(4)
S. R. Tendulkar c Fleming b McGrath	.139	(125)	Zaheer Khan not out	 7	(7)
V. V. S. Laxman run out			Harbhajan Singh not out	 9	(8)
(Symonds/Gilchrist)	.. 83	(88)			
*S. C. Ganguly c Bevan b Fleming	... 0	(3)	L-b 2, w 7, n-b 4	 18	
H. K. Badani run out (McGrath/Gilchrist)	23	(25)			
D. Mongia c and b McGrath	 4	(5)	(50 overs, 221 mins)	(8 wkts)	299
A. B. Agarkar lbw b Harvey	 1	(5)	Fall: 32 231 231 268 279 282 283 284		

J. Srinath did not bat.

Bowling: McGrath 10–0–52–3; Fleming 10–1–34–2; Harvey 10–0–48–1; Warne 10–0–64–0; Martyn 4–0–34–0; Symonds 4–0–37–0; Bevan 2–0–23–0.

Australia

†A. C. Gilchrist c Ganguly b Harbhajan			S. K. Warne run out (Srinath)	 18	(32)
Singh	.. 63	(70)	D. W. Fleming c Dahiya b Srinath	... 9	(8)
D. R. Martyn c Dahiya b Srinath	 19	(17)	G. D. McGrath not out	 0	(1)
R. T. Ponting c and b Agarkar	 23	(32)			
M. G. Bevan b Harbhajan Singh	 6	(11)	L-b 4, w 6, n-b 3	 13	
*S. R. Waugh c Tendulkar b Ganguly	. 23	(32)			
A. Symonds c Dahiya b Agarkar	 5	(6)	(35.5 overs, 175 mins)		181
D. S. Lehmann c Badani b Agarkar	... 1	(2)	Fall: 46 102 111 122 127 129 136		
I. J. Harvey c and b Harbhajan Singh	.. 1	(7)	171 172 181		

Bowling: Srinath 8.5–1–34–2; Zaheer Khan 6–0–51–0; Agarkar 8–0–38–3; Harbhajan Singh 9–0–37–3; Ganguly 4–0–17–1.

Umpires: V. Chopra and K. Hariharan.
TV Umpire: S. J. Phadkar.
Referee: C. W. Smith (West Indies).

†INDIA v AUSTRALIA

Fourth Limited-Overs International

At Indira Priyadarshini Municipal Cricket Ground, Visakhapatnam, April 3, 2001. Australia won by 93 runs. Toss: Australia.

After being rested in Australia's team rotation process, the in-form Matthew Hayden helped Australia to square the series and keep the climax for the final match. With his imposing sweeps and cover drives, Hayden made 111 while his partner in a 219-run stand, Ricky Ponting, burst back to batting life and displayed his customary sweet footwork and timing. The duo equalled Australia's highest second-wicket limited-overs stand, by Ponting and Mark Waugh against Zimbabwe at Delhi in 1998. After their departures, Michael Bevan, Steve Waugh and Shane Lee blasted 92 off the last 10.3 overs from the hapless Indian bowlers to set India an enormous target. Sachin Tendulkar started the innings off with the clear intention of batting to win, hitting 11 fours before his dismissal in the 16th over, but after that the innings lost direction in the steamy heat. Shane Warne maintained pressure on the batsmen throughout his ten overs, taking three wickets, while Mark Waugh chipped in for another three. Harbhajan Singh hit three sixes and three fours, and his stand of 59 in seven overs with Zaheer Khan entertainingly delayed Australia's victory.
Man of the Match: M.L. Hayden.

Australia

†A.C. Gilchrist c Dahiya b Srinath	6	(5)	S. Lee not out	25	(11)
M.L. Hayden st Dahiya b Harbhajan					
Singh	111	(112)	L-b 7, w 7, n-b 3	17	
R.T. Ponting c Tendulkar b Agarkar	101	(110)			
M.G. Bevan not out	43	(41)	(50 overs, 227 mins) (4 wkts)	338	
*S.R. Waugh c Srinath b Zaheer Khan	35	(24)	Fall: 6 225 246 304		

D.R. Martyn, S.K. Warne, D.W. Fleming, N.W. Bracken and G.D. McGrath did not bat.

Bowling: Srinath 10–0–61–1; Zaheer Khan 10–0–71–1; Agarkar 9–0–63–1; Harbhajan Singh 10–0–58–1; Singh 6–0–37–0; Ganguly 4–0–29–0; Tendulkar 1–0–12–0.

India

*S.C. Ganguly c Warne b Bracken	9	(36)	Zaheer Khan c Waugh b McGrath	29	(28)
S.R. Tendulkar c Waugh b Bracken	62	(38)	Harbhajan Singh c Lee b McGrath	46	(32)
V.V.S. Laxman st Gilchrist b Warne	11	(26)	J. Srinath not out	7	(4)
R.S. Dravid c and b Warne	7	(10)	L-b 2, w 12, n-b 3	17	
H.K. Badani c Warne b Waugh	25	(35)			
R.R. Singh c Gilchrist b Waugh	16	(31)	(45 overs, 195 mins)	245	
†V. Dahiya c Hayden b Warne	7	(15)	Fall: 47 85 87 102 135 144 149 169		
A.B. Agarkar lbw b Waugh	9	(16)	228 245		

Bowling: McGrath 8–0–62–2; Fleming 8–1–53–0; Bracken 7–1–21–2; Warne 10–0–38–3; Lee 3–0–11–0; Waugh 6–0–29–3; Bevan 3–0–29–0.

Umpires: G.A. Pratapkumar and S.K. Tarapore.
TV Umpire: A. Bhattacharia.
Referee: C.W. Smith (West Indies).

†INDIA v AUSTRALIA

Fifth Limited-Overs International

At Jawaharlal Nehru Stadium, Margoa, April 6, 2001. Australia won by four wickets. Toss: India.

Australia snatched a sweet 3-2 victory in this limited-overs series, winning a tense encounter on a deteriorating wicket with 12 balls to spare. Indian expectations had been high after Saurav Ganguly (nine fours and two sixes) and a century from V. V. S. Laxman (ten fours) carried them to 265. Ganguly's dispute over his dismissal, caught off a bouncer from Glenn McGrath, did nothing to diminish the Australian determination to win. Adam Gilchrist (ten fours and a six) and Matthew Hayden gave Australia a rocket-fuelled start with 70 off the first ten overs, and Michael Bevan (five fours and a six) steadily accumulated runs after Gilchrist's dismissal. At six for 202 Australia looked fragile, but Bevan's slashing six off Harbhajan Singh with five overs to go broke the run-a-ball target, and Bevan and Ian Harvey hit the last 67 off 8.5 overs to take Australia to victory. Hayden, who had top-scored in the Tests, completed the double by beating Laxman for most runs in the limited-overs series – 303 at 75.75, and deservedly took the Man of the Series award. Perhaps the difference between the results of the Tests and the limited-overs series was the fact that Harbhajan, Australia's nemesis in the Tests, took only four wickets at 59.25 from 47 overs in the five limited-overs matches.

Man of the Match and *Man of the Series:* M. L. Hayden.

India

*S. C. Ganguly c Ponting b McGrath	. 74	(81)	†V. Dahiya not out	15	(15)
S. R. Tendulkar c Gilchrist b Bracken	. 12	(15)	Zaheer Khan not out	0	(0)
V. V. S. Laxman c Gilchrist b Harvey	.101	(106)	L-b 3, w 3	6	
R. S. Dravid c Waugh b Symonds	. . . .	31 (49)			
H. K. Badani b Harvey	7	(14)	(50 overs, 213 mins) (6 wkts)	265	
Yuvraj Singh run out (Gilchrist/Bracken)	19	(21)	Fall: 16 121 218 230 230 262		

A. B. Agarkar, Harbhajan Singh and J. Srinath did not bat.

Bowling: McGrath 8–0–37–1; Bracken 10–1–37–1; Harvey 10–1–49–2; Warne 8–0–62–0; Symonds 8–0–40–1; Lehmann 6–0–37–0.

Australia

M. L. Hayden c Ganguly b Srinath	. . .	36 (41)	A. Symonds c Badani b Srinath	7	(9)
†A. C. Gilchrist b Tendulkar	76	(60)	I. J. Harvey not out	25	(26)
R. T. Ponting c Dahiya b Srinath	4	(4)			
M. G. Bevan not out	87	(108)	B 4, l-b 9, w 1, n-b 2	16	
*S. R. Waugh c Agarkar b Tendulkar	. 17	(30)			
D. S. Lehmann c Yuvraj Singh			(48 overs, 237 mins) (6 wkts)	269	
	b Tendulkar . .	1	(6)	Fall: 70 74 142 187 195 202		

S. K. Warne, G. D. McGrath and N. W. Bracken did not bat.

Bowling: Srinath 10–1–62–3; Zaheer Khan 9–0–43–0; Agarkar 6–0–45–0; Harbhajan Singh 10–0–55–0; Tendulkar 10–0–35–3; Yuvraj Singh 3–0–16–0.

Umpires: F. Gomes and S. K. Porel.
TV Umpire: K. Murali.
Referee: C. W. Smith (West Indies).

THE AUSTRALIANS IN KENYA, 2000-01

By KEN PIESSE

A typically cavalier century from Chris Cairns lifted New Zealand to its first major international limited-overs trophy when it won the final of the ICC Knockout Trophy against Pakistan in Nairobi. New Zealand had previously made the semi-finals of four World Cups without reaching a final.

It was the second mini-World Cup, following the inaugural competition held in Bangladesh and won by South Africa in 1998-89. Eleven countries took part this time, raising funds for cricket in developing areas. Conditions at the Gymkhana Ground, which can accommodate a crowd of 8,000, generally favoured the batsmen, while the outfield was green and almost lush despite a severe drought. Australia, the tournament favourites, were beaten in their only game, a quarter-final, by India.

Australia sent its strongest available team. Colin Miller, named for the first time at international limited-overs level, had to withdraw with a calf injury on the eve of the squad's departure. Another of the original 14, Shane Warne was absent with an injured knee following his season with Hampshire. With Stuart MacGill staying at home to get married, the selectors named New South Wales all-rounder Mark Higgs and South Australian Brad Young as the two spinners. Before their match against India, the Australians played two warm-up matches, against Kenya and England.

AUSTRALIAN TOURING PARTY

S.R. Waugh (New South Wales) (*captain*), A.C. Gilchrist (Western Australia) (*vice-captain*), M.G. Bevan (New South Wales), J.N. Gillespie (South Australia), I.J. Harvey (Victoria), M.A. Higgs (New South Wales), B. Lee (New South Wales), S. Lee (New South Wales), D.R. Martyn (Western Australia), G.D. McGrath (New South Wales), R.T. Ponting (Tasmania), A. Symonds (Queensland), M.E. Waugh (New South Wales), B.E. Young (South Australia).

Manager: S.R. Bernard. *Coach:* J.M. Buchanan. *Physiotherapist:* E.L Alcott. *Fitness adviser:* D. Misson. *Cricket analyst/assistant manager:* M.J. Walsh.

WARM-UP MATCH

KENYA v AUSTRALIA

At Simba Union Ground, Nairobi. September 30, 2000. Australia won by 93 runs. Australia elected to bat first.

Australia

M.E. Waugh c Odumbe b Odoyo	....	5	(14)	M.A. Higgs b A.O. Suji	17 (22)
†A.C. Gilchrist c Tikolo b Odoyo	....	7	(10)	B.E. Young b A.O. Suji	1 (6)
R.T. Ponting c Onyango b A.O. Suji		26	(39)	B. Lee not out	4 (6)
*S.R. Waugh retired		72	(74)	B 4, l-b 2, w 3, n-b 3	12
D.R. Martyn c and b Ababu		11	(27)		
A. Symonds b Onyango		14	(22)	(50 overs, 207 mins) (8 wkts)	246
S. Lee not out		77	(81)	Fall: 5 24 52 79 96 165 222 233	

J.N. Gillespie and I.J. Harvey did not bat.

Bowling: M.A. Suji 5–1–14–0; Odoyo 10–0–51–2; Ochieng 3–0–15–0; A.O. Suji 7–1–33–3; Abadu 3–0–13–1; Sheikh 8–0–43–0; Onyango 8–1–36–1; Odumbe 6–0–35–0.

Kenya

†K.O. Otieno c Gillespie b Young	...	31	(60)	L.N. Onyango c Gilchrist b Gillespie	6 (15)
R.D. Shah lbw b B. Lee		0	(3)	C. Otieno not out	5 (23)
J.K. Kamande b B. Lee		0	(2)	P. Ochieng b Gillespie	18 (11)
H.S. Modi c Symonds b Gillespie	....	7	(9)	J. Ababu b Higgs	4 (5)
S.O. Tikolo c and b Young		35	(60)		
*M.O. Odumbe lbw b Young		15	(28)	B 4, w 6, n-b 3	13
T.M. Odoyo c S. Lee b Higgs		12	(16)		
A.O. Suji b B. Lee		5	(6)	(43.2 overs, 184 mins)	153
M.A. Suji c M.E. Waugh b B. Lee	...	2	(18)	Fall: 5 9 20 70 93 106 113 117 119	
M. Sheikh c Symonds b B. Lee		0	(8)	121 126 146 153	

Bowling: Gillespie 9–1–25–3; B. Lee 7–0–22–5; Young 10–3–36–3; S. Lee 5–2–12–0; Symonds 5–0–27–0; Higgs, 7.2–3–27–2.

Umpires: L Bhudia and R. D'Mello.

WARM-UP MATCH

AUSTRALIA v ENGLAND

At Simba Union Ground, Nairobi. October 3, 2000. Tied. Toss: Australia.

Australia

†A.C. Gilchrist c Hick b White	......	40	(47)	S. Lee c Alleyne b Gough	1 (3)
M.E. Waugh c Trescothick b Caddick		1	(22)	B. Lee not out	9 (13)
R.T. Ponting lbw b Caddick	....	4	(13)	M.A. Higgs not out	3 (2)
M.G. Bevan c and b Giles	....	14	(32)		
D.R. Martyn b White		71	(89)	L-b 2, w 8, n-b 3.	13
A. Symonds run out (Thorpe)	....	27	(22)		
*S.R. Waugh retired		50	(39)	(50 overs, 212 mins) (9 wkts)	236
I.J. Harvey c Hussain b Trescothick	..	3	(3)	Fall: 10 24 55 82 116 195 207 216 231	

Bowling: Caddick 7–2–19–2; Gough 8–1–32–1; White 7–0–23–2; Ealham 7–0–38–0; Hick 9–0–58–0; Giles 0.5–0–2–1; Solanki 4.1–0–28–0; Trescothick 3–0–15–1; Hoggard 4–0–19–0.

England

M. E Trescothick c S. Lee b B. Lee	... 27	(28)	V. S. Solanki not out	3	(10)
†A.J1. Stewart c Gilchrist b Higgs	.. 38	(48)	M. W. Alleyne lbw b Symonds	.....	9	(8)
*N. Hussain c and b Harvey	 21	(43)	A. R. Caddick c B. Lee b Symonds	.. 0	(1)
G. A. Hick run out (Gilchrist)	 28	(27)	B 2, l-b 10, w 16, n-b 1 29		
G. P. Thorpe b B. Lee	 28	(62)			
A. Flintoff lbw b B. Lee	 17	(20)	(49.4 overs, 218 mins)	236	
C. White lbw b Symonds	 18	(25)	Fall: 45 85 122 150 178 181 214		
M. A. Ealham c Gilchrist b Gillespie	.. 18	(20)	220 236 236		

A. F. Giles, M. J. Hoggard and D. Gough did not bat.

Bowling: B. Lee 10–1–51–3; Gillespie 8–1–42–1; Harvey 6–0–17–1; Higgs 6–1–49–1; Young 8–1–29–0; S. Lee 5–0–20–0; Symonds 6.4–1–16–3.

Umpires: Ebrahim and Lalji.

AUSTRALIA v INDIA

At Nairobi Gymkhana Ground, Nairobi, October 7, 2000. India won by 20 runs. Toss: Australia.

Enjoying noisy crowd support from the local Indian population, India eliminated the Australians in a high-scoring game. Yuvraj Singh's 84 from just 80 balls was the cornerstone of the Indian innings, which during the opening onslaught by Sachin Tendulkar bubbled along at more than six an over. Tendulkar hit three fours and three sixes, two of which came from the bowling of Glenn McGrath, whose nine overs cost 61. Yuvraj, an 18-year-old left-hander from Punjab playing in only his second limited-overs international, reached 50 from 46 balls and shared a stand of 64 for the fifth wicket with veteran Robin Singh. Despite being docked two overs because of their slow over rate, the Australians seemed in control as Ricky Ponting and Michael Bevan took the score from three for 86 after 16 overs to 159 in the 29th. But Ponting was caught brilliantly on the leg side by Singh and Bevan was run out by Yuvraj, triggering a collapse. With 74 needed from eight overs, Brett Lee took 15 from an over from Anil Kumble before falling to Ajit Agarkar, and the game ended in the 47th over with Australia 20 runs short.

India

*S. C. Ganguly c Gilchrist b Gillespie	. 24	(42)	A. R. Kumble run out (Ponting)	 12	(21)
S. R. Tendulkar c Martyn b B. Lee	... 38	(37)	Zaheer Khan not out	 13	(13)
R. S. Dravid c S. Lee b Gillespie	 9	(18)	B. K. Venkatesh Prasad not out	... 6	(1)
V. G. Kambli c Gilchrist b S. R. Waugh	29	(40)			
Yuvraj Singh c and b S. Lee	 84	(80)	B 1, l-b 12, w 8, n-b 2 23		
R. R. Singh b Harvey	 19	(30)			
†V. Dahiya c M.E. Waugh b B. Lee	.. 5	(11)	(50 overs, 234 mins)	(9 wkts)	265
A. B. Agarkar c McGrath b S. Lee	.. 3	(9)	Fall: 66 76 90 130 194 215 222 239 258		

Bowling: McGrath 9–0–61–0; B. Lee 10–0–39–2; Gillespie 8–0–39–2; Harvey 9–1–54–1; S. Lee 10–0–31–2; S.R. Waugh 4–0–28–1.

Australia

M.E. Waugh c Kumble b Agarkar	 7	(24)	B. Lee c Ganguly b Agarkar 31	(28)

M.E. Waugh c Kumble b Agarkar 7 (24)
†A.C. Gilchrist c Ganguly b Zaheer Khan 33 (23)
I.J. Harvey c Yuvraj Singh b Venkatesh
                           Prasad .. 25 (24)
R.T. Ponting c Singh b Tendulkar 46 (59)
M.G. Bevan run out (Yuvraj Singh) .. 42 (52)
*S.R. Waugh b Zaheer Khan 23 (34)
D.R. Martyn b Singh 1 (8)
S. Lee run out (Ganguly) 4 (6)

B. Lee c Ganguly b Agarkar 31 (28)
J.N. Gillespie c Singh b Venkatesh
                           Prasad.. 14 (16)
G.D. McGrath not out 6 (8)
     L-b 4, w 7, n-b 2 13

(46.4 overs, 219 mins)   245
Fall: 43 51 86 159 163 169 189 224
     226 245

Bowling: Zaheer Khan 10–0–40–2; Agarkar 8–1–59–2; Venkatesh Prasad 7.4–0–43–2; Kumble 8–0–42–0; Tendulkar 7–0–31–1; Singh 6–0–26–1.

Umpires: S.A. Bucknor and D.R. Shepherd.
TV Umpire: P. Willey.
Referee: R.S. Madugalle (Sri Lanka).

THE AUSTRALIANS IN ENGLAND, 2001

By GIDEON HAIGH

To lose one Ashes series could be thought of as misfortune. To lose seven, as England now have, looks like carelessness, and an awful lot of it. The 2001 Ashes series will be remembered not so much as a series in its own right but as a continuation of the Australian hegemony that was established in August 1989. Ashes series remain a protected species, fought over five Tests when series of that duration are increasingly rare, but the results can scarcely be said to justify the procedure: England have won only one "live" Ashes Test since the 1986-87 series.

The margin of Australian superiority, moreover, appeared no nearer to narrowing in 2001. As in all six preceding series, custody of the Ashes was decided long before the end of proceedings, leaving the teams to compete only over the scoreline. Australian eagerness to sweep the series clean allowed England to pull back a win at Headingley, thanks largely to a remarkable 173 not out by Mark Butcher, but Australia made it an emphatic 4-1 with an overpowering victory at The Oval in which they expended only four wickets.

The series represented a twilight of the idols, with a number of eminent players unlikely to be seen again in Ashes competition, at least by English audiences: Steve and Mark Waugh and Shane Warne for Australia, Michael Atherton and Alec Stewart for England. The quality of the *materiel* coming forward, however, did not suggest that the gap between the two countries would close soon. Glenn McGrath, Adam Gilchrist, Ricky Ponting and Jason Gillespie are at the height of their powers. Marcus Trescothick, Michael Vaughan and Alex Tudor, the best of England's coming men, still have much to prove.

The tone of the series was set even before hostilities commenced, when both Vaughan and Graham Thorpe sustained injuries which largely excluded them from both the NatWest Series and the Tests. This was bad luck, but there was also a bad vibe to it all. Though Steve Waugh was stretchered from Trent Bridge with an incapacitating calf injury, he was *hors de combat* for only one Test before returning for a fat hundred at The Oval. "I'm a professional cricketer and I love playing for Australia," he said. "What else was I going to do?" Yet finding 11 fit, competent and committed cricketers at a time was again a task that regularly stretched England. After England's captain Nasser Hussain broke a finger during the First Test, we saw the comical sight of the various candidates to replace him disqualifying themselves. Steve Waugh expressed his puzzlement at this, though he must inwardly have exulted: the Australians, who draw strength from the psychological frailty they perceive in others, seized the Second Test by eight wickets, abetted also by a string of dropped catches.

Australia's victory was built around the accomplishments of Glenn McGrath and Shane Warne, who not only took 11 more wickets between them than all of England's bowlers put together, but were the only bowlers on either side to concede under three runs an over. For McGrath, this was merely more of the same; for Warne, a remarkable redemption after the travail of his Indian tour. It is amazing to recall that he was viewed at the outset as lucky to have retained his place at Stuart MacGill's expense. Both bowlers achieved significant landmarks. By dismissing Mark Ramprakash at The Oval, Warne passed Curtly Ambrose's wicket total, moving to fifth on the Test list. By dismissing Usman Afzaal in the same game, McGrath left Dennis Lillee behind, moving to second on the Australian list. It is strange that we think of bowling partnerships only in terms of new-ball attacks: Hall and Griffith, Lindwall and Miller *et al*. In fact, with both Warne and McGrath in his charge, Steve Waugh has had perhaps the ideal coupling, covering all possible conditions and contingencies. They even worked in complementary fashion: 25 of McGrath's 32 victims were in England's top seven, 13 of Warne's 31 in England's last four.

The feats of McGrath and Warne were all the more notable for the fact that they often lacked support. After bowling manfully on occasions in the first three Tests, Jason Gillespie appeared in need of the shade of a coolabah tree during the last two; Brett Lee was an expensive disappointment. More prolonged resistance from England's batsmen, in fact, might have tested the robustness of the four-bowler formula on which Australia relied unvaryingly, but it never arose. The Australian fielding was good enough rather than downright good, especially considering the exalted standards that Australian teams have sustained in recent years. But the catches missed were seldom crucial, and the team's confidence in its attack's ability to generate chances unwavering. Certainly, mistakes never seemed to have the same ruinous effect on morale as they did on England's.

The Australian batting was built round the core of its middle order. The Waughs were the acme of consistency, scoring two centuries each, and Adam Gilchrist the incarnation of audacity, his 152 from 143 deliveries at Edgbaston with 20 fours and five sixes perhaps the most extraordinary innings by a No. 7 batsman in cricket history. The player who gave greater aesthetic pleasure than any other player on either side, however, was Damien Martyn. He is one of those batsmen who renders the game so simple that you want to pick up your bat and start your career all over again. "So that's how it's done," you are tempted to think. His footwork is precise, his balance balletic. To say that he is a textbook batsman is not to flatter him; it is to flatter the textbook. At Headingley, he provided a master class in the back-foot drive, meeting the ball at the top of the bounce and repeatedly perforating point and cover. It was like watching a batsman rehearse his strokes in a mirror, the bat and every point of his anatomy in the right place.

Australia's top three proved more permeable, although Ponting exerted his authority at Headingley and The Oval, and Justin Langer redeemed an otherwise mediocre tour with a therapeutic hundred in the Fifth Test. Matthew Hayden was troubled when the ball moved because of a tendency to plant his front foot, and Michael Slater was perhaps the greatest disappointment of all. He batted as though unaware that you get four for a boundary regardless of how hard you hit it. His lithe and crisp strokeplay in

England eight years ago seems a distant memory. Now he positively belabours the ball, the bottom hand coming through like a clenched fist socking a disagreeable jaw. At Edgbaston, Slater played a spectacular innings, with strokes so *avant garde* that they could have been hung in Tate Modern. It set Australia's series off on the right foot, though not perhaps his own. Too many starts later were squandered through misplaced confidence and poor shot selection.

England's performance in this rubber was a deep disappointment. Considering that it had won four and tied one of its preceding five series, supporters had every right to expect better. The whole affair seemed to run off the rails in the NatWest Series, when there were some grotesque selections in the name of formulating a specialist one-day side. Edgbaston was then a walkover from which there was no going back.

Injuries explained only so much. The irony was that the two best English batsmen, Butcher and Ramprakash, were both replacements. England's policy on injury management, moreover, underwent some bizarre fluctuations: they committed the folly of picking two players who were transparently unfit, Ashley Giles and Craig White, but also let go from their squads bowlers whose problems appeared largely psychological, Alex Tudor and Chris Silverwood.

The 23-year-old Tudor could have made a difference. When he bowled with spirit and control at Trent Bridge, England looked fleetingly formidable. But the general lack of an effective second string imposed an absurd burden on the new-ball attack of Darren Gough and Andy Caddick, and the challenge of seven Tests in a summer seemed to exhaust them both. What was lacking most of all was slow bowling: Giles, Robert Croft and Philip Tufnell played a Test each and proved nugatory. To be fair, their support in the field was usually meagre, and England's catching at Trent Bridge and Lord's was execrable. This seemed a question of confidence and concentration rather than of technique. When an Englishman reprieved an Australian, his inner rage was almost palpable; it was as though he immediately projected into the future and saw himself ruefully applauding the escapee's 150.

Butcher and Ramprakash scored the only English centuries of the series, one grand, one exceedingly good. Stewart also had his moments, especially in the first innings at Leeds, in addition to keeping wicket tidily. But probably the best English prospect remained the 25-year-old Marcus Trescothick, who demonstrated excellent temperament at Edgbaston and Trent Bridge while the Australians were running rampant. He has technical problems on the line of leg and middle stumps when the ball is bowled across him, but is as still at the crease as some of his team-mates are skittish, and seems more permanent as a result. It is easy to imagine us still watching him in ten years. But who will be holding down the other end?

AUSTRALIAN TOURING PARTY

S. R. Waugh (New South Wales) (*captain*), A. C. Gilchrist (Western Australia) (*vice-captain*), N. W. Bracken (New South Wales), D. W. Fleming (Victoria), J. N. Gillespie (South Australia), M. L. Hayden (Queensland), S. M. Katich (Western Australia), J. L. Langer (Western Australia), B. Lee (New South Wales), D. R. Martyn (Western Australia), G. D. McGrath (New South Wales), C. R. Miller (Victoria), R. T. Ponting (Tasmania), M. J. Slater (New South Wales), S. K. Warne (Victoria) and M. E. Waugh (New South Wales).

W. A. Seccombe (Queensland) was called to join the touring party on standby for Gilchrist, A. A. Noffke (Queensland) was called in as a replacement for N. W. Bracken.

The Australian touring party for the international limited-overs series was as follows: S. R. Waugh (New South Wales) (*captain*), A. C. Gilchrist (Western Australia) (*vice-captain*), M. G. Bevan (New South Wales), N. W. Bracken (New South Wales), D. W. Fleming (Victoria), J. N. Gillespie (South Australia), I. J. Harvey (Victoria), M. L. Hayden (Queensland), D. R. Martyn (Western Australia), G. D. McGrath (New South Wales), R. T. Ponting (Tasmania), A. Symonds (Queensland), S. K. Warne (Victoria) and M. E. Waugh (New South Wales).

Manager: S. R. Bernard. *Coach:* J. M. Buchannan. *Physiotherapist:* E. L. Alcott. *Fitness adviser:* J. Campbell. *Cricket analyst:* M. J. Walsh.

AUSTRALIAN TOUR RESULTS

Test matches – Played 5: Won 4, Lost 1.
First-class matches – Played 11: Won 8, Lost 2, Drawn 1.
Wins – England (4), Worcestershire, MCC, Somerset, Sussex.
Losses – Hampshire, England.
Draw – Essex.
Limited-overs internationals – Played 7: Won 5, Lost 1, Abandoned 1.
Wins – England (3), Pakistan (2). Losses – Pakistan (1). Abandoned – Pakistan (1).
Other matches – Played 3: Lost 1, No-Result 1, Tied 1.
Loss – Middlesex. *No result* – Ireland. *Tied* – Northamptonshire.

TEST MATCH AVERAGES

ENGLAND – BATTING

	M	I	NO	R	HS	100s	50s	Avge	Ct
M. A. Butcher	5	10	1	456	173*	1	1	50.67	4
M. R. Ramprakash	4	8	0	318	133	1	0	39.75	3
N. Hussain	3	6	1	177	55	0	2	35.40	0
A. J. Stewart	5	9	1	283	76*	0	2	35.38	13
M. E. Trescothick	5	10	0	321	76	0	3	32.10	4
M. A. Atherton	5	10	0	221	57	0	2	22.10	7
J. Ormond	1	2	0	35	18	0	0	17.50	0
U. Afzaal	3	6	1	83	54	0	1	16.60	0
A. R. Caddick	5	9	2	101	49*	0	0	14.43	1
D. Gough	5	9	3	82	39*	0	0	13.67	0
I. J. Ward	3	6	1	68	23*	0	0	13.60	0
D. G. Cork	1	2	0	26	24	0	0	13.00	0
G. P. Thorpe	1	2	0	22	20	0	0	11.00	1
C. White	3	6	1	38	27*	0	0	7.60	1
P. C. R. Tufnell	1	2	1	7	7*	0	0	7.00	0
A. J. Tudor	2	3	0	14	9	0	0	4.67	0
A. F. Giles	1	2	0	7	7	0	0	3.50	0
R. D. B. Croft	1	2	0	3	3	0	0	1.50	0
A. D. Mullally	1	1	0	0	0	0	0	0.00	0

* Denotes not out.

BOWLING

	O	M	R	W	BB	5W/i	10W/m	Avge
R.D.B. Croft	3	0	10	1	1/8	0	0	10.00
M.A. Butcher	14	4	63	4	4/42	0	0	15.75
A.J. Tudor	44.5	7	195	7	5/44	1	0	27.86
D. Gough	155.1	24	657	17	5/103	1	0	38.65
U. Afzaal..............	9	0	49	1	1/49	0	0	49.00
A.D. Mullally..........	30.3	10	99	2	1/34	0	0	49.50
A.R. Caddick	177.4	24	748	15	5/101	1	0	49.87
D.G. Cork.............	23	3	84	1	1/84	0	0	84.00
A.F. Giles.............	25	0	108	1	1/108	0	0	108.00
J. Ormond.............	34	4	115	1	1/115	0	0	115.00
C. White	46.4	7	189	1	1/101	0	0	189.00
P.C.R. Tufnell	39	2	174	1	1/174	0	0	174.00
M.R. Ramprakash	8	0	31	0	–	0	0	–

AUSTRALIA – BATTING

	M	I	NO	R	HS	100s	50s	Avge	Ct/St
S.R. Waugh.........	4	5	2	321	157*	2	0	107.00	2
M.E. Waugh	5	8	3	430	120	2	1	86.00	9
D.R. Martyn	5	7	2	382	118	2	0	76.40	0
A.C. Gilchrist	5	5	0	340	152	1	2	68.00	24/2
R.T. Ponting........	5	8	0	338	144	1	2	42.25	7
M.L. Hayden........	5	8	1	234	68	0	1	33.43	4
M.J. Slater.........	4	7	0	170	77	0	1	24.29	1
S.M. Katich.........	1	2	1	15	15	0	0	15.00	1
J.N. Gillespie	5	4	1	41	27*	0	0	13.67	2
G.D. McGrath.......	5	4	3	11	8*	0	0	11.00	1
B. Lee	5	4	0	24	20	0	0	6.00	0
S.K. Warne	5	4	0	13	8	0	0	3.25	6
J.L. Langer	1	1	1	102	102†	1	0	–	1

* Denotes not out.   † Retired hurt.

BOWLING

	O	M	R	W	BB	5W/i	10W/m	Avge
G.D. McGrath	194.2	56	542	32	7/76	4	0	16.94
S.K. Warne............	195.2	41	580	31	7/165	3	1	18.71
J.N. Gillespie	174	42	652	19	5/53	1	0	34.32
B. Lee	120.5	18	496	9	2/37	0	0	55.11
M.E. Waugh...........	13	1	69	1	1/40	0	0	69.00
R.T. Ponting...........	4	0	8	0	–	0	0	–

AUSTRALIAN FIRST-CLASS MATCHES TOUR AVERAGES

BATTING

	M	I	NO	R	HS	100s	50s	Avge	Ct/St
D. R. Martyn	9	14	5	942	176*	5	3	104.67	3
A. C. Gilchrist	8	10	2	663	152	3	2	82.88	28/4
S. M. Katich	5	7	3	288	168*	1	1	72.00	7
M. E. Waugh	9	15	6	644	120	2	2	71.56	12
S. R. Waugh	7	11	2	583	157*	3	0	64.78	5
R. T. Ponting	9	15	1	844	147*	3	5	60.29	11
M. L. Hayden	10	17	1	636	142	1	3	39.75	6
M. G. Bevan	1	2	0	67	34	0	0	33.50	0
J. L. Langer	6	11	2	285	104*	2	0	31.67	5
W. A. Seccombe	4	5	0	157	76	0	1	31.40	8/2
S. K. Warne	8	10	2	237	69	0	2	29.63	13
M. J. Slater	8	13	1	341	77	0	2	28.42	1
A. A. Noffke	3	3	0	69	28	0	0	23.00	1
C. R. Miller	5	4	1	68	62	0	1	22.67	2
B. Lee	8	7	0	127	79	0	1	18.14	0
G. D. McGrath	7	6	3	53	38	0	0	17.67	1
J. N. Gillespie	8	9	3	94	27*	0	0	15.67	3
D. W. Fleming	5	6	0	49	20	0	0	8.17	0
N. W. Bracken	1	2	2	10	9*	0	0	–	1

* Denotes not out.

BOWLING

	O	M	R	W	BB	5W/i	10W/m	Avge
N. W. Bracken	24	5	61	5	3/29	0	0	12.20
G. D. McGrath	234.5	74	624	40	7/76	4	0	15.60
S. K. Warne	263	56	784	42	7/165	3	1	18.67
D. W. Fleming	138	32	390	19	6/59	1	0	20.53
M. J. Slater	3.2	0	23	1	1/23	0	0	23.00
S. M. Katich	24	2	106	4	3/21	0	0	26.50
D. R. Martyn	9	1	53	2	2/38	0	0	26.50
J. N. Gillespie	228	54	801	29	5/37	2	0	27.62
C. R. Miller	157.2	37	586	18	4/41	0	0	32.56
A. A. Noffke	67.4	16	258	6	3/66	0	0	43.00
B. Lee	186.5	30	752	17	3/17	0	0	44.24
M. E. Waugh	24	2	121	2	1/33	0	0	60.50
J. L. Langer	2	0	5	0	–	0	0	–
R. T. Ponting	7.3	1	15	0	–	0	0	–
M. G. Bevan	5	0	28	0	–	0	0	–
M. L. Hayden	11	2	44	0	–	0	0	–

LIMITED-OVERS INTERNATIONALS

ENGLAND – BATTING

	M	I	NO	R	HS	100s	50s	Avge	Ct	S-R
N. V. Knight	6	6	1	213	84	0	2	42.60	2	57.57
M. E. Trescothick	6	6	0	249	137	1	1	41.50	3	83.84
O. A. Shah	5	5	1	104	62	0	1	26.00	2	68.42
B. C. Hollioake	6	6	1	118	53	0	1	23.60	2	81.38
A. R. Caddick	4	4	1	60	36	0	0	20.00	0	67.42
R. D. B. Croft	2	1	0	20	20	0	0	20.00	1	66.67
A. J. Stewart	6	6	0	79	25	0	0	13.17	6	43.41
D. Gough	6	5	1	49	40*	0	0	12.25	2	42.98
D. G. Cork	5	4	0	42	18	0	0	10.50	0	79.25
V. A. D. Brown	3	3	0	21	12	0	0	7.00	0	58.33
P. D. Collingwood	4	4	0	20	9	0	0	5.00	0	48.78
A. D. Mullally	6	5	2	13	6	0	0	4.33	1	16.46
M. A. Ealham	3	2	0	4	4	0	0	2.00	1	21.05
M. P. Vaughan	4	4	0	7	5	0	0	1.75	1	24.14

* Denotes not out.

BOWLING

	O	M	R	W	BB	Avge
D. Gough	54	5	244	9	2/31	27.11
A. R. Caddick	38	4	161	5	2/37	32.20
A. D. Mullally	54	5	248	7	3/50	35.43
D. G. Cork	41.5	0	215	6	2/32	35.83
R. D. B. Croft	14	2	67	1	1/21	67.00
M. A. Ealham	25.3	0	127	1	1/32	127.00
M. P. Vaughan	2	0	17	0	–	–
P. D. Collingwood	7.1	0	49	0	–	–
B. C. Hollioake	31	0	179	0	–	–

AUSTRALIA – BATTING

	M	I	NO	R	HS	100s	50s	Avge	Ct/St	S-R
S. R. Waugh	6	4	2	200	64	0	3	100.00	0	77.52
R. T. Ponting	5	5	2	298	102	1	2	99.33	2	98.68
M. G. Bevan	5	4	2	102	56*	0	1	51.00	3	66.23
A. C. Gilchrist	6	6	1	248	80	0	3	49.60	7/5	90.18
D. R. Martyn	5	3	1	99	51*	0	1	49.50	0	70.71
M. E. Waugh	5	4	0	129	47	0	0	32.25	2	82.69
S. K. Warne	5	2	1	28	14*	0	0	28.00	5	73.68
A. Symonds	5	3	0	69	35	0	0	23.00	1	87.34
I. J. Harvey	5	2	1	19	19*	0	0	19.00	1	135.71
B. Lee	5	1	0	10	10	0	0	10.00	0	55.56
J. N. Gillespie	3	1	0	9	9	0	0	9.00	1	34.62
M. L. Hayden	4	3	0	8	8	0	0	2.67	2	32.00
D. W. Fleming	2	1	1	22	22*	0	0	–	1	100.00
G. D. McGrath	5	0	0	–	–	0	0	–	1	–

* Denotes not out.

BOWLING

	O	M	R	W	BB	Avge
M.G. Bevan	3.2	0	16	1	1/4	16.00
G.D. McGrath	47.5	12	141	8	2/19	17.63
I.J. Harvey	38.1	4	153	7	2/18	21.86
S.K. Warne	45	3	232	10	3/52	23.20
J.N. Gillespie	26	6	103	4	3/20	25.75
B. Lee	48	4	264	10	3/63	26.40
A. Symonds	23	0	129	4	2/24	32.25
D.R. Martyn	9	0	66	1	1/45	66.00
D.W. Fleming	20	3	75	1	1/37	75.00
M.E. Waugh	8	0	27	0	–	–

PAKISTAN – BATTING

	M	I	NO	R	HS	100s	50s	Avge	Ct/St	S-R
Yousuf Youhana	6	6	1	263	91*	0	2	52.60	0	64.62
Wasim Akram	3	3	2	49	28*	0	0	49.00	1	84.48
Saeed Anwar	5	5	0	197	77	0	1	39.40	1	71.90
Saleem Elahi	3	3	0	104	79	0	1	34.67	0	74.82
Rashid Latif	6	4	0	138	66	0	1	34.50	6/1	87.90
Azhar Mahmood	6	6	3	87	38*	0	0	29.00	2	129.85
Inzamam-ul-Haq	5	4	0	102	79	0	1	25.50	1	78.46
Abdur Razzaq	6	6	0	125	75	0	1	20.83	2	62.19
Younis Khan	6	6	1	96	41	0	0	19.20	5	71.64
Shahid Afridi	4	4	0	68	30	0	0	17.00	2	72.34
Faisal Iqbal	1	1	0	12	12	0	0	12.00	0	57.14
Shoaib Malik	1	1	0	9	9	0	0	9.00	0	112.50
Waqar Younis	6	4	1	19	14	0	0	6.33	0	95.00
Saqlain Mushtaq	6	3	2	3	2	0	0	3.00	2	37.50
Shoaib Akhtar	1	1	0	1	1	0	0	1.00	0	50.00
Fazl-e-Akbar	1	0	0			0	0		0	–

* *Denotes not out.*

BOWLING

	O	M	R	W	BB	Avge
Waqar Younis	46	2	219	17	7/36	12.88
Shahid Afridi	26.2	3	112	5	3/15	22.40
Saqlain Mushtaq	53	0	232	7	2/20	33.14
Abdur Razzaq	46.3	3	187	5	2/41	37.40
Shoaib Akhtar	5	0	41	1	1/41	41.00
Azhar Mahmood	46.3	1	231	4	2/46	57.75
Fazl-e-Akbar	10	2	29	0	–	–
Shoaib Malik	4	0	39	0	–	–
Wasim Akram	24	2	103	0	–	–

Note: Matches in this section that were not first-class are signified by a dagger.

WORCESTERSHIRE v AUSTRALIANS

At County Ground, Worcester, June 1, 2, 3, 2001. Australians won by 360 runs. Toss: Australians.

The Australians made short work of a county that defeated them in May 1997, winning comfortably with ten overs to spare. After finding themselves at an insecure six for 178 on the first day, they were revived by a seventh-wicket partnership of 148 in 30 overs between Damien Martyn – who started his tour in fine form, hitting 19 fours and two sixes off 149 balls – and Shane Warne. When Worcestershire batted, only Anurag Singh, who batted for nearly three hours, stayed at the crease for long, and before tea on the second day Australia had obtained a 188-run first-innings lead. Beginning with an opening stand of 103 in 70 minutes and ending with an unbeaten ninth-wicket stand of 51 in 17 minutes, Australia thundered along at nearly six an over, fulfilling their objective of gaining batting practice for the limited-overs series. Steve Waugh declared 548 runs ahead after 90 minutes on the third day and unleashed Glenn McGrath on his sometime county team-mates. Once Graeme Hick had perished first ball, caught at first slip, the only resistance was provided by the veteran David Leatherdale, who struck 11 fours in his 72.

Close of play: First day, Worcestershire (1) 1-50 (Singh 25, Hick 19); Second day, Australians (2) 4-236 (S. R. Waugh 15, Gilchrist 7).

Australians

M.L. Hayden c Pipe b Kabir Ali	20	– (2) b Rawnsley	65
M.E. Waugh c Singh b Sheriyar	13	– (1) b Sheriyar	48
R.T. Ponting lbw b Liptrot	24	– c Sheriyar b Solanki	65
M.G. Bevan c Weston b Kabir Ali	33	– c Kadeer b Solanki	34
*S.R. Waugh b Liptrot	30	– b Rawnsley	32
D.R. Martyn lbw b Rawnsley	108	– (7) st Pipe b Rawnsley	28
†A.C. Gilchrist c Leatherdale b Liptrot	21	– (6) lbw b Kabir Ali	13
S.K. Warne lbw b Rawnsley	68	– (9) not out	41
D.W. Fleming b Rawnsley	11	– (8) lbw b Liptrot	20
N.W. Bracken not out	1	– not out	9
G.D. McGrath c Leatherdale b Kabir Ali	4		
B 9, l-b 7, n-b 2	18	L-b 4, n-b 1	5

(87.2 overs, 330 mins) 351   (67 overs, 254 mins) (8 wkts dec) 360
Fall: 29 55 59 109 134 178 326 333 342 351   Fall: 103 143 189 218 254 266 305 309

Bowling: *First Innings*—Sheriyar 20–3–86–1; Kabir Ali 12.2–1–43–3; Liptrot 17–3–37–3; Leatherdale 5–0–46–0; Rawnsley 23–4–90–3; Solanki 10–3–33–0. *Second Innings*—Sheriyar 12–1–78–1; Kabir Ali 11–1–55–1; Liptrot 11–0–74–1; Rawnsley 24–3–108–3; Solanki 9–1–41–2.

Worcestershire

W.P.C. Weston c Warne b McGrath	6	– lbw b Bracken	22
A. Singh c Gilchrist b McGrath	62	– c M.E. Waugh b Fleming	11
*G.A. Hick c Warne b McGrath	19	– c Warne b Fleming	0
V.S. Solanki lbw b Fleming	3	– c Warne b McGrath	15
D.A. Leatherdale c Gilchrist b Bracken	22	– b Bracken	72
Kadeer Ali lbw b Bracken	5	– b McGrath	2
†D.J. Pipe b Warne	5	– c Bracken b Warne	8
Kabir Ali lbw b Bracken	11	– lbw b McGrath	39
M.J. Rawnsley b Fleming	8	– b McGrath	1
C.G. Liptrot not out	13	– not out	4
A. Sheriyar st Gilchrist b Warne	3	– run out (S.R. Waugh)	5
L-b 3, n-b 3	6	B 1, l-b 4, w 2, n-b 2	9

(63.4 overs, 245 mins) 163   (57.3 overs, 216 mins) 188
Fall: 6 50 67 109 115 120 134 138   Fall: 18 20 40 52 56 99 165 174
143 163   178 188

Bowling: *First Innings*—McGrath 13–6–31–3; Fleming 15–3–47–2; Warne 18.4–7–38–2; Bracken 13–2–29–3; Martyn 4–1–15–0. *Second Innings*—McGrath 12.3–4–31–4; Fleming 12–1–39–2; Bracken 11–3–32–2; Bevan 5–0–28–0; Warne 12–3–34–1; M.E. Waugh 5–0–19–0.

Umpires: M. Dixon and A.A. Jones.

†MIDDLESEX v AUSTRALIANS

At Lord's, June 5, 2001. Middlesex won by six wickets. Toss: Middlesex.

Playing rather carelessly by their standards, the Australians were comfortably defeated by a young Middlesex team, reaching a competitive total thanks only to Ricky Ponting's 57 with eight fours and a ninth-wicket stand of 75 between Ian Harvey and Jason Gillespie. The batsmen having left 34 deliveries of their allotment unused on a benign surface, Australia's bowlers were left with too much to do. With half-centuries from 71 and 76 balls respectively, 23-year-old Owais Shah and 24-year-old Ben Hutton were seldom troubled in a match-winning partnership. It was Australia's first defeat at the hands of Lord's county tenants since their first meeting on Australia's inaugural tour in 1878.

Australians

M. L. Hayden c Weekes b Hewitt	....	3	(15)	S. K. Warne c Nash b Weekes	......	7	(18)
M. E. Waugh c Hutton b Hewitt	....	14	(16)	J. N. Gillespie not out	....	19	(39)
R. T. Ponting c Nash b Weekes	......	57	(47)	N. W. Bracken b Hunt	....	1	(2)
*S. R. Waugh c Weekes b Keegan	....	4	(12)	L-b 4, w 3, n-b 4	....	11	
D. R. Martyn c Nash b Cook	....	19	(16)				
A. Symonds lbw b Cook	....	4	(16)	(44.2 overs, 183 mins)		232	
I. J. Harvey b Cook	....	84	(65)	Fall: 17 36 43 78 106 108 141 154			
†W. A. Seccombe c and b Weekes	....	9	(24)	229 232			

Bowling: Hewitt 9–2–43–2; Keegan 10–2–57–1; Hunt 4.2–0–32–1; Cook 8–0–39–3; Weekes 10–0–36–3; Hutton 3–0–21–0.

Middlesex

A. J. Strauss c Harvey b Bracken	.....	15	(24)	M. A. Roseberry not out	....	11	(16)
B. L. Hutton run out (D. R. Martyn)	...	73	(105)	B 3, l-b 5, w 15, n-b 5	....	28	
O. A. Shah st Seccombe b Warne	....	50	(72)				
R. M. S. Weston not out	....	36	(46)	(47.1 overs, 192 mins) (4 wkts)		233	
S. J. Cook c Martyn b Harvey	....	20	(25)	Fall: 33 146 170 204			

*P. N. Weekes, †D. C. Nash, C. B. Keegan, J. P. Hewitt and T. A. Hunt did not bat.

Bowling: Gillespie 9–0–38–0; Bracken 8–0–47–1; Warne 10–1–39–1; Harvey 10–1–36–1; Symonds 8.1–0–54–0; Martyn 2–0–11–0.

Umpires: B. Leadbeater and A. G. T. Whitehead.

†NORTHAMPTONSHIRE v AUSTRALIANS

At County Ground, Northampton, June 7, 2001. Tied. Toss: Northamptonshire.

Australia tied with an English county for the first time since 1930, and were somewhat lucky to do so. Apparently awed by the magnitude of the moment, Northamptonshire squandered three wickets in the last over from Ian Harvey when separated from victory by a single run while their captain David Ripley looked on helplessly. The cause of English cricket, nonetheless, was advanced little, the hosts' best batsman being Western Australian import Michael Hussey, who struck seven fours in a crisp 73. Earlier, after the loss of stand-in skipper Adam Gilchrist and Andrew Symonds from consecutive deliveries, Damien Martyn and Mark Waugh had righted the innings with an undefeated fourth-wicket partnership of 157 from 27 overs. Martyn's form already appeared to threaten the tenure of his state team-mate Justin Langer, who was not scheduled to arrive with other members of the Test squad until the end of the NatWest Series.

Australians

*†A. C. Gilchrist b Cousins	19 (47)			
D. R. Martyn not out	101 (131)	L-b 3, w 1, n-b 3		7
A. Symonds lbw b Cousins	0 (1)			
M. G. Bevan c G. P. Swann b Penberthy	19 (35)	(50 overs, 192 mins)	(3 wkts)	234
M. E. Waugh not out	88 (89)	Fall: 38 38 77		

M. L. Hayden, I. J. Harvey, J. N. Gillespie, D. W. Fleming, G. D. McGrath and W. A. Seccombe did not bat.

Bowling: Weekes 10–0–57–0; Cousins 10–3–27–2; Penberthy 10–0–41–1; Brown 10–0–41–0; Innes 7–0–46–0; G. P. Swann 3–0–19–0.

Northamptonshire

M. E. Hussey b Bevan	73 (106)	L. C. Weekes run out	11	(11)
M. B. Loye b McGrath	18 (21)	D. M. Cousins c Gilchrist b Harvey	0	(2)
J. W. Cook b Gillespie	12 (18)	J. F. Brown run out (Symonds)	0	(2)
G. P. Swann lbw b Gillespie	20 (24)	B 2, l-b 11, w 6, n-b 3	22	
A. J. Swann c Gilchrist b Bevan	24 (40)			
A. L. Penberthy run out (Symonds)	22 (35)	(50 overs, 202 mins)	234	
K. J. Innes c Gilchrist b Symonds	9 (18)	Fall: 29 56 91 155 156 173 217 234		
*†D. Ripley not out	23 (26)	234 234		

Bowling: McGrath 10–2–39–1; Fleming 4–0–19–0; Gillespie 10–0–51–2; Harvey 10–0–31–1; Symonds 10–0–43–1; Martyn 2–0–14–0; Bevan 4–0–24–2.

Umpires: N. G. Cowley and D. R. Shepherd.

NATWEST SERIES

†ENGLAND v PAKISTAN

First Limited-Overs International

At Edgbaston, Birmingham, June 7, 2001. Pakistan won by 108 runs. Toss: Pakistan. Limited-overs international debut: P. D. Collingwood.

Man of the Match: Saeed Anwar.

Pakistan

Saeed Anwar c Hollioake b Cork	77 (106)	Younis Khan c Stewart b Gough	9	(7)
Shahid Afridi c Ealham b Mullally	25 (24)	Wasim Akram not out	4	(4)
Abdur Razzaq run out (Hollioake)	9 (24)			
Inzamam-ul-Haq c Trescothick b Cork	79 (95)	B 4, l-b 5, w 9, n-b 2	20	
Yousuf Youhana run out (Stewart/Gough)	12 (18)	(50 overs, 210 mins)	(6 wkts)	273
Azhar Mahmood not out	38 (24)	Fall: 34 55 205 210 236 265		

†Rashid Latif, *Waqar Younis and Saqlain Mushtaq did not bat.

Bowling: Gough 10–0–53–1; Mullally 10–1–44–1; Ealham 10–0–35–0; Cork 10–0–44–2; Vaughan 2–0–17–0; Collingwood 2–0–18–0; Hollioake 6–0–53–0.

England

M. E. Trescothick c Younis Khan	
b Waqar Younis . . 28 (30)	
A. D. Brown c Rashid Latif	
b Waqar Younis . . 8 (13)	
N. V. Knight not out 59 (115)	
*†A. J. Stewart c (sub) Shoaib Malik	
b Azhar Mahmood . 10 (23)	
M. P. Vaughan c Saeed Anwar	
b Azhar Mahmood . . 5 (7)	
P. D. Collingwood lbw b Abdur Razzaq 2 (5)	
B. C. Hollioake c and b Saqlain Mushtaq 6 (13)	

D. G. Cork b Shahid Afridi 18 (21)	
M. A. Ealham b Saqlain Mushtaq . . . 4 (13)	
D. Gough lbw b Shahid Afridi 1 (6)	
A. D. Mullally c Rashid Latif	
b Shahid Afridi . . 3 (39)	
L-b 9, w 11, n-b 1 21	
(47.2 overs, 219 mins) 165	
Fall: 28 47 69 86 92 108 135 144	
147 165	

Bowling: Wasim Akram 7–2–20–0; Waqar Younis 6–0–31–2; Azhar Mahmood 10–0–46–2; Abdur Razzaq 7–0–24–1; Saqlain Mushtaq 10–0–20–2; Shahid Afridi 7.2–2–15–3.

Umpires: B. Dudleston and J. H. Hampshire.
TV Umpire: G. I. Burgess.
Referee: B. F. Hastings.

†AUSTRALIA v PAKISTAN

Second Limited-Overs International

At Sophia Gardens, Cardiff, June 9, 2001. Australia won by seven wickets. Toss: Pakistan.

After their indifferent beginning to the tour, the Australians' NatWest Series campaign began with an emphatic win against strong opposition. Pakistan's total was built round a seventh-wicket partnership of 124 from 127 deliveries by Yousuf Youhana and Rashid Latif, a limited-overs international record which created a respectable total out of a shaky six for 85. Brett Lee, unexpectedly included in the team 15 minutes before play because of injuries to Nathan Bracken, Jason Gillespie and Damien Fleming, conceded 85 from his ten overs, 37 of those in his last 18 deliveries, as the batsmen harnessed his pace on the small Cardiff ground. Shoaib Akhtar then bowled at breakneck speed, one delivery to Gilchrist being clocked at 97.7 mph, and was almost as expensive; Man of the Match Ricky Ponting hit five of his first 14 deliveries for four, and set the scene for a splendid partnership between Steve Waugh and Michael Bevan. Shane Warne's international summer began promisingly when his first ball dismissed Abdur Razzaq, the ball turning between the batsman's legs and bouncing onto the stumps from Gilchrist's gloves.

Man of the Match: R. T. Ponting.

Pakistan

Saeed Anwar c Warne b Harvey 35 (56)	
Shahid Afridi c M. E. Waugh b Lee . . . 11 (9)	
Abdur Razzaq st Gilchrist b Warne . . 9 (28)	
Inzamam-ul-Haq st Gilchrist b Warne . 0 (2)	
Yousuf Youhana not out 91 (103)	
Younis Khan lbw b Harvey 13 (19)	
Azhar Mahmood c Gilchrist b Warne . 0 (3)	
†Rashid Latif run out (S. R. Waugh/Lee) 66 (68)	
*Waqar Younis c Warne b McGrath . . 14 (10)	

Saqlain Mushtaq run out	
(S. R. Waugh/McGrath) . . 2 (3)	
Shoaib Akhtar c M. E. Waugh	
b McGrath . . 1 (2)	
L-b 3, w 6, n-b 6 15	
(49.5 overs, 211 mins) 257	
Fall: 14 44 45 65 83 85 209 241 254 257	

Bowling: McGrath 9.5–2–22–2; Lee 10–1–85–1; Harvey 10–2–39–2; Warne 10–0–52–3; Martyn 4–0–21–0; Symonds 4–0–23–0; Bevan 2–0–12–0.

Australia

M.E. Waugh c Younis Khan		*S.R. Waugh not out	54 (64)
b Abdur Razzaq	47 (51)		
†A.C. Gilchrist b Shoaib Akhtar	13 (13)	B 6, l-b 3, w 3, n-b 6	18
R.T. Ponting c Abdur Razzaq			
b Saqlain Mushtaq	70 (68)	(45.4 overs, 195 mins) (3 wkts)	258
M.G. Bevan not out	56 (84)	Fall: 20 112 142	

D.R. Martyn, A. Symonds, I.J. Harvey, S.K. Warne, B. Lee and G.D. McGrath did not bat.

Bowling: Waqar Younis 7–0–41–0; Shoaib Akhtar 5–0–41–1; Azhar Mahmood 8–0–37–0; Abdur Razzaq 9–0–42–1; Saqlain Mushtaq 8.4–0–45–1; Shahid Afridi 8–0–43–0.

Umpires: A.G.T. Whitehead and P. Willey.
TV Umpire: R. Julian.
Referee: B.F. Hastings.

†ENGLAND v AUSTRALIA

Third Limited-Overs International

At Ashley Down Ground, Bristol, June 10, 2001. Australia won by five wickets. Toss: England. Limited-overs international debut: O.A. Shah.

Australia's batsmen timed a testing chase adeptly, winning with three deliveries to spare after consecutive boundaries by their captain, the last ball of the penultimate over having been off-driven for six by Ian Harvey. Ricky Ponting's helter-skelter hundred, his eighth in limited-overs internationals, continued a convincing return to form after the travails of his tour to India. Earlier, Shane Warne had made the decisive contribution as a fielder: after a steady partnership of 124 between Marcus Trescothick and Nick Knight, Warne ran out Trescothick with a direct hit and caught Knight sharply at short mid-wicket. The momentum of the innings was not restored until Owais Shah and Ben Hollioake were united in the 43rd over. Their unbeaten fifth-wicket partnership was worth 70 in 45 deliveries, Shah making an impressive international debut and Hollioake reviving memories of his at Lord's four years earlier. But Australia were never seriously extended, and England's seventh consecutive limited-overs defeat equalled their worst losing streaks of the last 30 years.

Man of the Match: R.T. Ponting.

England

M.E. Trescothick run out		B.C. Hollioake not out	37 (26)
(Warne/Gilchrist)	69 (75)		
A.D. Brown c Gilchrist b McGrath	12 (16)	L-b 10, w 2, n-b 1	13
N.V. Knight c Warne b Lee	84 (115)		
*†A.J. Stewart lbw b Lee	25 (45)	(50 overs, 196 mins) (4 wkts)	268
O.A. Shah not out	28 (24)	Fall: 13 137 189 198	

D.G. Cork, M.A. Ealham, R.D.B. Croft, D. Gough and A.D. Mullally did not bat.

Bowling: McGrath 10–1–45–1; Lee 10–1–55–2; Harvey 10–0–59–0; Warne 9–0–48–0; Symonds 3–0–24–0; M.E. Waugh 8–0–27–0.

Australia

†A.C. Gilchrist c Shah b Gough	.....	4	(13)	*S.R. Waugh not out	....	26	(22)
M.E. Waugh b Cork	....	46	(61)	I.J. Harvey not out	....	19	(13)

†A.C. Gilchrist c Shah b Gough 4 (13)
M.E. Waugh b Cork 46 (61)
R.T. Ponting run out
    (Brown/Mullally/Stewart) . .102(116)
D.R. Martyn b Mullally 46 (57)
A. Symonds b Gough 23 (15)

*S.R. Waugh not out 26 (22)
I.J. Harvey not out 19 (13)
    B 1, l-b 4, w 1 6
                   ——
(49.3 overs, 208 mins)   (5 wkts) 272
Fall: 12 101 198 211 230

M.L. Hayden, S.K. Warne, B. Lee and G.D. McGrath did not bat.

Bowling: Gough 10–2–44–2; Mullally 10–1–50–1; Ealham 8.3–0–60–0; Cork 10–0–39–1; Croft 7–0–46–0; Hollioake 4–0–28–0.

Umpires: J.H. Hampshire and R. Julian.
TV Umpire: D.J. Constant.
Referee: B.F. Hastings.

†ENGLAND v PAKISTAN

Fourth Limited-Overs International

At Lord's, June 12, 2001. Pakistan won by two runs. Toss: England.
Man of the Match: M.E. Trescothick.

Pakistan

Saleem Elahi lbw b Gough 15 (25)
Shahid Afridi c Trescothick b Caddick 30 (44)
Yousuf Youhana c Shah b Mullally . . 81 (119)
Inzamam-ul-Haq b Caddick 0 (2)
Younis Khan c Knight b Cork 41 (56)
†Rashid Latif b Ealham 23 (26)
Abdur Razzaq c Gough b Mullally ... 3 (3)

Azhar Mahmood not out 27 (21)
Shoaib Malik b Gough 9 (8)
*Waqar Younis not out 2 (2)
    L-b 2, w 3, n-b 6 11
                   ——
(50 overs, 212 mins)   (8 wkts) 242
Fall: 28 59 60 140 190 195 208 237

Saqlain Mushtaq did not bat.

Bowling: Caddick 10–1–37–2; Gough 10–1–38–2; Mullally 10–0–47–2; Cork 7–0–50–1; Ealham 7–0–32–1; Hollioake 6–0–36–0.

England

M.E. Trescothick c Shahid Afridi
              b Saqlain Mushtaq . .137(142)
N.V. Knight run out (Shoaib Malik) . . 1 (7)
*†A.J. Stewart c Younis Khan
              b Abdur Razzaq .. 4 (19)
M.P. Vaughan c Azhar Mahmood
              b Waqar Younis . . 0 (4)
O.A. Shah run out (Younis Khan) 62 (94)
B.C. Hollioake b Waqar Younis 0 (1)
D.G. Cork run out (Yousuf Youhana) . 3 (7)

M.A. Ealham lbw b Shahid Afridi .. 0 (6)
D. Gough lbw b Abdur Razzaq 6 (9)
A.R. Caddick st Rashid Latif
              b Saqlain Mushtaq .. 10 (14)
A.D. Mullally not out 1 (1)
    L-b 5, w 5, n-b 6 16
                   ——
(50 overs, 237 mins)   240
Fall: 6 19 26 196 197 201 205 218
     237 240

Bowling: Waqar Younis 10–2–20–2; Abdur Razzaq 10–0–41–2; Azhar Mahmood 10–0–50–0; Saqlain Mushtaq 9–0–50–2; Shoaib Malik 4–0–39–0; Shahid Afridi 7–0–35–1.

Umpires: N.A. Mallender and K.E. Palmer.
TV Umpire: T.E. Jesty.
Referee: B.F. Hastings.

†ENGLAND v AUSTRALIA

Fifth Limited-Overs International

At Old Trafford, Manchester, June 14, 2001. Australia won on run rate. Toss: Australia.

Batting second as the ball seamed treacherously in an English twilight, the hosts stumbled to their lowest total in limited-overs internationals: 86 chasing a Duckworth/Lewis revised target of 212 from 44 overs after a rain delay. England lost their first six wickets in the space of 15 runs, pinioned by intelligent fast bowling and enterprising captaincy, Steve Waugh encircling the batsmen with close catchers. Shane Warne also found the conditions to his liking; in attempting to use his feet to him, Ben Hollioake was hopelessly marooned. Earlier, England had made a promising beginning, reducing Australia to three for 35 by the time rain first intervened. The visitors made up for lost time thereafter, Steve Waugh combining productively with Michael Bevan and Damien Martyn before another heavy shower brought their innings to a halt.

Man of the Match: J. N. Gillespie.

Australia

M. L. Hayden c Gough b Caddick	....	0	(4)	I. J. Harvey c Trescothick b Mullally	.	0	(1)
†A. C. Gilchrist c Hollioake b Gough	.	5	(22)	S. K. Warne not out	....	14	(13)
R. T. Ponting c Knight b Caddick	....	21	(24)			
M. G. Bevan c Stewart b Mullally	....	37	(50)	L-b 2, n-b 3	....	5
*S. R. Waugh lbw b Gough	....	64	(83)			
D. R. Martyn not out	....	51	(79)	(48 overs, 205 mins)	(7 wkts)	208
A. Symonds c Vaughan b Mullally	...	11	(15)	Fall: 0 23 27 93 161 188 189

J. N. Gillespie and G. D. McGrath did not bat.

Bowling: Caddick 10–2–45–2; Gough 9–0–31–2; Cork 9–0–50–0; Mullally 10–1–50–3; Hollioake 10–0–30–0.

England

M. E. Trescothick b McGrath	....	15	(43)	D. Gough lbw b Warne	....	2	(12)
N. V. Knight c Gilchrist b McGrath	...	12	(28)	A. R. Caddick not out	....	8	(12)
*†A. J. Stewart c Bevan b Gillespie	...	0	(3)	A. D. Mullally c Gilchrist b Harvey	..	6	(23)
M. P. Vaughan b Gillespie	....	0	(1)			
O. A. Shah c Ponting b Gillespie	.....	10	(23)	L-b 1, w 5, n-b 1	....	7
P. D. Collingwood c and b Symonds	..	9	(26)			
B. C. Hollioake st Gilchrist b Warne	..	0	(8)	(32.4 overs, 134 mins)		86
D. G. Cork c Hayden b Symonds	....	17	(18)	Fall: 25 26 26 40 40 40 65 69 69 86

Bowling: McGrath 9–3–19–2; Gillespie 9–5–20–3; Warne 7–2–16–2; Symonds 7–0–24–2; Harvey 0.4–0–6–1.

Umpires: J. W. Holder and J. W. Lloyds.
TV Umpire: M. R. Benson.
Referee: B. F. Hastings.

†AUSTRALIA v PAKISTAN

Sixth Limited-Overs International

At Riverside Ground, Chester-le-Street. June 16, 2001. Match abandoned due to rain.

Umpires: A. A. Jones and D. R. Shepherd
TV Umpire: M. J. Kitchen
Referee: B. F. Hastings.

†ENGLAND v PAKISTAN

Seventh Limited-Overs International

At Headingley, Leeds, June 17, 2001. Pakistan won after a crowd invasion ended play early and Alec Stewart conceded the match. Toss: Pakistan.

Man of the Match: Waqar Younis.

England

M. E. Trescothick b Waqar Younis	...	0	(1)	D. G. Cork c Rashid Latif		
N. V. Knight c Shahid Afridi				b Waqar Younis	..	4 (7)
b Waqar Younis		9	(23)	D. Gough not out	....	40 (86)
*†A. J. Stewart c Abdur Razzaq				A. R. Caddick c Rashid Latif		
b Waqar Younis	..	18	(47)	b Azhar Mahmood	..	6 (19)
M. P. Vaughan c Younis Khan				A. D. Mullally run out (Rashid Latif)		0 (5)
b Waqar Younis	..	2	(17)			
O. A. Shah c Inzamam-ul-Haq						
b Waqar Younis		3	(7)	L-b 6, w 8, n-b 7	....	21
P. D. Collingwood c Younis Khan						
b Waqar Younis	..	0	(1)	(45.2 overs)		156
B. C. Hollioake b Shahid Afridi	......	53	(66)	Fall: 0 23 30 38 39 51 58 125 142 156		

Bowling: Waqar Younis 10–0–36–7; Fazl-e-Akbar 10–2–29–0; Abdur Razzaq 7–2–24–0; Azhar Mahmood 7–1–25–1; Saqlain Mushtaq 7.2–0–17–0; Shahid Afridi 4–1–19–1.

Pakistan

Saeed Anwar c Stewart b Gough	.....	24	(29)	Azhar Mahmood not out	....	6 (4)
Shahid Afridi c Stewart b Gough	.....	2	(17)	W 3, n-b 9	....	12
Abdur Razzaq c Stewart b Cork	.....	75	(103)			
Yousuf Youhana c Stewart b Cork	...	24	(74)	(59 overs)	(4 wkts)	153
Younis Khan not out	....	10	(21)	Fall: 21 34 128 147		

Inzamam-ul-Haq, †Rashid Latif, Fazl-e-Akbar, *Waqar Younis and Saqlain Mushtaq did not bat.

Bowling: Gough 10–2–39–2; Caddick 10–1–28–0; Mullally 10–1–30–0; Cork 5.5–0–32–2; Hollioake 3–0–14–0; Collingwood 1–0–10–0.

Umpires: J. W. Holder and M. J. Kitchen.
TV Umpire: J. W. Lloyds.
Referee: B. F. Hastings.

†AUSTRALIA v PAKISTAN

Eighth Limited-Overs International

At Trent Bridge, Nottingham, June 19, 2001. Pakistan won by 36 runs. Toss: Pakistan.

A pitch invasion by Pakistan's supporters during their team's innings, banishing players from the field for 20 minutes, spoiled a game full of spectacle and event. Security measures again proved inadequate – despite similar scenes having taken place at Pakistan's meeting with England at Edgbaston on June 7 – prompting calls for legislation to deal with such trespassers. Spectators had little need for the fireworks they persisted in letting off in the stands: once Pakistan's batsmen had set a challenging target, captain Waqar Younis gave thrilling demonstrations of swing bowling under lights at each end of Australia's innings. Waqar dismissed Mark Waugh and Matthew Hayden in his first over and Michael Bevan in his third, then returned to dismiss Steve Waugh and Andrew Symonds in the space of four deliveries before ending Australia's hopes by toppling Brett Lee's off stump. Waqar was also expensive, Adam Gilchrist poaching four boundaries from his second over on the way to an exhilarating half-century from 29 balls. But the loss of Gilchrist and Martyn in the same over to Saqlain Mushtaq was costly and, despite a sixth-wicket partnership of 77 between Steve Waugh and Andrew Symonds, 102 in 19 overs proved a target beyond the Australian tail once Waqar returned.

Man of the Match: Waqar Younis.

Pakistan

Saeed Anwar lbw b Lee	34	(43)
Saleem Elahi lbw b Warne	79	(91)
Abdur Razzaq c Fleming b Lee	5	(10)
Yousuf Youhana st Gilchrist b Warne	44	(56)
Younis Khan c Gillespie b Martyn	23	(28)
Faisal Iqbal run out (M.E. Waugh/Gilchrist)	12	(21)
†Rashid Latif run out (S.R. Waugh)	26	(25)
Azhar Mahmood st Gilchrist b Symonds	15	(9)

Wasim Akram not out	28	(15)
*Waqar Younis b Symonds	3	(4)
Saqlain Mushtaq not out	1	(1)
B 1, l-b 2, w 14, n-b 3	20	

(50 overs, 221 mins) (9 wkts) 290

Fall: 61 71 164 190 207 233 257 261 274

Bowling: Fleming 10–2–38–0; Gillespie 10–0–58–0; Lee 10–1–41–2; Warne 9–1–60–2; Symonds 6–0–45–2; Martyn 5–0–45–1.

Australia

†A.C. Gilchrist b Saqlain Mushtaq	70	(44)
M.E. Waugh c Rashid Latif b Waqar Younis	0	(1)
M.L. Hayden c Rashid Latif b Waqar Younis	0	(5)
M.G. Bevan b Waqar Younis	5	(9)
*S.R. Waugh c Saqlain Mushtaq b Waqar Younis	56	(89)
D.R. Martyn c Azhar Mahmood b Saqlain Mushtaq	2	(4)
A. Symonds c (sub) Imran Nazir b Waqar Younis	35	(49)

S.K. Warne c Wasim Akram b Azhar Mahmood	14	(25)
B. Lee b Waqar Younis	10	(18)
D.W. Fleming not out	22	(22)
J.N. Gillespie b Abdur Razzaq	9	(26)
L-b 6, w 12, n-b 13	31	

(46.3 overs, 224 mins) 254

Fall: 5 6 35 111 113 190 190 208 223 254

Bowling: Wasim Akram 10–0–68–0; Waqar Younis 8–0–59–6; Saqlain Mushtaq 10–0–50–2; Abdur Razzaq 8.3–1–16–1; Azhar Mahmood 10–0–55–1.

Umpires: N.A. Mallender and G. Sharp.
TV Umpire: V.A. Holder.
Referee: B.F. Hastings.

†ENGLAND v AUSTRALIA

Ninth Limited-Overs International

At The Oval, June 21, 2001. Australia won by eight wickets. Toss: England.

A balmy day and a blameless Oval pitch were wasted on this unequal contest, meaningless in terms of the NatWest Series. Unable to qualify for the Lord's final, an inexperienced England line-up never recovered from the loss of Marcus Trescothick, who played a ball onto his stumps in Glenn McGrath's first over. Nick Knight and Andy Caddick showed resilience, and Ben Hollioake could consider himself unlucky – he was run out at the bowler's end when Robert Croft's straight drive brushed the fingers of Damien Fleming on his follow-through. Adam Gilchrist and Ricky Ponting quickly set about exploiting excellent batting conditions and a fast outfield, hitting half-centuries from 54 and 45 balls respectively. Croft held a sharp return catch with Australia 20 runs from victory, but Ponting was unconquered at the finish with his third individual award of the tournament. It was England's 11th consecutive limited-overs defeat: their worst sequence in history.

Man of the Match: R.T. Ponting.

England

M. E. Trescothick b McGrath	0	(6)	
*†A. J. Stewart c Bevan b Lee	22	(46)	
N. V. Knight c Gilchrist b Fleming	48	(81)	
O. A. Shah c Gilchrist b Harvey	1	(3)	
A. D. Brown c Ponting b Lee	1	(7)	
P. D. Collingwood c Harvey b McGrath	9	(9)	
B. C. Hollioake run out (Fleming)	22	(31)	
R. D. B. Croft c McGrath b Harvey	20	(30)	

D. Gough b Lee	0	(1)	
A. R. Caddick c Hayden b Bevan	36	(44)	
A. D. Mullally not out	3	(11)	
L-b 1, w 3, n-b 10	14		
(43.2 overs, 197 mins)	176		
Fall: 0 51 53 59 81 109 119 119 155 176			

Bowling: McGrath 9–4–27–2; Fleming 10–1–37–1; Harvey 10–2–31–2; Lee 10–0–63–3; Symonds 3–0–13–0; Bevan 1.2–0–4–1.

Australia

†A. C. Gilchrist c and b Croft	80	(90)	
M. L. Hayden c Mullally b Caddick	8	(16)	
R. T. Ponting not out	70	(71)	
M. G. Bevan not out	4	(11)	

W 6, n-b 9	15	
	—	
(30.1 overs, 135 mins)	(2 wkts)	177
Fall: 39 163		

M. E. Waugh, *S. R. Waugh, A. Symonds, I. J. Harvey, B. Lee, D. W. Fleming and G. D. McGrath did not bat.

Bowling: Gough 5–0–39–0; Caddick 8–0–51–1; Mullally 4–1–27–0; Croft 7–2–21–1; Hollioake 2–0–18–0; Collingwood 4.1–0–21–0.

Umpires: D. J. Constant and G. Sharp.
TV Umpire: N. A. Mallender.
Referee: B. F. Hastings.

QUALIFYING TABLE

	Played	Won	Lost	No-result	Points	Net run-rate
Australia	6	4	1	1	9	0.930
Pakistan	6	4	1	1	9	0.698
England	6	0	6	0	0	–1.329

Net run-rate was calculated by subtracting runs conceded per over from runs scored per over.

†AUSTRALIA v PAKISTAN

Final

At Lord's, June 23, 2001. Australia won by nine wickets. Toss: Pakistan.

Two years after they met in the World Cup Final at the same venue, Australia and Pakistan staged a virtual rerun of the game, Australia taking the honours by an identical margin after keeping their opponents to a puny total. The crucial moment in Pakistan's innings came when Yousuf Youhana, finding striker Inzamam-ul-Haq flat-footed, was thrown out from point by Ricky Ponting while trying to regain his ground at the bowler's end. It was the first of five wickets to fall for 50 runs, and Pakistan were to leave 45 deliveries of their allocation unused despite a steady eighth-wicket partnership of 41 between Rashid Latif and Wasim Akram. When Australia began their reply Adam Gilchrist was more circumspect than during his spectacular innings in the World Cup Final, but he twice pulled Abdur Razzaq for six, and his 50 partnership with Ricky Ponting required only 33 balls. Australia lost Mark Waugh, run out attempting a third, but only Wasim of Pakistan's attack threatened even momentarily. The crowd were, for once, generally well behaved, although the presentation ceremony on the pavilion balcony was marred when a beer can thrown from below struck Michael Bevan in the face. Though Bevan escaped injury, Steve Waugh described the incident as a "cowardly act", and there were calls for future ceremonies to be held in private. ICC referee Brian Hastings, meanwhile, suspended Inzamam for two matches and fined him half his match fee for dissent; given out leg-before while stretching forward to a Warne top-spinner, the Pakistani batsman was clearly reluctant to leave the scene, as Hastings said he had been on at least three other occasions in the last three years.

Man of the Match: A.C. Gilchrist. *Man of the Series:* Waqar Younis.

Pakistan

Saeed Anwar c Bevan b Harvey	27	(40)
Saleem Elahi c Gilchrist b McGrath	10	(23)
Yousuf Youhana run out (Ponting)	11	(37)
Inzamam-ul-Haq lbw b Warne	23	(31)
Younis Khan c Warne b Lee	0	(3)
Abdur Razzaq c Warne b Lee	24	(33)
†Rashid Latif b Warne	23	(38)
Azhar Mahmood b Warne	1	(6)

Wasim Akram b Gillespie	17	(39)
*Waqar Younis lbw b Harvey	0	(4)
Saqlain Mushtaq not out	0	(4)
B 2, l-b 3, w 8, n-b 3	16	
	—	
(42.3 overs, 189 mins)	152	

Fall: 28 47 60 60 92 102 110 151 152 152

Bowling: McGrath 10–2–28–1; Gillespie 7–1–25–1; Harvey 7.3–0–18–2; Lee 8–1–20–2; Warne 10–0–56–3.

Australia

†A.C. Gilchrist not out	76	(93)
M.E. Waugh run out		
(Yousuf Youhana/Rashid)	36	(43)
R.T. Ponting not out	35	(23)

L-b 1, w 8	9	
	—	
(26.3 overs, 124 mins) (1 wkt)	156	

Fall: 78

M.G. Bevan, S.R. Waugh, D.R. Martyn, I.J. Harvey, S.K. Warne, B. Lee, J.N. Gillespie and G.D. McGrath did not bat.

Bowling: Wasim Akram 7–0–15–0; Waqar Younis 5–0–32–0; Saqlain Mushtaq 8–0–50–0; Abdur Razzaq 5–0–40–0; Azhar Mahmood 1.3–0–18–0.

Umpires: D.R. Shepherd and P. Willey.
TV Umpire: R. Palmer.
Referee: B.F. Hastings.

MCC v AUSTRALIANS

At Arundel Castle, Arundel, June 25, 26, 27, 2001. Australians won by 280 runs. Toss: Australians.

The Australians beat a multi-national MCC at a canter, the chief source of interest being the continued jockeying for position in their Test top order. Michael Slater, Matthew Hayden and Justin Langer all disappointed – Langer also having the misfortune to sustain a heavy blow on the wrist while fielding at short leg – while Western Australian reservists Simon Katich and Damien Martyn made strong claims for consideration. Katich hit 27 fours and a six in his first century for Australia during the first innings, while Martyn took three hours over an accomplished 80 in the second innings. Steve Waugh also coasted to a century, facing 127 balls in all and scoring 80 in boundaries, while Shane Warne contributed healthily to both innings. For the hosts, New Zealander Mark Richardson carried his bat in MCC's first innings in a hand of two and a half hours, while West Indian Jimmy Adams was undefeated in the second after hitting 11 fours and a six. Queenslander Joe Dawes, playing league cricket in Kent, claimed five good wickets. Before the start of the game, both teams observed a minute's silence in honour of Sir Donald Bradman and Lord Cowdrey.

Close of play: First day, MCC (1) 6-82 (Richardson 31, Metson 0); Second day, Australians (2) 8/294 (Warne 30, Gillespie 2).

Australians

M. J. Slater lbw b Dawes	7	– (2) c Amin-ul-Islam	
		b Azhar Mahmood	17
M. L. Hayden c Kruis b Dawes	31	– (1) c Kruis b Willoughby	16
J. L. Langer c Adams b Dawes	4	– b Dawes	0
*S. R. Waugh b Willoughby	45	– c Asif b Kruis	105
D. R. Martyn b Dawes	8	– lbw b Shahid Afridi	80
S. M. Katich not out	168		
†W. A. Seccombe c Metson b Willoughby	17	– (6) c Ward b Willoughby	20
S. K. Warne c Shahid Afridi b Adams	69	– not out	30
J. N. Gillespie c Ward b Amin-ul-Islam	1	– (10) not out	2
D. W. Fleming c and b Amin-ul-Islam	6	– (7) c and b Shahid Afridi	1
C. R. Miller c Adams b Amin-ul-Islam	4	– (9) b Willoughby	0
B 4, l-b 12, w 7, n-b 7	30	B 10, l-b 7, w 1, n-b 5	23

(74.5 overs, 308 mins)   390   (78 overs, 304 mins)   (8 wkts dec) 294
Fall: 11 27 54 64 126 175 365 378 386 390   Fall: 29 30 55 213 251 253 259 273

Bowling: *First Innings*—Dawes 19–5–74–4; Willoughby 14–4–43–2; Azhar Mahmood 14–2–76–0; Kruis 10–2–56–0; Shahid Afridi 3–0–28–0; Asif Mujtaba 6–0–38–0; Adams 6–0–45–1; Amin–ul–Islam 2.5–0–14–3. *Second Innings*—Dawes 12–1–51–1; Willoughby 21–4–66–3; Azhar Mahmood 9–2–31–1; Kruis 13–1–52–1; Asif Mujtaba 10–1–39–0; Amin–ul–Islam 3–0–8–0; Shahid Afridi 10–2–30–2.

MCC

M. H. Richardson not out	64	– b Gillespie	17
Asif Mujtaba lbw b Fleming	0	– lbw b Miller	22
Amin-ul-Islam lbw b Fleming	1	– (4) c Seccombe b Martyn	20
D. M. Ward c Warne b Gillespie	4	– (3) c Waugh b Warne	57
*J. C. Adams lbw b Miller	0	– not out	81
Shahid Afridi c Warne b Miller	2	– c Katich b Martyn	28
Azhar Mahmood lbw b Warne	30	– run out (Waugh)	10
†C. P. Metson lbw b Gillespie	0	– lbw b Miller	3
G. J. Kruis lbw b Warne	2	– c Hayden b Miller	0
J. H. Dawes b Miller	1	– b Slater	10
C. M. Willoughby b Miller	0	– run out (Hayden/Slater)	8
B 1, l-b 12, n-b 7	20	B 2, l-b 14, w 1, n-b 7	24

(38.3 overs, 150 mins)   124   (72.2 overs, 260 mins)   280
Fall: 2 12 29 33 35 82 95   Fall: 33 109 109 155 193 215 232
115 124 124   232 253 280

Bowling: *First Innings*—Gillespie 11–2–32–2; Fleming 12–4–28–2; Miller 8.3–2–41–4; Warne 7–2–10–2. *Second Innings*—Gillespie 10–3–24–1; Fleming 10–4–17–0; Miller 23–3–87–3; Hayden 6–2–12–0; Warne 12–1–48–1; Martyn 5–0–38–2; Katich 4–0–15–0; Slater 3.2–0–23–1.

Umpires: N. L. Bainton and A. Clarkson.

ESSEX v AUSTRALIANS

At County Ground, Chelmsford, June 29, 30, July 1, 2001. Drawn. Toss: Australians.
    Keener on batting practice than a result, stand-in captain Adam Gilchrist let Australia's last engagement before the First Test peter out with his team 743 runs ahead. Gilchrist and Damien Martyn revived Australia on the first day from an uncertain four for 154 with a counter-attacking partnership of 251 in 49 overs. Laced with 21 fours and

three sixes, Gilchrist's 150 required only 149 deliveries, while Martyn cruised along in his slipstream, taking 182 deliveries over his 114 with 16 fours and a six. Jason Gillespie then produced a fierce spell for Nasser Hussain, resuming cricket after breaking a finger during the First Test against Pakistan: after opening his account by pulling Gillespie for six, England's captain was scratchy and tentative, finally offering a chance to short leg. Keeper James Foster, who shared a sixth-wicket partnership of 104 with Graham Napier, saw the hosts past the follow-on, hitting 11 fours in an attractive stay of 115 balls. Australia were clearly intent on keeping the hosts in the field thereafter. Matthew Hayden and Michael Slater opened with 138 in less than two hours, and Brett Lee and Gillespie added a partnership of 61 in 56 minutes to which Gillespie contributed two runs. In his first first-class innings on tour, Lee hit two sixes, one of them from Peter Such into the River Can. After that the interest of spectators and bowlers waned. The only Australian to derive nothing from his visit to Chelmsford was Justin Langer, caught at the wicket second ball in the first innings, and bowled playing down the wrong line after an uncomfortable stay of 72 deliveries in the second; his omission from the First Test was confirmed two days later. Interestingly, both umpires in this game had represented England against Australia during the World Series Cup of 1982-83.

Close of play: First day, Essex (1) 1-16 (Hussain 7, Robinson 8); Second day, Australians (1) 2-188 (Langer 10, Lee 7).

Australians

M.J. Slater c Foster b Ilott	15	– (2) c Ilott b McGarry 58
M.L. Hayden c Foster b Bishop	23	– (1) c Grayson b Such 98
J.L. Langer c Foster b Ilott	0	– b Such 17
M.E. Waugh c Napier b Bishop	25	– (6) lbw b Bishop 0
R.T. Ponting b Such	63	– (7) st Foster b Such 79
D.R. Martyn not out	114	– (10) not out 46
*†A.C. Gilchrist not out	150	– (11) not out 25
J.N. Gillespie (did not bat)		– (5) c Foster b Such 22
B. Lee (did not bat)		– (4) st Foster b Such 79
C.R. Miller (did not bat)		– (9) c Ilott b Clinton 62
G.D. McGrath (did not bat)		– (8) c McGarry b Clinton 38
B 4, l-b 10, n-b 1	15	B 14, l-b 16, n-b 15 45

(87 overs, 353 mins) (5 wkts dec) 405	(120 overs, 481 mins) (9 wkts dec) 569
Fall: 36 36 46 108 154	Fall: 138 175 210 271 272 372
	379 477 490

Bowling: *First Innings*—Ilott 19–4–83–2; Irani 8–3–11–0; Bishop 18–5–70–2; McGarry 11–0–86–0; Such 23–3–99–1; Grayson 8–2–42–0. *Second Innings*—Ilott 13–2–62–0; Bishop 15–0–80–1; McGarry 19–2–121–1; Such 39–11–131–5; Grayson 13–2–54–0; Robinson 10–0–54–0; Clinton 8–0–30–2; Foster 2–0–6–0; Hussain 1–0–1–0.

Essex

N. Hussain c Langer b Gillespie	16		M.C. Ilott lbw b Miller	7
A.P. Grayson c Gilchrist b McGrath	0		P.M. Such lbw b Gillespie	0
D.D.J. Robinson st Gilchrist b Miller	34		A.C. McGarry not out	0
R.S. Clinton lbw b Gillespie	0			
R.C. Irani c Ponting b Miller	18		L-b 7, n-b 16	23
†J.S. Foster c Gillespie b Lee	74			
G.R. Napier c Miller b Gillespie	59		(64 overs, 264 mins)	231
J.E. Bishop c Martyn b Gillespie	0		Fall: 7 29 33 74 79 183 183 190 202 231	

Bowling: McGrath 15–8–20–1; Gillespie 16–5–37–5; Lee 7–1–41–1; Miller 21–4–94–3; Hayden 5–0–32–0.

Umpires: I.J. Gould and T.J. Jesty.

ENGLAND v AUSTRALIA

First Test Match

At Edgbaston, Birmingham, July 5, 6, 7, 8, 2001. Australia won by an innings and 118 runs. Toss: Australia. Test debut: U. Afzaal.

Coinciding with the Second Rugby Union Test in Melbourne between the Lions and the Wallabies, and the appearance in the Wimbledon semi-final of English player Tim Henman, this Test could have been part of a triple national sporting celebration. Instead, it became part of a circle of mourning: like the Lions and Henman, England were brutally disposed of, with almost five sessions to spare. The *coup de grace* was a spell of 63 deliveries in which England lost their final seven wickets for 22 runs, though it was probably the rampaging 152 from 143 balls with 110 runs in boundaries by Adam Gilchrist that did most to sap the home team's spirit. It was four years to the day since he had been flown home from Australia's last Ashes tour after suffering a serious knee injury: now he brought England to their knees. Two of his seniors also grew in stature: Steve Waugh's hundred was his 26th in Tests, equalling Sir Garfield Sobers' tally; Shane Warne's 8/100 made him sixth on the Test wicket-taking list, overtaking Ian Botham.

England's pre-Test plans were thrown awry by injuries to Graham Thorpe, Michael Vaughan and first reserve Mark Ramprakash, resulting in the inclusion of Mark Butcher and 24-year-old debutant Usman Afzaal from Nottinghamshire. Ashley Giles and Andy Caddick also brought injuries into the game, while both Nasser Hussain and Craig White were returning from spells on the sidelines, boding ill for a team whose presence in the NatWest Series had been largely superfluous. If anything, the Australians were even stronger than during their limited-overs campaign, finally rewarding the in-form Damien Martyn with his first Ashes Test cap, and packing their strongest attack, to whom Steve Waugh offered the incentive of a sultry morning and a dry pitch of sometimes discomfiting bounce when he won the toss.

In fact, after the loss of Marcus Trescothick to Jason Gillespie's first delivery, Michael Atherton and Butcher added an affirmative 104 for the second wicket from 138 deliveries, setting the tone for a day of batting so positive it sometimes bordered on the riotous. Australia regained the ascendancy through Warne who, having described himself wryly before the match as no more than a "back-up bowler", commenced a teasing spell by inducing a bat–pad catch from Butcher with his second delivery in the last over before lunch. When Atherton's last Ashes fifty in 17 innings was ended by a clinking delivery from Gillespie, and Hussain misjudged Glenn McGrath's line in playing no shot, Warne clinically disposed of Afzaal, White, Giles and Darren Gough in the space of 19 deliveries, securing five wickets in a Test innings for the 17th time. The left-handed Ian Ward escaped him, only to chop McGrath onto his stumps. At nine for 191 shortly after tea, England's early assertiveness seemed a distant memory. The final session was to prove one of the most hectic in recent Ashes history, runs pouring forth at almost seven an over. Caddick, despite a broken finger, struck Warne over mid-wicket for a defiant six to commence an hour-long partnership with Alec Stewart of 103 in 76 deliveries. Caddick's unbeaten 49 in 40 deliveries was comfortably his best Test score, Stewart's 65 in 82 deliveries a timely return to form, and their last-wicket partnership England's best for 98 years.

Michael Slater and Matthew Hayden then set off in pursuit of England's 294 at a clip, Slater looting 18 from Gough's first over, Hayden pulling Gough for a huge six, and their first-wicket partnership of 98 spanning only fifteen overs. White's sprawling catch at mid-wicket stopped Hayden, and after trapping Ricky Ponting cheaply late on the first day, Gough bowled Slater for a blazing 76 in 82 deliveries with his first ball on the second. But there was much more batting to come. The Waugh brothers settled securely against an attack that, while keen, seemed to offer at least one half-volley or long-hop every over; Giles in particular was frequently astray in length. Aware this was too good an opportunity to miss, Steve Waugh appeared immovable throughout his sixth Test century in England on a second day abbreviated by rain and bad light. He found an able partner in Damien Martyn, who celebrated his promotion by parading his simple and elegant technique, and who with Adam Gilchrist piloted Australia into the lead once his captain had been dismissed by a ball that kept low. After negotiating a maiden from Butcher in the last over before tea while on 99, Martyn posted a memorable maiden Test century in three and a half hours with 15 boundaries. It was fully 3,012 days since his Test debut against West Indies. England had opportunities to curtail their partnership at several stages, particularly with the second new ball. After Stewart had culpably spared Martyn at 65 and White just got a hand to a flying edge in the gully when Gilchrist was 14, England's fielding then disintegrated completely when Gilchrist was left with the tail for company and tore into a tiring attack with abandon. He was 93 when joined by McGrath, reached his hundred with a suitably extravagant thick edge over Stewart's head, then took only a further 25 deliveries to move from 103 to 152 with six fours and four sixes. This included 22 from an over by Mark Butcher, an Ashes record. Like Fleetwood-Smith with McCabe at Trent Bridge in 1938, McGrath contributed one stoical single to the last-wicket stand of 63 in 36 minutes.

Rain was the only possible salvation for the hosts once Atherton perished during the last hour, and the fourth day began cloudy but dry with England 234 runs in arrears. The composure of Trescothick and Butcher at first suggested serious resistance. McGrath for once was below par while Brett Lee again struggled with his direction, and Trescothick in particular showed excellent judgment outside off stump, in between pulling both bowlers for six. But when Lee then unseated Butcher with a steepling lifter and induced Ward to drag on for the second time in the match, England's lower order succumbed timidly. Hussain, incapacitated by a blow on the little finger of his left hand from Gillespie, did not return to the crease. After the defeats of the Lions and Henman, he must have felt as though he was resisting not just a great Australian team but the tide of history itself.

Close of play: First day, Australia (1) 2-133 (Slater 76, M. E. Waugh 0); Second day, Australia (1) 4-332 (S. R. Waugh 101, Martyn 34); Third day, England (2) 1-48 (Trescothick 21, Butcher 15).

Man of the Match: A.C. Gilchrist.

England

M. A. Atherton c M.E. Waugh b Gillespie	57	– c M.E. Waugh b McGrath		4
M. E. Trescothick c Warne b Gillespie	0	– c M.E. Waugh b Warne		76
M. A. Butcher c Ponting b Warne	38	– c Gilchrist b Lee		41
*N. Hussain lbw b McGrath	13	– retired hurt		9
I. J. Ward b McGrath	23	– b Lee		3
*†A. J. Stewart lbw b McGrath	65	– Gillespie		5
U. Afzaal b Warne	4	– lbw b Gillespie		2
C. White lbw b Warne	4	– b Gillespie		0
A. F. Giles c Gilchrist b Warne	7	– c M.E. Waugh b Warne		0
D. Gough c Gillespie b Warne	0	– lbw b Warne		0
A. R. Caddick not out	49	– not out		6
B 10, l-b 8, n-b 16	34	B 1, l-b 5, n-b 12		18

(65.3 overs, 304 mins)	294	(42.1 overs, 200 mins) (9 wkts dec) 164

Fall: 2 106 123 136 159 170 174 191 191 294

Fall: 4 99 142 148 150 154 155 155 164

Bowling: *First Innings*—McGrath 17.3–2–67–3; Gillespie 17–3–67–2; Lee 12–2–71–0; Warne 19–4–71–5. *Second Innings*—McGrath 13–5–34–1; Gillespie 11–2–52–3; Warne 10.1–4–29–3; M.E. Waugh 1–0–6–0; Lee 7–0–37–2.

Australia

M. J. Slater b Gough	77	B. Lee c Atherton b Butcher	0
M. L. Hayden c White b Giles	35	J. N. Gillespie lbw b Butcher	0
R. T. Ponting lbw b Gough	11	G. D. McGrath not out	1
M. E. Waugh c Stewart b Caddick	49		
*S. R. Waugh lbw b Gough	105	B 3, l-b 7, n-b 23	33
D. R. Martyn c Trescothick b Butcher	105		
†A. C. Gilchrist c Caddick b White	152	(129.4 overs, 565 mins)	576
S. K. Warne c Atherton b Butcher	8	Fall: 98 130 134 267 336 496 511 513 513 576	

Bowling: Gough 33–6–152–3; Caddick 36–0–163–1; White 26.4–5–101–1; Giles 25–0–108–1; Butcher 9–3–42–4.

Umpires: S. A. Bucknor and G. Sharp.
TV Umpire: K. E. Palmer.
Referee: Talat Ali.

SOMERSET v AUSTRALIANS

At County Ground, Taunton, July 13, 14, 15, 16, 2001. Australians won by 176 runs. Toss: Australians.

Led by Ricky Ponting, the Australians made short work of Somerset despite the surprise reinforcement by the Pakistani Test players Shoaib Akhtar and Aamir Sohail. From the tourists' point of view, the most satisfactory developments were the performances of two players outside their Test team. Justin Langer groped his way towards a semblance of form with a hundred from 176 deliveries, painstaking in its early stages, gaining in fluency as he spent just over four hours in the middle. On a pitch that provided little encouragement, Damien Fleming took 8/97 from 36 hostile overs. The Australians were handicapped by injuries to Matthew Hayden's knee and Michael Slater's wrist which prevented them from batting or fielding on the second and third days, but others also made the most of the opportunities. Ponting's 128 in 130 deliveries included three fours and a six from an over by Shoaib, and Damien Martyn hit an undefeated 176 with 25 boundaries and put on 156 in 137 minutes with deputy keeper Wade Seccombe, representing Australia for the first time. The match was also the first appearance of Queenslander Ashley Noffke, recently arrived as a replacement for the injured Nathan Bracken. Somerset's resistance on the last day was prolonged by captain Michael Burns and 20-year-old Matthew Wood, who provided the most accomplished local batting in a team missing five of its regular players by reaching his second-innings fifty in 47 balls. But the match was ended quickly by Simon Katich's seldom-used left-arm spin, permitting an early escape to London for the Lord's Test.

Close of play: First day, Australians (1) 3-348 (Langer 104, Waugh 55); Second day, Somerset (1) 267 all out; Third day, Somerset (2) 1-52 (Aamir Sohail 20, Burns 19).

Australians

M. L. Hayden c Parsons b Grove	6		
M. J. Slater lbw b Kerr	28		
*R. T. Ponting b Shoaib Akhtar	128		
J. L. Langer not out	104	– (1) lbw b Shoaib Akhtar	10
M. E. Waugh not out	55	– (6) not out	41
S. M. Katich (did not bat)		– (2) c Turner b Shoaib Akhtar	3
†W. A. Seccombe (did not bat)		– (4) c Holloway b Blackwell	76
D. R. Martyn (did not bat)		– (3) not out	176
A. A. Noffke (did not bat)		– (5) c and b Blackwell	22
L-b 15, w 2, n-b 10	27	L-b 3, w 2, n-b 2	7

(74 overs, 296 mins)	(3 wkts dec) 348	(81 overs, 320 mins) (4 wkts dec) 335
Fall: 9 62 230		Fall: 12 15 171 213

D. W. Fleming and C. R. Miller did not bat.

Bowling: *First Innings*—Shoaib Akhtar 14–0–81–1; Grove 16–0–96–1; Kerr 17–3–52–1; Parsons 9–1–42–0; Blackwell 8–0–25–0; Burns 7–1–21–0; Aamir Sohail 3–0–16–0. *Second Innings*—Shoaib Akhtar 7–3–9–2; Grove 14–1–77–0; Kerr 19–0–89–0; Parsons 13–1–61–0; Burns 4–1–8–0; Blackwell 24–3–88–2.

Somerset

Aamir Sohail c Hayden b Noffke	50	– c Ponting b Miller	36
P.C.L. Holloway c Katich b Fleming	0	– c Ponting b Noffke	7
*M. Burns c Miller b Fleming	9	– lbw b Fleming	59
P.D. Bowler b Fleming	2	– (7) not out	26
M.J. Wood c Katich b Miller	39	– (4) lbw b Miller	51
K.A. Parsons c Martyn b Waugh	38	– (5) lbw b Fleming	3
†R.J. Turner c Langer b Fleming	42	– (6) lbw b Noffke	9
I.D. Blackwell c Ponting b Fleming	30	– c Noffke b Katich	28
J.I.D. Kerr c Seccombe b Fleming	13	– c Martyn b Katich	0
J.O. Grove c Waugh b Miller	6	– c Katich b Miller	0
Shoaib Akhtar not out	4	– st Seccombe b Katich	10
B 6, l-b 3, w 13, n-b 12	34	W 5, n-b 6	11

(68.2 overs, 265 mins)	267	(70 overs, 255 mins)	240

Fall: 1 15 33 111 132 189 243
     250 263 267

Fall: 13 93 118 122 173 175 228
     228 229 240

Bowling: *First Innings*—Fleming 17–2–59–6; Noffke 15–1–71–1; Miller 27.2–2–90–2; Ponting 3–1–5–0; Waugh 6–1–33–1. *Second Innings*—Fleming 19–6–38–2; Noffke 22–3–92–2; Miller 25–10–89–3; Katich 4–0–21–3.

Umpires: M. Dixon and M.J. Kitchen.

ENGLAND v AUSTRALIA

Second Test Match

At Lord's, July 19, 20, 21, 22, 2001. Australia won by eight wickets. Toss: Australia.

Australia's mortgage on Lord's, where they have not lost a Test since 1934, never seemed remotely in danger. This time England were handicapped not merely by uneven batting or nugatory second-string bowling, but also by inept fielding. Once Australia's first-innings lead of 214 had been fattened by a string of missed chances – Adam Gilchrist alone was dropped four times – there was no escape for the home team. It is a distinguishing skill of this Australian team that it leaves no error unpunished.

England's captaincy overshadowed the match's preliminaries. Both Alec Stewart and Mark Butcher ruled themselves out of consideration in the absence of the injured Nasser Hussain, leaving a reluctant Michael Atherton to take charge. This pass-the-parcel exercise puzzled Steve Waugh, who expressed surprise that the honour of leading their country should mean so little, and made him all the keener to insert the hosts on winning the toss beneath a cloudy sky and after rain had delayed the start by 75 minutes.

Rain after tea further curtailed play on the first day, but Australia struck four crucial blows in the 40.1 overs possible, the most important being Atherton who, in playing no stroke to a ball that seamed back wickedly, succumbed to Glenn McGrath for the 14th time in 15 Tests. England's hopes of a worthwhile first innings were left with Graham Thorpe, but after weeks of inactivity through injury he was not surprisingly unequal to the task. A telling spell by McGrath, including three wickets in nine deliveries, restricted England's last six wickets to 66 runs, six of them at a single hooked blow by Dominic Cork, who hit lustily until well held by Ricky Ponting at point. Australia's fielding was flawless throughout, a factor as material as England's later mistakes.

Australia's reply began tentatively against some fine new-ball bowling by Andy Caddick and Darren Gough, and when Michael Slater's uneasy vigil ended ten minutes before tea, it required a fine innings by Mark Waugh to recover the situation. He was abetted by an English attack that lapsed onto too short a length, and by Atherton's reluctance to post a third man, which allowed a regular leakage of boundaries. Waugh's was never a dominant innings, simply a calm, professional contribution to Australia's ascendancy, laced with attractive moments in its three and a half hours. Steve Waugh proved the ideal escort as his brother Mark edged through the nineties – sustaining a blow on the helmet from Caddick at 98 – towards his 19th Test century. A single to mid-on completed it, from 165 deliveries and including 13 fours; an attempted single to mid-on 12 minutes later ended it. Gough's direct hit was all the more remarkable for coming amid consecutive sessions in which England squandered two years of effort to dispel their reputation as the worst fielding side in the world by plunging straight to the bottom of the class again. The Waughs had already benefited, Mark having been missed at 59 by Craig White in the gully, Steve at 14 off a return catch to Gough. The Yorkshireman then had Gilchrist missed on four occasions in a single session: at 13 by Butcher at slip, at 33 by Ian Ward at cover, at 49 by Butcher at slip and at 73 by Atherton at slip. Between times, Gilchrist made hay, adding 78 in 148 balls with his Edgbaston accomplice Damien Martyn, then laying about him as the tail struggled against Caddick with the second new ball. His 90 from 121 deliveries, as at Birmingham, again had the effect of putting the game beyond England's reach.

Jason Gillespie removed Marcus Trescothick with a peach of a delivery seaming away down the slope. Shane Warne conjured a wicket from the rough, Atherton failing to cover leg stump as he attempted a sweep, and Thorpe was beaten for pace on the stroke of tea after a loquacious spell by Brett Lee. The crowd was in a surprisingly buoyant mood on this third day, drawing some solace from the 20th anniversary of the day England wrested victory from Australia at Headingley after following on. Australia's first-innings score being the same on this occasion, the partnership of 96 from 171 balls between Butcher and Ramprakash was felt to presage greater deeds. Four wickets in 16 deliveries on the fourth morning, however, including Butcher after a determined innings from 159 deliveries with a dozen boundaries, showed such fancies for what they were. In catching Gough, Mark Waugh set a record for Test catches of 158, underlining the splendid support that Australia's bowlers have enjoyed from their fielders for the last decade and which England's have usually lacked. Gillespie's figures were slightly spoiled when White took 19 from one over, but otherwise his pace and the sheer regularity with which he hit the seam were too much for batsmen deficient in both confidence and technique.

Caddick and Gough claimed consolation wickets before Australia collected the required runs in 19 deliveries; they at least could escape censure in what was England's 22nd defeat in the last 35 Ashes Tests.

Close of play: First day, England (1) 4-121 (Thorpe 16, Stewart 0); Second day, Australia (1) 5-255 (Martyn 24, Gilchrist 10); Third day, England (2) 4-163 (Butcher 73, Stewart 13).

Man of the Match: G. D. McGrath.

England

*M. A. Atherton lbw b McGrath	37	– b Warne	20
M. E. Trescothick c Gilchrist b Gillespie	15	– c Gilchrist b Gillespie	3
M. A. Butcher c M. E. Waugh b McGrath	21	– c Gilchrist b Gillespie	83
G. P. Thorpe c Gilchrist b McGrath	20	– lbw b Lee	2
M. R. Ramprakash b Lee	14	– lbw b Gillespie	40
†A. J. Stewart c Gilchrist b McGrath	0	– lbw b McGrath	28
I. J. Ward not out	23	– c Ponting b McGrath	0
C. White c Hayden b McGrath	0	– not out	27
D. G. Cork c Ponting b Gillespie	24	– c Warne b McGrath	2
A. R. Caddick b Warne	0	– c Gilchrist b Gillespie	7
D. Gough b Warne	5	– c M. E. Waugh b Gillespie	1
B 7, l-b 8, w 2, n-b 11	28	L-b 3, w 2, n-b 9	14

(63.3 overs, 297 mins) 187
Fall: 33 75 96 121 126 129 131
178 181 187

(66 overs, 286 mins) 227
Fall: 8 47 50 146 188 188 188
193 225 227

Bowling: *First Innings*—McGrath 24–9–54–5; Gillespie 18–6–56–2; Lee 16–3–46–1; Warne 5.3–0–16–2. *Second Innings*—McGrath 19–4–60–3; Gillespie 16–4–53–5; Lee 9–1–41–1; Warne 20–4–58–1; M.E. Waugh 2–1–12–0.

Australia

M. J. Slater c Stewart b Caddick	25	– (2) c Butcher b Caddick	4
M. L. Hayden c Butcher b Caddick	0	– (1) not out	6
R. T. Ponting c Thorpe b Gough	14	– lbw b Gough	4
M. E. Waugh run out (Gough)	108	– not out	0
*S. R. Waugh c Stewart b Cork	45		
D. R. Martyn c Stewart b Caddick	52		
†A. C. Gilchrist c Stewart b Gough	90		
S. K. Warne c Stewart b Caddick	5		
B. Lee b Caddick	20		
J. N. Gillespie b Gough	9		
G. D. McGrath not out	0		
L-b 9, w 1, n-b 23	33		

(101.1 overs, 449 mins) 401
Fall: 5 27 105 212 230 308 322 387 401 401

(3.1 overs, 15 mins) (2 wkts) 14
Fall: 6 13

Bowling: *First Innings*—Gough 25–3–115–3; Caddick 32.1–4–101–5; White 18–1–80–0; Cork 23–3–84–1; Butcher 3–1–12–0. *Second Innings*—Gough 2–0–5–1; Caddick 1.1–0–9–1.

Umpires: S. A. Bucknor and J. W. Holder.
TV Umpire: J. W. Lloyds.
Referee: Talat Ali.

HAMPSHIRE v AUSTRALIANS

At Hampshire Rose Bowl, Southampton, July 28, 29, 30, 2001. Hampshire won by two wickets. Toss: Hampshire.

Playing only four specialist batsmen, Australia were bundled out before lunch on the first day by Alan Mullally, who at one stage had 4/7, and 22-year-old swing bowler James Schofield. With his first ball in first-class cricket, Schofield had Matthew Hayden caught at second slip, then trapped Justin Langer with a full toss and elicited a lapse of concentration from Steve Waugh. It was Australia's lowest score against Hampshire since their 76 in 1985. After Brett Lee had struck twice in an over, Hampshire demonstrated that the batting conditions were far from difficult, Robin Smith adding 102 in 28 overs with Derek Kenway and 182 in 51 overs with Neil Johnson. The 37-year-old Smith, peppered with bouncers from Lee and Jason Gillespie, reached the first century against the Australian tourists in an innings spanning six hours and including 15 boundaries, causing one to wonder why his Test career had been cut so peremptorily short five years earlier. When Australia batted again, 257 in arrears, there was no sign of the swing witnessed on the first day. Hayden made hay against the county he represented four years earlier, reaching his century early on the final day. But the home side maintained its resolve. Giles White, an aspiring leg-spinner, took the prize wicket of Australia's captain, and John Francis, acting as substitute fielder, took an outstanding boundary catch to dismiss Damien Fleming, left hand stretched over his head with both feet off the ground. Hampshire then went after Waugh's generous target of 133 from 26 overs with alacrity. Shane Warne, also a former Hampshire representative, produced a virtuoso spell from the northern end, but with nine balls remaining Iain Brunnschweiler coolly scooped a ball to the fine-leg boundary to guide his side home.

Close of play: First day, Hampshire (1) 3-283 (Smith 79, Johnson 64); Second day, Australians (2) 1-176 (Hayden 92, Katich 49).

Australians

M. L. Hayden c Johnson b Schofield	1	– c Johnson b Udal	142
J. L. Langer lbw b Schofield	2	– c Kenway b Johnson	30
S. M. Katich c Prittipaul b Mullally	3	– c (sub) J. D. Francis b Udal	59
*S. R. Waugh c Johnson b Schofield	10	– c and b White	40
†W. A. Seccombe c Kenway b Mullally	13	– b Udal	31
S. K. Warne c Brunnschweiler b Mullally	1	– c Brunnschweiler b Schofield	15
B. Lee c Brunnschweiler b Mascarenhas	22	– c Brunnschweiler b Johnson	2
A. A. Noffke c Brunnschweiler b Mullally	28	– (10) c Prittipaul b Schofield	19
J. N. Gillespie b Mullally	1	– (8) not out	27
D. W. Fleming c Johnson b Udal	6	– (9) c (sub) J. D. Francis b Udal	5
C. R. Miller not out	2		
B 4, l-b 2, w 1, n-b 1	8	B 10, l-b 8, w 1	19

(30.4 overs, 135 mins) 97   (109.1 overs, 442 mins)(9 wkts dec) 389
Fall: 1 10 16 20 23 47 63   Fall: 72 198 271 283 321 333
     72 95 97   333 345 389

Bowling: *First Innings*—Mullally 11.4–3–18–5; Schofield 6–2–25–3; Mascarenhas 8–2–17–1; Johnson 4–0–25–0; Udal 1–0–6–1. *Second Innings*—Mullally 8–3–20–0; Schofield 28.1–3–106–2; Mascarenhas 1.5–0–8–0; Udal 47.1–10–149–4; Johnson 16–4–50–2; White 8–0–38–1.

Hampshire

D. A. Kenway c Waugh b Warne	70	– (2) c Katich b Lee	22
G. W. White c Seccombe b Lee	0	– (1) c Seccombe b Lee	8
W. S. Kendall lbw b Lee	0	– b Warne	9
*R. A. Smith lbw b Noffke	113	– (6) c Langer b Miller	10
N. C. Johnson b Gillespie	88	– lbw b Warne	37
†L. R. Prittipaul c Seccombe b Gillespie	10	– (4) b Lee	0
A. D. Mascarenhas c Seccombe b Noffke	10	– b Warne	14
S. D. Udal c Warne b Noffke	15	– b Warne	2
†I. Brunnschweiler c Waugh b Miller	1	– not out	10
J. E. K. Schofield c Katich b Miller	0	– not out	1
A. D. Mullally not out	4		
B 7, l-b 12, w 2, n-b 12	43	B 3, l-b 10, w 5, n-b 3	21

(114.1 overs, 445 mins) 354   (24.3 overs, 121 mins)   (8 wkts) 134
Fall: 13 14 116 298 321 328 339 350 350 354   Fall: 27 38 42 90 99 111 121 128

Bowling: *First Innings*—Lee 19–6–54–2; Fleming 21–6–53–0; Noffke 22.1–11–66–3; Gillespie 14–2–37–2; Miller 21–8–55–2; Warne 13–2–43–1; Katich 4–0–17–0. *Second Innings*—Lee 7–2–17–3; Fleming 4–0–22–0; Gillespie 3–0–19–0; Miller 5.3–0–32–1; Warne 5–0–31–4.

Umpires: J. F. Steel and R. A. White.

ENGLAND v AUSTRALIA

Third Test Match

At Trent Bridge, Nottingham, August 2, 3, 4, 2001. Australia won by seven wickets. Toss: England.

Australia won a record seventh consecutive Ashes series at 4 p.m. on the third day, after a match with more twists than the first two Tests but a fundamentally unaltered plot. On a pitch of uneven bounce and in conditions conducive to sideways movement, it was the first Ashes Test since Brisbane in December 1990 to feature four innings under 200, and as then Australia proved the side with the greater recuperative powers. At the end of the first day they were under acute pressure, but by the end of the second they had more than regained parity, and England in the end succumbed rather meekly.

England won their first toss in ten attempts but lost their captain to the second ball of the match in the worst possible circumstances. Michael Atherton, attempting to drop his wrists, was judged by umpire John Hampshire to have gloved to second slip – a decision soon revealed as incorrect, the ball having actually rebounded from his forearm guard. Marcus Trescothick filled the role of bulwark in a determined stay of more than two hours, striking 13 fours with a fluency none of his team-mates could mimic. Glenn McGrath gave a masterful display of seam bowling, even swinging the ball when it aged a little: his 20th bag of five wickets at Test level was also his fifth against England. Jason Gillespie also bowled expertly, while Shane Warne sneaked in to claim his 100th wicket against England when he had Robert Croft caught at silly point.

Australia were none for 48 in the blink of an eye, and the patrons eerily quiet. England's revival was led by Alex Tudor, playing his first Test for two years but confirming the impression he had made on Australians on his debut at Perth in December 1998. Falling at once onto a testing length, he trapped Matthew Hayden, and staunched the flow of runs. Darren Gough dismissed Michael Slater and Ricky Ponting, both driving diffidently, and Andy Caddick redeemed an insipid first spell with an inspired second that swept Steve Waugh, Damien Martyn and Shane Warne away in 11 balls. With Mark Waugh also fending Tudor to slip, Australia had lost seven for 54 in 93 minutes of penetrative bowling and surprisingly clean-handed catching. Adam Gilchrist, however, remained, and the resistance he organised with Gillespie on the second morning proved decisive. As ever, he enjoyed some luck, twice inside-edging narrowly past the stumps. But he drove thrillingly: two strokes on the up through cover brought a hasty curtailment to Gough's experiment with bowling round the wicket, and he needed only 49 balls to bolt to his fifty. Gillespie was a poised and deliberate foil, deflecting into gaps with aplomb, and showing a customary relish for the fight. Australia's five-run lead would have been beyond their wildest dreams 18 hours earlier.

Sixty-seven overs remained of the second day, and for 37 of those Atherton was at his cussed best. He was lucky to survive a leg-before-wicket appeal at 12, playing no shot to McGrath, but otherwise was imperturbable, even surviving a glancing blow on the jaw from Brett Lee at 91.8 mph from which he elegantly pirouetted to avoid hitting his stumps. Trescothick again showed his class, but was unlucky to be caught off Warne by Gilchrist, the ball having rebounded from a full-blooded sweep that connected with Hayden's ankle at short leg. Television replays also demonstrated that he was twice cursed: Warne's front foot was clearly over the crease. Under darkened skies, and rain from which the umpires gave the batsmen periodic respite, a patient partnership of 56 between Atherton and Mark Ramprakash from 117 balls kept them in the match until Warne interposed again. Atherton was given out caught at the wicket pushing forward – another dubious decision – beginning a spell of 4/11 from 36 balls. Alec Stewart dragged on rather casually, Ramprakash charged down the wicket crazily, and the anxious Craig White popped the last ball of the day to silly point. When Gillespie scooped 3/6 from his first 14 balls on the third morning, including Caddick as his 100th Test victim, custody of the Ashes looked safe, had it ever been in doubt. Warne's 6/33 was his 17th bag of five in a Test, his sixth against England, and his best figures since November 1995, before the finger and shoulder operations that had threatened his career. Gilchrist made six catches and a stumping to complement his priceless innings.

Australia's chase might have been more tentative had umpire Srinavas Venkataraghavan upheld Gough's leg-before-wicket appeal against Hayden from the second ball. As it was, some punchy shots, judicious calling and a stream of boundaries to the untenanted third man soon set them on their way. The fourth and last fifty partnership of the match was the largest and fastest, a 69-run 66-ball scamper for the fourth wicket by Mark Waugh and Martyn. By then their captain had succumbed to a strained left calf – sustained while setting off for a run from his first ball and requiring a stretcher to remove him – which was the only event to mar some full-blooded victory celebrations. The Australians performed a lap of Trent Bridge, during which Warne was the subject of fulsome tributes, and also the odd boo from a small contingent of Barmy Army irregulars, which was a form of tribute in itself.

Close of play: First day, Australia (1) 7-105 (Gilchrist 4, Lee 3); Second day, England (2) 6-144 (Ward 13).

Man of the Match: S. K. Warne.

England

*M. A. Atherton c M. E. Waugh b McGrath	0	–	c Gilchrist b Warne	51
M. E. Trescothick c Gilchrist b Gillespie	69	–	c Gilchrist b Warne	32
M. A. Butcher c Ponting b McGrath	13	–	lbw b Lee	1
M. R. Ramprakash c Gilchrist b Gillespie	14	–	st Gilchrist b Warne	26
†A. J. Stewart c M. E. Waugh b McGrath	46	–	b Warne	0
I. J. Ward c Gilchrist b McGrath	6	–	lbw b Gillespie	13
C. White c Hayden b McGrath	0	–	c S. R. Waugh b Warne	7
A. J. Tudor lbw b Warne	3	–	c Ponting b Warne	9
R. D. B. Croft c Ponting b Warne	3	–	b Gillespie	0
A. R. Caddick b Lee	13	–	c Gilchrist b Gillespie	4
D. Gough not out	0	–	not out	5
B 1, l-b 9, w 1, n-b 7	18		B 4, l-b 3, n-b 7	14

(52.5 overs, 230 mins) **185**

Fall: 0 30 63 117 142 147 158 168 180 185

(57 overs, 251 mins) **162**

Fall: 57 59 115 115 126 144 144 146 156 162

Bowling: *First Innings*—McGrath 18-4-49-5; Lee 6.5-0-30-1; Gillespie 12-1-59-2; Warne 16-4-37-2. *Second Innings*—McGrath 11-3-31-0; Gillespie 20-8-61-3; Lee 8-1-30-1; Warne 18-5-33-6.

Australia

M. J. Slater b Gough	15	–	(2) c Trescothick b Caddick	12
M. L. Hayden lbw b Tudor	33	–	(1) lbw b Tudor	42
R. T. Ponting c Stewart b Gough	14	–	c Stewart b Croft	17
M. E. Waugh c Atherton b Tudor	15	–	not out	42
*S. R. Waugh c Atherton b Caddick	13	–	retired hurt	1
D. R. Martyn c Stewart b Caddick	4	–	not out	33
†A. C. Gilchrist c Atherton b Tudor	54			
S. K. Warne lbw b Caddick	0			
B. Lee c Butcher b Tudor	4			
J. N. Gillespie not out	27			
G. D. McGrath c Butcher b Tudor	2			
L-b 3, w 1, n-b 5	9		L-b 4, n-b 7	11

(54.5 overs, 257 mins) **190**

Fall: 48 56 69 82 94 102 102 122 188 190

(29.2 overs, 137 mins) (3 wkts) **158**

Fall: 36 72 88

Bowling: *First Innings*—Gough 15–3–63–2; Caddick 20–4–70–3; Tudor 15.5–5–44–5; White 2–1–8–0; Croft 2–0–2–0. *Second Innings*—Gough 9–1–38–0; Caddick 12.2–1–71–1; Tudor 7–0–37–1; Croft 1–0–8–1.

Umpires: J.H. Hampshire and S. Venkataraghavan.
TV Umpire: D.J. Constant.
Referee: Talat Ali.

SUSSEX v AUSTRALIANS

At County Ground, Hove, August 8, 9, 10, 2001. Australians won by eight wickets. Toss: Australians.

The Australians stormed home to beat the seaside county having been, if not embarrassed, certainly uncomfortably extended on the first day. Misled by the pitch's greenish tinge, Adam Gilchrist invited Sussex to take first innings, but Australia's second-string attack was heavily manhandled by probably the County Championship's best opening partnership, Zimbabwe-born West Australian Murray Goodwin and 30-year-old Richard Montgomerie. Their first-wicket stand of 202, their sixth three-figure stand of the season, was the best for any wicket against the Australians so far, and Montgomerie's five-hour 157 with 19 fours comfortably the highest score. Goodwin's attractive hundred, studded with 17 fours, took only 135 balls, and was finally ended by Simon Katich's first ball. Chris Adams struck a six and seven fours in expediting his own declaration. Less than an hour was possible on the second day, and two quick declarations left Australia starting on a chase for 337 at 12.25 p.m. Adam Gilchrist and Ricky Ponting tore into an anodyne attack, adding 151 in 23 overs. Dropped at 12 and 98, Gilchrist cruised to his third century of the tour, needing only 102 balls to commandeer 114 with 88 in boundaries. Ponting's second century of the tour lasted 170 deliveries and included three sixes and 17 fours, the last of which brought Australia victory with 4.1 overs to spare. Katich, who helped him add 131 in 22 overs for the third wicket, was now favourite to replace the injured Steve Waugh for the Fourth Test.

Close of play: First day, Australians (1) 2-19 (Slater 16, Waugh 0); Second day, Australians (1) 2-86 (Slater 46, Waugh 32).

Sussex

M.W. Goodwin st Seccombe b Katich	105	– (7) not out	28
R.R. Montgomerie c Gilchrist b Fleming	157	– (6) lbw b Fleming	2
*C.J. Adams not out	66		
B. Zuiderent c Langer b Fleming	0	– (2) lbw b Fleming	6
M.H. Yardy run out (Langer)	6	– (1) not out	21
U.B.A. Rashid not out	0	– (4) c Seccombe b Lee	7
M.J.G. Davis (did not bat)		– (5) c Seccombe b Fleming	1
†N.J. Wilton (did not bat)		– (3) c Waugh b Lee	1
L-b 4, n-b 17	21	N-b 1	1

(91 overs, 347 mins)   (4 wkts dec) 355
Fall: 202 328 330 355

(20 overs, 85 mins)   (5 wkts dec) 67
Fall: 11 12 24 29 31

J.D. Lewry, B.V. Taylor and M.A. Robinson did not bat.

Bowling: *First Innings*—Lee 23–2–117–0; Fleming 20–4–67–2; Noffke 8.3–1–29–0; Miller 24–8–78–0; Ponting 0.3–0–2–0; Katich 13–2–53–1; Langer 2–0–5–0. *Second Innings*—Lee 10–1–27–2; Fleming 8–2–20–3; Miller 2–0–20–0.

Australians

M. J. Slater not out	46			
J. L. Langer lbw b Taylor	2	– c Adams b Lewry	14	
R. T. Ponting c Montgomerie b Taylor	0	– not out	147	
M. E. Waugh not out	32			
S. M. Katich (did not bat)		– (4) not out	40	
*A. C. Gilchrist (did not bat)		– (1) st Wilton b Davis	114	
L-b 1, n-b 5	6	B 10, l-b 5, n-b 9	24	

(21 overs, 87 mins)	(2 wkts dec) 86	(63.5 overs, 248 mins)	(2 wkts) 339
Fall: 14 16		Fall: 57 208	

†W. A. Seccombe, B. Lee, D. W. Fleming, A. A. Noffke and C. R. Miller did not bat.

Bowling: *First Innings*—Lewry 7–0–22–0; Taylor 10–1–39–2; Robinson 4–0–24–0. *Second Innings*—Lewry 11–2–52–1; Taylor 16.5–1–93–0; Robinson 13–1–71–0; Davis 12–1–56–1; Rashid 10–0–46–0; Montgomerie 1–0–6–0.

Umpires: G. I. Burgess and N. J. Llong.

IRELAND v AUSTRALIANS

At Ormeau, Belfast, August 12, 2001. No result. Toss: Ireland.

This friendly match at Ormeau fell foul of the weather not quite a quarter of the way through its allotted span, though that was long enough for Justin Langer to miss out again with the bat. His scratchy 22 ended with a slash to Dominick Joyce at point from the bowling of Conor Armstrong. Matthew Hayden, whose last innings against Ireland had been an unbeaten 133 eight years earlier, hit eight fours in his undefeated 52 from 74 balls. Most impressive of the local bowlers was Adrian McCoubrey, who beat all batsmen in his abbreviated spell before rain sent the crowd of 4,000 home disappointed.

Australians

J. L. Langer c Joyce b Armstrong	22	(50)
M. L. Hayden not out	52	(74)
S. M. Katich not out	5	(18)
L-b 3, w 4	7	

(23.4 overs, 99 mins) (1 wkt) 86
Fall: 66

M. E. Waugh, *R. T. Ponting, D. R. Martyn, S. K. Warne, †W. A. Seccombe, B. Lee, C. R. Miller and G. D. McGrath did not bat.

Bowling: Mooney 7–0–35–0; McCoubrey 7–1–15–0; Heasley 5–0–12–0; Armstrong 4.4–0–21–1.

Ireland

J. A. M. Molins, A. White, P. J. Davy, D. Joyce, *W. K. McCallan, †A. D. Patterson, D. Heasley, P. J. K. Mooney, M. D. Dwyer, A. G. A. M. McCoubrey, C. Armstrong.

Umpires: E. Cooke and T. Henry.

ENGLAND v AUSTRALIA

Fourth Test Match

At Headingley, Leeds, August 16, 17, 18, 19, 20, 2001. England won by six wickets. Toss: Australia. Test debut: S. M. Katich.

A match seemingly destined for a dishonoured grave late on the fourth day was suddenly resurrected, first by a sporting declaration from Australia's stand-in captain Adam Gilchrist, then by an innings of style and scale, destined to become an Ashes classic, by Mark Butcher. His undefeated 173 in five and a quarter hours, with a six and 23 fours, piloted England to what became a comfortable victory with almost 20 overs to spare, continuing the pattern established in recent Ashes series of Australian defeats in "dead" Tests. England's four for 315 was the highest fourth-innings total they had made to win a home Test, and only the eighth time a team had won a Test after a declaration by their opponents.

The Australians gave Simon Katich his first Test cap, then took first innings on a balmy summer's day, which was then dominated by Ricky Ponting. Having aggregated a paltry 77 in his previous ten Test innings, he finally experienced the glimmer of good fortune necessary in any return to form: his third ball, edged to Mark Ramprakash at third slip, was judged not have carried by third umpire Neil Mallender. The reprieve seemed to stall England's momentum as surely as it added to Ponting's. He bolted to his fifty in 66 deliveries, his century in 113, and his 144 from 154 balls in three and a half hours was studded with 20 fours and three meaty pull shots for six off the fast bowlers. He was chaperoned by Mark Waugh in a third-wicket partnership of 221 spanning only 273 deliveries; Waugh, himself a recipient of selectors' indulgence in the past, passed 2,000 runs against England in an attractive stay of 147 balls. England's bowlers extracted little life from a pitch that already looked as if it had hosted three days' play, and had the entirely undeserved fortune to pick up Ponting and Waugh in the last half-hour. With Katich feeling his way the next morning, Damien Martyn continued his prodigious advances as a Test batsman on this tour, powerful off the back foot, and offering not the ghost of a chance; the first 14 deliveries with the second new ball produced half a dozen boundaries. Fortunately for England, Darren Gough took advantage of the cloud cover, and found the accuracy that had eluded him the previous day, amputating a tail that added only 51 runs for the last five wickets in 58 balls. Martyn continued playing his strokes until the end to reach a hundred in 125 balls during the first over after lunch. Only the stroke that cost him his wicket and ended Australia's innings was other than completely orthodox: drawing away to slog, he was caught by Alec Stewart after Michael Atherton had parried the ball upwards. Gough's ninth bag of five wickets in a Test innings was also his fourth in Ashes Tests.

Atherton and Marcus Trescothick survived the 18 overs before tea, although Glenn McGrath obtained discomfiting lift, and might have had Trescothick had the third umpire not again ruled against a slips catch claimed by Mark Waugh. McGrath had both openers caught at the wicket in the first 20 minutes after tea, but the rest of the day was England's, Butcher and Nasser Hussain joining in a composed and enterprising stand of 91 in 137 minutes. Hussain was in remarkably good form for a batsman who had played only one match – for Essex Second Eleven – since his injury in the First Test. When three quick wickets fell next morning, too, the retreat was orderly rather than abject. After adding a careful 78 in 140 balls with Ramprakash, Stewart rallied the tail with a vivid array of strokes, including ten fours and a flat six over extra cover played from well outside leg stump. Stewart's best Test score for a year enabled England's last four to sell themselves for 57 runs in 65 deliveries: a somewhat chaotic interlude, though an improvement on recent performances. McGrath became the third Australian to take 350 Test wickets in the course of his 7/76, his 21st bag of five wickets in an innings and sixth against England, which guaranteed him a voluble following in the new West Stand. The pitch, dry but hard, was providing the fast bowlers with often discomfiting bounce. Brett Lee, whose fastest delivery of the day touched 92.5 mph, struck Ramprakash and Andy Caddick bruising blows on their left forearms.

Another event on the third day, perhaps unprecedented, also befell Caddick: having been bowled by a Lee no-ball, he was later called for overstepping in the course of bowling Michael Slater. Australia began a rain-shrouded fourth day with a lead of 205, but rain and bad light restricted their efforts to set an overpowering target. Ponting, dropped at four by Atherton off Gough, again made the most of his 90 minutes at the crease. But once most of the afternoon had been occupied by pitch inspections and the deployment and withdrawal of covers, Gilchrist set England the generous target of 315 to win in a day plus 20 overs.

Further rain left England only 15 deliveries to survive that evening: just sufficient to prevent the England Cricket Board from having to make another expensive refund to spectators. Spectators take pot luck, of course, and the 13,000 faithful souls who turned up on the fifth day will bless their foresight in years to come. It began inauspiciously. Atherton pulled the first ball of the last day for four, and gloved the third, a vicious lifter, to Gilchrist: the 18th time McGrath had claimed his wicket. Trescothick then played his worst shot of the summer, feet anchored, bat adrift, to leave England at two for 33 after 10 overs. Yet thereafter the pitch seemed to flatten out, the ball grew softer, and Butcher and Hussain tackled the Australian attack with vigour. Hussain pulled Jason Gillespie for a six over the wall that separates the ground from Cardigan Road, while Butcher grew in stature every ball: their 100 partnership arrived in a speedy 139 deliveries. After lunch, Lee bowled a fiery spell, touching almost 95 mph and hitting Butcher on the helmet; Butcher replied with a series of upper cuts to the untenanted third man and point region. Hussain was caught down the leg side after a stay of 117 balls, but Ramprakash played with immediate fluency. The pair added 75 in 17 overs until Mark Waugh claimed a catch at slip from Shane Warne which replays later demonstrated had not carried. Ramprakash walked without remonstrance, testament to the excellent feeling between the two teams throughout the match, which was also evident when the Australians warmly and unanimously applauded Butcher's hundred. The match ended on another tide of boundaries at 5.20 p.m., leaving Gilchrist to commend Butcher on "something special", and Hussain to compliment Gilchrist on playing the game "the right way".

It had been a match exciting, satisfying, frustrating and amusing by turns, the funniest instalment being when Hussain came to the wicket in the first innings, and an intruder convincingly attired as an English batsman followed him out the gate to walk a third of the way to the wicket. The burlesque was completed when he looked up to discover Hussain, and stripped off his helmet and turned back to the dressing room, talking on a mobile phone. Karl Power, an unemployed labourer from Droylsden, was applauded by spectators but ejected from the ground; a known sporting prankster, he had in April posed as a Manchester United player, lining up for the team photograph before its Champions League tie in Munich. The real surprise of this match, however, was the way England revealed themselves as a genuine international cricket team.

Close of play: First day, Australia (1) 4-288 (Martyn 19); Second day, England (1) 2-155 (Butcher 47, Hussain 45); Third day, Australia (2) 1-69 (Hayden 12, Ponting 30); Fourth day, England (2) 0-4 (Atherton 4, Trescothick 0).

Man of the Match: M. A. Butcher.

Australia

M. J. Slater lbw b Caddick	21	– (2) b Gough	16
M. L. Hayden lbw b Caddick	15	– (1) c Stewart b Mullally	35
R. T. Ponting c Stewart b Tudor	144	– lbw b Gough	72
M. E. Waugh c Ramprakash b Caddick	72	– not out	24
D. R. Martyn c Stewart b Gough	118	– lbw b Caddick	6
S. M. Katich b Gough	15	– not out	0
*†A. C. Gilchrist c Trescothick b Gough	19		
S. K. Warne c Stewart b Gough	0		
B. Lee c Ramprakash b Mullally	0		
J. N. Gillespie c Atherton b Gough	5		
G. D. McGrath not out	8		
B 5, l-b 15, w 1, n-b 9	30	B 5, l-b 7, n-b 11	23

(100.1 overs, 450 mins)   447   (39.3 overs, 184 mins) (4 wkts dec) 176
Fall: 39 42 263 288 355 396 412 422 438 447   Fall: 25 129 141 171

Bowling: *First Innings*—Gough 25.1–4–103–5; Caddick 29–4–143–3; Mullally 23–8–65–1; Tudor 18–1–97–1; Butcher 1–0–7–0; Ramprakash 4–0–12–0. *Second Innings*—Gough 17–3–68–2; Caddick 11–2–45–1; Tudor 4–1–17–0; Mullally 7.3–2–34–1.

England

M. A. Atherton c Gilchrist b McGrath	22	– c Gilchrist b McGrath	8
M. E. Trescothick c Gilchrist b McGrath	37	– c Hayden b Gillespie	10
M. A. Butcher run out (Lee)	47	– not out	173
*N. Hussain lbw b McGrath	46	– c Gilchrist b Gillespie	55
M. R. Ramprakash c Gilchrist b Lee	40	– c Waugh b Warne	32
U. Afzaal c Warne b McGrath	14	– not out	4
†A. J. Stewart not out	76		
A. J. Tudor c Gilchrist b McGrath	2		
A. R. Caddick c Gilchrist b Lee	5		
D. Gough c Slater b McGrath	8		
A. D. Mullally c Katich b McGrath	0		
B 2, l-b 3, n-b 7	12	B 14, l-b 16, n-b 3	33

(94.2 overs, 430 mins)   309   (73.2 overs, 329 mins)   (4 wkts) 315
Fall: 50 67 158 158 174 252 267 289 299 309   Fall: 8 33 214 289

Bowling: *First Innings*—McGrath 30.2–9–76–7; Gillespie 26–6–76–0; Lee 22–3–103–2; Warne 16–2–49–0. *Second Innings*—McGrath 16–3–61–1; Gillespie 22–4–94–2; Warne 18.2–3–58–1; Lee 16–4–65–0; Waugh 1–0–7–0.

Umpires: D. R. Shepherd and S. Venkataraghavan.
TV Umpire: N. A. Mallender.
Referee: Talat Ali.

ENGLAND v AUSTRALIA

Fifth Test Match

At The Oval, August 23, 24, 25, 26, 27, 2001. Australia won by an innings and 25 runs. Toss: Australia. Test debut: J. Ormond.

The Oval was the final fastness of English cricket – Australia had not won there since 1972 – yet it crumbled like all the citadels before it. The Australians lost only four wickets, and almost an entire day to rain, yet won this Fifth Test with more than a session to spare. Steve and Mark Waugh repeated the feat of Ian and Greg Chappell 29 years earlier by taking a hundred each from England's attack, while Shane Warne and Glenn McGrath again grew a cubit each: Warne moved to fifth on the Test wicket-taking list, McGrath to second on the Australian list. Warne became the first spin bowler in history to take 400 Test wickets, and the second-fastest bowler to that landmark: only Richard Hadlee, who performed the deed in his 80th Test, has taken fewer Tests than Warne's 92. His 11/229, moreover, represented his first match bag of ten wickets outside Australia.

The return of the Australian captain, who judged himself sufficiently recovered from his torn calf at Trent Bridge, added an urgency to Australian preparations. As selectors, Steve Waugh and Adam Gilchrist also omitted Michael Slater, in favour of Justin Langer as an ersatz opener: a surprising choice, considering Langer's tour record of barely 200 runs, but an investment in character that was fully rewarded. On the occasion of his first Test in England, Langer enabled Australia to dominate the first day with a disciplined century in just over four hours, beginning with a stand of 168 for the first wicket with Matthew Hayden, and raised with three consecutive boundaries from Philip Tufnell shortly after tea. Although conditions were muggy, the ball swung for only a few overs from the debutant medium-pacer Jimmy Ormond. The Australian left-handers, meanwhile, never let Tufnell settle, sweeping him repeatedly from on or outside off stump. A bouncer from Andy Caddick struck Langer's helmet with the score on one for 263, compelling Langer's retirement, but first Ricky Ponting then Mark Waugh timed the ball exquisitely.

Steve Waugh joined his brother half an hour before the close and, though clearly uncomfortable, was also ominously sound. The batting jamboree recommenced the next morning. Mark Waugh offered an early chance and Steve played and missed twice, but thereafter they were irresistible. Their partnership dawned gradually, the first fifty taking 114 balls and the second fifty 75, then blossomed, a further 97 needing only 116 balls. It was their ninth hundred partnership in Tests, and their second-largest. Mark struck Darren Gough and Tufnell down the ground for disdainful sixes, Steve slog-swept another; each played an extraordinary variety of drives and drubs, cuts and carves. Only the running between wickets was less than urgent, Steve's calf forcing him to stroll his singles like a gouty laird taking in his estate. Mark was out slogging at Gough after reaching his 20th Test century in ten minutes under four hours. Steve was still on 98 and, in a tense little passage of play, took 27 balls to raise his hundred with a single from a misfield: it was his 27th Test century, tenth as captain and ninth against England. Gilchrist played a smart little cameo until he hit Usman Afzaal's third ball in Test cricket – a wide full toss – to cover. Then Damien Martyn came in to help his captain add a spirit-breaking 107 from 105 balls, 54 of them turned by the West Australian into a swaggering unbeaten 64. The captain called it quits after batting 313 minutes and striking 21 fours and a six, and his declaration came not a moment too soon for England's bowlers, although at an uncomfortable juncture for their batsmen.

In the end England negotiated the day's remaining 20 overs positively. They lost Atherton to a magical Warne delivery that jagged from outside leg stump to strike the top of off stump, but were sustained by a bold half-century from Marcus Trescothick in 49 balls. Trescothick succumbed to Warne's skidder from the fifth ball next morning and Mark Butcher followed swiftly, but Nasser Hussain played with impressive poise and Afzaal with something approaching audacity in their half-centuries. Warne might have had Afzaal as his 400th Test wicket, but third umpire Mervyn Kitchen rejected a stumping appeal to which either verdict seemed possible depending on the camera angle. The leg-spinner finally became the sixth bowler to overtake the landmark when, given sixth over with the second new ball, he had Alec Stewart caught at the wicket, then trapped Caddick next ball. This was the cue for Mark Ramprakash, who had played with immense care and determination for almost four hours, to take the initiative, and he rallied the tail-enders to their best performance of the series. Ormond helped him add 37 in 40 minutes, and Gough 74 in 98 minutes, extending England's innings into the fourth morning. Ramprakash brought up only the second century of his 46-Test career by sweeping a Warne full toss for his 15th four, and was immediately engulfed by Gough's fraternal hug. It had taken 196 deliveries, and earned a standing ovation from the 18,000 crowd. England's innings was terminated after 40 minutes of the fourth morning, with Warne achieving his best Test analysis in England. Gilchrist's stumping of Gough provided him with his 100th dismissal in his 21st Test: another speed record for a cricketer who has done everything in his career in a hurry.

The fourth day was terminated an hour later by unexpected rain and gloom, England having lost Atherton to his nemesis McGrath for the 19th time in what was expected to be the former captain's final Test innings. As the fifth morning commenced, England had nine second-innings wickets available and needed 169 to make Australia bat again; they did not even go close. Four wickets fell in the first hour: Warne confounded Butcher and Hussain, while McGrath produced a ball of steepling bounce to unseat Trescothick and angled another across Afzaal. Steve Waugh attacked relentlessly, with five and six men round the bat for Warne, and six in the cordon for McGrath. Ramprakash again suggested composure before Hayden took a smart slip catch, and Stewart lingered, then played no stroke at a baffling leg break that ripped out of the rough to strike off stump. The pitch on which wickets had cost more than 74 runs each on the preceding four days could take no blame, and an hour and a quarter of assured batting after lunch by Gough and Ormond implied that a more determined team would have found sanctuary. In some respects this was the most abject English capitulation of the summer: a category of performance in which there was some competition.

Close of play: First day, Australia (1) 2-324 (M. E. Waugh 48, S. R. Waugh 12); Second day, England (1) 1-80 (Trescothick 55, Butcher 10); Third day, England (1) 8-409 (Ramprakash 124, Gough 17); Fourth day, England (2) 1-40 (Trescothick 20, Butcher 11).

Man of the Match: S. K. Warne. *Players of the Series:* G. D. McGrath (Australia) and M. A. Butcher (England).

Australia

M. L. Hayden c Trescothick b Tufnell	68	D. R. Martyn not out	64
J. L. Langer retired hurt	102		
R. T. Ponting c Atherton b Ormond	62	B 10, l-b 13, w 1, n-b 19	43
M. E. Waugh b Gough	120		—
*S. R. Waugh not out	157	(152 overs, 628 mins) (4 wkts dec)	641
†A. C. Gilchrist c Ramprakash b Afzaal	25	Fall: 158 292 489 534	

B. Lee, S. K. Warne, J. N. Gillespie and G. D. McGrath did not bat.

Bowling: Gough 29–4–113–1; Caddick 36–9–146–0; Ormond 34–4–115–1; Tufnell 39–2–174–1; Butcher 1–0–2–0; Ramprakash 4–0–19–0; Afzaal 9–0–49–1.

England

M. A. Atherton b Warne	13	– c Warne b McGrath	9
M. E. Trescothick b Warne	55	– c and b McGrath	24
M. A. Butcher c Langer b Warne	25	– c S. R. Waugh b Warne	14
*N. Hussain b M. E. Waugh	52	– lbw b Warne	2
M. R. Ramprakash c Gilchrist b McGrath	133	– c Hayden b Warne	19
U. Afzaal c Gillespie b McGrath	54	– c Ponting b McGrath	5
†A. J. Stewart c Gilchrist b Warne	29	– b Warne	34
A. R. Caddick lbw b Warne	0	– b Lee	17
J. Ormond b Warne	18	– c Gilchrist b McGrath	17
D. Gough st Gilchrist b Warne	24	– not out	39
P. C. R. Tufnell not out	7	– c Warne b McGrath	0
B 3, l-b 13, w 1, n-b 5	22	L-b 2, n-b 2	4

(118.2 overs, 514 mins)	432	(68.3 overs, 283 mins)	184

Fall: 58 85 104 166 255 313 313 350
    424 432

Fall: 17 46 48 50 55 95 126 126
    184 184

Bowling: *First Innings*—McGrath 30–11–67–2; Gillespie 20–3–96–0; Warne 44.2–7–165–7; Lee 14–1–43–0; Ponting 2–0–5–0; M. E. Waugh 8–0–40–1. *Second Innings*—Lee 10–3–30–1; McGrath 15.3–6–43–5; Warne 28–8–64–4; Ponting 2–0–3–0; Gillespie 12–5–38–0; M. E. Waugh 1–0–4–0.

Umpires: R. E. Koertzen and P. Willey.
TV Umpire: M. J. Kitchen.
Referee: Talat Ali.

AUSTRALIAN WOMEN IN ENGLAND AND IRELAND, 2001

The Australian women's team, playing under the title of the Southern Stars, had an outstanding tour of England and Ireland. They not only won every match, but played with such dominance that they were never threatened by any of their opponents. Unfortunately, the games were so one-sided that they lacked the tactical ploys and the tension that can accompany cricket between well-matched teams.

A glance at the statistics emphasises the story. In the two Tests Australian vice-captain Karen Rolton averaged 218 and Michelle Goszko 102, while England's best was 39.75 from Claire Taylor. Australia dismissed England four times, while England were able to take only 15 Australian wickets. Cathryn Fitzpatrick, with 17 at 10.23, took more wickets than the entire England attack. In the three limited-overs internationals the difference was just as evident, although the spread of performances by the Australians made the numbers less striking.

The future strength of Australian teams was indicated by the performances of the three Test debutants, Louise Broadfoot, Goszko and Therese McGregor. Goszko had an amazing opening, equalling the Test record with 204 out of a team total of 344. All-rounder McGregor bowled well in both Tests and limited-overs matches and contributed with the bat, while Broadfoot made a fine 71 in the Second Test. In the First Test Goszko became the second Australian to compile a Test double-century, after Joanne Broadbent's 200 in 1998, and a third followed when Rolton made 209 not out in the Second Test, setting a new Test record.

The First Test win was Australia's first since 1992 and the first on English soil since 1987, and Rolton won the Peden-Archdale Medal for her overall performances. Veteran bowler Charmaine Mason, the inaugural medallist in 1999-00, retired from senior cricket at the end of the tour.

Australia finished the tour with three limited-overs games in Ireland, winning all matches handsomely.

AUSTRALIAN TOURING PARTY

B. J. Clark (New South Wales) (*captain*), K. L. Rolton (South Australia) (*vice-captain*), L. Broadfoot (Victoria), S. A. Cooper (Queensland), A. J. Fahey (Western Australia), C. L. Fitzpatrick (Victoria), M. A. J. Goszko (New South Wales), J. Hayes (New South Wales), L. M. Keightley (New South Wales), O. J. Magno (South Australia), C. L. Mason (Victoria), T. A. McGregor (New South Wales), J. C. Price (Queensland) and L. C. Sthalekar (New South Wales).

Coach: S. Jenkin. *Manager:* J. Stainer. *Physiotherapist:* L. Ross. *Assistant coach:* C. Matthews. *Physical fitness co-ordinator:* S. Bailey.

AUSTRALIAN TOUR RESULTS

Test matches – Played 2: Won 2.
Limited-overs internationals – Played 6: Won 6, England (3), Ireland (3).
Other matches: Played 3: Won 3 – MCC Invitation XI, ECB Development XI (2).

TEST MATCH AVERAGES

ENGLAND – BATTING

	M	I	NO	R	HS	100s	50s	Avge	Ct
S. C. Taylor	2	4	0	159	137	1	0	39.75	0
S. V. Collyer	1	2	0	60	37	0	0	30.00	0
L. Harper	2	4	0	100	31	0	0	25.00	1
K. Lowe	2	4	0	60	23	0	0	15.00	0
D. Holden	2	4	1	40	24	0	0	13.33	1
C. J. Connor	2	4	0	40	16	0	0	10.00	2
A. Thompson	2	4	0	29	18	0	0	7.25	1
C. E. Taylor	2	4	1	21	9	0	0	7.00	0
C. Atkins	2	4	0	26	10	0	0	6.50	1
N. Shaw	2	4	0	8	8	0	0	2.00	0
J. Cassar	1	2	0	2	1	0	0	1.00	1
L. C. Pearson	2	4	2	0	0*	0	0	0.00	1

* Denotes not out.

BOWLING

	O	M	R	W	BB	5W/i	Avge
C. J. Connor	47	14	101	5	5/65	1	20.20
C. E. Taylor	48.1	12	123	4	2/87	0	30.75
D. Holden	25	4	79	2	2/62	0	39.50
S. V. Collyer	19	6	50	1	1/50	0	50.00
N. Shaw	24	3	106	1	1/60	0	106.00
L. C. Pearson	46.1	10	139	1	1/56	0	139.00
L. Harper	21	1	80	0	–	0	–

AUSTRALIA – BATTING

	M	I	NO	R	HS	100s	50s	Avge	Ct
K. L. Rolton	2	3	2	218	209*	1	0	218.00	2
M. A. J. Goszko	2	2	0	204	204	1	0	102.00	0
L. C. Broadfoot	2	2	0	95	71	0	1	47.50	2
L. M. Keightley	2	3	0	76	40	0	0	25.33	4
T. A. McGregor	2	1	0	23	23	0	0	23.00	2
A. J. Fahey	2	1	0	11	11	0	0	11.00	0
C. L. Fitzpatrick	2	1	0	10	10	0	0	10.00	1
J. C. Price	2	2	1	9	9*	0	0	9.00	6
B. J. Clark	2	3	1	15	9	0	0	7.50	1
O. J. Magno	1	1	0	4	4	0	0	4.00	1
C. L. Mason	2	1	1	0	0*	0	0	0.00	0
J. Hayes	1	–	–	–	–	–	–	–	3

* Denotes not out.

BOWLING

	O	M	R	W	BB	5W/i	Avge
O. J. Magno	30	18	29	5	3/16	0	5.80
T. A. McGregor	54	29	77	8	2/7	0	9.62
C. L. Fitzpatrick	96	36	174	17	5/29	2	10.23
C. L. Mason	82	35	139	6	4/66	0	23.16
A. J. Fahey	45	20	76	2	1/12	0	38.00
J. Hayes	22	8	48	1	1/28	0	48.00
K. L. Rolton	8	5	5	0	–	0	–

LIMITED-OVERS INTERNATIONAL AVERAGES
ENGLAND v AUSTRALIANS

ENGLAND – BATTING

	M	I	NO	R	HS	100s	50s	Avge	Ct	S-R
S.C. Taylor	3	3	1	97	50*	0	1	48.50	3	55.42
S.V. Collyer	3	3	0	60	26	0	0	20.00	1	40.81
D. Holden	3	3	1	34	22*	0	0	17.00	1	47.22
C. Atkins	1	1	0	17	17	0	0	17.00	0	20.98
A. Thompson	3	3	0	42	20	0	0	14.00	2	40.38
C.J. Connor	3	3	0	36	23	0	0	12.00	2	45.00
J. Cassar	3	3	0	31	21	0	0	10.33	1	39.74
C.E. Taylor	3	3	2	8	5*	0	0	8.00	1	20.51
L. Harper	1	1	0	6	6	0	0	6.00	0	33.33
J. Hawker	2	2	0	11	10	0	0	5.50	1	44.00
L.C. Pearson	3	2	0	4	4	0	0	2.00	0	30.76
H. Lloyd	2	2	0	1	1	0	0	0.50	0	4.00
K. Lowe	2	2	0	1	1	0	0	0.50	1	6.66
N. Shaw	1	1	0	0	0	0	0	0.00	0	0.00

* Denotes not out.

BOWLING

	O	M	R	W	BB	5W/i	Avge
C.J. Connor	29	3	106	6	2/33	1	17.66
S.V. Collyer	30	1	134	5	2/30	0	26.80
D. Holden	28	0	129	4	3/48	0	32.25
C.E. Taylor	29	3	113	3	2/30	0	37.66
L.C. Pearson	27	1	125	3	2/41	0	41.66
J. Hawker	4	0	38	0	–	0	–
N. Shaw	3	1	12	0	–	0	–

AUSTRALIA – BATTING

	M	I	NO	R	HS	100s	50s	Avge	Ct/St	S-R
K.L. Rolton	3	3	0	176	79	0	2	58.66	0	97.23
L.M. Keightley	3	3	0	163	75	0	2	54.33	1	59.48
B.J. Clark	3	3	0	118	69	0	1	39.33	2	61.45
T.A. McGregor	3	3	2	28	15	0	0	28.00	0	90.32
M.A.J. Goszko	3	3	0	64	35	0	0	21.33	1	80.00
L.C. Broadfoot	1	1	0	13	13	0	0	13.00	0	81.25
J.C. Price	3	3	1	20	13*	0	0	10.00	3/3	43.47
O.J. Magno	1	1	0	10	10	0	0	10.00	0	58.82
S.A. Cooper	2	2	0	17	9	0	0	8.50	0	48.57
C.L. Fitzpatrick	3	3	0	14	6	0	0	4.66	1	66.66
C.L. Mason	2	1	0	0	0	0	0	0.00	0	0.00
J. Hayes	3	1	1	4	4*	0	0	–	1	100.00
L.C. Sthalekar	2	2	2	4	3*	0	0	–	0	66.66
A.J. Fahey	1	–	–	–	–	–	–	–	1	–

* Denotes not out.

BOWLING

	O	M	R	W	BB	5W/i	Avge
T.A. McGregor	30	16	47	8	4/15	0	5.87
K.L. Rolton	15	4	46	4	3/14	0	11.50
A.J. Fahey	9	1	24	2	2/24	0	12.00
L.C. Sthalekar	18	4	49	3	2/25	0	16.33
C.L. Fitzpatrick	29	9	77	4	2/21	0	19.25
C.L. Mason	18.5	6	47	2	2/22	0	23.50
J. Hayes	25.3	5	80	2	1/19	0	40.00

LIMITED-OVERS INTERNATIONAL AVERAGES
IRELAND v AUSTRALIANS

IRELAND – BATTING

	M	I	NO	R	HS	100s	50s	Avge	Ct/St
C. M. O'Leary	2	2	0	72	42	0	0	36.00	1
M. E. Grealey	3	3	0	69	57	0	1	23.00	1
C. M. Beggs	3	3	0	46	45	0	0	15.33	1
S. A. Young	3	3	1	20	13*	0	0	10.00	0
N. Squire	3	3	1	16	11*	0	0	8.00	0
A. M. Budd	2	2	1	6	3*	0	0	6.00	0
C. J. Metcalfe	2	2	1	4	4*	0	0	4.00	0
I. M. Joyce	3	3	0	9	5	0	0	3.00	0
C. N. Joyce	2	1	0	3	3	0	0	3.00	1
A. Linehan	3	3	0	8	8	0	0	2.66	2/1
L. D. Molins	1	1	0	2	2	0	0	2.00	0
G. Leagy	2	2	0	3	2	0	0	1.50	0
C. M. A. Shillington	1	1	0	1	1	0	0	1.00	1
B. M. McDonald	3	1	0	0	0	0	0	0.00	0

BOWLING

	O	M	R	W	BB	5W/i	Avge
C. J. Metcalfe	12	0	50	3	3/43	0	16.66
S. A. Young	20.4	1	82	4	2/47	0	20.50
B. M. McDonald	25	5	64	1	1/15	0	64.00
M. E. Grealey	24	3	107	1	1/30	0	107.00
I. M. Joyce	25	4	113	1	1/40	0	113.00
C. N. Joyce	6.4	1	45	0	–	0	–
A. M. Budd	1	0	13	0	–	0	–

AUSTRALIA – BATTING

	M	I	NO	R	HS	100s	50s	Avge	Ct/St
L. M. Keightley	2	2	1	79	51*	0	1	79.00	1
K. L. Rolton	2	2	1	63	51*	0	1	63.00	0
M. A. J. Goszko	2	2	1	53	36*	0	0	53.00	2
B. J. Clark	2	2	0	96	80	0	1	48.00	2
S. A. Cooper	3	2	0	87	85	0	1	43.50	0
J. Hayes	3	2	1	20	15*	0	0	20.00	1
C. L. Fitzpatrick	2	1	0	13	13	0	0	13.00	1
J. C. Price	3	1	0	12	12	0	0	12.00	2
L. C. Broadfoot	3	2	0	17	9	0	0	8.50	0
L. C. Sthalekar	3	2	0	8	8	0	0	4.00	0
C. L. Mason	3	1	0	1	1	0	0	1.00	1
T. A. McGregor	2	1	1	9	9*	0	0	–	2
A. J. Fahey	3	1	1	0	0*	0	0	–	0

* Denotes not out.

BOWLING

	O	M	R	W	BB	5W/i	Avge
T. A. McGregor	16	6	29	7	4/8	0	4.14
C. L. Fitzpatrick	16	3	34	8	5/14	0	4.25
J. Hayes	20	10	37	4	2/14	0	9.25
C. L. Mason	24	4	49	3	2/24	0	16.33
L. C. Sthalekar	16.1	2	52	2	2/30	0	26.00
K. L. Rolton	3	0	16	0	–	0	–
A. J. Fahey	27	2	67	0	–	0	–

MCC WOMEN'S INVITATION XI
v AUSTRALIANS

At John Walker's Ground, Southgate, June 18, 2001. Australians won by 142 runs. Toss: Australia.

Australia were led by a talented all-round performance from leg-spinner Olivia Magno as they went to an easy limited-overs win against the MCC Eleven. After a good start by Louise Broadfoot and Michelle Goszko, wicket-keeper Julia Price and Magno joined in the free scoring to help the team to a formidable total. Broadfoot and Price retired when they reached their half-centuries. Magno's spin was too much for the invitation team, who struggled throughout, apart from New Zealand all-rounder Haidee Tiffen, who top-scored with 34 after taking 2/46.

Australia

L. M. Keightley b Tiffen 13 (28)	T. A. McGregor not out 12 (12)
L. C. Broadfoot retired 51 (68)	A. J. Fahey lbw b Tiffen 5 (4)
M. A. J. Goszko c Stock b Richards ... 35 (42)	C. L. Mason run out 2 (3)
S. A. Cooper b Richards 13 (24)	B 7, l-b 4, w 14 25
†J. C. Price retired 51 (64)	
K. L. Rolton c Morgan b Stock 10 (13)	(50 overs, 172 mins) (9 wkts) 251
O. J. Magno retired 34 (42)	Fall: 39 91 109 126 142 217 235 248 251

*B. J. Clark did not bat.

Bowling: Morgan 5–1–25–0; Tiffen 10–1–46–2; Handley 10–0–41–0; Richards 10–0–38–2; Stock 10–0–44–1; Rainford-Brent 5–0–46–0.

MCC Women's Invitation XI

M. Godliman lbw b Magno 15 (79)	B. Morgan lbw b Magno 0 (6)
†E. Donnison c Price b Mason 0 (1)	G. Richards lbw b Mason 0 (11)
J. L. Godman c Magno b Fahey 17 (51)	C. Ward not out 0 (6)
H. M. Tiffen c McGregor b Magno ... 34 (66)	
*P. te Beest c and b Magno 4 (7)	L-b 6, n-b 2, w 3 11
E. J. Rainford-Brent b Fahey 5 (16)	
D. A. Stock b Magno 7 (16)	(44.4 overs) 109
C. Handley b Magno 16 (12)	Fall: 2 30 52 56 66 81 101 108 108 109

Bowling: Mason 7.4–2–7–2; McGregor 7–2–9–0; Fahey 10–0–32–2; Rolton 6–2–14–0; Magno 10–4–34–6; Goszko 4–1–7–0.

Umpires: V. Gibbens and J. Hayes.

ECB DEVELOPMENT WOMEN'S XI v AUSTRALIANS

At John Walker's Ground, Southgate, June 19, 2001. Australians won by 170 runs. Toss: ECB Development Women's XI.

Australia won by 170 runs in their second tour match, after a solid team effort in both batting and bowling. Sent in to bat, they batted strongly right down the order, amassing another huge total off their 50 overs. Karen Rolton top-scored with 56 off 51 balls, and of the eight bowlers only leg-spinner Kathryn Leng offered any challenge to the Australians. The Australian bowlers, led by the pace of Charmaine Mason and Julie Hayes, then dominated the ECB XI, who had trouble scoring at all, though they almost batted out their 50 overs.

Australia Women

*B. J. Clark c Lloyd b Richards	34	(55)	
M. A. J. Goszko b Shaw	3	(8)	
K. L. Rolton retired	56	(51)	
S. A. Cooper b Leng	22	(31)	
L. M. Keightley c Lloyd b Walker	36	(46)	
C. L. Fitzpatrick st Joyce b Leng	14	(42)	
J. Hayes b Oakenfold	24	(24)	

C. L. Mason not out	30	(27)	
A. J. Fahey st Joyce b Clark	10	(19)	
O. J. Magno not out	1	(3)	
B 4, l-b 7, w 9, n-b 7	27		
(50 overs)	(8 wkts)	257	
Fall: not details available			

†. C. Price did not bat.

Bowling Shaw 6–0–41–1; Spragg 5–0–23–0; Richards 7–1–37–1; Reynard 8–0–38–0; Leng 9–1–32–2; Walker 6–2–20–1; Oakenfold 5–0–28–1; Clark 4–0–27–1.

ECB Development Women's XI

K. M. Leng c Rolton b Magno	12	(58)	
K. Oakenfold c Clark b Hayes	2	(7)	
H. Lloyd b Mason	29	(74)	
S. Redferd c Keightly b Fahey	5	(30)	
L. Spragg c Clark b Fahey	2	(17)	
N. Shaw c Keightley b Hayes	5	(23)	
*M. Reynard c Fitzpatrick b Hayes	5	(33)	
†L. Joyce b Mason	8	(25)	

A. Walker b Mason	0	(8)	
S. Clark not out	8	(13)	
G. Richards c Price b Mason	0	(4)	
B 4, l-b 4, w 2, n-b 1	11		
(48.4 overs)	87		
Fall: no details available			

Bowling: Fitzpatrick 10–4–15–0; Hayes 10–5–11–3; Mason 9.4–3–22–4; Magno 10–3–11–1; Fahey 6–2–7–2; Rolton 3–0–13–0.

ECB DEVELOPMENT WOMEN'S XI v AUSTRALIANS

At Brunton Memorial Ground, Radlett, June 21, 2001. Australians won by 88 runs. Toss: Australia Women.

In the second match against an England Cricket Board team, Australia's regular openers Belinda Clark and Lisa Keightley sharpened their game for the First Test with a century opening stand, paving the way for another big total. Karen Rolton hit 69 off 56 balls before retiring. After losing the top order cheaply, this time the ECB eventually made a better fist of their innings, some robust batting from the tail enabling them to bat out their 50 overs against a persistent Australian attack. Cathryn Fitzpatrick took two wickets in successive balls. Team rotation allowed all the Australians to play at least one tour match before the First Test.

Australia

L. M. Keightley c Richards b Reynard	40	(56)	
*B. J. Clark retired	67	(94)	
K. L. Rolton retired	69	(56)	
L. C. Broadfoot b Leng	15	(29)	
†J. C. Price c Godliman b Clark	8	(19)	
T. A. McGregor c and b Clark	14	(16)	
O. J. Magno c Reynard b Morgan	15	(16)	

L. C. Sthalekar lbw b Morgan	11	(17)	
C. L. Fitzpatrick not out	1	(3)	
B 2, l-b 4, w 5, n-b 4	15		
(50 overs, 184 mins)	(8 wkts)	255	
Fall: 103 121 179 203 224 225 254 255			

J. Hayes and C. L. Mason did not bat.

Bowling: Shaw 7–1–31–0; Spragg 7–0–37–0; Leng 7–1–35–1; Morgan 8–0–46–2; Richards 3–0–22–0; Reynard 10–1–32–1; Clark 8–0–46–2.

ECB Development Women's XI

H. Lloyd c Price b Mason 19 (48)	S. Clark c Price b Fitzpatrick 43 (43)
K. M. Leng c Sthalekar b Fitzpatrick . . 18 (37)	B. Morgan not out 7 (31)
M. Godliman c Clark b Fitzpatrick . . . 0 (1)	G. Richards not out 10 (17)
S. Redfern run out 29 (61)	
N. Shaw c Rolton b Magno 4 (14)	L-b 5, w 6, n-b 1 12
*M. Reynard lbw b Mason 0 (4)	
L. Spragg c and b Magno 0 (7)	(50 overs, 171 mins) (9 wkts) 167
†L. Joyce st Price b Sthalekar 25 (36)	Fall: 34 34 49 54 54 65 84 115 152

Bowling: Fitzpatrick 10–2–39–3; McGregor 10–2–28–0; Mason 5–3–9–2; Magno 7–2–13–2; Hayes 8–0–33–0; Sthalekar 10–3–40–1.

ENGLAND v AUSTRALIA

First Test Match

At Denis Compton Oval, Shenley, June 24, 25, 26, 2001. Australia won by an innings and 140 runs. Toss: England Women.

Australia achieved their largest winning margin in any Test – by an innings and 140 runs, with a day to spare – as they completely dominated England, whose match total of 204 could only equal the score of one Australian player, Michelle Goszko, who equalled the Test record held by Kirsty Flavell of New Zealand.

The England first innings was brought down by fast bowler Cathryn Fitzpatrick. She struck first when Louise Broadfoot took a brilliant diving catch in the slips to dismiss Arran Thompson, then bowled Jane Cassar. When Therese McGregor trapped Clare Connor in front to take her first Test wicket, England were three for 17 after an hour and a half. Test debutant Caroline Atkins resisted for two and a half hours for her ten runs.

After two early wickets fell, Goszko scored powerfully, hitting 24 fours to all parts of Denis Compton Oval as Australia swept passed the England total with only two wickets down. Apart from a solid 36 from opener Lisa Keightley, most of the other batters failed to get a start, but fellow debutants Louise Broadfoot and Therese McGregor provided Goszko with useful support as the score mounted. Goszko's was the last wicket to fall; she had batted for six and a half hours under hot sun and scored 204 out of 323 before a ball from Clare Taylor struck her on the pad. Connor's 5/65 was a just reward for her persistent left-arm spin.

The England second innings followed a similar pattern to the first, with only minor resistance to Australia's varied and accurate five-pronged attack. When Olivia Magno's leg-spin snared Lucy Pearson for the ninth leg-before-wicket dismissal of the match, Australia had won before 3 p.m. on the third day of a scheduled four.

Players of the Match: M. A. J. Goszko and C. J. Connor.
Close of Play: First day, England 103, Australia 2-60 (Keightley 19, Goszko 21); Second day, England 1-8 (Thompson 4, C. E. Taylor 0).

England

C. Atkins lbw b Fitzpatrick	10	– lbw b Magno	0
A. Thompson c Broadfoot b Fitzpatrick	1	– c McGregor b Fahey	18
†J. Cassar b Fitzpatrick	1	– (4) lbw b Mason	1
*C.J. Connor lbw b McGregor	8	– (5) b McGregor	16
K. Lowe b Fitzpatrick	23	– (6) c Broadfoot b Fitzpatrick	18
S.C. Taylor run out	18	– (7) lbw b McGregor	0
L. Harper c Magno b McGregor	19	– (8) b Fitzpatrick	20
N. Shaw c Keightley b Magno	0	– (9) c Keightley b Magno	8
D. Holden b Fitzpatrick	7	– (10) not out	4
C.E. Taylor c Price b Magno	5	– (3) b Fitzpatrick	6
L.C. Pearson not out	0	– lbw b Magno	0
B 4, l-b 7	11	B 4, l-b 6	10

(83.1 overs, 271 mins)   103
Fall: 7 9 17 41 50 90 90 90 103 103

(61 overs, 189 mins)   101
Fall: 0 15 16 45 45 45 82 91 101 101

Bowling: *First Innings*—Fitzpatrick 18.1–6–29–5; Mason 18–12–15–0; McGregor 15–10–13–2; Magno 17–11–13–2; Fahey 14–6–22–0; Rolton 1–1–0–0. *Second Innings*—Magno 13–7–16–3; Fitzpatrick 19–6–33–3; Mason 10–6–17–1; McGregor 7–5–7–2; Fahey 12–6–18–1.

Australia

*B.J. Clark lbw b Pearson	9	C.L. Fitzpatrick c Connor b Holden	10
L.M. Keightley c Thompson b Connor	36	A.J. Fahey lbw b Connor	11
K.L. Rolton b Shaw	0	C.L. Mason not out	0
M.A.J. Goszko lbw b C.E. Taylor	204		
L.C. Broadfoot c Pearson b Connor	24	B 9, l-b 8, w 4, n-b 2	23
†J.C. Price c Cassar b Connor	0		
O.J. Magno c Atkins b Holden	4	(115.1 overs, 404 mins)	344
T.A. McGregor c Harper b Connor	23	Fall: 14 21 128 178 178 216 282 319 338 344

Bowling: Shaw 11–0–60–1; Pearson 24–5–56–1; C.E. Taylor 17.1–4–31–1; Holden 21–4–62–2; Harper 14–1–53–0; Connor 28–6–65–5.

Umpires: L. Elgar and N.A. Mallender.

ENGLAND v AUSTRALIA

Second Test Match

At Headingley, Leeds, July 6, 7, 8, 2001. Australia won by nine wickets. Toss: Australia.

The Second Test looked as if it might develop into a contest until Karen Rolton stepped in to play her finest innings and overtake the Test record that Michelle Goszko had equalled in the First Test. England had hoped that their first innings of 144 might be competitive, and saw a glimmer of hope when Belinda Clark was back in the pavilion with the score at 16 and their First Test tormentor Goszko fell for a duck. Rolton, however, continuing her dominant form of the limited-overs series, was as devastating to the England bowling as Goszko had been in the First Test, hitting 29 fours and a six in six hours at the crease. Louise Broadfoot played a supporting role, scoring a stylish 71 as a counterpoint to Rolton's hard-hitting 209 not out as the pair added 253 for the fourth wicket in four hours.

The pace of Cathryn Fitzpatrick had wrecked England's first innings with another haul of five wickets; at that stage she had taken 13/93 in the series from 60 overs. Facing a deficit of 239, however, England put in a solid effort. Claire Taylor shook off her poor Test form to play a defiant innings, hitting 21 fours off 232 balls in 251 minutes at the crease. Apart from another useful knock from 17-year-old Laura Harper, Taylor's was a lone hand. She ensured that Australia had to bat again before she was last out, bowled by Charmaine Mason's last ball in Test cricket. Fittingly, Rolton hit the winning boundary, and Australia again won with a day to spare..

Players of the Match: K. L. Rolton and S. C. Taylor.

Close of Play: First day, Australia 1-68 (Keightley 29, Rolton 26); Second day, England 0-10 (Atkins 3, Thompson 6).

England

C. Atkins c Price b Fitzpatrick	8	– lbw b Mason	8
A. Thompson c Keightley b Fitzpatrick	4	– c Rolton b Fitzpatrick	6
S. V. Collyer c Rolton b McGregor	37	– c and b McGregor	23
†S. C. Taylor c Price b Mason	4	– b Mason	137
*C. J. Connor b Fitzpatrick	16	– b McGregor	0
K. Lowe c Clark b McGregor	11	– lbw b Fitzpatrick	8
L. Harper c Keightley b Fahey	31	– c Hayes b Fitzpatrick	30
N. Shaw c Price b Hayes	0	– c Price b Fitzpatrick	0
D. Holden b Fitzpatrick	24	– c Hayes b Mason	5
C. E. Taylor not out	1	– c Price b Mason	9
L. C. Pearson c Hayes b Fitzpatrick	0	– not out	0
B 6, l-b 1, w 1	8	B 7, l-b 10, w 2	19

(80.5 overs, 255 mins)	144	(112 overs, 351 mins)	245
Fall: 11 12 17 53 78 85 103 131		Fall: 12 37 55 55 80 161 161 212	
144 144		236 245	

Bowling: *First Innings*—Fitzpatrick 22.5–10–31–5; Mason 20–8–41–1; Hayes 13–5–28–1; McGregor 15–6–25–2; Fahey 7–2–12–1; Rolton 3–3–0–0. *Second Innings*—Fitzpatrick 36–14–81–4; Mason 34–9–66–4; McGregor 17–8–32–2; Fahey 12–6–24–0; Hayes 9–3–20–0; Rolton 4–1–5–0.

Australia

*B. J. Clark c Holden b C. E. Taylor	6	– (2) not out	0
L. M. Keightley run out	40	– (1) b C. E. Taylor	0
K. L. Rolton not out	209	– not out	9
M. A. J. Goszko b C. E. Taylor	0		
L. C. Broadfoot c Connor b Collyer	71		
†J. C. Price not out	9		
B 7, l-b 34, w 6, n-b 1	48		

(112 overs, 389 mins)	(4 wkts dec) 383	(3.1 overs, 11 mins)	9
Fall: 16 93 105 358		Fall: 0	

T. A. McGregor, C. L. Fitzpatrick, J. Hayes, A. J. Fahey and C. L. Mason did not bat.

Bowling: *First Innings*—Pearson 21–4–79–0; C. E. Taylor 29–7–87–2; Shaw 13–3–46–0; Collyer 19–6–50–1; Harper 7–0–27–0; Connor 19–8–36–0; Holden 4–0–17–0. *Second Innings*—C. E. Taylor 2–1–5–1; Pearson 1.1–1–4–0.

Umpires: A. Roberts and A. G. T. Whitehead.

ENGLAND v AUSTRALIA

First Limited-Overs International

At County Ground, Derby, June 29, 2001. Australia won by 99 runs. Toss: England.

In the limited-overs series which split the two Test matches Australia did not let up in their punishment of the demonstrably weaker England team. The selectors substituted Lisa Sthalekar and Julie Hayes for Olivia Magno and Avril Fahey in the limited-overs side, but the top order soon made it clear that any combination would bring victory. Lisa Keightley and Karen Rolton shared a second-wicket partnership of 124, Rolton blasting 11 fours in her 79 off only 68 balls. The duck of captain and opener Belinda Clark, after her failure in the First Test, was the only shadow cast on her innings. England lost early wickets and never looked like building a competitive reply. Therese McGregor took 4/15 to be the best of a very unyielding group of bowlers, and Lisa Sthalekar's off-spin took two key wickets on her international debut.

Players of the Match: K.L. Rolton and S.C. Taylor.

Australia

L.M. Keightley c S.C. Taylor b Collyer	75 (127)	C.L. Fitzpatrick run out	4	(9)
*B.J. Clark b Pearson	0 (7)	L.C. Sthalekar not out	1	(1)
K.L. Rolton c S.C. Taylor b Collyer	79 (68)			
M.A.J. Goszko c Holden b Pearson	35 (45)	L-b 2, w 12, n-b 1	15	
L.C. Broadfoot lbw b Connor	13 (16)			
†J.C. Price b Connor	6 (14)	(50 overs)	(7 wkts) 238	
T.A. McGregor not out	10 (14)	Fall: 3 127 196 204 213 220 237		

J. Hayes and C.L. Mason did not bat.

Bowling: Pearson 10–1–41–2; C.E. Taylor 10–0–54–0; Collyer 10–0–57–2; Connor 10–1–33–2; Hawker 2–0–17–0; Holden 8–0–34–0.

England

H. Lloyd lbw b McGregor	1 (19)	D. Holden not out	22	(36)
A. Thompson c Hayes b McGregor	17 (37)	C.E. Taylor b Fitzpatrick	0	(2)
K. Lowe lbw b Fitzpatrick	0 (5)	L.C. Pearson run out	4	(11)
S.C. Taylor b Sthalekar	39 (88)			
*C.J. Connor lbw b McGregor	2 (8)	B 1, l-b 4, w 9, n-b 2	16	
J. Hawker c Keightley b Sthalekar	10 (23)			
†J. Cassar st Price b McGregor	8 (11)	(47.5 overs)	139	
S.V. Collyer run out	20 (49)	Fall: 22 23 23 27 48 60 101 115 124 139		

Bowling: Fitzpatrick 9–3–21–2; McGregor 10–6–15–4; Mason 8.5–2–25–0; Sthalekar 8–2–25–2; Hayes 8–2–32–0; Rolton 4–0–16–0.

Umpires: P. Adams and J. Hayes.
TV Umpire: V. Gibbens.

ENGLAND v AUSTRALIA

Second Limited-Overs International

At County Ground, Derby, July 2, 2001. Australia won by 118 runs. Toss: Australia.

Sally Cooper made her debut, becoming the 164th player to represent Australia and the 94th in limited-overs internationals, while Julia Price became the sixth Australian to play 50 limited-overs internationals. Australia elected to bat on the flat wicket and again started brightly, with Belinda Clark hitting form at last, and Lisa Keightley and Karen

Rolton (61 off 65 balls) continuing their dominance of the England attack. The English batting never threatened to get on top of the Australian attack, and Karen Rolton displayed her all-round class, taking 3/14 with her left-arm medium pace.

Players of the Match: K. L. Rolton and D. Holden.

Australia

*B. J. Clark b Holden	69	(110)	C. L. Fitzpatrick b Connor	6	(7)
L. M. Keightley c Lowe b Holden	34	(55)	J. Hayes not out	4	(4)
K. L. Rolton c Thompson b Collyer	61	(65)	L. C. Sthalekar not out	3	(5)
M. A. J. Goszko c Hawker b Pearson	5	(11)	L-b 5, w 4, n-b 1	10	
S. A. Cooper c and b Connor	9	(11)			
O. J. Magno b Holden	10	(17)	(50 overs) (9 wkts)	227	
†J. C. Price run out	1	(3)	Fall: 101 144 158 179 191 194 203		
T. A. McGregor lbw b C. E. Taylor	15	(15)	215 219		

Bowling: Pearson 10–0–39–1; C. E. Taylor 9–2–29–1; Connor 9–1–38–2; Collyer 10–1–47–1; Holden 10–0–48–3; Hawker 2–0–21–0.

England

H. Lloyd b Fitzpatrick	0	(6)	D. Holden lbw b Sthalekar	9	(27)
A. Thompson c Price b Fitzpatrick	5	(22)	C. E. Taylor not out	5	(22)
S. V. Collyer c Price b Rolton	26	(74)	L. C. Pearson run out	0	(2)
S. C. Taylor lbw b McGregor	8	(10)			
*C. J. Connor c Goszko b McGregor	23	(54)	B 1, l-b 6, w 3	10	
K. Lowe c Fitzpatrick b Rolton	1	(10)			
†I. Cassar st Price b Hayes	21	(56)	(47.3 overs)	109	
J. Hawker c Clark b Rolton	1	(2)	Fall: 0 16 32 55 67 67 69 92 109 109		

Bowling: Fitzpatrick 10–4–27–2; McGregor 10–4–18–2; Hayes 9.3–3–19–1; Sthalekar 10–2–24–1; Rolton 8–4–14–3.

Umpires: K. J. Lyons and K. Taylor.
TV Umpire: A. Fox.

ENGLAND v AUSTRALIA

Third Limited-Overs International

At Lord's, London, July 3, 2001. Australia won by 66 runs. Toss: Australia.

The final match of the series at Lord's did nothing to disturb the triumphant progress of Australia or the distress of England. Again the big three, Belinda Clark, Lisa Keightley and Karen Rolton, ripped the England bowling apart, but once again the efforts of the lower order were disappointing. England's target of 207 was well beyond them, though this time they batted out their 50 overs. Claire Taylor held out until the end, top-scoring for the second time in the series. Karen Rolton finished the series with 176 runs (off 181 balls), while Therese McGregor was the best bowler, taking 8/47 off 30 overs.

Players of the Match: C. E. Taylor and T. A. McGregor. *Players of the Series:* C. J. Connor and K. L. Rolton.

Australia

L. M. Keightley c Connor b Holden	.. 54	(92)
*B. J. Clark c and b Collyer	 49	(75)
K. L. Rolton c Thompson b Collyer	... 36	(48)
S. A. Cooper c C. E. Taylor b Connor	. 8	(24)
M. A. J. Goszko c S. C. Taylor		
b C. E. Taylor	.. 24	(24)
†J. C. Price not out	 13	(29)

J. Hayes and A. J. Fahey did not bat.

C. L. Mason c Cassar b C. E. Taylor	. 0	(1)
C. L. Fitzpatrick b Connor	 4	(5)
T. A. McGregor not out	 3	(2)
B 5, l-b 2, w 8	 15	
(50 overs)	(7 wkts)	206

Fall: 102 112 147 180 190 192 201

Bowling: Pearson 7–0–45–0; C. E. Taylor 10–1–30–2; Connor 10–1–35–2; Shaw 3–1–12–0; Holden 10–0–47–1; Collyer 10–0–30–2.

England

C. Atkins c Price b Hayes	 17	(81)
A. Thompson lbw b Mason	 20	(45)
S. V. Collyer st Price b Fahey	 14	(24)
S. C. Taylor not out	 50	(77)
D. Holden b Fahey	 3	(9)
L. Harper c Fahey b McGregor	 6	(18)
N. Shaw lbw b McGregor	 0	(3)

L. C. Pearson did not bat.

*C. J. Connor c Clark b Rolton	 11	(18)
†J. Cassar b Mason	 2	(11)
C. E. Taylor not out	 3	(15)
B 2, l-b 4, w 7, n-b 1	 14	
(50 overs)	(8 wkts)	140

Fall: 37 55 65 72 99 99 127 131

Bowling: Fitzpatrick 10–2–29–0; McGregor 10–6–14–2; Mason 10–4–22–2; Fahey 9–1–24–2; Hayes 8–0–29–1; Rolton 3–0–16–1.

Umpires: N. J. Llong and J. West.

IRELAND v AUSTRALIA

First Limited-Overs International

At Rathmines, Dublin, July 12, 2001. Australia won on run rate. Toss: Ireland.

The home side's innings was marked by solid contributions from Clare O'Leary 89 balls, five fours) and Catriona Beggs (93 balls, five fours), but they were never able to score quickly enough against a persistent Australian attack to set the visitors anything but a nugatory target. Rain, however, during the Australian innings saw the total required adjusted to 117 from 36.4 overs. The accuracy of Barbara McDonald's ten overs caused a flurry of activity at the end from Michell Goszko and Julie Hayes which saw Australia home, albeit narrowly.

Ireland

C. M. O'Leary c Price b Hayes	 42
*A. Linehan c Goszko b McGregor	 8
G. Leahy lbw b Hayes	 2
C. M. Beggs c Price b McGregor	 45
M. E. Grealey run out	 1
S. A. Young c McGregor b Sthalekar	 6
L. D. Molins lbw b McGregor	 2
†N. Squires b Mason	 3

I. M. Joyce b Mason	 2
C. J. Metcalfe not out	 4
B. M. McDonald c Goszko b Sthalekar	...0
B 2, l-b 6, w 8, n-b 1	 17
(49.1 overs)	132

Fall: 24 40 83 84 104 108 124 124 126 132

Bowling: Mason 10–1–24–2; McGregor 10–3–21–3; Hayes 10–5–23–2; Fahey 10–0–26–0; Sthalekar 9.1–1–30–2.

Australia

*B. J. Clark c O'Leary b McDonald	16	J. Hayes not out	15
L. M. Keightley run out (Joyce)	28		
M. A. J. Goszko not out	36	W 5	5
S. A. Cooper c Beggs b Grearley	2		—
L. C. Broadbent c Linehan b Young	9	(5 wkts)	119
L. C. Sthalekar run out (McDonald)	8		

Fall: 46 46 49 64 77

T. A. McGregor, †J. C. Price, C. L. Mason and A. J. Fahey did not bat.

Bowling: McDonald 10–3–15–1; Joyce 10–2–47–0; Young 6.4–1–20–1; Grealey 8–3–30–1; Metcalfe 2–0–7–0.

Umpires: R. Cutland and M. Mellroy.

IRELAND v AUSTRALIA

Second Limited-Overs International

At Trinity College, Dublin, July 14, 2001. Australia won by nine wickets. Toss: Ireland.
    Ireland were quickly scorched by the pace of Catherine Fitzpatrick who had clean bowled three batters by the time the score had inches its way to seven. Clare O'Leary (118 balls, one four) then resisted stoutly, while Miriam Grealey (89 balls, four fours) drew on all her experience in making a pleasant contribution to a stand of 85. The Australian bowlers, however, kept the rest of the batting on a tight a leash and Fitzpatrick returned to cap off he best figures in one-day international cricket. Lisa Keightley (96 balls, three fours) and Karen Rolton (53 balls, six fours) teamed in a confident unbroken second wicket partnership of 85 which saw Australia home in an untroubled fashion.

Ireland

C. M. O'Leary c and b Hayes	30	(118)	I. M. Joyce lbw b Fitzpatrick	2	(8)
*A. Linehan b Fitzpatrick	0	(4)	A. M. Budd not out	3	(17)
G. Leahy b Fitzpatrick	1	(10)			
C. M. Beggs b Fitzpatrick	0	(9)	L-b 3, w 8	11	
M. E. Grealey c Fitzpatrick b Hayes	57	(89)		—	
S. A. Young not out	13	(36)	(50 overs, 156 mins)	(7 wkts)	119
†N. Squire c Keightley b Fitzpatrick	2	(8)	Fall: 2 4 7 92 97 109 113		

C. N. Joyce and B. M. McDonald did not bat.

Bowling: Fitzpatrick 10–3–14–5; Hayes 10–5–14–2; Mason 10–1–21–0; Fahey 10–0–29–0; Sthalekar 7–1–22–0; Rolton 3–0–16–0.

Australia

L. M. Keightley not out	51	(96)
M. A. J. Goszko lbw b Young	17	(36)
*K. L. Rolton not out	51	(34)
W 1	1	

(27.4 overs, 93 mins)   (1 wkt) 120

Fall: 35

C. L. Fitzpatrick, J. Hayes, C. L. Mason, A. J. Fahey, L. C. Sthalekar, †J. C. Price, S. A. Cooper and L. C. Broadfoot did not bat.

Bowling: McDonald 8–1–27–0; I. M. Joyce 5–1–17–0; Young 4–0–15–1; Grealey 6–0–30–0; C. N. Joyce 4.4–1–31–0.

Umpires: L. Hewson and M. Mellroy.

IRELAND v AUSTRALIA

Third Limited-Overs International

At Trinity College, Dublin, July 15, 2001. Australia won by 201 runs. Toss: Australia.

Belinda Clark (102 balls, six fours) and Sally Cooper (119 balls, five fours) stamped their authority on the bowling in an opening partnership of 157. The run feast, however, became a famine as the next eight wickets fell for only 90 runs. The leg-spin of Ciara Metcalfe was both controlled and effective, and she snared the wickets of both of the openers. Ireland were then overwhelmed in just 23 overs for their lowest-ever total against Australia. Therese McGregor secured her best one-day international cricket figures, and was ably assisted by Catherine Fitzpatrick. This match was the final of Charmaine Mason's 46 one-day internationals, which brought her 83 wickets at 13.83; in six Tests she took 13 wickets at 26.08.

Australia

*B. J. Clark c Grealey b Metcalfe	....	80 (102)
S. A. Cooper c Shillington b Metcalfe		85 (119)
L. C. Broadbent c Linehan b Young	..	8 (10)
K. L. Rolton run out	....	12 (9)
L. C. Sthalekar run out	....	0 (8)
†J. C. Price c C. N. Joyce b I. M. Joyce		12 (25)
C. L. Fitzpatrick b Young	....	13 (14)
J. Hayes run out	....	5 (5)

C. L. Mason st Linehan b Metcalfe	..	1 (3)
T. A. McGregor not out	....	9 (7)
A. J. Fahey not out	....	0 (0)
B 3, l-b 9, w 8, n-b 2	....	22
(50 overs, 186 mins)	(9 wkts)	247

Fall: 157 175 201 202 208 231 233 235 242

Bowling: McDonald 7–1–22–0; I. M. Joyce 10–1–49–1; Grearley 10–0–47–0; C. N. Joyce 2–0–14–0; Young 10–0–47–2; Budd 1–0–13–0; Metcalfe 10–0–43–3.

Ireland

*A. Linehan c Clark b McGregor	....	0 (6)
C. M. Beggs b McGregor	....	1 (8)
C. M. A. Shillington c and b McGregor		1 (10)
M. E. Grealey c Clark b Fitzpatrick	...	11 (27)
S. A. Young b McGregor	....	1 (21)
†N. Squire not out	....	11 (39)
I. M. Joyce c and b Mason	....	5 (18)
A. M. Budd b Fitzpatrick	....	3 (4)

C. J. Metcalfe b Fitzpatrick	....	0 (1)
C. N. Joyce run out	....	3 (5)
B. M. McDonald (absent injured)		
L-b 2, w 7, n-b 1	....	10
(23 overs, 82 mins)	(9 wkts)	46

Fall: 0 2 5 15 25 37 40 40 46

Bowling: McGregor 6–3–8–4; Fahey 7–2–12–0; Fitzpatrick 6–0–20–3; Mason 4–2–4–1.

Umpires: D. Walsh and D. Watson.

PART SIX: ADMINISTRATION AND LAWS

INTERNATIONAL CRICKET COUNCIL

On June 15, 1909, representatives of cricket in England, Australia and South Africa met at Lord's and founded the Imperial Cricket Conference. Membership was confined to the governing bodies of cricket in countries within the British Commonwealth where Test cricket was played. India, New Zealand and West Indies were elected as members on May 31, 1926, Pakistan on July 28, 1952, Sri Lanka on July 21, 1981, Zimbabwe on July 8, 1992 and Bangladesh on June 26, 2000. South Africa ceased to be a member of ICC on leaving the British Commonwealth in May, 1961, but was elected as a Full Member on July 10, 1991.

On July 15, 1965, the Conference was renamed the International Cricket Conference and new rules were adopted to permit the election of countries from outside the British Commonwealth. This led to the growth of the Conference, with the admission of Associate Members, who were each entitled to one vote, while the Foundation and Full Members were each entitled to two votes, on ICC resolutions. On July 12, 13, 1989, the Conference was renamed the International Cricket Council and revised rules were adopted.

On July 7, 1993, ICC ceased to be administered by MCC and became an independent organisation with its own chief executive, the headquarters remaining at Lord's. The category of Foundation Member, with its special rights, was abolished. On October 1, 1993, Sir Clyde Walcott became the first non-British chairman of ICC.

On June 16, 1997, ICC became an incorporated body, with an executive board and a president instead of a chairman. Jagmohan Dalmiya became ICC's first president. He was succeeded at ICC's annual meeting on June 22–26, 2000 by former Australian Cricket Board chairman Malcolm Gray AM.

Officers

President: M. A. Gray. *Chief Executive:* M. Speed.
Chairman of Committees: Cricket: Sunil Gavaskar; *Development:* no appointment; *Finance and Marketing:* E. Mani; *Associate Members:* J. Rayani.

Executive Board: The six officers listed above sit on the board ex officio. They are joined by Sir John Anderson (New Zealand), P. Chingoka (Zimbabwe), S. H. Chowdhury (Bangladesh), Raj Singh Dungarpur (India), R. van Ierschot (Holland), HRH Tunku Imran (Malaysia), Lord MacLaurin (England), Khalid Mahmood (Pakistan), R. Merriman (Australia), The Rev. W. Hall (West Indies), J. Ryani (Kenya), V. Malasekera (Sri Lanka), R. White (South Africa).

Constitution

President: Each Full Member has the right, by rotation, to appoint ICC's president. In 1997, India named J. Dalmiya to serve until 2000. M. A. Gray of Australia will now serve until 2003. Subsequent presidents will serve for two years.

Chief Executive: Appointed by the Council. M. Speed was appointed in June 2001.

Membership

Full Members: Australia, Bangladesh, England, India, New Zealand, Pakistan, South Africa, Sri Lanka, West Indies and Zimbabwe.

Associate Members*: Argentina (1974), Bermuda (1966), Canada (1968), Denmark (1966), East and Central Africa (1966), Fiji (1965), France (1998), Germany (1999), Gibraltar (1969), Hong Kong (1969), Ireland (1993), Israel (1974), Italy (1995), Kenya (1981), Malaysia (1967), Namibia (1992), Nepal (1996), Netherlands (1966), Papua New Guinea (1973), Scotland (1994), Singapore (1974), Tanzania (2001), Uganda (1998), United Arab Emirates (1990), USA (1965) and West Africa (1976).

Affiliate Members*: Afghanistan (2001), Austria (1992), Bahamas (1987), Bahrain (2001), Belgium (1991), Belize (1997), Bhutan (2001), Botswana (2001), Brunei (1992), Cayman Islands (1997), Cook Islands (2000), Croatia (2001), Cyprus (1999), Czech Republic (2000), Finland (2000), Greece (1995), Indonesia (2001), Japan (1989), South Korea (2001), Kuwait (1998), Lesotho (2001), Luxembourg (1998), Maldives (2001), Malta (1998), Morocco (1999), Norway (2000), Oman (2000), Philippines (2000), Portugal (1996), Qatar (1999), St Helena (2001), Samoa (2000), Spain (1992), Sweden (1997), Switzerland (1985), Thailand (1995), Tonga (2000) and Vanuatu (1995).

* Year of election shown in parentheses.

The following governing bodies for cricket shall be eligible for election.

    Full Members: The governing body for cricket recognised by ICC of a country, or countries associated for cricket purposes, or a geographical area, from which representative teams are qualified to play official Test matches.

    Associate Members: The governing body for cricket recognised by ICC of a country, or countries associated for cricket purposes, or a geographical area, which does not qualify as a Full Member but where cricket is firmly established and organised.

    Affiliate Members: The governing body for cricket recognised by ICC of a country, or countries associated for cricket purposes, or a geographical area (which is not part of one of those already constituted as a Full or Associate Member) where ICC recognises that cricket is played in accordance with the Laws of Cricket. Affiliate Members have no right to vote or to propose or second resolutions at ICC meetings.

AUSTRALIAN CRICKET BOARD

Officers

Chairman: D. W. Rogers.   *Chief Executive:* J. Sutherland.

Board of Directors: D. W. Rogers (*chairman*), Dr A. C. Battersby, J. Clarke, W. Edwards, B. F. Freedman, M. A. Gray, R. E. Horsell, W. J Jocelyn, R. F. Merriman (deputy *chairman*), D. G. Mullins, F. C. O'Connor, T. J. Robertson, B. K. Shepherd, G. L. Tamblyn (*finance director*).

AUSTRALIAN CRICKETERS' ASSOCIATION

The Australian Cricketers' Association was incorporated in February 1997. It represents the collective voice of all first-class cricketers in Australia. The ACA has recently completed negotiating a Memorandum of Understanding with the Australian Cricket Board, which formalises remuneration and welfare issues between the players and their respective cricket boards within Australia. The ACA is actively involved in protecting and providing benefits to all members, particularly in the area of professional advice and secular career training.

President and Chief Executive Officer: T. B. A. May.

ADDRESSES

INTERNATIONAL CRICKET COUNCIL

M. Speed, The Clock Tower, Lord's Cricket Ground, London NW8 8QN (44 20 7266 1818; fax 44 20 7266 1777; website www.icc.cricket.org; e-mail icc@icc.cricket.org).

Full Members

AUSTRALIA: Australian Cricket Board, J. Sutherland, 60 Jolimont Street, Jolimont, Victoria 3002 (61 3 9653 9999; fax 61 3 9653 9911; website www.acb.com.au).

BANGLADESH: Bangladesh Cricket Control Board, Syed Ashraful Huq, Bangabandhu National Stadium, Dhaka 1000 (880 2 966 6805; fax 880 2 956 3844; e-mail bcb@bangla.net).

ENGLAND: England and Wales Cricket Board, T. M. Lamb, Lord's Ground, London NW8 8QZ (44 20 7432 1200; fax 44 20 7289 5619; website www.ecb.co.uk).

INDIA: Board of Control for Cricket in India, J. Y. Lele, Sanmitra, Anandpura, Baroda 390 001 (91 265 431233; fax 91 265 428833).

NEW ZEALAND: New Zealand Cricket Inc., C. Doig, PO Box 958, 109 Cambridge Terrace, Christchurch (64 3 366 2964; fax 64 3 365 7491; website www.nzcricket. org.nz).

PAKISTAN: Pakistan Cricket Board, Brig. Munawar Rana, Gaddafi Stadium, Ferozepur Road, Lahore 546(92 42 571 7231; fax 92 42 571 1860).

SOUTH AFRICA: United Cricket Board of South Africa, M. G. Majola, PO Box 55009, North Street, Illovo, Northlands 2116 (27 11 880 2810; fax 27 11 880 6578; website www.ucbsa.cricket.org; e-mail ucbsa@ucb.co.za).

SRI LANKA: Board of Control for Cricket in Sri Lanka, V. Malalasekera, 35 Maitland Place, Colombo 7 (94 1 691439/689551; fax 94 1 697405; e-mail: cricket @sri.lanka.net).

WEST INDIES: West Indies Cricket Board, G. Shillingford, Factory Road, PO Box 616 W, Woods Centre, St John's, Antigua (1 268 481 2452; fax 1 268 481 2498; e-mail wicb@candw.ag).

ZIMBABWE: Zimbabwe Cricket Union, D. Ellman-Brown, PO Box 2739, Harare (263 4 704616; fax 263 4 729370; website www.zcu.cricket.org; e-mail zcu @samara.co.zw).

Associate and Affiliate Members

AFGHANISTAN Afghanistan Cricket Federation, PO Box 970, Kabul.

ARGENTINA: Argentine Cricket Association, D. Lord, ACA Sede Central, J. M. Gutierrez 3829, 1425 Buenos Aires (54 11 4802 6166; fax 54 11 4802 6692; website cricketargentina@mail.com).

AUSTRIA: Austrian Cricket Association, A. Simpson-Parker, Apollogasse 3/42, A-1070 Vienna (43 1 524 9366; fax 43 1 524 9367; e-mail 10747.740@compuserve.com).

BAHAMAS: Bahamas Cricket Association, S. Deveaux, Government House, PO Box 1001, Nassau (1 242 322 1875; fax 1 242 322 4659).

BAHRAIN Bahrain Cricket Association, PO Box 2400, Manama.

BELGIUM: Belgian Cricket Federation, M. O'Connor, Koningin Astridlaan 98, B-28 Mechelen (32 15 331 635; fax 32 15 331 639).

BELIZE: Belize National Cricket Association, Mrs V. Parks, Burnham Manse, 88 Albert Street, PO Box 619, Belize City (501 2 72201; fax 501 2 30936).

BERMUDA: Bermuda Cricket Board of Control, R. Horton, PO Box HM992, Hamilton HM DX (1 441 292 8958; fax 1 441 292 8959; website bcb@ibl.bm).

BHUTAN Bhutan Cricket Association, PO Box 242, Thimphu.

BOTSWANA Botswana Cricket Association, Private Bag 00379, Gaborone.

BRUNEI: Persatuan Keriket Negara Brunei Darussalam, S. Langton, PO Box 931, MPC-Old Airport, Berakas-BB 3577 (673 873 3737; fax 673 242 4088).

CANADA: Canadian Cricket Association, G. Edwards, 46 Port Street East, Mississauga, Ontario L5G 1C1 (1 905 278 5000; fax 1 905 278 5005).

CAYMAN ISLANDS: Cayman Islands Cricket Association, C. Myles, PO Box 1201 GT, George Town, Grand Cayman (1 345 945 5589; fax 1 345 945 5558).

COOK ISLANDS: Cook Islands Cricket Association, G. Hoskings, PO Box 139, Raratonga (682 29 312; fax 682 29 314).

CYPRUS: Cyprus Cricket Association, S. Carr, PO Box 3293, Limassol, Cyprus CY 3301 (357 5 354 371; fax 357 5 342 996).

CZECH REPUBLIC: Czech Republic Cricket Association, J. Locke, Na Berance 7, 160 Praha 6 (420 22 481 1672; fax 420 22 481 1608).

DENMARK: Dansk Cricket-Forbund, C. B. S. Hansen, Idraettens Hus, 2605 Brøndby (45 4326 2160; fax 45 4326 2163; e-mail dcf@cricket.dk).

EAST AND CENTRAL AFRICA: East and Central African Cricket Conference, T. B. McCarthy, PO Box 34321, Lusaka 1010, Zambia (260 1 226 228; fax 260 1 224 454).

FIJI: Fiji Cricket Association, P. I. Knight, PO Box 300, Suva (679 301 499/3321; fax 679 301 618).

FINLAND: Finnish Cricket Association, A. Armitage, Coats Opti Oy, Ketjutie 3, Fin-04220, Kerava (358 927 487 327; fax 358 927 487 371).

FRANCE: Fédération Française de Cricket, D. Marchois, La Saunerie, 41 rue de Fecamp, 75012 Paris (33 5 5354 4095; fax 33 5 5354 2783).

GERMANY: Deutscher Cricket Bund, B. Fell, Luragogasse 5, D-94032 Passau (49 851 34307; fax 49 851 32815; e-mail fell02@fsuni.rzuni.passau.de).

GIBRALTAR: Gibraltar Cricket Association, T. J. Finlayson, 23 Merlot House, Vineyards Estate (350 79461; also fax).

GREECE: Greek Cricket Federation, C. Evangelos, Cat. Pappa 8, Corfu 491(30 661 47753; fax 30 661 47754).

HONG KONG: Hong Kong Cricket Association, J. A. Cribbin, Room 1019, Sports House,1 Stadium Path, So Kon Po, Causeway Bay (852 250 48101; fax 852 257 78486; website www.hkabc.net; e-mail hcca@hkabc.net).

INDONESIA Indonesia Cricket Federation, Gedung BRI II, 19th Floor, Suite 1907, Jl Jend Suirman No. 44-46, Jakarta.

IRELAND: Irish Cricket Union, J. Wright, The Diamond, Malahide, Co Dublin 18 (353 1 845 0710; fax 353 1 845 5545; e-mail info@typetest.ie).

ISRAEL: Israel Cricket Association, S. Perlman, PO Box 65085, Tel-Aviv 61650 (972 3 642 5529; fax 972 3 641 7271).

ITALY: Federazione Cricket Italiana, S. Gambino, Via S. Ignazio 9, 00186 Roma (39 06 689 6989; fax 39 06 687 8684).

JAPAN: Japan Cricket Association, T. Bayley, Nankitsu Machi 15-5, Maebashi City 371-0043 (81 3 5772 3470; fax 81 3 5772 3471; website www.jca@cricket.ne.jp).

KENYA: Kenya Cricket Association, H. Shah, PO Box 45870, Nairobi (254 2 766447/764579; fax 254 2 765057; e-mail kcricket@iconnect.co.ke).

KUWAIT: Kuwait Cricket Association, Abdul Muttaleb Ahmad, PO Box 6706, Hawalli-32042 (965 572 6600; fax 965 573 4973).

LESOTHO Lesotho Cricket Association, 9 Erasmus Street, Ladybrand 9745, South Africa.

LUXEMBOURG: Federation Luxembourgeoise de Cricket, T. Dunning, 87 rue de Gasperich, L-1617 Luxembourg-Ville (352 430 12964).

MALAYSIA: Malaysian Cricket Association, K. Selveratnam, 1st Floor, Wisma OCM, Jalan Hang Jebat, 50150 Kuala Lumpur (60 3 201 6761; fax 60 3 201 3878).

MALDIVES Cricket Control Board of Maldives, Kulhivaru Ekuveni, 1st Floor, Cricket Indoor Hall, Male.

MALTA: Malta Cricket Association, P. Naudi, c/o Marsa Sports Club, Marsa HMR 15 (356 233 851; fax 356 231 809).

MOROCCO: Moroccan Cricket Association, C. Laroussi, 6 Rue Sefrou A8, Hassan-Rabat (212 7 766 453; fax 212 7 766 742).

NAMIBIA: Namibia Cricket Board, L. Pieters, PO Box 266, Windhoek 90(264 61 263128/263129; fax 264 61 215149).

NEPAL: Cricket Association of Nepal, B. R. Pandey, Heritage Plaza, 5th Floor, Kamaldi, PO Box 20291, Kathmandu (977 1 247485 ext. 252; fax 977 1 247946).

NETHERLANDS: Royal Netherlands Cricket Board, A. de la Mar, Nieuwe Kalfjeslaan 21-B, 1182 AA Amstelveen (31 20 645 1705; fax 31 20 645 1715; e-mail adelamar@kncb.nl).

NORWAY: Norway Cricket Association, R. Gibb, Geologsvingen 11, 0380 Oslo (fax 47 22 73 0653).

OMAN: Oman Cricket Association, A. M. Yousef, PO Box 3948, Ruwi 112, Muscat, Sultanate of Oman (968 79 6655; fax 968 70 6372).

PAPUA NEW GUINEA: Papua New Guinea Cricket Board of Control, W. Satchell, PO Box 83, Konedobu NCD (675 321 1070; fax 675 321 7974; e-mail imcsghai @loxinfo.co.th).

PHILIPPINES: Philippine Cricket Association, c/o Davies, Langdon & Search Philippines Inc., 4th Floor, 2129 Pasong Tamo, Makati City, Metro Manilla (63 2 524 1426; fax 63 2 525 2171; e-mail cjh@dls.com.ph).

PORTUGAL: Associação de Cricket de Portugal, J. Simonson, Largo de Academia Nacional de Belas Artes 16, Lisboa P-12(351 1 346 2277; fax 351 1 346 5079).

QATAR: Qatar Cricket Association, F. H. Alfardan, PO Box 339, Doha (974 433 461; fax 974 435 2978).

ST HELENA St Helena Cricket Association, Nia Roo, New Bridge Road, Jamestown.

SAMOA: Samoa Cricket Association, S. Kohlhasse, Seb & Rene Sports, PO Box 9599 (685 22 480; also fax).

SCOTLAND: Scottish Cricket Union, R. W. Barclay, National Cricket Academy, MES Sports Centre, Ravelston, Edinburgh EH4 3NT (44 131 313 7420; fax 44 131 313 7430; website www.scu.org.uk; e-mail admin.scu@btinternet.com).

SINGAPORE: Singapore Cricket Association, A. Kalaver, 31 Stadium Crescent (South Entrance) Singapore 397639 (65 348 6566; fax 65 348 6506).

SOUTH KOREA Korea Cricket Association 60-25 Hannam-Dong, Yongsan-Ku, Seoul 140 210.

SPAIN: Asociacion Española de Cricket, M. de Careaga, Casa Desiderata, VA 153, 03737 Javea, Alicante (34 96 686 6965; also fax).

SWEDEN: Sweden Cricket Board, Mrs I. Persson, Hjulstabackar 19BV, SE16365 Spånga (46 8 6496167; fax 46 8 7188850).

SWITZERLAND: Swiss Cricket Association, A. MacKay, Wingertlistrasse 22, 8405 Winterthur (41 52 233 4601; fax 41 1 839 4999; e-mail alex_mackay@ibi.com).

THAILAND: Thailand Cricket League, R. Sharma, 25-27 Soi 32/1, Charoen Nakhorn Road, Klongsan, Bangkok 10600 (66 2 862 7101; fax 66 2 862 4407; e-mail imcsghai@loxinfo.co.th).

TONGA: Tonga Cricket Association, c/o PO Box 1278, Nuku' Alofa (676 23 066; fax 676 26 011).

UGANDA: Uganda Cricket Association, J. Ligya, c/o National Council of Sports, Lugogo Stadium, PO Box 8346, Kampala (256 41 349550; fax 256 41 231478).

UNITED ARAB EMIRATES: Emirates Cricket Board, M. Khan, Sharjah Cricket Stadium, PO Box 88, Sharjah (971 6 532 2991; fax 971 6 533 4741; e-mail cricket@emirates.net.ae).

USA: United States of America Cricket Association, K. Prasad, The Cricket Pavilion, Hoverford College, 387 West Lancaster Avenue, Hoverford, Pennsylvania 19041 (1 6101 896 3633; fax 1 6101 896 7122).

VANUATU: Vanuatu Cricket Association, M. Stafford, c/o BDO, PO Box 240, Port Vila, Vanuatu (678 22280; fax 678 22317; e-mail stafford@vanuatu.com.vu).

WEST AFRICA: West Africa Cricket Conference, Miss G. Ekwempu, Tafawa Balewa Square, Race Course, Lagos, PO Box 9309, Nigeria (234 1 545 4472; fax 234 1 585 0529).

UK ADDRESSES

ENGLAND AND WALES CRICKET BOARD: T. M. Lamb, Lord's Ground, London NW8 8QZ (44 20 7432 1200; fax 44 20 7289 5619; website www.ecb.co.uk).

MARYLEBONE CRICKET CLUB: R. D. V. Knight, Lord's Ground, London NW8 8QN (44 20 7289 1611; fax 44 20 7289 9100. Tickets 44 20 7432 1066; fax 44 20 7432 1061).

AUSTRALIAN STATE CRICKET ASSOCIATION ADDRESSES

AUSTRALIAN CAPITAL TERRITORY: ACT Cricket, PO Box 3379, Manuka, Australian Capital Territory 2603 (61 2 6239 6002; fax 61 2 6295 7135).

NEW SOUTH WALES: Cricket NSW, PO Box 333, Paddington, New South Wales 2021 (61 2 9339 0999; fax 61 2 9360 6877).

QUEENSLAND: Queensland Cricket, PO Box 575, Albion, Queensland 4010 (61 7 3292 3100; fax 61 7 3262 9160).

SOUTH AUSTRALIA: South Australian Cricket Association, Adelaide Oval, North Adelaide, South Australia 5006 (61 8 8300 3800; fax 61 8 8231 4346).

TASMANIA: Tasmanian Cricket Association, PO Box 495, Rosny Park, Tasmania 7018 (61 3 6211 4000; fax 61 3 6244 3924).

VICTORIA: Victorian Cricket Association, VCA House, 86 Jolimont Street, Jolimont, Victoria 3002 (61 3 9653 1100; fax61 3 9653 1196).

WESTERN AUSTRALIA: Western Australian Cricket Association, PO Box 6045, East Perth, Western Australia 6892 (61 8 9265 7222; fax 61 8 9221 1823).

Other Bodies

ASSOCIATION OF CRICKET UMPIRES AND SCORERS: G. J. Bullock, PO Box 399, Camberley, Surrey, GU16 5ZJ, UK (44 1276 27962).

AUSTRALIAN CRICKETERS' ASSOCIATION: Tim B. A. May, Level 46, 525 Collins Street, Melbourne, Victoria 3000 (61 3 9614 8456; fax 61 3 9620 0601).

AUSTRALIAN SCHOOLS' CRICKET COUNCIL INC: A. A. K.Gifford, 29 George Street, Avalon, New South Wales 2107 (61 2 9918 3103; fax 61 2 99187211).

BRADMAN MUSEUM: R. Mulvaney, PO Box 9994, Bowral, NSW 2576 (61 2 4862 1247; fax 61 2 4861 2536).

CRUSADERS, THE: Swan Richards, 25–31 Rokeby Street, Collingwood, Victoria, 3066 (61 3 9415 6924; fax 61 3 9417 6911)

LORD'S TAVERNERS AUSTRALIA: Keith Jones, Townhouse 1, 1-3 Wells Street, Brighton, Victoria 3186 (61 3 9593 5301)

WOMEN'S CRICKET AUSTRALIA: Belinda Clark, 90 Jolimont Street, Jolimont, Victoria 3002 (ph/fax 61 3 9654 1490).

CRICKET ASSOCIATIONS AND SOCIETIES

AUSTRALIAN CRICKET SOCIETY INC., Mr Richard Elvins (President), 19 Acacia Avenue, Blackburn, Victoria 3130 (61 3 9877 4528). There are branches of the Society in each state.

THE LAWS OF CRICKET

As updated in 2000. World copyright of MCC and reprinted by permission of MCC. Copies of the "Laws of Cricket" may be obtained from Lord's Cricket Ground or from the MCC website at www.lords.org

INDEX TO THE LAWS

THE PREAMBLE – THE SPIRIT OF CRICKET

Cricket is a game that owes much of its unique appeal to the fact that it should be played not only within its Laws but also within the Spirit of the game. Any action which is seen to abuse this spirit causes injury to the game itself. The major responsibility for ensuring the spirit of fair play rests with the captains.

1.   There are two Laws which place the responsibility for the team's conduct firmly on the captain.

        Responsibility of Captains
        The captains are responsible at all times for ensuring that play is conducted within the Spirit of the Game as well as within the Laws.

        Player's Conduct
        In the event of a player failing to comply with instructions by an umpire, or criticising by word or action the decisions of an umpire, or showing dissent, or generally behaving in a manner which might bring the game into disrepute, the umpire concerned shall in the first place report the matter to the other umpire and to the player's captain, and instruct the latter to take action.

2.   **Fair and Unfair Play**
        According to the Laws the umpires are the sole judges of fair and unfair play. The umpires may intervene at any time and it is the responsibility of the captain to take action where required.

3.   **The Umpires are Authorised to Intervene in Cases of:**
        • Time wasting
        • Damaging the pitch
        • Dangerous or unfair bowling
        • Tampering with the ball
        • Any other action that they consider to be unfair

4.   **The Spirit of the Game involves RESPECT for:**
        • Your opponents
        • Your own captain and team
        • The role of the umpires
        • The game's traditional values

5.   **It is Against the Spirit of the Game:**
        • To dispute an umpire's decision by word, action or gesture
        • To direct abusive language towards an opponent or umpire
        • To indulge in cheating or any sharp practice, for instance:
          a) to appeal knowing that the batsman is not out
          b) to advance towards an umpire in an aggressive manner when appealing
          c) to seek to distract an opponent either verbally or by harassment with persistent clapping or unnecessary noise under the guise of enthusiasm and motivation of one's side

6.   **Violence**
        There is no place for any act of violence on the field of play.

7.   **Players**
        Captains and umpires together set the tone for the conduct of a cricket match. Every player is expected to mke an important contribution to this.

LAW 1. THE PLAYERS

1. Number of Players

A match is played between two sides, each of 11 players, one of whom shall be captain. By agreement a match may be played between sides of more or less than 11 players, but not more than 11 players may field at any time.

2. Nomination of Players

Each captain shall nominate his players in writing to one of the umpires before the toss. No player may be changed after the nomination without the consent of the opposing captain.

3. Captain

If at any time the captain is not available, a deputy shall act for him.

(a) If a captain is not available during the period in which the toss is to take place, then the deputy must be responsible for the nomination of the players, if this has not already been done, and for the toss. See 2 above and Law 12.4 (The Toss).

(b) At any time after the toss, the deputy must be one of the nominated players.

4. Responsibilities of Captains

The captains are responsible at all times for ensuring that play is conducted within the spirit and traditions of the game as well as within the Laws. See The Preamble – The Spirit of Cricket and Law 42.1 (Fair and Unfair Play – Responsibility of Captains).

LAW 2. SUBSTITUTES AND RUNNERS: BATSMAN OR FIELDER LEAVING THE FIELD: BATSMAN RETIRING: BATSMAN COMMENCING INNINGS

1. Substitutes and Runners

(a) If the umpires are satisfied that a player has been injured or become ill after the nomination of the players, they shall allow that player to have

(i) a substitute acting instead of him in the field

(ii) a runner when batting.

Any injury or illness that occurs at any time after the nomination of the players until the conclusion of the match shall be allowable, irrespective of whether play is in progress or not.

(b) The umpires shall have discretion, for other wholly acceptable reasons, to allow a substitute for a fielder, or a runner for a batsman, at the start of the match or at any subsequent time.

2. Objection to Substitutes

The opposing captain shall have no right of objection to any player acting as substitute on the field, nor as to where the substitute shall field. However no substitute shall act as wicket-keeper. See 3 following.

3. Restrictions on the Role of Substitutes

A substitute shall not be allowed to bat or bowl nor to act as wicket-keeper or as captain on the field of play.

4. A Player for whom a Substitute has Acted

A player is allowed to bat, bowl or field even though a substitute has previously acted for him.

5. Fielder Absent or Leaving the Field

If a fielder fails to take the field with his side at the start of the match or at any later time, or leaves the field during a session of play

(a) The umpire shall be informed of the reason for his absence.

(b) He shall not thereafter come on to the field during a session of play without the consent of the umpire. See 6 following. The umpire shall give such consent as soon as is practicable.

(c) If he is absent for 15 minutes or longer, he shall not be permitted to bowl thereafter, subject to (i), (ii) or (iii) below, until he has been on the field for at least that length of playing time for which he was absent.

> (i) Absence or penalty for time absent shall not be carried over into a new day's play.

> (ii) If, in the case of a follow-on or forfeiture, a side fields for two consecutive innings, this restriction shall, subject to (i) above, continue as necessary into the second innings but shall not otherwise be carried over into a new innings.

> (iii) The time lost for an unscheduled break in play shall be counted as time on the field for any fielder who comes onto the field at the resumption of play. See Law 15.1 (An Interval)

6. Player Returning Without Permission

If a player comes onto the field of play in contravention of 5(b) above and comes into contact with the ball while it is in play

> (i) the ball shall immediately become dead and the umpire shall award five penalty runs to the batting side. See Law 42.17 (Penalty Runs)

> (ii) the umpire shall inform the other umpire, the captain of the fielding side, the batsmen and, as soon as practicable, the captain of the batting side of the reason for this action.

> (iii) the umpires together shall report the occurrence as soon as possible to the Executive of the fielding side and any Governing Body responsible for the match, who shall take such action as is considered appropriate against the captain and player concerned.

7. Runner

The player acting as a runner for a batsman shall be a member of the batting side and shall, if possible, have already batted in that innings. The runner shall wear external protective equipment equivalent to that worn by the batsman for whom he runs and shall carry a bat.

8. Transgression of the Laws by a Batsman Who has a Runner

(a) A batsman's runner is subject to the Laws. He will be regarded as a batsman except where there are specific provisions for his role as a runner. See 7 above and Law 29.2 (Which is a Batsman's Ground)

(b) A batsman with a runner will suffer a penalty for any infringement of the Laws by his runner as though he himself had been responsible for the infringement. In particular he will be out if his runner is out under any of Laws 33 (Handled the Ball), 37 (Obstructing the Field) or 38 (Run Out).

(c) When a batsman with a runner is striker he remains himself subject to the Laws and will be liable to the penalties that any infringement of them demands. Additionally if he is out of his ground when the wicket is put down at the wicket-keeper's end he will be out in the circumstancs of Law 38 (Run Out) or Law 39 (Stumped) irrespective of the position of the non-striker or the runner. If he is thus dismissed, runs completed by the runner and the other batsman before the dismissal shall not be scored. However, the penalty for a No Ball or a Wide shall stand, together with any penalties to either side that may be awarded when the ball is dead. See Law 42.17 (Penalty Runs).

(d) When a batsman with a runner is not the striker

(i) he remains subject to Laws 33 (Handled the Ball) and 37 (Obstructing the Field) but is otherwise out of the game.

(ii) he shall stand where directed by the striker's end umpire so as not to interfere with play.

(iii) he will be liable, notwithstanding (i) above, to the penalty demanded by the Laws should he commit any act of unfair play.

9. Batsman Leaving the Field or Retiring

A batsman may retire at any time during his innings. The umpires, before allowing play to proceed, shall be informed of the reason for a batsman retiring.

(a) If a batsman retires because of illness, injury or any other unavoidable cause, he is entitled to resume his innings subject to (c) below. If for any reason he does not do so, his innings is to be recorded as "Retired – not out".

(b) If a batsman retires for any reason other than as in (a) above, he may only resume his innings with the consent of the opposing captain. If for any reason he does not resume his innings it is to be recorded as "Retired – out".

(c) If after retiring a batsman resumes his innings, it shall only be at the fall of a wicket or the retirementr of another batsman.

10. Commencement of a Batsman's Innings

Except at the start of a side's innings, a batsman shall be considered to have commenced his innings when he first steps onto the field of play, provided Time has not been called. The innings of the opening batsmen, and that of any new batsman at the resumption of play after a call of Time, shall commence at the call of Play.

LAW 3.   THE UMPIRES

1. Appointment and Attendance

Before the match, two umpires shall be appointed, one for each end, to control the game as required by the Laws, with absolute impartiality. The umpires shall be present on the ground and report to the Executive of the ground at least 45 minutes before the scheduled start of each day's play.

2. Change of Umpires

An umpire shall not be changed during the match, other than in exceptional circumstances, unless he is injured or ill. If there has to be a change of umpire, the replacement shall act only as the striker's end umpire unless the captains agree that he should take full responsibility as an umpire.

3. Agreement with Captains

Before the toss the umpires shall

(a) ascertain the hours of play and agree with the captains

(i) the balls to be used during the match. See Law 5 (The Ball).

(ii) times and durations of intervals for meals and times for drinks intervals. See Law 15 (Intervals).

(iii) the boundary of the field of play and allowances for boundaries. See Law 19 (Boundaries).

(iv) any special conditions of play affecting the conduct of the match.

(b) inform the scorers of the agreements in (ii), (iii) and (iv) above.

4. To Inform Captains and Scorers

Before the toss the umpires shall agree between themselves and inform both captains and both scorers

(i) which clock or watch and back-up time piece is to be used during the match.

(ii) whether or not any obstacle within the field of play is to be regarded as a boundary. See Law 19 (Boundaries).

5. The Wickets, Creases and Boundaries

Before the toss and during the match, the umpires shall satisfy themselves that

(i) the wickets are properly pitched. See Law 8 (The wickets).

(ii) the creases are correctly marked. See Law 9 (The bowling, popping and return creases).

(iii) the boundary of the field of play complies with the requirements of Law 19.2 (Defining the boundary – boundary marking).

6. Conduct of the Game, Implements and Equipment

Before the toss and during the match, the umpires shall satisfy themselves that

(a) the conduct of the game is strictly in accordance with the Laws.

(b) the implements of the game conform to the requirements of Laws 5 (The ball) and 6 (The bat), together with either Laws 8.2 (Size of stumps) and 8.3 (The bails) or, if appropriate, Law 8.4 (Junior cricket).

(c)   (i) no player uses equipment other than that permitted. See Appendix D.

        (ii) the wicket-keeper's gloves comply with the requirements of Law 40.2 (Gloves).

7. Fair and Unfair Play

The umpires shall be the sole judges of fair and unfair play.

8. Fitness of Ground, Weather and Light

The umpires shall be the final judges of the fitness of the ground, weather and light for play. See 9 below and Law 7.2 (Fitness of the Pitch for Play).

9. Suspension of Play for Adverse Conditions of Ground, Weather of Light

(a)   (i) All references to ground include the pitch. See Law 7.1 (Area of pitch).

        (ii) For the purpose of this Law and Law 15.9(b)(ii) (Intervals for Drinks) only the batsmen at the wicket may deputise for their captain at any appropriate time.

(b) If at any time the umpires together agree that the condition of the ground, weather or light is not suitable for play, they shall inform the captains and, unless

        (i) in unsuitable ground or weather conditions both captains agree to continue, or to commence, or to restart play, or

        (ii) in unsuitable light the batting side wish to continue, or to commence, or to restart play, they shall suspend play, or not allow play to commence or to restart.

(c)   (i) After agreeing to play in unsuitable ground or weather conditions, either captain may appeal against the conditions to the umpires before the next call of Time. The umpires shall uphold the appeal only if, in their opinion, the factors taken into account when making their previous decision are the same or the conditions have further deteriorated.

        (ii) After deciding to play in unsuitable light, the captain of the batting side may appeal against the light to the umpires before the next call of Time. The umpires shall uphold the appeal only if, in their opinion, the factors taken into account when making their previous decision are the same or the condition of the light has further deteriorated.

(d) If at any time the umpires together agree that the conditions of ground, weather or light are so bad that there is obvious and foreseeable risk to the safety of any player or umpire, so that it would be unreasonable or dangerous for play to take place, then notwithstanding the provisions of (b)(i) and (b)(ii) above, they shall immediately suspend play, or not allow play to commence or to restart. The decision as to whether conditions are so bad as to warrant such action is one for the umpires alone to make. The fact that the grass and the ball are wet and slippery does not warrant the ground conditions being regarded as unreasonable or dangerous. If the umpires consider the ground is so wet or slippery as to deprive the bowler of a reasonable foothold, the fielders of the power of free movement, or the batsmen of the ability to play their strokes or to run between the wickets, then these conditions shall be regarded as so bad that it would be unreasonable for play to take place.

(e) When there is a suspension of play it is the responsibility of the umpires to monitor the conditions. They shall make inspections as often as appropriate, unaccompanied by any of the players or officials. Immediately the umpires together agree that conditions are suitable for play they shall call upon the players to resume the game.

(f) If play is in progress up to the start of an agreed interval then it will resume after the interval unless the umpires together agree that conditions are or have become unsuitable or dangerous. If they do so agree, then they shall implement the procedure in (b) or (d) above, as appropriate, whether or not there had been any decision by the captains to continue, or any appeal against the conditions by either captain, prior to the commencement of the interval.

10. Exceptional Circumstances

The umpires shall have the discretion to implement the procedures of 9 above for reasons other than ground, weather or light if they consider that exceptional circumstances warrant it.

11. Position of Umpires

The umpires shall stand where they can best see any act upon which their decision may be required.

Subject to this over-riding consideration the umpire at the bowler's end shall stand where he does not interfere with either the bowler's run up or the striker's view.

The umpire at the striker's end may elect to stand on the off side instead of the on side of the pitch, provided he informs the captain of the fielding side, the striker and the other umpire of his intention to do so.

12. Umpires Changing Ends

The umpires shall change ends after each side has had one completed innings. See Law 14.2 (Forfeiture of an Innings).

13. Consultation between Umpires

All disputes shall be determined by the umpires. The umpires shall consult with each other whenever necessary. See also Law 27.6 (Consultation by Umpires).

14. Signals

(a) The following code of signals shall be used by umpires.

(i) Signals made while the ball is in play

Dead Ball   – by crossing and re-crossing the wrists below the waist.

No-ball	– by extending one arm horizontally.
Out	– by raising the index finger above the head. If not out, the umpire shall call "not out".
Wide	– by extending both arms horizontally.

(ii) When the ball is dead, the signals above, with the exception of the signal for Out, shall be repeated to the scorers. The signals listed below shall be made to the scorers only when the ball is dead.

Boundary 4	– by waving an arm from side to side.
Boundary 6	– by raising both arms above the head.
Bye	– by raising an open hand above the head.
Commencement of last hour	– by pointing to a raised wrist with the other hand.
Five Penalty Runs to be Awarded to the batting side	– by repeated tapping of one shoulder with the opposite hand.
Five Penalty Runs to be Awarded to the fielding side	– by repeated tapping of one shoulder with the opposite hand.
Leg-bye	– by touching a raised knee with the hand.
New Ball	– by holding the ball above the head.
Revoke last signal	– by touching both shoulders, each with the opposite hand.
Short run	– by bending one arm upwards and touching the nearer shoulder with the tips of the fingers.

(b) The umpires shall wait until each signal to the scorers has been separately acknowledged by a scorer before allowing play to proceed.

14. Correctness of Scores

Consultation between umpires and scorers on doubtful points is essential. The umpires shall satisfy themselves as to the correctness of the number of runs scored, the wickets that have fallen and, where appropriate, the number of overs bowled. They shall agree these with the scorers at least at every interval, other than a drinks interval, and at the conclusion of the match. See Laws 4.2 (Correctness of Scores), 21.8 (Correctness of Result) and 21.10 (Result not to be Changed).

LAW 4.   THE SCORERS

1. Appointment of Scorers

Two scorers shall be appointed to record all runs scored, all wickets taken and, where appropriate, number of overs bowled.

2. Correctness of Scores

The scorers shall frequently check to ensure that their records agree. They shall agree with the umpires, at least at every interval, other than a drinks interval, and at the conclusion of the match, the runs scored, the wickets that have fallen and, where appropriate, the number of overs bowled. See Law 3.15 (Correctness of Scores).

3. Acknowledging Signals

The scorers shall accept all instructions and signals given to them by the umpires. They shall immediately acknowledge each separate signal.

LAW 5.   THE BALL

1. Weight and Size

The ball, when new, shall weigh not less than 5 ½ ounces/155.9g, nor more than 5 ¾ ounces/163g; and shall measure not less than 8 ¹³⁄₁₆ inches/22.4cm, nor more than 9 inches/22.9cm in circumference.

2. Approval and Control of Balls

(a) All balls to be used in the match, having been approved by the umpires and captains, shall be in the possession of the umpires before the toss and shall remain under their control throughout the match.

(b) The umpire shall take possession of the ball in use at the fall of each wicket, at the start of any interval and at any interruption of play.

3. New Ball

Unless an agreement to the contrary has been made before the match, either captain may demand a new ball at the start of each innings.

4. New Ball in Match of More than One Days' Duration

In a match of more than one day's duration, the captain of the fielding side may demand a new ball after the prescribed number of overs has been bowled with the old one. The Governing Body for cricket in the country concerned shall decide the number of overs applicable in that country, which shall not be less than 75 overs.

The umpires shall indicate to the batsmen and the scorers whenever a new ball is taken into play.

5. Ball Lost or Becoming Unfit for Play

If, during play, the ball cannot be found or recovered or the umpires agree that it has become unfit for play through normal use, the umpires shall replace it with a ball which has had wear comparable with that which the previous ball had received before the need for its replacement. When the ball is replaced the umpires shall inform the batsmen and the fielding captain.

6. Specifications

The specifications, as described in 1 above, shall apply to men's cricket only. The following specifications will apply to

(i) *Women's*

   Weight: from 4 $^{15}/_{16}$ ounces/140g to 5 $^{5}/_{16}$ ounces/151g.

   Circumference: from 8 $^{1}/_{4}$ inches/21.0cm to 8 $^{7}/_{8}$ inches/22.5cm.

(iii) *Junior*

   Weight: 4 $^{11}/_{16}$ ounces/133g to 5 $^{1}/_{16}$ ounces/144g.

   Circumference: 8 $^{1}/_{16}$ inches/20.5cm to 8 $^{11}/_{16}$ inches/22.0cm.

LAW 6.   THE BAT

1. Width and Length

The bat overall shall not be more than 38 inches/96.5cm in length. The blade of the bat shall be made solely of wood and shall not exceed 4 $\frac{1}{4}$ inches/10.8cm at the widest part.

2. Covering the Blade

The blade of the bat may be covered with material for protection, strengthening or repair. Such material shall not exceed $^{1}/_{16}$ inch/1.56mm in thickness, and shall not be likely to cause unacceptable damage to the ball.

2. Hand or Glove to Count as Part of Bat

In these Laws,

   (a) reference to the bat shall imply that the bat is held by the batsman.

   (b) contact between the ball and either

      (i) the striker's bat itself, or

      (ii) the striker's hand holding the bat, or

      (iii) any part of a glove worn on the striker's hand holding the bat

   shall be regarded as the ball striking or touching the bat, or being struck by the bat.

LAW 7.   THE PITCH

1. Area of Pitch

The pitch is a rectangular area of the ground 22 yards/20.12m in length and 10ft/3.05m in width. It is bounded at either end by the bowling creases and on either side by imaginary lines, one each side of the imaginary line joining the centres of the two middle stumps, each parallel to it and 5ft/1.52m from it. See Laws 8.1 (Width and pitching) and 9.2 (The bowling crease).

2. Fitness of the Pitch for Play

The umpires shall be the final judges of the fitness of the pitch for play. See Laws 3.8 (Fitness of Ground, Weather and Light) and 3.9 (Suspension of Play for Adverse Conditions of Ground, Weather or Light).

3. Selection and Preparation

Before the match, the Ground Authority shall be responsible for the selection and preparation of the pitch. During the match, the umpires shall control its use and maintenance.

3. Changing the Pitch

The pitch shall not be changed during the match unless the umpires decide that it is unreasonable or dangerous for play to continue on it and then only with the consent of both captains.

4. Non-turf Pitches

In the event of a non-turf pitch being used, the artificial surface shall conform to:

(a) Length: a minimum of 58 feet/17.68m.

(b) Width: a minimum of 6 feet/1.83m.

See Law 10.8 (Non-turf pitches).

LAW 8. THE WICKETS

1. Width and Pitching

Two sets of wickets shall be pitched opposite and parallel to each other at a distance of 22 yards/20.12m between the centres of the two middle stumps. Each set shall be 9 in/22.86cm wide and shall consist of three wooden stumps with two wooden bails on top.

2. Size of Stumps

The tops of the stumps shall be 28 inches/71.1cm above the playing surface and shall be dome shaped except for the bail grooves. The portion of a stump above the playing surface shall be cylindrical, apart from the domed top, with circular section of diameter not less than 1 ⅜ in/3.49cm nor more than 1 ½ in/3.81cm .

3. The Bails

(a) The bails, when in position on top of the stumps,

      (i) shall not project more than ½ in/1.27cm above them.

      (ii) shall fit between the stumps without forcing them out of the vertical.

(b) Each bail shall conform to the following specifications

Overall length:	4 ⁵⁄₁₆ inches/10.95cm
Length of barrel:	2 ⅛ inches/5.40cm
Longer spigot:	1 ⅜ inches/3.49cm
Shorter spigot:	1 ³⁄₁₆ inches/2.06cm

4. Junior Cricket

In junior cricket, the same definitions of the wickets shall apply subject to the following measurements being used.

Width:	8 inches/20.32cm
Pitched for under 13:	21 yards/19.20m
Pitched for under 11:	20 yards/18.29m
Height above playing surface:	27 inches/68.58cm
Stump diameter:	not less than 1 ¼ inches/3.18cm nor more than 1 ⅜ inches/3.49cm
Each bail:	
Overall length:	3 ¹³⁄₁₆ inches/9.68cm
Length of barrel:	1 ¹³⁄₁₆ inches/4.60cm
Longer spigot:	1 ¼ inches/3.18cm
Shorter spigot:	¾ inches/1.91cm

LAW 9. THE BOWLING, POPPING AND RETURN CREASES

1. The Creases

A bowling crease, a popping crease and two return creases shall be marked in white, as set out in 2, 3 and 4 below, at each end of the pitch.

2. The Bowling Crease

The bowling crease, which is the back edge of the crease marking, shall be the line through the centres of the three stumps at that end. It shall be 8ft 8 in/2.64m in length, with the stumps in the centre.

3. The Popping Crease

The popping crease, which is the back edge of the crease marking, shall be in front of and parallel to the bowling crease and shall be 4ft/1.22m from it. The popping crease shall be marked to a minimum of 6ft/1.83m on either side of the imaginary line joining the centres of the middle stumps and shall be considered to be unlimited in length.

4. The Return Creases

The return creases, which are the inside edges of the crease markings, shall be at right angles to the popping crease at a distance of 4ft 4 in/1.32m either side of the imaginary line joining the centres of the two middle stumps. Each return crease shall be marked from the popping crease to a minimum of 8ft/2.44m behind it and shall be considered to be unlimited in length.

LAW 10. PREPARATION AND MAINTENANCE OF THE PLAYING AREA

1. Rolling

The pitch shall not be rolled during the match except as permitted in (a) and (b) below.

(a) Frequency and Duration of Rolling

During the match the pitch may be rolled at the request of the captain of the bat ting side, for a period of not more than seven minutes, before the start of each innings, other than the first innings of the match, and before the start of each subsequent day's play. See (d) below.

(b) Rolling After a Delayed Start

In addition to the rolling permitted above, if, after the toss and before the first innings of the match, the start is delayed, the captain of the batting side may request to have the pitch rolled for not more than seven minutes. However, if the umpires together agree that the delay has had no significant effect on the state of the pitch, they shall refuse the request for the rolling of the pitch.

(c) Choice of Rollers

If there is more than one roller available the captain of the batting side shall have the choice.

(d) Timing of Permitted Rolling

The rolling permitted (maximum seven minutes) before play begins on any day shall be started not more than 30 minutes before the time scheduled or rescheduled for play to begin. The captain of the batting side may, however, delay the start of such rolling until not less than ten minutes before the time scheduled or rescheduled for play to begin, should he so desire.

(e) Insufficient Time to Complete Rolling

If a captain declares an innings closed, or forfeits an innings, or enforces the follow-on, and the other captain is prevented thereby from exercising his option of the rolling permitted (maximum 7 minutes), or if he is so prevented for any other reason, the extra time required to complete the rolling shall be taken out of the normal playing time.

2. Sweeping

(a) If rolling is to take place the pitch shall first be swept to avoid any possible damage by rolling in debris. This sweeping shall be done so that the 7 minutes allowed for rolling is not affected.

(b) The pitch shall be cleared of any debris at all intervals for meals, between innings and at the beginning of each day, not earlier than 30 minutes nor later than 10 minutes before the time scheduled or rescheduled for play to begin. See Law 15.1 (An Interval).

(c) Notwithstanding the provisions of (a) and (b) above, the umpires shall not allow sweeping to take place where they consider it may be detrimental to the surface of the pitch.

3. Mowing

(a) The Pitch

The pitch shall be mown on each day of the match on which play is expected to take place, if ground and weather conditions allow.

(b) The Outfield

In order to ensure that conditions are as similar as possible for both sides, the outfield shall be mown on each day of the match on which play is expected to take place, if ground and weather conditions allow.

If, for reasons other than ground and weather conditions, complete mowing of the outfield is not possible, the Ground Authority shall notify the captains and umpires of the procedure to be adopted for such mowing during the match.

(c) Responsibility for Mowing

All mowings which are carried out before the match shall be the responsibility of the Ground Authority.

All subsequent mowings shall be carried out under the supervision of the umpires.

(d) Timing of Mowing

(i) Mowing of the pitch on any day of the match shall be completed not later than 30 minutes before the time scheduled or rescheduled for play to begin on that day.

(ii) Mowing of the outfield on any day of the match shall be completed not later than 15 minutes before the time scheduled or rescheduled for play to begin on that day.

4. Watering

The pitch shall not be watered during the match.

5. Re-marking Creases

The creases shall be re-marked whenever either umpire considers it necessary.

6. Maintenance of Foot-holes

The umpires shall ensure that the holes made by the bowlers and batsmen are cleaned out and dried whenever necessary to facilitate play. In matches of more than one day's duration, the umpires shall allow, if necessary, the re-turfing of footholes made by the bowler in his delivery stride, or the use of quick-setting fillings for the same purpose.

7. Securing of Footholds and Maintenance of Pitch

During play, the umpires shall allow the players to secure their footholds by the use of sawdust provided that no damage to the pitch is caused and that Law 42 (Fair and Unfair Play) is not contravened.

8. Non-turf pitches

Wherever appropriate, the provisions set out in 1 to 7 above shall apply.

LAW 11. COVERING THE PITCH

1. Before the Match

The use of covers before the match is the responsibility of the Ground Authority and may include full covering if required. However, the Ground Authority shall grant suitable facility to the captains to inspect the pitch before the nomination of their players and to the umpires to discharge their duties as laid down in Laws 3 (The Umpires), 7

(The Pitch), 8 (The Wickets), 9 (The Bowling, Popping and Return Creases) and 10 (Preparation and Maintenance of the Playing Area).

2. During the Match

The pitch shall not be completely covered during the match unless provided otherwise by regulations or by agreement before the toss.

3. Covering Bowlers' Run-ups

Whenever possible, the bowlers' run ups shall be covered in inclement weather, in order to keep them dry. Unless there is agreement for full covering under 2 above the covers so used shall not extend further than 5ft/1.52m in front of each popping crease.

4. Removal of Covers

(a) If after the toss the pitch is covered overnight, the covers shall be removed in the morning at the earliest possible moment on each day that play is expected to take place.

(b) If covers are used during the day as protection from inclement weather, or if inclement weather delays the removal of overnight covers, they shall be removed promptly as soon as conditions allow.

LAW 12.   INNINGS

1. Number of Innings

(a) A match shall be one or two innings of each side according to agreement reached before the match.

(b) It may be agreed to limit any innings to a number of overs or by a period of time. If such an agreement is made then

> (i) in a one innings match it shall apply to both innings.

> (ii) in a two innings match it shall apply to
> either   the first innings of each side
> or   the second innings of each side
> or   both innings of each side.

2. Alternate Innings

In a two-innings match each side shall take their innings alternately except in the case provided for in Law 13 (The Follow-on) or Law 14.2 (Forfeiture of an Innings).

3. Completed Innings

A side's innings is to be considered as completed if

(a) the side is all out, or

(b) at the fall of a wicket, further balls remain to be bowled, but no further batsman is available to come in, or

(c) the captain declares the innings closed, or

(d) the captain forfeits the innings, or

(e) in a two innings match it shall apply to
> either   (i) the prescribed number of overs has been bowled
> or   (ii) the prescribed time has expired.

4. The Toss

The captains shall toss for the choice of innings on the field of play not earlier than 30 minutes, nor later than 15 minutes, before the scheduled or any rescheduled time for the match to start. Note, however, the provisions of Law 1.3 (Captain).

5. Decision to be Notified

The captain of the side winning the toss shall notify the opposing captain of his decision to bat or to field, not later than 10 minutes before the scheduled or any rescheduled time for the match to start. Once notified the decision may not be altered.

LAW 13.   THE FOLLOW-ON

1. Lead on First Innings

(a) In a two innings match of 5 days or more, the side which bats first and leads by at least 200 runs shall have the option of requiring the other side to follow their innings.

(b) The same option shall be available in two innings matches of shorter duration with the minimum required leads as follows:

(i) 150 runs in a match of 3 or 4 days;

(ii) 100 runs in a 2-day match;

(iii) 75 runs in a 1-day match.

2. Notification

A captain shall notify the opposing captain and the umpires of his intention to take up this option. Law 10.1(e) (Insufficient time to complete rolling) shall apply.

3. First Day's Play Lost

If no play takes place on the first day of a match of more than one day's duration, 1 above shall apply in accordance with the number of days remaining from the actual start of the match. The day on which play first commences shall count as a whole day for this purpose, irrespective of the time at which play starts.

Play will have taken place as soon as, after the call of Play, the first over has started. See Law 22.2 (Start of an over).

LAW 14.   DECLARATION AND FORFEITURE

1. Time of Declaration

The captain of the batting side may declare an innings closed, when the ball is dead, at any time during a match.

2. Forfeiture of an Innings

A captain may forfeit either of his side's innings. A forfeited innings shall be considered as a completed innings.

3. Notification

A captain shall notify the opposing captain and the umpires of his decision to declare or to forfeit an innings. Law 10.1(e) (Insufficient Time to Complete Rolling) shall apply.

LAW 15.   INTERVALS

1. An Interval

The following shall be classed as intervals.

> (i) The period between close of play on one day and the start of the next day's play.

> (ii) Intervals between innings.

> (iii) Intervals for meals.

> (iv) Intervals for drinks.

> (v) Any other agreed interval.

All these intervals shall be considered as scheduled breaks for the purposes of Law 2.5 (Fielder Absent or Leaving the Field).

2. Agreement of Intervals

> (a) Before the Toss:

>> (i) the hours of play shall be established

>> (ii) except as in (b) below, the timing and duration of intervals for meals shall be agreed.

>> (iii) the timing and duration of any other interval under 1(v) above shall be agreed.

> (b) In a one-day match no specific time need be agreed for the tea interval. It may be agreed instead to take this interval between the innings.

> (c) Intervals for drinks may not be taken during the last hour of the match, as defined in Law 16.6 (Last hour of match – number of overs). Subject to this limitation the captains and umpires shall agree the times for such intervals, if any, before the toss and on each subsequent day not later than 10 minutes before play is scheduled to start. See also Law 3.3 (Agreement with Captains).

3. Duration of Intervals

> (a) An interval for lunch or for tea shall be of the duration agreed under 2(a) above, taken from the call of Time before the interval until the call of Play on resumption after the interval.

> (b) An interval between innings shall be 10 minutes from the close of an innings to the call of Play for the start of the next innings, except as in 4, 6 and 7 below.

4. No Allowance for Interval Between Innings

In addition to the provisions of 6 and 7 below,

> (a) if an innings ends when ten minutes or less remain before the time agreed for close of play on any day, there will be no further play on that day. No change will

be made to the time for the start of play on the following day on account of the ten minutes between innings.

(b) if a captain declares an innings closed during an interruption in play of more than ten minutes duration, no adjustment shall be made to the time for resumption of play on account of the ten minutes between innings, which shall be considered as included in the interruption. Law 10.1(e) (Insufficient Time to Complete Rolling) shall apply.

(c) if a captain declares an innings closed during any interval other than an interval for drinks, the interval shall be of the agreed duration and shall be considered to include the ten minutes between innings. Law 10.1(e) (Insufficient Time to Complete Rolling) shall apply.

5. Changing Agreed Time for Intervals

If for adverse conditions of ground, weather or light, or for any other reason, playing time is lost, the umpires and captains together may alter the time of the lunch interval or of the tea interval. See also 6, 7 and 9(c) below.

6. Changing Agreed Time for Lunch Interval

(a) If an innings ends when ten minutes or less remain before the agreed time for lunch, the interval shall be taken immediately. It shall be of the agreed length and shall be considered to include the ten minutes between innings.

(b) If, because of adverse conditions of ground, weather or light, or in exceptional circumstances, a stoppage occurs when ten minutes or less remain before the agreed time for lunch then, notwithstanding 5 above, the interval shall be taken immediately. It shall be of the agreed length. Play shall resume at the end of this interval or as soon after as conditions permit.

(c) If the players have occasion to leave the field for any reason when more than ten minutes remain before the agreed time for lunch then, unless the umpires and captains together agree to alter it, lunch will be taken at the agreed time.

7.   Changing Agreed Time for Tea Interval

(a)   (i) If an innings ends when 30 minutes or less remain before the agreed time for tea, then the interval shall be taken immediately. It shall be of the agreed length and shall be considered to include the ten minutes between innings.

(ii) If, when 30 minutes remain before the agreed time for tea, an interval between innings is already in progress, play will resume at the end of the ten minute interval.

(b)   (i) If, because of adverse conditions of ground, weather or light, or in exceptional circumstances, a stoppage occurs when 30 minutes or less remain before the agreed time for tea, then unless either there is an agreement to change the time for tea, as permitted in 5 above or the captains agree to forgo the tea interval, as permitted in 10 below the interval shall be taken immediately. The interval shall be of the agreed length. Play shall resume at the end of this interval or as soon after as conditions permit.

(ii) If a stoppage is already in progress when 30 minutes remain before the time agreed for tea, 5 above will apply.

8. Tea Interval – Nine Wickets Down

If nine wickets are down at the end of the over in progress when the agreed time for the tea interval has been reached, then play shall continue for a period not exceeding 30 minutes, unless the players have cause to leave the field of play, or the innings is concluded earlier.

9. Intervals for Drinks

(a) If on any day the captains agree that there shall be intervals for drinks, the option to take such intervals shall be available to either side. Each interval shall be kept as short as possible and in any case shall not exceed five minutes.

(b)   (i) Unless both captains agree to forgo any drinks interval, it shall be taken at the end of the over in progress when the agreed time is reached. If, however, a wicket falls within five minutes of the agreed time then drinks shall be taken immediately. No other variation in the timing of drinks intervals shall be permitted except as provided for in (c) below.

    (ii) For the purpose of (i) above and Law 3.9(a)(ii) (Suspension of Play for Adverse Conditions of Ground, Weather or Light) only, the batsmen at the wicket may deputise for their captain.

(c) If an innings ends or the players have to leave the field of play for any other reason within 30 minutes of the agreed time for a drinks interval, the umpires and captains together may rearrange the timing of drinks intervals in that session.

10. Agreement to Forgo Intervals

At any time during the match, the captains may agree to forgo the tea interval or any of the drinks intervals. The umpires shall be informed of the decision.

11. Scorers to be Informed

The umpires shall ensure that the scorers are informed of all agreements about hours of play and intervals, and of any changes made thereto as permitted under this Law.

LAW 16.   START OF PLAY; CESSATION OF PLAY

1. Call of Play

The umpire at the bowler's end shall call "Play" at the start of the match and on the resumption of play after any interval or interruption.

2. Call of Time

The umpire at the bowler's end shall call Time on the cessation of play before any interval or interruption of play and at the conclusion of the match. See Law 27 (Appeals).

3. Removal of Bails

After the call of Time, the bails shall be removed from both wickets.

4. Starting a New Over

Another over shall always be started at any time during the match, unless an interval is to be taken in the circumstances set out in 5 below, if the umpire, after walking at his normal pace, has arrived at his position behind the stumps at the bowler's end before the time agreed for the next interval, or for the close of play, has been reached.

5. Completion of an Over

Other than at the end of the match,

(a) if the agreed time for an interval is reached during an over, the over shall be completed before the interval is taken except as provided for in (b) below.

(b) when less than 2 minutes remain before the time agreed for the next interval, the interval will be taken immediately if either

(i) a batsman is out or retires, or

(ii) the players have occasion to leave the field

whether this occurs during an over or at the end of an over. Except at the end of an innings, if an over is thus interrupted it shall be completed on resumption of play.

6. Last Hour of Match – Number of Overs

When one hour of playing time of the match remains, according to the agreed hours of play, the over in progress shall be completed. The next over shall be the first of a minimum of 20 overs which must be bowled, provided that a result is not reached earlier and provided that there is no interval or interruption in play. The umpire at the bowler's end shall indicate the commencement of this 20 overs to the players and the scorers. The period of play thereafter shall be referred to as the last hour, whatever its actual duration.

7. Last Hour of Match – Interruptions of Play

If there is an interruption in play during the last hour of the match, the minimum number of overs to be bowled shall be reduced from 20 as follows.

(a) The time lost for an interruption is counted from the call of Time until the time for resumption of play as decided by the umpires.

(b) One over shall be deducted for every complete three minutes of time lost.

(c) In the case of more than one such interruption, the minutes lost shall not be aggregated; the calculation shall be made for each interruption separately.

(d) If, when one hour of playing time remains, an interruption is already in progress,

(i) only the time lost after this moment shall be counted in the calculation

(ii) the over in progress at the start of the interruption shall be completed on resumption of play and shall not count as one of the minimum number of overs to be bowled.

(e) If, after the start of the last hour, an interruption occurs during an over, the over shall be completed on resumption of play. The two part-overs shall between them count as one over of the minimum number to be bowled.

8. Last Hour of Match – Intervals Between Innings

If an innings ends so that a new innings is to be started during the last hour of the match, the interval starts with the end of the innings and is to end ten minutes later.

(a) If this interval is already in progress at the start of the last hour, then to determine the number of overs to be bowled in the new innings, calculations are to be made as set out in 7 above.

(b) If the innings ends after the last hour has started, two calculations are to be made, as set out in (c) and (d) below. The greater of the numbers yielded by these two calculations is to be the minimum number of overs to be bowled in the new innings.

(c) Calculation based on overs remaining.

(i) At the conclusion of the innings, the number of overs that remain to be bowled, of the minimum in the last hour, to be noted.

(ii) If this is not a whole number it is to be rounded up to the next whole number.

(iii) Three overs to be deducted from the result for the interval.

(d) Calculation based on time remaining.

(i) At the conclusion of the innings, the time remaining until the agreed time for close of play to be noted.

(ii) Ten minutes to be deducted from this time, for the interval, to determine the playing time remaining.

(iii) A calculation to be made of one over for every complete three minutes of the playing time remaining, plus one more over for any further part of three minutes remaining.

9. Conclusion of a Match

The match is concluded

(a) as soon as a result, as defined in sections 1,2,3 or 4 of Law 21 (The Result), is reached.

(b) as soon as both

(i) the minimum number of overs for the last hour are completed and

(ii) the agreed time for close of play is reached unless a result has been reached earlier.

(c) if, without the match being concluded either as in (a) or in (b) above, the players leave the field, either for adverse conditions of ground, weather or light, or in exceptional circumstances, and no further play is possible thereafter.

10. Completion of Last Over of Match

The over in progress at the close of play on the final day shall be completed unless either

(i) a result has been reached, or

(ii) the players have occasion to leave the field. In this case there shall be no resumption of play, except in the circumstances of Law 21.9 (Mistakes in Scoring), and the match shall be at an end.

11. Bowler Unable to Complete an Over During Last Hour of Match

If, for any reason, a bowler is unable to complete an over during the last hour, Law 22.8 (Bowler Incapacitated or Suspended During an Over) shall apply.

LAW 17.   PRACTICE ON THE FIELD

1. Practice on the Field

(a) There shall be no bowling or batting practice on the pitch, or on the area parallel and immediately adjacent to the pitch, at any time on any day of the match.

(b) There shall be no bowling or batting practice on any other part of the square on any day of the match, except before the start of play or after the close of play on that day. Practice before the start of play

> (i) must not continue later than 30 minutes before the scheduled time or any rescheduled time for play to start on that day.

> (ii) shall not be allowed if the umpires consider that, in the prevailing conditions of ground and weather, it will be detrimental to the surface of the square.

(c) There shall be no practice on the field of play between the call of Play and the call of Time, if the umpire considers that it could result in a waste of time. See Law 42.9 (Time Wasting by the Fielding Side).

(d) If a player contravenes (a) or (b) above he shall not be allowed to bowl until at least five complete overs have been bowled by his side after the contravention. If an over is in progress at the contravention he shall not be allowed to complete that over nor shall the remaining part-over count towards the five overs above.

2. Trial Run-Up

No bowler shall have a trial run up between the call of Play and the call of Time unless the umpire is satisfied that it will not cause any waste of time.

LAW 18.   SCORING RUNS

1. A Run

The score shall be reckoned by runs. A run is scored

> (a) so often as the batsmen, at any time while the ball is in play, have crossed and made good their ground from end to end.

> (b) when a boundary is scored. See Law 19 (Boundaries).

> (c) when penalty runs are awarded. See 6 below.

> (d) when Lost ball is called. See Law 20 (Lost Ball).

2. Runs Disallowed

Notwithstanding 1 above, or any other provisions elsewhere in the Laws, the scoring of runs or awarding of penalties will be subject to any disallowance of runs provided for within the Laws that may be applicable.

3. Short Runs

(a) A run is short if a batsman fails to make good his ground on turning for a further run.

(b) Although a short run shortens the succeeding one, the latter if completed shall not be regarded as short. A striker taking stance in front of his popping crease may run from that point also without penalty.

4. Unintentional Short Runs

Except in the circumstances of 5 below,

(a) if either batsman runs a short run, unless a boundary is scored the umpire concerned shall call and signal Short run as soon as the ball becomes dead and that run shall not be scored.

(b) if, after either or both batsmen run short, a boundary is scored, the umpire concerned shall disregard the short running and shall not call or signal Short run.

(c) if both batsmen run short in one and the same run, this shall be regarded as only one short run.

(d) if more than one run is short then, subject to (b) and (c) above, all runs so called shall not be scored.

If there has been more than one short run the umpire shall inform the scorers as to the number of runs scored.

5. Deliberate Short Runs

(a) Notwithstanding 4 above, if either umpire considers that either or both batsmen deliberately run short at his end, the following procedure shall be adopted.

> (i) The umpire concerned shall, when the ball is dead, warn the batsman or batsmen that the practice is unfair, indicate that this is a first and final warning and inform the other umpire of what has occurred.

> (ii) The batsmen shall return to their original ends.

> (iii) Whether a batsman is dismissed or not, the umpire at the bowler's end shall disallow all runs to the batting side from that delivery other than the penalty for a No ball or Wide, or penalties under Laws 42.5 (Deliberate Distraction or Obstruction of Batsman) and 42.13 (Fielders Damaging the Pitch), if applicable.

> (iv) The umpire at the bowler's end shall inform the scorers as to the number of runs scored.

(b) If there is any further instance of deliberate short running by either of the same batsmen in that innings, when the ball is dead the umpire concerned shall inform the other umpire of what has occurred and the procedure set out in (a)(ii) and (iii) above shall be repeated. Additionally, the umpire at the bowler's end shall

> (i) award 5 penalty runs to the fielding side. See Law 42.17 (Penalty Runs).

> (ii) inform the scorers as to the number of runs scored.

> (iii) inform the batsmen, the captain of the fielding side and, as soon as practicable, the captain of the batting side of the reason for this action.

(iv) report the occurrence, with the other umpire, to the Executive of the batting side and any Governing Body responsible for the match, who shall take such action as is considered appropriate against the captain and player or players concerned.

6. Runs Scored for Penalties

Runs shall be scored for penalties under 5 above and Laws 2.6 (Player Returning Without Permission), 24 (No Ball), 25 (Wide Ball), 41.2 (Fielding the Ball), 41.3 (Protective Helmets Belonging to the Fielding Side) and 42 (Fair and Unfair Play).

7. Runs Scored for Boundaries

Runs shall be scored for boundary allowances under Law 19 (Boundaries).

8. Runs Scored for Lost Ball

Runs shall be scored when Lost ball is called under Law 20 (Lost ball).

9. Batsman Dismissed

When either batsman is dismissed

(a) any penalties to either side that may be applicable shall stand but no other runs shall be scored, except as stated in 10 below. Note, however, Law 42.17(b) (Penalty Runs).

(b) 12(a) below will apply if the method of dismissal is Caught, Handled the ball or Obstructing the field. 12(a) will also apply if a batsman is Run out, except in the circumstances of Law 2.8 (Transgression of the Laws by a batsman who has a runner) where 12(b) below will apply.

(c) the not out batsman shall return to his original end except as stated in (b) above.

10. Runs Scored When a Batsman is Dismissed

In addition to any penalties to either side that may be applicable, if a batsman is

(a) dismissed Handled the ball, the batting side shall score the runs completed before the offence.

(b) dismissed Obstructing the field, the batting side shall score the runs completed before the offence.

If, however, the obstruction prevents a catch from being made, no runs other than penalties shall be scored.

(c) dismissed Run out, the batting side shall score the runs completed before the dismissal.

If, however, a striker with a runner is himself dismissed Run out, no runs other than penalties shall be scored. See Law 2.8 (Transgression of the Laws by a Batsman Who Has a Runner).

11. Runs Scored When a Ball Becomes Dead

(a) When the ball becomes dead on the fall of a wicket, runs shall be scored as laid down in 9 and 10 above.

(b) When the ball becomes dead for any reason other than the fall of a wicket, or is called dead by an umpire, unless there is specific provision otherwise in the Laws, the batting side shall be credited with

> (i) all runs completed by the batsmen before the incident or call, and

> (ii) (ii) the run in progress if the batsmen have crossed at the instant of th incident or call. Note specifically, however, the provisions of Laws 34.4(c) (Runs Permitted From Ball Lawfully Struck More Than Once) and 42.5(b)(iii) (Deliberate Distraction or Obstruction of Batsman), and

> (iii) any penalties that are applicable.

12. Batsman Returning to Wicket he has Left

(a) If, while the ball is in play, the batsmen have crossed in running, neither shall return to the wicket he has left, except as in (b) below.

(b) The batsmen shall return to the wickets they originally left in the cases of, and only in the cases of

(i) a boundary;

(ii) disallowance of runs for any reason;

(iii) the dismissal of a batsman, except as in 9(b) above.

LAW 19. BOUNDARIES

1. The Boundary of the Field of Play

(a) Before the toss, the umpires shall agree the boundary of the field of play with both captains. The boundary shall if possible be marked along its whole length.

(b) The boundary shall be agreed so that no part of any sight-screen is within the field of play.

(c) An obstacle or person within the field of play shall not be regarded as a boundary unless so decided by the umpires before the toss. See Law 3.4(ii) (To Inform Captains and Scorers).

2. Defining the Boundary – Boundary Marking

(a) Wherever practicable the boundary shall be marked by means of a white line or a rope laid along the ground.

(b) If the boundary is marked by a white line,

> (i) the inside edge of the line shall be the boundary edge.

> (ii) a flag, post or board used merely to highlight the position of a line marked on the ground must be placed outside the boundary edge and is not itself to be regarded as defining or marking the boundary. Note, however, the provisions of (c) below.

(c) If a solid object is used to mark the boundary, it must have an edge or a line to constitute the boundary edge.

> (i) For a rope, which includes any similar object of curved cross section lying on the ground, the boundary edge will be the line formed by the innermost points of the rope along its length.

(ii) For a fence, which includes any similar object in contact with the ground, but with a flat surface projecting above the ground, the boundary edge will be the base line of the fence.

(d) If the boundary edge is not defined as in (b) or (c) above, the umpires and captains must agree, before the toss, what line will be the boundary edge. Where there is no physical marker for a section of boundary, the boundary edge shall be the imaginary straight line joining the two nearest marked points of the boundary edge.

(e) If a solid object used to mark the boundary is disturbed for any reason during play, then if possible it shall be restored to its original position as soon as the ball is dead. If this is not possible, then

(i) if some part of the fence or other marker has come within the field of play, that portion is to be removed from the field of play as soon as the ball is dead.

(ii) the line where the base of the fence or marker originally stood shall define the boundary edge.

3. Scoring a Boundary

(a) A boundary shall be scored and signalled by the umpire at the bowler's end whenever, while the ball is in play, in his opinion

(i) the ball touches the boundary, or is grounded beyond the boundary.

(ii) a fielder, with some part of his person in contact with the ball, touches the boundary or has some part of his person grounded beyond the boundary.

(b) The phrases "touches the boundary" and "touching the boundary" shall mean contact with either

(i) the boundary edge as defined in 2 above

(ii) any person or obstacle within the field of play which has been designated a boundary by the umpires before the toss.

(c) The phrase "grounded beyond the boundary" shall mean contact with either

(i) any part of a line or a solid object marking the boundary, except its boundary edge, or

(ii) the ground outside the boundary edge, or

(iii) any object in contact with the ground outside the boundary edge.

4. Runs Allowed for Boundaries

(a) Before the toss, the umpires shall agree with both captains the runs to be allowed for boundaries. In deciding the allowances, the umpires and captains shall be guided by the prevailing custom of the ground.

(b) Unless agreed differently under (a) above, the allowances for boundaries shall be six runs if the ball having been struck by the bat pitches beyond the boundary, but otherwise four runs. These allowances shall still apply even though the ball has previously touched a fielder. See also (c) below.

(c) The ball shall be regarded as pitching beyond the boundary and six runs shall be scored if a fielder

(i) has any part of his person touching the boundary or grounded beyond the boundary when he catches the ball.

(ii) catches the ball and subsequently touches the boundary or grounds some part of his person beyond the boundary while carrying the ball but before completing the catch. See Law 32 (Caught).

5. Runs Scored

When a boundary is scored,

(a) the penalty for a No Ball or a Wide, if applicable, shall stand together with any penalties under any of Laws 2.6 (Player Returning Without Permission), 18.5(b) (Deliberate Short Runs) or 42 (Fair and Unfair Play) that apply before the boundary is scored.

(b) the batting side, except in the circumstances of 6 below, shall additionally be awarded whichever is the greater of

(i) the allowance for the boundary.

(ii) the runs completed by the batsmen, together with the run in progress if they have crossed at the instant the boundary is scored.

When these runs exceed the boundary allowance, they shall replace the boundary for the purposes of Law 18.12 (Batsman Returning to Wicket He Has Left).

6. Overthrow or Wilful Act of Fielder

If the boundary results either from an overthrow or from the wilful act of a fielder the runs scored shall be

(i) the penalty for a No ball or a Wide, if applicable, and penalties under any of Laws 2.6 (Player Returning Without Permission), 18.5(b) (Deliberate Short Runs) or 42 (Fair and Unfair Play) that are applicable before the boundary is scored, and

(ii) the allowance for the boundary, and

(iii) the runs completed by the batsmen, together with the run in progress if they have crossed at the instant of the throw or act.

Law 18.12(a) (Batsman Returning to Wicket He Has Left) shall apply as from the instant of the throw or act.

LAW 20. LOST BALL

1. Fielder to Call Lost Ball

If a ball in play cannot be found or recovered, any fielder may call Lost Ball. The ball shall then become dead. See Law 23.1 (Ball is Dead). Law 18.12(a) (Batsman Returning to Wicket He Has Left) shall apply as from the instant of the call.

2. Ball to be Replaced

The umpires shall replace the ball with one which has had wear comparable with that which the previous ball had received before it was lost or became irrecoverable. See Law 5.5 (Ball Lost or Becoming Unfit for Play).

3. Runs Scored

(a) The penalty for a No Ball or a Wide, if applicable, shall stand, together with any penalties under any of Laws 2.6 (Player Returning Without Permission), 18.5(b) (Deliberate Short Runs) or 42 (Fair and Unfair Play) that are applicable before the call of Lost Ball.

(b) The batting side shall additionally be awarded, either

> (i) the runs completed by the batsmen, together with the run in progress if they have crossed at the instant of the call, or

> (ii) six runs,

whichever is the greater.

4. How Scored

If there is a one-run penalty for a No Ball or for a Wide, it shall be scored as a No Ball extra or as a Wide as appropriate. See Laws 24.13 (Runs Resulting from a No Ball – How Scored) and 25.6 (Runs Resulting from a Wide – How Scored). If any other penalties have been awarded to either side, they shall be scored as penalty extras. See Law 42.17 (Penalty Runs).

Runs to the batting side in 3(b) above shall be credited to the striker if the ball has been struck by the bat, but otherwise to the total of Byes, Leg byes, No Balls or Wides as the case may be.

LAW 21. THE RESULT

1. A Win – Two Innings Match

The side which has scored a total of runs in excess of that scored in the two completed innings of the opposing side shall win the match. Note also 6 below. A forfeited innings is to count as a completed innings. See Law 14 (Declaration and Forfeiture).

2. A Win – One Innings Match

The side which has scored in its one innings a total of runs in excess of that scored by the opposing side in its one completed innings shall win the match. Note also 6 below.

3. Umpires Awarding a Match

(a) A match shall be lost by a side which either

> (i) concedes defeat, or

> (ii) in the opinion of the umpires refuses to play and the umpires shall award the match to the other side.

(b) If an umpire considers that an action by any player or players might constitute a refusal by either side to play then the umpires together shall ascertain the cause of the action. If they then decide together that this action does constitute a refusal to play by one side, they shall so inform the captain of that side. If the captain persists in the action the umpires shall award the match in accordance with (a)(ii) above.

(c) If action as in (b) above takes place after play has started and does not constitute a refusal to play

> (i) playing time lost shall be counted from the start of the action until play recommences, subject to Law 15.5 (Changing Agreed Times for Intervals).

> (ii) the time for close of play on that day shall be extended by this length of time, subject to Law 3.9 (Suspension of Play for Adverse Conditions of Ground, Weather or Light).

> (iii) if applicable, no overs shall be deducted during the last hour of the match solely on account of this time.

4. A Tie

The result of a match shall be a Tie when the scores are equal at the conclusion of play, but only if the side batting last has completed its innings.

5. A Draw

A match which is concluded, as defined in Law 16.9 (Conclusion of a Match), without being determined in any of the ways stated in 1, 2, 3 or 4 above, shall count as a Draw.

6. Winning Hit or Extras

(a) As soon as a result is reached, as defined in 1, 2, 3 or 4 above, the match is at an end. Nothing that happens thereafter shall be regarded as part of it. Note also 9 below.

(b) The side batting last will have scored enough runs to win only if its total of runs is sufficient without including any runs completed before the dismissal of the striker by the completion of a catch or by the obstruction of a catch.

(c) If a boundary is scored before the batsmen have completed sufficient runs to win the match, then the whole of the boundary allowance shall be credited to the side's total and, in the case of a hit by the bat, to the striker's score.

7. Statement of a Result

If the side batting last wins the match, the result shall be stated as a win by the number of wickets still then to fall. If the other side wins the match, the result shall be stated as a win by runs. If the match is decided by one side conceding defeat or refusing to play, the result be stated as Match Conceded or Match Awarded as the case may be.

8. Correctness of a Result

Any decision as to the correctness of the scores shall be the responsibility of the umpires. See Law 3.15 (Correctness of Scores).

9. Mistakes in Scoring

If, after the umpires and players have left the field in the belief that the match has been concluded, the umpires discover that a mistake in scoring has occurred which affects the result, then, subject to 10 below, they shall adopt the following procedure.

(a) If, when the players leave the field, the side batting last has not completed its innings, and either

(i) the number of overs to be bowled in the last hour has not been completed, or

(ii) the agreed finishing time has not been reached,

then unless one side concedes defeat the umpires shall order play to resume.

If conditions permit, play will then continue until the prescribed number of overs has been completed and the time remaining has elapsed, unless a result is reached earlier. The number of overs and/or time remaining shall be taken as they were when the players left the field; no account shall be taken of the time between that moment and the resumption of play.

(b) If, when the players leave the field, the overs have been completed and time has been reached, or if the side batting last has completed its innings, the umpires shall immediately inform both captains of the necessary corrections to the scores and to the result.

10. Result Not to Be Changed

Once the umpires have agreed with the scorers the correctness of the scores at the con-clusion of the match – see Laws 3.15 (Correctness of Scores) and 4.2 (Correctness of Scores) – the result cannot thereafter be changed.

LAW 22.   THE OVER

1. Number of Balls

The ball shall be bowled from each wicket alternately in overs of six balls.

2. Start of an Over

An over has started when the bowler starts his run up or, if he has no run up, his deliv-ery action for the first delivery of that over.

3. Call of Over

When six balls have been bowled other than those which are not to count in the over and as the ball becomes dead – see Law 23 (Dead Ball) – the umpire shall call "Over" before leaving the wicket.

4. Balls Not to Count in the Over

(a) A ball shall not count as one of the 6 balls of the over unless it is delivered, even though a batsman may be dismissed or some other incident occurs before the ball is delivered.

(b) A ball which is delivered by the bowler shall not count as one of the six balls of the over

(i) if it is called dead, or is to be considered dead, before the striker has had an opportunity to play it. See Law 23 (Dead Ball).

(ii) if it is a No Ball. See Law 24 (No Ball).

(iii) if it is a Wide. See Law 25 (Wide Ball).

(iv) if it is called dead in the circumstances of either of Laws 23.3 (vi) (Umpire Calling and Signalling Dead Ball) or 42.4 (Deliberate Attempt to Distract Striker).

5. Umpire Miscounting

If an umpire miscounts the number of balls, the over as counted by the umpire shall stand.

6. Bowler Changing Ends

A bowler shall be allowed to change ends as often as desired, provided only that he does not bowl two overs, or parts thereof, consecutively in the same innings.

7. Finishing an Over

(a) Other than at the end of an innings, a bowler shall finish an over in progress unless he is incapacitated, or he is suspended under any of Laws 17.1 (Practice on the field), 42.7 (Dangerous and Unfair Bowling – Action By the Umpire), 42.9 (Time Wasting By the Fielding Side), or 42.12 (Bowler Running on the Protected Area After Delivering the Ball).

(b) If for any reason, other than the end of an innings, an over is left uncompleted at the start of an interval or interruption of play, it shall be completed on resumption of play.

8. Bowler Incapacitated or Suspended During an Over

If for any reason a bowler is incapacitated while running up to bowl the first ball of an over, or is incapacitated or suspended during an over, the umpire shall call and signal Dead Ball. Another bowler shall complete the over from the same end, provided that he does not bowl two overs, or parts thereof, consecutively in one innings.

LAW 23.   DEAD BALL

1. Ball is Dead

(a) The ball becomes dead when

(i) it is finally settled in the hands of the wicket-keeper or the bowler.

(ii) a boundary is scored. See Law 19.3 (Scoring a Boundary).

(iii) a batsman is dismissed.

(iv) whether played or not it becomes trapped between the bat and person of a batsman or between items of his clothing or equipment.

(v) whether played or not it lodges in the clothing or equipment of a batsman or the clothing of an umpire.

(vi) it lodges in a protective helmet worn by a member of the fielding side.

(vii) there is a contravention of either of Laws 41.2 (Fielding the Ball) or 41.3 (Protective Helmets Belonging to the Fielding Side).

(viii) there is an award of penalty runs under Law 2.6 (Player Returning Without Permission).

(ix) Lost ball is called. See Law 20 (Lost Ball).

(x) the umpire calls Over or Time.

(b) The ball shall be considered to be dead when it is clear to the umpire at the bowler's end that the fielding side and both batsmen at the wicket have ceased to regard it as in play.

2. Ball Finally Settled

Whether the ball is finally settled or not is a matter for the umpire alone to decide.

3. Umpire Calling and Signalling Dead Ball

(a) When the ball has become dead under 1 above, the bowler's end umpire may call Dead Ball, if it is necessary to inform the players.

(b) Either umpire shall call and signal Dead ball when

(i) he intervenes in a case of unfair play.

(ii) a serious injury to a player or umpire occurs.

(iii) he leaves his normal position for consultation.

(iv) one or both bails fall from the striker's wicket before he has the opportunity of playing the ball.

(v) he is satisfied that for an adequate reason the striker is not ready for the delivery of the ball and, if the ball is delivered, makes no attempt to play it.

(vi) the striker is distracted by any noise or movement or in any other way while he is preparing to receive or receiving a delivery. This shall apply whether the source of the distraction is within the game or outside it. Note, however, the provisions of Law 42.4 (Deliberate Attempt to Distract the Striker). The ball shall not count as one of the over.

(vii) the bowler drops the ball accidentally before delivery.

(viii) the ball does not leave the bowler's hand for any reason other than an attempt to run out the non-striker before entering his delivery stride. See Law 42.15 (Bowler Attempting to Run out Non-striker Before Delivery).

(ix) he is required to do so under any of the Laws.

4. Ball Ceases to Be Dead

The ball ceases to be dead – that is, it comes into play – when the bowler starts his run up or, if he has no run up, his bowling action.

5. Action on Call of Dead Ball

(a) A ball is not to count as one of the over if it becomes dead or is to be considered dead before the striker has had an opportunity to play it.

(b) If the ball becomes dead or is to be considered dead after the striker has had an opportunity to play the ball, except in the circumstances of 3(vi) above and Law 42.4 (Deliberate Attempt to Distract Striker), no additional delivery shall be allowed unless No ball or Wide has been called.

LAW 24.   NO BALL

1. Mode of Delivery

(a) The umpire shall ascertain whether the bowler intends to bowl right handed or left handed, over or round the wicket, and shall so inform the striker. It is unfair if the bowler fails to notify the umpire of a change in his mode of delivery. In this case the umpire shall call and signal No ball.

(b) Underarm bowling shall not be permitted except by special agreement before the match.

2. Fair Delivery – The Arm

For a delivery to be fair in respect of the arm the ball must not be thrown. See 3 below. Although it is the primary responsibility of the striker's end umpire to ensure the fairness of a delivery in this respect, there is nothing in this Law to debar the bowler's end umpire from calling and signalling No Ball if he considers that the ball has been thrown.

(a) If, in the opinion of either umpire, the ball has been thrown, he shall

(i) call and signal No Ball.

(ii) caution the bowler, when the ball is dead. This caution shall apply throughout the innings.

(iii) inform the other umpire, the batsmen at the wicket, the captain of th fielding side and, as soon as practicable, the captain of the batting side of what has occurred.

(b) If either umpire considers that after such caution a further delivery by the same bowler in that innings is thrown, the umpire concerned shall repeat the procedure set out in (a) above, indicating to the bowler that this is a final warning. This warning shall also apply throughout the innings.

(c) If either umpire considers that a further delivery by the same bowler in that innings is thrown,

(i) the umpire concerned shall call and signal No Ball. When the ball is dead he shall inform the other umpire, the batsmen at the wicket and, as soon as practicable, the captain of the batting side of what has occurred.

(ii) the umpire at the bowler's end shall direct the captain of the fielding side to take the bowler off forthwith. The over shall be completed by another bowler, who shall neither have bowled the previous over nor be allowed to bowl the next over. The bowler thus taken off shall not bowl again in that innings.

(iii) the umpires together shall report the occurrence as soon as possible to the Executive of the fielding side and any Governing Body responsible for the match, who shall take such action as is considered appropriate against the captain and bowler concerned.

3. Definition of Fair Delivery – The Arm

A ball is fairly delivered in respect of the arm if, once the bowler's arm has reached the level of the shoulder in the delivery swing, the elbow joint is not straightened partially or completely from that point until the ball has left the hand. This definition shall not debar a bowler from flexing or rotating the wrist in the delivery swing.

4. Bowler Throwing Towards Striker's End Before Delivery

If the bowler throws the ball towards the striker's end before entering his delivery stride, either umpire shall call and signal No ball. See Law 42.16 (Batsmen Stealing a Run). However, the procedure stated in 2 above of caution, informing, final warning, action against the bowler and reporting shall not apply.

5. Fair Delivery – The Feet

For a delivery to be fair in respect of the feet, in the delivery stride

    (i) the bowler's back foot must land within and not touching the return crease.

    (ii) the bowler's front foot must land with some part of the foot, whether grounded or raised, behind the popping crease.

If the umpire at the bowler's end is not satisfied that both these conditions have been met, he shall call and signal No Ball.

6. Ball Bouncing More Than Twice or Rolling Along the Ground

The umpire at the bowler's end shall call and signal No ball if a ball which he considers to have been delivered, without having previously touched the bat or person of the striker, either

    (i) bounces more than twice, or

    (ii) rolls along the ground

before it reaches the popping crease.

7. Ball Coming to Rest in Front of Striker's Wicket

If a ball delivered by the bowler comes to rest in front of the line of the striker's wicket, without having touched the bat or person of the striker, the umpire shall call and signal No Ball and immediately call and signal Dead Ball.

8. Call of No Ball for Infringement of Other Laws

In addition to the instances above, an umpire shall call and signal No Ball as required by the following Laws.

Law 40.3 – Position of wicket-keeper

Law 41.5 – Limitation of on side fielders

Law 41.6 – Fielders not to encroach on the pitch

Law 42.6 – Dangerous and unfair bowling

Law 42.7 – Dangerous and unfair bowling – action by the umpire

Law 42.8 – Deliberate bowling of high full pitched balls.

9. Revoking a Call of No Ball

An umpire shall revoke the call of No ball if the ball does not leave the bowler's hand for any reason.

10. No Ball to Over-ride Wide

A call of No ball shall over-ride the call of Wide ball at any time. See Law 25.1 (Judging a Wide) and 25.3 (Call and Signal of Wide Ball).

11. Ball Not Dead

The ball does not become dead on the call of No Ball.

12. Penalty for a No Ball

A penalty of one run shall be awarded instantly on the call of No ball. Unless the call is revoked, this penalty shall stand even if a batsman is dismissed. It shall be in addition to any other runs scored, any boundary allowance and any other penalties awarded.

13. Runs Resulting from a No Ball – How Scored

The one run penalty for a No Ball shall be scored as a No Ball extra. If other penalty runs have been awarded to either side, these shall be scored as in Law 42.17 (Penalty Runs). Any runs completed by the batsmen or a boundary allowance shall be credited to the striker if the ball has been struck by the bat; otherwise they also shall be scored as No Ball extras. Apart from any award of a five-run penalty, all runs resulting from a No Ball, whether as No Ball extras or credited to the striker, shall be debited against the bowler.

14. No Ball Not to Count

A No Ball shall not count as one of the over. See Law 22.4 (Balls Not to Count in the Over).

15. Out from a No Ball

When No ball has been called, neither batsman shall be out under any of the Laws except 33 (Handled the Ball), 34 (Hit the Ball Twice), 37 (Obstructing the Field) or 38 (Run Out).

LAW 25.   WIDE BALL

1. Judging a Wide

(a) If the bowler bowls a ball, not being a No ball, the umpire shall adjudge it a Wide if according to the definition in (b) below, in his opinion, the ball passes wide of the striker where he is standing and would also have passed wide of him standing in a normal guard position.

(b) The ball will be considered as passing wide of the striker unless it is sufficiently within his reach for him to be able to hit it with his bat by means of a normal cricket stroke.

2. Delivery Not a Wide

The umpire shall not adjudge a delivery as being a Wide

(a) if the striker, by moving, either

(i) causes the ball to pass wide of him, as defined in 1(b) above, or

(ii) brings the ball sufficiently within his reach to be able to hit it with his bat by means of a normal cricket stroke.

(b) if the ball touches the striker's bat or person.

3. Call and Signal of Wide Ball

(a) If the umpire adjudges a delivery to be a Wide he shall call and signal Wide Ball as soon as the ball passes the striker's wicket. It shall, however, be considered to have been a Wide from the instant of delivery, even though it cannot be called Wide until it passes the striker's wicket.

(b) The umpire shall revoke the call of Wide ball if there is then any contact between the ball and the striker's bat or person.

(c) The umpire shall revoke the call of Wide ball if a delivery is called a No Ball. See Law 24.10 (No Ball to Over-ride Wide).

4. Ball Not Dead

The ball does not become dead on the call of Wide Ball.

5. Penalty For a Wide

A penalty of one run shall be awarded instantly on the call of Wide ball. Unless the call is revoked (see 3 above), this penalty shall stand even if a batsman is dismissed, and shall be in addition to any other runs scored, any boundary allowance and any other penalties awarded.

6. Runs Resulting From a Wide – How Scored

All runs completed by the batsmen or a boundary allowance, together with the penalty for the Wide, shall be scored as Wide Balls. Apart from any award of a five-run penalty, all runs resulting from a Wide Ball shall be debited against the bowler.

7. Wide Not to Count

A Wide shall not count as one of the over. See Law 22.4 (Balls Not to Count in the Over).

8. Out From a Wide

When Wide Ball has been called, neither batsman shall be out under any of the Laws except 33 (Handled the Ball), 35 (Hit Wicket), 37 (Obstructing the Field), 38 (Run Out) or 39 (Stumped).

LAW 26.   BYE AND LEG BYE

1. Byes

If the ball, not being a No Ball or a Wide, passes the striker without touching his bat or person, any runs completed by the batsmen or a boundary allowance shall be credited as Byes to the batting side.

2. Leg Byes

(a) If the ball, not having previously touched the striker's bat, strikes his person and the umpire is satisfied that the striker has either

       (i) attempted to play the ball with his bat, or

       (ii) tried to avoid being hit by the ball,

then any runs completed by the batsmen or a boundary allowance shall be credited to the batting side as Leg Byes, unless No Ball has been called.

(b) If No Ball has been called, the runs in (a) above, together with the penalty for the No Ball, shall be scored as No Ball extras.

3. Leg Byes Not to Be Awarded

If in the circumstances of 2(a) above, the umpire considers that neither of the conditions (i) and (ii) has been met, then Leg Byes will not be awarded. The batting side shall not be credited with any runs from that delivery apart from the one-run penalty for a No Ball if applicable. Moreover, no other penalties shall be awarded to the batting side when the ball is dead. See Law 42.17 (Penalty Runs).

The following procedure shall be adopted.

(a) If no run is attempted but the ball reaches the boundary, the umpire shall call and signal Dead Ball, and disallow the boundary.

(b) If runs are attempted and if

(i) neither batsman is dismissed and the ball does not become dead for any other reason, the umpire shall call and signal Dead Ball as soon as one run is completed or the ball reaches the boundary. The batsmen shall return to their original ends. The run or boundary shall be disallowed.

(ii) before one run is completed or the ball reaches the boundary, a batsman is dismissed, or the ball becomes dead for any other reason, all the provisions of the Laws will apply, except that no runs and no penalties shall be credited to the batting side, other than the penalty for a No Ball if applicable.

LAW 27.   APPEALS

1. Umpire Not to Give Batsman Out Without an Appeal

Neither umpire shall give a batsman out, even though he may be out under the Laws, unless appealed to by the fielding side. This shall not debar a batsman who is out under any of the Laws from leaving his wicket without an appeal having been made. Note, however, the provisions of 7 below.

2. Batsman Dismissed

A batsman is dismissed if either

(a) he is given out by an umpire, on appeal, or

(b) he is out under any of the Laws and leaves his wicket as in 1 above.

3. Timing of Appeals

For an appeal to be valid it must be made before the bowler begins his run up or, if he has no run up, his bowling action to deliver the next ball, and before Time has been called.

The call of Over does not invalidate an appeal made prior to the start of the following over provided Time has not been called. See Laws 16.2 (Call of Time) and 22.2 (Start of an Over).

4. Appeal of "How's That?"

An appeal "How's That?" covers all ways of being out.

5. Answering Appeals

The umpire at the bowler's end shall answer all appeals except those arising out of any of Laws 35 (Hit Wicket), 39 (Stumped) or 38 (Run Out) when this occurs at the striker's wicket. A decision Not Out by one umpire shall not prevent the other umpire from giving a decision, provided that each is considering only matters within his jurisdiction.

When a batsman has been given Not Out, either umpire may, within his jurisdiction, answer a further appeal provided that it is made in accordance with 3 above.

6. Consultation By Umpires

Each umpire shall answer appeals on matters within his own jurisdiction. If an umpire is doubtful about any point that the other umpire may have been in a better position to see, he shall consult the latter on this point of fact and shall then give his decision. If, after consultation, there is still doubt remaining the decision shall be Not Out.

7. Batsman Leaving his Wicket Under a Misapprehension

An umpire shall intervene if satisfied that a batsman, not having been given out, has left his wicket under a misapprehension that he is out. The umpire intervening shall call and signal Dead Ball to prevent any further action by the fielding side and shall recall the batsman.

8. Withdrawal of an Appeal

The captain of the fielding side may withdraw an appeal only with the consent of the umpire within whose jurisdiction the appeal falls and before the outgoing batsman has left the field of play. If such consent is given the umpire concerned shall, if applicable, revoke his decision and recall the batsman.

9. Umpire's Decision

An umpire may alter his decision provided that such alteration is made promptly. This apart, an umpire's decision, once made, is final.

LAW 28.   THE WICKET IS DOWN

1. Wicket Put Down

(a) The wicket is put down if a bail is completely removed from the top of the stumps, or a stump is struck out of the ground by

   (i) the ball.

   (ii) the striker's bat, whether he is holding it or has let go of it.

   (iii) the striker's person or by any part of his clothing or equipment becoming detached from his person.

   (iii) a fielder, with his hand or arm, providing that the ball is held in the hand or hands so used, or in the hand of the arm so used.

The wicket is also put down if a fielder pulls a stump out of the ground in the same manner.

(b) The disturbance of a bail, whether temporary or not, shall not constitute its complete removal from the top of the stumps, but if a bail in falling lodges between two of the stumps this shall be regarded as complete removal.

2. One Bail Off

If one bail is off, it shall be sufficient for the purpose of putting the wicket down to remove the remaining bail, or to strike or pull any of the three stumps out of the ground, in any of the ways stated in 1 above.

3. Remaking The Wicket

If the wicket is broken or put down while the ball is in play, the umpire shall not remake the wicket until the ball is dead. See Law 23 (Dead Ball). Any fielder, however, may

(i) replace a bail or bails on top of the stumps.

(ii) put back one or more stumps into the ground where the wicket originally stood.

4. Dispensing With Bails

If the umpires have agreed to dispense with bails, in accordance with Law 8.5 (Dispensing with Bails), the decision as to whether the wicket has been put down is one for the umpire concerned to decide.

(a) After a decision to play without bails, the wicket has been put down if the umpire concerned is satisfied that the wicket has been struck by the ball, by the striker's bat, person, or items of his clothing or equipment separated from his person as described in 1(a)(ii) or 1(a)(iii) above, or by a fielder with the hand holding the ball or with the arm of the hand holding the ball.

(b) If the wicket has already been broken or put down, (a) above shall apply to any stump or stumps still in the ground. Any fielder may replace a stump or stumps, in accordance with 3 above, in order to have an opportunity of putting the wicket down.

LAW 29.   BATSMAN OUT OF HIS GROUND

1. When Out of His Ground

A batsman shall be considered to be out of his ground unless his bat or some part of his person is grounded behind the popping crease at that end.

2. Which is a Batsman's Ground

(a) If only one batsman is within a ground

(i) it is his ground.

(ii) it remains his ground even if he is later joined there by the other batsman.

(b) If both batsmen are in the same ground and one of them subsequently leaves it, (a)(i) above applies.

(c) If there is no batsman in either ground, then each ground belongs to whichever of the batsmen is nearer to it, or, if the batsmen are level, to whichever was nearer to it immediately prior to their drawing level.

(d) If a ground belongs to one batsman, then, unless there is a striker with a runner, the other ground belongs to the other batsman irrespective of his position.

(e) When a batsman with a runner is striker, his ground is always that at the wicket-keeper's end. However, (a), (b), (c) and (d) above will still apply, but only to the runner and the non-striker, so that that ground will also belong to either the non-striker or the runner, as the case may be.

3. Position of Non-Striker

The batsman at the bowler's end should be positioned on the opposite side of the wicket to that from which the ball is being delivered, unless a request to do otherwise is granted by the umpire.

LAW 30. BOWLED

1. Out Bowled

(a) The striker is out Bowled if his wicket is put down by a ball delivered by the bowler, not being a No ball, even if it first touches his bat or person.

(b) Notwithstanding (a) above he shall not be out Bowled if before striking the wicket the ball has been in contact with any other player or with an umpire. He will, however, be subject to Laws 33 (Handled the ball), 37 (Obstructing the Field), 38 (Run Out) and 39 (Stumped).

2. Bowled to Take Precedence

The striker is out Bowled if his wicket is put down as in 1 above, even though a decision against him for any other method of dismissal would be justified.

LAW 31. TIMED OUT

1. Out Timed Out

(a) Unless Time has been called, the incoming batsman must be in position to take guard or for his partner to be ready to receive the next ball within three minutes of the fall of the previous wicket. If this requirement is not met, the incoming batsman will be out, Timed out.

(b) In the event of protracted delay in which no batsman comes to the wicket, the umpires shall adopt the procedure of Law 21.3 (Umpires awarding a match). For the purposes of that Law the start of the action shall be taken as the expiry of the three minutes referred to above.

2. Bowler Does Not Get Credit

The bowler does not get credit for the wicket.

LAW 32.   CAUGHT

1. Out Caught

The striker is out Caught if a ball delivered by the bowler, not being a No Ball, touches his bat without having previously been in contact with any member of the fielding side and is subsequently held by a fielder as a fair catch before it touches the ground.

2. Caught to Take Precedence

If the criteria of 1 above are met and the striker is not out Bowled, then he is out Caught, even though a decision against either batsman for another method of dismissal would be justified. Runs completed by the batsmen before the completion of the catch will not be scored. Note also Laws 21.6 (Winning Hit or Extras) and 42.17(b) (Penalty Runs).

3. A Fair Catch

A catch shall be considered to have been fairly made if

(a) throughout the act of making the catch

(i) any fielder in contact with the ball is within the field of play. See 4 below.

(ii) the ball is at no time in contact with any object grounded beyond the boundary.

The act of making the catch shall start from the time when a fielder first handles the ball and shall end when a fielder obtains complete control both over the ball and over his own movement.

(b) the ball is hugged to the body of the catcher or accidentally lodges in his clothing or, in the case of the wicket-keeper, in his pads. However, it is not a fair catch if the ball lodges in a protective helmet worn by a fielder. See Law 23 (Dead Ball).

(c) the ball does not touch the ground, even though the hand holding it does so in effecting the catch.

(d) a fielder catches the ball after it has been lawfully struck more than once by the striker, but only if the ball has not touched the ground since first being struck.

(e) a fielder catches the ball after it has touched an umpire, another fielder or the other batsman. However, it is not a fair catch if the ball has touched a protective helmet worn by a fielder, although the ball remains in play.

(f) a fielder catches the ball in the air after it has crossed the boundary provided that

(i) he has no part of his person touching, or grounded beyond, the boundary at any time when he is in contact with the ball.

(ii) the ball has not been grounded beyond the boundary. See Law 19.3 (Scoring a Boundary).

(g) the ball is caught off an obstruction within the boundary, provided it has not previously been decided to regard the obstruction as a boundary.

4. Fielder Within the Field of Play

(a) A fielder is not within the field of play if he touches the boundary or has any part of his person grounded beyond the boundary. See Law 19.3 (Scoring a Boundary).

(b) six runs shall be scored if a fielder

(i) has any part of his person touching, or grounded beyond, the boundary when he catches the ball.

(ii) catches the ball and subsequently touches the boundary or grounds some part of his person over the boundary while carrying the ball but before completing the catch.

See Laws 19.3 (Scoring a Boundary) and 19.4 (Runs Allowed for Boundaries).

5. No Runs to Be Scored

(a) If the striker is dismissed Caught, runs from that delivery completed by the batsmen before the completion of the catch shall not be scored, but any penalties awarded to either side when the ball is dead, if applicable, will stand. Law 18.12(a) (Batsman Returning to Wicket He Has Left) shall apply from the instant of the catch.

LAW 33.   HANDLED THE BALL

1. Out Handled the Ball

Either batsman is out Handled the ball if he wilfully touches the ball while in play with a hand or hands not holding the bat unless he does so with the consent of the opposing side.

2. Not Out Handled the Ball

Notwithstanding 1 above, a batsman will not be out under this Law if

(i) he handles the ball in order to avoid injury.

(ii) he uses his hand or hands to return the ball to any member of the fielding side without the consent of that side. Note, however, the provisions of Law 37.4 (Returning the Ball To a Member of the Fielding Side).

3. Runs Scored

If either batsman is dismissed under this Law, any runs completed before the offence, together with any penalty extras and the penalty for a No Ball or Wide, if applicable, shall be scored. See Laws 18.10 (Runs Scored When a Batsman is Dismissed) and 42.17 (Penalty runs).

4. Bowler Does Not Get Credit

The bowler does not get credit for the wicket.

LAW 34.   HIT THE BALL TWICE

1. Out Hit the Ball Twice

(a) The striker is out Hit the ball twice if, while the ball is in play, it strikes any part of his person or is struck by his bat and, before the ball has been touched by a fielder, he wilfully strikes it again with his bat or person, other than a hand not holding the bat, except for the sole purpose of guarding his wicket. See 3 below and Laws 33 (Handled the Ball) and 37 (Obstructing the Field).

(b) For the purpose of this Law, "struck" or "strike" shall include contact with the person of the striker.

2. Not Out Hit the Ball Twice

Notwithstanding 1(a) above, the striker will not be out under this Law if

(i) he makes a second or subsequent stroke in order to return the ball to any member of the fielding side. Note, however, the provisions of Law 37.4 (Returning the Ball to a Member of the Fielding Side).

(ii) he wilfully strikes the ball after it has touched a fielder. Note, however, the provisions of Law 37.1 (Out Obstructing the Field).

3. Ball Lawfully Struck More Than Once

Solely in order to guard his wicket and before the ball has been touched by a fielder, the striker may lawfully strike the ball more than once with his bat or with any part of his person other than a hand not holding the bat.

Notwithstanding this provision, the striker may not prevent the ball from being caught by making more than one stroke in defence of his wicket. See Law 37.3 (Obstructing a Ball from Being Caught).

4. Runs Permitted from Ball Lawfully Struck More Than Once

When the ball is lawfully struck more than once, as permitted in 3 above, only the first strike is to be considered in determining whether runs are to be allowed and how they are to be scored.

(a) If on the first strike the umpire is satisfied that either

(i) the ball first struck the bat, or

(ii) the striker attempted to play the ball with his bat, or

(iii) the striker tried to avoid being hit by the ball

then any penalties to the batting side that are applicable shall be allowed.

(b) If the conditions in (a) above are met then, if they result from overthrows, and only if they result from overthrows, runs completed by the batsmen or a boundary will be allowed in addition to any penalties that are applicable. They shall be credited to the striker if the first strike was with the bat. If the first strike was on the person of the striker they shall be scored as Leg Byes or No Ball extras, as appropriate. See Law 26.2 (Leg Byes).

(c) If the conditions of (a) above are met and there is no overthrow until after the batsmen have started to run, but before one run is completed,

(i) only subsequent completed runs or a boundary shall be allowed. The first run shall count as a completed run for this purpose only if the batsmen have not crossed at the instant of the throw.

(ii) if in these circumstances the ball goes to the boundary from the throw then, notwithstanding the provisions of Law 19.6 (Overthrow or Wilful Act of Fielder), only the boundary allowance shall be scored.

(iii) if the ball goes to the boundary as the result of a further overthrow, then runs completed by the batsmen after the first throw and before this final throw shall be added to the boundary allowance. The run in progress at the first throw will count only if they have not crossed at that moment; the run in progress at the final throw shall count only if they have crossed at that moment. Law 18.12 (Batsman Returning to Wicket He Has Left) shall apply as from the moment of the final throw.

(d) If, in the opinion of the umpire, none of the conditions in (a) above have been met then, whether there is an overthrow or not, the batting side shall not be credited with any runs from that delivery apart from the penalty for a No Ball if applicable. Moreover, no other penalties shall be awarded to the batting side when the ball is dead. See Law 42.17 (Penalty Runs).

5. Ball Lawfully Struck More Than Once – Action By The Umpire

If no runs are to be allowed, either in the circumstances of 4(d) above, or because there has been no overthrow and

(a) if no run is attempted but the ball reaches the boundary, the umpire shall call and signal Dead Ball and disallow the boundary.

(b) if the batsmen run and

(i) neither batsman is dismissed and the ball does not become dead for any other reason, the umpire shall call and signal Dead Ball as soon as one run is completed or the ball reaches the boundary. The batsmen shall return to their original ends. The run or boundary shall be disallowed.

(ii) a batsman is dismissed, or if for any other reason the ball becomes dead before one run is completed or the ball reaches the boundary, all the provisions of the Laws will apply except that the award of penalties to the batting side shall be as laid down in 4(a) or 4(d) above as appropriate

6. Bowler Does Not Get Credit

The bowler does not get credit for the wicket.

LAW 35. HIT WICKET

1. Out Hit Wicket

The striker is out Hit wicket if, while the ball is in play, his wicket is put down either by the striker's bat or person as described in Law 28.1(a)(ii) and (iii) (Wicket Put Down either

(i) in the course of any action taken by him in preparing to receive or in receiving a delivery, or

(ii) in setting off for his first run immediately after playing, or playing at, the ball, or

(iii) if he makes no attempt to play the ball, in setting off for his first run, providing that in the opinion of the umpire this is immediately after he has had the opportunity of playing the ball, or

(iv) in lawfully making a second or further stroke for the purpose of guarding his wicket within the provisions of Law 34.3 (Ball Lawfully Struck More Than Once).

2. Not Out Hit Wicket

Notwithstanding 1 above, the batsman is not out under this Law should his wicket be put down in any of the ways referred to in 1 above if

(a) it occurs after he has completed any action in receiving the delivery, other than as in 1(ii), (iii) or (iv) above.

(b) it occurs when he is in the act of running, other than in setting off immediately for his first run.

(c) it occurs when he is trying to avoid being run out or stumped.

(d) it occurs while he is trying to avoid a throw-in at any time.

(e) the bowler after starting his run up, or his bowling action if he has no run up, does not deliver the ball. In this case either umpire shall immediately call and signal Dead Ball. See Law 23.3 (Umpire calling and signalling Dead Ball).

(f) the delivery is a No Ball.

LAW 36.   LEG BEFORE WICKET

1. Out LBW

The striker is out LBW in the circumstances set out below.

(a) The bowler delivers a ball, not being a No ball and

(b) the ball, if it is not intercepted full pitch, pitches in line between wicket and wicket or on the off side of the striker's wicket and

(c) the ball not having previously touched his bat, the striker intercepts the ball, either full-pitch or after pitching, with any part of his person and

(d) the point of impact, even if above the level of the bails, either

(i) is between wicket and wicket or

(ii) is either between wicket and wicket or outside the line of the off stump, if the striker has made no genuine attempt to play the ball with his bat and

(e) but for the interception, the ball would have hit the wicket.

2. Interception of the Ball

(a) In assessing points (c), (d) and (e) in 1 above, only the first interception is to be considered.

(b) In assessing point (e) in 1 above, it is to be assumed that the path of the ball before interception would have continued after interception, irrespective of whether the ball might have pitched subsequently or not.

3. Off Side of Wicket

The off side of the striker's wicket shall be determined by the striker's stance at the moment the ball comes into play for that delivery.

LAW 37. OBSTRUCTING THE FIELD

1. Out Obstructing the Field

Either batsman is out Obstructing the field if he wilfully obstructs or distracts the opposing side by word or action. It shall be regarded as obstruction if either batsman wilfully, and without the consent of the fielding side, strikes the ball with his bat or person, other than a hand not holding the bat, after the ball has touched a fielder. See 4 below.

2. Accidental Obstruction

It is for either umpire to decide whether any obstruction or distraction is wilful or not. He shall consult the other umpire if he has any doubt.

3. Obstructing a Ball from Being Caught

The striker is out should wilful obstruction or distraction by either batsman prevent a catch being made.

This shall apply even though the striker causes the obstruction in lawfully guarding his wicket under the provisions of Law 34.3 (Ball lawfully struck more than once).

4. Returning the Ball to a Member of the Fielding Side

Either batsman is out under this Law if, without the consent of the fielding side and while the ball is in play, he uses his bat or person to return the ball to any member of that side.

5. Runs Scored

If a batsman is dismissed under this Law, runs completed by the batsmen before the offence shall be scored, together with the penalty for a No ball or a Wide, if applicable. Other penalties that may be awarded to either side when the ball is dead shall also stand. See Law 42.17(b) (Penalty Runs).

If, however, the obstruction prevents a catch from being made, runs completed by the batsmen before the offence shall not be scored, but other penalties that may be awarded to either side when the ball is dead shall stand. See Law 42.17(b) (Penalty Runs).

6. Bowler Does Not Get Credit

The bowler does not get credit for the wicket.

LAW 38. RUN OUT

1. Out Run Out

(a) Either batsman is out Run out, except as in 2 below, if at any time while the ball is in play

(i) he is out of his ground and

(ii) his wicket is fairly put down by the opposing side.

(b) (a) above shall apply even though No Ball has been called and whether or not a run is being attempted, except in the circumstances of Law 39.3(b) (Not Out Stumped).

2. Batsman Not Run Out

Notwithstanding 1 above, a batsman is not out Run out if

(a) he has been within his ground and has subsequently left it to avoid injury, when the wicket is put down.

(b) the ball has not subsequently been touched again by a fielder, after the bowler has entered his delivery stride, before the wicket is put down.

(c) the ball, having been played by the striker, or having come off his person, directly strikes a helmet worn by a fielder and without further contact with him or any other fielder rebounds directly on to the wicket. However, the ball remains in play and either batsman may be Run out in the circumstances of 1 above if a wicket is subsequently put down.

(d) he is out Stumped. See Law 39.1(b) (Out Stumped).

(e) he is out of his ground, not attempting a run and his wicket is fairly put down by the wicket-keeper without the intervention of another member of the fielding side, if No Ball has been called. See Law 39.3(b) (Not Out Stumped).

3. Which Batsman is Out

The batsman out in the circumstances of 1 above is the one whose ground is at the end where the wicket is put down. See Laws 2.8 (Transgression of the Laws by a batsman who has a runner) and 29.2 (Which is a Batsman's Ground).

4. Runs Scored

If a batsman is dismissed Run out, the batting side shall score the runs completed before the dismissal, together with the penalty for a No Ball or a Wide, if applicable. Other penalties to either side that may be awarded when the ball is dead shall also stand. See Law 42.17 (Penalty runs).

If, however, a striker with a runner is himself dismissed Run Out, runs completed by the runner and the other batsman before the dismissal shall not be scored. The penalty for a No Ball or a Wide and any other penalties to either side that may be awarded when the ball is dead shall stand. See Laws 2.8 (Transgression of the Laws by a Batsman Who Has a Runner) and 42.17(b) (Penalty Runs).

5. Bowler Does Not Get Credit

The bowler does not get credit for the wicket.

LAW 39.   STUMPED

1. Out Stumped

(a) The striker is out Stumped if

        (i) he is out of his ground and

        (ii) he is receiving a ball which is not a No Ball and

        (iii) he is not attempting a run and

(iv) his wicket is put down by the wicket-keeper without the intervention of another member of the fielding side. Note Law 40.3 (Position of Wicket-keeper).

(b) The striker is out Stumped if all the conditions of (a) above are satisfied, even though a decision of Run Out would be justified.

2. Ball Rebounding from Wicket-keeper's Person

(a) If the wicket is put down by the ball, it shall be regarded as having been put down by the wicket-keeper if the ball

(i) rebounds on to the stumps from any part of his person or equipment, other than a protective helmet, or

(ii) has been kicked or thrown on to the stumps by the wicket-keeper.

(b) If the ball touches a helmet worn by the wicket-keeper, the ball is still in play but the striker shall not be out Stumped. He will, however, be liable to be Run Out in these circumstances if there is subsequent contact between the ball and any member of the fielding side. Note, however, 3 below.

3. Not Out Stumped

(a) If the striker is not out Stumped, he is liable to be out Run out if the conditions of Law 38 (Run Out) apply, except as set out in (b) below.

(b) The striker shall not be out Run out if he is out of his ground, not attempting a run, and his wicket is fairly put down by the wicket-keeper without the intervention of another member of the fielding side, if No Ball has been called.

LAW 40.   THE WICKET-KEEPER

1. Protective Equipment

The wicket-keeper is the only member of the fielding side permitted to wear gloves and external leg guards. If he does so, these are to be regarded as part of his person for the purposes of Law 41.2 (Fielding the Ball). If by his actions and positioning it is apparent to the umpires that he will not be able to discharge his duties as a wicket-keeper, he shall forfeit this right and also the right to be recognised as a wicket-keeper for the purposes of Laws 32.3 (A Fair Catch), 39 (Stumped), 41.1 (Protective Equipment), 41.5 (Limitation of On Side Fielders) and 41.6 (Fielders Not to Encroach on the Pitch).

2. Gloves

If the wicket-keeper wears gloves as permitted under 1 above, they shall have no webbing between fingers except that a single piece of flat non-stretch material may be inserted between index finger and thumb solely as a means of support. This insert shall not form a pouch when the hand is extended.

3. Position of Wicket-keeper

The wicket-keeper shall remain wholly behind the wicket at the striker's end from the moment the ball comes into play until

(a) a ball delivered by the bowler either

(i) touches the bat or person of the striker, or

(ii) passes the wicket at the striker's end

or

(b) the striker attempts a run.

In the event of the wicket-keeper contravening this Law, the umpire at the striker's end shall call and signal No ball as soon as possible after the delivery of the ball.

4. Movement By the Wicket-keeper

It is unfair if a wicket-keeper standing back makes a significant movement towards the wicket after the ball comes into play and before it reaches the striker. In the event of such unfair movement by the wicket-keeper, either umpire shall call and signal Dead Ball. It will not be considered a significant movement if the wicket-keeper moves a few paces forward for a slower delivery.

5. Restriction on Actions of Wicket-keeper

If the wicket-keeper interferes with the striker's right to play the ball and to guard his wicket, the striker shall not be out, except under Laws 33 (Handled the Ball), 34 (Hit the Ball Twice), 37 (Obstructing the Field) or 38 (Run Out).

6. Interference with Wicket-keeper by Striker

If, in playing at the ball or in the legitimate defence of his wicket, the striker interferes with the wicket-keeper, he shall not be out, except as provided for in Law 37.3 (Obstructing a Ball from Being Caught)

LAW 41. THE FIELDER

1. Protective Equipment

No member of the fielding side other than the wicket-keeper shall be permitted to wear gloves or external leg guards. In addition, protection for the hand or fingers may be worn only with the consent of the umpires.

2. Fielding the Ball

A fielder may field the ball with any part of his person but if, while the ball is in play he wilfully fields it otherwise,

(a) the ball shall become dead and 5 penalty runs shall be awarded to the batting side. See Law 42.17 (Penalty Runs).

(b) the umpire shall inform the other umpire, the captain of the fielding side, the batsmen and, as soon as practicable, the captain of the batting side of what has occurred.

(c) the umpires together shall report the occurrence as soon as possible to the Executive of the fielding side and any Governing Body responsible for the match who shall take such action as is considered appropriate against the captain and player concerned.

3. Protective Helmets Belonging to the Fielding Side

Protective helmets, when not in use by fielders, shall only be placed, if above the surface, on the ground behind the wicket-keeper and in line with both sets of stumps. If a helmet belonging to the fielding side is on the ground within the field of play, and the ball while in play strikes it, the ball shall become dead. Five penalty runs shall then be awarded to the batting side. See Laws 18.11 (Runs Scored When Ball Becomes Dead) and 42.17 (Penalty Runs).

4. Penalty Runs Not Being Awarded

Notwithstanding 2 and 3 above, if from the delivery by the bowler the ball first struck the person of the striker and if, in the opinion of the umpire, the striker neither

    (i) attempted to play the ball with his bat, nor

    (ii) tried to avoid being hit by the ball,

then no award of five penalty runs shall be made and no other runs or penalties shall be credited to the batting side except the penalty for a No Ball if applicable. See Law 26.3 (Leg Byes Not to Be Awarded).

5. Limitation of On Side Fielders

At the instant of the bowler's delivery there shall not be more than two fielders, other than the wicket-keeper, behind the popping crease on the on side. A fielder will be considered to be behind the popping crease unless the whole of his person, whether grounded or in the air, is in front of this line. In the event of infringement of this Law by the fielding side, the umpire at the striker's end shall call and signal No Ball.

6. Fielders Not to Encroach on the Pitch

While the ball is in play and until the ball has made contact with the bat or person of the striker, or has passed the striker's bat, no fielder, other than the bowler, may have any part of his person grounded on or extended over the pitch. In the event of infringement of this Law by any fielder other than the wicket-keeper, the umpire at the bowler's end shall call and signal No Ball as soon as possible after the delivery of the ball. Note, however, Law 40.3 (Position of Wicket-keeper).

7. Movement by Fielders

Any significant movement by any fielder after the ball comes into play and before the ball reaches the striker is unfair. In the event of such unfair movement, either umpire shall call and signal Dead ball. Note also the provisions of Law 42.4 (Deliberate Attempt to Distract Striker).

8. Definition of Significant Movement

    (a) For close fielders anything other than minor adjustments to stance or position in relation to the striker is significant.

    (b) In the outfield, fielders are permitted to move in towards the striker or striker's wicket, provided that 5 above is not contravened. Anything other than slight movement off line or away from the striker is to be considered significant.

    (c) For restrictions on movement by the wicket-keeper see Law 40.4 (Movement By Wicket-keeper).

LAW 42. FAIR AND UNFAIR PLAY

1. Fair and Unfair Play – Responsibility of Captains

The responsibility lies with the captains for ensuring that play is conducted within the spirit and traditions of the game, as described in The Preamble – The Spirit of Cricket, as well as within the Laws.

2. Fair and Unfair Play – Responsibility of Umpires

The umpires shall be the sole judges of fair and unfair play. If either umpire considers an action, not covered by the Laws, to be unfair, he shall intervene without appeal and, if the ball is in play, shall call and signal Dead Ball and implement the procedure as set out in 18 below. Otherwise the umpires shall not interfere with the progress of play, except as required to do so by the Laws.

3. The Match Ball – Changing Its Condition

(a) Any fielder may

(i) polish the ball provided that no artificial substance is used and that such polishing wastes no time.

(ii) remove mud from the ball under the supervision of the umpire.

(iii) dry a wet ball on a towel.

(b) It is unfair for anyone to rub the ball on the ground for any reason, interfere with any of the seams or the surface of the ball, use any implement, or take any other action whatsoever which is likely to alter the condition of the ball, except as permitted in (a) above.

(c) The umpires shall make frequent and irregular inspections of the ball.

(d) In the event of any fielder changing the condition of the ball unfairly, as set out in (b) above, the umpires after consultation shall

(i) change the ball forthwith. It shall be for the umpires to decide on the replacement ball, which shall, in their opinion, have had wear comparable with that which the previous ball had received immediately prior to the contravention.

(ii) inform the batsmen that the ball has been changed.

(iii) award 5 penalty runs to the batting side. See 17 below.

(iv) inform the captain of the fielding side that the reason for the action was the unfair interference with the ball.

(v) inform the captain of the batting side as soon as practicable of what has occurred.

(vi) report the occurrence as soon as possible to the Executive of the fielding side and any Governing Body responsible for the match, who shall take such action as is considered appropriate against the captain and team concerned.

(e) If there is any further instance of unfairly changing the condition of the ball in that innings, the umpires after consultation shall

(i) repeat the procedure in (d)(i), (ii) and (iii) above.

(ii) inform the captain of the fielding side of the reason for the action taken and direct him to take off forthwith the bowler who delivered the immediately preceding ball. The bowler thus taken off shall not be allowed to bowl again in that innings.

(iii) inform the captain of the batting side as soon as practicable of what has occurred.

(iv) report this further occurrence as soon as possible to the Executive of the fielding side and any Governing Body responsible for the match, who shall take such action as is considered appropriate against the captain and team concerned.

4. Deliberate Attempt to Distract Striker

It is unfair for any member of the fielding side deliberately to attempt to distract the striker while he is preparing to receive or receiving a delivery.

(a) If either umpire considers that any action by a member of the fielding side is such an attempt, at the first instance he shall

(i) immediately call and signal Dead Ball.

(ii) warn the captain of the fielding side that the action is unfair and indicate that this is a first and final warning.

(iii) inform the other umpire and the batsmen of what has occurred. Neither batsman shall be dismissed from that delivery and the ball shall not count as one of the over.

(b) If there is any further such deliberate attempt in that innings, by any member of the fielding side, the procedures, other than warning, as set out in (a) above shall apply. Additionally, the umpire at the bowler's end shall

(i) award 5 penalty runs to the batting side. See 17 below.

(ii) inform the captain of the fielding side of the reason for this action and, as soon as practicable, inform the captain of the batting side.

(iii) report the occurrence, together with the other umpire, as soon as possible to the Executive of the fielding side and any Governing Body responsible for the match, who shall take such action as is considered appropriate against the captain and player or players concerned.

5. Deliberate Distraction or Obstruction of Batsman

In addition to 4 above, it is unfair for any member of the fielding side, by word or action, wilfully to attempt to distract or to obstruct either batsman after the striker has received the ball.

(a) It is for either one of the umpires to decide whether any distraction or obstruction is wilful or not.

(b) If either umpire considers that a member of the fielding side has wilfully caused or attempted to cause such a distraction or obstruction he shall

(i) immediately call and signal Dead Ball.

(ii) inform the captain of the fielding side and the other umpire of the reason for the call.

Additionally,

(iii) neither batsman shall be dismissed from that delivery.

(iv) Five penalty runs shall be awarded to the batting side. See 17 below. In this instance, the run in progress shall be scored, whether or not the batsmen had crossed at the instant of the call. See Law 18.11 (Runs Scored When Ball Becomes Dead).

(v) the umpire at the bowler's end shall inform the captain of the fielding side of the reason for this action and, as soon as practicable, inform the captain of the batting side.

(vi) the umpires shall report the occurrence as soon as possible to the Executive of the fielding side and any Governing Body responsible for the match, who shall take such action as is considered appropriate against the captain and player or players concerned.

6. Dangerous and Unfair Bowling

(a) Bowling of Fast Short Pitched Balls

(i) The bowling of fast short pitched balls is dangerous and unfair if the umpire at the bowler's end considers that by their repetition and taking into account their length, height and direction they are likely to inflict physical injury on the striker, irrespective of the protective equipment he may be wearing. The relative skill of the striker shall be taken into consideration.

(ii) Any delivery which, after pitching, passes or would have passed over head height of the striker standing upright at the crease, although not threatening physical injury, is unfair and shall be considered as part of the repetition sequence in (i) above. The umpire shall call and signal No Ball for each such delivery.

(b) Bowling of High Full Pitched Balls

(i) Any delivery, other than a slow paced one, which passes or would have passed on the full above waist height of the striker standing upright at the crease is to be deemed dangerous and unfair, whether or not it is likely to inflict physical injury on the striker.

(ii) A slow delivery which passes or would have passed on the full above shoulder height of the striker standing upright at the crease is to be deemed dangerous and unfair, whether or not it is likely to inflict physical injury on the striker.

7. Dangerous and Unfair Bowling – Action by the Umpire

(a) In the event of dangerous and/or unfair bowling, as defined in 6 above, by any bowler, except as in 8 below, at the first instance the umpire at the bowler's end shall call and signal No ball and, when the ball is dead, caution the bowler, inform the other umpire, the captain of the fielding side and the batsmen of what has occurred. This caution shall continue to apply throughout the innings.

(b) If there is a second instance of such dangerous and/or unfair bowling by the same bowler in that innings, the umpire at the bowler's end shall repeat the above procedure and indicate to the bowler that this is a final warning. Both the above caution and final warning shall continue to apply even though the bowler may later change ends.

(c) Should there be a further instance by the same bowler in that innings, the umpire shall

(i) call and signal No Ball.

(ii) direct the captain, when the ball is dead, to take the bowler off forthwith. The over shall be completed by another bowler, who shall neither have bowled the previous over nor be allowed to bowl the next over. The bowler thus taken off shall not be allowed to bowl again in tha innings.

(iii) report the occurrence to the other umpire, the batsmen and, as soon as practicable, the captain of the batting side.

(iv) report the occurrence, with the other umpire, as soon as possible to the Executive of the fielding side and to any Governing Body responsible for the match, who shall take such action as is considered appropriate against the captain and bowler concerned.

8. Deliberate Bowling of High Full Pitched Balls

If the umpire considers that a high full pitch which is deemed to be dangerous and unfair, as defined in 6(b) above, was deliberately bowled, then the caution and warning prescribed in 7 above shall be dispensed with. The umpire shall

(a) call and signal No Ball.

(b) direct the captain, when the ball is dead, to take the bowler off forthwith.

(c) implement the remainder of the procedure as laid down in 7(c) above.

9. Time Wasting by the Fielding Side

It is unfair for any member of the fielding side to waste time.

(a) If the captain of the fielding side wastes time, or allows any member of his side to waste time, or if the progress of an over is unnecessarily slow, at the first instance the umpire shall call and signal Dead Ball if necessary and

(i) warn the captain, and indicate that this is a first and final warning.

(ii) inform the other umpire and the batsmen of what has occurred.

(b) If there is any further waste of time in that innings, by any member of the fielding side, the umpire shall either

(i) if the waste of time is not during the course of an over, award five penalty runs to the batting side. See 17 below, or

(ii) if the waste of time is during the course of an over, when the ball is dead, direct the captain to take the bowler off forthwith. If applicable, the over shall be completed by another bowler, who shall neither have bowled the previous over nor be allowed to bowl the next over. The bowler thus taken off shall not be allowed to bowl again in that innings.

(iii) inform the other umpire, the batsmen and, as soon as practicable, the captain of the batting side of what has occurred.

(iv) report the occurrence, with the other umpire, as soon as possible to the Executive of the fielding side and to any Governing Body responsible for the match, who shall take such action as is considered appropriate against the captain and team concerned.

10. Batsman Wasting Time

It is unfair for a batsman to waste time. In normal circumstances the striker should always be ready to take strike when the bowler is ready to start his run up.

(a) Should either batsman waste time by failing to meet this requirement, or in any other way, the following procedure shall be adopted. At the first instance, either before the bowler starts his run up or when the ball is dead, as appropriate, the umpire shall

> (i) warn the batsman and indicate that this is a first and final warning. This warning shall continue to apply throughout the innings. The umpire shall so inform each incoming batsman.

> (ii) inform the other umpire, the other batsman and the captain of the fielding side of what has occurred.

> (iii) inform the captain of the batting side as soon as practicable.

(b) if there is any further time wasting by any batsman in that innings, the umpire shall, at the appropriate time while the ball is dead

> (i) award five penalty runs to the fielding side. See 17 below.

> (ii) inform the other umpire, the other batsman, the captain of the fielding side and, as soon as practicable, the captain of the batting side of what has occurred.

> (iii) report the occurrence, with the other umpire, as soon as possible to the Executive of the batting side and to any Governing Body responsible for the match, who shall take such action as is considered appropriate against the captain and player or players and, if appropriate, the team concerned.

11. Damaging the Pitch – Area to be Protected

(a) It is incumbent on all players to avoid unnecessary damage to the pitch. It is unfair for any player to cause deliberate damage to the pitch.

(b) An area of the pitch, to be referred to as "the protected area", is defined as that area contained within a rectangle bounded at each end by imaginary lines parallel to the popping creases and 5ft/1.52m in front of each and on the sides by imaginary lines, one each side of the imaginary line joining the centres of the two middle stumps, each parallel to it and 1ft/30.48cm from it.

12. Bowler Running on the Protected Area After Delivering the Ball

(a) If the bowler, after delivering the ball, runs on the protected area as defined in 11(b) above, the umpire shall at the first instance, and when the ball is dead,

> (i) caution the bowler. This caution shall continue to apply throughout the innings.

> (ii) inform the other umpire, the captain of the fielding side and the batsmen of what has occurred.

(b) If, in that innings, the same bowler runs on the protected area again after delivering the ball, the umpire shall repeat the above procedure, indicating that this is a final warning.

(c) If, in that innings, the same bowler runs on the protected area a third time after delivering the ball, when the ball is dead the umpire shall

    (i) direct the captain of the fielding side to take the bowler off forthwith. If applicable, the over shall be completed by another bowler, who shall neither have bowled the previous over nor be allowed to bowl the next over. The bowler thus taken off shall not be allowed to bowl again in that innings.

    (ii) inform the other umpire, the batsmen and, as soon as practicable, the captain of the batting side of what has occurred.

    (iii) report the occurrence, with the other umpire, as soon as possible to the Executive of the fielding side and to any Governing Body responsible for the match, who shall take such action as is considered appropriate against the captain and bowler concerned.

13. Fielder Damaging the Pitch

(a) If any fielder causes avoidable damage to the pitch, other than as in 12(a) above, at the first instance the umpire shall, when the ball is dead,

    (i) caution the captain of the fielding side, indicating that this is a first and final warning. This caution shall continue to apply throughout the innings.

    (ii) inform the other umpire and the batsmen.

(b) If there is any further avoidable damage to the pitch by any fielder in that innings, the umpire shall, when the ball is dead,

    (i) award five penalty runs to the batting side. See 17 below.

    (ii) inform the other umpire, the batsmen, the captain of the fielding side and, as soon as practicable, the captain of the batting side of what has occurred.

    (iii) report the occurrence, with the other umpire, as soon as possible to the Executive of the fielding side and any Governing Body responsible for the match, who shall take such action as is considered appropriate against the captain and player or players concerned.

14. Batsman Damaging the Pitch

(a) If either batsman causes avoidable damage to the pitch, at the first instance the umpire shall, when the ball is dead,

    (i) caution the batsman. This caution shall continue to apply throughout the innings. The umpire shall so inform each incoming batsman.

    (ii) inform the other umpire, the other batsman, the captain of the fielding side and, as soon as practicable, the captain of the batting side.

(b) If there is a second instance of avoidable damage to the pitch by any batsman in that innings

    (i) the umpire shall repeat the above procedure, indicating that this is a final warning.

    (ii) additionally he shall disallow all runs to the batting side from that delivery other than the penalty for a No Ball or a Wide, if applicable. The batsmen shall return to their original ends.

(c) If there is any further avoidable damage to the pitch by any batsman in that innings, the umpire shall, when the ball is dead,

(i) disallow all runs to the batting side from that delivery other than the penalty for a No Ball or a Wide, if applicable.

(ii) additionally award 5 penalty runs to the fielding side. See 17 below.

(iii) inform the other umpire, the other batsman, the captain of the fielding side and, as soon as practicable, the captain of the batting side of what has occurred.

(iv) report the occurrence, with the other umpire, as soon as possible to the Executive of the batting side and any Governing Body responsible for the match, who shall take such action as is considered appropriate against the captain and player or players concerned.

15. Bowler Attempting to Run Out Non-striker Before Delivery

The bowler is permitted, before entering his delivery stride, to attempt to run out the non-striker. The ball shall not count in the over. The umpire shall call and signal Dead ball as soon as possible if the bowler fails in the attempt to run out the non-striker.

16. Batsmen Stealing a Run

It is unfair for the batsmen to attempt to steal a run during the bowler's run up. Unless the bowler attempts to run out either batsman – see 15 above and Law 24.4 (Bowler Throwing Towards Striker's End Before Delivery) – the umpire shall

(i) call and signal Dead ball as soon as the batsmen cross in any such attempt.

(ii) return the batsmen to their original ends.

(iii) award five penalty runs to the fielding side. See 17 below.

(iv) inform the other umpire, the batsmen, the captain of the fielding side and, as soon as practicable, the captain of the batting side of the reason for the action taken.

(v) report the occurrence, with the other umpire, as soon as possible to the Executive of the batting side and any Governing Body responsible for the match, who shall take such action as is considered appropriate against the captain and player or players concerned.

17. Penalty Runs

(a) When penalty runs are awarded to either side, when the ball is dead the umpire shall signal the penalty runs to the scorers as laid down in Law 3.14 (Signals).

(b) Notwithstanding any provisions elsewhere in the Laws, penalty runs shall not be awarded once the match is concluded as defined in Law 16.9 (Conclusion of a Match).

(c) When 5 penalty runs are awarded to the batting side, under either Law 2.6 (Player Returning Without Permission) or Law 41 (The Fielder) or under 3, 4, 5, 9 or 13 above, then

(i) they shall be scored as penalty extras and shall be in addition to any other penalties.

(ii) they shall not be regarded as runs scored from either the immediately preceding delivery or the following delivery, and shall be in addition to any runs from those deliveries.

(iii) the batsmen shall not change ends solely by reason of the five-run penalty.

(d) When five penalty runs are awarded to the fielding side, under Law 18.5(b) (Deliberate Short Runs), or under 10, 14 or 16 above, they shall be added as penalty extras to that side's total of runs in its most recently completed innings. If the fielding side has not completed an innings, the 5 penalty extras shall be added to its next innings.

18. Players' Conduct

If there is any breach of the Spirit of the Game by a player failing to comply with the instructions of an umpire, or criticising his decisions by word or action, or showing dissent, or generally behaving in a manner which might bring the game into disrepute, the umpire concerned shall immediately report the matter to the other umpire.

The umpires together shall

(i) inform the player's captain of the occurrence, instructing the latter to take action.

(ii) warn him of the gravity of the offence, and tell him that it will be reported to higher authority.

(iii) report the occurrence as soon as possible to the Executive of the player's team and any Governing Body responsible for the match, who shall take such action as is considered appropriate against the captain and player or players, and, if appropriate, the team concerned.

REGULATIONS OF THE INTERNATIONAL CRICKET COUNCIL

Extracts

1. Standard Playing Conditions

At the May 2000 Cricket Committee meeting, the playing conditions for all Test Matches and One Day Internationals Matches were amended to include the new Laws of Cricket. These apply for one year commencing 1st October 2000, and include the following:

Duration of Test Matches

Test Matches shall be of five days scheduled duration, and of two innings per side. The two participating countries may:

(a) Provide for a rest day during the match, and/or a reserve day after the scheduled days of play.

(b) Play on any scheduled rest day, conditions and circumstances permitting, should a full day's play be lost on any day prior to the rest day.

(c) Play on any scheduled reserve day, conditions and circumstances permitting, should a full day's play be lost on any day. Play shall not take place on more than five days.

(d) Make up time lost in excess of five minutes in each day's play due to circumstances outside the game other than Acts of God.

Hours of Play, Intervals and Minimum Overs in the Day

1. Start and Cessation Times: To be determined by the Home Board, subject to there being six hours scheduled for play per day (Pakistan a minimum of five hours), and subject to:

(a) Play shall continue on each day until the completion of a minimum number of overs or until the scheduled or re-scheduled cessation time, whichever is the later. The minimum number of overs to be completed, unless an innings ends or an interruption occurs, shall be:

(i) on days other than the last day – a minimum of 90 overs (or a minimum of 15 overs per hour).

(ii) on the last day – a minimum of 75 overs (or a minimum of 15 overs per hour) for playing time other than the last hour of the match when Clause (e) below shall apply.

(iii) Additional Hour: Subject to weather and light, except in the last hour of the match, in the event of play being suspended for any reason other than normal intervals, the playing time on that day shall be extended by the amount of time lost up to a maximum of one hour. In these circumstances, the minimum number of overs to be bowled shall be in accordance with the provisions of this clause i.e. a minimum of 15 overs per hour and the cessation time shall be rescheduled accordingly.

(iv) If play has been suspended for 30 minutes or more prior to the commencement of the scheduled tea interval, the tea interval shall be delayed for half an hour.

(v) Experimental Condition – subject to both Boards agreement prior to the start of the Tour.

If any time is lost and cannot be made up under (iii) above, additional time of up to a maximum of one hour per day shall be added to the scheduled playing hours for the next day, and subsequent day(s) as required (to make up as much lost time as possible). Of this additional time the first 30 minutes (or less) shall be added prior to the scheduled start of the first session, and the remainder shall be added to the last session.

When additional time is added to subsequent day(s), no scheduled days play shall exceed seven hours. The length of each session of play under this experimental condition is subject to the provisions of Law 15.

Under Law 15.5 timings can be altered at any time on any day if playing time is lost, not necessarily on that day. The captains, umpires and the referee can agree different timings under those circumstances before play starts on any day.

(b) When an innings ends a minimum number of overs shall be bowled from the start of the new innings. The number of overs to be bowled shall be calculated at the rate of one over for each full four minutes to enable a minimum of 90 overs to be bowled in a day. The last hour of the match shall be excluded from this calculation when Clause (e) shall apply.

Where a change of innings occurs during a day's play, in the event of the team bowling second being unable to complete its overs by the scheduled cessation time, play shall continue until the required number of overs have been completed.

Where there is a change of innings during a day's play (except at lunch or tea), two overs will be deducted from the minimum number of overs to be bowled.

(c) Except in the last hour of the match, for which Clause (e) makes provision, if play is suspended due to adverse weather or light for more than one hour in aggregate on any day, the minimum number of overs shall be reduced by one over for each full 4 minutes of the aggregate playing time lost.

(d) On the last day, if any of the minimum of 75 overs, or as recalculated, have not been bowled when one hour of scheduled playing time remains, the last hour of the match for the purposes of Clause (e) shall be the hour immediately following the completion of those overs.

(e) Law 16.6, 16.7 and 16.8 will apply except that a minimum of 15 overs shall be bowled in the last hour and all calculations with regard to suspensions of play or the start of a new innings shall be based on one over for each full four minutes (refer (i) below). If, however, at any time after 30 minutes of the last hour have elapsed both Captains (the batsmen at the wicket may act for their Captain) accept that there is no prospect of a result to the match, they may agree to cease play at that time.

2. Extra Time

The umpires may decide to play 30 minutes (a minimum of eight overs) extra time at the end of any day (other than the last day) if requested by either captain if, in the umpires opinion, it would bring about a definite result on that. If the umpires do not believe a result can be achieved no extra time shall be allowed.

3. Use of lights

Experimental Condition (two years from August 1999) - subject to both Boards' agreement prior to the Tour.

If in the opinion of the umpires, natural light is deteriorating to an unfit level, they shall authorise the ground authorites to use the available artificial lighting so that the match can continue in acceptable conditions. The lights are only to be used to enable a full days play to be completed.

Note: The following Laws refer to the 2000 Code of the Laws of Cricket

Fitness of Ground, Weather and Light: Law 3.8

Law 3.8 shall apply, but in addition

If conditions during a rain stoppage improve and the rain is reduced to drizzle, the umpires must consider if they would have suspended play in the first place under similar conditions. If both on-field umpires agree that the current drizzle would not have caused a stoppage, then play shall resume immediately.

The umpires shall disregard any shadow on the pitch from the stadium or from any permanent object on the ground.

The Pitch: Law 7

Law 7.3 shall apply, but in addition

Captains, umpires, the referee and Groundsmen should co-operate to ensure that, prior to the start of any day's play, no-one bounces a ball on the pitch or strikes it with a bat to assess its condition or for any other reason, or causes damage to the pitch in any other way.

Prior to the start of play on any day, only the Captain and team Coach may walk on the pitch to assess its condition. Spiked footwear is not permitted.

The Over: Law 22

Law 22.5 shall apply, but in addition

Whenever possible the third umpire or TV umpire shall liaise with the scorers and if possible inform the on-field umpires if the over has been miscounted.

Judging a Wide: Law 25.1

Law 25.1 will apply, but in addition:

For bowlers whom umpires consider to be bowling down the leg side as a negative tactic, the One Day International Wide interpretation will be applied as follows:

Any offside or legside delivery which in the opinion of the umpire does not give the batsman a reasonable opportunity to score shall be called a wide. As a guide, on the leg side a ball landing clearly outside the leg stump going further away shall be called wide (refer Law 42.6).

Deliberate attempt to distract striker: Law 42.4

No penalty runs shall be awarded under this Law. If the umpires consider that any action by a member of the fielding side is a deliberate attempt to distract the striker the incident shall be reported to the referee under the Code of Conduct.

Deliberate distraction or obstruction of batsman: Law 42.5

Law 42.5 shall apply, and penalty runs shall be awarded, for any wilful attempt to obstruct the batsman as defined in the Law. However, no penalty runs shall be awarded if the umpires consider that a member of the fielding side wilfully attempts to distract the batsman under this Law. Instead, the incident shall be reported to the referee under the Code of Conduct.

Dangerous and Unfair Bowling – The Bowling of Fast Short Pitched Balls: Law 42.6

Law 42.6 (a) (ii) shall be replaced by the following:

    (a) A bowler shall be limited to two fast short pitched deliveries per over.

    (b) A fast short pitched ball is defined as a ball which passes or would have passed above the shoulder height of the Batsman standing upright at the crease.

In the event of a bowler bowling more than two fast short pitched deliveries in an over, either umpire shall call and signal no ball on each occasion.

ICC CODE OF CONDUCT

1. The captains are responsible at all times for ensuring that play is conducted within the spirit of the game as well as within the Laws.

2. Players and/or team officials shall not at any time engage in conduct unbecoming to their status which could bring them or the game into disrepute.

3 Players and/or team officials must at all times accept the umpire's decision and must not show dissent at the umpire's decision.

4. Players and/or team officials shall not verbally abuse, assault, intimidate, or attempt to assault or intimidate any umpire, spectator, referee, player or team official.

5. Players and/or team officials shall not use crude or abusive language nor make offensive gestures.

6. Players and/or team officials shall not disclose or comment publicly upon any alleged or actual breach of this Code, whether by themselves or any other person to whom the Code applies, or upon any hearing, report or decision arising from such an alleged or proven breach.

7. Players and/or team officials shall not at any time breach any ICC regulation which may be in force from time to time.

8. Players and/or team officials shall not make any public pronouncement or media comment which is detrimental either to the game in general; or to a particular tour whether or not they are personally involved with the tour; or to relations between the home boards of the competing teams.

9. Players and/or team officials shall not bet on matches nor otherwise engage in conduct referred to in Appendix A of the ICC Code of Conduct Commission Terms of Reference.

10. Players and/or team officials shall not use or in any way be concerned in the use or distribution of illegal drugs.

AUSTRALIAN CRICKET BOARD
PLAYING CONDITIONS, 2000-01

Note: This section is an abridged version of the full Playing Conditions Booklet of the Australian Cricket Board. Some parts have been omitted.

TEST MATCH
PLAYING CONDITIONS 2000-01

Except as modified for one-day internationals and in the section on other tour matches, these playing conditions shall apply to all tour matches.

1.   Laws of Cricket

Except as varied hereunder the Laws of Cricket (2000 Code) shall apply.

2.   Duration of Matches

Test matches shall be of five days scheduled duration, and of two innings per side. The two participating countries may:

- (a)   Provide for a rest day during the match, and/or a reserve day after the scheduled days of play.
- (b)   Play on any scheduled rest day, conditions and circumstances permitting, should a full day's play be lost on any day prior to the rest day.
- (c)   Play on any scheduled reserve day, conditions and circumstances permitting, should a full day's play be lost on any day. Play shall not take place on more than five days.
- (d)   Make up time lost in excess of five minutes in each day's play due to circumstances outside the game other than acts of God.

Other tour matches shall be as scheduled as in the tour program authorised by the Australian Cricket Board.

3.   Hours of Play, Intervals and Minimum Overs in the Day

3.1   Start and Cessation Times

3.1.1   Test Series
New South Wales, South Australia, Tasmania and Victoria

Session 1	11.00 a.m. – 1.00 p.m.
Lunch	1.00 p.m. – 1.40 p.m.
Session 2	1.40 p.m. – 3.40 p.m.
Tea	3.40 p.m. – 4.00 p.m.
Session 3	4.00 p.m. – 6.00 p.m.

Queensland

Session 1	10.00 a.m. – 12.00 p.m.
Lunch	12.00 p.m. – 12.40 p.m.
Session 2	12.40 p.m. – 2.40 p.m.
Tea	2.40 p.m. – 3.00 p.m.
Session 3	3.00 p.m. – 5.00 p.m.

Western Australia

Session 1	10.30 a.m. – 12.30 p.m.
Lunch	12.30 p.m. – 1.10 p.m.
Session 2	1.10 p.m. – 3.10 p.m.
Tea	3.10 p.m. – 3.30 p.m.
Session 3	3.30 p.m. – 5.30 p.m.

3.1.2 Minimum Overs in the Day in Test Matches

(a)   Play shall continue on each day until the completion of a minimum number of overs or until the scheduled or re-scheduled cessation time, whichever is the later. The minimum number of overs to be completed, unless an innings ends or an interruption occurs, shall be:

(i)   On days other than the last day – a minimum of 90 overs (or a minimum of 15 overs per hour).

(ii)   On the last day – a minimum of 75 overs (or a minimum of 15 overs per hour) for playing time other than the last hour when Clause (e) below shall apply.

(iii)   **Additional Hour:** Subject to weather and light, except in the last hour of the match, in the event of play being suspended for any reason other than normal intervals, the playing time on that day shall be extended by the amount of time lost up to a maximum of one hour. In these circumstances, the minimum number of overs to be bowled shall be in accordance with the provisions of this clause, i.e. a minimum of 15 overs per hour and the cessation time shall be re-scheduled accordingly.

(iv)   If play has been suspended for 30 minutes or more prior to the commencement of the scheduled tea interval, the tea interval shall be delayed for half an hour.

(v)   **Experimental Condition:** subject to both boards' agreement prior to the start of the tour.

If any time is lost and cannot be made up under (iii) above, additional time of up to a maximum of one hour per day shall be added to the scheduled playing hours for the next day, and subsequent day(s) as required (to make up as much lost time as possible). Of this additional time the first 30 minutes (or less) shall be added prior to the scheduled start of the first session, and the remainder shall be added to the last session.

When additional time is added to subsequent day(s), no scheduled day's play shall exceed seven hours. The length of each session of play under this experimental condition is subject to the provisions of Law 15.

Under Law 15.5 timings can be altered at any time on any day if playing time is lost, not necessarily on that day. The captains, umpires and the referee can agree different timings under those circumstances before play starts on any day.

(b)   When an innings ends a minimum number of overs shall be bowled from the start of the new innings. The number of overs to be bowled shall be calculated at the rate of one over for each full four minutes to enable a minimum of 90 overs to be bowled in a day. The last hour of the match shall be excluded from this calculation when Clause (e) shall apply.

Where a change of innings occurs during a day's play, in the event of the team bowling second being unable to complete its overs by the scheduled cessation time, play shall continue until the required number of overs have been completed.

Where there is a change of innings during a day's play (except at lunch or tea), two overs will be deducted from the minimum number of overs to be bowled.

(c)   Except in the last hour of the match, for which Clause (e) makes provision, if play is suspended due to adverse weather or light for more than one hour in aggregate on any day, the minimum number of overs shall be reduced by one over for each full four minutes of the aggregate playing time lost.

(d)   On the last day, if any of the minimum of 75 overs, or as recalculated, have not been bowled when one hour of scheduled playing time remains, the last hour of the match for the purposes of Clause (e) shall be the hour immediately following the completion of those overs.

(e)   Law 16.6, 16.7 and 16.8 will apply except that a minimum of 15 overs shall be bowled in the last hour and all calculations with regard to suspensions of play or the start of a new innings shall be based on one over for each full four minutes (refer (i) below). If, however, at any time after 30 minutes of the last hour have elapsed both captains (the batsmen at the wicket may act for their captain) accept that there is no prospect of a result to the match, they may agree to cease play at that time.

(f)   Notwithstanding any other provision, there shall be no further play on any day, other than the last day, if a wicket falls or a batsman retires or if the players have occasion to leave the field during the last minimum over within two minutes of the scheduled or re-scheduled cessation time or thereafter.

(g)   An over completed on resumption of a new day's play shall be disregarded in calculating minimum overs for that day.

(h)   Except on the final day, if in the event of ground, weather or light conditions causing a suspension of play and/or if the players are already off the field at the re-scheduled cessation time or any time thereafter, stumps shall be drawn.

(i)   Fractions are to be ignored in all calculations regarding the number of overs, except where there is a change of innings in a day's play, when the over in progress at the conclusion shall be rounded up.

(j)   The scoreboard shall show:
         – the total number of overs bowled with the ball currently in use; and
         – the minimum number of overs remaining to be bowled in a day.

(k)   Penalties shall apply for slow over-rates (refer ICC Code of Conduct).

3.2   Extra Time

The umpires may decide to play 30 minutes (a minimum of eight overs) extra time at the end of any day (other than the last day) if requested by either captain if, in the umpires' opinion, it would bring about a definite result on that day (this is in addition to the maximum one hour's extra time provided for in 3.1.1 (a) (iii) above). If the umpires do not believe a result can be achieved no extra time shall be allowed.

If it is decided to play such extra time on one or more of these days, the whole period shall be played out even though the possibility of finishing the match may have disappeared before the full period has expired.

Only the actual amount of playing time up to the maximum 30 minutes extra time by which play is extended on any day shall be deducted from the total number of hours of play remaining, and the match shall end earlier on the final day by the amount of time by which play was previously extended under this clause.

3.3 Use of Lights: Experimental Condition

(2 years from August 1999) – subject to both boards' agreement prior to the tour.

If in the opinion of the umpires, natural light is deteriorating to an unfit level, they shall authorise the ground authorities to use the available artificial lighting so that the match can continue in acceptable conditions. The lights are only to be used to enable a full day's play to be completed as provided in Clause 3 – Hours of Play, Intervals and Minimum Overs in the Day.

In the event of power failure or lights malfunction, the existing provisions of Clause 3 "Hours of Play, Intervals and Minimum Overs in the Day" shall apply. Once the lights have been turned on, they must remain on for the remainder of the day's play.

3.4 Luncheon Interval: Lunch shall be as provided in Clause 3.1. Where an innings concludes, or there is a break in play, within ten minutes of the scheduled interval, the interval will commence at that time and be limited to 40 minutes.

3.5 Tea Interval: Tea shall be of 20 minutes duration from the scheduled commencement time for the interval as provided in Clause 3.1, or at the conclusion of the over in progress at the above time subject to the provisions of Law 15.

Law 15.8 shall be replaced by the following:

If at the scheduled time for the tea interval, the ninth wicket of the innings in progress is already down, and it falls at, or after that time, or falls when less than two minutes remain before that time, play will continue for a period of 30 minutes unless the players have cause to leave the field of play, or the innings is concluded earlier.

3.6 Intervals for Drinks: The provisions of Law 15.9 shall be strictly observed except that under conditions of extreme heat the umpires may permit extra intervals for drinks.

An individual player may be given a drink either on the boundary edge or at the fall of a wicket, on the field, provided that no playing time is wasted. No other drinks shall be taken onto the field without the permission of the umpires. Any player taking drinks onto the field shall be dressed in proper cricket attire.

3.7 Time Keeping: Law 3.4 to apply. A clock on the ground shall be used to regulate the hours of play and intervals. The umpires must notify the ground authority which clock is to be followed, so that the spectators and representatives of the media may be informed. If the clock on the ground is out of order, the watches of the umpires shall determine the time.

3.8 Other Matches

Wherever possible, the above conditions have been applied to all other tour matches. However in the case of one-day matches, starting and finishing times (and interval times) may be altered on any scheduled playing day with the prior approval of the state authority, the ACB and the touring team manager.

4. Law 1.3 Captain

The following shall apply in addition to Law 1.3 (a):

The deputy must be one of the nominated players.

5. Appointment of Umpires

The following shall apply in place of Laws 3.1 and 3.2:

For as long as ICC maintains an international panel of umpires, the following rules for the selection and appointment of Test match umpires shall be followed as far as it is practicable to do so:

(a)   ICC will establish each year a panel of up to 20 umpires nominated by the Test countries and will appoint one umpire from that panel to stand in each Test match.

(b)   The home board shall appoint a committee for the purpose of nominating the other umpire to officiate in each Test match in its country.

(c)   Test match umpires will be nominated by this committee from those umpires officiating in first-class matches during the current season.

(d)   As long as possible before each Test match, ICC will advise the home board of the name of its appointee and the home board will advise the manager of the touring team of both umpires' names.

(e)   The home board shall also appoint a third umpire who shall act as the emergency umpire and officiate in regard to TV replays. Such appointment must be made from the panel of umpires used by the home board for international matches.

(f)   Neither team will have a right of objection to an umpire's appointment.

(g)   The sole authority for handling media enquiries shall be the ACB Media Manager or a nominee appointed by the board.

6.   Substitutes

6.1   Law 2.1 (b) will apply as modified:

(b)   The umpires shall have discretion, for other wholly acceptable reasons, to allow a substitute for a fielder, or a runner for a batsman, at the start of a match or at any subsequent time subject to consent being given by the opposing captain.

6.2   Law 2.5 Fielder Absent or Leaving the Field

Law 2.5 shall apply as modified:

If a fielder fails to take the field with his side at the start of the match or at any later time, or leaves the field during a session of play, the umpire shall be informed of the reason for his absence, and he shall not thereafter come onto the field during a session of play without the consent of the umpire. (See Law 2.6 as modified.) The umpire shall give such consent as soon as practicable. If the player is absent from the field for longer than eight minutes:

(i)   the player shall not be permitted to bowl in that innings after his return until he has been on the field for at least that length of playing time for which he was absent. In the event of a follow-on, this restriction will, if necessary, continue into the second innings.

(ii)   the player shall not be permitted to bat unless or until, in the aggregate, he has returned to the field and/or his side's innings has been in progress for at least that length of playing time for which he has been absent or, if earlier, when his side has lost five wickets.

The restriction in (i) and (ii) above shall not apply if the player has suffered an external blow (as opposed to an internal injury such as a pulled muscle) whilst participating earlier in the match and consequently been forced to leave the field. Nor shall it apply if the player has been absent for very exceptional and wholly acceptable reasons (other than injury or illness) and consent for a substitute has been granted by the opposing captain.

In the event of a fieldsman already being off the field at the commencement of an interruption in play through ground, weather or light conditions, he shall be allowed to count any such stoppage time as playing time, provided that he personally informs the umpires when he is fit enough to take the field had play been in progress.

6.3 Law 2.6 – Player Returning without Permission

Law 2.6 shall apply except that Clause 2.6 (iii) is deleted.

7. Law 3.8 and Law 3.9 – Fitness of Ground, Weather and Light

Add the following to Law 3.8:

If conditions during a rain stoppage improve and the rain is reduced to drizzle, the umpires must consider if they would have suspended play in the first place under similar conditions. If both on-field umpires agree that current drizzle would not have caused a stoppage, then play shall resume immediately.

The umpires shall disregard any shadow on the pitch from the stadium or from any permanent object on the ground.

8. Player Conduct

8.1 "Hitting Up"

Teams are required to observe ground authority regulations and to exercise the utmost care and caution when engaging in practice and pre-match warm-up and "hitting-up" activities so as to avoid the risk of injury to members of the public, damage to the centre wicket region and to perimeter fencing.

8.2 Test Matches

All players shall be bound by the terms of the ICC Code of Conduct for Players and Team Officials.

8.3 Other Matches

State players shall be bound by the terms of the ACB Code of Behaviour. Touring players shall be bound by Law 42.18 and/or the terms of the ICC Code of Conduct for Players and Team Officials.

8.4 Referee: Test Matches

The ICC will appoint an independent referee for all Test matches.

8.5 Other Matches

The local state association shall appoint a representative to meet with the umpires and captains prior to the commencement of the match to secure uniform interpretation of these playing conditions and to adjudicate, if necessary, should there be any dispute.

9. The Ball

9.1 Law 5 – The Ball

The following shall apply in place of Law 5.2:

The home board shall provide cricket balls of an approved standard for Test cricket and spare used balls for changing during a match which shall also be of the same brand. Wherever possible the home board will make available more than one make of approved ball and the captains may agree as to the make to be used. In the event of disagreement between the captains, the home board shall decide by the toss of a coin. The fielding captain or his nominee may select the ball with which he wishes to bowl from the supply provided by the home board. The fourth umpire (or third umpire when no fourth umpire is appointed) shall take a box containing at least six new balls to the dressing room and supervise the selection of the ball.

The umpires shall retain possession of the match ball(s) throughout the duration of the match when play is not actually taking place. During play umpires shall periodically and irregularly inspect the condition of the ball and shall retain possession of it at the fall of a wicket, a drinks interval, at the end of each over, or any other disruption in play.

Note: The Kookaburra "Turf" brand ball has been approved by the Australian Cricket Board.

9.2   Law 5.4 – New Ball in Match of More than One Day's Duration

The following shall apply in place of Law 5.4:

The captain of the fielding side shall have the choice of taking a new ball any time after 80 overs have been bowled with the previous ball. The umpires shall indicate to the batsman and the scorers whenever a new ball is taken into play.

9.3   Law 5.5 – Ball Lost or Becoming Unfit for Play

The following shall apply in addition to Law 5.5:

However, if the ball needs to be replaced after 110 overs for any of the reasons above, it shall be replaced by a new ball. If the ball is to be replaced, the umpire shall inform the batsmen.

9.4   Law 5.6 – Specifications

Law 5.6 shall not apply.

10. Law 6 – The Bat

Add the following sentence to Law 6.1:

The blade of the bat shall have a conventional "flat" face.

11. Law 7 – The Pitch

11.1   Law 7 – The Pitch

In addition to the Law 7.3, the following will apply:

Captains, umpires, the referee and groundsmen should co-operate to ensure that, prior to the start of any day's play, no-one bounces a ball on the pitch or strikes it with a bat to assess its condition or for any other reason, or causes damage to the pitch in any other way.

Prior to the start of play on any day, only the captain and team coach may walk on the pitch to assess its condition. Spiked footwear is not permitted.

Prior to the commencement of a day's play, one TV commentator and camera crew of the official licensed TV broadcaster(s) (but not news crew) may be permitted to inspect the pitch and surrounds subject to the following:

- a ball must not be bounced on the pitch
- a key or knife may only be inserted in the pitch in the area between the popping and bowling creases

In the event of any dispute, the referee in consultation with the home board will rule and his ruling will be final.

11.2   Law 7.4 Changing the Pitch

The following shall apply in place of Law 7.4:

1   In the event of a pitch being considered too dangerous for play to continue in the estimation of the match umpires, they shall stop play and immediately advise the match referee.
2   The match umpires and referee shall consult with both captains.
3   If the captains agree, play shall resume.
4   If the decision is not to resume play, the match umpires shall consider one of the following options:
    - whether the existing pitch can be repaired. Repair work will only be considered if there has been malicious damage to a non-crucial part of the pitch;
    - whether the alternative pitch can be used (but see above);
    - whether the match has to be abandoned.
5   When such a decision is made, the ground authority shall make a public announcement as soon as possible following that decision.

6   In the event of a decision being taken in favour of 4(a) or 4(b) above, the supervision of the remedial or new preparatory work shall be the responsibility of the match umpires and the representative of the ground authority.

7   The re-scheduled starting time and the re-scheduled cessation time, together with any make-up procedures in either the existing or experimental regulations, shall be the responsibility of the match umpires.

8   In the event that the existing pitch can be made playable after suitable remedial work (4(a) above) the match shall continue from the point stopped.

9   If a new pitch is prepared (4(b) above), the match shall be re-started from the first ball (but see above).

10   If the decision is to abandon the match (4 (c) above), the relevant officials from the boards involved shall agree on whether the match can be replayed within the existing tour schedule.

11.3 Law 7.5 – Non-turf Pitches
Law 7.5 shall not apply.

12. Law 8 – The Wickets

The following shall apply in addition to Law 8.2:
For televised matches the home board may provide a slightly larger cylindrical stump to accommodate the stump camera. When the larger stump is used, all three stumps must be exactly the same size.

13. Law 9.3 – The Popping Crease

Law 9.3 shall apply, except that the reference to "a minimum of 6 ft" shall be replaced by "a minimum of 15 yards".

14. Law 10 – Preparation and Maintenance of Playing Area

10.6 Maintenance of Foot Holes – Law 10.6 will apply but add:
The umpires shall see that wherever possible and whenever it is considered necessary, action is taken during all intervals in play to do whatever is practicable to improve the bowlers' foot holes. As soon as possible after the conclusion of each day's play, bowlers' foot holes will be repaired.
Note: Watering the Outfield
In order that the condition of the outfield can be maintained throughout the duration of a match, oval managers/curators must first be granted approval by both captains to water the outfield after any day's play.
Such approval shall not be unreasonably withheld.

15. Law 11 – Covering the Pitch – Before and During a Match

In place of Law 11.2, 11.3 and 11.4, the following shall apply:
In all matches, the pitch shall be entirely protected against rain up to the commencement of play and for the duration of the period of the match. It shall be wholly covered at the termination of each day's play or providing the weather is fine, within a period of two hours thereafter.

     The covers shall be removed no earlier than 5.00 a.m. and no later than 7.00 a.m. on each morning of the match (including the rest day) provided it is not raining at the time, but they will be replaced if rain falls prior to the commencement of play.

     Note: The covers must totally protect the pitch and also the pitch surroundings, a minimum five metres either side of the pitch and any worn or soft areas in the outfield, as well as the bowlers' run-ups to a distance of at least 10 metres.

     Attention is drawn to Clause 7.

16. Drying of Pitch and Ground

(a)   Prior to tossing for choice of innings the artificial drying of the pitch and outfield shall be at the discretion of the groundsman. Thereafter and throughout the match the drying of the outfield may be undertaken at any time by the groundsman, but the drying of the affected area of the pitch shall be carried out only on the instructions and under the supervision of the umpires. The umpires shall be empowered to have the pitch dried without reference to the captains at any time they are of the opinion that it is unfit for play.

(b)   The umpires may instruct the groundsman to use any available equipment, including any roller for the purpose of drying the pitch and making it fit for play.

Note: An absorbent roller may be used to remove water from the covers including the cover on the match pitch.

17. Law 12 – Innings

Law 12.1 (a) shall apply as modified:
(a)   A match shall be two innings per side subject to the provisions of Law 13.1.
Law 12.1 (b) and 12.3 (e) shall not apply.

18. Law 13 – The Follow-On

Add the following to Law 13.1:
If the provision of Clause 3.1 (a) (v) is applied the additional time is regarded as part of that day's play for the purpose of Law 13.3, i.e. it is the number of days remaining and not the total number of hours available.

19. Law 17 – Practice on the Field

The following shall apply in place of Law 17.1:
At no time on any day of the match shall there be any bowling or batting practice on the pitch or the square, except in official netted practice pitch areas. In addition there shall be no bowling or batting practice on any part of the square or the area immediately parallel to the match pitch after the commencement of play on any day. Any fieldsman contravening this Law may not bowl his next over.

   No practice may take place on the field if, in the opinion of the umpires, it could result in a waste of time. In this circumstance Law 42.9 shall apply.

20. Law 18 – Scoring Runs

Law 18.5 shall apply, except Clause (b) (iv) which is deleted.

21. Law 19 – Boundaries

Add the following to Law 19.1:
The playing area shall be a minimum of 140 yards from boundary to boundary square of the pitch. The pitch shall be a minimum 60 yards from one boundary square of the pitch. When this minimum distance is used, the pitch has to be a minimum 80 yards from the opposite square boundary. The straight boundary at both ends of the pitch shall be a minimum of 60 yards. Distances shall be measured from the centre of the pitch to be used.

   Any ground on which a Test or one-day international has been played prior to July 1, 1995 which does not conform with these minimum dimensions shall be exempt from this playing condition. Any new ground must conform to these minimum dimensions.

   If an unauthorised person enters the playing arena and handles the ball, the umpire at the bowler's end shall be the sole judge of whether the boundary allowance should be scored or the ball be treated as still in play or called dead ball if a batsman is liable to be out as a result of the unauthorised person handling the ball. See Law 19.1 (c).

Sight screens shall be provided at both ends of all grounds. Advertising shall be permitted on the sight screen behind the striker, providing it is removed for the subsequent over from that end.

22. Law 21 – The Result

Law 21 shall apply with the following:
Any query on the result of the match as defined in Law 21.1, 21.3, 21.4, 21.5, 21.8 and 21.10 shall be resolved as soon as possible and a final decision made by the umpires at close of play.

23. Law 22 – The Over

Law 22.5 shall apply with the following:
Whenever possible the third umpire or TV umpire shall liaise with the scorers and if possible inform the on-field umpires if the over has been miscounted.

24. Law 24 – No Ball

Law 24.1 (b) shall be replaced by the following:
The bowler may not deliver the ball underarm. If a bowler bowls a ball underarm the umpire shall call and signal dead ball, and the ball is to be re-bowled overarm.

25. Law 24.2 – Fair Delivery – The Arm

Law 24.2 shall apply, except that the reference to "Governing Body" shall be replaced by "ICC Match Referee":

26. Law 24.6 – Ball Coming to Rest in Front of Striker's Wicket

Law 24.6 and Law 24.7 shall be replaced by the following:
In addition, the umpire at the bowler's end shall call and signal "no ball" if a ball which the umpire considers to have been delivered:
  (i)   bounces more than twice or
  (ii)   rolls along the ground or
  (iii) comes to rest
before it reaches the striker or, if not otherwise played by the striker, before it reaches the popping crease. If the ball comes to rest in such circumstances, the umpire will call "no ball" and Law 25.3 shall apply.

27. Law 25.1 – Judging a Wide

Law 25.1 will apply, but in addition:
For bowlers whom umpires consider to be bowling down the leg side as a negative tactic, the one-day international wide interpretation will be applied as follows:

Any offside or legside delivery which in the opinion of the umpire does not give the batsman a reasonable opportunity to score shall be called a wide. As a guide, on the leg side a ball landing clearly outside the leg stump going further away shall be called wide (refer Law 42.6).

28. Law 32 – Caught

Add the following to Law 32.1:
The striker is out under this Law if the ball is deflected from his bat onto the helmet he is wearing and a fair catch is taken. Runs may be scored off deflections from the batsman's or fielder's helmet.

29. Helmets

The following will apply to the batsman:

A batsman may call for a helmet to be brought out to him at any time. He must then wear or carry it personally all the time while play is in progress, or can have it taken off the field at the fall of a wicket, or at the end of an over, or at any drinks interval.

In all cases, no actions involving helmets are to waste playing time. Umpires are not to hold helmets.

30. Law 41 – The Fielder

Law 41 shall apply with the following:

The exchanging of protective equipment between members of the fielding side on the field shall be permitted provided that the umpires do not consider that it constitutes a waste of playing time. A batsman may only change other items of protective equipment (e.g. batting gloves, etc.) provided that there is no waste of playing time.

31. Law 41.2 shall apply, except that Clause (c) is deleted.

32. Law 42.3 – The Match Ball – Changing its Condition

No penalty runs will be awarded under this Law. In the event that any fielder changes the condition of the ball unfairly, the umpires shall report the incident to the referee under the Code of Conduct. Law 42.3 shall apply as modified:

The reference to "Governing Body" shall be replaced by "ICC match referee".

Delete Law 42.3 (d) (iii).

Delete Law 42.3 (e) (ii) and replace with the following:

inform the captain of the fielding side of the reason for the action taken.

And in addition to Law 42.3:

In the event that a ball has been interfered with and requires replacement the batsman at the wicket shall choose the replacement ball from a selection of six other balls of various degrees of usage (including a new ball) and of the same brand as the ball in use prior to the contravention.

33. Law 42.4 – Deliberate Attempt to Distract Striker

No penalty runs shall be awarded under this Law. If the umpires consider that any action by a member of the fielding side is a deliberate attempt to distract the striker the incident shall be reported to the referee under the Code of Conduct. Law 42.4 shall apply as modified:

The reference to "Governing Body" shall be replaced by "ICC match referee".

Delete Law 42.4 (b) (i).

Neither batsman shall be dismissed from that delivery and the ball shall not count as one of the over.

34.   Law 42.5 – Deliberate Distraction or Obstruction of Batsman

Law 42.5 shall apply, and penalty runs shall be awarded, for any wilful attempt to obstruct the batsman as defined in the Law. However, no penalty runs shall be awarded if the umpires consider that a member of the fielding side wilfully attempts to distract the batsman under this Law. Instead, the incident shall be reported to the referee under the Code of Conduct.

Law 42.5 is split into two components and shall apply as modified:

For obstruction:

> The reference to "Governing Body" shall be replaced by "ICC match referee".
>
> Delete Law 42.5 (b) (vi).

For deliberate distraction:

> The reference to "Governing Body" shall be replaced by "ICC match referee".
>
> Delete Law 42.5 (b) (iv).
>
> Neither batsman shall be dismissed from that delivery and the run in progress shall be scored whether or not the batsmen have crossed at the instant of the call.

35. Law 42.6 – The Bowling of Fast Short-Pitched Balls

Law 42.6 (a) (ii) shall be replaced by the following:

(a)   A bowler shall be limited to two fast short-pitched deliveries per over.

(b)   A fast short-pitched ball is defined as a ball which passes or would have passed above the shoulder height of the batsman standing upright at the crease.

(c)   In the event of a bowler bowling more than two fast short-pitched deliveries in an over, either umpire shall call and signal "no ball" on each occasion.

A differential signal shall be used to signify a fast short-pitched delivery. The umpire shall call and signal "no ball" and then tap the head with the other hand.

If a bowler delivers a third fast short-pitched ball in an over, not only must the umpire call "no ball", but he must invoke the procedures outlined in Clause 36 in regard to cautioning the bowler.

If a bowler is no-balled a second time in the innings for the same offence, the umpire shall advise the bowler this is his final warning as provided for in Law 42.7 (b).

A third such offence in the same innings shall cause the umpire to invoke Law 42.7 (c) i.e. the bowler shall be removed forthwith and cannot bowl again in that innings.

The above is not a substitute for Law 42.6 (a)(i) (as amended below) which umpires are able to apply at any time.

36. Law 42.6 (a)(i)

Law 42.6 (a) (i) shall be replaced by the following:

The bowling of fast short-pitched balls is unfair if the umpire at the bowler's end considers that by their repetition and taking into account their length, height and direction, they are likely to inflict physical injury on the striker, irrespective of the protective clothing and equipment he may be wearing. The relative skill of the striker shall also be taken into consideration.

In the event of such unfair bowling, the umpire at the bowler's end shall adopt the following procedure:

(a)   In the first instance the umpire shall call and signal "no ball", caution the bowler and inform the other umpire, the captain of the fielding side and the batsmen of what has occurred.

(b)   If this caution is ineffective, he shall repeat the above procedure and indicate to the bowler that this is a final warning.

(c)   Both the above caution and final warning shall continue to apply even though the bowler may later change ends.

(d) Should the above warnings prove ineffective the umpire at the bowler's end shall:
   (i) At the first repetition call and signal "no ball" and when the ball is dead direct the captain to take the bowler off forthwith and to complete the over with another bowler, provided that the bowler does not bowl two overs or part thereof consecutively. See Law 22.8 (Bowler Incapacitated or Suspended during an Over).
   (ii) Not allow the bowler, thus taken off, to bowl again in the same innings.
   (iii) Report the occurrence to the captain of the batting side as soon as the players leave the field for an interval.
   (iv) Report the occurrence to the executive of the fielding side and to any governing body responsible for the match who shall take any further action which is considered to be appropriate against the bowler concerned.

37. Law 42.6 (b) – The Bowling of Fast, High, Full-Pitched Balls

Law 42.6 (b) shall be replaced by the following:
The bowling of fast, high, full-pitched balls (i.e. beamers) is unfair. Any fast, high, full-pitched ball which passes or would have passed above waist height of the batsman standing upright at the crease shall be called and signalled "no ball" by the umpire at the bowler's end.

In the event of a bowler bowling a fast, high, full-pitched ball, the umpire at the bowler's end shall adopt the following procedure:
(a) In the first instance the umpire shall call and signal "no ball", caution the bowler and issue a first and final warning and inform the other umpire, captain of the fielding side and the batsmen of what has occurred.
(b) At the first repetition call and signal "no ball" and when the ball is dead direct the captain of the fielding side to take the bowler off forthwith and to complete the over with another bowler, provided that the bowler does not bowl two overs or part thereof consecutively.
(c) Not allow the bowler, thus taken off, to bowl again in the same innings.
(d) Report the occurrence to both captains and the ICC match referee responsible for the match who shall take any further action which is considered to be appropriate against the bowler concerned.

38. Law 42.7 – Dangerous and Unfair Bowling – Action by the Umpire

Law 42.7 shall not apply.

39. Law 42.8 – Deliberate Bowling of High Full-Pitched Balls

Law 42.8 shall apply, except that the reference to Clause 6 (b) and 7 be replaced by the procedures of Clause 37 above.

40. Law 42.9 – Time Wasting by the Fielding Side

No penalty runs will be awarded under this Law. In the event of time wasting the umpires shall report the incident to the referee under the Code of Conduct.
Law 42.9 (b) shall apply as modified:
If there is any further waste of time in that innings, by any member of the fielding side, the umpire shall:
Call and signal dead ball.
Inform the other umpire, the batsman and, as soon as possible, the captain of the batting side of what has occurred.

Report the occurrence, with the other umpire, to the ICC match referee, who shall take such action as is considered appropriate against the captain and team concerned.

41. Law 42.10 – Batsman Wasting Time

No penalty runs will be awarded under this Law. In the event of time wasting the umpires shall report the incident to the referee under the Code of Conduct.

Law 42.10 (b) shall apply as modified:

If there is any further waste of time in that innings, by any member of the fielding side, the umpire shall:

Call and signal dead ball.

Inform the other umpire, the batsman and, as soon as possible, the captain of the batting side of what has occurred.

Report the occurrence, with the other umpire, to the ICC match referee, who shall take such action as is considered appropriate against the captain and team concerned.

42. Law 42.12 – Bowler Running on the Protected Area after Delivering the Ball

Law 42.12 shall apply, except that the reference to "Governing Body" shall be replaced by "ICC match referee".

43. Law 42.13 – Fielder Damaging the Pitch

Law 42.13 shall apply, except that Clause (b) (iii) is deleted.

44. Law 42.14 – Batsman Damaging the Pitch

Law 42.14 shall apply, except that Clause (c) (iv) is deleted.

45. Law 42.16 – Batsmen Stealing a Run

Law 42.16 shall apply, except that Clause (v) is deleted.

46. Law 42.18 – Players' Conduct

Law 42.18 shall apply, except that the reference to "Governing Body" shall be replaced by "ICC match referee".

CARLTON SERIES
PLAYING CONDITIONS, 2000-01

Test Match Playing Conditions and the Laws of Cricket (2000 Code) shall apply, except as varied below.

1. Duration of Matches

One-day international matches shall be of one day's scheduled duration. The participating countries in a series may provide for a reserve day on which an incomplete match may be replayed (but not continued from the scheduled day). The matches will consist of one innings per side and each innings will be limited to 50 six-ball overs. A minimum of 25 overs per team shall constitute a match.

2. Hours of Play, Intervals and Minimum Overs in the Day

There will be two sessions of three and a half hours each, separated by a 45-minute break.

2.2   Interval Between Innings

The innings of the team batting second shall not commence before the scheduled time for commencement of the second session unless the team batting first has completed its innings at least 30 minutes prior to the scheduled interval, in which case a ten-minute break will occur and the team batting second will commence its innings and the interval will occur as scheduled.

Where play is delayed or interrupted the umpires will reduce the length of the interval as follows:

Time Lost	Interval
Up to 60 minutes	30 minutes
Between 60 and 120 minutes	20 minutes
More than 120 minutes	10 minutes

Note: Refer also to the provisions of Clause 4.2

2.3   Intervals for Drinks: Two drinks breaks per session shall be permitted, each one hour ten minutes apart. The provisions of Law 15.9 shall be strictly observed except that under conditions of extreme heat the umpires may permit extra intervals for drinks.

An individual player may be given a drink either on the boundary edge or at the fall of a wicket, on the field, provided that no playing time is wasted. No other drinks shall be taken onto the field without the permission of the umpires. Any player taking drinks onto the field shall be dressed in proper cricket attire.

2.4   Extra Time: Provision has been made for up to 15 minutes of extra official playing time in day matches and up to 45 minutes in day/night matches – refer 4.2.1 (a) and 4.2.3.

3.   Appointment of Umpires

(a)   The home board shall appoint both on-field umpires from those umpires officiating in first-class matches during their current season.

(b)   The home board shall also appoint a third umpire who shall act as the emergency umpire and officiate in regard to TV replays. Such appointment must be made from the panel of umpires used by the home board for international matches.

4.   Length of Innings

4.1   Uninterrupted Matches

(a)   Each team shall bat for 50 overs unless all out earlier. A team shall not be permitted to declare its innings closed.

(b)   If the team fielding first fails to bowl the required number of overs by the scheduled time for cessation of the first session, play shall continue until the required number of overs has been bowled.

Unless otherwise determined by the referee, the innings of the team batting second shall be limited to the same number of overs bowled by it at the scheduled time for cessation of the first session. The over in progress at the scheduled cessation time shall count as a completed over. The interval shall not be extended and the second session shall commence at the scheduled time.

The referee may increase the number of overs to be bowled by the team bowling second if, after consultation with the umpires, he is of the opinion that events beyond the control of the bowling team prevented that team from bowling the required number of overs by the scheduled time for the cessation of the innings of the team batting first.

(c)   If the team batting first is all out and the last wicket falls at or after the scheduled time for the interval, the innings of the team batting second shall be limited to the same number of overs bowled to the team batting first at the scheduled time for the interval (the over in which the last wicket falls to count as a complete over).

(d) If the team batting first is dismissed in less than 50 overs, the team batting second shall be entitled to bat for 50 overs except as provided in (c) above.

(e) If the team fielding second fails to bowl 50 overs or the number of overs as provided in 4.1 (b), (c) or (d) by the scheduled cessation time, the hours of play shall be extended until the required number of overs has been bowled or a result achieved.

(f) Penalties shall apply for slow over-rates (refer ICC Code of Conduct for Players and Team Officials).

4.2 Delayed or Interrupted Matches

4.2.1 General

(a) The object shall always be to re-arrange the number of overs so that both teams have the opportunity of batting for the same number of overs. A team shall not be permitted to declare its innings closed.

A minimum 25 overs have to be bowled to the side batting second to constitute a match, subject to the provisions of Clause 4.1 (b).

The calculation of the number of overs to be bowled shall be based on an average rate of 14.28 overs per hour in the total time available for play. If a reduction of the number of overs is required, any recalculation must not cause the match to be rescheduled to finish earlier than the original cessation time. This time may be extended to allow for one extra over for both teams to be added if required.

(b) If the team fielding second fails to bowl the required number of overs by the scheduled cessation time, the hours of play shall be extended until the overs have been bowled or a result achieved.

(c) The team batting second shall not bat for a greater number of overs than the first team unless the latter has been all out in less than the agreed number of overs.

(d) Fractions are to be ignored in all calculations regarding the number of overs.

4.2.2 Delay or Interruption to the Innings of the Team Batting First

(a) If the number of overs of the team batting first is reduced, a fixed time will be specified for the completion of the first session, as calculated by applying the provisions of Clauses 2.2 and 4.2.1 (a).

(b) If the team fielding first fails to bowl the required number of overs by the scheduled time for cessation of the first session, play shall continue until the required number of overs have been bowled, and 4.1 (b) shall apply.

(c) If the team batting first is all out and the last wicket falls at or after the scheduled time for the interval, 4.1 (c) shall apply.

4.2.3 Delay or Interruption to the Innings of the Team Batting Second

If there is a suspension in play during the second innings, the overs shall be reduced at a rate of 14.28 overs per hour for time lost, except that, when the innings of the team batting first has been completed prior to the scheduled or rescheduled time for the interval between innings, the reduction of overs will not commence until an amount of time equivalent to that by which the second innings started early has elapsed.

The hours of play shall be extended by the amount of time lost up to a maximum of 15 minutes in day matches and up to 45 minutes in day/night matches. Calculations because of any time lost thereafter shall be as per 4.2.1 (a).

5. Restrictions on the Placement of Fieldsmen

5.1   Two semi-circles shall be drawn on the field of play. The semi-circles have as their centre the middle stump at either end of the pitch. The radius of each of the semi-circles is 30 yards (27.5m). The ends of each semi-circle are joined to the other by a straight line drawn on the field on the same side of the pitch.

The field restriction area should be marked by continuous painted white lines or "dots" at five-yard (4.5 m) intervals, each "dot" to be covered by a white plastic or rubber (but not metal) disc measuring seven inches (18 cm) in diameter.

5.2 At the instant of delivery, there may not be more than five fieldsmen on the leg side.

5.3 For the first 15 overs only two fieldsmen are permitted to be outside the field restriction marking at the instant of delivery.

5.4 For the remaining overs only five fieldsmen are permitted to be outside the field restriction marking at the instant of delivery.

5.5 Two inner circles shall be drawn on the field of the play. The circles have as their centres the centre point of the popping crease at either end of the pitch. The radius of each of the circles is 15 yards (13.72 m). The field restriction area should be marked by "dots". The segment for the circles reserved for the slip positions shall not be demarcated.

In the first 15 overs there must be a minimum of two stationary fieldsmen within the 15-yard field restriction of the striker at the instant of delivery. When a fast bowler is bowling the two stationary fieldsmen may be permitted to stand deeper than 15 yards (in the undemarcated area) provided only that they are standing in slip, leg slip and gully positions.

5.6 In circumstances where the number of overs for the team batting first is reduced, the number of overs in regard to the restrictions in 5.3 and 5.5 above shall be reduced proportionally in a ratio of 15:50 (30%) in accordance with the table below. Fractions are to be ignored in all calculations regarding the number of overs.

Total overs in innings	No. of overs for which fielding restrictions in 5.3 and 5.5 above will apply
25-26	7
27-29	8
30-33	9
34-36	10
37-39	11
40-43	12
44-46	13
47-49	14
50	15

5.7 Where the number of overs for the team batting second is reduced (including under the provisions of Clause 4.1 (b) and/or 4.1 (c) above), the restrictions in 5.3 and 5.5 above will apply for the same proportion of the second innings as applied in the first innings (fractions to be ignored).

5.8 In the event of an infringement of any of the above fielding restrictions, the square leg umpire shall call and signal "no ball".

6. Number of Overs per Bowler

No bowler shall bowl more than ten overs in an innings.

In a delayed or interrupted match where the overs are reduced for both teams or for the team bowling second, no bowler may bowl more than one-fifth of the total overs allowed. This restriction shall not apply to the team fielding second where the provisions of Clause 4.1(b) have been applied.

Where the total overs is not divisible by five, one additional over shall be allowed to the maximum number per bowler necessary to make up the balance.

In the event of a bowler breaking down and being unable to complete an over, the remaining balls will be bowled by another bowler. Such part of an over will count as a full over only in so far as each bowler's limit is concerned.

The scoreboard shall show the total number of overs bowled and the number of overs bowled by each bowler.

7. No Ball

Short-Pitched Bowling – if the ball passes or would have passed above the shoulder height of the striker standing upright at the crease, either umpire shall call and signal "no ball".

The penalty shall be one run for the no ball, plus any runs scored from the delivery.

8. Wide Bowling – Judging a Wide

Umpires are instructed to apply a very strict and consistent interpretation in regard to this Law in order to prevent negative bowling wide of the wicket.

Any offside or legside delivery which in the opinion of the umpire does not give the batsman a reasonable opportunity to score shall be called a wide. As a guide, on the leg side a ball landing clearly outside the leg stump going further away shall be called a wide.

A penalty of one run for a wide shall be scored. This penalty shall stand in addition to any other runs which are scored or awarded. All runs which are run or result from a wide ball which is not a no ball shall be scored as wide balls.

9. The Ball

The home board shall provide cricket balls of an approved standard for one-day international cricket and spare used balls for changing during a match which shall also be of the same brand.

The fielding captain or his nominee may select the ball with which he wishes to bowl from the supply provided by the home board. The fourth umpire (or third umpire when no fourth umpire is appointed) shall take a new box containing at least six new balls to the dressing room and supervise the selection of the ball.

The umpires shall retain possession of the match ball(s) throughout the duration of the match when play is not actually taking place. During play umpires shall periodically and irregularly inspect the condition of the ball and shall retain possession of it at the fall of a wicket, a drinks interval, at the end of each over, or any other disruption in play.

Where day/night matches are scheduled, white balls shall be used in all matches (including day matches) in a series. Each fielding team shall have one new ball for its innings.

In the event of a ball being lost during play or, in the opinion of the umpires, being unfit for play through normal use, the umpires shall allow it to be replaced by one that in their opinion has had a similar amount of wear.

In the event of a ball becoming wet and soggy as a result of play continuing in inclement weather or it being affected by dew, or a white ball becoming significantly discoloured and in the opinion of the umpires being unfit for play, the ball may be replaced by a ball that has had a similar amount of wear, even though it has not gone out of shape.

If the ball is to be replaced, the umpire shall inform the batsmen. Either bowler or batsman may raise the matter with the umpires and the umpires' decision as to a replacement or otherwise will be final.

Kookaburra "Turf" (white) brand balls as approved by the Australian Cricket Board will be used in all matches.

10. The Result

10.1   A result can be achieved only if both teams have had the opportunity of batting for at least 25 overs, subject to the provisions of Clause 4.1(b) and 4.2.2

(b), unless one team has been all out in less than 25 overs or unless the team batting second scores enough runs to win in less than 25 overs.

All matches in which both teams have not had an opportunity of batting for a minimum of 25 overs shall be declared "no result".

10.2 Tie

In matches in which both teams have had the opportunity of batting for the agreed number of overs, subject to the provision of Clauses 4.1 (b) and 4.2.2 (b), the team scoring the higher number of runs shall be the winner. If the scores are equal, the result shall be a tie and no account shall be taken of the number of wickets which have fallen.

10.3 Delayed or Interrupted Matches – Calculation of the Target Score

Experimental Condition (two years from August 1999) – if, due to suspension of play after the start of the match, the number of overs in the innings of either team has to be revised to a lesser number than originally allotted (minimum 25 overs unless the provisions of 4.1 (b) or 4.2.2 (b) apply), then a revised target score (to win) should be set for the number of overs which the team batting second will have the opportunity of facing. This revised target is to be calculated using the current Duckworth/Lewis method. The target set will always be a whole number and one run less will constitute a tie.

11. Points

11.1 Preliminary Matches

In a competition with three or four Full Members and with a final match or series, the home board may institute a points system as follows:

Win	2
Tie or No Result	1
Loss	0

In the event of the teams finishing on equal points, the right to play in the final match or series will be decided by the most wins in the preliminary matches or, when teams both have equal wins and equal points, the team which was the winner from the preliminary match(es) (played between them) will be placed in the higher position or, if still equal, the higher net run-rate in the preliminary matches. In a match declared no result, run-rate is not applicable.

11.2 Net Run-Rate

A team's net run-rate is calculated by deducting from the average runs per over scored by that team throughout the competition, the average runs per over scored against that team throughout the competition.

In the event of a team being all out in less than its full quota of overs, the calculation of its net run-rate shall be based on the full quota of overs to which it would have been entitled and not on the number of overs in which the team was dismissed.

Only those matches where results are achieved and where the Duckworth/Lewis method for recalculating the target score was not utilised will count for the purpose of net run-rate calculations.

11.3 Final Match or Series

If no result is achieved in a final on the scheduled day of play, the match shall be replayed on the scheduled reserve day. If no result is achieved in the replay on the reserve day, the match shall be declared drawn.

In the event of a drawn final, the prize money will be shared equally between the two competing teams.

In a best of three-final series, a third match will always be played where neither team has a clear two-match advantage after the scheduled completion of the second match.

For the determination of the final series no reference will be made to preliminary match results, wins or run-rates.

In the event of a tied final series, the prize money will be shared equally between the two competing teams.

12. Day/Night Matches

(a) Pads and players' and umpires' clothing shall be coloured.

(b) Sightscreens shall be black.

(c) If during a day/night or a day match played with black sightscreens and white balls, in the opinion of the umpires, natural light is deteriorating to an unfit level, they may authorise the ground authority to use the available artificial lighting so that the match can continue in acceptable conditions.

PURA CUP COMPETITION
PLAYING CONDITIONS, 2000-01

13. Interpretation of Playing Conditions

13.1 Uniform Interpretation

The local state association shall be responsible to ensure uniform interpretation of these playing conditions and to adjudicate, if necessary, should there be any dispute.

13.2 Contrived Result

1. The ACB shall have the power to investigate a game or the actions of the captains of the teams or any player involved in a match, if it suspects reasonably that the competing states with or without the assistance of any other person or club have colluded to contrive the result of a match. If the ACB decides to carry out an investigation, it will conduct such inquiries as it sees fit and invite submissions about the match or the conduct of either captain or any player, and will give the opportunity to be heard to interested parties, including representatives of both teams involved.

2. If the ACB finds that the teams, officials, captains or players have colluded unfairly to contrive the outcome of a match, to the detriment of any other team in the competition, the ACB may in its absolute discretion do one or more of the following:

    (a) fine a team, captain or player;

    (b) suspend a captain from playing in any match or matches;

    (c) disallow any points earned by a team in respect of the match;

    (d) amend any points earned by a team in the match; or

    (e) take such other action as is deemed appropriate by the ACB.

    For the purpose of this playing condition, "colluded unfairly to contrive the outcome of a match" means an agreement designed to contrive the outcome of a match in favour of a particular team or to achieve a result which is unfair to any of the other teams in the same competition. The operation of this playing condition is not intended to prevent competing captains from making aggressive declarations with a view to giving either side the chance of achieving an outright win.

14. Minimum Over-Rates

14.1 Play shall continue on each day until the completion of a minimum number of overs or until the scheduled cessation time, whichever is the latest. The minimum number of overs to be completed, unless an innings or an interruption occurs, shall be:

(a) on days other than the last day – minimum of 96 overs.

(b) on the last day – a minimum of 80 overs (or 16 overs per hour) for playing time other than the last hour when Clause 14.5 below shall apply.

14.2   When an innings ends, a minimum number of overs shall be bowled from the start of the new innings. The number of overs to be bowled shall be calculated at the rate of one over for each full 3.75 minutes to enable a minimum of 96 overs to be bowled in a day, and the time for close of play shall be re-scheduled accordingly.

The last hour of the match shall be excluded from this calculation, when Clause 14.5 shall apply.

Where a change of innings occurs during a day's play, in the event of the team bowling second being unable to complete its overs by the scheduled cessation time, play shall continue until the required number of overs has been completed.

Where there is a change of innings during a day's play (except at lunch or tea), two overs will be deducted from the minimum number of overs to be bowled.

14.3   Except in the last hour of the match, for which Clause 14.5 makes provision, if play is suspended due to adverse weather or light for more than one hour in aggregate on any day, the minimum number of overs shall be reduced by one over for each full 3.75 minutes of the aggregate playing time lost.

14.4   On the last day, if any of the minimum number of 80 overs, or as recalculated, have not been bowled when one hour of scheduled playing time remains, the last hour of the match for the purposes of Law 16.6 shall be the hour immediately following the completion of those overs.

14.5   Laws 16.6, 16.7 and 16.8 will apply except that a minimum of 16 overs shall be bowled in the last hour and all calculations with regard to suspensions of play or the start of a new innings shall be based on one over for each full 3.75 minutes.

If, however, at any time after 30 minutes of the last hour have elapsed both captains (the batsmen at the wicket may act for their captain) accept that there is no prospect of a result to the match, they may agree to cease play at that time.

14.6   Notwithstanding any other provision, there shall be no further play on any day, other than the last day, if a wicket falls or a batsmen retires or if the players have occasion to leave the field during the last minimum over within two minutes of the scheduled or re-scheduled cessation time or thereafter.

14.7   An over completed on resumption of a new day's play shall be disregarded in calculating minimum overs for that day.

14.8   Except on the final day, if in the event of ground, weather or light conditions causing a suspension of play and/or if the players are already off the field at the rescheduled cessation time or any time thereafter, stumps shall be drawn.

14.9   Fractions are to be ignored in all calculations regarding the number of overs, except that, where there is an over in progress at the conclusion of an innings, it shall be rounded up.

14.10   The scoreboard shall show:
  – the total number of overs bowled with the ball currently in use.
  – the minimum number of overs remaining to be bowled in a day.
  – the number of overs above or below the target overs for the day.

15. Penalties for not Achieving Over-Rates

Subject to the provisions of Clause 14 (Minimum Over-Rates), over-rates shall be assessed on 16 overs per hour, i.e. a minimum of 96 overs in a six-hour day, subject to the following deductions:

2 minutes	per wicket taken
4 minutes	for drinks breaks in excess of one per session
actual time	where treatment by authorised medical personnel is required on the ground and/or for a player leaving the field due to serious injury.

Overs will be calculated at the end of the match. For each over short of the target number, 0.1 shall be deducted from the team's match points.

For the purpose of calculation of penalties:

(a) the scheduled last hour of the match, as defined in Clause 14.4, shall be excluded.

(b) a maximum allowance of 20 overs in any hour shall apply.

In the event of a match finishing within three scheduled playing days, penalties for not achieving the required over-rates shall not apply, regardless of the hours played on those days.

16. The Result

16.1 Match Points

(i)	For an outright win after leading on the first innings	6 points
(ii)	For an outright win after a tie in the first innings	6 points
(iii)	For an outright win after being behind on the first innings	6 points
(iv)	For a tie where both teams have completed two innings (irrespective of the first innings result)	3 points
(v)	For a first innings lead (to be retained even if beaten outright)	2 points
(vi)	For an outright loss after leading on the first innings	2 points
(vii)	For a tie on the first innings (and no outright result)	1 point each
(viii)	For an outright loss after a tie in the first innings	1 point
(xi)	For a loss on the first innings	Nil
(x)	For an outright loss after being behind on the first innings	Nil
(xi)	Abandoned or drawn matches with no first innings result	Nil

Law 21 shall apply with the following:

Any query on the result of the match as defined in Law 21.1, 21.3, 21.4, 21.5, 21.8 and 21.10 shall be resolved as soon as possible and a final decision made by the umpires at the close of play.

11.2 Qualifying for the Final

The two teams which have highest aggregate of points at the end of a season shall play off in a final for the Pura Cup for that season (refer Clause 40).

In the event of an equality of points the higher number of outright wins will determine the positions on the Pura Cup table.

Should there be equality in both points and wins, the positions shall be determine by average calculated thus:

(i) divide the total number of runs scored by a state by the total number of wickets lost by it.

(ii) divide the total number of runs scored against a state by the total number of wickets taken by it.

(iii) divide the former (i) by the latter (ii); the team having the higher percentage shall be considered to have the better performance.

For the purpose of the calculations and for individual averages a team declaring its innings closed shall be deemed to have lost only the number of wickets which have actually fallen.

For the purpose of the calculations the provisions of Clause 15 shall apply.

Note: It is possible for a team to record a negative points tally on the Pura Cup table as a result of penalties incurred under the provision of Clause 15 (above).

40.7　Result

The team finishing second must defeat the team finishing first outright to win the Pura Cup; except where 40.1 (c) above applies, whereby the match shall revert to a first innings result.

Note: If the Final is drawn or tied, the team finishing at the top of the points table prior to the Final shall be declared the winner of the Pura Cup.

MERCANTILE MUTUAL CUP
PLAYING CONDITIONS, 2000-01

Pura Cup Playing Conditions and the Laws of Cricket (2000 Code) shall apply except as varied below.

1.　Duration of Matches and Composition of Team

1.1　Mercantile Mutual Cup matches shall be of one day's scheduled duration. The matches will consist of one innings per side and each innings will be limited to 50 six-ball overs. A minimum of 15 overs per team shall constitute a match (finals a minimum of 25 overs per team).

1.2　A team shall consist of twelve players.

Eleven fieldsmen only shall be on the field of play at any one time.

One player in each side shall not be permitted to bat.

Interchange of fieldsmen without restriction is permitted, provided no playing time is wasted.

There will be two sessions of three and a half hours each, separated by a break as per 2.1.1 and 2.1.2.

2. Hours of Play

2.2　Interval between Innings

The innings of the team batting second shall not commence before the scheduled time for commencement of the second session unless the team batting first has completed its innings at least 30 minutes prior to the scheduled interval, in which case a ten-minute break will occur and the team batting second will commence its innings and the interval will occur as scheduled.

Where play is delayed or interrupted the umpires will reduce the length of the interval as follows:

Time Lost	Interval
Up to 60 minutes	30 minutes
Between 60 and 120 minutes	20 minutes
More than 120 minutes	10 minutes

Note: Refer also to the provisions of Clause 4.2.

2.3　Intervals for Drinks

Two drinks breaks per session shall be permitted, each one hour ten minutes apart. The provisions of Law 15.9 shall be strictly observed except that under conditions of extreme heat the umpires may permit extra intervals for drinks.

An individual player may be given a drink either on the boundary edge or at the fall of a wicket, on the field, provided that no playing time is wasted. No other drinks shall be taken onto the field without the permission of the umpires. Any player taking drinks onto the field shall be dressed in proper cricket attire.

2.4　Extra Time

Provision has been made for up to 15 minutes of extra official playing time and up to 45 minutes in day/night matches – refer 4.2.1 (a) and 4.2.3.

11. Points

11.1 Preliminary Matches

Win	4
Tie or No Result	2
Loss	0

11.2 Bonus Points

The team that achieves a run-rate of 1.25 times that of the opposition shall be awarded one bonus point.

A team's run-rate will be calculated by reference to the runs scored in an innings divided by the number of overs faced.

Where matches are shortened and targets revised using the Duckworth/Lewis system, bonus run-rates and defensive targets are derived as a function of the revised target score and maximum overs.

In the event of the teams finishing on equal points, the right to play in the final match will be determined as follows:

- The team with the most number of wins
- The team with the most number of wins over the other team(s)
- The team with the highest number of bonus points
- The team with the highest net run-rate

In a match declared no result, run-rate is not applicable.

A team's net run-rate is calculated by deducting from the average runs per over scored by that team throughout the competition, the average runs per over scored against that team throughout the competition, that is,

net run-rate = Team run-rate per over minus Opponents' run-rate per over.

In the event of a team being all out in less than its full quota of overs, the calculation of its net run-rate shall be based on the full quota of overs to which it would have been entitled and not on the number of overs in which the team was dismissed.

In matches where play is delayed or interrupted, and the match becomes less than a 50-over per team match, the team run-rates will be calculated as follows:

(a) The team run-rate for the team batting second will be the rate achieved in its innings, with such rate being based on the number of overs as set in Clause 10.4.

(b) The team run-rate for the team batting first will be that which was achieved from the same number of highest-scoring overs as set in Clause 10.4 to be bowled to the team batting second.

12. Penalty for not Bowling Required Overs (Second Innings)

If the team fielding second fails to bowl the required number of overs by the scheduled time for cessation of the second session, play shall continue until the required number of overs has been bowled or a result achieved.

Unless determined otherwise the referee, after consultation with the match umpires and the scorers, shall award a penalty of six runs per over to the batting side for each over short of the required number at the scheduled, or re-scheduled, cessation time.

13. Final

13.1 Venue

The Final shall be played at a venue to be determined by ACB.

13.2 Tie

If there is a tie in the Final, the teams competing in the Final shall be declared joint winners.

13.3 No Result

If no result is achieved in the Final on the scheduled day of play, the match shall be replayed on the reserve date as scheduled.

In the event of a no result in the Final (including the reserve day), the team finishing on top of the points table at the end of the preliminary matches shall be declared the winner.

CHANGES TO ICC PLAYING CONDITIONS 2001-02

A summary of the approved changes to the ICC playing conditions for the 2001-02 season is as follows:

Test Matches

- Lost playing time can now be made up on subsequent playing days.
- Minimum number of overs not completed on one day can be made up on the next or subsequent days.
- The use of artificial lighting is to be mandatory where the natural lighting is deteriorating to an unfit level.
- The shadow from a fielder may fall across the striker's half of the pitch as long as the fielder remains still from the time the bowler commences his run-up until the striker has received the ball.
- The umpires shall periodically and irregularly inspect the ball. It is not necessary for the umpires to receive the ball at the end of every over.
- The use of the square for practice will be restricted to any netted area.
- Boundaries shall be designated by a rope or similar object as authorised by the ICC. Where appropriate the rope should be three yards inside the perimeter fencing or advertising signs.
- The legside wide law has been amended so that if a bowler is attempting to utilise the rough, not necessarily as a negative tactic, the strict limited-over wide interpretation shall apply.
- All five-run penalties to apply. In the event of a five-run penalty being awarded, the offending player is also reported under the Code of Conduct.
- Any short-pitched delivery that clearly passes above head height of the batsman standing upright at the crease shall be a no ball.

One-Day Internationals

- A bowler shall be allowed to bowl one short-pitched delivery per over.
- In a competition with three or more Full Members and with a final match or series, the match points shall be Win – 4, Tie or No Result – 2, Loss – 0.
- A bonus point is available to the team that achieves a run-rate 1.25 times that of the opposition (in a competition of three or more Full Members).

Recommendation:

Having regard for the decision made by ACB Directors to adopt ICC playing conditions it is recommended that ICC approved playing conditions for 2001-02 be adopted.

Pura Cup

The Playing Conditions Committee recommends that the following changes apply for the 2001-02 season:

- That four minutes be allowed for one drinks break in any session. This reflects the corresponding ICC playing condition.

ING Cup

- That the available extra time of 15 minutes in day matches and 45 minutes in day/night matches be available in both innings.
- That the six-run penalty for failing to bowl the required number of overs by the scheduled cessation of the second session shall also apply in the first innings.

ACB Cup

- That the captain of the fielding side shall have the choice of taking the new ball any time after 80 overs have been bowled with the previous ball.
- That the delivery following a no ball be a free hit to the batting side.

General

The Playing Conditions Committee has considered the following matters affecting the conduct of the game and recommends as follows:

- That the points demerit system (red/yellow/white card) not be proceeded with as the system was proposed as an alternative to the application of five-run penalties.
- That "ice vests" be permitted to be worn in matches provided that the vests are white, display no branding and are worn under the shirt.
- That the third umpire will not be used in Pura and ING Cup competitions to determine whether a clear catch has been taken.
- That the restrictions applying to under-age bowlers in ACB Youth Championships, ACB Cup and domestic competitions will apply in Pura and ING Cup competitions.
- That in the event of a match being abandoned because of negligent pitch and/or ground preparation it is considered that the match be awarded to the visiting side.

For the purposes of this clause, the home state will be deemed to have been negligent if the match is abandoned as a direct or indirect result of the home state (or any of its employees, contractors or agents) failing to take proper precautions in the circumstances to ensure that:

- the pitch was properly prepared; or
- the pitch was properly protected against the elements or other acts of God, vandalism or foul play, machinery or equipment failure or other reasonably foreseeable events.

The ACB Cricket Operations Department to arrange and ensure that a thorough investigation of the circumstances into the abandonment of the match is conducted and that a report be presented to a forum (to be determined) for decision and penalty if appropriate.

The Committee is strongly of the view that maximum points be awarded where negligence is proven as follows:

Pura Cup	6 points
ING Cup	4 points (no bonus point)

- That the Cricket Operations Department review the guidelines for alternative venues.
- Further to the recommendations on playing conditions included in the Board paper the following be added to the role of the Playing Conditions Committee
  - To brief the ACB representative on ICC Cricket Committee-Playing.
  - To appoint the ACB representative on ICC Cricket Committee-Playing as a member of the Playing Conditions Committee.
  - To receive recommendations from States, ACA, and the Technical Committee for changes to the ICC/ACB Playing Conditions.

AUSTRALIAN CRICKET BOARD
CODE OF BEHAVIOUR

PREAMBLE

Cricket is a game that owes much of its unique appeal to the fact that it is to be played not only within its Laws, but also within the spirit of the game. Any action seen as abusing this spirit causes injury to the game itself.

Embracing the spirit of the game means playing fairly and exhibiting respect for opponents, fellow team members, the umpires and the game's traditional values such as graciousness in defeat and humility in victory.

Cricket has a distinct place in Australian society and history. As an element in Australia's national identity, cricket plays a significant role. This status brings with it particular responsibilities for players and officials to conform to high standards of fair play and personal behaviour on and off the field.

This Code of Behaviour is intended to protect and enshrine such important qualities and standards so that all may continue to enjoy the game of cricket now and in the future.

SECTION 1: RULES FOR BEHAVIOUR

Laws of Cricket and spirit of the game
1. Players must obey the **Laws of Cricket** and play within the spirit of the game.
2. The captain and team coach must use their best efforts to ensure that their team complies with Rule 1 of this Section.

Unbecoming behaviour
3. Players and officials must not at any time engage in behaviour unbecoming to a representative player or official that could bring the game of cricket into disrepute or be harmful to the interests of cricket.

Assaults
4. Players and officials must not assault or attempt to assault:
   a) another player or official, or
   b) a spectator or other person attending a match to which this Code applies.

Intimidation of umpires and dissent
5. Players and team officials must not intimidate an umpire and must accept the umpire's decision. Players and team officials must not show dissent from the umpire's decision.

Crude or abusive behaviour and racial or religious vilification
6. (a) Players and officials must not use crude or abusive language or make crude or abusive gestures.
   (b) Players and officials must obey the Racial and Religious Vilification Code.

Anti-doping policy
7. Players and officials must obey the Anti-Doping Policy.

Betting, match-fixing and corruption

8. Players or officials must not, directly or indirectly, engage in the following conduct:

(a) bet, gamble or enter into any other form of financial speculation on any cricket match or on any event connected with any cricket match;

(b) induce or encourage any other person to bet, gamble or enter into any other form of financial speculation on any cricket match or on any event connected with any cricket match or to offer the facility for such bets to be placed;

(c) be a party to contriving or attempting to contrive the result of any cricket match or the occurrence of any event connected with any cricket match in exchange for any benefit or reward (other than a benefit or reward received from his home board);

(d) fail to perform on his merits in any cricket match for any reason whatsoever (including, in particular, owing to an arrangement relating to betting on the outcome of any cricket match or on the occurrence of any event connected with any cricket match) other than for legitimate tactical reasons in relation to that cricket match;

(e) induce or encourage any player not to perform on his merits in any cricket match for any reason whatsoever (including, in particular, owing to an arrangement relating to betting on the outcome of any cricket match or on the occurrence of any event connected with any cricket match) other than for legitimate tactical reasons in relation to that cricket match;

(f) for benefit or reward (whether for himself or any other person), provide any information concerning the weather, the state of the ground, a team or its members (including, without limitation, the team's actual or likely composition, the form of individual players or tactics), the status or possible outcome of any cricket match or the possible occurrence of any event connected with any cricket match other than in connection with bona fide media interviews and commitments;

(g) engage in any other form of corrupt conduct in relation to any cricket match or event connected with any cricket match;

(h) fail to promptly disclose to the Chief Executive Officer of the ACB that he has received an approach from another person to engage in conduct such as that described in paragraphs (a) to (g) above (such disclosure to be in writing and include full particulars of any such approach);

(i) fail to promptly disclose to the Chief Executive Officer of the ACB that he knows or reasonably suspects that any current or former player or official or any other person has engaged in conduct, or been approached to engage in conduct, such as that described in paragraphs (a) to (g) above (such disclosure to be in writing and include full particulars of any such knowledge or suspicion);

(j) fail to promptly disclose to the Chief Executive Officer of the ACB that he has received, or is aware or reasonably suspects that another player or official or any other person has received, actual or implied threats of any nature in relation to past or proposed conduct such as that described in paragraphs (a) to (g) above (such disclosure to be in writing and include full particulars of any such knowledge or suspicion); or

(k)   engage in conduct that relates directly or indirectly to any of the conduct described in paragraphs (a) to (j) above and is prejudicial to the interests of the game of cricket.

Clothing, footwear and equipment

9.   While playing matches, training, attending official functions or acting in an official or representative capacity for cricket, players and officials must wear and use only that clothing, footwear and equipment approved by or on behalf of the ACB. The wearing or display of a motif or logo not approved by or on behalf of the ACB is not permitted.

Detrimental public comment

10.   Players and officials must not make any public or media comment which is detrimental to the interests of the game or to a tour or series of matches in which they are or are likely to be involved. In particular, they must not:

(a)   denigrate a country in which they are or are likely to be touring or officiating;

(b)   denigrate the home country of a touring team against which they are or are likely to be playing or in respect of which they are or are likely to be officiating;

(c)   make detrimental comment upon the prospects of selection in any team of any player or upon the selection of any team when made; or

(d)   make detrimental comment upon the prospects of appointment of any team official or to the appointment of that person to another official capacity or upon the appointment when made.

Comment on disciplinary proceedings

1.   Players and officials must not make any public disclosure of or any public or media comment upon:

(a)   any report made to the Commission alleging a breach of this Code or of any appeal from a decision of the Commission;

(b)   he proceedings of any hearing of a report or appeal before the Commission; or

(c)   the decision of the Commission in relation to a report or appeal.

SECTION 2: THE CODE OF BEHAVIOUR COMMISSION

Establishment

1. A Code of Behaviour Commission is established.

Powers

2. The Commission is empowered to:

(a)   hear and decide reports and appeals brought under this Code and penalise any breaches;

(b)   hear and decide complaints referred to it under the Racial and Religious Vilification Code and penalise any breaches; and

(c)   deal with any other matter referred to it by the ACB.

SECTION 4: HEARINGS

Procedure

1.   The Commission will hold a hearing into each report made to it. Where appropriate, the Commission may hear more than one report simultaneously where those reports are in respect of the same or related behaviour.

2. The hearing of a report in relation to on-field behaviour (other than a report made by the Chief Executive Officer of the ACB pursuant to Rule 2 of Section 3) will be held promptly after the person against whom the report is made has been informed of the making of the report and its details. In the normal course of events and subject to the availability of a Commissioner, such reports will be heard on the day of the making of the report and no later than the commencement of the next match in which the player or official is scheduled to participate. The Commission may grant an adjournment of the hearing where the player or official demonstrates that an adjournment is essential in order to be given a fair opportunity to prepare a defence. The hearing of a report by the Chief Executive Officer of the ACB pursuant to Rule 2 of Section 3 will be held as soon as practicable after the report has been lodged, having regard always to the requirements to accord procedural fairness to the player or official concerned.

SECTION 5: PENALTIES

1. Subject to Rule 5 of this Section, in the event the Commission decides that any person has breached this Code of Behaviour, it will apply one or more of the following penalties:
    (a) Ban the person from representing Australia in international competition or in any other cricket activity;
    (b) Ban the person from (in the case of a player) being selected in a team or (in the case of an official) being involved in any team or match;
    (c) Ban the person from holding any position within the ACB;
    (d) Fine the person;
    (e) Direct that the person make reparation for damage caused by that person to any property;
    (f) Require the person to undergo counselling for a specified time;
    (g) Require the person to perform voluntary service to cricket or the community;
    (h) Reprimand the person.

2. Subject to Rule 3 and Rule 5 of this Section, when imposing any penalty upon a person who has breached the Code, the Commission may take into account any circumstance it considers relevant, including the following:
    (a) the seriousness of the breach;
    (b) the harm caused by the breach to the interests of cricket;
    (c) the person's seniority and standing in the game;
    (d) remorse shown by the person and the prospect of further breaches;
    (e) the prior record of the person in abiding by this Code, the ICC Code of Conduct and any similar code of behaviour; and
    (f) the impact of the penalty on the person, including the person's capacity to pay a fine as evidenced by the proportion of the person's annual income from the ACB or a state or territory cricket association that the proposed fine represents.

RACIAL AND RELIGIOUS VILIFICATION CODE

1. Purpose of Code

The purpose of this Code is to:

1. Recognise the commitment of the Australian Cricket Board to the elimination of racial and religious vilification of players.
2. Establish a framework for handling complaints made by players who believe they have been subjected to racial or religious vilification by another player.

2. Conduct Covered by the Code

A player who is participating in a match under the jurisdiction or auspices of the ACB will not engage in any conduct, act towards or speak to any other player in a manner which offends, insults, humiliates, intimidates, threatens, disparages or vilifies the other player on the basis of that player's race, religion, colour, descent or national or ethnic origin.

THE ACB'S POSITION ON DOPING

2.1 The ACB condemns the use of performance-enhancing drugs and doping practices in sport. The use of performance-enhancing drugs and doping practices is contrary to the ethics of sport and potentially harmful to the health of athletes.

The only legitimate use of drugs in sport is under the supervision of a physician for a clinically justified purpose.

2.2 The ACB aims to prevent the use of performance-enhancing drugs and doping practices in cricket by:

(a) imposing effective sanctions on persons who commit doping offences;
(b) educating and informing persons about drugs in sport; and
(c) supporting the drug-testing programs and education initiatives of the ASDA and other drug-testing authorities.

SRI LANKA FOURTH ON ICC TABLE

Sri Lanka's 2-1 series win over India moved them into clear fourth place on the revised ICC Test Championship table at September 3, 2001. Prior to this series Sri Lanka shared fourth position with the West Indies, but are now .08 of a point ahead of them.

The updated Championship table shows:

ICC Test Championship Table, September 2001

Team	Played	Won	Lost	Drawn	Points	Average
Australia	13	10	2	1	21	1.62
South Africa	15	10	3	2	22	1.47
England	14	7	5	2	16	1.14
Sri Lanka	13	6	5	2	14	1.08
West Indies	13	6	6	1	13	1.00
New Zealand	15	6	7	2	14	0.93
Pakistan	15	3	7	5	11	0.73
India	13	3	7	3	9	0.69
Zimbabwe	14	2	10	2	6	0.43
Bangladesh	1	0	1	0	0	–

PART SEVEN: MISCELLANEOUS

CHRONICLE OF 2000-01

By NABILA AHMED

AUGUST

19 Steve Waugh blasts ICC's new five-run penalty rule whereby five runs are awarded against a player for breaches of conduct, including sledging. **20** South Africa win final Melbourne's Docklands Stadium limited-overs match by eight wickets to level the series 1-1. Steve Waugh angered by decision to dock Australia two batting overs for taking nine minutes too long to bowl their overs, when South Africa were fined ten per cent of their match fee for being 5.5 overs behind. "The whole thing's ridiculous. Someone's got to look at changing those rules," he said.

SEPTEMBER

1 Three Pakistani cricketers appear before a Pakistan Cricket Board inquiry after they allegedly invited women to their Lahore hotel room before flying out for a tri-nation tournament in Singapore. **4** For the first time in 31 years, West Indies lose a Test series in England, 3-1. **19** Glenn McGrath ends debut season with English county Worcestershire with 114 wickets in all at 11.8. South Australia's Darren Lehmann top-scores in the county competition, with 1,477 runs at 67.13. In Division Two, Hampshire's Shane Warne is the third-highest wicket-taker, with 70 wickets at 23.14. **23** Shane Warne withdraws from October's ICC Knockout Trophy in Kenya to have minor knee surgery. New South Wales all-rounder Mark Higgs is the surprise replacement.

OCTOBER

1 Kenya field three extra players in their warm-up match against Australia, but lose by 93 runs, with Brett Lee taking 5/22. **5** ICC hires Melbourne-based public relations firm Porter Novelli to attend to its image. **6** ACB introduces changes to Mercantile Mutual Cup rules to encourage "brighter" cricket: teams achieving a run-rate one and a half times that of their opposition will receive a bonus point, and slow over-rates will be penalised with six runs for each over not completed on time. Queenslander Carl Rackemann named Zimbabwean coach. Rackemann had been the country's bowling coach since December 1999. **7** Umpire Darrell Hair removed from Sri Lanka's quarter-final match against Pakistan in Nairobi following an ICC administration bungle. ICC chief executive David Richards says Hair, who has not umpired a match involving Sri Lanka since no-balling Muttiah Muralidaran in 1995, will officiate in another match. **8** Nineteen-year-old Yuvraj Singh dominates Australia's pace attack in Australia's first match in the ICC Knockout Trophy, blasting 84 runs off 80 balls. India win by 21 runs, knocking Australia out of the tournament. **10** ACB announces a name change for the domestic first-class tournament, from Pura Milk Cup to Pura Cup, less than 12 months after the Sheffield Shield was cast aside. **13** Prime Minister John Howard introduces a "Bradman clause" as part of Corporations Law to stop commercial exploitation of Sir

Donald's name. Previously, only members of the royal family, people of royal patronage and ex-servicemen's organisations had such protection clauses. John Bradman had asked the Prime Minister to help after Adelaide businesses applied to register names including "Erotica on Bradman". **15** Needing 17 Test wickets to reach a record 500, veteran West Indian paceman Courtney Walsh puts off retirement for another tour of Australia. **17** Former New Zealand captain John Wright named Indian coach after Geoff Marsh pulls out of the race. **18** ICC rules out amnesty for cricketers involved in match-fixing, as former South African captain Hansie Cronje threatens to sue the United Cricket Board of Control for his life ban. The ICC executive board sends declaration forms to all international players, umpires, referees, officials, administrators, employees and curators in an attempt to gather more information about corruption in cricket. **26** Shane Warne to miss six to eight weeks after breaking a finger on his bowling hand during Victoria's Pura Cup match against New South Wales at Richmond Cricket Ground. Warne, who misjudged a skied catch, will require a screw to be inserted in his finger. **30** Michael Slater hospitalised after complaining of shortness of breath and feeling unwell at a national players' camp in Mooloolaba. Steve Waugh announces his intention to continue playing until the next World Cup in South Africa in 2003.

NOVEMBER

1 Indian police arrest three bookmakers who they say were involved in a cricket match-fixing operation. ACB to launch an investigation into Mark Waugh after Indian Central Bureau of Investigation's report on cricket match-fixing and "other related malpractices" suggests the batsman may not have been totally honest with previous inquiries. In the report Mukesh Gupta, believed to be "John" the bookie who paid Waugh for weather and pitch information in 1994, says Waugh was given $US20,000 – five times more than the batsman had previously admitted receiving. Gupta supports Dean Jones' claims that he was offered and rejected $US40,000 for weather and pitch information during Australia's tour of Sri Lanka in 1992. Gupta also implicates captains from all Test-playing nations except Australia, Zimbabwe and Bangladesh. **2** Mark Waugh denies the allegations. **6** Victoria lose six for 20 in less than an hour to be all out for 249 in their Pura Cup match against Queensland at Allan Border Field. Play is ended 23 overs early by a spectacular electrical storm. Victorian vice-captain Darren Berry makes a fourth-ball duck, drops two catches and misses a stumping before vomiting and leaving the field with a viral infection, all in one afternoon. **7** West Indians begin tour of Australia with match against ACB Chairman's XI in Perth, where heavy rain causes play to be abandoned after lunch. Brian Lara and Sherwin Campbell both score centuries, with the slightly overweight Lara blasting three sixes and 11 fours. **8** South Africa's Jonty Rhodes, 31, retires from Test cricket after 52 Tests. Michael Slater shrugs off mystery illness to post a century against Tasmania in a Pura Cup match in Hobart. **9** Playing his first innings since the fresh bribery allegations, Mark Waugh scores 152 for New South Wales against Tasmania in their Pura Cup match at Hobart. With Brian Lara not playing, West Indians are bowled out for 132 by Western Australia in Perth. West Indian bowler Kerry Jeremy receives a fracture in his left jaw when a Matthew Nicholson bumper misses the grill on his helmet. **10** Bangladesh make their Test debut, playing India at the Bangabandhu National Stadium in Dhaka. **12** After a seven-wicket loss in the first-class match against Western Australia, the West Indian cricketers head straight for a net session at the WACA. **13** Indian police register case against former ICC president Jagmohan Dalmiya after a sports promoter and six television executives from the Indian government television network are accused of abusing their positions and engaging in criminal conspiracy. **14** The West Indians beat a Northern Territory Invitational XI by 57 runs in Alice Springs. **15** Dangerous pitch at the WACA Ground forces Mercantile Mutual Cup match between Western Australia and Queensland to be abandoned after just five overs. **17** Left-armer Mathew Inness takes a career-best 6/26 as Victoria bowl out West Indians for 167. The tourists go on to lose the match by an innings and 63 runs inside three days. **18** The Weekend Australian newspaper calls on Mark Waugh and Brian Lara to stand down from the First Test "in the best interests of the sport". Cricket writer Malcolm Conn says England captain Alec Stewart and Pakistan's Wasim Akram, Mushtaq Ahmed, Saeed Anwar and Inzamam-ul-Haq should not take part in their Test match at Lahore. **20** South Africa's Allan Donald becomes the 15th player to reach 300 Test wickets when he traps New Zealand's Shayne O'Connor leg-before. **21** A hamstring strain keeps Jason Gillespie out of First Test. At a Brisbane dinner marking the 40th anniversary of the 1960 Tied Test between Australia and West Indies, the ACB announces Garry Sobers, Alan Davidson, Joe Solomon and Norman O'Neill would be immortalised alongside Sir Frank Worrell, with awards for batsman, bowler, fieldsman, and outstanding individual performance of the series named after them respectively. **22** The Australian women's cricket team flies out to New Zealand to defend the World Cup trophy. **23** Glenn McGrath takes 6/17 off 20 overs as West Indies are dismissed for 82 on the first day of the First Test. Australia go on to win the match by an innings and 126 runs inside three days. **24** Mathew Inness posts return of 6/26 for the second time in five days as South Australia are bowled out for 96 against Victoria at the MCG. **26** South Australia's Shane Deitz becomes the slowest first-class century-maker at the MCG, his hundred against Victoria coming in 438 minutes off 338 deliveries. **29** All-rounder Karen Rolton (51 and 2/41) and debutante Therese McGregor (4/18) lead Australia to a six-wicket win over New Zealand in the first match of the World Cup in Christchurch. **31** West Indies Cricket Board disciplinary committee chairman Lennox John is dismayed at Brian Lara travelling with 18-year-old lingerie model girlfriend Lynssey Ward. "If persons leave to go and play cricket then that must be the objective, not activities that are sure to act as distractions," he says.

DECEMBER

1 In his 64th Test, Glenn McGrath becomes the third Australian cricketer to take 300 Test wickets when he dismisses Brian Lara for a duck on the first day of the Second Test in Perth. Next ball, McGrath becomes the eighth Australian to take a Test hat-trick. **2** After scoring his 18th Test century Mark Waugh says he never felt any pressure from within the Australian team to step down from international cricket following fresh bribery allegations. **3** Australia claims cricket's greatest winning streak: their victory over West Indies by an innings and 27 runs is their 12th consecutive Test victory, eclipsing the 11-game winning sequence posted by West Indies from 1983-84 to 1984-85. Steve Waugh rules himself out of the Third Test in Adelaide with a buttock strain. Michael Bevan becomes New South Wales' highest run-scorer in first-class cricket, edging past Mark Taylor's record of 6,090 runs in the Pura Cup match against Western Australia at North Sydney Oval. Veteran Zoe Goss snares 4/10 off 9.3 overs to lead Australia to their third straight victory at the women's World Cup in New Zealand. **4** Nathan Bracken takes 5/22 as New South Wales rout Western Australia for 89 runs in the second innings to claim outright victory in their Pura Cup match. **5** Uncapped 19-year-old Jamaican Marlon Samuels flies to Australia to replace the injured Shivnarine Chanderpaul. **7** West Indies lose to Prime Minister's XI by four wickets at Manuka Oval despite a heartening 97 by Daren Ganga. West Indies are so depleted by injury that fielding coach Julian Fountain has to take the field. **9** Australia A pile on four for 306 after West Indian captain Jimmy Adams opts to bowl upon winning the toss in a match that was supposed to give his team some much-needed batting practice. **10** Back injury rules Brett Lee out of Third Test. Australian women continue their unbeaten run in New Zealand, beating England by 54 runs to advance to the semi-finals of the World Cup. **11** Brian Lara scores 231 against Australia A, striking 172 in boundaries. **12** In

Johannesburg, groundsman Chris Scott is awarded Man of the Match as South Africa and New Zealand draw a rain-affected Test match. **13** David Boon replaces Geoff Marsh as a national selector. Karen Rolton blasts the quickest limited-overs international century in women's cricket, posting her hundred off 57 deliveries in 66 minutes as Australia race to a nine-wicket win over South Africa. **15** The Third Test begins in Adelaide with Adam Gilchrist in his 12th Test becoming only the third wicket-keeper to captain Australia, after Jack Blackham and Barry Jarman. Brian Lara notches his 15th Test century. **17** Paul Reiffel becomes Victoria's highest wicket-taker in first-class cricket, with 298 wickets. In Adelaide, Stuart MacGill is reported for a breach of discipline after he shoulders West Indian Ramnaresh Sarwan at the foot of the walkway near the players' gate. **18** Colin Miller takes a career-best 5/32 to add to his 5/81 from the first innings as Australia prepares for victory in the Third Test. Australian women again beat South Africa by nine wickets, this time in the semi-final of the World Cup. **19** Australia win the Third Test by five wickets to retain the Frank Worrell Trophy. **23** Australian women lose World Cup final to New Zealand by four runs despite an innings of 91 from captain Belinda Clark. **26** Boxing Day Test gets under way in Melbourne in front of a crowd of 73,233. **27** West Indian wicket-keeper Ridley Jacobs equals the Test record for most catches in an innings with seven catches. Steve Waugh notches up his 23rd Test century. **29** Australia extend their winning streak to 14, defeating West Indies by 352 runs. **30** West Indian Mervyn Dillon, who stepped on a bottle during the First Test, is ruled out of the Fifth Test with an ankle injury.

JANUARY

1 Steve Waugh says Australia are the only team in Test cricket who play to win right from the start. **2** Sherwin Campbell and Wavell Hinds share in a record 147-run opening partnership on the first day of the Fifth Test in Sydney. Shane Warne marks his return to state cricket with three wickets against Western Australia in a Mercantile Mutual Cup match at the WACA Ground. He demonstrates a new delivery – the bouncer. **3** Michael Slater is dismissed in the nineties for the ninth time in Test cricket, equalling Steve Waugh's record. Colin Miller unveils his contribution to Australia's Centenary of Federation celebrations: bright, "Federation blue" hair, prompting gales of laughter from batsman Courtney Walsh, who has to step away from the crease to compose himself. **4** Steve Waugh brings up his 24th Test century. **5** Australia complete first whitewash of a series against West Indies, winning by six wickets. Courtney Walsh is given a guard of honour by the players and a warm ovation from the spectators as he completes his last match on Australian soil. Asked after the match what keeps him going, Walsh, 38, replies, "Utter madness." Warne takes 5/49 off 20 overs to lead Victoria to a Pura Cup win against Western Australia. **9** Australia defeat Victoria by two runs in a friendly match at Junction Oval attended by 7,000 people. In Adelaide, West Indies beat Australia A by four wickets, with Marlon Samuels contributing 45 runs. **11** Steve Waugh celebrates his 300th limited-overs international with a victory over West Indies in the Carlton Series opener. Allan Border says ICC should invest money in West Indian cricket before Asian regions. "I know the ICC are trying to develop the game globally and take it into the Japans and Chinas and those sort of areas but I think we should shore up what we have first," he says. **12** Zimbabwe begin their Australian tour with a 216-run loss against Australia A. **13** Led by an unbeaten 83 from Ricardo Powell, West Indies beat Zimbabwe by one wicket in Brisbane. **14** After being dropped on two, acting captain Adam Gilchrist (98) shares in a 206-run first-wicket partnership with Mark Waugh (112 not out) as Australia defeat West Indies by nine wickets. **16** ACB announces Mark Waugh will be questioned over alleged involvement with bookmaker. The announcement is followed by revelations that South Australia's Darren Lehmann and Peter McIntyre had been interrogated and cleared about betting on the outcome of the Third Test. **17** Brian Lara blasts an unbeaten 116 as torrential downpour leads to an Australian win in Sydney. **18** In the light of the lack of competition in the Carlton Series, Peter Roebuck calls for a quadrangular tournament of 25-over matches, with four teams playing on the same night. **19** Zimbabwe are beaten by an Australian Country XI in a limited-overs match at the Bradman Oval in Bowral. Led by an innings of 167 from former Zimbabwean player Murray Goodwin, Western Australia post a massive 352 in the Mercantile Mutual Cup against New South Wales, who fall short by 72. **22** Mark Waugh refuses to be interviewed in joint ACB and ICC inquiry into allegations that he took bribes from Mukesh Gupta. Waugh's manager releases a statement saying his lawyers have told the ACB the batsman would not meet investigators in February as planned. ACB chief executive Malcolm Speed says Australians were not implicated in claims by former Pakistani cricketer Qasim Omar that bookmakers provided Australian prostitutes for players as part of a match-fixing scam in the 1980s. **23** Captain Heath Streak takes 4/8 off eight overs to lead Zimbabwe to their first victory on tour, beating a West Indian team that was all out for 91. **24** ACB issues Mark Waugh a 24-hour ultimatum, saying in a letter that the batsman will be axed if he does not agree to co-operate with investigations. The letter also details issues over which Waugh will be questioned. The ultimatum angers the Australian Cricketers Association, with president Tim May saying Waugh has been denied basic rights. **25** Mark Waugh cleared to continue playing after his lawyers accede to ACB demands. Waugh says he doesn't believe his reputation has been damaged. **26** West Indies record their fifth single-figure opening partnership from seven limited-overs internationals as Australia win at Adelaide. **27** Belinda Clark fires 76 runs off 93 balls at Bankstown Oval as New South Wales win fifth straight Women's National Cricket League trophy. **28** Australia win sixth limited-overs match in a row after amassing highest total of the summer's Carlton Series. Channel Nine's telecast of the match includes Shane Warne's multiple obscenity in response to Zimbabwean Stuart Carlisle's shot through the covers. **30** Australia complete highest successful limited-overs run chase on domestic soil, losing only four wickets to reach Zimbabwe's 279. Mark Waugh scores an unbeaten century.

FEBRUARY

2 West Indies defeat Zimbabwe by 44 runs in Perth. England Cricket Board left red-faced after its official Cricinfo-run website criticises several team members, including captain Nasser Hussain. **4** Zimbabwe out of Carlton Series after their one-run defeat by Australia. Damien Martyn scores 144 – the fourth-highest limited-overs international innings by an Australian. **6** Brett Lee receives surgery on a severe elbow injury that will keep him out of Australia's tour of India. **7** Australia win first Carlton Series final by 134 runs. **8** Michael Kasprowicz is announced as Lee's replacement. **9** Australia take the Carlton Series, with proceeds from the match to help World Vision raise funds for India's earthquake victims. Brian Lara controversially named Man of the Series. **10** Mark Waugh tells anti-corruption investigators he doesn't recognise Mukesh Gupta. **11** West Indian Marlon Black requires ten stitches to a head wound after he was bashed with a plank of wood outside Sirens nightclub in Melbourne. **12** Steve Waugh awarded the second Allan Border Medal at a Melbourne function. A purple-haired Colin Miller is named Test player of the year, Glenn McGrath limited-overs international player of the year and Darren Lehmann state player of the year. **18** Colin Miller takes a six-wicket haul against India A as Australia begin their tour. **25** Michael Bevan's unbeaten 135 takes New South Wales to victory in Mercantile Mutual Cup final against Western Australia. Sir Donald Bradman passes away at his Adelaide home, aged 92. **27** Wearing black armbands, Australia and India begin their three-Test series with a minute's silence for Sir Donald. **28** Adam Gilchrist scores the second-fastest Test century by an Australian, bringing up his hundred from 84 balls.

MARCH

1 Australia complete 16th successive Test win, beating India by ten wickets in three days in the First Test. Michael Slater, who had a catch appeal dismissed by third umpire Narendra Menon, argued with umpire Srinivas Venkataraghavan before verbally clashing with batsman Rahul Dravid. Steve Waugh describes Slater's behaviour as "over the top" and Slater later apologises to Dravid. The match referee takes no action. **2** England seek a shorter, four-Test Ashes series in 2002-03, ahead of the World Cup in South Africa. **3** ICC ranks Australia equal third with India on incidents requiring action by the match referee as at the end of 2000. Pakistan's Inzamam-ul-Haq heads the individual indiscretion list. For the first time in history, a batsman is stranded on 99 by a declaration in domestic competition when Victorian captain Paul Reiffel declares with Michael Klinger one run short of his maiden century. **5** New South Wales wicket-keeper Brad Haddin flies to India as reinforcement for Adam Gilchrist, who has a strained hip. **6** Slater blames the media for blowing up the Dravid incident. "What I was actually saying was very constructive and in no way abusive to anyone," he recalled. Tom Moody retires from cricket having played 300 first-class matches, including eight Tests. Moody, who with 9,520 runs is Western Australia's all-time leading first-class run-scorer, will take up a position as director of coaching at English county Worcestershire. **7** A Sri Lankan magistrate orders the arrest of former Test captain Arjuna Ranatunga for alleged assault on students who hit a cricket ball into the grounds of his family home. **8** Saurav Ganguly turns up late for a tour match between Australia and Indian Cricket Board President's XI and then does not take the field for 35 minutes. **9** Bishen Bedi says Steve Waugh is the "most outstanding captain" in modern cricket. **10** Michael Slater fined half his match fee for the First Test and given a one-match suspended ban for six months for publicly commenting about the handling of the Dravid clash. **11** Off-spinner Harbhajan Singh takes India's first Test hat-trick as Australia lose seven for 98 in the final session on the first day of the Second Test. **14** V. V. S. Laxman and Rahul Dravid bat through the entire fourth day of the Test. **15** V. V. S. Laxman makes India's highest Test score of 281. India become only the third Test side to win a match after following on, after breaking Australia's winning sequence with a 171-run defeat. **16** Australian coach John Buchanan raises the possibility of dropping Shane Warne for the Third Test, saying the spinner may not be fully fit. **17** Andrew Symonds in doubt for limited-overs series in India after he sustains a freak injury while packing. Standing on an esky to reach up, he fell and hurt his shoulder. **19** Matthew Hayden scores 203 to help Australia to a first-innings total of 391 on the first day of the Third Test. Steve Waugh becomes the sixth man in Test cricket to be given out handling the ball. **20** Courtney Walsh becomes the first to reach 500 Test wickets with his dismissal of Jacques Kallis on the third day of the Second Test between West Indies and South Africa. Australian Malcolm Speed named new ICC chief executive. **23** India beat Australia by two wickets to win Border-Gavaskar Trophy. With 35 wickets at 16.69, 20-year-old Harbhajan Singh is named Man of the Series. **25** In front of 650 people at the Sir Donald Bradman memorial service at Adelaide's St Peter's Cathedral, John Bradman pleads with the public to let his father "go free". "Don't enslave him with worship," he says. **26** Australia lose first limited-overs international by 60 runs despite a 90-ball 99 from Matthew Hayden, who successfully persuaded the selectors to let him stay on in India after the completion of the Test series. **27** In Brisbane, Victoria lose Pura Cup final by seven wickets amid controversy surrounding the umpiring. Queensland captain Stuart Law, who was dropped twice, caught off a no-ball and had an appeal for a low catch by Michael Klinger ruled in his favour by the third umpire, marvels at his luck: "Fourteen million, isn't it – Powerball Thursday night? I'll go and buy a ticket tonight," he says. **28** Mark Waugh posts his 18th limited-overs international century as Australia win by eight wickets. Champions Cup, a round-robin tournament involving domestic limited-overs winners from India, New Zealand, South Africa and Australia, begins in Western Australia. **31** Sachin Tendulkar passes 10,000 runs in limited-overs cricket as India defeat Australia by 118 runs. Steve Waugh thought Saurav Ganguly had tried to claim the toss even though the coin came down on the Australian's call, heads. "It was a different coin today and I couldn't figure out whether it was heads or tails. I don't know what the fuss is about. I never said I won the toss," says Ganguly.

APRIL

4 After a 219-run partnership between Matthew Hayden and Ricky Ponting – an Australian record limited-overs partnership outside Australia – the tourists thrash India by 93 runs to level the limited-overs series 2-2. Saurav Ganguly turns up for the toss 15 minutes early wearing an Indian training shirt, in breach of ICC regulation which stipulates captains must wear match clothes at the toss. Coached by Trevor Chappell, Bangladesh arrive in Zimbabwe promising to perform "as well as we possibly can" on their first Test tour. **6** Wisden attacks ICC over match-fixing inaction, accusing the body of being "besotted by the opiate of their importance". **7** Australia win the limited-overs series despite a maiden century from V. V. S. Laxman. At the toss this time, Saurav Ganguly was already out on the field when Steve Waugh was getting ready to walk out. Referee Cammie Smith calls Ganguly back to the boundary rope where he has to join Waugh for the captains' walk to the wicket. **8** Ganguly says he is happy to see Australia go. "It just pissed me off. They are complaining just about anything and everything. They are supposed to be a good team but to see them complain every time is just schoolboy stuff," he says. **14** Australia's team for the Ashes tour is announced. With the average age of 30, the touring party is said to be the oldest ever, with the exception of the post-war teams of 1921, 1926 and 1948. **19** Western Australian fast bowler Duncan Spencer becomes the first cricketer to be banned for using an illicit substance. Spencer, who tested positive to nandrolone, is banned for 18 months after a seven-hour hearing in Melbourne. In a Centenary of Federation celebration match, an Aboriginal and Torres Strait Islander Commission XI defeat a Prime Minister's XI by six wickets with three balls to spare. West Indian cricket authorities introduce a fine for dropped catches in the Fifth Test against South Africa. **26** Pakistani fast bowler Shoaib Akhtar cleared over the legality of his action with the aid of a report from the University of Western Australia. **28** Harbhajan Singh is offered the post of deputy superintendent of police by his home state of Punjab as well as 500,000 rupees and a small plot of land as reward for his bowling in the Test series victory against Australia.

MAY

1 Martin Love, Nathan Bracken and Ashley Noffke are included in the new list of ACB contract players. Matthew Elliott, Michael Hussey, Michael Kasprowicz and Andy Bichel are dropped. ICC anti-corruption chief Sir Paul Condon hands match-fixing report to the head of ICC conduct commission. The report concludes that some players, umpires and officials are so deeply involved in match-fixing that they cannot stop for fear of losing their property and lives. It finds match-fixing may have occurred as recently as Pakistan and New Zealand's limited-overs series which finished in April. **7** Australian coach John Buchanan's role is under review after he cast doubt on Shane Warne's involvement in the Third Test in India. **8** In his book *Retired Hurt*, Sri Lanka's Roshan Mahanama alleges Glenn McGrath called him a "black monkey" during the second limited-overs final of the 1995-96 season in Australia. **9** ACB reveals Colin Miller, Adam Gilchrist and John Buchanan received suspicious phone calls from an Indian man on the morning of India's victory in the Third Test. The man allegedly inquired about the general state of the match and pitch. **10** ACB announces the highest-paid Australian cricketer will receive projected potential payments of $1.162 million by the end of season 2002-03. **11** ACB sacks John Buchanan as selector on the Ashes tour but Steve Waugh says the decision is wrong. **23** Steve Waugh welcomes the idea of a Test championship but questions the wisdom of a system that awards series wins rather than every Test win. Ansett Airlines announced as the major sponsor of Australian Test cricket for the next five years. **24** Sir Paul Condon says the previously publicised inquiry is "only the tip of the iceberg" as ICC releases its report into match-fixing. The report's recommendations include plans for the ICC to implement training programs to raise awareness of the risks of corruption, the appointment of full-time security managers by full member nations to prevent and detect improper approaches to players, and restrictions on mobile phone usage by players during international matches. **25** On the eve of the Ashes tour, Steve Waugh says Australia go to England as underdogs after losing their last two Tests; he later says it was just a "throwaway line". **28** The Australian team re-enacts at Gallipoli a match played by ANZAC troops on Shell Green during the 1915 Gallipoli campaign.

JUNE

5 Nathan Bracken's Ashes tour is endangered by a shoulder injury during Australia's loss to Middlesex in a limited-overs match. **7** England's Nick Knight is struck by a spectator during a pitch invasion that mars Pakistan's 108-run win in the opening limited-overs international of the tri-nation series. Shane Warne ends his seven-year association with Nike. **8** James Sutherland appointed chief executive of the ACB. The 35-year-old former Victorian fast bowler takes over from Malcolm Speed, who replaces David Richards as the chief executive of ICC. **9** Australia defeat Pakistan by seven wickets in their first limited-overs match of the series. **12** England suffer their eighth limited-overs defeat in a row, losing to Pakistan by three runs despite 137 runs from Marcus Trescothick – the highest limited-overs score by an Englishman at Lord's. **14** England are dismissed for their lowest score in limited-overs cricket, managing just 86 runs as Australia win by 125 runs under the Duckworth/Lewis method. Steve Waugh pledges players will not question any umpiring decision during the Ashes tour. **17** A steward is hospitalised with broken ribs and a damaged spleen after he is trampled and kicked as Pakistani fans try to souvenir stumps with their team still four runs short of victory. Play cannot be resumed; England's captain Alec Stewart concedes the match. **18** At a London meeting, ICC unanimously endorses interim report of Sir Paul Condon's anti-corruption unit. **19** Steve Waugh takes his team off after a firecracker explodes within metres of Brett Lee in the outfield during Australia's match against Pakistan. Play resumes after 17 minutes, and Pakistan win by 36 runs. **21** England lose an unprecedented 11th successive limited-overs international, going down by eight wickets against Australia. **23** Australia cruise to a nine-wicket victory over Pakistan in the final of the tri-nation series. Michael Bevan is hit in the face by a full beer can hurled onto the balcony during the presentation ceremony. Christopher Bassano, who played for the Tasmanian Second XI in 2000-01, scores 186 not out and 106 on his first-class debut, playing for Derbyshire. **24** Cathryn Fitzpatrick's career-best return of 5/29 leads Australia to a commanding position on the first day of the First Test against England at Shenley. **25** Simon Katich brings up his maiden century for Australia against MCC at Arundel. Australia's Michelle Goszko strikes a stunning 204 to equal the record Test score by a woman. **26** Australian women win first Ashes Test by an innings and 140 runs an hour after lunch on the third of four scheduled days. **28** Brendon Julian retires from representative cricket. The 30-year-old Western Australian, who played seven Tests in a 12-year career, will be the newest reporter on the Nine Network's *Getaway* program.

JULY

2 Damien Martyn replaces Justin Langer in the Test team after Langer's four first-class innings on tour bring just 21 runs. **4** Steve Waugh is presented with ICC Test World Championship trophy at Edgbaston. **5** England begin the Ashes campaign without key batsmen Michael Vaughan and Graham Thorpe because of injury. Nathan Bracken undergoes arthroscopic surgery in Sydney to determine the extent of damage to his injured left shoulder. **6** Australian women begin the Second Test, with Karen Rolton striking a Test record of 209 not out against England at Headingley. **7** Adam Gilchrist dazzles with 152 on the third day of the First Test. He sets a new record for the number of runs scored by one player in an Ashes Test over, taking 22 runs off Mark Butcher, who saw the first, third and final ball go for six, the fourth for four and the second deflect off his hands in a difficult caught-and-bowled chance. Steve Waugh later declares Gilchrist's hand the best he has seen in Test cricket. **8** Australia win the First Test by an innings and 118 runs. Australian women claim the Ashes series with a nine-wicket victory over England. **9** Nasser Hussain ruled out of the Second Test because of a broken little finger suffered during the First Test. Malcolm Speed takes over as ICC chief executive. Soon after, Speed writes personally to each of the ten Test captains, asking for their support in upholding standards of conduct on the field of play. **12** Alec Stewart supports decision to appoint Michael Atherton England's stand-in captain. **13** Carl Rackemann says he will leave his coaching position in Zimbabwe when his contract ends in August due to "commitments back home, especially my farm". **14** Damien Fleming takes 6/59 on the second day of the tour match against Somerset. **15** Australian women dismiss the Irish for 46 in a crushing 201-run win, the 11th victory of their 11-match tour of the British Isles. **19** The on-again off-again Super Challenge limited-overs series between Australia and India set down for September is cancelled after ACB receives advice from the Board of Control for Cricket in India that it is unable to send a team. **22** England crash to an eight-wicket defeat at Lord's in the Second Test after a dramatic batting collapse – the last six wickets fell in 39 minutes and 48 balls – leaves Australia with just 14 runs to win. **24** Jack Russell, at 37, offers to come out of retirement from Test cricket for the remainder of the Ashes series. "If the England selectors want me to come back for one, two or three Tests against the Australians this summer, then I would love to help," he tells London's *Daily Mail*. **25** Speaking at the Trafalgar Square launch of the year-long countdown to the Commonwealth Games, Steve Waugh defends the England team. "England aren't playing that badly. The results look very one-sided but we know it's a good contest out in the middle," he says. Women's Cricket New South Wales announces Julie Hayes as the new state captain after Belinda Clark decides to play for Victoria in the 2001-02 season of the Women's National Cricket League. Clark, who played for New South Wales for 17 years, had moved to Melbourne in 2000 to take up a position as the chief executive officer for Women's Cricket Australia. **28** Alan Mullally strengthens his Ashes claims by taking five Australian wickets as the tourists are dismissed for 97 in a morning by Hampshire. Western Australia's Mike Hussey scores 329 not out for Northamptonshire, a record for the county. **29** Rod Marsh resigns as the head coach of the AIS Cricket Academy to take up a position with the England and Wales Cricket Board as director of its new National Cricket Academy. Hampshire inflict the first defeat of the Australians in a first-class match on the Ashes tour with a thrilling two-wicket victory. It was Hampshire's first win over the Australians since 1912. **31** Australian coach John Buchanan denies a document proclaiming "psychological control" over England was intentionally leaked to the media ahead of the

Third Test. His memo, which relates theories from fifth-century BC Chinese warrior Sun Tzu's book *The Art of War* to Australia's Ashes campaign, was slipped under the door of journalists as well as players by a receptionist at the team's Southampton hotel.

AUGUST

1 Two letters written by the late Sir Donald Bradman to former Australian Test captain Greg Chappell are sold for $6,700 at a Melbourne auction. The letters, which were written shortly after Chappell joined Kerry Packer's World Series Cricket in 1977 and revealed a wide rift between the two, were bought by a local buyer. Chappell's decision to sell the letters had been opposed by the Bradman Foundation, with Bradman's son John claiming his father would have been unhappy that his private letters were being sold in public for profit. **4** At 4 p.m. on the third day of the Third Test, Australia reach their 158-run victory target to clinch the series and win the Ashes for the seventh time in a row. Captain Steve Waugh, who tore a calf muscle while attempting a single, is expected to miss the rest of the series. Waugh says Australia should now be allowed to take the original Ashes urn home. **6** Tim Lamb, chief executive of the England and Wales Cricket Board, says, "There is absolutely no question of the original Ashes urn leaving Lord's – it belongs at Lord's." Alec Stewart disagrees. "They deserve it, and the Australian public should have the chance to see exactly what their team's been winning," he writes in his Cricinfo column. Bob Simpson announces he will quit as Lancashire coach at the end of the season. **7** Mark Waugh is cleared of corruption allegations following ACB's Anti-corruption Investigator Greg Melick's investigations into allegations made by Indian bookmaker Mukesh Gupta. "Mark has consistently denied any wrongdoing and I can find no basis on which to recommend that any charge be laid," Melick says.

OBITUARIES

By WARWICK FRANKS

BASSANO, BRIAN STANLEY, died on July 10, 2001 at Launceston. Born at East London, South Africa, on March 21, 1936, Brian Bassano was widely known and respected in the cricket communities of South Africa, England and Australia as a forthright and perceptive writer with a deep and abiding commitment to the best traditions of the game. He moved to England in the 1960s to further his career as a journalist and also played club cricket with the Sussex Martlets. Back in South Africa, in the 1970s he made a practical gesture against apartheid by forming the Rainbow Cricket Club, one of the first multi-racial cricket clubs, one of whose members was the journalist Donald Woods. Simultaneously, he spent some seasons managing the Border side in the Currie Cup competition. After moving to Port Elizabeth in 1981 Bassano was also involved in the promotion of township cricket for the Eastern Province and South African Cricket Associations, also putting his experience to good use as a radio commentator. In 1988 he moved to Launceston where he continued his journalism, again mainly in a freelance capacity, although he did celebrate spending five years with that city's *Examiner*, the longest period for which he held himself in bond as a salaried journalist. His encyclopaedic knowledge of the game in his homeland is contained in *South Africa in International Cricket 1888-1970* (1979), out of which came a 30-part television series, and is also reflected in *The MCC in South Africa 1938-39* (1997). He teamed with Rick Smith in writing *The West Indies in Australia 1930-31* (1990), *A Springbok Down Under: South Africa on Tour 1931-32* (1991) and *Vic's Boys: Australia in South Africa 1935-36* (1993), books which were crucial additions to previously neglected episodes in Australian cricket. His last work, which appeared at the time of his death, was a monograph on Aubrey Faulkner in the ACS *Famous Cricketers* series. Fascinated by the intricacies of cricket such as leg-spin, and enthralled by the history of the game and those who played it, Bassano interviewed countless cricketers of the past and present, all of whom responded warmly to his enthusiasm, knowledge and tact. His son, Chris (1975-), a product of the Launceston Cricket Club, made a spectacular entry to the English county scene by becoming the first player to score a century in each innings on debut in a County Championship match, when he made 186 not out and 106 for Derbyshire against Gloucestershire at Derby in June 2001.

BEARD, BARRY ALLAN, died on June 9, 2001, at Ulverstone, on Tasmania's north-west coast. Born at Bothwell, in Tasmania's Midlands, on December 21, 1941, Barry Beard was educated at Ulverstone High School. A slimly-built left-hander with an array of stylish strokes, his moment came in January 1975, when the state selectors finally paid attention to his claims, by selecting him at the age of 33 for the two games against the MCC tourists. The first, at Hobart, was rain-affected, and Beard had the mortification of being run out for one. Immediately afterwards, the two teams met again at Launceston, on an underdone and spiteful pitch. He went in with the score at four for 74 which quickly became eight for 82, but Beard then made a composed 49 in 130 minutes, being well supported by Gerry Davies (26) in a ninth-wicket partnership of 61. His handling of Derek Underwood was particularly adept, and his judicious shot selection brought him five fours and two sixes. The day after this game finished, he played in the semi-final of the Gillette Cup, against New Zealand at the MCG, but he made only two on the losing side. A consistent player for the Ulverstone club in the North West Tasmania Cricket Association competition, he was still making runs in the 1982-83 season when he scored 316 at 79.00. Beard's long service to the club as player, secretary and treasurer was recognised by the award of life membership. He spent many years in the employment of the farm machinery firm of William Adams Proprietary Limited.

	M	I	NO	R	HS	100s	50s	Avge	Ct	St	W	Avge	BB
First-class	2	3	0	51	49	0	0	17.00	1	0	0	–	–

BEDFORD, ALBERT AUSTEN, died on March 25, 2001, at Noarlunga in the southern suburbs of Adelaide. Born at Rose Park, Adelaide on September 12, 1932, Bert Bedford played some lower-grade cricket for Glenelg before moving to the Adelaide club in 1952-53. Over the next four seasons, he played a small number of first-grade games as an orthodox left-arm spinner yet, at the beginning of the 1956-57 season, he was promoted to the state side to cover the absence of Jack Wilson, who was still on his way back from the 1956 tour of England, Pakistan and India. It was during this season that he secured his best first-class bowling figures when he took 4/80 against New South Wales at Sydney, his victims being Jim Burke, Ian Craig, Richie Benaud and Alan Davidson. Possessing a distinctive slinging action, Bedford was not a big spinner of the ball, instead relying on line and length to pin down and frustrate batsmen. These virtues of his bowling were seen to advantage against Western Australia at Adelaide in 1957-58, when his 32.6 overs in the visitors' first innings produced a return of 3/45. Curiously, although he was an extremely modest left-handed batsman in grade cricket, he made something of a specialty of useful late-order contributions at the first-class level. He joined in five partnerships of over 50, the highest coming when he made 28 of an eighth-wicket partnership of 85 with Phil Ridings (86 not out) against Queensland at Adelaide in 1956-57. Bedford became an expert drinks carrier, being twelfth man for South Australia on seven occasions before he was finally dropped from the side after an unproductive three matches in the first half of the 1958-59 season. Between 1952-53 and 1972-73, he scored 944 runs at 12.25 and took 298 wickets at 18.43 for his club, with best figures of 6/20 against Glenelg in 1958-59. On the Saturday following his death, the Adelaide A-grade team members wore black armbands as a mark of respect.

	M	I	NO	R	HS	100s	50s	Avge	Ct	St	W	Avge	BB
First-class	15	22	5	277	32*	0	0	16.29	10	0	33	41.60	4/80
Domestic first-class	13	19	3	266	32*	0	0	16.63	9	0	28	42.39	4/80

BRADMAN, DONALD GEORGE, died at his home in the Adelaide suburb of Kensington Park on February 25, 2001. See full obituary earlier in this volume.

	M	I	NO	R	HS	100s	50s	Avge	Ct	St	W	Avge	BB
First-class	234	338	43	28,067	452*	117	69	95.14	131	1	36	37.97	3/35
Domestic first-class	62	96	15	8,926	452*	36	20	110.20	38	1	12	37.00	3/54
Test	52	80	10	6,996	334	29	13	99.94	32	0	2	36.00	1/8

CLEMENTS, SHANE CLIFTON, died on April 22, 2001, at his home in the southern Perth suburb of Inglewood. Born on June 28, 1958, at Middle Swan, in Perth, Shane Clements was an opening batsman of style and purpose who had to vie for a place in the state team with the likes of Bruce Laird, Graeme Wood, Geoff Marsh and Mike Veletta. Educated at John Forrest High School, he made an immediate impact as a teenager with the Bassendean–Bayswater club from whence he was selected for Western Australia's Colts side. Clements started his first-class career magnificently when, playing against Queensland in Western Australia's last home match of the 1981-82 season, he made 73 and 86, sharing in opening stands of 127 and 171 with his club team-mate Geoff Marsh. Next season, he failed to capitalise on this start and only appeared in four games, but in 1983-84 batted with real consistency, scoring fifties in each of his first three games. He followed this with an innings of prolonged resistance and capable strokeplay when, against Tasmania at Launceston, his 151 helped Western Australia to snatch the first-innings points which ensured a home Sheffield Shield final. In that final, his 28 in the second innings, while being small numerically, was an important psychological contribution to his side's win, as it blunted the pace of Jeff Thomson and Craig McDermott. He made 480 first-class runs at 40.00 for the season. In 1984-85, Clements again batted usefully without playing a big innings, his highest score of the season being the 60 he made against Sri Lanka in his last match before being dropped permanently from the state side. He subsequently played grade cricket with the Mount Lawley and Wanneroo clubs.

	M	I	NO	R	HS	100s	50s	Avge	Ct	St	W	Avge	BB
First-class	20	33	1	1,114	151	1	8	34.81	15	0	0	–	–
Domestic first-class	18	29	0	1,017	151	1	7	35.07	15	0	0	–	–
Dom. limited-overs	7	7	0	123	35	0	0	17.57	2	0	1	61.00	1/61

COLLINS, FRANK HENRY KENNETH, died on January 24, 2001, at Penola, in the south-east of South Australia. Born in the Port Adelaide district of Queenstown on December 16, 1910, Frank Collins was educated at Woodville High School. He made his initial first-grade appearance for the Port Adelaide club at the age of 17 during the 1928-29 season, marking the occasion by taking a wicket with his first ball. After a season with the Colts side, he returned to Port Adelaide to establish a reputation as a lively medium-pace bowler who was difficult to get away and a lower-order batsman who was capable of scoring useful runs. Early in the 1933-34 season he took 6/27 and 6/21 against Kensington, the latter return including a spell of 5/1 during which he took a hat-trick. Performances such as this led to his selection in the state side against New South Wales at Adelaide in December. He made an excellent start by bowling Don Bradman for one, while in his next match, against Queensland, he made 36, joining with "Perka" Lee (55) in adding 54 in 36 minutes for the seventh wicket. The slightly built Collins spent most of the next three seasons in the South Australian side but, although maintaining admirable accuracy (13 of his 24 first-class victims were bowled), he found regular hauls of wickets difficult to maintain. His best return came against Victoria at Adelaide during the 1934-35 season when he took five of the first six wickets to fall for 78 in the first innings and then helped his side to a comfortable victory by removing both Len Darling and Jackie Scaife in the second when they were building a partnership which offered their team a faint sniff of victory. By 1939 he was living and working in the Penola district, although he continued to appear for Port Adelaide until 1946-47. He took a total of 234 first-grade wickets at 19.48 and made 2,034 runs at 17.60, including a century against Glenelg during the 1933-34 season. His son, Dean (1942–), played for South Australian Country against the West Indians at Berri in 1960-61 and emulated his father by taking a wicket with his initial ball in first-grade for Port Adelaide against East Torrens in 1964-65.

	M	I	NO	R	HS	100s	50s	Ct	St	W	Avge	BB
First-class	15	23	4	311	37*	0	0	9	0	24	45.83	5/78
Domestic first-class	13	19	4	279	37*	0	0	9	0	22	45.23	5/78

COSGROVE, ERNEST WILLIAM, died at Concord General Hospital, Sydney, on October 18, 2000. Born in the inner-western Sydney suburb of Annandale on June 12, 1949, Ern Cosgrove had a distinguished career as a scorer whose work became synonymous with speed, accuracy and comprehensiveness. His skills had their genesis when, as a 13-year-old, he began scoring for his brother's Saturday morning team. In 1967-68 he began his formal association with his beloved Balmain, initially as scorer, then as secretary and delegate to the New South Wales Cricket Association from 1980 to 1985, and, finally, as delegate to the Sydney Cricket Association from 1988 to 1993. From 1977-78 he began scoring for visiting teams at the Sydney Cricket Ground, learning from and working with the masterful Dave Sherwood until the latter's death in 1985. Cosgrove then succeeded to the position of both Australian and New South Wales scorer until chronic ill-health caused by kidney failure forced his retirement in 1996. A teacher of commerce and geography, in the late 1980s Cosgrove was posted to Moree High School, in the remote north-west of New South Wales. His scoring duties necessitated an eight-hour drive to Sydney the night before the match and a return as soon as the game finished, but a later appointment to North Sydney Boys' High School eased this situation considerably. Shortly before his death he was one of the recipients of the Australian Sports Medal awarded in conjunction with Sydney's hosting of the

Olympic Games and directed to recognising a cross-section of those who had contributed to the creation of the nation's sporting excellence.

COWDREY of TONBRIDGE, Baron, died at Littlehampton, West Sussex, England, on December 5, 2000. Although Michael Colin Cowdrey's death is more fully memorialised in the 2001 English edition of *Wisden*, it is fitting that his Australian connection should be mentioned in these columns, given that his Test career opened and closed in Australia and that 27 of his 114 Test matches were played here on six tours. Moreover, his cricket and his demeanour inspired the warmest affection and the most unalloyed respect in Australian players and the cricketing public. He first toured Australia in 1954-55 as a 21-year-old and quickly made his presence felt with a century in each innings against a strong New South Wales attack. In the second innings of the Second Test, at Sydney, he made a calmly determined 54 in 193 minutes, and his fourth-wicket partnership of 116 with Peter May (104) set England on the road to the first of three successive victories and the retention of the Ashes. In the next Test, at Melbourne, he dominated his side's innings of 191 with 102 made in four hours of batsmanship of the highest quality. As Australians saw more of Cowdrey, there grew a feeling of bafflement that such an elegant player, who had the ability to dominate any attack, could seemingly drift into a becalmed state of introspective strokelessness. In the Second Test at Melbourne in 1965-66, in only 197 minutes, he made a felicitous and stroke-filled 104. The beauty of this innings was in stark contrast to his wearisome effort in the Third Test of the 1958-59 series where he took 365 minutes to make 100 not out, an innings characterised by his repeated and ugly thrusting of the pad at Benaud's leg-spin. On the 1962-63 tour, he made the highest score by a player on tour in Australia when he made 307 against South Australia in only 389 minutes and was joined by Tom Graveney (122 not out) in a fifth-wicket partnership of 344. After the First Test of the 1974-75 series, when the bruising pace of Lillee and Thomson injured John Edrich and Dennis Amiss, Cowdrey's presence was requested and he thus equalled the record of the mercurial Johnny Briggs in making a sixth visit to Australia. Nearly forty-two years of age, he epitomised Maurice Leyland's reported dictum on facing fast bowling: "None of us likes it but not all of us lets on." Almost straight off the plane, he played in the Second Test at Perth, making 22 and then resisting defiantly for 137 minutes in scoring 41 against the Australian pace attack at its most frighteningly destructive. Even the most rabidly chauvinistic Australian supporter responded warmly to the dignified courage and self-deprecating charm of this perennially popular English player.

	M	I	NO	R	HS	100s	50s	Avge	Ct	St	W	Avge	BB
First-class	692	1,130	134	42,719	307	107	231	42.89	638	0	65	51.21	4/22
Test	115	188	15	7,624	182	22	38	44.06	120	0	0	–	–
Int. limited-overs	1	1	0	1	1	0	0	1.00	0	0	0	–	–

FITZMAURICE, DUDLEY JAMES ANTHONY, died on June 28, 2001, in Melbourne. A capable all-rounder, Dud Fitzmaurice spent much of the 1930s on the fringes of the powerful Victorian team of that time, four matches spread over six seasons being scant reward for his talents. Born on May 21, 1913, in the Melbourne suburb of Carlton, his batting was marked by a liking for powerful straight and cover driving, while he bowled accurately at a lively pace, with the ability to swing the ball both ways. After playing two matches against Tasmania in 1933-34, he did not get another chance until the Melbourne game against the island state in the February of the next season. Even then, it was as a late replacement, but he showed his capabilities by scoring 102 in 162 minutes from the No. 9 position. Coming in with the score at seven for 134, partnerships of 140 for the eighth wicket with Stan Smith (92) and 78 for the ninth wicket with Harry Britt (37) allowed Victoria to total 370. He had to wait until 1938-39 for his final game. Fitzmaurice played with South Melbourne from 1930-31 to 1945-46, a period which included five games with the Colts side in 1932-33, scoring a total of 2,808 runs at 23.1 and taking 198 wickets at 23.6. Subsequently, he moved to captain Brighton in the sub-district competition for a few seasons and, in 1947-48, his astute leadership, particularly of an unknown spinner named Jack Iverson, was an important factor in the club winning their first premiership for over 20 years. His younger brother, Des (1917–81), played two matches for Victoria in 1947-48 and toured India with the Commonwealth team in 1949-50.

	M	I	NO	R	HS	100s	50s	Avge	Ct	St	W	Avge	BB
First-class	4	7	3	230	102	1	0	57.50	0	0	134	67.00	1/24

FRANCIS, JOHN CHARLES, died on July 6, 2001, at Camberwell, Melbourne. Jack Francis spent the major portion of his long life in the suburb of Hawthorn, where he was born on June 22, 1908, and for whose Australian Rules team he played six games in 1926, the year after the club had entered the Victorian Football League competition. He also played cricket for the Hawthorn–East Melbourne Cricket Club from 1926-27 to 1937-38, scoring 2,666 runs at 26.39 and taking 23 wickets at 26.93. During a period of enormous strength in Victorian cricket, he was tried as a specialist batsman in only three matches, all against Tasmania in the 1932-33 season. In the first of these, at Launceston in December, he opened the innings and claimed the distinction of making a century on debut, his 135 occupying 193 minutes of pleasant strokeplay, he and Hector Oakley (53) adding 108 for the third wicket. Francis played baseball with the Melbourne Cricket Club and later played over 800 games with the lawn bowls section of the MCC, continuing to play until only several months before his death. A younger brother, Jim (1911-), played football for Carlton and was later a well-known coach of both Carlton and St Kilda.

	M	I	NO	R	HS	100s	50s	Avge	Ct	St	W	Avge	BB
First-class	3	4	0	186	135	1	0	46.50	1	0	0	–	–

GEHAN, RODNEY ARTHUR HOWARD, died on February 8, 2001, at Hope Island, on Queensland's Gold Coast. Born at Werribee, Victoria, on November 12, 1942, the powerfully built Rod Gehan burst onto the Adelaide scene with the Woodville club in the 1960-61 season. Lightning fast, he could intimidate batsmen with sheer speed, their discomfiture being enhanced by his wildly erratic approach. In a match against East Torrens during his first season, he delivered 19 wides and three no-balls during his 11 overs in the first innings and followed this with seven no-balls in three overs in the second innings. He was given one state game, against Victoria in Melbourne, at the beginning of the 1962-63 season, when he took 2/51 in the second innings, including Colin McDonald in his final appearance in first-class cricket. Doubts about his action culminated in being called for throwing during the 1964-65 season and he was dropped, although the club selectors later recalled him when they were convinced that he had rectified the problem. Next season he transferred to the Sturt club but was again called after several matches, and this time he was unable to return to the side. In his six seasons of Adelaide cricket he took 110 wickets at 18.82. In 1967-68, he made one appearance for Randwick in the Sydney grade competition in a rain-interrupted match before moving to such areas as Papua New Guinea, Indonesia and north Queensland in the course of his employment.

	M	I	NO	R	HS	100s	50s	Avge	Ct	St	W	Avge	BB
First-class	1	2	1	4	2*	0	0	4.00	0	0	2	44.00	2/51
Domestic first-class	1	2	1	4	2*	0	0	4.00	0	0	2	44.00	2/51

GULLIVER, KENNETH CHARLES, died on June 11, 2001, at the northern Sydney beachside suburb of Collaroy. Ken Gulliver's cricket was an expression of the values which were the core of his being. His skill and scrupulous fairness sprang from his commitment to a belief that the game enshrined some of the important moral and religious values that should shape a well-lived life. Born at East Maitland in the Hunter Valley of New South Wales on August 14, 1913, he was educated at Sydney Technical High School, and in 1927 began an association with the Mosman club that was to last

for the rest of his life. Having made
his initial first-grade appearance in
1930-31, he quickly became a fixture
in the side and his all-round skills
were vital components of the three
premierships Mosman secured
during the 1930s. The slightness of
his frame (167 cm and 65 kg) did not
hinder the free-stroking aggression of
his left-handed batting, while his
method as a big-turning leg-spinner
was, as usual, caught to perfection by
Ray Robinson: "His arm comes right
over the top, and he clears a passage
for it by tucking his head over, like a
fowl going to roost." Gulliver
captained New South Wales Colts in
each of the three games in which he
played against the Queensland Colts
side. On the first of these occasions,
at the beginning of the 1935-36
season, he made 129 not out and
joined Jack Walsh in adding 126
entertaining runs for the seventh
wicket in only 63 minutes at the
Sydney Cricket Ground No. 2.

Gulliver appeared at a time when
competition for a place in the New
South Wales side as a spinner was
particularly keen, so his chances were sporadic at best. After two games in 1936-37, he
did not appear for the state again until 1938-39, when he was appointed captain against
Queensland at Sydney, after New South Wales found that its four Test players were
unavailable. Despite making 31 and 40 he was dropped immediately, only to lead the
New South Wales Second XI against Victoria shortly after, his figures of 5/22 and 4/23
being crucial in his side's comfortable victory. He played three games during the 1940-
41 season and, in the first of these, against a Combined Queensland–Victorian side at
Brisbane, he returned his best first-class analysis of 5/80, each of his dismissals being
caught behind by Ron Saggers. During World War II he saw service in both the Army
Medical Corps and as a welfare officer with the War Service Department of the YMCA.
He was a regular member of the state side when first-class cricket resumed in the 1945-
46 season and made his highest score of 72 not out against the Australian Services side,
joining Ken Grieves (102 not out) in a rollicking partnership of 151 for the eighth wicket
in 104 minutes.

He then returned to his monumental career with the Mosman club. During the war he
had been unstoppable: in 1941-42 he took 98 wickets and, two seasons later, followed
this up with 660 runs and 88 wickets. Gulliver played first-grade uninterruptedly from
1930-31 to 1962-63, scoring 9,309 runs at 35.80, while his 1,028 wickets at 18.30 place
him second among Sydney grade wicket-takers behind Hugh Chilvers, who claimed
1,153 victims. That his potency remained undiminished is highlighted by the fact that
in both 1956-57 and 1957-58, when he was in his mid-forties, he made more than 400
runs and took 40 wickets. Furthermore, his fielding in front of the wicket was a thing of
wonder – fearless, with a sure pair of hands and a bullet-like throw, his presence was as
good as having an extra bowler. Gulliver, however, still had another quarter-century of

service to give to his club. Drawing on his playing experience and the tactical skills he had gained in his 15 years as first-grade captain, he gave invaluable advice and guidance to a legion of younger players in the lower grades. He finally retired at the age of 76 when, playing for the club's B Reserve side in the local competition, he had not been dismissed for two seasons. By that stage he had lifted his aggregate for the club to 14,275 runs and 1,533 wickets, while the club had accorded him life membership in 1957 and enshrined his name in the gates leading to Mosman Oval.

He had a parallel career in baseball which was as substantial as his cricket achievements. He captained Mosman, New South Wales and Australia and went on to a long period of involvement as an administrator of the sport, besides giving commentary on ABC radio. His service to sport was recognised in 1985 when he was awarded the Medal of the Order of Australia. Gulliver spent many years as a company representative and sales co-ordinator in the engineering industry but it was his active involvement in all facets of the life of the Anglican Church which was particularly important to him. His business background and church commitment were expressed through his work with the Gideons International organisation.

	M	I	NO	R	HS	100s	50s	Avge	Ct	St	W	Avge	BB
First-class	12	16	3	451	72*	0	3	34.69	10	0	22	40.13	5/80
Domestic first-class	3	5	0	111	40	0	0	22.20	6	0	3	43.33	1/4

GUY, JAMES JOHN, died on August 2, 1999 at Launceston, the city where he had been born in 1914. Having been educated locally at St Patrick's College, Prospect, he played cricket in Launceston but his career was cut short when a bale of wool fell on his leg, causing permanent damage to his knee. He took up umpiring after World War Two, officiating in eight first-class games between 1946-47 and 1962-63, including matches against visiting MCC, West Indian, South African and Australian touring teams. Guy's long period of service in local cricket continued until 1980 and was recognised by the award of life membership of the Northern Tasmanian Cricket Umpires' Association in 1974 and the Northern Tasmanian Cricket Association in 1977. Further endorsement of his contribution to the community came in 1986 when he was appointed as an Officer of the Order of Australia. He began his working life as a clerk in the Tasmanian Railways, before becoming, successively, paymaster at the Examiner newspaper and an officer with the Launceston Bank for Savings.

HANLIN, DAVID WALTER, died suddenly on June 6, 2001, at Chester, Cheshire, while on a trip to the United Kingdom. Born in the inner-western Sydney suburb of Ashfield on December 8, 1928, Dave Hanlin was educated at North Sydney Boys' High School and played first-grade for Manly at the age of 16. Having enrolled as an engineering science student at the University of Sydney, he quickly became an important member of the cricket club's attack, his height (185 cm) and powerful build allowing him to bowl with pace and control. In his first full season, 1947-48, he took 9/51 against Petersham, and more wickets in the next season saw him play for the state second eleven and then the Sheffield Shield side against South Australia at the SCG as a late replacement for Keith Miller. Hanlin played in the first two matches of the 1949-50 season, his best performance coming against Western Australia at Sydney. In his side's first innings, he scored 19, the 42 he added for the ninth wicket with Fred Johnston being crucial in pushing his side towards a modestly respectable total. With the wind behind him, he then took two quick wickets, finishing the innings with 3/26, but this was his last first-class outing, as he acted as twelfth man in both matches of the ensuing southern tour. He continued to be a force in grade cricket, taking 8/70, including a hat-trick, against North Sydney in 1951-52, his last season in Sydney where he took a total of 200 first-grade wickets at 16.48. Having joined the regular army, Hanlin was transferred to Perth, where he spent four seasons with Claremont–Cottesloe as an effective opening partner to the former state player Peter Dunn.

From 1962 to 1969, he served as a construction engineer in south-east Asia, including Vietnam. He was promoted to the rank of colonel in 1975 and retired in 1983 as Chief Engineer, Headquarters 1st District, having been awarded the Medal of the Order of Australia in the Military Division in 1981 for his service to the Australian Army in the field of Army construction. The sporting interests of his wife and daughters saw him take an active part in the administration of sports in which they were involved, culminating in his appointment as manager of the Australian diving team at the 1982 Commonwealth Games in Brisbane. A brother, Peter (1931–2000), was Australian shot put champion on seven occasions and was a member of the Australian team at the 1956 Olympic Games in Melbourne.

	M	I	NO	R	HS	100s	50s	Avge	Ct	St	W	Avge	BB
First-class	3	5	1	46	19	0	0	11.50	1	0	8	23.75	3/26
Domestic first-class	3	5	1	46	19	0	0	11.50	1	0	8	23.75	3/26

HAWKE, NEIL JAMES NAPIER, died at North Adelaide on December 25, 2000, after two decades during which he conducted a series of prolonged and courageous battles against debilitating and extreme ill-health. Born in the Adelaide suburb of Cheltenham on June 27, 1939, he was educated at Woodville High School and made his mark as an 18-year-old Australian Rules footballer with the Port Adelaide club. Despite kicking 15 goals from full-forward in his third game, he was dropped two games later, so it was not surprising that he accepted an offer from East Perth for the 1958 season. Having been a dominant factor in successive premierships for the club and representing Western Australia in 1959, Hawke's cricketing ability as an all-rounder with North Perth saw him called into the state side at the beginning of the 1959-60 season. He celebrated the occasion by making a determined 89 against Victoria at Perth but, thereafter, runs and wickets proved to be elusive and he was dropped for the last match of the season. He then returned to Adelaide where he became a fixture in both the Port Adelaide and state sides for the next eight seasons. Despite an ungainly, sidling approach to the wicket, his strong shoulder action and a full follow-through allowed him to swing the ball late and cut the ball sharply. Inevitably known as "Hawkeye", he constantly varied his line of attack, often bowling around the wicket, while his tall, robust frame allowed him to bowl for long spells at a lively fast-medium pace. He was a capable batsman with a well-organised defence whose strength was his ability to drive powerfully and with discernment. This all-round ability was seen to advantage during the 1961-62 season when, as South Australia crushed his former state by 274 runs, he followed an undefeated 58 with figures of 7/38 and 5/44.

Early in the next season, he reaffirmed his value by making 46 and 37 not out and taking 6/130 against the MCC tourists. Continued useful performances led to his Test debut in the last match of the series, at Sydney. He continued his advance during 1963-64 when he played in four of the five Tests against South Africa. In the Fourth Test, at Adelaide, Hawke was both persistent and economical as he took 6/139 as the South African batsmen flayed the other bowlers in amassing a total of 595. In the final Test, at Sydney, he came to the crease as last man with three hours of play remaining and Australia only 120 runs in front. He kept a cool head for 75 minutes in making 16 not out, as he and Tom Veivers (39) added 45 and made the game safe for their side. When he was selected for the 1964 tour to England it was widely predicted that he would relish the conditions there; prediction became achievement as he took 34 wickets in May, including 6/19 from 21 overs against Nottinghamshire on a docile Trent Bridge pitch. On the tour as a whole, Hawke was second in the bowling aggregates with 83 wickets. He took 6/47 in the first innings of the final Test, at The Oval, the match in which he became Fred Trueman's 300th Test dismissal. In the previous Test, at Headingley, he had come in with Australia struggling at seven for 178 in reply to England's 268. With Peter Burge (160) playing an innings of power and authority, Hawke batted sensibly for 99 minutes as he made 37 of a partnership of 105 which was

the prelude to a comprehensive English defeat.

The 1964-65 season saw Hawke at the height of his powers as in nine matches he scored 560 runs at 70.00 and topped the national aggregates with 41 wickets at 24.31, figures which made him an obvious choice for Australian Cricketer of the Year. His value was epitomised in South Australia's traditional Christmas match against Queensland, when he followed figures of 5/92 with his only first-class century. In the second innings, with his side at six for 196 and still 17 short of making the visitors bat again, Hawke proceeded to bat so forthrightly for the remaining 218 minutes of the game that he made an undefeated 141 with 19 fours, his rousing straight driving completely quelling the Queensland attack.

He continued his good form on the subsequent tour of the West Indies, where he was Australia's best bowler, claiming 24 Test wickets at 21.83 as he made skilful use of normally unpropitious conditions for his type of bowling. In the Third Test, at Georgetown, he took 6/72 and 4/43 in a losing cause, although he was able to contribute six wickets to Australia's lone victory, in the Fifth Test, at Port of Spain. In addition, he played several innings of real fortitude, most notably in scoring 45 not out and 33 to record the highest aggregate for Australia in the First Test, at Kingston.

In 1965-66, Hawke was again the season's most successful bowler with 49 wickets at 25.73. In the Third Test against England, at Sydney, he returned his best Test bowling analysis of 7/105 from 33.7 overs, an unremitting effort which could not prevent Australia losing by an innings. When the result was reversed in the next Test, at Adelaide, he contributed 5/54 in the second innings. He toured South Africa in 1966-67, but was largely ineffective and took only four wickets in the two Tests in which he appeared. Next season, he was back at his potent best, taking 48 wickets at 19.54, although in a season of experimental Test selection against India, he was only called on for the last of the four Tests. Against New South Wales, however, at Sydney he produced his best first-class bowling performance in taking 8/61. Again taken to England in 1968, his powers seemed to desert him and he only took 35 wickets for the tour, managing but a single wicket in the first two Tests. He appeared twice for Tasmania in 1968-69, making him one of the small group of cricketers to have represented three states, and then returned for a season to the Lancashire League club, Nelson, for whom he had played in 1967. He toured Pakistan with a Commonwealth team in 1970-71 before transferring to East Lancashire for whom he played between 1971 and 1974.

When he had returned to Adelaide in 1961, he played football for the West Torrens club, thrilling the crowds with huge kicks, using the drop punt style that he had made his trademark. Hawke was part of the South Australian team which in 1963 gained its first home win over Victoria since 1926. He is still the only player to have represented both Western Australia and South Australia at football and cricket. While living in England in the 1970s and running a sports store, he honed his golfing skills to the point where, with a handicap of two, he was able to enter the British Amateur Golf Championship. A journalist by profession, he wrote for the now-defunct Adelaide papers the News and the Sunday Mail, prior to undertaking television commentary on Sheffield Shield matches for Channel Nine.

In July 1980, following bowel surgery, he suffered complications involving two years of massive infection and failure of the major organs, together with repeated cardiac arrest. He faced the necessity of extensive surgical intervention and a prolonged period of intensive care and drip-feeding, supported by the selfless devotion of his wife, Beverley, and the consolations of his religious faith. Having defied the odds with courage almost beyond mortal ken, his litany of suffering continued in the last decade when he was subjected to heart failure, blood poisoning, damage to the central nervous system, cirrhosis of the liver and hepatitis B and C. Hawke had always been a gregarious and generous man who had embraced life to the full, and his unflinching and uncomplaining struggle only increased the universal love and respect in which he was held. His former team-mate Terry Jenner spoke for Hawke's friends and admirers when he said: "His ability to go through barriers that kept coming in front of him was remarkable. The fact that he still kept his sense of humour and was able to absorb pain and press forward was an inspiration to us all." As a mark of respect, the Australian team wore black armbands on the second day of the Second Test against West Indies. His autobiography, *Bowled Over*, was published in 1982.

	M	I	NO	R	HS	100s	50s	Avge	Ct	St	W	Avge	BB
First-class	145	198	57	3,383	141*	1	11	23.99	85	0	458	26.39	8/61
Tests	27	37	15	365	45*	0	0	16.59	9	0	91	29.42	7/105
Domestic first-class	50	82	24	1,812	141*	1	9	31.24	29	0	169	29.74	8/61

HONOUR, VICTOR GERALD, died on January 3, 2001, at the western Brisbane suburb of Brookfield. Born in the village of Bierton, near Aylesbury in Buckinghamshire, Vic Honour was educated at The King's School in the Lincolnshire town of Grantham. In 1927 his father's health dictated that the family seek a warmer climate; Queensland was chosen as a result of the family's befriending an Australian serviceman from Yandina who was on leave in England during World War One. Having played with both Northern Suburbs and Toombul, in 1932-33 he began an association with the University club that lasted until he left Brisbane in 1948 and during which he compiled 4,942 first-grade runs at an average of 28.54, including eleven centuries. A productive 575 runs at 52.28 in 1933-34 was rewarded with state selection during the next season but, despite an extended trial, he was unable to reproduce his grade form at the higher level. His best game was against New South Wales at Sydney when, batting at No. 4, he scored 30 in the first innings and added 66 for the third wicket with Cassie Andrews (118). He followed this with his highest first-class score of 34 in the second innings, while, in the next match, against South Australia at the Gabba, he made his side's second top score of 32 in the first innings. In 1935-36 he was chosen for his second Colts match against New South Wales and compiled a solid and organised 81, while in 1937-38 he made 141 in the annual Intervarsity match with Sydney. He scored another century (112 not out) in 1946-47 in the last of his six appearances in these matches. Captain of the University side from 1937-38, his leadership was an important factor in his side's A-grade premiership in 1940-41. Honour was extensively involved in administering the game. Having been a member of the University club's committee over a number of seasons, he was president from 1940-41 to 1945, in addition to being a club delegate to the Queensland Cricket Association. From 1944 to 1949 he was a member of the association's Executive Committee and served as a state selector in 1942-43 and again from 1945-46 to 1948-49. Importantly, he was entrusted with the completion of A History of Queensland Cricket (1946), which had been commenced by

E. H. Hutcheon prior to his death in 1937 and continued by T. J. Bale until his death in the year of the book's publication.

Originally a primary school teacher, Honour transferred to the secondary service while he was studying part-time at the University of Queensland, from whence he graduated in arts in 1940. After a long term at Brisbane State High School, he was promoted as Deputy Principal of Rockhampton High School and Technical College in 1953 before opening the new North Rockhampton High School as its inaugural principal in 1956. In 1958 he transferred to Townsville High School before returning to Brisbane where he later opened Corinda High School, a position he held until his retirement in 1975. In all of his postings he established a reputation as an energetic and inspiring teacher and administrator who was committed to a broad and inclusive philosophy of education. He collaborated with his teaching colleague George Lockie, who also played cricket for Queensland, in the production of a large number of social studies and geography texts which were used widely throughout Australia. He also played a major part in the preparation and publication by Jacaranda Press of a popular school atlas. His outstanding record of service to the community through education was recognised with the British Empire Medal in 1988 for services to education and sport.

	M	I	NO	R	HS	100s	50s	Avge	Ct	St	W	Avge	BB
First-class	6	10	0	147	34	0	0	14.70	3	0	0	–	–
Domestic first-class	6	10	0	147	34	0	0	14.70	3	0	0	–	–

LANCASTER, JOHN LINDSAY, died in Melbourne on February 2, 2001. Born at North Fitzroy on October 15, 1905, John Lancaster began umpiring district cricket during the 1930s. In the first season after the war he officiated in the Victorian XI v The Rest match at Carlton, while in 1947-48 he received his only first-class appointment when he umpired the game between Victoria and Queensland at the Melbourne Cricket Ground. Rain ruined the match as a contest, the second and fourth days being completely blank. At this stage, the demands of his accountancy practice forced Lancaster's retirement from cricket but he continued his long association with Australian Rules football. He had already officiated in 11 VFL Grand Finals between 1934 and 1944 as a boundary umpire, plus the 1947 game as a goal umpire. Lancaster then spent 25 years on the VFL Umpires Appointments Board, followed by three years as its chairman, a record of service which led to his life membership of the VFL in 1977. In 2000 he received a special Australian Sports Medal.

LANGLEY, GILBERT ROCHE ANDREWS, died on May 14, 2001, in the Adelaide suburb of Fullarton. To the casual observer, Gil Langley may have lacked the feline artistry of Don Tallon or the predatory skill of Wally Grout, yet for 26 Tests in the 1950s he was an unfailingly safe wicket-keeper who moved with an anticipation which belied his amply comfortable build. This ability to be ahead of the play was allied to sharp reflexes and the surest of hands. He was immediately recognisable with his ruddy complexion, thinning fair hair and a shirt which delighted in working free of the confines of his trousers. Born at North Adelaide, on September 14, 1919, he was originally a free-scoring batsman with the Sturt club who did not take up keeping until he had been in the side for some seasons. He played his first two matches with the state in 1945-46 as a specialist batsman. South Australia found it difficult to settle on a regular keeper, and when Langley next appeared for the state in December 1947, he was the fifth glove man tried in just over two seasons. He settled to the role so quickly that, with 31 dismissals, he was the most prolific keeper in Australia in 1948-49. In addition, he batted consistently and made the first of his four first-class centuries, a combative 141 not out in only 220 minutes, against Queensland, at Brisbane, during which he dominated an eighth-wicket stand of 141 with Bob McLean (42). Because of Tallon's unavailability, Langley went to South Africa in 1949-50 as understudy to Ron Saggers and, with the arrival of the West Indians in Australia in 1951-52, he gained Test selection when Tallon's health caused him to miss a season's first-class cricket. He was an immediate success and his 21 dismissals (16 catches and five stumpings) equalled the existing series record of Saggers and Herbert Strudwick.

He toured England in 1953, where he established his ascendancy over Tallon as the preferred national keeper. During the 1954-55 Ashes series, he had to miss the last three Tests after he suffered a serious injury to his eye when, in a Sheffield Shield match against Queensland, he was struck by a ball from Jack Wilson which had bowled Ron Archer. The injury caused so much trouble that he did not play until the Second Test of the ensuing inaugural tour to the West Indies. Langley was quickly back to his best and in the remaining games he twice equalled Bert Oldfield's 1924-25 record of five dismissals in an innings. It was on this tour, in the Fourth Test, at Bridgetown, that he made his only Test fifty, a reminder that his batting at this level was strangely unproductive, given his obvious capability with the bat. During the next season, against Queensland at Adelaide, he batted with great circumspection for 250 minutes in making 97 as a makeshift opener, joining Les Favell (80) in a partnership of 119.

Langley's presence was one of the few rays of light in the gloom of the 1956 Australian tour of England. Having claimed six victims in the First Test, he created a new record of nine dismissals (eight catches and a stumping) in the next Test, at Lord's. He then strained tendons in his hand while fielding in the outfield against Glamorgan and had to miss the next two Tests. Such was his omnipresence behind the stumps that his 19 dismissals in three Tests were made out of the 44 wickets which fell to bowlers while he was keeping; moreover, he caught ten of Keith Miller's 21 dismissals in the series. *Wisden* recognised his contribution by naming him as one of its Cricketers of the Year. Langley closed his Test career by playing against Pakistan and India on the way back to Australia and then chose the match against New South Wales at Adelaide in December 1956 to mark his farewell to first-class cricket. Appropriately, he made 100 out of 156 in three hours during the second innings, albeit in a losing cause.

In earlier years, Langley had made a name for himself as a gargantuan run-scorer in that distinctive feature of the Adelaide sporting scene, electric light cricket. In a period of three years in the early forties, he made 7,000 runs in this form of the game and was joined in playing it by his wife, his two brothers and his sister. He is also remembered as one of South Australia's most skilled footballers, playing 163 senior games as a mobile rover for the Sturt club in the South Australian National Football League, captaining the side for a number of seasons and winning the Best and Fairest award in 1945 and 1946. Langley played for South Australia on 11 occasions and also captained the team. Because he saw service in the munitions industry in Melbourne during World

War Two, he played a few games with Essendon, including being on the reserves bench during the 1943 grand final. He subsequently played lawn bowls, naturally with the Sturt club and, equally naturally, with great skill.

Langley entered state politics in 1962 as Australian Labor Party member for the seat of Unley, which he held until he retired in 1982, his constituents responding to his sincerity and hard work by according him the kind of affectionate respect his team-mates had felt for him. His political service drew partly on his public profile but was also an expression of his commitment to the best traditions of his party. A qualified electrician, he often used his trade skills to carry out small maintenance jobs while he was campaigning. He was speaker of the House of Assembly from 1977 to 1979 and his many contributions to public life were recognised by the award of the Medal of the Order of Australia in 1984. His nephew Jeff Langley (1948–) played 28 matches for South Australia and Queensland as a batsman between 1969-70 and 1979-80.

	M	I	NO	R	HS	100s	50s	Avge	Ct	St	W	Avge	BB
First-class	122	165	39	3,236	160*	4	12	25.68	292	77	0	–	–
Tests	26	37	12	374	53	0	1	14.96	83	15	0	–	–
Domestic first-class	46	77	12	1,859	141*	3	7	28.60	111	24	0	–	–

LEE, ROBERT WILLIAM, died on June 9, 2001, in Adelaide, after a long battle with mesothelioma, the result of coming into contact with asbestos when he was an apprentice fitter and turner at the Islington Railway Workshops. Born in the Adelaide suburb of Hindmarsh on January 31, 1927, Bob Lee was educated at Adelaide High School. He had a long and productive career as an opening batsman with the Adelaide club from 1943-44 to 1963-64, during which time he scored 6,508 runs at 29.71 and spent a number of seasons as captain and coach. Despite his consistency, he had to wait until 1956-57 for state selection, when he was given the consolation of being part of South Australia's first team to visit Tasmania. He made a competent 86 in just under three hours, the 114 he added for the fifth wicket with Colin Pinch (101) helping his side out of a minor predicament. Lee played in the last Sheffield Shield match of the season and then had to wait until 1959-60 for one more fleeting inclusion in the state side. He was particularly well known and highly regarded in the world of Australian Rules football, playing 96 games for West Adelaide between 1944 and 1957. He received the reserves Magarey Medal in his last season, following which he was involved in coaching for the club in both reserve and first grade, becoming president of the club in 1965. Subsequently, he joined the management committee of the South Australian National Football League and moved the motion that the league develop its own ground away from the Adelaide Oval, the culmination of which was the building of Football Park in the late 1960s. His administrative skills were utilised on the South Australian Football Commission, the Australian National Football Council and the inaugural board of the Adelaide Crows. After leaving the service of the railways, Lee became a wine merchant before taking up a career in real estate.

	M	I	NO	R	HS	100s	50s	Avge	Ct	St	W	Avge	BB
First-class	3	6	2	142	86	0	1	35.50	3	0	0	–	–
Domestic first-class	2	4	1	34	19*	0	0	11.33	0	0	0	–	–

LOXTON, COLIN CAMERON, died on September 2, 2000, at Greenslopes, Brisbane. Born in the Sydney suburb of Beecroft on New Year's Day, 1914, Col Loxton received his primary education in Brisbane before being sent to Melbourne Grammar where he played in the school's First XI. From 1934 to 1936 he was a student at Pembroke College within Cambridge University from whence he received the degree of Master of Arts. As well as playing for the Crusader's XI, he represented the University once in 1935 and, in addition, received an athletics Blue for hurdling. Returning to Brisbane, he made an important contribution to the University club in 1936-37 when his 502 runs of pleasant strokeplay included two centuries. At the end of the season, the tall (185 cm), well-built

Loxton captained Combined Universities in a rain-interrupted two-day game against the touring MCC team in which he made 39. Early next season, he led the Queensland Colts side against New South Wales at the Gabba. Having opened and been dismissed by the seventh ball of the match for a duck, he batted at No. 4 in the second innings and top-scored with 53. He then played four Sheffield Shield matches where, although tried as an opener and as low as No. 8, he was unable to produce an innings of substance. His best effort came in his initial match, against Victoria at the Melbourne Cricket Ground, when, in the second innings, he resisted for 133 minutes in making 25, adding 72 for the second wicket with Jim Coats (46). Ironically, he was more successful as a lively fast-medium bowler, taking one more wicket in these four games than he did in his two seasons of grade cricket. His most productive figures were against New South Wales at Sydney where he took 1/39 and 2/27, the latter return including the wickets of Bert Oldfield and Sid Barnes, clean bowled in quick succession.

During World War Two, he was a pilot in the Royal Australian Air Force, serving in the Pacific region and rising to the rank of squadron leader. In June 1943 he received a bullet wound to the knee which ended his cricket-playing career. After the war he turned his attention to administration, serving as president of the University Cricket Club and also spending a decade as vice-president of Western Suburbs. In addition, he was delegate for the Proserpine Cricket Association to the Country Committee of the Queensland Cricket Association from 1958 to 1967. During this period he served as a Country member of the QCA Executive Committee (1963–66), while in 1962-63 he was both a Country delegate to the QCA General Committee and a Country selector. Having started in the retail industry with Pennys Ltd in 1938, he joined the trading firm of Burns Philp in 1946 before moving to TAA and Ansett Airlines in the early 1960s. His son, John (1945–), played 22 matches for Queensland between 1966-67 and 1970-71.

	M	I	NO	R	HS	100s	50s	Avge	Ct	St	W	Avge	BB
First-class	4	4	0	61	25	0	0	7.63	4	0	6	34.33	2/27
Domestic first-class	4	4	0	61	25	0	0	7.63	4	0	6	34.33	2/27

THOMAS, MAXWELL RAYMOND, died on May 20, 2001, at the Hobart suburb of Lenah Valley. A substantial batting presence in the Tasmanian teams of the decade immediately following World War Two, Max Thomas was an obdurate left-hander who reined in his strokes in the service of his side. His nickname of "Wacker" was an ironic tribute to his approach to batting, an approach whose solidity reflected his deliberate and considered personal demeanour. Born at Launceston on May 28, 1921, he made an impact in his initial first-class appearance at Hobart, against the Australian Services team in January 1946, when he batted for 330 minutes in compiling 164 which included one six and 14 fours. He was the less flamboyant presence in an opening partnership of 136 with Ron Morrisby (82) in just under two hours. Next season, against Victoria at Launceston, Thomas came to the crease when the first wicket fell in the opening two minutes of play. He then defied the attack for 266 minutes before being last out for 74 of his side's total of 176. Subsequently, he found first-class runs more difficult to garner, and disappeared from the state side for the two seasons from 1949-50. He made a successful return in 1951-52, scoring 43 and 48 as an opener against the touring West Indians, innings whose combined time totalled nearly five hours. In 1953-54, he was listed as twelfth man against Victoria at Hobart, but came into the side after Ray Stokes had to withdraw. Coming in at number three, Thomas stood firm for 368 minutes as he made 136, an innings which included an eighth-wicket partnership of 121 with Bertie Brownlow (46). A few days later, at Launceston, he reminded the Victorians of his adhesiveness by making an undefeated 86 in the second innings in 233 minutes.

Thomas was a dominating presence in local cricket for the South Launceston club, scoring 7,085 runs and taking 416 wickets with a mixture of right-arm medium pace and off-spinners. His skill was exemplified by the 599 runs he made at an average of 99.84 in the 1953-54 season and also by the fact that he was an automatic selection for the northern representative team from 1939 to 1956. Although his bowling was used only sporadically at first-class level, he took 5/54 against Victoria at Launceston in 1948-49 and opened the bowling at Melbourne in 1951-52. A teacher of manual arts in secondary schools, he was transferred to Hobart in the late 1950s where he took up umpiring so successfully that he officiated in four first-class matches, all against touring teams, between 1965-66 and 1970-71. His older brother, Ron (1915–1987), played 26 first-class matches between 1933-34 and 1950-51, scoring 1,304 runs by methods which were as carefree as his younger brother's were careful and deliberate.

	M	I	NO	R	HS	100s	50s	Avge	Ct	St	W	Avge	BB
First-class	19	37	3	955	164	2	3	28.08	8	0	7	23.42	5/54

WALTON, DOUGLAS JOHN, died on February 18, 2001, in Hobart. Born in the Derwent Valley town of New Norfolk on April 9, 1927, Doug Walton was a left-handed batsman whose capable and organised approach drew the plaudits of Tasmania's best bowler, Terry Cowley. He played for the Hobart club Glenorchy from 1947-48 to 1963-64, scoring 6,585 runs at 35.03, his prolific consistency reflected in his recent selection in the club's Team of the Century. Walton first appeared for Tasmania against Victoria at Hobart in 1950-51 when he scored 23 and 25 but he had to wait another six years to be selected again at the state level. In 1959-60 he did well in the two matches against the Victorians; at Hobart he enlivened the closing stages of a Tasmanian defeat by unleashing a ferocious burst of strokeplay, hitting 31 in only 26 minutes with six fours, mostly from the bowling of Alan Connolly. At Launceston he twice top-scored; in the first innings he made 66 (135 minutes, nine fours) and was joined by Terry Cowley (59) in a rousing eighth-wicket partnership of 108 in only 89 minutes which pulled Tasmania back from a parlous seven for 84. In the second innings, he showed composure in making 48 out of his side's 113. Next season, he was part of the first Tasmanian side to visit Adelaide since 1935-36 and made a fluent 54. At the end of 1960-61, in his last match for Tasmania, he played attractively against the Australian team on its way to England in making 51 in 79 minutes, the highest score in an innings of 147.

	M	I	NO	R	HS	100s	50s	Avge	Ct	St	W	Avge	BB
First-class	9	16	2	381	66	0	3	27.21	6	0	0	–	–

WARD, RONALD EGBERT, died on November 8, 2000, at Launceston. Born on May 7, 1905, in Adelaide, Ron Ward was educated at Woodville High School before winning a scholarship to the South Australian Teachers' Training College. He played both cricket and football for West Torrens and it was his skill in football which, in 1930, won him a coaching position in Launceston, where he also played club cricket for both North Launceston and Esk. His five matches for Tasmania were spread over five years, but his highest innings came in his second match, against Victoria at Launceston in 1930-31, when he made 47 not out at No. 8, joining Neil Davis (42) in a seventh-wicket partnership of 69 in Tasmania's substantial total of 446. Later that season, he also appeared against South Australia at Adelaide where his useful medium-pacers dismissed Cec Starr and Mervyn Hutton with successive balls. Several months earlier, Ward and Ray Ferrall (whose obituary appeared in last year's *Wisden Australia*) had been co-commentators for radio station 7LA in presenting Tasmania's first live cricket commentary in hour-long shifts. In his final appearance, against Victoria at Launceston over New Year 1936, he made 39 of a second-wicket partnership of 94 with Ted Smith (90). Ward was on the staff of Launceston Grammar from 1932 to 1938 and was coach of the school's First XI. He then joined the staff of 7LA, ultimately becoming the station's general manger. Having joined the RAAF in 1942, he served in New Guinea before being seconded to General Douglas MacArthur's Advanced Headquarters. As a result of his intelligence work in New Guinea and the Philippines, he was awarded the Bronze Star by the United States.

	M	I	NO	R	HS	100s	50s	Avge	Ct	St	W	Avge	BB
First-class	5	9	1	155	47*	0	0	19.37	5	0	3	33.66	2/31

WATKINS, ATHOL GEORGE, died on April 9, 2001, at Berkley Vale, on the central coast of New South Wales. Born on a dairy farm at Ulmarra, on the Clarence River in northern New South Wales, on April 11, 1919, Athol Watkins left school at the age of 13 to go droving before working with the butcher in his home town. Later in the 1930s, he became a dogman at the Port Kembla steelworks, south of Sydney, before his equestrian experience was utilised in the Australian Army's Light Horse. In late 1944, he began an association of 40 years with the Sydney Cricket Ground when he was given three days' casual work there. Initially, his duties included cleaning toilets, sweeping grandstands and raking down the Hill but he graduated to groundwork and was later given the SCG No. 2 wicket to maintain. He succeeded Bill Watt as curator when Watt accepted an appointment to the Melbourne Cricket Ground in 1958. At this time, pitches were prepared using a horse-drawn roller on a ground at which time seemed to have stood still. Watkins, however, was required to cope with the complete transformation of the ground through such features as the advent of day-night cricket in 1978-79 and the erection of the electronic scoreboard in 1983. During the 1960s he procured the last 800 tonnes of the Bulli soil which was integral to the preparation of the quality pitches for which Sydney was renowned. His work history is instructive in our age of obsession with credentials; although he started a greenkeeper's course, his extensive duties prevented him from ever completing it. Nevertheless, he was widely regarded as a world-class curator whose attention to detail was such that he habitually worked on Christmas Day so that the pitch in preparation would be properly watered. A man of few words, he set himself high standards of achievement and worked ceaselessly in the service of the ground he loved. His severing of links on retirement, however, was total and he never returned to his old workplace. Watkins subsequently endured blindness stoically for the last decade of his life.

CRICKET BOOKS, 2000-01

By JAMIE GRANT

It is ironic that the cricket book from the past 12 months which should be most likely to give pleasure to real cricket lovers will not be easily available in all bookshops. That is to say that Jim Young, having written in **Any Old Eleven** precisely the kind of book which has been needed for many years, has been unable (or perhaps unwilling) to find a mainstream publisher for what is a comic masterpiece. The publisher would no doubt be happy to fill any orders from those unable to find the book in conventional retail outlets (Cape Weed Press, PO Box 63, Warburton, Vic, 3799, $16.95).

To judge from the stock of cricket books held by those retailers, and from the titles listed in publishers' catalogues, it is the accepted wisdom in the publishing mainstream that the only cricket that readers should be interested in is at the international level. As a result, cricket writing has been pushed toward extinction – most cricket books these days are not so much written as dictated by former international players who rely heavily on the services of ghost-writers. Yet this accepted wisdom is based on a fallacy. It assumes that those who play cricket, those who watch it, and those who read about it are exactly the same people. Though there is of course some overlap, this is not on the whole the case; many of those who play cricket scarcely watch it at all (not even when their own team is batting), while the majority of cricket-watchers do not bother to read books about it. To confuse the issue further, many of those who buy cricket books do not actually read them, if only because they are often bought as presents by non-reading relatives. (I make this assertion with the authority of one who has worked as a bookshop assistant.)

The name of Jim Young does not figure among lists of former Australian Test cricketers; instead, he took the field in the Northern and Combined Churches Cricket Association, a suburban competition played on matting in Melbourne. The cricket he writes about is what is generally known as "park cricket". There is a distinction to be made, which Young is careful to draw, between "park cricket" and "a casual hit with the kids, or scratch matches and social games arranged *ad hoc*". It is a form of cricket where the standard is often laughable, and yet is played with the utmost seriousness by "formally constituted bodies", divided into numerous descending grades.

Humour arises, in cricket, out of the tension between the seriousness of the participants and the essential absurdity of the activity they are engaged in (considered objectively, or seen by an outsider, the game is ridiculous, after all, as even its terminology of "deep" and "fine" and "silly" tends to confirm); the game only ceases to be funny when players try to make a joke of it. These are principles Jim Young understands implicitly, and perhaps the greatest of his book's various virtues is its perfectly deadpan tone. The team he played for, Naughton's Old Boys, was named after the well-known Melbourne University pub of that name. "Some may perceive an anomaly in the participation of a pub team in a Churches cricket competition," he remarks in an example of his understated humour.

None of the cricketers Young writes about will be familiar to his readers from endless television replays of every dismissal, boundary stroke and abusive outburst in their careers; instead, they are nondescript characters he succeeds in bringing to life with all the skill of a novelist. In addition to his skills of characterisation and as a humorist, though, Young makes an important contribution to what might be described as the philosophy of cricket. Test cricketers are a tiny minority of the vast body of individuals who play the game in parks and pastures and village greens all over the world: the real meaning of the game is to be found among that majority. Thus while some of the incidents he describes are unique – an elephant on the pitch, and female prison escapees

running over the field, for example – many more, and many of his more general observations on the game, have the quality of universality: "A wise Frenchman – hard to believe he didn't know something about cricket – once remarked that 'in the misfortunes of our best friends we always find something not entirely displeasing'." This maxim is well-illustrated by a story about Young himself facing a bowler known as "The Beast" and being twice "smacked on the back leg around about an inch and a half from where it really hurts", while listening to "the howls of glee coming from my team mates at the boundary line". He adds later, "Though you take the field as a team, you play alone."

By the ends of Young's book, figures such as Clem Simonetto, Max Radcliffe and Pat O'Connor seem as familiar to the reader as Shane Warne and Glenn McGrath – or at least Clarrie Grimmett and Bill O'Reilly. Yet even though the leading characters in the book rise to no greater heights than C Grade in the Northern and Combined Churches, Young has many shrewd observations to make about the Test cricketers of the past and the present, pointing out that on the one hand much of the decline in the standard of behaviour among Test players ("sledging", gambling, disputing umpires' decisions) is the result of the behaviour of D Grade church players working its way up through the ranks, while on the other remarking that Andrew Hilditch would not have been dismissed "handled the ball" in the Perth Test against Pakistan in 1979 if he had "played a bit more park cricket". If he had, he would have "known not to give an aggravated opposition even the smell of a chance of cheating you out".

Also outside the mainstream is **Passport to Nowhere** (Walla Walla Press, at specialist outlets or c/o author PO Box 403, Kent Town, SA, 5071; $32.95), by Bernard Whimpress. Subtitled "Aborigines in Australian Cricket 1850–1939", this is essentially a critical review of two previous books on the same subject, *Cricket Walkabout* by D. J. Mulvaney (later revised in collaboration with Rex Harcourt) and *Obstacle Race* by Colin Tatz. Whimpress takes issue with Mulvaney and Tatz because he regards their conclusions as being too generalised, the result of "little (if any) additional primary research on cricket".

Whimpress has thoroughly examined the primary evidence, including newspapers, manuscripts and annual reports of cricket associations, and has thus produced much fascinating material in which the focus is on actual cricket matches for which records exist. Mulvaney and Tatz, he feels, are less interested in cricket as a game than in issues of racial discrimination and Social Darwinism which can be discussed in a cricketing context; Whimpress puts these issues into a more balanced perspective – without dismissing them – while showing a persuasive concern for cricket in itself.

Passport to Nowhere had its origin as a PhD thesis, and some general readers may be deterred by a sentence like this one: "In seeking to account for the adoption of cricket by Aborigines and their progress and decline in the game I have used a particular model of diffusion theory known as the diffusion of innovations." They should, however, persist. The well-researched chapter-length biographies of the five most prominent Aboriginal cricketers of the period – Johnny Mullagh, Bullocky, Jack Marsh, Albert Henry and Eddie Gilbert – contain enough cricketing detail to hold the attention even of those who are not persuaded by the somewhat ambiguous conclusions Whimpress reaches on the topic of racial relations and throwing.

Another book which appears, at first glance, to belong outside the commercial mainstream is Kersi Meher-Homji's **Famous Cricketing Families** (Kangaroo Press, $29.95). The mainstream thinks otherwise: mountainous quantities of this title can be discovered in every book outlet from the neighbourhood independents to K-Mart. Meher-Homji – two of whose uncles played for Indian teams in the early 20th century – is perhaps best known as a collector of cricketing oddities, having published books on subjects such as six-hitters and duck-scorers, and being a frequent contributor of newspaper items about statistical coincidences. He is clearly one of those who find the mathematics of cricket an important aspect of its appeal (the existence and the ongoing popularity of *Wisden* are a further testament to this aspect), and thus belongs among that considerable proportion of long-time cricket lovers for whom the one-day version of the game, with its limited numbers, is a disappointment.

There are few mentions of limited-overs cricket in *Famous Cricketing Families*, if only because most of the players discussed in the book had completed their careers long before the late 1970s. Members of two of the families discussed – the Bannermans and the Gregorys – played in the very first Test match in 1877, while more than half of the 34 families discussed at length had members who appeared in first-class cricket between the two world wars. Yet Meher-Homji is nothing if not thorough and up-to-date, so that his final full-length chapter is about Australia's Lee brothers, and he notes the family connections of current Test players Justin Langer and Stuart MacGill, as well as the Australian-born England players Adam and Ben Hollioake (whose father, John, played for the Fitzroy district club made famous by another of the families he includes, the Harveys).

If Meher-Homji has a fault as a writer, it may be his inability to resist puns such as this one (referring to the family of Hanif, Mushtaq, Shoaib *et al.*): "mountains of runs kept coming to the Mohammads". Yet however packed with fascinating and little-known facts his books are, they leave one wondering as to their point.

What, then, does this year's mainstream of cricket publishing comprise? There are certain kinds of books which recur with the regularity of a monsoon: the annual instalment of Steve Waugh's diary, two or three books written by, and two or three more ghost-written by, Ken Piesse, the latest reissue under another title to make it seem like a new book of an old book by Roland Perry. Shane Warne's autobiography will be published again, as will Ian Healy's, while Shane and Brett Lee have combined in a ghost-written dual autobiography which doubtless covers much the same material as can be found in Kersi Meher-Homji's chapter on the brothers. None of these could be said to have literary merit: they might bring to mind the famous Truman Capote remark about Jack Kerouac's work, "That's not writing, it's typing."

Few stenographers could surpass the words-per-minute rate of Ken Piesse, among whose productions are **The Complete Shane Warne** (Viking, $27), a book which might be made redundant by the reissue of Warne's autobiography, and, perhaps somewhat improbably, **Mahanama – Retired Hurt** (published by the author, $39.95 hardback, $29.95 paperback, available from 8 Aranmore Cr, Narre Warren North, Vic, 3804). The latter, a ghost-written autobiography of the Sri Lankan player Roshan Mahanama, attracted media attention for its comments on what he calls "this business of sledging". He protests, "I cannot understand how any sportsman indulging in this noble game can stoop so low as to insult a member of the opposing team in foul language." Mahanama needs to consult Jim Young: "Well, back in the park we know the answer to that: 'Stick it up him, Slugger', 'Too good for this bludger', 'Let's have another', 'Knock his stumps over', 'Knock his bloody head off', 'Give 'em buggery'. And of course, 'Talk it up, Towners, this ain't no turkey shoot!'"

Though it comes from the mainstream publisher HarperCollins, **Test Team of the Century** (edited by Garrie Hutchinson; $25.50) is a more unusual – and original – idea than might at first appear. When the 20th century came to an end, the Australian Cricket Board took it upon themselves to nominate 12 players who would be regarded as the "Test Team of the Century". Unsurprisingly, there were many notable omissions. Garrie Hutchinson, seeing the "impossibility of the task", decided to pick a team of his own which "might give the 'officials' a run for their money". Modestly, he says, "Perhaps my team isn't as well balanced as the official one," though his, unlike the Cricket Board's side, includes a left-arm bowler for variety. Having chosen a team of players, Hutchinson then chose another team, of writers. He commissioned – or, in the case of those of his contributors who are long-deceased, reprinted – a short essay on each of the players in the official Test Team of the Century, and on each of the players in his alternative team.

The writers' team Hutchinson has chosen could be regarded as a definitive list of the best Australian cricket writers, from figures in the past such as A. G. Moyes, Ray Robinson and Jack Fingleton to present-day journalists Mike Coward, Philip Derriman, Greg Gowden and Gideon Haigh. More significantly, there are also contributions from two distinguished historians in Ross McMullin and Don Watson, and from novelists and playwrights Alex Buzo, Steven Carroll, Laurie Clancy and Barry Dickins (Hutchinson himself has been a poet and playwright among his other accomplishments), as well as from two actors in Graeme Blundell and the one-time Channel Nine commentator Kate Fitzpatrick. The result is a collection with as much variety and balance as the two teams of players. Some contributors write as much about themselves as they do about their nominal subject, others approach the topic glancingly, while others still write directly (and insightfully) about the career of a player. The point of this book is to be found in the writing, so that it would be pedantic to complain about the occasional typographical error among the figures it includes.

Other Australian cricket books published in 2000-01 included:

A Century Partnership, Rob Hansen (A History of Upper Beaconsfield CC in Victoria), $27.00
An Unforgettable Summer, Alf Batchelder et al., (A 40th Anniversary Tribute to the Australia–West Indies 1960-61 series), $15.00
Australian Cricket Annual 2000, (ed) Allan Miller, $40.00
Australian Test Cricketers, Rick Smith, $29.95
Bradman's Band, Ashley Mallett, $25.00
Calypso Summer, Mike Coward, $40.00
Captain Australia, Roland Perry, $36.00
Cricket's Greatest Scandals, Ken Piesse, $25.00
Dusky Legend, Maurice Ryan (Biography of Sam Anderson, Aboriginal Cricketer), $16.50
For Club and Country, Ken Williams (On Melbourne Cricket Club's Test players), $15.00
Hands & Heals, Ian Healy, $36.00
140 Years in the East, Craig Reece, $10.00
Never Satisfied: Diary of a Record-Breaking Year, Steve Waugh, $30.00
Taylor & Beyond, Malcolm Knox, $25.50
The Best of Keepers: The Life and Artistry of Don Tallon, Philip Derriman, Standard edition, $15.00, Leather-bound limited edition, $190.00
The Best of the Best: A New Look at Test Cricket, Charles Davis, $27.00
The Dominators, Allan Border et al., $32.00
Waugh's Way, Roland Perry, $25.00
Wisden Cricketers' Almanack Australia 2000-01, (ed) Gideon Haigh, $45.00

With thanks to Roger Page Cricket Books for information on the above titles.

Any publishers who would like to have books noticed in these pages should write to Wisden Australia, c/o Hardie Grant Books.

CRICKET AND THE MEDIA, 2000-01

By ALEX BUZO

KEYHOLES AND BUTTONHOLES

While the blowtorch of investigative journalism was applied to cricket by the *Australian*, over at Channel Nine it was show business as usual. In the *Sydney Morning Herald* and the *Age* the roles of reporter and expert were largely combined, and there was no shortage of censorious opinion. The *Sunday Telegraph* may be a tabloid, but it outdid them all with a highly original investigation into the number of runs Mark Waugh scored when his model girlfriend was present, and the bigger total – as their documented and scholarly research proved – when she was absent. As Norman May might have said, the season was a pot pourri with mixed ingredients.

The panel on Foxtel's *The Back Page* voted match-fixing in cricket as the major sports story of 2000, and the *Australian* obviously agreed. Their inquiry led them to call for the standing down of Mark Waugh and Brian Lara. The response from Peter Roebuck in the Fairfax press was predictably furious. A great admirer of the quieter Waugh twin, Roebuck described the investigative journalists as "scavengers" and called for them to back off: "the puffed-up blowhards had scented blood and had long ago divided the world into black and white, the better to make hysterical conclusions" (*Sydney Morning Herald*, February 2).

The secret of the Waugh–Warne fines had been kept for five years, a tribute to the game's cult of "omerta", or silence. It was finally broken by an alert non-player journalist, Malcolm Conn of the *Australian*. Many bookmakers would have accepted bets that the story would break on Channel Nine, happy in the knowledge that the ex-player commentators on Nine would be unlikely to involve themselves in such a violation of the *Mates Act*. The *Australian*'s Dossier team, composed entirely of non-players, made further investigations into cricket, including such issues as the low participation of Aborigines, falling television ratings and what it takes to become an official. They also commissioned and published a Newspoll that found "20 per cent of cricket lovers are no longer confident that one-day games are not rigged".

Investigating charges that cricket is mono-cultural, the Dossier team found that Jason Gillespie was the only "avowedly indigenous" player to wear the baggy green cap, many years after Faith Coulthard-Thomas won selection in the women's team in 1958. They managed to winkle out a wonderful statement from a cautious Rod Marsh – "Might I suggest that some cultures like to play a shorter sport?" – and an even more cautious un-named ex-player who set out the golden pathway to a place on the Australian Cricket Board: "Start with stacking balls for the Under-13s, graduate to pads, move on to raffling chooks in the bar..."

Meanwhile, that indomitable Englishman, Peter Roebuck, encapsulated some of the multicultural uncertainty of the times when he wrote of the First Test of the 2001 Ashes series: "The Poms relied too much upon a couple of bowlers and gave too much away, dishing out boundaries as if it were Christmas in the Hussain household." (*Sun-Herald*, July 8).

Despite the campaign in the *Australian*, Mark Waugh did not stand down, and the paper moved on to other issues, such as the perennial canard that it is harder to get out of the Australian team than it is to get in: "Discarding a struggling Justin Langer for Damien Martyn at the very peak of his form represents a major breakthrough in selection policy which suggests anyone out of form will no longer be safe – not even Mark Waugh ... the Langer Principle has replaced the Tubby Principle" (Malcolm Conn, July 4). This was accompanied by a table, "Batting Performances under Steve Waugh", which had Martyn on top with 60.25 and Mark Waugh – never far from their thoughts – on the bottom with 33.51.

The *Australian*, which is probably not the favoured reading matter in dressing rooms, continued to raise issues related to the game, but also co-opted Adam Gilchrist to write a column, which was about as newsworthy as Channel Nine's *Postcards from Sri Lanka*. "For a touring cricketer it can be an emotional roller-coaster" was one revelation.

For the first time since 1981, Kerry Packer's "cricket channel" announced it would not be covering an Ashes tour. The job was left to Channel Seven, which copied the faltering Nine format by hiring a commentary team made up of ex-players from the eighties, such as Bob Willis, Ian Botham, Paul Allott, David Gower and Jeff Thomson. The incomparable Thommo, who is at home in any medium, promptly let fly with the magic word when he believed the microphone was off.

This team quickly proved that the number one blood sport in England was not fox hunting, it was finding the no-ball after a batsman has been dismissed. The camera at crease level is intended to adjudicate on run-outs, but the boys had great fun using it after a dismissal to highlight any no-balls. "The line doesn't belong to the bowler, it belongs to the umpire," said Ian Botham, but Beefy was being a little disingenuous; the line quite clearly belonged to the commentators.

One complaint about recent players doing commentary is that they won't make any critical remarks; this was not true of Bob Willis, who pronounced on a run-out involving the Pakistani Falstaff, Inzamam-ul-Haq, a noted ambler between the wickets. "That's self-preservation, as regards Inzamam," said Willis.

Peter Roebuck was also not afraid to sink the talons in where he felt it necessary: "Warne was his artful self. Lately he has been bluffing, as the dreadful Ian Botham did towards the end of his career."

Roebuck has carved out a unique career as a year-round prose writer on the summer game for the Fairfax press as well as English publications. With the signing of Mark Ray as the principal cricket writer, Fairfax made a breakthrough on many fronts. Ray has an honours arts degree and was a Sheffield Shield player; now in the age of job-shedding and rationalisation, he combines the roles of reporter and expert, mastering both description and censorious judgment: "After 22 overs England were one for 99 yet were nowhere near comfortable, let alone in control. At least the two batsmen were playing positively rather than waiting passively for the inevitable as previous England teams have done far too often."

Ray was mirrored perfectly by Mike Selvey in the *Guardian*, whose mixture of reportage and ex-player scorn is slightly more succinct: "The tactics against Caddick were bewildering, where a legitimate attempt to tickle him up turned into a posturing bombardment that served no purpose."

Other parts of newspapers have worked hard to separate and label clearly what is news and what is comment; in the sports section the pair have bonded. It is no use looking back to the era of *Sydney Morning Herald* legend Tom Goodman (temper democratic, bias non-existent), who was the master of objective reporting and the style without any style. He was often accompanied on the page by the cantankerous buttonholing ex-player Bill O'Reilly, whose hobbyhorses kicked up huge clouds of dust.

The public does respect ex-players, and the phenomenon of the non-playing sports writer such as Ian Wooldridge, Red Smith or Mike Lupica is not so much a part of the Australian scene. The high ratings of Channel Nine until recently demonstrate this, with Tony Cozier being the only journalist allowed into the ex-players' sanctuary that was the commentary box. We don't expect them to break stories or raise issues, but we do look to them for authority.

The lingering final image of the Second Test in Kolkata is of Glenn McGrath standing his ground, the last man out and the fourth leg-before-wicket on the final day. All four were plumb, wrote Peter Roebuck, and you believe this man who led England to defeat in the Netherlands because whatever the stains on the record might be, he is an ex-player. The Kolkata Test, which India won after following on, was described by Roebuck as the best he has seen in 25 years, and you respect that, too.

The commentary team for Foxtel was led in India by David Hookes, who is both a journalist and an ex-player, so there was something of a Third Way about the coverage. Hookesy even attempted a bit of analysis, opining that Matthew Hayden's improvement was due to self-belief and improved footwork. The big question was how did this fringe player – Mr Pura Cup, Mr Suspect Temperament, Mr No Test Technique – suddenly become Australia's leading run-scorer, making the Indian fast bowlers feel the pain of the full face of his bat and sweeping the spinners into the dustbin of square leg? He's improved, said the Channel Ninepins who were on board. Yep, no doubt about it.

One unexpected source of stories was Steve Waugh himself. He either generated or kept rolling the issues of crowd control, doctored pitches, coaching, four-day tests, 12-player limited-overs teams, and on the subject of Pakistan tanking in New Zealand, he was full of fraternal loyalty: "You're never too sure what to believe coming out of there [Pakistan]." On that chestnut about the coach being dropped as a selector because players would be reluctant to approach him for advice about a weakness: "I hope not, because that means they won't be coming to me because I'm a selector and I'm captain."

One issue Steve Waugh did not raise was player behaviour, which was dealt with by Dossier at length, and by the rest of the press during the Slater–Dravid imbroglio in Mumbai. Waugh himself is a known sledger and was not at the forefront when this issue came up. It was the women's team which had to bear the brunt of criticism, an interesting development in an era when people are quick to claim moral superiority on a flimsy basis. England manager Gill McConway took the high ground when she told the *Guardian*, "Australia are probably the most uncouth team in world cricket and while we encourage our girls to respond, we do not want any bad language."

If match-fixing was the biggest of these stories, it was not the one that occupied the most space; this honour went to the death of Sir Donald Bradman on February 25. This was the cue for untold numbers of supplements to be printed by all papers. They colourised photos, tracked down spectators, and commissioned articles on everything to do with the Don – his religion, his kinship with Mozart and Joe DiMaggio, his endless centuries – except for one tiny thing: what was he like as a batsman? You would never guess that he was a predominantly back-foot player who favoured the cross-bat strokes. Perhaps in the era when "on the back foot" has become a political cliche meaning "forced to be defensive" it was inconvenient to mention that when bowlers saw Bradman (or O'Neill or many others) go on to the back foot, they went a paler shade of white. Many of the tributes that "poured in" were of course well-meaning, but most were windy woofs.

A curious aspect of the flurry of supplements honouring Bradman was that in a nominally egalitarian society most of the supplicants tried to outdo each other in elevating the great man way above his team-mates. Arthur Morris was at the other end when Bradman made his final duck, sitting on a small matter of 196 runs, and he was lost in the rush to puffment, both in 1948 and especially now. "Not since Shakespeare," wrote Peter Roebuck, "has anyone been so far ahead of his colleagues." Bernard Shaw protested about the "Bardolatry" of Shakespeare, but that had nothing on the Bradolatry that followed the fading of the Don. In the land of Supplementaria, it seems, there is a god rather than a king.

Strangely enough, one of the most delightful pieces of writing was not generated by any of these big issues. It was by Andrew Ramsey in the *Australian* and it dealt with a kind of cricket that is not much seen on television: the Pura Cup. Dean Jones held the record for the slowest century in state competition, and as Shane Deitz approached a new "long-playing record" (© W. Grout 1957), Jones left the press box and went down to the boundary, clapping each dot ball and urging the South Australian not to have a go. In an age where the line between reportage and opinion has become blurred, Jones set an example by isolating his partisanship. This is how Ramsey (*Australian*, November 27) introduced his tale of Time and Victorian Man: "While those who were unable to sleep during Shane Deitz's marathon maiden century hope to expunge it from their memories, one former Australian batting legend will recall it with a clarity he usually reserves for his own epic innings."

If in general terms there was an "up there for thinking, down there for dancing" divide between the print media and television, the scribes did have some lighter moments. Euphemism of the year undoubtedly went to Malcolm Conn. Under the somewhat cruel headline "Softly, softly for Warne comeback" appeared the following: "Australian officials said Warne had made a commitment to watch his weight despite looking comfortable in the television commentary box during the First Test in Brisbane" (*Australian*, November 28).

The University of Western Australia's description of Shoaib Akhtar's "uniquely flexible right arm" was an interesting coinage, as was Damien Martyn's "It's good to be fully picked" (instead of just replacing an injured player). Now that Warwick Hadfield has been retired there were no real bloopers or cringe-making phrases, although a Foxtel reporter did keep the spirit of Haddles alive when he stated, "Australia were only 161 runs in a rear". Otherwise, 2000-01 was the year the print media got serious.

A collection of beanpole quicks and runt-like batsmen, the Australian team became known as The Dominators, despite the hiccup in India. Whether they were being puffed or dissected, no one in any medium denied them the title. On that, at least, there was agreement.

AUSTRALIAN CRICKET MEMORABILIA, 2000-01

By STEPHEN W. GIBBS

As Sir Donald Bradman is believed to have signed some one million items during his lifetime there will always be a Bradman item available. The only upbeat aspect of his death in February 2001 is that the supply side of the market for his autograph has finally peaked, although rumours have been circulating of signed copies of his funeral service brochure! The Bradman items with a strong associative element (for example, a bat used in a famous innings) will continue to bring surprising prices and the rest will have a ready, if modest, market appeal.

In March Australia Post reissued its Bradman stamps, which were originally released in January 1997 as part of the Australian Legends series, this time with his life years overprinted. The Royal Australian and Perth mints produced another Bradman series (the first coming in March 1996) of legal tender coins in June 2001 to commemorate his life: a 20-cent, two $5 coins and a $20 gold/silver coin, with a special three-coin packaged limited set selling for around $450.

Some items offered at the Charles Leski auctions in Melbourne during the period under review were appealing. The 1878 tour account by Reynolds *(Padwick: 4968)* fetched $12,815; Cohen's *NSW Cricketers' Guide & Annual Report* for 1877-78 *(Padwick: 3372)* $6,400; *The Cricketer's Guide* for the season 1857-58 by William Fairfax *(Padwick: 3360)* $5,535; and a doubly rare Sydney 1883 edition of *St Ivo and the Ashes (Padwick: 4408)* realised $4,660. These are some of the seminal Australian cricket bibliographical items and it is unusual to see such a collection come to market in one season.

A collection of 97 items from the Test cricketer Alan Connolly was offered in October 2000. The clearance rate and prices realised were disappointing, with the only lot bringing more than $1,000 ($1,050 plus 16.5 per cent) being two Victorian jumpers and a Victorian cap. Seven items linked with the Australian player Ross Gregory were unsold at a reserve of $2,400. Jack Fingleton's Australian 1935-36 blazer did, however, attract interest and was sold for $4,600. A "baggy green" came to auction: Neil Harvey's 1956 cap was offered by Lawson's in their February 2001 sale. It was passed in at a bid of $4,250 (estimate $10,000-12,000).

Timing is crucial in cricket and, it seems, auctions also. The bat signed by both teams in the 1921 series was offered at auction in May 2000 (estimate $1,500-1,600) but passed in. It was subsequently offered in September 2000 and realised $3,145. The reverse was the case for a 1909 A. G. Spalding bat with 15 Australian signatures, first offered with an estimate of $5,000-$10,000 and passed in; it later sold for $3,785.

Cricket bats used in Test matches are generally deemed desirable but it depends: a bat used by Graeme Wood to score a Test century was passed in (estimate $600-800) and Craig Serjeant's Test hundred bat was sold for $465. The pads Colin McDonald used during the 1958-59 Ashes series were passed in after having an estimate of $500-600. The local market for such items seems yet to find its buyer demand and commensurate price levels.

Strong performers continue to be items connected with the Golden Age (1890-1914), where signed postcards of Hill, Darling, Howell, Noble, Gregory and Kelly went for prices ranging from $420 to $575 (plus 16.5 per cent buyer's costs). An infrequently offered set of 14 cricket badges, the 1901 Cameo English Cricketers, attracted $1,690, after costs.

Another buyer favourite, Arthur Mailey, had a signed, hand-written letter from 1921, in which he detailed his sketching activities, sell for $505. An item with a connection with a current player, Shane Warne, being a set of Victorian car registration plates –

WARNEY – had no offers at an estimate of $1,500-1800. What consequences did the potential buyers see in the display of these plates on their car?

Continuing use of the Internet is evident, with eBay always offering a myriad of cricket items starting from very low prices. Sports Memorabilia Australia now conducts its regular sporting (including cricket items) auctions through the eBay facility, looking for a wider buying audience for its established electronic auctions.

The shock of the memorabilia season was the auction price paid for two press-clipping scrapbooks compiled on the Bodyline series by Hugh Buggy, the cricket writer. This lot was offered at the same auction as similar scrapbooks compiled by him on other interesting series such as the 1911-12 MCC tour to Australia and the Triangular series of 1912 (offered in one lot and realising just $120 plus 16.5 per cent). The Bodyline items went for a total cost of $6,700 to a buyer rumoured to be from the subcontinent.

Modern memorabilia issuing from firms such as Art of Cricket in the Australian Capital Territory feature both current and recently retired cricketers and historical themes such as the limited edition print of the 1868 Aboriginal Team to the UK, which was issued to commemorate the inaugural Prime Minister's XI versus the ATSIC Chairman's XI match played in Canberra in April 2001.

The Australian collecting market generally was affected by the attention and money directed to the Sydney Olympics in September 2000, but with disposable income now becoming available after the Games and the interest always generated by an Ashes tour to England the prospects are looking bright for an active memorabilia season for 2001-02.

Prices stated include, where applicable, auction buyer's premium and GST.

FIXTURES, 2001-02

Note: At time of publication all fixtures were correct.
Timetables are subject to change without notice.

NEW ZEALAND AND SOUTH AFRICA TO AUSTRALIA
2001-02 INTERNATIONAL SEASON

2001
November

Thur 1 – Sun 4	Queensland v New Zealanders	Brisbane
Wed 14	Prime Minister's XI v New Zealanders	TBC
Fri 16 – Mon 19	South Australia v New Zealanders	Adelaide

December

Wed 5	ACB Chairman's XI v South Africans	Perth
Fri 7 – Mon 10	Western Australia v South Africans	Perth
Thur 20 – Sun 23	New South Wales v South Africans	Sydney

2002
January

Tue 8	Australia A v New Zealanders (day/night)	Brisbane
Thur 10	Australia A v South Africans (day/night)	Adelaide
Wed 23	Australian Country XI v New Zealanders	Bowral

Test Series

2001
November

Thur 8 – Mon 12	First Test – Australia v New Zealand	Brisbane
Thur 22 – Mon 26	Second Test – Australia v New Zealand	Hobart
Fri 30 – Tue 4	Third Test – Australia v New Zealand	Perth

December

Fri 14 – Tue 18	First Test – Australia v South Africa	Adelaide
Wed 26 – Sat 30	Second Test – Australia v South Africa	Melbourne

2002
January

Wed 2 – Sun 6	Third Test – Australia v South Africa	Sydney

VB Series

2002
January

Fri 11	Australia v New Zealand (day/night)	Melbourne
Sun 13	Australia v South Africa (day/night)	Melbourne
Tue 15	New Zealand v South Africa	Hobart
Thur 17	Australia v New Zealand (day/night)	Sydney
Sat 19	New Zealand v South Africa (day/night)	Brisbane
Sun 20	Australia v South Africa (day/night)	Brisbane
Tue 22	Australia v South Africa (day/night)	Sydney
Sat 26	Australia v New Zealand (day/night)	Adelaide
Sun 27	New Zealand v South Africa (day/night)	Adelaide
Tue 29	Australia v New Zealand (day/night)	Melbourne

February

Fri 1	New Zealand v South Africa (day/night)	Perth
Sun 3	Australia v South Africa	Perth
Wed 6	First Final (day/night)	Melbourne
Fri 8	Second Final (day/night)	Sydney
Sun 10	Third Final (if required) (day/night)	Sydney

2001-02 PURA CUP

2001
October

Wed 17 – Sat 20	New South Wales v Tasmania	Sydney
Wed 17 – Sat 20	Queensland v Western Australia	Brisbane
Wed 17 – Sat 20	South Australia v Victoria	Adelaide
Wed 24 – Sat 27	Victoria v Queensland	Melbourne
Fri 26 – Mon 29	Western Australia v Tasmania	Perth
Fri 26 – Mon 29	New South Wales v South Australia	Sydney

November

Thu 8 – Sun 11	Western Australia v Queensland	Perth
Thu 8 – Sun 11	Victoria v New South Wales	Melbourne
Fri 9 – Mon 12	Tasmania v South Australia	Hobart
Sun 25 – Wed 28	South Australia v Western Australia	Adelaide
Sun 25 – Wed 28	Queensland v New South Wales	Brisbane

December

Wed 5 – Sat 8	Tasmania v Victoria	Hobart
Thu 13 – Sun 16	Victoria v South Australia	Melbourne
Thu 13 – Sun 16	Queensland v Tasmania	Brisbane
Fri 14 – Mon 17	New South Wales v Western Australia	Sydney

2002
January

Thu 17 – Sun 20	South Australia v New South Wales	Adelaide
Thu 17 – Sun 20	Tasmania v Queensland	Hobart
Fri 18 – Mon 21	Western Australia v Victoria	Perth
Fri 25 – Mon 28	New South Wales v Victoria	Sydney
Fri 25 – Mon 28	Tasmania v Western Australia	Hobart
Fri 25 – Mon 28	Queensland v South Australia	Brisbane

February

Wed 13 – Sat 16	South Australia v Queensland	Adelaide
Fri 15 – Mon 18	Western Australia v New South Wales	Perth
Sun 17 – Wed 20	Victoria v Tasmania	Melbourne
Thu 28 – Sun 3	Victoria v Western Australia	Melbourne
Thu 28 – Sun 3	New South Wales v Queensland	Sydney

March

Fri 1 – Mon 4	South Australia v Tasmania	Adelaide
Wed 13 – Sat 16	Queensland v Victoria	Brisbane
Wed 13 – Sat 16	Tasmania v New South Wales	Hobart
Wed 13 – Sat 16	Western Australia v South Australia	Perth
Wed 20 – Sun 24	Final	

2001-02 ING CUP

October

Sun 7	New South Wales Blues v Victorian Bushrangers	North Sydney
Fri 12	Western Australia v Southern Redbacks (day/night)	Perth
Sun 14	New South Wales Blues v Tasmanian Tigers	North Sydney
Sun 21	Southern Redbacks v Victorian Bushrangers	Adelaide
Sun 21	Queensland Bulls v Western Warriors	Brisbane
Wed 24	Western Warriors v Tasmanian Tigers (day/night)	Perth
Sun 28	Victorian Bushrangers v Queensland Bulls	Melbourne

November

Sat 3	Tasmanian Tigers v Western Warriors	Hobart
Sun 4	Victorian Bushrangers v Southern Redbacks	Melbourne
Sat 17	Victorian Bushrangers v Western Warriors	Melbourne
Sun 18	New South Wales Blues v Queensland Bulls	Sydney
Fri 30	Southern Redbacks v Western Warriors (day/night)	Adelaide
Fri 30	Queensland Bulls v New South Wales Blues (day/night)	Brisbane

December

Sat 8	Southern Redbacks v New South Wales Blues	Adelaide
Sun 9	Tasmanian Tigers v Victorian Bushrangers	Hobart
Tue 18	Queensland Bulls v Tasmanian Tigers (day/night)	Brisbane

2002
January

Fri 4	Western Warriors v Queensland Bulls (day/night)	Perth
Sun 6	Tasmanian Tigers v Southern Redbacks	Launceston
Sun 6	Victorian Bushrangers v New South Wales Blues	Melbourne
Sat 12	New South Wales Blues v Southern Redbacks	Coffs Harbour
Sun 13	Tasmanian Tigers v Queensland Bulls	Hobart
Wed 16	Western Warriors v Victorian Bushrangers (day/night)	Perth

February

Fri 1	Southern Redbacks v Tasmanian Tigers (day/night)	Adelaide
Fri 1	Queensland Bulls v Victorian Bushrangers (day/night)	Brisbane
Sun 3	New South Wales Blues v Western Warriors	Sydney
Fri 8	Queensland Bulls v Southern Redbacks (day/night)	Brisbane
Sun 10	Tasmanian Tigers v New South Wales Blues	Devonport
Wed 13	Western Warriors v New South Wales Blues (day/night)	Perth
Sat 16	Victorian Bushrangers v Tasmanian Tigers	Melbourne
Sun 17	Southern Redbacks v Queensland Bulls	Adelaide
Sun 24	Final	

WOMEN'S CRICKET AUSTRALIA
2001-02 PROGRAMME

National Matches

2001
November

Sat 3 – Sun 4	New South Wales v South Australia	Dalton Park, Wollongong, NSW
Sat 3 – Sun 4	Queensland v Victoria	Allan Border Field, Qld
Sat 24 – Sun 25	Western Australia v South Australia	Abbett Park, Scarborough, WA

December

Sat 1 – Sun 2	New South Wales v Queensland	Drummoyne Oval, NSW
Sat 8 – Sun 9	Victoria v Western Australia	Central Res, Glen Waverley, Vic
Sat 22 – Sun 23	South Australia v Victoria	Adelaide Oval, SA
Sat 29 – Sun 30	Western Australia v New South Wales	WACA Ground, WA

2002
January

Sat 12 – Sun 13	South Australia v Queensland	Adelaide Oval No. 2, SA
Sat 19 – Sun 20	Queensland v Western Australia	Allan Border Field, Qld
Sat 19 – Sun 20	Victoria v New South Wales	tba, Vic
Sat 2	Semi Final	Bankstown Oval, NSW
Sun 3	Semi Final	Bankstown Oval, NSW

February

Mon 4	Final	Bankstown Oval, NSW

International Matches

2002
February

Sat 16	New Zealand v Australia Youth	Melbourne tbc
Mon 18	New Zealand v South Australia	Adelaide
Wed 20	Australia v New Zealand	Adelaide
Thur 21	Australia v New Zealand	Adelaide
Sat 23	Australia v New Zealand	Melbourne
Wed 27	Practice Game	New Zealand
Thur 28	Practice Game	New Zealand

March

Sat 2	Australia v New Zealand	New Zealand
Sun 3	Australia v New Zealand	New Zealand
Wed 6	Australia v New Zealand	New Zealand

FUTURE TOURS

AUSTRALIA IN SOUTH AFRICA, 2001-02

2002
February
Fri 15 – Mon 18	v South Africa A	Potchefstroom
Fri 22 – Tue 26	First Test v South Africa	Johannesburg

March
Fri 1 – Mon 4	v South Africa A	Port Elizabeth
Fri 8 – Tue 12	Second Test v South Africa	Cape Town
Fri 15 – Tue 19	Third Test v South Africa	Durban
Fri 22	First Limited-Overs International v South Africa	Johannesburg
Sun 24	Second Limited-Overs International v South Africa	Centurion
Wed 27	Third Limited-Overs International v South Africa	Potchefstroom
Sat 30	Fourth Limited-Overs International v South Africa	Bloemfontein

April
Wed 3	Fifth Limited-Overs International v South Africa	Durban
Sat 6	Sixth Limited-Overs International v South Africa	Port Elizabeth
Tue 9	Seventh Limited-Overs International v South Africa	Cape Town

PROPOSED FUTURE TOURS INVOLVING AUSTRALIA

2002
Australia to Zimbabwe

2002-03
Australia to Pakistan
England to Australia
International Limited-Overs Series
(Australia, England and Sri Lanka)
World Cup in South Africa
Australia to West Indies

2003-04
Australia to Bangladesh
Zimbabwe to Australia
India to Australia
International Limited-Overs Series
(Australia, India and Zimbabwe)
Australia to Sri Lanka

2004-05
Australia to India
West Indies to Australia
Pakistan to Australia
International Limited-Overs Series
(Australia, Pakistan and West Indies)
Australia to New Zealand

2005
Australia to England

2005-06
Bangladesh to Australia
South Africa to Australia
International Limited-Overs Series
(Australia, Bangladesh and South
Africa)
Australia to South Africa

2006-07
Australia to Zimbabwe
New Zealand to Australia
England to Australia
International Limited-Overs Series
(Australia, England and New Zealand)
Australia to West Indies
World Cup in West Indies

2007-08
Sri Lanka to Australia
India to Australia
International Limited-Overs Series
(Australia, India and Sri Lanka)
Australia to Pakistan

2008-09
Australia to Sri Lanka
Pakistan to Australia
West Indies to Australia
International Limited-Overs Series
(Australia, Pakistan and West Indies)
Australia to New Zealand

2009
Australia to England

2009-10
Zimbabwe to Australia
South Africa to Australia
International Limited-Overs Series
(Australia, South Africa and Zimbabwe)
Australia to South Africa

2010-11
Australia to India
England to Australia
Australia to West Indies